SCOTTISH EDUCATION
SECOND EDITION: POST-DEVOLUTION

Edited by T. G. K. Bryce and W. M. Humes

Section editing by
Brian Boyd
Tom Bryce
John Halliday
Walter Humes
Sue Kleinberg
Malcolm L. MacKenzie
Lindsay Paterson
Mary Simpson

Edinburgh University Press

© in this edition Edinburgh University Press, 2003
Copyright in the individual contributions
is retained by the authors

First edition published 1999

Edinburgh University Press
22 George Square, Edinburgh

Typeset in 10 on 12pt Ehrhardt
by Hewer Text Limited, Edinburgh, and
printed and bound in Spain
by GraphyCems.

A CIP record for this book is available from the British Library

ISBN 0 7486 1625 X (paperback)

The right of the contributors to be identified as authors
of this work has been asserted in accordance with the
Copyright, Designs and Patents Act 1988.

This project is supported by
The Carnegie Trust for the Universities of Scotland.

Contents

The Contributors

Frank R. Adams is Director of Undergraduate Studies in the Moray House School of Education, University of Edinburgh.

Julie Allan is Professor of Education in the Institute of Education, University of Stirling and Director of the Participation, Inclusion and Equity Research Network.

Professor Robert Anderson is a Professor in the History Department at the University of Edinburgh.

Rowena Arshad, OBE, is the Director of the Centre for Education for Racial Equality in Scotland (CERES), Equal Opportunities Commissioner (Scotland) and Senior Lecturer in Equal Opportunities in the University of Edinburgh.

Mr David Betteridge was formerly Headteacher of Pollokshields Primary School, Glasgow and a Senior Lecturer in the Faculty of Education, University of Paisley.

Keir Bloomer is Chief Executive of Clackmannanshire Council and Vice Chair of Learning and Teaching Scotland.

Dr Brian Boyd is Reader in Education at the University of Strathclyde.

Linda Boyes is a Policy and Research Manager at the Scottish Council Foundation.

Bob Brewer is a Lecturer in Physical Education in the Moray House School of Education, University of Edinburgh.

Karen Bryce is Principal Teacher of Home Economics at Shawlands Academy, Glasgow.

Professor Tom Bryce is Professor of Education in the Faculty of Education, University of Strathclyde and was Faculty Vice Dean (Research) from 1997 to 2002.

Dr Douglas Buchanan is a Lecturer in the Department of Curriculum Research and Development, Moray House School of Education, University of Edinburgh.

Charles Byrne is Senior Lecturer in Music Education in the Faculty of Education, University of Strathclyde.

Mel Cadman is a Lecturer in the Department of Social Work in the Faculty of Education, University of Strathclyde.

Mr David Caldwell is Director of Universities Scotland, the representative body for all Scottish higher education institutions.

Ms Alison Cameron is a Policy Adviser in the Department of Education, North Lanarkshire Council.

Professor David Carr is Professor of Philosophy of Education in the Moray House School of Education, University of Edinburgh.

Mono Chakrabarti is a Professor in the Department of Social Work at the University of Strathclyde.

Donald Christie is Vice Dean (Research) in the Faculty of Education of the University of Strathclyde.

Dr Rae Condie (formerly Stark) is a Reader in the Faculty of Education, University of Strathclyde and was Faculty Vice Dean (Academic) from 1998 to 2002.

Dr Tom Conlon is a Senior Lecturer in the Moray House School of Education, University of Edinburgh and was Principal Assessor for CSYS Computing Studies with the SEB and SQA from 1995 to 2001.

Graham Connelly is a Senior Lecturer in the Department of Educational Support and Guidance in the Faculty of Education, University of Strathclyde.

James C. Conroy is Head of the Department of Religious Education at the University of Glasgow.

Glen Coutts is Senior Lecturer in Art and Design Education in the Department of Applied Arts, Faculty of Education, University of Strathclyde.

Dr Linda Croxford is Senior Research Fellow at the Centre for Educational Sociology, University of Edinburgh.

John Dakers is a Lecturer in the Department of Educational Studies at the University of Glasgow and is Course Leader for the educational component of technological education.

Dr John Darling (1942–2002) was Co-director of the Centre for Educational Research in the University of Aberdeen.

Christine De Luca is Head of Assessment Research and Development at the Scottish Qualifications Authority.

Fernando Almeida Diniz recently retired from the Moray House School of Education, University of Edinburgh where he was Senior Lecturer in Social Justice in Educational Studies.

Robert Doherty is a Lecturer in the Department of Educational Studies, University of Glasgow.

Dr Gari Donn is Chief Programme Officer (Higher Education), Commonwealth Secretariat, London.

Ms Anne Donovan is a writer and teacher, presently job-sharing as APT English at Hillhead High School, Glasgow.

Dr Paul Dougall is Senior Lecturer in the Department of Applied Arts at the University of Strathclyde.

Aline-Wendy Dunlop is a Senior Lecturer in the Department of Primary Education, University of Strathclyde and Course Director for the Postgraduate Diploma in Early Education.

Sue Ellis is a Senior Lecturer in the Department of Primary Education, University of Strathclyde.

John Fairley is a Professor in the Strathclyde Business School.

Barry Finlayson is a Senior Lecturer in the Department of Business and Computer Education, Faculty of Education, University of Strathclyde.

Professor Gerry P. T. Finn is Professor in the Department of Educational Studies, Faculty of Education, University of Strathclyde.

Dr Tom Fitzpatrick was formerly Vice Principal, Notre Dame College of Education, Glasgow.

Joan Forrest is a Senior Lecturer in Health Education in the Department of Social Studies Education in the Faculty of Education at the University of Strathclyde.

Fred Forrester is an educational consultant and journalist. Until his retirement in 2000, he was Depute General Secretary of the Educational Institute of Scotland, the largest Scottish teachers' organisation.

Gill Friel is Headteacher of St Ninian's Primary School, Stirling.

Dr Bill Gatherer was HMI and Chief Adviser in Lothian and is now a consultant in education for citizenship and character education.

Eleanor Gavienas is a Lecturer in Primary Education in the Faculty of Education, University of Strathclyde.

Tony Gavin was formerly Headteacher of St Margaret's Academy, Livingston.

Judith Gillespie, who has been involved as a parent in Scottish education since 1985, is currently the Development Manager for the Scottish Parent Teacher Council.

Dr Bob Glaister is Senior Lecturer and Staff Tutor (Education) with the Open University in Scotland and was Dean of the OU's School of Education from 1990 to 1998.

Rothwell Glen is Principal Teacher of Physics at Park Mains High School, Erskine, Renfrewshire.

Professor John Halliday is Professor of Education in the Department of Educational Studies, University of Strathclyde.

Professor David Hartley is Professor of Educational Theory and Policy in the Education and Social Work Department of the University of Dundee.

Dr Peter Higgins has extensive teaching experience in outdoor centres as well as at university level and is Head of Outdoor and Environmental Education in the Moray House School of Education, University of Edinburgh.

Peter Hillis is Reader in History Education in the Faculty of Education at the University of Strathclyde and President of the Scottish Association of Teachers of History.

Cathy Howieson is a Senior Research Fellow in the Centre for Educational Sociology at the University of Edinburgh.

Anne Hughes is a Senior Lecturer in the Faculty of Education, University of Strathclyde. She is currently Vice Dean (Academic) and was for four years Head of Primary Education.

Professor Walter Humes is Professor of Education and Head of the Department of Educational Studies in the Faculty of Education, University of Strathclyde.

Gordon Jeyes is Director of Children's Services in Stirling and General Secretary of the Association of Directors of Education in Scotland.

Mr Derek Johnston is a Lecturer in the Faculty of Education at the University of Glasgow.

Joyce Johnston is a former HMI (Education) and has been Principal of Fife College of Further and Higher Education since 1996.

Professor Richard Johnstone is Vice Dean (Research) in the Faculty of Human Sciences and Director, Scottish Centre for Information on Language Teaching and Research, Institute of Education, University of Stirling.

Dr Elizabeth Jordan is a Senior Lecturer in Edinburgh University and Director of the Scottish Traveller Education Programme.

George Kerevan is Associate Editor at *The Scotsman*. He was an academic economist for twenty-five years.

Professor Gordon Kirk is a Vice Principal at the University of Edinburgh. From 1991 to 1998 he was Principal of Moray House Institute of Education and from 1998 to 2002 Dean of the Faculty of Education at the University of Edinburgh.

Dr Margaret Kirkwood is a Senior Lecturer in Educational Studies in the Faculty of Education, University of Strathclyde.

Sue Kleinberg is a Senior Lecturer in the Department of Primary Education, University of Strathclyde.

Graham Leicester is Director of the International Futures Forum.

Frank Lennon is Headteacher at St Modan's High School, Stirling.

Dr Kay Livingston is the Director of the Quality in Education Centre at the University of Strathclyde.

Lesley Low is a Lecturer in Initial Teacher Education at the University of Stirling and was a Research Fellow in the Institute of Education from 1991 to 2002.

Andrew Lyon, interested in the relationship between thinking and doing, acts as Converger for the International Futures Forum, based at the Scottish Council Foundation.

Professor John MacBeath OBE, holds the Chair of Educational Leadership, University of Cambridge and is Director of Leadership for Learning, the Cambridge Network.

Mr Donald MacDonald was formerly Head of Geography in the Department of Social Studies Education, Faculty of Education, University of Strathclyde.

John MacGregor is Senior Lecturer in the Department of Mathematics, Science and Technological Education, Faculty of Education, University of Strathclyde.

Matthew MacIver is Chief Executive and Registrar of the General Teaching Council for Scotland.

Gilbert MacKay is Professor of Special Education, University of Strathclyde.

Dr Tommy MacKay is Director of Psychology Consultancy Services and an Honorary Lecturer in Psychology at the University of Strathclyde.

Jeannie Mackenzie is Integration Manager for New Community Schools in East Renfrewshire.

Mr Malcolm L. MacKenzie was formerly a Senior Lecturer in Education at the University of Glasgow.

Dr Effie Maclellan is a Reader in Educational Studies at the University of Strathclyde.

George A. T. MacBride is Principal Teacher, Support for Learning, in Govan High School, Glasgow. He is currently Convenor of the Education Committee of the EIS and a member of the Advisory Council of LT Scotland.

Dr Judith McClure is Headteacher of St George's School, Edinburgh and Chairman of the Management Committee of the Scottish Council of Independent Schools.

James McCormick is Director of the Scottish Council Foundation and was Research Director from 1997 to 2002.

Professor David McCrone is a Professor in the Department of Sociology at the University of Edinburgh.

Dr James McGonigal is Head of Language and Literature in the Faculty of Education, University of Glasgow.

Dr David J. McLaren is a Senior Lecturer in the Department of Educational Studies in the Faculty of Education at the University of Strathclyde.

Mrs Marion McLarty is a Senior Lecturer in the Department of Educational Support and Guidance in the Faculty of Education at the University of Strathclyde.

Henry Maitles is Senior Lecturer in the Faculty of Education and Head of Department of Social Studies Education, University of Strathclyde.

Joan Menmuir was formerly a Senior Lecturer in the Department of Educational Studies in the Faculty of Education at the University of Strathclyde.

Arthur Midwinter is Emeritus Professor of Politics at the University of Strathclyde and Budget Adviser to the Finance Committee of the Scottish Parliament.

Professor Ted Milburn is Professor of Community Education in the Faculty of Education, University of Strathclyde and Director of the Centre for Youth Work Studies.

Brian Morris is a Lecturer in Educational Management in the Institute of Education, University of Stirling.

Professor Pamela Munn is Professor of Curriculum Research and Dean of the Moray House School of Education, University of Edinburgh.

Robert Munro is a Reader in the Department of Business and Computer Education in the Faculty of Education at the University of Strathclyde.

Lillian Munro is an Assessment Manager with the 5–14 Assessment Unit at the Scottish Qualifications Authority.

Angela Napuk is a researcher in the Educational Assessment Unit of the Moray House School of Education, University of Edinburgh.

David Newall is Director of Planning at the University of Strathclyde.

Liz Niven is a poet based in south-west Scotland where she has been a teacher, Scots Language Development Officer and Writer-in-Residence. Her last collection, in 2001, was published by Canongate.

Professor Jenny Ozga is Professor of Educational Research and Director of the Centre for Educational Sociology, University of Edinburgh.

Dr Pauline Padfield is a Research Fellow in the Scottish Travellers Education Programme, Moray House School of Education, University of Edinburgh.

Lindsay Paterson is Professor of Educational Policy at the Moray House School of Education, University of Edinburgh.

Professor Michael Peters is Research Professor of Education at the University of Glasgow and holds a personal chair at the University of Auckland.

Dr Willis Pickard was formerly Editor of the *Times Educational Supplement Scotland*.

Ms Aileen Purdon is a Lecturer in the Department of Educational Studies in the Faculty of Education at the University of Strathclyde.

Professor David Raffe is the Director of Research in the Moray House School of Education at the University of Edinburgh and was the Director of the Centre for Educational Sociology from 1987 to 2001.

Sheila Riddell is Professor of Social Policy at Glasgow University and Director of the Strathclyde Centre for Disability Research.

Boyd Robertson is Senior Lecturer in Gaelic in the Faculty of Education, University of Strathclyde.

Isobel J. Robertson was formerly a Senior Lecturer in the Department of Mathematics, Science and Technological Education in the Faculty of Education, University of Strathclyde and Co-director of the AAP Mathematics projects between 1990 and 1996.

Mrs Pam Robertson was formerly a Senior Lecturer and Director of the B.Ed. (Hons) Music Course, University of Aberdeen, and an Expressive Arts contributor to both the B.Ed. and P.G.C.E. Primary Courses.

Mr Alex Rodger was formerly Development Director for Secondary Education and Convenor of the Religious and Moral Education Unit at Northern College.

Dr Angela Roger is a Senior Lecturer in Education at the University of Dundee.

Sheila Semple is currently Director of the Centre for Guidance, Careers and Personal and Social Development at the University of Strathclyde.

Dr Bob Sharp is a Reader in the Scottish School of Sports Studies, Faculty of Education, University of Strathclyde.

Professor Richard Shaw was formerly Principal of the University of Paisley.

Mark Sheridan is Head of the Department of Applied Arts, Faculty of Education, University of Strathclyde.

Professor Mary Simpson holds the Chair in Classroom Learning in the Moray House School of Education at the University of Edinburgh and is Programme Coordinator of the Ed.D.

Dr Rebecca Soden is a Reader in the Department of Educational Studies, Faculty of Education, University of Strathclyde.

Nicky Souter is a Senior Lecturer in Science Education at the University of Strathclyde Faculty of Education and has been Course Director for the Post Graduate Certificate of Education (Secondary) since 1999.

Paul Standish teaches and researches in the philosophy of education at the University of Dundee, and is Editor of the *Journal of Philosophy of Education*.

Lord Sutherland was formerly Principal of Edinburgh University.

Dr Craig Thomson is Principal, Glenrothes College.

David Wallace is a Lecturer in Community Education in the Faculty of Education, University of Strathclyde.

Professor Douglas Weir is in the Department of Social Studies Education at the University of Strathclyde. He was Dean of the Faculty of Education from 1997 to 2001.

Graham White is Head of the Department of Primary Education in the Faculty of Education, University of Strathclyde. Previously he was Course Director of the PGCE Primary course.

Tony Williams is Senior Lecturer in Classics in the Department of Language Education in the Faculty of Education, University of Strathclyde.

Mr Jim Wilson is Principal Teacher of Mathematics in Williamwood High School, East Renfrewshire.

Dr Valerie Wilson is the Director of the Scottish Council for Research in Education Centre at Glasgow University.

I

Introduction and Overview

1

An Introduction to Scottish Education, 2nd edition: Post-devolution

Tom Bryce and Walter Humes

PURPOSE AND ORIGINS

With the first edition of this text, we set out to provide a detailed, informed and critical account of Scottish education at the turn of the century. It was timely to attempt such an undertaking not simply because of the approaching new millennium but, more importantly, to coincide with the formation of the new Scottish Parliament. Inevitably that would bring change to education, we reasoned, and, while admitting that the directions of that change would not be easy to predict, we believed that an understanding of education at the time, appropriately contextualised, would be important to any sensible evolution of educational practice in the future. An effort was made therefore to address each of the sectors in the Scottish educational system and to set out the professional thinking which relates to practice. A comprehensive treatment was given of pre-school, primary, secondary, further, adult and higher education, together with observations concerning the important contexts – historical, cultural, political, social and economic – within which education was pursued in Scotland. The various chapters were written by specialists who drew upon up-to-date research and contemporary analysis to give fresh insights into educational developments and professional practice throughout the Scottish educational system. Each of the chapters was specially commissioned for the volume.

The text combined material written by educationists with first hand experience of their own organisations and fields of influence (individuals able to give 'insider' perspectives) with commentary and analysis written by academics whose researches enabled them to offer illuminating interpretations of how particular aspects of education were conducted in Scotland (individuals able to take 'outsider' perspectives). A deliberate effort was made to combine concise description with a critical perspective. That is, detailed information was supplemented by an outline of the issues of contention and debate among the professionals concerned with each area. Inevitably the balance of description to critique varied across the chapters, it being more difficult for 'insiders' to be as detached as 'outsiders'. Conversely, the knowledge and insight which the 'insiders' brought to the text was substantial and, in some respects, could not be matched by the 'outsiders'. The book was therefore intended to inform all those who sought to understand educational practice and convey what Scottish educators themselves thought about their own educational system; its strengths and achievements, as well as its weaknesses; their pride in it and their concerns for it.

We hoped that *Scottish Education* would be of particular use to students and scholars, native and foreign, as well as to those professionals who were keen to look beyond their own sector or particular specialism, to see how education 'works' in Scotland. The need for a book of this sort had been evident to us for some time, not least in our day-to-day work in teacher education. Student teachers (and indeed experienced teachers engaged in professional development) must come to terms with complex ideas and practices. Sharing the broad spectrum of thinking which relates to policy and action is an important step in becoming an effective teacher (or in extending one's field of influence and competence).

At the time of preparing the first edition, short, introductory or overview texts about Scottish education were few in number, there being a near-thirty year gap between Leslie Hunter's excellent study *The Scottish Educational System* (1968) and Clark and Munn's *Education in Scotland* (1997). And although there had been a steady increase in well-researched books concerned with particular aspects of provision, informed accounts spanning the broad front of education were still thin on the ground. This remains so today.

Furthermore, educational practice has become more complex over the decades and differences between Scottish circumstances and their equivalents elsewhere in the UK and in Europe have become difficult to summarise with ease. Educationists who address audiences outwith Scotland frequently find themselves required to say what is particularly Scottish about Scottish education. How is it distinctive? What do we do that is different from practice elsewhere? The important point is that while Scotland is a part of Europe, it is not a part of England. Foreigners often assume that what takes place in schools, colleges and universities in Scotland is the same as in England. Perhaps such assumptions have been diminishing since devolution and the establishment of the Scottish Parliament. However, and as we wrote in the introduction to that first edition, we would be the last to claim that everything about Scottish education is distinctive. Rather we sought to provide a wide range of material which would allow others to make their own judgements as to what was unique; what was similar but different; and what was indeed comparable to practices elsewhere. In the final analysis, the reader must weigh things up and form judgements in the light of the evidence.

We were delighted when the first edition met with acclaim from both academics and students. Reviewers in many journals commended the authors for their informed and well-researched accounts; the content was both authoritative and critical in setting out what matters to educators. Student teachers and post-graduates (teachers and other professionals pursuing higher degrees as part of their continuing professional development) alike welcomed the accessibility which the text brought; not only that, it was in 'bite-sized' pieces and covered a considerable amount of relevant material. It was heartening also to learn of how many others, researchers, organisations, individuals in central and local government, journalists, and even some politicians, found the text to be a useful source of essential information.

When we created the first edition, we knew that some things would date of course. Education, along with other parts of civic society, is subject to change and evolution, perhaps even more so. However we reckoned that what was expressed by the authors in response to our suggested guidelines would have lasting value, and was certainly worth recording. Our words were: 'with an appropriate formulation, much could and should be written as a substantive and critical record of current activities which would both inform readers and provide a basis upon which subsequent revisions could be made; the volume would provide a reference point for future writers and researchers'.

Four years on, we judged that there should be a second edition of *Scottish Education*. The first years of the Scottish Parliament have witnessed more changes than we predicted, many but not all of them deriving from the operations of the Parliament itself. New departments of central government have introduced reform and local government has continued to evolve, despite fears that centralisation of educational control might quickly result. Key bodies have changed or merged. Important initiatives have been brought about through the passing of the Parliament's first Act in 2000 (fittingly an Education Act). Primary, secondary and tertiary education have all encountered major shifts, particularly secondary and further education, with the implementation of Higher Still. Universities struggle with ever-increasing student numbers and related financial difficulties. Scottish education saw the worst ever catastrophe with the SQA exam debacle of 2000, the reverberations from which are still being felt.

We decided that a revision of the text should reflect education post-devolution; that it should, wherever appropriate, track the effects of new parliamentary thinking and opera-tions in all that goes on in education. Moreover, it should bring everything up to date. And some holes should be filled; we had set out to be as comprehensive as possible, but were quick to be reminded of some crucial gaps. A number of the original authors had changed field (or in some cases retired) and some of the changes required new researchers and writers. In the end, we commissioned forty-two new authors and there are nine new topics. (Some of the 'old' topics have been dropped as a consequence of change; thus Learning and Teaching Scotland is described, that organisation having resulted from the merger of the Scottish Consultative Council on the Curriculum and the Scottish Council for Educational Technology, for example (LTS = SCCC + SCET, but with some differences . . .)).

As for the first edition, for each of our contributors we drew up (or revised) a list of content guidelines; a set of headings which specified the subject matter to be addressed in the chapter concerned. Typically, these amounted to ten or twelve points, sometimes expressed in professional 'shorthand', and no doubt something of our own values and orientation was contained in these headings. To take one example, the draft specification for Chapter 45 was as follows:

Section VII Chapter 45.   Guidance, Personal and Social Education and Pastoral
                             Care in the Secondary School
- What guidance is (and is not) and how it operates in the typical school, making brief reference to the key documents in the evolution of guidance practice.
- The role of different staff vis-à-vis duties and specific inputs to Personal and Social Education (PSE) programmes typically provided.
- The preference for vertical systems of guidance.
- Conflict for teachers ('wearing two hats') and the considered effect of guidance upon school ethos.
- Distinctions in practice between guidance and counselling; growing interest in counselling.
- Links between guidance staff and parents, social work, police, etc.
- Personal and Social Development (PSD) and PSE; typical programmes available in schools – drugs education, sex education, health education.
- The continuity of guidance provision from 5–14 to S6.
- The increased demands resulting from Higher Still; changing priorities in vocational and/ or curricular and/or personal guidance?
- Issues of confidentiality, data-protection and legality.
- Staff development needs and their fulfilment (or not).
- Future scenarios for guidance provision.

We explicitly encouraged each of the contributors to regard such specifications as a guide and to develop their chapter content as they, as experts, saw fit. (The reader might like to match Chapter 45 against the guideline points given above.) They did so, in some cases negotiating shifts of emphasis and content. Only one saw fit to rewrite the entire specification to achieve a better conception of the area in question.

The detailed specifications served several purposes. As for the first edition, in drawing them up we were able to keep a check on the structure of the text (with two of the original sections being combined – see below). The full set convinced us of the sheer amount which must be written to give something of the real flavour of Scottish education; and we were again reminded of areas where our own knowledge was patchy and uneven. The specifications also enabled us, and subsequently contributors, to set boundaries around particular areas, knowing that related topics and complementary treatments would feature elsewhere. While the chapter specifications helped to minimise duplication and overlap, we felt it essential from the outset that, in particular areas, writers coming from quite different perspectives would serve to illuminate the complexity of certain topics. Last, the full set of chapter specifications enabled us to share with our section editors how we had conceived the sections, the contributory chapters and the work as a whole; as a team, we were able to improve the coherence of the text and to ensure that gaps were filled. The nine new topics are:

- Chapter 11: Parliament, SEED and the Administration of Scottish Education after Devolution
- Chapter 12: ELLD and the Scottish Parliament
- Chapter 24: The Scots Language in Education
- Chapter 27: The Financing of Educational Provision
- Chapter 28: School and Work: The Employers' Perspective
- Chapter 66: Outdoor Education
- Chapter 84: Baseline Assessment
- Chapter 93: Education at the Margins: Outsiders and the Mainstream
- Chapter 114: Scottish Education: An International Perspective

Many of the other chapters have changed in emphasis. The extent of the revision is therefore substantial.

SECTIONS AND SECTION EDITING

II	Policy and Provision in Scottish Education	*Lindsay Paterson*
III	The Administration and Control of Scottish Education	*Tom Bryce and Walter Humes*
IV	The Historical, Cultural and Economic Context of Scottish Education	*Malcolm MacKenzie, Walter Humes and Tom Bryce*
V	Pre-school and Primary Education: Organisation and Management	*Sue Kleinberg*
VI	Pre-school and Primary Education: Curriculum	*Sue Kleinberg*
VII	Secondary Education: Organisation and Management	*Brian Boyd*

Some aspects of the structure of the text will be self-evident from the section titles; however certain emphases merit explicit comment at this stage.

SECTION II POLICY AND PROVISION IN SCOTTISH EDUCATION

This section is intended as an overview of the whole field and contains introductory chapters for each of the four main sectors: primary, secondary, further and higher education. The opening chapter contains up-to-date statistics on patterns of provision in Scottish education, on trends and priorities. It contextualises the provision for education and outlines the changing pattern of governance. Chapter 3 sets out the philosophy and practice of primary education and provides an indication of the extent to which Scottish primary education is child-centred. The reader who wishes to focus upon primary schooling should read this chapter prior to those in Sections V and VI. Chapter 4 looks at Scottish secondary schools, noting the senses in which they may still be said to be 'comprehensive' in character, having been subject to a variety of pressures to change over the last twenty years or so. The reader who is focusing upon secondary schooling should read this chapter prior to those in Sections VII and VIII. Scotland's further education colleges, which provide post-school education, were until 1993 the responsibility of local government; now colleges are run independently on the basis of a direct block grant from central government and with expectations to diversify. Chapter 5 provides an introduction to further education and analyses the difficult ten years since 'incorporation'. It also emphasises the very significant blurring of the further education/higher education divide.

An introduction to Scottish university education and something of the character and provision in tertiary education is described in Chapter 6. Very significant changes have taken place in tertiary education in Scotland, as elsewhere, and the overall institutional framework is analysed in this chapter. Following these five chapters are two which contextualise the statutory provision of education in Scotland. Chapter 7 looks critically at the policy process itself, highlighting post-devolution changes and the several interpretations of how change is brought about. Chapter 8 examines the politics of education during the early years of the new Scottish Parliament, noting the altered dynamics of the main political parties. Scotland has a small but not insignificant private school sector and this, and its influence, is described in Chapter 9. The section ends with our own analysis of the distinctiveness of Scottish education; this chapter (10) endeavours to get behind the myths and traditional claims made about education in Scotland.

SECTION III THE ADMINISTRATION AND CONTROL OF SCOTTISH EDUCATION

Section III is devoted to an examination of how education is controlled and managed at central and local government levels, post-devolution. It also looks at the key organisations which provide support for teachers at national level, several of which have undergone significant change in recent years. The Scottish educational system has always been separate from its counterpart in England and Wales. Pre-devolution, the Secretary of State for Scotland had overall responsibility for education (amongst other things) and was a minister in the UK Government. With the formation of the Scottish Parliament in 1999, overall responsibility resides with the First Minister in the Scottish Executive, day-to-day management lying with two ministers who hold education portfolios. There are now two departments with responsibilities for education, the Scottish Executive Education Department (SEED) and the Scottish Executive Education and Lifelong Learning Department (SEELLD or ELLD). Chapters 11 and 12 respectively deal with their operations, their relationships with the two parliamentary committees concerned, and with Parliament itself. These chapters provide detailed analyses of how the challenging first years have been handled and the complex of relations between politicians and officials who administer the system. Higher education in the UK is the responsibility of four separate councils (one each for England, Scotland, Wales and Northern Ireland) and Chapter 13 looks at Scottish higher education funding and the operations of the Scottish Higher Education Funding Council (SHEFC), established in 1992. Her Majesty's Inspectorate of Education (HMIE) has a reputation for significant influence and central direction in Scottish education. Its status was changed in 2001 to an executive agency in the wake of the examinations crisis of 2000 (with the title shift from HMI to HMIE) and Chapter 14 sets out the new responsibilities and duties of this small group of people (now numbering under 100). Scotland's school educational system involves a partnership between central and local administration, as Chapter 15 explains. Chapters 15 and 16 give clear analyses of the details, from political and operational perspectives, respectively. Chapter 17 outlines the recent and current provision of local educational development services in Scotland, this work having been subject to upheaval through periods of change in local government organisation and, most recently, as a consequence of the McCrone settlement.

Until recently, responsibility for advising on the curriculum of Scottish schools lay with the Scottish Consultative Council on the Curriculum (SCCC) and responsibility for technology support lay with the Scottish Council for Educational Technology (SCET). These bodies were merged in 2000 to form Learning and Teaching Scotland (LTS) and Chapter 18 looks closely at the reality of that new organisation's work. The section concludes with a careful scrutiny of the responsibilities and actions of Scottish parents, their involvement and influence on key aspects of education having been significant for many years (Chapter 19).

SECTION IV THE HISTORICAL, CULTURAL AND ECONOMIC CONTEXT OF SCOTTISH EDUCATION

This section contains several chapters analysing the principal contexts of education in Scotland. Two chapters deal with the historical context, in quite different ways. A Conservative government was elected in the UK in 1979 (under Margaret Thatcher) and there followed eighteen years of Conservative rule, which brought many challenges to teachers and schools. Chapter 20 charts the history of Scottish education up to 1980, therefore, and Chapter 21 deals with the troubled years which followed, as well as the recent period under New Labour in Scotland. Scottish culture and the growth of nationalism is explored in Chapter 22; it shows how Scottish culture impinges upon education and extends some of the arguments presented in Chapter 10 in Section II. Gaelic education is, of course, significant in Scotland, despite the size of the minority so affected by it. Chapter 23 describes the provision for Gaelic (at primary, secondary, tertiary levels and beyond). Some parts of this chapter could have been included in the primary and secondary curriculum sections (VI and VIII) but the very nature of the language and the spirited drive to maintain and develop its use are better expressed in a single chapter. With regard to the majority of the population, Scottish people certainly use a variety of accents and dialects, and many claim that the spoken language is significantly different from Standard English. The Scots language is the subject of Chapter 24 in which the authors carefully analyse the challenges presented to teachers where pupils can have different speech habits at home from those they exercise in the more formal parts of schooling. Catholic education merits a chapter in its own right and the character of denominational schools is given in Chapter 25. (Scotland's state schools are, properly, described as denominational and non-denominational, not Catholic and Protestant as is sometimes crudely stated.) Proportionately more primary and secondary Catholic schools are located in the West of Scotland, in and around Glasgow, for historical reasons. Their distinctive ethos is conveyed in Chapter 25, though reference is made to them in a number of chapters throughout the volume.

In every country, the relationship between education and the economy is complex. Chapter 26 presents a penetrating analysis of the situation as it pertains in Scotland. There is very little *educational* literature on how educational provision is financed; few know what it costs to run schools and educate children, far less the actual mechanisms in operation at central and local government levels to determine grants and allocations. Chapter 27 provides detailed insights into how it all works in Scotland. Employers are bound to have diverse views on the effectiveness of the education system. At the end of the day, it might be difficult to claim that consensus exists, even regarding the utility of qualifications used to certify capability and prospects for the world of work. In Chapter 28, four members of the Scottish Council Foundation offer their analysis of the employer's perspective on Scottish education. National aspirations, in Scotland as elsewhere, are to widen access and opportunities, particularly to further and higher education and amongst groups tradition-ally subject to barriers and/or discrimination; Chapter 29 deals with access in the Scottish context. The final chapter (30) in Section IV looks critically at what is fashionably called values education, often said to be implicit in teaching methodologies and materials but sometimes given separate curricular treatment.

SECTIONS V TO VIII PRE-SCHOOL, PRIMARY AND SECONDARY SCHOOL EDUCATION

At the heart of the volume, in Sections V to VIII, are chapters concerned with pre-school, primary and secondary school education. They deal with how schools are organised and managed, and with what is taught in Scottish schools. Children in Scotland go to primary school at age five and authorities are required by statute to provide that primary education. With regard to pre-five education, political agendas have varied considerably during the last decade. With the incoming Labour government in 1997 aspirations for wider provision than previously available (in local authority nursery schools or playgroups, or in some cases private nurseries) took hold. Chapter 31 opens Section V with an examination of current provision and the issues surrounding pre-five education. This is followed by chapters concerned with how nursery and primary schools are organised and managed, their ethos and how teachers work with young children. Pupils spend seven years in primary school and at age twelve move from primary to secondary school. The efforts made by teachers to smooth the transition from P7 to S1 (which for some pupils is difficult) are described in the chapter on primary–secondary liaison (34).

The curriculum sections (VI for primary and VIII for secondary) do not simply replicate official documentation about what ought to be in the curriculum. They endeavour to describe what is actually taught; the approaches used by teachers; the emphases to be encountered in pupil activity; and the influences of government policy and assessment requirements upon what takes place in Scottish classrooms. While these curriculum chapters are mostly short (approximately 2,500 words) they encapsulate much that is distinctive about Scottish school teaching today. The first chapters in these sections (Chapters 35 and 47), each approximately 5,000 words (as are most others in the volume), give an overview of the curriculum of primary and secondary schools. Thereafter there are chapters for each of the curriculum programmes (or subjects) and these are placed alphabetically within each section. In the secondary curriculum section (VIII), three cross-departmental, or whole-school, curriculum areas are included alongside the traditional subject areas (viz. Career Education, Information Technology and Health Education) together with a topic not dealt with in the first edition, Outdoor Education (Chapter 66).

In Section VII there are chapters concerned with the organisation, management and discipline of secondary schools. Scotland's secondaries incorporate hierarchical management structures and the roles and duties of teachers at the various levels are set out and related to the operation and ethos of the typical school. (The McCrone settlement will result in a flattening of the structure of promoted posts in schools; that is discussed in the final chapter of the book, Chapter 115.) The pastoral care of pupils is organised by guidance teachers in Scotland's secondary schools, there being in each school a team of teachers, part of whose remit is to deal specifically with the Personal and Social Education of pupils (Chapter 45). The demands and complexities of the new Higher Still curriculum and the consequences of the McCrone settlement present significant challenges to Guidance teachers. The section concludes with a chapter (46) devoted to the organisation of teaching within classrooms, with a particular focus on what is known as the differentiation of the curriculum (to suit differing abilities, achievements and rates of progress).

SECTION IX FURTHER AND HIGHER EDUCATION

Children may leave secondary school at sixteen years of age (at the end of S4) though staying-on rates have increased dramatically in recent years. The majority of pupils continue to be educated in secondary schools, in S5 and in smaller, but growing, numbers in S6, though some will choose to continue their education in a further education (FE) college. From 1985, vocational education programmes were certificated within a national framework of modular provision. Although this originated in the FE sector, up to a quarter of such national certificates were being taken in schools by the end of the 1990s, pupils working towards both general and vocational educational qualifications. Inevitably the character of further education colleges is different from that of secondary schools, even allowing for the implementation of Higher Still which affects FE as much as secondary education. The section begins with an outline of the current priorities in FE: something of the diversity and variation in provision in this sector is indicated in Chapter 72, extending the material introduced in Chapter 5. The distinctions between the intentions for liberal and vocational education are carefully set out in Chapter 73. The response of educators to the rapidly changing world of work and the need for tailor-made programmes of study and marketable certificates is conveyed in the chapter which follows; FE has been considerably influenced by the needs of industry and commerce in Scotland (Chapter 74).

Able pupils in secondary schools will elect to enter higher education (HE) from S5 or S6 and, in line with UK government policy, the proportion of the cohort studying at university has risen steadily over the decades, to over 50 per cent in Scotland. Very significant numbers of young people therefore attend Scotland's universities – both traditional and 'new' (including those which were formerly central institutions or 'polytechnics', to use the more commonly understood English term). There is an increasing blurring between FE and HE and a trend towards co-operation between the two sectors in course provision. Chapter 75 examines how students are taught in both FE and HE.

Higher education institutions have become increasingly subject to public scrutiny and audit and Chapters 76–8 view their development in this context, Chapter 76 looking at the curricular structures of universities. Scotland's universities have long traditions of service to their communities; the nature of these links, their increasing diversification and the challenges presented to, and the response of, the FE and HE sector is set out in Chapter 77. Following the publication in 1997 of key government reports on Higher Education (Dearing and Garrick), and the importance of Research Assessment Exercises (RAEs), the priorities for HE continue to be subject to great pressure and Chapter 78 critically assesses the predicament of the university system in Scotland. The section finishes with two chapters concerned with adult and continuing education, lifelong learning (79) and the distinctive operation of the Open University in Scotland (80).

SECTION X ASSESSMENT, CERTIFICATION AND ACHIEVEMENTS

Assessment and certification constitute the greatest sources of influence upon the curriculum and this section is devoted to the very considerable changes which have taken place in recent years in Scotland, not only to the conduct of assessment but to the organisational structures through which formal certification is carried out. The section opens with two chapters which describe the changing patterns in primary and secondary schools. Chapter 81 explains how different assessment is for teachers now compared to a generation ago, innovative grading arrangements, reporting formats and internal assessment having all become a source of challenge and demanding workloads. Chapter 82 looks at how difficult it has been to increase the amount of ongoing assessment in classrooms intended directly to influence learning and teaching (formative assessment), and the recent indications of progress.

Scotland was long used to one single examination body for the certification of general education awards achieved by pupils at the end of secondary school – the Scottish Examination Board (SEB). The certification of vocational awards was the responsibility of the Scottish Vocational Education Council (SCOTVEC) between 1985 and 1997. These bodies had quite different origins, characters and modi operandi. Concomitant with the bringing together of general and vocational certificate arrangements under Higher Still (implemented from 1999 onwards), the two examination bodies were merged into one single authority – the Scottish Qualifications Authority (SQA) – in 1997. Many of the operations of the new SQA derive directly from the practices of SEB and SCOTVEC. Chapter 83 examines the activities of the SQA from an external perspective. Baseline assessment, that is making early judgements of pupils' abilities and skills with a view to how they might be taught in primary school (and, particularly from a political point of view, how that subsequent teaching might be held to account) is the subject of Chapter 84. It is followed by a careful analysis of national testing in Scotland, something brought about under Conservative UK legislation but very differently effected in Scotland compared to England and Wales. At the time of writing the national testing of pupils in primary and secondary schools is not a mandatory requirement in Scotland in the way that it is in England. Schools throughout the country do not conduct tests upon pupils uniformly: teachers choose when to conduct testing and draw from item banks specifically designed for the purpose; their use is therefore 'confirmatory' in character. Chapter 85 provides the detail of how this came about and its present operation (albeit in the climate of a Labour government still wedded to standards and accountability) and sets out the changes about to be brought in under the title 'national assessment'.

In the section concerned with the secondary curriculum (VIII), some of the authors draw on firm evidence to attest to the competence of pupils in their subjects. A book concerned with the education of young people ought, however, to say something about achievements as demonstrated in national certification results and in the evidence from major research surveys. The remaining chapters of Section X deal with these in several ways. First, Chapter 86 gives something of the character of pupils in Scotland's primary and secondary schools. It draws both upon teachers' views of pupils and pupils' views of themselves, concentrating upon their conceptions of schooling. The chapter uses both research evidence and popular images of children and their behaviour.

Chapter 87 describes Scotland's programme of national achievement monitoring, the Scottish Executive's Assessment of Achievement Programme (AAP), whose annual surveys of what pupils know and can do at three key stages of education (P4, P7 and S2) have been conducted by independent researchers since the early 1980s. The findings in the three main surveyed areas, English language, mathematics and science, and the trends emerging from inter-survey comparisons, are analysed (and related to international comparisons in the case of mathematics and science). The chapter which follows (88) reflects critically upon the national achievements found in SQA (and previously SEB and SCOTVEC) results over a number of years. The trends concerning pupils' capabilities, evident in the steadily increasing presentations at Standard Grade (S4) and the various Higher Grade levels (S5, S6 and FE) are explored in detail.

The Centre for Educational Sociology at Edinburgh University has conducted a wide range of surveys relating the achievements of young people to a variety of factors including social class, gender and schooling; some of the rich seam of data concerning Scotland's youngsters is set out in Chapter 89. The section finishes with an examination of the research into school effectiveness and school improvement. The Centre for Quality in Education (QIE) at the University of Strathclyde, amongst other things, carried out the nationally funded Improving School Effectiveness Project (collaborating with staff from the London Institute for Education). Chapter 90 relates findings about pupils from that project, and others, to various measures of how education is conducted in Scottish primary and secondary schools.

SECTION XI CHALLENGES AND RESPONSES: EDUCATION FOR ALL?

Educational systems are challenged by the particular difficulties and needs of varied groups of pupils and different systems respond in different ways. Section XI contains a range of professional perspectives in this regard, allowing the reader to see both how we construe the challenges in Scotland and what teachers do in schools, supported by the work of other professional colleagues (in psychological services, in social work, in community education). The first chapter (91) tracks the changing definitions of special educational needs and disabilities across two decades and examines the current roles of teachers and other agencies in identifying and providing for special needs. Chapter 92 looks at the evolution of thinking on social inclusion and describes and contextualises the actions of teachers currently designated Learning Support teachers. Their predecessors a generation ago would have been termed Remedial Teachers: the changed discourse indicates that educational practice and its rationale is now different and promises to change further. A rather heterogeneous group of youngsters is referred to in 'Education at the Margins' (Chapter 93). Travellers' children (themselves a mixed group) present special challenges to state schools, owing to their irregular patterns of attendance. So too do 'looked after' children and long-term hospitalised young people. Other groups effectively reject state education, notably the growing numbers of home-educated children. The authors of Chapter 93 give consideration to the many issues involved. 'Child Guidance' and the work of educational psychologists has changed significantly in orientation over the years and Chapter 94 analyses the present operations of the psychological services; how educational psychologists relate to teachers and their impact upon the educational system.

Both social work and community education are local authority service provisions quite separate from school education. Social workers do have close links with schools, however, largely through their connections with the guidance system. Where a pupil's difficulties are rooted in problematic family or wider social circumstances, referrals will be made to the local social work department. For some schools, there is necessarily close co-operation between the two professional groups. Chapter 95 describes social work with teachers specifically in mind. Community educators, to some extent because their service constitutes non-statutory provision, operate with a quite different rationale and ethos. On the whole, they try to tailor their work to perceived and expressed community needs. Chapter 96 explains what community education is about and again the details are set out with teachers specifically in mind.

Not all pupils find school satisfactory and Chapter 97 explores the nature and origins of disaffection, including those which might derive from the system itself or how it operates, together with the characteristics of youth culture and anti-school sub-cultures. The final three chapters in Section XI deal with areas where, in Scotland as elsewhere, challenges derive from prejudice and discrimination, again sometimes within the education system itself. One chapter (98) takes up the issue of gender, a second (99) looks at religious prejudice, so-called sectarianism, and the third (100) considers racial discrimination. Each of these areas has been the focus of research, earnest efforts in schools and elsewhere to counter bias, and of course the subject of policy initiatives at government and local level.

SECTION XII SCOTTISH TEACHERS, TEACHER EDUCATION AND PROFESSIONALISM

This section of the book concentrates upon the teaching profession in Scotland; upon Initial Teacher Education (ITE) and subsequent Continuing Professional Development (CPD) and with matters concerned with the competence of the workforce. The first chapter (101) is about the teacher education institutions (TEIs) themselves, formerly all distinct and distinctive colleges of education and now parts of the university sector. The largest, formerly known as Jordanhill College, is now the Faculty of Education of the University of Strathclyde (in Glasgow). The chapters which follow deal with the programmes of professional studies in ITE (Chapter 102) and with the varied and changing ways in which post-initial CPD is carried out. A significant part of the latter has been reshaped by the requirements of the McCrone settlement and Chapter 103 closely scrutinises issues currently of great concern to teachers. The competence of teachers was among the measures of educational accountability made prominent during the Conservative regime and remained on the agenda through the change to the Labour administration in 1997. Competences for teachers (followed by benchmarks for courses) were drawn up for ITE and their detail has become the subject of scrutiny and debate. These and related standards for later stages of a teaching career are examined in Chapter 104. The European dimension has been promoted steadily in the past decade, with a number of Scottish schools developing close working links with Europe through projects, exchanges, curricular inserts and permeating devices. There are important implications for teachers in all of this and these are explored in Chapter 105. Issues of interchangeability (concerning work opportunities as well as qualifications) also increasingly affect teachers. The courses which students, of all kinds, are able to pursue in higher education institutions, including TEIs, have become subject to credit ratings and transferability. Chapter 106 spells out how these now operate in Scotland (SCOTCAT Arrangements). The next four chapters in Section XII are all concerned with research and education, though in different ways. The first (Chapter 107) looks at the relationship between research and practice and highlights some of the studies designed to explore and improve aspects of schooling in Scotland. Chapter 108 describes the Scottish Educational Research Association (SERA) which has been in existence for more than a quarter of a century; Chapter 109 the Educational Journals which are available in Scotland (including the *Scottish Educational Review* (*SER*) which is the centrepiece of scholarly publication for teachers and lecturers); and Chapter 110 the Scottish Council for Research in Education, founded in 1928, and now known as the SCRE Centre, having merged with the University of Glasgow. The next three chapters focus upon professionalism. The teaching unions are described in Chapter 111. The General Teaching Council for Scotland (GTCS), established in 1965, is responsible for entry to the profession: it accredits ITE courses and formally controls assessment during the probationary period (Chapter 112). The last chapter in this section (113) provides a view of Scottish teachers drawing from a wide range of literary, historical and contemporary sources.

SECTION XIII FUTURE

The concluding section offers two perspectives on the challenges facing Scottish education in the future. Chapter 114 steps outside the system and offers an international perspective on Scottish education, questioning whether global forces will lead to increasing similarities between education in Scotland and elsewhere, or to greater determination to remain distinctive. In the last chapter (115), entitled 'The Future of Scottish Education', we review the current situation in the light of the salient changes since 1999, when the first edition of this book was published. We take account of the evidence and analysis that has been presented in the preceding sections of the book, and identify a number of key themes that are likely to remain important in the immediate future. We also reflect on the strengths and limitations of the project as a whole, now sustained across two editions.

REFERENCES, ABBREVIATIONS AND SOME QUALIFICATIONS

The above overview of the chapter contents might be taken to suggest that our conception of the text and what it should contain was easily determined and straightforward. This was not so. There is no self-evidently correct or ideal structure for a book of this scope and scale. Any structure is problematic and the one we have created has probably ensured more coherence in some areas than in others. We hope that it will work well enough for the reader intent upon understanding the range and diversity of education in Scotland. The structure of the second edition is identical to that of the first, save that the chapters concerned with assessment and certification have been combined with those on achievements (to create section X here).

With regard to coherence in another sense, it should be recognised that with so many contributing authors there are some conflicts and a few tensions evident in the text itself; it would be unreasonable to expect complete consistency of view and interpretation from everyone. In some instances the editors do not share the line taken by the author, nor would we expect to do so. Many issues in education are highly contestable and a healthy system requires vigorous debate. While we drafted all 113 specifications (leaving aside this first and the last chapter) we did encourage the writers to develop them by incorporating their own views. That has happened and we believe the text is much the richer as a result.

Given the general propensity for academics to incorporate as many references in support of their writing as possible, we imposed upon our contributing authors the limit of just six key references per chapter. The six so identified by each writer constitute those texts/articles which it is suggested the reader should consult if keen to pursue the area in question and to develop further understanding. Many of the writers (including ourselves in Chapters 4, 7, 10, 81, 83 and 115) felt it necessary to incorporate additional references and these have been built into the text itself. (The disincentive to clutter the writing as a result was that this counted against the text length which could be submitted!) There is one exception to the 'rule of six, maximum' and this relates to Chapter 27, 'The Financing of Educational Provision'. As indicated earlier, the paucity of educational writing in this field makes its contribution particularly welcome and the author has provided an extended list of references.

All educationists share a professional shorthand well known by the profusion of abbreviations and acronyms. We have endeavoured to have these spelled out within each chapter where they are first encountered – for example, the Scottish Executive Education Department (SEED) – but an additional glossary of terms and abbreviations has been supplied at the end of the volume. This lists all of the items found in the text and it is included in addition to the conventional index.

ACKNOWLEDGEMENTS

At the beginning of this chapter we expressed some of the thinking which lay behind the creation of this text. While we have endeavoured to provide a definitive text on Scottish education, we have done so in the explicit recognition of the very considerable contributions by individuals and groups, by researchers, organisations and institutions throughout Scotland, particularly in the last fifty years. Scholarship concerning Scottish education by Scots men and women has increased steadily over recent years. This volume is intended to complement the endeavour, not only through the inclusion of new contributions by seasoned Scottish writers but also by others who are less well known. We are indebted to them all. Sadly, during the early stages of work on the second edition, John Darling of Aberdeen University died. He was a much liked and respected colleague and a good friend. There was no opportunity for him to revise Chapter 3 of the first edition and, with a small number of changes which we made ourselves, it has been included in this volume. We are sure that he would have wished us to do so.

With regard to the editing, from the outset the advice given to us was not to contemplate editing the complete work ourselves but to work with a team. That proved to be valuable and important advice, for the editing turned out to be extremely demanding and time-consuming. Like the first edition, this volume would not have seen the light of day had it not been for the good efforts of those friends and colleagues who shared the editing with diligence, patience and care, in some cases taking material from rough first draft, through several revisions, to the final published version contained in the text. To all we express our sincere personal gratitude.

Many others are due our thanks. Secretaries Delsia Maddocks and May Habbick at Jordanhill coped brilliantly with varied manuscripts, disc formats and e-versions of draft chapters; their fortitude and talents over an extended period are much appreciated. Donald Gray helped assemble the glossary of abbreviations for the first edition and Suzanne Buck extended it for this second edition. Library staff at Jordanhill were immensley helpful in response to a wide range of enquiries about sources and references. We are grateful to The Carnegie Trust who provided financial support in the form of a grant to us for the research involved in the project, and to SEED who made a contribution towards the production costs which have ensured the text's availability in paperback format, amenable to student purchase. And we must thank staff at Edinburgh University Press, in particular Nicola Carr. Her reactions during the project ranged from sheer incredulity when we put our proposal forward for the first edition, to friendship and solid support as we steadily moved to its completion, then, four years on, to the creation of this second edition. Nicola Wood, EUP's copy-editor, worked swiftly and skilfully with us to prepare the final text for production. There are others without whose help the book would not have been produced but formal acknowledgement must stop somewhere. Let us therefore conclude by thanking the many pupils, students, teachers and colleagues who have, over the years, taught us about Scottish education and for whom this book might be seen as an expression of gratitude.

II

Policy and Provision
in Scottish Education

2

Educational Provision: An Overview

Lindsay Paterson

STRUCTURES AND SECTORS

Scottish educational provision is dominated by four large sectors – primary schooling, secondary schooling, further education colleges, and higher education institutions. Almost everyone progresses from primary at about age five to secondary at about age twelve, and leaves secondary between the ages of sixteen and eighteen. Most people then move to a college or a university for some post-school education. Alongside these main areas of activity are diverse other sectors – notably, pre-school education, special education, and community education. Nearly all of special education, over 90% of the primary and secondary sectors, about three quarters of the pre-school sector, and most of community education are governed by thirty-two locally elected education authorities. The remainder of these sectors is provided by private and voluntary organisations, most of which charge fees. Schools associated with particular religious denominations fully joined the public sector in Scotland in the 1920s, and now are governed and funded in almost exactly the same way as non-denominational schools. The Church retains a say in the curriculum and in appointments to senior posts. All the denominational schools in the public secondary sector are Roman Catholic, as are all but two in the public primary sector.

All but two of the forty-five further education colleges are independent incorporated bodies funded by central government via the Scottish Further Education Funding Council, by student fees, and by a variety of private sources (see Chapter 5). These forty-three were removed from the governance of the education authorities in 1993 (but the two small colleges in Orkney and Shetland remained with their education authorities). The higher education institutions are self-governing and subject to the general oversight of the Scottish Higher Education Funding Council, and receive their funds from public grants, student fees, and private sponsorship of research and teaching (see chapter 6). The whole Scottish education system costs about £4.5bn in public expenditure, to which can be added about £600–800m in private expenditure on independent schools and on aspects of higher education – in total about 8% of Scottish Gross Domestic Product.

The main changes in provision in recent decades have concerned post-compulsory education and pre-school education, both having expanded significantly. As far as the broad pattern of provision is concerned, the primary years and the first four years of secondary have not changed nearly so markedly. This contrasts with the 1960s and 1970s when the early years of secondary were transformed by the introduction of comprehensive education, so that selection by measured ability for different types of secondary course was ended in the public sector. Nevertheless, stability of provision has been accompanied by great changes in practice. This chapter is concerned with the statistics of participation in the various sectors of education; it is mostly not concerned with the details of what goes on when students enter. (See Chapters 4 and 5, and Sections V–VIII.)

Statistics quoted are from Scottish Executive and Scottish Office Statistical Bulletins. Guides to further statistical information can be found in the list of references. Throughout this chapter, the term 'public school' is used with the meaning that it conventionally has in Scotland (as in North America), in other words a school managed by public authorities. The other types of provision are referred to as independent or voluntary.

PROVISION AND PARTICIPATION

Pre-school

Pre-school education has expanded steadily over the past decade and a half. In 1986, 40% of four-year-old children had an education authority nursery place, as did one fifth of three-year-olds. In 2000, the proportions were 97% of four-year-olds and 80% of three-year-olds, representing 98,837 places for children aged three and four years, 72,797 provided by education authorities. The provision for four-year-olds was at a uniformly high level throughout the country, but for three-year-olds there were large variations by region. For example, in 2000, only 58% of three-year-olds had education authority places in Falkirk and West Lothian.

Supplementing nursery schools is a variety of day-care arrangements that probably involve some education. In 1997, for example, a total of 58,510 children aged 0–4 were attending formal day-care institutions other than nurseries – such as play-groups and family centres – and there were also 34,983 children aged 0–8 who were looked after for part of the week by registered child-minders. In that same year, nurseries contained 35,162 children, and so non-nursery care was numerically very significant. Not counted here, moreover, is unregistered care, and, indeed, the dividing line between formal and informal care is vague. Around a half of all day-care institutions were paid for in part by parental fund-raising.

The expansion of nursery education has been encouraged by research evidence that it improves children's educational progression later on – for example, from the Head Start programme in the USA. Developing reading skills at this age has apparently been effective in reducing the educational disadvantage suffered by children in socially deprived areas of the cities. Despite these educational reasons for expanding nursery provision, probably the single biggest influence has been the growth in the proportion of mothers who work outside the home, for whom pre-school education is a form of good-quality childcare.

Primary

Changes in the pattern of primary provision have been largely driven by demographic trends. Numbers of primary pupils reached a peak of half a million in the late 1970s, dipped to about 430,000 in the 1980s, rose to nearly half a million again in the mid-1990s, and were back to 432,250 in 2001, 97% of whom were attending public schools. In 2001, there were 2,336 primary schools, 97% of them public; this was about 200 fewer than in 1980, closures having been forced by falling rolls and by shifts of population away from rural areas. There were the equivalent of 23,191 full-time primary teachers (96% of them in the public schools). Public expenditure on primary schools was £2,228 per pupil in 2001.

Some closures were also caused by the effects of parental choice, the legislation inaugurated in 1980 that allowed parents to choose the school to which their child would go. The incidence of these placing requests has steadily risen since then, from 10% of primary one pupils in 1985 to 20% in 2000. A school is in danger of closure if a large proportion of its potential pupils have chosen to go elsewhere. Most of the placing requests are for entry to primary one, but in 2000 about 2% of pupils in primaries two to seven had moved directly into one of these years as a result of a placing request. There is a great deal of regional variation in the level of placing requests. It is highest in the cities and towns where there is a genuine choice of accessible schools. Thus, in 2000, the incidence in primary one was one quarter or more in Angus, Dundee, East Dunbartonshire, East Renfrewshire, Edinburgh, Glasgow, Inverclyde, Perth and Kinross, and Renfrewshire. By contrast, in predominantly rural areas, the rates were low: they were one in ten or fewer in Aberdeenshire, East Lothian, Fife, Highland, Moray, Orkney, and Shetland.

The public schools ranged in size in 2001 from 6% with fewer than twenty pupils to 8% with more than 400. The average size was 185. The small schools are mostly in rural and island areas, and the cost of running them is reflected in the range of average recurrent costs per pupil among the education authorities: for example, in 2001, the expenditure was £4,051 per pupil in Eilean Siar (Western Isles) but only £1,929 in Falkirk. Many of the small schools have to organise their teaching into composite classes (where children from different year groups are taught together): in 2001, 27% of primary classes were composite, affecting 23% of pupils.

Among the education authority primary schools, 15% are associated with the Roman Catholic Church; they educate 18% of primary pupils. There is one primary associated with the Episcopal Church, and one Jewish primary.

Secondary

The size of the secondary sector has been driven by two contradictory trends. The dominant effect has been demographic, as in the primaries; but partly offsetting this has been a sharp rise in the rate of staying on in school beyond age sixteen.

Numbers of pupils in secondary school reached a peak in 1980 at over 400,000, and then fell by over one quarter to under 300,000 by 1990. In 2001, they had recovered again to 334,003 (95% in public schools). In that year, there were 444 secondary schools (87% of them public), with the equivalent of 24,333 full-time teachers (92% in the public schools). About fifty schools closed between 1980 and 2001. The cost of providing the public schools in 2001 was £3,311 per pupil.

As with primaries, one of the reasons for school closures was placing requests. The incidence of placing requests is lower than in primary, partly because more communities have just one secondary school and so have no practicable choice on offer: in 1985, 10% of pupils in the first year of secondary school were there as the result of placing requests, and this had grown to 13% in 2000. A further 1% of pupils in later secondary stages entered these directly as a result of a placing request. The regional pattern was similar to that for primaries.

Statistics on the size of secondary schools have not been published since 1996, when 1% had fewer than 100 pupils and 11% had more than 1,000. On the whole, the smaller schools are in rural areas, although size can also reflect an education authority's policies over several decades. Most notably, Fife decided to have large comprehensive schools in an attempt to avoid the concentration of social classes into particular schools. As a result, the average size of their schools in 2001 was 1,212, far above the national average of 817. The same authority has also had a complementary policy of keeping primary schools small, and so its average roll in that sector was just 201, quite close to the average of 185. Small schools cost more to run. Thus, in 2001, the recurrent cost per pupil of secondary education in Fife was £3,192, one of the lowest. In Shetland, by contrast, with an average roll of only 181, the cost per pupil was £5,651.

The only denominational public schools in the secondary sector are Roman Catholic, educating 17% of pupils. There is one grant-aided secondary school which did not transfer to either the education authority sector or the independent sector along with all the other such schools in 1985.

The main changes in the structure of secondaries have been in the fifth and sixth year, as a result of rising rates of staying on into full-time post-compulsory education, up from 54% in 1985 to 72% in 2000. There has also been a large increase in the proportion staying on for six years, from 25% in 1985 to 51% in 1998. Most of the staying on in full-time education beyond age sixteen is in schools: about 13% of the age group enter full-time courses in Further Education Colleges at this stage, although this is a doubling since the early 1990s. The rate of staying on in school varied regionally. In 1997, it was under two-thirds in Aberdeen, Dundee, East Lothian, Glasgow, Midlothian, Orkney, Shetland and West Lothian, and was over 75% in Argyll and Bute, East Dunbartonshire, East Renfrewshire, Eilean Siar and Stirling.

The immediate cause of rising staying-on rates is improving attainment in the fourth year of secondary school. The Scottish Young People's Survey showed that, in 1991, people who had seven or more Standard Grades at levels 1–3 were almost certain to stay on, whereas two-thirds of people with no Standard Grades at levels 1–3 left. That rising attainment is encouraged, in turn, by rising levels of parental education, well-educated parents being more likely to encourage their children to succeed at school. It is also shaped by the growing gap between boys' and girls' attainment: in 2001, 76% of girls stayed on, but only 68% of boys. The gender gap is most evident among low-attainers: girls' propensity to stay on is less affected by low attainment than is boys'.

Youth unemployment has only a limited effect on staying-on rates: rates rise when unemployment rises, but do not fall back when unemployment falls. More important than these external influences are the positive attractions of the flexible structures of curriculum and examinations in the fifth and sixth years: when people stay on, they do not feel that they are committing themselves irrevocably to two years of schooling, because there are worthwhile awards to be gained in the meantime. The character of the fifth and sixth year is discussed fully elsewhere in this volume, for example in Chapter 89.

Spanning secondary and primary is special education, for children with severe learning difficulties. In 2001, there were 230 such schools, catering for about 9,000 pupils. The size of this sector has remained almost the same since 1980, despite policies of trying to incorporate children with special educational needs into mainstream primary or secondary schools.

Post-school

After leaving school, increasing proportions enter further stages of education. The proportion entering any education after leaving school was 35% in 1980; continuous data compiled on the same basis are not available to the end of the century, but in 2001 the proportion of eighteen-year-olds who were still in education was 57%. There are two broad sectors which the leavers enter. On the one hand is vocational further education, taking place in forty-five further education colleges. The majority of people in FE colleges are not school leavers, however: in 1999, only 23% of students in vocational further education were aged under eighteen. Most students take part time technician courses while they are working. Indeed, 84% of students at FE colleges attend part-time. The total number of students in FE colleges rose from about 150,000 in the middle of the 1980s to around 220,000 between the late 1980s and the mid-1990s, and then to around 430,000 by the end of the century. In 2000, the total recurrent costs (including bursaries for students) of the forty-three FE colleges which are the responsibility of the Scottish Further Education Funding Council was £321m.

The other post-school sector is higher education, which has grown rapidly since the early 1990s. It takes place in both higher education institutions and further education colleges. There are twenty higher education institutions, with (in 2000) 16,255 staff. In 2000, higher education institutions cost £752m in recurrent grants from various public sources and £591m of private funds (including privately funded tuition fees).

In 2000, 50% of people entered any higher education by the time they were aged twenty-one, up from 26% in 1990 and 18% in 1975. The number of students in higher education rose from 109,000 in 1980 to 263,000 in 2000. The proportion of undergraduates who entered part-time courses was 52% in 1980 but 45% in 2000, because full-time numbers rose more rapidly than part-time ones. But part-time postgraduate study has grown in significance: the proportion of postgraduates who entered part-time courses was 19% in 1980 and 41% in 2000. An increasing proportion of undergraduates was aged over twenty-one – 23% in 1980, but 41% in 2000.

Rising rates of entry by school leavers have been influenced by rising levels of attainment in the final years of secondary school. But there are other explanations as well. Young women used to be less likely to apply to higher education (despite having good enough school attainment), but this difference has declined. Thus, in 1980, only 43% of undergraduates were female; in 2000, it was 57%. Although social class differences remain in rates of entry, they too have declined. Thus, whereas in 1980 school leavers whose fathers were in professional occupations were six times more likely to enter higher education than leavers whose fathers were in manual occupations, by 1994 that had narrowed to a ratio of 2:1. Furthermore, young people from minority ethnic groups in Scotland are proportionately more likely to enter higher education than young people who are white.

Rates of entry to higher education by school leavers vary by region. They are highest in the rural areas and in the wealthier areas, and lowest in Glasgow. People are now much less likely than they were even two decades ago to enter their local institution: they travel all over Scotland. But nine out of ten entrants to higher education stay in Scotland. Because Scottish higher education provides 12.5% of higher education places in the UK, while Scotland provides only 9.8% of higher education students, about one in five students at Scottish institutions comes from outside Scotland. In some of the older universities (such as Edinburgh) the proportion from outside is one half.

Scottish higher education differs from that elsewhere in the UK in having a high proportion of students doing higher education courses in further education colleges: the proportion among undergraduates in 1999 was 34% in Scotland, but around 12% in England. Among all students in FE colleges, 17% are on higher education courses. The type of course in FE colleges is quite different from the courses in universities. Whereas 81% of undergraduates in universities take degree courses, 98% of undergraduates in FE colleges do diplomas. Moreover, 58% of undergraduates in FE colleges study part time, compared to just 18% in the universities. FE colleges are not only good at offering part-time courses; they also are better than the universities at attracting working-class students, partly because they mainly serve the communities in which they are based.

Community education is a much more diverse sector, and has no statutory basis. It is therefore vulnerable to contraction whenever budgets are tight (see also Chapter 96). Nevertheless, it has a significant impact. In 1995, it attracted about half a million participants, about 60% of whom were adults. Most community education takes place in school evening classes or in community centres. But there has also been a slow growth in the number of adults attending secondary-school classes during the day along with teenage children. In 1990, 4.5% of students in secondary schools were adults, but in Lothian this was 7.5% and in Glasgow it was 10%. Further education colleges are in direct competititon with schools for this type of student. The Open University in Scotland meets similar needs at a more advanced level: it has grown at much the same rate as the rest of higher education, from 5,994 students in 1980 to 13,775 in 2000. In the early 1990s, about four-fifths of adult participants in general community education were women, but about 58% of students in the Open University were men (see Chapter 80). In both community education and the Open University, people who already had a lot of initial education were more likely to take part than people who had left school at the first opportunity.

POLICIES ON PROVISION AND PARTICIPATION

Each sector has been affected by changes in governance and in policy over the last couple of decades, and this is likely to continue, especially as a consequence of the setting up of the Scottish Parliament in 1999.

Although all political parties favour the expansion of nursery education, there have been deep divisions over how best this is to be done. The Conservative government until 1997 proposed to use a system of vouchers, which parents of children aged four would receive as an entitlement, and which they could then spend in return for a nursery place. Vouchers have long been favoured by the educational right, and this scheme (for the whole of Britain) was believed by some to be a pilot for voucher schemes affecting all education.

The other political parties opposed the vouchers, and the new Labour government moved to abolish them by the session 1998–9. Nevertheless, even some Labour-controlled education authorities until then used the vouchers to expand nursery provision beyond the level it had been at. Since only three-quarters of pre-school places are provided by the education authorities, the non-Conservative majority in Scotland has not shown any sign of insisting on universally public provision. (See Chapter 31 for pre-5 provision.)

Both primary and secondary schools have undergone significant changes in governance. These include general supervision by school boards made up of the elected representatives of parents and teachers (with parents in a majority), devolved school management and the Conservative government provisions for public schools to leave the control of education authorities and become self-governing. The Scottish Parliament repealed the almost unused self-governing legislation in 2000, but the devolution of power to headteachers will continue. The school boards, too, have become widely accepted, and, indeed, became allies of the school professionals in their resistance to certain Conservative government policies in the late 1980s (see also Chapter 19). Devolved management and school boards are likely to make the system less governable than previously. Because they also can be presented as a form of devolution of power, they are consistent with the principle of decentralisation that was one motive behind the setting up of the Scottish Parliament.

Some likely future directions of policy have further significant implications for the structure of secondary education. The inspectorate recommended in 1996 that more setting of pupils by ability be adopted in the first two years of secondary. If that recommendation is widely adopted – and the Scottish Executive has not disagreed with it – then the character of the transition from primary to secondary could change substantially. It is also likely to be proposed that pupils should experience fewer discrete subjects in secondary one and some discrete subjects in primary seven, to smooth the present transition from essentially one teacher of all subjects in P7 to as many as fifteen teachers in S1.

None of these changes would exacerbate the differences among secondary schools. But some commentators believe that the Higher Still reforms at the other end of secondary school could reintroduce the distinction between academic and non-academic schools which comprehensive education was supposed to have ended. The fear is that only a few, highly academic schools would teach the Advanced Higher, and that some schools would not be able to teach beyond the Intermediate levels in any but a few subjects. Creating such divisions is not the intention of the policy, but they could emerge by default, partly driven by the effects of parental choice of school, so that academically well-motivated pupils might tend to be concentrated in a minority of schools.

Beyond school, the expansion of higher education is likely to continue. Given the importance of the FE colleges in providing higher education in Scotland, and given also their capacity to attract working-class and part-time students, they are generally favoured by the majority in the Scottish Parliament as a main route to expansion, in contrast to England. It is already planned, for example, that a new University of the Highlands and Islands will be based on the network of FE colleges in the area. The Scottish consensual support for broadening access was also seen in the Parliament's voting in 2000 to abolish tuition fees for Scottish students in undergraduate higher education courses and to reintroduce grants for Scottish students on low incomes.

The Scottish Office had established a funding council for FE colleges, to entrench their independence from government. The Scottish Higher Education Funding Council has attracted consensual support since it was established, and is widely seen as a model for guiding all post-school institutions under the Parliament. But, because FE remains much closer to the labour market than does higher education, its governance is likely to remain distinct. For example, compared to their reaction to the pre-school voucher scheme, the non-Conservative parties were less hostile to the voucher scheme which the Conservative government introduced for some further education provision (Skillseekers). Vocational education has always had elements of private provision within it, and has always had to respond to market pressures for skills.

The content of further education itself will be changed by the Higher Still proposals. Breaking down the barriers between academic and vocational education at this stage might eventually lead to the abolition of the distinction between further and higher education.

There would then be a continuum of post-school courses, provided in institutions with a variety of styles and ethos. For example, the Parliament's Enterprise and Lifelong Learning Committee recommended in 2002 that everyone be entitled to public funding for attending educational courses up to the equivalent of the second year of a university degree, as a step towards the possible unification of all kinds of education up to that level.

Both further and higher education will contribute to the development of lifelong learning, as is currently favoured by all political parties. Lifelong learning is seen not only as a good in itself, but also as a way in which a new democracy could be underpinned by knowledgeable and critical citizens. To harness community education to that purpose, it is likely that the Scottish Parliament will eventually want to give it a statutory basis. This would guarantee a relatively secure future for it, but at the expense of tighter control by the inspectorate, and probably also closer association with colleges and universities.

REFERENCES

Paterson, L. (2003), *Scottish Education in the Twentieth Century*, Edinburgh: Edinburgh University Press.
Scottish Executive statistics at www.scotland.gov.uk/stats
SFEFC at www.sfefc.ac.uk
SHEFC at www.shefc.ac.uk
Scottish Parliament at www.scottish.parliament.uk

3

Scottish Primary Education: Philosophy and Practice

John Darling

HISTORICAL THEORY

In the middle of the twentieth century, to have completed the Froebel course at a training college was to become one of the elite in what is now called 'early stages' teaching. If the course content had rather tenuous links with the philosophy of Friedrich Froebel, it is nonetheless significant that the name of a mid-European theorist should be used to confer status on a professional qualification. Twentieth-century primary education in Scotland did not fight shy of theory.

Froebel developed his ideas from watching Pestalozzi teaching in his innovative school where much of the learning was experiential, a principle which Pestalozzi acquired from reading Rousseau's *Emile*. Another visitor to Pestalozzi's school was Scotland's Andrew Bell who saw no merit in such progressive methods. Bell's own method was monitorialism: one master instructed pupil monitors who then instructed the rest of the children. At best, learning could only have been superficial and mechanical. But if the system was clearly ineffective, it was cheap. By the time Froebel published his *Pedagogics of the Kindergarten* in 1840, monitorial schools had been established in Scotland for some time. According to an inspector's report (in the Committee of Council on Education Minutes 1841–42), one of the better ones seems to have been in Bon Accord parish, Aberdeen:

> On the day of my visit 287 pupils present; and it must be admitted that arrangements enabling a teacher, with only one adult assistant, to conduct with any amount of success the studies of so many, must be characterised by no ordinary degree of skill . . .
> . . . this system, properly understood and efficiently worked, supplies the only means at present within our reach of rendering the schools for the poor in large towns places where instruction can be efficiently given. I am not insensible to its inherent and necessary defects, or to the greater advantages which might be secured by other but more expensive arrangements.

Monitorialism offered a solution to the economic problem of providing schooling for the labouring classes in Scotland's burgeoning cities. For these children, education was seen as being urgently required to combat the three 'I's – ignorance, irreligion and immorality.

Thirty years later, after considerable pressure from the teachers' union, the Educational Institute of Scotland (EIS), Andrew Bell's money was made available to fund another significant development in Scottish education – the founding at two universities (Edinburgh and St Andrews) of chairs in the 'theory, history and practice of education'. The Bell professors were formally required to include in their lectures the occasional discourse on the merits of monitorialism, but the incumbents seem to have neglected this part of their duties. The foundation of the first university chairs of education speaks volumes for the standing of education in Scotland, and of the school teachers themselves. Again, John Gibson, HMI:

> I have examined 16 parochial schools. The teachers are, generally speaking, highly accomplished men. Eight of them are preachers of the Church of Scotland, five are students of divinity, and the remaining three have gone through a complete course of study at the University of Aberdeen.

The book which set the tone for one important strand in Scotland's educational philosophy was written by an Aberdeen professor of logic. In 1879, Alexander Bain, one of the founding fathers of psychology, published *Education as a Science*. If the religious origins of Scottish schools ensured that combating the three 'I's became a mission to be pursued with zeal, educators themselves seemed to think it prudent to put their faith in the new science of psychology as well as in God. As psychology developed, so did the psychology of education. In people like Godfrey Thomson, Scotland made significant contributions to the study of measurement and the theory and practice of testing; and the importance of these was conveyed to teachers in the course of their training. These preoccupations have often been portrayed as linked to teaching policies which are unenlightened or even oppressive. But in Scotland measurement and testing have often been thought of primarily as tools of diagnostic assessment and aids for pupil guidance. This was perhaps most obvious in the work of William Boyd who taught at Glasgow University from 1907 to 1945 and who pioneered child-guidance clinics. Boyd appeared to see no tension between promoting new techniques of assessment and preaching the ideals of Rousseauesque progressivism. He was a prominent member of the New Education Fellowship, an international organisation formed to promote liberal educational practice. Himself a committed member of the EIS, Boyd encouraged his fellow members to press for and participate in educational research.

The high point of primary education's interest in educational science was its preoccupation in the 1950s and 1960s with the work of Jean Piaget. Seldom read, but endlessly referred to, Piaget's work purported to demonstrate that children went through a stage of 'concrete operations' in which they were unable to think in abstract terms. During this time learning had to be rooted in experience. Not only did the age range identified by Piaget accord with the age of pupils in Scottish primary schools, but the implications to be drawn appeared to match the progressive pedagogical principles in which teachers had already become interested. Primary education had acquired an educational science of its own. The vehicle for transmitting Piaget's teaching was the teachers' training college through which everyone wishing to teach in a primary school had to pass. Reflecting the long-established Scottish interest in educational science, colleges all had psychologists in post. The explication of Piaget became their new calling.

THE MEMORANDUM PHILOSOPHY: SCOTLAND'S EMILE?

The critical policy document, which was built around Piaget, was the Primary Memorandum, published in 1965. Officially called *Primary Education in Scotland*, it was written by a committee consisting of three college staff, eight teachers and eight inspectors. The

Primary Memorandum constitutes a landmark which has from the time of publication dominated the developing primary education scene. It was given a notably positive endorsement by the Secretary of State for Scotland whose foreword (after giving the obligatory recognition to Scotland's 'great tradition in education') argues that:

> we owe it to our successors to keep our educational thinking and practice abreast of the needs of our day and to lay foundations on which they can build. In education as well as in industry, science and the arts, progress depends on willingness to push beyond familiar horizons. (SED, 1965, p. iii)

The thinking of the memorandum has permeated Scottish primary education: its tone still remains a dominant influence, despite some inimical trends in UK politics. Two decades after its publication, a report called *Education 10–14 in Scotland* (Consultative Committee on the Curriculum, 1986) characterised primary education as having been learner-centred ever since the Primary Memorandum. To this day, the primary education experienced by many Scottish children is very much as envisaged in this seminal document.

One attraction of identifying Piaget as the major influence is that this conferred on the committee's thinking the suggestion of principles built upon modern scientific findings; but the truth is that much of the argument sounds more like Rousseau than Piaget. Significantly, the opening chapter of the memorandum is called 'The Child'; and it is argued that taking as a starting point what is known about children will lead to certain pedagogical conclusions. In particular, teachers must be sensitive to the way in which children grow and develop: consequently it is the responsibility of the memorandum to provide an account of this. This is done in a pretty broad way: children are said to develop along similar lines, but at different speeds. The teacher's job is to 'stimulate progress' or to 'supply means of assisting (the pupil's) natural development'. As in Rousseau's *Emile*, it is claimed that 'by satisfying the needs of one stage she (the teacher) provides for development more efficiently than by trying to anticipate or prepare for the next' (SED, 1965, p. 3). And attention is drawn to the fact that:

> there are many attainments and skills which children achieve spontaneously, and many things which they discover for themselves at stages in their development when they are ready to do so. (SED, 1965, p. 3)

It is illuminating to note some specific points of indebtedness to the eighteenth-century French philosopher. In, for example, his discussion in *Emile* Book III (Dent/Everyman edn, trans. B. Foxley) of how to teach science, Rousseau counsels the teacher against trying to transmit scientific facts and theories.

> It is not your business to teach him the various sciences, but to give him a taste for them and methods of learning them when this taste is more mature. (Rousseau, 1762, pp. 134–5)

Exactly the same priorities are spelled out in the memorandum:

> The acquisition of knowledge and skills, once the main aim of education, is no longer as important as it was . . . Much more vital today . . . are the fostering of intellectual curiosity, and the development of the capacity to acquire knowledge independently. (SED, 1965, p. 18)

But for teachers to be successful in fostering enquiry, an appreciation is required of the ways in which children's thinking differs from that of adults. On the importance of avoiding the assumption that children are like adults in their styles of thought, the memorandum is again *Emile* clearly paraphrased.

> Nature would have them children before they are men . . . Childhood has its own ways of seeing, thinking and feeling; nothing is more foolish than to try and substitute our ways . . . (Rousseau, 1762, p. 54)

> She (the teacher) must realise that the child is not an adult in miniature: he does not feel, or act or think like an adult. (SED, 1965, p. 3)

In the memorandum, part, but only part, of this difference is understood in Piagetian terms: where possible, skills and processes should be learned in 'concrete' situations. 'Children should not be expected to achieve symbolic, abstract thinking before they are ready for it' (SED, 1965, p. 13). Again, in stressing the importance of understanding, the Primary Memorandum is following a point insisted upon by Rousseau. In the eighteenth century such an idea was innovative: the fact that in the early twenty-first century it is no longer necessary to argue in favour of understanding as an objective is an indication of how influential its proponents have been. And yet it is not so long since mindless monitorialism was in vogue, with rote learning dominating classroom practice long after the demise of Bell's system. The memorandum insists that children's school work 'should not be for them a mere meaningless manipulation of verbal and other symbols' (SED, 1965, p. 13). Two centuries earlier Rousseau had claimed that this was what learning inevitably became unless the curriculum was based on what was within the child's own experience.

In Rousseau's conceptual framework much is made of the distinction between the artificial/conventional and the natural, indicating that the former category was, if not invariably evil or harmful, at least less desirable: 'natural' was a term of commendation. In the memorandum there are references to 'natural development' and 'natural curiosity'; and also to 'unnatural silence'! Play is said to be the child's 'natural way of learning'; and it is regretted that this approach is given adequate scope only in the early years. This is explained in a section entitled 'The need for freedom', again echoing an eighteenth-century theme. (Arguably, Rousseau's most famous line is 'Man is born free'.)

The child, according to the memorandum, should have 'freedom to experiment with language', since, it is claimed, skills of communication and self-expression may be harmed 'by a too early insistence on conventional correctness' (SED, 1965, p. 13). In Mathematics there should be 'practical activities' instead of 'lengthy and repetitive mechanical computations'. And the reader of the memorandum is told – although the underlying reasoning is far from obvious – that if the curriculum is to be meaningful to the child it will have to be 'integrated': 'the curriculum is not to be thought of as a number of discrete subjects, each requiring a specific allocation of time each week or month' (SED, 1965, p. 37).

In the memorandum Mathematics has replaced 'Arithmetic'; but perhaps more significantly this is dealt with under the broader heading of 'Environmental Studies'. In passages like the one above, the term 'subject' is invested with an overtone of the repressive and the out-of-date. It is recommended that subject-centred curricula give way to methods and curricula based on the needs and interests of the child (SED, 1965, p. 60). The memorandum has sometimes been accused of being vague about what these methods are and how they might be deployed. It does, however, state:

- that whole class, group, and individual methods all have their place;
- that there is evidence that while group methods make demands on teachers, the effort required to make the change pays dividends; and
- that there is no place for seating pupils in formal rows (SED, 1965, pp. 67–8).

Arranging children in rows is often associated with the custom of seating pupils in order of 'merit', a practice which the memorandum specifically condemns. But the document's strictures on testing go beyond this. Tests, it claims, are accorded too much importance, take up too much time and have a deleterious effect on the curriculum. Poetry, art and music should never be examined, and testing is also inappropriate if History, Geography and Science are to proceed by way of discovery and enquiry. A distinction is drawn between testing (which is seen as dubious) and assessment (which is not): assessment is primarily to be conducted through the teacher's day-to-day observation. Such assessment is essential for the teacher's purposes, and the need for diagnosis is one factor which may legitimately require recourse to formal testing (SED, 1965, pp. 48–9).

Much of the memorandum philosophy has come to be accepted to the point where it constitutes a well-established norm. Arguably, it has influenced practice to the point where practitioners now see nothing distinctive in how they teach: it sometimes takes visitors from overseas to register surprise at the absence of the formal traditionalism which many expect to find in Scottish classrooms to remind practitioners that Scottish primary education is indeed child-centred. In the course of their initial teacher education, taken at one of a limited number of training institutions, all primary teachers are socialised into a child-centred approach whether they know it or not. As will be shown later, however, this fundamental philosophy has been subject to qualification in recent years.

THE POLITICS OF PROGRESSIVISM

The Primary Memorandum did not arrive in 1965 as news from nowhere. It has been noted that this kind of thinking had already been in evidence in colleges and universities, and that much of it was anticipated in the writing of Rousseau 200 years earlier. An explanation has to be found, however, for the child-centred approach being officially sanctioned and endorsed at this time, and for this it is necessary to look beyond schooling to consider some relevant social and political factors.

Acclaim for the memorandum philosophy required a particular kind of climate. The 1960s brought with them a sense of impending change on a radical scale. Everyone was to be liberated from repressive conventions and pointless pressures to conform. The insistence on the right to pursue one's individual lifestyle plus the newly available contraceptive pill led to a reaction against puritanical restrictions in a movement towards what was called 'permissiveness', a term which at that point was used for purposes of approbation. In 'Annus Mirabilis' Philip Larkin famously recorded:

Sexual intercourse began
In nineteen sixty-three
(Which was rather late for me) –
Between the end of the Chatterley ban
And the Beatles' first LP

Also in 1963 came the fall of Harold Macmillan, whose slogan 'You've never had it so good' was popularly paraphrased as 'We've never had it so often'. In this context the Conservative Party was beginning to appear woefully out of touch, an impression fatally confirmed by replacing Macmillan with a peer of the realm. Swiftly reduced from the House of Lords to become an elected MP with a Scottish seat, Douglas-Home was asked whether he would be buying a house in his new Perthshire constituency and replied that he owned too many houses already. The Conservatives lost power the following year.

The 'establishment' became a target to be challenged, rejected and mocked. To shock and to scandalise was easy, was fun and, for some, was also profitable. With hindsight, much of this 'radicalism' seems puzzlingly innocuous. Malcolm Muggeridge achieved massive notoriety from some mildly critical observations on the monarchy, remarks which he later claimed were 'sensible' and 'amiable'. And he himself turned censorious when he resigned as rector of Edinburgh University in protest against the new and decadent values of Edinburgh students, their offence being to campaign for the installation of contraceptive dispensers in their union.

Macmillan's legacy was a popular conviction that Britain had a prosperous future. The vaguely egalitarian sentiments of the subsequent Labour government converted this into a belief that some of the nation's apparently plentiful resources should be channelled into sections of society which had not to date received a fair deal. The widely held, if optimistic, belief was that such prioritising in education would unlock the potential not just of countless individuals but of society's future development.

It is not hard to see connections between this social climate and the philosophy being forged in primary education in Scotland. The Primary Memorandum represents a reaction against the old ways. People wanted a better, happier childhood for their offspring, and this included their schooling. The new philosophy appeared to be based on scientific findings about child development; and it took a positive view of the potential of each parent's child. Egalitarianism was also reflected in a major rethinking of a different sector of schooling: secondary schools were to become comprehensive (see Chapter 4). This had an important repercussion for the primary sector since the selectivity exercise involving examinations at the end of the primary years was no longer required. The 'qualifying' examination, like any such examination, dictated the form of the curriculum in the later years. When this straitjacket was removed, a curriculum vacuum was created, and was to be filled by the new primary philosophy.

This, however, is to make change seem easy; in fact there have been significant modifications to the thinking of the 1960s, often prompted by concerns about a struggling economy and rising unemployment. Reaction, though certainly evident in Scotland, has been much more strident south of the border where the Plowden Report (1967), which repeated much of the thinking of the Primary Memorandum, came to acquire demono-logical status in the 1990s.

One factor which helped to bring the new educational thinking under critical scrutiny was the change in atmosphere not in primary schools but in universities. The 1960s was a time of student unrest. Universities were criticised for seeing learning in terms of the expertise and interests of traditional university teachers. There was a demand for a more holistic view of knowledge crediting everyone with insight and understanding. There was a suspicion among British students that continental left-wing theory was not taken adequately into account; nor were Eastern forms of thought. Even rationality itself was viewed as constituting a limiting framework, at least in its most conventional forms. To some professors all this appeared as an appalling challenge, academically, professionally and personally, threatening all that they held dear, including their own positions. And some saw it as the logical extension of the new primary school philosophy with its apparently anti-authoritarian ideas and its rejection of a subject-centred curriculum.

Significant critical volumes appeared in 1969. One was *Perspectives on Plowden* edited by R. S. Peters who held the chair of Philosophy of Education at London University's Institute of Education and who was the most influential educational philosopher in the country. The book offered negative appraisals of some of the key concepts in child-centred thinking – growth, needs and interests. The other major publication in that year was the first of a series of Black Papers published by the Critical Quarterly Society and edited by two English dons, C. B. Cox and A. E. Dyson. This took a much more abrasive and confrontational line. While the first issue was primarily concerned with higher education, the link was already being made with primary education; and in subsequent issues this became a principal focus of concern. The thinking of the Black Papers was so much at odds with mainstream 1960s thinking that it was readily – too readily – ridiculed. What was not then foreseen was that many of its seemingly eccentric ideas would in the 1980s become adopted as policy by a Conservative government.

The Thatcher and Major governments played a role in education which was directive to an extent unimaginable in the period after the war. In England the single most striking development was the imposition of a detailed National Curriculum consisting of ten school subjects. Previously the curriculum had been treated as the preserve of teachers, but under the new arrangements there was said to be a division of spheres of influence: what was to be taught would be laid down, while how it was to be taught would be left to the professional judgement of teachers. In 1991, however, this differentiation seemed to be challenged when the government commissioned a report on English primary teaching from three educationists whose views were already well known. They recommended more whole-class teaching and more subject-based lessons; topic-based enquiry and discovery methods were said to have contributed to underachievement (Alexander et al., 1992). In the eyes of many, the Plowden Report was discredited. In 1992 C. B. Cox wrote in the *Sunday Times* (26 January) that from the very start he had seen it as a 'disaster'. And Rhodes Boyson declared: 'It destroyed the academic opportunities of two, if not three, generations of children.' At the Conservative Party Conference in 1991 John Major intoned: 'The progressive theorists have had their say, and they have had their day.' The *Sunday Times* itself pronounced that the Plowden Report had been 'laid to rest without mourners'.

The extreme, polemical and essentially primitive arguments against progressivism during this period were far from impressive. What was produced by politicians, journalists and academics was less a critique than an assault. If some of this was motivated by a belief that it would gain public support, such judgements seem at best to have been unreliable. In the course of the 1997 general election campaign, John Major declared his enthusiasm for reintroducing selective secondary schooling ('a grammar school in every town'); the Conservative Party was routed by the electorate.

CHANGE AND CONTINUITY

The pattern of the 1997 election results is instructive, with Scotland returning no Conservative Members of Parliament. This suggests a significant difference in the climate of ideas north and south of the border. The political situation throughout the Thatcher and Major regimes was that Scotland continued to return a majority of Labour MPs. There was, therefore, a real sense in which Conservative ideas were consistently rejected; and this had an important bearing on educational policy at the primary school stage. One of the most visible consequences of the disharmony between the government and the social culture of Scotland was the resistance in 1991 to the introduction of standardised testing for all pupils in primary four (eight-year-olds) and primary seven (eleven-year-olds): the Conservative education minister was forced to withdraw this proposal in the face of determined opposition from teachers and parents alike.

In Scotland, the central feature of the 1990s at the curriculum level was the development of the 5–14 programme. This envisaged a curriculum consisting principally of five broad areas, for each of which there was a set of guidelines intended to represent best practice. This programme evolved through a process of consultation, with Conservative ministers tending to exert pressure along relatively traditionalist lines; for example, one education minister was anxious to see history and geography taught as separate subjects. The programme has been implemented gradually by schools, which have characteristically devoted time set aside for in-service work to consider how the recommendations can best be adapted and fleshed out. The complete programme is now in place. In each curriculum area pupils progress through five defined 'levels', although it is recognised that pupils will advance at different rates. Externally devised tests are intended to confirm the teacher's judgement about the stage which the pupil has reached, and are used at whatever point the teacher thinks they are appropriate.

The 5–14 programme obviously extends beyond the primary school, and deliberately so, since it is intended to promote continuity between primary and secondary education. But clearly it also has the potential to ensure continuity within the primary school; there is no longer any possibility of individual teachers devising wholly individual or idiosyncratic curricula. Unlike the English National Curriculum, the Scottish programme does not have the force of law: for this to happen would require major change, since the statutory powers of the First Minister for Scotland are confined to the issuing of 'guidance' on the curriculum. In practical terms, however, observance of the guidelines is mandatory: they constitute an important part of the framework which the inspectorate uses to judge the work of a school, and no school can today afford to risk an adverse judgement.

The development of national guidelines has not been accompanied by a return to traditional teaching methods. The inspectorate's recommendation is that there should be variety in teaching methods, with teachers considering which method is most appropriate to each particular piece of learning. Echoing the Memorandum, the inspectorate publication, *5–14: A Practical Guide* (1994), states: 'Class, group and individual methods all have their place in promoting effective learning and teaching.' Activity methods and enquiry methods are seen as suitable. In the *Guide*, the inspectorate continues to employ the concept of 'child-centred learning', a phrase which, incidentally, never appears in the Primary Memorandum. The revision of *The Structure and Balance of the Curriculum* in 2000 continues to urge teachers to use flexible groupings to teach; 'using a variety of approaches' is elevated to being one of 'four key factors . . . widely accepted as the basis of good practice . . .' (LTS, 2000, p. 45).

The main change which has taken place in the practice of primary education has been one of curriculum structuring. While this is inevitably designed centrally, there remains scope for decision-making at the level of the school and the individual teacher. It seems reasonable to view this as child-centred education rendered systematic. The philosophy of Scottish primary education, as outlined in the Primary Memorandum, seems not to have been rejected, but continues to be seen as generally acceptable to both teachers and parents; and there is also continued recognition of the value of the Memorandum methods. It is recognised that different children develop at different speeds. And because there has been no adoption of a ten-subject curriculum, Scotland has been able to retain a relatively fluid and flexible curriculum, the interpretation and implementation of which depend heavily on the professional judgement of teachers, either individually or collectively.

If this assessment is correct, it has to be asked why the Scots have largely abstained from the disparagement of educational progressivism and the primary teaching profession which adopted it, which has characterised discussions of child-centred primary education in England. The answer seems to be that in Scotland there is no widespread tension between parents and teachers because in Scottish primary schools, however child-centred, teachers continue to be very much as parents expect them to be. Primary teachers in Scotland have traditionally enjoyed a significant measure of respect, and not without reason. Reflecting the importance attached to education in Scotland, these teachers have themselves been well educated people. From as early as 1926 all male primary teachers were required to hold university degrees, and Scotland's teaching force became all-graduate in advance of teachers in England. From 1966 onwards, with the advent of the General Teaching Council for Scotland, it became impossible to teach without a professional qualification.

It can further be argued that Scottish teachers, perhaps like Scots generally, are rather conservative: deviant thinkers find other occupations to pursue. This is not to say that there is in the profession a hostility to new ideas or an unwillingness to change; but innovations are adopted cautiously and judiciously (see Chapter 10). Child-centred education had to be tried and tested. In England this philosophy was occasionally given a libertarian inter-pretation; and this produced some outlandish school regimes which brought the new approach into disrepute. It is unsurprising that Scotland's primary teachers generated no such fiascos. It is true that the Primary Memorandum modified understanding of educational aims: pupils were to be independent learners, flexible thinkers and well-rounded people. But at the core remained the business of learning; and the child-centred approach was valued as an intelligent and efficient means to this end. In short, child-centred education has tended to be relatively well received in Scotland because it has been practised in a level-headed form. And teachers remained where they had always been – firmly in charge. The relatively high standing of teachers combined with a social culture which is supportive of trade unionism, brought about a powerful profession. One outcome of this is the agreement on class sizes forced through by the profession: no primary class can have more than thirty-three pupils. With such numbers not only are group methods possible, but order tends to prevail.

While the abandoning of classroom authority would be anathema to parents as well as to teachers, at least discipline is now exercised along more humane lines than previously. The eventual abolition of corporal punishment, however, is an achievement for which no-one in Scottish education can be given the credit. Pusillanimously, the educational progressives who wrote the Primary Memorandum refrained from pronouncing on what they described as 'a controversial issue', and contented themselves with recommending that the use of the belt should be reviewed by the profession. Children continued to be belted frequently throughout the 1960s and 1970s. In an enquiry conducted by the Scottish Council for Research in Education (*Pupils' Attitudes to School Rules and Punishments*, 1977) 84% of boys at secondary school reported that they had been belted in primary school, with 34 per cent saying they had been belted 'quite often'. For the girls the corresponding figures were 57% and 13%. In the spring term of 1972 the belt was used 4,000 times in Edinburgh's primary schools. The ready application of the belt was constantly glossed over by the profession, with teachers' unions falsely claiming that corporal punishment was used only as 'a last resort'. And if the frequency of belting was seldom reported, what was never remarked on was how hard children were struck. If an errant dog had been dealt such blows, the perpetrator could have been arrested.

Demand for change was confined to a minority amongst both teachers and parents. In the event, abolition was brought about from outside. Two Scottish mothers insisted that their education authority should guarantee that their children would not receive corporal punishment. When their request was refused, a complaint was lodged with the European Commission on Human Rights. In 1982 the European Court ruled that parental objections to corporal punishment had to be respected. Some Scottish authorities began to phase it out, and the House of Commons finally voted for abolition in 1986.

The profession's dragging of heels on this issue shows the conservatism of Scottish education at its worst. But the practice of corporal punishment alongside progressive teaching methods for the best part of two decades does seem to confirm the view that child-centred education was implemented in a way that allowed considerable continuity in the nature of primary schooling: children were to learn and teachers were to remain in authority. It seems likely that its adoption of a non-radical interpretation of child-centred education protected Scottish primary education from the kind of anti-progressive backlash experienced in England. Developments since the late 1980s designed to ensure that the child-centred approach is well structured and managed suggest that primary education will continue in this vein for the foreseeable future.

REFERENCES

Alexander, R., Rose, J. and Woodhead, C. (1992) *Curriculum Organisation and Classroom Practice in Primary Schools: A Discussion Paper*, London: DES.

LTS (2000) *The Structure and Balance of the Curriculum: 5–14 National Guidelines*, Edinburgh: Scottish Executive.

McEnroe, F. J. (1983) Freudianism, bureaucracy and Scottish primary education, in W. M. Humes and H. M. Paterson (eds), *Scottish Culture and Scottish Education 1800–1980*, Edinburgh: John Donald, pp. 244–66.

Paterson L. (1996) Liberation or control: what are the Scottish education traditions of the twentieth century?, in T. Devine and R. Finlay (eds) *Scotland in the Twentieth Century*, Edinburgh: Edinburgh University Press, pp. 230–49.

SED (1965) *Primary Education in Scotland*, Edinburgh: HMSO.

SOED (1994) *5–14: A Practical Guide*, Edinburgh: HMSO.

4

Scottish Secondary Education: Philosophy and Practice

Tom Bryce and Walter Humes

PHILOSOPHY AND HISTORY: 'COMPREHENSIVE' EDUCATION?

Some 95% of Scottish pupils receive their secondary education in all-through comprehensive schools catering for the age-range 12–18. This uniformity of provision can be interpreted in several ways. It can be seen as an expression of social unity enabling the vast majority of youngsters to share a broadly similar education prior to entering the adult world in which they will pursue different personal and occupational pathways. It can also be regarded as a manifestation of the democratic will, endorsed at successive elections (pre- and post-devolution) in Scotland and surviving even the attacks of the Thatcher years. And it can be viewed as a statement of belief in equality of opportunity whereby all secondary pupils, regardless of class, gender or ethnic background, have a chance to develop knowledge and skills, and experience a sense of achievement.

These three principles – social unity, democracy and equality – are sometimes linked to that rather amorphous idea of the Scottish tradition in education (see Chapter 10) which serves an important function in social and political consciousness. Scotland's national identity is defined partly in terms of communal solidarity, a belief in democratic processes and a commitment to social justice. There is, of course, an element of myth in this self-perception but, at the levels at which invocation of the Scottish tradition usually operates – political debate and journalistic rhetoric – strict adherence to reality, past or present, is not necessary. As McPherson and Raab note (in *Governing Education*, Edinburgh: Edinburgh University Press, 1988, p. 407) 'myth is simultaneously expressive and explanatory. It is about hearts and minds. It asserts identity, celebrates values, and explains the world through them.' The story (or myth) that Scots tell themselves about the principles underlying secondary education is not to be dismissed as fiction. Rather it is to be understood as one reading – a partial reading – of how the present system has evolved. Partial readings also manifest themselves in operational definitions of what comprehensive schooling means. For some it means non-selection on the basis of ability; for others it relates principally to neighbourhood schooling, and for others again it is most concerned with a common curriculum. Depending on which of these operational definitions is highlighted one will have a different conception of what a comprehensive school is or should be. A particular problem with the internal coherence of the comprehensive philosophy relates to the justification in terms of social unity. Generally, social unity applies in relation to class, gender and ethnic background but in Scotland it does not apply to religion where the principle of divided secondary education has been accepted and endorsed in law since 1918. In West Central Scotland in particular there is widespread provision for children to attend separate Catholic primary and secondary schools. These exist alongside non-denominational schools. Other chapters in this volume provide detail of this significant aspect of Scottish education (see Chapters 25 and 99 in particular).

A brief excursion into the recent history of Scottish secondary education will serve to indicate some of the other elements in the 'comprehensive' story that are often forgotten. It was not until 1936 that the right of all pupils to receive secondary education was officially recognised by the Scottish Education Department. Prior to that, various forms of post-elementary education were available up to the statutory leaving age of fourteen (later raised to fifteen and then sixteen) but it was believed that only a minority of pupils could benefit from advanced schooling. George Macdonald, secretary of the SED from 1922 to 1928, stated confidently that:

> the school population falls into two parts – the majority of distinctly limited intelligence, and an extremely able minority drawn from all ranks and classes who are capable of responding to a much more severe call. The type [of education] that is best for one is not necessarily the best for the other, and attempts to establish equivalence may result in harm to both' (quoted in Paterson, H. M. 'Incubus and ideology: the development of secondary schooling in Scotland, 1900–1939, in W. M. Humes and H. M. Paterson (eds) *Scottish Culture and Scottish Education, 1800–1980*, Edinburgh: John Donald, 1983, pp. 208–9)

Macdonald's statement that the able minority is 'drawn from all ranks and classes' can be seen as an attempt to counteract the criticism that SED policy at that time was class-based and elitist. Ability, not social origin, was to be the determining factor, thus enabling that part of the Scottish tradition which emphasises equality of opportunity to be maintained – at least at the level of political discourse. In this, educational administrators were aided by the work of psychologists who developed mental tests which, they claimed, provided reliable measurements of general intelligence of a kind that had predictive value in relation to pupil capability and achievement. Scotland, through the work of Sir Godfrey Thomson and others, was at the forefront of the mental testing movement. Policy makers eagerly embraced the claims of the psychometrists, seeing in them a ready justification for limited (or, later, divided) provision of secondary education. Sir Godfrey Thomson himself was disarmingly frank in his view of schooling:

> [It] acts as a sieve, or a succession of sieves, sorting out pupils into different kinds. In its crude form this idea presents the picture of a ladder of education, up which a competing crowd start, the weaklings to be elbowed off as they endeavour to climb . . . This picture is somewhat repellent . . . Since, however, people clearly differ in their qualities and abilities, it is certain that a period of education will always be a period of sorting. (quoted in Paterson, op. cit., p. 212).

Arguments of this kind continued to operate in the period after the Second World War when the junior/senior secondary system became formalised. Towards the end of their primary schooling, Scottish children were assessed by means of the so-called 'qualifying' examination which was used to determine the type of secondary school to which they would be sent. Junior secondary schools provided three-year courses, largely of a non-academic kind, for pupils who would cease their formal education at fifteen. Senior secondary schools provided five-year courses of academic education leading to Scottish Leaving Certificate examinations (the entry route to higher education). In the 1950s some 35% of the secondary school population in Scotland gained admission to senior secondary schools. In England during the same period only 20% of pupils gained places at grammar schools (the equivalent of Scottish senior secondary schools). Thus Scotland could claim to be relatively democratic in its provision. Furthermore, in small towns and rural communities, where numbers could not justify the creation of separate schools, 'omnibus' schools catered for the full ability range but with strictly demarcated courses for those who 'passed' and 'failed' the qualifying examination.

Politicians and administrators claimed that junior and senior secondary schools were accorded parity of esteem: they were simply catering for different needs. This was never a convincing argument. Senior secondaries always enjoyed much better provision in terms of buildings, equipment and teaching staff. Other arguments against selection began to emerge. Research evidence cast doubt on the fairness and reliability of the qualifying examination and its English equivalent (the 11–plus). Sociological research concluded that there was indeed a strong social class factor in the allocation of pupils to different types of secondary schooling: working-class pupils were disadvantaged in the process of selection. The whole notion of a limited pool of ability was disputed. Instead of early labelling, it was argued, a system which offered opportunity to as many young people as possible would reap benefits not only in terms of individual achievement but also in terms of wider social utility.

The case for fully comprehensive secondary education, admitting all pupils to the same school on a non-selective basis, was made with increasing force. As early as 1947 the Scottish Advisory Council on Education had recommended a comprehensive system together with a common curriculum core and a common examination. This recommendation was ignored by the SED but in the more egalitarian climate following the Second World War it was only a matter of time before the case was won. The process was not painless, however. It is often said that the prior existence of a significant number of omnibus schools north of the border made comprehensivisation much easier than in England, but here too there were bitter arguments about the alleged destruction of schools with fine academic traditions, as John Watt has shown (PhD thesis, University of Glasgow, 1992). And even after the formal decision was taken in 1965 to implement a fully comprehensive system (by which time one-fifth of secondary schools were already comprehensive, admittedly with streamed classes on entry, according to Gray, McPherson and Raffe, 1983) there was much debate about what precisely this should mean and many traditional practices persisted. The development of comprehensive education within secondary schools since then has been rather uneven, certainly during the years of the Conservative government (1979–97) where there were instances of policy change consistent with the concept of social unity (e.g. 'mainstreaming') but rather more where policy change was designed to counter it (e.g. parental choice). To an extent what pupils encounter in secondary schools varies with the relative affluence or poverty of the neighbourhood setting and in the conurbations of the Central Belt there is probably more variation amongst schools than elsewhere in the country. The parental choice legislation of the 1980s served to manipulate the intake of individual schools, such are the powerful perceptions of the curricula on offer and of the behavioural contagion of the pupils in particular areas. These perceptions have impacted upon the philosophy and practice of secondary education.

THE EFFECTS OF PARENTAL CHOICE

The Education (Scotland) Act of 1981 giving parents choice of school, subject to availability of places, has resulted in a substantial minority of pupils (around 13% on average at present) attending schools other than their local secondary, that is schools perceived to be desirable, the so-called 'magnet' schools. Inevitably this has altered the range of abilities of pupils attending particular schools and it is sometimes said that schools in certain communities have their tops 'creamed off' as a result. Coupled with legislation concerning standards and accountability, Scotland has had to contend with league tables of its secondary schools, especially those ranked according to academic results – for example, numbers of Standard Grade Credit awards gained by S4 candidates; numbers of Higher Grade C+ passes in S5 – and of course league table positions bolster public perceptions. (Unlike England and Wales, Scottish primary school national test results cannot be assembled for this purpose.) There is widespread belief in the teaching profession that league tables substantially reflect catchment intake rather than school output, and this is especially detrimental in circumstances where home support for scholastic effort by pupils is lacking. At the same time, league tables mask the determined and often successful efforts which schools now take to counter difficulties – supported study classes, study skill courses, tutoring arrangements during senior school examination preparation. It is also important to take account of the growing body of evidence deriving from school effectiveness and school improvement studies (see Chapter 90) that, even in disadvantaged areas, the efforts of teachers can make a difference.

Following the arrival of the Labour government in 1997 and the antipathy felt by the Scottish Education Minister towards league tables of raw results, schools are currently issued with 'added-value' measures (i.e. figures are provided to show what each subject department adds by way of value to pupil achievements as they move from Standard to Higher Grade, together with between-subject differences within schools and subject differences between schools across the country – an individual school is compared with similarly achieving schools). The hard facts are, however, that it is now no longer the case that Scottish secondary schools exclusively serve their local communities; the 'magnets' have become more attractive, while the so-called 'sink' schools have had to fight to stay open, the parental choice policy having coincided with the declining birth rate and falling school rolls. The revised ways of publishing academic results have done little to reverse this trend. Indeed a significant dimension to primary-secondary liaison in some urban schools has involved secondary principal teachers unashamedly touting for business during visits to their associated ('feeder') primaries.

It was noted earlier that the principle of social unity in comprehensive education was somewhat compromised by the denominational issue. One interesting consequence of parental choice legislation has been the willingness of some parents to put their perception of educational quality above denominational allegiance. For example, a few non-Catholic parents have been prepared to take legal action against local authorities in an attempt to secure places for their children at local Catholic schools perceived to be offering a high standard of education. As yet, these are isolated cases but they may prefigure a more general trend in which the religious question will cease to exercise the potency it has had in the past.

In the City of Glasgow, one reform of secondary provision has taken place which runs counter to the idea of the traditional comprehensive school. It was intended to effect nine school closures and to rationalise the remainder, so saving on an over-supply position of

40%. The reform plan developed the notion of specialisms for particular schools (dance, sport, international, etc.) and argued for more relevant and flexible curricula. Unashamedly, it ran counter to the concept of the neighbourhood school. However, in 2002, the First Minister restated Scottish government commitment to the comprehensive principle, signalling a difference from the encouragement of specialist schools in England.

From a different perspective, the 1981 Education (Scotland) Act made many secondary schools more comprehensive in pupil character by giving parents whose children would otherwise attend special schools the opportunity to have them taught in mainstream schools. Not only do many comprehensives now take pupils who were formerly educated outwith the mainstream, some have adapted their buildings (e.g. physical access for wheelchair pupils) or their facilities (e.g. specialised equipment for pupils with visual or hearing impairments). Some have completely integrated local special school provision; others have formed particular links with retained special schools, ensuring two-way benefits to pupils and the good use of specialist expertise. The actual pattern of provision varies throughout the country. (See Chapters 91 and 92 for aspects of learning support and specialised provision available in many schools.) Recent (UK) legislation has now come into play which requires schools, colleges and universities to be much more anticipatory of the needs of students with disabilities. The Special Educational Needs and Disability Act 2001 became part 4 of the Disability Discrimination Act (1995) and was implemented from 1 September 2002 (www.legislation.hmso.gov.uk/acts/acts2001.htm). Thus disabled students cannot be treated 'less favourably' and 'reasonable adjustments' must now be made to teaching to ensure that they are at no 'substantial disadvantage'. (Additional auxiliary aids and services must be in place by September 2003 and adjustments to the physical environment by September 2005.)

THE SUBJECT-CENTREDNESS OF THE SECONDARY CURRICULUM

It may be an international cliché to say that 'primary teachers teach children and secondary teachers teach subjects' but it is certainly true of Scotland where all-through (six-year) comprehensive secondary schools are marked by a subject-centredness of long-standing (and indeed some conservatism). Most of the subjects pre-date comprehensivisation and they were the hallmarks of the senior, but not the junior, secondary schools which preceded them. If the comprehensive ideal in Scotland is characterised by social unity, by equality of access and opportunity and one asks: Access to what?, then one would still have to say to an essentially academic diet driven by subject departments. Even the recent and largely successful moves to give more vocational emphasis to the upper secondary school have been, on the whole, delivered departmentally. Subjects seem to need departments and the working of departments preserves the status quo, resisting that which does not fit. In Scotland's secondary schools it is very evident that the curricular influences are top-down; what goes on in S1 is determined more by what goes on in S5 than by what goes on in P7. When the Munn Report addressed the S3–S4 curriculum in the 1970s, the effect was to rationalise and support the existence of subjects. So novel possibilities such as conceptualising the secondary curriculum in different ways, perhaps through issues or school-wide topics, or introducing new subject matter drawn from the social sciences, were not agreed to in Munn and the secondary curriculum has become justified in terms of, and dominated by, its (compulsory) core of traditional subjects. One of the main criticisms of schools by the rebellious R. F. Mackenzie was that 'conventional education . . . lacked coherence in being too subject-centred and had no rationale that linked it in a grand design that would fire the imagination . . . and free children from the rigidity of a curriculum dominated by the need for exams' (Murphy, P. A. 1998, *The Life of R. F. Mackenzie: A Prophet Without Honour*, Edinburgh: John Donald, pp. 158–9). While Mackenzie would have rejoiced in devolution, he would surely have been disappointed to see so little change to the curriculum of secondary schools.

The traditional core to the secondary curriculum has meant that book-knowledge has tended to be valued at the expense of much else, with the consequence that what is expected for less able pupils working at the Foundation levels of Standard Grade is less demanding but broadly similar in nature (at worst being criticised as merely 'watered-down academic knowledge'). Across the ability range, the innovations of Standard Grade in the 1980s to broaden what should be learned beyond 'knowledge and understanding' were fairly hard fought battles. Practical abilities, investigative skills, problem-solving, oral abilities and so forth got into the secondary curriculum, within subjects, but the strain they create for assessment and certification means they remain somewhat curtailed, indeed are under pressure to be reduced (see Chapter 81 on Assessment). While Higher Still has brought more vocational elements into the S5–S6 cuuriculum, and with them a wider range of capabilities to be developed, much of the curriculum remains conventional. Given recent challenges to educational thinking to view human potential as multi-dimensional, say from Howard Gardner's 'multiple intelligences' or from Daniel Goleman's 'emotional intelligence', one would have to admit to resistance in Scotland; Scottish educators remain fairly one-dimensional in their outlook (but are probably no different from their English or European counterparts). The emphasis in Scottish secondary education is and always has been upon subject-ability.

EVIDENCE ON THE SUCCESS OF SUBJECTS

Evidence on the success of this orientation is mixed. In 1996, Benn and Chitty's survey of UK schools led them to conclude that Scotland's comprehensives stood out from those in all other areas of the UK. On several indicators, including quality of academic results, staying-on rates and the achievement of vocational qualifications, Scotland was ahead (Benn and Chitty, 1996). This, they argued, was despite Conservative government policies intended to undermine the comprehensive system in Scotland as elsewhere. England may, however, be a poor comparator with which to assess the achievements of Scottish secondary school pupils. Successive reports of the Organisation for Economic Co-operation and Development (OECD) suggest that, on a number of criteria, Scotland compares badly with other developed industrial countries. International studics are notoriously difficult because it is not always possible to obtain data that can be compared directly. Nevertheless, the pattern over a five-year period consistently suggests that the traditional view that Scottish education is among the best in the world is now questionable. Part of the explanation offered by the OECD is under-investment but, post-devolution, this point has less validity.

Clearly these judgements about relative success involve many other factors than the structure of the curriculum. What is worth noting, however, is that the curriculum and assessment reforms in Scotland over more than two decades have not challenged subject-centredness in any fundamental way. Even the 5–14 programme, deliberately designed to bring the primary and secondary sectors together, adopted subjects as the basic curriculum unit. The terms used for the curricular areas were certainly primary-friendly (Expressive

Arts, Environmental Studies, etc.) but their actual content deliberately introduced the detail of secondary subject matter to primary schools.

The Scottish Office Report on *Standards and Quality in Scottish Schools 1995–98* (SOEID, 1999) summarises the strengths and weaknesses detected during that period through the inspections of 300 primary and 130 secondary schools by Her Majesty's Inspectorate (HMI). Breadth of the curriculum is a strength firmly identified in both sectors (and, appropriately, in accord with the first word in the 5–14 curriculum mantra: 'breadth, balance, continuity, coherence and progression'). Systematic self-evaluation was noted as 'taking root in schools' in both sectors. There were however weaknesses, notably that pupils were found to be underchallenged in many schools, 'a feature that was particularly evident at S1/S2' (p. ii). This point repeated a similar finding observed in the previous three-yearly report published in 1996. Later chapters in this volume set out the relatively disappointing pupil achievement data for S1–S2 revealed in a succession of national surveys in English language, in Mathematics and in Science (see Chapter 87). These results accord with the HMI findings and serve to underline the point that Scottish schools do have difficulties at these particular stages. Chapter 81 notes the determined response by SOEID in the case of mathematics teaching. The more general point is that subject specialisation (the main plank of the much vaunted 'breadth') in secondary schools fails to connect well with pupils and their demonstrated achievements (as shown in Assessment of Achievement Programme surveys) at P7.

It is tempting to deduce that the identity of subjects with departments, and therefore with teachers who work very much independently of teachers in other subjects, is a big part of the problem. Subjects occupy the high ground in secondary education; subject departments are the citadels of power; their structured independence is a serious obstacle in the way of 'continuity, coherence and progression'.

SOEID (1999) records other strengths of secondaries: the good standards in S3–S6 (e.g. the 4 per cent rise in Standard Grade Credit results over the period 1995–8); the steady picture at Higher Grade (with 20% of pupils gaining three or more at A – C); learning and teaching at the upper stages (in S5 and S6 described as 'good or very good' in 75% of schools); the positive ethos of schools; their resources; their leadership; the operations of school development planning and the commitment to promoting an ethos of achievement. HMI have issued separate reports on almost all of the subjects of the secondary curriculum, in each case drawing upon inspection evidence obtained across lengthy periods (in some cases over ten years). These appear in the series *Effective Learning and Teaching in Scottish Secondary Schools* and are worthy of close reading: publication dates are *Modern Languages* 1990; *History, Modern Studies, English,* all 1992; *Mathematics, Computing,* both in 1993; *Sciences, Religious Education,* both in 1994; *Geography* in 1995; *Home Economics* and *Guidance,* both in 1996; *Business Education and Economics* in 1997; *Art and Design, Physical Education,* and *Music* in 1998. In all of these, the dedication and commitment of teachers to their subjects is underlined.

THE QUALITY OF LEARNING

The five terms in the 5–14 curriculum mantra were of course coined to stress the desirably wide range of ideas and skills which pupils should learn as they progress through school. It seems a pity that other equally important terms were not added to 'the five', notably depth and choice. The depth or quality of one's learning, its meaningfulness and significance to the individual, is of vital consequence. As a principle for reflection upon the effectiveness of schooling, 'depth or quality of learning' surely deserves centre stage. Pupils' testimonies as well as research cast some doubts on the true significance of the expanding success rates in secondary certificate numbers at S4–S6. For example, the relative popularity of the three science subjects at S5 stands in contrast to the findings from research on adults' grasp of basic science concepts and processes, as revealed in all the 'public understanding of science' literature (see Bryce, T. G. K., 'Towards the Achievement of Scientific Capability', *Scottish Educational Review*, 28.2, 1996, pp. 90–9). In their everyday lives a few years away from school, people show a less than impressive grasp of much of their very specialised learning from the subjects they studied at school. Moreover, anecdotal evidence would suggest that very many pupils indulge in rote learning at the certificate stages, and get away with it. On this, however, Scotland is probably no different from any other country.

In this context the SCCC document *Teaching for Effective Learning* (SCCC, 1996) may be regarded as unusual. Designed to encourage critical reflection by teachers on their teaching strategies, this discussion paper outlined what is known about how people learn and how effective teachers operate. The achievement of meaningful learning where young people are able to reason confidently and use skills and knowledge in real settings are desired targets for education, which seem to sit uneasily with the plethora of certificates which mark the end of secondary school. The SCCC document could be said to have challenged the celebrated confidence traditionally held for the subject-dominated secondary curriculum. It asked teachers to address fundamental questions about their approaches to teaching. Encouraging teachers to reflect on such matters as part of the process of professional self-development involves shifting the focus from concerns about curriculum content to questions of pupil engagement and motivation, and pedagogical style.

A more recent document by SCCC's successor body, Learning and Teaching Scotland (LTS) also serves to challenge traditional assumptions. *Creativity in Education* (LTS, 2001) argues for a more open, experimental and risk-taking approach to learning, and links such an approach to personal development, economic growth and active citizenship. However, when set against the strong degree of intellectual and psychological attachment which most secondary teachers have to their subject, the recommendations of both *Teaching for Effective Learning* and *Creativity in Education* seem well-intentioned but weak. The capacity of the teaching force to resist cross-curricular approaches to learning should not be underestimated. They are likely to have the support not only of the Educational Institute of Scotland (EIS) but also of the General Teaching Council (GTC), whose history is in part a story of careful gatekeeping to ensure that entry to the ranks of secondary teaching is closely linked to formal qualifications in the subject(s) to be taught. This is still regarded as more important than any generic skill in teaching or understanding of the processes of learning.

Strong political will is required if this mind-set is to be shifted. There are a few signs of forces at work which may promote change in the medium term, if not immediately: the emphasis on cross-curricular 'core skills' in Higher Still; concerns about the negative effects of departmentalism in relation to the S1 and S2 stages of the 5–14 programme; managerial perceptions that excessive subject-mindedness on the part of teachers can be a barrier to change; the possible effects of the revised promotion structure for teachers brought about by the McCrone settlement.

MIXED-ABILITY TEACHING IN S1 AND S2

Any discussion of teaching for effective learning or of the problems in S1 and S2 is bound to raise the question of how teachers organise their pupils. For several decades the prevailing pattern has been for mixed-ability classes to be formed from the intakes from primary school. In official reports, encouragement has been given to teachers to vary their methods and grouping arrangements to suit their particular purposes (therefore sometimes exploiting 'whole class teaching', sometimes using group work, sometimes individualised schemes of instruction). A detailed examination of this matter is given in Chapter 46. It is useful at this juncture to note that secondary subjects vary somewhat in their preferences for mixed ability teaching. It has been common, for example, to find English and Science departments embracing it positively (using group and paired teaching methods not very different from those which most pupils will be comfortable with from their time in primary school) while the Mathematics departments in the same schools are more inclined to set pupils early. The assessment and reporting procedures developed for the 5–14 programme have had a significant impact, with P7 achievement grades accompanying pupils as they move into secondary school. Thus having detailed records of who has reached level D, who is only at C, etc. has heightened the debate at S1 as to how pupils should be grouped for teaching purposes. At national level, the Scottish Office took a forthright stance on the matter in *Achievement for All: A report on Selection within Schools by HM Inspectors of Schools* (SOEID, 1996). Its recommendations favoured much greater use of attainment groups and setting as the means of organising pupils; 'direct teaching' was encouraged and said to be more feasible when pupils are set by ability (within subjects). The report was published as a direct follow-on to *Standards and Quality in Scottish Schools 1992–1995* (SOEID, 1996) and set out the official reaction to the disappointments with S1–S2 performance. What is rather surprising is that the 'critical review of the literature pertaining to the ability grouping of classes and within classes' (Harlen, W., and Malcolm, H. (1997), *Setting and Streaming: A Research Review*, Edinburgh: Scottish Council for Research in Education) which the Scottish Office commissioned from the Scottish Council for Research in Education (SCRE) to inform the preparation of *Achievement for All* was not referred to in that publication. Harlen and Malcolm's summary of the somewhat conflicting international research, was that there is no consistent evidence in support of setting. The concerns about S1–S2 were further addressed in *Achieving Success in S1/S2. A Report on the Review of Provision in S1/S2 by HMI* (SOEID, 1997). The report defined 'direct teaching' in ways which most would describe as 'good teaching' and was notable for its defence of good practice preceding and following S1–S2; HMI wanted both the breadth advocated by the 5–14 curriculum and the specialisation which followed it, yet had difficulty in solving the problems encountered at the transition. They were forced to assert that the present S1–S2 framework (embraced in 5–14 principles and targets) both prepared pupils to continue with certain subjects and also served as a satisfactory exit point in relation to the subjects they discontinued. It seemed hard to reconcile both arguments. Perhaps the toughest line in the report was the contrast which HMI struck between the quality of the pastoral care which schools effected in the primary/secondary transfer, and the inadequacy of the subject monitoring which they found in so many schools. Thus:

> The monitoring and evaluation of pupils' academic progress in S1/S2 need to be improved in most schools. Although guidance and learning support staff generally deal well with pupils

whose performance is causing significant concern to subject teachers, few schools monitor the performance of all pupils sufficiently closely (*Achieving Success in S1/S2*, SOEID 1997, para. 3.10)

In the more recent *Standards and Quality* report (SOEID, 1999), and referred to previously, HMI were able to say that 'a growing number of schools were setting pupils in groups based on prior attainment, particularly in English language and mathematics' but 'arrangements for meeting pupils' needs showed some weaknesses or were unsatisfactory in 45% of subject departments' (p. 17). It is thus evident that discussion surrounding the somewhat disappointing achievements of pupils in S1 and S2 in Scotland is vigorous and lively. Teachers, researchers, inspectors and politicians hotly debate possible solutions. Interestingly the debate is now being conducted not in terms of ideological consistency with the comprehensive ideal but more in terms of the practical efficacy of alternative strategies.

There is much less argument about the organisation and arrangements in S3–S6, the Standard Grade programme having evolved three broad curriculum levels for S3 and S4, and the more recent Higher Still programme having put in place a rather more complex five levels arrangement for S5 and S6 (and beyond in FE). Chapter 47 provides detail of the practical structures which are found in all schools; the guiding principle is that of differentiated levels with safeguards in favour of pupils when it comes to the national examinations taken at S4 and beyond. By the middle years of secondary there would appear to be widespread acceptance of curricular and assessment patterns which have been designed to encompass the whole range of pupil ability.

SCHOOL AS COMMUNITY AND NEW COMMUNITY SCHOOLS

Secondary headteachers, even in schools which are judged successful by conventional indicators (examination success, entry to higher education, low figures for absenteeism, good discipline) would be quick to point out that the life of a secondary school involves much more than the work of subject departments. Schools provide systems of guidance and pastoral care to assist in the personal development of pupils, as well as to offer advice on curricular and vocational choice. Furthermore, they run social education programmes, which cut across subject divisions, and which deal with a wide range of issues of direct interest to young people – health, relationships, sexual behaviour, drugs, the law, personal finance. In most schools, there are well-developed links with the wider community through work experience schemes, environmental projects and charitable activities on behalf of the elderly, the handicapped and the homeless. Schools also offer the opportunity to take part in sports and hobbies, though teacher support for out-of-hours clubs and societies has never fully recovered from a period of industrial action in the 1980s when teachers withdrew from such activities. Nevertheless, it can reasonably be claimed that there is an 'informal' curriculum which supplements and extends the formal curriculum of subjects and departments.

The aim is to produce a climate which is felt by pupils to be supportive of their overall development. Such a climate is more likely to encourage effort and a positive outlook than one which is seen to be concerned only with academic success. Interestingly however, there is some evidence to suggest that in more deprived areas, Catholic schools achieve higher overall attainment levels than equivalent non-denominational schools (M. T. Thomson, EdD dissertation, University of Strathclyde, 2001). The concern with the values of the

school as an institution has always been a prominent feature of the Catholic
now accorded importance by all schools. There has been much interest in i
'ethos indicators' which are likely to show that the values of community a
institution. These include strong leadership, clear goals, open commun
links with parents and good teacher-pupil relationships.

All of this is undoubtedly well-intentioned and, where it is successful, it is be
of immense benefit to pupils. However, the notion of school as community should not be
overstated. Research evidence suggests that guidance provision invariably comes second
to subject requirements and that many pupils are sceptical about its effectiveness (see
Chapter 45). In some schools, guidance staff devote a disproportionate amount of their
time to dealing with 'problem' pupils and so the more positive aspects of their work are
underdeveloped. Again, social education programmes are variable in quality. Pupils
sometimes say that they know more about the topics under consideration (e.g. drugs) than
the adults leading the discussion. No doubt there is an element of teenage bravado in such
responses but they suggest that the self-reporting of schools about the success of these
programmes should be treated with caution. As far as extra-curricular activities are
concerned, teachers themselves often admit that it is a relatively small proportion of the
school population who are actively involved. Many pupils seek, and find, alternatives
outside school.

The New Community Schools pilot programme which got under way in 1999 involved
170 schools where additional funding was concentrated by central government in disadvantaged areas in which children face significant risk of social exclusion and formidable
barriers to learning in their everyday environment. A number of these schools comprise
clusters of nursery, primary and secondary schools, though some are single institutions. A
key feature of them is the attempted integration of school education, family support through
social work services, and health education promotion. Joint training as well as joint
operations by teachers, social workers, community educators, health professionals and
child-workers was envisaged by the SOEID initiative, somewhat akin to Education Action
Zones in England. In the interim evaluation findings published in July 2002, researchers
reported that 'cross-agency liaison and practice have been substantially enhanced', with a
number of case studies suggesting their powerful potential for overcoming the barriers
associated with multiple deprivation (SEED, 2002). Government has continued to 'roll out'
New Community Schools across Scotland and Issue 6 (August 2002) of the Newsletter by
the same name describes the different projects underway in different authorities despite the
reduced funding allocations 'agreed' between central and local government. In the case of
Glasgow's 'Learning Communities', the integration achieved has thus far not connected to
the pedagogy of secondary schools, according to Wilkinson et al. in their report to the
Scottish Educational Research Association's Annual Conference in 2002. It is likely that the
inflexibility of the current secondary curriculum remains a significant impediment to
progress.

THE FUTURE OF SECONDARY EDUCATION

It has long been taken for granted in Scotland that the 12–18 all-through comprehensive
school is the most rational way of organising post-primary education. The curriculum
reform programme, starting with Standard Grade then the 5–14 programme and finally
Higher Still, can be seen as a statement of confidence in existing structures. Scotland has no

tertiary or sixth-form colleges of the kind that exist in some parts of England. Demographic factors in many parts of the country provide compelling practical reasons for the comprehensive form of organisation: diverse provision would not be cost effective and would tend to reduce curricular choice within institutions. Furthermore, secondary headteachers argue that mixing older and younger teenagers has benefits for both in relation to progressive maturity, social responsibility and peer support.

There are, however, arguments and pressures which open up the possibility of alternatives. As the upper secondary school population increases (as a result of staying-on rates) the case for separate provision for post-compulsory students gains in strength. For some students the more informal climate of FE colleges will be attractive. This is a trend already in evidence in England. Another alternative has surfaced in the reopening of the debate about the merits of middle schools catering for the 10–14 or 10–16 age range. Scotland had a brief (and geographically very restricted) flirtation with middle schools in the 1970s but they never enjoyed much support. The current concerns with progression from P6 to S2, described above, have caused some policy makers to think again about the possible attractions of middle schools.

One encouraging development, the full impact of which will not be felt for a few years, is central and local government commitment to a major refurbishment and rebuilding programme for schools. The financing of this programme is a controversial issue with several authorities embracing public/private finance initiatives and others expressing a preference for traditional state funding. From an educational point of view, however, the important thing is that the learning environment for pupils is being significantly enhanced.

Under New Labour it has become permissible to 'think the unthinkable' in social policy. Comprehensive education was previously a non-negotiable item in the ideology of the political left. Judging by the changes that have taken place in health and social benefits, this may no longer be the case, though the evidence suggests that Scotland will require more persuasion than England to depart significantly from the all-purpose comprehensive school. Nevertheless the language of choice, quality, standards and effectiveness is as much part of Labour discourse as it was of the Conservatives. Against this background, it can be expected that the concepts of democracy, equality and social unity, as applied to secondary education, will be subject to further redefinition (perhaps beyond all recognition) as the twenty-first century advances, just as they were modified in the course of the twentieth century.

REFERENCES

Benn, C. and Chitty C. (1996) *Thirty years on: Is Comprehensive Education Alive and Well or Struggling to Survive?*, London: David Fulton Publishers.

Clark, M. M., and Munn P. (eds) (1997) *Education in Scotland. Policy and Practice from Pre-school to Secondary*, London: Routledge. (In particular see Chapter 4 by Brian Boyd, The statutory years of secondary education: change and progress; and Chapter 5 by David Raffe, Upper-secondary education.)

Gray, J., McPherson A. F. and Raffe D. (1983) *Reconstructions of Secondary Education: Theory, Myth and Practice since the War*, London: Routlege and Kegan Paul.

SCCC (1996) *Teaching for Effective Learning*, Dundee: SCCC.

SEED (2002) Interchange 76. Sammons, P. et al., *National Evaluation of the New Community Schools Pilot Programme in Scotland: Phase 1: Interim Findings*, Edinburgh: SEED.

SOEID (1999) *Standards and Quality in Scottish Schools, 1995–98: A Report by HM Inspectors of Schools*, Edinburgh: SOEID.

5

Further Education in Scotland

Craig Thomson

ONE SECTOR, MANY DIMENSIONS

The work of further education colleges in Scotland defies simple definition or description. It is here that vocational education meets and integrates with academic and recreational learning; employee training sits alongside personal development; and higher education finds seamless integration with further education. This is also the point in Scotland's lifelong learning infrastructure where many school-based learning experiences are extended and enhanced and where work-based and community-based learning are linked most effectively into the mainstream.

Colleges play a central role in developing the skills base of the economy both by providing vocational programmes for new entrants to the labour market and by integrating with and leading employee development programmes to update the skills of the current workforce. They stretch the work of schools, dealing with issues from disaffected youth to support for advanced school qualifications and integrate with and complement the work of universities. The diversity of the work of colleges is extended further by their provision of informal courses of study. Courses with diverse topics and titles such as 'Creative Writing', 'Digital Photography', 'Introduction to the Internet' and 'Sign Language' provide a wide range of new skills and knowledge for the adult population. While for some learners these courses are ends in themselves addressing a specific personal interest, for others they act as an important 'toe in the water' and first step back into learning, development and employment.

This chapter aims to provide an insight into the range of activities indicated above by describing the volume, funding and profile of colleges' work and the ways in which it is managed and supported. The picture that emerges is complex. Description is made difficult by the lack of agreed, clear and consistent terminology to indicate the diverse learning stages, sectors and locations involved and the institutional and funding arrangements that support these. To avoid confusion, it is important to clarify how a number of key terms will be used. 'Further education' and 'higher education' are taken as definitions relating to levels of learning. The principal locations in which learning is supported and the main basis on which funding is administered are referred to as 'colleges', 'universities' and 'schools.' The terms 'community education' and 'community-based learning' are taken in their literal sense, that is, relating to the location in which the learning is taking place. Where the body behind this is relevant (for example, distinguishing between local authority or college provision in the community) this is made clear at the time. Based on this set of definitions, the term 'college sector' is employed to refer to the area of work that is the primary focus of the chapter and the principal home of further education in Scotland.

A DECADE OF CHANGE

In 1993, colleges entered a new era as they became incorporated institutions in line with the arrangements set out in the Further and Higher Education (Scotland) Act (1992). These provided for colleges leaving local authority control and becoming corporate bodies. A board of management was established for each incorporated college and became the statutory body and the formal employer for all staff. Boards took on responsibility for governance, strategy and the operational effectiveness of their college. In effect, colleges moved from being administered bodies to managed ones with the role of the principal cast in a new light. Principals moved from 'head of service' roles to new, more demanding positions as academic leaders, accounting officers and chief executives.

In the years following incorporation the funding model used to determine the level of grant for colleges led to significant inter-college competition and rivalry. Student numbers grew but with little real increase in the overall funding for the sector. By the second half of the 1990s, the final years of the then Conservative government found the sector in the political wilderness facing significant reductions in real levels of overall funding and a rapidly declining level of funding for each learner.

The political context changed radically with the election of a Labour government in 1997 and the final two years of the twentieth century proved to be highly significant in shaping the future of the sector. Firstly, in 1998 the funding tide turned:

> In 1998, the then Secretary of State announced the allocation of an extra £214 million for further education in Scotland following the Comprehensive Spending Review, to widen access to further education, particularly for those from disadvantaged backgrounds, stabilise the colleges financial health and invest in information technology and college infrastructure (McLeish, H., *Foreword to Further Education in Scotland*, Edinburgh: Scottish Executive, 1999, p. 4).

Secondly, on 1 January 1999, the Scottish Further Education Funding Council was created, working in shadow form until 1 July when it formally assumed its full range of duties and responsibilities. Thirdly, and also in July 1999, the impact of the Scottish parliamentary elections began to take effect. Further education is a devolved matter. In July the new Minister for Enterprise and Lifelong Learning formally assumed responsibility for the sector.

In the financial year running from 1 August 2000 to 31 July 2001, colleges received a total of £284.3m in Grant in Aid (funding related to volumes of student activity). The amounts received by individual colleges varied from £17.6m for Aberdeen College to £0.27m for Newbattle Abbey College. In addition to this, the sector received just over £41m for disbursement to students in the form of bursary support.

The injection of new funding enabled the sector to maintain a strong underlying trend of growth and to play the central role in delivering the government's undertaking (Scottish Office 1998) to create 40,000 additional lifelong learning places within three years. Alongside this colleges responded positively to the minister's direction that they should extend and enhance their contribution to economic development, social inclusion and the widening of access to higher education. Colleges were urged to do this in a way that demonstrated increased efficiency and effectiveness; greater financial stability; higher levels of collaboration; and a rapid extension of the use of ICT both in course delivery and in college management.

In parallel with changes in funding levels and in the political context over the past decade, colleges have undergone significant changes in their overall profile as businesses. Each individual institution now contracts with SFEFC on an annual basis for delivery of a fixed volume of learning activity based on student units of measurement (SUMs) and while SFEFC remain the dominant source of income, others have grown significantly. Training and consultancy carried out on a commercial basis provide an important income stream. Contracts with Local Enterprise Companies (LECs) are also a growing source of income. These relate mainly to work carried out in support of Scottish Vocational Qualifications (SVQs) and Modern Apprenticeship programmes. Colleges also contract with LECs to support e-business, small business development and other economic development initiatives.

The changes of the late 1990s and the first few years of the new decade, in particular the allocation of additional funding and the creation of the Scottish Parliament, have led to increased scrutiny of the performance of colleges. On the one hand, this has had the very positive effect of making the achievements of the sector more visible. Colleges are increasingly recognised as central, effective agents in the delivery of government lifelong learning and social inclusion objectives. However, on the other hand, additional funds have come with demands for colleges to increase productivity and efficiency. The Audit Committee of the Scottish Parliament (see, for example, the committee's 7th report 2002 at www.scottish.parliament.uk/official_report/cttee/audit-02/aur02–07–02.htm) has made clear both to colleges and to SFEFC its desire to see continuing improvement in the financial health of the sector. Co-operation between the Funding Council and colleges has resulted in a number of initiatives addressing a broad agenda of improvement with financial health as the main current priority. Most significant among these initiatives has been the creation of a 'Further Education Development Unit' by SFEFC. Led by a college principal on part-secondment and drawing on expertise from across the sector, the unit is working with individual colleges where issues have been identified by SFEFC or by the colleges themselves.

A twist in the complex development of the sector came in 2002 as growth in funding and numbers stalled and colleges found themselves on a funding plateau. For the first time since incorporation, the 2002–3 learning year began with no planned growth in funded student numbers. Furthermore, despite the growth in spending on the college sector announced in the 2002 Strategic Spending Review (SSR), the timing of this growth is such that college funding from SFEFC and funded student numbers will experience no growth during 2003/04 (See Table 5.1).

While these figures are superficially clear, meaningful comparisons between years and with previous years are made extremely difficult by the complexity and the lack of transparency in the calculations that lie behind them. The total allocated to the college sector is a composite figure including elements that are applied to student support, capital expenditure and to funding for student places. Changes in the real unit of funding available to support tuition are lost in this complexity. The three years covered by the 2002 SSR run through to 2005–6 and it is not until the second and third year that colleges will again experience real growth in overall expenditure. Furthermore, plans for improvements in the unit of funding and investment in infrastructure in 2004–5 are likely to mean that there will be no significant growth in student numbers until 2005–6.

Table 5.1:   Funding from SFEFC 2002–6

Year	£m	Cash % increase	Estimated real % increase
2002–3	420		
2003–4	429	2.1	0
2004–5	466	8.6	6
2005–6	504	8.2	5.5

While the diversification of income sources noted earlier in this section has been a positive development, several elements of the 'other' (that is, non-SFEFC) income earned by colleges present particular potential problems. On the one hand, colleges are exposed to short-term 'stop/start' cycles in funding as new initiatives emerge and disappear. Individual Learning Accounts in their first period of use, mainly during 2001, provide an illustration of this. On the other hand, colleges are vulnerable to longer-term significant shifts in other funding. Over the past decade European Union (EU) Structural Funds and other programmes have provided a significant flow of both revenue and capital funding for many colleges. This funding is now in decline and the increase in core funding from SFEFC in the late 1990s coincided with a period of particular decline in the levels of EU funding achieved by colleges. A further rapid decline in finance from this source will take place in the middle of the current decade as EU funding programmes conclude. This decline is likely to coincide with and lessen the impact of the next stepped rise in income from SFEFC described above, presenting a further complex twist in the story of college funding.

THE SECTOR IN PROFILE

During 2000–1 enrolments in college courses totalled 487,341. These related to courses provided from a total of over 4,000 sites across Scotland including community and work-based locations. The most popular courses offered by colleges were in Information Technology with over 20% of enrolments falling into this area of study. A further 15% of enrolments were accounted for by Family Care, Personal Care and Personal Development.

The description of the sector presented in this section including the data in the previous paragraph draws on detailed statistical reports produced by the Scottish Executive (www.scotland.gov.uk/stats/bulletins/00196–09.asp) and the Association of Scottish Colleges (www.ascol.ac.uk). Unless otherwise stated, data relate to the 2000–1 academic year. The profile that is revealed confirms the broad and central role of colleges in lifelong learning. Table 5.2 provides an overview of male, female and total enrolments by mode and stage of study.

Any comparisons between full and part-time enrolments have to be made with some caution. In particular, two points have to be borne in mind. Firstly, courses do not fit neatly into one of two simple categories, that is, full-time and part-time. The wide spectrum of learning opportunities made available stretches from full-time study to very short part-time programmes and encompasses programmes that vary widely in duration and patterns of study. Secondly, the method of recording enrolments means that at the margins individual learners may enrol for more than one part-time course in any one year leading to an element of double counting (of individuals as opposed to learning episodes). Despite these caveats, the underlying picture revealed by Table 5.2 reflects the importance of part-time enrolments. These encompass a rich range of provision including short programmes, longer-term evening study, day release courses, work-based learning, distance learning, ICT supported remote study and flexible 'drop in' programmes for learners. In the 2000–1 academic year just over 85% of enrolments were for part-time study. Furthermore, as will be described below, the highest rate of growth in enrolments in the late 1990s and the first years of the new century was in this category.

Table 5.2: College enrolments 2000–1 by mode, stage and gender

	Further Education		
	Male	Female	Total
Full-time	20,763	20,730	41,493
Part-time	153,567	219,332	372,899
Total	174,330	240,062	414,392
	Higher Education		
	Male	Female	Total
Full-time	14,555	16,807	31,362
Part-time	19,224	22,363	41,587
Total	33,779	39,170	72,949
	All Students		
	Male	Female	Total
Full-time	35,318	37,537	72,855
Part-time	172,791	241,695	414,486
Total	208,109	279,232	487,341

Analysis of the gender balance in enrolments shows that on both full-time and part-time programmes the number of female learners outnumbered males. Overall, 57% of total enrolments were by females with the imbalance being particularly evident in part-time programmes where female and male enrolments were 58% to 42% respectively. Full-time programmes attracted 52% female and 48% male learners.

Figure 5.1 is based on ages of learners at the time of enrolment. This reveals that 22% of learners were under eighteen and that 20% fell into the eighteen–twenty-four bracket. Over half of enrolments, 58%, were twenty-five or over.

Earlier in this chapter, the underlying trend of growth in the college sector was noted along with the contribution that this had made to the government's commitment to the extension of lifelong learning. The trend of growth is indicated in Figure 5.2 which confirms both the trend and the acceleration that took place as colleges responded to the objectives set out in *Opportunity Scotland* (Scottish Office 1998).

Figure 5.1:   Age distribution of college students

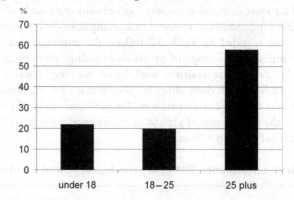

Figure 5.2:   College enrolments: 1995–6 to 2000–1

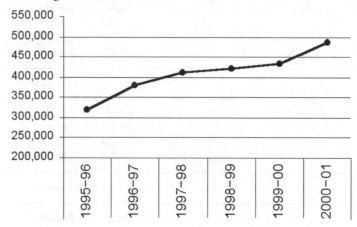

Figure 5.3:   Growth in enrolments between 1995 and 1996 and 2000 and 2001
(1995–6 = 100)

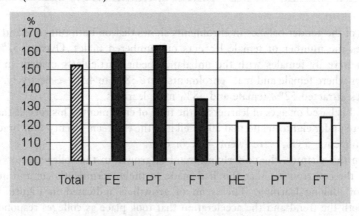

While growth in numbers during this period was evident in all main categories of college work, the rate of growth was uneven. Figure 5.3 indicates the relative growth in enrolments in full-time and part-time further and higher education between 1995 and 1996 and 2000 and 2001. Taking 1995–6 as 100, total enrolments grew by 52% over that six-year period. This was made up of 59% growth in further education and 22% growth in higher education enrolments. The most rapid increase was in part-time at 63% compared with a 34% increase in full-time further education. In higher education, growth in full-time and part-time enrolments grew relatively evenly at 21% and 24% respectively.

ASSESSMENT AND CERTIFICATION

Assessment and certification are further useful areas to explore in setting out the distinctive current features of the college sector and the changes that are shaping it for the future. The dominant group of qualifications offered is drawn from those awarded by the Scottish Qualifications Authority (SQA). These include National Qualifications (NQs), Higher National Certificates (HNCs) and Higher National Diplomas (HNDs), SVQs and specialist courses. Working with university partners, a number of colleges also offer ordinary degrees validated by their partners and provide courses leading to a wide range of professional qualifications awarded by bodies such as the Chartered Institute of Marketing, the Chartered Institute of Personnel and Development and the Institute of Operations Management. Other organisations involved in the validation and award of qualifications linked to college courses include City and Guilds and a large number of bodies providing passport qualifications in specific vocational areas as diverse as food hygiene, non-destructive testing and gas safety.

The early years of the twenty-first Century are a time of major change and development in the structure and content of Scottish qualifications. Three interlinked sets of changes are of particular relevance to colleges. Firstly, Higher Still which has been implemented from 1999 has had a major impact. Higher Still can be argued to have moved the focus of qualifications in a direction that is beneficial to the college sector. However, a number of problems and disappointments are evident. The Higher Still initiative was developed with a strong emphasis on parity of esteem between vocational and academic qualifications and with the declared aim of widening the range of routes and options open to learners. In addition to this, support and development of core skills, issues that had been in focus for some time in colleges, were given a formal place in certification with assessed levels of communication, numeracy, problem solving, information technology and 'working with others' all recorded.

Despite these and other potentially positive elements of the initiative, Higher Still has presented a range of problems to colleges. Changes to assessment have threatened to take colleges into a regime of rigid external assessment inconsistent with the flexible internally assessed and externally moderated approach that has served them and their clients well (see Chapter 81). In addition, the resources required to embrace Higher Still have proved difficult to find. The programme of funded Higher Still development has been unevenly balanced with, for example, support for the development of materials for vocational qualifications less comprehensively resourced than support for those for traditional academic areas.

While the qualifications offered by colleges have changed with SQA National Certificate qualifications being replaced in relatively large numbers, this process has been taken forward with increasing caution. Colleges have gone through a major change programme embracing the integrated certification system that Higher Still has promised. However, concerns about the flexibility of content and the rigidity of assessment have made them stop short of complete change. In parallel with these internal issues, colleges have had to respond to a secondary, external impact as schools have changed the qualifications that they offer. At worst, the impact of Higher Still at the schools/college interface has involved progression to college diminishing as a result of schools offering vocational programmes drawing on a poor and inappropriate resource base in subjects such as catering and other physical resource dependent vocational areas. At best, the initiative has opened up the opportunity for collaboration between schools and colleges resulting in a richer set of choices for school students with colleges providing support for vocational units, developing alternative routes to qualifications and providing Highers and Advanced Highers in specialist areas such as advanced IT and programmes of study, such as Psychology, not traditionally offered as part of the school curriculum.

The second major change in assessment and certification with a significant impact on colleges is the review of Higher National Qualifications, that is, HNCs and HNDs. This review, which is being undertaken by SQA as the awarding body, dates back to 1995 and has been slow and lengthy. The two main factors within the review have been relevance and desirability, that is, ensuring that the content of qualifications remains current and that Higher Nationals continue to enjoy a high level of fit with other parts of the qualifications structure. In particular, the HN review has been shaped by the Scottish Credit and Qualifications Framework (SCQF) which is touched on briefly below and is described elsewhere in this volume (see Chapter 106). There have been a number of controversial elements to the review. These have included the 'levelling' of credit-bearing units. In a departure from the more flexible arrangements within which HN units can be generally recognised as at HN level without being specified as either HNC or HND, levelling will result in them being assigned as either level 7 or level 8 in SCQF.

Controversy has also surrounded the proposed change in the number of credits required to earn an HNC from 12 to 15 (to half of the value of the 30-credit HND). Credits in this area as in the further education work of colleges are roughly equivalent to forty hours of learning. At the time of writing, solutions are being sought to address two problems that will be created if three additional credits are included. These relate to the additional costs of increasing the credit value and to the impact that the increase will have on part-time HNC programmes, a point of concern for many employers. This would be likely to lead to the loss of the two-year part-time HNC with a 15-credit qualification stretching into a third year of study. The scale of the problem is reflected in the fact that approximately 60% of HN enrolments are on HNC programmes and of these approximately 60% are part-time.

The third of the major changes in qualifications with an impact on the college sector is the implementation of the SCQF. The National Implementation Plan published by SCQF in 2002 (www.qaa.ac.uk/crntwork/nqf/scqf/scqf%5Fupdate08%02Do2.htm) indicates the principal objectives and action relating to this initiative, including the publication of an implementation plan for colleges. Given the many points of cross-boundary interaction and integration described above which characterise the sector, it is reasonable to predict that SCQF will continue to be welcomed by colleges. Implementation is likely to help to clarify the work of the sector and to smooth transition in a number of related dimensions including transition to college courses; from further education to higher education within colleges;

and on from college courses to later stages of study. Learners will increasingly be able to move and to transfer credit between different stages and forms of learning. The potential of SCQF is also indicated by the extent to which the development to date has helped to cast light on current fault lines in the qualification framework in Scotland. These are most evident at the interface between SVQs and other vocational qualifications at National Qualification and Higher National levels. It is at these points that current arrangements are characterised by low levels of credit transfer resulting in duplication of learning and assessment for many, particularly young learners in work-based programmes.

COLLEGES' CONTRIBUTION TO HIGHER EDUCATION

Reflection on the interweaving pattern of further and higher education provision across institutional boundaries provides a further insight into the complex role of colleges in Scotland. Taking further and higher education as levels of work and distinguishing these from the two sectors principally involved in their delivery produces the distribution set out in Table 5.3 which is based on analysis of enrolment figures for 2000–1 reported by the Scottish Executive (www.scotland.gov.uk/stats/bulletins/00196–09.asp). 'Higher education' and 'further education' are used in the sense defined by the Further and Higher Education (Scotland) Act 1992 which states that a course is classified as HE if it is at HNC/D level or above. This classification includes SVQ and NVQ courses at level 4 and above. Further education is defined as any activity up to but not including HNC/HND level and includes National Certificate units, SVQ/ NVQ to level 3, Access courses, Highers and Advanced Highers. It also includes courses that do not lead to a recognised qualification.

Unsurprisingly, Table 5.3 confirms the predominant roles of colleges in the delivery of further education and the university sector in the delivery of higher education. However, it also reveals the significant roles of colleges in the delivery of both full and, in particular, of part-time higher education programmes and of the university sector, or the higher education Institutions (HEIs), in the delivery of part-time further education.

Table 5.3: **Enrolments in further and higher education by sector (based on rounded figures)**

(000)	College Sector			University / HEI Sector			Total		
	Full-Time	Part-Time	Total	Full-Time	Part-Time	Total	Full-Time	Part-Time	Total
Further education	41	373	414	< 1	143	143	41	517	558
Higher education	31	42	73	134	56	190	166	97	263
Total	73	414	487	134	199	333	207	614	821

The positive and productive overlap between sectors is also illustrated by analysis of two characteristics of the flow of learners that lie behind these statistics. Firstly, the pattern of progression for young people into higher education reveals the extent to which the much vaunted achievement of a 50% rate of progression to higher education has been dependent on the joint efforts of the two sectors. Figures for academic year 2000–1 show that 43.2% of

Scots entering full-time HE for the first time did so in a college. As the Association of Scottish Colleges (ASC) have pointed out, the 50% figure for overall progression to higher education would be reduced very significantly if college-based higher education was removed from the calculation:

> The age-participation index for under-21s entering full-time higher education . . . would be only 31% were it not for the large numbers of young people who start HE studies in FE colleges. (ASC, 2002, p. 3)

Secondly, analysis of levels and locations of study confirms the central role that colleges play in the provision of part-time higher education. In 2000–1 over 70% of learners entering part-time HE for the first time did so in a college.

The dominant pattern for progression from Higher National courses in colleges to the later stages of higher education in the university sector is set within a large number of bilateral articulation agreements. These specify progression routes for (generally full-time) students moving from HNC or HND to an appropriate point of entry to a degree course. Where the curricular fit is good, progression can be from HNC to year two of a degree or from HND to year three. Where articulation is less exact, the point of progression is to an earlier stage of the degree programme. As relationships between the college and university sectors have matured, articulation agreements have also been established based on collaborative and innovative curriculum design. In a number of cases the university leaves the delivery of years one and two to the college. The creation of such programmes has played a significant role in developing routes and points of access for non-traditional university entrants.

   The central role of colleges in the development and delivery of higher education in Scotland is a major element in a vigorous debate going on at the time of writing into the nature, purpose and location of higher education. This debate has been framed by two parallel reviews. The first of these, the *Scottish Higher Education Review* (Scottish Executive 2002) has endeavoured to consider the core issues affecting higher education in Scotland in the early years of the new century. The second, the *Inquiry into Lifelong Learning* by the Scottish Parliament's Enterprise and Lifelong Learning Committee (Scottish Parliament 2002) has also cast light on higher education by setting it in context and by basing its deliberations on a more inclusive view of that level of learning. The further development of the SCQF and the continuing strong political and practical support for the Access to HE agenda have also helped to shape the political and practical context within which higher education is developing.

SUPPORT AND SELF-HELP FOR THE SECTOR

As reflected in the earlier sections of this chapter, the growth and development of colleges in the post-1993 era can be argued to result from a range of factors including the political context; the funding formulas applied both in times of tight and more generous funding; the energy, adaptability and inventiveness of college staff; and the central location of the sector in Scotland's developing lifelong learning infrastructure. Throughout this period, colleges have faced the challenge of managing and maintaining a broad range of roles, responsibilities and relationships both locally and nationally. Each individual college operates in a wide and diverse web of relationships, maintaining key partnerships with councils, principal local employers, local enterprise companies, the voluntary sector, schools, universities, chambers of commerce, community groups, other colleges and with bodies such as learndirect Scotland and Careers Scotland. Nationally, the further education sector operates in a similarly challenging environment managing demanding relationships with an equally diverse set of organisations and initiatives.

In the years since incorporation most individual colleges have proved adept at managing their boundaries by working creatively within these complex networks based on a range of loose alliances and more formal partnerships. At a national level, the success of the sector as a whole at developing its role and points of influence and at lobbying and influencing effectively results from a number of inter-linked factors.

These include:

- the creation and development of the ASC as a body supporting and representing the sector;
- the formation of the Principals' Forum as a body bringing together principals to share challenges and to develop their individual and shared positions on key developments with a Chairs' Forum playing a similar supportive role for the chairs of boards of management; and
- the involvement of college principals and other senior staff in key working groups, boards and other bodies dealing with specific initiatives and strategic issues relevant to the sector.

The ASC, which is the central cohering factor in these developments, is funded by the sector on a subscription basis and has in membership all but one of Scotland's colleges. It has a board of directors made up of college principals, chairs of boards and the organisation's chief officer. In addition to performing the functions covered by 1 above, it plays a central role in each of the others. Appointments to national working groups and other bodies are frequently sought via the ASC. The Principals' and the Chairs' Forums are supported by ASC staff.

The ASC is an example of the sector combining effectively to address its shared agenda. A further example is provided by the Scottish Further Education Unit (SFEU). The first three years of the new century were a time of significant change for the SFEU. Following a review of funding and organisation, the unit emerged as an independent company belonging to the sector with all colleges registered as members. In addition to earning income from its project work and staff development activities, the funding of SFEU is supported in part by way of a service level agreement with SFEFC.

Despite experiencing upheaval during this period as a result of changes in funding and organisation, SFEU has maintained its core purpose:

> to actively assist and support colleges in maintaining and developing (their) valued and crucial central role within Scotland – our vision being to work in partnership towards a world-class FE system in Scotland. (Hunter, 2001, p. 3)

The focus of the work of the SFEU remains on developing staff and the curriculum and on working with colleges to respond to new initiatives with an impact in these areas, working to develop 'people and practices in colleges' (p. 3).

Boards of management of colleges also represent an important element of the support enjoyed by the sector. The roles of boards can be defined in stark terms as simply concerned with setting strategic direction and monitoring progress and financial performance.

However, the role performed is generally much more widely supportive. The principal formal functions of boards of management are set out in an information pack published by ASC in 2000 for new members of college boards:

> The Board of Management of a college is, under the terms of the 1992 Act, a corporate body charged with the duty of
> - managing and conducting their college
> - ensuring that their college provides suitable and efficient further education to students of the college taking account of provision of education in the areas in which the college is situated and the likely needs of people who might wish to become students of the college. (p. 9)

The pack goes on to describe the role of the board in setting the strategy of their college by assessing the environment in which they operate. Based on this assessment, boards are charged with setting the scope of activities and ensuring that these are matched to the needs of the local area. These and related activities are described as enabling boards to:

- formulate a clear purpose and objectives
- understand the competitive environment
- match organisational resources to the environment
- monitor, review and adapt, where necessary, the activities. (p. 10)

In the years immediately following incorporation a considerable proportion of board time was spent on ensuring that colleges developed the capacity, experience and expertise necessary to manage key functions that had previously been provided by the local authorities; mainly personnel, estates and finance. By the final years of the 1990s the need to focus on these points had diminished leaving boards more opportunity to concentrate on their responsibilities for strategic planning. Significantly, many boards had also become more effective at supporting their colleges on a wider front and, in particular, in providing a further link between colleges and their commercial and wider communities.

2003 AND BEYOND

At the time of writing, colleges find themselves in familiar circumstances as they face demanding programmes of development in challenging and uncertain times. In concluding this chapter, it is possible to identify three main elements of the strategic backdrop that will shape the future of colleges through to the end of the decade and against which the pressures, relationships and priorities outlined above will develop and unfold.

Firstly, reorientation of policy will result from the various reports and recommendations on the future of school education, higher education and lifelong learning. As indicated earlier in the chapter both lifelong learning and higher education have been subject to national consultation and review. More recently these have been joined by a national review of the purposes of the school sector and a national debate on school education. Changes resulting from each of these will have significant implications for the college sector.

Secondly, structural reorientation of the sector as a whole is under way as mergers move forward in Glasgow. While the speed, nature and extent of reshaping in the number of colleges in Scotland is difficult to predict, it is clear that far-reaching change is on the horizon. In addition to mergers, the sector will also see a continuing increase in collaboration between and among individual initiatives. Work carried out on behalf of the Funding Council resulted in the publication in 2002 of a series of reports on the demand and supply of further education in Scotland (Collins and Wheelhouse, 2002). In addition to a national report, area reports were prepared for the North East, Tayside, Fife, Central, Edinburgh and the Lothians, Lanarkshire, the West and the South. The area reports provide a foundation on which searching questions can be posed relating to area patterns of provision, efficiency and opportunities for collaboration.

Finally, deeper-seated strategic review, stimulated by planning guidance received from SFEFC, is evident as individual colleges reflect on and develop their plans for the coming years. In addition to considering the first two sets of points above, colleges will be scanning their external environments and looking to the future with a view to continuing their roles at the centre of lifelong learning and vocational training for their various communities. Achieving this will involve securing the mix of staff, curriculum, supporting services, technology, equipment, relationships, income streams and the range of other components that will constitute a successful college as the first decade of the twenty-first century proceeds.

REFERENCES

Association of Scottish Colleges (2002) *ASC Response to Scottish Higher Education Review – 2nd Consultation*, Stirling: Association of Scottish Colleges.

Collins, R. and Wheelhouse, P. (2002) *Demand and Supply of Further Education in Scotland*, Edinburgh: SFEFC.

Hunter, C. (2001) 'SFEU and FE colleges: meeting the challenges and future together, *Broadcast* 54, Stirling: SFEU.

Scottish Executive (2002) *Scottish Higher Education Review, Second Consultative Paper: Shaping our Future*, Edinburgh: Scottish Executive.

Scottish Office (1998) *Opportunity Scotland*, Edinburgh: The Scottish Office.

Scottish Parliament (2002) *Enterprise and Lifelong Learning Committee, 2nd Report 2002 – Interim Report on the Lifelong Learning Inquiry*, Edinburgh: Scottish Parliament.

6

Scottish Higher Education: Character and Provision

David Caldwell

The purpose of this chapter is to describe the main characteristics of the Scottish higher education (HE) sector as it is constituted in the early years of the twenty-first century and to outline the educational provision available within it. This will be placed in the context of an examination of the major changes in the sector and its environment since the early 1990s, and particularly the impact of political devolution.

THE HIGHER EDUCATION INSTITUTIONS (HEIs)

In recent decades the number of HEIs in Scotland has rarely remained static for long, and the period between 1990 and 2002 has been one of significant change. Within this certain trends are clearly discernible. One of these is a reduction in the overall number, with a particularly large decline in the number of monotechnics. Another is an increase in the number with university title, which has the consequence that the universities now contain more than 90% of the student population of the sector as a whole.

In 1990 there were twenty-six HEIs. Only eight, fewer than one-third of the total, were universities, although between them these accounted for more than half the student population measured as full-time equivalents (FTEs). The remainder were central institutions (CIs) and colleges of education (CEs) funded directly by the Scottish Office and having the status of non-departmental public bodies (NDPBs). The group of CIs further divided into five larger institutions with a fairly broad subject base and a strong vocational focus, and eight smaller institutions each covering a narrower subject range. The five larger CIs all gained university title in the early 1990s, and by 2002 three of the smaller CIs and all five CEs had been absorbed into universities.

What is notable about these very substantial structural changes which have taken place in a relatively short time is that they have been led and managed by the institutions themselves, rather than having been externally imposed. While government and the funding body have become more interventionist in HE policy and planning during the last quarter-century, their interventions have been more supportive than directive. It is a telling illustration of how, with appropriate encouragement and incentives, a sector composed of autonomous institutions can respond effectively to changing circumstances and needs. It is doubtful whether simple central direction could have achieved as much.

Although the trend has been towards a reduction in the number of institutions, movement has not been exclusively in one direction: in 2001 two institutions (Bell College in Hamilton and the UHI Millennium Institute) were designated as HEIs for the first time. Thus in 2002 the Scottish HE sector comprised thirteen universities and six other HEIs, all having their primary bases in Scotland and eligible to receive funding from the Scottish Higher Education Funding Council (SHEFC). In addition, SHEFC funds the Scottish activities of the Open University, and there is one further HEI, the Scottish Agricultural College, which receives its funding not from SHEFC but from the Scottish Executive Environment and Rural Affairs Department (SEERAD).

Institutions have grown substantially during this period. Official figures collected by the Higher Education Statistics Agency (HESA) show that the sector's total student population in 2000–1 was approximately 190,000, compared with 105,000 a decade earlier. Part-time numbers more than trebled, from around 17,350 to 55,700, but though the rise in full-time numbers was less dramatic it still represented an increase of over 50%. Postgraduate numbers increased more quickly than undergraduate, more than doubling to reach over 40,000, a figure which rises to nearly 48,000 if continuing education students are included. The increase in the number of first degree students to around 116,000 represented a 55% increase. By 2000–1 the three largest Scottish universities each had over 20,000 students, and the smallest over 4,600.

There is considerable diversity among the institutions which make up the sector. Among the universities alone, at least three distinct groups can be identified: the four 'ancient' universities, all of which were established before the end of the sixteenth century; four 1960s universities; and five 1990s universities. Even within these groups there are significant differences.

Of the ancients, St Andrews, Glasgow and Aberdeen were fifteenth-century foundations created by papal bull, while Edinburgh was founded later, in 1583, as a civic university. In the case of Aberdeen, for a substantial period there were two universities, the original foundation, King's College, and a second institution founded in 1593, Marischal College. King's and Marischal merged in 1860. All the ancients have undergone huge changes during their long history, but this remains a coherent group of institutions retaining some distinctive common characteristics. One example of this is the system of faculty entry, and the encouragement to most students to study a number of different subjects in their first two years before deciding in which subject to specialise, or indeed whether to take a broadly-based non-specialist degree. Another example is to be found in the schemes of governance, within which the most idiosyncratic feature, though not one of the oldest since in its present form it dates only from the nineteenth century, is the office of rector. The rector is elected triennially by the students (or, in the case of Edinburgh, by staff and students), and chairs the university court, which is the name by which the governing bodies of most Scottish universities are known.

There is still greater diversity among the 1960s group. In fact only one of them, Stirling, was an entirely new foundation. Two others, Strathclyde and Heriot-Watt, had been CIs funded mainly by the Scottish Office, though also receiving significant funding from the University Grants Committee, and until they gained university title they did not have their own degree-awarding powers. The last of the four, Dundee, had (as Queen's College, Dundee) been an integral part of the University of St Andrews before gaining independent university status. A common feature of all four, and one which distinguishes them from all other Scottish HEIs, is that their governing instruments are royal charters.

The 1990s group (Napier, Glasgow Caledonian, Robert Gordon, Paisley and Abertay

Dundee) is more homogeneous. These were the five larger CIs and, like the English polytechnics, they were granted degree-awarding powers and university title in the early 1990s. The governing instruments for these institutions are statutory instruments approved by the privy council.

The smaller HEIs which do not have university title are similarly constituted under statutory instrument. Typically they cover a narrower range of subjects than the universities, but three (Queen Margaret University College, Bell College and the UHI Millennium Institute) are significantly more than monotechnics. Four others (Glasgow School of Art, Edinburgh College of Art, the Royal Scottish Academy of Music and Drama, and the Scottish Agricultural College) are smaller, specialist institutions.

DIVERSITY AND DISTINCTIVENESS

The diverse origins of Scottish HEIs are reflected in a corresponding diversity in missions. The main differentiation is between the pre-1992 universities on the one hand and the former CIs on the other. The eight older universities are characterised by strong research performance and a teaching subject mix biased towards traditional academic disciplines. In the other institutions teaching is concentrated on vocational subjects and most of the research undertaken is of an applied nature.

In the case of research the difference is particularly apparent in the SHEFC research grant allocations related to the results of the Research Assessment Exercise (RAE). Of the SHEFC grants for 2002–3 based on RAE 2001, amounting to more than £132m, over 93% was distributed to the eight older universities. However, even within this group there are significant differences, with just two institutions (Edinburgh and Glasgow) securing between them approximately £65m in RAE-based grants, or nearly 50% of the total. The £6.3m allocated for knowledge transfer activities is more evenly spread.

Similarly there are divergences in the composition of the student community. The former CIs recruit more heavily from their local populations than do the eight older universities, which recruit a higher proportion of students both from other parts of the UK and from overseas. However, as with research there is also differentiation within the subgroups. For example, St Andrews and Edinburgh are particularly successful in recruiting students from England, while Glasgow and Strathclyde recruit strongly from their own region. The social mix varies too, with wide disparities in the proportion of students drawn from social groups IIIM, IV and V, which have significantly below average participation rates, ranging in different institutions from less than 15% to over 40%. The former CIs have been generally more successful in recruiting students from these social groups and from geographical areas where participation rates have been low.

Despite these differences, one of the distinctive features of Scottish HE is its cohesiveness. In part this is to do with size: Scotland is a small country, making relationships closer and simpler to manage, and interactions easier and more frequent. There are also certain substantive distinguishing characteristics of the Scottish system. Some of these, like the broader school curriculum and differences in the school examination system, lie outwith HE. Although there has been criticism that the school curriculum and the HE curriculum have not always been well integrated, and even that the demands of the HE sector have sometimes distorted the school curriculum, the characteristics of school education have contributed towards the development of a distinctive framework of degree programmes and awards. The fact that pupils have usually taken the final school examination a year earlier than their English counterparts is one of the factors leading to the Scottish first degree pattern being of three-year ordinary and four-year honours degrees instead of the English three-year honours degree. However, more than half those entering HEIs direct from school stay on at school for a sixth year, and the introduction of Advanced Highers will lead to the learning undertaken during that year having a clearer purpose, which HEIs will have to recognise. The breadth of the school curriculum is reflected to some extent in a more broadly based HE curriculum, although the trend since the mid-twentieth century has been towards more specialisation. One measure of this is that those graduating from three-year ordinary degree programmes are now outnumbered by honours degree graduates by about four to one, where a generation earlier the numbers were broadly comparable.

Another factor which distinguishes Scottish HE is the high participation rate. In 2002 new Scottish Executive figures indicated that this rate had reached 50.4% (by age twenty-one), the first time it has crossed the 50% barrier. This represents a doubling of the rate in twelve years, and is one of the highest HE participation rates anywhere in the world, comparing with a rate of approximately 35% in England. Since successful completion rates are also among the best internationally, it can now be expected that around 40% of each age cohort of Scottish school leavers will achieve an HE qualification. Despite the higher participation rate, recruitment has remained buoyant, allowing the Scottish Executive's planned student numbers to be comfortably and consistently achieved.

An important contributory factor to the achievement of such high participation rates is the amount of HE delivered in further education (FE) colleges. In 2000–1 approximately 73,000 HE students in Scotland were studying in FE colleges, compared with 33,000 ten years earlier. Of the 73,000 figure, which represents nearly 28% of total HE numbers, 57% are studying part-time. Nearly all of the FE sector's contribution is in the form of Higher National Certificate and Diploma (HNC and HND) courses, which are at below degree level, but which often articulate with degree programmes in HEIs. This explains in part why nearly as many entrants to HEIs now come via FE colleges as come direct from schools.

Although in Scotland as elsewhere in the UK participation rates vary substantially between different social groups, the discrepancies in Scotland are smaller. One measure of this is that the proportion of the young full-time first degree entrants who came from low participation neighbourhoods in 1999–2000 was 18% in Scotland compared with 12% for the UK as a whole. Since the overall participation rate is already considerably higher, this means that a young person from a low participation neighbourhood in Scotland is almost twice as likely to gain entry to HE as someone in the same position in another part of the UK.

Among the other aspects of participation deserving mention is a striking shift in gender balance. In 1990–1 this was 55% to 45% in favour of male students, but by ten years later the figures were exactly reversed with female students accounting for 55% of the total. There has also been some movement in the relative participation rates of different age groups, where the number of students aged twenty-five and over has risen more rapidly, reaching 45% of total HE numbers by 2000–1.

Despite the many distinctive features of the Scottish system, it is neither inward-looking nor parochial. Most Scottish HEIs are building stronger international profiles, and all are well integrated into the larger UK system. Large numbers of non-Scots teach and research in Scottish HEIs, just as many Scots teach and research in HEIs outside Scotland. The research performance of Scottish HEIs is judged alongside that of all other HEIs in the UK, and for most research income they compete on a UK or international basis. Moreover they compete successfully: for example, they obtain around 13% of UK Research Council grants, or about half as much again as Scotland might expect on the basis of its population, although this may simply reflect the fact that Scotland has about 12.1% of all academics working in UK HEIs. Despite the different structure of undergraduate programmes in Scotland, there is substantial common ground on learning outcomes and on standards, facilitating healthy cross border traffic of students, of which Scotland is the net beneficiary. Each year there are 6,000 or so new undergraduate entrants to Scottish HEIs from other parts of the UK. This represents about one sixth of the full-time first degree intake to Scottish HEIs, although only around 2% of the total number of English, Welsh and Northern Irish entrants. Approximately 2,000, equivalent to about 5% of the Scottish total, leave Scotland each year to study elsewhere in the UK, where they constitute less than 1% of the student population. The regard in which Scottish qualifications are held outside Scotland is demonstrated by the substantial numbers of graduates who make their careers outwith Scotland.

AUTONOMY AND ACCOUNTABILITY

Of the features shared with other UK HEIs, one of the most highly valued by the institutions themselves is their autonomy. Of course the influence of government, as the single largest source of funds, is enormous, but HEIs remain legally independent. This is an important protection against inappropriate political intervention in the daily management of institutions, and it encourages, or avoids stifling, innovation and enterprise. So far UK governments have mostly resisted the temptation to impose highly directive central planning on HE, recognising that such experiments as have been attempted have been largely unsuccessful. The subject rationalisation initiative by the University Grants Committee in the 1980s is a good example. Had all its plans been implemented, some successful academic developments would have been thwarted. Even apparently simple tasks, such as planning the supply of certain professionals such as doctors and teachers, have had only limited success. On the other hand, when government has sought to influence rather than to direct, results have been much better. For example, the sector has met its student number targets consistently for the last ten years, and research performance has improved significantly during the same period. In both cases government encouraged and incentivised, but entrusted delivery to HEIs acting autonomously.

Of course institutions should be accountable for the use they make of the public funds which they receive, and there are mechanisms for ensuring that HEIs use these funds for the purposes for which they are provided, and that they secure best value for these funds. Accountability operates primarily through the funding councils, but the sector is also subject to oversight by Audit Scotland. The mechanisms have become increasingly systematic and rigorous. They are also onerous, placing a larger burden on institutions than is necessary to satisfy the requirements of public accountability, a view which was endorsed in July 2002 in a report by the Cabinet Office's Better Regulation Task Force, *Higher Education: Easing the Burden*. It is a challenge now for government and for the funding councils to ensure that their accountability mechanisms are as lean and efficient as they expect HEIs to be in their use of public funds.

The argument about the size of the burden is not limited to accountability for public funds. It has also arisen in connection with the assessment of the quality of both teaching and research.

In the case of teaching it became evident that the arrangements for quality assessment introduced when the funding councils were created in 1992 were costly relative to the benefit realised. The main purpose was to provide information to potential students and other stakeholders about the quality of teaching in HEIs. In Scotland the quality of teaching was found to be either excellent or highly satisfactory in most cases and at least satisfactory in all the others. Since this was an expensive way of demonstrating that confidence in the quality of provision was justified, a review was undertaken. The outcome is a new system which should be equally effective but less burdensome. It places greater reliance on institutions' own academic quality assurance systems, but a rigorous scheme of institutional audit conducted by a team of external reviewers, including a student, will test the robustness of these systems.

Issues about research accountability have also generated controversy. Cost has again been one of the issues, particularly in relation to one of the most important mechanisms, the RAE. Held roughly once every five years, this generates a huge volume of work for every institution. The financial rewards for success in the RAE, and correspondingly the financial loss arising from failing to achieve an optimal outcome, are such that HEIs are prepared to invest substantial effort and resources in trying to secure the best possible result. While the cost is high, the results of successive RAEs indicate impressive increases in the quantity (as measured by the number of active researchers) and even more markedly in the quality (as measured by the improvement in average grades) of research in UK universities. Therefore most HEIs have remained broadly supportive of the RAE approach.

However, new doubts have arisen following RAE 2001. These do not primarily concern the RAE itself but rather the fact that the increase in funding did not match the improvement in the results. In Scotland some additional funding was announced within weeks of the publication of RAE 2001 results, but much less than the results justified. The subsequent announcement of the outcome of the Scottish Executive's 2002 spending review included additional resource for science and research, but this does not become available until 2004 and, as only part of it will be distributed in relation to RAE performance, it will not fund the improvement fully. The problem associated with an exercise which encourages better performance but then fails to reward it adequately is certain to be one of the issues in the post-RAE review.

THE CHANGING ENVIRONMENT

The extent of the change to which Scottish HEIs have responded since 1990 is considerable. At the beginning of the 1990s there were two distinct sectors. The eight universities were part of a UK system, funded by the Universities Funding Council, which acted as a buffer between the universities and government. Only they had their own degree-awarding powers. The CIs and CEs constituted a separate Scottish system, with no buffer body between them and government, and with no degree-awarding powers. Although many of their programmes led to degree awards, the degrees were those of validating bodies, usually of the Council for National Academic Awards (CNAA) but sometimes of one of the existing universities.

Though change was a constant theme from 1990 onwards, its pace was not consistent. Three periods were of special significance.

The first of these was from 1992 until 1993. It was during this period that a sequence of important changes took place across the UK. The most fundamental of these was that the practice of separate funding arrangements for different types of institution (universities on the one hand, and polytechnics and other types of HEI on the other) was replaced by funding arrangements that were differentiated on the basis of territory. Primary legislation was enacted to create the new funding bodies and to establish a new framework for tertiary level provision. This included an Act specific to Scotland, the Further and Higher Education (Scotland) Act 1992.

The changes had a major impact on all Scottish HEIs. For the eight existing universities it meant their no longer being integrated within a UK-wide funding system. This was an outcome which the majority of them had vigorously opposed during the debate about devolution in the 1970s, but by the early 1990s opinions had altered, and the change was broadly welcomed. For the CIs and CEs it meant their achieving greater autonomy as part of a unified Scottish HE system funded by a single body. Moreover, that body acted as a buffer between them and government and thus liberated them from NDPB status. For the larger CIs there were the added benefits of university title and degree-awarding powers, the latter benefit being extended also to some of the smaller institutions. The wider grant of degree-awarding powers in the UK as a whole undermined the principal function of the CNAA, and it was dissolved.

The second of these periods was 1996 to 1997, during which a committee was established under the chairmanship of Lord Dearing to conduct a national inquiry into HE. This was a UK inquiry, but one which recogniced that Scottish circumstances were different. Therefore a Scottish committee, chaired by Sir Ron Garrick, was appointed. Its report was published as a separate volume alongside the main report and its supplements. The inquiry represented the most wide-ranging review of HE in the UK since the Robbins Report in 1963, and was the more significant because of the timing of its publication in July 1997, very soon after the new Labour government had taken office. Although the new administration by no means implemented all of Dearing's recommendations, the report was nonetheless influential in helping to shape its policy on HE issues.

The third crucial period was the arrival of political devolution in 1999. In part the ground had been prepared in 1992 by the creation of a single Scottish HE sector and the establishment of SHEFC as its funding body, and by the work of Sir Ron Garrick's committee. Nevertheless devolution has made such a large difference to the environment within which the sector works that it justifies detailed examination.

THE IMPACT OF DEVOLUTION

As already observed, long before devolution Scottish HE had a number of distinctive features marking it out from provision in other parts of the UK. Moreover, after 1992 funding for the whole sector was provided from the Scottish block grant, and differences began to appear between SHEFC's funding methodologies and those employed by the funding councils in England and Wales. For example, there were differences in the formulae used for allocating funds for teaching and research. However, these differences were relatively minor, as was to be expected when all the funding councils were receiving ministerial guidance from the same unitary UK administration, operating in the context of a well-established convention of collective responsibility. For the most part, HE policy was made for the UK as a whole.

Devolution changed this, and changed it more immediately than expected. However, there is also a danger of overstating the scale of the change, and of emphasising what is now done differently in Scotland at the expense of those features which remain common throughout the UK. The similarities still outweigh the differences. What devolution has done is to increase the likelihood that some differences will arise.

One obvious reason is that ministerial guidance to each of the funding councils now comes not just from a different minister but from a different administration. There is no certainty that the same party will be in government at both Westminster and Holyrood. Indeed the voting system for the Scottish Parliament, with its strong bias towards proportionality, makes it almost impossible for a single party to achieve an overall majority, with the consequence that coalition government must be the norm. In Westminster by contrast, single party government is the norm and coalition very much the exception. Even if the two governments were of the same political complexion, they would still be distinct bodies which must be expected, at least occasionally, to adopt different policy positions.

In practice one significant variation is to be found in the very way that government departments are structured. The Scottish Executive did not follow Westminster practice of a unified department to cover all levels of education. Instead it created one department to deal with school education, and another to handle FE and HE. The latter, the Scottish Executive Enterprise and Lifelong Learning Department (SEELLD), is also responsible for economic development. Of course there is some loss from not having an all-age education ministry. HE has vital interactions with school education, because of the high proportion of HE students who enter direct from school, and the fact that HEIs train those who teach in schools. While it is always possible that the Scottish Executive may revert to a more traditional pattern, the present arrangement forms an interesting example of the Executive's willingness to innovate. It also signals something substantive in policy terms, namely that the Executive sees HE as having a central role in its economic development strategy. The pairing of lifelong learning with enterprise does not arise from mere convenience or chance. There is purpose behind it, and it has won support from both the HE sector and the business community.

One key change is in the amount of governmental attention and scrutiny devoted to all the devolved areas, including HE. For the minister, notwithstanding the fact that his portfolio is considered a particularly large and demanding one, HE constitutes a significant part of it. This was not the case before devolution, when typically one junior minister in the Scottish Office would be responsible for all of Scottish education and at least one other major function.

Just as there are differences in governmental structures, so too there are in the parliaments. It is an aim of the Scottish Parliament that its committees should have a particularly influential role, which could even include the initiation of legislation. This is in keeping with the assumption that governments will normally be coalitions, and that it is therefore desirable to emphasise the kind of cross-party collaboration represented by the specialist committees. The Enterprise and Lifelong Learning Committee (E&LLC) has already demonstrated a keen interest in HE, spending many more hours on issues affecting Scottish HE than the equivalent committee at Westminster was able to do prior to devolution.

This more intensive scrutiny became particularly evident during 2001 when the then minister, Wendy Alexander, launched an SEELLD review of SHEFC and of the HE sector, and at about the same time the E&LLC began an inquiry into lifelong learning. This latter inquiry has confirmed that the spirit of cross-party collaboration need not inhibit vigorous debate. The committee's evidence sessions were robust, and its report published in

October 2002 (9 Report 2002, *Final Report on Lifelong Learning*, Scottish Parliament Paper 679) included a number of radical proposals, several of which concerned the relationship between FE and HE sectors. The committee made an especially strong case for better articulation between programmes in the two sectors, and recommended merger of the Scottish Further Education Funding Council (SFEFC) with SHEFC within five years.

The increase in attention and scrutiny from both government and parliament can be perceived as either opportunity or threat. The threat is of excessive political interference that might undermine the autonomy which HEIs cherish. It would be reckless to say that this could not happen, but to date it has not been borne out by events. Ministers have concentrated on broad strategic direction, and have resisted the temptation to become involved in the detailed management of the sector. The balance has favoured opportunity: we have parliamentarians, ministers and senior officials who are better informed about HE than their predecessors, and whose improved understanding of its potential should benefit both the sector and the country as a whole.

STUDENT SUPPORT

The issue which has demonstrated most powerfully the difference which devolution can make is that of student support. It emerged initially as a debate about tuition fees, which became one of the dominant issues in the Scottish Parliament elections in 1999. The introduction of tuition fees was the Labour government's response to one of the urgent problems it faced when it came to office in 1997, namely the fact that underfunding of HE had become acute following nearly two decades of cuts which had reduced the real value of funding per student by approximately 40%. The charging of means-tested tuition fees, equivalent on average to rather less than one-quarter of the actual cost of tuition, created an additional income stream for HEIs and reduced pressure on the public purse. Moreover, it appeared reasonable to ask that those who benefited from HE should make a contribution towards its cost, so long as there were safeguards to exempt low-income families. It was less logical for a government which declared itself to be in favour of widening access to those from less well-off families to accelerate the abolition of the means-tested maintenance grant, a move which was clearly to the disadvantage of less well-off students.

These policy shifts predated devolution and hence applied throughout the UK. They were not popular, but nor was there vociferous public opposition to them. It was significant, however, that tuition fees became a party political issue, and that all the major parties other than Labour opposed their introduction. This made no difference at Westminster where Labour enjoyed a large majority and there was no prospect of it being outvoted. On the other hand it could make a great deal of difference given a different electoral scenario, and this is precisely what the 1999 elections to the Scottish Parliament provided.

Scottish Nationalists, Conservatives and Liberal Democrats all campaigned for the abolition of tuition fees, believing them to be unpopular and seeing this as one of the issues on which they could differentiate themselves from Labour. The stance of the Liberal Democrats was particularly crucial, since they appeared to be Labour's only realistic coalition partner. The fact that they declared the abolition of tuition fees a non-negotiable objective was therefore highly significant.

When the elections took place Labour won fifty-three out of the seventy-three constituency seats, but the proportionality factor in the form of top-up seats left it too far short of an overall majority to govern alone. Therefore, as anticipated, the first Scottish Executive was Labour led but with the Liberal Democrats as coalition partners. This left the Executive with little option but to abolish fees. However, it was also recognised that this had to be achieved in a manner that did not damage two other priorities. The first was ensuring that the funding of the HE sector should not be further undermined: the abolition of tuition fees would do great damage unless equivalent funding was found from another source. The second was improving the HE participation rates of students from low income families: they would not benefit from the abolition of fees, since (fees being means-tested) they did not pay them anyway.

In an effort to find a solution that would be generally accepted, the Executive decided to establish an independent committee of inquiry into student finance to consider the issues at arms length from party politics. An Edinburgh lawyer, Andrew Cubie, who had good connections both with Scottish business and with HE, chaired the committee of fourteen members representing all the key interests. The committee worked quickly and intensively, publishing its report by the end of 1999, less than six months after its establishment. It offered an ingenious solution to the two policy dilemmas mentioned above.

Its answer to the problem of funding the sector was that, while tuition fees would be abolished, an alternative mechanism would be created to ensure that those who benefited most from HE would make a contribution towards its cost. Because the Committee did not consider it appropriate to collect the contribution until graduates had felt the benefit, it proposed a scheme whereby they would begin repaying part of the cost only once their salary levels were substantially in excess of national average earnings. This would provide an income stream to replace tuition fees, although there would be a time lag before it began to flow. In the short-term additional public money would have to be invested to compensate HEIs for the loss of tuition fee income. The committee addressed the second issue, that of widening participation, by proposing the reintroduction of means-tested grants to cover at least a significant part of the maintenance costs of students from low income families.

The response of the Scottish Executive to Cubie's recommendations was largely positive. It accepted the main principles, while making some detailed adjustments, of which the most serious was that the threshold salary level at which graduates are expected to begin repaying part of the cost of their education was set below and not above the national average earnings figure. Nonetheless, the overall outcome was that two important features of UK government policy, the introduction of means-tested tuition fees and the ending of means-tested student grants, had both been overturned in Scotland, demonstrating at a very early stage that devolution does make a difference.

CONCLUSIONS

The picture of the HE sector sketched above is generally a favourable one. That is justified, as Scottish HEIs have achieved great successes in many key areas, notably the growth of the system and the improvement in research performance. Even in instances where achievement has been more modest, such as the widening of access, the sector can argue legitimately that the failure to do better is not for want of effort on its part. However, the sector does have critics, and their views should be acknowledged.

Among the most frequently voiced criticisms is that there is insufficient collaboration within the system itself and between HE and other sectors. In part this reflects a failure by HEIs to publicise the extensive and increasing amount of collaboration and partnership in which they are involved, but equally most would accept that there are more such opportunities yet to be taken up.

A more fundamental criticism is that the sector has failed to state as clearly as it should its view of the purposes of HE and their relevance to current circumstances. The scale of growth of the system, the speed of change in the environment, and the diversity of institutional missions have all contributed to making it more difficult to articulate these purposes. However, they have also made the task more urgent. The fact that there is a growing tendency for government, employers and significant numbers of students to see the production of employable graduates as the primary purpose means that it is vital that the case is made for those other purposes which are equally or even more important. In its submission in 2002 to the SEELLD review of HE, Universities Scotland, the representative body for the sector, attempted to tackle the issue, listing the following main purposes: the provision of high quality advanced education available to all those capable of benefiting from it; leading the advancement of knowledge and facilitating knowledge transfer; supplying well-educated graduates to the employment market; sustaining lifelong learning needs; the development and transmission of culture; providing an informed critique of public policy; and contributing to establishing Scotland's place in the world.

The sector may also have been too passive in its acceptance of governmental actions, especially over its tolerance of very large growth in student numbers without a corresponding increase in resources. As a result, despite the fact that for Scottish HE the experience of the early years of devolution has been mainly positive, a large question remains concerning the underfunding of the system. That there is serious underfunding is no longer in doubt. It is acknowledged by government right up to the level of the Prime Minister. There is no longer any argument that something needs to be done to rectify matters. The debate has moved on to how it will be achieved. The funding gap does not have to be met wholly from public sources, and in England one leading option is to increase tuition fees, or even deregulate them altogether. The particular dilemma faced by the Scottish Executive is that it has ruled out tuition fees as an option for the foreseeable future, and has thus limited the sector's ability to draw on alternative sources of income.

The problem is exacerbated by ever increasing public policy demands on the sector, for which resources are not increased correspondingly. Government would like to add social inclusion and commercialisation of research to the sector's traditional missions of learning and teaching and research, but the funding streams to support these are minimal. Worse, there is justified suspicion that part of the modest funding which has been allocated has been found by diverting some existing funding which would otherwise have been available for the traditional missions. Scottish HEIs already draw an increasing proportion of their income from non-governmental sources, but there is a limit to the extent to which they can exploit these sources to subsidise work that is undertaken for public benefit and in response to explicit government requirements.

Much will depend on the considered view taken by the Scottish Executive about the significance for Scotland's future of a vigorous, enterprising and well-resourced HE system. So far its rhetoric has been positive, even if the resources provided have not fully matched it. However, in the early years of devolution financial circumstances were relatively benign. Now the Executive has made a number of additional spending commitments which mean that more difficult choices have to be made. One test of the seriousness of the Executive's aim to create a 'smart successful Scotland' will be its willingness to make investment in HE a priority.

REFERENCES

Higher Education Funding Council for England, SHEFC, Education and Learning Wales, Northern Ireland Department for Employment and Learning (2001) *Performance Indicators in Higher Education in the UK 1999/2000*, Bristol: HEFCE.

Higher Education Funding Council for England, SHEFC, Education and Learning Wales, Northern Ireland Department for Employment and Learning (2001) *2001 Research Assessment Exercise: The Outcome*, Bristol: HEFCE.

Higher Education Statistics Agency (2002) *Students in Higher Education Institutions 2000/01*, Cheltenham: HESA.

Independent Committee of Inquiry into Student Finance (1999) *Student Finance: Fairness for the Future* (The Cubie Report), Edinburgh: Independent Committee of Inquiry.

National Committee of Inquiry into Higher Education (1997) *Higher Education in the Learning Society*, Report of the National Committee (The Dearing Report), Norwich: HMSO.

National Committee of Inquiry into Higher Education (1997) *Higher Education in the Learning Society*, Report of the Scottish Committee (The Garrick Report), Norwich: HMSO.

7

Policy Making in Scottish Education

Walter Humes

The corresponding chapter in the first edition of this volume offered an account of policy making in education before the establishment of the Scottish Parliament. The present chapter seeks to bring the account up to date by considering what difference the Parliament has made and, in particular, whether there is evidence of the 'new politics' that was promised as devolution approached. Lynch (2001, p. 89) has observed that: 'the Scottish Parliament was designed to fulfil an ambitious agenda of participatory politics by the public and pressure groups as well as power-sharing between parties and legislators and the pursuit of consensus politics'. The expectations associated with this agenda raise a series of interesting questions:

- To what extent, within the educational sphere, has the intention of participation and power-sharing been realised?
- In what ways has the traditional policy community in Scottish education been affected?
- Have relations between the Scottish Executive and Non-Departmental Public Bodies (NDPBs) differed significantly from those that characterised the operations of the Scottish Office?
- What changes, if any, can be detected in the role of important professional groups, such as the inspectorate and directors of education?
- Have new constituencies of people been involved in the various stages of policy making, from conception through to implementation?
- Can major changes of style and substance be detected, or has it been very much 'business as usual'?

The answers that will be proposed in this chapter – some of which should be regarded as highly provisional – must be considered alongside the new chapters on the Scottish Executive Education Department (SEED) and the Enterprise and Lifelong Learning Department (ELLD), as well as the substantially revised chapters on the politics of Scottish education and the inspectorate (Chapters 11, 12, 8 and 14 respectively).

Policy making in education (as in other fields) can be approached from several perspectives. It can be explained in terms of manifesto commitments by political parties, the ideological framework which informs those commitments, the plans which are drawn up to translate policy intentions into practical action, and the legislative and other forms of power which are required to ensure that this happens. Likewise, the study of policy making can proceed in a variety of ways. It is possible to focus on the content of policies, the processes by means of which broad policy intentions are refined, the language which is used to promote policies, the individuals, groups and institutions that play a part in the consultation and development phases that normally form part of a policy initiative, or on some combination of these. Moreover, in advanced democratic societies, policy making is rarely a straightforward business. Debates about policy are generally marked by conflict, negotiation and compromise, and hard decisions have to be taken about priorities, funding, and timing. At best, according to Ball, the exercise is likely to be 'unwieldy and complex', at worst 'unscientific and irrational' (*Politics and Policy Making in Education*, Routledge, 1990, p. 3). These observations point to the need to dig beneath the surface of official statements about the origins and intentions of particular policies, and the justifications which are offered for their introduction.

The analysis that follows is concerned principally with policy processes, though it will be illustrated with reference to particular developments for there has been no shortage of policy initiatives in the post-devolution period. Reference will also be made to the way in which policies have been managed and to their reception by teachers at the implementation stage. First, however, it is necessary to give a brief summary of what happened prior to devolution. This will serve as a reference point for some of the judgements that will be offered later.

POLICY MAKING PRE-DEVOLUTION

There was no universally-held view of educational policy making prior to the establishment of the Scottish Parliament: 'official' and 'unofficial' readings of the situation existed. According to official accounts, the making of educational policy occurred in a variety of ways and involved a range of people operating in different circumstances. Sometimes it emerged after mature consideration and reflection, informed by evidence and research; at other times it was a response to immediate events that were perceived as requiring attention. Furthermore, although policy was primarily the responsibility of politicians (in particular the Education Minister acting on behalf of the Secretary of State), many others were involved in the successive stages of policy making. Senior civil servants (administrators) and members of Her Majesty's Inspectorate (HMIs) had an important part to play (though, as will be seen, the role of inspectors became a controversial issue post-devolution). In addition, the views of a number of agencies outside government were fed into the process: Learning and Teaching Scotland (LTS); the Scottish Qualifications Authority (SQA); the Association of Directors of Education in Scotland (ADES); the Convention of Scottish Local Authorities (COSLA); the General Teaching Council for Scotland (GTCS); the Educational Institute of Scotland (EIS); the Scottish Parent Teacher Council (SPTC); and primary and secondary headteachers' associations.

Underlying this official account was a belief in the efficacy of certain fundamental principles – notably, partnership, consultation and consensus. On this view educational provision depended on the co-operation of central and local government, teachers and parents, curriculum and assessment bodies. Consequently, in the framing of new policies, it was essential that they worked in partnership with each other. This required that all those concerned had an opportunity to make representations and express opinions on policy proposals – thus the importance of consultation. As a result of consultation exercises – so the argument continued – policies were adjusted and the outcome was a broadly agreed consensus which took account of the legitimate concerns of a wide range of people. In all of this, the stewardship of those entrusted with formulating, developing and implementing policies was seen as unproblematic: it was assumed that they could be relied upon to act in the public interest.

From the mid-1980s onwards this account was challenged by a number of researchers who suggested that it was necessary to look in more detail at the distribution and exercise of power in policy-making, at the management styles that were employed, and at the forms of discourse that were used in promoting policies. These researchers offered an 'unofficial' account of what happened. Prominent among them were McPherson and Raab (*Governing Education*, Edinburgh: Edinburgh University Press, 1988) and Humes (*The Leadership Class in Scottish Education*, Edinburgh, John Donald, 1986).

McPherson and Raab used the term 'policy community' to describe the network of people inside and outside government who, collectively, helped to determine the educational agenda. At the centre of this process were politicians, administrators and inspectors within the Scottish Office, although the precise relationship and relative power of these three groups was subject to change over time. In terms of links with the wider educational policy community outside government, HMIs were especially important because of the extensive range of contacts (with schools, local authorities and teacher education institutions) their inspection work allowed them to develop. Moreover, as far as advising on policy was concerned, they had an important 'intelligence gathering' function, identifying issues that merited attention and producing reports that informed ministerial thinking. HMIs also had considerable powers of patronage in making recommendations for membership of the working parties, committees and development groups that were used to plan and flesh out the details of policies. McPherson and Raab suggested that expertise was not the only criterion for admission to the policy community. Recipients of patronage had to exhibit the qualities of 'deference and trust', including a respect for the traditional bureaucratic virtues of discretion and confidentiality, and a willingness to proceed through 'proper channels' rather than engage in public debate that might be politically embarrassing. In other words, these 'outsiders' were expected to come to share the 'assumptive worlds' of government officials. The permitted discourse of the policy community was thus controlled from the outset.

Humes presented an even sharper critique by suggesting that there was a 'leadership class' in Scottish education that employed a rhetoric of democratic participation but actually operated in its own interests. The management style of the leadership class was fairly authoritarian, though the nature and extent of the control was disguised through various presentational devices or 'strategies of containment'. These included the following: careful control of the flow of information relating to policy initiatives; the marginalisation of dissent; skilful circumscribing of the scope of government-funded research enquiries; promotion of a cult of managerialism which encouraged concentration on 'how?' rather than 'why?' questions; initiation of those admitted to the policy community into a conformist bureaucratic ideology, with the honours list used as a reward system (see also Bryce & Humes 1999).

As devolution approached, others took up some of these concerns, placing them in a wider political context and expressing the hope that the new parliament would allow for more open forms of policy-making to develop. Paterson (2000), for example, predicted that there might be an upsurge of 'civic activism' which would challenge the 'democratic deficit' in the traditional policy process. Instead of relying on selective consultation with favoured partners and on compliant NDPBs, a Scottish parliament would have to be more transparent in its dealings with a 'new active citizenry'. To what extent have such aspirations been realised? Are there signs of greater openness and increased accountability?

Before attempting to offer a judgement on this it is necessary to provide some information about the content of educational policies in the period since the establishment of the Scottish Parliament. (For much more detailed information on the Parliament's debates on education see Donn 1999–2002.)

POLICY INITIATIVES

Just as Tony Blair's UK government made education a priority when the Labour Party was elected in 1997, so the Scottish Executive under the leadership of the First Minister Donald Dewar placed education at the top of its agenda when the new Scottish Parliament first met in July 1999 (a position reinforced by Dewar's successors as First Minister, Henry McLeish and Jack McConnell). There followed a number of major policy developments. The McCrone Committee produced a series of important recommendations on teachers' pay and conditions, and outlined a new framework for the induction, registration and continuing development of teachers. Although the implementation of the McCrone proposals has not been without difficulties, its general approach was widely regarded as signalling a desire to place Scottish education on a firm footing by according value and status to teaching as a profession. Likewise, the Cubie Committee on student tuition fees produced a well-received report and, although its recommendations were subsequently watered down, the outcome placed Scottish students at an advantage compared to their English counterparts. Up-front tuition fees were abolished and subsistence support was provided for priority groups (see Chapter 13). On the legislative front, the Standards in Scotland's Schools etc. Act of 2000 imposed additional duties on education authorities and made them subject to inspection. The role of the General Teaching Council was also extended to include responsibility for assessing the competence of registered teachers. The Scottish Executive itself was required to justify policy decisions on the basis of the contribution they would make to the improvement of quality in education. As part of this, National Priorities had to be set out and these were approved by the Scottish Parliament in December 2000 as follows:

Achievement and Attainment
- To raise standards of educational attainment for all in schools, especially in the core skills of literacy and numeracy, and to achieve better levels in national measures of achievement including examination results.

Framework for Learning
- To support and develop the skills of teachers, the self discipline of pupils and to enhance school environments so that they are conducive to learning and teaching.

Inclusion and Equality
- To promote equality and help every pupil benefit from education, with particular regard paid to pupils with disabilities and special educational needs, and to Gaelic and other lesser used languages.

Values and Citizenship
- To work with parents to teach pupils respect for self and one another and their interdependence with other members of their neighbourhood and society and to teach them the duties and responsibilities of citizenship in a democratic society.

Learning for Life
- To equip pupils with the foundation skills, attitudes and expectations necessary to prosper in a changing society and to encourage creativity and ambition.

The seriousness of intent with regard to education was signalled in other ways too. The failure of the Scottish Qualifications Authority to produce the 2000 examination results in a timely and efficient manner led the Education Minister to move swiftly to draft in external staff to sort out the crisis and the SQA board was reconstituted. As part of the fallout from this episode, the role of the inspectorate was redefined. Policy making and inspection processes were clearly separated. The function of the renamed HMIE (Her Majesty's Inspectorate of Education) was restricted to inspection and it became an executive agency in April 2001. It was also physically relocated at some distance from both the Parliament and from senior administrators within the civil service. A subsequent attempt by Her Majesty's Senior Chief Inspector to present this reduction of status as a development which was 'overdue and . . . a response to the changes in roles and functions brought about by devolution' (HMIE, Annual Report 2001–2, p. 2) was not entirely convincing. It was widely perceived as an acknowledgement of the inspectorate's previous involvement in policy making and, more specifically, of the conflict of interest which arose from its responsibility to judge the success of policies which it had helped to promote in the first place.

More recently the current Minister for Education and Young People (Cathy Jamieson) launched a national debate which sought to canvass public views on future policy. In her foreword to the launch document (March 2002) the minister said, 'I want to hear as many views as possible from a wide range of people about the kind of education system we want to see for future generations.' A briefing pack posed a series of questions covering both theoretical and practical issues, ranging from why we educate children and young people in the first place to where and when education is best delivered. A separate enquiry, initiated by the Education, Culture and Sport Committee, canvassed views on the purposes of Scottish education and an analysis of responses was presented to the committee in September 2002. (For a more detailed discussion of this enquiry see Chapter 8.)

These initiatives are subject to more than one interpretation. They could be seen as attempts to soften the hard-edged character of some New Labour policies, such as the continuing emphasis on standards, targets and outcomes (a theme taken over from the New Right). Other efforts at striking a balance between progressive and traditional perspectives on educational policy include the work on citizenship and creativity undertaken by Learning and Teaching Scotland. Alternatively, the national debate and the parliamentary committee enquiry could be seen as genuine attempts to seek new ideas from non-traditional sources and to promote dialogue between politicians, professionals and members of the public. The fact that these two separate exercises took place also suggests interesting tensions between the Executive and the backbench MSPs who constitute the membership of parliamentary committees. Such tension might be regarded as healthy for democracy even if it makes the life of ministers more difficult.

It should also be noted that information about policy initiatives is now more easily accessed, thanks to advances in information technology. The Scottish Executive website contains a vast amount of material relating to education – discussion papers, reports, consultation documents, press releases and so on. However, there is a need to review guidelines on publication as there are confusing inconsistencies between (and sometimes within) departments in the format and content of documents. The same criticism applies to some hard-copy material issued by SEED and ELLD.

Taken together these developments certainly seem to indicate a strong political commitment to the importance of education in post-devolution Scotland. But does the substance match up to the official rhetoric? The Scottish Parliament has been in existence for a relatively short time and so it would be premature to offer anything more than a provisional assessment. Nevertheless, there is some evidence that enables a few conclusions to be drawn.

THE POLICY PROCESS POST-DEVOLUTION

One of the justifications for the establishment of the Scottish Parliament was that it would require politicians and officials to be more accountable to the Scottish people than had been possible under the previous system. Prior to devolution the Scottish Office had been subject to criticism on a number of grounds, most notably a perception that ministers and civil servants owed their first loyalty to Westminster and Whitehall rather than to Scotland and often acted in ways that prevented proper scrutiny of their actions. Accordingly, when the operational principles for the new Parliament were being drawn up, a number of important values were asserted as essential characteristics:

> 'the Scottish Parliament should embody and reflect the sharing of power between the people of Scotland, the legislators and the Scottish Executive; the Scottish Executive should be accountable to the Scottish Parliament and the Parliament and Executive should be accountable to the people of Scotland; the Scottish Parliament should be accessible, open, responsive and develop procedures which make possible a participative approach to the development, consideration and scrutiny of policy and legislation:' (Scottish Office, *Shaping Scotland's Parliament*, Edinburgh: The Stationery Office, 1998, p. 3)

An important part of trying to ensure that these principles are upheld is the role of parliamentary committees. In the case of education there are two – the Education, Culture and Sport Committee and the Enterprise and Lifelong Learning Committee. Both have remits which enable them to examine educational matters, call ministers and officials to account, and initiate enquiries and reports. However, the extent to which these powers are effectively exercised depends on the balance of committee membership, party loyalties and expertise in areas under discussion. Reference will be made later to the role of the Education, Culture and Sport Committee in relation to the passage of the Standards in Scotland's Schools etc. Act.

A research study of the effects of devolution in Scotland, with particular reference to its impact on local government, provides interesting insights into the changing configurations of some (but not all) of the key players in policy-making (Bennett, Fairley and McAteer, 2002). The study was based on 120 interviews with Scottish Executive ministers, civil servants and senior councillors and officials from eleven local authorities. It found that the great majority of those in local government were supportive of the Parliament and devolution. 'Generally, local government reported that, post devolution, government was more open and inclusive, and ministers and civil servants had become more accessible' (p. v). However, those in local government tended to be less positive about the Executive than about the Parliament and some interviewees were critical of the attitude of senior civil servants, one commenting that 'They are high in arrogance – they have a command view of the world' (p. v). Equally, some civil servants expressed doubt about the capacity of local government to deliver certain political priorities. On communication between the Executive and COSLA, the body which represents the collective interests of local authorities, there was a feeling among local government interviewees that the relationship was inclined to be 'too cosy', thereby compromising COSLA's campaigning role.

These points relate to the overall picture. What about education specifically? The study found that devolution had impacted differentially on different local government services. Directors of education were more positive than any other professional group. They 'felt very supportive of the Executive and enthusiastic about their role in working in partnership' (p. v). One senior member of ADES remarked, 'We are well connected to policy-making circles,' and stated that there was now a 'more open exchange of views across and between actors' (p. 35). Chief executives and representatives of other local government services (housing, economic development) were less favourable in their comments, some claiming that the civil service did not really understand local government because it had never carried responsibility for the actual delivery of services. It is one thing to frame policy: it is quite another to carry it through to the point of implementation.

How are these findings to be interpreted? On the face of it they seem to indicate – albeit with some reservations – that things are moving in the right direction towards greater transparency and responsiveness on the part of Executive (compared to the Scottish Office). First, however, it should be noted that the findings were based on elite interviews: that is, the respondents were people who enjoyed a measure of relative power in the political and professional worlds they inhabit. Most of them would also have had similar status pre-devolution and indeed some would have been involved directly in preparing for devolution. In other words, they had a stake in ensuring the success of the exercise. This may go some way towards explaining the generally positive attitudes to the political changes that accompanied the creation of the Parliament. At the same time, the setting up of the Parliament inevitably involved redrawing the political map in a way that repositioned many of the key players. Politicians now owe their first loyalty to Holyrood rather than Westminster. Civil servants have had to come to terms with a more overtly political environment in which they are subject to the scrutiny of backbench MSPs and parlia-mentary committees, as well as ministers within the Executive. Local government personnel (both elected members and officials) would naturally be concerned to make representations to the new Parliament to try to ensure that their influence was at least maintained and, if possible, strengthened. Some of the statements reported in the study should, therefore, be regarded both as genuine attempts to understand the new situation and as claims about the importance of their own contribution (compared to that of other players). In other words, the respondents were well placed to comment on what had been happening but could not be considered as neutral, disinterested observers.

A second interpretative point relates to the political congruence between central and local government in Scotland. Although the Scottish Executive is formed from a coalition of Labour and Liberal Democrat ministers, the Labour Party is easily the more dominant partner having secured fifty-six MSPs compared to seventeen by the Liberal Democrats in the 1999 election. Similarly at local government level Labour has enjoyed dominance for many years. There is, therefore, a natural tendency for the two levels of government to support each other on most issues. With regard to officials, civil servants are expected to give neutral advice while policies are being developed but, once they are approved, their role is to promote whatever the government of the day wants to achieve (e.g. the National Priorities in education). Local government officials are expected to operate in a similar way but the record of some local authorities in Scotland has led to concerns both about the role of officials and about the basis on which some senior appointments are made. The 'correct' political sympathies and an appropriately deferential attitude to leading councillors may be just as important as ability. 'Independence of mind' is rarely found on job descriptions. It is unlikely, therefore, that the conformist ideology which prevailed pre-devolution has been set aside in favour of something more critical and questioning.

This observation leads into a third point of explanation arising from the devolution study. The positive response of directors of education can partly be attributed to the political importance attached to education as a policy priority and the relatively generous financial settlement which education has enjoyed compared to other public services. But it is also important to note that educational policy was already largely devolved before the establishment of the Scottish Parliament and directors of education were already key players in the policy community. Their position has, if anything, been strengthened post-devolution because of the need to consult them on the implications of all the policy initiatives that have been pursued by successive Education Ministers (each concerned to make their mark). Furthermore, the track record of directors of education in exhibiting those qualities of 'deference and trust' which ensured their admission into the inner councils of state continued well after the study undertaken by McPherson and Raab in the 1980s. Their 'assumptive world' took it for granted that it was in their interests to 'go with the grain' of whatever happened to be the dominant policy discourse. More charitably, their actions might be interpreted as a perception of their role as being principally concerned with managerial and operational matters rather than with fundamental issues of meaning and purpose in educational policy, though their submission to the parliamentary enquiry into the SQA exam crisis did show a welcome awareness of the need for 'philosophical underpinning' to support educational reform (see Paterson, L., *Crisis in the Classroom*, Mainstream, 2000, pp. 137–8).

Further insight into the conduct of educational policy in Scotland post-devolution is provided by an interesting unpublished study by Gillies (2001), looking specifically at the various stages of the Standards in Scotland's Schools etc. Act of 2000. Gillies sought to assess the handling of this important piece of legislation using the Parliament's own stated commitment to open, inclusive government. He focused particularly on the requirement to have pre-legislative scrutiny before the formal processes of legislation and on the role of the Education, Culture and Sport Committee in amending the proposals. His main source was the official record of Parliament but he also secured interviews with SEED officials and obtained questionnaire responses from MSPs.

What were the origins of the Act? Prior to the 1999 elections to the Scottish Parliament, civil servants, in accordance with usual practice, produced a number of position papers based on the manifestos of the main political parties. Post-election a relatively small group of people consisting of Labour ministers, SEED officials and advisers took the decision to proceed from policy paper to legislation. There was no proper pre-legislative scrutiny. Gillies concludes that this had 'all the hallmarks of elitist policy-making' (p. 21). He also suggests that the primary motivation was political rather than educational. The main driver was the high priority attached to education by the Labour Party during the election campaign and the need to be seen to be doing something that publicly demonstrated that commitment.

The decision having been taken, the next stage was the issuing of a consultation document, *Improving Our Schools* (which also included the draft bill). The consultation exercise ran from July to October 1999 and the results were published in January 2000 along with an amended draft Bill (known at that stage as the Improvement in Scottish Education Bill), taking on board some of the comments that had been received. There is no doubt that the consultation exercise was extensive and on a scale unmatched under the old Scottish Office regime. More than 27,000 copies of the document were sent out, sixty-five meetings involving ministers and senior officials were held across Scotland, an internet website was set up, and a special effort was made to consult children and young people. Some 320 responses were received. Two important questions arise from this process. How were the responses assessed? And what difference did they make to the legislative proposals? According to Gillies, officials he interviewed were vague about how submissions were handled and admitted that there was no specific methodology in processing them. He concludes that there is a need for an open system so that the criteria by means of which submissions are judged are transparent. With regard to the impact of the consultation, Gillies states, 'In effect, very few changes were made as a result of the consultation stage' (p. 26). There was greater recognition of the rights of children but this was motivated as much by international pressures (from the European Union and the United Nations) as by views submitted by respondents. Other changes gave stronger emphasis to the role of parents and to the education of children with significant health difficulties. In general, however, the practical consequences of the consultation exercise seem to have been limited. This led to charges of tokenism and Gillies suggested that this stage was, 'of more value to the Executive in terms of policy promotion, public relations and political campaigning' (p. 31) than an example of genuine democratic participation which made a difference.

This view was reinforced by members of the Education, Culture and Sport Committee who had to produce a report on the nature of the consultation stage. They drew attention to discrepancies between the procedures drawn up by the consultative steering group (and endorsed by the Parliament) and what actually happened: the lack of pre-legislative scrutiny came in for particular criticism. The committee also had responsibility to subject the legislation to a 'line by line' examination and suggest further amendments. A total of 141 amendments were proposed but only five in the name of committee members were accepted. However, some of the committee discussion was taken on board and the Executive itself brought forward a number of additional changes in its own name. A final opportunity to influence the legislation arose at the meeting of the Scottish Parliament on 7 June 2000 when a debate lasting three hours took place. Opportunity for backbench MSPs to contribute was limited and this led to a feeling of being sidelined. Gillies describes this stage as 'defective' (p. 41) and 'unduly precipitate' (p. 42) and states that it 'cannot be thought of as a paradigm of reflective policy-making' (p. 42).

Can any wider conclusions be drawn from this particular case? It is evident that the major players (ministers, chairs of committees, MSPs, civil servants) are still finding their feet in the new political environment. They are having to work under pressure because of public expectations and are subject to a greater degree of scrutiny than applied pre-devolution. If they are perceived as failing, then the credibility of the Parliament is seriously weakened. The evidence of public opinion polls suggests that while most Scots are pleased to have a parliament in Edinburgh, they are still to be convinced of the quality of political and administrative leadership. This uncertainty is reinforced by a perception that sometimes attention is being deflected from the substantive issues by power-plays involving the main players. Tensions within the Executive (e.g. the resignation of Wendy Alexander as Minister for Enterprise and Lifelong Learning early in 2002), between the Executive and committee members, and between MSPs and the civil service all create the impression of a system that is still in transition. With regard to the last point, one MSP, the Liberal Democrat, Donald Gorrie, has expressed frustration about what he sees as the 'stranglehold which the Civil Service has over the Executive's policy development . . . Ministers currently listen to civil servants and ignore MSPs. This must change. We must persuade the civil servants to change many years of secretive "knowledge is power" mentality – that everyone outside . . . is an enemy to be kept in the dark' (cited in Gillies, p. 8). A continuing task for the Parliament is to find effective means of challenging and changing the ways in which the civil service operates.

As far as the wider policy community is concerned – those individuals, groups and institutions outside government that have traditionally had some role in shaping the policy agenda or, at least, the development of policy once its broad framework has been decided at a political level – it is rather early to judge the effect of devolution. However, some preliminary observations can be offered.

In post-devolution Scotland, the notion of a single educational policy community has become rather questionable, though the tendency towards fragmentation pre-dated the creation of the Parliament. As educational provision has expanded and become more complex, so it has become difficult for any one group to penetrate all sectors of the system. The inspectorate, traditionally the key agency in gathering intelligence and maintaining networks, has been weakened (at least for the time being) and, in any case, has a limited remit in relation to some sectors, particularly higher education. This means that it might be more meaningful to refer to a number of overlapping policy *communities*, rather than a single, coherent entity. Thus it might make sense to speak of a range of policy communities, each with a particular focus – pre-school and primary education, secondary education, special education, further education, higher education, teacher education, community education. There will be points of convergence between these but, for many purposes, they will remain separate. It is, of course, the job of the Scottish Executive to maintain an overview of the system as a whole, but the difficulty of doing so should not be under-estimated. Even within SEED and ELLD there are different divisions and sections, and maintaining satisfactory communication between them can be problematic. These complexities mean that the old patronage system is likely to come under some strain and be less straightforward to manage. There is, in fact, a need for a serious research study of changing patterns of patronage pre- and post-devolution. Some of the familiar faces from the past have certainly been able to secure continuing access to the corridors of power, but their positions are less secure than they were and new channels of influence are emerging. As yet, however, there has been no 'bonfire of the quangos' and the system of appointments has been subject to charges of cronyism (see 'Quango watchdog filled by Labour', *Scotsman*, 30 January 2002, p. 8).

One way of conceptualising the present position would be to say that a looser set of social networks – some professional, some political, some personal – is now in evidence, and their relative importance is likely to vary over time and be dependent on the particular arena under consideration. For example, whereas some policy communities (such as secondary education) are largely home-grown, in the sense of drawing mainly from within Scotland, others (notably higher education) operate within a broader UK and international framework and this is reflected in their composition. It is also important to note the emergence of some interesting new players in the shape of independent 'think tanks' seeking to contribute to the climate of ideas in post-devolution Scotland. These generally have interests that include, but extend beyond, education. Examples are the Scottish Civic Forum, Big Thinking and the Scottish Council Foundation. The last has produced a series of thoughtful publications, especially on economic and educational issues (see, for example, Bloomer, K., *Learning to Change: Scottish Education in the 21st Century*, Edinburgh: Scottish Council Foundation, 2001). Insofar as these groups do succeed in stimulating serious debate, they will serve as a counterweight to the pragmatic (some would say anti-intellectual) tendencies of the dominant twentieth-century approaches to educational policy-making in Scotland. In doing so, they may recapture something of the spirit of the Sixth Scottish Advisory Council on Education which produced enlightened and theoretically robust ideas in the middle decades of the twentieth century, not least in its 1947 report on secondary education.

FROM INTENTION TO IMPLEMENTATION

Whatever the origins and intentions of educational policies, in the final analysis their success or failure depends on the expertise and commitment of individual teachers in schools and other educational institutions across the country. Communicating with practitioners at all levels involves the efforts of a wider range of people than those who might be regarded as central players within the relevant policy community. Here the role of development officers and in-service trainers is important. All the major programmes of reform both pre- and post-devolution – such as Higher Still and the Chartered Teacher initiative – have depended on substantial inputs from 'intermediate' staff of this kind, often seconded from local authorities or teacher education institutions on temporary or part-time contracts, who have produced materials and explained and promoted approved policies to groups of teachers up and down the country. Within local authorities, advisers and staff tutors attached to educational development services have also made a vital contribution. It is at this point that the 'unwieldy and complex' nature of policy implementation becomes particularly apparent. Levels of initial awareness among school staff vary, schools may be more or less receptive to new ideas, and demand for back-up in the form of equipment and resources is rarely matched by supply. The 'intermediate' staff generally do not have an easy task in their efforts to ensure that policy initiatives get off to a good start. Their power is limited and, while they can convey concerns at local level back to the central agencies, they cannot guarantee that there will be an adequate response. They thus occupy a somewhat ambivalent position, trying to satisfy two audiences – policy-makers at national level and classroom teachers at local level. Their ambivalence serves as a reminder of the untidy, and sometimes frustrating, nature of policy development, a feature that official accounts tend to ignore. Teachers can be provided with all kinds of support and staff development to acquaint them with the requirements of new programmes – but that is not enough. They need to be convinced that the reforms which they are asked to implement are sound in principle and consistent with their own professional standards and values. There is no short cut or 'quick fix' in this process.

Decisions about the nature and extent of educational provision in any society are inescapably decisions about the value system which that society is seeking to promote. Educational institutions embody social messages about fundamental principles such as freedom, authority, equality, justice and community. Thus policy decisions are never purely technical matters about the most efficient means of reaching stated objectives. They are always expressive of a social philosophy that, in a democracy, should be contestable and open to argument. The official rhetoric of post-devolution Scotland has made some substantial claims about the opportunities for democratic debate which the new constitutional arrangements allow. What the evidence of this chapter suggests is that the possibilities inherent in the Scottish Parliament – through the democratic mandate which it represents, the powers of parliamentary committees and the increased accountability of officials – are still at an early stage of development and, while there are some grounds for cautious optimism, there is still a fair way to go in terms of extending opportunities for the genuine involvement of people outside the traditional political, bureaucratic and professional elites.

REFERENCES

Bennett, M., Fairley, J. & McAteer, M. (2002) *Devolution in Scotland: The Impact on Local Government*, York: Joseph Rowntree Foundation.

Bryce, T. G. K. & Humes, W. M. (1999) *Policy Development in Scottish Education*, Synergy for the Scottish Parliament: Perspectives on Policy No. 1, Glasgow: Universities of Glasgow and Strathclyde.

Donn, G. (1999–2002) Education in the Scottish Parliament: Parliamentary Reports 1–6, *Scottish Educational Review* 31–4.

Gillies, D. J. M. (2001) The Scottish Parliament and educational policy making, unpublished MEd. dissertation, University of Strathclyde.

Lynch, P. (2001) *Scottish Government and Politics: An Introduction*, Edinburgh: Edinburgh University Press.

Paterson, L. (2000) *Education and the Scottish Parliament*, Edinburgh: Dunedin Academic Press.

8

The Politics of Scottish Education

Derek Johnston and Malcolm L. MacKenzie

It is not easy to define politics. One of the most famous attempts is Easton's 'the authoritative allocation of values'. A similar, more recent, definition is Ball's 'operating statements of values'. However defined, the subject involves policies, decision making, ideologies and conflict, the implementation process and the micro-politics which take place in small groups in all organisations. Many educationists are wary of politics, not least because it can involve them in what Humes has described as 'getting their hands dirty'. Yet in recent years the study of the relationship between politics and education has become very prominent because of the obvious impact of political thinking on educational change. It is particularly true in contemporary Scotland in terms of the relationship between the education system and the governance of Scotland which has been subjected to radical change as a consequence of the creation of a Scottish parliament.

THE SCOTTISH PARLIAMENT.
THE WHITE PAPER (1997) AND THE SCOTLAND ACT (1998)

In his preface to Scottish New Labour's party manifesto for the Scottish Parliament elections (May 1999) the late (and much lamented) Donald Dewar reminds us that the first section of the Scotland Act had just six words, 'There shall be a Scottish Parliament.' He indicates that for him the creation of the Parliament was 'the fulfilment of a lifetime ambition' and claims that, like his friend, the late John Smith, he knew it to be the 'settled will' of the Scottish people. He also describes it as 'a parliament fit for a new century'.

References to the Parliament are made throughout this volume, especially since the passage of time enables analysis to be made of the Parliament's achievements as well as its aspirations. However, consider first what the Parliament was set up to do, noting in particular the significance of the key word 'devolution'. To explain this term, it is necessary to put it in context by looking at what preceded the passing of the Scotland Act 1998.

In July 1997 the newly elected British Labour government, led by Prime Minister Tony Blair, presented to the Westminster Parliament a White Paper containing its proposals for the creation of a Scottish parliament to which clearly defined powers would be devolved, including education and training. These powers incorporated school education, including pre-five, primary and secondary education; the functions of Her Majesty's Inspectorate of Schools; teacher supply, training and conditions of service; further and higher education, including policy, funding, the functions of the Scottish Higher Education Funding Council

(SHEFC) and student support; science and research funding where supported through SHEFC and where undertaken in support of other devolved matters; training policy and lifelong learning, including all the training responsibilities which had been exercised by the Scottish Office; vocational qualifications, including the functions of the Scottish Qualifications Authority (SQA); careers advice and guidance. The White Paper proposed to reserve certain matters to the United Kingdom Parliament, including the United Kingdom Research Councils. It should be noted that, in the words of the White Paper, the UK Parliament 'is and will remain sovereign'. As it is customary with government White Papers put out initially for discussion, the aforementioned proposals were followed by legislation, in this case the Scotland Act 1998. The point about 'sovereignty' is crucial. The sovereign Westminster Parliament has devolved some of its powers to another body, in this case the Scottish Parliament. This is not the same as restoring the Parliament which ended in 1707. The debate about sovereignty or independence remains in Scotland and may well be given added impetus by the existence of a devolved parliament. This point should be put in an historic context.

Following the union of the Crowns of Scotland and England in 1603, the union of the Scottish and English Parliaments in 1707 created a parliament of Great Britain, meeting in London. In its first chapter the White Paper provides a short historical account of the development of the government of education in Scotland. It points out that the office of Secretary of Scotland was created in 1885, and enhanced in 1926 to Secretary of State. St Andrew's House in Edinburgh became the headquarters of the Scottish Office in 1939 and functions of the Scottish Office in London were transferred to Edinburgh. This was administrative devolution as distinct from parliamentary devolution. The White Paper also indicated that in the years preceding parliamentary devolution, further administrative devolution to the Scottish Office had taken place, resulting in the addition of major functions such as industrial support, training, higher education and the arts.

In pre-devolution times, before the transfer of power on 1 July 1999, the central government of education was, therefore, conducted through the Scottish Office, headed by the Secretary of State for Scotland. The government department with the administrative responsibility for the Secretary of State's functions prior to the Act was the Scottish Office Education and Industry Department (SOEID) headed by a junior minister accountable to the Secretary of State and a member of the team of ministers, all elected politicians, accountable to the Westminster Parliament.

So what has changed? The following is intended as a short guide to some of the structural changes, most of which will be more fully discussed in other chapters in this volume.

- The office of Secretary of State for Scotland remains, although many of its functions, including education, are devolved to the new Parliament. It is significant that the Secretary of State has remained a member of the British Cabinet. Some English MPs have questioned whether Scottish MPs at Westminster should have the right to vote on matters pertaining to English education or on other matters devolved to the Scottish Parliament on which English MPs are not allowed to vote. This 'West Lothian' question, as it has been dubbed, will, one ventures to predict, continue to reassert itself.
- The Scottish Parliament is elected by a system of proportional representation. This had led to a formation of an alliance between Scottish New Labour and the Liberal Democrats (Scotland). Thus, at the time of writing, the First Minister is Jack McConnell (Labour) while the Deputy First Minister and Minister for Justice is Jim Wallace (Lib. Dem.).

- The Scottish Executive (SE) is the devolved government for Scotland. As its title implies, the SE has the powers to go beyond that of placing a legislative programme before Parliament and can in fact take executive decisions on matters relating to the administration of devolved affairs.
- Operational relations between the Scottish Executive, UK government departments and the Cabinet of the National Assembly of Wales are regulated by a series of Concordants. While collectively the twenty-three Concordants can be viewed as a mechanism to ensure that UK inter-governmental relations are conducted in an amicable manner, these formal agreements do in effect place certain constraints on the day-to-day policy activities of the Scottish Executive. As Lynch (2001) has indicated, the Concordants can be construed as 'political mechanisms to bind the Scottish Executive into UK government structures' (p. 150).
- The Scottish National Party are well represented in the Parliament. Their voice has been strengthened in Scottish education by the new system. Should future elections result in their holding a majority in the Parliament, the issue of Scottish independence and the ability of Westminster to devolve in the way designed will become of national importance and may decide the future of Scotland.
- Devolution did not create a separate Scottish civil service. However, the Scottish Executive is permitted to have considerable access to civil service personnel and expertise in order to assist in the task of governing devolved matters.
- The Scottish Executive Education Department (SEED – see Chapter 11) has direct responsibility for policy concerning pre-five, school and community education; tourism, culture and sport; and a range of additional services and programmes that affect the lives of young people in Scotland.
- The Enterprise and Lifelong Learning Department (ELLD) is responsible for the country's economic and industrial development, transport infrastructure, tourism, further and higher education, student support and the promotion of lifelong learning. It has a role in funding the Scottish Further Education Funding Council (SFEFC) and the Scottish Higher Education Funding Council (SHEFC).
- The Scottish Parliament is a unicameral committee-based legislature. There is no second chamber and the committees are multi-party. The committees combine both legislative and scrutiny functions (Lynch, 2001). Individual committees of the Scottish Parliament do, therefore, potentially hold a significant amount of power and influence in relation to policy formation.
- Currently, therefore, the committee system of the Parliament contains two committees that have direct relevance to educational policy formations – the Education, Culture and Sport Committee and the Enterprise and Lifelong Learning Committee, both with MSPs as conveners. (Given the power of parliamentary committees to influence Scottish Executive policy matters it is worth highlighting the fact that the Enterprise and Lifelong Learning Committee is, at the time of writing, convened by Alex Neil of the Scottish National Party, not a member of the Executive coalition.)

PARTY POLITICS

Just as the Secretary of State for Scotland is a politician, elected as a candidate on behalf of a political party, so is the First Minister in the Scottish Parliament and his ministers, including the Minister for Education and Young People, with responsibilities for pre-school education, children and young people, and the Minister for Enterprise, Transport and Lifelong Learning who, in terms of education, has responsibility for further and higher sectors, as well as being Minister for Science.

While the Scottish Executive has national oversight of education and a major role in the inspection of schools, through Her Majesty's Inspectorate of Education, the provision and delivery of school education, as in pre-devolution times, is the responsibility of thirty-two unitary authorities, which are known as education authorities, who have a statutory duty to provide adequate and efficient school education. The duty of providing further education was removed from education authorities by the Further and Higher Education (Scotland) Act 1992, as a consequence of which further education colleges became accountable directly to the Secretary of State through a process known as incorporation. They are now accountable to the Minister for Enterprise, Transport and Lifelong Learning. Other functions of education authorities include the making of provision for special educational needs and for the teaching of Gaelic. They also have a duty to provide adequate facilities for recreational and sporting activities. They are responsible for the construction of buildings, the employment of teachers and other staff, and the provision of equipment and materials. They exercise responsibility for the curriculum taught in schools, taking account of national guidance.

As previously indicated, the First Minister and his ministers are politicians, elected as candidates on behalf of a political party. At local authority level, most elected councillors are party political, although some stand on an independent ticket. Thus, the governance and policy process of education in Scotland are imbued with political debate. This is not to discount the vital role of professionalism in delivery of the education service, a profes-sionalism for which Scottish teachers and lecturers have an international reputation and which is expressed not only in the classroom and lecture hall but through bodies such as the General Teaching Council for Scotland (GTCS) and Learning and Teaching Scotland (LTS). The relationship between teacher autonomy, professionalism and politics is an important, controversial and increasingly sensitive one, not least in respect of curriculum and methods. One of the most notable developments in post-war Britain has been the growing importance which politicians of all political parties attach to education, both in their policies and in their public pronouncements. Indeed, the leader of the Labour Party, Tony Blair announced before the 1997 British general election that the main theme of his campaign was to be 'Education, Education, Education', an emphasis reiterated in his campaign during the 2001 general election. This contrasts significantly with the position in immediate post-war Britain when education, although important, undoubtedly took second place in the minds of politicians to other issues such as the economy, foreign affairs, and, in terms of personal social services, health and housing. Although more recently health and, to some degree, transport, not to mention foreign affairs consequent upon 11 September 2001, have re-emerged as major players, the key importance attached to education policy in respect of its contribution to the national economy, changing technology and the culture and fabric of society, renders it necessary that students and practitioners of education make themselves familiar not only with the policies of the political parties but with their underlying theories and ideologies. This is especially true of Scotland where it is important to consider whether or not the creation of a Scottish parliament has brought the political and educational processes closer together.

THE ELECTION OF THE SCOTTISH PARLIAMENT
AND THE PARLIAMENT IN ACTION

A term increasingly used in describing political policy in recent years is 'discourse'. Ball (1990), acknowledging his debt to the work of Michel Foucault, says that discourses embody meaning and social relationships, and constitute both subjectivity and power relations. As he puts it: 'Discourses are, therefore, about what can be said, and thought, but also about who can speak when, where and with what authority' (p. 17). The relationship between knowledge, language and power is central to any analysis of discourse. Individuals or groups who can change, control or 'set' the discourse are exercising real power. The source of the discourse may not be immediately apparent. The parameters of the discourse may, in fact, determine a person's perception and creation of reality so that, as Ball puts it, 'we do not speak the discourse. The discourse speaks us' (p. 18).

In the era of the government headed by Margaret Thatcher, the discourse in education changed. In common parlance one might say that 'the goalposts were moved'. Whereas in the immediate post-war era the emphasis was on structures, notably the reorganisation of secondary education on comprehensive lines, expansion and equality, after 1979 a new language appeared and this is reflected in the manifestos put forward to the electorate by all the political parties in the British general elections of 1997 and 2001. Taken collectively, what is evident is a concern with standards and teacher appraisal, accountability, co-operation with the private sector and a respect for the market model of delivery. There is also an emphasis on skill, school discipline, pre-school education and parental choice and the rights of the consumer, usually defined as the parent, not the child.

Discourse is important, not only for what it says but often even more importantly for what it does not say. There is sparse reference to equality, structures or social engineering of the kind endemic in the pre-Thatcher era. Some commentators take the view that the entire policy discourse in education, including that in Scotland, is dominated by a neo-liberal, New Right, 'Thatcherite' paradigm; that, to put it another way, the Thatcher party may be over but the discourse lingers on, effectively controlling what people think and do. However, this view could be disputed by questioning the true extent to which Scottish education has in fact been influenced by the New Right. While major initiatives such as 5–14, Standard Grade, the Action Plan and Higher Still were to a certain degree guided by New Right thinking, such crucial curriculum and assessment developments do not represent a simple manifestation of the ideology. Moreover, New Right policies in Scotland continually received an inhospitable reception from both the teaching profession and the general public alike, inevitably leading to substantial difficulties. The argument that New Right discourse continues to have a major influence over Scottish education does, therefore, require a certain level of analysis. As a step in this direction, it is worth looking at some of the central policy proposals presented to the electorate by Scotland's four major political parties in the May 1999 elections to the Scottish Parliament.

A reading of the documentation presented to the Scottish people by Scottish New Labour, the Scottish Conservative and Unionist Party, the Scottish Liberal Democrats and the Scottish National Party reveals the extent to which Scotland's major political parties have embraced the discourse of neo-liberalism in relation to their respective educational policy proposals. Although this evidently reflects the continuing influence of the Conservative years, it should be also be observed that the policies tendered by the Scottish political community are akin to those found throughout the developed world – what is commonly referred to as the 'globalisation process'. While much is made of the traditional autonomous nature of education in Scotland and the special place that it has in the hearts and minds of its people, the increasing influence of global politics on this valued aspect of Scottish civic society cannot be overestimated. Scotland may now have its own parliament in order that 'Scottish solutions to Scottish problems' can be formulated, but the country is not immune from the effects of ideology that has its roots on the world stage.

Throughout all four party manifestos it is not surprising, therefore, to find educational policies that correspond to this new trend. The raising of standards, for example, is very much to the fore with all four major parties making policy commitments in this area. While attempting to increase the quality of Scottish education is nothing new (it could, for example, be argued that the establishment of comprehensive schools was linked to the nation's strong desire to raise the standard of education for working-class children), the nature of the policy proposals presented in the party manifestos reveals an altogether different bias relating to the issue of quality improvement in education. These range from the setting of targets through to initiatives such as the strengthening of school leadership. Developing what has become known as the 'culture of lifelong learning' – by expanding access to education at both pre- and post-compulsory level – can also be identified as a common thread throughout all of the party's policy commitments.

While there are many points of convergence in the manifesto commitments of Scotland's four main political parties, it would be wrong to suggest that there is uniformity throughout their various educational ideas. In terms of raising standards it is interesting to note, for example, the alternative slant placed on this policy commitment by Scottish Labour in comparison to their Conservative opponents. The New Labour tendency to 'soften the edges' of potentially difficult policy proposals, by choosing to employ non-confrontational language while at the same time failing to specify precisely what course of necessary remedial action would be taken ('in our drive for excellence we will set targets, and develop appropriate measures to allow all schools to gauge their progress') is very much present. In contrast, the Conservatives are much more direct in their pronouncements. In addition, the Liberal Democrat tradition of supporting greater access to higher education is reflected in its Scottish Parliament manifesto commitment to quadruple student access funds to £14m to help the poorest students obtain a university education. A further issue worthy of note is the manner in which Scottish Labour makes extensive use of its UK counterpart's already established terminology, readily employing key New Labour phrases such as 'social exclusion', 'partnership' and 'knowledge economy'. Adopting the neo-liberal phraseology of Tony Blair (often referred to as the politics of the 'Third Way') allows the party in Scotland to reap the benefits of UK Labour's electoral success. Scottish Labour's capacity to get two bites at the electoral cherry is something that the other parties north of the border have struggled to come to terms with.

The study of political manifestos represents one important means whereby analysts can gain an understanding of a political party's direction in relation to educational policy. However, it was not until the new Parliament was up and running that the country obtained a more accurate picture concerning the manner in which the new democratic institution would preside over Scotland's highly-valued education service. An initial indication of how this would be accomplished came with the Scottish Executive's decision to create separate ministerial posts for school education and the post-compulsory sector. Denholm and Macleod (2002) have highlighted how this move on behalf of the Executive 'acknowledged the key and increasing role of further and higher education institutions in equipping the workforce with skills and generally powering the so-called knowledge economy' (p. 121). In spite of various alterations to the make-up of the Cabinet, this distinction is, at the time of writing, still in place with the Executive possessing a ministry for Education and Young People and a corresponding government department for Enterprise, Transport and Lifelong Learning. The splitting of ministerial duties has had an influence on how the Parliament itself generates and debates the formation of educational policy, with two corresponding parliamentary committees being established to examine and report on any issue that falls within the responsibility of the relevant department. Both committees have played a key role in scrutinising and shaping Scottish educational policy and the multi-party nature of their make-up has ensured that healthy political discussion has been a constant characteristic of this process. As one would expect, lively political debate has similarly been a never-ending feature of events in the Parliament's main chamber, with educational matters being attended to in plenary sessions such as the deliberation of parliamentary motions, debates relating to Scottish Executive legislative proposals or issues raised during question time.

With regard to the educational policy output of the Scottish Parliament, the above procedural mechanisms have given rise to a range of major initiatives during the institution's first term in operation. These have included legislation to abolish up-front tuition fees for students in higher education, an attempt to enhance the quality of local authority educational provision through the passing of the Standards in Scotland's Schools etc. Act 2000 (an Act that also made provision for the ministerial establishment of national priorities in education as well as the abolition of self-governing schools), and the endorsement of an agreement designed to improve the professional conditions of service and pay for teachers in the school sector. Both Parliament and the Executive's commitment to improving the quality of provision in Scottish education was further reinforced by an announcement in the chamber on 20 March 2002 by the Minister for Education and Young People that there was to be the launch of a national debate on education. The magnitude of this initiative can be underlined by the fact that around 20,000 responses were received from all sectors of Scottish life, covering an array of issues relating to the nation's private and state-funded educational provision. The debate is currently in its 'reflection' stage with responses being collated and reviewed by researchers from the University of Edinburgh. Thereafter, there will follow an official 'response' period, at which point the Executive will identify key themes from the debate process (this is scheduled to occur in 2003) before finally deciding upon an overall strategy to take forward educational provision in Scotland.

In respect of Scottish education, the above is a necessarily selective review of both policy commitments by the major political parties and the subsequent work of the new democratic institution during its initial term. Yet by what route did they evolve? What do they say about the relationship between education and society? Above all, what do they reveal about discourse? Is a discourse from furth of Scotland determining the agenda? If so, who is in control? Is the discourse changing? Is 'on to independence' creating a new discourse or would an independent Scotland still be strongly influenced by discourses emanating not only from south of the border but from the impact of globalisation? These are difficult issues to which there are no easy answers. But in order to approach a better understanding of them it is necessary to place recent policy pronouncements and initiatives in context. The first step in achieving this is to consider their antecedents and it is necessary to go back some way in time.

THE NEW RIGHT

In the summer of 1968 an event occurred whose significance was only appreciated much later, namely a speech by Conservative MP, Enoch Powell, to the Conservative's Party's

National Advisory Committee on Education. In his speech Powell claimed that, of all sacred cows, education was both the most sacred and 'the most cowlike'. He dismissed the conventional wisdom that there was a direct causal relationship between educational expenditure and economic growth as 'bunkum' and attacked the 'Robbins principle' that those with requisite entrance qualifications had a 'right' to higher education. Powell believed that education was a 'good' which society should distribute only to the extent that it wished or could afford to do so, not in anticipation of some measurable economic return or in accordance with some mythical right of the individual.

The following year, 1969, saw the publication of the first Black Paper edited by C. B. Cox and A. C. Dyson. It was a pamphlet, the first in a long series, containing articles by prominent literary figures, academics and politicians which criticised the consensus in contemporary education. The first Black Paper entitled *Fight for Education* attacked, among other things, comprehensive schools, alleged falling educational standards, the end of selectivity, a perceived breakdown in discipline, both in schools and higher education. The first shots in the battle about to be waged by the New Right had been fired. Scottish academics, politicians and members of various pressure groups were to participate in the battle, but its nature and effects can only be understood by looking at education and politics in a British and international context.

Carr and Hartnett (1996) argue that the central aim of the New Right was to break the consensus about education policies. The crucial event was the election of Margaret Thatcher as leader of the Conservative Party. As Carr and Hartnett put it, 'the real change came when Mrs. Thatcher was elected leader of the party in 1975: that event allowed the educational counter-revolution to be staged' (p. 154). Levitas (1986) in her book *The Ideology of the New Right* (Polity Press, 1986) identifies two strands in its thought. One is a neo-liberal, laissez-faire economism devoted to the principle of the free market, associated with a wide range of authors, including J. S. Mill, Adam Smith, F. A. Hayek and Milton Friedman. The second strand Levitas identifies is the puritanism of the American 'moral majority' associated in the 1980s with spokespersons such as Irving Kristol and the Reverend Jerry Falwell, and in Britain with the emphasis on cultural transmission advocated by Roger Scruton.

In Carr and Hartnett's view the New Right coalition operated 'with consummate political, media and rhetorical skills' (p. 158). They refer to Knight's research (1990) which, they state, analyses how the New Right coalition 'moved from the periphery of educational policy making to its centre'. Perhaps most important is what they say about discourse:

> The New Right, through its techniques of persuasion and, by hard work and the imaginative use of language and the media, created a new populist form of discourse based on pamphlets and the 'findings' of its Think Tanks. The discourse was directed not at educational experts or teachers but at parents and voters. It also developed and exploited close links with the media, especially newspapers and television. This gave far greater coverage to its claims, assertions, fictions, myths and proposed policies. (p. 159)

The following policies might all be seen as evidence of the impact of New Right thinking on Scottish education during the years of Conservative government at Westminster which ended with Labour's landslide victory in the 1997 general election and its repeat in the general election of 2001. The reader is invited to consider the extent to which these policies and their underlying discourse have been replicated in the policies adopted by the Scottish Executive as well as the extent to which they are reflected in the manifestos described above. Examples of the policies might include: the parents' charter; the growing power of parents in Scottish school management, encouraged by the School Boards (Scotland) Act 1988; the transfer to Scottish schools of power over their budgets by devolved management of resources; the opting-out legislation contained in the Self-Governing Schools etc (Scotland) Act 1989; the abolition of Strathclyde Region and the hostility directed towards it, for example, in Prime Minister John Major's description of it as a 'monstrosity'; the ending of the two-tier system of local government, reinforced by a distrust of the role of local politics and administration in the government and management of schools; the privatisation of services through 'contracting out'; the encouragement via the curriculum of a risk-taking, entrepreneurial culture; public – private sector financial partnerships, notably in the building of new and the modernisation of old schools; the emphasis on skill acquisition and wealth creation; positive school-industry links; national testing and the publication of school test results; a concern to raise and, if necessary, enforce standards through an emphasis on targets, measurable outcomes and, above all, a belief in accountability reflected, for example, in the 5–14 programme; a strong line on appraisal and the dismissal of incompetent teachers and an increased role for the GTCS in helping attain these managerial objectives. The requisitioning of this discourse, albeit with modifications (for example, the termination of 'opting-out' in Scotland) by New Labour, explains in part the landslide victories gained in the 1997 and 2001 general elections, the loss of all Conservative Westminster seats in Scotland in 1997 and the regaining of only one in 2001, and the possibility of Labour hegemony (perhaps in alliance with the Liberal Democrats) in Scottish political life, whether at Westminster or in the Scottish Parliament. What is New Labour? Why has it, hitherto, been so successful in electoral terms.

NEW LABOUR

In 1988 in the publication *The Social Market Economy* (Social Market Foundation) Robert Skidelsky wrote:

> The most hopeful political development of recent years is revival of belief in the market system. It has become worldwide, uniting rich and poor, capitalist and socialist countries in a common language and the beginnings of a common practice. In Russia, China and Eastern Europe, the monoliths of state socialism have started to crumble, in the West the army of officials is in retreat. (p. 4)

Skidelsky argues that a social market economy is, above all, embedded in social arrangements regarded as 'fair'. This analysis may give a clue to the electoral success of New Labour and the abandonment of state socialism, as witnessed by the excision of clause 4 pertaining to the common ownership of the means of production, distribution and exchange from its constitution. The quest for fairness embedded in the social market approach may also explain the apparent paradox that, in a post-Thatcherite world, the worth of market forces has been accepted while the harsher, socially unconcerned aspects of classical liberalism have been rejected by the British electorate, above all in Scotland.

Not everyone accepts this analysis. To some, the revival of market forces and a move to globalisation dominated by international capitalism means that New Labour, in spite of its protestations, is not speaking the discourse of social justice but is itself 'being spoken' by the discourse of neo-liberalism. Such critics might note the emphasis, for example, in the major piece of legislation produced by the Scottish Executive, Standards in Scotland's Schools etc. Act, 2000, on measurable outcomes, accountability, and targets as redolent of the language of classical management and its accompanying authoritarianism. Advocates of New Labour might reply that in his preface to New Labour's manifesto (1999) the much respected Donald Dewar wrote that the Scottish Parliament would work for 'what we used to call the common weal'. Such a defender might point to the policy of tackling social exclusion by the creation of New Community Schools throughout Scotland. It is suggested here that the social market concept has replaced socialism as the central plank of Labour ideology to the dismay of Old Labour and of neo-Marxists.

NEW POLITICS?

Espousing the principles of the social market does not, however, represent the sole means by which key figures in New Labour have attempted to transform the party. With the assistance of several notable political allies, Tony Blair has successfully managed to drill his administration into a highly-organised political machine in which significant emphasis is placed on both the central co-ordination of government activity and the presentation of policy initiatives. Much has been made of New Labour's ability to put a particular 'spin' on policy announcements – rightly so. Modern-day politics is such that the inception, presentation and implementation of governmental policy represents a vital means whereby the party in power can command the political landscape and set the policy agenda. (Although in terms of the implementation stage, it is interesting to note that central government has become well-versed in the act of delegating this task to other bodies, thus avoiding ultimate responsibly for any shortcomings as policy is put into practice.)

Dominating the news agenda, continually introducing new policy initiatives in order that day-to-day news coverage of political events matches government priorities, creating what is in effect a 'political spectacle' (Edelman, M., *Constructing the Political Spectacle*, Chicago: Chicago University Press, 1988) has become an art form in modern-day politics and New Labour has continually demonstrated that it can command its execution in masterly fashion. Indeed, as the New Labour machine has become aware of the political benefits of carefully orchestrating every stage of the policy process, so too have individual politicians. In an age when politics is viewed very much as a career rather than a civic duty, ministers are keen to shape and present their own message in such a way that they are seen to be effective political operators. Consequently, those wishing to understand the reasons for the introduction of a specific policy initiative should begin to look beyond conventional factors in relation to issues appearing on the policy agenda (for instance, that of traditional political ideology or the responding to the concerns of a particular social group) and instead begin to consider factors such as the desire of political parties – or indeed individual politicians – to use policy in order to gain advantage in the political landscape.

It could be argued that in this new era of Scottish politics, one of the most noticeable exponents of 'political spectacle' has been the MSP for Motherwell and Wishaw (and now Scotland's First Minister), Jack McConnell. Indeed it was during his period as Minister for Education, Europe and External Affairs (October 2000 – November 2001) that McConnell displayed his credentials as an effective and energetic modern-day political operator. While clearly McConnell's achievements during his short period as education minister are worthy of praise (most noticeably dealing with the crisis in the Scottish Qualifications Authority and steering through the McCrone settlement), it should not go unnoticed that his period in office also involved extensive use of policy briefings to the Scottish media. Whether it was on the front page of the *Times Educational Supplement Scotland*, or a personal interview in *The Herald*, McConnell was continually setting out his own policy agenda. The benefit of this approach is that those who use it are able to identify their own issues to address and have the confidence to believe that a related successful political resolution may be formulated. This question and answer dialectic process (identification of policy issues followed by associated policy solutions) can then be carefully orchestrated using a range of instruments of dissemination. The individual politician is subsequently viewed as carrying out his ministerial duties in a effective manner. Although Ian MacWhirter has recently highlighted that, as First Minister, Jack McConnell has made an attempt to follow the lead of Westminster and move away from 'sophisticated media presentation' (p. 32), the fact that skilful politicians can use the policy process for their own career advancement must still not be ignored by those wishing to gain an understanding of the matrix of government. The 'political spectacle' is now very much a part of UK politics and researchers of all aspects of government policy must make themselves aware of the manner in which it can be assembled and put into service.

NEW SCOTLAND

According to Skidelsky, the movement of ideas in favour of a more decentralised, competitive and entrepreneurial economy is driven by the force of new technology, as a consequence of which the 'social market economy' recognises the 'instrumental efficiency of decentralised decision-making'. The move to decentralisation seen in the decision to create a Scottish parliament raises questions about Scottish national identity and consciousness and whether recent constitutional changes will inevitably trigger radical developments along nationalist lines.

Scotland, as a nation, chose to merge its parliament with that of England in 1707. Now, what it has is not the restoration of that parliament but a 'devolved' one, denied sovereignty, which, for the time being at least, remains at Westminster. Is Scotland still a nation? In their analysis of the question, Brown, McCrone and Paterson (1996) describe Scotland as a 'civil society' partly because the Scots are a group of people who are aware of having an identity distinct from other groups around them. They argue that Scotland is not simply a piece of geography but a 'transcendent idea which runs through history, reinterpreting that history to fit the concerns of each present' (p. 35). Thus Scotland, England and Wales are 'figments of the imagination'.

That nationhood has its existence in consciousness more than in law and economics can be readily agreed; hence the political importance of education because it, above all, forms consciousness. It is of course true that Britain, and the sense of being British, is also a figment of the imagination. The future of Scotland will be determined by which forms of consciousness prevail. The Scottish Conservative and Unionist Party, from its base in the Scottish Parliament, afforded by proportional representation, may revive, especially if it returns to its One Nation compassionate tradition compatible with Scottish culture. Or it may cling to a neo-classical liberalism alien not only to the Scottish people but to its own traditions. New Labour, perhaps in alliance with the Scottish Liberal Democrats, may hold sway with an essentially social market philosophy. The devolved Parliament may prove not a bulwark against but a stepping stone towards an independent, increasingly nationalistic Scotland. One is reminded that the consistent theme running through the Scottish National Party's 1999 manifesto was 'on to independence'. The road to independence may lie not only in votes and policies but in the SNP contributing to, even creating, the discourse of Scottish policies. This is already seen in the emphasis on support for Scottish culture, including Gaelic, by all the parties. One would anticipate Scottish culture featuring prominently in all future political manifestos in Scotland, combined with commitments to social justice, all within the context of a free market economy. Devolution has given Scottish nationalists not, at least so far, the independence they seek but a power-base which they are still learning how to use.

Perhaps in the long run things will only appear to change, even in an independent Scotland. The Scottish 'policy community' and 'leadership class' may, like the Sicilian aristocracy in Guiseppe di Lampedusa's novel *The Leopard* continue to filter, interpret and regroup in the face of the radical changes of New Labour/Social Democrat policies, or the potentially even more radical policies of the Scottish National Party, just as they did in response to the New Right. In any event, education, as Prime Minister Blair has stated, will remain centre stage in the political debate, contributing both to the discourse and to who is actually speaking it.

REFERENCES

Ball, S. J. (1990) *Politics and Policy-Making in Education. Explorations in Policy Sociology*, London and New York: Routledge.

Brown, A., McCrone, D. and Paterson, L. (1996) *Politics and Society in Scotland*, London and New York: Macmillan Press.

Carr, W. and Hartnett, A. (1996) *Education and the Struggle for Democracy. The Politics of Educational Ideas*, Buckingham: Open University Press.

Denholm, J. W. and Macleod, D. (2002) Educating the Scots: the renewal of the democratic intellect, in G. Hassan and C. Warhurst (eds), *Anatomy of the New Scotland: Power Influence and Change*, Edinburgh: Mainstream Publishing.

Lynch, P. (2001) *Scottish Government and Politics: An Introduction*, Edinburgh: Edinburgh University Press.

MacWhirter, I. (2002) The new Scottish political classes, in G. Hassan and Warhurst (eds), *Anatomy of the New Scotland: Power Influence and Change*, Edinburgh: Mainstream Publishing.

9

The Independent Sector

Judith McClure

RECENT DEVELOPMENTS IN THE INDEPENDENT SECTOR IN SCOTLAND

Although independent school pupils represent just 4% of the total school population in Scotland, the independent sector has entered the new millennium as a strong player in the development of Scottish education. There are over seventy schools in membership of the Scottish Council of Independent Schools (SCIS) with a total number in the year 2000 of 30,904 pupils, plus a number of specialist schools. SCIS schools represent over 96% of the pupils in the independent sector in Scotland. The strength of the sector lies not only in the coherence lent to it by the support and leadership of SCIS, but also in the cherished independence of the individual schools. Each one was founded with a commitment to meet the needs of a distinctive set of pupils, and this diversity of origin and sense of history has encouraged a determination to maintain high educational standards and personal and social values. The necessity of attracting fee-paying parents gives an edge to the efforts of the leaders and managers of each school in maintaining and improving its educational standards and in satisfying the needs of individual pupils.

As Scottish education in 2002 embraces the challenge of national debate, the strong leadership, diversity and innovation characteristic of many independent schools are of particular interest. In the last decade of the twentieth century SCIS schools sought to improve their responsiveness to pupils and parents as they faced the anticipated fall in the school-age population at the same time as the phasing-out of the Assisted Place scheme. They welcomed the quality initiative led by HMI and their teachers participated increasingly in the SCIS programme of staff development. SCIS headteachers, like their colleagues in the state sector, deprecated the popular use of league tables and preferred to focus on improving the attainment of their own pupils. In its strategic analysis 2000, the board of SCIS, elected from governors, heads and bursars, took the view that Scotland provides a differentiated system of education, in which independent schools form a distinctive element. Each school should understand its own distinctiveness but also recognise its part in Scottish education and its development. Nationally opinion may still be divided over what can be seen as the privileges of the independent schools, particularly in relation to charitable status, and some would argue that their very existence is inconsistent with a policy of social inclusion; but there seems to be a constructive acceptance by ministers and the Scottish Executive of the independent sector and its place in Scottish education.

The shift in the political view of the independent sector has been matched by developments in social attitudes and behaviour. The survey 'The State of the Nation 2001' (*Scotsman*, 30 April – 4 May 2001) showed that for the first time ever the number of Scots who think private education is a good thing has overtaken those who think private schools should be abolished by the government. Prior to the May 1999 general election, as many as 29% of Scots wanted private education banned, compared with only 19% in England. The 2002 figure was 15%. Positive support for private education was strongest among the middle classes (37%) and those in the main childbearing group of ages 25–34 (30%). The west and east of Scotland were united in greater support (30% each) compared with the north and south, where it was only around a fifth. Many Scots still feel uncomfortable about private education: a third of them viewed it as socially divisive, but nevertheless still a matter of personal choice. It is always risky to put together figures from different sources, as happened in the 2001 survey, but the views recorded probably do reflect broadly the range of opinion and suggest significant changes in social attitudes.

In the 'State of the Nation' survey, the three reasons for choosing an independent education which received the most support were a better standard of education, individual attention in smaller classes, and the opportunity for pupils to realise their full potential. These areas scored almost twice as highly as a wider curriculum, better discipline and examination success, which themselves were significantly higher than facilities and extra-curricular activities. These public perceptions have not been tested by any study, and except for examination comparisons, can only be judged by the performance of individual schools, all of which are subject to inspection by HMIE. Certainly all these areas are priorities for the leaders and managers of independent schools, many of which have thrived for several generations through constant improvement and innovation and increasingly through partnerships with the local community.

TRADITIONS AND GOVERNANCE

The seventy and more schools of the independent sector represent a very wide range of educational models. Large city day schools often include pre-school departments as well as primary and secondary education. Although most schools are co-educational, there are schools for girls or boys, day and boarding schools, preparatory schools (which end at age eleven, twelve or thirteen), and rural schools. Like their English counterparts, many Scottish independent schools have long traditions, some tracing their origins to the middle ages, others to the generosity of seventeenth- or eighteenth-century benefactors, such as George Heriot, the Hutcheson brothers, George Watson, Robert Gordon and Mary Erskine, who opened schools for poor boys and sometimes girls. Once state provision of education for all developed in the late nineteenth century, there were controversies over the use to which charitable endowments should be put, and there was a strong view that they were originally intended for the children of the poor. The non-public school sector included both independent schools, which depended on fee income and in some cases on endowments, and grant-aided schools, which received a proportion of their income from public authorities, until the 1970s. Modern independent schools now have to seek to reconcile their commitment to education and to individual pupils with the need to raise the income necessary to provide high quality education. This challenge is tackled by offering bursaries to those who need financial support, through values which encourage pupils to contribute to society, and by charitable activities. Independent schools of nineteenth-century and later foundation were often born of deeply felt hopes, such as the campaign for the education of women, the particular needs of a locality or the educational philosophy of an individual or group. The loyalty and sense of purpose that are at the heart of many independent schools are rooted in their foundation and history.

One of the factors in the success of independent schools throughout their history has been capable and sometimes visionary leadership, visible in the quality of individual headteachers and members of staff. There has been no study of this area in Scotland, though the Institute of Education of the University of London's *Establishing the Current State of Leadership in Independent Schools in England* (2002) has interesting conclusions and draws comparisons with a similar study of state sector headteachers. As in England, the great majority of independent schools in Scotland operate with a governing body, often as the directors of a charitable company limited by guarantee. There is ongoing controversy over the definition of independent schools as charities and their claim to operate for the public benefit in the provision of education and access to their facilities will be tested. The role of the governors of each independent school is well defined. All schools strive to ensure that their governors are committed to the institution, have close contacts with parents and pupils, and are prepared to contribute their own expertise to its governance and above all to its strategic leadership. The dependence of each school on fee income and its status as a charity have necessitated a great deal of attention to financial and estate management, and the marriage of educational and business leadership in senior management teams is worthy of note. The strength of the governance and management of the most effective independent schools, which binds them to their parents and the local community, provides an interesting model at a time when the state sector is devolving more responsibility and freedom of action to individual headteachers and their schools.

INDEPENDENT SCHOOLS AND THE COMPETITIVE ENVIRONMENT

The figures for the overall numbers at the start of session in SCIS schools over the last seven years show a remarkably stable number of pupils, in the region of 31,000. This reflects a small increase in the percentage of pupils in the independent sector, as the total pupil population in Scotland has fallen significantly from an estimated 847,287 in 1995 to 781,434 in 2000. The corresponding numbers in the independent sector were 32,341 in 1995, 3.82% of the whole, and 30,191 in 2000, 3.86%. Whilst the overall percentage of independent school pupils hovers around 4%, there is considerable variation in different areas, as shown in Table 9.1.

Table 9.1: Independent schools percentages

Council	Percentage of independent school pupils overall in 2000	Percentage of secondary independent school pupils in 2000
Edinburgh City	18.1%	23.6%
Glasgow City	8.4%	12.3%
Perth and Kinross	11.5%	16%
Dundee City	5%	7.8%
Aberdeen City	10.5%	12.9%

The figures for Edinburgh are striking, and reflect not only the strong traditions of the city's large number of distinctive independent schools, but growth in the Lothians, which accounts for an increasing proportion of Scotland's population and households, according to the Edinburgh and the Lothians Structure Plan, Major Issues Report 2000. However, the figures produced annually by SCIS in its *Directory of Independent Schools* reveal a downward trend of boarding, which has always been of relatively less significance in Scotland, against the recent stabilisation in England. Few predominantly boarding schools have been able to resist this trend, though there are powerful exceptions. Other schools are using various strategies to improve boarding, for instance by more flexible arrangements, by penetrating overseas markets, or, for those in urban centres, by increasing their attraction to day pupils. On the other hand many schools are full to capacity and have waiting lists, and in general the independent sector has maintained its position despite declining demographic trends. The growth of nursery departments for children aged 3–5 has been a significant feature of the last decade in many Scottish independent schools. The national provision for children of this age has produced partnership arrangements with local authorities in some areas, and this trend looks certain to continue.

COSTS AND FEES

The audit of the cost of pre-school education in Scotland prepared by Audit Scotland in 2000 and the publication of budgeted running costs per pupil in Scottish publicly-funded schools in the SEED statistical bulletin have made it possible to draw some conclusions about costs in the maintained and independent sectors. Direct comparisons have not been attempted because of the difficulty of estimating costs of capital works, which in the independent sector have to be borne by each individual school but are not included in running cost expenditure for publicly-funded schools. As would be expected, the major cost drivers in both sectors are the teacher–pupil ratio and the size of the school: in general, the smaller the school, the higher the cost per pupil. The influence of size on running costs is less marked among larger schools in the state sector, and it seems that the same applies to independent schools and partly accounts for the continued strength of the large urban all-through schools. There is no doubt that the lower teacher–pupil ratio in the independent sector contributes substantially to the higher annual cost per pupil and hence to the size of fees (see Table 9.2).

Table 9.2: Teacher–pupil ratios

Figures for 2000	Independent sector in Scotland	Publicly funded Schools in Scotland
Teacher–pupil ratio in primary education	1:13.1	1:19
Teacher–pupil Ratio in secondary education	1:8.8	1:13

Although the lower teacher–pupil ratio contributes to the public perception revealed in the 'State of the Nation 2001' survey, it is important to note that while many independent schools do have very small classes, in large urban schools the class average in the early years of secondary education can be in the region of twenty-seven pupils, closer to that of their publicly-funded counterparts. The lower teacher–pupil ratio is related much more to the wide range of subjects and specialist teachers available throughout the school, and especially in the top four examination year groups.

While the average fee increases in the independent sector for senior day pupils was 5.9% in 1999 and 7.00% in 2000, it reached 10% in 2001 as a direct result of the impact on the budget for teachers' salaries after the national agreement following the McCrone Report. Independent schools attempt to make their fees more accessible for pupils from a wider range of backgrounds by offering bursaries. A few have endowments for this purpose, but for many a percentage of fee income is used to fund bursaries, an average of 7.66% in a 1999 UK survey undertaken for the Independent Schools Bursars' Association. Overall it is clear that the cost of independent education is substantially more, perhaps as much as one and a half times more, than the average cost per pupil in publicly-funded schools. The more substantial costs of independent sector schools are largely accounted for by the lower teacher–pupil ratio, something that is clearly appreciated by parents, and by their programme of capital expenditure, not included in the SEED figures. One of the major challenges for the independent sector is the need for heavy and continued capital investment, particularly in information and communications technology, to provide constantly improving facilities for learning in an increasingly complex and differentiated market.

THE ROLE OF THE SCOTTISH COUNCIL OF INDEPENDENT SCHOOLS

In the decade since its foundation, SCIS has become of increasing importance to independent schools in Scotland and has played a crucial role in gaining recognition for the sector in Scottish education. While conscious always of the independence of its member schools, SCIS fulfils the role of an education authority in disseminating information, encouraging partnerships, stimulating debate and organising a substantial programme of professional development courses for governors, headteachers and both teaching and support staff. SCIS, not least through its director Judith Sischy, has a recognised place in Scottish education and is able to represent the views of the sector and to ensure that its interests are considered. SCIS functions also as a support network for schools and staff, and is able to provide the accurate data upon which successful school management depends. It has taken the initiative in bringing together working groups of member headteachers to produce guidelines in areas of mutual concern, such as in child protection, complaints procedures, and teachers' contracts. Its advisory service provides impartial advice to parents who are seeking to find an appropriate independent school, which will meet the needs of their children. SCIS exemplifies the tension between the independence of schools founded as individual institutions and ultimately responsible for their own survival, and the need for them to work together in order to develop, improve and meet the challenges of a period of great educational change.

THE DIVERSITY OF INDEPENDENT SCHOOLS

The wide range of independent schools in Scotland is perhaps of increased interest in a time of educational innovation and experiment. While single-sex education has virtually disappeared from the public school sector in Scotland, there are eight girls' schools in Scotland and three boys'. The accelerating success of girls at all levels of education is observable in

Scotland as well as elsewhere, but there has not been an interest in the particular strengths of single-sex schools here as there has been in England, where they are very strong in both the state and independent sectors and some of the oldest boys' schools and girls' schools regularly gain positive publicity for their performances in academic league tables. In Scotland the aim of the new Scottish Girls' Schools group is not to denigrate co-education but to point out the importance of choice and the especial strengths of girls' schools, which have played a distinguished role in encouraging the education of women since the late nineteenth century. Today some of the issues associated with educating the sexes together are being recognised, and the long-standing experience of single-sex schools is important. It is interesting to note that there are fewer boys' schools than girls' schools, and that in recent years, whilst most girls' schools have maintained a strong single-sex tradition, several boys' schools have become co-educational or established a co-educational sixth form. Those highly-regarded single-sex schools that are clearly very successful in recruitment should continue to do well. As the importance of gender differentiation in pupil progress is becoming more prominent in the analysis of attainment it may be that the distinctive contribution of all single-sex schools will be increasingly recognised. There are interesting findings in the study by Dr M. T. Thomson (2001) of trends and gender issues in examination performance in both state and independent schools from 1997 to 1999. There are other areas of diversity in the independent sector: some, for instance, are religious foundations and others retain the distinctive educational traditions of their foundation.

Boarding education continues to play a significant part in the independent sector, despite the decline in numbers. Boarding schools have adapted to a profound change in social attitudes, and their boarding houses have become more home-like, comfortable places where staff and pupils live together on friendly terms and account is taken of pupil opinion. The Care and Welfare of Residential Pupils Inspections undertaken by HMIE and the work of the newly-formed Care Commission and its care standards have reflected an increasing concern for the happiness and well-being of the individual pupil living away from home, and independent boarding schools have contributed to the national guidelines and taken part in new initiatives in staff training. The nature of boarding has become more linked with family need, more flexible, and multi-cultural. Although a demand still exists for a traditional, all-embracing boarding school life, most families want schools to be responsive to their needs, and schools have recognised the importance of ensuring that boarders keep closely in touch with their parents and live as normal a life as possible. While it is unlikely that boarding numbers will rise substantially, there is no doubt that the nature of family life and work still makes it necessary for some children to have the stability of a boarding school life. Such a time can be happy and enriching, and provide a diversity of opportunities and an experience of independence which lead to special confidence and maturity.

THE STAFFING OF INDEPENDENT SCHOOLS

There has been increasing mobility of teachers between the state and independent sectors in recent years, though a feeling that teachers in independent schools work in a privileged and elitist environment still lingers. Independent schools expect their staff to be registered with the GTC, to be involved in personal professional development, and to take part in extra-curricular activities. A strong feature of the independent sector has always been its pastoral care, and teachers must play a full part in that in both primary and secondary education. Although the demands are high, the advantages of working with smaller class sizes in schools with a strong sense of tradition and purpose and a commitment to personal and social values are clear. In general SCIS schools remunerate teachers according to the national salary scales, though some schools pay a percentage more and all have an expectation of involvement in extra-curricular activities both in and out of school. Scottish independent schools probably have a higher proportion of teachers who move from England, and in general they attract large numbers of applicants for vacant posts, particularly in urban centres. SCIS schools are committed to continuing professional development for their staff and have their own professional review and development guidelines, and they have embraced induction schemes for newly-qualified teachers which accord well with their natural practice of supporting staff. The challenge for independent schools is not the motivation and retention of teachers, but the need to ensure that they all have the range of experience which is necessary for development in the profession, and particularly of experience outside their own schools.

THE INDEPENDENT SECTOR AND THE COMMUNITY

The modernisation of boarding and the broader background of teaching staff are both features of an important change in independent schools: their willingness to engage more readily in the community and with public sector schools and to seek such experiences for their pupils, recognising them to be an essential element in their education. In Scotland there has been no central policy to match the independent/state school partnership initiative begun in England in 1997, reviewed after five years by Chris Parker in *Two Sectors, One Purpose* (2002). Even so, links between state and independent schools are growing: some are long established, for instance in sport or in open schemes such as Young Enterprise or the Duke of Edinburgh's Award; others are tentative new growths as pupils mingle at student conferences. Once contacts are made, the social backgrounds of the pupils in independent schools can be found to be very similar to those in many state schools, except for those with catchment areas of great social deprivation. Teachers, too, benefit from contacts; and exchange arrangements, visits and mutual shadowing by headteachers are beginning to take place. Parents who have chosen independent education for their children are supportive and committed, and many facing times of financial difficulty may make sacrifices to afford the fees. Many plan their children's education years ahead, and clearly feel that the experiences given to them add value to their education. Independent school pupils are also increasingly engaged with the local community, in work experience and shadowing schemes, in links with business and industry, in charitable activities and in community service. It is likely that this trend will continue and develop.

Involvement in the local community is also brought about by contact with further and higher education. Independent schools have regularly played their part in the training of student teachers, and many have strong links with an institution of teacher education. Arrangements for the induction of newly qualified teachers will increase these connections, and the concern of the sector to develop its staff has seen many bonds forged between individual teachers pursuing higher degrees and university departments. The role of SCIS as a provider of development courses has furthered contacts with those involved in teacher education and research in school improvement and the development of pastoral care. The post-McCrone encouragement of continuing professional development, which includes a new emphasis on development opportunities within schools and on practitioner research, should bring about more substantial links between independent as well as state schools and universities, to the advantage of all. As the curriculum diversifies and schools look to develop their provision, higher and further education will have their parts to play in partnership with the independent as well as the state sector.

THE INDEPENDENT SECTOR AND GOVERNMENT

The independent sector enjoys a constructive relationship with the Scottish Executive, with ministers and with the Scottish Parliament. The duty placed on ministers under the Standards in Scotland's Schools etc. Act 2000 to secure improvement in schools extends to the independent sector. The explanatory document to the Act states that in exercising their functions in respect of the inspection and registration of independent schools, Scottish ministers will take full account of their new duty to secure higher standards and improvement in quality. They look forward to developing a positive relationship with independent schools directly and through the Scottish Council of Independent Schools to ensure that this is achieved. The director of SCIS meets regularly with ministers and with officials from SEED as well as HMIE, and is a member of the GTCS. SCIS headteachers are represented on national bodies, such as Learning and Teaching Scotland, the ministerial group reviewing National Qualifications and the Ministerial Strategy Committee on Continuing Professional Development for Teachers. The UK government accepted the inclusion of the independent sector in the Prime Minister's initiative to increase the number of overseas students in the UK. Independent schools are able to use the UK and Scottish Education brand devised for universities and colleges and to secure the support of Education Scotland in attracting overseas students. Whilst they cherish their independence and individuality, independent schools in general see themselves as part of Scottish education and are keen to take part in educational development and add to the richness of provision for pupils in Scotland.

CURRICULUM AND EXAMINATIONS

Independent junior schools and preparatory schools normally adopt the holistic approach of their state counterparts and use the 5–14 guidelines flexibly. However they are able to make use of more subject specialists, often from a very early stage in areas such as Music, Physical Education and Modern Languages. Some prepare their pupils for the common entrance examination, a means of assessment and selection used by some independent senior schools. At early secondary level and sometimes before, pupils can be set for certain subjects, principally Mathematics, and a broad curriculum generally includes a choice of Modern Languages and sometimes Latin. In recent years there has been a strong focus on the individual needs of pupils, and support for learning has been increased by the employment of teachers specialising in this area. In all schools the curriculum is enhanced by clubs and societies, and by sporting events and musical and dramatic productions.

Independent schools in Scotland espouse the same mission as their state sector counterparts of preparing their senior pupils as individuals for the challenges of adult life and work, and in many cases they follow the same core curriculum and framework of qualifications. They have had the enviable freedom, however, to use their lower teacher–pupil ratio to respond to the needs of pupils in including a wider range of subjects in the curriculum and in offering a substantial number of examination courses. A large minority of schools provide courses leading to English qualifications as well as to those offered by the SQA. In general

Scottish independent schools are proudly Scottish as well as British: their students are involved in a broadly Scottish curriculum framework and many of their teachers play their part in marking for the SQA. A particularly interesting area, which has not received study, is the remarkable success of candidates from independent schools in external assessments. The SCIS figures for the diet of 2002, for instance, show a Higher Grade A–C pass rate of 89% in SCIS schools, with 45% at A. The substantial difference between this and the national average is worthy of investigation. Professor Lindsay Paterson, in his unpublished article 'Attainment in public-sector and independent schools in Scotland, 1994, by social class and parental education: some results for discussion' (Paterson, 2002), has started an informed debate. He argues that a large part of the sector difference may be explained by the socio-economic status of the families from which the students come, and that the high rates of examination success in independent schools are probably in large measure due to the parents of the students who attend them. He concludes also that the sector difference is particularly small for students who might be expected to do well in any sector, because they can draw on a great deal of parental support at home, as their fathers work in a professional occupation and they live with two parents both of whom stayed on at school to at least age 17. Professor Paterson's statistical analysis and his conclusions will engender further debate, but they do not necessarily conflict with the general view that important factors in the high levels of attainment in independent schools are their ethos of achievement, and the high expectations and support of each pupil by teachers and parents. A large majority of pupils from independent schools gain university places and a significant proportion choose universities in England, including Oxford and Cambridge. Although the 'State of the Nation Survey' did not suggest that the examination results of independent schools are in the forefront of public perceptions, in practice they are the single most important hard indicator of the success of the education offered by schools in the sector.

CURRENT ISSUES AND FUTURE PRIORITIES

Throughout their history, the independent schools of Scotland have had to change to secure their place in Scottish education, offering excellent teaching and facilities and concentrating on the welfare of the individual pupils – thereby persuading parents that it is worth investing a considerable sum in educating their children privately. Independent schools will continue to be vulnerable to a downturn in the economy, and to their need to meet the costs of their educational provision, including capital development, from fee income. The substantial fee increases of recent years which have been caused by the settlement in *A Teaching Profession for the 21st Century* (*The McCrone Report*, Scottish Executive, 2000) cannot be replicated forever without making it impossible for a significant number of parents to meet the fees of independent education. Yet the sector must keep pace not only with nationally agreed teaching salaries but with the continued improvement in state education, especially the investment in information and communications technology and in the training of staff in the new teaching and learning styles which it makes possible. Parental expectations have increased as society changes and all manner of facilities for pupil learning, eating, playing and comfort improve. To these must be added the costs of meeting the demands of health, safety and security regulations and the new requirement for an accessibility strategy. Independent schools have to be well managed to anticipate such expenditure and to identify and mitigate the risks facing their schools. It is important to them that charitable status is preserved, and as the definition of public benefit becomes clearer, schools need to ensure that they are developing their links with the local community while preserving their independence and security.

But with these challenges come substantial opportunities. The very independence of the sector has encouraged its schools to innovate and to respond to pupil needs and parental requests. Independent schools are no strangers to widening access to subjects and courses, to offering numerous opportunities, and to encouraging pupils to compile a portfolio of qualifications. There is much to be gained from participating in the national education debate and in having a voice in developments in the curriculum, and in the welfare of pupils and of the teaching profession. The sector is responding to these challenges and rejoices in the strength and support of SCIS. Experience and history suggest that the sector overall will remain strong and that independent schools will continue to flourish, although some individual changes will be inevitable. Schools will succeed through constant improvement, innovation and partnership, through the quality of the education they offer and the care they give to the development of the individual pupil. The opportunities for each school lie in a real understanding of its place in Scottish education and its local community, or its wider constituency in the case of the boarding sector. The diversity of the independent sector, its commitment to education and its pupils, and its capacity to change and improve, make it a worthy contributor to the developments in Scottish education which lie ahead.

REFERENCES

Parker, C. (2002) Five years on: partnership reviewed in Bernard Stafford (ed.), *Two Sectors, One Purpose: Independent Schools in the System*, Leicester: SHA.

Paterson, L. (2002) Attainment in public-sector and independent schools in Scotland, 1994, by social class and parental education: some results for discussion, unpublished article.

SCIS, *Directory of Independent Schools 2002–2003*, Edinburgh: SCIS (published annually).

SEED Statistical Bulletin 2001, Edinburgh: SEED.

Thomson M. T. (2001) Trends and gender issues in SCE examination performance in all state and independent schools in Scotland 1997–1999, unpublished EdD dissertation, University of Strathclyde.

10

The Distinctiveness of Scottish Education

Walter Humes and Tom Bryce

It is instructive for any nation to re-examine from time to time the fundamental values which its major social institutions are said to embody. Education has traditionally been identified as one of the three institutions which mark the social and cultural life of Scotland as distinctive, especially when compared to England. (The other two are the law and the Church.) With the election of a Scottish parliament in 1999 a new focus for the political identity of Scotland was created, which has strengthened the separate character of the nation's defining institutions. Scotland has entered a new era and it is timely, therefore, to take stock of the particular contribution which the educational system has made to the life of the nation in the recent past and, potentially, will make in the future. This will involve looking not only at the formal ways in which Scottish education is distinctive but also at the beliefs which underlie its institutional structures.

A useful reference point for the discussion that follows can be found in James Scotland's two-volume history of Scottish education, published in 1969. In his final chapter, Scotland attempted to define the Scottish tradition in education. He first identified a number of key components which helped to shape that tradition, for instance, pietism, poverty, militant democracy, academic bias, conservatism, authoritarianism, economy. None of these components, he acknowledged, 'has been entirely for the good of the people; each in its own way is open to severe criticism' (Scotland, 1969, vol. 2, p. 274). Nevertheless, 'the general impression is of a heritage worth remembering and building upon' (p. 274). He summed up his interpretation in six propositions which, he suggested, encapsulated the essence of Scottish attitudes towards education:

- education is, and always has been, of paramount importance in any community;
- every child should have the right to all the education of which he is capable;
- such education should be provided as economically and systematically as possible;
- the training of the intellect should take priority over all other facets of the pupil's personality;
- experiment is to be attempted only with the greatest caution; and
- the most important person in the school, no matter what theorists say, is not the pupil but the (inadequately rewarded) teacher. (p. 275)

Much has changed in the period since this list was drawn up and a few of the items no longer seem persuasive, but some at least (the first three?) would still receive widespread endorsement. And although the pride which Scottish people traditionally have had in the quality of their educational system is now held less confidently, belief in the importance of education, its value both for the individual and for society as a whole, remains unshaken. Thousands of Scots, many from modest backgrounds, can testify to the power of education to enrich (in some cases, transform) their lives, and even those who have not themselves done particularly well at school are often anxious that their own children should take advantage of the improved opportunities now open to them.

These attitudes help to ensure that the position of education in the national consciousness remains strong. Moreover, belief in the worth and purpose of education is linked to the sense of national identity which is regularly invoked to draw attention to the differences between Scottish and English society (see Chapter 22). This takes the form of a story or 'myth', shaped by history but not always supported by historical evidence, to the effect that Scottish society is relatively egalitarian and meritocratic; that ability and achievement, not rank, should determine success in the world; that public (rather than private) institutions should be the means of trying to bring about the good society; and that, even where merit does justify differential rewards, there are certain basic respects – arising from the common humanity of all men and women – in which human beings deserve equal consideration and treatment. Taken together, these features can be summed up in the phrase used by George Davie for the title of his famous book, *The Democratic Intellect* (1961). To describe the democratic intellect as constituting a 'myth' is not to dismiss it as untrue. Gray, McPherson and Raffe make the point that a myth is a narrative that people tell themselves for two reasons: 'first, to explain the world and, second, to celebrate identity and to express values' (*Reconstructions of Secondary Education*, London: Routledge, 1983, p. 39). The extent to which the values are actually achieved in practice is a matter for analysis and interpretation. So too is the question of who promotes the myth and who benefits from it. These are crucial issues that will be revisited later in the chapter.

First, however, it is necessary to ground the discussion in some factual information about those features of the day-to-day workings of the Scottish educational system which mark it out as distinctive. How are the differences between Scottish and English education reflected in the experiences of pupils, teachers and parents? What is the significance of these differences? And how do they connect with broader questions of consciousness, identity and values?

FORMAL DISTINCTIVENESS

Perhaps the most potent expression of the distinctiveness of Scottish education is the separate legislative framework which sets out the nature of provision and the agencies responsible for its delivery. Legislation is now framed by the Scottish Executive and formal responsibility for the system as a whole rests with the First Minister. Prior to devolution, Scottish legislation often (but not always) post-dated statutory provision in England, but it did not always follow an identical pattern. A clear example was the legislation relating to parental choice of school enshrined in the Education Act of 1980 (England and Wales) and the Education (Scotland) Act of 1981. The Scottish Act gave stronger rights of choice to parents. Exceptions to the granting of parental rights had to be specific and had to relate to such things as the need to employ an additional member of staff or to alter school buildings. Furthermore, Scottish parents had the right to appeal to a sheriff and, where an appeal was upheld, the education authority was required to review all similar cases (Adler et al:

Parental Choice and Educational Policy, Edinburgh: Edinburgh University Press, 1989). Partly as a result of the Scottish experience, the rights of parents in England were strengthened in the 1988 Education Reform Act.

One of the first Acts of the Scottish Parliament was the Standards in Scotland's Schools etc. Act 2000. It introduced a new school improvement framework, one part of which set out five national priorities for education. Whether through the direct influence of parliamentarians in debate or as a result of the wide consultation exercise conducted in conjunction with it, the process led to a firm emphasis upon equality and inclusion. Social learning and citizenship figure prominently and government accepts the advantages to be gained from joint working with agencies other than education, as in the multi-professional approach to New Community Schools. The priorities concerned with achievement and attainment are for all pupils; the needs of the disabled and those with special educational needs figure centrally. While it has been left to schools and authorities to implement the national priorities, the legislative framework requires them to formulate improvement and development plans accordingly. Arguably the thrust of this Scottish parliamentary thinking represents a genuine inclusiveness in thinking, backed by imperatives and controls. This constitutes a familiar combination of typically Scottish appeal to democratic sentiments allied to firm central direction of policy.

Other examples of important legislative differences prior to devolution can be seen in the arrangements for school boards in Scotland compared to governing bodies in England, devolved school management in Scotland compared to local financial management in England, and the circumstances which require the opening and maintenance of a Record of Needs for children requiring special educational provision in Scotland compared to the Statement of Needs in England.

Provisions for the testing of pupils are also different north and south of the border. The Conservative government tried to put national testing in place in Scotland as it did in England and Wales but considerable resistance from parents, teaching unions and local authorities (particularly Strathclyde Region) resulted in different legislation being enacted in Scotland. As described elsewhere in this volume, teachers carry out national testing at times of their choosing to check their classroom assessment judgements, and do so by drawing upon available national item-bank test materials. There is, therefore, no centralised capacity to assemble data such as has been used for league tables in England and Wales.

Further evidence of Scottish distinctiveness can be seen in the separate institutional apparatus which maintains the system. There is one national examination body, the Scottish Qualifications Authority (SQA), whereas in England there are several examination boards, ostensibly serving different parts of the country though schools are not confined to entering candidates in the board located in their geographical area. Other important bodies expressive of the separate character of the Scottish system include Learning and Teaching Scotland (LTS) and the General Teaching Council (GTC). LTS advises the First Minister on all matters relating to the curriculum as they affect the age range 3–18. It issues guidance to local authorities and schools, carries out programmes of curriculum development and produces a wide range of publications covering many aspects of pre-school, primary and secondary education. In Scotland, unlike England, there is no formally prescribed national curriculum though, in practice, most schools follow closely the recommendations contained in national documents such as those deriving from the 5–14 development programme.

The GTC, established by statute in 1965, is a body containing a majority of teacher representatives, which controls entry to the profession, accredits initial training courses for teachers and has responsibility for the assessment of probationary teachers. Formally independent, the GTC has strong links with the Scottish Executive Education Department (SEED) and some teachers are sceptical of the degree of real autonomy which it possesses. Its very existence, however, is testimony to the relative status of teaching as a profession in Scotland, compared to England. Only recently has an English GTC been established (by a 1998 Act of the UK parliament), with powers that are significantly weaker than those enjoyed by the GTC in Scotland.

The way in which the institutional apparatus of Scottish education functions helps to explain a somewhat ironic feature of the system. Although the educational workforce consistently exhibits anti-Conservative tendencies (in a party-political sense), the process of educational advancement nonetheless reflects a kind of determined conservatism. As Brian Boyd's 1996 *Herald* Essay observes ('The Scottishness of our Schools', *The Herald*, 28 January 1996), Scotland has never been extreme with its educational innovations; the Scottish approach 'has always been to integrate innovation firmly into traditional approaches'. Boyd's analysis is consistent with James Scotland's observation that a feature of the Scottish tradition is that 'experiment is to be attempted only with the greatest caution'. National bodies such as LTS and the SQA operate as bureaucracies with established ways of doing things and a concern to ensure that safeguards are built into the system. Their officers often have a strong commitment to particular areas of the curriculum and, although important cross-curricular developments are taking place in both primary and secondary schools, most developments start from existing practice rather than a radical review of the curriculum as a whole. This approach is strongly promoted by Her Majesty's Inspectors of Education, a small but powerful group concerned to identify and disseminate 'good practice'. Through the exercise of their very considerable informal power, HMIEs influence many of the activities not only of LTS and SQA staff but also of the diminishing group of teacher educators who contribute to educational reform by helping to develop and deliver programmes of staff training. For major initiatives, the co-ordinated efforts of all of these groups is important and the small size of Scotland is often seen as an advantage in this respect. People tend to know each other and a consensus is perhaps easier to reach than it would be in a larger, more anonymous system. This consensus is often presented as a distinctive and positive feature of Scottish education but it has a downside as well. It can lead to complacency and a failure to question existing practice in the fundamental way that may be needed. The 'practice-driven' approach to curriculum development helps to explain the relative conservatism identified by writers such as Boyd and Scotland.

Another feature of Scottish education for which claims are made in respect of distinctiveness is the breadth of the curriculum available to pupils in schools, and it would be fair to say that all the national programmes – Standard Grade, 5–14 and Higher Still (the last being subsumed under 'new National Qualifications') – have preserved breadth of study. A common Scottish–English comparison has been between the number of Higher subjects taken by the typical S5–S6 pupil and the fewer subjects taken in England by the typical A-level pupil. A careful distinction should be made, however, between courses followed and actual qualifications gained. Analysis of the pattern of Higher results carried out for the Howie report (*Upper Secondary Education in Scotland*, Scottish Office Education Department, 1992, Edinburgh: HMSO), and which informed the thinking that led to Higher Still, indicated that too few Higher passes were achieved by the end of S5, and S5–6 courses were not genuinely two-year courses where they needed to be; breadth in opportunity to take Highers there may have been, breadth in achievement there was not. Higher Still has now brought about a five-level framework for qualifications in S5 and beyond and early indications (rapid uptake and success of sub-Higher courses, particularly at Intermediate 2 – see Chapter 81) suggest that improved patterns of achievement can be combined with the broad range of subjects studied at this level. It is still early days, there having been only four years of implementation, each seeing progressively fuller uptake across schools and subjects, and further analysis will be required.

Compared with the school system, the formal distinctiveness of Scotland's universities is less clear cut. For most of the twentieth century Scottish universities were seen primarily as United Kingdom institutions and the body responsible for their funding – originally the University Grants Committee (later the Universities Funding Council) – was accountable to the Department of Education and Science (DES) in London. This position was reviewed from time to time but the consistent message from Scottish university principals was that they were against the Scottish Office taking over responsibility. Part of the explanation was a desire to retain international standing and a fear that the Scottish Office might try to interfere with academic freedom. These attitudes began to change in the 1980s when, following a major financial exercise involving severe cutbacks, in which there was a feeling that the UGC's understanding of and sympathy for the Scottish dimension was deficient, demands for the establishment of a separate Scottish sub-committee of the UGC were voiced. These were initially rejected but the climate had altered and it was only a matter of time before the funding arrangements were revised. Since 1992 the Scottish Higher Education Funding Council (SHEFC) has been responsible for distributing grants for teaching, research and associated activities in all Scottish higher education institutions. Matters relating to quality assurance, however, continue to be adminstered on a UK-wide basis under the direction of the Quality Assurance Agency (QAA), a body established in 1997. QAA's role has been criticised as excessively bureaucratic and it is now attempting to operate 'light touch' systems of accountability.

UNDERLYING VALUES

The extent to which the various manifestations of formal distinctiveness embody a particularly Scottish vision of the nature and purpose of education is a matter of continuing analysis and debate. G. E. Davie (1961) argued that the special character of Scotland's educational system has been progressively weakened by a process of assimilation to English norms, notwithstanding the separate legislative framework. According to Davie, the Scottish university curriculum, with an emphasis on curricular breadth and philosophical enquiry, was steadily weakened during the nineteenth century by a narrow English empiricism which led to specialisation and fragmentation of knowledge. This process was aided by the introduction of English-style examinations and the appointment of English candidates to key university chairs in Scotland. Secondary schools were required to adapt to the changes in order to prepare candidates for university entrance and so the anglicising tendencies gradually entered the whole system. One manifestation of the trend was the disparagement of Scots and Gaelic as legitimate forms of language for learning. A restatement and updating of Davie's analysis was offered by A. L. Walker in his highly polemical study *The Revival of the Democratic Intellect* (Edinburgh: Polygon, 1994).

The pessimism of Davie and Walker would now be challenged. Cameron Harrison, writing about attitudes to Scots and Gaelic says that 'the age of hostility is past' ('How Scottish is the Scottish curriculum?', in M. M. Clark and P. Munn (eds), *Education in*

Scotland, London: Routledge, 1997, p. 160). Similarly, it is possible to point to the development of curricular materials with a strong Scottish flavour across a range of subjects in primary and secondary schools. Scottish history is now well-established as a field of study in schools and universities, and the use of Scottish texts in drama and literature courses is widespread. Add to this the wider cultural renaissance in Scotland, which includes art, music and media, and the argument that Scottish society and Scottish education are dominated by English values and institutions seems hard to sustain.

It is, however, not a simple either/or issue, with the 'purity' of Scottish values being set against the 'contamination' from south of the border. A significant number of Scots feel themselves to be both Scottish and British (and in some cases European as well) and they want the next generation to enjoy the freedom to enter different cultural worlds. They certainly want Scottish identity and culture to be given proper recognition within the curriculum but they also want their children to be able to cope with the globalisation of knowledge. The international character of many areas of learning and the employment markets associated with them (e.g. technology, computing, economics, banking, law, government) is now recognised. These are cross-national trends which cannot be resisted. To the extent that any educational system must try to prepare young people for the future, Scotland cannot afford to construct a curriculum on the basis of romantic retreat to an imagined golden age of the past. Scottish distinctiveness has to be shaped and redefined in a way that is compatible with the realities of the modern world.

This is not an easy task and it has as much to do with maturity and confidence as with knowledge. Evidence for such an attitudinal shift is patchy. It is perhaps strongest in those fields associated with the artistic renaissance referred to above. But in other spheres of activity there are still many instances of Scottish defensiveness, inarticulateness and embarrassment when faced with the seemingly greater social confidence of the English. Even worse, there have been a number of ugly examples of anti-English racism in different parts of Scotland. Self-confidence about one's own national identity should not be incompatible with tolerance of diversity in other people. That is a mark of cultural maturity. A useful first step would be a recognition of the diversity inside Scotland itself. In September 2002 however, as the Scottish Executive launched its campaign to tackle racism ('One Scotland, Many Cultures'), a System Three survey of 2000 people commissioned by the Executive revealed high proportions of self-reported racist tendencies (with nearly one-quarter of Scots admitting to being racist and 52% being worried if the numbers of people from other cultural or ethnic backgrounds living in Scotland were to increase). Figures like these are higher than the public would like to believe. Should one interpret them to be an indication that Scots are becoming more racist? Or, might people now be willing to recognise racist tendencies for what they actually are? (see Chapter 100).

From another perspective, there always has been considerable cultural variation within Scotland – between Highlands and Lowlands, Edinburgh and Glasgow, cities and rural communities, Catholics and Protestants. This diversity has often been submerged in a standardised and idealised model of Scottish life which, with staggering improbability, manages to combine elements of Knox, Burns, Hampden, Red Clydeside and a kailyard version of community life (Humes, 1984). Stripping away these internal mythologies may serve to counteract the easy recourse to demonising the English. Blaming England for Scotland's ills prevents the hard thinking that is needed now that Scotland has assumed greater responsibility for its own affairs.

CRITICS OF THE SCOTTISH TRADITION

One way of extending the demythologising process is to examine what critics of the Scottish educational tradition have had to say. The accounts of that tradition which receive greatest attention and which help to shape popular consciousness tend to be those which are written by members of the educational establishment. James Scotland is a case in point. He was principal of Aberdeen College of Education, convener of the GTC, and a long-standing member of the policy community. It is not surprising that interpretations coming from such sources should give more prominence to the achievements of the system, rather than its shortcomings. However, there is a counter-tradition – albeit a minor one – of radical twentieth-century criticism which casts interesting light on the cherished principles identified by James Scotland. It is an interpretation, moreover, that raises important questions about the relation between schooling, society and values.

One early critic was Patrick Geddes (1854–1932), a botanist and environmentalist, who described elementary and secondary schools as 'prisons for body and mind' whose main function was to serve the needs, not of children, but of 'text-book perpetrators' and 'examination-machine bureaucrats' (quoted in Boardman, P., *Patrick Geddes: Maker of the Future*, Chapel Hill, NC: University of North Carolina Press, 1944, pp. 269, 266). Underlying this criticism was a profound awareness of the ways in which schooling, the provision of which was intended to open up opportunities, could become an oppressive institutional apparatus for stifling genuine interest in children. Geddes was a keen advocate of getting children out of the classroom and encouraging them to discover things for themselves: his advocacy led to the introduction of nature study in primary schools. A similar philosophy was evident in the writings of A. S. Neill (1883–1973) who became a key figure in the progressive movement, attracting enthusiasm and notoriety in almost equal measure for his school Summerhill. Neill left Scotland because he disagreed fundamentally with the emphasis on discipline and authority, and the centrality of the teacher rather than the pupil. Strongly influenced by Freudian psychology, he based his school on the principle of freedom and saw modern society as hostile to individuality and creativity. Yet another critic, R. F. Mackenzie (1910–87) tried, ultimately unsuccessfully, to establish a regime within the state system which challenged traditional ideas on curriculum content and pupil learning. Like Neill, he saw attitudes to schooling as symptomatic of wider social attitudes: 'The crisis in Scottish schools is a crisis in Scottish life . . . Scotland's schools are at the centre of Scotland's perplexity, one of its main causes' (*The Unbowed Head*, Edinburgh: EUSPB, 1977, p. 6). Mackenzie believed that for many Scottish youngsters the experience of schooling was largely negative. They were given few opportunities to explore and enjoy learning in creative ways that connected with life outside school; they were constantly reminded of their inadequacies and failures; and they were ill-equipped to meet the challenges they would face as adults. These deficiencies, Mackenzie believed, helped to explain the cultural malaise from which he felt Scotland suffered – a malaise evident in a lack of drive and intiative, a passivity in the face of officialdom and an impoverished sense of life's possibilities. It is a bleak picture of institutional failure and missed opportunities. Harry Reid, in his foreword to Murphy's biography of R. F. Mackenzie, reflects on what he would have made of the Scottish Parliament and of education in particular. Mackenzie would certainly be '. . . teaching, always teaching us to reject the mendacious and the meretricious, to discard the conventional, to reject the divisive and – above all – to be kind, and to think well and think big' (Murphy 1998, p. vi).

The current generation of teachers and headteachers would certainly disagree with the critics and claim that modern schools are much less oppressive places where pupil achievements are celebrated and the richness of learning in all its forms is recognised and encouraged. That may be so – though it would be a matter for debate – but it does not diminish the responsibility to confront past practices and to reflect on their significance for the present and future. The value attached to schooling in Scotland (identified by James Scotland as one of the tradition's defining characteristics) makes it doubly important to consider its wider social impact and here the need to confront uncomfortable truths remains strong. In a statement which resonates powerfully with the critics, the historian T. C. Smout comments:

> It is in the history of the school more than in any other aspect of recent social history that the key lies to some of the more depressing aspects of modern Scotland. If there are in this country too many people who fear what is new, believe the difficult to be impossible, draw back from responsibility, and afford established authority and tradition an exaggerated respect, we can reasonably look for an explanation in the institutions that moulded them. (Smout, 1986, p. 229)

Even if the radical educational philosophies of Geddes, Neill and Mackenzie are not accepted, it is possible to recognise the validity of what Smout is saying about Scottish society. The situation may be improving post-devolution but it is a slow process. Resistance to change in working practices, reluctance to take on new challenges, unwillingness to accept leadership roles, reticence in the face of professional and bureaucratic authority – these are still recognisable features of life in Scotland. They are by no means universal but they are sufficiently widespread to have attracted the attention of social commentators. In the Thatcher years they led to the phrase 'dependency culture' being coined, a concept that implied an expectation that the state would provide when personal responsibility failed. Under New Labour an attempt is being made to address the problems associated with passivity and defeatism through an emphasis on civic involvement, entrepreneurship and creativity – all designed to reduce dependence on state benefits and encourage people, particularly young people, to become active citizens, contributing not only to personal advancement and the economic life of the country but also to attitude sets in families and communities.

The Scottish Parliament certainly has the potential to serve as a positive focus for significant economic, social and cultural reform. For that to happen on the scale that is needed, however, would require a major transformation encompassing not only education but a wide range of other public and private services as well. The capacity of children to benefit from schooling is profoundly affected by issues of housing, employment, poverty and health. It is in the inter-connection of these forces that solutions to the sort of cultural defects which Smout describes must be found. A major test of the Scottish Parliament, therefore, will be its success in tackling these problems in an innovative and coordinated way – in other words, in showing that 'joined up government' can make a difference. Prior to the reorganisation of local government in 1996 some of the larger regions (notably Strathclyde and Lothian) tried to co-ordinate social strategy on a multi-disciplinary basis but, with the fragmentation of services involved in the creation of thirty-two councils, some ground was lost. The importance of developing policies which locate educational provision in the context of broader social issues is, however, now well understood by both politicians and professionals. Even so, the choices they face are daunting.

SOCIAL POLARISATION AND THE KNOWLEDGE UNDERCLASS

The sheer scale of the task should not be underestimated, as consideration of the case of a comprehensive school serving a disadvantaged housing scheme on the outskirts of Glasgow or Edinburgh will demonstrate. Such a school is affected by social polarisation, in the sense that it is cut off from the amenities of more affluent districts, and by the legacy of ill-judged housing and planning policies in the 1950s and 1960s. The community is likely to suffer from higher levels of poverty, unemployment, ill-health and crime than other areas within the city. What are the choices open to parents, teachers and politicians in such a case? Some parents might exercise the right of choice and send their children to a 'better' school further afield. That could have individual advantages but it might deprive the neighbourhood school of the children and parents who, potentially, could make the greatest contribution to its ethos and level of achievement. To the extent that that happens, the comprehensive principle – a central plank in Scottish distinctiveness – is weakened. One response to these problems has been the creation of New Community Schools which seek to bring about more effective inter-agency provision covering education, health and social work services (see Chapter 4). It remains to be seen whether in the longer term such initiatives ensure that comprehensive schooling meets the needs of all pupils, not least those who live in areas of multiple deprivation.

The teachers in a school serving a socially disadvantaged area might make a strategic decision to offer a curriculum that is different from the mainstream curriculum in most Scottish secondary schools. This is unlikely to be as radical as that recommended by Neill or Mackenzie but it might well involve giving particular attention to issues which children will face outside school. Thus a programme with a substantial input on social education, covering topics such as health and diet, sexual behaviour, relationships, parenting skills, the use and abuse of drugs and alcohol, living within a budget and awareness of the law, might occupy a significant part of the timetable. A programme of this kind would be well-intentioned but it could, paradoxically, convey a message of social stereotyping and intensify, rather than reduce, the 'ghettoisation' of the community. Furthermore, insofar as it leads to a reduction in the amount of time spent on more conventional subjects, it could help to expand what has recently been called the 'knowledge underclass' – those who lack the understanding and skills to be able to function effectively in an information-rich environment.

For politicians, both local and national, the key question is what kind of social intervention is likely to pay the greatest dividends. The current government is committed to putting education at the top of its priority list. But might it not be that greater employment opportunities or improved housing would actually be a sounder investment in that they would improve individual and community self-esteem which, in turn, might encourage greater responsiveness to what education has to offer, in a way that schooling alone could not do? Once again, the interpenetration of the various aspects of social policy is apparent.

There are, of course, no simple answers to these questions, but it is in schools such as these that the strongest test of Scottish educational principles is to be found. If democracy and equality mean anything, then they must offer hope to children and families experiencing multiple disadvantage. Around 40 per cent of pupils attending Glasgow schools live in poverty, as measured by their entitlement to free school meals, and the evidence is that this poverty is increasingly concentrated in a few areas. If the trend towards community segregation continues, the credibility of that part of the Scottish tradition in education which emphasises opportunity for all (never mind achievement for all) will be difficult to maintain. The ideal of social inclusion is easy to state. Achieving it is another matter.

COMPETING INTERPRETATIONS

In earlier sections of this chapter a contrast has been drawn between celebratory interpretations of the Scottish educational tradition (such as James Scotland's) and critical interpretations (such as R. F. Mackenzie's). To polarise these inevitably over-simplifies the forces at work, not least by failing to take account of the particular circumstances at any given time in the evolution of the tradition. Lindsay Paterson has claimed that an analysis of the ways in which Scottish education has been subject to reform suggests that a highly complex blend of traditional and radical thinking can be detected at various points in recent educational history (Paterson, 1996). He argues that it is misleading to interpret the development of Scottish education in terms of a crude dichotomy between control and liberation. Depending on the circumstances of the time, different educational philosophies were mobilised in a variety of ways. Referring to the introduction of comprehensive education, he states that, 'the single act of abolishing selection [was] a real victory for progressive educational thought' and that its radical effect can be seen 'in the slow revolution it has brought about in the educational aspirations of the whole community'. Significantly, however, the switch to comprehensivisation was not a peculiarly Scottish development, though it is often claimed that comprehensive schools had their roots in the old 'omnibus' schools found in small towns and rural communities in Scotland. This claim ignores the extent of selection and streaming within omnibus schools. Recent evidence from public consultation as part of the National Debate on the future of Scottish education carried out in 2002 indicates continuing support for the comprehensive principle, however defined.

A better test of Paterson's thesis would be to look at a specifically Scottish policy, such as Higher Still, which has been represented as a bold attempt to address recognised weaknesses in upper secondary education. To what extent does it embody continuity with traditional values and to what extent does it break new ground? At one level, Higher Still can be seen as a strategy to extend the principle of equality of opportunity by making it easier for a larger proportion of the school population than hitherto to gain awards for achievement, in the form of national certificates, across a wider range of curriculum content. Furthermore, in its explicit rejection of a 'twin track' approach, which would have separated academic and vocational cohorts of pupils, Higher Still seeks to end the divisiveness of the stratification of knowledge. It aims to provide a unified system of post-compulsory education which offers a fair measure of flexibility and choice to users.

All this can be regarded as enlightened but, at another level, the Higher Still programme might be seen as driven by professional and bureaucratic interests rather than the interests of learners. It fails to challenge the autonomy of subject departments in secondary schools (see Chapter 4) and this might well make it difficult to achieve success in promoting cross-curricular core skills, which employers regard as valuable. The modular structure on which Higher Still is based has brought with it a bureaucratic system which teachers find oppressive and pupils find confusing (thus the heavy emphasis on guidance in negotiating the system). Moreover, the whole programme is assessment-led, a feature which some would see as fundamentally anti-educational. The emphasis on assessment and certification has produced what might be called a 'technical' approach to development and implementation. What is lacking is a wider vision of how Higher Still impacts on the lives of students and on Scottish society in the twenty-first century. There is, in other words, a philosophical vacuum at the heart of Higher Still. Any attempt at serious epistemological debate about the nature and structure of knowledge appropriate to the upper secondary school has long since been abandoned. Pragmatism has taken over.

The fact that Higher Still can be subject to alternative readings goes some way towards bearing out Paterson's point about the complexity and malleability of traditions. In a similar fashion, it is possible to tell the bigger story of the distinctiveness of Scotland's educational tradition in more than one version. New 'myths' can replace the old ones and the task of deconstruction is never-ending. What can be said is that the claims made for the quality of Scottish education, past and present, have been substantial and that they have sometimes led to an unjustifiable degree of complacency. Increasingly, international comparisons suggest that Scotland needs to do better on a number of fronts. The value attached to education, both by policy makers and by ordinary Scots, remains high but the ideals expressed in the official discourse need to be constantly tested against the realities as experienced by pupils, teachers, parents and employers. As the Scottish Parliament continues to grapple with these challenges, Scottish education needs both its advocates and its critics.

REFERENCES

Davie, G. E. (1961) *The Democratic Intellect*, Edinburgh: Edinburgh University Press.

Humes, W. M. (1984) The cultural significance of Scotland's educational system, in D. McCrone (ed.), *The Scottish Government Yearbook 1984*, Edinburgh: Unit for the Study of Government in Scotland, pp. 149–66.

Murphy, P. A. (1998) *The Life of R. F. Mackenzie: A Prophet without Honour*, Edinburgh: John Donald.

Paterson, L. (1996) Liberation or control: what are the Scottish education traditions of the twentieth century? in T. M. Devine and R. J. Finlay, eds, *Scotland in the 20th Century*, Edinburgh: Edinburgh University Press, pp. 230–49.

Scotland, J. (1969) *The History of Scottish Education*, vol. 2, London: University of London Press.

Smout, T. C. (1986) A Century of the Scottish People 1830–1950, London: Collins.

III

The Administration and Control of Scottish Education

11

Parliament, SEED and the Administration of Scottish Education after Devolution

Gari Donn

In 1999 Scotland achieved its devolved parliament introducing the first Scottish parliament and administrative system for 300 years. Based on the principles of power sharing (between the people of Scotland, the legislators and the Scottish Executive), accountability (between the Executive and Parliament and between these and the people), access and participation and equal opportunities, the 129 elected Members of the Scottish Parliament (MSPs) took their seats in Edinburgh to consider 'devolved business' (education and lifelong learning issues, transport, environment, rural affairs, health and community care, legal affairs and finance and public services) but not 'reserved matters' (areas of macro economic policy, foreign affairs or defence). So, 'devolution' being the delegation of powers from central government to local bodies, Scotland's devolved Parliament began business with a restricted legislative agenda (albeit with the power to alter the rate of tax). After all, this was not 'independence'. The question was: would this mean that Scottish education is 'no longer administered by a political party whose policies are at variance with the views of the majority of the Scottish people, as expressed in elections' (Brown, 1999)? The past few years have indicated that the governance of Scottish education is a complex and, at times, a perplexing socio-political activity. It may take more than a change of name at the level of administration to demonstrate that Scottish education is, truly, in the hands of those upholding Scottish interests.

The following analysis focuses upon post-devolution developments in education and particularly the administration of education through various parliamentary, civil service and agency arrangements. Attention is drawn to the fascinating relationships between key players, interest groups and organisations overseeing policy developments in Scotland's education: it is noted that these relationships may have harboured within them the old and well-established set of factions and particularities so characteristic of the 'old Scottish education community' which existed in the pre-devolution educational environment. Through portrayal of the Official Record of parliamentary debates and accounts from the Committees overseeing education, an understanding is presented of discourses involving education during the first three years of the Scottish Parliament. It is argued that the new political settlement appears to counter-pose underlying social justice philosophies of education with the more mercurial requirements of financial management. It suggests that it will be in everyone's interests if Scotland's devolutionary environment can enhance historic commitments to collective welfarism whilst helping to develop new and relevant political and administrative liaisons.

THE MACHINERY OF ADMINISTRATION OF EDUCATION

Central to administration of education in Scotland is the Scottish Executive Education Department (SEED) which emerged out of the Scottish Office Education and Industry Department (already, in 2003, an apparent anachronism – so there is success for Scotland's educational agenda!), which itself emerged out of the Scottish Office Education Department (SOED) and that from the long-established Scottish Education Department (SED), so well remembered in many education policy texts. Yet SEED of 2002 has a huge remit: not only does it address education for Scotland, but also tourism, culture and sport, children and young people (early education and childcare; children and families) but also is the reporting Ministry for Social Work Services Inspectorate (a Scottish Executive Professional Unit), Historic Scotland (a Scottish Executive Agency) and, another Agency, Her Majesty's Inspectorate of Education (HMIE).

It can be seen that with this large portfolio the scope of the SEED is wide. In relation to the field of education per se, SEED plays a major role in the efficacious administration of Scotland's education system, particularly over the school and young persons sectors. Its remit is to ensure that every child or young person is able to work to their fullest potential, that all children have access to early learning education and care, that social justice is promoted, and that standards are raised and achievement broadened. Within the SEED, the Schools Group (with the 'Teachers Division', 'New Educational Developments Division', and 'Qualifications, Assessment and Curriculum Division') is responsible for policy covering priorities in education, teachers and schools, social justice, school ethos, support and special educational needs, and curriculum assessment and qualifications developments.

Until 2001 the inspectorate, the HMI, was tightly interwoven within SEED: after April 2001 the HMIE came to operate as an executive agency of the Scottish Executive but with the HMIE directly accountable to ministers for the standards of its work, and the promotion of standards and quality at schools. Its independent inspections, reviews and reporting on educational establishments, community outreach relations and relations with local authorities are said to ensure standards in Scotland's schools are maintained (see Chapter 16).

In addition, SEED sponsors the national non-departmental public body (NDPB), Learning and Teaching Scotland (LTS). This body, formed in 2000 from the merger of the SCCC and SCET, provides advice, support and staff development to enhance lifelong learning. In particular it provides advice to ministers regarding the use of ICT to support the school curriculum; advice to the Funding Councils on matters related to the use of ICT in Scottish schools and establishments for lifelong learning; and researches on work related to school and pre-school curriculum use of ICT. Although concerned with school-based activities, part of its remit involves lifelong learning: many of its contacts are key players and organisations under the remit of the Enterprise and Lifelong Learning Department (see chapter 12). It may be that there will be advantage in restructuring the administrative divisions so that all educational concerns come under one department. However, this change has yet to happen.

Alongside the many shifts and innovations in nomenclature were continuing changes in the philosophical context of education (education by the 1990s had become that key factor in preparation for work, fore-fronted at the expense of other cultural, social and personal purposes of education); there were changes, also, in the domicile of top civil servants, post-1999, these persons and positions no longer based in London at Dover House (the

'Scotch Office' of old), but in Edinburgh. Nevertheless, after devolution, the Scotland Office still existed, albeit with reduced powers; coming to represent Scotland's interests in matters that are reserved to the UK Parliament. It is headed by the Secretary of State for Scotland who remains a member of the UK Cabinet and is not a member of the Scottish Executive.

Devolution required the return to Scotland not only of these officials and their administrative machinery – met at the Leith Scottish Executive building by those of lesser ranks already within the SOEID and positioned in Scotland – but also the UK-raised budgets through which education can be administered efficaciously. Throughout the 1980s and 1990s education had been at the centre of government policy, and this period came to be known as a time of intense 'politicisation of education'. Indeed, various researches note (Paterson 1997) the strained relationship between the civil servants and their political masters of SOEID, frequently the result of differing approaches to spending and accounting.

DEVOLUTION AND DIFFERENCE

So devolution in 1999 was seen as an opportunity for Scotland to reclaim Scotland's education; to harvest once again the human capital produced through a social welfarist approach to education policy and to distance, with great – astonishing? – speed, the education policies of Scotland from those of the more commercially oriented, consumerist and managerialist policies said to be being developed and adopted south of the border.

In leaving the south behind, politicians wishing to identify with Scotland's educational agenda, and those civil servants of the new era, also wishing to justify their newly-acquired status and nomenclature, began to revel in the differences: no OFSTED here; no assisted places scheme needed here; no – well, perhaps no – public private partnerships in the building of schools; little demand for schools to 'opt out' of local authority (LA) control: indeed, the opposite, a desire to ensure the maintenance of the education–local authority relationship, much confused though it had been by twenty years of central government castigation and change. Yet the local authorities (there being twelve regional councils pre-1996, these having become thirty-two unitary councils in local government reorganisation in 1996) had begun to develop their own and diverging approaches to, and agendas for, education. Further, many LA positions had become staffed by newly appointed officials, not those from the confrontational days of the 1980s and early 1990s, when Scottish local authorities frequently opposed education policies of the Conservative government: no longer were LAs clear-cut in their opposition to teacher appraisal, standard attainment tasks (tests), publication of league tables for schools: no, those 'older combative officials' were now part of the cadre of MSPs (constituency and list) in the new Scottish Parliament. So new relationships had to be forged and developed between the Scottish Executive, the Scottish Parliament and the local authorities.

In a similar way, new relationships had to be forged between the inspectorate and the Scottish Executive, the necessary result of a confusion in the historical role of the HMI in Scotland. Instead of developing a system as in England and Wales of inspection separate from a government department, Scotland's educational policy community cherished HMI as providing information to politicians and civil servants about what was happening on the ground. As part of the Scottish Executive, HMI staff continued to work closely with administrators and, in fact, to interchange with administrators as senior civil servants on committees or in advisory roles; to engage in both policy making and practice; to take the lead in areas of research and to manage research programmes; and thereby to maintain much greater contact between research communities, administration and political processes than became possible in England and Wales with the generation of OfSTED, its reports and encyclicals. However, this cosy relationship also harboured the origins of the most disruptive 'debacle' in Scottish education, the SQA examinations crisis of 2000: an occurrence that happened less than two years after devolution.

But before this episode there were positive developments for Scotland's devolved governance of education. It was central to the post-devolution education discourse that the Scottish Executive continued to expound its commitment to education as a social good; education as a vehicle to help to achieve the goals of equity, access, participation and individual entitlement to education after schooling (Bryce and Humes, 1999, p. 1010). Support was given to the General Teaching Council for Scotland (GTCS) which was entrusted to oversee and enhance the standards of teachers in schools, and the accreditation and review of courses for initial teacher training, and to provide structures to support probationary teachers (see Chapter 112).

In fact, issues concerning teachers have formed a substantial part of the work of the Scottish Parliament. Following the McCrone Committee Report into the pay and conditions of teachers, it became apparent that teachers were being seen as part of the problems of education, rather than part of the solutions. The period of praise for the teaching profession, throughout the years from the end of the nineteenth century until the 1970s had been superseded in the 1980s (during the years of the Conservative govern- ment) by a politically intense agenda of denigrating the 'quasi-profession'. Recent debates in Parliament have indicated that because education has many roles to play, teachers also have to become multi-faceted in their approaches to teaching and learning. Had education continued to be seen as a force for social justice, perhaps teachers would have retained some of their aura of professionalism. But because the Parliament requires education to become a force for the provision of human capital into organisations, the companies of the knowledge economy, and is seen to be failing at that, teachers frequently have felt that they are being castigated for failures not of their making. McCrone's recommendations concerned payment (increased pay for more time spent in specific tasks) and restructuring of leadership positions in schools (a 'senior management team' not necessarily very different in remit from that of Scotland's companies). How these changes will impact on performance remains to be seen.

Performance has been the watchword of those charged with managing the Scottish Qualifications Authority (SQA). The SQA, established in 1996, out of the merger of the Scottish Examination Board (SEB) and the Scottish Vocational Education Council (SCOTVEC), like the HMI, became part of the 'debacle'. It had been given responsibility for the development, assessment and certification of qualifications – other than those for higher education; although that, too, would alter when, in 2002, the frameworks of Scottish Higher Education's Quality Assurance and SQA merged to become the Scottish Credit and Qualifications Framework (SCQF). SQA's remit has been to devise, develop and validate and accredit qualifications, approve education and training establishments, arrange for, assist in and carry out the assessments for those taking SQA qualifications, quality assure education and training establishments hosting SQA examinations and issue certificates to candidates (see Chapter 83). How different the situation is from that in the south with its three competing examinations and qualifications authorities. And how much easier, perhaps, for something to go wrong, very badly wrong, when there is only one SQA and when there is no 'independent' OfSTED-like brake on incestuous educational relations between players in policy and practice.

However, one might have hoped that the Scottish Parliament with its debating chamber and its two education committees would have performed that brake-like function. But, there too, less than critical appraisals of the possibilities of 'catastrophe' brought about through the continuation of historical educational relationships allowed the problem to occur. The two committees acted after the event, but perhaps that was understandable and a result of their mandates. The Education, Culture and Sport Committee (EC&SC) was given responsibility for the consideration and reporting on matters related to school and pre-school education, those matters falling within the remit of the Minister for Education and Young People; and the Enterprise and Lifelong Learning Committee (E&LLC) has responsibility to consider and report on matters relating to the Scottish economy, industry, training and further and higher education, these matters falling within the remit of the Minister for Enterprise and Lifelong Learning (see Chapter 12).

Perhaps the dearth in forms and structures within which to articulate critical reflection on the part of the Parliament and its two education committees was the result, also, of the changes in personnel in top political positions. It has been unfortunate that some changes and transfers became necessary following the death of the first First Minister, Donald Dewar and then following the resignation of the second First Minister, Henry McLeish. Within the first few years of the devolved Parliament there have been frequent changes in Ministers of Education (at the time of writing, three: Galbraith, McConnell, Jamieson) and their deputies and Ministers for Lifelong Learning (McLeish, Gray) and their deputies. Although convention allows, indeed requires, changes in political portfolios, there are grounds for suggesting that a newly devolved parliament with relocated and restructured civil service machinery, required, indeed necessitated, continuity in the development of relationships: to remove political (and administrative) staff after just months in their posts may have been 'normal practice' elsewhere but certainly proved a problematic procedure in the recently-devolved environment of Scottish education (Donn, 2001, p. 97).

FURTHER AND HIGHER EDUCATION

As in other countries, further education (FE) and higher education (HE) in Scotland fall under the responsibility of a ministry with many other concerns. Indeed, the remit for the Ministry of Enterprise and Lifelong Learning covers the economy (what is left after 'reserved' macro-economic decision making is addressed), transport – roads, lifeline air and ferry services, public transport, business and industry (including Scottish Enterprise, Highlands and Islands Enterprise, trade and inward investment), energy and science as well as further and higher education and lifelong learning. It is a portfolio allowing only a certain percentage of policy making and civil service time to be allocated to 'education'. One result, however, from these portfolios being under the one ministry, is that further and higher education, together, come to be seen very clearly under the rubric of the new knowledge economy.

In one E&LLC meeting after another views have been expressed by MSPs of the great Scottish 'world out there' (Stone, E&LLC: 1.11.2001 col. 3558) just waiting to be made more economically efficient and being made possible, in part, by more relevant HE and FE systems for Scotland's knowledge (Stephen, E&LLC: 9.2.2001 col 859). Nicol Stephen, Deputy Minister for Enterprise and Lifelong Learning advised:

> There have been major changes in Scotland over the past 50 years, from a reliance on heavy manufacturing . . . to the new industries such as electronics and biotechnology. in 1997 electronics accounted for more than half of Scottish manufacturing exports. Scotland must produce people of talent, creativity, innovation and passion, focusing upon skills, learning and knowledge. (Stephen, E&LLC: 9.2.2001 col. 859–60)

As various MSPs noted, the role of education, both FE and HE as well as schooling, is central in this drive to the knowledge economy. In light of this, the Scottish Executive itself must be aware that it 'is failing to deliver or galvanise or co-ordinate action. There is a fundamental lack of clarity about the responsibilities of the UK Government and the Scottish Executive' (Mundell, E&LLC. 9.2.2001 col. 871). This absence of decipherable and transparent lines of authority is a theme repeated in various debates throughout the first years of the Parliament. One area of educational activity has been less beset with the critique of opacity, that being the FE sector.

By 2002 Scotland had forty-seven FE colleges, all self-standing financially since 1992 and, in the market place crowded with agencies and providers, all having to compete ferociously for student numbers. In addition, the Scottish Executive delivers £1bn per annum for lifelong learning, some of which funds specific courses at FE Colleges. Yet, as MSPs note, 'there is no coherent national strategy,' but rather a confused and overlapping array of services, often targeting the same potential or actual unemployed individuals and which can be provided by a social inclusion partnership, the employment service, a local enterprise company, a voluntary association, an FE college or a department of a LA (E&LLC news release 28.9.2001). It is to be hoped that as the 'political and educational settlement' of post-devolution Scottish education becomes more established and confident, there will be diminution of such crass over-kill on providers and more money for those for whom the funds are raised.

In the field of HE, Scotland's devolution settlement may have had less immediate impact although change appears imminent. The Scottish Higher Education Funding Council (SHEFC) had been established in 1992 (under the Further and Higher Education (Scotland) Act) to provide financial support for teaching, research and associated activities in Scottish higher education institutions. Following devolution, it became a non-departmental public body responsible to the Scottish Executive through the Enterprise and Lifelong Learning Department. In 2001, following the Dearing Committee Report on higher education for the twenty-first Century, and the Garrick Report on Scotland's higher education, changes in and controversy about the SHEFC higher education research and teaching reviews became commonplace. The E&LLC reported that there was an annual grant of £440m to HEIs (1999–2000) which was allocated 66:34 teaching:research (the budget for 2003–4 was increased to £700m). Argument occurred when SHEFC had proposed to reduce from twenty-two to six the number of subject areas open to the Research Assessment Exercise. This was seen by the E&LLC as producing a less transparent funding environment as well as introducing a situation that would benefit the disciplinary area of medicine (it being in receipt of vast research grants and gaining, thereby, high research ratings). Other subjects, perhaps '3–rated in the Exercises', and perhaps taught in small groups and using new technology, were seen by the E&LLC as central to the Scottish economy, yet would have been losers in the battle for scarce HE funds. As the convenor of the E&LLC noted at the time, '(The Report of the E&LLC is) a far-sighted view of how university teaching and research should integrate with the wider economic, cultural and social life of the nation.' (Neil, E&LLC: 1.11.2001 col. 3542).

However, although the Scottish Executive is the parliamentary guardian of all those principles underlying state-funded education – equity, equality of opportunity, social justice – it appears that they are much easier to proclaim in committee than to put into practice in higher education. Alongside the issue of research funding (although, interestingly never addressed by any MSPs as the 'legitimisation of the demise of the arts and social science' these disciplinary areas being peopled by specialists in self-funded, or no-funded, research) there came the contentious policy issue of student fees – the Education (Graduate Endowment and Student Support) (Scotland) (No 2) Bill. This came to play a large part in parliamentary and committee discussions during the first years of devolution.

The devolved Parliament inherited the mechanism for debate on student finance – the Cubie Report, emerging from the Cubie Committee. This had been an independent committee of inquiry established to investigate student finance; to complete a comprehensive review of student fees and financial support for students; to report on the desirability of promoting access to FE and HE, particularly for those under-represented groups (E&LLC Session 1 (2000) SP Paper 252: 9–10). It took a number of MSPs by surprise, but the Cubie report recommended the abolition of tuition fees for all students; the continuation of non-repayable bursaries for FE students; the reintroduction of an endowment scheme for post-graduation contributions of £3,075 towards tuition costs, payable (once salary is above £25,000) at a rate of 2% per annum of income; the abolition of the student loan entitlement for students with parents earning more than £47,000 per annum; the introduction of wider access and mature student bursaries and the introduction of additional support for lone parents, mature students with children and for students with disabilities. Of course, not all these recommendations were accepted by the Parliament.

The debates on student loans and their collection became fraught and drew attention to the complex relationship between the UK government and the Scottish Executive and their separate, and sometimes overlapping, sometimes conflicting, realms of responsibility. The E&LLC was asked why the Student Loans Company and the Student Awards Agency for Scotland were involved in distributing and collecting student loans (MacAskill, E&LLC: 7.3.2001 col. 1634). It fell to an official of the Enterprise and Lifelong Learning Department of the Scottish Executive to inform the members of the committee that collection had to be through the UK Inland Revenue (not a Scottish student loans company) because 'in conjunction with other UK departments we have a relationship with the Inland Revenue. The Scottish Executive does not have the competence to form a relationship with the Inland Revenue outwith the UK scheme'. (E&LLC: 7.3.2001 col. 1638) 'The reality is the collection is a reserved area,' the minister, Mr Henry McLeish added (McLeish, E&LLC: 7.3.2001 col. 1639).

It is an interesting facet of devolution that more interest seems to be engendered in the Parliament by this fees issue than the announcement of a national education debate (Jamieson, official report 20.3.2002 col. 10,365) on the future of school education and the importance of the 'unique partnership' between the Scottish Executive and the Education, Culture and Sport Committee. The form of the 'partnership' dialogue may change, but it can usually be seen to involve finance. When discussion erupted on the Education (Disability Strategies and Pupils' Records) (Scotland) Bill, this 'unique partnership' quickly turned to discuss costs of developing and maintaining facilities in schools for disabled children. The Executive announced a £9m resource allocation, perhaps expecting praise. However, South Lanarkshire Council, for example, had worked out that of the council's 124 primary schools, forty would require lifts at a cost of £3.2m, ramps and toilets at a cost of £5m, induction loop systems or individual micro-link systems at a cost of between £500,000 and £1m. This council alone would require the £9m in one year. But it was not just finance involved: it seems that devolution comes with built-in 'partnerships'. Like the UK Inland Revenue and the student fees issue, disability tends to be treated as a 'reserved' matter (the Special Educational Needs Act 2001 being UK legislation) but special educational needs are the responsibility of the Scottish Parliament (recent legislation being the Standards in Scotland's Schools, etc., Act 2000) (Stephen, EEC&SC: 22.1.2002 col. 2990).

THE PROBLEMS AND POLITICS OF DEVOLVED EDUCATION

In retrospect, the 'debacle' was, of course, almost inevitable. There had been pressure on policy makers to ensure that those students in the upper years of the secondary school were given opportunities to achieve a wide range of academic and vocational qualifications. These came to be known as Access, Intermediate 1, Intermediate 2, Highers and Advanced Highers. All qualifications adopted new forms of continuous assessment alongside the formal, summative, end of session examinations (see Chapter 81).

At the same time as these new curricula, assessment and qualifications were being introduced, the SEB and SQA were entering into their first years of merged existence. And alongside these developments the old, centralised and not-devolved HMI continued to exert immense pressures on the stages and stances of the new Highers curriculum and its qualifications.

How important therefore was the new computerised system to support all these changes and especially the new forms of assessment. How important that in the new dawn of devolution, the new political settlement, all players should be willing to – and be seen to – work together. Yet, how unfortunate that this didn't happen. The HMI continued to exude their aura of control over innovations yet had little knowledge of the actual processes in the implementation of those innovations. The SEB and SCOTVEC, now in the SQA, continued to have doubts about the sense of its merged existence and each body kept a wary distance between their historic domains (academic education or vocational education) whilst being called upon to integrate all knowledge and developments on curricula, assessment, examinations and qualifications. The Scottish Executive policy makers, frighteningly up-beat and fearfully optimistic about the new era, were new to their posts, hardly in various doors before they were moved to other departments. The Scottish Executive Education Department assumed that all was 'as before devolution', after all, education had been administered by the SOEID personnel, by many now in SEED, and there would be no problems – there hadn't been, so why should there be now: little wonder therefore that no-one knew what had happened and who to blame, when the class of 2000 were sent wrong copies or failed to receive their Higher and Standard Grade examination certificates.

This was devastating not only for the students and parents but also for the Scottish education community. John Elvidge, then head of the SEED, noted that Higher Still had been built on the foundation of a strong belief in social inclusion and that 'integration of academic and vocational education was the one guiding principle that should shape our work' (Elvidge, EC&SC: 29.9.2000: col. 1412). Douglas Osler, Senior Chief HMI referred to the need to ensure 25,000 or so young people would gain intermediate certificates, something no previous generation had had (Osler, EC&SC: 29.9.2000 col. 1413).

So whilst students and parents bemoaned the lack of certificates, and the failure to produce these resulted in problems with university entrance and post-school activities, the two committees sought to clarify their responsibilities. SQA as an agency within the remit of the Ministry for Enterprise and Lifelong Learning came to the attention of the Enterprise and Lifelong Committee. Concern was also expressed by the Education Culture and Sport Committee as most of the issues relating to SQA referred to schools and, 'the failure to award certificates timeously and correctly to students requires answers' (Mulligan (Convenor), EC&SC: 6.9.2000 col. 1311). Therefore the trail of culpability started with the questions: On what basis did ministers decide to move on Higher Still in one go? On whose advice was that decision made? On what information were ministers acting? How has that decision impacted upon the crisis that we now face? What trials of the computer system were undertaken? Why were the markers paid lower rates this year? Were they under-qualified? If so, why did that situation arise? Did the exam papers go missing? Was the crisis due to operational failure, or were policy makers to blame? (Gillon, EC&SC: 6.9.2000 col. 1324).

Undoubtedly one aspect of the 'disaster' in Scottish education (Russell, EC&SC: 6.9.2000 col. 1318) was the relationship between the various key players – the HMI, teachers' unions, SEED, SQA, the Higher Still development unit. The SQA, at the centre of the 'shambles' (Stone, EC&SC: 6.9.2000 col. 1315) was seen to have produced 'a serious failure' for Scottish education (McLeish, E&LLC: 4.10.2000 col. 1214). Its board was castigated as being 'unwieldy', lacking in clarity, unaccountable, out of touch, unwilling to listen to people. 'Its minutes are never accurate because they do not record everything discussed and there is no real flow of information between the ad hoc groups and the liaison groups' (Peattie, E&LLC: 4.10.2000 col. 1206). That may be the case, Galbraith noted, but SQA 'do make much of their own income – perhaps to the detriment of their other activities' (Galbraith, E&LLC: 4.10.2000 col. 1206).

Keir Bloomer, president of the Association of the Directors of Education in Scotland (ADES) drew attention to both Higher Still and quality issues:

> ADES is in no doubt that the difficulties that brought the system close to collapse derive from the implementation of Higher Still. (T)he overload in demand for data . . . lead[ing] to a large number of errors in the handling of data, huge demands for the checking and re-checking of error-strewn data, and, ultimately, to failures to incorporate particular internal assessment elements into certification . . . [also] . . . poor management of the marking process . . . Their origins lie in the over-complexity of the programme . . . many of the data are required to generate certification information that is itself not needed, not wanted, not understood and intrinsically worthless.' (Bloomer, EC&SC: 25.10.2000 col. 1752)

Teachers' union leader John Kelly (NASUWT) drew attention to the 'reluctance to accept professional judgements of teachers and a reluctance on the part of HMI of schools, and possibly, the Higher Still development unit to give Ministers messages they might not have wanted to hear' (Kelly, EC&SC; 4.10.2000 col. 1540). But, as noted, teachers had come to be seen not as part of 'solutions' but 'problems': so why would their views be of any necessary relevance? Mr Jeyes of the Convention of Scottish Local Authorities (COSLA) summarised wisely when he said that:

> People tend to be more lenient about something they and their colleagues have been involved in designing. They are pre-disposed to supporting it, to making it work and to smoothing its implementation. There is a need to introduce a system of independent regulators . . . who would be in a position to intervene in a way the HMI, the Executive and the SQA directors were unable to. (Jeyes, EC&SC: 25.10.2000 col. 1779)

But the absence of this advice, at an appropriate time, was compounded by the transfer and movement of ministers: Brian Wilson was moved, Helen Liddell came to be in charge, but she, too, lasted months before Sam Galbraith was in post. By the time he was moved and Jack McConnell became Minister of Education, there was a degree of anxious stability: then McConnell became First Minister and Scotland's education came under a new Minister of Education, Cathy Jamieson. Little wonder, then, that even had 'words been heard' they may have been spoken to a departing back.

The resulting decisions regarding the HMIE and SQA may aid the process of the 'educational and political settlement' in Scotland: in November 2000 the SQA (with a new board and chief executive) was moved to the portfolio of the Minister for Education, Europe and External Affairs, although the minister and officials for Enterprise and Lifelong Learning will continue to have an interest in SQA, especially given their policy responsibility for FE and HE sectors and for vocational qualifications and training policy.

CONCLUSIONS

Whether this new 'political settlement' for the SQA works in practice is debatable. The foregoing account has indicated that departmental divisions may well impede efficacious implementation of policy decisions. It may be that future devolved education business will require the Parliament to reassess the lines of administrative accountability and increase transparency in its relationships to educational organisations. This may come to be seen as best undertaken by one department responsible for education.

However, for that to occur, the role of education may also need to be reassessed. If schooling, FE, HE and lifelong learning are to be seen as more than a bridge between Scotland's people and their role as human capital in the knowledge economy, the Parliament may have to reflect on its definition of 'education' and, importantly, have the confidence to differentiate itself from any UK definitions.

The reports of the first few years of devolution, Cubie, McCrone, and the introduction of the national education debate, indicate that redefining the educational agenda for Scotland will not necessarily be easy. It has been seen that there are many muddied waters between 'reserved' and 'devolved' business. Education – seemingly 'devolved' and part of an historic political settlement involving Scotland's own policy community – is actually very much part of and interwoven into more UK-based and mercurial definitions of what it means to educate in the twenty-first century. It may take considerable political confidence for any settlement regarding education to come to reflect the wishes of the Scottish people as 'expressed in elections'. Scotland is, after all, a country with people from diverse backgrounds and holding diverse educational ambitions. To see education as the development of economic human capital more than – perhaps even instead of – the building of the social, personal and humanistic enterprise, may well be selling Scotland's people short.

REFERENCES

Brown S. (1999) *The Scottish Office Education and Industry Department*, Edinburgh: SOEID.
Bryce T. G. K. & Humes W. M. (eds) *Scottish Education*, Edinburgh: Edinburgh University Press, ch. 11.
Donn G. (2000) Education in the Scottish Parliament, *Scottish Educational Review*, 32(2), 180–1.
Donn G. (2001) Education in the Scottish Parliament, *Scottish Educational Review*, 33(1), 93–7.
McPherson A. and Raab C. D. (1988) *Governing Education: A Sociology of Policy since 1945*, Edinburgh: Edinburgh University Press.
Paterson L. (1994) *The Autonomy of Modern Scotland*, Edinburgh: Edinburgh University Press.
Paterson L. (1997) Policy making in Scottish education: a case of pragmatic nationalism, in Clark M. M. and Munn P. A. (eds), *Education in Scotland: Policy and Practice from Pre-school to Secondary*, London: Routledge.

12

The Enterprise and Lifelong Learning Department (ELLD) and the Scottish Parliament

John Fairley

This chapter outlines the main activities and structures of ELLD in education and training, discusses the Parliament's recent review of lifelong learning, and considers the future for this area of policy.

The creation of ELLD was one of the major organisational changes to the Civil Service to follow the arrival of the Parliament. Post-school education and enterprise came under the new ELLD, while school and pre-school provision remained with the Scottish Executive Education Department (SEED – see Chapter 11). The new department gave more prominence to lifelong learning, which the Scottish Executive believes vital to levels of employment, economic performance and social inclusion. The prominence of lifelong learning appeared to be further enhanced by its appearance in a ministerial portfolio. The first Minister for Enterprise, Transport and Lifelong Learning was Wendy Alexander. Sections of the media quickly dubbed her the 'Minister for Everything'. At the time of writing the minister is Iain Gray, and the tag has remained with him. Critics of his portfolio have argued that it is too big, and that events could see lifelong learning downgraded in priority. Some have also argued that while lifelong learning and enterprise should be closely linked, perhaps transport would sit better with environmental policy.

There is a cross-party Parliamentary Enterprise and Lifelong Learning Committee (E&LLC). Its first convenor was John Swinney MSP. At the time of writing Alex Neil MSP is convenor. The committee is widely reckoned to be one of the more effective in the Parliament. It is consensual and inclusive in its approach. It has sought to engage key sectors of civil society through innovative devices such as the 'Business in the Chamber' discussion. The E&LLC has tackled some very large and 'cross cutting' issues. The Committee's remit, as agreed by the Parliament in June 2002, is:

To consider and report on matters relating to the Scottish economy, industry, training and further and higher education and such other matters (excluding transport) as fall within the remit of the Minister for Enterprise, Transport and Lifelong Learning; and on matters relating to tourism which fall within the responsibility of the Minister for Tourism, Culture and Sport.

The committee's first enquiry was into business support services. As a result of its recommendations, twenty-two local economic forums were set up across Scotland. These aimed to bring the partners together at local level, to streamline service delivery, and to bring educational institutions into the process. In September 2001 the committee launched a year-long enquiry into lifelong learning. The enquiry's main findings and recommendations are discussed below.

ELLD'S INITIAL STRATEGY

The Scottish Executive adopted a definition of lifelong learning as: 'the continuous development of the skills, knowledge and understanding that are essential for employability and personal fulfilment' (ELLD, 2001, p. 3). ELLD is the main (but by no means the only) part of the Executive responsible for taking this forward and making it operational. ELLD set out to implement *Opportunity Scotland* which provided a lifelong learning strategy for 1998–2002. The five key themes of this document were: raising awareness; improving access; extending participation; encouraging progress; ensuring quality. In addition, the Executive has adopted three themes to improve the processes of policy development and delivery, namely: stimulating demand; improving the range and quality of information and guidance; enhancing skills levels.

Opportunity Scotland was adjusted in the light of the Executive's contribution and response to the processes which resulted in the European Commission's *Memorandum on Lifelong Learning* which was published in October 2000. It seems likely that the report by the E&LLC, and the Executive's response, will lead to the development of a new strategy for Scotland.

THE RESOURCES AND ACTIVITIES OF ELLD

The mapping of lifelong learning undertaken for the Parliament (Blake Stevenson 2001), ELLD's evidence to the Parliament's enquiry (ELLD, 2001), and SEED's (2002) National Dossier all document a very wide range of activities that are overseen or undertaken by ELLD. Some of these are policies or programmes that began before the Parliament was created, others are newer. Some are devolved, and distinctively Scottish, while others are reserved. ELLD's roles in job-related training, some aspects of which have been reserved to Westminster, led to the establishment of a concordat between the Scottish ministers and the Secretary of State for Education and Skills.

The planned ELLD budget for 2001–2 totalled £2,153.4m. Some £1,500m (69.7%) of this was for FE and HE, including student support. By contrast some £455m (21%) was available for the enterprise networks, and only one-third of that was for training programmes (ELLD 2001, p. 15). In terms of budgetary allocations, the colleges and universities have the lion's share. ELLD liaises and consults the universities through Universities Scotland (see Chapter 6). The principals of FE colleges are consulted by ELLD, often through the Association of Scottish Colleges (see Chapters 5 and 72).

However, some of the Executive's priorities are pursued by the enterprise networks, by other parts of the ELLD framework, and indeed by other parts of the Executive. ELLD's main spending programmes are carried out at arm's length from the department, by a range of Non Departmental Public Bodies (NDPBs). The largest of these is the Scottish Higher Education Funding Council (SHEFC) which was established in 1993 (see Chapter 13). SHEFC had some £659.6m in the planned budget for 2001–2. It funds twenty-one higher education institutions (HEIs) (including the 13,600 places in Scotland offered by the Open

University) and the equivalent of 132,550 full-time student places. A twenty-second HEI, the Scottish Agricultural College, with three campuses, is funded by the Scottish Executive Rural Affairs Department (SERAD).

In July 1999, the Scottish Further Education Funding Council (SFEFC) began operating under powers in the Further and Higher Education (Scotland) Act 1992. The SFEFC replaced the former FE funding unit of ELLD. The SFEFC funds the forty-two Colleges which are incorporated under the 1992 Act. Local authority colleges were retained in Orkney and Shetland, and others are run by trusts, giving a total of forty-seven. These colleges oversee a network of community and work-place based learning centres in addition to their main campuses. This FE college network enrolled 434,435 students in 1999–2000 (Blake Stevenson, 2001, p. 19) on a range of courses including higher education. In the ELLD plans for 2001–2, the SFEFC budget was £418.4m.

In relation to HE and FE, ELLD drew the Parliament's attention to a number of positive trends, including:

- Student numbers up by 25% since 1994–5
- The participation of women rising faster than men in both sectors
- An increase in students over 30 of 84% since 1994–5
- An age participation index for young people of 48%, with the equivalent for England being 30% (ELLD 2001, p. 10).

The second largest category of spending relates to the Student Awards Agency for Scotland (SAAS), with its planned budget of £421.9m for 2001–2. While the agency is little discussed, the issue of student support provided a significant and early innovation by the Parliament. The Executive's response, in May 2000, to the independent committee of enquiry chaired by Andrew Cubie, proved controversial for failing to implement the committee's report in full. However, significant changes were made giving Scotland a unique system of student support. Notably the means-tested contribution to tuition fees was abolished for eligible Scottish domiciled and EU students, and additional investment was targeted on students from the lowest income groups (see also Chapter 6). The Education (Scotland) Act 1980 was amended to allow support for HE distance learning students. From 2000–1 the income levels for calculating student support, and the levels of support, were aligned for FE and HE students. The methods of payment remain different with FE paying college bursaries, while in HE students have a loan entitlement. A pilot scheme of educational maintenance allowances (EMA) was introduced in East Ayrshire in the autumn of 1999, with further pilots in Dundee, Glasgow and West Dunbartonshire in the autumn of 2001. These are designed to encourage and support 16–19-year-olds from low income households to stay in education and will run until 2004. A maximum of £40 per week was made available in cases where parental income was less than £13,000 per year.

Clearly these data, programmes and initiatives in the main relate to areas of policy continuity, and developments which began before the Parliament was formed. It is not clear how the arrival of the Parliament affected these, if at all. The major exception to this is the overhaul of student support which followed the Cubie Report. However, consitutional change did lead to significant changes in the institutional framework, notably the creation of ELLD and the SFEFC, to new levels of scrutiny and to new forms of institutional cooperation. The numbers of HE students in the FE sector, and the fact that they share a chief executive, mean that the two funding councils co-operate closely. The Executive encouraged still wider co-operation by establishing a joint lifelong learning group (JLLG) made up of the chief executives of the funding councils and the enterprise agencies. This was intended to make recommendations for bringing the work of agencies in lifelong learning and enterprise development closer together through joint strategies and initiatives. The JLLG reported in December 2000. The role of the JLLG led to fears being expressed in some HEIs that the Executive's view of economic development might come directly to influence funding council resource allocation decisions. This was felt by some to pose a threat to institutional autonomy and possibly even to academic freedom.

A third institutional development was the creation of the Scottish University for Industry (SUfI) in October 2000. This may be seen as the implementation in Scotland of a UK policy. It was a key commitment in the Scottish Executive's first programme for government (ELLD 2001, p. 21). SUfI operates under the brand name *learndirect Scotland*. It is not a university in the sense of providing HE. Rather it will work to increase demand for education by putting individuals and employers in touch with the most appropriate provider. It is establishing a Scotland-wide network of accredited learning centres. Through these, its freephone helpline, and its website, it aims greatly to improve access.

THE ENTERPRISE NETWORKS

Two of ELLD's NDPBs, Scottish Enterprise (SE) and Highlands and Islands Enterprise (HIE), oversee two networks of Local Enterprise Companies (LECs). In the planned budget for 2001–2, £386m was allocated to SE, and £69.5m to HIE. SE and HIE were set under specifically Scottish legislation of 1990. SE combined the previous functions of the Scottish Development Agency and the Training Agency, both of which were abolished by the Act. HIE took over the functions of the Training Agency and Highlands and Islands Development Board, which was also abolished. The Act required SE and HIE to decentralise their functions to local companies or partnerships, and the then Scottish Office chose the company route. The formation of SE and HIE was part of a more general policy switch away from economic intervention towards encouraging enterprise. A key element in this was getting employers involved at board level in SE, HIE and the LECs, in particular so that they could influence strategy and bring business methods into public policy. When they were set up, the largest part of the budgets of SE and HIE came with the 'volume' training programmes developed in response to mass unemployment. As unemployment has declined, so has the need for these programmes, and the emphasis has shifted to training which is designed to improve employability. Again this is part of an international trend.

The Scottish Executive inherited these institutions. It quickly moved to centralise control over the LECs in the SE network, something which Labour had advocated for some time. (The generally small HIE LECs had needed central direction from the outset.) This was reflected in name changes. As an example, the LEC for Glasgow had been called the Glasgow Development Agency, and this was changed to Scottish Enterprise Glasgow. In January 2001, the Executive set out directions and priorities in *A Smart Successful Scotland, Ambitions for the Enterprise Networks*. This document set out priorities for the labour market and skills development:

- improving the operation of the labour market to better match supply and demand;
- providing the best start for young people by equipping them with skills to take advantage of lifelong learning opportunities;

- narrowing the gap in unemployment between local areas across Scotland;
- improving demand for high quality in-work training. (ELLD 2001, p. 18)

A joint performance team made up of SE, HIE and the Executive developed targets for each of these priorities, and these will be used to assess network performance. SE and HIE pursue these priorities through a range of initiatives, and as purchasers rather than providers. In this purchasing role, LECs have often seen themselves as agents of change in the public education system, seeking to influence the form and content of provision. However, this has varied across Scotland.

In 1997 Labour introduced its 'flagship' policy for welfare to work. While similar Conservative proposals had encoutered fierce criticism, there was very little criticism of Labour's policy in Scotland (Fairley, 1998). Welfare to work is reserved because it links education and training, job creation, and reform of the benefits system. In 1997, Scottish Enterprise took a paper to the Westminster committee that was examining Labour's plans, in which it argued for a 'lifelong learning approach' to the same social issues. Labour's policy produced a number of 'New Deal' schemes targeted on different social groups, some of which are partly defined by age. There are currently schemes for lone parents, disabled people, partners of the unemployed, and long-term unemployed people aged eighteen to twenty-four, over thirty, and over fifty. Each of these has some learning component. Approximately £47m is spent on these schemes in Scotland each year.

The largest New Deal is for 18–24-year-olds unemployed for six months or more. It offers each entrant an initial period of individual assessment, known as the 'Gateway', which may include some educational provision, and may last up to four months. There are then four options; these may not all be available in each area. Each option has a learning dimension, and one of them is in full-time education or training. A study of this last option for the Executive in 2000 found that non–completion rates were 50% in FE and 60% in the private sector (Blake Stevenson, 2001, p. 28). This New Deal is the only area of provision for young people over sixteen which is compulsory. Failure to enter or to participate adequately, or dropping out – all carry the threat of full loss of welfare benefits.

The New Deal is run by the Employment Service. This was widely criticised in the late 1990s, because the body was largely concerned with policing benefits, and hardly seemed 'fit for purpose', and because Scotland already had the LECs with several years' experience of providing training for the unemployed. The eventual solution was to run New Deal through complex partnership and contracting regimes. Generally, for the learning elements, the Employment Service contracts with the LEC which in turn contracts with the provider. There are twenty-three New Deal 'delivery areas' – the LEC areas plus West Lothian.

Training for Work (TfW) is described by ELLD (2001, p. 24) as 'the main devolved programme which links and supports welfare to work'. With the arrival of the main New Deal, TfW was revamped to focus on the skills needs of over twenty-fives who have been unemployed for six months. TfW is also used by the LECs to respond to the retraining needs of redundant workers.

SKILLSEEKERS

Skillseekers is also described as a 'devolved programme'. It was introduced in 1995, as the replacement for Youth Training. All 16- and 17-year-olds were guaranteed entry to

Skillseekers. While older people could be admitted, this was at the discretion of the LECs which implemented it. The main features of Skillseekers are that: each trainee should have an individual training plan; employers should be involved; and training should lead to a recognised qualification, up to SVQ level III.

A National Audit Office enquiry into Skillseekers in 1998/9 was critical of the poor links betweeen the training provided and the needs of the economy, but positive about other aspects of the programme. An estimated £81m is spent each year on Skillseekers. In 2002, E&LLC recommended that Skillseekers be abolished, and that steps be taken to improve Modern Apprenticeship. In 1995 the UK government introduced Modern Apprenticeship (MA), which focused on the same age group as Skillseekers. There was some resistance to MA in Scotland, primarily because of the desire to avoid competition between programmes. The compromise solution was to develop MA within Skillseekers.

MA offers 16–24-year-olds paid employment plus the opportunity to train at craft, technician and trainee management level. In 1999, the UK Chancellor of the Exchequer announced a new target of 20,000 MAs in Scotland. At the time many in Scotland thought that the existing target was already too high. The proportion of MAs taken up by women is low and varies between the LEC areas. The low point is 4% in the Western Isles, while the highest is Glasgow at 27%.

A new SE/HIE unit, Future Skills Scotland will focus on improving labour market intelligence, particularly with regard to changing demand for skills. The unit will collate labour market information gathered from a wide range of bodies – including the LECs, local authorities and Careers Scotland – and this will be made available to employers and others who need to know about changing skill requirements. In 2002, a new Careers Scotland was established by the Executive, following the Duffner Review. Careers Scotland brings together roles played by the former Careers Service, Adult Guidance Networks, Education Business Partnerships and Local Learning Partnerships. It will provide a unified and all-age service. The new organisation operates on the same boundaries as the LECs.

INDIVIDUAL LEARNING ACCOUNTS (ILAS)

ILAs were adminstered by the Enterprise networks. An ILA was a 'virtual account' to be used to fund training. ILAs were available to anyone in employment. The individual would pay in £25, the LEC would add £150 (with more available for priority groups), and the employer could make a contribution. The Scottish target was to achieve 100,000 operational ILAs with a public expenditure cost of £22m. In 2002, the scheme was abandoned, first south of the border then later in Scotland, amid allegations over abuses and fears that management arrangements were not sufficiently robust to prevent these from occurring.

E-LEARNING

SE has given priority to e-learning and has an e-business group. In 2001, SE had committed some £840,000 to a number of initiatives, including: establishing its own e-learning team, benchmarking Scotland against other countries, stimulating research, and setting up a Challenge Fund.

NATIONAL TRAINING ORGANISATIONS (NTOS) AND EMPLOYERS

The NTOs mostly operated on a UK or Britain-wide scale, though a small number were Scottish. In 2001, there were seventy-three of these, covering over 90% of the workforce. They provided the main collective voice for employers regarding vocational education and training. They were responsible for developing the national occupational standards on which vocational training and qualifications are based, and for aspects of labour market intelligence. In operational terms, partnership working between the NTOs and the LECs was very important, although in some sectors it appears not to have been very effective. Most of the NTOs had a sector focus, but some focused on particular skills or occupations across sectors. In the latter it proved more difficult effectively to engage employers. Most of the NTOs were small, and some simply lacked the capacity to be effective. In 2001, twenty-one of the NTOs had at least one employee in Scotland, and a further twenty employed a consultant to represent their interests (Blake Stevenson, 2001, p. 30). The NTOs were co-ordinated and supported by a Scottish Council. In 2001, the NTOs were collectively spending around £0.5m in Scotland, each year, for a three-year funding round (against a UK allocation of £45m).

Three of the NTOs were NDPBs with statutory duties to raise levies to fund training – the Construction Industry Training Board (CITB), the Engineering Construction Industry Training Board (ECITB) and the Seafish Authority. The first two raised per capita levies, while the third raised levies on the catch landed. These levies were used primarily to fund training activity, and the CITB operated training centres in Scotland. As cross-border public authorities, the NDPBs had some accountability to the Parliament. In 2001–2, the Ministers for Lifelong Learning in the four UK territories conducted a review of the NTOs with a view to some degree of rationalisation in order to improve their effectiveness. This led to NTOs being replaced by a smaller network of Sector Skills Councils.

TRADE UNIONS AND LIFELONG LEARNING

In 2000, the Executive set up the Trade Union Working Party on Lifelong Learning (TUWPLL), which is chaired by the Enterprise Minister, and the Trade Union Fund for Learning (TUFL). The fund is largely based on a similar scheme which was set up in England in 1998. In Scotland £400,000 has been made available each year, for four years. This is recognition of the important roles which trade unions can play in encouraging their members to get involved in work-based learning, and, at times, in promoting learning in the workplace through collective bargaining. The TUFL has supported a range of initiatives and projects. These are also supported by the STUC's Lifelong Learning Unit. Examples of projects include: a £44,750 grant to UCATT to train workplace learning representatives and SVQ assessors, and to conduct training needs assessments; a £47,800 grant to EQUITY to provide actors with the skills needed for screen acting; a £49,650 grant to ASLEF to promote lifelong learning in the rail industry.

A MODERN LEARNING INFRASTRUCTURE

ELLD has overseen attempts to modernise the learning infrastructure, and to improve co-ordination of its parts. SUfI is seen as a key part of this process. There are four key elements of the new learning infrastructure:

- structures, processes and financial incentives to underpin demand;
- a qualifications system which is flexible and integrated and suits the needs of both the individual and employers;
- the availability of learning to best suit the needs of the modern learner;
- delivery systems facilitated by e-learning (ELLD, 2001, p. 16).

THE RECOMMENDATIONS OF THE E&LLC AND THE FUTURE FOR LIFELONG LEARNING

The committee began an inquiry into lifelong learning in July 2001 and launched its final report and recommendations in October 2002 (E&LLC, 2002b). The Parliament commissioned background research to help the committee get started (Blake Stevenson, 2001). The E&LLC received written evidence from over 120 organisations and individuals, and oral evidence from a further fifty-eight organisations. Members of the committee undertook case study visits to the UHI Millennium Institute in Inverness, the Crichton University Campus in Dumfries, the John Wheatley College in Glasgow, the European Commission and Parliament in Brussels, the Dundee Partnership, FAST-TRAC in Fife, and the Glasgow Partnership. A seminar was organised with the Scottish Council Development and Industry to help canvass the views of business, and in April 2002, the E&LLC hosted a Lifelong Learning Convention. Following the convention, the committee received a further fifty-four items of written evidence. In short, the inquiry was the most thorough and comprehensive overview of post-school education and training ever in Scotland.

The consideration of evidence led the committee to modify its definition of lifelong learning, which became: 'the continuous development of knowledge and skills aimed at enhancing the individual's quality of life and society's wellbeing.' The committee reached a number of important conclusions. It came to the view that Scotland lacks a single lifelong learning system, and that HE, FE, vocational training and community education tend to function as separate sectors. It recommended that a strategy should be developed with a focus on the linkages between the four main sectors.

The committee found that the funding of post-school education and training was extremely complex. It also found that the ability of individuals to secure public funding varied enormously, and that funding had a clear tendency to be regressive, with those most in need encountering the lowest levels of provision. And it found that lifelong learning tended to be shaped by producer interests. The committee's response to this situation is the most radical part of the final report.

The E&LLC proposed that the new strategy for lifelong learning should be based on the principle of entitlement. It argued that this would have a number of advantages over the current situation, in particular that entitlements would empower individual learners and reduce the control exercised by producer interests; that it would lead to more flexible learning patterns, with less emphasis on the immediate post-school years; that it would encourage new patterns of learning with individuals more able to move horizontally, as well as vertically, through the system; and that it would encourage greater parity of esteem between the sectors. The practical proposal is that each citizen should be entitled to 720 SCQF credits. This is broadly equivalent to two years of post-compulsory schooling plus four years of higher education. However, an entitlement system would allow the individual greater control over when, where and how to study, and would require greater flexibility on the part of providers. This approach would open up lifelong learning to everyone.

In total the E&LLC report makes seventy-nine recommendations for improving lifelong learning and these cannot all be discussed here. However, when they are considered together it is clear that the committee is proposing a major shake-up of existing arrangements to achieve much wider access to learning and fairer access to resources within the context of a long-term strategy for Scotland's economy and society. In order to get the process under way a number of changes are proposed for the short term. These include merging the HE and FE funding councils; increasing the HE wider access premium from 5% to 25%; improving support for part-time learners; better focused support for equalities policies in education; the abolition of Skillseekers which is perceived to have failed in its objectives; and a reorientation for the enterprise networks to focus on improving employers' capacity for supporting workforce development.

CONCLUSIONS

It is clear that ELLD oversees a wide range of education and training providers and activities. While there is planning and monitoring of effectiveness in some areas of provision, there is no overall strategy. And the evolution of provision has produced very complex funding arrangements and huge inequalities in the allocation of resources to support individuals' learning. The E&LLC has conducted an in-depth review of this situation. It has proposed a new philosophical basis for developing a strategy. And it has set out a radical set of recommendations for moving the system on, making it more coherent, empowering learners, and improving access to learning and to resources. The Scottish Executive will take time to consider this report and make its response. However, if it goes with the grain of the recommendations then there is likely to be considerable change to the institutions and activities currently overseen by ELLD, and it may be that lifelong learning is developed in ways that are more distinctively Scottish.

REFERENCES

Blake Stevenson Ltd (2001) *Mapping of Lifelong Learning Provision in Scotland*, Scottish Parliament Information Centre (for ELLC), September.

E&LLC (2002a) *Inquiry on Lifelong Learning*, Interim Report, March, Edinburgh: The Scottish Parliament.

E&LLC (2002b) *Report on Lifelong Learning*, October, Edinburgh: The Scottish Parliament.

ELLD (2001) *Inquiry by the Committee on Enterprise and Lifelong Learning into Lifelong Learning*, Evidence from the SEELLD, October.

Fairley, J. (1998) Labour's New Deal in Scotland, *Scottish Affairs*, 25, Autumn.

SEED (2002) Education and Training in Scotland – National Dossier, Edinburgh: The Stationery Office.

ACKNOWLEDGEMENT

The author would like to thank ELLD for documentation and briefings. Any errors in the text are the author's responsibility.

13

Scottish Higher Education Policy and Funding

David Newall

STUDENT FINANCE

In the campaign for the first Scottish parliamentary election in May 1999, higher education found itself, unusually, in the political spotlight. Scottish Labour defended the means-tested undergraduate tuition fees just introduced by the Blair government. Every other party demanded their abolition. When the election left Labour requiring a partnership with the Liberal Democrats to govern, something had to be done about tuition fees. But that might leave Labour advocating one policy in Scotland and another elsewhere in the UK. To buy time, the incoming Executive referred student finance to an independent committee, chaired by Andrew Cubie. It was the first independent committee of inquiry created by Scotland's Parliament.

Cubie helped the government out of its difficulty, and not just through buying time. His report was notable for its directness, for the clarity of its principal recommendations, and for the warmth with which it was received across Scotland. 'We have no doubt,' it said, 'that the student or parental contribution to tuition fees in full-time higher education should be abolished for Scottish students . . . the present arrangements are badly discredited, add to anxieties about debt and create undue anomalies.' (Independent Committee of Inquiry into Student Finance, 1999). Cubie was firm also in stating that funds to assist students with living costs must be better targeted; at young people from low income backgrounds, lone parents, mature students and students with disabilities. The Executive implemented Cubie's main recommendations. The up-front tuition fee was abolished and instead employed graduates would now contribute to a Scottish Graduate Endowment, a source of support for future students. And new bursaries and supplementary grants were introduced, targeted at the priority groups identified by Cubie. The new system was not without problems. There were apparent inequities (a non-Scottish UK undergraduate, for example, would be charged a tuition fee by a Scottish university, whereas students from all other EU nations would not). And the arrangements had become complex, with so many new measures introduced in successive years. Perhaps the greatest challenge facing university entrants in Scotland would now be that of understanding the system of student finance. But overall the post-Cubie reforms improved Scotland's system of student support. It is more generous than that elsewhere in the UK, and that goes down well in a country which traditionally has viewed higher education as a national strength.

HIGHER EDUCATION IN SCOTLAND

That is not to say that Scots necessarily have a clear idea of what higher education is. The meaning of the term has changed over the years, and currently it is used to mean two different things. Higher education can be defined as academic activity equivalent to, or more advanced than, the first level of undergraduate study. By this definition, 30% of Scotland's higher education is provided by its forty-six further education colleges, which deliver most sub-degree qualifications (Higher National Certificates and Diplomas). A second definition – used here – relates to institutions rather than levels of study. Scotland's higher education institutions (HEIs) are the eighteen members of the higher education sector. They include thirteen universities; four dating from medieval times (Aberdeen, Edinburgh, Glasgow and St Andrews); four given university status in the 1960s (Dundee, Heriot-Watt, Stirling and Strathclyde); and five which became universities in the 1990s (Abertay, Glasgow Caledonian, Napier, Paisley and Robert Gordon) – see Chapter 76. The remaining five HEIs are smaller non-university institutions; Bell College, Edinburgh College of Art, Glasgow School of Art, Queen Margaret University College and the Royal Scottish Academy of Music and Drama). This is a diverse group, with annual turnovers ranging from £8m to £300m. It includes research-intensive universities with a broad portfolio and an international profile, and smaller institutions whose focus is specialist or whose work is more closely related to their regional community. What defines the institutions as a group is that they are funded from Scotland's higher education budget (which also finances the Open University in Scotland and the embryonic University of the Highlands and Islands), with grants distributed by the Scottish Higher Education Funding Council, or SHEFC (http:// www.shefc.ac.uk). The same institutions have a representative body called Universities Scotland (see Chapter 6). Its title is inaccurate, as some of its members are not universities, but the word is a convenient shorthand and is used in that sense below.

SHEFC is a Non-Departmental Public Body (NDPB, or 'quango') and in terms of the resources it controls (£725m per annum) is the most significant in Scotland. Its 12–15 members hold senior positions in universities and other public and private sector organisations and it is a powerful body. As well as administering public funds and monitoring the financial health of the universities, it has a fundamental influence on the shape of higher education in Scotland. The universities are sometimes reluctant to acknowledge this influence. They enjoy greater powers than their counterparts on mainland Europe and set store by their institutional autonomy, enshrined in various papal bulls, royal charters and Acts of Parliament. But, without exception, the universities are crucially dependent on Government funding. In practice their autonomy is constrained by whatever conditions the Funding Council may attach to their grant.

FUNDING FOR TEACHING

Undergraduate teaching is the most significant activity undertaken by Scotland's universities, and accounts for around 75% of funds distributed by SHEFC. For students resident in the EU, the Funding Council supports a certain number of 'funded places' at each institution (expressed as full-time equivalents) and each funded place is worth a 'unit of resource'. These vary by discipline and have two components, tuition fee and grant. Table 13.1 illustrates funding levels for three subject groups in 2003–4. There are thirteen groups.

Table 13.1: SHEFC units of resource, 2003–4 (£)

	Tuition Fee	Fee Grant	Unit of Resource
Social Sciences	1,125	2,345	3,470
Science	1,125	5,665	6,790
Clinical & Veterinary Practice	1,125	12,160	13,285

Following Cubie, undergraduate tuition fees are paid – for Scottish and non-UK EU students – by the Student Awards Agency for Scotland. Students from elsewhere in the UK may have fees paid in whole or part by their local authorities, depending on their financial circumstances. For all these students, the fee (currently £1,125) is prescribed annually by the government, with universities prohibited from charging 'top-up fees'. Postgraduate teaching involves similar units of resource, but with a tuition fee element of £2,940. Top-up fees are not prohibited for postgraduate study, and many universities offer programmes such as MBAs which charge much higher fees.

SHEFC has no role in determining which subjects universities teach, or the nature or length of courses, and – except for Medicine, Veterinary Science and Teacher Education, whose numbers are controlled by the Scottish Executive – it allows resource transfers between subjects, so assisting universities in keeping their course portfolios under review. However, SHEFC's enforcement of the government's policy of 'consolidation' means that the overall full-time undergraduate population in each HEI has effectively been frozen at 1995–6 levels. The freeze does not apply to postgraduate study, and there is a small cash incentive to increase part-time numbers – undergraduate and postgraduate – in line with the Executive's encouragement of wider access to higher education.

While not deciding which subjects are taught, SHEFC has a duty to ensure that teaching is of satisfactory quality. The Further and Higher Education (Scotland) Act 1992 introduced an onerous teaching quality assessment regime by which the Funding Council was required to assess teaching quality in every university department in Scotland. This first took place in the period 1993–8, with review panels producing public reports on each department's teaching, including a score on a four-point scale. Departments achieving the highest score ('Excellent') were awarded a 5% grant increase by SHEFC: the few departments afforded the lowest score ('Unsatisfactory') were given a year to address their shortcomings with the threat that, if they did not, funding would be withdrawn.

Teaching quality assessment encouraged universities to examine afresh their teaching methods and to make students better aware of course requirements, but it did so at great expense. At the universities' insistence, a peer review system operated, with assessments undertaken by academic staff. This placed a huge imposition on academics' time but did not necessarily give the academic community confidence in the process. Top academic staff were invariably reluctant to serve on panels, and staff in old and new universities often had different views on how to assess quality. The system of assessment has been in flux in recent years, with universities arguing for a 'lighter touch' to be employed. That does appear to be the thrust of SHEFC's outline proposals for a new quality assessment regime, beginning in 2003–4. The approach will be institution-wide, with individual subjects assessed exceptionally, and emphasis will be placed on measures universities are taking to achieve 'quality enhancement'. The system will be operated on SHEFC's behalf by the UK's Quality Assurance Agency (QAA).

FUNDING FOR RESEARCH

Around 15% of SHEFC funds are distributed in support of research. As with teaching, the Funding Council does not prescribe what research should be undertaken, but its approach strongly promotes a policy of 'research selectivity', with funds directed to departments whose research has been highly regarded through the UK-wide Research Assessment Exercise.

Throughout the 1980s every UK university received a research grant, irrespective of the volume or quality of its research. The government became dissatisfied with this and sought to develop a mechanism for directing resources at areas of proven excellence. The first Research Selectivity Exercise took place in 1986, with university departments ranked 1, 2 or 3 by panels of academic experts. In 1989, a more extensive exercise employed a five-point scale. Then in 1990, the Research Assessment Exercise (RAE), as it now was, became suddenly much more serious. The government announced that the following year's distribution of research grant must have regard to the 1989 RAE results. It also confirmed that a further Research Assessment Exercise would take place in 1992, and that university departments awarded the lowest rating – of 1 on the five-point scale – would receive no research grant in the years thereafter. Following 1992, and the Research Assessment Exercises of 1996 and 2001, the distribution of research funds has become much more selective.

Table 13.2 shows the relative amounts of research grant awarded to departments in Scotland in the years following the last three RAEs. SHEFC policy has been to maintain a constant level of funding for departments with the highest rating. As more departments have achieved high ratings, funding for the others has declined.

Table 13.2:   Relative levels of research grant (£)

RAE Rating*	1992	1996	2001
5*		1.00	1.00
5	1.00	1.00	0.88
4	0.71	0.65	0.48
3a		0.42	0.20
3	0.51		
3b		0.27	0.00
2	0.36	0.00	0.00
1	0.00	0.00	0.00

The rating scale was extended in 1996 from a 5-point to a more complex 7-point scale.

The RAE is managed jointly by the UK's Higher Education Funding Councils (in England, Scotland, Wales and Northern Ireland). It involves sixty-nine subject panels with academic and non-academic members. Universities make a submission, covering the previous five years, for each department they wish to have assessed. This identifies the most significant publications produced, and shows the department's record in winning research grants and contracts and training research students. It also describes how the department manages its research and sets out its research strategy. The RAE panels are required to read publications and to determine each department's rating following a published methodology, a process which takes about six months. Departments have no right of appeal.

With the strong reputational and financial value associated with RAE ratings, this exercise is having a powerful effect on management decisions in the universities. Choices are being made about whether to invest in or withdraw from research in areas of relative weakness. Department heads are having to determine what contribution each member of staff can make to research. And research profile is playing a crucial – possibly disproportionate – role in decisions on staff appointments.

ACCOUNTABILITY

Teaching Quality Assessment and Research Assessment have served well the government's desire that universities should be accountable for their performance, providing numbers which allow comparisons to be made. In addition, the Funding Council publishes annual performance indicators, focusing on three areas: admission of students from disadvantaged backgrounds; undergraduate success rates; and graduate employability. These indicators have aroused little interest, partly because they are highly technical, but universities will view them more seriously if they become more significant in funding decisions. This has happened only to a small extent so far, with SHEFC introducing a funding premium related to the number of students each university admits from disadvantaged neighbourhoods.

Teaching and research assessment data, performance indicators and annual statistical returns (on staff, students and finance), provide a wealth of numerical information on UK higher education. Several newspapers have used this resource to compile 'league tables', ranking universities according to their performance. In doing so, they claim to provide helpful information to prospective applicants. Each league table is different, and a university's position can alter dramatically depending on the indicators selected, the weight afforded to each, and the ways in which journalists interpret – and all too frequently misinterpret – statistical data. League tables tend to rank Oxbridge and other prestigious research-intensive institutions most highly, placing post-1992 universities well down the table. The universities are hostile to them, arguing that they have diverse missions and that attempts to rank them are therefore misguided.

Universities are thus accountable in several ways for their outputs. In addition, they account for the strategic objectives to which they apply public funds, and for the systems by which they ensure these funds are used properly. Annually, SHEFC requires each university's governing body – or 'court' – to submit a strategic plan setting out objectives in teaching, research and resource management over the next four years. Strategic plans allow the Funding Council to open a dialogue with an institution whose objectives appears to conflict with Executive policy. They are a tool of accountability, showing how public funds for higher education are being managed strategically. How these funds are used at operational level is the concern of a financial memorandum between SHEFC and each institution. This requires the governing body to ensure that funds are used in ways consistent with the purposes for which they have been provided, and that arrangements are in place for sound financial administration. Courts must appoint a chief accounting officer – in practice, the university principal – and must have an audit committee which, complying with a SHEFC code of practice, oversees arrangements for internal and external audit. Courts must also manage universities' finances so as to ensure continuing viability. Where a university is identified as having financial difficulties, the Funding Council will demand a financial recovery plan.

Should SHEFC determine that a university is in breach of its financial memorandum, it may decide to suspend – temporarily or permanently – grant payments, or to demand repayment of funds it determines have been spent inappropriately. There is in fact a difficulty with this second sanction. Unless income is earmarked, accounting systems are generally unable to identify which source of funds has been used to finance a particular item of expenditure. Universities derive significant funds from sources other than the Funding Council, and the financial memorandum does not apply to these other revenues.

UNIVERSITY FINANCES

SHEFC grant makes up just 43% of the universities' income. They generate revenue from sources such as overseas and postgraduate tuition fees, research contracts, and residences and catering operations. Some also derive significant amounts from endowments and from the sale of intellectual property. This income funds a range of activity and adds to the impact universities have on the economy. But most of it is 'tidal'. It comes in from a purchaser of a service, and it goes out in meeting the additional costs of providing that service. Rarely does it contribute much to core costs. Indeed charities and some public bodies contract with universities on the basis that the service they purchase will be subsidised by the provider. If they operated on a simple commercial basis, universities would undertake much less research.

Despite these private sources of revenue, universities are therefore crucially dependent on SHEFC grant to meet their core costs and when public funding is cut they feel the consequences. This was a continuing state of affairs throughout the 1990s, with successive annual reductions ('efficiency gains') in higher education funding. The situation came to a head when the funding announcement for 1996–7 included a 6% cut and the prospect of a further 6% in 1997–8. The outgoing Conservative and incoming Labour governments had already agreed they would use this Treasury-created cash crisis as the pretext for charging undergraduates tuition fees but, with the 1997 general election approaching, they post-poned political debate by referring university finance to Lord Dearing's national committee of inquiry. Dearing's full remit was wide-ranging, and he addressed it conscientiously, producing a huge report (National Committee of Inquiry into Higher Education, 1997). He was treated with great disrespect by the new government when, within a week of his report being published, it announced its own plans for undergraduate fees, which were sub-stantially different from his proposals.

Over time, Dearing's report has had greater impact. He argued that universities could not continue to bear the sort of cuts they had faced through the 1990s, and his observations on wider access and research infrastructure have encouraged the government to invest additional funds in higher education. Recent years have seen nothing quite like the funding crisis of 1996–7, but budgets remain under pressure and campuses show the effects of a 50% reduction in the unit of funding over the last twenty-five years.

THE SOCIAL AND ECONOMIC ROLE OF THE UNIVERSITIES

The last twenty-five years have posed financial challenges for universities, but they have also seen growing appreciation of their significance to the nation's social and economic well-being. Dearing described higher education as 'fundamental to the social, economic and cultural health of the nation', and stressed the importance to a civilised society of *'values that characterise higher education; respect for individuals and their views; and respect for truth'*. Dearing's view of higher education as a force for social cohesion has chimed well with the Labour government's concern for social inclusion. In England and Wales, it aims to expand higher education participation to 50% of the population. In Scotland, where that figure has been achieved, concern has focused on promoting opportunities for people who have been deterred from university study. Following Cubie, improved financial support is available for disadvantaged students, and SHEFC's wider access scheme now encourages universities to admit more students from disadvantaged backgrounds. They have responded enthusiastically, working in partnership with local authorities and with schools which have low rates of progression to higher education. Pupils' aspirations are being raised through student role models and campus activities, and support is being provided to make the transition to higher education less daunting. With secondary school rolls projected to fall by 12% in the next decade, it makes sense for the universities to broaden their recruitment base in this way.

The government is conscious also of the contribution universities make to the Knowledge Economy. A 'smart successful Scotland' will have as its foundation a highly skilled and well educated workforce. Universities are no longer ivory towers, but 'engines of the economy', an image they have been happy to cultivate: their submission for funding to the 2002–3 Scottish Budget was headed 'Recession-Proofing Scotland'. But if Scotland is not as smart and successful as it would like to be, that might then suggest the problem lies with the universities. Employers frequently voice concerns that they cannot recruit enough well qualified graduates in their fields, and that graduates' general employment skills are lacking, and SHEFC and Scottish Enterprise ask whether the nation could not be smarter at providing for labour market needs. Now, employers' complaints need to be taken with some caution. Some employers will always complain about graduates' skills, just as some farmers will always complain about the weather. The frequent assertion that graduates are not 'hitting the ground running', is a meaningless metaphor. And few commentators seriously advocate a system of national workforce planning. In those sectors – primarily health and education – where workforce planning models operate in Scotland, they have not allayed employers' concerns about labour supply; arguably they have made things worse. Scotland's universities are in fact producing more highly skilled graduates than ever before. The tragedy is that every year 24% of them leave Scotland for jobs elsewhere in the UK. Allowing for graduate migration to Scotland, there is still a net annual haemorrhage of 10%, equivalent to 4,000 highly skilled graduates, in whom Scotland's education system has invested over £250m.

DEVELOPMENTS IN UNIVERSITY RESEARCH

Universities have a role in creating high-skill jobs to retain graduates in Scotland and there are now several government initiatives promoting commercial exploitation of research, often through funds to nurture 'spin-out companies'. But the activity is not on a scale that will transform the Scottish economy. Spin-out companies require, crucially, the engagement of an academic champion. Few academics have the skills and interest to commercialise research, and universities would be worried if it were otherwise, because they need their top research staff to boost their RAE ratings.

It is a perverse consequence of its success, but the Research Assessment Exercise may now be doing serious damage to UK research. Since its cautious beginnings it has achieved a great deal. There is widespread acceptance of the need for selectivity, and the process has credibility with academic staff, who view RAE ratings as important performance indicators. As a result the exercise has become too dominant an influence. Academic appointments are often made with a view to the next RAE result, sometimes at the expense of longer-term investment in staff development. And the RAE is a powerful force for conservatism. Staff are encouraged to pursue lines of research which will receive ready recognition from peers, applying for prestigious awards and publishing in the right journals. Research, by its nature, should challenge convention, not be directed by it. SHEFC is conscious of the conservative pressures associated with RAE-based funding and, through its Research Development Initiative, has sought to pump-prime novel programmes to enhance Scotland's overall research portfolio. A continuing scheme of this sort may be valuable but, when public money is invested in unconventional initiatives, there are inevitably concerns about accountability. It has been difficult for SHEFC to demonstrate that there are sound, objective reasons for funding some research development proposals and not others.

The future shape of Scotland's research will be decided as much outside the country as inside, much depending on the policies of the UK's Research Councils which provide time-limited funds for specific research projects. Selectivity is a fact of life, and the question is the extent to which funding may be focused on a few universities. Will the RAE continue? There is a feeling that the 2001 exercise was onerous and that surely the government's requirements for accountability can be met in a less painful way? There is concern, too, about grade inflation. In 1992, 27% of staff assessed were in departments rated 4 or above. In 1996 this figure had risen to 59%. In 2001 it was 80%. While the universities demand additional funds to reward this improvement, the government wonders whether it is genuine. But there is no certainty that the RAE will be reformed. A similar post-mortem took place after the 1996 RAE, and served simply to reinforce the system. And the radical alternative sometimes mooted – of funding all research through the Research Councils – is now less likely since, post-devolution, it would require a transfer from the Scottish to the UK Budget.

FUNDING MODELS

If RAE-based funding continues, so will controversy about the degree of selectivity produced by the funding model. SHEFC has provoked discussion about funding methods, and to some extent defined its scope, through the transparent model it employs in distributing funds for teaching and research. The approach has important strengths. It is accountable, provides open incentives, and allows recipients to check the sums. But transparency also exposes a range of imperfect statistics to scrutiny. The proportion of funds distributed for teaching and research, for example, bears no relation, unless by accident, to the costs of each. And the spurious exactitude of the teaching units of resource, expressed to the nearest pound, masks the fact that they are simply based on historical convention, subjected to annual increments over decades. Yet, while universities may take issue with specific factors in the funding model, there is no collective will to see the model change. When SHEFC recently undertook a review of teaching funding, the exercise failed to develop a more rational method of distribution and the universities' principal concern was for stability in institutional allocations. Currently, the funding model is being challenged from outwith the universities. The Executive's higher education review argues for a system 'which would recognise and value more clearly the diversity in the sector, (Scottish Executive, 2002) a theme echoed in a recent SHEFC-commissioned report which criticises formula-based funding for 'encouraging convergent institutional strategies' (SHEFC, 2002). But neither document makes practical proposals for addressing these perceived failings. In fact SHEFC's funding model *does* recognise and value diverse factors, and surely it is right that this is done openly, through a published formula. Funding formulae are never perfect. There are always shortcomings in the statistics, and the recipients (usually all of them simultaneously) feel they are being short-changed. But how much happier would they be if the formula was abandoned and funding decisions were made instead in smoke-filled rooms?

Or perhaps they could be made by students? Dearing favoured a move in this direction, recommending that 60% of teaching funds should be distributed through student choice rather than by formula. Some of Dearing's recommendations have had an important influence on government policy, but this is not one of them. In Scotland, the Executive ultimately funds the cost of university education and, through SHEFC, it has been able to budget for and control that cost by capping the full-time undergraduate population. If university funding was driven by student choice, the system of control would be weakened and the Executive could find itself writing a blank cheque for higher education. That is not about to happen.

SCOTLAND'S HIGHER EDUCATION STRATEGY

The Executive controls public investment in higher education, but it takes the view that a high degree of institutional autonomy is desirable, and Scottish universities enjoy more autonomy than most. They are free to hire and fire staff, to determine which teaching and research they will undertake, to decide which students they will admit – and which they will not – and, subject to national guidelines, to buy and sell real estate and to merge with other institutions. Autonomy encourages a dynamic and diverse university sector, and inter-university competition promotes quality and student choice. But institutional autonomy has its shortcomings. It can result in needless duplication, with universities keen to compete in areas of growth, but less inclined to withdraw from subjects in decline. It can involve 'academic drift', with institutions aspiring to operate at higher academic levels and neglecting the nation's need for less advanced qualifications. And autonomous institutions, acting in competition, may not be best placed to respond to growing business opportunities in E-learning and in international markets.

The Funding Council has sought to counter some of the negative features of autonomy through special initiatives, funded outwith the standard teaching and research formulae. These have allowed SHEFC, while not challenging their autonomy, to encourage universities to move in certain directions, usually involving collaboration. Special initiatives have, for example, helped finance institutional mergers and a small number of subject rationalisations. But universities have misgivings about special initiatives. Sometimes they involve time-consuming bidding arrangements, and they always involve 'top-slicing' – withholding an element of financial control from the universities themselves. Initiatives to enhance the national IT infrastructure, and to promote the Executive's policy on wider access have generally been welcomed. But where special initiatives are not directed towards established national priorities, the rationale for top-slicing funds, and the processes by which the funds are awarded, are questioned.

Some would argue that established national priorities are what is lacking. The Garrick Committee (Dearing's Scottish sub-committee) felt the need for 'a more strategic vision for the higher education sector' (National Committee of Inquiry into Higher Education, 1997) and proposed a Scottish Forum for Higher Education to advise on issues such as subject rationalisation. A similar concern is evident in the current review of higher education, which seeks 'the right balance between co-operating and competing, between local provision and global aims,' and considers the Executive should 'clarify the role of SHEFC and, without compromising the autonomy of the sector, enhance its capacities to facilitate change across institutions' (Scottish Executive, 2002). And yet, if the Executive wishes to see change in higher education, it already has the financial levers to make it happen. The main impediment is not institutional autonomy, but a lack of confidence to drive national strategy forward. And that may be no bad thing, because previous attempts to strengthen national planning in UK higher education have been unsuccessful. Where the government has succeeded in delivering strategic change, such as increased participation and research selectivity, it has done so, not through central planning, but by introducing competitive funding mechanisms and allowing institutional self-interest to do the rest. An effective balance does need to be struck between institutional autonomy and central steer, and in this Scotland appears to have been relatively successful. The ease with which its universities interact with the Executive and the Funding Council is a source of envy elsewhere in the UK. And in some respects the higher education system itself is envied. Scotland outperforms the rest of the UK in widening access and in research. It produces a higher proportion of graduates than any other European nation. And the universities have a profound impact on the national community. That impact was evident as the Scottish Parliament began its work and it has been reinforced by the actions of the Executive since 1999.

REFERENCES

Independent Committee of Inquiry into Student Finance (1999) *Student Finance: Fairness for the Future* (The Cubie Report), Edinburgh: Independent Committee of Inquiry.

National Committee of Inquiry into Higher Education (1997) *Higher Education in the Learning Society. Report of the National Committee* (The Dearing Report), Norwich: HMSO.

National Committee of Inquiry into Higher Education (1997) *Higher Education in the Learning Society. Report of the Scottish Committee* (The Garrick Report), Norwich: HMSO.

Scottish Executive (2002) *Shaping Our Future, Scottish Higher Education Review*, Edinburgh: Scottish Executive.

SHEFC (2002) *Higher Education in Scotland, Orchestrating an Adaptive Knowledge Based system*, PA Consulting, Edinburgh: SHEFC.

14

Her Majesty's Inspectorate of Education (HMIE)

Douglas Weir

THE ORIGIN AND DEVELOPMENT OF THE INSPECTORATE

In 1840 John Gibson was appointed as the first of Her Majesty's Inspectors of Schools in Scotland. At that time the government was particularly indebted to the Church of Scotland for providing most schools and thus Gibson's appointment (and those of his colleagues for some time to come) was subject to the approval of the Church. Although the state was intervening in the quality assurance of schools from that date it was doing so because of the growing desire to ensure accountability for the public funding which was given to schools and not as an aggressive statement to Church schools that their standards were poor. Indeed as Bone (1968, p. 22) indicates, citing the Privy Council minutes, the charge on Gibson and his colleagues was 'that you should bear in mind that (this) inspection is not intended as a means of exercising control, but of affording assistance'. For the past 160 years, that balance between control and assistance has been the dominant point of tension between the state and school inspectors on the one hand, and between inspectors and teachers on the other hand.

The state rhetoric has consistently portrayed HM Inspectors as independent, a notion most heroically restated by Ian Lang, as Secretary of State for Scotland, in December 1992 when he pronounced to Parliament that:

> The distinctive and central role of HM Inspectorate in Scottish education and the value of its worth to the education system in the past has been widely recognised. I endorse its role as primarily responsible for independent and objective evaluation of the standards of the education system.

Teachers on the other hand have generally seen inspectors as agents of state control. No matter how personable the inspector (and many are), when they are facing teachers in their official capacity, the teachers' instinctive reactions are that they are to be measured, judged and controlled. Whilst not in such an extreme fashion, numerous policy analysts share the same suspicions of the inspectorate, arguing that state appointees, most of whose remit is at least approved or at most prescribed by ministers, cannot avoid being seen as agents of the state rather than allies of the teachers. As Humes describes it in *The Leadership Class in Scottish Education* (Edinburgh: John Donald Publishers, 1986), HMI reflects 'the tendency of well-established bureaucracies to place the interests of members above those of the public'.

In their early years, HM Inspectors had three major tasks – to scrutinise applications for aid to build schools; to inspect schools in receipt of state grants; and to evaluate the state of education in specific districts! As local government evolved, the first of these became redundant. The second function remains the core task of HMI to this day. The third has been apparent in numerous forms and has recently (1999) re-emerged in a more formal guise through the statutory responsibility of HM Inspectors to judge the quality of education provision made by each local council in Scotland and to report on it.

While HMIs currently in post would typically have a national remit as well as a geographical base (Northern, Western or Eastern) they do not have the same length of service in a particular locality nor such an intimate knowledge of their local schools as their early predecessors had. While some nineteenth-century HMIs were feared rather than respected locally, there are many instances of testimonials and generous gifts to those with distinguished long service and a reputation for successful advocacy of the interests of 'their' schools. Bennett (2001, p. 73) draws attention to a regular criticism made by teachers of today's HMI in that the inspectors 'inevitably knew less of the context in which the school was operating and of circumstances which were unique in each school'. The question of central versus local has embedded within it another matter which has been actively debated since HM Inspectors were first appointed. In the early days the crucial criterion for appointment as HM Inspector was scholarship. Today it is significant and successful practice as a teacher. The movement from one position to the other has been gradual but steady.

Talking about the expansion in the inspectorate following the introduction of compulsory schooling in 1872, Bone (1968, p. 82–3) says, 'The [new] Inspectors were all young [and] . . . though some of them had taught, it had not been in ordinary schools, and scholarship was now being considered more necessary than teaching experience.' For some years after this, the Educational Institute of Scotland was highly critical of inspectors without significant experience of school teaching, arguing that they would not recognise good teaching unless they themselves had been good teachers. Each time there was new recruitment to the inspectorate as a result of expansion the tension rose again, only to subside after a few years as the new recruits' 'on the job' experience overtook their lack of initial experience. The Scotch Education Department view was made very clear in 1906 by Sir John Struthers, its secretary (quoted in Bone, 1968, p. 61), when he stated that 'It was also a fact that scholarship goes further than anything else to secure the respect even of the ordinary teacher.' Nevertheless the pressure from teachers' organisations continued. By the early 1930s the department's criteria for appointment to the inspectorate were a good honours degree, some postgraduate experience, and five years service as a teacher.

Gradually the requirement that inspectors should demonstrate their scholarship has been eroded and replaced by a requirement to demonstrate their professionalism – whatever that might mean. The clearest recent description of one of HM Inspectors of Education comes from a former Senior Chief Inspector (Gallacher, 1999, p. 137).

> Recruits to the Inspectorate must therefore be highly respected and experienced professionals in their field. They are recruited to provide an appropriate balance of expertise across the various sectors and subject specialisms. They must offer an outstanding track record in teaching or lecturing or informal education; have occupied one or more posts of responsibility in education

or a relevant field with distinction, and demonstrate the ability and adaptability to extend their range of professional interests and sphere of activity.

The evidence suggests that this is more a recipe for perpetuating a particular type of recruit than ensuring that the inspectorate reflects the whole education profession. The inspectorate has been slow to appoint and promote women, slow to appoint and promote primary teachers, slow to appoint and promote representatives of minority communities, and is under-representative of those with experience in local authorities or higher education or even those with advanced degrees in education. As a consequence, their leadership has been called into question most notably in the official Rayner Report of 1981.

At present (September 2002) there are ninety-two inspectors in Scotland. By age, seventy of them are over fifty and only one is aged under forty. By gender, thirty-one are female. In the senior ranks there are six men and one woman. While all HMI can undertake duties across the whole of the inspectorate's remit, twenty-three HMI are in post because of their particular specialist expertise in secondary education and only eight because of their specialised primary education roles. For reference it is salutary to compare this governing elite against all teachers. Of Scotland's 50,000 teachers in state schools, 35,000 are female and 22,000 teach in primary schools, and at least one-quarter of all teachers are over the age of fifty. Even taking headteachers as a comparison group by age and status, more than eight of every ten are female. The composition of the inspectorate moves slowly towards being more representative of the upper reaches of the teaching workforce but still under-represents women and primary education. The drift away from scholarship as a criterion for appointment has inevitably reduced the ability of HMI to influence policy and practice through intellectual argument (see Humes, 1986, p. 79), and instead, as will be seen below, they have tended towards finding solutions based on technicist or managerialist approaches.

A further duty of inspection from inception was awarding certification to novice teachers. This, together with the initial task of approving state funding for schools, was the key measure for improving the quality of school education. Until 1965 when legislation setting up the General Teaching Council for Scotland was passed, this measure ensured that all teachers were visited by an HMI at the beginning of their careers for the purpose of assessing their competence to teach. It also gave HMI considerable authority for approving and monitoring programmes of initial teacher education.

While this author is one of the last remaining teachers to have had such an HMI visit at the beginning of his career and remembers the anxiety which it engendered, there are at least two positive advantages of such a system. Firstly it gave HMI a keener, personal, appreciation of the (then) colleges of education and their staffs and it gave the beginning teacher a face and name to associate with national responsibility in their subject or sector. Furthermore the HMI visit was an independent confirmation of competence as a teacher which has certain advantages over the current system where recommendations for full registration as a teaching professional are the responsibility of school management alone. The question of school and teacher autonomy versus central control remains the crucial point of tension today, raising questions over exactly what positive purpose is served by HM Inspectors.

With regard to the changing remit and duties of HM Inspectors, there is the matter of their involvement in national programmes of curriculum and assessment. At the outset, the reports from HMI on the state of education in particular districts were the only source of accurate data on which government could base policies for school curriculum and assessment. In assessment, from 1864 and the introduction of the first 'payment by results' code, HMI were assessing pupil attainment on a systematic basis. From 1888 in secondary schools and from 1903 in primary schools, HMI also controlled the national assessment of 'leaving' performance of pupils, to the point where, from 1911, they were responsible for setting and marking the Secondary Leaving Certificate. By 1922, selection for secondary education passed to the local authorities, but HMI domination of the Secondary Leaving Certificate did not end until the Scottish Certificate of Education Examination Board came into existence in 1965. Even then, the national examinations body and its subject panels continued to be indebted to HMI who were a cornerstone of such groups and highly influential in the development of syllabus and assessment, both in the secondary school where they played a key role in developing Standard Grade, and in the primary school where they led the 5–14 programme. Only when the Scottish Qualifications Authority was set up in 1996 was this umbilical relationship between HMI and secondary school assessment severed.

In curriculum, the earliest phase dominated by 'payment by results' ensured that the curriculum consisted mainly of 'teaching to the test'. But when the prescription of courses from the centre ended in 1899, inspectors were quickly able to reinforce the advisory dimension of their work and commence a series of documents designed to support the curriculum and its development. This aspect of the inspectors' work became so well respected that the famous Report on Secondary Education (Edinburgh, HMSO) issued by the Advisory Council on Education in Scotland in 1947 even said that the title 'Inspector' should become 'Education Officer' and routine inspection be discontinued so that HM Inspectors could 'devote their time to more constructive functions.' The Advisory Council vision was of a service comprising 'consultants and collaborators . . . to stimulate by discussion and suggestion, to spread ideas and be a link between school and school, to provoke the unreflective to thought and to awaken healthy doubts as to the sufficiency of familiar routines . . .' (para. 656). Indeed from the mid-1950s development work led by HMI, but including many others from within schools and local authorities, increased so much as to reduce significantly the time spent on routine inspections. Even when the Consultative Committee on the Curriculum was set up in 1965, the secretary of SED was its chair and HMI continued to play prominent roles.

In the 1980s, however, civil servants and HMI had become unhappy with what now was the Scottish Consultative Council on the Curriculum (SCCC) and its tendency to offer advice which was in conflict with the prevailing (Thatcherite) political rhetoric. HMI again asserted their influence over curriculum through taking control, explicitly and implicitly, of the 5–14 programme and the Higher Still development programme. Ultimately, SCCC and the Scottish Council for Educational Technology (SCET) were merged in 2000 to form Learning and Teaching Scotland (see Chapter 18). That new body has a public profile which shows a greater emphasis on the technical and communications (ICT) dimensions of curriculum delivery and a smaller contribution at present on the development of curricular practice in schools. HMIE on the other hand, as a consequence of this struggle for dominance over the curriculum, has flooded the market with its series of publications on Standards and Quality, on Effective Learning and Teaching, and on Improving Subjects at 5–14. However, the source of evidence for HMI advice on curriculum is their own inspections of schools rather than the collegial working party of the 1965–85 period. Given the artificial nature of a school's behaviour during an inspection and given the restrictive remit which HMI follow during an inspection, it is difficult to judge the reliability of the evidence upon which HMI base their curricular advice. In many cases it is the quality of individual specialist HMI which produces helpful curricular guidance rather than the collective activity of HMI as an agency.

Having now looked at the ebb and flow over 160 years of the battle between control and support in the work of HMI, it is time to focus on the work of what is now Her Majesty's Inspectorate of Education (HMIE) in Scotland.

INSPECTION TODAY

Since April 2001, inspectors have been put at arms' length from the Scottish Executive Education Department in the form of an executive agency, but are still directly accountable to the Scottish ministers for the standards of their work. This change of status does not alter the core tasks of the inspectorate as described on their website (www.scotland.gov.uk/hmie): 'HMI are maintaining their rigorous annual programme of independent inspections and reviews. This evidence will enable us to provide independent professional advice to Scottish Ministers, and relevant Departments of the Scottish Executive to inform educational developments and assist in policy formulation.'

Inspection is by far the largest part of the HMIE remit, occupying around two-thirds of the staffing capability of the inspectorate. It includes inspection of pre-school centres, primary, special and secondary schools, community learning, residential provision, local authorities, initial teacher education and further education colleges. It is also highly visible as, since 1983, inspectors' reports have all been published. Most of the inspections of schools are of the 'Standards and Quality' type which look at the school as a whole – ethos, resources (including staffing and accommodation), curriculum, learning and teaching, support for learning, care and welfare and leadership. For primary schools the process of inspection is normally contained within one week. For secondary schools the process is normally two periods of four days' inspection, separated by a brief interval. In each case a report is issued within sixteen weeks to the school, and widely published within twenty weeks. Finally HMI revisit the school about two years after the report has been published to see what progress has been made and then to report their conclusions to parents.

HMIE now also undertakes more limited Care and Welfare inspections typically of residential provision in schools and hostels. These inspections concentrate on the school's ethos and links with the community; accommodation, staffing and resources devoted to pupil care and welfare; support for pupils; and the management of care and welfare.

Possibly the most important additional function in recent years is the inspection of the thirty-two local authorities. The reports of these inspections have now provoked such an interest and are available in sufficient numbers for league tables to have been produced by the press, ranking local authorities by the number and quality of positive references made on them by HMIE. The official purpose of such inspections is outlined thus on the HMIE website:

> Local authorities have a duty to seek to improve the quality of education and raise standards. An inspection will evaluate how well schools in your council are being supported and challenged to improve standards of education and how well the council's staff and other resources achieve Best Value in helping schools. Overall, it will evaluate how well education in this area is being managed for the benefit of the community. Inspections evaluate existing performance and identify points for action where improvement is needed.

The various forms of inspection consume two-thirds of inspectorate time and this may increase as a result of moving towards the Scottish Executive's target of each primary school being inspected once in every seven years and each secondary school being inspected once in every five years. HMIE does not inspect on its own. Most inspection teams include a lay member (from a national panel of 100 people 'whose experience is not in education') and one or more associate assessors 'who are experienced practitioners in the relevant field.' The first group are to help ensure that accountability to the public interest is maintained and to allay any suspicion of a cosy relationship between inspection and teachers. The second group give a reassuring peer dimension to the inspection but are also there as a form of staff development 'within the context of quality assurance developments in Scottish schools and colleges . . . provid[ing] a means of increasing the number of staff with expertise in evaluation.'

Even with an increased frequency of inspection, HMIE is anxious that is quality message becomes a continuous feature of school planning. Its philosophy is that the possibility of tension between teachers and inspectors is reduced if schools are continually made aware of criteria for successful schools, both in documentation and through 'hands-on' experience as associate assessors. Then, it is presumed, schools will build their own internal quality processes around HMIE guidance and not be surprised by or suspicious of the periodic Standards and Quality inspections which will hopefully confirm, from the external perspective, that the school is keeping up to the mark.

This quality improvement strategy is driven by the Audit Unit of HMIE, under its own Chief Inspector. That unit takes the lead in quality assurance by recording collating, analysing and reporting on quality matters, and by setting performance targets for schools and local authorities. Its best known means of involving schools in this process is the document *How Good is Our School?*, revised by HMIE Audit Unit in 2002 and commonly known as *HGIOS*.

HGIOS asks schools to critically examine themselves by reference to national priorities and targets, taking account of local authority and school specific targets, and measured against the school development plan. *HGIOS* processes involve taking a broad view of performance across key areas of curriculum; attainment; learning and teaching; support for pupils; ethos; resources and management; leadership and quality assurance. The quality (or performance) indicators also require schools to take a closer look at specific areas viewed as successful or causing concern. By using the guidance in *HGIOS*, schools can evaluate their whole provision, generating quality or performance indicators (or using HMIE's own exemplars) on each aspect of provision, and rating each on a scale from 4 (very good) to 1 (unsatisfactory). The school's own self-evaluation then becomes a key document when HMIE conducts a Standards and Quality inspection and tests its observations and analyses against the school's own.

THE FUTURE OF INSPECTION

It is difficult to reach a dispassionate view on HMIE and its processes from inside the system. Recently, however an inspector from Northern Ireland, seeking to understand her own province's inspection processes and those of other countries, undertook doctoral studies entitled 'Inspection: A Catalyst for School Improvement' (Bennett, 2001). This thesis provides a helpful context for evaluating school inspection in Scotland. At the macro level, Bennett has concerns about the manner in which inspection is presently contextualised. For her, the last fifteen years have seen increasing control on schools from the centre which reduces the power of teachers and deprofessionalises them. That control is exemplified by processes of inspection, performance indicators and target setting which together provide external constraints on the autonomy of schools and teachers, telling them what standards they should reach rather than giving them freedom to negotiate local standards with their local communities.

Talking about herself and the Scottish HMIE whom she met, Bennett regrets the climate of competitiveness which exists between teachers and inspectors and the shift from 'ally' to 'judge' which she believes is increasing.

> The increase in inspection duties and the reduction in pastoral duties meant that inspections took place less often as part of an ongoing relationship with the school and were, therefore, not well-founded on trust and shared values. As inspectors became more exclusively involved in inspection, we knew inevitably less of the context in which the school was operating and of circumstances which were unique in each school. (Bennett, 2001, p. 73)

From interviews with teachers, Bennett identifies a number of positive features of inspection such as delivering public accountability, providing an external perspective and forcing schools to pay more attention to their ongoing development. The interviews did, however, generate more negative than positive comments, including the following: the inspection time was too short; class teachers did not have sufficient contact with HMIE; inspectors lacked a knowledge of the school in its context; the process was too stressful and adversarial.

In her work, she notes that primary school teachers had more negative feelings about inspection than secondary teachers, partly because of the lack of specific advice that they received, partly because they misconstrued inspection as leading to school improvement when it was really about system judgements, and partly because in a small school (which most primaries are) the identity of the individual teacher is more easy to guess (and therefore judge) from the published HMIE report.

Bennett does, however, produce evidence to support *HGIOS* as a useful tool for school self-improvement while nevertheless pointing to the inconsistency between self-improvement (using the Audit Unit's *HGIOS*) and the global targets for achievement set by the same Audit Unit. She comments that 'the whole concept of self-evaluation, so much heralded by HMI, is still too controlled and too inflexible to encourage teachers to innovate and follow their own convictions' (p. 463). Her conclusion therefore is that the Scottish system of inspection is weak in not engaging teachers with each other and with external advice in pursuit of a school's own development priorities and evaluation strategies.

While there have been a number of criticisms levelled at what is now HMIE, the public debate about its role has been less vociferous than in England where the parallel body, the Office for Standards in Education (OfSTED) has become more heavily criticised. OfSTED is a non-ministerial government department whose inspectorate has a remit similar to HMIE. The differences between the two are, however, important. OfSTED has proportionately fewer inspectors of its own, with most of the work of inspection being contracted out to casual workers, taking on inspections for a fee and naturally anxious to accord with OfSTED views in order to gain future fees. In addition, the cycle of inspection is not as even-handed as in Scotland because inspection in England targets so-called failing schools and spends more time with them. Furthermore OfSTED practises a highly intensive and prescriptive role in the inspection of teacher education, which is perceived to be a reaction against any tendency to liberal thinking. Finally the role of Chief Inspector of Schools in England and the Inspectorate itself are heavily politicised. Particularly when Chris Woodhead was England's Chief Inspector of Schools from 1994 to 2000, the impression was conveyed that the Chief Inspector was the mouthpiece of government rather than the independent arbiter that Scots politicians claim the Scottish Senior Chief Inspector and his team to be.

It is as an executive agency, at arms length from government, that HMI in Scotland will be judged over the next few years. The first full year of working was reported in the HMIE *Annual Report 2001–2002* (The Stationery Office, Edinburgh, 2002). The outgoing Senior Chief Inspector, Douglas Osler, pronounced himself satisfied by the progress made in the first year and expressed his view that the change in status 'was overdue'. For Mr Osler the cornerstone of HMIE and that by which it presumably can be judged is the link between inspection and self-evaluation in driving up standards. Yet, as all the preceding text has demonstrated, that link between control and self-regulation has never been easy or comfortable.

A careful reading of the HMIE *Annual Report* also illustrates the dominant role of inspection itself and the subordinate role of advising. Politicians and their civil servants have created a constitutional and geographical distance between themselves and HMIE. Other groups in the Scottish educational system may receive advice or enter into discussions with inspectors but will seldom now have them on the inside of their governing bodies or advisory councils. It might be expected that HMIE will continue to have significant influence on the development of Scottish education but this is by no means inevitable. As has always been the case, individual inspectors will remain influential if they have a personal credibility based on intellect and expertise. HMIE as a body, however, is now very dependent for its influence on its publications in the form of inspection reports and other compilations of advice taken from the same reports.

If the trends apparent in the *Annual Report* continue, teachers will have very little contact with HMIE except through the still-feared cycle of inspections. The hopes for school self-evaluation will remain largely unrealised because schools are in awe of the perceived power of HMIE. This leads them to create their self-evaluations and development plans on the basis of what they think HMIE will want to see when conducting their Standards and Quality inspections. But if schools and teachers are to receive acceptable advice towards self-improvement which is based on knowledge of their local circumstances, the present inspectorate model does not fit these needs. It inevitably creates an impression of control rather than development. How to reconcile the political need for schools to be accountable with the professional need for collegial support therefore remains unresolved.

REFERENCES

Bennett, M. E. J. (2001) Inspection : a catalyst in school improvement, unpublished PhD thesis, Glasgow: University of Strathclyde.
Bone, T. R. (1968) *School Inspection in Scotland 1840–1966*, London: University of London Press.
Gallacher, T. N. (1999) The Scottish inspectorate and their operations in T. G. K. Bryce and W. M. Humes (eds), *Scottish Education*, Edinburgh: Edinburgh University Press.
HMIE www.scotland.gov.uk/hmie
Humes, W. M. (1986) *The Leadership Class in Scottish Education*, Edinburgh: John Donald Publishers.

15

The Local Governance of Education: A Political Perspective

Keir Bloomer

POLITICAL MANAGEMENT AT NATIONAL LEVEL

Since the first edition of this book appeared in 1999, the political governance of Scottish education has changed profoundly. The opening of the Scottish Parliament in July 1999 and the parallel establishment of the Scottish Executive in both its political and administrative guises represent, perhaps, the biggest changes since the creation of state education in Scotland following the Act of 1872.

Scottish education has always been distinct from that in England and the remainder of the United Kingdom. Attempts to provide a national, although by no means universal, system go back over 500 years. The distinctiveness of Scottish education was maintained by the Act of Union in 1707. Indeed, along with the Church and the law, education became one of the defining characteristics of continuing Scottish tradition and separateness (see Chapter 10).

Autonomous management was built into Scottish state education from the outset. A key feature of the 1872 Act was the establishment of the Scotch (sic) Education Department which became part of the Scottish Office when it was set up in its turn in 1885. The growth in independence of the Scottish Office during the early twentieth century ensured that the education system north of the border enjoyed almost complete autonomy.

Under the pre-devolution system, political responsibility at cabinet level rested with the Secretary of State for Scotland. Except on relatively rare occasions, such as the Scottish teachers' strike of the 1980s, when events in Scotland might have been considered to have implications for education in the remainder of the UK, it seems unlikely that Cabinet attention was often focused on this area of the Secretary of State's responsibilities. More immediate accountability formed part of the remit of one or other of the Scottish Office junior ministers. In those days, the amount of parliamentary time devoted to Scottish education was relatively small. Finding time in the legislative programme tended to be problematic. The passing of Education Acts in successive years in 1980 and 1981 was, in this respect, exceptional. Not surprisingly, parliamentary scrutiny of affairs of no direct relevance to nearly 90% of MPs was relaxed.

In other words, prior to 1999, political direction of Scottish education at national level largely lacked the element of democratic accountability. Scottish Office ministers played an important role in the direction of the system but in a manner which passed largely unregarded by Parliament. All of this was, of course, a critical part of the argument of those who supported devolution and the establishment of a Scottish parliament. It was argued that administrative devolution without political devolution meant that the various activities of the Scottish Office, including education, were largely free of democratic scrutiny. New arrangements under which Scottish ministers would be directly accountable to a Scottish parliament which would undoubtedly devote significant amounts of time to the national education system would, it was maintained, improve both the quality and the transparency of decision-making (see Paterson et al., 2001).

Clearly, there is room for debate about whether educational management and policy making at national level has improved since 1999. What is not open to question is that the new Parliament has devoted considerable time to education and both the number of accountable ministers and their visibility in Scotland have markedly increased.

The management structure of the new Scottish Executive – a term which is unhelpfully used to describe both Scottish ministers and the Scottish civil service – split responsibility for education in two. The Scottish Executive Education Department (SEED) deals with schools, early education and childcare while further education and higher education fall within the remit of the Scottish Executive Enterprise and Lifelong Learning Department (SEELLD). Each of these departments has a minister in the Cabinet and SEED also has a junior minister with specific responsibility for schools. Thus, from being merely part of the remit of one Junior Minister, education is now the concern of three ministers, one of whom is of Cabinet rank.

The committee structure also reflects this divide with the Education, Culture and Sport Committee dealing with schools while the Enterprise and Lifelong Learning Committee is concerned with universities and colleges.

This division has been the subject of some controversy. Several contributors to the recent national debate on education observed that to look at schools in isolation was misguided. Furthermore, the extension of the Enterprise and Lifelong Learning Department's remit to include transport seems to render the existing arrangements less coherent. Nevertheless, the existence of two committees has obviously increased the number of MSPs who are closely involved with educational discussion and increased the amount of time made available for it.

The new structures have certainly been active. The first major Bill submitted to the Scottish Parliament concerned school education. It was the subject of an unprecedented effort to consult. Public consultation became an explicit part of the legislative process. A well-produced consultation paper containing not only the text of the Bill as originally proposed but also explanatory notes and specific invitations to comment was widely circulated. Evidence was taken from a range of bodies and at the end of the consultation process another document was issued, summarising the comments received and giving the reactions of the Executive. In important respects, the resulting Standards in Scotland's Schools etc. Act 2000 incorporated changes arising from this consultation.

Furthermore, the discussions on the Bill led directly to a further consultation on the national priorities for education and less directly to the national debate initiated in the spring of 2002.

Both committees have also held important inquiries. The investigation of the Education, Culture and Sport Committee into the failures of the Scottish Qualifications Authority in connection with the 2000 diet of examinations offered an unprecedented degree of scrutiny of shortcomings in the education service. Such a detailed inquiry would not have been possible under the pre-devolution arrangements and it is quite possible that important outcomes such as the reorganisation of the inspectorate would not have occurred. Similarly, the lifelong learning inquiry which published its report in October 2002, seems set to exert a major influence on policy for some time to come. The less extended inquiry into the purposes of education by the Education, Culture and Sport Committee may emerge as being of comparable importance.

All of this activity has influenced the way in which educational policy making in Scotland takes place. The Scottish public as a whole may, as successive opinion polls suggest, be disappointed in the performance of the new Parliament but civic Scotland has little reason to complain of the extent of its involvement (see Hassan and Warhurst, 2002a, 2002b). Whether all of the scrutiny, consultation and evidence giving constitute, as was predicted by some of the supporters of devolution, 'a new form of politics', can be debated. The increased access enjoyed by the broader education community would be hard to dispute.

Prior to the establishment of the Parliament, political involvement in the management of Scottish education at a national level was largely focused on the Convention of Scottish Local Authorities (COSLA). Not surprisingly, therefore, devolution has had an impact on that body. As the body representing Scottish local authorities collectively (although currently only twenty-nine of the thirty-two are in membership), COSLA has not only had the opportunity to influence national policy-making but has also been directly involved in important aspects of management. In particular, councillors selected by COSLA have formed the employers' sides of the various national negotiating bodies including that dealing with teachers' salaries and conditions of service.

The new arrangements have brought about closer partnership working between COSLA and the Scottish Executive than existed previously with the Scottish Office. Negotiations with teachers provide an interesting instance. Previously, all discussions were bilateral, with COSLA speaking for management and the Scottish Office present, if at all, in an observer role. Because of its control over resources, the Scottish Office's influence was enormous, but was exercised away from the negotiating table. By contrast, in the negotiations leading to the McCrone agreement on teachers' pay and conditions, the Scottish Executive was present as an active third force. Collaboration (or, on occasion, differences) between the local authorities and the Executive thus became more explicit.

Partly in consequence, COSLA has come to see itself less as a lobbying organisation and more as a partner, pursuing a common agenda with the Executive. Instances would include 'Modernising Government', a government programme focused on improving business processes and the use of new technology in the public sector, and 'A Joint Future', involving collaboration between health and social work agencies, as well as the discussions on professional development and management structures which have followed the McCrone settlement. Increasingly, COSLA comes close to acting as a national agency promoting collaboration within local government and between local government and other bodies. This development has been viewed differently according to political perspective. Not surprisingly, supporters of opposition parties see in it a loss of COSLA's political independence and a failure to represent the interests of local government.

It is perhaps worth noting in passing that much of the collaboration between COSLA and the Executive is undertaken at an officer rather than a political level. The role of directors of education in, for example, the resolution of the exam crisis or the various post-McCrone discussions has been crucial. It is, perhaps, therefore, not surprising that the Association of Directors of Education in Scotland (ADES) emerged from a recent study by the Rowntree Foundation as, of all local government professional associations, the one most satisfied with its dealings with the Executive and Parliament. ADES, more than most, thus symbolises the civic Scotland which enjoys enhanced influence under the new arrangements.

POLITICAL MANAGEMENT IN LOCAL AUTHORITIES

Since 1929, the management of school education has been the statutory responsibility of local authorities. Councils have interpreted this responsibility as giving them local discretion in important policy matters. As Malcolm Green pointed out in the previous edition of this book, few of them would have accepted the definition commonly offered of education in England as 'a national service locally administered'.

In 1996, when local government in Scotland was reorganised, many people doubted whether this degree of independence could be sustained. The main concern lay in the small size of most of the new authorities. Where there had been twelve authorities, there were to be thirty-two. As the three islands councils were unchanged and four of the new unitary authorities were to have the same boundaries as their regional predecessors, in effect, five large and medium-sized regions were to be replaced by twenty-five new councils. Would they be able to manage a complex large-scale service such as education effectively? Perhaps equally importantly from a political perspective, would they be able to sustain a pluralist notion of the direction of Scottish education or would they become, in practice, merely agents of government policy?

This concern became more acute after the general election of 1997 brought devolution firmly back onto the agenda. Would the new Scottish Parliament and Executive draw powers away from local government? Would there really be space in a small country for political decision-making at two levels (or four if the influence of the UK and EU are suitably recognised)? The fate of education, as the largest local government function, was obviously a critical test case.

In the event, the new local authorities have both contributed to and benefited from the increasingly open intellectual climate which surrounds Scottish education. Several of the new authorities were openly critical of what they portrayed as a 'compliance agenda' driven forward by national development programmes and by the inspectorate. They pointed to lack of independent innovation and lack of diversity as critical weaknesses in the system. Such authorities took advantage of the lack of any legally enforceable national curriculum in Scotland and pursued development agendas which were, at least in some significant respects, independent. Not surprisingly, they welcomed the government's Early Intervention programme, not only because it addressed a widely shared priority to improve standards of early literacy and numeracy, but also because it provided additional funding without detailed national prescription regarding its use. Some aspects of the Excellence Fund were similarly well-received although others appeared as instruments of centralisation.

By the beginning of the new century, the notion of a broad national sense of direction with increased encouragement for experiment and diversity at local level had become quite firmly established. Some of the new local authorities can legitimately claim to have helped steer thinking in this direction. It would, however, be wrong to attribute the change in climate solely to the influence of local government. Important figures within the Executive had also become convinced that micro-management by central government did not offer the best way forward. In any event, the scale of economic, technological and social change and the need to ensure that education kept pace was promoting a more questioning attitude towards the future of education, and of schools in particular, in most developed countries. Furthermore, even insofar as local authorities played a significant part in this change in climate, the extent to which this was the result of political as opposed to professional opinion is perhaps open to question.

The political decision-making structures of local authorities are in most respects similar to those existing before 1996. After reorganisation, all authorities bar one established education committees although some used other titles. In the interim, the exception, Clackmannanshire, has come into line. On the other hand, two councils, East Renfrewshire and Edinburgh, have developed political executive structures along lines which have become quite popular south of the border.

Whenever a council establishes an education committee, even if it is described in some other way such as 'Children's Services Committee', places have to be provided on it for Church representatives. Most of the former regional councils also provided for teacher representation. In the post-1996 period, some councils have included representatives of parents, of young people or of other constituencies such as local business or non-teaching employees. There has thus been some movement towards a more corporatist and ostensibly consensual approach to political decision making at a local authority level.

A further significant change has been a broadening of the remit of education committees (and education directorates). From the outset, most of the new, smaller authorities chose not to establish separate management structures for services such as leisure and libraries. Over the ensuing years, a trend towards much more radical restructurings has developed. In at least three councils, education now forms part of a single department including also social work and housing. Only a third of the chief officers in charge of education now hold posts answering to the traditional description of a director of education. While the responsibilities of committees and their conveners do not now always reflect management structures, their remits too have also frequently expanded.

The overall picture is of increasingly diverse authorities pursuing highly complex and largely professional agendas in closer collaboration with a range of stakeholders and in response to increasingly ambitious government objectives. The following sub-sections illustrate this in relation to some of the major issues currently affecting Scottish education.

PUBLIC SERVICE REFORM

Public service reform is top of the national political agenda. The major services, especially health and education, are widely portrayed as inefficient and resistant to change. Opinion polls suggest that the public believes that services have actually deteriorated during the term of the current government despite new resources increasingly being available. There is said to be much scepticism that funding in itself will bring improvement.

Much of this debate, particularly in relation to education, is conducted in terms relevant only to England. Concern about 'bog standard' or 'bargepole' comprehensives does not seem to affect Scotland. The A-level fiasco of 2002 (which eclipsed SQA's failures of two years earlier) did not affect Scottish schools. Nevertheless, the McCrone settlement was supposed to be about modernisation and there are critical aspects of government thinking which are unquestionably impinging on Scottish education.

The most important of these is the pursuit of 'customer focus'. Services, it is said, should be shaped around users' needs not providers' convenience or traditional habits of thought.

This view has prompted models of public service shaped around groups of clients, such as children, or 'life events', such as moving house (and therefore school).

Critical to customer focus is the idea of 'joined-up services'. Its first – and so far, most influential – expression in educational terms has been the New Community School. This concept, based on the notion of 'full service schools' found in the US, is a relatively unthreatening one. Other public services relating to young people and their families could be located in schools or could be accessed through them. Apart from convenience to the public, there should be benefits arising from increased interaction between different groups of professionals. The building, however, remains a school and educational interests predominate. The agenda is thus set by the local council as education authority.

Much more politically problematic is the idea of community planning. At the time of the 1999 Scottish Parliament elections, this was undoubtedly one of the Labour Party's 'big ideas'. It is somewhat unclear whether it remains so or whether more limited and focused collaborations such as that between social services and health in the Joint Future programme are now seen as offering a better route forward.

Community planning is intended to bring together a wide range of public agencies (and potentially others) which, in consultation with the community, will jointly plan for the future. Although by no means solely concerned with service delivery, the creation of more coherent and customer-focused services is undoubtedly a key objective. Unlike community schools, however, community planning involves difficult issues of accountability. Councils may tend to assume a lead role based on democratic legitimacy. However, a range of factors such as lack of credibility because of low voter turnout or the strong imperative of central government direction in services such as health may well undermine this position. To date, most community planning partnerships have focused on issues such economic development or promoting healthy lifestyles. While education is certainly relevant to both of these, it has not generally surfaced as a key area of partnership activity in its own right. As a result, difficult issues such as pooled budgets and conflicting service priorities have not had to be faced.

Collaboration in the design and delivery of public services is a central government priority. Partnership working is a way of taking it forward in circumstances where central government is unwilling to extend the remit of local authorities. It remains to be seen whether voluntary co-operation will suffice or whether the centralising tendencies which are believed by many to be inherent in the 1999 settlement will take the form of imposing joint planning and joint service delivery in a way which would undoubtedly alter the political governance of education.

PUBLIC PRIVATE PARTNERSHIPS

If public service reform may contain the seeds of future political disputes between local and central government, PPP offers plenty of examples of conflict now. Constraints on public sector borrowing by traditional routes combined with substantial incentives to develop private partnerships have ensured that a growing number of local authorities have embarked on ambitious school building programmes using the PPP routes. Falkirk, then under Labour control, was the first council to put forward a scheme which replaced a significant proportion of its secondary schools at a single stroke. Subsequently, Glasgow completely refurbished or replaced all of its secondaries. Other substantial projects are under way and more are promised. Generally, Labour-run councils have been prepared to go down the PPP road (although some would probably find traditional methods both easier to manage and more congenial). Other councils have been more reluctant with some developing alternative models such as 'Not For Profit Trusts' which may, or may not, meet the Executive's criteria for support.

Criticism of PPP is of two distinct types. There is a pragmatic argument that long-term cost will be greater and that future generations will pay heavily for a temporary capital spending spree. Secondly, there is a more ideological objection that PPP represents an extension of privatisation.

So far as the first argument is concerned, the jury is still out. The Accounts Commission produced a report which, in several respects, was sceptical about aspects of the scheme. There has also been research suggesting that PPP is a less satisfactory source of finance for schools and hospitals than for, for example, roads and prisons. Furthermore, there is growing concern that PPP produces conservative thinking and buildings obsolete from the start. On the other hand, there is no doubt that the physical infrastructure of the Scottish Education system is being transformed at a pace never previously seen.

The ideological argument is more easily pinned down. Services such as cleaning, catering, grounds maintenance or technician support are undoubtedly transferred to the private sector. Whether this constitutes privatisation in any important sense depends upon two further considerations. Firstly, do such changes affect the core purposes of the school? After all, school transport and major maintenance have always been privately provided. Secondly, if a service is publicly funded and thus, in terms of strategic policy, publicly directed, does it matter if it is not publicly managed?

Opinions on these questions will inevitably differ. What appeared to emerge from the Prime Minister's stance at the 2002 Labour Conference was a view that the major public services must remain free at the point of use and open to all but could be managed in any of a variety of ways. Of course, this view does not directly affect a devolved Scottish education system. Critics of PPP, however, will fear that it might.

PPP and, of course, the broader question of what constitutes a public service, clearly have the capacity to affect profoundly the political management of education. At the most benevolent, entering into a partnership arrangement for the delivery of a range of important but ancillary services allows senior management in schools to concentrate on issues of learning and teaching. At the same time, the attention of education directorates and of education committee members can be directed towards educational support, quality improvement and putting into practice that broad concept of education which the national debate has indicated commands public support. An alternative view might be that if the element of operational responsibility were reduced, such strategic concerns could be dealt with at national level.

QUALITY IMPROVEMENT

Much of the political interest in education over the past fifteen years is derived from the view that, in the knowledge economy, raised educational standards are essential to economic competiveness. At the same time, spreading high levels of attainment as widely as possible furthers the cause of social inclusion by increasing earning power and the prospects of securing employment.

In common with many other developed countries, therefore, Scotland has been putting in place a quality assurance framework designed to raise achievement. Although less rigid and less brutal than its counterpart in England, this framework has also emphasised a range of measurable outcomes, generating league tables which allow comparisons to be made. The indicators contained in *How Good is Our School?* (SOEID, 1995) have allowed for a more focused inspection regime. At the same time, the range of areas covered in the attempt to measure less tangible aspects of school activity has resulted in a framework less rigidly focused on testing and examination success. Furthermore, there is a welcome emphasis on self-evaluation and continuous improvement.

The most recent addition to this apparatus has been the inspection of local authorities. This is not, as some councillors may imagine, an inspection of the director of education and his/her department but an evaluation of the way in which the council as a whole, including its political dimension, carries out its educational functions. Two significant issues arise.

Firstly, the connection between local authority performance and pupil experience is extremely attenuated. The report recently compiled by OfSTED on completion of its first round of inspections of the 150 English education authorities confirms the work of earlier researchers in suggesting that local authorities can do little directly to raise standards. There are certainly risks in passing judgements in areas where the causal connections are scarcely established.

Secondly, and far more importantly from a political perspective, are the implications of having elected bodies with their own mandates inspected by a national agency using national objectives and criteria of quality as the basis of its evaluations.

BROADENING THE AGENDA

Some 25,000 people took part in the national debate on education. Many of these participated through consultations and events organised by local authorities. This was, therefore, very much a collaborative exercise. Early indications suggest that the debate showed a high level of public confidence in Scottish education but paradoxically an understanding of the need for quite far reaching change. Rapidly changing circumstances, global as well as local, seemed to have persuaded people that the status quo, however good in its own terms, would not meet the needs of the future. Respondents were clear in their support for a broad concept of education. They want young people to have a wider range of experiences although they are aware of the problems of a crowded curriculum. There were demands for less emphasis on subject content but more on the promotion of higher-order intellectual skills, personal qualities and inter-personal skills.

It is possible to present the findings of the national debate as a ringing endorsement of Scotland's comprehensive system which, therefore, stands in little need of change. Alternatively, attention can be focused on the widespread concerns expressed about the curriculum, the excessive influence of examinations and the perceived narrowness of the educational experience taken as a whole. In other words, Scottish education might be facing the period of stability which many people undoubtedly want but could equally well be on the brink of very far-reaching change. For the short term, the decision is a matter of political preference by the Scottish Executive. In the longer term, it is difficult to avoid the impression that far-reaching social, economic and technological change will need to be reflected within the education system. This has two important implications for the governance of education.

The first, and less significant, relates to working in partnership. Developments such as New Community Schools are already pioneering the idea that education services can work in collaboration with others to provide, in effect, a one-stop shop for children and their families. Other developments, such as community planning, may require education to work in a more equal partnership to deliver broader, more corporate objectives. The very extended concept of educational purpose emerging from the debate and necessitated by contemporary circumstances may further advance this idea of partnership working. If so, the political governance of education will become more complex and the lines of account-ability less clear.

The second implication is more fundamental and relates to the pace of change. The major public services are often criticised for the slowness of their response to altering circum-stances. Politicians, both national and local, experience great difficulty in translating policy imperatives into altered services at the level of the individual classroom (or, for that matter, the individual hospital ward).

This presents the paradox of governments seemingly unable to achieve a transforming modernisation of education but at the same time forced to concede that there have been too many initiatives and that the burden of change lies heavily on staff. A harsh judgement would be that the system is exhausted by tinkering and cannot make the effort for real change.

In conclusion, it is perhaps worth contemplating if this problem is inherent in the current system of governance. Politically driven change normally requires high levels of consent. An adversarial parliamentary (or council) system and media anxious to exploit conflict makes such consensus difficult to achieve. A rapidly changing world demands speed and effectiveness in response. Can a politically managed system keep up with the pace? Time will tell.

REFERENCES

Hassan, G., and Warhurst, C. (eds) (2002a) *Anatomy of the New Scotland: Power, Influence and Change*, Edinburgh: Mainstream Publishing.
Hassan, G., and Warhurst, C. (eds) (2002b) *Tomorrow's Scotland*, London: Lawrence and Wishart.
Paterson, L. et al. (2001) *New Scotland, New Politics?* Edinburgh: Polygon.

16

The Local Governance of Education: An Operational Perspective

Gordon Jeyes

It is likely that the first term of Scotland's devolved Parliament 1999–2003 will be considered a transitional period. Consequently, even description is difficult at present as the significant changes of recent years contradict to some extent previous arrangements which remain in force. Such contradictions may emanate from legislation having a different political or philosophical provenance or from the fact that the process of legislation all too often drags the past with it and surviving pieces of legislation add to the complexity. Examples of survivals are contained in the only partially repealed 1956 School Code; or the tortuous complexity of placing request legislation which not only becomes harder to follow and easier to challenge with each change but, as recently evidenced, more difficult to revise; or the various attempts to modernise teachers' disciplinary procedures.

The first parliamentary term's transition has attempted to take forward an enlightened approach based on individual human rights, integrated and co-ordinated government, and an enabling, inclusive approach to governance. Nevertheless contradictions and tensions are clear in the emerging framework. For example,

Section 1 of the Standards in Scotland's Schools etc. Act 2000 states clearly that every child of school age has the right to school education. This would appear to place the child, rather than the education authority or the parent at the heart of the education system.

Section 2 (1) of the Standards in Scotland's Schools etc. Act 2000 attempts a definition of the purpose of education, referring to 'the development of the personality, talents and mental and physical abilities of the child or young person to their fullest potential'.

Primary legislation for education authorities remains section 1 of the Education (Scotland) Act 1980 which in section 28 states 'in the exercise and performance of their powers and duties under this Act, the Scottish Ministers and education authorities shall have regard to the general principle that, so far as is compatible with the provision of suitable instruction and training and the avoidance of unreasonable public expenditure, pupils are to be educated in accordance with the wishes of their parents.'

Section 1 (1) of the Education (Scotland) Act 1980 remains in force and it speaks not of the needs of individual young people, but educational provision which is 'adequate and efficient'.

A model based on community engagement, integrated service provision and a clear relationship with civic society as a whole (*New Community Schools Prospectus*, SEED, 1999).

A clear commitment to a school effectiveness model based on standards, league tables and targets (SOEID letter, 13.2.1998, from HMSCI to all schools).

These contradictions are exacerbated by the lack of clarity regarding the role of parents. This was described in the first edition of Scottish Education (Bryce and Humes (eds), 1999) by Keir Bloomer in Chapter 14 on the local governance of education. He referred to the confusion between the application of free market principles to benefit consumers and the involvement of local communities through establishment of school boards. Thus is Scotland building an education tradition based on parent as customer or as manager? Is the country moving towards an individualised, more bespoke system, recognising the right of each child to school education or the wishes of parents? Are duties relating to adequate provision or the development of the personality, talents and mental and physical abilities of the child or young person to fullest potential? Is Scotland promoting straightforward models of school effectiveness or encouraging schools to understand that their own effectiveness is dependent on the effectiveness of civil society as a whole: families, playgroups, community centres, youth clubs, neighbouring schools?

Of course it is not as if arrangements pre-devolution were without paradox.

- Local authorities had a free hand provided the education on offer was 'adequate and effective', could devise their own syllabuses and seek accreditation for learning from wherever might seem appropriate. The expectation however was that they would conform, and they did.
- Policy making covering curriculum specification, learning and teaching advice and examination / assessment syllabuses was dominated by those charged with independently inspecting the effectiveness of the system.
- The emphasis has been on devolved management and self-evaluation but advice and prescriptions regarding the methods to be used were invariably detailed and regular from both government and local authority.
- Parents were advised that they had a choice of schools when at best they could state preference, a preference usually inhibited by geography, poverty or popularity.

Devolution provided an opportunity to clarify national and local roles in education policy making, in line with statutory and other agreed procedures. This clarification has begun. Quality assurance and policy-making functions at national level have been separated. A system of external scrutiny for education authorities in line with the principles of a best value regime has been put in place and can evolve satisfactorily. There remains, however, considerable confusion between means and ends, process and outcomes, control and encouragement / empowerment.

DUTIES AND RESPONSIBILITIES

The Education (Scotland) Act 1980 as amended remains the primary piece of education legislation for Scotland. Nevertheless the Standards in Scotland's Schools etc. Act 2000 may come to be seen as a watershed, and its impact will continue for a number of years potentially making a significant difference to the way that education is delivered. The requirement to ensure full compliance with the European Convention of Human Rights meant the Act was more similar to the 1995 Children (Scotland) Act than previous education legislation. The recognition of the individual and the rights of children were in contrast to duties for adequate provision and efficiency. The central purpose of the Act in 2000 was to establish a new improvement framework for Scottish education and thus clarify roles and responsibilities for school improvement among the minister, the Parliament, local authorities, headteachers and parents. The legal basis for children's rights within the education system would relate to: the right of each child to school education; agreed statements on the purpose of education; the importance of the child's views.

These and the detailed elements within the Act require to be considered when undertaking duties as described in The Education Scotland Act 1980, under principles covering:

- The right of pupils to be educated as far as is reasonable in accordance with the wishes of their parents.
- The duty of parents to provide efficient education by ensuring that their children regularly attend school or by other means.
- The duty of education authorities to secure adequate and efficient provision of school education.

This balancing act makes it difficult thus far to judge whether or not the child, rather than the education authority or the parent has yet been placed at the heart of the education system.

The Improvement Framework

The improvement framework is set out in sections 3–7 of the Act (Scottish Executive, 2000). The framework operates at three levels – national government, local government and individual schools. The framework aims to set the key outcomes for education at a national level and devolve responsibility for finding the best solutions to a local level so that account can be taken of particular circumstances. At each level a plan or set of objectives will be produced so that schools, education authorities and the Scottish ministers can be held accountable for their efforts in trying to improve educational standards. Figure 16.1 shows how different groups can influence the framework at the different levels.

School Development Plans

It is envisaged that preparation of school development plans will go hand in hand with preparation of the education authority statement.

Content: has to take account of the annual statement of improvement objectives from the education authority.
has to include an account of ways and the extent to which the headteacher will consult the pupils at the school and seek to involve them in decisions regarding the everyday running of the school.

Figure 16.1:   The improvement framework

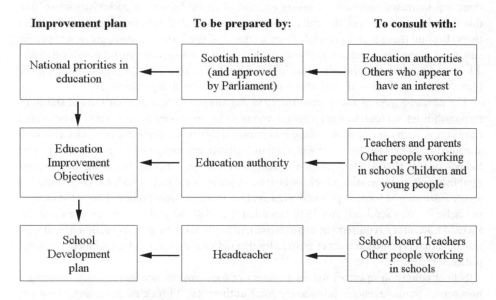

Improvement plan	To be prepared by:	To consult with:
National priorities in education	Scottish ministers (and approved by Parliament)	Education authorities Others who appear to have an interest
Education Improvement Objectives	Education authority	Teachers and parents Other people working in schools Children and young people
School Development plan	Headteacher	School board Teachers Other people working in schools

Consult with: the school board;
the teachers employed in the school;
persons employed or working in the school on an unpaid basis;
local bodies that are representative of parents, pupils, teachers or those
employed or working in the school on an unpaid basis;
there must also be an opportunity for pupils to make their views known

Prepared by: the headteacher

Frequency: will be produced annually (also annual report on progress)

In the Standards in Scotland's Schools etc. Act 2000, school education has been expanded to mean not only primary and secondary education and where necessary special education, but also nursery education as defined for 3- and 4-year-olds. The responsibilities of local authorities for post-school education are limited to areas such as adult basic education and the provision of a range of opportunities in an informal, community setting. These are carried out in liaison with Communities Scotland and further education colleges, universities and voluntary bodies.

Councils, (usually referred to as authorities) have a range of responsibilities and powers which can be seen as supportive of the main duty of ensuring the provision of adequate and efficient school education. Thus they must maintain a psychological service, collaborate with parents in the recording of special educational needs, provide school catering at least for those entitled to free meals, issue grants to poorer families for school clothing and footwear and arrange for the provision of school transport where children have relatively long journeys to school. They also have, under section 69 of the Local Government (Scotland) Act 1973, a fairly general power to take action which can be legitimately seen as supportive of their statutory responsibilities.

As well as the detailed elements within the Standards in Scotland's Schools etc. Act 2000, there was increased emphasis on taking account of views. Education authorities must have due regard to the views of the child or young person in decisions that significantly affect them. Beyond that general principle from section 2 of the 2000 Act, there are other specific situations where the education authority or the school is required to consult pupils carefully. These are in relation to the education improvement objectives and the school development plan. Such consultation should also include staff and the full parent body.

The phrasing quoted above from the 1980 Act suggests a Scottish tradition of statutory responsibilities set out in very general terms. The requirement to arrange free school transport is often quoted as one of the exceptions to this as it is particularly precise although amended in Education Scotland Act 1996 to facilitate provision on grounds of safety. The School Boards (Scotland) Act 1988 is also extremely prescriptive regarding the present establishment and operation of school boards. It presents a statute which has contributed to a very institutional form of parental participation through these bodies. The Self-Governing Schools etc. (Scotland) Act 1989 amended the 1980 Act and prescription reached the stage of a statutory requirement to advertise nationally the first promotion opportunity for teachers, that is principal teacher posts, a level of detailed involvement unparalleled in other public services.

School education operates within a system of local governance increasingly covering a number of public agencies not merely local authorities. Through community planning, liaison will be of crucial importance with: Communities Scotland; Scottish Enterprise; Careers Scotland; FE colleges; universities; voluntary sector; Youth Scotland; Sportscotland; Arts Council. A number of responsibilities of the these bodies previously rested with local authorities. The tendency to remove responsibilities from local authorities matches the increasing trend to prescribe how local authorities should undertake their duties.

The Education (Scotland) Act 1981 set out the framework in great detail how special educational needs should be assessed and provided for. The process of assessing special educational needs has sometimes got in the way of the resourcing and the provision. It is recognised that this is ripe for reform but there has been considerable difficulty in reaching agreement between parent groups and local authorities regarding the best way to proceed. In addition to the main education legislation in the period 1988 to 2000 there has been considerable other legislation which education authorities have to consider carefully. These are listed in the appendix to this chapter.

DEVOLUTION

In considering the impact of devolution on the local governance of education, it is important to remember that there were three principal imperatives, viz: 1. the requirement to scrutinise Scottish government more precisely; 2. the need to increase the capacity for debate and policy-making; 3. resources to update Scottish legislation more expeditiously.

While the nature of the policy debate and the legislative process has been closely observed, it can be argued that increased scrutiny particularly by the Parliament, was the most necessary and perhaps the most successful change. Scotland has gone from being the least scrutinised part of UK government, to among the most transparent and carefully observed. The new constitutional settlement sought to establish scrutiny, policy debate and law making in an open and inclusive way. As the Scottish Parliament is a single chamber with no revising opportunities, scrutiny at the law making stage is vital. Thus pre-legislative scrutiny was introduced and debate entered with civic Scotland. Education's first experience of pre-legislative scrutiny was impressive and widely welcomed. There was genuine debate to prepare legislation and make an effective contribution to school improvement and to enhance the rights and entitlement of each school student. The outcome of the consultation process was thoroughly reported and the parliamentary committee took evidence from a wide range of sources. This process worked well on the big ideas but was perhaps less successful in the nitty gritty of legislative detail. The process did lead to strong support for an inclusive and unequivocal statement of the right of each child to school education.

This has been followed up by the publication of the National Priorities. These are:

- to raise standards of educational attainment for all schools, especially in the core skills of literacy and numeracy and to achieve better results in national measures of achievement, including exam results;
- to support and develop the skills of teachers, the self-discipline of pupils and to enhance school environments so that they are conducive to learning and teaching;
- to promote equality and help every pupil benefit from education, with particular regard paid to pupils with disabilities and special educational needs, and to Gaelic and other lesser-used languages;
- to work with parents to teach pupils respect for self and one another and their interdependence with other members in their neighbourhood and society and teach them the duties and responsibilities of citizenship in the democratic society;
- to equip pupils with the foundation skills, attitudes and expectations necessary to prosper in a changing society and to encourage creativity and ambition.

These National Priorities were generally welcomed and seen as a reasonable attempt to begin discussion of the definition of education beyond a narrow attainment agenda. It could be argued that National Priority 2 is a different type of priority, a condition of success rather than an objective but they present a helpful starting point. The process of turning these National Priorities into outcomes and targets is altogether more problematic and has at times illustrated a continuing commitment to managerial control from the centre.

Before leaving the issue of devolution it is relevant to mention the crisis of confidence arising from the difficulties with the processing of data by the Scottish Qualifications Authority in the school examination diet of 2000. This illustrated the dangers in the Scottish model of policy development where consultation leads to systems becoming ever more complex and when there is dependence on a single examination authority delivering a template designed by Her Majesty's Inspectorate. The new status for HMIE as an agency concentrating solely on inspection and advice would probably have occurred without the challenge to our complacency in 2000 but these events probably brought that change forward. There were several enquiries into the difficulties. The Education, Culture and Sport Committee held open, lengthy and detailed investigations. Their conduct was rigorous and impressive. If the crisis had happened prior to devolution, the Scottish Select Committee may have set some time aside but would probably have heard only from SQA, senior Scottish civil servants, a minister and the Senior Chief HMI. Post-devolution, the committee took evidence from a wide range of professional and political groups and also, crucially, from parents and students. The openness of the committee system that will take evidence in public and then weigh the quality and wisdom of this openly is considerable progress.

UNITARY COUNCILS

Local government in Scotland was reorganised with effect from 1 April 1996. The reorganisation involved no change in the three Island areas where unitary authorities had been established twenty years before. However, in mainland Scotland, twenty-nine new unitary authorities assumed responsibility for all local government functions. These twenty-nine thus replaced the nine regional councils, which had previously been responsible for education, and fifty-three district councils. Four of the new councils have the same boundaries as the predecessor regions. These include the three smallest in population terms – Borders, Dumfries and Galloway and Highland – as well as Fife. Central, Grampian and Tayside regions were each divided into three new authorities; Lothian into four and Strathclyde into twelve.

Thus, in about one-sixth of Scotland, the reorganisation necessitated only a fairly limited change so far as education was concerned. In the remainder of the country, existing large services had to be divided into much smaller organisations. The complexities of change were not as great as in the case of former district services, at least in some instances. No new authority took over educational responsibilities from more than one predecessor regional council. By contrast, services were often acquired from two, three or even four predecessor districts. The removal of certain powers and duties from local authorities and the introduction of unitary councils was an attempt to reduce the influence of councils as they had been perceived by the government as resistant to change. The suspicion was that the government wished major public services such as education to operate to a national system, locally administered.

Such suspicion did not go away with the election of a Labour government in 1997. Tensions are still being played out since the introduction of devolution and the desire of either the Parliament or the ministers to take more direct action. The first impact of the introduction of unitary councils was immediate budget pressures for certain councils, exacerbating reduced levels of funding which had deteriorated over the previous fifteen years. It appeared initially that the only diversity was for each council to follow the same guidance but with significantly different levels of resources. It was no longer statutory for each council to have a specific director of education although initially all thirty-two councils had a chief officer clearly identified as fulfilling that role. Six years on, the position is more mixed and many directors have additional responsibilities, usually either for some or all aspects of social work or leisure and recreation. Others have a clearly defined executive director role in a very small management team.

Nevertheless all chief officers currently leading education services in whatever role in each of the thirty-two councils come from an education service background. An exception to this was Perth and Kinross where education and children's services were for a brief time led by a chief officer with a social work background. Given the on-going financial pressures and the need to keep the service lean and enabling, further rationalisation of director and heads of service posts is likely.

COUNCIL STYLE/RELATIONS BETWEEN OFFICIALS AND ELECTED MEMBERS

There are numerous layers of accountability for local authorities in post devolution Scotland;

- as upholders of the rights of children;
- as providers for parents as consumers and as school board members;
- as service providers to schools who enjoy devolved school management by statute;
- as part of community planning within the general power of community initiative.

It is within this complex context that the chief officer with responsibility for education is accountable within the local government structure to the council executive or designated committee. The chief officer remains very significant and can influence the content and style of education service management locally to a considerable extent. The skills required, however, are more subtle or at least different from those apparent in regional Directors of Education. Moreover it remains the case that individual elected members cannot instruct officers. Only the council, through executive cabinet or committee to which it has delegated decision making powers has this capacity. Instructions which are given, are to the director who remains responsible for how they are carried out and can delegate tasks while retaining the line of responsibility and accountability.

There has been considerable consultation on best practice in forms of local government management, with initial advice following the 1994 Local Government Act and further reports: Scottish Office (1999), Scottish Executive Development Department (2000). The emphasis has been on streamlining local government accountability and challenging elected members to concentrate on strategy and scrutiny. At the time of the creation of unitary councils it was a reasonable generalisation to suggest that district councils had a closer working relationship with officers and more involvement in operational or day to day matters. Regions, not least as a consequence of size and function, had adapted to strategic guidance and intervention. Consequently, unitary councils have a wide range of political accountability styles dependent on their provenance. Cabinet-style executives have been introduced in, for example, East Renfrewshire and Edinburgh. Councils such as Stirling and Fife have a small number of cross-cutting policy committees while the committee structure elsewhere remains traditional, complete with a considerable number of sub-committees. In line with the committee structure, the range of delegation to chief officers also varies considerably, as does the amount of member involvement in, for example, responses to technical papers from Scottish Executive Education Department, GTCS or other national education bodies.

Within regional councils, education departments were never particularly comfortable within corporate management structures. Within these large organisations corporate management often seemed to exist for its own sake emphasising policy issues which appeared to have little impact in communities. Corporate management since reorganisation has been much more focused on co-ordinated working and service delivery. In these circumstances education services are more fully engaged although as noted below the relationship between the council and schools remains ambiguous. In providing the detailed guidance of implementing a political strategy such as the establishment of a children's service or a corporate commitment to social inclusion, officers have considerable influence in policy development although, of course, in theory members make policy. As with the decision-making structure and schemes of delegation, there is wide variety. Some members have strategic vision and are comfortable as policy makers, many others are much happier functioning solely as an advocate for constituent interest. At the level of the individual service, policy tends to originate as a political idea but in terms of action is designed by officers, frequently in response to government initiatives, with members functioning in an ombudsman role. The one area of progress for members in recent years is a realisation that scrutiny is an important function and can lead to considerable influence. The 1990s was a difficult time to be a councillor in Scotland as most had not come into public life to decide on an annual basis which service should be cut, nor did they see their function as merely to administer the latest government initiative. Add to that the fact that the workload of elected members increased considerably in 1996 with the reduction in the number of councillors in Scotland from 1,611 to 1,216.

RELATIONS WITH STAKE HOLDERS

Children and Young People

There has been a considerable increase in good practice with regard to consulting and listening to and valuing young people's views. There is formal reference to this within the Standards in Schools etc. Act 2000. In addition, most secondary schools in Scotland have pupil councils and in many authorities pupil councils are now also a key feature in primary schools. This is supported by authority-wide discussions in various youth forums and young persons' representation on working groups and even council committees. Young people are given the opportunity to influence and take responsibility for their day-to-day environment and schools are beginning to take their views into account with regard to timetabling and, at a very general level, appointment procedures. Such activity is supported nationally through the publication on citizenship by Learning and Teaching Scotland and the work of the Schools Ethos Network and the Anti-Bullying Network.

Parents

Parental involvement can be viewed as a straightforward hierarchy. Firstly, all parents should be encouraged to take an interest in their child's learning and schools should make efforts to ensure that activities between the home and school are complementary. Secondly, parents should be encouraged to support the school in a general way, to comment on policies, to lobby and participate and, from time to time, to fund-raise. Thirdly, parents should be recognised as co-educators and the work between home and school operated as a seamless partnership. In this way, achievement can be maximised and the welfare of the child taken fully into account. In addition to a general commitment to partnership there is a clear commitment to parental rights. That children should be educated in accordance with the wishes of their parents has been translated into full engagement with parents if their child has special educational needs and into choice of school. These were set out in the Education (Scotland) Act 1981.

The aspects of the 1981 Act dealing with choice of school have been fairly significant with regard to school effectiveness, particularly in urban areas. Parents are not bound to use their local school but have the right to put in a placing request to the school of their choice. Choice is, however, limited, as popular schools fill up. Choice is also limited by isolation or cost of transport. Amendments to the placing request legislation were contained in the Education (Scotland) Act 1995 as well as in the Act of 2000 enable authorities to reserve some places for expected population changes within the catchment area.

In most cases, however, an authority would have to demonstrate that enrolling the additional child would require significant, otherwise avoidable public expenditure, normally in the form of an additional teacher or extra accommodation. In practice, some 90% of placing requests are granted. The legislation has enabled consumer choice for a substantial minority of Scottish families. The choice is often made on social grounds on the basis of seeking effective peer group influences. Thus there has been a drift away from schools in areas of deprivation to schools in suburbs or small towns on the edge of cities.

Another form of parental right was the School Boards (Scotland) Act 1988 which sought to involve parents to a modest extent in the management of schools. The Standards in Scotland's Schools etc. Act 2000 redefined school board involvement in the appointment of senior staff, giving final say in a leet to the local authority. School boards were also given the general duty to assist the headteacher in raising standards. The boards also have always had the right to seek additional powers but few have pursued that option. Given the over-prescriptive nature of the initial legislation, boards from time to time become entangled in a bureaucracy and some, including other major parent bodies, have argued that school boards can inhibit rather than enhance parental involvement. There is currently a national review.

At the time of consultation on the 2000 Act, the Convention of Scottish Local Authorities and the Association of Directors of Education in Scotland argued that there should be a full overhaul of school board legislation. The level of bureaucracy arising as a direct result of the 1989 legislation seemed disproportionate to the influence available to school boards. Schools should be empowered to establish more radical forms of participation for parents. Parental involvement could be expressed as a general duty on local authorities and schools and if they can demonstrate support for models which make participation easier, then school boards should be unnecessary. In other words it was argued that school boards should be the default position if parent participation is not being given full expression (see Chapter 19).

Headteachers

The efficient management of the education service is critically dependent upon the relationship between senior officers of the authority and headteachers. That relationship has become ambiguous particularly with regard to lines of accountability. As opposed to England and Wales, headteachers are employed by local authorities and responsible for carrying out the duties of authorities as defined in the 2000 Act. Headteachers, however, are appointed by an appointment committee made up of equal numbers from the school board and the authority. Thus the headteacher is employed by the authority but not appointed directly by them.

Headteachers are managed by a Director of Education or Head of Schools but have a varying degree of independence for the day-to-day management of the school within the scheme of devolved school management which was given statutory backing in the 2000 Act. This is supported by an insistence on each school having a school development plan. A Scottish Executive review of devolved school management suggested that the picture varied widely across the country (*Review of Devolved School Management*, SEED, 2001). In some parts of the country there was a lack of headteacher confidence and in others, schemes were narrow, limited and contained considerable amounts of notional devolution. Devolved school management has been successful with regard to headteacher involvement in all appointments and in efficient and effective use of resources. There has, however, been little evidence of using even such powers of virement as exist, or of strategic budgeting over a number of years. Headteachers leading effective schools often argue that there remains far too much constraint and, even in authorities where there is considerable delegation and freedom, national resources come in ring-fenced forms with HMIE seeking evidence in tightly specified forms (see SEED Support Packs for National Priorities in Education, 2002).

The ambiguity about the role of the headteacher became clear during discussions on revising teachers' conditions of service for the twenty-first century, following the report by Gavin McCrone. The EIS, as Scotland's largest teaching union, continues to argue that headteachers are merely the leading teacher in a school, while local authorities seek to stress their crucial management role and responsibility for very significant budgets. Headteacher Associations remain disenchanted because they are not directly represented on the Scottish Negotiating Committee for Teachers (SNCT) which replaced the Scottish Joint Negotiating Committee (Teachers Side School Education) – SJNC (TSSE). They are however represented on the General Teachers' Panel. The main teachers' trade unions would argue that the numbers in the headteacher groups do not justify their place on SNCT. In strict trade union terms this is correct, and it should be noted that local authority representatives on the SNCT are elected members, not chief officers some of whom provide support solely in an advisory capacity. It is however clear that headteachers should be involved in the detailed national negotiations but probably through recognition of their important management role and thus should be involved in the group advising elected members along with directors and heads of service. These tensions are reflected in the McCrone Agreement (SEED, 2001) some of which has not been phrased to give full recognition to the importance of the headteacher as school manager and leader. The headteacher is accountable to the council through the chief officer responsible for education and responsible for the quality of teaching and learning in schools. On the other hand the education service is accountable to the headteacher for the quality of support services on offer. The authority, within an enhanced quality assurance role, seeks to support the school but also to challenge; while headteachers, when local authorities are inspected by HMIE, can assist in the evaluation of the support provided. The relationship is thus not a straightforward line management one, but involves a degree of inter-dependence and mutual respect. There are aspects which clearly require further clarification.

Teachers

The agreement reached in January 2001 would have benefited from more careful and considered editing. Indeed, the enthusiasm to conclude an agreement was so great once the general principles had been agreed, that final progress was dependent on ambiguity. Consequently the first phase of the complex change in teachers' pay and conditions of service changes has been marked by a search for meaning. Discussions had centred around legitimate trade union concerns about workload and morale and management desire for flexibility and diversity. In pursuit of diversity there should have been common cause to enhance the opportunities for teachers to exercise independent professional judgement and to pull back from the sometimes excessive detail inherent in managerial forms of accountability. The difficulty was that the agreement reached (SJNC (TSSE) SE40) in 1987 institutionalised a lack of trust and tightly defined conditions of service which included precisely demarcated time zones in an anti-professional way. By 2003 there has been significant progress, but in many parts of the country there remains insufficient trust or independent professional judgement prepared to be held to account.

There was, perhaps, a lack of strategic management of change and all attention focused on detail. However, the opportunity was created to build on outstanding teacher professionalism in Scotland through:

- a contractual commitment by each teacher to continuing professional development;
- a structure of standards and benchmarks from initial teacher education through standard for full registration to standards for chartered teachers and headship;
- enhanced and high quality induction/probation arrangements the detail of which require refining if the national guarantee is to be sustainable;
- the avoidance of top down solutions such as performance related pay;
- a system whereby classroom teachers can obtain realistic salaries without seeking managerial responsibilities by entering the chartered teachers programme.

In addition it has been helpful that collective bargaining in an open and transparent way has been moved to the centre of school organisation. Issues regarding teacher availability during the working week and accountability for time remain less resolved. Too often teachers felt criticisms of their professionalism were merely slogans to lengthen the working week. It is, nevertheless, reasonable to presume that, at times of harmonious industrial relations teachers can make individual decisions regarding their contribution to the whole life of the school, in areas such as sports, arts and culture and regarding the level and speed with which individual classes get feedback following marking.

It is also the case that a full debate regarding an appropriate and collegiate management structure for a twenty-first century school has yet to take place. A further trend to be noted in Scottish schools is the increasing range of staff. This has come about through government initiatives such as alternatives to exclusion and classroom assistants. Additional resources of some £50m for support staff by the third year of the settlement (2003–4) were also earmarked within the settlement on teachers' conditions of service. In many authorities the increased range of staff is taken further through New Community Schools activity and with the recognition that raising achievement can take twenty-four hours a day and cannot be achieved by teachers alone. Sustaining the nurture and progress of a child involves close working with the family and for many communities further progress depends on close working among education, community services, health and social work.

PUBLIC PRIVATE PARTNERSHIP

Fortunately this chapter is not the occasion to evaluate the macro-economics of the private finance initiative (PFI) and the impact on the public sector borrowing requirement. It is nevertheless worth noting the enormous impact on school estate through this means initially in Falkirk and Glasgow followed by other authorities, and then a massive £1.1bn announced in 2002 with further resources allocated in March 2003. Issues associated with PFI contracts are covered in the Accounts Commission publication *Taking the Initiative, Using PFI Contracts to Renew Council Schools*, published 12 June 2002. Some of the benefits identified included:

- a clear focus on service with comprehensive, detailed and output focused contracts;
- in the larger projects, fresh thinking about the basic configuration of project schools (Edinburgh and Glasgow);
- competition which enabled education services to concentrate on matters of learning and teaching and to seek to realise a set of ideas;
- enhanced partnership by avoiding renegotiations arising from cost problems and delays.

Issues still to be examined include the impact on the service when a number of schools have their facilities privately managed and the rest do not; and the changing pattern of facilities management involving public sector unions. This latter issue sits in the context of considerable change in direct service organisations as the transition from compulsory competitive tendering to the best value regime is completed.

THE KEY ISSUES

The most significant issue regarding the local governance of education remains the future role of local authorities in the management of school education. This can be set in the context of on-going tensions between local authorities and the Scottish Parliament as increasing amounts of guidance, some with force of statute, are issued and funding is ringfenced and tightly specified. Some believe that local authorities should merely administer a national system while others support the view that there is a need for an alternative policy voice which supports and challenges schools and creates the capacity for creativity and diversity.

The last Conservative government sought to create market-place solutions to encourage efficiency and promote higher standards. In private transactions, competition can operate to the consumers benefit. However, in the absence of a transparent price to each family for a place at a school, and without competition in many parts of Scotland, the search for a market has merely spawned stifling efforts to quantify and compare performance. More-over, education remains a common good, the overall quality of which matters to all of us in a way in which the purchase of white goods by individuals does not. Management in schools and local government can and has learned from the private sector. It is, however, a mistake to model leadership in the public sector solely on the managerial practice of the private sector. Effective management does require analysis of specific purposes, conditions and tasks. Business concepts such as strategy, performance management, quality control and marketing can have their value for a public institution such as a school but the meaning must vary. The challenge to manage schools is to relate this discipline to its unique purpose, conditions and tasks. The weakness of much current management thinking and the use of misleading language is a failure to take account of the distinct characteristics of public service. In the public domain, judgement among priorities is required because objectives, interest and values can conflict and need to be balanced.

In policy terms the case for local authority leadership or co-leadership of education in the twenty-first century is based on:

- linking community schools to community planning;
- social inclusion, not least through effective integration of services for children;
- local democracy through participatory mechanisms and schools as democratic institutions; training for citizenship;
- sustainability, both through active citizenship and environmental awareness.

In considering these roles of an education authority, reflection is required as to whether a national framework rigidly established would achieve as much. The evidence suggests otherwise. Success in raising standards, in looking at the interests of the whole child has come through local initiatives. The 2000 Act has assisted in clarifying who does what. If local authorities are clear about their role in education and give it full importance, their future involvement is secure. Given a very difficult ten-year period, however, there are issues about confidence, recognising the successful, avoiding complacency and, indeed succession planning. A key role for the local authority is entirely compatible with an extension of devolved school management. The authority would be well placed to provide a challenge and support role proportionate to need and to take account of the full range of a school's contribution to a community covering issues relating to social justice as well as achievement. Thus it is appropriate for the government to continue to emphasise integrated service delivery and co-ordinated policy and strategic planning (see Scottish Executive, 2001).

Nixon (2001) has identified key links between the development of New Community Schools in parts of Scotland with research in the United States on school practice engaging with community and democratic renewal. He challenged the assumption that an improved link between inter-agency provision and community provision was of itself sufficient. He wrote:

> this paper challenges that assumption and argues that there are serious difficulties in attempting to collapse a potentially radical agenda into a mildly progressive agenda emphasising co-ordinated service provision and professional collaboration. New Community Schools have the potential for multi-professional work to re-state the principles of the Scottish comprehensive tradition. Schools have to, however, consider the democratic way in which they operate and how democratic schools engage effectively with their local community. Thus local authorities can assist schools to enable each pupil to live their life to the full, to be stretched to full capacity and with society realising its collective potential.

At the end of his paper on New Community Schooling in Scotland, Nixon makes some general conclusions: 'without the backing of the statutory powers invested in the local authority the project (New Community Schools in Stirling) we are studying would be unsupportable . . . without a continuing commitment to enablement and negotiation by that local authority in exercise of its power the project would be unsustainable' (Nixon, 2001).

Given the continuing uncertainty within political quarters regarding the role of local authority management of schools this point is crucial. Equitable settlements across the wide variety of local interests that children's needs require would be unthinkable without local governmental authority (and increasingly within the context of community planning). The task for the local authority, however, is not to exercise power but to exercise authority through the sharing of power.

It was striking when considering the evidence to the Education, Culture and Sport Committee (June 2002) regarding the purposes of education in Scotland to note the commonality among evidence from parents, unions, directors and students that the obsessive emphasis on the school improvement agenda, league tables, targets and attainment required to be counter-balanced. Systems, structures and data can and have assisted, indeed are essential, but when delivering the common good of education, public services for children or support for teachers as creative professionals, there is a need to ensure reflection on values, attitudes and relationships. There is scope for new models of change that go beyond the work on school effectiveness. Increasingly, schools need to understand that their own effectiveness is dependent on the effectiveness of civil society as a whole. Schools need to develop practices and structures to square up to that understanding. They must play a full part in the pattern of local governance providing services to meet the needs of all children in an holistic, integrated and co-ordinated way.

On the basis of the above agenda, local authorities can remain crucial to enhancing services support for children. There is however a need to strengthen the capacity to make available best practice on education policy matters. More joint work across council boundaries has to be encouraged. There is a need for an alternative voice to the Executive regarding policy and it is insufficient for this voice to be developed solely in the universities and in the voluntary sector. There should be increasing investment by local authorities, perhaps via COSLA, in leading, developing and improving education policy. Failure to do this leaves local authorities open to the accusation of merely administering education. In addition as the pattern of inspections of local authorities moves forward there is a need to think about the ways in which local authorities support each other. It is not a competition. It is not a league table. If there is an area where assistance can be provided local authorities should be structured to give that assistance and to function as an improvement agency.

Bob Downes, director of BT Scotland, kicked off a CBI contribution to the education national debate with a reference to Arthur Herman's book *The Scottish Enlightenment: The Scots Invention of the Modern World* (London: Fourth Estate, 2002) praising the merchants' commitment to well-rounded education and the high standards achieved in the eighteenth century. This was, of course, before mass production capitalism in the nineteenth century which changed the needs of the market place. Perhaps the most encouraging sign to emerge from the national debate is that the needs of the economy and the benefits of a liberal education can coincide and provide an effective driving force for change.

APPENDIX

The Human Rights Act 1988
Regulation of Care 2001
Ethical Standards in Public Life etc. (Scotland) Act 2000
Data Protection Act 1998
Draft Data Protection (Miscellaneous Subject *Access Exemptions*) Order 2000
Race Relations Act 1976, as amended by the Race Relations (Amendment) Act 2000
Disability Discrimination Act 1995, as amended by the Special Educational Needs and
    Disability Act 2001
Education (Disability Strategies and Pupils' Educational Record) (Scotland) Act 2002
Freedom of Information Act 2000
The Education (School and Placing Information) (Scotland) Amendment Regulations 2000
    – updating information to be in handbooks to take account of SQA and Higher Still
The Education (Provision of Information as to Schools) (Scotland) Amendment Regula-
    tions 2000 – exam pass rates no longer need to be provided to Scottish ministers; schools
    to provide information on staying-on rates
The Education (Assisted Places) (Scotland) Amendment Regulations 2000 – adjusts the
    level of parental income required to qualify

The Children (Protection at Work) (Scotland) Regulations 2000 – updates previous legislation

Added to the above will be an average of 250 principal pieces of correspondence, advice or accountability / audit trails from Scottish Executive Education Department to local authorities per year.

REFERENCES

Nixon, J. (2001) Education renewal as democratic practice: 'new' community schools in Scotland, *International Journal of Inclusive Education*, 5. (4), 329–52.

SEED (2001) *A Teaching Profession for the 21st Century. Agreement reached following recommendations made in the McCrone Report*, Edinburgh: SEED.

Scottish Executive (2000) Standards in Scotland's Schools etc. Act 2000, Edinburgh: Scottish Executive.

SEDD (2000) *Renewing Local Democracy: You should be . . . taking part . . . getting involved . . . making a difference*, Report of the Local Democracy Working Group, chaired by Richard Kerley, Edinburgh: SEDD.

Scottish Executive (2001) *For Scotland's Children*, Edinburgh: Scottish Executive.

Scottish Office (1999) *Moving Forward: Local Government and the Scottish Parliament*. Report of the Commission on Local Government and the Scottish Parliament (The McIntosh Report), Edinburgh: The Stationery Office.

17

Educational Development Services

Alison Cameron

Educational development services in Scottish local authorities have gone through various metamorphoses since they began to emerge in the 1960s, and at the time of writing, are still shape-shifting. Variously named advisory, educational development, educational support, quality development and quality support services (the list is not exhaustive), a new breed of quality improvement officers is waiting in the wings to 'support and challenge schools in a context of continuous improvement'.

Advisers, to use the most generic and least acronym-ridden (if somewhat old-fashioned) term, have traditionally occupied a middle ground in the business of delivering an education service at local authority level, and may be described as neither fish nor fowl: that is to say, involved neither in direct delivery of education, nor in the direct management of schools. Instead, they have operated in a support and development capacity, most obviously supporting schools, and perhaps less obviously, supporting directorate teams. Inevitably, operating in this middle ground has its difficulties and its ambiguities. It also has some surprising strengths: arguably, it has been the finely-honed chameleon tendencies and preparedness of advisers to deal in both camps which has enabled the survival of something akin to a development service in most authorities, even in the wake of local government reorganisation in 1996. Regarding themselves first and foremost as teachers whilst understanding the processes of the centre, acting as buffers and advocates for both sides, they have proved to be worth retaining even in the face of financial constraints.

While it is the business of this chapter to attempt to describe the role of educational development services in Scotland from early days to the present, it is as well to flag up from the outset that the picture will not be clear-cut, and that it is set to change significantly. The Standards in Scotland's Schools etc. Act 2000 made the duty of education authorities to 'challenge and support' schools quite unequivocal, and lent urgency to ensuring that advisory staff, traditionally comfortable with 'support', became equally adept at 'challenge'. Further, in the aftermath of the McCrone Report which set its sights on producing 'A Teaching Profession for the 21st Century', steps were taken to disabuse advisory staff of their commonly-held view of themselves as 'teachers first'. The pay and conditions settlement which emerged for advisers broke the (*de facto* if not *de jure*) link with teachers' pay, heralded a new spinal pay structure subject to job evaluation, and stipulated that advisers (or their equivalents) would be known as quality improvement officers with effect from August 2002.

EMERGENCE OF EDUCATIONAL DEVELOPMENT SERVICES

While there has never been uniformity in the shape of advisory/development services across Scottish authorities, snapshots of provision as developed in response to changing circumstances over the last four decades may help with an appreciation of current issues and concerns.

Throughout the 1960s, specialists in 'practical' subjects (Physical Education, Technical Education, and Music) were increasingly employed to organise swimming venues, sports fixtures, concerts, or the deployment of specialist equipment across the authority. These 'organisers' also had a responsibility for health and safety issues, and had a major say in the appointment of staff in schools. With substantial resources at their disposal, they were regarded by staff in schools as fairly influential figures.

It was not until the early 1970s, however, that the need became apparent for subject specialists to be appointed at local level in other 'non-practical' subjects, for the purposes of curricular and staff development. The introduction of the Primary Memorandum (1965) had heralded major changes in the curriculum and in teaching approaches; at secondary level there was the development of 'O' Grade and the raising of the school leaving age. Teachers in schools needed support and advice to help them negotiate their way through new curricula and respond to a different set of demands. Staff tutors and advisers, usually effective and innovative principal teachers, were appointed to develop the subjects being introduced, and at secondary level the advisory service gradually came to replicate the departmental structure in schools. Primary advisers, often drawn from the ranks of primary headteachers, fulfilled a more generalist function, able by dint of their previous experience to provide not only curriculum and staff development, but also management advice to their former colleagues.

By the mid-to-late-1980s, advisory services were probably at the height of their power. Dependent on size, local authorities could count on fairly complete cohorts, with teams of primary and secondary advisers, and at least one special needs and pre-five adviser. In Strathclyde, the largest of the authorities, each of the six sub-regional divisions replicated this pattern. This meant that there was potential across Scotland for cross-fertilisation of ideas and good practice, and national committees of advisers were formed to act as support networks and to influence the development of the curriculum. At local level, advisers had a fair degree of control over the allocation of resources. By and large, their support was welcomed (if not always uncritically) by teachers struggling to survive the onslaught of continual curricular change. Within local authorities, furthermore, a career structure was beginning to emerge. An adviser might graduate to a post as sector or senior adviser within the service, be promoted into the directorate, join Her Majesty's Inspectorate or alternatively, return to school as head or depute head. Despite niggles to do with individual personalities not pulling their weight, or having lost touch with the reality of the classroom, advisers were generally valued as useful intermediaries between education authority and schools. Behind the scenes, they may have been oiling the wheels of the educational bureaucracy locally and nationally, but out in schools, they were seen as counsellors, subject (or sector) leaders and (essentially) as friends.

In the 1990s, however, external influences began to impact on the provision of this service within local authorities. It became clear that any support delivered 'free' from the centre would be viewed more critically once resources were delegated to schools. To survive, a less 'ad hoc' and more accountable service would be required.

The example of Strathclyde, where a major restructuring of the advisory service took place in the early 1990s, illustrates this trend. While the restructuring appeared at the time to be largely to do with nomenclature – the educational development service replaced the old advisory service – the move was an attempt to make the service more flexible and responsive. Reflecting the realisation that the pace of educational change demanded a continuous transfusion of new blood into the service, a substantial budget was made available for the secondment of practising teachers to supplement the existing permanent cohort of staff. And in response to the directorate's requirement for ready access to expertise on a range of policy matters, a clutch of regional advisers was appointed to lead on cross-curricular issues such as special educational needs, health education, guidance, religious education, outdoors education, the arts, education-industry links and the European dimension.

If the first restructuring within Strathclyde Region had been mainly about managing an increasingly complex service more efficiently, the second, which took place in 1993, was an attempt to impose the principles of the market economy, and carried with it even more radical and painful implications. Instead of accessing help when and as they wished, schools started the year with an allowance of credits, which they could 'spend' on the purchase of services – centralised or in-house staff development, curriculum development, management consultancy – delivered by members of the development service. This transfer of development staff salaries to schools may have been notional (no money changed hands) but the conceptual shift it carried with it was profound. For the first time, there was a sense that schools paid the piper and could therefore expect to call the tune. The shift of emphasis was reinforced by the establishment of the title of educational development officer as the generic term for a member of the educational development service. The days of 'advisers' dispensing expertise and largesse as the need arose were waning fast.

There were several serious purposes behind the restructuring within Strathclyde Region, however unpopular it may have been. First, it tried to resolve a tension inherent in every local authority advisory service, namely that of reconciling the adviser's responsibilities to schools with the vying demands of the administrative centre. The notional transfer of funds was designed to make it clear that the prime task of an adviser was school-based. Second, it attempted to make service provision to schools more equitable, ensuring that every establishment was able to gain access to the resource on offer, and encouraging less proactive establishments to take advantage of this and to be more discriminating in their use of it. Third, however, and most significantly, it attempted to preserve a service which was in danger of disappearing altogether, by applying some reality therapy as part of a hard message: advisers/development officers were not there as of right, and would not continue to exist unless their services were perceived as valuable by schools and centres. The precedent had already been set south of the border, where the influence of local authorities (and the services they offered) had radically diminished with the delegation of financial management to schools. This was in fact part of a wider movement which would affect not only service delivery mechanisms but the nature of the service to be delivered. The move mirrored the changes in the funding of the teacher education institutions (TEIs) in relation to the specific grant made available from central government for the provision of in-service training for teachers. The substantial proportion of this grant previously ringfenced to the TEIs had been transferred to authorities in a phased arrangement which gave staff in the TEIs a chance to adapt to meeting the needs of clients, and to compete in the market place along with other providers.

In the same way, members of the advisory/development services were required to adapt to a changing economic climate and to some unpalatable truths. The distress evident in long-serving and even recently appointed advisers to the change in title from adviser to educational development officer bore witness to the fact that the old title carried a prestige and a status which the new term did not. Losing the title seemed like a demotion. Similarly, the idea that development services had a cash value attached to them was a major culture shock to both advisers and schools. It offended the then prevalent view that education should be removed from such considerations, it disturbed the established client/provider relationship, and it imposed a bureaucracy (as well as a certain rigour) in which few could see any advantage. Yet although the 1993 Strathclyde restructuring may have stemmed from financial imperatives, in retrospect it may be seen to have set in motion a necessary transition from an unwieldy, permanent, secondary-dominated, subject-focused service to a more flexible and needs-related model.

In most of the authorities to be substantially affected by reorganisation, in fact, steps had been taken to rationalise provision prior to 1996. While the break-up of the regional structures offered the opportunity to rewrite history missing out this last distasteful chapter (the changes had by no means bedded down), the enormous disruption to existing patterns allied to competing political considerations and funding cuts meant that in some cases educational development services virtually disappeared.

IMPACT OF LOCAL GOVERNMENT REORGANISATION (1996)

Local government reorganisation in April 1996 created thirty-two unitary authorities where in terms of educational provision there had previously been twelve local providers: nine regional and three island authorities. The implications for educational development services were profound. However unwieldy the regions had been in terms of size and geographical diversity – Strathclyde Region alone covered half of Scotland in terms of population – economies of scale had compensated for a certain lack of sensitivity to local need. Further, the very diversity in terms of socio-economic profile, geography and scale of regions such as Grampian, Lothian and Strathclyde had meant that resources could be dispensed more equitably across pockets of affluence and ghettos of deprivation. Given the cost of reorganisation as it impinged at every level and in every area of local government, any services which were non-statutory were going to be regarded as standing on extremely shaky ground. Even where the political will existed, the smaller unitary authorities simply could not afford to provide such services. And, at the very point where co-operation and a sharing of resources might have been sensible, there was an equal and opposite pressure to 'go it alone'. When the dust settled, a very uneven picture emerged across Scotland in terms of support services. Factors of geography, size, past history, funding base and political will influenced whether and/or in what degree a development service as such was built into the new structures. The unitary authorities may have been new, but their coats had to be cut from old cloth, and at least initially, the individuals 'disaggregated' from their regional base to their chosen unitary authority determined the type and function of the service on offer.

The results of a survey carried out by the Association of Educational Advisers in Scotland (AEAS) in August 1997 provide some sense of the pattern which emerged. Highland Council, less affected by reorganisation, had retained a large advisory team with subject specific remits, as had Glasgow and North Lanarkshire, where advisers offered curricular support in their subject specialism, had a functional responsibility within the authority, and had a pastoral role with regard to schools. In stark contrast, certain of the smaller authorities, such as Aberdeenshire, Moray and Midlothian, had no educational development service staff as such. In Aberdeenshire, development work was taken forward by Curriculum Networks made up of practitioners in schools, and facilitated by education officers who were not themselves subject specialists but who acted as lead officers for the authority.

More typically, however, the 1997 survey showed educational development services in Scotland comprising anything from three to ten individuals whose remits ranged widely across subject specialisms and age ranges, and included any number of authority respon-sibilities. In the smallest of these, three or four advisers/development officers acted in a consultancy role with respect to schools, brokering staff development needs whilst also supporting the directorate. In the middle were a number of education development services whose members tended to carry many more roles than would hitherto have been the case. An English Adviser, for example, might also have curricular responsibility for Drama, Modern Languages, and Personal and Social Education, operational responsibility for Higher Still developments and pastoral responsibility for a number of schools. He or she might also be involved in development planning and in quality assurance.

Other emergent themes included the diversity in terminology employed. Out of nineteen authority responses to the survey, ten had retained (or reverted to) the job title of adviser, although the service was more usually referred to as educational development, quality development, curriculum support, or services to schools. This may have been part of the 're-writing history' already alluded to, an attempt to restore a status which was perceived to have been lost, or to suggest a return to pre-market economy days. It had no great bearing on the degree of responsibility assumed or the type of work undertaken. (It will be clear by now that the use of the term 'adviser' in this chapter as a generic term for a member of a local authority educational development service, carries no particular implication as to role or status in the post-1993 context.)

This pattern has tended to be maintained up to the time of writing (autumn 2002), although in some authorities those individuals employed previously as advisers became subsumed into the ranks of administrative, professional, technical and clerical (APT & C) staff as service managers or equivalent principal officer posts. This may have been due to political expedience – education departments are often under pressure to slim down structures and large advisory staffs can be embarrassing when budget cuts need to be made – or to the view that the work being carried out was closer to that of an education officer than that of a traditional 'adviser'. Another trend has been the temporary second-ment of school staff as curriculum development officers to support particular areas of the curriculum, or to respond to national initiatives. The advent of the government's Excellence Fund (now Action Fund) in 1997 released additional funding for posts to co-ordinate, for example, out of school hours learning, early literacy, or work with parents. The plethora of single-issue posts of this kind has increased the overall number of support staff in recent years, although this has been counterbalanced by a dwindling number of permanent staff who cope with an increasing number of cross-authority responsibilities, whilst often overseeing the specific work of less experienced, temporary staff.

These observations are reflected in an analysis carried out in North Lanarkshire Council in 2001 as part of a Best Value Review of its quality development service. From the responses made by some twenty Scottish authorities to a range of questions relating to size, structure and function of educational development services, the following snapshot emerged:

- The number of advisers varied hugely, and not only in respect of size of authority. At that time, August 2001, North Lanarkshire itself had 22.5 FTE including externally funded and temporary posts; Glasgow had 21.5 FTE and Falkirk 30 FTE. On the other hand, the City of Aberdeen had 2 FTE and Aberdeenshire and Midlothian had no staff employed in this capacity.
- Most typically, primary advisers had been headteachers (HTs) and secondary advisers had been principal teachers (PTs) or assistant headteachers (AHTs) in their previous lives.
- While certain authorities provided a comprehensive menu of in-service opportunities to staff, elsewhere (for example, in Dumfries and Galloway), a network of headteachers and principal teachers co-ordinated staff and curriculum development requests, and this pattern was fairly common in authorities where advisory staff were few or non-existent. Charges for providing such services centrally varied also from free to a nominal daily rate to cover venue costs.
- Duties were equally varied. Typically, however, in addition to their curricular, pastoral and functional roles, permanent advisory staff would be called upon to prepare committee papers, carry out Best Value Reviews, undertake investigations, contribute to corporate strategy, represent the authority on national bodies and organise cross-authority events.
- Most authorities developed curricular materials for their own consumption; others generated income by selling these on. The same pattern applied to staff development.

It is interesting to note that the roles occupied by advisory staff and education officers had considerable overlap. In Aberdeen City, for example, where there were only two advisers, education officers carried out pastoral and functional support roles, as part of their line management responsibility. In Moray, on the other hand, quality assurance staff and Curriculum Development Officers had a line management responsibility for all schools, including supporting development planning and standards and quality monitoring. In Orkney, the advisorate and directorate worked together, carving up schools between them and offering a range of support.

A further theme which emerged from the North Lanarkshire analysis, however, was the growing tendency to divert advisers away from their traditional subject-based and support role, towards a generic 'challenge'/quality assurance role. South Lanarkshire, for example, had formed a Challenge and Support Team with responsibility for all aspects of development planning and staff development and review. Similarly, East Renfrewshire saw the emphasis for its quality development officers as being 'challenging and supporting schools', and accordingly, the delivery of in-service courses had been 'radically reduced'. Schools were expected to arrange their own school-based in-service from their delegated budget.

The picture emerging from the survey is usefully supplemented by a profile of advisory services which appeared in the *Times Educational Supplement Scotland* on 8 March 2002 as part of the media attention which followed the post-McCrone pay dispute. In Renfrewshire, at that point, the seven permanent advisers were reported as having 'overall responsibility for quality development, linking to schools, subject areas and project management covering primary, secondary, pre-five and special educational needs.' A team of seconded staff tutors worked to these permanent advisers, delivering in-service training and support in schools, and feeding back information to them.

The seven permanent advisers are reported as 'increasingly . . . [working] in quality development, looking at exam analysis, 5–14 targets, attendance (as part of target-setting), helping to draw up each school's three year authority review and compiling HM Inspectorate of Education reports and performance data, which they draw together for their own standards and quality reports'. In performing this function, the importance of the close link with schools is stressed. One adviser interviewed is quoted as saying, 'We know our schools and their staff and we share good practice with them. In our pastoral role we are critical friends for senior management, challenging and suggesting improvements. Without us, schools would be insular.' The same article details the duties of advisers in Clackmannanshire, Scottish Borders, Dumfries and Galloway and City of Edinburgh; nearly all included a generic planning and monitoring role in respect of schools in addition to (or instead of) their subject role, and the headteachers interviewed all appeared to value their advisers, stressing both subject specific support and the 'critical friend' approach to monitoring quality.

While, then, it may be true that the educational development services post-reorganisation had been formulated not so much in response to strategy as to exigency, the indications were that five years on, the focus had shifted to a much more generic role, and was already modelling the quality improvement role to be formalised in the aftermath of the McCrone agreement.

QUALITY IMPROVEMENT, AND
A TEACHING PROFESSION FOR THE 21ST CENTURY

The protracted negotiations over pay and conditions for teachers, which culminated in February 2001 in the McCrone settlement, offered a substantial pay increase for teachers (23.4% over three years) in return for an array of changes in conditions. The settlement, subtitled *A Teaching Profession for the 21st Century*, was designed to enable a more flexible and responsive education service sufficient to meet changing needs. Advisers and psychologists, however, who until that point had been on a teachers' pay scale and had received the same increases as teachers, found themselves excluded from the settlement. Promise of an early review group to consider claims for parity of treatment did not materialise, and in fact a full year passed before reluctant agreement was reached via EIS ballot.

In April 2002, the Scottish Negotiating Committee for Teachers finally published its Salaries and Conditions of Service Agreement for Education Advisers (Circular SNCT/12). In addition to national pay scales which broke the traditional link with teachers' pay (15.7% over three years as opposed to 23.4%), the conditions of the agreement included a directive that the title of adviser would change to that of Quality Improvement Officer with effect from August 2002, and that this would be subject to job-sizing a year later, in August 2003.

Thus while the only change to the conditions of advisers was to add a further contractual thirty-five hours per annum for continuing professional development (CPD), for the first time, the duties for members of the educational development services were laid down nationally. Appendix 3 of the circular outlined the role of Quality Improvement Officers in the education service as follows:

> Quality Improvement Officers will require to
> • Analyse and use performance information to challenge schools to improve
> • Ensure that local authority (and national) priority areas and targets are taken forward appropriately by schools
> • Draw on the knowledge of schools to support and inform strategic planning and policy development
>
> (Circular SNCT/12, April 2002)

While space does not permit further elaboration of the list of knowledge, skills and abilities which the SNCT stipulates will be necessary to carry out the duties effectively (they include knowledge of National Priorities and developments, the ability to support schools in development planning and in the application of performance information, the identification of good practice and promotion of improvement strategies, the writing of reports and the application of procedures associated with HMIE inspections) it is significant that none of the three broad duties listed above relates directly to the traditional foci of advisers: curricular and staff development. All three duties, moreover, can be seen to relate closely to the now statutory duty of the authority to secure school improvement, and are couched in terms of national and authority rather than school priorities. It is perhaps worth noting that teacher status (GTC registration) is no longer required.

Exit stage right, the traditional adviser – teacher, subject specialist, advocate, critical friend; enter stage left, Quality Improvement Officer – performance monitoring data in one hand, development planning pro forma in the other? Before the death knell rings out for a gentler, less accountable age of development and support, it is worthwhile looking at the new backcloth which is emerging from the shadows. For in setting out its vision for a teaching profession for the twenty-first century, the McCrone settlement also heralded in a major overhaul of what has become known as continuing professional development (CPD), with teachers aspiring to chartered teacher status or to a management role having to go through a modularised programme of accredited development, and with all teachers expected to commit themselves to an additional thirty-five hours of professional development annually. Most recently, learndirect Scotland has been commissioned to set up a national register of providers, with local authorities and other agencies invited to apply for registration with a view to possibly to becoming accredited national providers of CPD, in partnership with colleges and universities. Clearly, a role still exists for staff development, and despite doubts in 1996 that local delivery of staff development could be maintained, the signs are there for a federal structure, nationally co-ordinated, but locally delivered, playing to local strengths though offered beyond authority boundaries.

Where does this take educational development services, now quality improvement services, in the local authority context? Have they been transformed overnight, as at August 2002, into a 'Securitate' (one of the more affectionate terms for Strathclyde's Quality Assurance Unit) or into the 'Adspectors' of south of the border? Or is this simply a necessary refocusing of support services to enable local authorities to perform their duty to secure school improvement more effectively?

It is too soon to say the extent to which the traditional ability of the adviser to work effectively with schools from a basis of common identity will be undermined, if at all. As suggested earlier, authorities were already responding to the duties contained in the Standards in Scotland's Schools Act by refocusing their educational development service staff away from curricular and staff development duties and towards performance monitoring and quality assurance. Falkirk Council has responded to Circular SNCT 12 by re-allocating its curriculum support officers to clusters of schools in a new Quality Improvement Officer role which is largely to do with development planning and review. North Lanarkshire Council has responded by restructuring its comparatively large quality development service into a service which continues to fill a tripartite link, curricular and functional role, whilst offering both the 'challenge' and the 'support' functions. In other places, earlier evidence would suggest that the generic role already being performed will not take much realignment to fit with the steer given in the SNCT circular.

ISSUES

The history of the emergence, influence and subsequent chequered fortunes of educational development services over the past four decades has already occasioned discussion of issues and concerns which the current reformation appears to be attempting to address. The following are unresolved at the time of writing:

- whether a distinctive education development/quality improvement service will continue to exist within a local authority structure, after job-sizing has taken place, and now that the link with teachers has been broken, or whether, as the *TESS* article suggested, quality improvement officers will simply join the lower rungs of the directorate;
- whether quality improvement officers will continue to fulfil both a generic quality improvement role and the curricular/staff development role, or whether the roles will be split; and critically, affecting both of the above,
- the issue of recruitment and retention now that the salary differential has been eroded.

The McCrone debacle has been a painful reminder for advisers of the precarious position they hold in the twilight zone between local authorities and schools. It was clear that the management side wished the link with teachers to be broken. The EIS which ostensibly represented advisers as well as teachers at the McCrone negotiating table, appeared at best indifferent to defending the advisers' claim to be teachers.

Following the settlement, in fact, and actively encouraged by the AEAS, a number of advisers have gone across to the National Association for Educational Advisers, Inspectors and Consultants (NAEIAC). For longstanding EIS members, the move represents both anger at the EIS's denial of there ever having been a link with teachers (see, for example, *Sunday Herald*, 3 February 2002), and an acknowledgement that the link was now broken.

A leader in the *TESS* offers a useful comment on the place of advisers, post McCrone:

> Yet at issue remains the future role of advisers. It will have to be settled over the next two years through the post-McCrone job-sizing exercise. Advisers say they are teachers, which is as important in how they want to be perceived by classroom colleagues as in how their pay is calculated. The employers see them as part of the quality control apparatus.
>
> Before too long all advisers may find themselves on the bottom rung of education directorates. That at least would stop them being at the EIS's mercy.
>
> (*TESS*, 15 March 2002)

A major question is flagged up in the *TESS* leader – is an advisorate role compatible with a directorate role, or should the functions be kept separate? As already discussed, the dividing line between advisory/developmental and directorate activities was often finely drawn, with advisers acting on the one hand in a pastoral capacity with respect to schools, and on the other performing a sort of sub-development officer role in respect of drawing up policies and attending meetings on behalf of the authority. And yet, when the chips were down, as they certainly were at the time of local government reorganisation, many advisers discovered that experience in supporting the business of learning and teaching was not seen as a particularly valuable commodity when it came to running the service overall: few were successful in gaining posts in the management structure. Similarly, during the McCrone debacle, education directorates (with some notable exceptions) remained curiously silent in the face of COSLA's insistence that the opportunity was taken to break the link between advisers and teachers. The two elements of the service may be complementary but are probably not yet ready to merge.

The reticence to support the advisers' claim for parity with teachers was largely, it may be surmised, because salary anomalies in local authority structures created by McCrone did not end with advisers. Allowing advisers to receive a salary increase in line with teachers would solve the problem of recruiting teachers into the advisorate and keeping them there, but would create a new problem by reducing the differential between advisers and third tier (education officer) posts, who in turn have suffered an even worse erosion of pay differential in relation to second tier officers. In fact, the McCrone settlement has brought this to crisis level for both advisers and third tier officers.

In 1991, an adviser's salary was commensurate with that of a depute headteacher of a large school, and slightly more than that of a primary headteacher, making the job an attractive prospect for a primary head, or an AHT or principal teacher (secondary). Since then, the differential has been steadily eroded and by April 2003, that will mean that a primary head would have to take a drop in salary to become a quality improvement officer, as would a secondary depute head (the AHT position having disappeared). This also means that staff seconded from schools to provide the up-to-the-minute knowledge and credibility for specific tasks may be earning more than the permanent staff to whom they report. The same argument applies in respect of third tier directorate posts: it is likely to prove difficult in the future to attract in the kind of relevant up-to-the minute school-based expertise which has proved so valuable in the past. Given that the new look advisorate is specifically charged with performance monitoring, requiring a degree of credibility, this may prove particularly problematic.

LIKELY FUTURE DEVELOPMENTS

It may be that the outcome of the McCrone negotiations leading to a formalised role for educational development services will to a large extent resolve some of the major tensions and issues surrounding educational development services in the mid to late 1990s. Certainly, any ambiguity of role is removed, although it begs the question of what will be lost if the 'challenge' role undermines the critical friend dimension of peers speaking to peers. It regularises the *de facto* position of the development service servicing the directorate, although the job specification does not make it clear where the job of a quality improvement officer ends and the job of an education officer begins.

One thing the McCrone settlement may have done is to safeguard the future of educational development services, always a soft target while front line delivery is at stake. However, while it justifies the need for a service which monitors and challenges, it does not offer a framework for the provision of the many other tasks which an education authority must undertake to secure school improvement. Taking forward the National Priorities, improving learning and teaching, and developing educational policy, will all have to be fitted in around the margins.

It is likely that the dissatisfactions and the creativity made possible by a patchwork of secondments and a stretching of job remits will continue to flourish. It is also likely that the job-sizing scheduled for August 2003 will prove painful and divisive, and will further erode the goodwill and teamwork which has proved so important in making the service work. Ultimately, it is to be hoped that through time this will also help to reveal the scale of the tasks undertaken by advisers, and to iron out some of the anomalies present for both advisers and education officers.

A major influence on the future of educational development services must be the emergence of the National Register of Providers, and the delivery of in-service as authorities sign up as national providers of continuing professional development. National curricular initiatives demand massive amounts of development work at authority level in order to be implemented. At institutional level, HMI inspections, school development planning and the pursuit of the National Priorities give rise to a consistent need for establishment-focused, localised support. This traditional locus for educational development services cannot afford to be overlooked in the drive for 'challenge'.

The previous version of this chapter (in the original 1999 edition of *Scottish Education*) suggested that the agenda for educational development would be increasingly nationally driven and managed. With Circular SNCT/12 and the proposals for a national register of accredited providers, this may turn out to be the case. However, in the wake of numerous inspections of local authorities – the majority of which have referred positively to the support provided by educational development services – and in the light of the duty placed on authorities to secure school improvement under the 2000 Act, the stage also seems set for a locally provided and managed, if more centrally orchestrated, 'quality improvement' service. Such a service will continue to play its part in taking forward both national and local agendas with scope for creativity and innovation at authority level.

ACKNOWLEDGEMENTS

The author is grateful to colleagues across Scotland for sharing information on local and national provision, and in particular wishes to acknowledge the contributions of Vivien Casteel (co-author of the previous chapter in the 1999 edition of this book), and of North Lanarkshire colleagues Sandra Love, Mary Devine and Ellen Doherty in offering valuable insights into current provision, and for commenting on the draft.

18

Learning and Teaching Scotland

George A. MacBride

FORMATION, CONSTITUTION AND REMIT

Learning and Teaching Scotland (LTS) is an executive Non-Departmental Public Body, established by Scottish ministers on 1 July 2000, sponsored by the Scottish Executive Education Department (SEED). LTS was formed as the successor to the Scottish Consultative Council on the Curriculum (SCCC) and the Scottish Council for Educational Technology (SCET). Following quinquennial reviews of the two bodies in January 1998, the Minister for Education carried out a consultation exercise on options for the future of the two bodies which resulted in their amalgamation and the development of the new organisation's five part remit:

- to provide support, resources and staff development which enhance the quality of educational experience, thereby improving pupil and student achievement and attainment, and to promote learning throughout life;
- to review all matters relating to the school and pre-school curriculum, including the use of ICT to support the delivery of the curriculum, and to provide independent advice to Scottish ministers;
- to review all matters relating to the use of ICT in Scottish education and provide independent advice to Scottish ministers and, as appropriate, to the funding councils;
- to undertake, manage, quality assure and support a programme of research and development work relating to the school and pre-school curriculum and to the use of ICT in Scottish education as agreed with the Scottish Executive;
- to provide advice and carry out development work, including staff development, in relation to ICT and the curriculum, where agreed with the organisations providing or responsible for education in Scotland.

LTS is funded from various sources: by a core grant from the Scottish Executive; through specific programmes from a variety of sources, notably from SEED; through the sale of products and services to teachers, schools and other education providers. LTS is a moderate sized organisation with an annual turnover of some £17m and a staffing complement of nearly 200. A permanent staff, headed by the chief executive, is supplemented by additional members of staff appointed as required on a short-term contract or secondment basis to undertake duties relating to particular projects. Responsibility for the corporate governance and strategic management of LTS is vested in a board appointed by ministers; the organisation's activities are informed by an advisory council, also appointed by ministers.

Such a bald description of the organisation and its remit begs questions relating to effectiveness and coherence but should not prevent a consideration of the fundamental question as to whether there is any need for such a body within the education system of a small country like Scotland.

PREDECESSOR ORGANISATIONS

The two predecessor organisations were very different from each other, not only in terms of remit but in terms of governance and in terms of institutional culture. SCCC had its origins within the structures of the Scottish Office Education Department. Although it formally became more independent as a Non-Departmental Public Body, its funding, and indeed its continued existence, remained directly dependent on the department and on ministers. Such a dependency relationship carried the risk that the organisation would be constrained in its consideration of views at variance with government policy.

It is worthy of note that the organisation, its staff and its Council contributed to and, perhaps more importantly, sustained an influential critique of government educational policy throughout the 1990s. This was achieved partly by developing its credibility in carrying out effectively the review and development tasks remitted to it by government; partly by developing a distinctive vision of Scottish education; partly by maintaining dialogue with a wide range of partners; and partly by skilful maintenance of personal relationships with key members of the relatively small Scottish educational leadership class. It could of course be argued that such a strategy would result in the incorporation of SCCC into the views of the department. However the the work of the SCCC in its last years, perhaps most notably the *Revised Guidelines on the Secondary Curriculum* and the revised *Guidelines on the Balance and Structure of the Curriculum 5–14*, has played a significant part in taking forward thinking about the curriculum and the organisation of our schools.

Both documents moved well away from the orthodoxies of the then government as interpreted by such bodies as the inspectorate which placed very strong and very public constraints on the ability of schools to organise the curriculum as they thought fit. Both guidelines are premised on the principles that planning for effective learning is more important than the delivery of inherited curricular structures and that schools and teachers have a right and duty to plan to meet the needs of their pupils. Even before this, however, the SCCC had supported the view that national curricular guidelines did not form a curriculum specification but rather a framework within which teachers should think for themselves. While SCCC's ability to support Scottish teachers was limited by a remit which precluded any formal staff development, this did not prevent the organisation from providing support through the dissemination of material to teachers.

SCET had a very different background in that its promotion of information and communications technology was largely carried out through commercial means. While the freedom required for successful commercial operations afforded the organisation greater independence from government and enhanced opportunities to pursue a range of initiatives, SCET seems to have found it difficult to develop the sort of coherent ideology that marked SCCC. Much of SCET's work was devoted to the development, provision and promotion of software that could be used within schools and classrooms. This was supported by the provision of staff development to teachers, support for the dissemination of hardware, and support for management information systems. The highly effective way in which SCET carried out these activities is reflected in the extent to which its work has come to permeate all sectors of the educational community of Scotland. There can be few schools which do not use its software; few teachers who have not had an opportunity to develop their skills through SCET inservice; few development plans which have not been informed by SCET's often pioneering work on relating ICT to learning. However the impression remains that in responding to developments in technology, in promoting a wealth of initiatives, in working across all sectors of education, and in dealing with learning, curriculum, management and administrative, SCET did not have the space or time to reflect and offer a critical perspective on practice in its field. This is to be regretted since all too often in recent years governments have treated ICT as a panacea.

RELATIONSHIPS WITH THE EXECUTIVE

The existence of organisations like LTS as Non-Departmental Public Bodies (NDPBs) raises issues about democratic governance. Why should a small country like Scotland (in which school education is provided by clearly accountable elected bodies and is monitored by agencies responsible to these bodies) require an NDPB such as LTS?

The context and framework for school education is ultimately established by legislation through the elected Parliament; those responsible for policy are therefore clearly accountable to the electorate. Most commentators agree that this electoral accountability has been enhanced through the use of proportional representation, through the committee system, through the enhanced roles afforded back-bencher members, and through improved access and proximity, both literal and metaphorical, for the public. Such developments are rightly claimed as the practical manifestations of a widely accepted political commitment in Scotland to openness and democracy. Two very different public debates have demonstrated the ability of the Executive and Parliament to lead and respond to educational issues without the need for any intervening body. The first of those arose from the principled decision of ministers to introduce legislation to remove section 2(a) of the Local Government Act which prohibited any 'promotion' of homosexuality. The ill-informed myths promoted through an expensive public relations campaign hostile to this proposal were countered through the promotion of informed discussion. A less prominent example is afforded through the on-going debate on the best means of providing for special educational needs which has led to reflection on what thinking should underpin practice. Such examples of the ways in which elected politicians can initiate debate on educational matters challenge the need for any intermediary body such as LTS.

Pressure to consider such a question has been raised through the commitment of the Executive to a 'bonfire of the quangos' in the interests of enhanced democracy. Quasi Autonomous Non-governmental Organisations (quangos) had acquired, fairly or not, a reputation for the worst sorts of bureaucracy, for secrecy in decision taking, for lack of responsiveness to public views, for being filled by place men (occasionally women), and for being inefficient and ineffective.

There are of course powerful arguments for the existence of such a body as LTS. The first of these is the need for the Executive to be well informed. There has been, however, a well established mechanism for so doing – Her Majesty's Inspectorate for Education (HMIE). Concerns that HMIE as a body was too close to ministers were addressed by the establishment of HMIE as an executive agency, which formally ensures that monitoring of policy and practice and any advice arising from monitoring is perceived to be independent of policy formation. Further, it is always open to the Executive to set up short-term working groups of various types or to commission outside organisations to carry out studies. Several examples of this are evident in the aftermath of the report of the McCrone inquiry: *A Teaching Profession for the 21st Century*. The Executive commissioned consultants to report on aspects of initial teacher education, commissioned a consortium to develop the chartered teacher programme, set up a ministerial standing committee on continuing professional development and a steering group on the development of the chartered teacher programme. These groups have been set up for specific purposes and are answerable to ministers.

The troubled history of the Higher Still programme provides a further example of the means by which policy formation within Scottish education can be informed through public debate. The failure of ministers at earlier stages to take into consideration professional views, which has been attributed to the role of the inspectorate in filtering these, led to a belated dialogue with the educational community (as opposed to the incorporation of that community into decisions already taken). This resulted in the establishment of a review group with wide ranging membership which made a number of recommendations to ministers who, accountable to the Parliament and ultimately to the electorate, took the final decision on which recommendations to progress immediately and on which recommendations there should be further consultation. It could again be argued that there was no need for any intervening body.

OPERATION OF BOARD AND COUNCIL

LTS was set up with both a board and an advisory council each of which has very different remits and roles. To ensure co-ordination and coherence, the chair and vice-chair of the board carry out the same roles for the advisory council. The chair and board are appointed by the Scottish Executive to oversee and direct organisational affairs; the board is responsible for management of the organisation, both through responsibility for staffing and for the management of finance and through establishing and monitoring the annual plan. This board consists of persons with experience in relevant areas of Scottish education and with experience of management systems. In an innovation for educational NDPBs, the chair is afforded three paid days per month to undertake duties associated with the post. Currently some of this time is used to permit the chair and the chief executive to meet regularly to agree and monitor achievements targets; further the chair, ex officio, may also attend meetings of the organisation's senior management team. It could well be argued that such a board system should help to prevent the failures in management and in perceived public accountability that afflicted the Scottish Qualifications Authority at the very time at which LTS was being established. Through an annual planning process which ensures that the views of schools and teachers are taken into consideration, the board seeks to deliver value for money and effort in terms that the educational community might perceive to be relevant.

The advisory council is appointed by ministers to provide independent advice to the Executive, whether requested or not. The council can undertake consultations on draft documents; the council is not responsible for the annual plan although it considers and comments on the draft of the plan. Membership of the advisory council is representative in that it includes a wide range of those involved in education: teachers, parents, higher education representatives, advisers. In accordance with principles of transparency applications for membership were widely and openly sought and all applicants, however nominated, were interviewed. The word 'representative' is of course open to various interpretations.

There is a strong political case to be made that within an informed democracy, civic society must contribute to the formation of policy and the development of practice. This has been strongly argued within Scotland by various bodies involved in public life: a range of mechanisms has been developed for so doing, including representation on NDPBs. Propositions within the debate about the nature of democracy in Scotland are not simply the property of pressure groups and potential contributors can be very different from the concept of 'stakeholders' frequently used by New Labour. One argument assumes that the governance of society will be enhanced through the contribution of civic society to policy critique and development; while another appears close to the Thatcherite view which reduces citizens to consumers. It was argued explicitly by Thatcherites (and implicitly New Labour in England appears to accept this) that education is a consumer good and that the views of parents as consumers must be afforded a central place in monitoring practice, but not in developing policy which is located within central government; New Labour in England has extended this to recognise that the voice of pupils as consumers may be heard. A related concept (or propaganda myth) is that of 'producer capture' which implies that the influence of 'producers' (here teachers and providers) in decision making should be significantly reduced.

Clearly stakeholders will seek to make their views known to decision makers. Teacher unions, parent organisations, groups such as the Association of Directors of Education (ADES), all regularly meet with senior civil servants, with ministers and with political party representatives. This is part of an open society but there continues to be concern more generally that lobbying, even within the clear rules set up by the Parliament, can tip over into attempts to exert undue influence behind closed doors. Such lobbying also prevents discussion among the various partners as it is almost always bilateral. This is likely to leave the individual stakeholders in the position of petitioners rather than partners; more importantly it prevents the effective synergy of discussion and debate.

It can be argued that the advisory council of LTS is a means of ensuring that participants in civic society are heard. The considerable delay in setting up the advisory council could be perceived as an attempt to downgrade the organisation but, more probably, simply reflects the pressures on an Executive seeking to carry out a wide range of functions with limited resources. More substantially, the advisory council is open to the criticism that it reflects a cosy consensus. The usual suspects are present: ADES, the major teacher unions, higher education, primary and secondary heads, an industrialist, parent organisations. It could be further argued that the decision to implement and introduce greater transparency in appointments to such bodies (Nolan procedures) in fact removes no real power from the Executive. Interviews carried out by senior civil servants may be perceived to be little more transparent than direct appointment. The proof of the independence of the council can ultimately only lie in its actions.

REFERENCE GROUPS

LTS has devised a number of means of ensuring that within the complexities of our society it can draw on a wide range of views in other ways. Most obviously, there is the decision to set up five reference groups to deal with specific aspects of Scottish school education. Each group is chaired by a member of the advisory council, includes another two or three members of council within its membership but most significantly also includes some fifteen practitioners. While three focus on phases of school education, one has the remit of inclusive education and one the future of school education in Scotland. This allows for a range of expertise to be drawn upon and ensures that stakeholders have a greater input into the deliberations of the council and board. However the selection of members of these groups is open to the same sorts of criticism as the appointment of council members and forces us to consider what is meant by the involvement of civic society.

Because of the comparatively short period in which the organisation has existed it is not easy to judge its independence by the work it has carried out. However, the conference organised by LTS as its contribution to the current national debate may provide some clues to this. This conference drew its starting points from a range of papers summarising research within and outwith Scotland and through presentations from its own officers, from speakers from outside Scotland, from academics and from trade unionists. The paper submitted by LTS following discussion at and among members of the advisory council demonstrates lines of thought which are not constrained by Executive policy: in particular the paper argued that '[t]here should be a process of working towards a restructuring of schools, especially secondary, both physically . . . and in terms of their internal organisation [less hierarchical management; alterations to class-size; changes to the school day; 'core plus specialist' teams of teachers; . . .]' (National Debate on the Future of School Education: Initial Response from the Advisory Council of LT Scotland, 2002).

DEVELOPMENT WORK

Apart from this new work LTS has continued curriculum development work that the former SCCC had been engaged in. In early years education, development work was started on continuity and progression from pre-school to primary. In addition to the curricular guidelines within the 5–14 curriculum noted above, LTS has published major reviews of the national guidelines for environmental studies, including health education and ICT, and guidelines on modern languages. Practitioners have been involved in this work through direct participation and through consultation. Importantly, these reviews have been undertaken within an ethos which recognises that teachers deserve support as they take decisions on the best means of meeting their pupils' needs; hence these guidelines have been accompanied by support materials which outline a range of good practice but make clear that this is indicative, not restrictive or prescriptive.

LTS also continued to develop a range of generic issues during 2000–1, including education for work, where the last of several sets of support materials was completed and made available to schools; education for citizenship, where the work of a review group was completed; creativity in education, where work was started with the IDES Network to foster creativity in schools; and the National Grid for Learning (NGfL). A wide range of partners has been involved in the dialogues leading to these developments which are not restricted to detailed priorities set by the Executive.

LTS has more directly, through commissions, contributed to the support of Executive initiatives, but in so doing has maintained a dialogue with the rest of the education community. A ready example is provided in the *Guidance on Sex Education in Scottish Schools* which was published on behalf of the Scottish Executive in March 2001 within the context of the debate noted above on section 2(a); again this drew on the contributions of a wide range of practitioners. When ministers considered it necessary to review the purposes of assessment for pupils up to the age of certification, they made use of the inspectorate to carry out the initial review, followed this with consultation and subsequently established an action group to manage a programme of work. Stakeholders have been involved both through the consultation and through membership of the action group chaired by the deputy minister. LTS has responsibility for managing the projects required by this programme, informing this process by seeking input from the profession through a newsletter and website, as well as through participation in the action group. In supporting new National Qualifications ('the Higher Still Programme') through the publication of teaching materials, LTS has endeavoured to ensure that there is co-ordination among all potential providers and has sought feedback from the profession on its requirements. These examples would suggest that even when directly commissioned (and paid) to carry out functions on behalf of the Executive, LTS seeks as a minimum to be responsive to the needs of professional users.

EXAMPLES OF RECENT PUBLICATIONS AND RESOURCES

During the first year of its existence LTS published a wide range of documents. In addition to the publication of revised 5–14 national guidelines, along with the accompanying support materials, work was done in partnership with the Nuffield Foundation and several local authorities to produce a substantial pack of support materials for primary teachers which met the specification for technology in the revised guidelines; this was designed to help teachers develop children's technological capability effectively and with confidence during every primary stage. For the post-14 stage, LTS continued to develop new National Qualifications support materials, working with the Higher Still Development Unit (HSDU), the Scottish Further Education Unit (SFEU), local authorities and others. Parallel work on producing flexible learning materials – the Open, Flexible and Distance Learning (OFDL) project – was also continued through this period. An example of more routine work was the publication of a third set of materials in the Education for Work series, which relates education for work to learning and teaching in individual subjects in secondary schools.

In addition, LTS provided a wide range of production services from multimedia and website development to video production and consultancy, including: redesign of the National Grid for Learning Scotland website; release of Streetwise CD-ROM; launch of the Scottish Road Safety Campaign website; work on installation of interactive multimedia kiosks for Scotland Street Museum; development of a website for Stòrlann (the Gaelic Resource Catalogue); creation of a National Assessment Bank CD-ROM for the Scottish Qualifications Authority; and online learning events for schools.

STAFF DEVELOPMENT

From the start LTS managed an extensive programme of staff development including: fifty-five training courses; twenty Software in Focus days; the geographic coverage of the Learning Schools Programme at 31 March 2001 included all schools in twelve education authorities and a number of other schools, in total around 8,000 teachers. It secured funding from the Special Educational Needs Innovations Grant Programme for a mobile training unit which travelled around Scotland taking ICT training to teachers in their own locality. The Software in Focus days have been developed into curriculum workshops which cover different aspects of the 5–14 curriculum, each event taking an in-depth look at four software titles and exploring how they could be integrated into the classroom. This demonstrates one way in which the work of the two predecessor organisations has been brought together.

It can fairly be asked whether this amount of work could be undertaken by any other body within Scottish education. But it could also be asked whether this work has had any impact on education in Scotland. The evidence strongly suggests that it has in fact so done. LTS has had to take on two radically different cultures in terms of disseminating materials and supporting teachers. SCET was an organisation operating within a commercial environment, if not within a freely operating market: it was able to sell its own software, others' software and offer staff development to teachers, all at a price (though often a highly advantageous price). SCCC on the other hand could not directly offer staff development (though it could provide dissemination and consultation conferences or events) but could provide a range of support materials. Since these were often related to national developments or government initiatives, their provision to schools had to be free of cost to the establishment. To ensure that materials were in fact positively selected rather than simply arriving in schools, much was distributed by a voucher system through which members of staff had to make a positive decision to obtain materials which suited their needs. Evidence gathered by SCCC suggested that this was both popular and effective; figures for attendance at commercial events suggest also a continuing meeting of perceived needs.

CONTRAST WITH CORRESPONDING BODIES ELSEWHERE IN UK

There is a notable difference in the public ethos and culture of LTS when compared with the other three parallel bodies within the United Kingdom. These three have a statutory foundation and have a responsibility for assessment and qualifications as well as the curriculum. The Qualifications and Curriculum Authority (QCA) in England describes itself as 'a guardian of standards in education and training . . . work[ing] with others to maintain and develop the school curriculum and associated assessments, and to accredit and monitor qualifications in schools, colleges and at work' (http://www.qca.org.uk). As a statutory body, QCA has responsibilities for developing and monitoring the statutory national curriculum and national assessment system and for developing, regulating and monitoring the National Qualifications System. QCA stresses its mission to 'give pupils, students, trainees, parents, teachers, further and higher education tutors and employers increased confidence in the standards that underpin the curriculum and the national assessment and qualifications systems'. There is little reference to any aspect of teaching or learning. Interestingly the organisation sees its partner in Scotland as another 'regulatory authorit[y]', the Scottish Qualifications Authority (SQA).

Although the Northern Ireland Council for the Curriculum, Examinations and Assessment (CCEA) has a remit for the development of educational technology and the production of multimedia resources and has produced materials for teachers' continuing professional development, its statutory responsibility is primarily concerned with curriculum, examinations and assessment, including giving advice to the Department of Education on these matters, including specifically the Transfer Procedure tests for children moving from primary to secondary education. There seems little direct reference to the maintenance of standards.

The Qualifications, Curriculum and Assessment Authority for Wales (ACCAC) appears to lie between these two bodies 'and works particularly closely with Estyn, Her Majesty's Inspectorate for Education and Training in Wales'. ACCAC is responsible in Wales for ensuring quality and standards in external general and vocational qualifications; for keeping under review all aspects of the school curriculum and statutory assessment arrangements for maintained schools; and for publishing and disseminating information relating to qualifications, curriculum and assessment in Wales. There is a responsibility on the body to commission classroom materials but only in regard to supporting the teaching of Welsh, other subjects through the medium of Welsh and Wales-specific aspects of the curriculum. While bodies can create their own spaces within statutory and political constraints there seems little doubt that these bodies have a much smaller role than LTS in supporting, managing and developing change.

CURRENT PRIORITIES AND FUTURE TARGETS

Scotland is a country whose views on its education system are marked by a number of myths. These myths are important in that they help determine views both on what the education system is like and on what it should be like. A myth is one means of expressing our ideology or philosophy. However there is a consensus that an acceptance of mythology has led to complacency. This complacency of Scottish education is all too often linked with an approach that stresses pragmatism at the expense of philosophical enquiry. Pragmatism allows people to do better what is already being done. The actions of previous administrations in setting up league tables, and in focusing on tightly specified performance indicators, has undoubtedly contributed to improving standards in these narrowly defined terms. More importantly, pragmatism does not encourage the community to consider whether this is in fact a worthwhile enterprise. It limits, indeed encourages people not to extend, their horizons.

It could be argued that the work of LTS is a supportive response to the changes initiated by others. Under this heading one could list many of the publications of LTS intended for use in the classroom or in supporting classroom practice; support publications within the Higher Still programme; staff development to improve practice in the use of ICT; even the revisions of National Guidelines may fall into this category. But other publications go well beyond this. Work on citizenship, on creativity, the contribution to the national debate, all break new ground. More fundamentally LTS, particularly through the work of its advisory council, contributes to the development of thinking about possibilities for the future of education and learning. If there were no such body as LTS with the duty and opportunity to go beyond pragmatism in this way, there would be a serious risk of ossification and of lowered expectations within Scottish education.

Currently, LTS has four strategic objectives, an examination of which demonstrates the organisation's commitment to development. One is concerned with its own internal organisation and management:

- to ensure that LTS demonstrates a culture of openness, accountability and care, adhering to the disciplines of continuous improvement and critical self-evaluation and optimising its use of available resources – human, technological and financial.

One could be described as largely pragmatic and lying within Executive policy though it is readily capable of a broader definition:

- to provide advice on, and support for, the identification and implementation of National Priorities in Scottish education and in learning throughout life.

The other two are unambiguously concerned with a broader and ambitious mission:

- to foster and support informed debate on a long-term vision for the future of education and encourage evolution towards the realisation of such a vision by promoting creativity and innovation;
- to pursue, in collaboration with the Scottish Executive, local authorities and others, a coherent, sustainable and long-term approach to the management of change in learning and teaching.

In carrying out the Executive commission on the implementation of the National Priorities improvement framework, LTS could appear to be no more than the servant of the Executive. But LTS has ensured that work on developing performance indicators has been informed by debate at advisory council, by continuing dialogue with education authorities and schools and by the employment of practitioners to carry out the required work. The other two objectives demonstrate even more clearly the commitment to work to extend thinking and to involve a wide range of partners in this process.

Change is an essential feature of the education system. It is easy to produce clichés about the need for change, the need for modernisation, the need for competitiveness. More fundamentally one has to consider the ways in which education is designed to bring about change, and to manage change, and to prepare its recipients to live with and to bring about that change. Change over which we feel little control is in fact harmful, while change which we control can be a source of creativity and fulfilment. The need to recognise the complexity of the education system underpins the work of LTS. In particular it is not possible to impose simple solutions on every school throughout the country; to do so would not draw on the strengths of all participants. Rather staff must be supported as they contribute their thinking to the development of solutions.

LTS makes space for this sort of wider thinking. But it is not happenstance. The structure of the organisation recognises the validity of a range of points of view; the development of partnership agreements and minutes of understanding with a wide range of organisations; the provision of support to the teaching profession; the involvement of the teaching profession in development; the development of an annual plan in which support for change is essential; and perhaps above all the development and expression of an ethos of support and challenge mark out an organisation different from similar bodies elsewhere within the United Kingdom. Making space for such thinking is easier in an education system which is not constrained by a legally imposed curriculum and which commits the Executive to consult on its improvement plans. In so doing, LTS ensures that the views and priorities of teachers, schools and other bodies are communicated to its board and the Scottish Executive through its annual planning process, thereby demonstrating its determination to be not only accountable and transparent but also relevant to its community.

ACKNOWLEDGEMENTS

This chapter has been informed by a reading of recent annual plans and reports of LTS and its predecessor organisations, discussion with the organisation's chief executive and the author's membership of the Council of SCCC and of the Advisory Council of LTS [LTS website: http://www.LTScotland.com].

REFERENCES

LTS (2001) *Creativity in Education*, Dundee: LTS.
LTS (2002) *Education for Citizenship in Scotland – A Paper for Discussion and Development*, Dundee: LTS.
Paine, N. (1999) The Scottish Council on Educational Technology (SCET), in T. G. K. Bryce and W. M. Humes (eds) *Scottish Education*, Edinburgh: Edinburgh University Press.
Ross, H. (1999) The Scottish Consultative Council on the Curriculum (SCCC), in T. G. K. Bryce and W. M. Humes (eds) *Scottish Education*, Edinburgh: Edinburgh University Press.
SCCC (1996) *Teaching for Effective Learning*, Dundee: SCCC.
SCCC (1999) *Curriculum Design for the Secondary Stages – Guidelines for Schools*, Dundee: SCCC.

19

The Parent Dimension in Education

Judith Gillespie

THE EARLY YEARS

Parents have always been slightly tangential to schools. Sure they provide the children – the raw material of the education system – but they have no direct role in the day-to-day working of schools, as this tends to be a two-way dialogue between teachers and pupils. Parents do have a role as advocates of their children's interests but even this gets eroded as the youngsters get older. Once pupils are sixteen, they are legally responsible for their actions, for their subject choice and attendance, and the school is required to deal directly with them. Consulting parents at this stage is more by way of habit and courtesy than legal requirement.

However, going back to the introduction of universal compulsory education, parents were seen, in some sense, as the enemy. Prior to the 1872 Act, many children worked and their very modest earnings were an important part of the family income. The introduction of compulsory schooling hit poor families hard. Not only did they have to pay – education was compulsory, but not free – they also lost income from the children's earnings. Consequently, parents were given the legal duty to ensure that their children were educated so that action could be taken against them if they tried to keep them out of school and in work. This legal obligation, once introduced, has been maintained in successive Education Acts, but the understanding of its purpose has shifted somewhat. Subsequent generations have used it to argue for an active role for parents in running schools and determining the curriculum.

From the school's point of view, if parents produced the children and ensured their attendance, that was the end of the story. Indeed, some even went the length of having wide white lines drawn across their playgrounds with the legend No Parents Beyond This Point written in large clear letters, and, for many years, parents were quite accepting of this approach. Whilst the very first parent teacher associations were formed in the 1920s, it was not until 1948 that there were enough such associations for them to come together and form a national organisation. This was the Council of Parent and Parent Teacher Associations of Scotland which was subsequently renamed the Scottish Parent Teacher Council (SPTC) and is still around today (see SPTC, 1998). The purpose of this national body was to encourage closer co-operation between home and school, but the organisation was very much the child of a few activists, had very modest membership and frequently came close to folding. Reading the minutes of the early years, it is clear that the organisation's biggest problems were to get ordinary members to participate actively and to get some kind of official recognition. The latter only arrived in the early 1970s in the form of a modest £50 grant for a conference from the then named Scottish Education Department. This coincided with greater recognition for parent teacher associations (PTAs) at school level as, where they existed, they were used to select parent representatives for the newly formed school councils.

School councils were set up following the 1973 Local Government (Scotland) Act. They were usually based on a secondary school and included parent and teacher representatives from all the schools – primary, special, nursery and hospital schools – within the secondary school catchment area. School councils were enormous, varyingly effective but official and attended by representatives of the relevant education department. They had little power but provided an important forum for discussion of issues that affected all the different schools. Most significantly they gave parents' views recognition and an official status that was reinforced by the fact that they were chaired by a parent.

COMING OF AGE

However it was in the 1980s that the big change to parental involvement really happened. There were two drivers. The first was a growing realisation that children did better if their parents were somehow involved in their education. This led to calls for more active parental involvement in schools and advocates of this approach were delighted by the 1980 Education (Scotland) Act. They focused on two sections:

- section 28 which stated, 'Education authorities shall have regard to the general principle that . . . pupils are to be educated in accordance with the wishes of their parents.'
- section 30 (surviving from the 1872 Act) which stated, 'It shall be the duty of the parents of every child of school age to provide efficient education for him [sic] suitable to his age, ability and aptitude.'

They interpreted these to mean that parents should have a more active role in running schools and determining the curriculum. They failed to point out that both sections carried important caveats. Section 28 stated that parents' wishes should be observed as long as they were 'compatible with the provision of suitable instruction and training and the avoidance of unreasonable public expenditure', whilst section 30 continued beyond the much-quoted section to add, without so much as a comma, that the parental duty could be discharged 'by causing him [sic] to attend a public school regularly or by other means'. However, then as now, very few people read the actual legislation, so the lobby for more parent power appeared to have unambiguous legislative backing.

One keen advocate of this approach was Dr Alastair Macbeth of Glasgow University's Education Department and he also acted as an adviser to the SPTC (Macbeth, 1989). His ideas matched with the organisation's original purpose so the SPTC was quick to take advantage of this change in attitude. It was into this changing climate that the second more powerful driver for a change in the parental dimension arrived. This was overtly political and came from the then Conservative government's policy of putting faith in the market system to deliver efficiency in public services.

The first step was the introduction of the first parents' charter in 1981, which gave parents the right to choose schools outwith their own locality. Technically, parents were given the right to express a preference for an out-of-area school although their request could be turned down on a number of grounds, including if granting it would cause any extra expense, such as of an extra teacher, at the designated school. In practice, the charter was sold as giving parents an absolute right to choose their child's school and the permitted reasons for rejecting such a request were often ignored by the education authority and more often by sheriffs when parents took any rejection to appeal.

However, the real period of parent power came after the 1987 election when Michael Forsyth, the new minister with responsibility for Scottish education, came along with proposals for individual school boards to replace the area councils. He found a natural and willing partner in SPTC which saw boards as a means of increasing parents' influence over schools. Forsyth's purpose was more about politics than about simply involving more parents. He saw boards as a stepping stone along the way to self-governing schools. This was a proposal to take schools out of local authority control and place them under small boards of management with parental majorities – a process universally referred to as 'opting-out'. It would have had the added consequence of undermining the authority – and hence power – of the local authorities, whose largest service was education and who were the power-base of political opposition in those days. With different aims in mind, a natural partnership was formed between the politician and the SPTC on the delivery of boards. SPTC was duly rewarded with section 12 of the School Boards (Scotland) Act 1988, which placed a duty on school boards 'to encourage the formation of parent teacher or parents' associations'.

Another Forsyth parent-focused initiative, directed at providing the necessary consumer discipline to the education market, was the publication of so called 'league tables'. These provided a school by school comparison of Highers results. Ostensibly, they were to help parents make more informed decisions on their choice of school. However, they fitted Forsyth's bigger political purpose and this, in turn, was fuelled by the media when it ranked schools in order of achievement and picked out the best and worst. It is no accident that use of the parents' charter, which had until this time been modest, suddenly took off now that parents essentially had a government-provided guide to good schools.

Ironically, the political agenda stirred parents to mass participation. There were 8,000 responses to the consultation on school boards – a figure that is way off the Richter scale of responses to similar consultations, which normally attract replies from only a few hundred individuals and groups. Moreover, whatever the SPTC's views on the desirability of boards, over 90% of respondents rejected the proposal, largely on the grounds that they didn't trust other parents to run their child's school and they particularly didn't trust the type of parent who would put themselves forward! Despite this opposition, the scheme went ahead and so ensured that the members of the first school boards, set up in 1989, were themselves quite political. Many found the most certain way to get elected was to state clearly in their election statements that they would always oppose opting-out.

It is not really surprising that these first generation 'political' boards continued the pattern of parental opposition to government policy and were key in the next fight, which was to prevent the introduction of national tests. This was another step in the government's market agenda, designed to introduce the rigour of comparative exams into the primary sector. The proposal was that all children in primary four and primary seven would take a national test to see what stage they were at in the new 5–14 curriculum. Parents were concerned that the tests would reintroduce streaming and that their own individual children would not come out on the winning side. Thousands therefore took up invitations to sign a simple note withdrawing their children from the tests on the assurance that there would be no disadvantage either to them or their children. Meanwhile, at national level, an action group – the Parents' Coalition – sprang up to spearhead the campaign. As the Tory policy was based on parental choice, the government was politically unable to act against this and Michael Forsyth had little option but to sanction the 'voluntary' nature of the tests in January 1991. The eventual settlement of the testing standoff, which followed the 1992 election, actually imposed a more rigorous testing regime. The tests in primaries four and seven were replaced by tests at the end of each of the five stages of the 5–14 curriculum but, because pupils reached these stages at different times, it was not possible to use the test results to compare schools or teachers.

Parents also showed they were very political in the way that they used the opting out legislation, which was introduced in 1989. As repeated consultations proved, there was very little desire on the part of parents actually to run schools so when the legislation was invoked this was generally as a means of winning some or other battle. In most cases the battle centred round a proposed school closure. An authority was not allowed to close a school whilst there was an ongoing ballot on self-governing status. Parents therefore set up ballots simply to thwart local authorities' rationalisation plans. The most successful campaign was around St Gerard's High School in Glasgow, where parents refined the process into a rolling ballot. As an authority could not go ahead with a closure if any associated school had a ballot pending, the Southside Parents' Action Group organised a series of ballots in St Gerard's and its associated primaries. In the end the government had to face reality – they were being outsmarted by parents – and in 1996 the legislation was amended to close this loophole.

In the end, only two schools ever became self-governing. With one of these, Dornoch Academy, it was the result of a fight to reverse the authority's decision to change the school from a four-year to a two-year secondary. In fact, as a self-governing school Dornoch achieved six-year status and then the parents were quite happy, when the opting-out legislation was rescinded in the 2000 Education Act, to come back under local authority control. Only in St Mary's in Dunblane have parents lived up to Forsyth's ideal of running a school because they feel they can do it better. Here parents are still fighting through the courts against a return to local authority control although, as yet, without any success – but causing a lot of delay!

The government suffered much at the hands of parents in this highly political period of parental involvement and so it then started a new tack and emphasised parents' responsibilities. The agenda moved on to issues like attendance, homework and school uniform and the important part parents had to play in such matters. The idea of parents' contracts was even mooted but never really got beyond the pilot stage in Scotland. Meanwhile boards became involved in decision making at school and, just in case they thought they had any spare time, they were swamped with consultation documents and information – always a useful way of silencing all but the most determined opposition. Subsequent generations of school board members have arrived on the scene with little awareness of the early history and without the political imperative of their predecessors. They have got stuck into the workload, if not with enthusiasm, then with diligence.

Meanwhile schools have been left to cope with two in-house parent committees – the board and PTA – and find it difficult. In small schools, the membership of the boards and of the PTA is often more or less identical; it's just that they operate under different hats. In the majority of schools, the solution to the two-committee structure has been to give them each different roles: the board is responsible for education issues and the PTA has been reduced to fund-raising and not much else. However, some schools cannot support both in any real sense and here it is usually the board that survives. Its statutory status and the recognition given to it by the education authority makes it seem more important. Meanwhile individual parents are now becoming more generally aware of their legal rights and responsibilities (see Welsh, 2001).

THE FORMAL PARENT DIMENSION IN SCHOOLS

School Boards

Membership and organisation

The original purpose of boards was to be embryonic boards of management for opted-out schools. They were therefore set up on a business management model – a small efficient committee with formal arrangements and outside co-opted 'expertise'. The position of co-opted members causes problems. The original idea was to involve some local businessmen and so on, but such people have little real interest in school matters so, even when a board can find people willing to be co-opted, they rarely turn up to meetings. On the other hand, the co-opted role does allow some former parents to keep a tight grip on boards. There are cases where the same person has been chairman of the school board since inception, first as parent, then as co-optee.

The bulk of the legislation covers membership and methods of appointment. The format of boards has always been alien to the normal pattern of parental involvement in schools, which tends to be more spasmodic, ad hoc and focused on the child. Inevitably, boards have been attractive to people who feel comfortable working in formal committee structures and research has shown that, in every school, board members are drawn from the top social grouping at that school. In secondary schools they often represent the most academic group whilst the majority of chairpersons are men. The corollary of this is that board members tend to enjoy being board members and like the formal arrangements. They tend to support the continuation of the current arrangements and, as 'boards' are taken to mean 'parents', this is often represented as the 'parental view', although typically it is the view of six out of 1,500 parents – or even of just the chairperson. In short, school boards are a middle-class construct, which are most appealing to and work best in middle-class schools. In contrast, many non-board parents are totally confused about boards. They either ignore their existence or think they are the same as English school governing bodies, which they hear about on the national news.

Function

Because boards' main purpose was to opt out – and very few went down this road – the majority have floundered to know what they are really there for. They quickly established that they did not have a proper management role and could not run the school according to their own diktats. Their principal powers are to approve the headteacher's spending proposals, discuss the school development plan (annual actions) and to appoint senior staff (an occasional action). They also have a duty to keep parents informed, but as this can be a very time-consuming job and most parent board members are busy people, this duty tends to have been only minimally fulfilled. Indeed, as regards the wider parent body, boards often act as a sort of black hole for information.

Outside these duties, boards have developed three main forms of activity:

- They are a focus group for the school – discussing school policies and issues. In this they most properly exercise their 'parents' representative' role.
- They act as a lobbying group for the school, taking up school needs with outside bodies, usually the education authority.
- They act as a consultation group for the Scottish Executive, although boards themselves rarely take such consultations wider than their own membership. In this they are responding to the Executive/authority's agenda rather than pursuing the agenda of parents in the school. Some boards have served a useful service in carrying out these activities although, counting the number of responses to any Executive consultation against the full number of boards, this is only the minority.

However, through such activities a small group of parents have become relatively well informed about education issues.

Official Status

School boards have come to be viewed as the 'official' way parents are involved in schools and in many respects it is this 'official recognition' which is their greatest asset. It has forced some reluctant heads to allow parental involvement for the very first time.

- Boards have a right to information.
- Headteachers have a clearly defined responsibility towards boards.
- Boards have financial support to run their affairs, for clerking service, to cover members' transport costs, attendance at conferences etc.
- The formal postal elections are funded by the authority.
- Both Scottish Executive and local authority consultations are directed to school boards.
- Boards are the general recipients of mailings, invitations etc.
- Boards are invited to send representatives to authority-wide consultative committees/ education committees.
- Most authorities have a school board unit – or an official with responsibility for school boards – which offers support.
- Boards are agents of the authority and members are indemnified against prosecution.
- The SEED gives further recognition to boards by issuing a newsletter.
- Authorities are required to consider the views of school boards.

In return, this official recognition has given parents the courage to ask questions and challenge the system.

Parent/Parent Teacher Associations

Parent teacher and parent associations (PTAs/PAs) are essentially the same type of body and are similar enough to be treated together. PTAs/PAs pre-date boards and it is worth noting that many of the incredible 8,000 responses to the original school board consultation came from PTAs. Prior to boards, they exercised many of the consultation/ lobbying functions of boards, although in a more random way.

Membership and Organisation

PTAs/PAs are 'home grown'. Their membership and organisation are determined locally. They usually have a constitution but this tends to be no more than a simple description of the organisation. All the parents (and teachers) are members by default although the committee is often taken as being the PTA/PA. However, even this committee tends to involve more parents than the school board, to be less formal and to attract a wider range of parents, though mostly women.

Functions

- PTAs have traditionally varied in what they do but have usually had a fund-raising and social dimension.
- Many see themselves as having a role in providing information, running extra curricular activities for pupils, acting as a channel for parents' concerns etc.
- PTAs are independent of the school and are publicly liable. They need insurance and have to provide this for themselves.
- PTAs are self-financing and get no money from the authorities.
- They get no official recognition from the authorities – they are rarely included in consultation exercises or asked to participate in consultative committees.
- What they are 'allowed' to do is totally determined by the headteacher. A head who is genuinely interested in partnership can help develop a really vibrant PTA. Other heads regard them simply as the fund-raising arm of the school that should hand over money without asking any questions.

PARENTS BEYOND SCHOOLS

The two-committee structure at school level quickly led to questions about the nature of parental representation at national level. Initially, the Scottish Parent Teacher Council made a bid to represent both PTAs and school boards, but the constitutional changes necessary for this to proceed were rejected by its members at the 1988 AGM, leaving the way open for a new national body. In 1991, Ann Hill, a parent activist from Dumfries and Galloway, strongly supported by the then Director of Education there, Bill Fordyce, set about establishing a new national organisation, the Scottish School Board Association (SSBA). Although the SSBA is a voluntary organisation, it has acquired virtual statutory status by its association with the statutory boards. Many authorities have built links with the SSBA as part of their process of supporting boards and organise SSBA membership of boards on an authority-wide basis.

One outcome of this new focus on parents through the introduction of boards and the policy of parental choice was an understanding, throughout the education service, that parents should be consulted more. Local authorities approached this in a number of ways. Some, like Fife, had a parent representative on their education committee, but the majority set up some form of consultative group drawing parents from local boards. Meanwhile parents were also routinely involved in national committees and task groups. This first started in the early 1980s when George Jackson, chairman of the SPTC, was appointed by the Secretary of State to the General Teaching Council for Scotland. It has continued apace and is now almost obligatory for a parent to be involved on all national committees, task groups and quangos. However, these often work at such a technical level and in such obscure officialese that it is very difficult for all but the most dedicated parent to cope.

Not surprisingly, the two national parents' organisations were usually asked to nominate suitable parents for membership of national bodies and this in turn gave the SSBA and SPTC increased status. Ministers suddenly became willing participants at conferences organised by the two bodies and the press eagerly sought parents' views, which often resulted in controversial headlines.

THE SPONTANEOUS PARENT DIMENSION

However, for the majority of parents, the real focus of their involvement is their child – not school management or what might happen to the curriculum ten years from now. It is the immediate that matters. At school level, the parent–teacher interview is the most important form of involvement for most parents and it is easy to get a cheer by suggesting that time for this should be increased. In 1998, the SPTC and the main teachers' union, the EIS, responded to a government consultation on partnership with parents, which had focused on school boards, with a joint leaflet emphasising the importance of the personal contact between parents and teachers. However, in reality this is the part of their work that teachers like little and it is perhaps not unexpected that the parent–teacher interview is currently falling foul of the new thirty-five hour working week agreed in the recent McCrone pay deal.

This focus on the individual child does sometimes spill over into a national dimension. And then parents do not wait to go through any committee. They organise themselves and act directly. As has already been pointed out, opposition to boards was based on distrust of other parents running 'my child's' school and resulted in a massive response to the consultation. The thousands of parents who withdrew their children from the national tests when these were first introduced in 1990 did so because they were concerned that they would be unfair to their own individual children. It was also typical that the opposition was spearheaded by a new, single-issue group, the Parents' Coalition, that sprang up outside the constraints of the established SPTC. Ultimately, it was cumulative individual concern that scuppered Michael Forsyth's plans for testing in primary schools.

The Southside Parents' Action Group (SPAG) was another spontaneous, single-issue group, this time focused on stopping the closure of St Gerard's High School in Glasgow. Proposals to shut a school are almost always guaranteed to provoke a hostile reaction from the school's parents and packed-out, angry meetings. The action by SPAG was merely a high profile case of what commonly happens in such circumstances. Their cleverness was in exploiting the government's opting-out legislation for their own ends.

Forsyth was more successful with promoting use of the parents' charter because this time he managed to appeal to the interests of individual parents. Whilst at the formal level, parents' groups voiced their opposition to the publication of league tables of exam results, at the individual level many parents took advantage of the information to choose what they saw as better schools for their own children and use of the parents' charter increased enormously.

School transport is a parent issue but one which rarely makes it on to official agendas. It did come to prominence in 1994 when a school bus crashed just outside Biggar and two children were killed. This led to a vigorous campaign by parents for improvements in the safety of school transport and in particular for seat belts to be fitted. The organising group –

Belt Up School Kids – was another voluntary group which showed very professional skills but was run from the home of an individual parent at Biggar High School. The vigour of the campaign led to a change in legislation so that in 1997 it became law for all school contract coaches and minibuses to be fitted with seat belts.

In 1996, parents, tired of years of cuts in education spending which had resulted in tatty textbooks, limited equipment, few computers, decrepit buildings and a shortage of staff, joined the teachers in a massive march of protest. The volume and spontaneity of the protest took the government by surprise and forced them to announce some extra funding.

More recently, when the Scottish Qualifications Authority messed up the exam results in the summer of 2000, parents acted directly by contacting schools, MSPs, education departments, the press, and so on. They did not bother waiting for school boards or PTAs to get their act together. And in 2001, parents in the Scottish Borders, faced with proposals for education cuts as the result of a £3.9m over-spend by their local education department, were quick to get organised and force the authority to think again.

Many slogans have been attached to the parental dimension in education – choice, power, partnership (see Wolfendale and Bastiani, 2000) – but in truth the parent dimension has tended to operate on two levels. There is the organised form, working through committees and fitting in with management and government structures. And then there is the organic natural form when parents focus on their own children, but every now and then combine in rage into a massive and unstoppable force. Measuring parental involvement by participation in the formal structures will always underestimate the true level of parental interest.

THE SIGNS OF CHANGE

However, now there are signs that even the formal methods of involving parents are changing. Moreover, the Executive is moving beyond parents to pupils. Every consultation is now extended to include pupils. Nearly every ministerial and parliamentary statement has to include a comment about the wisdom provided by such pupils and pupils are beginning to find themselves invited to join the endless national committees. The Standards in Scotland's Schools etc. Act 2000 stated that education was henceforth the right of every child and formalised youngsters' involvement in the decision making process by requiring all schools to set up a pupil council and to consult that council over policy matters, including the development plan.

Similarly the Act confirmed that boards were now part of management structure. It gave them a duty to further the Executive's policy of raising standards but did nothing to suggest how this duty might be fulfilled. At the same time the Act effectively acknowledged that the current structure of boards is unpopular. It increased the power of boards to co-opt parents to fill vacancies left by a shortage of parents willing to stand for election. More fundamentally, there is also a growing realisation that the current formal system of parental involvement is not working. The two-committee structure in schools has compartmenta-lised parental involvement unhelpfully. School boards have become totally swamped with management issues and are invited to comment on a range of government and local authority policies, which may not be the slightest bit relevant to them as parents. They are involved in discussion about school funding and development plans which, whilst slightly more relevant, may not cover real parents' issues. Meanwhile many PTAs have been reduced to little more than fund-raising bodies often instructed by teachers on how much they need to raise and what they should buy. New Community Schools, recently set up to involve a range of services in the education system and to provide a community focus, are trying out new forms of involvement. These range from using outreach staff for visiting parents at home to providing parents with classes at the school in topics that are of interest to them.

Meanwhile parents have become less good at their number one function within the education service – providing the children. The number of live births has fallen from a post-war high of just over 104,000 in 1964 to a mere 51,000 in 2001. The parents of school children are becoming an endangered species.

REFERENCES

Macbeth, A. (1989) *Involving Parents: Effective Parent Teacher Relations*, London: Heinemann Educational.

SPTC (1998) *50th Anniversary of the Scottish Parent Teacher Council 1948–1998*, Edinburgh: SPTC.

Welsh, J. (ed.) (2001) *A–Z of Scots Education Law: A Guide for Parents*, Norwich: Scottish Consumer Council; The Stationery Office.

Wolfendale, S. and Bastiani, J., (eds) (2000) *The Contribution of Parents to School Effectiveness*, London: David Fulton.

IV

The Historical, Cultural and Economic Context of Scottish Education

20

The History of Scottish Education, pre-1980

Robert Anderson

Scottish education has been characterised by a peculiar awareness of its own history. Since 1707 its distinctness has been a mark of national identity to be defended against assimilation with England, and its supposed superiority has been a point of national pride. Two achievements were especially notable: the early arrival of universal or near-universal literacy, and a precociously developed university system; on these was founded the 'democratic' myth of Scottish education, later expressed in the literary and popular image of the 'lad o' pairts', the boy of modest social origins from a rural or small-town background climbing the educational ladder to such professions as the ministry, schoolteaching, or the civil service. Like other national myths, this idealises reality, but has a core of truth, though most historians would agree that it represented an individualist form of meritocracy, rather than reflecting a classless society. For all the virtues of the rural parish school, the chief features of modern Scottish education were created in the few decades following the Education (Scotland) Act 1872, and as a pioneering urban and industrial country Scotland was deeply marked by the class divisions of the nineteenth century. The 1872 Act was a political and administrative landmark, but (as we shall see) the basic task of schooling the new working class had already been largely overcome, and the increased intervention of the state was not so much a reaction against the previous dominance of religion and the Church, but rather a modernised and secular form of an ideal of 'national' and public education, aimed at imposing cultural uniformity, which can be traced to the Reformation, if not before, and which is itself a strong constituent of the Scottish tradition.

THE PARISH SCHOOL AND LITERACY

The leaders of the Scottish Reformation had an unusually clear vision of the role of education in creating a godly society. *The First Book of Discipline* of 1560 sketched out an articulated educational structure, from parish school to university, and aimed at providing basic religious instruction and literacy in each parish. Achieving this was the work of several generations, but it is today generally agreed that by the end of the seventeenth century the network of parish schools was largely complete in the lowlands, though not in the highlands. The Act of 1696 passed by the Scottish Parliament, which was strengthened in 1803 and remained the legal basis of the parish schools until 1872, consolidated this structure. The landowners (heritors) were obliged to build a schoolhouse and to pay a salary to a schoolmaster, which was supplemented by the fees paid by parents; ministers and presbyteries were responsible for the quality of education and the testing of schoolmasters. This was a statutory system, but one run by the church and the local notables rather than the state.

Schooling did not become compulsory until 1872, and attendance in the early modern period depended partly on the perceived advantages of education (which were greater for boys than girls), and partly on the pressure of landowners, ministers, and community opinion. Attendance was clearly not universal, and recent studies of literacy have challenged the traditional optimistic picture. Houston (1985, pp. 56–62) estimates male literacy (defined as the ability to write a signature rather than a mark) at 65% in the lowlands in the mid-eighteenth century, and female at no more than 25–30%. This put the Scottish lowlands among the more literate areas of Europe, but was not a unique achievement. As elsewhere, literacy varied regionally (the borders and east central Scotland being the most advanced), was higher in towns than in the countryside, and was correlated with occupation and prosperity, reaching artisans, small merchants or farmers before labourers, miners, factory workers or crofters.

It is very likely that the early stages of the industrial revolution, with the accompanying phenomena of urbanisation and migration from the highlands and Ireland, worsened overall rates of literacy. But exact figures are lacking until the official registration of marriages was introduced in 1855. At that time 89% of men and 77% of women could sign the registers – compared with 70% and 59% respectively in England. But signature evidence may underestimate the basic ability to read, for writing was taught as a separate skill, with higher fees, and many children, especially girls, did not advance beyond reading. Taken as a whole, the evidence on literacy suggests that by 1800 Scottish lowland communities had made the fundamental transition to written culture. Illiteracy survived, but was stigmatised and deplored by the Church and the secular authorities, and the ability to read was broad enough to support the beginnings of a tradition of working-class self-education and self-improvement.

None of this applied to the highlands, where attempts to create schools suffered from adverse economic and geographical conditions, the slow penetration of the Church's basic parochial organisation, and the resistance of an oral Gaelic culture. After 1715, and even more after 1745, Church and state combined to enforce loyalty and orthodoxy, and it was axiomatic that this must be through the medium of English. Parish schools were supplemented by those of the Society in Scotland for Propagating Christian Knowledge, founded in 1709, but the refusal to teach in Gaelic (except initially as an aid to learning English) created a formidable cultural barrier between family and school. Nevertheless, by the early nineteenth century conditions in the more prosperous parts of the highlands and islands were not so different from the lowlands, though usually with scantier resources, and illiteracy was being driven into its last redoubts in the western isles.

A notable feature of the parish school was its connection with the universities. Schoolmasters were expected to have some university experience, and taught enough Latin to allow boys to pass directly into university classes. This system had evolved to encourage the recruitment of ministers, and there were bursaries to give promising pupils financial support. This was the origin of the tradition of the 'lad o' pairts', and though in practice most such boys came from the middle ranks – the sons of ministers, farmers and artisans – rather than the really poor, the educational opportunities offered in the countryside made Scotland unusual.

BURGH SCHOOLS AND UNIVERSITIES

The parish school legislation did not apply in burghs. It was normal for royal burghs to maintain burgh schools, whose existence can be traced back into the middle ages. Originally these were grammar schools, teaching Latin with an eye to the universities, but town councils began to appoint additional teachers for modern and commercial subjects, and by the late eighteenth century there was a move to consolidate the various schools in an 'academy', usually housed in impressive new buildings. The expanding middle class of the towns was thus well catered for, and outside the big cities the burgh schools and academies were open to both sexes, an unusual feature at the time. But town councils had no statutory duty to provide education for the mass of the population, and most basic education in the towns was given by private teachers. Although Scotland has a strong tradition of public education, private schools once had a vital role, in rural areas as well as in the towns, being squeezed out only in the nineteenth century by competition, from churches and charitable bodies as well as the state. These schools have been underestimated as they left few traces in historical records. They ranged from the 'dame school' where a woman taught reading to young children in her own home, through the 'private adventure' school which at its best could give the same sort of education as a parish school, to expensive boarding and day schools in the cities, training boys for the university or a commercial career, or 'young ladies' in the accomplishments expected of a middle-class bride.

The vigorous state of urban education by 1800 reflected the prosperity of the age of improvement, as did the striking success of the universities, of which Scotland had five. Three were founded in the fifteenth century (St Andrews, Glasgow and King's College Aberdeen), and two after the Reformation (Edinburgh and Marischal College Aberdeen), but the Reformation did not change their fundamental character, as inward-looking institutions teaching arts and theology, whose core task was the training of the clergy. The political and religious upheavals of the seventeenth century were damaging, but after 1700 the universities embarked on a notable revival culminating in the age of the Enlightenment, when Scotland was for a time in the van of European thought. The lecture-based curriculum had a broadly philosophical approach embracing modern subjects like science and economics, and directly expressed enlightened ideals of politeness, improvement and virtue. The universities could thus offer a liberal education to the social elite, while simultaneously developing professional training, especially at Edinburgh, in law and medicine. Medical education was especially important in securing the universities' reputation and in attracting students, as was to remain the case in the nineteenth century. Socially, the fact that all the universities except St Andrews were situated in large towns kept them in touch with contemporary demands and made them accessible to the new commercial and professional classes; the sons of the aristocracy and gentry, no longer sent abroad to universities like Leyden, rubbed shoulders with a more modest and traditional contingent aiming at the ministry or schoolteaching.

THE INDUSTRIAL REVOLUTION AND MASS EDUCATION

By the end of the eighteenth century Scots were aware of the distinctive character of their educational system, and already saw it as a point of superiority over England. But it had evolved within a predominantly agrarian society, dominated by its traditional elites, and committed to religious uniformity. Industrialisation, the appearance of modern class divisions, the rise of political democracy, and the growth of religious pluralism posed formidable challenges, and required far-reaching adaptations. The working of the Scottish system had not been affected by the union of 1707, but the practical and political response to industrialisation was inevitably similar in Scotland and England, and required legislation which brought them closer together.

The problems of educating the new urban working class were first tackled around 1810, initially by philanthropists advocating the 'Lancasterian' method of monitorial instruction, but mainly by the Church. Supporting schools became a standard activity for church congregations, and there were many religiously-inspired committees and societies which promoted special types of school – infant schools, schools in the highlands, schools for girls, schools for the 'ragged' children of the streets, evening schools for factory workers. These activities were co-ordinated locally by the church's presbyteries, and nationally by the General Assembly's influential Education Committee. But hopes of a continuing partnership between Church and state were shattered by the Disruption of 1843, after which the Church of Scotland was a minority Church. Shortly afterwards, in 1846, state aid to education (which had started in the 1830s with building grants, and was supervised from 1840 by a Scottish inspectorate) was reorganised to give annual grants to schools which followed the state's curricular 'Code'. The grant system encouraged the professional training of teachers through the 'pupil-teacher' system of apprenticeship, linked with the 'normal' or training colleges run by the Churches. In dispensing its grants, the state did not discriminate between denominations. The new Free Church threw itself into an ambitious educational programme, while Episcopalians and Roman Catholics concentrated on providing for their own adherents. The growth of Catholic schools, especially in Glasgow and the west, was fuelled by Irish immigration, and state support was especially important because of the poverty of the Catholic community. The Catholic system also had distinctive cultural features such as teaching by religious orders, and separate boys' and girls' schools.

There thus developed a dual system: the statutory parish schools, still limited to rural parishes, and a very diverse sector of denominational and voluntary but state-aided schools. Attempts to merge the two systems and achieve a more rational use of resources preoccupied politicians for many years, but always foundered on the rocks of party-political and religious dissension. The 1872 Act was thus a considerable achievement. It created a 'state' system by giving control of most schools to an elected school board in each burgh and parish, and persuaded the Presbyterian churches to hand over their schools to the boards. This contrasted with the situation in England and Wales, where the Education Act 1870 inaugurated a bitter rivalry between board and Church schools, requiring further legislation in 1902 and 1944.

The 1872 Act created two new agencies which, in different forms, were to share the direction of education thereafter. The school boards gave new scope to local opinion. They were elected by a form of proportional representation, and the franchise included women if they were independent property-holders; women could also be members of the boards, and made a distinctive contribution in the larger towns. School boards lasted until the Education (Scotland) Act 1918, when they were replaced by ad hoc education authorities on a county basis; only in 1929 was education transferred to the all-purpose local authorities. The second creation of 1872 was the Scotch Education Department (SED; not renamed Scottish until 1918). From 1885 the SED was attached to the new Scottish Office, and its early secretaries Henry Craik (1885–1904) and John Struthers (1904–23) turned it into a powerful bureaucracy, giving Scotland a more centralised and uniform state system than England. The balance between central and local control was weighted from the start towards the SED, since school boards and local authorities, despite their rating powers, still depended on state grants and had to meet the conditions laid down centrally.

BEFORE AND AFTER THE EDUCATION ACT 1872

The creation of state systems of popular education was a general feature of the nineteenth century, related to broader movements of democratisation (the franchise was extended to urban workers in 1867), to the needs of a developing economy, and to the rise of the nation state and national rivalries. Legislation reflected the desire of the state to control a vital agency of citizenship and national efficiency, as much as to promote mass literacy. In fact both school attendance and literacy were already at a high level in Scotland, as the reports of the Argyll Commission in 1867–8 revealed. The practical significance of the 1872 Act was that it established common standards and filled the gaps which the voluntary system had been unable to reach.

The first gap was between men and women. In 1870 90% of bridegrooms could sign their names, but only 80% of brides. The idea that girls needed a less complete schooling than boys lingered, but in the mid-nineteenth century there had been a growth of separate schools for girls, which probably helped to accelerate female literacy. It was associated with the rise of the woman teacher, and although it was well after 1872 before women outnumbered men in the profession, the training colleges offered women a significant path to independence and social mobility. After 1872 school boards usually abolished the small girls' schools, and mixed education became the norm. By 1900, when formal literacy was virtually complete, there was only one point between men (98%) and women (97%), and girls stayed slightly longer at school than boys (Anderson, 1995, pp. 234, 305).

A second gap was within the working class. Under the voluntary system, skilled and 'respectable' workers, who could afford to pay the standard school fee of about threepence a week, had access to schools of reasonable quality, and their children could stay long enough to master the basics, as did nearly all children in the rural lowlands. But the urban poor usually had access only to inferior schools, charging a penny a week or giving a charitable free education. In factory and mining districts, and in the big cities, child labour was a major disincentive to education. Factory legislation, as well as compulsory schooling, progressively removed this obstacle, and though school fees were not abolished until 1890, school boards offered an education of equal quality to all their constituents. The huge urban schools which remain the symbol of the Victorian era in education became part of the homogeneous working-class experience which had evolved by 1900.

A third gap was between Lowlands and Highlands. The Argyll report revealed the poverty and backwardness of education in the Western Isles, Skye and some mainland districts, though these conditions were by now untypical of the Highlands as a whole. For some years Highland school boards were to struggle with inadequate resources, but the problems were overcome within a generation. Part of the price was a further retreat of Gaelic. The 1872 Act has often been blamed for this, and it is true that official policy made only minor concessions to the language; but there was nothing new in this, for Highland educational initiatives had always insisted on the primacy of English. It was not until after 1945 that serious efforts were made to promote bilingualism.

A fourth gap, which the 1872 Act did not remedy, was the situation of Catholic schools.

Illiteracy persisted in the Catholic community, and helped make the western counties a problem area. The religious settlement of 1872 was not accepted by Catholics or Episcopalians, and they continued to receive direct state grants, which covered running costs but not capital expenditure. The Episcopalian schools stagnated and eventually withered away, but the Catholic sector expanded, from sixty-five schools in 1872 to 226 in 1918; about an eighth of all Scottish children were in Catholic schools. Lack of resources meant that schools were under-equipped, teachers poorly paid, and secondary education under-developed. This was increasingly felt as an injustice, and the 1918 Act transferred Roman Catholic schools to the education authorities, to be supported on the same financial basis as other schools, with safeguards for religious instruction and the denominational affiliation of teachers. Protected and promoted by the hierarchy, often in alliance with the new Labour electorate, Catholic schools soon acquired an entrenched position in the public system (see Chapter 25).

The 1872 Act made education compulsory from age five to thirteen, raised to fourteen in 1883. But this was theoretical, as children could leave earlier if they had mastered the 'three Rs'. From 1901, however, fourteen was enforced as the effective leaving age, and by then the elementary curriculum included subjects like History, Geography, Elementary Science, Physical Training, and some semi-vocational elements: Woodwork for boys, Cookery and 'Domestic Economy' for girls. Once every child passed through the school, governments also saw its value as an agency of social welfare: school meals and medical inspection were put on a statutory basis in 1908. The daily routines of the elementary school were not to change fundamentally thereafter until the 1960s.

THE REMODELLING OF ELITE EDUCATION

While elementary education developed on its own lines, having an essentially working-class character which contrasted with the lack of sharp social differentiation in the old parish schools, secondary schools and universities were remodelled to meet the needs of the expanding middle class for professional qualifications and examination credentials. The movement for university reform began early, and was often controversial. There were royal commissions of inquiry in 1826 and 1876, and reforming Acts of Parliament in 1858 and 1889, which overhauled both constitutions and curricula. In the early nineteenth century the universities had no entrance examination, and although there was a recommended curriculum, many students stayed for only a year or two, chose which lectures to attend, and took no examinations – formal graduation had become the exception. But this no longer suited the needs of the age, and the outcome of reform by the 1890s was a standardised pattern of graduation, with the arts curriculum offering a choice between three-year ordinary and four-year honours degrees. Specialised courses, including separate faculties of Science, replaced the old MA curriculum with its compulsory Latin, Greek and Philosophy. The typical age of entry rose from fifteen or sixteen, as it still was in the 1860s, to seventeen or eighteen, and free entry gave way to an entrance examination equivalent to the School Leaving Certificate introduced by the SED in 1888. These changes were only possible because secondary schools had been reformed and given an extended academic curriculum.

A 'secondary' system (the term itself appeared only in the 1860s) was constructed from disparate elements. The 1872 Act transferred the burgh schools to school boards, but otherwise did little for secondary education. Resources were found instead from endowments, and in the 1870s and 1880s many older endowed schools, including the former residential 'hospitals' like George Heriot's in Edinburgh, were modernised. Further gaps were filled by 'higher grade' schools, founded by school boards as extensions of elementary schools, especially in Glasgow. In 1892 the first state grants for secondary education appeared (ten years earlier than in England), and were used to build up schools in smaller towns as well as to strengthen existing ones. The result was that although schools differed in prestige and legal status, they formed an effective national network able to prepare both for the universities and for business careers. The Argyll Commission in the 1860s had identified fifty-nine public secondary schools with 14,879 pupils. By 1912 there were 249, with 38,312 pupils (19,611 boys and 18,701 girls). Of these 143 gave a full five-year course, and 106 a three-year or 'intermediate' one; 171 of the schools charged no fees (Anderson, R. D. *Education and Opportunity in Victorian Scotland: Schools and Universities*, Clarendon Press: Oxford, 1983, pp. 134, 243–6). This pattern was to change little until the 1940s.

Two points were especially significant. Firstly, though Scotland was not a pioneer in university education for women – because of legal obstacles, their admission was delayed until 1892 – mixed secondary education became firmly established, at least outside Edinburgh, Glasgow and Aberdeen, where high schools and endowed schools remained single-sex. Middle-class parents now had as good a choice of education for their daughters as for their sons, and this was reflected in the percentage of women students at the universities, which was high by contemporary standards: 23% by 1914, rising to 34% in the 1920s, though it fell again in the 1930s to 26–7%.

Secondly, the schools served a wide social range. The road to the university now lay only through the secondary school, but analysis of the social origins of university students suggests that opportunities for mobility were not narrowed. Although Scotland had a few English-style 'public schools' like Fettes College, and some exclusive day schools like Edinburgh Academy and its equivalents in Glasgow (see Chapter 9), the Scottish middle class were generally content to use their local schools. At the other end of the social scale, accessibility was wide because many secondary schools charged no fees, and bursaries were fairly widely available. Transfer from elementary to secondary schools around the age of twelve became an accepted if still limited phenomenon. The 1918 Act required education authorities to make free secondary education available to all, though they could and did retain fee-paying in designated schools.

THE TWENTIETH CENTURY: TOWARDS AN INTEGRATED SYSTEM

By 1900, the extension of the elementary curriculum and the increasing number of children staying at school after age twelve raised the question of relations between the two sectors. The SED was now using the term 'primary' for the early stages of education, but the underlying social conception was still that true secondary education was only for an academically gifted minority, and it was official policy (formalised in 1903) to draw a sharp distinction between secondary and advanced elementary education. A 'qualifying exam-ination' at twelve identified the exceptional talents who might climb the educational ladder (a favourite image of the time), but the majority stayed on in the primary school and took 'supplementary courses'. After leaving school, they were encouraged to attend evening 'continuation' classes, mostly vocational. The reforming mood created by the First World War raised hopes of an end to this dualism, especially as the 1918 Act proposed raising the leaving age from fourteen to fifteen. But financial crisis suspended this provision – and also plans for compulsory continuation classes for adolescents – and the SED resisted pressures for 'secondary education for all', continuing to insist that the different types of course should be rigidly separate. Its controversial regulations of 1923 renamed the supplementary courses 'advanced divisions', but these were denied secondary status, and most had only a two-year curriculum.

In practice the inter-war years saw a blurring of the distinction between courses. In smaller towns, both types were given in 'omnibus' schools which took all older children, and elsewhere the authorities usually grouped advanced education in 'central' schools, replacing all-age schools with a redistribution at age twelve (the 'clean cut'). The Education Act 1936 proposed raising the leaving age to fifteen in 1939, and although this was postponed because of the war (until 1947) the SED finally accepted that all post-primary courses should be called secondary, divided where necessary between 'senior' (five-year) and 'junior' (three-year) schools. This system was consolidated and developed in the 1940s. Most senior secondary schools were old-established secondaries, with superior buildings, equipment and staffing, while junior secondaries were either former central schools or new foundations. All-age primary schools finally disappeared except in remote rural areas. Thus apart from places served by bilateral omnibus schools, Scotland now had a selective secondary system based on the 'twelve-plus' examination, given new scientific authority by the intelligence testing developed in the 1930s.

Secondary schools were the most dynamic sector of Scottish education between the wars: numbers rose to about 90,000 by 1939. But low birth rates and the collapse of traditional industries had a generally negative and depressing effect. Despite a few initiatives like the creation of the Scottish Council for Research in Education in 1928, official thinking remained conservative. There was, for example, no vigorous promotion of scientific and technical education, of a kind which might have helped revive the Scottish economy. The Second World War changed this, directly by underlining the importance of science and advanced education, indirectly by creating long-term social aspirations which broke the fetters of the selective system. Even for the political left, selection seemed acceptable after the war as an expression of equality of opportunity, and the more idealistic vision expressed in the 1947 report of the Scottish Advisory Council on Education was rejected by the SED. But the breaking down of the old industrial economy, with its relatively small elite and its mass working class, undermined the assumption that academic education and examination qualifications could be reserved for a quarter or a third of the population. There was also a fundamental change in the career expectations of women. Thus by the 1960s there was an increasing demand to stay on at school, and to gain qualifications which the junior secondaries were unable to offer. One response was the introduction of the Scottish Certificate of Education in 1962, with a Higher Grade which was less university-oriented than the old Leaving Certificate, and a new Ordinary Grade offering a wider range of subjects for fourth-year pupils.

These pressures paved the way for the eventual raising of the leaving age to sixteen in 1973, and more immediately for the abolition of selection in 1965, a policy which aroused some controversy at the time, but which soon achieved wide acceptance, as it failed to do in England. The pattern of mixed, six-year comprehensives was almost universal in Scotland. Difficulties arose chiefly in the cities, where it meant the end of the remaining fee-paying schools, and where residential segregation strongly influenced the character and achievement of schools. A further consequence of the policy, also concentrated in the cities, was the withdrawal of the state's direct grants to old-established endowed schools, which now passed with their middle-class clientele into the independent sector.

The organisation of secondary schooling and its relation with primary schools was the most politically sensitive issue in Scottish education for much of the twentieth century. But primary education had its own revolution after 1945. An expanding birth-rate, and the shift of the population from central districts to suburbs and new towns, required a massive programme of new building and teacher training. So did the introduction of more child-centred educational methods, and the SED's 1965 Memorandum, *Primary Education in Scotland*, gave these official sanction.

Expansion was also marked at the post-secondary level. Government policy after 1945 accepted the need for more students in both traditional universities and technical colleges, and the Robbins Report of 1963 only endorsed a trend already well under way. A new university opened at Stirling, and Strathclyde and Heriot-Watt universities were created from existing advanced technical colleges. Technical colleges had their roots in the nineteenth century, and the leading ones had been financed directly by the SED as 'central institutions' since 1900. Now full-time and degree-level work was encouraged, and local technical and adult education were combined in a network of 'further education' colleges. The old teacher-training colleges, renamed colleges of education in 1958, were also encouraged to expand their remit and award degrees. By 1980, therefore, the concept of a 'tertiary' education of which traditional universities were only one part was well accepted, and it attracted more than 15% of the age-group; but the general extension of university status remained in the future.

CONCLUSION

The growth of secondary and higher education since 1945 can be seen as the latest stage in a continual expansion of education, and of its place in the lives of individuals, which began in the mid-nineteenth century and shows no sign of coming to an end. At its outset most working-class children, if they attended school at all, left at ten or eleven, while middle-class children, apart from a small minority who went to the universities, left at fourteen or fifteen. By 1980, the age of leaving full-time education, though still conditioned by social class, ranged from sixteen to twenty-two or more. In responding to the problems created by the industrial revolution, Scotland was given a good start by its tradition of national education and by a cultural disposition, with religious, political and social roots, to value educational achievement. But as other countries caught up, Scotland ceased to be so exceptional, though some indicators (notably the rate of participation in higher education) remained very favourable. Many historians would argue that while the system promoted meritocracy, and allowed individual Scots to move upwards into both Scottish and British elites, the education offered to the ordinary child was less impressive. The structure of schooling which developed after 1872 reflected class divisions in Scotland much as elsewhere, and twentieth-century progress towards greater equality of opportunity, though perhaps made smoother by an idealised conception of the educational past, had still to contend with social inequalities which the formal integration of educational institutions achieved by 1980 could not itself remove.

REFERENCES

Anderson, R. D. (1995) *Education and the Scottish People, 1750–1918*, Oxford: Oxford University Press.

Gray, J., McPherson, A. and Raffe, D. (1983) *Reconstructions of Secondary Education: Theory, Myth and Practice since the War*, London: Routledge.

Houston, R. A. (1985) *Scottish Literacy and the Scottish Identity: Illiteracy and Society in Scotland and Northern England, 1600–1800*, Cambridge: Cambridge University Press.

Humes, W. and Paterson, H. (eds) (1982) *Scottish Culture and Scottish Education, 1800–1980*, Edinburgh: John Donald.

Scotland, J. (1969) *The History of Scottish Education*, 2 vols, London: University of London Press.

Withrington, D. J. (1988) Schooling, literacy and society, in T. M. Devine and R. Mitchison (eds), *People and Society in Scotland. I. 1760–1830*, Edinburgh: John Donald.

21

The History of Scottish Education, 1980 to the Present Day

Willis Pickard

LABOUR LEGACY, TORY AGENDA

Changes of government do not affect day-to-day teaching in schools and colleges. Yet over time they make a difference. It is convenient to start the most recent story of Scottish education in 1979 when a Conservative government led by Margaret Thatcher took over from Labour. The new ministers at the Scottish Office inherited an education system in transition and arrived with their own agenda. Decisions that had to be taken because of matters in the pipeline were at least as significant as those emanating from the Conservative manifesto.

The most poisoned chalice handed to Thatcher, in her own opinion, was the Clegg Commission which was studying UK public sector pay and which in 1980 recommended rises for teachers ranging from 17% to 25%. The effects of wage inflation on economic policy and political direction were dire. They were also to lay the foundations for an intensifying argument about teachers' pay and conditions which in Scotland led to the long and bitter industrial dispute from 1984 to 1986.

A second inheritance from Labour was in the secondary school curriculum. The Labour government had reached no final conclusions about the Munn and Dunning Reports of 1977. Together these had recommended new courses and examinations for all S3 and S4 pupils to replace the Ordinary Grades which had been designed for 30% of the school population and which were clearly unsuitable for a large number of the pupils staying on till sixteen following the raising of the leaving age in the early 1970s. The new Secretary of State, George Younger, and his Education Minister, Alex Fletcher, decided in 1980 to pursue the Munn and Dunning agenda. By 1982 that took final form in a paper, *A Framework for Decision*, as the Standard Grade development programme.

The two-year courses were based on the belief, enshrined in the report of the committee chaired by a headteacher, Sir James Munn, that all pupils should follow a curriculum based on eight modes of learning. Following the recommendations of the committee under Joseph Dunning, then principal of Napier College, they would achieve Standard Grade qualifications – partly assessed within schools – at three levels, Credit, General or Foundation. Although five years had elapsed between the original reports and the launch of the development programme, the speed with which teachers were then expected to implement changes and the reliance placed on them to develop suitable course-work were to have some unfortunate results. The government's strategy was to retain direction of the programme, coupled with extensive involvement of practising teachers. But the extra demands fuelled the wider discontents about pay levels and conditions of service. They also gave the teachers a weapon. Because Standard Grade needed their co-operation, it could be jeopardised by a withdrawal of goodwill that fell far short of a withdrawal of labour. The two-year dispute was to postpone full implementation for virtually the remainder of the decade.

Unusually for a Scottish Education Minister, Fletcher won legislative time in two successive parliamentary sessions. His 1980 Education (Scotland) Act restated longstanding principles such as the duty of parents to educate their children, but it also took forward another non-partisan legacy from the previous government. The Warnock Report of 1978 had recommended sweeping changes at UK level in the education of children with special needs. Its principles had accorded with the views of the inspectorate in Scotland and the upshot was legislation which established rights for parents and children to education within either a special setting or a mainstream school. Early identification and assessment of need were emphasised, and for children with more pronounced difficulties a Record of Needs would be opened and regularly reviewed.

The new ministers wanted to make their own mark as well as carry forward an inheritance. In 1978 Fletcher, along with fellow MP and teacher John MacKay, later himself to be an education minister and latterly member of the House of Lords, had published an opposition pamphlet, 'Scottish education – regaining a lost reputation'. It denounced standards in schools and demanded greater accountability to and more opportunities for parents. In government this had two immediate consequences. As in England, an assisted places scheme was instituted by which children of less well-off families qualified for free or subsidised places in independent schools. Secondly, Fletcher, as an Edinburgh MP, had been influenced by parents who had brought court cases, such as one involving the 'Leith Ten', to challenge the rigid school catchment areas in Labour regions. So the Education (Scotland) Act of 1981 was framed to include the so-called 'parents' charter'. Those who did not want their child to go to the school in their catchment area could nominate another which was obliged to take a pupil unless it could show that it was overcrowded. Since the 1980s most parents who have sought a placing request have been successful. But some schools have become oversubscribed.

SPEEDY ACTION

Less well remembered than the Standard Grade development programme but at least as important was the Action Plan launched in 1983. It charted the way to a curriculum for 16–18-year-olds not going on to higher education. In effect it was a bold plan to transform the whole of further education, and the contrast has been drawn between how quickly the FE colleges responded to the challenge while the schools dragged their heels over Standard Grade.

The Action Plan led to the establishment of the Scottish Vocational Educational Council (SCOTVEC) with a completely new system of curriculum delivery, assessment and certification. For the SCOTVEC National Certificate every course had to be redesigned in the form of forty–hour modules, each of which was accompanied by detailed 'descriptors', of which there came to be many hundreds. The advantage of modularised courses lay in their flexibility. They could be used to build coherent curricula of increasing difficulty and they gave students far greater choice.

Whereas previous governments had had to tackle overcrowding of schools and lack of qualified teachers, the 1980s saw a different challenge: a drastically reduced birth-rate leading to smaller pupil numbers and pressure to close under-used schools in the face of parental opposition. But despite the reduced numbers, there was a growing tide of youth unemployment as unskilled jobs disappeared and traditional avenues from school to work, such as apprenticeships, had to be replaced by a succession of national measures starting with the Youth Opportunities Programme, which was intended to focus on training but looked more like a stop-gap response to unemployment. When the government launched the Youth Training Scheme in 1983, the Sheffield-based Manpower Services Commission, which was charged with UK training initiatives, appeared to have more clout at the summit of government than the national education departments.

Teaching children about business and preparing them for the world of work was not new, but it received greater emphasis from a government wedded to ideas of self-help and entrepreneurship. In Scotland teachers remained suspicious of the politics behind enterprise education but co-operated in, for example, the great expansion of work placements for pupils, especially in the final year of compulsory schooling. The Technical and Vocational Education Initiative which offered government cash to locally devised schemes was initially regarded with suspicion by the Scottish Office Education Department, but the pool of money was irresistible. TVEI schemes were especially beneficial to schools in deprived urban areas, and teachers became adept at making bids which found a vocational and entrepreneurial slant for almost any kind of secondary school project.

A 1981 report, *Teaching and Learning in P4 and P7*, by the inspectorate showed how traditional had remained methods of teaching and curriculum content despite innovative thinking dating back to the Primary Memorandum of 1965. Having instituted changes in the middle years of secondary, the government and its advisers in the Scottish Consultative Council on the Curriculum turned their attention to the lower secondary and its relationship to the upper primary. After a starter paper in 1980 a committee was set up two years later under the chairmanship of David Robertson, Director of Education in Tayside. Its attempt to pilot ideas in schools was frustrated by the teachers' dispute, but in 1986 it published *Education 10–14 in Scotland*.

This was an ambitious and widely acclaimed attempt to find a philosophy that would unify the education of the age group and counter discontinuities between the generalist approach of primary teachers and the subject specialisms of secondary. The admirers of the report did not, however, include the government. The inspectorate published a 'costing' of implementation, which the new Minister of Education, Allan Stewart, found excessive. The report was buried, but the belief remained that cost was less of an obstacle than the insistence by Robertson and his colleagues that every secondary and its associated primaries be involved in translating a recommended model for learning into a detailed curriculum. That would have placed too much power in teachers' hands, and they were already holding the whole system to ransom.

THE LONGEST DISPUTE

The teachers' dispute was to alter everyone's thinking. Both sides, government and unions, had much to lose during the two years, and after it was over, each vowed for different reasons never to let disagreement become a damaging standoff. At root from the unions' point of view, and especially that of the Educational Institute of Scotland (EIS) whose dominant position with almost 80% of school teachers in membership meant it controlled the teachers' side of the direct-bargaining Scottish Joint Negotiating Committee (with the local authority employers on the other side of the table) was a belief that the pay gains of the mid-1970s had been lost. The Clegg award of 1981 may have been too much for the Prime Minister, but it clearly failed to restore the position following the earlier inquiry, by Lord Houghton, in 1974. Restoration of Houghton-levels of pay award, coupled with refusal to trade off conditions of service for money, was the rallying cry.

The strategy was to call for an independent pay review. The government repeatedly rejected the demand. By 1984 the EIS was ready for action, and a rolling programme of short strikes was set in train. In addition, work on curricular development was halted. The annual timetable of preparation for the Scottish Examination Board's Standard Grade and Highers awards was threatened, and this was to cause particular anxiety for two years. In the event the external exams went ahead and were marked as normal. Whether any pupils got poorer marks because of disrupted teaching, no-one could later prove.

The EIS, backed by the smaller Scottish Secondary Teachers' Association, neither wanted nor could have afforded an all-out strike. The teachers needed outside support. They had it in principle from the local authorities, the largest of which were Labour-controlled. They had to ensure parental backing as well, and too much disruption to classes would have sacrificed that sooner rather than later. So a new form of action was devised. It concentrated disruption on schools in Conservative-held seats, especially those of govern-ment ministers. John Pollock, the wily as well as charismatic general secretary of the EIS, knew the tactic was risky. It came close to contempt of Parliament. But it limited the number of days' teaching lost and largely excused schools in poorer areas.

The public remained convinced the teachers had a case – that they were, in the view of a joint local authority-union study, over-worked, under-valued and under stress. The government could only hope that the teachers' resolve would crumble under public pressure because the Prime Minister refused to budge. She was after all in prolonged and bitter dispute with trade unionists traditionally more militant and more capable of causing national damage. But it was a sign of a changed economy that a formerly moderate white-collar profession could retain public sympathy and remain undefeated while the miners found themselves isolated and ultimately powerless.

The deadlock was not broken until March 1986. Two events prompted a change of attitude by the government and allowed the unions to call off their action. The first was that Malcolm Rifkind had replaced George Younger as Secretary of State. Allan Stewart lost his job as Minister of Education, the victim of the Cabinet's no-surrender policy which he had defended manfully but with no effect on public opinion. The new team of Rifkind and John MacKay as his junior convinced the Prime Minister that the dispute had to be resolved well before the next election, which took place in the spring of 1987. They were helped by a second factor – the ending of a similar dispute with teachers south of the border. Mrs Thatcher reluctantly accepted a Scottish committee of inquiry headed by Sir Peter Main, former chairman of Boots.

If *An Unlikely Anger*, the title of a journalist's contemporary account of the struggle is correct, most teachers accepted that they had won an unlikely victory and could not count on continued public patience. Six months later the Main Committee proposed limits on the hours teachers were contracted to work, a new grade of senior teacher to reward those who stayed in the classroom and a simplified pay structure. There was no recommended increase to compensate for previous losses. In other words the claims about pressure of work had had a more sympathetic response than those for a pay rise. Both sides in the dispute could accept Main without loss of face.

From the dispute the unions took two important lessons. Firstly, all-out, countrywide stoppages were no longer practicable, especially because of restrictions imposed by Conservative trade union legislation. Power should be devolved from union headquarters to local associations. The council reforms of 1996, creating thirty-two education authorities out of the twelve previous ones, encouraged the EIS to a more locally based structure. Secondly, winning public support had been the key to maintaining the dispute over two years. In future, sympathy would be turned into alliance. The government learned lessons, too. It felt it had been held to ransom because too much reliance had been placed on a profession which had behaved as a militant trade union. The relaunched Standard Grade programme now relied on centrally produced materials and not those devised (latterly, not devised) at classroom level.

Meanwhile the teachers had had to adjust to another expression of consumer pressure. In 1984 a Bill was introduced to ensure that no child in a state school received corporal punishment if his parents objected. Due to take effect in 1986, the legislation did little more than recognise a fait accompli. The European Court of Human Rights had ruled in the 1982 Campbell and Cosans case that the philosophical convictions of parents against the use of corporal punishment had to be respected. To avoid further legal challenges all but four of the twelve education authorities had abolished the belt by the time the government introduced its bill. Teachers who had supported corporal punishment as the best last resort accepted that times had changed. But there was widespread concern about the effectiveness of alternative sanctions, especially exclusion from school.

IDEOLOGY TAKES OVER

The election of 1987 reduced the number of Scottish Conservative MPs to ten. Among the casualties was John MacKay. Malcolm Rifkind found a new Education Minister in Michael Forsyth, the right-wing young MP for Stirling. Immediately Forsyth, who had trained in public relations, set out to make his mark. His gospel was a pamphlet, *Save Our Schools*, which he and other members of the Thatcherite No Turning Back group of back-bench MPs had published during the last Parliament. It argued the consumerist message for education. Schools should be removed from local authority control, power should pass from professionals to parents, and vouchers should be introduced to allow parents to 'buy' education where they chose.

Despite upsetting civil servants and even the Secretary of State by his impetuosity, Forsyth got his way. His first affront to the educational establishment came with legislation to create school boards. The measure could have been uncontroversial since all four political parties had included in their election manifestos a pledge to reform existing school councils. In most parts of the country a council existed for a secondary school and its associated primaries. It therefore was not felt to belong to an individual school. Had Forsyth limited his legislation to creating a board (or council) for every school, he would have had little opposition. But he cloaked his proposals in consumerist garb, arguing the case for parents to become involved in the practice of education as well as in supporting and working with the school as part of the community. Parents soon made it clear they had no wish to interfere with teachers' professional judgements or to take over the running of a school from its headteacher. In the first elections to boards in 1989, where parents formed a majority of members, most candidates stood on a minimalist platform, tacitly or explicitly rejecting the government's philosophy.

The Self-Governing Schools Act of 1989 illustrated the difficulty which increasingly became one of credibility for the Conservative Party north of the border. Following English example, the Scottish Office introduced legislation to allow schools to leave local authority control if parents voted to opt out. Such schools would then be funded directly by the Scottish Office. Forsyth was enthusiastic, the Secretary of State much less so. Opposition MPs found themselves wrongfooted by Forsyth's debating skills and the legislation was always destined to pass because of the weight of English Tory MPs. But the irrelevance of the measure to Scottish conditions was clear. Only two schools were to opt out compared with many hundreds in the south of England. The statute was used most by schools trying to resist closure proposals from their local authority.

The balance of power between local authority and schools was changing for another reason. In England local management, by which financial and administrative decisions were devolved from councils to heads and lay governors, became universal by the end of the 1980s. The Scottish Office followed suit with a scheme for devolved management of schools, but not before the Labour fiefdom of Strathclyde had embarked on its own scheme for 'delegated management of resources'. Frank Pignatelli, Strathclyde's Director of Education, determined not to wait for an imposed Scottish Office scheme and devised one which avoided many of the problems of the one south of the border, where funding formulas proved too rigid and encouraged school governors, for example, to remove experienced teachers and replace with them cheap young ones. The Scottish Office was unable to promote devolved management as a route to greater school efficiency and accountability to parents. But espousal of devolved powers within the local authority structure undermined the case for opting out.

A MORE NATIONAL CURRICULUM

The government also turned its attention to the primary and lower secondary. In a 1987 consultation paper, *Curriculum and Assessment: a Policy for the 90s*, it argued that there was a lack of precision in what primary schools offered and that parents were puzzled. Reflecting on the messages of the discarded 10–14 report it also pointed to discontinuity between primary and secondary. The Consultative Council on the Curriculum was asked to draw up guidelines, with priority for English, Mathematics and Environmental Studies including Science. Here was an example of the Scottish Office taking a firm lead. Primary schools had had little direction about what to teach. Inspectors had not been able to assess them against an agreed programme. The question was how far the new intervention stemmed from Scottish conditions – including ministers' resentment at teachers' autonomy and the power of education authorities – and how far it reflected a UK strategy. On the one hand it was argued that Forsyth was in thrall to the forces which produced a statutory national curriculum south of the border through Education Secretary Kenneth Baker's Education Reform Bill, which passed through Parliament in 1988. On the other hand there was no attempt to base the 5–14 programme (as the new curriculum came to be called) on statute or to prescribe, for example, texts suitable for 7-year-olds or episodes of glorious history to be studied, as Thatcher insisted in England and Wales.

The 5–14 curriculum eventually evolved in five areas – English, Mathematics, Environmental Studies (including History, Geography, Science and Technology), Expressive

Arts (including Physical Education) and Religious and Moral Education. Was the generic primary teacher expected to become a polymath? There were concerns, especially about Science and Technology and Religious Education. But many teachers welcomed a structure to their curriculum and the detailed guidance offered. The inspectorate emphasised repeatedly in the 1990s that not all aspects were to be introduced at once.

If the philosophy and content of the changes were widely accepted, the proposals for assessment were not. The curriculum was divided into five levels. Most pupils were expected to achieve level A in the first or second year of primary, level E in S1 and S2. Forsyth insisted that parents wanted an external gauge against which individual pupils' progress could be measured, but he said he was not wanting league tables of primary schools or of teacher performance. National tests would be set for pupils in P4 and P7.

The response was national resistance. An alliance to boycott the tests sprang up. Teachers defied their local authorities, though some authorities were themselves in defiant mood. Parents withdrew their children on test days. The government was powerless, caught again by unexpected consumer support for the teachers' case, which basically was that the tests would tell them nothing they did not already know about their pupils and that the curriculum would be narrowed as inevitably pupils were prepared to face the banks of test items prepared by the Scottish Examination Board.

By this time Forsyth had gone off to chair the Scottish Conservatives. Ian Lang, his successor and later the Secretary of State, was more emollient but also less committed. He realised that compliance with government wishes was impossible to ordain. Winning the 1992 election was the priority. Unexpectedly the Conservatives not only held on to power but regained modest ground in Scotland. The government, with the gentlemanly Lord James Douglas-Hamilton installed as Education Minister, stopped defending the indefensible. Instead of every P4 and P7 child being tested, teachers would use the tests to check on every pupil as he or she moved from one 5–14 level to the next. So there would also be tests in secondary schools, though the introduction of these proved hard to achieve since teachers were reluctant and local authorities unwilling to apply pressure.

THE STANDARDS DEBATE

In 1988 the centenary of the Highers was celebrated, but it was clear that all was not well with the benchmark of dependability in the Scottish assessment system, preferable though its breadth was to the much criticised narrowness of English A levels. With an increased number of pupils staying on at school, too many found the Highers an impossible or dispiriting challenge and the alternative diet of SCOTVEC modules lacked coherence and esteem. For all candidates there was too short a period between Standard Grade and Higher exams, with cramming taking precedence over education. For able pupils the sixth year offered too little challenge: they were accepted for university entrance on the basis of Highers, with the Certificate of Sixth Year Studies not being recognised. In 1992 a government committee chaired by John Howie, a St Andrews University Mathematics professor, found that although Scotland continued to compare well with England in terms of school leavers qualified for higher education, we had been overtaken by other west European countries.

The Howie Committee, much impressed by the Danish model in particular, suggested a twin-track system by which pupils would opt for an academic or vocational route with a common terminus in higher education entry for those who wanted it and with opportunities for transfers along the way. Able pupils would prepare for a Scottish baccalaureat in sixth year. Although the report was initially welcomed, its academic-vocational division was soon declared divisive. In 1994 Michael Forsyth as Secretary of State produced an alternative model known as the Higher Still development programme, which retained the Highers but added an Advanced sixth-year version to challenge the ablest and established, for slower learners, Access and Intermediate levels. Further education as well as schools would use the programme which would seek parity of esteem between courses derived from the SCOTVEC experience and those from an academic tradition. The Scottish Examination Board and SCOTVEC would merge.

The thrust of the programme proved acceptable to most teachers; the short time for preparation and alleged lack of resources did not. Twice the government conceded a year's delay. The second postponement was among the first acts of the Labour administration in 1997. The first Higher Still exams were set in 2000 with Advanced Higher a year later.

Concern about standards extended beyond S5 and S6. Michael Forsyth believed that schools should be publicly challenged. So tables of exam performance were published, though teachers said the results showed the social composition of the school rather than the 'valued added' between S1 and S4–S6. Tables of attendance and absence, leavers' destinations and school costs were also made public. Schools were expected to prepare and make available to parents their development programmes. Schemes of self-evaluation supplemented inspectors' reports which had been made public since the 1980s. Teachers were to be appraised by their seniors, although with the aim of enhancing staff development rather than identifying the incompetent. The agents of change were to be central government, through the inspectorate, and school managers themselves. Distrust of education authorities continued even after local government reorganisation in 1996 saw the end of the large Labour regions and the creation of thirty-two councils, none of which returned a Conservative administration in the first elections.

Fittingly, the last major reform by Forsyth introduced parental vouchers, a cause he had propounded through the No Turning Back group. Across the UK universal pre-school education for 4-year-olds was to be achieved by offering parents a voucher which could be used in a local authority, voluntary or private establishment. In the session 1996–7 four Scottish councils piloted a scheme which was then made national from August 1997. Parents welcomed an increase in nursery places but were unimpressed by the bureaucracy attached to vouchers. Labour opposed the scheme in the 1997 election campaign and on taking office announced its abolition, but the new Scottish Office team of Donald Dewar as Secretary of State and Brian Wilson as Education Minister said it should run for a year until an alternative could be devised. Wilson later made clear that local authorities should have responsibility for implementing the pledge that free part-time places would be available in one setting or another for all 4-year-olds. (By 2002 a place was made available for all 3-year-olds as well.)

The Conservatives lost all their Scottish seats in 1997. Distrust of their education policies contributed to the debacle. A sign of looming trouble was the march and rally in Edinburgh in 1996 against cuts in school funding which attracted 40,000 parents and teachers. When Labour took office, the education community breathed a sigh of relief and the atmosphere lightened, but ministers made clear that money would remain tight. An early popular initiative was extra funding for a scheme to help young primary pupils who were struggling with reading.

Over twenty years the balance of power that influences classroom practice had changed.

The role of central government and of parents had increased; that of local government and the teacher unions diminished. Further education shows more starkly than schools the shifting of power. In 1993 as a result of the Further and Higher Education (Scotland) Act, which also allowed central institutions to seek university status, the FE colleges were removed from their local authorities and given a form of self-government. Their boards were expected to look for profit-making courses. Funding now came from the Scottish Office, which strove to find formulas that would reward enterprise and student success. The needs of the consumer, that is the student, reigned over those of the provider. National pay and conditions were challenged. The unions found themselves confronting individual boards and college managers rather than a nationally uniform structure.

TESTS FOR DEVOLUTION

From 1997, against a background of financial constraint that for three years disappointed hopes of investment in buildings and resources, Labour ministers planned for devolution. The legislation establishing the Edinburgh Parliament in 1999 was, for education, straightforward: virtually everything from pre-school to university (with the exception of research funding) was handed over to the new MSPs and the Scottish Executive.

The procedures of the new Parliament and Executive were given an early education test: the Standards in Scotland's Schools etc. Bill was, fittingly, the first major piece of legislation, since it focused on the rights of the youngest citizens and sought to tap into their views as part of the new extensive consultation process underpinning the making of laws. The Bill provided for the return of self-governing schools to education authorities, which themselves were now to be subject to HMI inspection. The presumption that children with special needs would attend a mainstream school was also written in, prelude to a further initiative by the Executive that would abolish the record of needs.

The governing coalition of Labour and Liberal Democrats was put to the test when the minority partner was challenged to fulfil an election pledge to abolish student tuition fees imposed by Labour at Westminster. After the Cubie Committee in late 1999 recommended a graduate levy and bursaries for the hardest-up students, the Executive was able to pronounce the end to fees, though payments would be made by graduates once they were earning a modest annual £10,000. The coalition had survived an educational crisis that was basically political. But the new proximity of Parliament, people and press threw up another challenge when campaigners against the abolition of a measure aimed at safeguarding pupils from the promotion of homosexuality in schools wrongfooted ministers.

What has been described as the most serious crisis in Scottish education of modern times saw the Parliament at its most exposed and yet at its best. In 2000 the Scottish Qualifications Authority, a recent conjunction of the Examination Board and SCOTVEC, failed accurately to process thousands of Higher and Standard Grade papers. It had succumbed to the extra pressures of Higher Still, an untried computer system and poor management controls. The Parliament sought and failed to bring the Schools Minister, Sam Galbraith, to book, and with him the inspectorate which had been heavily involved in promoting Higher Still and working with the SQA. But the inquiries by MSPs, who were particularly keen to hear the evidence of exam candidates, were of an intensity and determination that would not have been possible in the Westminster Parliament.

In the ministerial reshuffle following the death of First Minister Donald Dewar in the autumn of 2000, Sam Galbraith was moved to the environment brief, to be replaced by Jack

McConnell. He immediately responded to the criticism, led by education authorities, that the HMI was increasingly initiator of controversial policies and then invigilator of how they were carried out in schools. The inspectorate was now detached from government and turned into an executive agency. If this was seen by councils as a victory in their long-running struggle with central government, Mr McConnell and his successor from 2001, Cathy Jamieson, were to go further, making clear that provided standards were monitored, maintained and raised, education authorities should be freer to adapt the curriculum and organise schools according to local need. One model was no longer deemed to fit all; specialist schools for the arts and sport were grafted onto the comprehensive stalk. New Community Schools were financed, though to no single pattern, to bring social service and health facilities under one roof. The Labour-dominated councils responded by ignoring long-held ideology and accepting public-private partnerships as the way to find money for new buildings.

Another achievement by McConnell before he became First Minister in 2001 was to persuade the councils and teacher unions to accept a deal, based on the findings of an inquiry led by Gavin McCrone, into teachers' pay and conditions. Salaries would go up by around 21% between April 2001 and August 2003; the promotion structure of schools was to be simplified and teachers agreed to continuing professional development throughout their careers, starting with a guaranteed probation year after initial training. Dispensing with the small minority of incompetents would become easier.

Such changes will not be complete until at least 2006 by which time the Executive hopes another of its initiatives will bear fruit: in 2002 Cathy Jamieson launched a national debate on what education for the next ten years should be about and how it should be provided.

REFERENCES

Clark, M. M. and Munn, P. (eds) (1997) *Education in Scotland: Policy and Practice from Pre-School to Secondary*, London: Routledge.
Paterson, L. (2000) *Crisis in the Classroom*, Edinburgh: Mainstream Publishing.
Ross, D. (1986) *An Unlikely Anger*, Edinburgh: Mainstream Publishing.
SOED (1992) *Upper Secondary Education in Scotland* (The Howie Report), Edinburgh: HMSO.
SOED (1994) *Higher Still: Opportunity for All*, Edinburgh: HMSO.
SEED (2001) *A Teaching Profession for the 21st Century*, Edinburgh: HMSO.

22

Culture, Nationalism and Scottish Education: Homogeneity and Diversity

David McCrone

At the core of this chapter is a puzzle. Scottish education is central to Scottish national identity. The movement for statehood in most Western countries was about mobilising a strong sense of national identity. Why, then, did it take until the closing years of the twentieth century for a Scottish parliament to be re-established? How is this apparent Scottish exceptionalism to be explained?

EDUCATION AND SCOTTISH NATIONAL IDENTITY

The first premise can be stated simply: that education has been and is vital to the sense of Scottishness. In the words of the historian Robert Anderson: 'Education has become a marker of Scottish identity, associated with various supposed qualities of the Scottish character such as individualism, social ambition, respect for talent above birth, or 'metaphysical' rationalism' (1997, pp. 2–3). In many ways, education in Scotland has this capacity to be the carrier for so many and often contradictory meanings of who Scots are (McCrone, 2001). That is the first clue to the puzzle. It prompts a more detailed exploration of the ideas associated with education. What is involved here are myths. The term 'myths' does not mean the same as untruths, such as, for example, that the earth is flat. It can be proved that it is not. The point about myths, however, is that they are not amenable to proof. In the words of the United States Constitution, 'We hold these beliefs to be self-evident.'

Myths, in other words, operate on a different plane from 'facts'. By their nature they are a collection of symbolic elements organised to explain and validate sets of social institutions. The social anthropologist, Geoffrey Duncan Mitchell, defined them as follows: 'Myths operate to record and present the moral system whereby present attitudes and actions are ordered and validated' (*A Dictionary of Sociology*, London: Routledge and Kegan Paul 1968, p.122). Myths are general guides to help interpret complex social reality. They operate as reservoirs of beliefs and values which allow individuals to interpret the world and their place within it. All human beings are subject to this process. There is a natural human tendency to think of myths as something that other people require. Anthropologists or sociologists of religion show the ways sacred or transcendent beliefs act as guides for others, but most people think that as rationalists they have little need of such symbolic supports. Such a view would be mistaken. Everybody is affected, including academic writers who seek to uncover the myths others live by.

Consider again the case of the United States of America and its self-evident truths. One central one is the American Dream. This holds that the raw materials of success are hard work and talent. However, a critic might point out that success in the USA seems to come to those who have inherited capital, whether in material or cultural form. Cynically, it might be said that rich and successful people tend to have rich and successful parents. Rags to riches, it might be concluded, is a myth (to revert expediently and temporarily to the common-sense usage of the term).

THE LAD O' PAIRTS

In Scotland, there is an equivalent myth, the lad o' pairts, and it too is centred upon 'getting on', and education is central to it. The lad o' pairts (note that there is no 'lass o' pairts' in this pervasive myth: getting on is for boys to do) was, according to David Murison writing in the *Scottish National Scots Dictionary*, a talented youth, usually the son of a crofter or peasant who had ability but insufficient means to benefit from schooling. Murison traces its usage to the late nineteenth century in a story 'Domsie', published in the collection, *Beside the Bonnie Brier Bush*, (1894) by the Kailyard novelist, 'Ian MacLaren' (in real life a Free Church minister, the Rev. John Watson, born in Essex). The 'Domsie' of the title is the schoolteacher or dominie who skilfully wheedles sufficient capital out of the purses and pocket-books of local worthies to allow his talented charges to go on to university. Domsie is so successful that in MacLaren's words: 'Seven ministers, four schoolteachers, four doctors, one professor and three civil service men had been sent out by the auld schule in Domsie's time, besides many that had given themselves to 'mercantile pursuits'.' Clearly, the professions are what matter – teaching, ministering and administering. Trade is of lesser importance in this scale of values (indicated by the quotation marks and the lack of precision in numbers). The short story is cut shorter by the early death of Domsie who receives this panegyric:

> Domsie, as we called the schoolmaster behind his back in Drumtochty because we loved him, was true to the tradition of his kind, and had an unerring scent for 'pairts' in his laddies. He could detect a scholar in an egg, and prophesied Latinity from a boy that seemed only fit to be a cowherd.

KAILYARDISM AND SCOTTISH CULTURE

It might, not unreasonably, be tempting to relegate such stories to sentimentalised history, issuing as they did from the popular literary style called Kailyard which flourished from about 1880 until 1914, and described by the *Penguin Guide to Literature* as consisting of 'minor writers who pursued Scottish country quaintness into whimsical middens'. This tradition is often blamed for sins much worse than affronts to literature; some saw it as laying down a distorted image of Scotland as a couthy, parochial backwater. Tom Nairn, in *The Break-Up of Britain*, commented:

> Kailyardism was the definition of Scotland as wholly consisting of small towns full of small-town 'characters' given to bucolic intrigue and wise sayings. At first the central figures were usually Ministers of the Kirk (as were most of the authors) but later on schoolteachers and doctors got

into the act. Their housekeepers always have a shrewd insight into human nature. Offspring who leave for the big city frequently come to grief and are glad to get home again (peching and hosting to hide their feelings) (1977, p. 158).

At this point it may seem easy to dismiss Kailyardism and its narratives as of little importance beyond the cultural genre of the turn of the century. After all, as Willie Donaldson has pointed out in his book *Popular Literature in Victorian Scotland* (1986), even at its height it was by no means as hegemonic as was once thought, and took second place in Scotland to a much more popular genre of newspaper writing with a more radical and less complacent edge.

Kailyardism, however, cannot be dismissed so easily. First, it generated its own mythology in the second half of the twentieth century insofar as many critics blamed it for laying down a reactionary and defensive view of Scotland. Such a critique argued that Scotland's failure to strike out for a parliament of its own could be traced to the supposedly insidious effects of this dominant discourse. Quite simply, Scots were feart, and blame lay with the distorting imagery of cultural formations like the Kailyard. Critics spun their own versions. In the 1970s the historian Christopher Harvie identified two historical Scottish personality-types the 'red' and the 'black' (remember that it was a Scot, R. L. Stevenson who invented Dr Jekyll and Mr Hyde):

> The red Scots were cosmopolitan, self-avowedly enlightened, and, given a chance, authoritarian, expanding into and exploiting bigger and more bountiful fields than their own country could provide. Back home lurked their black brothers, demotic, parochial and reactionary, but keeping the ladder of social promotion open, resisting the encroachments of the English governing class. Together, they controlled the rate of their own assimilation to the greater world, the balance which underlay the Union. (*Scotland and Nationalism*, London: Allen and Unwin 1977, p. 17)

There was, in truth, little empirical evidence for Harvie's distinction, but it caught the imagination at the time (especially after the failure of the Devolution Bill in 1979) of those seeking to explain why Scots for much of the history of the Union did not strive for political independence, or even a home rule parliament.

The second reason why the Kailyard mattered was that it captured and amplified the key social icon of late nineteenth and early twentieth century Scotland, the lad o' pairts. If and when the Kailyard declined, the iconography of the lad o' pairts did not. This was because it was embedded in a wider tradition of social egalitarianism. Few myths are more powerful and prevalent in and about Scotland than that it is a more egalitarian society than England, and that it is less class-bound. The late historiographer-royal Gordon Donaldson put it this way: 'It is true to this day that Scotland is a more egalitarian country than England, but as a result of class consciousness horizontal divisions into classes have become . . . more important than vertical divisions into nations' (*Scotland: The Shaping of a Nation*, Newton Abbot: David and Charles 1974, p. 117). Scottish literature and culture have made considerable play of this set of ideas. D. Wittig in his book *The Scottish Tradition in Literature* (Edinburgh: Oliver and Boyd, 1958) made it the central motif from the poetry of the fourteenth and fifteenth century, through Robert Burns and even Walter Scott, and on into the twentieth century with novelists like Neil Gunn and Lewis Grassic Gibbon. Wittig depicted the movement as follows:

The democratic element in Scottish literature is one of its most striking characteristics. 'Democratic' is not really the correct word; it is rather a free manliness [the gendering of core values once more – author], a 'saeva indignatio' against oppression, a violent freedom, sometimes an aggressive spirit of independence and egalitarianism. (p. 95)

This generic Scottish myth of egalitarianism has at its core the iconography of the lad o' pairts, and is the key to explaining why educational values appear so central to a sense of Scottish culture. In defining Scotland and its distinctiveness vis-à-vis the 'Other' – in this case, England – it helps to confirm a sense of identity by saying who Scots are and what they value. It connects, of course, with other typifications such as 'We're a' Jock Tamson's bairns.' David Murison gives the origin and meaning of this saying as 'the human race; common humanity; also with less universal force, a group of people united by a common sentiment, interest or purpose' (*Compact Scottish National Dictionary*, Aberdeen: Aberdeen University Press, 1986, vol.v, p. 337). 'Jock Tamson' also stands for whisky, and for 'John Thomas' with its sexual connotations.

THE AMBIGUITY OF TRADITION

Myths, like traditions, draw upon the past, but they have an active, contemporary significance which involves processes of selective inclusion and exclusion. Traditions and myths, as Raymond Williams observed, provide meaningful though partial interpretations of social reality.

Tradition has been commonly understood as a relatively inert historicised segment of social structure; tradition as the surviving past. [However] what we have to see is not just a 'tradition', but a selective tradition – an intentionally selective version of a shaping past and a pre-shaped present, which is then powerfully operative in the process of social and cultural definition and identification. It is a version of the past which is intended to connect with and ratify the present. What it offers in practice is a sense of predisposed continuity. (*Marxism and Literature*, Oxford: Oxford University Press, 1977, p. 115)

Traditions, then, legitimise institutions, symbolise group cohesion and socialise others into appropriate beliefs and values. They do so in a complex and ambiguous way so that they lend themselves to a variety of cultural and political ideologies. This can be seen when the Scottish – egalitarian – myth is examined more closely. It has an asociological, almost mystical element (similar in purpose to the American Dream). Scots are deemed to be egalitarian almost by dint of racial or ethnic characteristics. On the other hand, social inequality – the actual distribution of society's resources – may well be, and of course usually are, unequal. The myth has, in fact, two versions, which might be labelled the 'idealist' and the 'radical'. In the former, the objective existence of social inequality matters far less than the shared common humanity of (in this case) being Scottish. Inequality is man-made, set against the basic egalitarianism. That, after all, is the point of Burns' poem 'man's a man for a' that'. Social rank – the guinea's stamp – matters less than common humanity. There is, however, ambiguity in Burns' message. There is no calling for the end of social inequality, simply the proper appreciation of 'the pith o' sense and pride o' worth'. Indeed, 'a man's a man for a' that' is an appeal to the virtues of fraternity rather than equality in a sociological sense.

It is true that in the strong – the 'radical' – sense of the poem, Burns is making a revolutionary appeal for radical social change, and that is possibly the sense which those on the Left wish to give it. There is however the idealist version which implies that the objective facts of social inequality and rank matter far less than basic common humanity. Why change the superficial?

When the Scottish myth and its incumbent lad o' pairts is examined in this way, its sociological significance begins to emerge. Egalitarianism does not assume social equality. As Allan MacLaren pointed out:

> The egalitarianism so often portrayed is not that emerging from an economic, social or even political equality; it is equality of opportunity which is exemplified. All men are not equal. What is implied is that all men are given an opportunity to be equal. Whatever the values attached to such a belief, if expressed today, it would be termed elitist not egalitarian. (*Social Class in Scotland; Past and Present*, Edinburgh: John Donald 1976, p. 2).

This is familiar territory. The two senses of the myth refer to, on the one hand, equality of opportunity – the idealist version; and equality of achievement – the radical version. The latter refers to measuring equality of outcomes: class, race, gender and so on. The former refers in essence merely to formal opportunity afforded to the able student to proceed through the educational system from school to university.

It can also be seen how the lad o' pairts would have been a creature of his time. In eighteenth-century Scotland a small elite was being catered for in a limited number of professions – school teaching, the law, the ministry and medicine. The failure of the 'lad' to make it could readily be explained in personal rather than structural terms: in short, it was his own fault. In this respect, egalitarianism was a conservative ideology which congratulated itself on the openness of Scottish society and its social institutions. It could even be employed, as it was in the 1970s, to defend fee-paying local authority schools on the grounds that they afforded the lad o' pairts an educational and social opportunity not given in the comprehensive sector.

To connect together the idealist and the radical versions of the myth is to give them a coherence which they do not normally have. Nevertheless, it can be seen more clearly how flexible, ambivalent and multi-stranded the myth is. It lends support to the conservative seeking assurance that existing institutions are for the best; while for nationalists it provides a vision of a Scotland which is democratic and different from its southern neighbour; and for socialists it confirms the radical predispositions of Scotland. The myth matters because of its framing assumptions rather than its substance. It confers legitimacy on both idealist and radical interpretations alike.

The myth is also addressing a former social order. As MacLaren points out: 'There is some evidence to suggest that the 'Scottish Myth' is a product of a former rural paternalism rather than an urban industrialism in which class identity and economic individualism overruled a declining concern for communal and parochial obligations.' (1976, p. 9). It largely derives from a typically pre-industrial, even pre-capitalist social order where social identity is conferred by community not class. In strict sociological terms, the lad o' pairts belongs to a defunct Scotland. Ian Carter in his analysis of the Kailyard school commented:

> MacLaren's novels share important features with the parish histories that poured off the presses in such numbers in the 1880s and 1890s. Both rest on an ideology of community – parish life as

harmonious – and both tell pawky stories of local characters to demonstrate that sense of shared community. (*Scottish Journal of Sociology*, 1976, p. 1).

The egalitarianism bred of an attachment to peasant values and the social organisation of small towns could make little sense of the new urban industrial experience. Should then the iconography of the lad o' pairts be dismissed as a historical legacy of the Scottish conservative imagination? It cannot be simply this, because it consistently runs up against counter-evidence, and so is difficult to debunk. As Robert Anderson observes:

> Most observers agree that the myth of the lad of parts [sic] corresponds to some underlying reality, albeit idealized. It expressed a nineteenth-century ideal of meritocracy, which did allow for individual social mobility, yet also legitimized the reproduction through schooling of the inequalities of industrial society; even when meritocratic concepts challenged class barriers, they hardly acknowledged those of gender. (1997, pp. 53–4).

Anderson's evidence *(Education and Opportunity in Victorian Scotland*, Oxford: Oxford University Press; Edinburgh: Edinburgh University Press, 1983) shows that as late as the third quarter of the nineteenth century, many students at Scotland's universities came from peasant or working-class origins. Aberdeen admitted a large proportion from agricultural backgrounds (as much as 20% in 1910), while Glasgow had a relatively high percentage of students from manual working class origins (24% in 1910) .

Myths do not survive and flourish unless they connect with the realities of life, or are at least not wholly contradicted by them. In the post-war period, there is evidence that educational opportunity was unusually present in Scotland. Keith Hope's re-analysis of the 1947 Scottish Mental Study led him to conclude that 'Scotland, as we would expect, is more merit-elective than the United States' (*As Others See Us*, Cambridge: Cambridge University Press, 1984, p.30). The surviving potency of the myth does not simply rely, however, on such evidence, but above all on the institutional carriers which sustained it. McPherson and Raab (1988) have been able to show that Scotland's administrative elite gave it voice through the educational system. Andrew McPherson has spoken of the 'Kirriemuir Career' among the Scottish schools inspectorate to show how small-town Scotland predominated in these circles, to the detriment of the urban west. Robert Anderson uses McPherson's findings to conclude that the Welsh and Scottish 'democratic myths' had some substance, and that as members of the British elite, they may have had broader social origins than their English equivalents. In other words, the Scottish myth is kept alive in large part because it was and is a key ideology to the Scottish education system and its cadres. It also helps to explain why a perceived attack on the Scottish education system is perceived as an attack on Scottish culture and identity itself.

EDUCATION AND NATIONAL IDENTITY

It will be instructive at this point in the argument to return to the puzzle with which the chapter began. We have tried to show how central education and its iconography is to Scottish national identity. Our next task is more straightforward, namely to show how this was in no sense unique to Scotland but a central feature of all Western industrial societies. The late Ernest Gellner showed that nationalism is not the result of sentiment or historical folk-memory, but is an essential part of the modern condition. Being national is the modern condition, and the natural form of political loyalty. 'Every man is a clerk,' in his words, because there is an assumption of universal literacy, and secondly, that clerks are not horizontally mobile because they cannot move from one language-zone to another very easily. The condition of language in which he/she is reared and operates is commonly the vernacular, the language of home, school and state, which in turn reinforces nationalist tendencies.

Modern loyalties correspond in large part with political units defined by language which is the dominant mode of instruction and expression in the education system. In other words, the state is in these terms a cultural system, but one in which the population actively attests to its nationality. This is a key point in Gellner's book *Nations and Nationalism* (Oxford: Blackwell, 1983), as it permitted him to argue that nationalism derives not from atavistic and sentimental attachment, but is made and mobilised by the conditions of modernity themselves. That is why Gellner had no truck with either pro- or anti-nationalists who wish to essentialise nationality, and why he is frequently associated with a modernist position which sees nationalism as a form of secular religion for the modern state.

Because change is the characteristic feature of such societies, people have to be ready for change, and the main agency for sensitising people to this is the education system which becomes the central institution in society. Modern society is both more homogeneous (everyone gets the same basic training), and yet more diversified (the complex division of labour). The key motor in all this is education which furnishes a generic training, and shapes society like an army in terms of its integrated and fine-tuned organisational features. However, the key difference in terms of social order is that modern society is largely self-regulating. At its centre is the professor, not the executioner; the doctorate rather than the guillotine the emblem of state power. The monopoly of legitimate education is now more important, more central than is the monopoly of legitimate violence. Hence, nationalism grows in the medium of this rational, egalitarian ethos.

In the translation of society from rural to urban, peasants had to be turned into citizens. Eugene Weber in his book *Peasants into Frenchmen: The Modernisation of Rural France, 1870–1914* (London: Chatto and Windus, 1977) shows why this was necessary so soon after a thoroughgoing revolution only a century before. The startling fact was that as late as the 1860s, fully a quarter of the French population did not speak the language. 'In short', says Weber, 'French was a foreign language for a substantial number of Frenchmen, including almost half the children who would reach adulthood in the last quarter of the century' (p.67). The key institutions which 'made Frenchmen', according to Weber, were the village school system of the Third Republic, the fact that education became useful as a means of social mobility up and away from the countryside, and above all, the sequence of wars with Prussia/Germany which induced conscription. The French state also supplied the first modern maps of the country soon after the Franco-Prussian war, so that 'by 1881, few classrooms however small, appear to have lacked a map' (1977, p. 334), and the image of the national hexagon began to be both recognised and hegemonic. Weber comments that the famous geographical icon can be seen as a colonising symbol reflecting a complex of internal territories conquered, annexed and integrated into the political and administrative whole.

The idea of 'France' which began as an elite concept was extended by a process akin to colonisation through communication (roads, railways, and above all by the newspapers – *le papier qui parle*) so that by of the end of the nineteenth century popular and elite culture had come together after a break of two centuries. Three major cultural innovations had helped to bring this about: education – the development of the secular equivalent of the Church, sometimes both competing with and complementing it; the invention of public ceremonies such as Bastille Day; and the mass production of public monuments.

SCOTTISH OR BRITISH?

How does Scotland fit into this model? Here the third and final part of the puzzle is encountered. The main purpose of schooling everywhere was to imbue pupils with the new patriotism rather than simply teaching them new technical skills such as reading, writing and counting. This can be seen in the mobilisation of 'national' history and geography, and the 'national' curriculum.

The social construction of history can often be seen in cases where there are competing accounts on offer or changes over time. For example, as Robert Anderson shows, the curriculum for teaching (especially History) in Scottish schools in the late nineteenth century reflects these shifts rather well. The 1873 Code drawn up by (as it was known then) the Scotch Education Department (SED) had a greater emphasis on Scottish (over British) history than the 1886 Code which abandoned Scottish and local emphases. The political aims of at least one schools inspector was clear: 'one must question the value of a school history that lands a child in the midst of loose laws and looser passions, and unquestionably helps . . . to maintain sentimental Scotch antipathy to England' (Anderson, R. *Education and the Scottish People, 1750–1918* Oxford: Clarendon Press, 1995, p. 214). However, in the 1880s, there was resistance to the use of the term 'English' rather than 'British' in history textbooks, and by 1907, the SED was stressing that Scottish history was central to the curriculum, with an emphasis on Scotland's contribution to empire. The general message was that Scotland and England, once historic enemies, now formed the basis for a world empire (pp. 219–20).

In like manner, the icons of history are redrawn according to the political and cultural needs of the day. For example, that icon of Scottish national identity, William Wallace, was resurrected in the 1990s by Hollywood and turned into 'Braveheart'. In many ways the survival of mere fragments of history is a boon to heritage makers, because it allows more easily the re-presentation of national myth. Graeme Morton shows how, despite his execution by the English state in 1305, Wallace could be refocused in the nineteeth century as the fusion of nationalism and unionism. During the age of nationalism, he argues, William Wallace secured his position as Scotland's most efficacious patriot, fulfilling the agenda of friends and foes of the Union.

The completion of the puzzle is now close. Why, if Scotland's identity was inextricably bound up with its education system, and it can be shown that in the nineteenth century similar processes were happening in Scotland as elsewhere, did education and national identity not generate the demand for self-determination? The short answer is that Scotland had already achieved this. In many ways it had little need for a formal parliament as long as its needs were met by other social institutions – what is called civil society – and as long as the British state did not interfere unduly with the internal mechanisms of self-governance.

AUTONOMY AND CIVIL SOCIETY

The term 'civil society' refers to those areas of social life – the domestic world, the economic sphere, cultural activities and political interaction – which are organised by private or voluntary arrangements between individuals and groups outside the direct control of the state. In other words, whereas the state can be treated as a unitary entity which functions externally (through warfare) and internally (through law), society is composed of an extensive though bounded network of self-activated individuals and groups. State and society are not wholly independent of each other, but are largely formed and maintained within the context of the other.

The concept of civil society is not without dispute, particularly concerning its relationship between state on the one hand and market on the other. As regards the first, civil society should be understood as the sphere of that which is relatively but autonomously private within a modern polity. In other words, given the way state and civil society operate across each other today, they cannot easily be differentiated. To take the Scottish example, institutional autonomy as regards law, education and local politics is now underwritten and managed by the state, albeit a Scottish 'semi-state'.

'Civil society' indicates that there is a sphere which is autonomous from the state. Neither is it simply the economy writ large. Similarly, what is meant by the state and society have themselves changed over time, as well as the relationship between them. The distinction between the two was probably much more meaningful to Victorians than it is to us today. That is because the last century or so has seen an increasing fudging of the boundary between state and society. Notably, the extension of the franchise has brought to bear new political and social pressures on the state, and increasingly the state is constituted to exercise rule over society. The state is required to address the concerns of its citizens more directly, and this presents the task of societal management for modern governments.

In short, for so long as Scottish civil society was in charge of its education system, and Scots found it worthwhile to compete in the British imperial labour market, then there was little need to mobilise a political nationalism to win what freedoms one already actually had. This was also the context in which educational reforms had taken place at the end of the nineteenth century. As regards the reform of university education in 1876, George Davie has famously argued in his book *The Democratic Intellect* (1961) that it was driven by pressure to anglicise the curriculum the better to compete in the wider British market place, and that in the process Scotland's 'democratic intellect' was sacrificed. Lindsay Paterson in his book *The Autonomy of Modern Scotland* (1994) points out that such a view does not explain why the universities never generated the same degree of nationalist agitation which took place elsewhere. In other words, the nationalist dog did not bark because it already had what it wanted. This is a view shared by Robert Anderson who argues that as a result of the reforms: 'Intellectual standards were raised, and the middle class demand for qualifications allowing Scots to compete for jobs on a British basis was well satisfied' (1997, p. 38).

IDENTITY, EDUCATION AND THE SCOTTISH PARLIAMENT

What impact has the establishment of the Parliament in 1999 had on the sense of Scottish national identity? In particular, has the devolved education system led to a reinforcement of people's sense of being Scottish? Policy divergence has indeed been a feature of post-1999 Scottish education. One area has been with regard to university tuition fees. The scrapping of up-front fees in 2000, and the creation of post-graduate endowments, was the most obvious difference north and south of the border, and resulted by and large from Labour's minority status in the Scottish Executive. Better to accede with reasonable grace to the abolition of fees than suffer the loss of its Liberal Democrat partners in government. By

2002, Scotland's First Minister had affirmed a vision for secondary schooling in which 'every school is excellent' rather than creating a few schools as 'centres of excellence' (*The Herald*, 6 November 2002). On both the fees issue and on the vision of secondary schooling, Scotland was asserting difference from England.

It would, in truth, be difficult to argue that these differences were the result of any straightforward increase in Scottish, over British, identity, or that such policy divergences were themselves generating assertions of national identity. This is because, firstly, that Scotland had long been 'different' with regard to education in particular; indeed, one might even argue that, if anything, Scottish and English educational policy and practice have been converging for about a century. In the second place, 'identity' is not a simple variable which waxes and wanes in any straightforward way as a result of policy shifts. The argument in this chapter has been that Scotland's institutional autonomy acts as a cultural prism through which matters of policy and issues of identity are refracted. Thus, a shared commitment to common schooling is itself generated by institutional difference, and in turn reinforces a set of social and political values which are interpreted as the 'Scottish way'. What the Scottish Parliament has done is to give political voice to these values, and to translate them into institutional practice, which is more directly politically accountable in the light of perceived electoral pressures. While Scotland has long been 'different' in educational terms, the new political structures reinforce and institutionalise these differences, and make them more directly answerable to Scottish public opinion. The old order has withered away.

CONCLUSION

What, in the last resort, has brought this state of affairs to an end is what Neil MacCormick called in his 1997 British Academy lecture, the 'Scottish anomaly' – the capacity of an archetypal 'nation-state' to operate in a federal way – can no longer be contained within the unitary state structure. Scotland's autonomy in educational as in other institutions of civil society can no longer operate in its traditional way. MacCormick observes:

> It is an autonomy that has made possible the continuing assertion of a submerged constitutional tradition of a distinct Scottish stamp. The continuing claim to a historically attested sovereignty of the people is part and parcel of that. It includes the implication that assent to the union involves a continuing '*plebiscite de tous les jours*'. So long as the will of the majority sustains it, it will continue. If it ceases to do so, it will cease.

And it has ceased: at least in its post-1707 Union form. The puzzle is solved. Scottish education is central to Scottish national identity. The movement for statehood in most Western countries was about mobilising a strong sense of national identity. Only in the late twentieth century did people in Scotland find it necessary to defend and extend their civil autonomy with a parliament, albeit within the British state, at least for the time being. The old bargain – the marriage of convenience, as it were – which was struck in 1707 to give Scotland civil self-government but within the British state, and crucially its empire, has run its course.

REFERENCES

Anderson, R. (1997) *Scottish Education since the Reformation*, Edinburgh: Economic and Social History Society of Scotland.

Davie, G. (1961) *The Democratic Intellect*, Edinburgh: Edinburgh University Press.

McCrone, D. (2001) *Understanding Scotland: The Sociology of a Nation*, London: Routledge.

McPherson, A. and Raab, C. (1988) *Governing Education*, Edinburgh: Edinburgh University Press.

Nairn, T. (1977) *The Break-Up of Britain*, London: Verso.

Paterson, L. (1994) *The Autonomy of Modern Scotland*, Edinburgh: Edinburgh University Press.

23

Gaelic Education

Boyd Robertson

Gaelic is the longest-established of Scotland's languages. It was brought to Scotland by settlers from Ireland in the fifth and sixth centuries AD. These immigrants, known to the Romans as Scotti, gave the country its name and their Celtic language penetrated almost every part of Scotland and became, for a brief period, the language of the Crown and of government. From the twelfth century onwards, the status of the language was eroded by anglicising influences from the south and it became increasingly marginalised.

Today, only 1.2% of Scots speak Gaelic. These 58,652 Gaelic speakers are to be found mostly in the Western Isles and on the western fringes of the mainland but there are also significant communities of Gaelic speakers in urban centres such as Glasgow, Edinburgh and Inverness. The last twenty years have, however, seen a remarkable renaissance of the language and culture, reflected in the arts, the media, the socio-economic sphere and education. The following account of current provision and recent developments charts the progress made in meeting the educational needs and aspirations of Gaelic speakers and learners.

PRE-SCHOOL EDUCATION

It is singularly appropriate to begin an overview of Gaelic education with the pre-school sector because this has been the seedbed for much of the regeneration and growth in Gaelic in, and beyond, education.

Increasing exposure to the English language and to Anglo-American cultural influences caused concern amongst parents and Gaelic activists about the detrimental effect this would have on young children's fluency in, and attitude towards, the language. It was considered essential to counteract this trend by seeking to associate the minority language with positive and enjoyable experiences and this led in the late 1970s to the formation of the first Gaelic playgroups and to demands for children's programmes in Gaelic on television. A national association, Comhairle nan Sgoiltean Araich (CNSA), was set up in 1982 to promote the development of Gaelic-medium playgroups. The existence today of over 150 pre-school groups throughout, and in a few instances beyond, Scotland suggests that CNSA has been successful in its mission. CNSA is a voluntary sector provider with limited resources and has not, hitherto, seen a major role for itself in delivering nursery education. This has been regarded as the province of local authorities and, up until 1995, there were only three Gaelic nursery units in the whole of Scotland. The introduction by the government of an entitlement to funded nursery education for 4-year-olds in 1998–9 led to a mushrooming of provision and over 400 children now attend the thirty-six Gaelic nurseries, most of which are located in schools with Gaelic-medium streams.

PRIMARY EDUCATION

Provision for Gaelic in primary schools has been transformed in the last three decades. Before the reorganisation of local government in the 1970s, Gaelic had a minor role in the primary curriculum. Even in schools in strong Gaelic-speaking communities, the teaching medium was almost exclusively English, the home language of most of the pupils being reduced to the status of a subject to be studied.

The position of Gaelic changed radically in 1975 with the launch of a bilingual education project by the newly-formed local authority for the Outer Hebrides, Comhairle nan Eilean. This initiative received government backing with the Scottish Office jointly funding the first two three-year phases of the project which sought to build on the home language of the majority of pupils and used Gaelic as a teaching and learning medium along with English. This was the first time that Gaelic was used officially as a medium of instruction in state schools and represented a major advance for the language in education. There was a favourable parental response to the project in its early years but, by the early 1980s, concern was being expressed about the level of fluency in Gaelic being attained by pupils in some schools after several years of bilingual schooling. Parents also voiced dissatisfaction with the progress being made by certain schools in implementing the bilingual model.

A similar bilingual scheme was piloted in 1978 in five Skye schools by Highland Regional Council and was eventually extended to all primary schools on the island. The lower incidence of Gaelic-speaking children on Skye required a rather different bilingual approach with greater emphasis placed on the needs of learners. Doubts about the ability of bilingual models to deliver fluency in Gaelic comparable to that in English and a growing awareness of the erosion of the language amongst the school age population made parents, educationalists and language activists realise that another approach was needed. Developments in Welsh and in other minority languages were studied and the findings suggested that use of the minority language as the medium of education had to be maximised to ensure language maintenance and transmission. The first Gaelic playgroups had demonstrated the viability of this approach and convinced parents that it should be continued in primary school.

Highland and Strathclyde Regional Councils responded to parental pressure for Gaelic-medium education and set up units in schools in Inverness and Glasgow in 1985. The success of these first units and the continuing spread of the playgroups, fuelled demand for provision in other areas. By 2002–3, fifty-eight schools and 1,928 pupils were engaged in Gaelic-medium education. Most units are in the Highlands and Islands but there are several in non-Gaelic-speaking areas such as Aberdeen, Cumbernauld, Edinburgh, Kilmarnock and Stirling. Gaelic-medium units or streams are generally situated in local schools in which the majority of pupils are educated in English, but 1999 saw the beginning of a new phase in Gaelic-medium education with the opening of Scotland's first all-Gaelic school in Glasgow and the designation of five schools in the Outer Hebrides as Gaelic schools.

In virtually all Gaelic-medium classes there is a mix of fluent speakers and learners. The proportions vary depending on the type of community the school serves. In rural, island schools, many of the pupils come from Gaelic-speaking homes while in urban, mainland schools few pupils have that home background. Research shows that factors which influence parents to opt for Gaelic-medium education include maintenance and development of the mother tongue, restoration to a family of a language that has skipped a generation or two, acquisition of a second language, the perceived advantages of bilingualism and access to Gaelic culture and heritage.

The Gaelic-medium curriculum follows the National Guidelines on Gaelic 5–14 produced by the Scottish Office Education Department in 1993. These guidelines set out attainment targets and programmes of study for five levels of primary and early secondary education. They provide teachers with a curricular framework that identifies 'the aims of study, the ground to be covered, the way that learning should progress and how pupils' attainment should be monitored and recorded' (Gaelic 5–14 Preface). The guidelines for Gaelic-medium education have been formulated along similar lines to those for English but there are significant differences between the two, especially in respect of the scheduling of attainments in certain linguistic skills. This arises from the fact that Gaelic-medium education begins with a two-year language immersion programme.

The immersion phase is designed 'to provide children from non-Gaelic backgrounds with basic oral competence in Gaelic' (para. 1.3) and 'to reinforce the existing skills of Gaelic-speaking children whose competence in the language may diminish in a predominantly English-speaking environment' (para. 1.3.) During this phase, the teacher uses Gaelic almost exclusively and the emphasis is on the development of listening and speaking skills. It is anticipated that 'pupils should be able to communicate with the teacher and other pupils in social interaction and classroom routines on a range of topics' (para. 1.1) by the end of the two years. The emphasis on oral skills, which continues beyond the immersion phase, means that pupils in Gaelic-medium classes attain targets in these and in literacy skills in a different sequence and time frame to those in English-medium classes.

The 5–14 guidelines state that Gaelic-medium education should aim 'to bring pupils to the stage of broadly equal competence in Gaelic and English, in all the skills, by the end of P7' (para. 1.1). It is left to the discretion of local authorities and schools how this should be achieved. There is considerable variation in practice between authorities in the use made of English as a teaching medium beyond the immersion phase. The balance between Gaelic and English ranges from 60:40 through to 90:10 and there is concern amongst parents that the weaker Gaelic model inhibits the development of fluency. Most schools introduce reading and writing in English in P3 and increase the weighting given to English in P6–7.

There is little doubt that Gaelic-medium education has been a success. An HM Inspectors of Schools report, *Provision for Gaelic Education in Scotland*, published in 1994, acknowledged that the Gaelic-medium approach had 'worked well' and was more effective than bilingual provision in achieving fluency. Research into the attainments of pupils receiving Gaelic-medium primary education, conducted by a team led by Professor Richard Johnstone of Stirling University, concluded that 'In many, though not all instances, they out-performed English-medium pupils and, in addition, gained the advantage of becoming proficient in two languages' (Johnstone, 1999).

Gaelic features in the curriculum of primary schools in another two forms. In the Outer Hebrides, some schools which do not have Gaelic-medium units offer pupils a form of bilingual education developed from the earlier project model. Schools which have units also provide a measure of bilingual education to pupils outwith the unit. In other schools, Gaelic is taught as a second language for a short time each week by a specialist itinerant teacher or by a member of staff with the appropriate skills. This type of provision has been offered in schools in parts of Argyll and Perthshire, in Inverness and in areas such as Lochaber, Skye and Lochalsh and Wester Ross for the best part of three decades, but it is now being superseded by a model based on the Modern Languages in the Primary School scheme in which class teachers are given a period of tuition in the language to enable them to teach it at a basic level.

SECONDARY EDUCATION

The use of Gaelic as a medium of education in secondary schools has not kept pace with developments in the primary sector. The language was first used in the teaching of secondary subjects in 1983 when Comhairle nan Eilean set up a pilot project as an extension to its primary bilingual programme. The two-year pilot involved two small secondary schools in Lewis, Lionel and Shawbost, and concentrated on the social subjects. Pupils responded positively to the use of their mother tongue and the pilot was deemed a success by all concerned. The two, two-year schools continued to teach History and Geography through Gaelic following the pilot phase.

The first Gaelic-medium unit on the mainland opened at Hillpark Secondary in Glasgow in 1988. Further provision was established in 1992 in Millburn Academy, Inverness and Portree High School thus ensuring that there was continuity of Gaelic-medium education for pupils of the three largest primary units. By 2002–3, Gaelic-medium education had been introduced into another sixteen schools.

The use of Gaelic as a medium in secondary is restricted to a few subjects. History is the most widely available subject while Geography, Personal and Social Education, Mathematics, Science, Home Economics, Computing, Technical Education and Art are taught in Gaelic in one or more of the schools. Candidates may elect to sit Gaelic versions of Standard Grade examinations in History, Geography and Maths at present and other subjects and levels will be added as the sector grows.

The development of Gaelic-medium education in secondary has been hampered by a number of factors. One of the most significant of these is the fragmented nature of the secondary curriculum with its specialist subject structure. To operate economically and effectively, this requires a substantial cohort of pupils in any one year. The typical primary school structure with one teacher per class lends itself more readily to a smaller cohort and the level of subsidy required is significantly less. It will be some considerable time before the Gaelic-medium cohort in most receiving secondaries reaches the point of economic viability in a range of subjects and expansion of provision will be contingent on central government funding being available.

Financial considerations were probably uppermost in influencing HMI to conclude in their 1994 report that 'the provision of Gaelic-medium secondary education in a number of subjects, determined by the vagaries of resource availability, is neither desirable nor feasible in the forseeable future' (para. 1.12). This recommendation, which contrasted with the report's commendation of Gaelic-medium primary education, was accepted by the then Conservative government and became Scottish Office policy. It provoked an indignant response from the Gaelic community which highlighted the absence of any educational rationale for the decision, the disjunction it would cause in children's education and the illogicality and absurdity of abandoning a scheme in which so much had been invested. One of the earliest actions of the Labour government in 1997 was to overturn this policy and the inspectorate was instructed by the Minister for Education and Gaelic at the Scottish Office,

Brian Wilson, to enter into discussions with local authorities about ways 'to support and extend Gaelic-medium teaching in specified subjects in the secondary curriculum'.

Pupils in Gaelic-medium classes also study the language as a subject. They take the Gàidhlig course which is designed for fluent speakers and leads to certificate examinations at Standard Grade, Intermediate 1 and 2, Higher and Advanced Higher. In 2002, 138 candidates sat the Standard Grade exam and 72 were presented for Higher. The fluent speakers cohort includes pupils who have been in bilingual programmes in primary, and a small number who may not have had access to Gaelic-medium education and had little or no exposure to the language in primary, but who come from Gaelic-speaking homes and begin formal study of the language in secondary.

A Gaelic (Learners) course leading to separate certificate examinations was instituted in 1962. This followed a campaign by prominent Gaelic teachers who highlighted the inequity of asking learners of Gaelic to sit the same examination as native speakers. The new course brought provision for pupils learning Gaelic broadly into line with that for pupils learning other modern languages.

Classification of pupils as learners or fluent speakers is a recurrent issue. The Scottish Qualifications Authority (SQA) Gaelic Assessment Panel has recently produced revised guidelines on categorisation but the interpretation and implementation of the guidelines is sometimes challenged by parents. This usually arises where a school has adjudged a pupil to be a fluent speaker and parents feel that categorisation as a learner would improve the child's chances of success in certificate examinations.

Less than 10% of state schools offer the Gaelic (Learners) option. Most of these are located in the Highlands and Islands. The number of schools has remained at around forty for many years, although there have been regional fluctuations with expansion in the Inverness area and contraction in Glasgow. Four Glasgow schools have ceased to offer Gaelic in the recent past and there is now only one school where Gaelic is taught in a city with some 6,000 Gaelic speakers. Some schools in the independent sector occasionally present pupils for National Qualification examinations. The number of presentations for the Gaelic (Learners) exams in 2002 was 331 at Standard Grade, 72 at Access and Intermediate levels and 141 at Higher.

In schools in the Outer Hebrides, Skye and the western part of the Highland mainland, it is council policy that all first and second year pupils study Gaelic and another modern language. In most other parts of Scotland, pupils typically have to choose between Gaelic and French, or German, from first year or take Gaelic as a second language option in second or third year. These option arrangements militate against a large uptake of the subject.

The teaching of Gaelic has changed radically in the last thirty years. Where it was once a subject of study and analysis with an approach not unlike the classical languages, it progressed through a stage where the emphasis was on vocabulary, grammar and structure using English as the medium of instruction, to a methodology today which aims to produce learners with communicative competence in the language and uses the target language extensively in the classroom.

The last ten years have seen a marked improvement in teaching/learning resources. Before then, teachers had to adapt courses geared for the adult independent study market but now they have access to a substantial corpus of materials designed for learners in school. A similar advance has been made in respect of materials for the fluent speakers course, much of it produced by local authorities, sometimes on an individual, but more often on a collaborative, basis.

In addition to the long-term courses outlined above, there are also short-term modular courses for both learners and fluent speakers. There are five levels of National Certificate (NC) modules for Learners which adhere closely to Modern Languages module specifications. Fluent speakers can choose from twenty-nine modules on a range of topics that embraces communication, literature, the media and economic development. Short courses in Celtic or Gaelic Studies feature as pre-language or introductory courses in the first year curriculum of a few schools and there is scope for the introduction of modules in these subjects within the Higher Still framework.

SUPPORT STRUCTURES

Recent developments have been facilitated and sustained by the creation of enabling mechanisms and support structures. Chief among these has been the Scheme of Specific Grants for Gaelic Education initiated by the government in 1986. Under this scheme, local authorities submit project proposals to the Scottish Office and receive 75% funding for approved projects. Grants are only awarded for new or additional provision and authorities are expected to meet the full costs of developments after three years. The scheme's initial budget of £250,000 had risen to £2.8m in 2001–2. Authorities can bid for funding on an individual or collective basis, but the Scottish Executive Education Department (SEED) expects authorities to allocate a proportion of total funding to collaborative projects.

The Scheme of Specific Grants and the impulse to collaborate created a need for co-ordinated action by local authorities and led to the formation of an inter-authority network. A structure, affording co-operation at political, managerial and curriculum development levels, was put in place by the three local authorities with the largest concentrations of Gaelic-speakers – Highland and Strathclyde Regional Councils and Comhairle nan Eilean. Other authorities with Gaelic provision joined the network's management review group which prioritised development proposals submitted by primary, secondary and community education review groups. This review process resulted in projects such as the production of Maths and Science schemes for primary schools, a learners' course for secondary schools and the creation of a database for modern Gaelic terminology.

Despite the impressive progress of recent years, there is still an urgent need for more and better resources for schools. In recognition of this, a national resource centre for Gaelic was established by the government on Lewis in 1999. The new centre, Stòrlann, has put in train a planned programme to address the deficit in most curricular areas.

National agencies such as the Scottish Qualifications Authority and Learning and Teaching Scotland (LTS), an amalgamation of the Scottish Consultative Council on the Curriculum (SCCC) and the Scottish Council for Educational Technology (SCET), play significant roles in supporting Gaelic education. The SQA has a Gaelic assessment panel which nominates setters, examiners, moderators and markers for national examinations and provides advice on matters relating to syllabus and assessment. The panel has recently produced a revised and extended set of guidelines on Gaelic orthography which update and further exemplify the Gaelic Orthographic Conventions published in 1981 by the predecessor body, the Scottish Examination Board. SQA and LTS representatives participate in working parties which prepare subject guidelines and advice for national curriculum development programmes.

Teachers today have access to a range of computer programmes in Gaelic. Some are original Gaelic programmes but many are Gaelic versions of programmes produced in

English. Teachers can also access a bank of radio and television programmes designed for use in school. Scottish Television, Grampian and Channel 4 have each produced schools programmes but the BBC is the main provider. It produces programmes on radio and television, caters for learners and fluent speakers and addresses various stages within both primary and secondary. The Comataidh Craolaidh Gàidhlig, the Gaelic Broadcasting Committee, which administers an £8.5m Gaelic Television Fund set up by the government in 1991, funds some educational output.

Language development bodies and community organisations also play a key role in bolstering and promoting Gaelic in education. The language development agency, Comunn na Gàidhlig (CNAG), employs an education officer who participates in the inter-authority network referred to earlier and liaises extensively with community groups, service providers and national agencies. CNAG was instrumental in setting up Comann nam Pàrant (Nàiseanta), a national association of parents involved in Gaelic education, which has branches in most places where there is a Gaelic-medium unit.

TEACHER EDUCATION

Three teacher education institutions (TEIs) make provision for Gaelic – the University of Strathclyde in Glasgow, Aberdeen University and the University of Glasgow. Strathclyde's Faculty of Education, formerly Jordanhill College, is the only TEI that has consistently provided training in each of the main pre-service courses with permanent specialist staff.

Each TEI offers some training in Gaelic within the BEd and Post-Graduate Certificate in Education (Primary) (PGCE(P)) courses. The University of Strathclyde and Aberdeen University have Gaelic pathways in the BEd course and Gaelic-speaking students receive tuition in linguistic skills and teaching methods throughout the course. Periods of school experience in a Gaelic unit are built into the pathway and into the training of students on the PGCE(P) course. Provision for Gaelic at the University of Glasgow Faculty of Education, which services the Roman Catholic sector, is more ad hoc but includes a Gaelic school placement. Most of the training in Gaelic at each TEI is optional and outwith core elements of the course. The concentrated nature of the one-year PGCE course affords little scope for additional classes and Gaelic input is, therefore, very limited.

There is widespread dissatisfaction amongst teachers, education managers and parents about the nature and extent of training provided for Gaelic-medium teachers. Surveys have shown that newly-qualified teachers are highly critical of pre-service arrangements and feel inadequately prepared for the Gaelic-medium classroom with its additional demands and specialised requirements. The present situation where students receive no certification or formal qualification for Gaelic-medium teaching is deemed increasingly anomalous and was highlighted in a report published by the General Teaching Council for Scotland (GTCS) in 1999. The report, *Teaching in Gaelic-Medium Education*, made a series of recommendations for change, including the development of a dual English/Gaelic-medium route in BEd and PGCE courses which would confer a qualification to teach in either medium and be formally recognised by certification.

Pre-service training arrangements for secondary teachers of Gaelic are more satisfactory. Gaelic is one of the subject specialisms in which students undertaking the Postgraduate Certificate in Education (Secondary) course (PGCE(S)) can qualify and they receive training in Gaelic teaching methods as a core part of the course. Their training enables them to engage in teaching both the Gàidhlig and Gaelic (Learners) courses. Strathclyde

University is the only TEI that offers the PGCE(S) Gaelic course each year and it is also the sole provider of any training in Gaelic-medium secondary education, a field set to assume greater significance.

Most inservice training in Gaelic is organised and delivered at local authority and school level with occasional input from TEI staff. The inter-authority network arranges in-service courses annually and there are national training events as part of curriculum development initiatives like Higher Still. Teachers wishing to convert from secondary to primary or to gain a qualification to teach another secondary subject can do so by means of a one-term Additional Teaching Qualification (ATQ) course at a TEI. Several teachers have entered Gaelic-medium teaching by this route and the ATQ has helped authorities address staffing shortages more immediately than otherwise possible.

A number of steps have been taken to increase the supply of Gaelic-medium teachers. Recruitment drives have been undertaken by SEED and CNAG and the Scottish Higher Education Funding Council (SHEFC) has funded places for Gaelic-medium students at the Universities of Aberdeen and Strathclyde. A distance-learning version of the PGCE (Primary) course is being developed by the University of Strathclyde in partnership with Lews Castle College, Stornoway and local authorities in the Highlands and Islands. These measures have helped to reduce the gap between supply and demand but the throughput of trained personnel is still insufficient to sustain, let alone expand, the Gaelic-medium service.

FURTHER AND HIGHER EDUCATION

The use of Gaelic as a medium of education extends into the tertiary sector and is, indeed, at its most comprehensive in one further education (FE) college. Sabhal Mòr Ostaig was founded in 1973 as a Gaelic college in the Sleat area of Skye. Initially, the college ran a programme of short courses in Gaelic language and culture but, ten years on, it embarked on full-time provision.

Today, the college offers certificate, diploma, degree and postgraduate courses in Business Studies, Information Technology, Management, Communications, Broadcasting and the Arts. All these courses, and others in Gaelic language and Gàidhealtachd Studies, are delivered and assessed in Gaelic and the administration of the college is also conducted in Gaelic. Sabhal Mòr has considerably expanded its portfolio of short courses and over 500 students enlist annually for tuition in a range of language and culture classes. The college campus houses a Gaelic research agency, Lèirsinn, a Gaelic theatre company, Tosg, and a marketing and communications company, Cànan, which publishes educational material. Sabhal Mòr is also home to the Columba Initiative designed to foster closer cultural, educational and linguistic links between Scotland and Ireland.

In 1997–8 a full-time Gaelic immersion course was introduced at Sabhal Mòr. The first such immersion course, sponsored by CNAG, was piloted in Lochaber in 1995–6 by Inverness College. The pilot was adjudged a success and the 600-hour course was repeated in Lochaber, in Inverness and in Clydebank College the following session. The effectiveness of learning a language through immersion is now widely attested and demand for this model amongst adult learners is such that a further five colleges mounted the course in 2001–2.

Sabhal Mòr, Lews Castle, Inverness and other FE establishments in the north have joined forces to form the University of the Highlands and Islands Millennium Institute

(UHIMI) which aims to win university status for the federal, collegiate institution. An award of £33m from the Millennium Fund, supplemented by European money, is being used to upgrade facilities and to develop degree level courses at the thirteen participating colleges and institutes. It is envisaged that UHIMI will reflect the character and culture of the region and give Gaelic a higher profile and an enhanced role as a specialist subject of study and as a medium of learning and assessment. Sabhal Mòr is likely to be the main centre of Gaelic provision within UHIMI but Lews Castle will also play a prominent part.

Traditionally, students wishing to study Gaelic at university have had to go to Aberdeen, Edinburgh or Glasgow, each of which has a Celtic department. These three departments offer a range of undergraduate courses in Gaelic and Celtic Studies and students can take an Honours degree in Celtic or a joint honours in Celtic and another subject. Celtic Studies encompasses the study of other Celtic languages, particularly Irish Gaelic and Welsh. Provision is made for those wanting to learn the language and Celtic Civilisation classes cater for those with an interest in cultural heritage. Some Celtic Studies classes are taught in Gaelic but the language is not yet deployed as a medium in other subject areas. Postgraduate study opportunities are also available in the discipline. The University of Strathclyde has, since its merger with Jordanhill College, established Gaelic classes for learners.

COMMUNITY EDUCATION

Time spent in school is but a fraction of the time spent in the home and the community, and the contribution of these domains to the education of the child is being recognised increasingly in the development of Gaelic education.

Local authorities throughout Scotland arrange evening classes for parents who wish to learn Gaelic in order to assist, and keep in step with, the linguistic progress of their offspring. Some authorities also provide language packs for parents who are not Gaelic speakers so that they can help their children with homework. Reinforcement of the language beyond the school is regarded as a vital part of the Gaelic-medium education strategy, especially for children from non-Gaelic-speaking homes, and a nationwide network of Gaelic youth clubs has been set up by CNAG. Over 1,500 children between the ages of five and twelve attend the fifty-two Sradagan clubs.

Another community initiative, Fèisean nan Gàidheal, seeks to reinforce the link between the language and the culture. A fèis, or festival, is typically a week-long event which offers children tuition in Gaelic and in a variety of Gaelic arts including drama, storytelling, song and music. The fèis movement began in Barra and has evolved into a national agency which assists with the organisation of thirty-two separate fèisean in communities in, and beyond, the Highlands and Islands. Two of the fèisean provide all tuition through the medium of Gaelic.

In addition to the classes for parents mentioned above, a number of agencies run classes and short courses for adult learners. The community education departments of local authorities and FE colleges continue to be the principal providers. Most of the classes are designed for beginners and follow an SQA modular scheme or have a less defined conversational format. University departments of continuing education also offer similar kinds of classes. Intensive short courses for learners are organised by a number of public and private agencies.

RESEARCH

While a great deal of research has been conducted on linguistic, socio-linguistic, demo-graphic and literary topics by university Celtic departments, the School of Scottish Studies at Edinburgh University, the Lèirsinn Research agency at Sabhal Mòr and individuals such as Kenneth MacKinnon and Charles Withers, Gaelic education has not received the attention it warrants. There was, until lately, little available in published form.

The Department of Education at Stirling University has been the locus for three important research projects into aspects of Gaelic education. The first of these was an evaluation of the Western Isles Bilingual Project, led by Donald MacIntyre and Ros Mitchell, published in 1987. The findings were generally favourable to the project and supportive of the bilingual scheme. There followed, in 1994, Professor Richard Johnstone's review of research, the *Impact of Current Developments to Support the Gaelic Language*. The report gave a comprehensive account and perceptive analysis of developments in education and other fields of Gaelic activity. The previously referred to HMI report, *Provision for Gaelic Education in Scotland*, also published in 1994, provided a more detailed review of each sector of education but was heavily criticised by the Gaelic community for some of its conclusions and recommendations in respect of secondary education. The third government funded Stirling project was a three-year programme of research into the attainments of pupils in Gaelic-medium primary education in Scotland. The research, conducted in collaboration with the Scottish Council for Research in Education (SCRE) and Lèirsinn, and published in 1999, confirmed that pupils educated in Gaelic 'were not being disadvantaged in comparison with children educated through English' and were, in many instances, outperforming English-medium pupils, while also gaining the advantage of proficiency in two languages (Johnstone, 1999).

Like Stirling, Lèirsinn has been involved in a number of research projects concerned with Gaelic education. The agency was commissioned by the Inter-Authority Standing Group for Gaelic (IASG) to undertake a review and assessment of support and provision for Gaelic-medium education and produced two reports, one on teacher training and another, Critical Skills, in 1996. More recently, Lèirsinn has investigated emergent identities in bilingual education and patterns of Gaelic speech in secondary education.

PROSPECTS

It will be apparent from the foregoing review that substantial progress has been made in Gaelic education, particularly in the provision of Gaelic-medium pre-school and primary education. Buoyant and burgeoning as the Gaelic-medium development would appear to be, it is, nevertheless, a tender and fragile flower. This was graphically illustrated in 1996 when cutbacks in local authority funding led to a proposal to close a thriving Gaelic-medium unit in East Kilbride. A concerted campaign by parents and language agencies averted closure but the proposal underlined the insecurity of provision for Gaelic and highlighted once more the lack of a national policy on Gaelic education and the language's vulnerability in the absence of official recognition and status.

CNAG has been at the forefront of a campaign to win for the language a 'secure status' which it is envisaged would consolidate current provision, confer additional linguistic rights on Gaelic speakers and lead to greater use of the language in official domains. The Scottish Executive has committed itself to 'working towards secure status' and the First Minister,

Jack McConnell, has pledged to introduce legislation on Gaelic early in the next Parliament. The establishment by the Executive of an official Board for Gaelic, Bòrd na Gàidhlig, in September 2002 has been widely welcomed by the Gaelic community and it is hoped the new board will expedite progress towards a Gaelic Language Act.

One of the policy areas that the new board will have to tackle will be the development of a national strategy for Gaelic education. Gaelic agencies have long advocated the development of a national plan to bring coherence to the ad hoc, piecemeal and unco-ordinated provision for Gaelic education. The production of a national strategy should be facilitated by the Scottish Executive's identification of Gaelic education as one of the 'National Priorities' in the Standards in Scotland's Schools etc. Act 2000 which created a new statutory framework for schools' education and requires local authorities and schools to plan, monitor and report on improvements in education.

Teacher recruitment and training will be key elements of a national strategy for Gaelic education. The GTCS report, referred to earlier, set out the main requirements in this field and would, if acted upon, overcome most of the shortcomings of the present system.

Remarkable as the growth in Gaelic-medium education has been, a great deal remains to be done. Seventeen years after the establishment of the first Gaelic-medium units in primary schools, there is still only one dedicated Gaelic-medium school anywhere in Scotland. Parental campaigns for similar schools in Edinburgh and Inverness have met with different responses from the local authorities concerned. This, and attempts by some councils to cap the number of pupils entering Gaelic-medium education, reinforces the need for a national strategy.

Good practice in maximising the use of the language as the vehicle of instruction needs to be more uniformly adopted if the 5–14 target of attaining broadly equal competence in both languages by P7 is to be achieved. While nursery education is now much better integrated with primary provision, properly planned progression across all sectors of Gaelic-medium education remains an aspiration. In particular, the issues around the primary/secondary interface which lead to a significant drop in the number of pupils following the Gaelic-medium curriculum in secondary have yet to be resolved. The planning process should be informed by the experience and expertise available in Wales and Ireland where similar problems have been encountered and overcome. Different models of provision might be required in secondary schools in urban and rural settings but sustained incremental development of subject specialist teaching through the medium of Gaelic will be needed throughout Scotland in order to generate greater parental confidence in Gaelic-medium education as a whole. Expansion of the secondary sector and enhancement of further and higher education provision will be needed to create a sufficient pool of trained personnel to maintain and develop the system.

Local authorities will require an assurance of continued government funding for new initiatives and projects and specific funding for Gaelic will have to be extended to further and higher education institutions if they are to meet the increased demand for training in the language in an overall context of fiscal constraints. This is particularly true of the TEIs where an extension of Gaelic-medium training would have considerable financial implications because of the specialist nature of the provision and the small numbers involved.

Access to the language and culture should not be confined to the Gaelic-medium sector. Over 90% of secondary school children in Scotland are denied the opportunity to learn Gaelic in their local school. Research, attitudinal surveys, audience figures for learners programmes on television and the uptake of learners' classes in continuing and higher education all suggest that there is considerable potential for the development of provision for learners within secondary schools. If the decision to make Gaelic a national priority is to have real substance, local and central government should collaborate in framing a phased programme of development which might include identifying one school in urban areas which would offer tuition in Gaelic and measures such as harnessing information technology and open-learning to provide access in areas with little Gaelic provision or presence.

Celtic and Gaelic elements of Scottish heritage, life and culture continue to be neglected in Scottish schools and it is an indictment of the education system that so few pupils have any awareness of Celtic civilisation and Gaelic culture. It is to be hoped that the Scottish Parliament will address this issue, perhaps within the context of an overall review of the place of Scottish culture in the curriculum, and find an appropriate way of informing every pupil in Scotland about a core element of their heritage.

REFERENCES

HMI, (1994) *Provision for Gaelic Education in Scotland*, Edinburgh: SOED.

Johnstone, R. (1994) *The Impact of Current Developments to support the Gaelic Language: Review of Research*, Stirling: Scottish Centre for Information on Language Teaching and Research.

Johnstone, R. (1999) *The Attainments of Pupils Receiving Gaelic Medium Primary Education in Scotland*, Stirling : Scottish Centre for Information on Language Teaching and Research.

Robertson, B. (2001) *Gaelic : The Gaelic Language in Education in the UK*, Leeuwarden: Mercator-Education.

Robertson, B. (2001) *Gaelic in Scotland*, in G. Extra and D. Gorter (eds) *The Other Languages of Europe*, Cleveden: Multilingual Matters.

SOED (1993) *Curriculum and Assessment in Scotland: National Guidelines: Gaelic 5–14*, Edinburgh: HMSO.

24

The Scots Language in Education

Anne Donovan and Liz Niven

THE SCOTS LANGUAGE – ITS HISTORY AND DEVELOPMENT

Scots is an Indo-European language descended from a northern form of Anglo-Saxon. By the seventh century AD, this Germanic branch of the language had reached the south-east of what is now Scotland and by the eleventh century AD was firmly established across central and southern Scotland. In addition to such Anglo-Saxon vocabulary as *bairns*, *thrawn*, *bide* and *byre*, strong Scandinavian, French and Dutch influences can still be heard in words such as *lass*, *lug*, *lowse*, *braw*, *douce*, *fash*, *scone* and *redd* respectively. Latin remains in, for example, *janitor* and *dux*; Irish and Scots Gaelic have provided further lexical items such as *bens*, *glens* and *straths*. Thus, as with the English language, contact with other countries and the legacy of loan words from several nations have contributed to the formation of the Scots language.

Much written Scots was produced in the late fourteenth-century court of James IV by the King's commissioned poets and dramatists, and by the early sixteenth century Scots was developing as an all-purpose national language. This was the nearest point at which Scots came to adopting a written standard, accepted, on equal terms, with other European languages. However English began to wield greater influence around the time of the Reformation in 1560 when the Geneva Bible was translated into English rather than Scots. Anglicisation increased after the departure of James VI to London and the Union of the Crowns in 1603, particularly among the Scots nobility. Finally, after the Treaty of Union in 1707, English became the official language of government and the court, even though Scots was almost universally spoken throughout lowland, central and north-east Scotland, and Gaelic in the Highlands and Islands.

CONTEMPORARY SCOTS

Contemporary spoken Scots embraces a wide variation in language on a continuum from Scottish Standard English to broad Scots. The possible range of pronunciation, vocabulary, grammar and idiom is wide, and nuances can be so subtle that its speakers are unaware that they are not actually speaking English. While examples of overt Scots might be demonstrated in vocabulary such as *aye* or *wee*, *kye* or *yowe*, covert Scots might be employed in the use of words such as *pinkie* or *outwith*.

In some situations, words have different meanings in English than in Scots. For example, *a chap at the door* or *going for the messages* are common Scottish phrases with different meanings when spoken by English speakers. Similarly, grammatical constructions such as the use of the indefinite article and possessive pronoun (*I have the flu and I'm away to my bed* rather than 'I have flu and I am going to bed') are typically Scottish while the use of *yous* as a second person plural pronoun emulates the 'vous' of French grammar. Yet these are often regarded as 'bad grammar' rather than examples of legitimate Scots. Frequently, speakers will shift between speech forms depending on their current audience and purpose. The Scottish writer Andrew Greig succinctly expresses this in his novel *Electric Brae*.

> His accent was moving in and out of focus like his finger. Who are we? I wondered. We don't even speak consistently. We'll say 'yes' and 'aye' in the same conversation, alternate between 'know' and 'ken', 'bairn' and 'wean' and 'child' and not even know why. Even the old man did it, and I've lost half his tongue, the better half. We're a small country with blurry boundaries.

SCOTS LANGUAGE – LANGUAGE OR DIALECT?

As stated in the Mercator-Education Dossier, *The Scots Language in Education in Scotland*,

> One of the greatest barriers to Scots being acknowledged as a distinct language in Scotland is its close proximity to English. As both are Germanic languages, from a common root and sharing much vocabulary, modern Scots tends to exist on a continuum with broad Scots at one end and Scottish Standard English (SSE) at the other. This situation is roughly similar to the continuum that exists in Dutch/German and Danish/Norwegian. No controversy exists with these languages in establishing whether they are dialects or languages.

The Scottish language dictionaries list ten dialect areas. All have their own particular pronunciation and dialect variations. For example, 'good' might be written and pronounced as *guid* or *geed* or *gweed*. Opinions vary widely as to whether an agreed written standard is desirable; some creative writers and readers fear a dilution in individuality while some language activists would prefer an agreed written language, not necessarily spoken by any particular region of the country. The argument as to whether Scots is a language or a dialect frequently provides a diversion from productive discussion about Scots language issues. However, several factors contribute to a widespread belief that Scots is indeed a language: it is widely spoken throughout Scotland, it has all the elements of a language (that is, accent, dialects, grammar, idiom), it has a clear geographical boundary within a nation state and it has a centuries-old pedigree of literature. The only missing element is the lack of a standardised written form.

COMMON PERCEPTIONS OF SCOTS

The perception of Scots as an inferior version of English has led to its lack of official recognition, as well as confused and conflicting attitudes. Worryingly, it is often those who are themselves Scots speakers who perceive their voice as less acceptable. Various studies, mostly university based, have been conducted on attitudes towards Scots. When interviewed, a vast number of speakers refer to their speech as slang rather than Scots. The implications of these beliefs for Scottish national identity are considerable. In a study of Glasgow dialect it was noted that:

To move into the realms of 'proper' speech holds national significance as well as class significance for the Scot. Even if the English dialect speaker takes lessons to perfect an RP accent, he will still be English. If the Scots does this, he may throw away more in the loss of an outward, recognisable national identity . . . both may disguise their regional origins but only one belies his national identity.' Yet many Scots speakers continue to feel inferior about their voice thus perpetuating the phenomenon kent as The Scottish Cringe. Janet Menzies: *An Investigation of Attitudes to Scots and Glasgow Dialect among Secondary School Pupils*, p.3 http://www2.arts.-gla.ac.uk/COMET/starn/lang/menzies/menzie1.htm)

Trial questions for the 2001 National Census revealed that there are at least 1.5 million Scots speakers while an Aberdeen University study (whose questions were more detailed, including prompts as to specific dialects of Scots) suggested a figure nearer 3 million. At an anecdotal level much more Scots across the continuum is heard at all levels of society, both formal and informal. Scottish voices are evident in the media though their distinctiveness lies in their strong accents rather than in the use of vocabulary and grammar. Spoken Scots is heard in radio and television interviews conducted with the public although the voice of the interviewer tends to remain Scottish-accented English. Occasionally, programmes are presented by Scots speakers but they are still in the minority.

OFFICIAL ATTITUDES

Ambivalence towards Scots language issues is often evident in official policy and practice. However, the formation of a cross-party group for Scots language in the Parliament indicates positive support for the language at a national level: this group has compiled a Statement of Linguistic Rights for Scots. The Scottish Executive also maintains a website outlining its support for the language and, in 2001, the United Kingdom government ratified the Charter for Minority Languages for Scots. Theoretically, this supports several practical conditions for Scots language in education, 'the provision of appropriate forms and means for the teaching and study of regional or minority languages at all appropriate stages' (PART 11, article 7, para 1.f). Nevertheless, a parliamentary response stated in early 2002 that the Executive 'does not consider that any action is necessary to comply with the European Charter for Regional or Minority Languages' and 'has not formulated any policy on the numbers of speakers of Scots'. However, in November 2002, Parliament adopted the McGugan Report which recommends increased support for the language.

Furthermore, at parliamentary level there has been debate about the issue of signage for the new Parliament building under construction. Gaelic and English have been determined as the only two languages appearing on signs, the reason supplied being that two languages was the maximum possible. (In several European countries, including Switzerland, signs are printed in more than two languages.) On the other hand, at the formation of the Parliament, the Scottish equivalent of Hansard liaised with the Scottish National Dictionary and Glasgow University to establish an agreed orthography in which to record speeches by MSPs in Scots where appropriate. (In previous years, the Westminster Hansard had found it necessary to translate words such as *stushie*.)

SCOTS IN EDUCATION – POLICY

In spite of apparently contradictory signals from officialdom, the place of Scots language and literature in the curriculum looks assured, to judge from various policy documents. Certainly attitudes from HMI have altered since it was observed that Scots 'is not the language of educated people anywhere.' More recently, Her Majesty's Inspector of Schools' report on English in the series *Effective Learning and Teaching in Scottish Secondary Schools* (1992) states: 'It should be the aim of English teaching throughout the secondary school to develop the capacity of every pupil to use, understand and appreciate the native language in its Scots and English forms.' Supportive statements about Scots in the curriculum exist in several 5–14 documents with the greatest emphasis found in English language. In the section devoted to Scottish culture, it states:

> The first tasks of schools are therefore to enable pupils to be confident and creative in this language and to begin to develop notions of language diversity, within which pupils can appreciate the range of accents, dialects and languages they encounter. This will involve teachers in valuing pupils' spoken language, and introducing them to stories, poems and other texts which use dialect in a positive way.

Scots language and literature has also been included in the examination syllabus. Candidates are encouraged to 'write in Scots where appropriate' as part of their creative writing paper in English at Higher level. (While there is no specific advice in the guidelines, it has always been possible to do this at Standard Grade.) Until recently some texts were prescribed at Higher level; *Sunset Song* was one of the most popular, ensuring that many young people read literature in Scots, while the Scottish literature options at Advanced Higher include many in Scots. The introduction of an optional Scottish Language paper at Advanced Higher Level in 2000 allows candidates to select from topics such as the use of Scots in contemporary literature, the difference between the Scots of young and old people, its use in the media. All these developments indicate changed attitudes to the use of Scots in education. However, in the three years since the exam's inception, no pupil has yet been presented for it, suggesting that teachers must be trained in and confident about Scots language issues, as well as Scots literature, before the shifts in attitude by official bodies is matched by practical action.

SCOTS IN EDUCATION – PRACTICE

On paper, all would seem to be well, but what is the current reality of the classroom? In practice it would be fair to say that the experience of any individual child will depend very much on the teachers she/he happens to get and their attitude to the Scots language. In some primary schools the situation is similar to that described by Robert Tyson in 'Scots language in the classroom: viewpoint 1' (Niven and Jackson, 1998, pp. 71–5) where Scots language and culture is an everyday feature of the whole school experience of the pupils. As well as studying Scots literature and celebrating St Andrew's day, signs around the school have been printed in Scots as well as English, a local dictionary of Scots has been compiled and those pupils who come from outwith the area can actually learn Scots. However in many primary schools Scots features only in the study of poetry and prose and in some places that still means learning a poem for Burns night. Similarly, in secondary English departments, listening to, reading, writing, and speaking in Scots are part of each day's experience in some classrooms, while next door there can be teachers who feel they have to 'get through' at least one Scottish text at Higher, and that is not necessarily one written in Scots.

Traditionally the Scottish teacher has had a great deal of freedom in selecting what is taught and the methods employed in the classroom, and in spite of increased bureaucracy this is still the case. The curriculum in Scotland is largely regulated by guidelines to be interpreted rather than by mandate. While there are many positive features associated with it, this freedom, allied to the problematic attitudes towards Scots outlined earlier, has led to somewhat disparate provision. No formal assessment has been carried out to establish how widespread the teaching of Scots is in Scottish primary schools. Any evidence has been gathered through the study of schools offering in-service training to staff, the responses of teachers to random questioning and the results of a few optional studies by students in teacher education. It is widely accepted that the inclusion of Scots varies greatly across the country, with interested individuals teaching pupils about Scots (though not necessarily in Scots) and non-interested teachers omitting it entirely from the curriculum. Similarly in secondary education, since Scots language teaching is subsumed under the English subject area, the extent to which it is studied in the classroom is unsupported by statistical evidence and the range of provison is patchy.

Teacher training institutions, hampered by ever shortening contact time with students, include some discussion about Scots within language and literature classes. Some allow students to select Scots language as their area for specialist study while others, for example, Strathclyde University Faculty of Education, now include a compulsory Scots language element in its four year BEd degree (albeit two hours in a four-year course). However, as long as there is no compulsory study of Scots language and literature for all teachers in training, practitioners with limited knowledge about and confidence in these areas will continue to appear in the classroom, thus perpetuating the current anomalous situation.

SCOTS LITERATURE

One area where Scots is alive and vigorously kicking is in contemporary literature. As has been stated previously, Scotland has a rich literary heritage, much of it in Scots, and in the early part of the twentieth century, the so-called 'Scottish renaissance', is well represented by poets such as MacDiarmid (who observed in 1958 that: 'if Scottish writers use English, they must be content to play a very subordinate role') and prose writers like Nan Shepherd and Lewis Grassic Gibbon (who stated that Scots would 'adorn his meaning with a richness, a clarity and a conciseness impossible in orthodox English'.) In the later part of the twentieth and into the twenty-first century a similar resurgence has been noted, resulting in a clear confidence in the way that writers use the languages of Scotland in whatever ways they choose, whether these languages are English, Scots, Gaelic, Punjabi or a mixture of these or any other languages heard in Scotland. Also there is increasing interest in and respect for writing in Scots (though it may not necessarily be called that). James Kelman's Booker Prize for *How Late It Was, How Late*, and the international reputation of *Trainspotting* by Irvine Welsh, are two of the most obvious examples of this, but there is an increasing appetite by publishers, reviewers and translators furth of Scotland for Scots writing. This can only have an effect on the perceptions of the Scottish people, especially, perhaps, young people.

EDUCATIONAL RESOURCES

The existence of suitable resources with which to teach Scots language and literature is crucial, especially since many teachers have not had specific or thorough training in these areas. Increased burdens of assessment have meant that teachers have less time to prepare new materials and therefore look to texts which have commercially or centrally produced worksheets for them. This has tended to favour texts in Standard English and it is clear from the publishing experiences of the last twenty years that the production of curricular materials for Scots language is an ongoing problem. Commercial British publishers have been reluctant to produce materials for a relatively small market while the few Scottish publications emerging over the last twenty years have been faced with the dilemma of short print runs followed by out-of-print titles in a very short space of time. Support from bodies such as Learning and Teaching Scotland or the ringfencing of funds for Scots Language resources (paralleled in other countries with minority languages) would still seem to be necessary if the curriculum demands resources. A major factor in determining how much demand there actually is for Scots language teaching materials is the influence of the Scottish Executive. As has been noted, this remains weak despite occasional supportive statements in documents.

However there is no doubt that things are changing and the number of high quality resources has increased. One of the most popular and widely used of these is *The Kist/A Chiste*, published jointly by SCCC and publisher Nelson Blackie in 1996. This package (which resulted from the Scottish Language Project, a major initiative launched by the SCCC) consists of a richly illustrated anthology of poetry, prose and dramatic excerpts in Scots and Gaelic, audio cassettes of all the anthology's content, teacher notes and two books of photocopiable classroom worksheets. The materials were highly praised and awarded the TESS/Saltire Education prize. Currently, the anthology is still available from Learning and Teaching Scotland though the other materials have been allowed to go out of print. *The Kist* remains very popular among both teachers and pupils in primary and secondary schools.

Channel 4 television produced, in 2000, a five-part series of programmes, called *Haud Yer Tongue*, available on video tape and accompanied by a teacher's book of curricular activities. This is a highly valuable resource since it is accessible, lively and up to date. In 2001, *Turnstones 1*, the first of a series of textbooks for secondary English Departments published by Hodder & Stoughton, received the TESS/Saltire award. It integrates Scots and English in poetry, prose and drama-related work as well as exercises in debating skills and formal language skills. One of the advantages of this series is that the work is in both Scots and English, which means it is a highly flexible resource. Like *The Kist*, *Turnstones* also addresses the issue of lack of confidence which prevents some teachers from using Scots materials, since it provides a clear framework and extensive glossary, with teachers' notes available on an accompanying CD.

Very recently, with substantial Scottish Arts Council Lottery funding, the Itchy-Coo Project has produced its first set of books of classroom material in Scots for all stages of the primary and secondary curriculum. These include Scots versions of a child's alphabet book and a history of the Scots Parliament. Over a three-year period there will be a series of books in and about Scots as well as translations such as the Greek myths. These look set to be another useful asset to the classroom. The Association of Scottish Literary Studies (ASLS) and small Scottish publishers such as Merlin Press, Watergaw, and Scotsoun, also produce curricular materials, including cassettes of Scots poetry and song, worksheets and language exercises. *A Braw Brew* (Watergaw) is a collection of stories in Scots for 10–14-year-olds accompanied by a set of photocopiable classroom worksheets. The Scottish Language Dictionaries have produced Scots dictionaries, classroom-related materials, a CD Rom of interactive language activities and a grammar workbook. SCCC has provided Support Notes and Bibliographies for Scots language elements of Higher Still English and Communication.

CLASSROOM PRACTICE

How is this material used in the classroom? A typical starting point for many teachers in both primary and the early stages of secondary, is to introduce poetry in Scots, often in the variety most familiar to the area. *The Kist* has a wealth of such material and is popular. The focus is often on getting the pupils to become more comfortable about reading in Scots. Depending on their previous experience, some pupils will have already seen written Scots and may find it easier to read than English, while for others it will be unfamiliar.

Another typical lesson is to increase vocabulary using word banks and dictionaries. One of the most important points about this apparently very simple exercise is that it shows pupils that Scots words are actually words in their own right, not simply corruptions of English. Knowledge about language, grammar and linguistic concepts can all be taught through the medium of Scots. Opportunities for pupils to write in Scots would usually be offered and, depending on the confidence and experience of pupils (and perhaps the teacher), this may take the form of a dialogue or short play.

Often the greatest challenge pupils find in writing Scots is how to spell it. Since there is no standardised version of Scots spelling, and since literary models use different variations, this can provoke anxiety in both teachers and pupils, since correct spelling is a cornerstone of learning to write. The use of a Scots dictionary can help, offering various spellings from which a pupil may choose the one nearest to the form of Scots she or he wishes to write. However for some children, the dictionary can be a hindrance, particularly if they are, perhaps for the first time, writing in their own 'voice' and teachers may wish to suggest that the pupil leaves the dictionary aside till he or she has written that voice in what seems the most appropriate way. In fact the process of writing in Scots and the linguistic and cultural questions which arise from such lessons provide opportunities for highly sophisticated language issues to be aired and discussed.

At later stages, models of increasing sophistication will be used and while poetry is still popular, there are increased opportunities for studying work in drama and prose. Prose fiction still tends to be represented by short stories, and it is an example of the increasingly established position of Scots in the curriculum, that anthologies of short stories produced specifically for use in schools (such as the *Heinemann New Windmill Book of Scottish Short Stories*) now include a far greater proportion of stories in Scots than was the case even ten years ago. With the exception of *Sunset Song*, it is still rare to find classes tackling a novel written entirely in Scots. However, the opportunities for senior students to explore texts of their own choice in the Personal Study of Literature can often be the focus for a contemporary Scots text. Talking about the issues surrounding Scots can also be used to provoke discussion and in S3–4 often prove lively topics for talk assessments.

SCOTS LITERATURE VS SCOTS LANGUAGE?

However much user-friendly Scots material becomes available in classrooms, however many policy documents are produced supporting Scots, is it the case that, while Scots literature is acceptable in the classroom, Scots language is still barely tolerated? Scots is the first language of many pupils (and often the second language of many whose first language is other than English) and, informally, many teachers in both primary and secondary classrooms (of all subject areas) may speak Scots or use Scots vocabulary or grammatical constructions. But the prevailing perception of Scots as an 'inferior' version of English, fit perhaps for comedy programmes or the intimacy of family life but not for the serious, public face of language, means that very few would actually teach lessons in Scots, even when the lesson is about Scots. And it is still the case that pupils may be corrected if they speak Scots in the classroom, thus breaching linguistic rights outlined in the UK-ratified Charter for European Minority Languages.

Since English is perceived as the most important of the languages of Scotland, some questions continue to raise their heads. Does encouraging pupils to become fluent in Scots in some way hamper their ability to communicate in English? Does time spent on Scots language activities mean less time available to teach them Standard English? Research suggests that those who are fluent in their mother tongue and whose linguistic competences are developed in that language are more easily able to learn other languages. This applies to speakers of Scots as well as other languages. As Gordon Gibson says in 'Teacher training viewpoint' (Niven and Jackson, 1998, p. 102):

> Evidence from research seems to all point in one direction, telling us that familiarity with a range of languages and dialects enhances the language development of children, extends their metalinguistic awareness and is of positive benefit to them in their education.

This parallels the experience of other bilingual children in Scotland, those who are speakers of community languages such as Punjabi and Urdu. In fact many of the conclusions of the authors of *Education of Minority Ethnic Groups in Scotland : A Review of Research* (Powney, J., McPake, J., Hall, S. and Lyall, L. SCRE, 1998, http://www.scre. ac.uk/summary/rr88.html) could apply to those children who are Scots speakers.

> While many different languages are spoken by some pupils in Scotland, there is little research investigating the effects of bilingualism on learning. More attention has been paid to provision of English as a second language (ESL) than to providing opportunities for pupils to develop their skills in community languages. Bilingualism has been shown to have positive effects on children's educational development. However American research suggests that failure to develop children's skills in both languages can have detrimental effects. In the UK, bilingual education for Welsh and Gaelic speakers is well established but has never been a serious proposition for bilingual children from minority ethnic backgrounds. (p. 2)

Not only has Scots-medium education never been a serious proposition, but many parents and some teachers seem to feel that teaching pupils in their own language and about their own language will actually disadvantage them. The cultural and historical reasons why this is so have already been discussed at length. And in spite of support for Scots in the primary and secondary school curricula, at pre-school and nursery level there is no official policy regarding Scots. Furthermore, the dearth of books, tapes and video materials in Scots suitable for very young children means that the dilution of a Scots-speaking child's vocabulary as well as a failure to develop language skills in Scots takes place at an even earlier stage, especially where parents view the acquisition of Standard English as a way of 'getting on'.

However it must also be asked what is the effect on the achievement and progress of children and young people throughout their lives of the failure genuinely to value and foster their first language, whether that language is Scots or another commuity language. Furthermore, genuine commitment to Scots language implies an obligation on the part of those involved in education to value the languages of all pupils and develop their skills in those languages. Theoretically, the Scottish Executive seems to support this:

> Pupils should be allowed to use their mother tongue throughout the school . . . Teachers should therefore build on the diversity of culture and language . . . fostering respect for and interest in each pupil's mother tongue and its literature (Diversity of language and culture *English Language 5–14*, (Edinburgh: SOEID, 1991, p. 59).

PROSPECTS

It is difficult to predict the future for the Scots language in education. On the one hand it would seem to be optimistic given the re-formation of a Scottish Parliament and its inclusion of a cross-party group for the language. However in 2000 the Scottish Executive published its National Cultural Strategy in which support for Scots language and culture seems lacklustre seen in the light of its highly supportive stance towards Gaelic culture. There continue to be major difficulties for Scots to become accepted at a formal level when no standardisation of the written language has emerged and its non-inclusion in the judiciary or in parliamentary documents prevents its ratification in Part I of the European Charter of Minority Languages, which would give it greater status and protection.

Judging by the language's ability to survive in its rich diversity of forms across the country, despite centuries of difficulties and obstacles in both education and in official circles, it might be accurate to predict its future prospects as being highly promising. Its greatest hope of survival might be in its proximity to the English language and thus its adaptability to contemporary needs. Greater public awareness of Scots in its twenty-first century forms, and clearer support from the Scots-speaking public might be required to bring about increased inclusion in education. However, this may well require more knowledge about Scots language in the curriculum to raise the status of the Scots language in the minds of Scots themselves. In a typically democratic manner, the fate of Scots language will possibly be decided by the Scottish people and not imposed from above. Unlike English dictionaries which can be read as prescriptive, Scots dictionaries are descriptive. However, many educationalists and activists, aware of the implications of language repression, would prefer to see a more concerted, structured approach with language maintenance and planning debated at a national level. It would seem that the Scottish Executive, the Scottish education system, its teachers and pupils, as well as parents are still uncertain as to how to proceed with their treatment of twenty-first century Scots language. On the one hand, there is widespread support for the inclusion (though not necessarily compulsory) of Scots literature in the curriculum. On the other hand, there is still unease about the encouragement of spoken Scots in education and in formal society.

The puzzle remains, why is there such reluctance about the value or the consequences of 'allowing' a nation to hear its own voice?

Meanwhile, between 1.5 million and 3 million Scottish people continue to speak the language at some point on the linguistic continuum. Most remain illiterate in this language, a somewhat unusual situation in a nation with a highly developed educational system.

REFERENCES

Corbett, John (1997) *Language and Scottish Literature*, Edinburgh: Edinburgh University Press.
Kay, Billy (1986) *Scots the Mither Tongue*, Darvel: Alloway Publishing.
McClure, J.Derrick (1988) *Why Scots Matters*, Edinburgh: Saltire Society.
Niven, L. (2002) *The Scots Language in Education in Scotland*, Leeuwarden: Mercator-Education: European Network for Regional or Minority Languages and Education.
Niven, L. and Jackson, R. (eds) (1998) *Scots Language: Its Place in Education*, Dumfries: Watergaw.
SOEID (1991) *English Language 5–14: National Guidelines*, Edinburgh: HMSO.

25

Catholic Education in Scotland

Tom Fitzpatrick

THE EDUCATION (SCOTLAND) ACT 1918

The Education (Scotland) Act, 1918 aimed at promoting an educational system marked by religious tolerance and equal opportunity for all. It enshrined a concept of secondary education 'for all fit to profit from it'. It provided financial aid to make that a reality for a greatly increased spectrum of the population, thereby remedying long-standing grievances affecting the voluntary schools – Catholic and Episcopalian – that had opted to remain outside the national system instituted in 1872.

Two hundred and twenty-six Catholic schools transferred into the education authorities set up under the Act. The vast majority were elementary schools managed by parish priests, located in industrial areas of the south-west and west central belt, and in populous centres of the Lothians, Fife, Tayside and Aberdeenshire. A few existed in Speyside, Banffshire, Galloway and the West Highlands and Islands, where Catholic communities had survived from pre-Reformation times. Post-primary education, apart from that given in supplementary classes in some parochial schools, was in the hands of religious teaching orders – Marist Brothers, Christian Brothers, Society of Jesus, Benedictines, Ursuline and Franciscan Sisters, Sisters of Mercy, Congregation of Notre Dame, Society of the Sacred Heart, Faithful Companions of Jesus and the Sisters of the Cross and Passion – who managed some fifteen independent schools in Glasgow, Edinburgh, Ayrshire, Renfrewshire, Dumbarton, Dundee, Dumfries, Bothwell, Fort Augustus and North Berwick. The number of secondary pupils was a tiny fraction of the primary population. Other orders, among them the Vincentians, Sisters of Charity and Good Shepherd Sisters, contributed to the education of the community by work of a social nature including the housing of orphans, supervision of delinquents and teaching the deaf and blind.

For centuries, before and after the Reformation, Scotttish culture was nurtured by an education based on the Christian ideals and values that moulded European civilisation. During the first millennium of the Christian era it was theocentric in essence. In the second, the emphasis shifted towards an anthropocentric mode, in which understanding of the human condition and of the natural world became principal goals. A Christian humanist culture grew throughout Europe, in which Scotland shared. According to T. C. Smout in *A History of the Scottish People 1500–1830* (London: Fontana, 1967, p. 81), in Scotland 'by the year 1500 three universities existed . . . song schools and grammar schools existed in all the main burghs, and in many small towns like Kirkwall, Montrose, Brechin and Musselburgh.'

Religious reformation and scientific advance broke the cultural unity of Europe. According to M. Lynch, in *Scotland – A New History* (London: Century, 1991, p. 106) 'the generations after 1560 saw the consolidation rather than the establishment of an elementary national system of education: schools were refounded or recast rather than created as new foundations.'

After 1707 an educational partnership was established between the Church of Scotland and the state. No freedom was allowed to others. Catholic education, apart from that given in seminaries overseas, ceased until the beginning of the nineteenth century, when the population began to increase rapidly, particularly in the coalfield areas. New parishes were founded, sometimes with a school attached. A rudimentary system formed, which was stimulated by the Education Act of 1847 and the introduction of the pupil–teacher system, and then more importantly by the advent of religious teaching orders. For an analysis and assessment of their work, see F. J. O'Hagan, *The Contribution of the Religious Orders to Education in Glasgow during the Period 1847–1918* (PhD thesis, Glasgow, 2001); and T. A. FitzPatrick, *The Marist Brothers in Scotland before 1918*, (Innes Review, vol.XLIX: I, 1998 1–10).

By 1872, when the civil authority took control of education, a secular spirit was making rapid headway in Scotland. According to O. Chadwick, in *The Secularisation of the European Mind in the Nineteenth Century*, (Gifford Lectures, Edinburgh, 1973–4; Cambridge University Press, 1975, p.232), 'even the most militant of nineteenth-century French anti-clericals, who advocated non-religious education in schools, recognised the need for moral education, holding that fundamental moralities are natural to humanity, and that a code of ethics could be found on which all men could agree.' Catholics held that moral and religious education are inextricably linked, and the Catholic schools remained outside the national scheme. Because of their limited resources they could not keep pace with expanding needs. By 1918 the parochial schools were overcrowded, ill-equipped and suffering a serious shortage of qualified teachers. Fewer than 3% of their pupils went on to any form of secondary education.

The settlement of 1918 made possible the evolution of a Catholic sector within the national system, in which the hierarchy had a measure of control through its statutory power to approve teachers and appoint supervisors of religious education. Catholic teachers had to be qualified under the national regulations and also be approved by a bishop as to 'religious belief and character'.

For a detailed account of the outcome of this settlement, see FitzPatrick, T. A. *Catholic Secondary Education in South West Scotland before 1972: Its Contribution to the Change in Status of the Catholic Community* (Aberdeen: Aberdeen University Press, 1986). Studies in the Innes Review relating to the institution and operation of the 1918 Act are: Bro. Kenneth FMS, *The Education (Scotland) Act 1918 in the Making*, vol. XIX:2 (1968) pp. 19–128; Treble, J. H. *The Development of R. C. Education in Scotland, 1878–1978*, vol. XXIX:2 (1978) pp. 111–39; Treble, J. H. *The Working of the 1918 Act in the Glasgow Archdiocese*, vol. XXXI:1 (1980) pp. 27–44; Darragh, J. *The Apostolic Visitations of Scotland, 1912 and 1917*, vol. XLI: 1 (Glasgow: Scottish Catholic Historical Association, 1990) pp. 7–118; FitzPatrick, T. A. *The Catholic Teachers' Union, 1917–1919*, vol.XLI:I (1990) pp. 132–5; Aspinwall, B. *Catholic Teachers for Scotland*, vol.XLV:1 (1994) pp. 47–70; Fitzpatrick, T. A. *Scottish Catholic Teacher Education: the Wider Context*, vol. XLV:2 (1994) pp. 147–70; Zwolinski, F. A. *The Congregation of the Christian Brothers in Scotland, 1951–1983*, vol. XLIX:1 (1998) pp. 11–40.

BETWEEN THE WARS

After 1918 there was an upsurge in demand for secondary education. If the benefits of the Act were to be fully achieved, its legal requirements had to be met and the hierarchy satisfied in respect of the education to be provided to a much wider spectrum of the population than before. In the parochial schools, the spiritual and moral formation of the child lay at the heart of the educational process, whereas in the national system intellectual development and attention to utilitarian values took precedence. The associated problems, felt most acutely at secondary level, were exacerbated by changes in school organisation and by the rising academic attainments being asked of all teachers.

Within two decades, some parochial schools progressed to junior secondary or inter-mediate status; existing secondary schools expanded and others were founded. To meet the demand for teachers, Craiglockhart College for women was opened in Edinburgh in 1920. Dowanhill College in Glasgow, also for women, was already well established. Special provision had to be made for the training of Catholic men. As well as following the prescribed course at a provincial centre, they had to attend a course in Religious Education, provided by the Hierarchy, which led to the award of a Religious Teaching Certificate. All who sought to teach in Catholic schools were required to hold this certificate and be approved by the bishop of the diocese.

A new degree of social mobility was experienced within the community, with teachers the backbone of an emerging middle class. Throughout Strathclyde, and in Edinburgh, Fife and Dundee, schools increased in size and number. The flow of Catholic students to the universities, previously minuscule, mushroomed. By 1939 the number of graduates seeking to enter teaching had outstripped the provision of posts, and many newly qualified teachers found themselves surplus to requirements. The emphasis in the schools on producing teachers, which had had a restrictive effect on educational objectives, diminished, and more former pupils began to find their way into other professions and occupations. The outbreak of the Second World War halted this progress.

THE WAR YEARS

The impact of war-time conditions on the schools was severe. In 1939 some 70% of the Catholic population was located in the most congested areas of the south-west, the majority in the city of Glasgow itself. When evacuation became necessary, most Catholic schools were in sending or neutral zones, with very few in receiving areas. One objective of the scheme, 'to match householders and evacuees according to social class and religion', was impossible of achievement, so that the disruption bore heavily on a major part of the Catholic sector.

As the war progressed the number of teachers completing training fell drastically. A significant proportion of the teaching force consisted of recently qualified young men who were called up for national service. Staffs were depleted, and recently-founded schools were disrupted before becoming properly established. A statement from the 1947 SED *Report on Education in Scotland* was particularly true of the Catholic sector: 'great efforts were made . . . to maintain ordinary standards at least in the basic subjects . . . this aim was not fully achieved . . . at the primary stage proficiency in written composition, arithmetic and power to comprehend was not yet up to pre-war standard.'

REVOLUTION

The Second World War ended, as had the first, with the passing of an Education (Scotland) Act of historic significance. Primary and secondary education were to be redefined as progressive courses of instruction appropriate to the age, aptitude and ability of the pupils concerned. Secondary education was seen to be a stage in the life of every child, rather than a particular type of schooling provided for some but not for all. This changed view, stemming at least in part from the national experience of common suffering in war-time, required that a new system be evolved that would suit the majority of pupils as well as the old had fitted the few.

The school leaving age was to be raised at once to fifteen, and later to sixteen; adequate and efficient provision of free primary, secondary and further education was to be made; junior colleges were to be set up for the compulsory part-time education of young persons aged fifteen to eighteen; milk and meals were to be provided in all schools.

A vast expansion of school accommodation was urgently needed. The shortage of teachers, a legacy of war, was exacerbated by the raising of the leaving age, and by a dramatic rise in the school population resulting from a greatly increased birth-rate. Inevitably, this shortage would become progressively more acute as secondary and further education developed. In 1958 the regulations governing the training of teachers were revised. Training colleges were given increased powers, and several new ones were founded. As the children born in the immediate post-war years progressed through the primary, secondary and further education stages, these sectors experienced in turn rapid expansion followed by equally dramatic contraction. The resultant strains on the educational system were compounded by large movements of population, the breakdown of old communities, the emergence of new towns and an unprecedented explosion of knowledge and communication technology. Along with these went a decline in religious faith and practice, and a loss of certainty in previously accepted moral absolutes. Particularly damaging was the erosion of the Christian concept of the family as the basis of society.

Catholic education had to adjust to these changes, as well as to the insights of the Second Vatican Council, which ended in December 1964. Its findings had implications not only for formal religious instruction, but also for all aspects of Christian education.

In 1965 the Scottish Education Department required county authorities to implement a comprehensive system of secondary education, hoping thereby to minimise the divisiveness associated with the separate categories of schools in the existing system. The Catholic community on the whole felt that the demands of social justice would be better served by this rather than the former selective approach, which appeared to run counter to its view of the value of every individual. It was also clear that its continuing need for expansion at secondary level would only be met by the implementation of this government policy.

The schools had to adapt to this revolution while preserving their distinctive religious character. The ensuing problems, associated particularly with the persistent shortage of teachers, were felt acutely. *Scottish Education Statistics, Secondary Schools Staffing Survey 1970*, vol.3 (1972) points out that in the industrial west Roman Catholic schools especially were understaffed by any reasonable standard, as evidenced by high pupil-teacher ratios, large classes, high turnover, curtailed curriculum and part-time education. Counties in the east fared better through their ability to attract non-Catholic staff. The capacity of the schools to offer an adequate programme of religious education diminished. Periods of religious instruction were shortened, their number reduced, and more of their time taken up with secular tasks. The presence of the religious orders in the schools declined, in line with a decrease in vocations to the religious life and in religious observance generally . . . There was a growing reluctance amongst Catholic secondary teachers to undertake religious instruction, which had become more fragmented and more arduous than before. The difficulties were further aggravated when the leaving age was raised to sixteen in 1972.

INCREASE

By 1972 the Catholic sector was almost commensurate with the population it served. A comprehensive system was emerging, albeit at different rates throughout the country. Glasgow's seven full secondary schools had increased to twenty-seven comprehensives, and comparable progress was being made particularly in the neighbouring counties, and in Edinburgh and Dundee.

The fundamental philosophical shift enshrined in the Education (Scotland) Acts of 1945 and 1946 demanded revision both in the content of the curriculum and the methods used; the emergence of ultra-large comprehensive schools brought to light a range of pupils' needs heretofore unsuspected or neglected; emphasis on child-centred education encouraged new teaching approaches; changes in child–parent relations had repercussions within the schools. A greatly increased corps of teachers was required, able to focus on the personal, moral and spiritual needs of individual pupils of a wide range of intellectual ability and social experience.

From 1967 – when the Bearsden campus of Notre Dame College came into use – the teacher-training system expanded. Men were admitted to the primary diploma course. By 1970 there were ten colleges of education in Scotland, under pressure to meet a continually rising demand in an increasingly wide range of subjects and activities. New teaching qualifications were introduced, including a college-based Bachelor of Education degree in which academic development and professional training were carried out concurrently, validated in the case of Notre Dame College by the Council for National Academic Awards. The vast changes in curriculum content required by the special needs of the comprehensive system and by the ongoing explosion of knowledge were met by an embryonic structure of in-service training, a statutory responsibility of the colleges.

The turbulence in the national educational system reflected a deep-seated malaise in society at large. A loss of moral certainties in the adult population resulted in the erosion of parental authority and confusion in the minds of the young, and led to a crisis in moral and religious education which demanded responses from civil and ecclesiastical authorities. Following the publication by the SED of two seminal memoranda, *Guidance in Scottish Secondary Schools* (1968) and *The Structure of Promoted Posts in Scottish Secondary Schools* (1971), outlining the underlying philosophy and the practical issues involved, a structure of personal, vocational and curricular guidance was introduced in all secondary schools, which led to a widening of commitment to pastoral aspects of the teacher's work.

Because of its long involvement in child guidance and its concept of education as necessarily concerned with the moral and spiritual as well as the intellectual development of children, Notre Dame College was able to co-operate vigorously and give a lead in this area. From 1971 residential, non-denominational in-service courses in guidance were mounted at Bearsden during the summer vacation, which prepared the way for the introduction, at the national level, of special qualification courses.

In 1972 the Millar Report, *Moral and Religious Education in Scottish Schools* other than

Roman Catholic, appeared. In the same year the Catholic Education Commission, composed of representatives nominated by the bishop of each diocese, was instituted to advise the Hierarchy on educational matters. In 1974 a Teaching Qualification in Religious Education for Secondary Education was introduced, regulations governing qualifications to teach religious subjects were formulated, and Specialist Teachers of Religious Education began to be trained to meet the demands that followed. This led to the development of examinable Religious Studies, which required that the teaching be subject to inspection. Section 66(2) of the Education (Scotland) Act 1980, which forbade inspection of Religious Instruction by HMI, was repealed by the Education (Scotland) Act 1981, and in 1983 inspection of Religious Education began. Parallel to these developments full-time chaplains were appointed to Catholic secondary schools, diocesan catechetical centres were set up, and in-service courses in Religious Education were introduced. In 1976 an Advanced Diploma in Religious Education offered by Note Dame gained recognition as a teaching qualification. It developed into an Advanced Teaching Qualification in Religious Education (ATQRE) provided through distance learning.

DECREASE

By the middle of the 1970s, a fall in the birth-rate, as dramatic within the Catholic community as in the nation as a whole, led to a decline in the primary school population, with a similar consequence at higher levels to follow. The endemic shortage of teachers suddenly disappeared. The educational expansion of the post-war period went into reverse, and many primary and secondary schools contracted or closed. The teacher-training system was again overhauled. A proposal that Craiglockhart might forge a link with another college in the east was not acceptable to the Catholic community. The view prevailed that what was required was one college located in the west where the bulk of the Catholic population was situated, while a presence was retained in the east. The only real option was a merger of the two existing colleges, with one board of governors, one staff, and unified control of resources. The two Catholic colleges were dissolved, and in 1981 a new institution, St Andrew's College of Education, was founded at Bearsden in the building formerly occupied by Notre Dame College. The rule that the principal of a Catholic college should belong to a religious teaching order was abrogated. For an account of the merger see T. A. FitzPatrick, *No Mean Service: Scottish Catholic Teacher Education 1895–1995* (Glasgow: St Andrew's College, 1995) p. 155–85.

TRANSFORMATION

Between 1918 and 1980 Catholic education was transformed, mainly through the greater understanding of the needs of the community shown by the civil authorities and a major shift in education policy by government. Children of a wider segment of the population were being taught in smaller classes and in better surroundings than ever before. Teachers were better qualified, and the shortage that had so long haunted the system had ended. The level of academic attainment was comparable with that of the non-denominational sector. The number of former pupils going on to further and higher education had mushroomed, and was contributing to the common good in a multitude of ways, in medicine, nursing, the law, the civil service and in the expanding world of finance, as well as in higher education, administration, politics, journalism and the arts. A Catholic middle class had emerged, the fruit of the expanded educational service, and the traditional image of the Catholic layman as 'a hewer of wood and drawer of water' no longer applied. Something, however, had been lost. Before 1918 the Catholic community had a unity of outlook based on a common culture that distinguished it in many ways from the country as a whole. By 1980 that unity was eroding, and division based on social distinctions was growing. The tradition of Catholic intellectualism dwindled, and with it that integration of culture and faith which might be taken to be the hallmark of an educated Catholic community.

THE ETHOS OF CATHOLIC SCHOOLS

The ethos or characteristic spirit of any community is a function of its fundamental and essential beliefs, a reflection of its value-system and of its view of its place in the universe. It is related to the prevalent tone of the community, and is the result of the manner and degree to which practical expression is given to its beliefs. The ethos of an educational system can be understood only in relation to the community it serves.

Scottish Catholic schools have therefore to be seen in the context of the history and spiritual disposition of the local Catholic community. They bear witness to the Catholic view of the nature and condition of the human person, as imperfect but redeemed, and of infinite value. The extent to which expression is given to this view may vary in time and place, depending on the degree of understanding of and commitment to that view which prevails.

In 1918 Catholic schools accepted the academic standards and organisational structure of the national system, and subsequently absorbed many of its positive aspects, as for example recognition of the contribution of education to the common good, the right of the young to an education from which they are capable of profiting, and access to it unhindered by class, gender or other distinctions. However, Catholic schools belong to an older, faith-centred tradition that aims to bring faith, culture and life into harmony; in which the rhythm of school life is in tune with the Church's liturgical year, and within which academic content is illuminated with the spirit of the Gospel. This tradition holds that education must be directed towards the development of the moral as well as the intellectual faculties of the child, and that personal development is incomplete when spiritual and religious growth is neglected. It strives to achieve its aims through the implanting of the motives and practices of the Catholic religion. It is this religious dimension that gives the Catholic school its distinctive character. The Christian message, enshrined in the two great commandments of love, should animate the school community, and infuse secular teaching with religious awareness and understanding.

The religious dimension finds its principal expression in the classroom in the relationship between teacher and taught, and also in the relative value of the goals that are being pursued. The respect accorded to the pupil by the teacher, and to the teacher by the pupil, find their justification in a belief about the nature of persons, just as the respect towards subjects of study is founded on a belief about the nature of reality itself. These beliefs form the guiding principle at the heart of the educational process. If they command the commitment of both teacher and taught – conveyed in the case of pupils by their parents – they provide the common ground on which sound relationships can grow, and a disciplinary framework without which learning cannot take place. This is what makes the difference between a school where education is permeated by the Christian spirit and one in which religion is regarded as an academic subject like any other. Teachers committed to the first philosophy accept a responsibility for the moral and spiritual welfare of their pupils that extends beyond the satisfying of their intellectual needs. In this tradition moral and religious education are inseparable. The distinctiveness of Catholic education therefore rests ultimately on the faith, doctrine and sacramental practice of the Catholic Church.

BY WHAT AUTHORITY?

In the natural order parents are the first teachers of their children, and the source of authority over them. Children have a right to be nurtured by their parents, and a corresponding duty to respect them. Parents have a duty to care for their children, and a corresponding right to be respected. In our democracy, parents devolve some of their authority to the schools where, in the Scottish tradition, the teacher stands *in loco parentis*.

A religion is more than a philosophy, and education more than the passing on of an ideology. The consequence for teachers is spelt out in the Roman document *The Catholic School*: 'The acheivement . . . of the Catholic school depends not so much on subject matter or methodology as on the people who work there . . . The extent to which the Christian message is transmitted through education depends greatly on the teacher, by whom the integration of faith and culture is mediated.' For a successful outcome, a consensus of outlook between parents and teachers is essential. (*Mutatis mutandis*, the same could be said of any system.) The demeanour and life-style of teachers proclaim their outlook and attitudes. It is the quality of integration of faith and life in the person of the teacher that ennobles the work of education.

PAST HISTORIC

After 1918, in order to gain a licence to teach, Catholics had to satisfy the requirements of both civil and ecclesiastical authorities. All prospective teachers had to gain, by written examination, a preliminary religious certificate at the end of their secondary schooling. Women aspirants then had to train at either of the two residential Catholic colleges, Dowanhill or Craiglockhart. Men had to train at a provincial college – usually Jordanhill or Moray House – and also follow a parallel course in Religious Education laid down by the Church. This involved attendance at a series of extra-mural lectures taken concurrently with the university or college course, together with a series which took place during the training year with the co-operation of the college authority. A full Religious Certificate was awarded on the satisfaction of all these requirements, the complexity of which indicated the importance in the Church's eyes of the teacher's role. When in 1967 men were admitted to the non-graduate diploma course in primary education, the Catholic colleges opened their doors to male students. Thereafter Catholic men could meet all requirements during their college training. For a detailed account, see T. A. FitzPatrick, *No Mean Service: Scottish Catholic Teacher Education 1895–1995*, (Glasgow: St Andrew's College, 1995), pp. 79–82.

With the massive expansion of education in the 1960s the training system came under great strain. The preliminary religious certificate examination was abandoned. Notre Dame College expanded into a new building at Bearsden, while retaining its original premises at Dowanhill. Craiglockhart expanded *in situ*. Degree-awarding powers were extended to colleges of education, and Notre Dame gained validation for its courses from the Council of National Academic Awards. With the introduction of national qualifications for Special Teachers of Religious Education, agreement was reached between the Catholic Education

Commission and the Scottish Education Department that HM Inspectors had the right to inspect professional aspects of religious education in Catholic schools.

In 1981 St Andrew's College of Education became the National Catholic College, and all prospective Catholic teachers were require to follow the course in Religious Education provided there. To meet the difficulties of students unable for geographical or other approved reasons to undertake the training, distance learning courses were provided, backed by in-service courses at bases in Edinburgh and Dundee.

In 1982 HH Pope John Paul II, in the course of his historic visit to Scotland, spoke in St Andrew's College to a group representative of every level of Scottish ecclesiastical, academic and civil life. He stressed the need in education for the development of the whole person, and commented on the purpose of a university and the relevance of the school, not merely as a recruiting ground for university students, but as an essential part of the continuous process of education.

Because of the many changes in the field of religious education, the Catholic Education Commission sought an amendment to the Education (Scotland) Act 1980, reaffirming the right of the local bishop to approve 'as to religious belief and character' any teacher appointed to a post in a Catholic school. This amendment became part of the Self-Governing Schools etc. (Scotland) Act 1989.

As the second millennium of the Christian era drew to a close, the rate of change that characterised the post-war educational scene accelerated. The presence of the religious teaching orders in the schools declined to near vanishing point. Convent schools of the Franciscan Sisters and the Sisters of Mercy in Glasgow, in existence since 1847, Sacred Heart Convent School in Girvan and the Benedictine Abbey School at Fort Augustus were among those that closed. St Joseph's College in Dumfries, a Marist boarding school for boys, became a local authority comprehensive school. In Glasgow lay men and women took charge of St Mungo's Academy and Notre Dame High School. Private schools in the archdiocese of St Andrew's and Edinburgh founded by the Ursuline Sisters, the Sacred Heart Society, the Christian Brothers and the Benedictines, all closed. The Catholic tradition of single-sex education all but disappeared. The independent Kilgraston Convent School founded by the Society of the Sacred Heart, and Notre Dame High School in Glasgow, continued as schools for girls only, but St Aloysius' College, founded in Glasgow in 1859 and still under Jesuit management, began to cater for both boys and girls. For contributions to this aspect of the history of Scottish Catholic education, see Handley, J. E. *A History of St. Mungo's Academy, 1858–1958* (Paisley: Aitken, 1958); O'Hagan, F. J. *Catholic Education in Glasgow in the Nineteenth and Twentieth Centuries: Responding to Change*, (Glasgow: MEd thesis, 1994); McCabe, J. V. *The History of St. Aloysius' College, 1859–1999* (Glasgow: St Aloysius' College, 2000); Turnbull, M. T. R. *Abbey Boys: Fort Augustus Abbey Schools* (Perth: Corbie.com, 2000); Taylor, M. G. *The Blue and the Gold: A History of St. Joseph's College, Dumfries, 1875–2000* (Dumfries: St Joseph's College, 2000).

In 1991 the Council for National Academic Awards was wound up as part of a national restructuring of higher education, and St Andrew's College became an associate college of the University of Glasgow. In 1999, the University's Departments of Education, Adult and Continuing Education, the Teaching and Learning Service, the Centre for Science Education and St Andrew's College merged to form a Faculty of Education, in which existing teaching activities would be sustained, and provision made for undergraduate, postgraduate and research students and for professional development programmes for teachers and others in the educational field. It will continue to fulfil the traditional role of St

Andrew's College in the initial training of Catholic teachers, supervised by a Board of Catholic Education particularly concerned with the preparation of teachers for Catholic schools.

FUTURE

Historically, the Scottish pedagogical tradition, underpinned by the trinity of home, church and school, was consonant with the Catholic view that full educational development is a function not only of the school but also of the family and the whole Christian community.

Now, in the first years of the third millennium, changes in social mores that run counter to Christian values expose the young to confusing intellectual and spiritual influences. The Catholic sector has to operate in a structure in which utilitarian elements have priority over religious and moral aspects, and in a climate of scientific materialism unsympathetic to the values it tries to propagate. Its ethos is further endangered because of its openness to applicants from other religious and cultural traditions.

Catholic education is based on a concept of the nature of human beings that will not change. It represents a transcendental view of the cosmos as in essence contingent, and of human beings as imperfect, but redeemed. It holds that these views are not contrary to reason, but have been most clearly expressed through the revelation of God in history, and finally in the person of Jesus.

Scottish Catholic education was greatly dependent on the work of religious teaching orders. The continuation of the tradition now devolves more and more on a lay teaching cadre, at a time when traditional moral and spiritual verities are being questioned and many young people are alienated from mainstream religion.

REFERENCES

Abbott, W. (ed.) (1966) *The Documents of Vatican II*, London: Chapman.
HH Pope John Paul II (1998) *Fides et Ratio*, Rome: Vatican Press.
Notre Dame Sound Archive (NDSA): Oral evidence transcribed in FitzPatrick, T. A. (1982) *Catholic Secondary Education in South-West Scotland 1922–1972*, PhD thesis, vol.3, Glasgow.
McRoberts, D. (1979) *Modern Scottish Catholicism*, Glasgow: Scottish Catholic Historical Association.
Maritain, J. (1932) *The Things that are not Caesar's*, London: Sheed and Ward.
The Sacred Congregation for Education (1977) *The Catholic School*, London: Catholic Truth Society.

26

Education and the Scottish Economy

David Hartley

Scotland has a mature capitalist economy. In 1995 it contributed 8.5% of the UK's Gross Domestic Product. In March 1997, 74.7% of employees worked in the service sector, and 16% in manufacturing, a pattern similar to that in the other advanced industrial democracies. In 1999, about one in five of all Scottish employees worked according to some form of flexible working pattern, the figure for women being higher, at one in four. Weekly earnings in Scotland are lower than in Great Britain as a whole, a gap which has been increasing, both for women and men. In 2000, women earned 75% of men's earnings, but the gap is closing. About 10% of workers in Scotland are self-employed, about three percentage points below the average for Britain, and that proportion has recently started to decline. Contemporary capitalism in Scotland reveals a growing divide between the 'haves' and the 'have-nots'. The unemployment rate for those aged over sixteen in Scotland in 2000 was 7.6% (9.1% for men, 5.9% for women). Twenty-two per cent of all family types in Scotland had an income below the 60% median income level in 1999. Government statistics published in 2002 show that 20.1% of Scottish primary school children are entitled to free meals. In Glasgow city, the percentage was 40%. (A Bill to introduce free school meals for all children was rejected by MSPs in July 2002.)

Throughout the industrialised world, capitalism is being restructured. There are two broad trends emerging: globalisation; and post-Fordism. Take globalisation. Transnational corporations constantly seek to increase their profitability by relocating to those parts of the world where the rate of return on their investment is maximised. The production and consumption of goods and services is becoming globalised. Capital now flows around the world almost instantaneously, in digital form, without regard for national boundaries. Environmental pollution also ignores national boundaries. Speculators can cause a run on a currency which a national government would find difficult to curb. The Pacific-rim economies are developing rapidly, and they have access to capital, to an educated labour force, to very low wage levels, and to vast domestic markets; and they are not overly burdened by the costs of a welfare state.

But there is a paradox: whilst the globalisation of markets proceeds unchecked, there is a tendency for cultural forms to assert themselves around the banner of national identity. Indeed one could say that this collection of essays is an example of that very assertion of national identity. A White Paper published in 1997 underlines the point. Its title, *Raising the Standard*, seems ambiguous: not only to raise standards in education so that the country can become economically competitive, but also to fly the flag, to raise the standard so to say, and assert national identity. Thus whilst at the economic level there is globalisation, at the cultural level there is a search for identity, and this can reveal itself in the affirmation of nationhood, or in the assertion of other community affiliations such as those based on religion, sexuality, gender, or ethnicity. The economic trends are towards homogeneity, but there are increasing fragmentations at the level of culture. And globalisation is not even: some countries globalise, others are globalised. There are what have been termed 'vernacular globalisations': that is, nation states attempt to interpret global economic forces, which is why there is still a range of different types of welfare state, some (like Denmark and Finland) well funded, others (like the USA) much less so.

What of post-Fordism? This logically requires a prior statement about Fordism. In the first two decades of this century empirical studies of the work-process were undertaken – notably by F. W. Taylor in the United States – so that its elements could be defined, and best practice documented. Taylor's ideas were taken further by Henry Ford who built the moving car-assembly line. The raw material went in at one end of the factory and the car emerged at the other. But what was so efficient about Ford's process was that the control of the workers was built into the very technology, the assembly-line, whose speed could be set by management. But that was in the 1920s. Since the 1960s a new management style has emerged: post-Fordism. The workers must be flexible, able to multi-task, to come and go as the needs of the business dictate. Although flexibility means being adaptable while actually in work, it also requires a readiness to move in and out of work. At work, employees must be able to supervise themselves, and to display a repertoire of social skills in order to deal better with the public. So this is emotional labour, not just manual labour. These workers are said to be empowered, to have a sense of ownership about what they do. But this ownership is usually of the means – of the tactics – whereby they will achieve management's goals and strategies, on time, to specification, with zero-defects, all this while revealing a pleasant have-a-nice-day disposition. And this post-Fordist workforce is divided into 'core' and 'peripheral' workers. At root, post-Fordism is a managerial style which is aimed at maximising efficiency and effectiveness, without workers having to succumb to highly bureaucratic directives. The idea is that they manage themselves. Government is confining itself more to strategy, and institutions more to 'owning' the tactics whereby that strategy (often defined as targets) is achieved. This is governance, not government as it used to be known. So much for globalisation and post-Fordism. How have these economic shifts impinged upon Scottish education in recent years?

Before considering education, a brief mention of the so-called 'new economy' is necessary. There is now an emerging view about the kind of worker which the new economy needs, and how that worker is to be educated. In his *End of Millennium* (Oxford: Blackwell, 2nd edn, 2000) Manuel Castells distinguishes between two kinds of labour: 'generic' and 'self-programmable'. Generic workers are the classic 'hands' of the nine-teenth-century factory floor. Generic workers are to be 'warehoused' as opposed to 'educated'. But not so the self-programmable worker: this worker has the ability to redefine constantly the skills required for tasks at hand. This is a learning worker. The implications of this for primary education have been hinted at by Richard Scase in his study *Britain Towards 2010: The Changing Business Environment* (London: DTI, 1999). He suggests that nursery and primary education will need to provide for effective inter-personal skills and personal creativity so that corporate creativity and innovation can be developed. It was stated earlier that about 75% of workers are employed in the service sector, and these tend to be local, not global, provisions. Most jobs now involve what has been called emotional and intellectual labour, rather than manual labour, as in the early twentieth century.

EDUCATION

Now part of the global economy, the Scottish economy faces financial pressures on its public services, including education. Would-be foreign investors (as well as existing domestic ones) are not usually willing to pay high levels of corporation tax. They do not need to; they can relocate to Asia, or to Eastern Europe. As far as government is concerned, more needs to be done with less money. This approach marked a considerable shift in policy when it was introduced in the early 1980s. Before then, governments had decided upon the social distribution of education, health-care and other benefits in society. Thereafter the New Right sought to subject the welfare state to market forces, for a number of reasons. In the first place welfare provision was said to be both inefficient and less than effective. Part of the reason for this was that there was too much bureaucratic interference, especially by local government, which was allegedly driven by petty politics rather than by the need to get the job done properly. In sum, the 'producers' – the professionals and bureaucrats – had allegedly 'captured' the welfare state for their own ends, leaving aside the needs of the clients, or 'consumers'. Under Thatcherism, however, consumers were to be placed in control. This meant that they had to be in a position to decide upon the best provider and product. Schools would have to compete for children, and in order to succeed in the market they had to be both efficient and effective, otherwise they might cease to 'trade'.

During the 1980s, therefore, education was, quite literally, called to account. Since then, too, there have been a series of high-profile international league-tables published, such as the Third International Mathematics and Science Study (TIMSS), which compared the performance of 13-year-olds' average scores for Mathematics and Science across forty-one nations. When the data for South Korea were compared with those for Scotland, it suggested that there was no simple correlation between achievement and per-pupil expenditure. In Mathematics, South Korea ranked second; Scotland, twenty-ninth. In Science, South Korea ranked fourth; Scotland, twenty-sixth. But South Korea spent only $2,000 per pupil compared to Scotland's $4,300. The government's interpretation of data such as this was that Scotland could well make large efficiency gains without necessarily lowering standards. Indeed throughout the 1980s, Conservative politicians in Scotland, led by Michael Forsyth, tried to devise ways of maximising effectiveness at the same time as increasing efficiency, thereby 'doing more with less'. In 2000, the PISA (Programme for International Student Assessment) assessed the performance of 15year-olds in thirty-two countries. In the combined reading scale, Scotland ranked sixth out of thirty-one, a little higher than England. The highest ranks were achieved by Finland, Canada and New Zealand. In mathematical literacy, Scotland ranked fifth, again a little higher than England. The top ranks were assigned to Japan, the Republic of Korea and New Zealand. In science, Scotland ranked ninth.

So the state would be rolled back, and Quasi-Autonomous Non-governmental Organisations (quangos) inserted between government and civil society in order to steer policy on the government's behalf. Individual freedom would replace social justice; quality would prevail over equality; business contracts would replace social contracts. In short, a completely new vocabulary began to suffuse education: gone were the egalitarian notions of the 1950s and 1960s; in their stead came accountability, consumer choice, audits, efficiency, effectiveness, enterprise, together with a range of metaphors drawn from industry. The story was being rewritten. According to Mrs Thatcher there is no such thing as society; only individuals and families. Paradoxically, what individuals share socially is that they are self-interested and all-consuming. They are urged to become active citizens: ever-ready workers, lifelong learners and ceaseless consumers, purposeful and prudential, with a can-do demeanour.

During the 1980s the elements of the market slowly began to emerge: first, the 'raw material' (the pupil); second, the 'producer' (the school); third, the 'product' (the examination results); fourth, the 'market place' (as symbolised in the league tables of results); and fifth, the all-important 'consumer' who 'shops around'. In education, however, the pupil is in the logically difficult position of being both a producer and a consumer: that is, pupils co-produce their learning with their teachers. Given all of these elements, what would ensue would be efficiency, effectiveness and excellence – in theory. But there is a caveat to be made about this market. It is rigged and regulated. As shall be argued below, its rules of exchange and currency are set by the government, and the 'players' are not evenly positioned to profit from it. It is not a free market; it is, as Julian Le Grand states, a 'quasi-market', and it is in Figure 26.1.

Figure 26.1:   The 'quasi-market' in education

Consumer choice	Output quality control
Parents charter	National curriculum guidelines, 5–14
Assisted Places Scheme	National testing
School boards	School league tables
Nursery school vouchers	
Process deregulation	Process quality control
Devolved school management	Reform of teacher training
Self-governing schools	School inspections

The two columns seem to contradict each other. On the left are those policies which have helped to redefine the parent as a consumer. The consumer is involved in the school and in some of the decisions which can be taken about it – whether or not, for example, it remains under the control of the education authority. On the right are listed a series of measures which enable the consumer to compare objectively the 'output quality' measures of the different schools in the local market place. Also on the right are those policies which might serve to ensure 'process quality' – that is, the quality of teaching. So, on the left-hand side there are appeals to choice and local democracy, and on the right-hand side there are measures which are controlled by central government. In a completely free market the controls put in place on the right-hand side would be absent. What emerges, therefore, is a quasi-market, a regulated market. Its two dimensions, choice and control, will now be examined.

The first part considers the extent to which market forces have influenced Scottish education. There have been changes in the organisational arrangements for governing and managing Scottish education. This is referred to as the 'marketisation of education'. The second part deals with curricular and pedagogical changes which both implicitly and explicitly are vocational in their purpose. This is referred to as the 'vocationalisation of education'. These two strands, of course, overlap, both logically and chronologically, and the nature of this intersection will be indicated.

EDUCATION AND THE ECONOMY: THE MARKETISATION OF EDUCATION

First, it is necessary to clarify why marketisation was regarded as important for the economy in the 1980s and early 1990s. Put simply, market processes were regarded as (there was no evidence for it at the time) being more efficient and effective for education. If it was more efficient, then it would be cheaper, with fewer calls upon the nation's coffers; and, if effective, then, so the argument ran, the nation could compete more effectively in global markets because the workforce would be more skilled. Crucial for a market are informed customers. Before 1979, 'parental involvement' had tended to mean that schools should establish a professional relationship with parents because research had shown that parental involvement correlated well with pupil achievement. In 1981, however, the professional relationship between home and school was redefined as more of a business or calculative relationship. Parents were to be consumers. They were enabled to choose a school which was not necessarily their local one. In a democracy, this notion of choice had a politically sound ring to it, and it resonated even more with parents who were part of a consumer society. Here, therefore, was the first dent in the 'social engineering' of the state education system which had been constructed since 1945. Now, calculation and self-interest would be the determinants of educational provision. There was, too, an impression given that the 'market' was somehow 'natural': that there was a Darwinian logic to it which saw the fittest survive and the weakest go to the wall.

Choice

The government assumed that parents would make rational choices on the basis of reliable information. In the early 1980s, league tables of school attainment were not available, so a school-by-school comparison based on objective data was not easy to make. The government had assumed further that all parents had available to them the same range of choices. This was clearly not the case, especially in rural areas, or when the costs of travelling to a desired school were in excess of what parents could pay, or when the costs of moving house nearer to that school were equally prohibitive. So although parents had the same 'right to choose', the available choices were by no means equally distributed. Furthermore, a certain cultural capital is required of parents when they come to decode the images and information which a school provides, and this capital – like financial capital – is not available equally to all. The ability to exercise a choice is therefore socially structured; it is not just a matter of rational choice.

The Education (Scotland) Act 1981 enabled open enrolment by allowing parents to express a preference for a school. This would be met if the education authority did not have to supply another teacher, or alter the architecture of the school, or if the incoming pupil was not overly disruptive. Government statistics published in May 2002 indicate that the opportunity to choose has been expanding. Some 30,227 'placing requests' were made in 2000–2, up 18.9% over ten years, with about two-thirds of them for primary schools. In

2000–2, about 85% of requests were granted. Even when parents do exercise their right to choose, they seem to do so for reasons which were not intended by the government: proximity; the presence of family and friends; or perceptions about the social composition of the catchment area, the more up-market the better. And notwithstanding all of this, when the demand for a school exceeded the supply, then instead of the consumer choosing the school, the school began to select the child.

A further policy which purported to widen parental choice was the Assisted Places Scheme (APS). This was introduced in 1981 and has been the object of much controversy. From the outset the Scottish Education Department was very careful in its rationale for the scheme not to imply a denigration of Scotland's much-esteemed comprehensive schools. Indeed, by claiming to widen educational opportunity, the scheme was said to complement the comprehensive system. It also had the convenient effect of injecting state funding into an independent sector which had been feeling the pinch in the wake of the demise of the grant-aided schools. In order to take advantage of the scheme, parents would have to be informed about it, but its availability seems not to have been widely known in the beginning, except, of course, if a pupil of limited means was already in the private sector. In 1994, only 45% of pupils on assisted places were receiving a full remission of fees in Scotland, and it is clear the poorest children were not taking up their full quota. Immediately before the 1997 general election, the Conservative government had proposed nearly to double the number of assisted places. The incoming Labour government withdrew the scheme in 1997.

According to Conservative thinkers in the 1980s, a market can only operate when schools are freed from the fetters of local authority control and placed in the hands of the parents and the staff. Only when local bureaucracy is by-passed can the schools be set free to perform as they would wish. To effect this, a conversion process was set in train. The first stage was to involve the parent in the school; and the second was to empower both the parents and the school by assigning to them greater financial powers in the hope that they would go on to opt out of education authority control.

Involvement and empowerment

This process began with the school boards, which were established in 1988 (see also Chapter 19). Unlike their English counterparts – the governing bodies – the Scottish school boards neither controlled the school budget nor did they have the right to hire and fire staff. And curriculum, pedagogy and assessment all remained under the control of central government. The main power of the school board was that it could ballot parents who could decide whether or not to apply to the Secretary of State for self-governing status. This power was conferred by the Self-Governing Schools etc. (Scotland) Act 1989. The number of schools which became self-governing in Scotland was only two. Even those schools which thought that, by opting out, they could avoid closure were dismayed to learn that the Education (Scotland) 1996 Act prevented them from doing so. The unwillingness of Scottish schools to opt for self-governing status may partly be explained by a curious procedural mistake by the government. In England and Wales, grant-maintained (or opted-out) status had been enabled at the same time as the legislation for local management of schools (LMS) was enacted, the reason being that schools should first have experience of managing their own budgets before seeking opted-out status. In Scotland, however, the government's policies for Devolved School Management (DSM, the counterpart to LMS) came nearly three years after the Self-Governing Schools etc. (Scotland) Act 1989. The Labour government has now withdrawn self-governing status. This has left a curious situation. The school boards were introduced with a central purpose of enabling a ballot of parents to decide whether or not to apply for self-governing status. Even though the opportunity for self-governing status has now been removed, the school boards remain, with 83% of eligible education authority schools having elected one, as at May 2000. Having considered the left-hand or 'choice' dimension of the marketisation model, the discussion now turns to the right-hand column of Figure 26.1: The 'quasi-market' in education.

Product and process quality control

A market needs a product for consumers to buy. But consumers have rights; they are to be protected. One way of protecting the consumer is to ensure that there is suffecnt quality control exercised by an independent agency. There must be ways for the consumer to distinguish between the products on offer. There must be reliable and valid information which is readily available and simple to understand. For the government this 'product' was in the form of an 'output measure', namely the school's aggregate attainment level on national tests and examinations. Each secondary school was ranked on a league table, thereby enabling the consumer to shop around. But before this assessment could take place there needed to be a standardisation of the curriculum so that national tests could be seen to be fair and comparable. One of the reasons – though not the only one – for the introduction of the 5–14 national curricular guidelines in Scotland was that it would allow for national testing across a given age-range (see Chapter 85). Its elaborate curricular structure facilitated the bureaucratic ordering of knowledge into discrete sections. In a sense, therefore, the national guidelines were assessment-driven. The point being stressed here is that the 'national curriculum' was a necessary pre-condition for the quasi-market in Scottish education.

   What of process control? This is much more difficult to achieve. The process is in effect the pedagogical relationship, which is a social process, and which is not easily freeze-framed into discrete assessable units, unlike the national 'product' tests. More to the point, the pupil and the teacher co-produce the product, so it is difficult to disentangle the teacher's pedagogical input from that of the pupil.

   The Conservative government was cautious about introducing teacher appraisal. It was first mooted in 1984 when the government was formulating its policy on staff development. Staff development was seen as the pre-condition of worthwhile staff appraisal: that is to say, unless the staff development needs of a teacher are known then it is difficult to define a worthwhile programme of professional development. Needs and programmes should be matched. By appraising the staff their needs would be made explicit. Needless to say, the teaching profession were less than pleased when in 1989 the Secretary of State proposed a hierarchical and somewhat judgemental system of staff appraisal, for they feared a link between it and merit-pay, a link which the Main Report had earlier denied, but which was later to be admitted by the government in January 1997 with the publication of *Raising the Standard*. More directly, the government intervened in the then colleges of education (all of them are now within the university sector) by defining the competences which must be taught. All that said, however, there is no counterpart in Scotland to England's OfSTED and Teacher Training Agency. And there is no legislated system of performance appraisal, as in England. In sum, the market experiment in Scottish education has largely failed, except for the 'parental choice' legislation. On the other hand, there remains central control. Insofar as the marketisation of education is concerned, the Scots have little truck with it, and are reluctant to undermine the notion of public provision, locally administered. Education in Scotland still retains high public esteem, and this may be further enhanced by the Scottish Parliament.

EDUCATION AND ECONOMY:
THE VOCATIONALISATION OF EDUCATION

The relationship between the economy and education can be taken a little further. In addition to the organisational changes which have been made to facilitate the operation of market principles in education, there has also been a series of other changes to education which purport to render it as being functional for the economy. First, there was the vocationalisation of the curriculum; and second, there was the emergence of new learner-centred pedagogies which prepare the pupil for post-Fordist management regimes in the workplace and for service-sector jobs. Taken together these substantive curricular and pedagogical changes have been found mainly in secondary and further education. Perhaps most important have been the profound pedagogical shifts which have taken place since 1983. In that year, the *Action Plan 16–18s in Scotland* hurriedly and comprehensively rationalised further education. The various credentials and examining bodies were incorporated within a new National Certificate validated by a new examining body, SCOTVEC. Completely new modes of assessment and teaching styles were also initiated. The curriculum was modularised. In sum, a learner-centred pedagogy was called for, one which would enhance the self-esteem and autonomy of the learner. SCOTVEC, the examining body for FE, has now been combined with the Scottish Examinations Board (SEB) to form the Scottish Qualifications Agency (SQA). This reveals yet another strengthening of the relationship between the economy and education.

There were sound vocationalist reasons for these changes. The importance of the service sector of the economy was becoming more apparent as traditional manufacturing industries declined. School-leavers were more and more required to manipulate words rather than materials. They needed to be taught – implicitly and explicitly – a new repertoire of personal and social skills which would also be functional for these emerging service industries. So, although 'personal and social development' (PSD) courses had the expressed intention of contributing to personal development, they also had the added benefit of being functional for the economy. They could be seen as both therapeutic and as vocational: therapeutic in the sense that the learner was taught not to feel a diminution of dignity even if she or he had 'failed to find work'; vocational in that the emergent service-sector economy required a sophisticated repertoire of social skills – skills not taught by the entrenched didactic pedagogy of the secondary school. Put another way, the learner-centred classroom management style was supposed to anticipate a future self-managing style at work. Just as in the classroom, students were to take responsibility for their own learning, so later in the workplace they would work with minimum supervision. The mode of social control became more reflective, more inner-directed, less bureaucratic. Even the school league-tables have been redefined as an aid to self-evaluation and management. In sum, both SCOTVEC modules and the school-based Technical Vocational Educational Initiative (TVEI) adopted this new pedagogical style, especially for the lower academic achiever. They initiated curricular and pedagogical changes which were functional for the new service industries and for an emerging post-Fordist managerial regime. TVEI was also very well resourced, its funding controlled not by the then Scottish Education Department but by a quango – the Manpower Services Commission (MSC) – which was a UK-wide agency of the Department of Trade and Industry. Later, both north and south of the border, the education and industry portfolios of government were combined, thereby underlining the tightened bond between them. It was the MSC, too, which initiated the contract culture in education: a new payment-by-results approach to funding.

The Compacts Initiative in the early 1990s was another explicitly vocationalist policy. Unlike TVEI, it did not seek to 'buy' the formal curriculum; rather, it sought to remove what were perceived as shortcomings in the transmission of the hidden curriculum. Whereas under TVEI the school entered into a contract with the Training Agency (the successor to the MSC), under the Compacts Initiative the individual pupil, the school and a local business consortium or college entered into a joint 'contract'. Though not a legally binding contract – more of a commitment – the pupil was 'guaranteed' a job, or training leading to a job, provided that the pupil met stringent behavioural and achievement targets. But what was curious about the compacts was their emphasis on rewarding what would be termed the 'work ethic' of old: neatness, time-keeping, diligence and deference. During a time of rising youth unemployment, the guarantee of a job seemed to be too good to be true; and it was, for there were no legal obligations on any of the parties to adhere to the 'contract'.

There have been other measures. The Scottish counterpart to the city technology college (CTC), the technology academy, failed to materialise. Colleges of further education were incorporated, thereby becoming detached from the control of local authorities. The Enterprise in Higher Education scheme was launched. Tax relief for vocational course fees was allowed in 1993–4, and a system of Youth Credits was introduced. But perhaps the most important decision yet to be taken is the extent of the use of information technology in education. This, in theory, would have a number of economic effects: it would drastically reduce 'delivery' costs, thereby lightening the fiscal burden on the welfare state; and it would widen access and maximise flexibility. Given the relatively higher costs of teaching in higher education – especially in the sciences – there may be some move towards first implementing it there. The MacFarlane Report *Teaching and Learning in an Expanding Higher Education System* (SHEFC, 1996) has already opened the debate on this in Scotland. However, if information technology is to be used as a pedagogical device, it would almost certainly require a standardisation of the syllabus in certain subjects, at a cost to academic freedom in higher education. The University of the Highlands and Islands is already being developed very much with a view to using information technology.

Finally, what are some implications of the new economy for education? It has been argued that recent decades have witnessed a search for the effective school. Standards have been to the fore of policy. Notwithstanding the notion of devolved school management, highly bureaucratic structures have been established. To this bureaucratic repertoire is now being added that which speaks of emotion and creativity. Having been consigned to the margin, the creative and expressive dimensions of education are being revived. If it is agreed that the new economy is becoming more of a cultural economy – that is, if culture itself is becoming commodified – then creativity is crucial for production. But it is equally important for consumption: within postmodern culture, with all of its contingencies, ambiguities, risks and uncertainties, the individual is prompted continually to create a makeover of the self. In the interface between the economy and the self is situated both the creative producer and the creative consumer. In order to be *e*ffective as a producer and a consumer, it is necessary to be *a*ffective. In a response to calls by business leaders, government is seeking to generate in the schools new kinds of emotional and creative capital. It is now a question of learning to labour; but to do so emotionally, creatively. The expressive seems set to be instrumentalised. At a recent conference organised by the DEMOS think-tank, Allan Wilson, MSP for Sport and Culture in the Scottish Executive, was reported as saying, 'We need creative workers in local government, we need creative managers in Scotland's voluntary sector and we need creative entrepreneurs in Scottish Industries. In fact we need every single Scottish citizen to tap in to their creativity. But in particular we do recognise the vital role played by the creative industries as part of a productive and successful economy.' The fifth of the government's six National Priorities states that it wishes, 'to equip pupils with the foundation skills, attitudes and expectations necessary to prosper in a changing society and to encourage creativity and ambition'. All this portends some difficulties for government. The emphasis has recently been on standards, and on more whole-class approaches to teaching. The fostering of creativity and emotional literacy, however, requires a pedagogy – a more expensive pedagogy – which has more of the characteristics of child-centred education. Even if government recognises the performative and instrumental effects of child-centred education (that is, creativity is good for the new economy), it may nevertheless decide not to fund it, because it would require pressure on the public purse.

CONCLUSION

The market-driven education policies of the Conservative governments between 1979 and 1997 changed the metaphors and meanings of education. In Scotland, where education is held in high public esteem, there was a mixed reception to them. So far as the marketisation of education is concerned, the attempt to produce a 'market' has been relatively unsuccessful. It has been argued above that, in order to bring about this quasi-market, the curriculum itself needed to be defined, and its transmission to be monitored by national testing, league tables and teacher appraisal. Here the government's gains were greater. The vocationalisation of education, both in terms of curriculum and of pedagogy, was also considered. Except in further education and in the education of the lower achievers in secondary schools, the vocationalisation of the formal curriculum has not been great. However, insofar as pedagogy is concerned, there are strong signs that Scottish education at all levels is shifting towards a learner-centred approach, except, paradoxically, in the primary school where the alleged 'excesses' of child-centredness are to be curbed. Many of these reforms – modularisation and continuous assessment – have their roots in further education, a sector which has always been closest to the world of work. This pedagogy is functional not only for a service sector economy, but also for post-Fordist management regimes. But – and here the link with efficiency looks questionable – it is also a much more expensive pedagogy than the old didacticism. What is evident, therefore, is an emerging tension between this relatively expensive learner-centred pedagogy and the increasing use of standardised curricula and information technology which are meant to cut costs. In the interests of economic efficiency, governments can be expected to try and claim that both consumer choice and learner-centred pedagogy are compatible with the greater use of information technology and a standardisation of the curriculum.

REFERENCES

DEMOS (2002) *Creativity in the New Scotland*, Scottish Labour Party Conference, Inverness. http://
www.demos.co.uk/creativityscotlandwilson.htm as at 10 July, 2002.

Scottish Executive (2001) *Scottish Economic Statistics*, Edinburgh: Scottish Executive.

SEED (2002) *Programme for International Student Assessment: Scottish Report*, (the PISA study 2000),
Edinburgh: SEED.

Scottish Statutory Instrument (2000) *The Education (National Priorities) (Scotland) Order 2000 no
443*, Edinburgh: The Stationery Office.

27

The Financing of Educational Provision

Arthur Midwinter

This chapter examines the financial mechanisms that require to be understood if professionals wish to grasp the process of resource allocation to Scotland's schools. In Scotland, the resource allocation process has become more complex with the establishment of the Scottish Parliament, and it is necessary to make some brief comments on the financial arrangements under devolution. Thereafter, the chapter describes the educational financial framework, analyses some of the emerging issues, and assesses whether education has become an Executive priority in resource allocation.

The British budgetary system is heavily incremental, focusing on change at the margins. Most of a new budget reflects past commitments including large scale investments such as schools or staff salaries which can only be changed at a heavy cost – such as redundancy. Public expenditure patterns can be changed but slowly. The Scottish Parliament largely inherited the system which evolved under the Scottish Office, in which the Treasury has overall responsibility for resource allocation across the UK, and the Executive has responsibility for resource allocation to services within budget totals, albeit with a modest tax-varying power.

It is often wrongly commented that the Scottish Budget is determined by the Barnett Formula, even by experienced journalists. In fact, the Barnett Formula only applies to a small proportion of new expenditure, and it is more accurate to describe the arrangements as a block and formula approach. The Scottish Budget is composed of the Departmental Expenditure Limit (DEL) which is set for three years; and Annually Managed Expenditure (AME) which is set annually to reflect current conditions. Not all of the Scottish Budget is funded by grant from Westminster, as elements of expenditure are funded by local taxation, borrowing and European Commission grants.

Within the DEL, the largest element (99.5%) is known as the Assigned Budget, to which the block and formula element applies. This is the main source of funding for schools. The block refers to the expenditure baseline – the previous year's budget – which forms the dominant part of the new budget. The formula element applies to changes (usually increases) in expenditure, and is based on population shares. These changes are based on decisions made regarding English allocations. For example, an increase of £100m on education in England, will result in an increase of around £10m in Scotland, based on Scotland's population as a proportion of England. The total increase for Scotland is built up in this way, but there is no requirement to allocate resources according to the formula in Scotland. The end product is a block grant, which Parliament can spend according to its priorities. Funding available for education spending can be further influenced by Local Authority Self-Financed Expenditure (LASFE), which is outwith the Scottish Budget, and not subject to the Barnett Formula. This has in fact been increasing less than in England in recent years (Midwinter, 2002) but powers do exist for the UK government to take it into account if:

- levels of self-financed spending have grown significantly more rapidly than equivalent spending in England over a period; and
- this growth is such as to threaten targets set for the public finances as part of the management of the United Kingdom. (HM Treasury, 2001)

Political arguments have persisted over the adequacy of the current financial arrangements and the fiscal powers in particular (Jamieson, 2001). In practice, however, this system has delivered a broadly stable share of public spending for Scotland since its introduction in 1979. The spending plans in Spending Review 2000 provided for three years of real increases, an average of 4.5%, which converted into increases of £3.8bn or over £1bn per annum, after the two-year spending freeze under New Labour prior to devolution. Further growth of 4.6% per annum until 2005–6 was announced in September 2002, creating the largest period of sustained growth in funding in recent history. For the most part, the focus of what follows will be with spending within the DEL and from local taxation. However, teachers' pensions are funded under Annually Managed Expenditure.

Around £438m of expenditure is controlled by the Executive within the Education and Young People budget, including £225m of Specific Grants. Of the £213m spent directly by the Executive, the allocations are Schools (£131m); Children and Young People (£63.5m) Social Work Training (£10m) and Information, Analysis and Communication (£2m). Some of this funding is targeted on deprived children; some is revenue funding support of public private partnership (PPP) projects; some goes to develop inclusive education; some goes to develop ICT infrastructure; and some to fund Her Majesty's Inspectorate (Scottish Executive 2002a, p. 56).

THE FRAMEWORK OF EDUCATION FINANCE

School expenditure is a significant element of the Scottish Budget and of local government expenditure. For 2003–4, it will be around £3.3bn, from a local government total of £7.7bn. Accountants distinguish between capital expenditure and revenue expenditure. Capital expenditure is defined as expenditure which creates a physical asset of long-term benefit to the community, such as school buildings or technology and equipment. It is conventionally funded by borrowing and repayment of interest but can also be funded by capital receipts or revenue. The Executive controls the total amount of capital expenditure, and contributes to repayments by grants to councils. Authorities receive a block allocation for spending on education, roads and transport, non-council housing, social work, flood prevention and other services, which authorities can allocate according to their priorities. In 2002–3, around 20% of the total of around £400m will be spent on education. Capital expenditure has been rising since devolution.

Capital allocations relate to conventional capital procurement and not PPPs. PPPs are a new method of funding capital investment, with provision by the private sector in the short-term which attracts grant support from the Executive. Projects totalling over £1.15bn were announced in June 2002 with support monies available for repairs and improvements to existing schools (Scottish Executive 2002b). Funding support for PPPs is provided through Aggregate External Finance, in the same way as for conventional loan charges at the moment. Priority is given to projects for major replacement and refurbishment of schools, located within an authority's own estate plans, which demonstrate the relevant considera- tion of the impact on the school environment of future learning and teaching needs, are clearly affordable, deliverable, and achieve value-for-money.

The financial watchdog, the Accounts Commission, published a major study of private finance initiative (PFI) contracts in education in 2002. In concluded that councils have managed the processes well, and that real benefits in terms of planning and project management have materialised. Whilst the funding was used to renew 'inadequate, redundant or dilapidated school buildings', financial considerations were dominant. The process delivers a strong focus on service provision – as the contractor is involved for a longer term than traditional suppliers – and also strong financial control. However, the report also highlighted significant weaknesses in the appraisal process. Firstly, it concluded that the cost of private finance is higher by around 8–10% per annum than traditional procurement in the public sector. Secondly, it challenged the validity of the public sector comparator (or PSC) which is the estimate that councils make of costs using traditional procurement. The PSC has 'inherent uncertainty' over the costings, and the methodology excludes the difference in costs arising from the lower borrowing rates available to councils. The Commission criticises this approach, noting that 'the actual costs of debt financing are a relevant if not necessarily decisive factor in testing the economy and ultimately the value-for-money of a PFI schools contract' (Accounts Commission 2002, p. 12).

The publication of this report at a time when political divisions are deepening over the issue – with the SNP opposed on principle – and when proposals to use PFI to renew the prisons estates and additional school projects were before the Parliament, has ensured this will be a major electoral issue in the 2003 Holyrood election. The Commission also notes that education authorities have no real choice over the type of procurement, but only whether to bid or not. Falkirk and West Dunbartonshire Councils have both voted not to enter any further PFI contracts, as they believe them to be too costly in the long term. Councils continue to press for a greater degree of local choice over forms of procurement through a prudential scheme of capital finance.

Revenue expenditure is the major component of school funding, which covers staff costs, heating and lighting, books, interest payments etc. Central support for such expenditure is paid through Aggregate External Finance which is made up of three elements, Specific Grants, Non-Domestic Rates and Revenue Support Grant. These are defined as follows:

- Specific Grants form part of the total grant support to local government. Their allocation and distribution are set centrally, linked to specific policy initiatives and expectations, and account for a decreasing proportion of AEF;
- Non Domestic Rates are collected by local authorities, paid into a central pool and redistributed to authorities in proportion to their populations;
- Revenue Support Grant makes up the balance of AEF. (Scottish Executive 2002a, p. 206)

The central element in the calculation of grant distribution to education authorities is Grant Aided Expenditure (GAE), which is the amount the Executive believes authorities need to spend in total on service provision. These are calculated on a service by service basis, but treated as a block assessment, which authorities are free to allocate, with the minor exception of specific grants such as Educational Special Needs grant.

The calculation of GAEs is through the client group method, which the Executive regards as an objective method of estimating authorities relative expenditure needs. It seeks to take into account variations in the need for and the cost of providing services to a similar standard with a similar degree of efficiency. The indicators selected to assess need must be outwith the control of local authorities; be plausible measures of need; and be associated with inter-authority expenditure variation. Primary indicators are identified for each service and regarded as the most significant single determinant of expenditure, whilst secondary indicators are regarded as reflecting additional need or costs. Primary indicators allocate 92% of the total GAE; secondary indicators only 2%; and a further 6% is allocated on the basis of adjusted budgets where it is difficult to identify appropriate indicators.

In education, the primary indicator is the number of school pupils, whilst there are secondary adjustments for the percentage of pupils in small rural schools; urban settlement pattern; and income support dependants (see Figure 27.1 for full list). Until recently, the client group assessments which underpin GAE have been under regular review in the Distribution Committee of the Working Party of Local Government Finance, composed of representatives of the Scottish Executive and COSLA. With the introduction of three-year settlements, however, a simplified approach was identified. The initial year was based on client group assessments, with future years increased by population projections.

Since devolution, the Executive has identified education as a spending priority. In the 2000–1 budget, all the growth in GAE was allocated to the four priority services (education, fire, police and social work) and these accounted for 80% of local budgets, putting pressure on other services. In 2001–2 this practice was stopped. Over the three-year period, the education GAE grew by 13.3%, 1% above the Scottish average – although McCrone funding was allocated in addition to this. From 2002–2003, spending totals for service GAEs continue to be provided on a national basis, but not to individual local authorities. It is therefore for local authorities to determine how much is spent on education. Table 27.1 sets out a comparison between education budgets and GAEs. This shows a close correspondence with local authorities consistently spending slightly more than the GAE provision since reorganisation. This gap broadly remains at outturn. Table 27.2 shows that the education share of GAE has grown since 1997, but at local level, education's share of the budget has remained stable. Within these totals, authorities vary in their budget estimates. Since devolution, education authorities have increased their budgets within a range of +6.9% to +23.4%, evidence of the continuing discretion offered by the block grant system. Expenditure plans for 2002–3 and 2003–4 were announced to authorities in 2001. The GAE for education for 2002–3 is £3022.2m, and for 2003–4 it will be £3099.7m. Allocations made by authorities for revenue spending in their 2002–3 budgets are also not yet available.

Specific Grants are mechanisms to deliver national priorities, and promote service development. These amount to 5.4% of GAE (See Table 27.3). In 2002–3, £137m of specific funding was transferred from the central education budget to the GAE. The

Figure 27.1: Client group assessments for education

SERVICE	PRIMARY INDICATOR	SECONDARY INDICATOR	OTHER TREATMENT	ADDITIONAL COMMENT
Nursery school teachers	Population aged 3–4			
Primary school teachers	Primary school pupils in education authority and self-governing schools	Percentage of pupils in small rural schools		
Secondary school teachers	Secondary school pupils in education authority self-governing schools. Including adults.		Adjustment for islands authorities	Adjustment for the difference of average cost per pupil & between island and mainland Authorities.
Special education	Population aged 2–19		Share of specific grant	
Gaelic			SEED allocation	
Education deprivation			SEED allocation	
Teachers for ethnic minorities				
School transport	Population aged 5–15	Population dispersal	GAE based on share of actual expenditure (most recent LFR)	
School bursaries				
School meals	Pupil meals	Seasonally adjusted Income Support dependents		Adjustment to remove variation in benefit data arising from seasonal employment patterns
School non-teaching staff, property etc.	Pupils in education authority and self-governing schools (including adults and pre-school provision, excluding special school pupils).	Urban settlement pattern (10,000)		
Hostels and clothing	Pupils in education authority and self-governing schools, including pre-school provision and excluding adults	Hostel places / Seasonally adjusted Income Support dependents	Adjustment to remove variation benefits arising from seasonal employment patterns	
Community education	Total population			
Residual further education	Population over 16			
Resident FE travel and Bursaries			GAE based on share of actual expenditure	Estimated budget enhancement to cover the FE and HE student support schemes alignment costs from autumn 2001
School security			GAE based on former share of specific grant	
Childcare strategy			A letter has been issued by SE Children & Young People's Group, to all chief executives confirming the allocation for 2001–2	Continuation of ministerial initiative arising from Comprehensive Spending Review (CSR)
Sure Start Scotland (formerly The Very Young)			A letter has been issued by SE Children & Young People's Group, to all chieg executives outlining the allocation for 2001–2	Continuation of ministerial initiative arising from CSR
Excellence Fund-Core Programme			GAE based on distribution set out in SEED letter of 22 Dec 2000 'Excellence Fund for Schools'	Continuation of ministerial initiative arising from CSR

Table 27.1:   Comparison of education budgets and GAE since local government
reorganisation

Year	Budgets £m	GAEs £m	% Difference
1996–7	2333.1	2305.8	1.18
1997–8	2349.0	2319.4	1.27
1998–9	2437.6	2414.0	1.00
1999–2000	2605.0	2572.9	1.25
2000–1	2717.1	2676.4	1.52
2001–2	2950.6	2937.1	0.46

Table 27.2:   Education share of local budgets and GAEs

Year	Budgets %	GAE %
1996–7	41.8	43.2
1997–8	42.2	43.2
1998–9	42.4	46.9
1999–2000	42.8	45.1
2000–1	42.8	45.3
2001–2	43.1	46.0

Table 27.3:   Specific grants within education GAE

	Specific Grant Total £m	Share of Total Education GAE
1996–7	12	0.5%
1997–8	4	0.2%
1998–9	4	0.2%
1999–2000	98	3.8%
2000–1	155	5.7%
2001–2	197	6.6%
2002–3	182	5.6%
2003–4	188	5.4%

Includes Special Education Needs, Inservice Training of Teachers Grant, Gaelic Specific Grant and, from 1999–0 Excellence Fund for Education.

Finance Minister said that the grant funding had 'allowed us to move from an uneven provision of nursery places between local authority areas' (Local Government Finance Announcement to the Scottish Parliament, 6 December 2001). The main education-specific grant is the Excellence Fund. The Local Government Committee recommended all specific grants, except the Police Grant. should be transferred to GAE (Scottish Parliament, 2002), and the Education Committee agreed this specifically for the Excellence Fund (Education Committee Report on Stage 1 of the Budget, 2002). In the 2003–4 budget, £64m is transferred to GAE.

RESOURCE ALLOCATION IN LOCAL GOVERNMENT

When local authorities receive notification of their grant support and capital allocations, they begin the process of balancing the budget and setting the council tax at a level sufficient to cover the gap between their expenditure estimates and grant income. This process is an incremental one, reflecting the high degree of committed expenditure in the budget. Choice is focused on the margins, with a few new developments or savings packages determined through political priorities.

The budget is not the place to make or review policy. Rather, it is the mechanism to provide the funding necessary to meet the cost of existing policies and programmes, and new developments. In the post-war period, advocacy of more extensive budget reviews has been commonplace, through systems such as programme budgeting, zero-based budgeting, or more recently outcome budgeting. These systems promise more than they deliver, facing constraints in the form of existing commitments – such as staff salaries, school buildings and equipment – which can be changed only slowly. Moreover, all such schemes have analytical constraints, in integrating resource allocation with objectives and outcomes, and the information overload which comprehensive approaches require. Classical incremental systems have greater political realism, using the base budget as precedent with choice concentrated on the margins where change is possible, and with in-depth analysis now carried out in best value reviews which can deal with service issues or corporate issues.

In education budgets, some 70% of spend is allocated through budgetary decentralisation to headteachers under Devolved School Management (DSM). This is a form of 'regulated autonomy' (Hoggett, 1996) whereby organisational control is exercised through a strategic resource framework within which heads have autonomy over the use of resources to meet agreed objectives and targets. The objectives of DSM were set out in Circular 6/93, and include providing flexibility, choice and quick responses to changing needs and priorities, and promoting greater efficiency in managing resources and better value-for-money. Under the delegation of budgets, authorities were expected to ensure that there was significant budgetary autonomy over staff costs, furniture and fittings, property costs, and supplies and services. Some 71% of education budgets are devolved in Scotland (CIPFA, 2002). In general, this shift has been welcomed by headteachers, but with concern for budgetary controls over virement or end-year flexibility, and budget constraints (Adler et al., 1997). However, the system was introduced in a period of severe financial restraint, with savings anticipated from local government reorganisation, and pay increases expected to be met from efficiency gains. Indeed, education staffing levels fell in the immediate post-reorganisation squeeze on budgets (Midwinter and McGarvey, 1997). Headteachers support for budgetary autonomy was countered by concern for the time consuming nature of controlling budgetary minutiae.

Problems of budgetary control in DSM was one of the factors contributing to the education budget overspend in Borders Region which finally resulted in the resignation of the council leader. The Controller of Audit (Accounts Commission, 2001) highlighted a number of weaknesses in financial management, particularly related to DSM. The Borders scheme permitted flexibility between years, and the council deemed £1.1m of its 2000–1 overspend to be early utilisation of the budget for 2001–2. The general practice in Scotland is for the staff costs to be controlled through 'staff weeks' rather than cash, which is controlled centrally. However, the staffing budget estimate included a 'staff turnover adjustment' of £0.5m, to reflect cost reductions which arise when staff leave and are replaced on a lower scale. The central administration budget, in which this was located, was not adequately monitored and overspending occurred. The Commission reported a lack of monitoring and control in the DSM system and a failure to appreciate fully its impact on the council's financial position. However, this accounted for only around 25% of the over-spend, and spending on special needs – which is an emerging problem across Scotland (Scottish Parliament Education Committee Stage 1 Report, Budget 2003–4) – overshot because of growth in demand, whilst the nursery budget overspend resulted from an over-assessment of income.

The parliamentary inquiry by the Education Committee went further, and criticised poor governance, when the leader of the council blamed inadequate funding from central government as the cause of the problem (Education, Culture and Sport Committee, 4th Report 2002, para. 26). The council has a reputation for fiscal prudence, having the lowest Band D council tax in Scotland until 2002–3, and now having the second lowest. Scottish Borders spent only 1.8% above its GAE figure, compared with a Scottish average of 6.4%. It receives the eighth highest per capita grant at £1306, some £45 above average. In 2000–1, its education budget was £513 per capita, about £18 per capita below average. The Education, Culture and Sport Committee expressed further concerns over the way in which a letter announcing earmarked funding from the Executive for repairs, maintenance and equipment was accompanied by a clawback of devolved budgets to reflect the failure to meet the staff turnover target. Although distinctive budget decisions, this appearance of virement was confusing to politicians and public (4th Report, pp 9–10). This is an example of the lack of clarity in education finance with the use of block grants and specific grants centrally, and departmental and devolved budgets locally.

EMERGING FINANCIAL ISSUES

Since 1998, a number of academics and journalists have been predicting a financial squeeze on public spending in Scotland. The argument is based on two assumptions both of which are highly questionable; that the operation of the Barnett Formula is squeezing public expenditure; and this squeeze is being exacerbated by the Executive making policy commitments, such as the McCrone funding for which there was no budgetary provision.

One problem with the squeeze theory is that it is based on predictions from the spending plans, and thus excludes supplementary allocations and interdepartmental transfers. In addition, Scotland has a falling share of the UK's population, so its budget share would be expected to decline modestly. A second problem is that in practice it refers to a relative squeeze, not a real squeeze on spending. Spending on Scottish education could both fall in relative terms (i.e. in comparison to the UK average) and grow in real terms at the same time.

In practice, no change in Scotland's relative position has occurred, although it may do so by 2003–4, as the spending increase is large. The Scottish Parliament inherited a position whereby Scotland, with around 8.6% of the UK population, received 11% of education spending, and that remains the position in the most recent outturn data (HM Treasury,

2002). Over the post-devolution period, education funding has continued to grow in real terms. The data presented in Table 27.1 on local budgets has been reworked into real terms in Table 27.3, for the post-devolution period. It shows spending has risen by 14% in real terms since the change of government, and by 8% since devolution. Real growth is now around 4% per annum.

There are similar weaknesses in the arguments over McCrone funding. Whilst it may be true that there was no provision for McCrone in the budget at the time the decision was taken, it has since been built into the budget. This was achieved firstly by the End-Year Flexibility arrangements, which now permit underspending to be carried forward to future years, and secondly from the growth in the budget since 1998.

The Executive has provided funding for McCrone of £174m in 2001–2; £276m in 2002–3; and finally £405m in 2003–4. This figure is £140m less than COSLA's estimate of £545m. Both sides agree on the pay and salary costs, but differ over the cost of absence cover, support staff, probationers and continuing professional development. Further problems have arisen from the mismatch between the calculation of costs, which is based on actual staff numbers, and the distribution of grant, which is based on the needs based formula. Roughly half the authorities receive more than the likely McCrone costs, whilst the others receive less. These shortfalls amount to nearly £10m, and for six authorities the sums are around £1m each. This issue was highlighted when a local authority in McCrone surplus reallocated funding to the social work budget, triggering protests from teaching staff (Buie and Ross, 2002). Under the block grant system, the authority was perfectly entitled to do so, but it raises issues about responsibility and accountability for education finance which merit further discussion.

Governments initially relied on specific grants to fund the education service, but more recently a process of consolidation resulted in the present position where most of the funding comes via the Revenue Support Grant. Specific grants often itemise controls over spending, and have a directive effect which encourages expenditure in a specific service (Davies et al., 1981). Grant consolidation was defended as a means of permitting local discretion in meeting needs. In education, there has been a long history of specific grants to promote service standards (Barlow, 1981). In the Thatcher era, the block grant was used mainly as an instrument of expenditure control, and central government's choice of grant form usually reflects its policy objectives. In 2002, however, the Executive has a commitment to reduce specific grants, but also to promote particular services. This reflects differing concerns within governments between finance ministers and spending ministers.

There is a strong case for rethinking these conventional orthodoxies in the post-devolution era. Firstly, there is now a more inclusive budgetary process, with a greater degree of scrutiny of the Executive's budget proposals than at Westminster (Midwinter and McGarvey, 2001). Secondly, the block allocation obscures serious parliamentary scrutiny of the proposals, yet local government accounts for nearly one-third of the Scottish Budget. Thus it is possible to tell how much grant support is provided for local government, but not what outputs the Executive expects to gain for such funding.

The Education Committee highlighted this concern over both McCrone funding, and the use by Scottish Borders Council of funding 'earmarked' for schools to tackle its budget problems (Scottish Parliament Education Committee, 2002). The McCrone funding, for example, which is central to the modernisation of the teaching profession, would not have resulted in mismatches if allocated through expenditure based specific grants. Block grants by their nature imply discretion, and make it more difficult for the Executive to exercise control, and the Parliament to exercise scrutiny.

It is also arguable that the arrangements for funding education are central to current debates about the fiscal autonomy of local government. The essence of a local service is that its level and quality can be left to local choice. If the Executive wishes to direct standards and developments, and increasingly treats education as a national service locally delivered, then the case for reinventing an Education Specific Grant is strengthened. Parliament needs to choose the form of grant which reflects the focus of accountability. If the Executive wishes to promote education, then it should be accountable for delivery and that requires a specific grant. Since devolution, local authorities have increased education budgets by 1% more than the average for Scottish local government. Spending increases vary between education authorities, but not so greatly as between social work, roads or leisure services which have a greater degree of policy discretion (Midwinter, 2002).

This writer's view is, however, that the Executive will not seek to clarify accountability for educational finance, preferring the capacity to take praise for additional funding when it suits it, and using the escape clause of local discretion when criticised. The problems of finance are at the margins, and it is clear that additional funding has been delivered, even if accountability is blurred by the existing arrangements.

SPENDING REVIEW 2002

The UK Spending Review was published in July 2002. It is only concerned with DEL expenditure, and it increased the resources available for 2003–4 by £500m, with further increases of £1,200m and £1,400m for the next two years. Including the already planned increase of £1,000m for 2003–4, these constitute an average real growth of 4.4% over the Spending Review period, continuing the trend established in Spending Review 2000.

The Scottish real increase is less than the UK average of 5.2%, and over the Spending Review period the Scottish share of DEL expenditure will fall from 7.59% to 7.40%. This is what would be expected from the operation of the Barnett Formula and Scotland's relative population decline. The fall in budget share of 0.06% per annum is in line with the decline in population share of 0.05%, so that Scottish spending per capita relative to the UK should be broadly maintained.

These growth figures reflect the UK government's decision to increase taxes. Education funding, of course, is determined mainly through GAE, and in September the Finance Minister announced growth in local government revenue funding of 8.7%. (Scottish Executive, 2002b) For education this would translate into additional funding of nearly £300m (including funding from council tax).

The foreword to the Executive's spending plans for the next three years committed it to ensuring 'pupils, teachers and parents will benefit from a dramatic investment in our schools and teaching' plus the provision of funding for the full implementation of the new pay and conditions agreement. New commitments over the three-year period included £25m for quality of life in schools; £10.5m to improve the education attainment of looked-after children; £21m to improve inclusion and access for children with special educational needs and disabilities; and £10m to improve discipline in schools. These will mainly be provided through Specific Grants, thereby increasing the use of these grants from £140m to £240m by 2005–6.

Further revisions to spending plans were announced in a parliamentary statement on 24

June 2000, through the End-Year Flexibility arrangements, which increased funding for local government by £95m, with guidance that priority should be given to Scotland's children.

The issue of education funding was highlighted in a *Herald* editorial (16 July 2002), which warned of the political consequences if the Executive decides to spend less of its cash on education than the Chancellor of the Exchequer, Gordon Brown, and argued that the Executive has to be seen to be improving public services at the same rate planned for England. Such an approach would make a nonsense of devolution, which is intended to permit Scottish determination of priorities. The Executive has already shown flexibility over UK guidance, for example, by announcing that the additional funding from the Chancellor for health would be spent on improving health, but not necessarily through the health budget. The provision of fruit in school for poor children was highlighted as a possible option (Finance Committee Official Report, June 2002).

In the final analysis, however, the resources allocated to education will reflect local decisions, and on past performance, Scotland's councils can be expected to spend broadly in line with the GAE provision, thereby adding further funding growth for Scotland's schools.

CONCLUSIONS

This chapter has analysed developments in education finance since devolution. The data show that the Conservative government's assumption that local government reorganisation would not result in service reductions is suspect, as spending fell in 1997–8. What is also clear is that spending began to grow under the Blair government, and that the rate of growth has increased since devolution.

A number of critics argue that there should be a needs assessment exercise over territorial spending. This reflects dissatisfaction with the outcomes of the current arrangement, and there is a view that this over-rewards Scotland (McCrone, 1999; Morgan 2001). This orthodoxy is most strongly held in Wales and north-east England. It is not based on any serious analysis of the evidence on relative expenditure needs, but on assumptions made in a 1979 HM Treasury study, which concluded that Scottish needs were 15% higher than England but expenditure was 22% higher at that time. The method used, however, was not foolproof, and included heavy caveats about the need for further work. Recent research showed that comparison of local education spending between Scotland and England is problematic, and the key causes of variation are accounting practice and the proportion of the school population educated in public schools. When this is taken into account, the Scottish excess falls from 30% to 9% (Midwinter, 1997). Further consideration of the impact of sparsity and poverty on educational spending needs would be required, but the key point is that it is rash to assume that Scotland would necessarily lose from a needs assessment exercise.

The chapter has also shown how the financial framework of devolved government operates, including central spending on education, and described how the system of local government finance effects the service. It has discussed some emerging issues over education expenditure shown that forecasts of a Barnett Formula-driven spending squeeze were wrong; that funding provision for the McCrone settlement is provided in the Scottish Budget; and that Spending Review 2002 has delivered a further period of spending growth until 2005–6. Nevertheless problems remain because of the shortfall between central and local estimates of the costs of McCrone and difficulties of distribution. Finally, the chapter has discussed the merits of differing forms of grant support, arguing that if Parliament wishes more rigorously to scrutinise the expenditure of education authorities, then the specific grant model should be considered. Nevertheless, the blurring of accountability at present has political advantages which the Executive may prefer to retain.

In summary, education expenditure has been significantly increased since devolution, although this is also true in England, but devolution allowed a quick response on teachers' pay which might not have occurred under Whitehall. Education finance has been a priority for the Executive. From 1997 to 2001 the growth in education spending was 25.6%, well above the average of 18.1% but less than the growth in the health budget of 27.5% over the same period. In practice, the amounts actually spent on education reflect the priorities of the Scottish Executive, the political preferences of local authorities, and the skills in budgetary politics of the service director. The return to growth has not removed the need to defend the education turf in the arguments for public money.

REFERENCES

Accounts Commission (2001) Scottish Borders Council Education Overspend, Special Report 2001–4, Edinburgh: Audit Scotland.

Accounts Commission (2002) Taking the initiative: using PFI contracts to renew council schools, Edinburgh: Audit Scotland.

Adler, M., Arnott, M., Bailey, L., McAvoy, L., Munn, P. and Raab, C. (1997) Devolved School Management, Report prepared for SOEID.

Barlow, J. (1981) Central-local government financial relationships and policy making in Education and Housing. Paper presented to the Political Studies Association Annual Conference, Hull, April.

Buie, E. and Ross, D. (2002) Council anger at McCrone shortfall, The Herald, 10 May.

CIPFA (2002) Rating Review, 2001–2 (CIPFA in Scotland, Edinburgh).

Davies, J., Gibson, J., Game, C. and Stewart, J. (1981) Grant characteristics and central-local relations. Report for the Economic and Social Research Council, University of Birmingham.

HM Treasury (2001) Statement of Funding Policy, London.

HM Treasury (2002) Public Expenditure Statistical Analyses, London.

Hoggett, P. (1996) New modes of control in the public service, Public Administration 74. 1, pp. 33–48.

Jamieson, B. (2001) Calling Scotland to Account: Policy Options for Spending and Taxation, Edinburgh: The Policy Institute.

McCrone, G. (1999) Scotland's public finances from Goschen to Barnett, Quarterly Economic Commentary, 24(2), March, pp. 30–45.

Midwinter, A. (1997) Local education spending in Scotland and England: problems of comparison in the LACE study, Scottish Educational Review 29(2), 146–53.

Midwinter, A. (2002) The new politics of local spending: central-local financial relations under Scottish devolution, Public Money and Management April–June, 1–9.

Midwinter, A. and McGarvey, N. (1997) Local government reform in Scotland: managing the transition, Local Government Studies 23(3), 73–89.

Midwinter, A. and McGarvey, N. (2001) The new accountability: devolution and expenditure politics in Scotland, Public Money and Management 21(3), 47–53.

Morgan, K. (2001) The new territorial politics: rivalry and justice in post-devolution Britain, Regional Studies 35(4), 343–8.

Scottish Executive (2002a) The Scottish Budget 2003–4, Edinburgh: Scottish Executive.

Scottish Executive (2002b) Building a Better Scotland: Spending Proposals 2003–2006. Edinburgh: Scottish Executive.

Scottish Parliament Education, Culture and Sport Committee (4th Report, 2002), Report on Scottish Borders Education, SP Paper 519, Edinburgh: Scottish Executive.

28

School and Work:
The Employers' Perspective

*Linda Boyes, Graham Leicester, Andrew Lyon
and James McCormick*

In Scandinavian countries the notion of a learning society is more developed and explicit than in Scotland. Education there tends to be viewed as a means to enhance citizenship, voluntary activities, parenthood, or political, social or cultural life. The proposition put forward by the Scottish Council Foundation is that Scotland should adopt a similar approach. Education for employment and education for life are not different; any divide between the two is unhelpful creating increased pressure on an already crowded curriculum. If there is a move towards an education system that prepares young people for their many roles in society, at home, in school or education, in the community, at work, in leisure time, and in relationships, this will provide them with the attributes and competencies necessary to be active participants in the world of work. This approach will enable young people to gain the skills required to compete in the employment market, to develop and manage their careers, and to make a valuable contribution to Scotland's economy and society.

Current education policy does make the link between education and its role in preparing young people for adult life, but however worthy the aims of policy are, it is only when policy and practice come together in a coherent way that lasting results are achieved. The education system operates in a complex demographic, social and economic environment, with many vested interests, and a wide range of contributors, sometimes with conflicting demands, but each with an opinion on what education should be about and how it should be delivered. There has to be a balance between existing constraints and the necessity for change. Looking to the future, there is an opportunity to blur the boundary between education for work and as a preparation for adulthood, and to develop a deeper relationship between education and society based on the development of human capacity. This chapter explores current reality and a possible future for Scottish education.

THE CURRENT CONTEXT

Schools are communities, not necessarily of interest but of necessity, as young people and their parents have limited choice over where and how education is delivered. Private or independent schools and home education, although available, are not a viable option for most families. To encourage diversity and widen choice, a 'charter schools' model has emerged in the United States. These schools are sponsor-created and administered, outcome-based public schools that operate under a contract between the school and the local school board or the state. Charter schools are exempt from most state and local laws and regulations, but to gain charter renewal the schools must prove that their students have gained the educational skills that the school and its sponsor specified in the initial contract. It is not self-evident that this is the only or best way to increase diversity within schooling, but it is a trend Scotland might explore further.

Schooling in its early stages is inclusive and seeks to create a nurturing ambience appropriate to the needs and stage of development of the child. Schools are places where all young people go from four or five years of age until at least sixteen, with increasing numbers staying on for a further one or two years. This is the time in their lives when they form their view of the world and their role in society. In the early part of the last century, when the promise of a state education was made to all young people, their time in school was more limited than today, entry into employment and society came at a much earlier age and schools did not have to deal with the wide ranging issues they do today. Nowadays young people and their families have more complicated needs than in the past. The concept of family has changed dramatically in recent decades. There are many more single parent households, and more dual earner households, thereby reducing the availability of family support systems. The demand for pre-school and after-school care has never been greater.

Stepping into the adult world of personal or family responsibility comes sooner for some young people than others. Adolescence and the way it affects teenagers is also a phenomenon of the later part of the twentieth century, which some secondary schools are struggling to cope with. There are concerns about the effects of schooling upon teenagers focused on issues such as bullying, drugs and the effects of peer group pressure, particularly on low-achieving boys. At this age, young people still need to be in a nurturing environment but there is a growing requirement to exert some control over their own lives as they move towards adulthood and independence. The education system also has to cope with the consequences of child and family poverty, which although high on the agenda of UK government and the Scottish Executive (notably through its Social Justice strategy) is still disturbing by European Union standards.

Scottish school education is characterised by a remarkable degree of uniformity. Although there is no statutory national curriculum, national guidelines and advice coupled with regular inspection have established a general standardisation of practice. State schools offer seven years of primary education and six of secondary education. Some parts of the system have tried to accommodate the differing needs of young people. However, because of this homogeneity the capacity to innovate and diversify is limited. It is difficult to balance individually tailored approaches with a standardised curriculum and there is now a growing realisation that the current model of 'mass production' has limited value in meeting a wide range of needs and academic ability.

Broadly speaking, the aim of education is to achieve a high level of success for every child. 'Where school education is provided to a child or young person by, or by virtue of arrangements made, or entered into by an education authority, it shall be the duty of that authority to secure that the education is directed to the development of the personality, talents and mental and physical abilities of the child or young person to their fullest potential' (Scottish Executive, 2000). But does it?

When young people enter secondary education content begins to take precedence over the development of skills. As children grow older, the institution becomes less capable of responding to individual need. Because the purpose is to 'pass', it ceases to matter to learners whether the process has any value in itself. The importance of content is enshrined in subject divisions and the end result examinations reinforce a subject-based approach to the curriculum and place heavy reliance on assessing subject content. Bayliss (1999) supports the assertion that schools cannot be creative in their teaching if the bulk of their energy is devoted to meeting targets or preparing for a volley of examinations, and has argued that 'the subject based curriculum and examination structure are the major obstacles to progress in education', and that 'transformation can only be secured if we are clear what it is students need to learn' (p. 7).

Qualifications essentially act as a series of filters to weed people out of the system so that ultimately a percentage of the population become disengaged from learning, school and society. The system appears to work for many, but for those who tend to be non-academic, or who cannot thrive in the current school environment, where is the alternative to wasted human potential? Those who feel disadvantaged or disenfranchised sometimes vote with their feet. During 2000–1, of the 38,656 exclusions from local authority schools, 86% were from secondary schools, and of those, 79% were boys. If a key objective in education is to promote equality and help every pupil benefit from education, that promise cannot be made to those who do not readily fit the current system. Government policy is now moving towards the goal of 50% of the population gaining access to higher education by the age of thirty. This drive is likely to push schools even more strongly towards being a filter into higher education and biased towards the entrance demands of these institutions.

The volume of published information on education, particularly school performance, has grown steadily. This information has been widely used, discussed and analysed, leading to performance improvement through increased target setting for individual institutions. Evidence from comparisons of educational performance across Scotland show variations from school to school but this can be because of a wide range of contextual factors that may not always be recognised or taken into consideration. Relying mainly on quantitative findings does not reflect the true picture and assumes that the measures are valid and reliable. This would be a workable proposition if educational qualifications were a good proxy for the qualities and skills people need to be effective in life and work. However, changing demands of both cannot be measured in a 'one-off' manner through the current examination system and this poses problems for leadership and management of education.

One of the issues that makes fundamental change difficult starts with the idea that parents want qualifications for their children. This is perceived as the key to good employment prospects. Policy-makers then set targets based on the belief that this is what people want. Many educators are frustrated by this approach: their feeling is that people learn where their energy and passion is, and this cannot be released as too much time and attention has to be paid to maintaining or increasing the numbers passing exams. There is a wider, but as yet vaguely articulated, sense that the system of mass education does not seem well suited to meeting today's needs, let alone those of the future.

At this stage, it is necessary to consider the issue of knowledge. Current arrangements are based on the assumption that there is a core of knowledge that young people should possess before leaving school. This knowledge is drawn from a broad field, reflecting the main ways in which people have sought to understand the world. The view that young people should experience a broad and balanced curriculum, in which traditional subjects embody the main ways of knowing, has underpinned official thinking in Scottish education for most of the period following the Munn Report of 1977. It has only recently been subject to serious challenge.

In theory, there is much to commend the Munn approach. Having all young people leave school with a worthwhile knowledge and understanding of language, the arts, sciences and social sciences is a worthy objective. The problem is that, for many learners, subject content is not knowledge; it is information. The element of understanding that would transform it into knowledge is missing. Its seeming irrelevance and relative lack of authenticity means that, far from shaping thinking through life, it may be quickly forgotten. What is lacking is the depth that produces understanding. This cannot be developed through content at a greater level of detail but requires an appropriate context and processes for learning, and depth gained through experience.

LEARNING AND EDUCATION

How people learn is equally as important as what people learn. The work of Howard Gardner, in developing the theory of 'multiple intelligences', suggests that learners absorb, retain, and manipulate information in different ways. Because individuals differ from one another, educators should try to understand the learners in their classrooms and implement teaching strategies based upon individual need. The concept of personal learning styles is at the heart of this approach.

According to the theory, individuals differ from one another in the relative strengths of the intelligences as well as the ease with which the intelligences are used to demonstrate understanding to themselves and others. Learners should be given opportunities to learn and exhibit their understanding using a wide variety of intelligences. Furthermore, there is an increasing awareness that people's learning styles vary and that, if everyone is to reach their full potential, account needs to be taken of this. More positive and formative approaches to assessment and self-assessment have been developed. Our concept of intelligence has become more sophisticated and diverse. A wider range of capabilities is now valued and promoted.

The discoveries made to date suggest that the human brain is not a logic machine but a living organism. Emotional and physical circumstances can help or hinder the process of learning. The brain does not readily follow sequences prescribed by those who already know. Rather, it excels at absorbing information in a variety of formats from a seemingly random range of sources and in making sense of it. The mind reacts well to rich and varied stimulation and thrives in an atmosphere of high challenge but low threat. Indeed, experiences characterised by uncertainty, anxiety and stress inhibit learning. Multi-sensory experience along with sustained mental and physical challenge develops enduring networks in the brain. Learning which integrates different areas of the brain is likely to be the most sustainable.

As yet, however, the impact of all these recent understandings in the classroom is slight. Teaching methods, curricular objectives and even the nature of school premises will need to change significantly before they properly reflect what is already understood about how to create the best circumstances for effective learning. The need for more individualised learning experiences is evident but the practicalities of schooling make it hard to implement such approaches. The implications for the roles of teachers and other educators have yet to be fully explored. The schools that are designed and built or remodelled today should inspire teachers and their students to meet their current needs, but should also be adaptable enough to meet the needs of tomorrow.

Through the introduction of the New Community Schools initiative in Scotland, there is recognition that schools on their own cannot address all the barriers to children's learning. Their focus is on the pupil and his or her family – addressing needs through integrated provision of services, teachers, social workers, community education workers, health professionals and others working together in a single location. New Community Schools seek to address the many factors that affect attainment at school – which should be more broadly defined – and look at achievement in the widest sense. Their success may be limited if the broader issues of content and delivery are not addressed.

CURRENT INITIATIVES AS PREPARATION FOR WORK

Education to work pathways are incorporated into curriculum design largely without recognition that the majority of time is spent on examination related subject specific activities. In Scotland the model in use is for young people to spend one week during their later secondary years in a working environment. With continuing education, exposure to the world of work is dependent on the type of course undertaken, the more vocational the greater need for workplace involvement. In the Netherlands, for example, some pupils, depending on need and aspirations, follow a more vocationally focused route, spending usually two days per week in school, or two weeks in school, followed by three weeks in the workplace. In Finland, those aged sixteen embarking on a vocational route spend three quarters of each programme within businesses. In both countries there is a long-standing culture of vocational education sitting alongside academic study based on the view that for many young people vocational study is more appropriate (see Clegg and Grayson, 2002).

Enterprise education is widely talked about in Scottish education and education policy. In the school system, it is expected that pupils from age five onwards should be able to develop enterprising skills and attitudes. The HMI Report *Education for Work in Schools* (HMI, 2000) stated that 'primary and secondary pupils have an entitlement to enterprise education and schools are encouraged to develop policies to ensure this entitlement is delivered.' However the gulf between policy and practice is evident from a recent National Centre: Education for Work and Enterprise report (Watt, 2002) which identified that no more than 10% of pupils in secondary schools experience enterprise education at any time during the S1–S6 years.

Efforts to encourage enterprise and entrepreneurship for those aged fifteen to twenty-five are available through Young Enterprise Scotland. Students, known as 'Achievers', create their own company with supported advice and guidance. They make all the key decisions including which products they will create and sell, how the business will be managed, which members of the newly formed company will be responsible for performing all essential activities from marketing and sales, to production and financial control. Each company is then linked with an Adviser from the business world who will act as their personal consultant. The activities are designed to make the transition from education to work easier for young people, but it is not part of the mainstream option for all young people.

Education for Work (EfW) is now widely available in schools across Scotland. Research findings (SEED, 2002) from those who had recently experienced this first hand showed that work experience was by far the most commonly identified activity as providing the most learning. A typical response was that the length of the work experience placement should be increased, or there should be more than one separate week. Very few students were able to make the link between school subjects and the world of work, and a recommendation in the report suggested young people need the opportunity to reflect on their experiences and to link them to a set of outcomes for EfW. One of the major benefits claimed by EfW is the capacity to make subjects real and meaningful to participants, yet this study at least suggests that is not yet being achieved in the minds of students. There is a lack of connectedness to lessons having value and meaning beyond the instructional context, and young people did not make a connection to the larger workplace or social context. Again this initiative appears to suffer the fate of other worthy policy ideas. As gaps occur between policy aims and practical application the desired objectives are not fully achieved.

JOBS AND THE ECONOMY

Scotland has a mainly micro or small firms business base. Although inward investment and the growth of Scottish companies have been promoted, the main jobs market can be found in the smaller business sector. Conditions in Scotland's labour market have improved significantly in recent years. Unemployment is low by historical standards, with both youth and long-term adult unemployment falling substantially, and the number of people in employment at or near record levels. There have been, of course, shifts in the quality of employment (working conditions, working time, access to training or overall workforce development strategies). The concept of 'job-specific' skills owes more to the 'older' economy, with broad based skills a necessity for the new ways of working and living. At one time a craft or technical skill or degree secured employment, but now, as the economy is changing, so are jobs and job requirements, resulting in a need for people to embark on a programme of lifelong learning to remain employable. The job for life employment contract has long gone and is now replaced with more short-terms jobs, linked to varying patterns of attendance. Careers are not only to be found in the private sector; the public and voluntary sectors are continuing to employ large numbers of people. Self-employment, although an attractive proposition for some, does not enter into career options for the majority of young Scots.

There has been a swing away from manufacturing to service industries, with a continuing shift of the occupational structure. There will be increased demand for higher skilled labour in professional and managerial jobs, but also a corresponding demand for lower levels of skill, with employment opportunities in service areas such as leisure, care and hospitality, as well as in a range of skilled trades such as those related to construction.

Higher-level skills are associated with a rise in professional and managerial jobs and lower level skills with a rise in consumer spending on leisure, social and personal care provision. Evidence shows that those with higher skill levels have the potential to earn higher salaries and move through employment with greater ease than those with lower skill levels. Access to workplace training is more limited for those with lower levels of education attainment, further compounding their inability to progress within employment and improve their living standards. A consequence of this is that in future the divide in terms of living standards and quality of life between the groups is also likely to increase.

Success in securing fulfilling employment is in turn linked to the speed of change in the economy and demand for skills and knowledge of the labour market. Work is being transformed by global competition and the growth in information and communication technologies. Future employment will become more concentrated in activities with unique, high human value content. Those activities which do not require this high human value content will be automated. For example, call centre employment is already beginning to be replaced by automated technology. Decentralisation of decision making, multi-tasking and teamworking are linked to the reorganisation of work and work practices. The skills required to be part of the workforce are changing – creative thinking, innovation, networking and the ability to seek out knowledge are at a premium.

Technology is continuing to impact on every aspect of life, including work. The use of computers and the internet in education is also a guide to how well prepared tomorrow's workforce will be in one of the basic skills for life and work. Over recent years the availability of ICT in schools has increased dramatically, but the extent to which this sits on the periphery of teaching and learning or is consistently integrated into mainstream delivery is debatable.

Much has been written about the pace of change and its impact on the economy, society and people over the last twenty years. Moves from an industrial age to a knowledge economy, new, digital or networked economy, and changes to the role of people in society all have a profound effect on the role of education and schools. This change has also found its way into the labour market resulting in shifting patterns of demand for labour and skill requirements. Work provides an opportunity to use and develop core skills and competence, not content-specific information or knowledge. There is a growing trend towards examination results being used in initial sifting rather than final selection decisions made by employers. Decisions on recruitment are increasingly based on the ability of potential employees to demonstrate specific talents and behaviours with job-specific skills viewed by employers as gained once in post. The diminishing relative value of academic attainment as a proxy for future success at work further supports the need to re-evaluate what is taught and measured. Young people need to leave school not just with sound subject-matter knowledge and skills, but ready to continue learning throughout life. In order to do so, they must be able to manage their own learning, rather than solely relying on teachers to do so. This means they must, on the one hand, be interested and engaged in learning and, on the other hand, have strategies for learning effectively.

A POSSIBLE FUTURE

Predictions by the Registrar General for Scotland estimate the number of young people entering the education system will reduce in the next 20 years. Scottish population figures show that the number of children aged under 16 is projected to fall to 85% of the 1999 level by 2019. If future investment in their education is viewed only as a means of achieving higher rates of employment and ultimately economic prosperity, their contribution to society more generally will be less effective than it could be.

The changes that have taken place outside schools, in society, the environment and the economy, have until now been slow to permeate the education delivery model. If the pace of change continues as it has, now is the time to reshape the education system to support the ideal of learning as a preparation for life in the twenty-first century. Some of the possible characteristics of such a system are identified below.

- There will be a move towards 'lifewide' as well as lifelong learning. Schools in the future can offer a controlled testing ground for developing a new kind of education and introduce new educational models with options to suit different learners and facilitators of learning. They can create an environment where learning is fun and young people are proud of their achievements. In essence it is necessary to bring schools to life and life to schools.

- There will be a sharper degree of awareness, not least in government circles, that the environment in which education is delivered symbolises the value society places on young people's learning. Projects such as School Works, a national project advocating the belief that the design and use of school buildings can raise educational achievement and support a culture of lifelong learning, can set guiding principles that will drive the design of learning environments. School will be reinvented as a hub of learning, and will link with other resources inside and outside the immediate school environment. This will allow for an evolving curriculum, more varied pedagogical styles and better use of space and time.

- Technology will have an enhanced role to play in connecting educational institutions with each other and with wider communities. It will also have a part to play in customised delivery, integrated within a range of options to provide ease of access to information and tools to develop a broad range of skills and knowledge. However, technology can only complement, not replace, the need for developmentally appropriate activities nurturing the physical, emotional and intellectual well-being of each young person.

- Understanding how children and young people learn will lead to progressive educational practices and learning which will develop the broad range of intelligences. A successful delivery model will be compatible with how the brain works. What is done will be based to a greater extent on what we know. This means as a minimum that schools must be safe, mentally stimulating, and active for learners and provide personal feedback to the learner. A corollary is that schools will become spaces of inquiry to explore what is not already known.

- A holistic model of delivery will be in place, to develop the whole person. The system will develop in a way that creates a meaningful and rewarding experience that the learner wants to repeat, with a strong interplay between practical experience and theoretical knowledge. Mass production delivery will be replaced by highly customised learning, which recognises that the most effective learning takes place when an individual is motivated and wants to learn. New relationships will be established. Most young people and their parents will become active and informed participants, not passive recipients.

- Interactions at all levels are based on communication with family, friends, work colleagues, customers or other members of the communities which individuals inhabit. The changing face of democracy, encouraged mainly by developments in technology and government, will move towards more consultation at national, local or community level, with greater potential to engage citizens in decisions. Young people will develop the ability to deliberate and contribute to decision making at all levels based on an understanding of the context and actions proposed. The educational value placed on the need to develop these critical skills will be clearly evident within the curriculum.

- Delivery of education for citizenship will recognise that citizenship is best learnt through experience and interaction with others and will better prepare young people for their roles in society. There will be more meaningful ways to integrate education, employability and work experience through closer involvement with the business community, coupled with earlier and extended participation in working environments. Set in this wider context, education for work and enterprise will be understood as an integral part of the school experience, not an interruption to what is often considered as 'real' learning (through core subjects with a secure place in the curriculum).

- There will be a willingness to embrace experimentation and uncertainty and to change course if policies are not delivering the desired results. Schools will be opening their doors to the community for all members to take advantage of the resources available and building strong links with families in ways that recognise young people's learning works best as a partnership between parents and teachers.

- Outcomes in future will be measured by a broader range of indicators, including confidence, trust, fulfilment, and competence in life skills as well as academic achievement. These will be delivered through powerful learning experiences beyond the school gates as well as within classrooms. The curriculum will be broad based with thematic interdisciplinary approaches linked to the interests of young people and life issues. Students will be able to solve problems through asking questions and seeking to understand rather than having to remember information. Time for reflection and questioning will be built into curriculum design. Policy and practice will combine in a coherent way to encourage innovation and continued learning at all levels of the education system.

In summary, education for work alone cannot meet the needs of society; however, if education actively promotes the skills and competencies which people require to be effective members of society, the needs of the workplace will also be met. Success will be limited only by everyone's creativity and willingness to change and restructure the 'traditional' model of education and education delivery. Should the future be about a continuing search for a system that provides a mass solution, or should it be about customised and tailored provision that builds individual capacity and capability?

REFERENCES

Bayliss, V. (1999) *Opening Minds, Education for the 21st Century*, London: Royal Society for the Arts.

Clegg, N., MEP, and Grayson, R. (2002) *Learning from Europe – Lessons in Education*, London: Centre for European Reform.

Scottish Executive (2000) Standards in Scotland's Schools etc. Act, *2000*. Edinburgh: Scottish Executive.

SEED (2002) *Learning Gains from Education for Work*, Interchange 74, Edinburgh: SEED.

Watt, D. (2002) *Enterprise Education in Secondary Schools: A Critical Enquiry*, Glasgow: University of Strathclyde: National Centre: Education for Work and Enterprise.

29

Access to Scottish Education

Angela Roger

WHO HAS ACCESS TO SCOTTISH EDUCATION?

Scottish education has achieved a great deal in terms of access in recent years. Primary and secondary schooling are a realisable expectation for the vast majority of young people. Significant progress has been made in overcoming barriers to participation in schools and in the curriculum for pupils from all social classes and for pupils with physical disabilities including autism and dyslexia. However, for children in families who suffer from a combination of problems such as unemployment, poor housing, high crime environments, poor health and family breakdown, a real possibility of social and educational exclusion still exists. Beyond the compulsory stages of education in Scotland, equity in provision and equality of opportunity is less widespread. Although government policy has put mass participation in further and higher education high on the political agenda, and participation in higher education in Scotland now exceeds 50%, this rate still falls short of some other developed Western nations. This chapter considers the extent to which Scotland has succeeded in expanding access to post-compulsory education in the latter half of the twentieth century, with a particular focus upon higher education, for it is here that there is still much to be done. In the second part of the chapter, some of the issues arising out of the existing pattern of progress are considered and it is argued that despite the expansion of provision, pride in the success to date may mask continuing inequalities in access to education. Furthermore expansion will be limited in future by under-investment in universities.

BACKGROUND TO EXPANSION

Expansion in post-compulsory education at school level was promoted assiduously by successive governments during the 1980s and 1990s. Two main sets of arguments were used to advocate the increase in numbers of students sought for recruitment to further and higher education: an aspiration for economic competitiveness and an appeal to social justice. The first set of arguments holds that Scotland as a nation requires to participate in a global market which is premised less upon manufacturing and more upon marketing of information in which competition is fierce. The 'knowledge economy' needs more highly skilled and more highly educated workers. Education is seen to be a crucial component in success. Nations with whom the UK competes in the global market, such as Germany and Japan, have higher participation rates in education than the UK and it is therefore believed that there is a causal link between economic success in those countries and the high numbers in their populations achieving higher levels of education. A simple causal link is, of course, open to dispute, though in the past it has been possible to show that higher achievement in education leads to greater success at an individual level in terms of job opportunity and professional status.

The social justice argument holds that access to education is an individual's right and that there are long-term benefits for society in having a well-educated citizenry, for educated people are more likely to participate in democracy and better able to contribute to the cultural life of the nation. In addition, under-representation in higher education of some groups of people – women, disabled people, minority ethnic groups, older people and people from lower socio-economic groups – suggests a waste of talent, since it is indefensible in the twenty-first century to believe that talent resides exclusively or even primarily in young, white, able-bodied, middle-class men.

The thrust of much government policy has been driven more by the economic competitiveness argument rather than by appeals to social justice, although the election of a Labour government in 1997 and its re-election in 2001, together with the re-establishment of a Scottish Parliament in 1999 have also meant that social justice arguments, especially in Scotland, have been intensified. There is a convenient convergence of aspiration among advocates of each argument which has permitted considerable progress to be made in providing greater access to higher levels of education.

EXTENT OF PROVISION

Paterson (1997a) traces the expansion of secondary education in the unprecedented period of change from 1980 to 1995. Four indicators are used: Ordinary and Standard Grade attainment; staying-on rates; attainment in Highers; and rates of entry to higher education. At Standard Grade the attainment rate for five or more passes at levels 1–3 reached 70% compared to 54% achieving five or more O Grades at levels A–C in 1981. In particular, the performance of girls has improved beyond the rate of boys. The gap between the performance of socially advantaged young people and socially disadvantaged narrowed, except at the top end of achievement.

Persistence in secondary education has also improved. By 1994, the staying-on rate had risen from 52% in 1983 to 70%, with reduced social class inequalities and girls being more likely to stay on than boys. Achievement at Higher, measured at three or more passes, the traditional entry qualification for higher education, also improved. This rose from 20% in 1981 to 29% in 1995. Clearly, the introduction of comprehensive education made a positive impact on social class inequalities during the early 1980s. Once again, girls increasingly out-performed boys.

ENTRY TO HIGHER EDUCATION

The most dramatic expansion in Scottish education has undoubtedly been in participation in higher education. From a 6% participation rate by the age of twenty-one in the 1960s, the rate rose to 45% in 1995 and has now exceeded 50%. Between the years 1988 and 1993 a very rapid rise in participation took place. Social class differences in entry rates have now begun to diminish though participation by young people from homes where the father is in manual work is still less than half that of children of professional fathers. Once again, females are more likely than males to enter higher education with the female participation rate now well over 50%. Another hitherto under-represented group has also achieved a considerable turnaround: participation in higher education by students from minority ethnic groups outstrips that of white students' participation by more than two to one. As Paterson (1997b) shows, some substantial inroads into social inequalities were made in Scotland in the past forty years, especially in gender but significantly also in social class and ethnicity.

However, there is no cause for complacency. While middle-class girls and mature women have made significant progress in gaining entry to higher education, the participation of working-class boys remains low. It is important, however, to recognise that an analysis of achievement by gender is insufficient in itself to address the multiple inequalities which affect some groups in society.

KEY ACCESS DOCUMENTS

Since the Education (Scotland) Act 1872 paved the way for universal secondary education, various government and non-governmental initiatives have been directed at further improving access to education. Whilst it might be argued that the battle for compre-hensive access had been won in secondary education by the 1980s using such evidence as quoted above, participation in further and higher education required new impetus because of the demographic downturn in the number of young school leavers. The Action Plan (*16–18s in Scotland: An Action Plan*, SED, 1983) called for renewed efforts to increase participation in further education. The Action Plan restructured the further education curriculum into a modular system and introduced a unified system of certification for post-compulsory education (the National Certificate). The reforms had far-reaching effects not only on the further education sector, but also in post-16 education in schools in Scotland. The Action Plan gave further education a more dynamic profile than had been the case before. It also had a significant impact on preparation for higher education, providing an alternative set of qualifications to the Higher for under-qualified school leavers and adult returners.

The Scottish Office embarked on an ambitious programme of reform of upper secondary education in setting up the Howie Committee which was charged with a review of upper secondary education. Its report argued for a twin track of vocational and academic qualifications, the 'ScotCert', a course which was primarily vocational in orientation, and the 'ScotBac' which was primarily academic in focus. However, Howie's proposed solution, though not the analysis underpinning it, was rejected in favour of the Scottish Office's alternative programme, Higher Still (*Opportunity for All*, SOEID, 1992). The Higher Still reforms of curriculum arranged for an integrated set of courses throughout the upper stages of secondary schooling and the introduction of a new examination, the Advanced Higher, to replace the Certificate of Sixth Year Studies. Both academic subjects and vocational subjects were to be offered to pupils and vocational subjects were to have 'parity of esteem' with academic. 'Group awards' comprising a cognate set of courses would be offered. All of these Scottish qualifications, including Standard Grade, the examination taken at age sixteen, National Certificate and Scottish Group Awards, were rebranded in 1999 as National Qualifications. In 2000–1 they were brought into a single unified framework, the Scottish Credit and Qualifications Framework (SCQF) (published jointly by the Quality Assurance Agency for Higher Education, Universities Scotland, the Scottish Qualifications Authority and the Scottish Executive in September 2001) which incorporated developments over the past twenty years. The framework encompasses qualifications gained at school, in further education, and higher education up to and including Master's degrees and is designed to make relationships between qualifications clearer, to clarify routes for progression throughout the Scottish system and to provide information on Scottish Credit Accumulation and Transfer (SCOTCAT) points for use to gain credit for learning within and beyond Scotland. In this regard it should be noted that some 40% of students entering higher education do so through a further education route and the SCQF framework should afford greater comparability between qualifications helping to break down barriers still further.

ACCESS TO FURTHER AND HIGHER EDUCATION

The most significant new recruiting ground for students for higher education is no longer the school-leaver population. The numbers of adult students gaining access to higher education have been increasing rapidly since the early 1980s showing a 193% increase in over 25s during the years 1982 and 1986. As a response to the 1987 White Paper *Higher Education: Meeting the Challenge* (DES, 1987) which called for widening participation in vocationally relevant education, the Scottish Office announced an initiative in April 1988, the Scottish Wider Access Programme (SWAP). SWAP was intended to 'stimulate developments aimed at increasing the number of mature students and those without traditional entrance qualifications entering higher education' (Scottish Information Office, 0643/88). Later in that year, the particular needs of employers facing the demographic decline in young workers was cited, together with the needs of the teaching and health-related professions for women graduates, as further reasons for those in higher education to adjust their attitudes to non-standard entry to higher education (Scottish Information Office, 1968/88). Significantly, SWAP arrangements provided guaranteed places in higher education for those who successfully completed their further education courses. Many further education colleges had also developed courses for access to higher education institutions. Universities' access summer schools for adult returners began in 1981. However, the difference between the SWAP courses and universities' access courses lay in SWAP's use of recognised national qualifications, especially the National Certificate. After completing a SWAP course, people could theoretically proceed to any course of higher education and not be confined to one particular institution.

As a result of these various initiatives, during the period from 1987 to 1994, the increase in over 21s entering full-time undergraduate and sub-degree courses was almost double (201.7%) that of the overall increase (104.7% overall). Adult returners more than compensated for the demographic downturn in numbers of school-leavers.

Whereas most of these special courses were organised for mature students, normally those over twenty-one who had experienced a significant break between school and return to study, a separate innovation took the form of summer schools for young people who had been educationally or socially disadvantaged during their final years at school. Traditionally, these young people would have had to follow a further education course to gain access to higher education. However, the new access courses speeded up entry to higher education through an intensive, university-based summer school with places offered to those who successfully completed the course. In the year 1999, just over 2.4% of students entered higher education through an access programme, whether through SWAP, another access course or an access summer school.

INSTITUTIONAL POLICIES

Motivated in part by the competition for students upon which funding is based, most Scottish universities now have policies in place which permit socially or educationally disadvantaged students to enter courses of study. It should be said that the pre-1992 universities have had a worse record of admission of students from groups that were previously disadvantaged. It should also be noted that some of the 'ancient' universities are less likely than the 1960s-established or later established institutions, to admit non-traditional students. Although the data of Osborne et al. (1997) are selective, they cite figures for 'non-standard' entrants as 1.7% of 'standard entrants' in one 'ancient' university, compared to 15.2% 'non-standard' to 'standard' entrants in a 1960s-established institution. In 1999, in one 'ancient' university, only 2% of students had no formal qualifications compared to other entrants, while in one post-1992 institution, the figure was 42.4%. It is clear that some universities have found it more in their interest to recruit from previously under-represented groups than others which have never experienced any lack of well-qualified traditional applicants to fill their places. Recognising this, the Scottish Higher Education Funding Council (SHEFC) instituted a series of targets for institutions to meet in relation to wider access issues. In 2002, institutions were required as a condition of grant to specify in their strategic plans, how they were going to meet demands for equality of opportunity and widening participation specifically in relation to social class, age, disability, gender, race and any other factor which might lead to unfair treatment of students.

ALTERNATIVES TO HE INSTITUTIONS

Higher education in Scotland is not exclusively provided by higher education institutions. Students in further education institutions follow courses of higher education aiming not for a degree but, for example, a Higher National Diploma. The proportion of students studying full-time in higher education courses in further education colleges in 1987 was 19.1% of overall numbers, whereas in 1994 it had grown to 33.1%. In 1999 it was 35%. The corresponding proportions of undergraduates in HEIs declined from 80.9% to 66.9% in the period 1987 to 1994, and was 65% in 1999, clearly indicating the significance of the further education sector in the higher education 'market'. The Open University in Scotland also provides opportunities to study to degree level for some 2,000 students. The University of the Highlands and Islands Millennium Institute (UHI), an initiative launched in 1996 with generous government funding, is based upon a consortium of further education colleges serving the north of Scotland. The UHI aims to develop a radical alternative to institution-based higher education. Both the UHI project and the well-established Open University provide a model of remote-access education to challenge the status quo both in terms of student access and the funding of higher education. It is no longer necessary, although it may continue to appear desirable, for a student to attend classes for face-to-face teaching in order to obtain a degree.

SUPPORT FOR ADULT RETURNERS: CHANGING PATTERNS OF LEARNING AND THE ACHIEVEMENT OF 'ACCESS' STUDENTS

Institutions have had to adapt as they admit new groups of students. Ball (1990) pointed out the responsibilities of those in higher education to recognise that new groups of students in higher education would create new demands in terms of learning and teaching methods and pastoral care (*More Means Different: Widening Access to Higher Education*, London: RSA/ Industry Matters). Most universities took the young, full-time undergraduate as the norm and have been slow to adapt by providing new modes of study, flexible teaching, additional support for people with child-care responsibilities or people with disabilities. Initial predictions that 'more means worse', that is, that students hitherto denied a place in the academy would perform poorly if admitted, have not, however, been borne out. Although research in this area is at an early stage, the indications are that students gaining access by non-traditional routes are just as likely to succeed in gaining a degree as their more traditional counterparts. Some further fears have been articulated that degree standards have fallen and therefore that a degree is now easier to obtain. Universities deny this and cite as evidence the various quality assurance processes which will now be considered.

STANDARDS AND QUALITY

The impetus in higher education to attract new groups of students coincided with the accountability movement which introduced into HE various quality and accountability measures such as student charters and the teaching quality assessment process (TQA). A new quality assurance mechanism based on internal processes is due for implementation in 2003–4. Driven by government's drive towards efficiency and value for money, TQA sought to assure the tax payer that higher education was maintaining standards and ensuring quality. The Lindop Report, *Academic Validation in Public Sector Education*, (Department of Education and Science, 1985) first raised the suggestion that 'standards' for access students were lower than for traditional students, although *Meeting the Challenge* (DES, 1987) reported that no evidence could be found to substantiate the fear of a drop in standards. However, in part due to the relative novelty of non-traditional access routes to higher education, little empirical evidence yet exists. The research also suffers from problems of comparability since systematic collection of statistics by the Higher Education Statistics Agency by mode of entry, which would allow comparisons to be made, only recently began. An extensive review of the research into the performance of non-traditional participants in higher education in Scotland was commissioned by SCOTVEC (Gallacher, J. and Wallis, W., *The Performance of Students with Non-traditional Qualifications in Higher Education: A Review of Research Literature*, 1993). This study concluded that 'non-traditionally qualified students perform at least as well as, and in some cases better than, traditionally qualified students'. There were, however, some subject differences. Over-21s performed better than their younger counterparts in Arts and Social Sciences, but this was less marked in Science, Engineering, Medicine and Health Studies. Whilst no national study of the performance of students entering higher education with non-traditional qualifications exists, studies in individual universities (such as the University of Dundee and the University of Stirling) confirm these trends. However, as Osborne et al. (1997) recognise, a significant gap in the research evidence about the performance of these new groups of students is an analysis of any factor other than route of entry, such as socio-economic status. As Gayle et al. (2002) appreciate in their study of participation in England and Wales, more research on these complex, inter-related factors needs to be done.

FUTURE PROVISION

Perhaps the most significant event in the past three decades in higher education was the report of the Dearing Committee of Inquiry into Higher Education, *Higher Education in the Learning Society* (1997). It signalled significant changes for Scottish education in the years to come. The Dearing Report stated as one of its main principles that higher education in the future must 'encourage and enable all students – whether they demonstrate the highest intellectual potential or whether they have struggled to reach the threshold of higher education – to achieve beyond their expectations'. The Dearing Report appeared to restate Robbins' comprehensive ideal for higher education and eschewed any pretensions to an elite system of education. In particular, the report recognised both the economic and social justice arguments for continuing to widen access. However, Dearing's recommendation to introduce fees for study was seen as a retrograde step. The introduction of student fees became a prominent issue in the elections for the Scottish Parliament and one of the first actions of the Scottish Executive was to set up an independent review of student finance under the chairmanship of Andrew Cubie. The subsequent report recommended the abolition of student fees and the introduction of an endowment which would be repaid when graduates earned over £25,000. Cubie's recommendations were not fully implemented with a compromise being reached whereby Scottish students' fees were paid and graduates' loans would be repayable when their income reached £10,000.

THE ISSUES

In the second part of this chapter, some of the issues arising out of the pattern of progress which has been traced above will be considered. It can be said with confidence that comprehensive compulsory secondary education has been virtually achieved and schools have been successful in achieving a better than 70% participation rate in post-compulsory stages. Much of this achievement is due to the efforts of teachers and schools themselves. Some of the explanation for the improved participation rate also lies in the success of government policy which has effectively insisted on school-leavers remaining in some form of education or training until the age of eighteen. More negatively, an explanation lies in the difficulties young people would experience in finding work if they were to leave school, and the inflation in qualifications required to achieve most kinds of employment. Nevertheless there are encouraging signs that staying on at school may be more than a good thing in itself. Achievement, for example, has kept pace with the higher participation rates. This means that young people derive a positive educational benefit out of staying on at school, though persistent social class inequalities in performance at the top end of achievement at Standard Grade can be distinguished.

New gender inequalities are, however, apparent. Whereas in the early part of the twentieth century it was the case that girls were at a disadvantage in educational terms, a growing trend is apparent in boys' under-performance compared to girls. While explanations for these differences vary, the most plausible explanation seems to lie in peer pressure for under-achievement among boys and their poor perception of prospects in the labour market.

In terms of participation in higher education, significant inroads have been made into the achievement of mass participation. If Robbins' notion of a place for anyone with the ability and aptitude to benefit from higher education is taken as a marker of a comprehensive ideal for access to higher education, Scotland is possibly not far short of the mark. However, there is no room for complacency. The probability of children with fathers in manual work being twice as unlikely to participate in higher education as children of professional fathers, gives grave cause for concern. Though Scotland is now a better educated society than ever before, unacceptable social class and other inequalities persist.

The overall picture of positive progress in higher education in overcoming inequalities does also mask some persistent problems. There exist significant pockets of under-representation in some subjects. In science, technology and engineering there are substantial gender differences in participation which are not wholly accounted for by schools' preparation of young people. Girls are less likely to choose these subjects and are less likely than their male counterparts to persist in them if they do. Entry qualifications do not present a barrier to participation since girls are achieving good grades in mathematics and science, but there may be hidden, cultural barriers, both in society at large and within higher education itself, which conspire to dissuade them from participation in science at university. Research into the factors which affect women's experience of higher education in science, engineering and technology, for example, suggests that the social context of these subjects, and the culture of the departments in which they are taught, are constructed according to a white, male, Euro-centric set of attitudes and values which is not conducive to the participation of excluded groups (Byrne, E., *Women and Science: The Snark Syndrome*, London: Falmer Press, 1993).

Despite schools' success in better preparing young people for higher education, the expansion of higher education provision and enhanced opportunities for adult returners to education, significant structural barriers exist. The costs of participation in terms of maintenance, family responsibilities (especially for mature students) must be overcome. An additional factor lies in the location of a suitable course and the feasibility of living away from home, which means extra resources. The quantitative increase in access provision continues to mask the underlying inequalities for those who are prevented either by life chances or family circumstances from taking advantage of the increases in provision.

The question of whether access to higher education affords the same opportunities in terms of quality of provision and future reward as in the past must also be posed. While the numbers of students in higher education have doubled over the last twenty years, this rapid rise has been achieved against a background of a reduction of more than 40% in funding for higher education over the same period. Furthermore, expansion may be confined to the past by under-investment in universities rather than be likely to progress into a new period of expansion in the years to come. It was precisely this crisis of resources which prompted the government to commission the review of finance in higher education published in the Dearing Report. The abolition of the maintenance grant also made student finance problematic. Many so-called full-time students are already working substantial numbers of hours necessarily to supplement their grants and loans (Smith and Taylor, 1999) with consequent effects on the amount of time available for study and even attendance at classes. Further encroachment into full-time study is likely; indeed, full-time study may become the exception rather than the norm as students in the UK adopt a mode of study prevalent in other countries such as the US, where 'working one's way through college' is commonplace.

Bernstein's definition of the university as 'an institution based on talk' may be all but gone. It can no longer be assumed that the undergraduates of the future will leave home to immerse themselves in study at an institution of their choice with all the social and cultural benefits this may bring. Although study at a home university appears more economical as the cost of maintenance is privatised within the family, it may reduce choice of course and relevance of qualification for an individual.

The opportunities offered by information technology for remote teaching and study such as those provided by the Open University or promised by UHI, and the growing use of virtual learning environments (VLEs) for learning in traditional universities, have the potential to change the dominant, full-time mode of study. The Open University has long recognised the benefits of face-to-face interaction with tutors and peers and has organised for it. While VLEs provide a fairly sophisticated medium for interaction among students and tutors they do not fulfil the need for social interaction.

The need for employment to supplement income may demand more flexible modes of study including modular degrees and the type of sandwich courses more familiar in vocational further education. While these modes of study offer an apparently economical alternative to full-time study, there is necessarily a loss of coherence and consistency in this fragmentation of experience which may be detrimental.

These factors all promise to shape the higher education of the future and it cannot be assumed that the progress of the last forty years will continue. Institutions themselves are changing. The competition for scarce research and teaching funds bring closer the prospect of a two-tier or even three-tier higher education system in which an elite group of universities specialises in research and teaches only an elite group of students; a middle-ranking group which strives to provide quality research and teaching; and a lower rank which cannot compete for research funding and teach large numbers of students. Under the current climate of competitive individualism and diminishing resources, the prospect of a comprehensive higher education system run on the same basis as the comprehensive school, that is, one which provides equity of provision and equality of opportunity, becomes more and more remote.

It appears then, that social justice is a prize which is as yet beyond the grasp of a country which nevertheless has high aspirations for its higher education system. While the economy of Scotland remains static, appeals to economic competitiveness will continue to be made and pressure on institutions to produce more and better graduates will be renewed. But further expansion is likely to be increasingly resource-limited and competitive, and it is more than likely that a return to increased selectivity – of and by students – will be seen. Increased selectivity spells a diminution of opportunity, not expansion. Until the economic position of universities is secured, social justice will remain an aspiration.

REFERENCES

Gayle, V., Berridge, D. and Davies, R. (2002) Young people's entry into higher education, *Oxford Review of Education*, 28 (11), 5–20.

Osborne, M., Leopold, J. and Ferrie, A. (1997) Does access work? The relative performance of access students at a Scottish university, *Higher Education*, 33, 155–76.

Paterson, L. (1997a) Student achievement and educational change in Scotland, 1980–1995, *Scottish Educational Review* 29 (1), 10–19.

Paterson, L. (1997b) Trends in higher education participation in Scotland, *Higher Education Quarterly*, 51, 29–48.

Raab, G. (1998) *Participation in Higher Education in Scotland*, Edinburgh: Napier University.

Smith, N. and Taylor, P. (1999) 'Not for lipstick and lager': students and part-time work, *Scottish Affairs*, 28, Summer.

30

Values Education in Scotland

David Carr

VALUES AND VALUES EDUCATION

The recent growth of interest in values and so-called values education in the UK and elsewhere itself undoubtedly calls for comment: as well as producing a rash of professional conferences, books and papers on the issue, this interest has drawn commentary from such official educational quarters as the National Curriculum Council (NCC), Office for Standards in Education (OfSTED) and Schools Curriculum and Assessment Authority (SCAA). It has also been a focus of widespread political and media attention. All the same, given that on certain fairly uncontroversial interpretations of 'education' and 'values', the expression 'values education' seems something of a pleonasm – what else could education be but a matter of communicating values? – it seems worth asking what has driven more recent interest in values in education. Briefly, it seems likely that three distinguishable but related concerns lie behind this current educational concern.

The first reflects a degree of public panic at what is widely regarded as the breakdown of traditional mores under the influence of liberal individualism and economic consumerism. This is usually held to be evident in a decline of discipline among the young – as exhibited in the drug or crime oriented hedonism of this or that youth culture – but it has been highlighted for many by a number of disquieting, if more sporadic, recent outbursts of individual murder and mayhem. A second related reason, however, seems more symptomatic of a professional concern that recent politically-driven educational reforms have focused more on the economic than the moral benefits of education: that recent emphases on raising standards have been upon the academic or vocational goals of schooling to the serious neglect of more fundamental issues concerning the humanisation of young people. At a more theoretical level, latter-day political preoccupations with the raising of academic and vocational standards might be regarded as simply one expression of those consumerist values of contemporary economic liberalism which have been (allegedly) directly responsible for the spread in Western society of selfish materialism and hedonism. Thus, a third reason echoes a filtering down of concerns – long a source of controversy in contemporary social and moral theory – about how a degree of common social co-operation and purpose might be sustained in that problematic fusion of cultural pluralism and liberal individualism which conditions both the social reality and the political ideology of developed democracies.

In consequence, despite an apparent cross-curricular concern throughout the values education literature with a wider range of human values – with social, intellectual, aesthetic and spiritual as well as moral values – the main focus has undoubtedly been upon the ethical dimension of human development. Recent values education initiatives seem to have been above all concerned to emphasise responsibility for the moral formation of their pupils as an integral part of the professional lives of all teachers – not just specialists in RE or PSD – in the interests of producing individually responsible, law-abiding and socially attached citizens.

But, of course, although it would be improper to suggest that teachers have generally been neglectful of this responsibility, any such emphasis does squarely confront educationalists with a web of conceptual and practical problems about the very character of moral education. So, although space does not here allow for any deep exploration of the moral philosophical complexities of such problems, it may be useful to identify a few key connected moral educational issues. First, there is an issue of freedom versus authority in relation to moral life: insofar as morality is thought of in terms of both obedience to law or rule and freedom of choice – what should be the right balance between moral authority and freedom? This also raises the difficult question of what moral freedom might, as such, mean.

On this matter, despite the denial of some moral theorists that morality is at all a rational matter, most have argued that a capacity to grasp moral reasons is crucially presupposed to any sort of free moral choice. But one must now ask about the logical status and authority of such reasons. On this, whereas some moral theorists would regard moral reasons as deriving from recognition of one's place in a socio-culturally determined network of attachments and responsibilities which sharply define one's moral identity, others – not least so-called 'non-cognitivists' – have regarded moral reasons as no more than personal constructs, by virtue of which individuals are entirely free to form (subject only to requirements of rational consistency) their own commitments and attachments. This, however, raises the issue of whether to construe moral conduct primarily in terms of individual autonomy or social responsibility. In the terms of a very broad distinction of contemporary moral and social theory, those who place the greatest emphasis on individual freedom are often called 'liberals,' whereas those who press more the social dimensions of morality may be referred to as 'communitarians'. Finally, it may be noted that all these issues overlap in interesting and complex ways with respect to the matter of whether any such thing as moral education – as opposed to moral indoctrination – is possible, and it is a common if not clearly justified complaint of liberals that those who locate moral authority in the received socio-cultural values of community are hard put to sustain this distinction.

At all events, given the clear moral educational interest of these difficult issues – which continue to be the focus of heated controversy in the complex literature of modern moral and social philosophy – it would appear that any serious professional interest in moral education must presuppose at least some working knowledge of contemporary ethical theory. However, insofar as modern empirical psychology has also been a source of influential views regarding the processes of moral formation, it is arguable that teachers *qua* moral educators also need to be knowledgeable about the psychology of moral development. It is also likely that many would regard the late American cognitive psychologist Lawrence Kohlberg as the greatest influence on post-war theorising about moral education. Under the initial influence of Piaget (and through him Kant), Kohlberg was the architect of a complex theory of moral formation which sought to track the growth of moral reason through a series of cognitive stages from infancy onwards. Briefly, Kohlberg's cognitive psychology is a constructivism of the sort philosophers would classify as morally 'non-cognitivist' – and, as such, it has strongly liberal individualist leanings.

That said, Kohlberg was from an early stage sensitive to criticisms that his account seriously sidelined the social and inter-personal dimensions of morality, and sought in response to supplement his psychology with a moral sociology of so-called 'communities of justice'. In drawing for this upon ideas in the contractarian tradition, however, Kohlberg could not be said to have departed significantly from a basic liberal position, and his ultimate account is a highly unstable mix of ideas from Dewey, Rawls, Habermas – as well as, as already mentioned, Kant and Piaget. To that extent, it is doubtful whether his various amendments adequately address the sorts of objections that have been raised over the years by, for example, communitarians, post-analytical social philosophers, virtue-theorists and feminists of the 'ethics of care' school. Of more recent challenges to Kohlbergian ideas, perhaps the largely American 'character education' movement has been the most widely influential – despite the lack of any strong theoretical basis to character education, and its alleged association with various forms of right wing reaction to the purported permissivism of contemporary liberalism. A philosophically more sophisticated response to cognitive developmentalism might well be expected from modern (Aristotelian and other) 'ethical naturalists' and 'virtue theorists': but despite evidence of growing educational philosophical interest in virtue theory, such interest is relatively embryonic and it is rather too early to assess its practical impact and implications.

VALUES EDUCATION IN THE SCOTTISH CONTEXT

Although attention to these and other questions currently exercising present-day proponents of values education have ever been high on the agenda of Scottish educationalists – it may here be worth noting that Scots (A. S. Neill and R. F. Mackenzie for two famous examples) have been very much in the vanguard of 'progressive' attempts to give education a more 'human face' – serious Scottish interest in values education as such is, as elsewhere, a relatively recent phenomenon. To be sure, concerns with moral, social, spiritual and religious formation have long featured conspicuously in major Scottish educational initiatives: in this connection, it is noteworthy that whilst these aspects of education were from the outset conceived as crucial components of Scotland's own 5–14 programme, much of the official values education documentation produced by NCC, OfSTED and SCAA south of the border seems to have been by way of compensation for the general failure of the English National Curriculum to give explicit recognition to such issues. Be that as it may, Scottish interest in values education in its current form is probably due in no small part to the timely appearance in the early 1990s of the Aberdeen-based Gordon Cook Foundation.

Although the Gordon Cook Foundation did not of itself create the widespread interest among Scottish teachers and academics in educational values and values in education, the emergence of a very well-endowed charitable trust dedicated precisely to the promotion of better personal and social values among the young – at the generous bequest of the late Aberdeen industrialist for whom the trust is named – has proved an enormous shot in the arm to research and development in fields that have less often been prime targets for funding from more conventional sources. Moreover, although one cannot be sure that Cook grants have invariably been awarded to projects that might have won the ready approval of their benefactor, and while there is always bound to be, in the nature of an enterprise of this sort, much controversy and disagreement about the worth of this or that enterprise, there can be no doubt that the foundation has supported a rich variety of theoretical and practical research and development under the broad heading of 'values education'. It is therefore worth devoting some space here to some of these projects – especially those that have involved collaboration with major Scottish educational institutions and organisations otherwise professionally involved with aspects of values education.

Perhaps the best place to start is with the work throughout the 1990s of the Scottish Consultative Council on the Curriculum (SCCC) which seems to have been one of first beneficiaries of Cook support. Although the council had certainly been exercised by questions about values in the curriculum in the ordinary course of its professional involvement with major Scottish curriculum initiatives from the 1970s onwards, its focus on value aspects of education certainly seems to have been intensified with Cook Foundation stimulus and a constant stream of challenging and sometimes controversial papers greatly helped to keep important issues of educational values and ethos in the spotlight. Hence, beginning with the 1991 publication of *Values in Education*, the SCCC has gone on to produce, with Cook Foundation assistance or under its own steam, a number of significant documents – such as *School Climate and Ethos* (1994), *A Sense of Belonging* (1995) and *The Heart of the Matter* (1995) – all addressed to important issues of personal and social development, school climate and ethos. In addition, the council commissioned works from individual authors researching into questions of values and moral education – including Elliot Eisner, Bart McGettrick and the present writer – for a wide ranging series of essays entitled *Perspectives: Occasional Papers on Values and Education*.

Given the direct concern of the Cook Foundation with educational research and development, it is hardly surprising that Scottish institutions directly concerned with educational research and the professional training of teachers have also received generous Cook funding – and, indeed, two principals of Scottish colleges of education have served on the board of trustees of the Foundation. At one time or another, then, all major Scottish teacher training institutions (now transformed into university faculties of education) have worked on Cook-funded projects concerned to investigate this or that aspect of values education – with particular reference to secondary education (Northern College, 1990, Moray House, 1991), primary education (St Andrews College, 1990), nursery education (Craigie College, 1991), professional teacher education and training (Jordanhill, 1991, Northern, 1990, St Andrews, 1990) and further education (Jordanhill/Strathclyde, 1994). At a level somewhat removed from first-hand professional concerns with teacher training and elementary schooling, however, the Cook Foundation has also supported more academic university ventures in Scotland and elsewhere. A particularly noteworthy initiative has been the impressive series of Victor Cook Memorial Lectures organised by the Centre for Philosophy and Public Affairs at the University of St Andrews. This has featured papers on values and education from Lord Quinton and Professor Anthony O'Hear (1992), Baroness Warnock and Professor Richard Pring (1994), Sir Stewart Sutherland (now Lord Sutherland) and Rabbi Jonathan Sacks (1996), and – in what would appear to conclude the series – Mary Midgely and Brian Appleyard (1998). With additional Cook assistance, however, the centre has also produced other short booklets (of two papers apiece) entitled *Values and Values Education* (David Carr and John Haldane, 1993) and *Values, Education and Responsibility* (Elizabeth Pybus and Terence McLaughlin, 1995).

In addition to its sponsorship of prestigious university lectures, the foundation has also supported the mounting of significant university and higher education conferences on aspects of values education in Scotland and elsewhere. Besides support for recent key conferences on moral and spiritual education outwith Scotland – not strictly within the scope of this chapter – the foundation assisted the University of Edinburgh Centre for Research in Child Development to mount a 1991 conference on the moral development of the child which brought together an international group of leading scholars in the field. However, it should also be noted that several significant Cook-sponsored conferences have been organised by the former colleges of education – Northern College (1995), St Andrews (1996), Moray House (1997), Strathclyde (1998) – for the express purpose of celebrating and monitoring the progress of foundation-funded projects. Once again, many of these have featured presentations and addresses from leading local, national and international lights in values and moral education.

It would be impossible to do full justice to the breadth and extent of Cook-funded work: much valuable assistance has been given to individual educational and/or teacher research-ers often operating in relative independence from major research agencies, institutions and organisations in Scotland and elsewhere. Indeed, as already noted, much Cook funding has gone to projects conceived and implemented well beyond the borders of Scotland. Thus, rounding off this brief Cook's tour in fairly short order, it must suffice to mention just a few of the notable associations and/or collaborations between significant Scottish agencies and the foundation. One such continuing collaboration has been with the Scottish Council for Research in Education (SCRE). As well as supporting a number of professional research projects into values aspects of education – concerning, for example, parents perceptions of values education (1991) and values in the primary school (1992) – the foundation has consulted SCRE in evaluating the effectiveness of its own activities as a funding agency (1996, 1997). Some of SCRE's work, as well as other research and development initiatives inside Scotland and beyond, were usefully highlighted in a special pull-out feature of the *Times Education Supplement Scotland* – also supported by the foundation – in June 1995.

Other instances of collaboration between the foundation and Scottish organisations have included support for initiatives mounted by the Scottish Environmental Council (1995), the Scottish Community Education Council (1996), the Scottish Parents Consultative Forum (1996), Glasgow City Council Education Department (1995), the Highland Award Project (1993), Grampian Police (1995) and the former Scottish Office Education Department (1995). This last collaboration is noteworthy insofar as the SOED and its recent successor SEED have continued to be – in virtue of their leadership and overseer roles with respect to educational provision in Scotland – authors of many values-implicated school initiatives. A key school values collaboration with the Scottish Office Education Department, has been the development of *Ethos Indicators* (1992) for use in self-evaluation by primary and secondary schools. In this connection, the longstanding experience of the Inspectorate in assessing the quality of school ethos and relationships has also proved invaluable in the development of diagnostic and other tools for school-based monitoring of the value dimensions of their work.

Indeed, since the development of ethos indicators, school-based work on the promotion of positive educational climate and relationships has progressed further with the establish-ment in 1994–5 of the Scottish Schools Ethos Network. In the course of encouraging innovative work on the improvement of educational ethos, the network has from 1997 to the present awarded ethos prizes on an annual basis to particular primary and secondary schools across the Scottish system, and the details of these achievements are to be found in *Building on Success: Case Studies of Ethos Award Winners 1997–2001* (2002). Such work on school ethos should also be seen as related to – indeed, as one practical expression of – a Scottish Executive concern to promote a revitalised sense of citizenship on the part of schoolchildren. A review group on citizenship education was set up in October 1999 and the results of its deliberations have now been published under the title *Education for Citizenship: A Paper for Discussion and Development* (2002).

One could not possibly conclude even a brief survey of the current state of values education in Scotland without appropriate recognition of the important role that the religious communities (of all major world faiths) have continued to play in the moral and spiritual formation of young people – both in the course of personal religious witness and via faith community initiatives. However, given the history of Scotland's cultural development – not least the major formative influence that patterns of immigration, particularly from Ireland, have had on that development – most substantial communities of faith in Scotland inevitably fall either side of the main Western Christian confessional divide. Several leaders of values education initatives and projects in Scotland are active Catholics or Protestants – but, more importantly, the main Christian denominations have continued to have significant influence on values education in mainstream state and independent schooling. What, of course, is immediately distinctive about Catholic values education in Scotland is that it has long been pursued in a relatively separate sector of state maintained schooling which continues to be a matter of some controversy. Nevertheless, there can be no doubt that the Catholic Church has in this context sought in both policy and practice to remain faithful to a particular vision of the inseparability of moral and other human values from the religious and divine which continues to offer a powerful challenge to contemporary secular materialism.

CRITICAL EVALUATION OF RECENT VALUES INITIATIVES

Nothing has so far been said about the overall character and quality of all these diverse values initiatives. The most general thing that might be said, however, is that there is no such overall character, and the quality appears to have been rather variable. A fair proportion of the work – that which, perhaps, falls most obviously under the heading of research – seems to have been fairly straightforwardly descriptive or fact-finding, though usually with a view to assisting the formulation of school or other educational policy proposals. Some other work has been of a more academic or theoretical kind, focused primarily upon the conceptual clarification of aspects of moral and evaluative discourse – though there has been some hesitance on the part of the Cook and other research funding agencies to target such work for support, given a questionable assumption that such investigations are of less urgent practical import than direct developmental work in schools. Apart from the implications any such assumption might have for the coherence of practical work lacking appropriate conceptual clarification, however, it is arguable that it also presupposes a questionable view of the actual relationship of moral philosophy, discourse or 'theory' to moral practice.

At all events, much recent work does seem to have been of a more practical developmental than philosophical or theoretical kind. Some seems to have been concerned, perhaps in the light of empirical research, to try to change or modify aspects of the educational environment – for example, school climate and discipline, teacher–student relationships or patterns of pupil motivation – in the interests of 'improving' institutional ethos or reducing what are perceived to be 'negative' aspects of juvenile behaviour. To that extent, however, it may be that at least some values initiatives have operated according to a more or less manipulative agenda of social engineering or behaviour modification – no matter how well-intentioned this may have been. By contrast, other work seems to have focused less on environmental conditioning or behaviour shaping and more on the education of moral reason and understanding. But such work raises rather different problems concerning the very character, point and purpose of moral and other evaluative deliberation.

Given the aforementioned post-war influence of Kohlberg, it is hardly surprising that many values education initiatives focused upon the development of moral reason – in Scotland as elsewhere – have pursued a quasi-Kohlbergian strategy of moral dilemma exploration broadly aimed at the resolution of moral problems. It is probably best to speak of a 'broadly' Kohlbergian strategy, since there may be some doubts about the methodological purity of much teacher-initiated work of this kind. Many other pedagogical approaches employed in values education – such as Values Clarification and Matthew Lipman's Philosophy for Children – utilise techniques of dilemma exploration and it seems likely that much street level values education pedagogy is a theoretically loose blend of ideas drawn from somewhat disparate sources. But the fact is that, mixed or pure, all such work raises familiar difficulties about the precise point and purpose of moral deliberation.

One point on which there is much agreement is that moral dilemmas are of a significantly different logical character from scientific or artistic problems, and therefore that moral reason does not function in relation to moral problems as scientific or artistic reasoning work for the resolution of theoretical or technical problems. Indeed, if it is a hallmark of a moral dilemma or conflict that it is precisely unsusceptible of any theoretical or technical solution, then it becomes difficult to see how moral reasoning – construed either as a moral decision procedure or as a form of values clarification – could have much, if any, rational or educational point. The trouble is that such 'reason' is liable to collapse either (on a values clarification interpretation) into a form of moral subjectivism or relativism, or (on a Kohlbergian constuctivist interpretation) into some kind of non-cognitivist personal commitment to self-legislated principles – neither of which provides much basis for genuine education in moral enquiry. What would therefore seem to be required for this purpose – as a legion of critics of liberal individualist moral theory have, in their different ways, argued – is a quite different conception of the role of practical reason in human affairs.

A more general problem with the current spate of new values education activity may lie with the wide diversity of educational and other aims which seem to have been included within its overall compass. From one viewpoint, such diversity might be welcome: one might regard the garden of values education as one in which a thousand flowers bloom (and one might tolerate the few weeds that also flourish as worth the diversity). It seems to be in some such spirit of openness that the Cook Foundation claims to eschew allegiance to any particular values agenda. But reluctance to co-ordinate diverse practical activities or bring them in line with some overall strategic plan may also be logistically problematic if the normative and evaluative foundations of different projects and initiatives differ to the point of practical inconsistency.

Hence, although it seems proper and laudable enough that a given values education initiative aims to promote morally-principled, law-abiding citizens who are also able to identify with some sort of community, such praiseworthy but nevertheless different aims may also be in some tension. First, there seems to be an enormous unresolved confusion at the heart of the values education movement between education and social control. It has already been seen that although some programmes appear to focus upon getting young people to think for themselves in the interests of forming their own personal values, others seem more concerned with negative modes of social engineering. Again, although some researchers seem busily occupied in trying to create some sense of cultural attachment for the promotion of a greater sense of human fellowship, others are just as busy trying to heal those social divisions which are, at home and abroad, in part the result of such attachment. In short, it is not obvious that moral education (in any robust sense) would be the best route to crime reduction; the most effective ways of reducing crime or producing socially conformist behaviour may well be subversive of moral development; a strong sense of cultural identification might inhibit rather than foster greater moral reflection; and so on. There is therefore at least a danger that any large-scale attempt to promote values education which does not systematically address the normative and conceptual questions underlying these potential conflicts of goals is liable, whatever good otherwise comes of it, to spend some of the time falling over its own feet.

REFERENCES

Advisory Council of Learning and Teaching Scotland (2002) *Education for Citizenship in Scotland: A Paper for Discussion and Development*. Dundee: LTS.

Carr, David (1996) *The Moral Role of the Teacher*, Perspectives on Values 3. Edinburgh: SCCC Publications.

Haldane, John (ed.) (1993) *Education, Values and the State* (Victor Cook Memorial Lectures by Baroness Warnock and Professor Richard Pring), University of St Andrews: Centre for Philosophy and Public Affairs.

Halstead, Mark and Taylor, Monica, J. (eds) (1996) *Values in Education and Education in Values*, London and Washington DC: Falmer Press.

Haydon, Graham (1997) *Teaching about Values: A New Approach*, London: Cassell.

SSEN (2002) *Building on Success: Case Studies of Ethos Award Winners* 1997–2001, Edinburgh: Scottish Executive.

V

Pre-School and Primary Education: Organisation and Management

31

Early Education and Childcare

Aline-Wendy Dunlop

The last decade has marked an unprecedented time of development in early education and childcare in Scotland. Most recently a number of changes anticipated by Watt in the first edition of *Scottish Education* (pp. 307–15) have come to fruition; other changes and the rate of change could not have been foreseen at the time of writing. This chapter sets out to summarise and trace the route by which the place of early education and childcare have become closely related and to record both the relationships and the distinctiveness of the services and the issues which surround them. It will focus on the youngest children: under-threes, and on the lives and experience of children from three to five years when they are not taking part in the twelve and a half hours per week of free pre-school education to which all 3- and 4-year-olds have become entitled since the end of the year 2002.

Early education and care is now widely seen as fundamental to lifelong learning and social change. The Thematic Review of Early Childhood Education and Care Policy undertaken by the Organisation for Economic Co-operation and Development (OECD, 2001), reports taking a broad and holistic approach to studying children's early development and learning. The review considered all education and care arrangements for children under compulsory school age, 'regardless of setting, funding, opening hours, or programme content' (p. 3). The review also investigated links between family support, health, employment, and social integration policy domains. It emphatically stated its consideration of care and education as inseparable and made recommendations for improving both quality and access to integrated services.

At the heart of these discussions lie the place and status of the child, the family and the education–care balance. The focus of this chapter emphasises early education and care rather than early schooling which is addressed in the following chapter.

LOOKING BACK: A HISTORICAL VIEW

An understanding of the legacy of early years traditions, themes in policy-focused early years research in Scotland, the position of women in the home and workplace, and the role of the local authority in supporting early education and childcare, are each important in considering change and weighing up its value. There is a strong tradition of early childhood practice in Scotland, from Robert Owen's day, through to the early years of the last century with the inner city child gardens which flourished in Scottish cities at that time, to the present with a continuing commitment to the child as an individual and to the uniqueness of early childhood (Dunlop, 2001).

Since the 1970s, priorities for what educational research was undertaken into provision for our youngest children have been focused on co-ordination of services for under-fives, the integration of children with special educational needs (SEN), the provision in rural areas, staff training, ethnic minority issues and parental needs, interest and involvement. However the first initiative to link education and care only came about in the mid-1980s when the then Strathclyde Region established policy to create community nurseries which were to provide both education and care in an integrated way under one roof, or through one service. Some of the challenges faced by that initiative have still to be resolved, for example: the different training backgrounds of early years personnel and the relative values placed on the different expertise.

Alongside these public sector debates ran the development of private and voluntary provision. Unless deemed to be in need, families had little access to extended day care unless they sought this privately: working parents found that early years education was set up to provide for their children, but not for family need as a whole, and certainly not to allow women to join the workforce. The playgroup movement which had started its campaign to promote more nursery education in Scotland in 1967, over the years developed services itself and became established in its own right, claiming a greater sensitivity to parents' needs and to ways of involving parents in their children's development and learning than was widely established in the public sector of the time.

The playgroup movement developed an infrastructure of training, of fieldworkers and of fundraising which fostered wide development. Playgroups grew up in locations where nursery education and care did not: government uncertainty in face of the costs of pre-school provision meant that other services grew up to fill the gap. In some cases these services also attracted government or local government grants.

The various services were characterised by their different aims, lack of uniformity, uncertainty as to their future and variability of the standard of experience offered to young children. From the late 1980s, with the increasing articulation of the primary school curriculum, debate ensued on what the pre-school curriculum should be like. Publicly provided nursery education began to define curriculum and by the mid-1990s most local authority areas had produced a curriculum document. The development of quality assurance mechanisms occurred in the public and independent sectors almost simultaneously. Such initiatives led to the publication of *Performance Indicators in Nursery School/Class/Pre-five Unit Self-evaluation* (Edinburgh: SOED, 1995) and of *A Curriculum Framework for Children in their Pre-school Year* (HMI, Edinburgh: Scottish Office, 1997) which was offered for consultation throughout Scotland. The development of a national curriculum framework has been marked by the willingness to consult at each stage of development. In 1999 the present version, *A Curriculum Framework for Children 3 to 5*, (SCCC, 1999) was published.

In considering the context of early education up to the early 1990s, Watt raised a key question: 'What is pre-five education outside the home for and how can it be justified?' and then identified four subsidiary questions (*Scottish Education*, 1st edn p. 307). She went on to consider each of these issues in turn, embedding them in their historical context and then relating them to the climate of development in 1999. In turning the corner into a new millennium these questions still hold a place, but the answers to them are now very different.

The new language of policy might ask: 'What is early childhood education and care for and how can it be justified?' In answer it is now possible to assert that the rationale for early childhood education and care ('pre-five' is no longer a useful description as it implies pre-schooling and only for the year immediately preceding entry to school) is now much more clearly understood and embedded in policy in Scotland than it was even three or four years ago. Government policy points clearly to the early years as a prime time to begin to make a difference: raising achievement, social inclusion, health needs, children's rights, the support of families of very young children in deprived areas, and the education and training of a suitable workforce to meet these policy needs have never been higher on the political agenda than they are today. It is clear that these various forms of early intervention into child and family life are deemed by government to hold a promise for what children will become and therefore how society itself may change (Fabian & Dunlop, 2002).

Central to developments, education and care are increasingly advocated as inseparable if not yet fully integrated services. Early education is now available to all 3- and 4-year-olds in Scotland, and additional services are aimed at those in social need. Partnership in provision is expected of local government which, in meeting the statutory duty to provide early years education and care, are expected to set up and support Childcare Partnerships of public, private and voluntary sectors. There is no doubt that early education is now seen as a legitimate contender for educational resources, and that these will continue to expand as indicated in the present government spending review (September 2002).

A PRESENT VIEW

Major changes to date include: the introduction of a national curriculum for 3–5 years, thus giving greater recognition to pre-school education; the provision of a pre-school education place for every 3- and 4-year-old and children in their deferred year with January/February birthdays, and the opportunity to have this combined with childcare; the establishment of Childcare Partnerships in every local authority area to work in partnership with private and voluntary providers; the requirement for an Early Education and Childcare Plan in every local authority area, and improved co-ordination of services through Out of School Childcare and Wrap Around Care.

The status of pre-school education has changed: for the first time there is a statutory duty on local authorities to provide pre-school education, and this is to be done through the development of Childcare Partnerships. Politically these developments are driven by concerns over under-achievement, the real difficulties experienced in attempting to integrate early education and care, the consideration of out-of-school care, social inclusion policies, the presumption of mainstream education for all and the present focus on the very young children: the under-threes.

The aims to develop services to meet the needs of families with young children, to expand quality early years and out-of-school care provision and to train the early years workforce has been matched by funding streams to make this possible through Sure Start Scotland funding, the Childcare Strategy Funding, the Pre-School Education Development Grant and the New Opportunities Fund. The flexibility of the additional resources has been useful in enabling a range of developments, for example: additional places for children aged 0–3 years; staffing to support parents through providing parent groups; individual support and the development of specialist services to work with families; greater commitment to quality and quality assurance; and the publication of national quality assurance material designed for both care and education.

The strength of political will to bring about change on this scale has led to a number of major changes. Nationally, the emphasis has been on the rising profile of childcare issues and attention to the childcare sector generally; a new focus on monitoring quality expressed by government as 'standards, benchmarks and outcomes', beginning with the Curriculum Framework and extending in 2002 to the care standards operated by the National Care Commission; new initiatives on 0–3s and the beginnings of a new partnership relationship amongst early years practitioners which aims eventually to support a fully integrated service.

The introduction of National Care Standards for Early Education and Childcare up to the age of sixteen was heralded in the Gulbenkian Foundation Report *Effective Government Structures for Children* (1996) which speculated on the development of a new focus on children for the Scotland of the future. The issues raised then included the setting up of a Care Commission: five years later legislation was passed to ensure this happened.

The Regulation of Care (Scotland) Act 2001 determined that the new national care standards would apply equally to public, private and voluntary sector services and in premises (domestic and non-domestic) which provide for care for over two hours a day and for six days or more each year. The range of services covered includes nursery classes, crèches, childminders, after-school clubs and playgroups. The consultation included the following groups: the Scottish Childminding Association; the Scottish Pre-School Play Association; the Scottish Independent Nurseries Association and the Scottish Out-of-School Care Network. The main focus of the standards is the quality of life experienced by users of the service: whether child, young person, parents or carer; so aiming to ensure a variety of perspectives on early education and childcare.

Further, the standards claim to reflect the rights of children and young people as set down by the UN Convention on the Rights of the Child. The main principles of the National Care Standards are: dignity, privacy, choice, safety, realising potential and equality and diversity.

Of the 188,000 children in Scotland attending 4,117 centres covered by census (nursery, playgroups, playschemes, out-of-school care, crèche or family centres), 59% were either 3- or 4-years-old. Twenty-nine per cent of the children covered by the census were under three: this figure represents 31,699 children (SEED, summary results of the 2002 Pre-school and Daycare Census, Education and Children's Statistics Unit, News Release, 10 September, 2002). In total, 98,769 children attended early years pre-school settings of some type.

At the time of publication, whilst nearly three-quarters of Scottish 3- and 4-year-olds as well as those on deferred entry to primary school make use of local authority provision, 26.5% of children aged three and four attend pre-school early education settings run by partnership providers in a range of community, workplace, private, independent, voluntary and playgroup provision (census statistics cited above). These centres must comply with conditions set for them in order to become providers: these include the development of a Profile of Provision, adherence to the 3–5 curriculum and to registration and inspection standards. Often such centres provide extended hours, two and a half hours daily of which the child may attend through a funded partnership place with additional paid-for hours in the same setting. Large numbers of children attend a variety of different provision during the course of the day or week, and these transitions may be a challenge to them (Fabian & Dunlop, 2002).

As Local Authorities worked to achieve targets for universal provision for 3- and 4-year-olds by the end of 2002, new developments have arisen. Care standards will be inspected annually, education inspection by HMIE becomes three yearly. The challenge to avoid uniformity, given that diversity and choice are seen as markers of quality, to provide parents with sufficient information and to consult with them over their control of choice are issues raised in a study of the *Effectiveness of One Scottish Local Authority in Providing a High Quality Pre-school Education Service to Meet the Varied Needs of Children and Families within a Context of Partnership* (McDonagh, MSc University of Strathclyde, 2002). The need for greater flexibility is highlighted, as is the need to find ways of providing equitably for all families by offering more than the thirty-three weeks of provision currently available in partnership settings, which contrasts sharply with the forty weeks in local authority provision. A relative concept, true partnership can only develop if it is based on mutuality as well as co-operation.

CONCEPTS OF LEARNING AND THE EDUCATION AND CARE RELATIONSHIP

As more and more young children enter group day care and education it is essential that the rhetoric of documentation can be translated into approaches which are favourable for children. Such discussion must go beyond how resources are provided or space is used, to the very core of the dynamics of human learning. Through national documentation, and individually we may all have the best interests of children at heart. Central to achieving their best interests are the relationships developed with children, between adults and children and between children themselves. The notion of learning in companionship (Trevarthen, 2001) has never been more important. The quality of interaction, the sustained involvement of children in matters which interest them and the development of self-confidence and positive dispositions to learning are crucial. Without companionship relationships, one cannot be sure of reaching the child: joint and mutual involvement fosters joint creation of meaning (Dunlop, 2002, current research).

'Those settings which see cognitive and social development as complementary achieve the best profile in terms of child outcomes' (Siraj-Blatchford et al., 2002, p. 10). Such approaches are especially effective when they are also encouraged in the home in terms of parental support. However this research also highlights that in more disadvantaged areas staff need to go beyond supporting parental needs and simply involving them as helpers, and become more dynamic in influencing and supporting the parents' role in developing the home learning environment. If children's learning is also supported at home, such shared and proactive enterprise promises to influence children's developmental progress. A concept of education as two and a half hours a day is clearly insufficient: this core element of planned learning is a beginning. Education is not confined to learning in institutions. Further, the developing recognition of pre-school children as learners, along with the recognition of the place of continuity and progression in children's learning, is likely to have an impact on the early stages of the primary school.

OUT-OF-SCHOOL CHILD CARE

In taking a closer look at the numbers of children in Scotland involved in out-of-school care, a number of issues are raised – 3,481 children under one; 7,754 1-year-olds and 20,434 2-year-olds are in out-of-home care, excluding those with childminders, nannies and other domestic provision. For these children it is important to know how their involvement in such settings affects them both day-to-day and in the longer term. Such experience is often highly favourable, but what are the features that make it so, and conversely what sorts of experiences should be avoided in the interests of the well-being, resilience and successful involvement of children in learning? In terms of out-of-school care, 28,500 6–8 + -year-olds attended such facilities at the time of the 2002 census.

The census also gives figures for the maximum number of pre-school and daycare places available at any one time to children in Scotland: this was 145,447 in school term time. This figure reduced to 53,806 in school holidays and this in itself raises issues about forms of care and whether young children are adequately provided for outside of the two and a half hours per day entitlement to free pre-school education and outside the forty weeks of term time.

In January 2002 there were over 4,100 centres offering pre-school education or daycare for children. Just over half of the centres described themselves as nurseries and a further 26% as playgroups. The remaining 23% of centres were made up of out-of-school care clubs (11%), playschemes (4%), crèches (4%) and family centres (4%). Broad headings may over-simplify the complexities of out-of-school care. It is likely that children are involved in a very wide range of experiences including out-of-school clubs such as breakfast clubs, study groups, and holiday clubs, childminder care, informal adult care, no care, self and sibling care, sitter/relative care, neighbour care, day-care centre care, school based programmes, activity-oriented programmes including a range of academic and curricular activities, TV viewing and what children and young people might describe as 'chilling out'.

Involvement in a range of provisions during the day or over a week or the year raises a number of key areas for further investigation. The model taken in the feasibility study of the impact of out-of-school-care, undertaken by the Thomas Coram Research Unit and The National Centre for Social Research (DfES, 2001) highlights certain key areas for investigation which are equally relevant in Scotland and could provide a model for investigation. The possible benefits and the outcomes for children, schools and communities in Scotland are not yet known.

THE VARIETY OF PEOPLE INVOLVED WITH YOUNG CHILDREN

Given the range of settings and the age and circumstances of the children involved, it is likely that not only are children experiencing a series of physical transitions from place to place, but also a series of approaches and a wide variety of people with whom to relate. The increased emphasis on the training of staff is needed and the development of a flexible framework for it has been helpful in enabling this workforce to access opportunities.

TRAINING BACKGROUNDS

The census found a total of just over 27, 000 people working in pre-school and daycare centres; 98% of these are women with a mix of part- and full-time working hours. Very few men work in early childhood education and care, slightly more work in out-of-school care and leisure time facilities. Anecdotal evidence of withdrawal of staff from the sector resulted in a survey commissioned by SEED: it was the first of its kind in Scotland. It is important to the development of the Childcare Strategy and is reported in SEED *Interchange 73*.

Significantly more staff are employed on a part-time basis than full-time. Around 60% hold some form of childcare related qualification, with most staff in pre-school centres (85%) and out of-school clubs (78%) employed on a permanent basis and jobs are often held for five years or more. Staff in the sector are not highly qualified, with those in early years service being more highly qualified than those in other parts of the sector. Approximately 60% of childcare staff across Scotland (around 20,000) hold some form of childcare related qualification (including some non-recognised qualifications such as modules). The most commonly held (33%) is at SVQ3/HNC level. SVQ4/HND level qualifications are held by only 3% of staff, and teaching/degree level by 10%. SVQ2 and SVQ modules are each held by fewer than one in ten staff.

The Training Challenge funding, which was initially for two years from 2000, has now been extended to four years: a fully qualified workforce is heralded for 2004. To what level will such a workforce be qualified? A significant finding of the Effective Provision of Pre-School Education (EPPE) project is the improved learning outcomes for children who experienced teacher involvement in their early education: both because of the direct contact with the teacher, but also because of the raised quality of learning interactions which occurred in teams of staff where teachers were included. In Scotland we need to consider very carefully the way in which teachers continue to play a part in early education and care settings, given the January 2002 *Guidance on Involvement of Teachers in Pre-School Education* (SEED, 2002), as well as the general level of qualifications achieved and aimed for, for all staff, by 2004 and beyond. In 2002 it was estimated that 1,882 teachers were employed in this sector in Scotland: current research would suggest that their role is crucial and should not be underestimated if government is to achieve its desired outcomes for early education and care.

STATUS OF STAFF AND RECRUITMENT

Average pay levels for this sector appear low but the responsibilities of childcare staff are significant and qualifications are desirable. Pre-school centres and out-of-school clubs continue to take on new staff. Of the 27% in the census who had recruited or attempted to recruit in the previous year, one third of pre-school centres and 60% of out-of-school clubs had had difficulty filling paid posts. As services develop and the need for staff grows, the challenge to maintain and develop quality will also grow.

LOOKING FORWARD: FUTURE DEVELOPMENTS

Since government now accepts that investment in early childhood services can be justified, the new broad, unanswered question is 'What difference will such interventions into children's present lives make in the long term?' Government has never been more certain that it can make a difference, but its ambitions raise both perennial and new subsidiary questions:

- Should the focus be on children's present experience or on what they should become and what are the implications of such a question?
- To what extent do the new provisions ensure satisfactory partnership, diversity, and choice?
- Is quality fully understood and can quality be ensured at the same time as increased coverage for 0–5 and out-of-school care?
- What are the effects of curriculum definition for 3- and 4-year-olds on the 5–14 programme and vice-versa?

- With the difficulties of recruitment and take-up of work in the early years and childcare services, how can their status and recruitment needs be met ?
- What is the place of parents and families in developments for their children?

The growth of confidence in the pre-school sector and its established place in government thinking and funding is now more evident. With a feeling that developments for 3- and 4-year-olds are now well in place, the new focus is likely to be on policy making and thinking about practice for 0–3-year-olds. Account will need to be taken of children's present experience and how change may influence future outcomes. This hope for the future is dependent on well-thought-through policy and considered allocation of funding and on asking all concerned what is indeed in the best interests of children. There is a sense in which the pressure on children to 'become' outweighs an appreciation of who they currently are. Positive approaches will value children for who they are now, as well as their potential as future citizens.

Care needs to be taken to understand children's learning and probably to avoid over-formalising it too early, however the move towards curriculum definition and a constructive assessment process with explicit attention to transition to school can support this focus on appropriate childhood experience. Part of this will be the recognition that education can be offered, whatever the location of provision or its funding source or sector.

The nature of the voluntary sector has already changed greatly as it moves towards the meeting of new standards and maintains its eligibility for funding. Can quality be defined universally, or should the context carefully be considered? The positive and distinctive features of voluntary sector provision need to be safeguarded if a mutually respectful partnership and collaboration is to be achieved. The home and community remain the most powerful influences on children: family needs are not static; diversity, flexibility and choice are needed to match the diversity in our communities.

With several sets of standards, the integration of education and care inspection is an important priority in the early years field. Integrated structures are needed if integrated services are to result. Present structures may sustain the care/education divide. There is a danger that a shift to thinking about inspection and less attention explicitly and directly to development, accompanied by a changing ethos among those carrying out the inspection and registration, could challenge the advances in educational provision and practice of recent years.

In terms of recruitment to early childhood services, the Training Challenge is aptly named. It has been seen that the status of workers in the sector is low and responsibilities high. Recognised professional pathways need to be introduced and could encourage take-up of training opportunities. A new initial training route, which will encompass the development of a broader range of skills and knowledge, required for working in the early years field, may be another important consideration. The very real responsibilities involved in early education and childcare demand a review of the age of entry to early childhood training and entry qualifications commensurate with the many demands of such work. Professionalism and respect for the profession are important concepts.

RESEARCH

'Research cannot make the decisions for policy makers and others concerned with improving the quality of education and services for children. Nor can it by itself bring about change. However, it can create a better basis for decisions, by providing information and explanation about policy and practice and by clarifying and challenging ideas and assumptions.'(SEED, *Interchange* 73, 2002).

Currently research in early education and care in Scotland has moved on from attempts to define and measure 'good or best quality' to a less prescriptive focus on the perspective of stakeholders and examination of the experience of children. This is an important development in terms of children's rights to be heard. It will be important to continue to ask, 'How is it for children?' and to ask that of the children themselves. So too further exploration of the child as a learner and the appropriate pedagogy (including ICT) to support that learning is needed.

REFLECTIONS

To what extent are childcare partnerships true partnerships, or are they just a maintenance of inequalities? To what extent are the evident training needs of the early education and care workforce being met in ways which are appropriate to the working context of the practitioners? To what extent will the contributions of the different training/education backgrounds continue to be valued or should moves be made towards the recognition that the higher the academic background of the worker, the higher the quality of interaction, and the more sustained learning opportunities and learning for children will be? At the time of writing the Scottish Executive has announced its approach to the three-year spending review which sets out policy commitments to 2005–6. The investment is welcome. Will the work done be more of the same or might the Scottish Education Debate generate a more radical set of approaches to early childhood education and care?

The Scottish Minister for Education and Young People is quoted as saying, 'We know we will do better in the school years if we get it right in the early years' (Cathy Jamieson, *TESS*, 20 September 2002). The debate about what 'getting it right' means in practice, must continue.

REFERENCES

Dunlop, A. W. A. (2001). The child at the centre. Early childhood provision and curriculum in Scotland, in V. Sollars (ed.), *Curricular Policies and Practices in Early Childhood Education*. Malta: University of Malta.

Fabian, H. and Dunlop, A. W. A. (eds) (2002) *Transitions in the Early Years. Debating Continuity and Progression for Children in Early Education*, London: Routledge Falmer.

Munton, A. G., La Valle, I., Barreau, S., Pickering, K. and Pitson, L. (2001) *Feasibility Study for a Longitudinal Survey of the Impact of Out-of-School Childcare on Children*, Research Report 319, London: Department for Education & Skills.

Organisation for Economic Co-operation and Development (2001) *Starting Strong: Early Childhood Education and Care*, France: OECD Publications.

Siraj-Blatchford, I., Sylva, K., Muttock, S., Gilden, R., Bell, D. (2002) *Researching Effective Pedagogy in the Early Years*, Research Report 356, London: Department for Education & Skills.

Trevarthen, C. (2001) Intrinsic motives for companionship in understanding: their origin, development and significance for infant mental health, *International Journal of Infant Mental Health*, 22(1–2) 95–131.

32

Early Education and Schooling

Anne Hughes and Sue Kleinberg

This chapter focuses on 3–8-year-olds in nursery and infant schooling. It may seem puzzling to have Chapter 31 on early education and childcare then to find this one overlapping by its inclusion of 3–5-year-olds. This is partly in response to Executive policy which deems two and a half days per week to constitute 'pre-school' education but also in recognition of the longstanding debate on the age range which constitutes early education. The education debate rests on the extent to which children in this age range have distinctive ways of learning and therefore might require distinctive educational provision. The debate is currently heightened by a government policy agenda to provide a 'joined up' response to issues such as universal pre-five attendance, raising standards in literacy and numeracy, social inclusion, adult employment and childcare. There is concern that pre-school and the early stages of primary schooling are conceptualised jointly as an early start to 'schooling' in terms of an early focus on literacy and numeracy and what children need to learn to progress in school as opposed to more traditional conceptualisations of holistic and developmental approaches to early education. This chapter will seek to outline current practice and to explore factors of importance.

THE DISTINCTIVENESS OF YOUNG CHILDREN'S LEARNING AND THE SCOTTISH RESPONSE

Why has early childhood been regarded as special? Traditionally it has been seen as a time of rapid development in all areas of learning. The acquisition and development of language, and social, physical, emotional, moral and spiritual intelligences/capabilities are all seen as inter-related, equally valuable and to be fostered, indeed nurtured, by a curriculum which is responsive to the child. Whilst not discarding the role of direct verbal instruction, recognition was given to the motivational power of curiosity, play, activity, interest, first-hand experience and the creation of meaningful contexts. The subject-centred curriculum and transmission models of pedagogy were seen as less appropriate for an age group which had not acquired the symbol systems used by older children. Propositional, 'know that', knowledge was deemed less important than process, 'know how', knowledge in laying the foundations for such learning. The learning environment should be health promoting, safe but challenging and leading to positive attitudes to learning, the self, and others.

Support for the views held by pioneers in the field of practice came from the work of

Piagetian psychologists. This suggested marked changes in the nature of logic a young child used which were seen as based on age-related stages. Whilst Piaget did not underestimate the influence of the environment on development, his work was interpreted by many as indicating that a loosely structured curriculum with varied and rich resources to explore was sufficient for such development to occur. The significance of later work in child development cannot be neglected. The work of Donaldson in *Children's Minds* (London: Fontana, 1978) showing the contextually embedded nature of children's learning, and Tizard and Hughes in *Young Children Learning* (London: Fontana, 1984) showing the competence of children in the home context are perhaps best known. More recently the work of such as Vygotsky and Rogoff has influenced understanding of the importance of relationships and social context on learning. The former's concept of the zone of proximal development draws attention to the things which a child can do only with the guidance and scaffolding help from a more expert person. Similar ideas are contained in the work on peer social learning and the metaphor of the child as an apprentice. It also has implications for the roles which educators might adopt in early education clearly highlighting facilitation, support and modelling rather than direct instruction.

Whilst such work in child development can be seen as endorsing the principles of early education, it can also be seen as showing the importance of the parent/carer in promoting learning. Studies show how, in the home context, the adult's contribution is more likely to be initiated by the child and be more readily interpreted through a shared culture and intimate knowledge of contexts. This work gives additional support to the concept of the parent as key educator providing continuity and having implications for partnership with schools.

Parents of children in primary school have certain rights to information and to representation on school boards. No such rights exist in the nursery sector. However, the involvement of parents in early education has been a feature across both sectors possibly because of the close proximity of staff and carers as young children are brought to and collected from the establishment. Innovations in the form of pre-entrant visits, workshops on specific curriculum aspects and parental assistance with classroom activities, materials and visits are now well established. However, it is probably true to say that genuine involvement in decision making and participation in curriculum and assessment remain largely a professional concern.

Two research traditions have helped build knowledge about how young children learn. The first were studies relating to the impact of provision and types of provision, the second to child development. Research in the first sought evidence of measurable and lasting gains for the disadvantaged, but many findings were difficult to generalise because of the designs of the studies. Much of the work in Scotland focused on examining learning in different pre-school settings with very little work on learning in the infant class (see Mooney, A. & Munton, A. G.,1999.

The SED memorandum, *Primary Education in Scotland* (Edinburgh: HMSO, 1950) recognised the distinctiveness of the infant years. It acknowledged that although nursery education was already seen as separated from infant provision both sectors should subscribe to the same principles, stating that it should 'in practice make little difference whether a child spent the two years, five to seven, at the top of a nursery school or the bottom of a primary school' (p. 130). As we will see, that statement could not now be made.

The potential conflict between the traditional responsive curriculum of early education and the subject-centred nature of the 5–14 reform has not gone unrecognised. In 1992 the

Scottish Consultative Council on the Curriculum produced *Reflections on Curriculum Issues – Early Education*. This document still used the term early education to cover pre-schooling and the infant stages but raised questions such as: should future advice focus on the 3–8 age group or pre-fives? How can continuity in learning in early education be addressed? Should advice be related to areas of the curriculum or should it focus on specific issues, for instance play, motivation and learning, parental involvement in early education? In the document HMI Boyle expressed concern that, 'There are dangers now in beginning to accept the term "pre-school", particularly in terms of it suggesting a downward extension of the primary school instead of an outward development of family education, with all that means in terms of differences in culture and values' (p. 25).

PROVISION

In the 1970s the pressure to provide pre-five places and the influence of the ideology of compensation for early disadvantage were tied to an increase in nursery provision per se. An increase in the number of children accessing provision was achieved by moving from full-day attendance to part-time half-day attendance with exceptions only for priority needs. By 1996 there were only 245 publicly funded nursery schools, 606 departments attached to primary schools and sixty-one schools and departments in the private sector. They provided provision for 37.9% of the population of 3- and 4-years-olds. Recent rapid expansion of provision can be seen in the comparable figure from 2002 of 96% of 4-year-olds and 85% of the 3-year-olds. (All statistics are taken from the Scottish Executive summary results of the 2002 Census of Pre-school and Day Care or from the 2002 Statistical Bulletin: Edn/B1/2002/3).

The policy context for provision has been widened by the inclusion of economic, cultural and employment factors. The expansion has become part of a wider childcare strategy to make available pre-five places both for the development of children and 'to help parents balance work and family life'.

Early education provision traditionally had two distinct forms, non-statutory nursery education for children under five years of age in schools or classes and statutory infant education in primary schools for 4½-year-olds to 8-year-olds. Nursery schools are now usually free standing with the most common size being up to fifty children. Nursery classes are, in the main, attached to a primary school with its headteacher assuming overall management responsibility. Over the last five years expansion had been concentrated in the less costly nursery class provision where many resources could be shared with the primary school.

More recently pre-school provision has developed a third route through local councils working in partnership with the private sector by funding children for two and a half days with parents paying for 'wrap-around' care sessions. Indeed, such provision is now a statutory duty; 23% of children attending pre-five provision are in partnership provision. Recent data show how children may be receiving many and different services during the week and increasingly these may be provided on the same site. As one might expect there is diversity in practice across the country particularly given the challenge of provision in sparsely populated rural areas. All nursery provision is non-denominational but on transfer to primary school parents may choose a Roman Catholic or a non-denominational school.

Entry to primary school occurs once a year and 96% of provision is publicly funded. In Scotland all children who are five before 1 March enter school in the preceding August.

This results in an entry age between four and five years old. The average school size is 185 children with the average class size being 24.3 and the teacher:pupil ratio being 1 : 18.9. There is considerable variation in this sector with, for example, an average school roll of 59 in the Western Isles. Private schools are more often a feature of the urban areas. Children transfer to secondary education after seven years.

Given the once-yearly entry to primary school and the arbitrary date for admission one child may be in pre-five provision and a counterpart could be in primary one and their experiences could be very different.

In the nursery provision experiences still tend to be play and activity based. Space is mostly open plan with freedom to move between different areas/resources, and a common pattern is to have periods of freely chosen activity and grouping interspersed with small group or whole group activities determined by the adults. There have been differences across the country in terms of the model used. In some areas the degree of adult determined activities through themes and topics has been more marked than in others. Increasingly in response to the introduction of the Curriculum Framework for Children 3–5 and the downward pressure of the Early Intervention initiative some of the play activities have become more structured and related to literacy and numeracy. Overall though, the nursery play way enables children to construct their own curriculum to a considerable extent choosing resources to explore their concerns.

Primary provision is structured by the 5–14 subject areas and suggested time allowances, as well as by commercial texts and schemes adopted as school policy. In the infant classes, time for free choice is more limited and progressively so across the three years. Where play does occur it is more frequently structured by the teacher to fit the literacy and numeracy programmes rather than selected or initiated by the child. The capacity to follow up an interest is undoubtedly made harder by the number of children and the pressure to cover the agreed curriculum in this setting. It may be as Clark (1988) suggested that the infant class does not provide opportunities to continue with the pursuit of challenging and creative activities because of its size as well as for other reasons.

The infant child is likely to spend a large part of the day working alone on individual tasks assigned by the teacher. Such tasks are carried out whilst seated in groups of four to eight. The child is periodically withdrawn to work with the teacher in small groups, commonly ability groups for Mathematics and Reading. This may then be followed up by differentiated tasks. Times for the whole class to work together are provided particularly for activities to do with news, story time and Literacy and Numeracy. In many schools the morning is still given over to Language and Mathematics activities particularly so where the council policy has been influenced by the English Literacy and Numeracy hours, which also place value on whole-class teaching. Most classrooms are self-contained and hold one age group, but composite classes made up of two or more age groups may be formed depending on the size of the school roll. Recently there has been a growth in setting children according to ability.

Not only may the curriculum differ but also the staffing. About 80% of staff in all forms of pre-five provision have a qualification most frequently in childcare and education. The title 'nursery nurse' although outmoded is still in use to describe the predominant staff group, but most settings will also have a qualified 'teacher'. Local authority nursery schools and classes have a staff ratio of 1:7.3 and a teacher:child ratio of 1:25.5. The partnership provision has comparable figures of 1:4 and 1:53.6, but, whilst in part this will reflect the attendance of under-threes, many partnership settings do not have a teacher. In local authority primary schools the teacher:child ratio is 1:18.9, so theoretically, each child has an increased chance to interact with the teacher.

In 1997 the government launched an Early Intervention programme to improve literacy and numeracy in primary one and two. This, along with the social inclusion policy and the intention to reduce teacher workload have led to a rapid increase in the number of adults in the primary classroom. Staff such as classroom assistants and special educational needs assistants give rise to a 1:14.2 adult:child ratio. The growth is such that, in full-time equivalents, one-fifth of staff are non-teaching staff. The impact of classroom assistants is seen by teachers as beneficial in that they have more time to plan and teach, as keeping children on task has become a major part of the role of the classroom assistant

The teacher, in both primary and nursery settings, is now likely to have gained a qualification in teaching either through a four-year BEd degree or by a one-year post-graduate course. Both routes meet the national Standard for Initial Teacher Education. From 2002 onwards they will then have a guaranteed induction year in which one-third of the time will be for professional development; and on completion of the year they must meet the standard for full registration which is linked to the standard for ITE. The nursery nurse is likely to have undertaken two years of further education leading to a Higher National Certificate in Child Care and Education. The nursery school headteacher will probably to have an additional qualification in early education. The promoted staff in the primary school which houses the nursery class will not necessarily have such a qualification although many local councils are seeking specific continuing professional development for head-teachers and the increasing number of newly appointed nursery class teachers. Tradition-ally the nursery class teacher was seen to operate in a 'team leader role' but the rapid expansion in nursery class provision and the management structures of primary schools have tended to question this assumption. Staff in partnership nurseries and centres may have a range of qualifications including SVQ 2, 3, or National Certificates and HNC.

The introduction of the assistant headteacher role (SED Circular 819, 1972) increased the number of promoted posts in primary schools and a shift to generic management ideology was subsequently evident in the erosion of the early education specialist with responsibility for primary one to three. The move to conceptualise the headteacher as manager grew in the 1980s and culminated in the SED-funded Management Training Modules for Headteachers produced in 1990. In 1998 a new national Scottish Qualification for Headteachers was introduced covering all sectors and open to aspirant heads who are recommended by their headteacher and selected by their local council. It is expected that all new headteachers will have the qualification by 2005. Currently a Chartered Teacher Standard and a framework for a continuing professional development programme to meet this is being piloted. This will provide an alternative route to career and salary progress by focusing on more effective classroom practice and contributing to the development of teaching and learning within a team. Options within this route can be age/stage related so could incorporate or build on existing postgraduate modules in early education. These existing routes which preserve an early education specialism are either in Early Education or Early Primary Education.

CURRICULUM LINKS

Although the nursery education sector is inspected and has set performance indicators, the curriculum was, until recently, largely structured and interpreted locally. The 1994 5–14 guidelines made no reference to this sector. By 1995 all authorities making provision had produced guidelines which, whilst broadly following national advice in subscribing to play and process approaches, also framed the curriculum in broad content areas and increasingly such guidelines sought to recognise the relationship with the 5–14 content framework. In contrast there has always been national guidance which covers the curriculum of the infant classes.

In order to ensure more continuity the government issued *A Curriculum Framework for Children in their Pre-School Year* in 1997 and its successor, *A Curriculum Framework for Children 3 to 5* in 1999. These can be seen as defining nationally appropriate content and assessment procedures which link all forms of pre-school curriculum ever more closely to the primary curriculum as can be seen in Figure 32.1.

Figure 32.1: From Curriculum 3–5 to 5–14 Curriculum

Curriculum Framework 3–5	5–14 Curriculum Guidelines
Emotional, Personal and Social Development	Personal and Social Development
Knowledge and Understanding of the World	Religious and Moral Education
	Environmental Studies
	Mathematics
Communication and Language	English Language
Expressive and Aesthetic Development	Expressive Arts
Physical Development and Movement	

The language of the pre-five and 5–14 documents has moved closer most notably in the use of 'should learn to' for the younger age group and 'learning outcomes' for the primary school. Alongside this there has been a growth in the use of transitional assessment records through which the pre-five sector passes on records to the primary school in an attempt to ensure both continuity and progression. In many councils this has been allied to the use of base line assessment techniques so that they can engage in value-added studies.

By virtue of the link to national testing the curriculum in the infant classes has become more age/stage graded with attainment targets being given for all curricular areas. Specific levels of achievement for Mathematics, Reading and Writing are set for individual schools in the light of characteristics such as the level of free school meals – an indicator of poverty – and past achievements. Children in primary one to three are subject to the expectation that all of them will cover and achieve level A targets and some will achieve level B. Concern with national mathematical targets led HMI in 1997 to suggest that most children should achieve level A by the end of primary two. In June 2001 73.5% reached level A or above in Mathematics, 48.8% in Reading and 33.3% in Writing. HMI Boyle's concern (referred to above) was mainly about the impact of 5–14 on the pre-five stage but developments like these highlight a similar concern about 'the death of infancy' in the early primary.

The National Evaluation of the Early Intervention Programme Final Report (Fraser et al.,

2001) was largely based on testing primary three classes in 1998 and three years later. The findings showed that there was an overall increase in Reading attainment but not in Mathematics. However despite the extra resources given to early intervention schools, their results were no different from those in non-early intervention schools unless the 'funding was focused in a smaller number of schools'. Given the history of differences in attainment related to pupil characteristics it is not surprising to see that Scotland, like many other nations, finds that being female affects reading; and being older and reporting having support from home are associated positively with both Reading and Mathematics. Where English is not the first language or the child receives free school meals the effect is negative. In its conclusions the report makes several important recommendations including that of the need to debate curriculum balance in the early stages with respect to the possible under-representation of play and self-directed learning opportunities.

PLANNING AND MANAGING THE CURRICULUM

The advice on planning for 5–14 is tied to the school development model in 1994, the SOED document, 5–14 *A Practical Guide*. Once the whole school audit for a curriculum area has been made, the individual teacher's role is seen as 'keeping the existing strengths of your classroom practice while trying to develop aspects which may be new or in which you lack confidence' (p. 9), and engaging in long- and short-term planning. Long-term is linked to the school year and framed by strands. Short-term is framed by a topic or block of teaching-linked targets and fleshed out to show if it is for class, group or individual and what will be assessed and recorded.

The role of the headteacher is to monitor and evaluate the implementation of the curriculum ensuring that within each classroom each strand is addressed, that teaching and learning builds on what was learned in earlier years and that children are making satisfactory progress in achieving the standards indicated in the attainment targets.

Changing roles and career development aspirations of staff in early education have created a context in which access to continuing professional development has become a key issue. Postgraduate courses at certificate, diploma and masters level which emphasise practitioner reflection have been developed in higher education. The multi-professional background of staff and their involvement in a range of provision for 3–8-year-olds is an innovative and enriching feature of these courses. The newer courses exist alongside or incorporate parts of the traditional infant and nursery teacher special qualifications. Recently the needs of nursery nurses for continuing professional development have been recognised by the introduction of a Professional Development award beyond the level of HNC in the FE sector.

Innovative modular BA degrees in Early Childhood Studies have been introduced in 1997 in the Universities of Strathclyde and Dundee and a wider focused childhood studies course in Paisley University integrates early childhood with wider care and education. Within these courses opportunities for part-time study, accreditation of prior learning and exit routes at diploma stages are helping to build a flexible structure of CPD providing access to graduate level study in early childhood care and education Indeed routes are now in place from an HNC to a diploma on to a BA and then to masters level.

Individuals have been keen to undertake this training and some employers have supported it financially. However, it is not clear what career development will be available to those undertaking these awards or what impact their increased expertise will have in practice. There is a move to ensure all heads of centres will have graduate level or SVQ4 qualifications by 2004.

Quality assurance in the pre-school sector was until recently the sole responsibility of HMIE. *The Child at the Centre* (Scottish Executive, 1999) provided guidance on performance indicators to be used as a tool for self-evaluation and inspection. In future this will be a shared responsibility. The establishment of the Scottish Commission for the Regulation of Care (2002) and the publication of National Care Standards (2002) will establish an alternative quality assurance regime with a focus on care rather than education. The partner body, the Scottish Social Services Council, will register those working in pre-school education and childcare and will oversee the training and regulation of the workforce. The publication of SEED Guidance on the Involvement of Teachers in *Pre-School Education* (2002) recognises that teachers can make a distinctive contribution to children's early learning but it highlights the wider role of the teacher in promoting a discourse with other staff on effective learning and practice. Given that teachers are the most expensive staffing resource in pre-school education, it may be that this wider role predominates rather than a direct role in facilitating the learning of individual children. Recent work by Siraj-Blatchford et al. (2002) notes that, 'trained teachers use the most sophisticated pedagogy including shared sustained thinking'.

ISSUES

Recent changes led to the raising of a number of issues particularly in relation to the distinctiveness of early learning.

Curriculum and methodology

The content pressure of the 5–14 reforms has eroded the concept of three to eight as a distinctive period of learning. Whilst the links may promote continuity and progression in content terms, which may be desirable, there remains a danger that the distinctive methodology of early education could be hard pressed by an emphasis on assessment and standards. The aim for pre-school education may be stated as 'preparation' but the government itself recognises that this intent could be subverted into 'an early start'.

Indeed, the curriculum may become narrowed, given the increased attention to literacy and numeracy for both sectors. The introduction of base-line assessment with its value added dimension may well have a similar impact if it leads to 'teaching to the test'. The fear expressed here is that an introduction to the technical rules/subskills of say reading, without first understanding the cultural rules and purposes of the skills, may lead to surface not deep learning and may be undermining dispositions to learn.

Roles and responsibilities

Increasingly there has been a blurring of aspects of the teacher's and nursery nurse's role in practice and policy documents. The HMI report, *Education of Children Under Five in Scotland* (SOED, 1994), adopted the generic term 'educator' to refer to those holding professional qualifications relating to the education of children and made few distinctions in role descriptions between staff other than to observe that some members of every staff team require 'depth of knowledge' (para. 7.2). Stephen (1999) has raised the issue of the wide range of values and perceptions of the curriculum held by those with different qualifications.

The expansion of pre-five provision has been costly and teachers are expensive. In 2000 SEED published a document, *The Role of the Teacher in Pre-Five Services,* stating that 'the cost of employing a teacher may lead to increased charges for child care which could, perversely, reduce parental access to services' and follows up with the market view that 'the teacher is the most expensive staff resource and needs to be used intensively and efficiently in line with best value.' The issue is what constitutes 'best value' for the child given Siraj-Blatchford's (op. cit.) findings on the significant impact of teacher–child interactions compared to others' interactions.

Accessibility

The expansion of provision has undoubtedly helped both parents and children, but in terms of adult access to the labour market it is questionable if part-time can be sufficiently flexible and affordable to meet the varying needs of the labour force – particularly women who often have unusual shift patterns.

Continuing professional development

The diversity of provision and the range of staff who work in the same context do suggest that there is a need for professional development and recognition of that development for all. Teachers now have an agreed framework for their professional development and standards are well developed and recognised in terms of additional qualifications, promotion prospects and monetary reward. Such access and recognition is not in place for other workers in both the pre-five and primary sector and there may be both educational and equity issues when only one group in the work force benefits from such provision, particularly in the context of both the expectation of team work and the need for interprofessional knowledge, skills and attitudes.

Given the development of an ethos of 'educare' rather than education and care, the role of the teacher does need further examination particularly in the pre-five sector. However this may also be the case in the primary school as new ideas such as the community school and consortia of establishments in a geographical area embody a concept of education in a broader context. The roles of all adults may need to be reconceptualised to include more recognition of the importance of interdisciplinary skills in the provision of services across sectors.

Quality Assurance

This may well be the central issue particularly with the respect to the curriculum children receive and we see two aspects which will need consideration. There is a need to examine the quality and use made of transition data to see if the systems for fostering continuity and progression are robust. In 2001 HMI produced an overview of their inspections in the pre-five sector and noted that there were differences between voluntary and partnership provision and within nursery schools and classes. Overall, but in not all cases, the partnership provision was deemed as only fair or unsatisfactory in at least 25% of these centres in the key curriculum areas of Knowledge of the World, Communication and

Language, Physical Development and Movement and Expressive and Aesthetic Development, compared to no unsatisfactory and an average of 6% fair in the local authority and independent sector nursery provision. The costs of ensuring a minimum common knowledge base in all forms of provision will be expensive. Quality assurance via school self-evaluation and inspection is well established in the primary sector.

IN CONCLUSION

Government concern to develop greater integration across services will have to balance the need to provide and promote both education and care. In the current context of expansion and the increased influence of new structures whose focus is care, this will be a major issue along with continuing concerns about the attainment focus in the early primary stages.

REFERENCES

Clark, M. (1988) *Children under Five:* Educational Research & Evidence, London: Gordon & Breach.

Fraser, H., MacDougall, A., Pirrie, A., Croxford, L. (2001) *National Evaluation of the Early Intervention Progamme Final Report*, University of Edinburgh, Edinburgh: KPMG.

Mooney, A. and Munton, A. G. (1999) pre-school educational research: in V. Wilson and J. Ogden-Smith (eds), *Pre-School Education and Childcare in Scotland – Setting the Scene* Edinburgh: SEED.

SCCC (1992) *Reflections on Curriculum Issues – Early Education*, Dundee : SCCC.

Siraj-Blatchford, I., Sylva, K., Muttock, S., Gilden, R., Bell, D. (2002) *Researching Effective Pedagogy in the Early Years*, Norwich: DfES.

Stephen, C., Brown, S., Cope, P., Waterhouse, S. (1999) Pre-school educational research in V. Wilson and J. Ogden-Smith (eds), *Meeting Children's Education Needs : The Role of Staff and Staff Development*, Edinburgh: SEED.

33

Ethos, Management and Discipline in the Primary School

Eleanor Gavienas and Graham White

Ethos and discipline are two closely related but separate aspects of the management of schools. Ethos, or the habitual character of primary schools, is quickly apparent both to professionals involved in education and to parents. Indeed the casual visitor to a school can rapidly gain an impression of the ethos of the establishment by merely observing playground behaviour, relationships between pupils and staff, relationships among staff members and the overall presentation of the building. Eisner (1994) usefully summarises what he considers ethos to be: 'Ethos for me is a term that refers to the underlying deep structure of a culture, the values that animate it, that collectively constitute its way of life' (p. 2).

To those outside education, discipline, in the sense of control and regulation, has long been regarded as an important part of a school's ethos and a key area of concern for teachers and school managers. Indeed, politicians are very quick to blame the ills of society on a supposed lack of discipline in our schools. This naive causal link ignores the complex and changing relationship between schools and the populations which they serve and, more critically, fails to recognise that if the ethos of an establishment is good, then discipline is much less of a problem.

In Scotland, during the last twenty years, there has been a shift in thinking about discipline and ethos in primary schools. Formerly teachers saw discipline as something to be imposed upon children if learning and teaching were to be productive. Teachers felt they had the right, indeed the duty, to impose particular rules and to ensure that these rules were adhered to by the pupils. When these rules were broken teachers saw it as part of their professional duties to punish the miscreants. Such punishments were devised to fit the misdemeanour rather than the child. Scottish teachers felt comfortable that this approach to discipline was fair, rational, logical and that it was sanctioned by the pupils' parents in particular and by Scottish society in general. Despite changing attitudes, the term 'ethos' was not in common currency until the 1980s when research into this aspect of school life burgeoned.

Before outlining current approaches to developing a policy on ethos and discipline and how schools put policy into practice there are important background factors to be considered which are particularly relevant to the Scottish context. These include cultural traditions, social changes which impinged upon schools, and the requirement for parental consultation and involvement.

CULTURAL TRADITIONS

The historical link between ethos and discipline can be explained, in the first instance, if one examines the development and traditions of Scottish primary education. Scotland has a long history of valuing education not just for an elite but also for the wider population, which stretches back to the time of John Knox. As documented by Cruickshank in the *History of the Training of Teachers in Scotland* (London: University of London Press, 1970), there was a democratic tradition in Scottish elementary education which preceded the demand for an educated workforce evident in other rapidly industrialising countries across Europe. Indeed the brightest pupils were encouraged to aspire to a university education, if possible, irrespective of ability to pay. Education was seen as the key to advancement in life, an attitude which permeated society at all levels. This resulted in considerable respect for teachers and the authority invested in them.

In the nineteenth century large classes were the norm and, in order to ensure control, rituals and routines were thoroughly established in schools. Discipline was strict, a fact acknowledged by Hunter in *The Scottish Educational System* (Oxford: Pergamon, 1972), but, generally, there was very little conflict with parents. This tradition of accepting that authority is largely in the hands of teachers can be witnessed in the attitudes of some parents over a century later. A historical legacy of support for the school and discipline is still there, to some extent, in the Scottish psyche.

SOCIAL CHANGES

By the 1960s, the writings of philosophers such as Montessori and Froebel and the evidence from research into learning by Piaget and others were beginning to influence mainstream primary education. These changes were formalised in the Scottish Education Department's publication of the watershed report *Primary Education in Scotland* (SED, 1965). To some extent this report was a product of its time. The 1960s was an era of great social change with, in particular, the emergence of individual freedom of expression and a questioning of traditional power structures. Freedom and respect for the individual, which starts in childhood, is a common thread in the writings of the great educational philosophers and, critically, was in tune with the prevailing mood of the decade. The ethos of society at large was reflected in recommendations made to schools.

Teachers were liberated from what was seen as too structured a curriculum, with too much central control of education, and were encouraged to adopt a child-centred approach to learning. The official view, as set out in the report, was that when such reforms were achieved children would assume much greater responsibility for their own conduct and discipline. Teachers in consultation with their professional bodies, for example the Educational Institute for Scotland and the General Teaching Council for Scotland, were also encouraged to review the use of corporal punishment in primary schools. The notion that learning should be pleasurable, with schools being places to which children should want to go, was actively upheld by Her Majesty's Inspectorate (HMI). To a considerable extent this has been one of the lasting legacies of the reforms. Most primary children now declare that they like school and are most anxious to attend.

PARENTAL INVOLVEMENT

The changes in schools in the 1960s became characterised under the generic term of 'progressive education' and left many experienced teachers feeling uncertain about their role. They had responsibility for the curriculum but only general guidance on its content and structure. Parents also seemed to lack an understanding about what schools were trying to achieve. As far as some teachers were concerned the whole process was made doubly difficult with the abolition of corporal punishment in 1981. Without physical sanctions, discipline had to be achieved using other systems of control such as deprivation of privileges. The ethos envisaged in the 1960s of teachers and pupils and parents working together in an atmosphere of mutual respect had not developed in many schools.

However, the traditional trust and respect, built up over the past century still lingered, but it could be argued that the decade between 1970 and 1980 was a time when increasing numbers of parents began to doubt some of the methods and activities within primary schools. In most schools parents were not consulted, nor even informed, about changes to the curriculum or to the discipline policy. The deficiencies of the situation were accurately summarised by the Committee on Primary Education (COPE, 1983) when reflecting upon the previous ten years. The authors of the COPE document wrote, 'neither the teacher nor the curriculum exists in a vacuum,' and further suggested that all of the members of a school community should accept the purposes and intentions of the organisation and 'work together in attempting to achieve the purposes'.

In the 1970s schools did not actively encourage parents to question teachers. The prevailing attitude at the time was exemplified by notices, displayed prominently at the door of primary schools, instructing parents to report directly to the headteacher, thereby discouraging any direct contact with a class teacher. Such an attitude was not conducive to the creation of the community spirit envisaged by COPE.

As a response to the uncertainties of the 1970s, the 1983 COPE publication was indeed important. Deliberately, it put considerable emphasis on the role of parents in the education process:

> formal arrangements for school parent contact cannot replace a school ethos which encourages a parental interest and encourages parents to come to the school at other times than those set aside for the formal transmission of information. (p. 61)

Schools were also encouraged to be more aware of the wider community which they served and to recognise that education would not necessarily lead to full employment:

> the situation in which children could be encouraged to do well at school so that they could do well in terms of a job and lifestyle is rapidly changing. Schools more than ever need to be seen to be relevant to the needs of the community and able to cope with a changing society. (p. 67)

The formal participation of parents was important for two reasons: firstly to play their part in school life and, secondly, to encourage parents, some of whom the educational system had failed, to look again at what schools were trying to achieve. However, a minority of schools were subject to parental pressure in the areas of discipline and control, with teachers challenged to explain why certain actions had been taken against their children. In this crucial area of school management and community liaison it was recognised that work had to be done.

It is now almost universally accepted by Scottish teachers that the level and nature of parental involvement will have a profound effect on a school's ethos. The introduction of school boards in the late 1980s formalised this process to some extent, with headteachers reporting on a regular basis to board members on matters of discipline, including exclusions. Many primary schools offer a range of opportunities, over and above the statutory parents' evenings, for teachers and parents genuinely to collaborate in their children's education. These often include the provision of a parents' room, interest classes, opportunities for parents to assist in classrooms and in outdoor activities, regular newsletters where the tone reflects a real partnership between home and school, and home visiting schemes whereby teachers visit parents in their homes to discuss their children's progress. The nature of opportunities will vary from school to school, but the quality of parental involvement will be characterised by the teachers' willingness to appreciate the concerns of the parents and to enter into truthful and non-condescending dialogue with the first educators of their pupils. There can be little doubt that the quality of the home–school relationship should mirror the quality of teacher–pupil relationships which are at the very heart of a school's ethos.

Since the advent of the Scottish Parliament, the Executive has established a high priority for its policy of Social Inclusion. Perhaps the best example of this policy in action are the New community Schools which have inclusion at the heart of what they are trying to achieve. Other professionals such as social workers, community education staff and health workers combine to ensure that, in collaboration with parents, as many pupils as possible are included in the educational process.

APPROACHES TO DEVELOPING A POLICY ON ETHOS AND DISCIPLINE

By the mid-1980s there was a general acceptance by teachers that effective learning can occur only when certain conditions exist. It was recognised that children learn best in a relaxed atmosphere where they feel free to question teachers in order to clarify their thinking. Teachers, and society in general, began to appreciate the reasons behind children's unacceptable behaviour, where it existed, and sought to understand rather than condemn. In such a climate inflexible rules and punishments would have no place and schools would now have to find other means of establishing and maintaining discipline. Schools, therefore, began to examine their discipline policies in light of this more enlightened thinking and sought to reach a common understanding of the issues.

Some senior management teams began this process by considering the 'hidden curriculum' of their schools. If the ethos of a school is the value system that underpins all the practices within a school then the hidden curriculum is a subset of this and refers to all the practices related to the transmitting of the formal curriculum. It could be said that the hidden curriculum makes manifest, perhaps unintentionally, the value system that underlies the curricular policies of a school. It might, therefore, include such things as the means of delivering the curriculum (e.g. class/group/individualised programmes of work), the manner in which it is delivered (e.g. whether the teacher takes a didactic/discursive approach), the condition of the resources, and the way in which the teachers address the pupils when teaching. The hidden curriculum, therefore, refers to the way the pupils are treated during lessons and could be said to be the aspect of school life that is, ironically, least hidden from pupils.

Examination of policies, both curricular and more general, is currently the overall responsibility of headteachers. Increasingly over the last ten years they have been charged with overseeing the planning and implementation of all school policies of which ethos and discipline are but two. A key to this process was the introduction of Development Planning, whereby staff together would analyse the strengths and weaknesses of a school and as a result establish priorities for action. Action could include formulation or revision of school policies, appropriate staff development and the purchase of any materials considered to be necessary to support the changes. Discussion of Development Planning was instigated by HMI who highlighted the importance of a team approach and of a consultative management style. To assist further in this process, *Using Performance Indicators in Schools' Self-Evaluation* (SOED, 1992) was produced and circulated to all schools. This working document contained advice on procedures for whole school development planning with one major section of the document entitled Ethos. Within this chapter there were subheadings entitled climate and atmosphere, pastoral care, effectiveness of staff and team work, partnership with parents, with school board, and links with other schools and agencies.

However, the most popular and accessible publication to date on the subject, which is currently widely used in Scottish primary schools, is *Using Ethos Indicators in Primary School Self-Evaluation* (SOED, 1992). This document identifies twelve ethos indicators related to different aspects of ethos and discipline in primary schools. The indicators identified are: pupil morale; teacher morale; teachers' job satisfaction; the physical environment; the learning context; teacher–pupil relationships; equality and justice; extra curricular activities; school leadership; discipline; information to parents; parent–teacher consultation. This useful publication also contains sample questionnaires for pupils, parents and teachers to be used to audit/monitor the development of a school's ethos. The extremely thorough approach to the analysis of a school's ethos from a range of standpoints has proved a useful starting point for many primary schools.

The two earlier documents of 1992 were, to some extent, brought together by HMI when they produced *How Good is Our School: Self-Evaluation Using Performance Indicators* (SOED, 1996). Within this publication, there are performance indicators relevant to ethos and discipline under the subheadings of support for pupils and ethos. The 2002 edition of this document is now the starting point for school inspections by Her Majesty's Inspectors, therefore making reflection upon ethos and discipline an important part of the quality assurance process, to be undertaken both within the school and by external assessors. A positive atmosphere for learning and teaching is now a vital aspect of every school. The way in which schools create it will now be considered.

POLICY INTO PRACTICE

Many schools have recognised the part the physical appearance of a school can play in enhancing a positive climate and have endeavoured to create and maintain a clean, warm, bright, welcoming environment for all who work in or visit the building. This basic but important aspect of school life is often one of the first tackled by headteachers and senior management teams wishing to improve the ethos of their schools, as change to the physical environment may be simple and relatively inexpensive. Such things as displaying children's work imaginatively, decorating rooms and corridors with pot plants and artefacts, ensuring that curtains/blinds are in good condition, all help to send the message that the people who run this school care for the comfort and aesthetic sensibilities of those who work there.

The presence of pupils' and parents' noticeboards in a school helps to create a climate where people's views and interests are valued. In the same way, 'Best Work Boards', where children's achievements are displayed in a prominent way, indicate that pupils' individual successes are important. Clear and friendly signs, in several languages, which direct people to the headteacher's room or school office, give the impression that those who work there recognise the possible insecurities of visitors and that they wish to put people at ease.

The environment immediately outside the school has also recently received much attention, in particular how the condition of the school playground can affect the climate of a school. As the Scottish Consultative Committee on the Curriculum has shown, in *Climate for Learning* (Dundee: SCCC, 1996), the physical environment of the playground can have an effect upon children's self-esteem and therefore their behaviour. In the accompanying audio tape, entitled *Grounds for Learning*, the issue of the design of the playground is discussed and the conclusion reached that fights and bullying are often an inevitable consequence of the physical design of the space. The same research has shown that children value quiet peaceful places in the school playground and many schools now provide areas with tables and benches where children can spend time chatting, reading or simply watching the world go by. The curtailing of football games to specified areas of the playground must count as one of the major blows for equality in recent years; in the past the football players (traditionally boys) dominated much of the space in playgrounds.

Perhaps the most fundamental shift in the practice of effective discipline in Scottish schools has been away from punishing unacceptable behaviour towards rewarding conduct which is acceptable. Regular assemblies where pupil successes are celebrated by the whole school are now a fairly common means of raising pupils' self-esteem and of creating a sense of belonging as well as reinforcing high expectations. This celebration of success is compatible with a system of discipline which rewards rather than punishes. Some schools have very precise means of rewarding children which entail tangible objects such as plastic tokens which can be 'cashed in' for symbolic rewards such as points or merits. Those pupils gaining an agreed amount of symbolic rewards are often then given some sort of treat at the end of the week such as a longer playtime or more time playing computer games. An accompanying certificate is often given to reinforce the school's approval and to inform parents of the success of their children.

Exactly who rewards pupils varies from school to school. Some may decide that only the class teacher should do this while in other schools all adults, including non-teaching staff, are encouraged to reward acceptable behaviour in all pupils. The definition of acceptable behaviour is also variable. Some schools reward those pupils whose behaviour has been exemplary whilst others reward those whose behaviour has improved over a period of time. The setting of very individual and focused goals (e.g. managing not to call out in class from nine o'clock until the morning interval) and then rewarding such behaviour, is now fairly common.

Some schools which have used extrinsic rewards for good behaviour are also giving attention to how they might develop the intrinsic values in children which go alongside behaving acceptably, which ultimately should be the aim of any positive discipline policy. This entails giving much time to listening to pupils' explanations of their actions and to explaining teacher actions to pupils. Such an apparently simple approach has been found to be effective in dealing with instances of bullying in schools. Pupils who are being bullied will confide in teachers if they know they will be listened to and those who are bullying will be more likely to change their behaviour after discussing the effects of their actions on others. The inclusive school which attempts to serve all pupils, including those who bully, also attempts to develop its pupils' ethical and moral sensibilities. Without devoting time to such development any reward may be only superficially successful in that it may modify children's behaviour but may not instil in pupils values such as justice, integrity and honesty.

Where rewarding acceptable behaviour has not been sufficient to ensure appropriate conduct, schools often enforce sanctions. In the past, practices such as denying children their interval or lunch breaks, although illegal, were fairly commonplace. It has been standard practice for many years for teachers to ask pupils to write lines, although both teachers and pupils recognise that this practice is usually ineffectual. In some schools the practice of sending pupils to a member of the senior management team is used frequently although precisely what the result of this course of action might be is not often discussed amongst staff. Perhaps this approach does have some merit in that it provides 'time out' for the pupil, his/her classmates and the teacher. The severest sanctions might include the withdrawal of some pleasurable experience such as attending class parties, end of term trips or playing for the school's netball or football team, but perhaps the action that works best when pupils behave unacceptably is the involvement of the child's parents, as verified by Munn et al. (1992):

> A letter home to parents, a parent being asked to come to the school, or a child being placed on 'report' with a parent having to sign a behaviour card, are examples of actions heartily disliked by pupils. (p. 104)

When a misdemeanour is deemed very serious schools can consider temporary exclusion for up to three days or, ultimately, permanent exclusion, the latter being fairly rare in Scottish primary schools. Temporary exclusions require the involvement of parents in that they are required by law to accompany the child on return to school and to enter into discussion with the headteacher on how the child can be encouraged to behave appropriately in future. This exercise will be of greatest benefit when the ongoing relationship between home and school is based on mutual trust and respect. The quality of home–school relationships is therefore crucial to the discipline policy which constitutes a very important part of the ethos of a school.

The role of the promoted staff will be vital in monitoring the implementation of any policy and teachers have the right to expect practical support in this. Support from the senior management team may take many forms, from modelling the agreed desired behaviours, to picking up the pieces when things go awry, as well as adapting the strategies to accommodate new or unforeseen situations.

Headteachers and their senior management teams may also be in need of support in establishing a positive ethos in their schools. The Scottish School Ethos Network was established in 1995 by the Scottish Office in order to provide such support. This network provides teachers with a platform to share ideas about how exactly they are improving the ethos of their schools and to offer advice and support to those who are finding the process of change difficult. It distributes regular newsletters and an annual conference helps to keep members in touch with the latest successful strategies for the creation and maintenance of a positive school ethos. The sharing of practices regarding positive discipline policies may be a part of the network's function but it is not its sole function. The Promoting Positive Discipline Initiative has been established to allow teachers to share their philosophies and the actual day-to-day strategies they use in effecting positive and humane discipline in their schools. The initiative encourages teachers to write about their practices in order that good practice in relation to discipline is recorded and disseminated.

Another widely used set of materials for staff development has been a pack entitled *Promoting Positive Behaviour in the Primary School* (Strathclyde Regional Council, 1991). This pack contains a video, case studies and structured tasks to help teachers analyse their current practices and to consider strategies for the development of policies on ethos and discipline.

CURRENT ISSUES

The all-embracing nature of the concept of a school's ethos can act both to complicate and to oversimplify what is meant by the term. The staff of one school may wish to view it as a complex set of messages which it sends to pupils, parents and the community. The staff of another may view the ethos of their school as being determined by how decently teachers and other adults behave towards pupils. Both definitions may be deemed appropriate but neither makes it easy to offer clear and unambiguous advice on how a positive ethos can be achieved. Ethos indicators merely indicate desired states, they do not define the routes to success. If teachers view the indicators as a recipe to be followed it is doubtful if a positive ethos will result. Each school must debate its own route to this end. That is the difficult part. Sharing a vision of what constitutes a positive ethos means examining personal values and being prepared to enter into genuine debate with colleagues about how exactly it can be achieved and maintained in a school. The quality of the debate will be dependent on the level of commitment that each member of staff can bring to the process. The complex nature of building a positive ethos and discipline system means that the process will be continuous and ever-changing – not an easy or comfortable position for those teachers or headteachers who seek absolutes.

Although many teachers are sharing the details of their policies and practices regarding ethos and discipline across Scotland through the Promoting Positive Discipline Initiative and the Scottish School Ethos Network, it is recognised that no two schools will share the same policy or practice in relation to ethos and discipline. The very different contexts of Scottish primary schools, particularly with regard to location, class and race, defy blueprints for success in the field of discipline and ethos. There can be little doubt that teaching children in areas of deprivation, where they are in receipt of free school meals and clothing grants and where the levels of unemployment are high, can be a very different job from teaching children in affluent suburbs. Children's poor living conditions will no doubt affect their self-esteem and their motivation to do well at school. In such situations the primary school must offer understanding and compassion with no lowering of its expectation that children will succeed with the appropriate support. Teachers in schools in deprived areas of Scotland may find it more difficult to create and maintain a positive climate for learning and teaching and therefore deserve a high level of support from their senior management teams who deserve the same from their education authorities.

Perhaps one of the most important aspects of current thinking about discipline concerns the examination of how teachers' behaviour can influence the discipline and therefore the ethos of a school. In *Teaching for Effective Learning*, (1996) SCCC states that:

> In the classroom the way teachers behave, determines the way learners behave. How teachers
> establish their authority, the tone of their voice, the little things they continually say and do on a
> daily basis, determines the climate in their classroom. (p. 19)

A common understanding of exactly how teachers should behave towards children, in order to facilitate effective learning and teaching, has not been achieved. This is not surprising and should not be viewed as disappointing. Schools which seek such recipes have missed the point. If a school is serious about improving discipline and its general climate, then the teachers must enter into debate about how and why they behave the way they do towards children and how their behaviour affects the learning and teaching process.

The difference between treating all pupils equally and treating all children equitably is still to be fully explored by all teachers. The fact that some children, by dint of their differing capacities to behave acceptably, may require slightly different rules or may require to be treated differently by teachers, is not fully appreciated by those teachers who seek easy answers. However, the notion of the inclusive school which demonstrates the desire to involve, care for and cater for all its pupils, not just those who present few challenges to teachers, is slowly gaining ground in Scottish primary schools. In turn, the senior management team must recognise and accept the differences there will be amongst staff in implementing any policy, and should not be disappointed when common purposes are interpreted slightly differently or when common strategies are executed in a variety of styles. Teachers can only work within the limitations of their personalities and to expect otherwise is to expect too much. It will be the duty of the senior management team to monitor the day-to-day procedures and to discuss any difficulties that individual teachers may have in putting the agreed policy into practice, before offering advice and practical support. This is not to say that any teachers should be exempt from attempting to establish good quality relationships with their pupils, far from it. All teachers should be willing to show care and concern for their pupils; and this should not be seen as something added on to the business of teaching effectively but as an integral and pivotal part of teaching and learning.

The manifestation of a primary teacher's care and concern for pupils takes many forms. She or he will be prepared to listen to pupils not merely to assess whether the key points of a lesson have been absorbed but to determine the pupils' opinions, misgivings, fears, misconceptions about the subject matter. She or he will ensure that all resources are carefully planned to meet the different needs of pupils. She or he will accept responsibility for the social and moral well being of pupils. In short, many Scottish primary schools attempt to get to know their pupils and will give something of themselves in return. As the SCCC document states: 'Giving of yourself to establish and maintain quality relationships in a classroom situation is one of the most challenging and stressful aspects of the job of teaching' (p. 16). The Scottish primary education system whereby teachers are in constant contact with their pupils for most of the school day, week, term, session offers tremendous opportunities for teachers to model decent and compassionate behaviours. Such behaviours from teachers are a prerequisite for the nurturing of the same behaviours in pupils.

Despite all the difficulties, it would appear that many Scottish primary schools are successful in their attempts to create a positive ethos in their schools. A great number of HMI reports contain evidence that Scottish primary teachers are aware of the multifarious aspects that constitute a school's ethos and are working to improve the pupils' experience of school life. The following statement exemplifies this:

The school has a very positive ethos. The atmosphere was welcoming, morale was high and there was a pervading sense of common purpose. Pupils' achievements were highlighted prominently through awards and displays and at weekly assemblies. There was a great range of extra-curricular activities. Older pupils often accepted responsibilities for aspects of the life of the school (David Livingstone Memorial Primary School, HMI, 1996).

REFERENCES

Committee on Primary Education (1983) *Primary Education in the Eighties: a COPE Position Paper*, Edinburgh: CCC.

Eisner, E. (1994) *Ethos and Education*, Dundee: SCCC.

Munn, P., Johnstone M. and Chalmers, V. (1992) *Effective Discipline in Primary Schools and Classrooms*, London: Paul Chapman.

SCCC (1996) *Teaching for Effective Learning*, Dundee: SCCC.

SOED (1992) *Using Ethos Indicators in Primary School Self-Evaluation*, Edinburgh: SOED.

SOED (1996) *How Good is Our School: Self-Evaluation Using Performance Indicators*, Edinburgh: SOED.

34

Primary–Secondary Liaison

Brian Boyd and Mary Simpson

PANTOMIME HORSE OR SEAMLESS ROBE?

> We take it as axiomatic that a young person's experience of education should be coherent, continuous and progressive. (*Education 10–14 in Scotland*, CCC, 1986)

The problems of continuity and progression between primary and secondary school are not new. In 1980, the then Depute Senior Chief Inspector of Schools, Andrew Chirnside, made a speech in which he used the metaphor of the pantomime horse in which the two sectors of education, while wishing to proceed in the same direction, failed to co-ordinate their approach to learning and teaching. They seemed not to be speaking the same language and as a result, he argued, the first two years of secondary, for many young people, brought the 'onset of failure'.

In 1983, a national Programme Directing Committee was established to look at the problem. The time was right to address it, since national committees had just reported on curriculum and assessment in the middle years of secondary (Munn and Dunning, 1977), the primary curriculum had undergone a major review in 1965 followed by an inspectorate update (1981), and following on from the Warnock Report in England and Wales (1977), there had been a national report on the education of children with learning difficulties in Scottish schools in 1978. What Chirnside and his colleagues could not have known was that the changing political landscape in the UK would have a dramatic effect on policy making within Scottish education and that the review of the late primary and early secondary curriculum would be the first to be affected by the new, accountability-driven agenda being pursued by the UK Government in the 1980s and 1990s.

The strategies for improvement of the transition arrangements between primary and secondary sectors suggested by the 10–14 report had been widely welcomed and, although its proposals were not formally adopted as national policy, within a few years many of the suggested strategies became commonplace in secondary schools, for instance the visits of primary pupils to the secondary classrooms to meet their future teachers, and the production of school brochures to inform parents, in non-technical language, of the circumstances and requirements of the secondary school. However, progress towards the more important objectives set out in the report, those of ensuring curricular continuity, and improving progression in the learning and development of individual pupils, was less in evidence. In the 1980s, there was no formal mechanism or generally accepted framework by means of which primary and secondary schools could come to agreements about key curricular components; in the absence of a nationally or regionally agreed common curricular structure and of effective mechanisms for cross-sector co-ordination, liaison activities were sporadic and many were of limited success.

The 5–14 development programme, launched by the ministerial paper *Curriculum and Assessment: a Policy for the 90s*, (SED, 1987) had as a central aim the promotion of continuity and progression in the learning and experiences of pupils, the stages P7–S2 being of particular concern. The mechanisms which were subsequently set in place to improve the situation included curriculum guidelines which all schools were enjoined to implement, described at five levels of attainment (A–E); and teacher assessment and national testing to monitor the progress of individual pupils within this common framework in primary and early secondary.

The key question is, to what extent have these initiatives resulted in improved continuity and progression, thereby replacing the pantomime horse by a seamless robe?

PRIMARY AND SECONDARY LIAISON: THE PROBLEMS AND CONCERNS

Continuity in the Curriculum

> A lot of difficulties in S1 are due to coverage, the pressure to get through the curriculum. (principal teacher of Learning Support, Boyd and Simpson, 2000, p. 27)

The curriculum guidelines provided, for the first time, a common language which would enable primary and secondary teachers to discuss common content and goals in teaching and learning. Terms such as 'strands', 'programmes of study', 'Levels A – E' (and later F) came into general usage across the primary–secondary divide, enabling school managers, teachers and advisers to work together to co-ordinate the curricular provision and the experiences and attainments of individual children. Many jointly devised schemes of work such as 'Link Schemes' – work started by pupils while in primary and continued in secondary school – were initiated. However, the curriculum content in the guidelines had been aggregated into five major areas: Language, Mathematics, Environmental Studies, Expressive Arts and Religious and Moral Education, which subsumed the wide variety of subjects considered by both primary and secondary teachers to be essential for a broad and balanced education. Unfortunately, while this gross division was fairly compatible with the pre-existing primary practices, which had been dominated by language, Mathematics and theme work, the five-fold division was not compatible with the equivalent curriculum of S1–S2 which was delivered by seventeen or more separate subject teachers located in different departments. The combination of the three sciences into 'integrated science', or of History and Geography into 'social subjects' had never been universally achieved. However, the recent advancement of Standard Grade into S2 is hastening their 'disaggregation' in some schools. In curricular terms, these first two years are seen by secondary teachers more as a preparation for the choices to be made at Standard Grade than a continuation of the primary experiences.

Continuity in Pedagogy

> I haven't been in a primary school since I was 11! They have a group approach there. We may need to find out more about P6 and P7. (principal teacher secondary, Boyd and Simpson, 2000, p. 15.)

When young people are asked about their experience of coming to the secondary school they cite the variety of teachers and subjects they experience as a definite plus (Boyd and Simpson, 2000). Pupils in P1 to P7 typically have one teacher for each of these years, or for two or more years in small schools, who will be teaching every subject across a range which is almost identical to that of the seventeen secondary school subjects, although some visiting specialists may occasionally be available to assist or advise with Music, Art or Physical Education. A change of teacher is bound to bring welcome novelty and variety. If there is an uncomfortable incompatibility between pupil and any subject, the teacher's style or personality, it will happily cease within the hour!

The pedagogy of the primary classroom typically still involves much group work on common topics, but with pupils set in groups for different levels of work. 'Finding things out' through activities, accessing CD-ROMs and so on, are commonly used strategies. In the secondary schools, such methodologies can occasionally be found, particularly in subjects such as English, or the social subjects, but the typical pedagogy is of whole class work such as questions and answers, with subject content transmission through teacher talk, or school-made workbooks used individually. Setting is being increasingly introduced as a means of pursuing the elusive 'homogeneity'which is clearly necessary for speedy 'coverage' by exposition through lock-step teaching.

The primary teachers' lack of knowledge and confidence in teaching the full range of subjects has been the focus of several studies. A commonly suggested remedy is that secondary teachers, especially in Science and Maths, should regularly visit and instruct their colleagues how to teach the subjects. However, the results of the AAP monitoring over the years points to a healthy progression from P4 to P7, with the slowing off of progress in P7 to S2 (see Chapter 87). Clearly there is more to promoting pupils' learning than just knowledge of the subject – an effective pedagogy is equally essential and perhaps the exchange of expertise needs to go in both directions.

Continuity in Pastoral Care and Pupil Support

> The secondary is very helpful with the Gala and the Athletics Championships because the kids have gone along and have seen the school. (primary headteacher, Boyd and Simpson, 2000, p. 15)

While the problems of curricular progression and continuity seem almost insuperable, it is important to acknowledge where there have been successes. As chapter 86 shows, the support provided across P7 to S1 is of a very high standard. Vulnerable young people, those with special educational needs and those whose parents choose to make placing requests to a secondary school other than the one associated with their child's primary, are almost always identified early and supported through the transition period. Throughout primary seven, there are meetings of guidance, learning support and subject staff to share information and plan programmes – vital in anticipating potential difficulties for both the pupils and staff in the secondary setting. There are often evening meetings where parents can visit the secondary school, meet staff and have questions answered. Documentation is aimed at pupils, parents and secondary staff. These are now fairly standard procedures and in individual schools are supplemented by sports events, mathematical challenges, residential summer schemes, study support classes and even weekly visits to the secondary schools by pupils and staff to use art, ICT or other facilities. The net effect for many pupils is that the move to secondary school is now smooth and unproblematic.

THE CONTRIBUTION OF ASSESSMENT AND MONITORING

My main concern is that the primary information should be acted on. I suspect that a few do, and many don't. (Assistant headteacher secondary, Boyd and Simpson, 2000, p. 19)

A central concern of the 5–14 programme was to promote the generation of records which would inform parents and professionals about the progression of individual children and the stages they had reached in order that the continuity of education could be smoothed. Of vital importance in this process is the written records which the primary teacher has assembled and passed to the secondary school. The early problems indicated were access of secondary teachers to the information, the use of a common format across the associated primaries, the trust which the secondary teachers had in these records, and finally the action which they subsequently took (Simpson and Goulder, 1998). The situation has now improved on all these fronts; for example, a national format for 5–14 progress reports has been devised. However, as the quotation above indicates, matters in many schools are still far from satisfactory.

With respect to the primary teachers' general appraisals of individual pupils, a perception in secondary schools was that they 'wrote in a code which maximises the positive and minimises the negative', and that the assessments of levels of attainment were consequently unreliable. This points towards a lack of opportunity for liaison in the form of cross-sector moderation meetings, essential for standardising judgements. While primary schools had generally grasped the concept of formative assessment and had been able to introduce it into the planning process in the way the 5–14 guidelines had proposed, secondary teachers still tended to see assessment as summative, consisting mainly of tests to be passed or failed at the end of units, terms or sessions. An attempt was made by authorities to reduce the number of teachers encountered by pupils each week in S1. However, the requirement to meet staged targets appeared to result in meeting the targets becoming the goal. Some reduction in the number of teachers has been achieved (to thirteen), but largely through the ingenuity of the timetablers rather than the development of any coherent curricular planning which actually met the aim of the process – teachers getting to know pupils better. Increasingly, the response given to the requirement to meet the needs of diverse pupils for progression and continuity, is setting on the basis of national tests – which teachers also indicate they distrust (Boyd and Simpson, 2000). Assessment and monitoring processes have thus failed to bridge the primary/secondary gap: each attempt fails to make the sectors more like each other.

PUPILS' AND PARENTS' VIEWS

In their study of S1 and S2, Boyd and Simpson interviewed groups of pupils in P7 about their expectations, and followed up by interviewing pupils in S1 and S2 about their experiences. Many of the issues which exercise professionals are of little concern to pupils. They like the variety of subjects, they like moving around from class to class and they seem to enjoy having a range of teachers. However, they echo the concerns of professionals when they claim that they are not doing work which is any more difficult than that in P7, that they get less regular homework and that there is much repetition of work which they have already done.

Their parents have similar concerns. While expressing general satisfaction with secondary school and the transition arrangements, they report concerns that pupils are going back over old ground in S1, that there is less proper homework and, importantly, that there is more unfinished class work that is to be completed at home. In many subjects, books, folders and jotters stay in the classroom, and concerned parents find it difficult to stay abreast of what their child is doing, particularly in the face of limited and fairly terse communications from teachers.

CHANGES IN THE SYSTEM AND FUTURE DEVELOPMENTS

The future of primary and secondary education in Scotland is, at the time of writing, the focus of a national debate. There are some straws in the wind. The Scottish Executive Education Committee's circular on flexibility in the curriculum has opened the door to changes which could potentially enable greater continuity and progression in the curriculum from P7 to S1 for some pupils. Already there are signs of changes being made to the S1/S2 curriculum, but they point towards the reinforcement of the subject and exam dominated secondary model of education. In other words, flexibility is being interpreted as a sector-specific matter and not one which will promote the negotiation of optimal learner-centred educational experiences or a common language for discussing pedagogy and curriculum. The pantomime horse lumbers on and for many pupils 'fresh start' is still the norm.

It is fairly clear that teachers in the two sectors do not yet, 5–14 notwithstanding, share a common culture. From the time of their teacher education courses, the differences appear to be reinforced and opportunities for liaison are not prioritised. Cluster groups of schools (known across Scotland by different names) involving a secondary and associated primary and, sometimes, pre-5 and special needs schools, work at different levels of effectiveness throughout the country. In one council, there are pioneering schemes where one of the headteachers is promoted to the level of principal and decision making is at the level of the cluster. In others, the arrangement is much looser and variations in effectiveness owe much to the personalities of the headteachers involved.

What is certainly true is that there is a growing realisation that the issues of progression and continuity need to extend beyond the completion of progress reports, agreement on content to be covered (when and by whom) and occasional bridging projects. The key focus has to be learning and teaching and there are some signs that issues such as 'thinking skills' and metacognition, along with the importance of motivation and self-esteem to pupils' success as learners, may be the common ground which 5–14 did not successfully provide.

REFERENCES

Boyd, B. and Simpson, M. (2000) *Developing a Framework for Effective Learning and Teaching*, Falkirk; Angus Council.

CCC (1986) *Education 10–14 in Scotland*, Dundee: CCC.

SED (1987) *Curriculum and Assessment in Scotland: A Policy for the 90s*, SED.

Simpson, M. and Goulder, M. (1998) Promoting Continuity and Progression: Implementing 5–14 in secondary school Mathematics and English departments, *Scottish Educational Review* 30(1), 15–28.

VI

Pre-School and
Primary Education: Curriculum

35

5–14: Origins, Development and Implementation

Frank R. Adams

ORIGINS

The Curriculum and Assessment 5–14 Programme can be seen as having two linked but distinctive origins. One was the political circumstances which led a government to seek central control over the school curriculum. The other was the professional imperatives which led to the curriculum for the primary and early secondary stages being more explicitly formulated than in the previous forty years. It is difficult to disentangle these sources given the commonality that existed between them in the professional role of the inspectorate in advising the Secretary of State for Scotland (pre-devolution) on the school curriculum.

Political priorities for the Conservative government, coping with the backlash from a damaging teachers' strike in the mid-1980s, were an increase in parental choice and in the provision of information on schools. The frequent expression of traditional concerns about alleged falling standards and the ideological distrust of so-called 'progressive' methods created the context for the introduction of a programme to provide a centralised initiative on the curriculum which would simultaneously limit teacher autonomy, promise clearer definition of the curriculum and better communication with parents, and exercise greater control over standards through national testing, thus creating a comprehensive, appropriate political response. The appearance of the Secretary of State's Consultative Paper (SED, 1987) was described as, 'a shift in policy making style in Scotland from debate followed by consensus to consultation followed by imposition' (Roger, in Hartley and Roger, 1990, p. 1).

The professional context for 5–14 can be traced through the range of reports produced by HM Inspectorate and the Scottish Education Department (SED) in the period from 1965 to 1987.

DEVELOPMENT

The starting point of the SED's *Primary Education in Scotland* (SED, 1965) is not arbitrary. The Memorandum, as it came to be known, was widely described, up to 1987, as the benchmark against which all progress in primary education was measured. It pre-dated by two years the English Plowden Report, regarded as the epitome of child-centredness, and set out a philosophy of primary education which started with the needs and was responsive to the interests of the child, was appropriate to age, aptitude and ability and saw pupils as active in their own learning.

The document emphasised consultation and debate: 'The memorandum avoids prescription of either subject-matter or methods' (p. viii), and variety rather than conformity:

> Much of the content of the curriculum will vary from school to school, from class to class within the same school, in certain instances from pupil to pupil within the same class . . . it is for each headteacher and his [sic] staff to determine . . . precisely what is to be included . . . (p. 38)

It challenged teachers, particularly headteachers, to reconceptualise their approaches to the education of primary school age children. This is in stark contrast to the prescription of current centralised arrangements.

Six years after publication of the Memorandum, the SED published *Primary Education: Organisation for Development* (SED, 1971) which was a 'progress report' on the guidance for teachers in implementing the Memorandum's suggestions offered by education authorities, colleges of education and headteachers.

The 1965 Memorandum had left provision of guidance on the curriculum to the education authorities but the wide variability found in the quality and impact of that guidance was ascribed to failure to take full account of school circumstances, being over-general in the advice given and even to the providers sometimes having lacked 'the opportunity to practise in the classroom the theories they were advocating' (pp. 8–9). A need for schools to have 'clearly defined curricular policies' was identified because of the evidence that 'few headteachers [had] done anything to formulate a policy for the planned implementation of the approaches suggested by the Primary Memorandum' (p. 16).

Significant weaknesses in primary–secondary liaison were identified with secondary teachers unable to appreciate the nature of work in primary and some primary teachers asking secondary teachers to tell them what to teach in upper primary leading to advice which was 'ill-advised and [which] has had a restricting effect on the curriculum of the primary school' (p. 22). Almost contemporary with the primary report, the SED published *The First Two Years of Secondary Education* (SED, 1972) which reported on a survey of just under half of secondary schools in Scotland and commented on 'a disconcerting absence of a clearly defined policy' on new forms of organisation and with the common course for S1 and S2 (p. 18).

Between 1972 and 1980 a number of SED reports were circulated to schools, developing specific aspects of the curriculum, the most significant of which was *Primary Education in Scotland: Mathematics* (SED, 1973). Known as Curriculum Paper 13, the document was presented as an updating and consolidation of the work outlined in the Primary Memorandum and might be seen as the first national guideline in a curricular area for primary schools. Advice was offered in relation to three stages, P1–P3, P3–P5, and P5–P7. Two short paragraphs on links with the secondary provided a foretaste of the attainment targets and levels of 5–14:

> The test of where a child should be at the end of P3 is his ability to understand and deal with the work he is doing, not his age nor the length of time he has been in school. The brightest pupils

will have covered more than is suggested here, while the slowest will not have reached the final point in the progression. (p. 5)

Learning and Teaching in P4 and P7 (SED, 1980) was a survey of primary education in 152 schools at P4 and P7 which also assessed, through the Scottish Council for Research in Education (SCRE), national standards in Reading and Mathematics. Rather than the broad, active curriculum proposed in 1965, *Learning and Teaching in P4 and P7* found a narrow curriculum comprising reading comprehension, language exercises and formal aspects of Maths with little or no Science, spoken English and Art. The inspectorate suggested that the curriculum was not meeting the expectations of 1965 and, in some cases, not even extending to the standards of the 1950 guidance to schools or the 1956 Code. Teachers favoured closed responses from pupils, very little discovery learning, open-ended questioning and discussion. Curricular integration was not common:

> The Scottish primary school teacher insists on making her pupils literate and numerate . . . The acquisition of a variety of modes of learning and a potential for creative activity appears to go largely unchallenged by the present curriculum. (p. 7)

In 1980, only seven years before the Curriculum and Assessment 5–14 Programme, the need for consensus still appeared important for policy makers. In calling for a major review of primary education, the SED felt that 'it would be unwise to undertake it without regard to a wider consensus about the nature and content of primary education' (pp. 49–50). Nevertheless, for the first time since 1965, the necessity, desirability and extent of national monitoring of standards was raised, setting the scene for battles to come over national testing.

Questioning the extent and desirability of teacher autonomy in determining the curriculum appears to have been a concern but, taken with Curriculum Paper 13 and later with the SED report on *Learning and Teaching: The Environment and the Primary School Curriculum* (SED, 1984), official thinking in the 1980s signalled a shift towards central direction in the curriculum.

An account of the origins of 5–14 would be incomplete without reference to the alternative proposals for a reconceptualised primary and early secondary curriculum developed by the Consultative Committee on the Curriculum's (CCC) Education 10–14 Programme (CCC, 1986). Challenged with the task of reconciling primary and secondary approaches to the curriculum, the Education 10–14 Committee proposed the same basic principles of continuity, progression, breadth and balance as the Curriculum and Assessment 5–14 consultative paper would do only eighteen months later, but the 10–14 concept of guidelines was combined with a recognition of the professional commitment of teachers and proposed 'autonomy within guidelines'. As commentators have noted (Boyd, in Humes and MacKenzie, 1994; Hartley and Roger 1990), 10–14 was the victim of a change in the political climate.

This change was reflected in the fact that the concept of guidelines in *Curriculum and Assessment in Scotland: A Policy for the '90s* (SED, 1987) was based on the threat that 'the Secretary of State would not rule out introducing legislation to ensure the proper implementation of national policy' (SED, 1987, para. 54). The consultative paper suggested that there were weaknesses in the curricular and assessment practices of primary and early secondary schools, identified as poor school policies for the curriculum, lack of definition of the curriculum and curricular discontinuity, insufficient challenge for pupils especially at P6 and P7, inconsistent assessment practices and poor communication with parents.

The paper set out a strategy to meet these weaknesses which was, in essence, to produce detailed guidelines on the aims, objectives and content for each aspect of the curriculum for P1–S2 and to put into place improved assessment practices and a national testing programme to give 'assurance about the progress that is being achieved.' (SED, 1987, p. 9). HMI reports, mainly on primary education, from 1973–1984 contained the elements of the official advice that was eventually crystallised in the conjunction of professional advice and political ideology that was represented by the 1987 consultative paper.

Continuity and progression between P7 and S1 was a major objective of both the Education 10–14 Report and the 5–14 proposals. It is significant, however, that the 5–14 programme in seeking to achieve linkage between two sectors of school education, traditionally different in rationale and assumptions, proceeded without any contextualising rationale or philosophy. This has been discussed elsewhere (Adams, 1988; Adams in Kirk and Glaister, 1994) and is common with events which have surrounded the development of the national curriculum in England, Wales and Northern Ireland. Advice to schools was expected to be as slim as possible in response to politicians' suspicion of so-called 'theory' and their more pragmatic fears about the impact on teacher workload. In Scotland, the response of politicians and some civil servants to the length of the Education 10–14 Report was rejection of the prolixity of professional educators and an apparent lack of confidence in the ability of the teaching profession to cope with the analysis of complex ideas in favour of a short, sharp, simple set of instructions presented as guidelines, a view disputed by many practising teachers.

Among the short, simple instructions of 5–14, the advice on the complex notion of balance in the primary curriculum stands out. In 1983, the National Committee on Primary Education (COPE), in *Primary Education in the Eighties* (COPE, 1983) had acknowledged the importance of the issue of balance and breadth in the primary curriculum but had rejected a simple arithmetical approach to balance: 'The idea of balance involves not just a balance of modes or curricular experiences, but balance of skills, activities, social experiences . . . balance of teaching approaches of different types,' (pp. 18–19). This kind of complexity was rejected by 5–14 where, late in the development process, a precise definition of balance as 'appropriate time . . . allocated to each area of curricular activity', was set out in *Structure and Balance of the Curriculum 5–14* (SOED, 1993). The overriding need to find a way of describing the primary curriculum balance that articulated with the existing timetabled structure of S1 and S2 appears to have forced this kind of simplistic approach to a complex issue.

Seven years on, in 2000, new advice on structure and balance became available in the form of a new guideline, *The Structure and Balance of the Curriculum: 5–14 National Guidelines* (Learning and Teaching Scotland, 2000). The scope of this new document is significant in that it includes the previously absent advice on a rationale for the 5–14 curriculum as well as more extended definitions of the key principles of 5–14. Also, significantly, the document reinterprets the advice on balance which was contained in the original 1993 guidelines.

The recommended balance in the 1993 and the 2000 guidelines is set out below in Table 35.1.

Table 35.1: Balance of minimum allocation of time

	1993		2000	
	Primary	Secondary 1 and 2	Primary	Secondary 1 and 2
Mathematics	15%	10%	15%	10%
Language	15%	20%	20% (including Modern Language from P6)	20%
Religious and Moral Education	10%	5%	15% (including Personal & Social Development and Health Education)	5%
Expressive Arts	15%		15%	15% (including Physical Education)
Environmental Studies	25%		15% (Society, Science & Technology)	30% (Society, Science & Technology)
Scientific Studies and Applications		10%		
Technological Studies and Applications		10%		
Social and Environmental Studies		10%		
Creative and Aesthetic Activities		10%		
Physical Education		5%		
Flexibility	20%	20%	20%	20%

The guidance emphasises that the allocations of time are minimum allocations. Early criticism based, for example, on the problems of specifying the 15% of the curriculum that is exclusively language development as distinct from the language development that takes place elsewhere have continued. (See, for example, Adams in Kirk and Glaister, 1994, pp. 4–6) Four years on from the publication of the time allocations there is evidence to suggest that, even given the flexibility factor, the profession is not satisfied that global allocations of time can be made. Differences between the needs of P1–P3 and P4–P7, for example, raise doubts about the minimum allocation of 25% to Environmental Studies throughout the primary years. Growing emphasis on, for instance, early literacy have caused some education authorities to issue guidance on balance which is different from the official line.

By late 1999 some education authorities, notably North Lanarkshire, had begun to issue local guidance on balance to primary schools which gave greater emphasis to Reading, Writing and Mathematics and developed proposals to move Standard Grade courses to S2 and S3 effectively making the 5–14 curriculum a 5–13 curriculum. Pressure on education authorities to increase the emphasis on the so-called 'three Rs' and on achievement at Standard Grade had become greater by the introduction of a target-setting regime in 1998 (*Raising Standards – Setting Targets* : SOEID, March 1998) as part of the new 'Quality

Initiative in Scottish Education' (see below). By early 2000, East Renfrewshire education authority had begun piloting a scheme which derived 5–14 targets from Standard Grade targets in order to 'drive up attainment' (*Times Educational Supplement Scotland*, 7 January 2000). There seems little doubt that the introduction of target-setting has had a significant impact on the implementation of 5–14, at least in the central areas of Reading, Writing and Mathematics.

The 5–14 programme applies only in Scotland while the National Curriculum is the statutory guidance on the curriculum in England and Wales. There have been marked similarities in the process of production of the national curriculum guidance in Scotland and England. In both cases subject based working groups were set up, each producing its 'ideal' curriculum, the sum of which is a vastly complex map of the primary curriculum with overload resulting from curriculum decisions made by isolated working groups using the strategy of include everything and cross-reference among curricular areas. Other similarities include the confidentiality of the working groups (lack of public access to minutes and working papers), tight time scales, tokenistic consultation and rapid introduction to schools.

The English National Curriculum differs principally from the Scottish 5–14 Curriculum and Assessment programme in its separation of the primary stages from the secondary through presentation of curriculum at Key Stages 1 and 2 (5–7 years and 7–11 years) for primary and Key Stages 3 and 4 (11–14 years and 14–16 years) for secondary. While 5–14 occupies the longest timespan in the Scottish curriculum made up of 5–14 years (P1–S2), which includes attainment targets grouped at six levels of progression A–F, followed by Standard Grade (S3–S4) and Higher Still (S4–S6), there is no overall perception of the Scottish curriculum as a seamless garment from P1 to S4. Differences also exist in the curriculum coverage at each of the stages. The 5–14 programme covers all of the areas of the curriculum and does not prescribe a core curriculum, while the English National Curriculum labels English, Mathematics and Science as core subjects with Technology, History, Geography, Art, Music and PE as foundation subjects at Key Stages 1 and 2 and, with the addition of a modern language, at Key Stage 3. There are similarities in terminology within both structures but differences in interpretation of the terms used is set out in Table 35.2, below.

Table 35.2: Balance of the allocation of time in 5–14

	Primary	Secondary 1 & 2
Mathematics	15%	10%
Language	15%	20%
Religious and Moral Education	10%	5%
Expressive Arts	15%	
Environmental Studies	25%	
Scientific Studies & Applications		10%
Technological Studies and Applications		10%
Social & Environmental Studies		10%
Creative and Aesthetic Activities		10%
Physical Education		5%
Flexibility	20%	20%

The nature of the 'programmes of study' in the two educational systems is of particular interest. The English National Curriculum is prescriptive in what is to be taught at each Key Stage while the Scottish 5–14 programme expects schools to use the information and advice contained in the 5–14 guidelines to review existing school programmes and to develop appropriate responses.

IMPLEMENTATION

It is a moot point as to when any development programme is complete and full implementation of the changes should be expected. The 5–14 development programme is no exception to this since final versions of the national guidelines appeared over a three-year period (1991–4) and then had to find their place in the existing development plans of schools. New editions of guidelines, specifically in aspects of Environmental Studies, appeared by 2000 reflecting to some extent the difficulties that schools had had in dealing with the Environmental Studies guidelines in 1993. The introduction, in 2000, of a set of documents entitled *Guide for Teachers and Managers* providing 'practical advice and exemplification' relating to the Environmental Studies national guidelines could be significant in implementation of this problematic curriculum area in the years to come. The order of publication and revision therefore continues to play a part in the implementation of 5–14 in schools as Table 35.3 shows:

Table 35.3:   Publication dates of 5–14 national guidelines

1991	English Language	Assessment	Mathematics					
1992	Expressive Arts	Religious and Moral Education	Latin	Modern Languages	Reporting			
1993	Structure and Balance of the Curriculum	Personal and Social Development	Environmental Studies	Gaelic				
1994	5–14: A Practical Guide							
2000	The Structure and Balance of the Curriculum: 5–14 (i) National Guidelines (ii) Guide for Teachers and Managers	Environmental Studies – Society, Science and Technology: 5–14 National Guidelines	Health Education: 5–14 (i) National Guidelines (ii) Guide for Teachers and Managers	Information and Communications Technology: 5–14 (i) National Guidelines (ii) Guide for Teachers and Managers	Modern Languages: 5–14 National Guidelines	Environmental Studies: Social Subjects: 5–14 Guide for Teachers and Managers	Environmental Studies: Technology 5–14 Guide for Teachers and Managers	Environmental Studies: Science 5–14 Guide for Teachers and Managers

There are three current sources of evidence about the extent and nature of the implementation of 5–14. One is the official SOED-funded evaluation programme co-ordinated by the Scottish Council for Research in Education (SCRE). The second source is evidence from school inspections summarised in the *Standards and Quality in Scottish Schools* series (1992–95, 1995–98 and 1998–2001). The third is independent research related to the 5–14 programme.

The official evaluation of the 5–14 programme (Harlen, 1996) focused initially on the years 1991–5 and was subsequently extended to take in the period 1995–7. Evidence from the primary school evaluation indicates that 5–14 documentation appears, increasingly, to be used as the main tool for curriculum audit and, as familiarity with the details of the documentation grow, 5–14 takes on the dominant role in forward planning. The overall tone of the SCRE evaluation suggests there is acceptance of the 5–14 framework by the profession despite some initial difficulties caused mainly by the apparent complexity of the documentation and the pace of change (Harlen, 1996, p. 32). Evidence from the secondary sector, however, indicates that there is less enthusiasm for the national guidelines as the basis for continuity from primary to secondary:

> . . . in terms of continuity of progress for the individual pupil, the entrenched preference for a 'fresh start' and lack of interest in records and work sent by pupils' previous teachers remain a cause for some concern. (Harlen, 1996, p. 31)

The preliminary public reports in the educational press (Simpson and Goulder in *Times Educational Supplement Scotland*, 12 September 1997) on the surveys carried out in 1995–6, indicate that implementation of the English and Mathematics guidelines was regarded as 'well under way' in most secondary schools but that other curricular areas were at 'the earliest stages of implementation, that of discussion and awareness raising' in half of the schools surveyed by the researchers. Clearly the existence of the 5–14 guidelines was not sufficient in itself to guarantee that there would be continuity between the primary and secondary stages. Commentators have continued to voice criticism of the apparent inability of the 5–14 initiative to guarantee an improvement in primary-secondary continuity and in the S1/S2 experience (see e.g. Forrester, *TESS*, December 2000; Boyd, *TESS*, January 2000).

5–14 is an essential plank in the 'Quality Initiative' that has been promoted by HM Inspectors in Scottish schools. The 1987 consultative paper did not rule out legislation to ensure the introduction of 5–14 and expected HMI to reinforce this in their inspection of schools (SED, 1987, p. 7). *Standards and Quality in Scottish Schools* (SOEID, 1996) and *Standards and Quality in Primary and Secondary Schools 1998–2001* (HMIE, 2002) have reported on standards of attainment in English Language and Mathematics in both primary and S1/S2 against the 5–14 attainment targets.

A key difference between the 1996 and the 2002 reports relates to the introduction and use of performance indicators in schools based on *How Good is Our School?* (1992, 1996 and 2002). The foreword to the 2002 edition by the HMSCI, Douglas Osler, catalogues the new quality initiative as including the Standards in Scotland's Schools Act (2000); new National Priorities with improvement plans and targets; and more extensive local authority quality assurance procedures. *The Standards and Quality Report 1998–2001* lists a range of improvements since 1998 in aspects of the 5–14 curriculum in primary schools but it is significant to note that improvements in the secondary context make no reference to S1 and S2, confirming the concerns expressed by critics of the implementation of the 5–14 curriculum.

Independent research on 5–14 has been very scarce since its implementation. Research has been commissioned by the Scottish Office Education Department (later the Scottish Executive Education Department) some of which has had a significant impact on teaching and learning, for instance studies leading to implementation of Early Literacy schemes.

Little research appears, however, to have been carried out independently which might have subjected the 5–14 initiative to critical analysis. The ESRC-funded research carried out by Swann & Brown in 1997 remains a significant exception. One source of independent thinking on the impact of 5–14 might have been research theses carried out for the award of PhD or masters degrees. In the period 1991–6, a key implementation period for 5–14, only ten theses were submitted to Scottish universities on aspects of 5–14. In contrast, aspects of the National Curriculum were the subject of at least three times as many submissions.

ISSUES

The 5–14 development programme has given rise to many issues for practitioners in both schools and teacher education institutions as well as those in education authorities. The final section of this chapter will identify some of these issues which remain problematic and which will continue to form the basis for considerable debate.

The 5–14 programme was promoted as being 'founded on widely accepted principles' (SED, 1987, p. 3) and 'built on the advice and teaching materials already available as a result of the work of the CCC' (p. 18). English Language 5–14, for example, could draw on the extensive work done in the 1980s on children's writing by the Scottish Committee on Language Arts (SCOLA) in the primary context and on similar work which had been going on in the secondary context but, even then, the resulting guidelines were open to criticism by the former chair of SCOLA:

> . . . the neat curricular tabulations of the 5–14 documents are . . . a denial of the innate complexity of learning and teaching. English Language 5–14, as a model, bears little if any relationship to how children acquire language. (Macdonald in Kirk and Glaister, 1994, p. 57)

This kind of criticism shows the problem that the totality of the experience of pupils in primary or early secondary schools is not reflected adequately in the simple assurance that the curriculum is broad, balanced, continuous and progressive, important as these concepts may be. Their importance is only matched by their problematic nature when attempts are made to turn them into day-to-day classroom experiences for pupils and teachers. The apparently straightforward presentation of the content of the national guidelines belies the complexity of the daily professional judgements required in teaching and reduces the role of competent, reflective practitioners in the successful application of any guidelines.

Where the basis of curricular agreement did not already exist, the potential for the exercise of professional judgement might appear greater, giving the teacher more flexibility and freedom to act. However, the complexities of the professional disagreements over Environmental Studies (see Adams in Kirk and Glaister, 1994, pp. 11–16) are such that more than four years after the publication of the national guidelines there is a continuing lack of consensus on the preferred curricular organisation, particularly at the S1/S2 ages. In 2000, Learning and Teaching Scotland, on behalf of the Scottish Executive, published revised guidelines on Environmental Studies which removed Health Education and Information Technology from Environmental Studies. The single Environmental Studies guideline of 1993 was replaced by a suite of three national guideline documents (Society, Science & Technology; Health Education; Information & Communications Technology) and five 'Guide for Teachers and Managers' documents (Social Subjects; Science; Technology; Health Education; Information and Communications Technology). The new guidelines and guides received a less than enthusiastic welcome from at least one education authority and from the EIS (*TESS*, 11 February, 2000) which described them as 'unmanageable and content-heavy' and as 'imposing unreasonable expectations on teachers'.

The extent to which integration should exist in the primary curriculum remains problematic (see, for example, Macdonald, in Kirk and Glaister pp. 50–68; Adams, pp. 15–16) for both schools and teacher education institutions seeking to prepare students for the often apparently conflicting demands of the modern primary school. Unfortunately the problem is more complex than whether to link subjects within a curriculum plan. The Committee on Primary Education (COPE) issued a 'starter paper' *Some Aspects of Thematic Work* (COPE, 1987) which emphasised the centrality of the processes of learning and the contexts in which learning took place. This was swamped by the 5–14 consultative documents which, while endorsing the modes of teaching first established by COPE in 1983, did little to examine the relationship between the processes of learning and the planned curriculum and it is in this vacuum that the issue of integrated work exists. Further debate on the issue of thematic work seems now to have disappeared. The fundamental question for primary practice today is not about how the curriculum is organised, described or reported on. It is about the conceptions of knowledge and how it is constructed and, in particular, the role that the teacher plays in partnership with his or her pupils in constructing that knowledge. It is to do with the relationship between the teacher and the taught; between teaching and learning.

The 5–14 curriculum has been in place for more than ten years and questions do arise about the shelf-life of that curriculum. Despite the assertion in 1991 that 5–14 was no more than a codification of existing good practice, there can be no doubt that its introduction was a significant upheaval in the professional experience of schools and teachers. While concerns continue to be expressed about the impact on curricular balance in primary with a significant increase in attention to basic literacy and numeracy coupled with a significant lack of impact on the early secondary curriculum, there can be little doubt that the 5–14 curriculum is the *de facto* national curriculum of Scotland.

The term '5–14 curriculum' no longer describes a new initiative but rather simply delineates the age-span that the national guidelines cover. No curriculum can be regarded as being final. It is always a compromise between the competing priorities of many stakeholders, including pupils, parents, politicians, and employers and should be subject to continual monitoring and development. The basis for the kind of curriculum change that took place in the late 1980s and early 1990s was, for many teachers, a negative assessment of the quality of their work and it is to be hoped that the new millennium has brought with it a changed attitude from those in authority to the contribution of teachers to the quality of education in Scotland. The focus on school-based self-evaluation should increase ownership of the curriculum and its development by teachers provided that the basis for that self-evaluation, for example *How Good is Our School?* (2000), is not seen as proxy for centralist direction by the Scottish Executive.

The initiation of a National Debate on Education in March 2002 by the Minister for Education and Young People has been presented as the first step towards formulating a long-term vision for Scottish Education. By July 2002, 1,200 responses had been received by the Scottish Executive which will, in due course, inform discussion by the Scottish Parliament. The range of responses is likely to be wide as the following examples indicate:

- Ideas from contributions by pupils to a national debate conference sponsored by the EIS (May 2002) include more specialist teaching in primary schools, more PE, sport and Home Economics and more opportunities for active learning.
- The Scottish Arts Council (July 2002) has called for greater emphasis on the arts in schools because 'the status of arts and culture remains low'.
- *Sportscotland* (July 2002) calls for at least two hours per week of PE in schools.
- The Scottish Parent Teacher Council, in a submission to the Scottish Parliament Education Committee (June 2002), calls for an extension of the school week with extra time given to Art, Music, PE and Drama taught by specialists.

A strategy document resulting from the national debate is scheduled for publication in 2003. The minister sees that document as 'our chance to look to the future – informed by the past and the present. Our experiences as children, as parents, as teachers, as managers and as leaders can all contribute to our shared vision of education for the 21st century' (May 2002). Beyond 2003, 5–14 may be a historical concept. If the post-2003 curriculum is genuinely informed by the views of all of those involved and if teachers are no longer the recipients of a top-down process and the victims of a blame culture, then we may have moved on from Hartley and Roger's 'consultation followed by imposition' and at last have achieved a consensus curriculum.

REFERENCES

Adams, F. R. (1988) Curriculum framework for the primary stages, *Scottish Educational Review*, 20(2), 93–6.

Harlen, W. (1996) *Four Years of Change in Education 5–14*, Edinburgh: SCRE.

Hartley, D. and Roger, A. (1990) *Curriculum and Assessment in Scotland: A Policy for the 90s*, Edinburgh: Scottish Academic Press.

Humes, W. M. and MacKenzie, M. L. (1994) *The Management of Educational Policy*, Essex: Longman.

Kirk, G. and Glaister, R. (1994) *5–14: Scotland's National Curriculum*, Edinburgh: Scottish Academic Press.

Swann, J. and Brown, S. (1997) The implementation of a national curriculum and teachers' classroom thinking, *Research Papers in Education*, 12.(1), pp. 91–114.

36

English Language

Sue Ellis and Gill Friel

Language is a key curricular area in Scottish primary schools. It has a minimum time allocation of 15% of the timetable but most schools also use time from their 20% flexibility-factor for Language. Implementation of the non-statutory *English Language 5–14: National Guidelines* (SOEID, 1991) is almost universal and the guidelines are used to frame policy development, planning, teaching, assessment and reporting to parents.

English Language 5–14 identifies aspects of learning, or strands, within four attainment outcomes: Listening, Talking, Reading and Writing (see Table 36.1). Within each strand, attainment targets describe minimum competencies for six broad levels of attainment, levels A-F. Since 1999 these levels have been used by schools and local authorities to set achievement targets. The 'programmes of study' within the guidelines are supplemented by advice and resources published by Learning and Teaching Scotland (http://www.ltscotland.com), formerly the Scottish Consultative Committee on the Curriculum. Pre-five practice is informed by the joint SEED/LTS publications *A Curriculum Framework for Children 3–5* (1999) and *A Child at the Centre* (2000).

In 1997, local education authorities were given Scottish Office funding and considerable autonomy to develop early intervention projects in P1 and P2. Projects adopted different perspectives on teaching, learning and staff development whilst emphasising broadly similar content (phonological awareness, emergent and independent writing, whole-class/interactive teaching, home-school links and increased staffing in the form of nursery-nurses, classroom assistants and additional teachers in early years classrooms). The initiative raised attainment, teacher expectations, confidence, knowledge and enthusiasm (Fraser et al., 2001) and has prompted debate, and some concern about, pre-5 literacy development, baseline assessment, pedagogical knowledge, staff development and curriculum balance in the early stages. Although funding in the most successful projects was targeted at disadvantaged groups, the attainment gaps associated with socio-economic advantage, gender and age of entry were not eliminated, nor was the gap in attainment between Reading and Writing. In 1999, target setting was used to focus attention on attainment in writing, resulting in local authorities developing policies, programmes and support materials for this (e.g. Glasgow Education Authority, 2000).

Table 36.1:   Attainment outcomes and strands in English Language 5–14

	Reading	Writing	Talking	Listening
	ATTAINMENT OUTCOMES			
S	Reading for Information	Functional Writing	Conveying Information, Instructions & Directions	Listening for Information, Instructions & Directions
		Imaginative Writing		
T	Reading for Enjoyment	Personal Writing		
R	Reading to Reflect the writer's Ideas	Handwriting & Presentation	Talking in Groups	Listening in Groups
A	and Craft	Spelling, Punctu-ation & Structure	Talking about Experiences, Feelings & Opinions	Listening in Order to respond to Texts
N	Awareness of Genre			Awareness of Genre
D	Reading Aloud	Knowledge about Language	Talking about Texts	Knowledge about Language
			Audience	
S	Knowledge about Language		Awareness Knowledge about Language	

MONITORING AND ASSESSMENT PROCEDURES

Her Majesty's Inspectorate of Education (HMIE) monitors the effectiveness of language programmes and standards of attainment through inspection reports of individual schools. HMIE also produces summary reports and reports on aspect inspections, which highlight general issues (SOEID, 1998; 1999) (http://www.scotland.gov.uk/hmie). It is the norm for children to sit national tests in Reading and Writing when the teacher judges them to have attained the relevant 5–14 level. Test items try to reflect classroom practice and are selected from a bank of items by the teacher, who administers and marks them against national criteria.

The Assessment of Achievement Programme (AAP), monitors national standards at P4, P7 and S2, enabling comparisons between stages and over time. English Language surveys were carried out in 1984, 1989, 1992, 1996 and 2001. The design of the national test and its relationship with the AAP is currently under review.

Policy and Practice Prior to 5–14

Prior to 5–14, curriculum development was influenced by the 'Primary Memoran-dum' (SED, *Primary Education in Scotland*, Edinburgh: HMSO, 1965), which promoted an integrated, contextualised language curriculum over rote-learning and book-based exercises. The Scottish Central Committee on Primary Education (SCCOPE/COPE) and its sub-committee for Language Arts (SCOLA) advised on language policy, teaching methodology and content (SCOLA, 1975). Its key concerns were poorly-focused teaching and progression in topic-based language work, poor awareness of talking and listening and the lack of good classroom resources and advice in this area. It wanted to promote reading for pleasure, less focus on purely secretarial skills in writing and a more structured approach to assessment and recording. The COPE documents *Hand in your Writing* (SCCC, 1981) and *Mr. Togs the Tailor* (SCCC, 1982) promoted context and purpose, audience awareness and redrafting. To ensure a clear teaching focus, *Responding to Writing* (SCCC, 1986) based assessment strictly on the written product, which unfortunately focused attention on the communicative adequacy of children's writing rather than on developmental issues or the writing process strategies to be taught. Pedagogical debate about the teaching of reading seems to have been widespread, vibrant and productive. Meetings of the United Kingdom Reading Association (West of Scotland Reading Association in Glasgow) were regular and well-attended. Classroom resources such as the *Edinburgh Reading Test* (London: Hodder and Stoughton, 1977), the *Scope for Reading* series (Edinburgh: Holmes McDougall, 1975) and COPE documents such as *The Reading Habit* (COPE, 1978) illustrate the desire to develop a coherent, skills-based curriculum beyond the infant stages.

READING AND WRITING

Currently, over 97% of primary schools use commercial resources such as reading schemes and phonics programmes to teach reading. Commercial resources for teaching handwriting, spelling, punctuation, grammar, reading for information and writing are also common. Whole-class reading activities generally include phonics teaching, listening to stories and discussion using big books. Many classrooms have book corners to promote reading for pleasure, although the quality and use of these varies. Despite anecdotal evidence of a recent general shift to whole-class teaching, reading tends to be taught in differentiated attainment groups. Differentiation is reflected in the level of text difficulty and the rate at which children move through the scheme rather than in the tasks or instruction given; once on the scheme all children work through broadly similar activities. In good practice, topic work provides a context for teaching Reading for Information and for writing, with differentiated worksheets to support those with literacy difficulties. Schools supplement core reading schemes with activities and alternative schemes, structured around the 5–14 strands and use group/class novels to extend (or occasionally, in the upper primary stages, to replace) the reading scheme.

Much writing is taught as a whole class activity. Following international trends, recent attention has been on non-fiction writing, peer feedback, scaffolded tasks and teacher-modelling. Many local authorities have adopted a genre-based approach to Functional Writing, leaving some teachers confused about how this relates to the formats (letters; instructions; posters etc.) specified in 5–14. Personal and Imaginative Writing are combined in the national test and there is anecdotal evidence of a decline in the frequency of open-ended imaginative writing tasks. Where writing is taught well, children are sometimes allowed to choose their own topic, format or genre, but generally, teachers specify these, even in Personal Writing. Desk-top publishing is encouraged. Reading-writing links are recognised in many local authority policy documents and infant teachers commonly link the teaching of phonological awareness, phonics and spelling.

In the pre-5 sector, play and group-time activities promote environmental print, stories, developmental writing, phonological awareness and home-school links. HMIE inspection evidence indicates huge diversity within the private sector and that local authority nurseries tend to be more consistent than private nurseries working in partnership with local authorities.

TALKING AND LISTENING

The emphasis on talking and listening in *English Language 5–14* was greeted with genuine surprise in schools despite policy documents since 1965 advocating that teachers should plan contexts for talk and accept and develop the language children bring to school. Standards in talking and listening, as measured by AAP surveys and HMIE inspection reports, improved after teachers adopted the 5–14 guidelines.

Now more schools have active policies for talking and listening, although some are still making opportunities available rather than actively teaching it. Most schools timetable the use of cassettes and listening tables. Some follow published schemes, others plan oracy into topic work, using assemblies and class presentations as opportunities for children to address a larger audience. Infant classes have a 'news' or 'circle' time and implement the group discussion activities of reading schemes. Burns Day celebrations and local festivals promote poetry recital, Scots language and choral speaking.

There is some evidence that schools are finding it difficult to support progression in the middle/upper stages and active teaching of group discussion skills remains problematic. A deeper understanding of collaborative group work and of how to adapt task structures to develop specific types of learning would ensure more effective use of group tasks across the curriculum. Without this understanding, teachers' perceptions of what is important in the language curriculum can be unduly influenced by the exclusion of talking and listening from national testing.

ISSUES OF CONCERN

English Language 5–14 presented a welcome return to a focus on the content of language teaching. However, unless used with understanding, it can distort rather than support the rich model that underpins best practice in Scottish schools. In particular, although the guidelines recognise language as a vehicle for learning, the strands, targets and programmes of study do not exemplify this. This can encourage a focus on 'knowledge-telling' tasks in which clear communication and transmission of knowledge are paramount, rather than 'knowledge transforming' ones in which language shapes meaning and is the means to achieve personal understandings.

Some schools and local authorities are finding it hard to get a productive balance between resource-driven programmes of work and the need for flexibilty. In best practice, teachers have sufficient flexibility to ensure children have time to understand things in depth and can get intellectual and emotional satisfaction from their work. However, the pressure for accountability can prompt an over-emphasis on schemes and worksheets to evidence coverage and progression. Whilst this supports weak teachers, it frustrates the best and can divert others from developing more complex models. It can fragment the curriculum and encourage teachers to 'think in boxes' rather than contextualise work and make links. In some cases, the sheer number of programmes to be covered creates stress, leading to mechanistic teaching, and time pressures which squeeze opportunities for play and self-directed learning, extended writing, poetry and reading for pleasure. Such approaches sit uneasily in an education system that values creativity, thinking skills and independent learning. The management, organisation and staff development strategies that create responsive, reflective practitioners, able to adapt teaching input and activities to meet the children's interests, needs and concerns within a contextualised, responsive curriculum need to be more clearly identified. We do not have robust data on the range and balance of teaching strategies adopted in literacy across Scotland and much evidence is anecdotal.

The use of national tests for target setting and the publication of school results within local authorities has inevitably raised the profile of those elements that are tested. In writing, this means a focus on the written product and on the forms of planning and teacher-support promoted by the tests rather than the wider range of strategies and tasks that create self-motivated, independent writers. The drive for a 'good finished product' means that it is rare for children, even in the upper primary, to write without support from the task or teacher. Yet teacher-free, independent writing opportunities are necessary if children are to learn to orchestrate their writing-knowledge effectively. In reading it is accepted that children should read without teacher/task mediation but evaluative questions, which are given little emphasis in the reading tests, tend to be overlooked. Talking and listening, are not tested, and require more explicit attention, having lost some of the status gained when 5–14 was first introduced.

Staff-development challenges remain. Although reading standards have improved and there have been significant gains in writing, continuity of attainment across the transitions from pre-five to primary and from primary to secondary schools is an issue currently being addressed. The Early Intervention Initiative is also being extended into the middle and upper primary stages to ensure children's long-term literacy success. Staff development to address underachievement needs to help teachers differentiate tuition to coach effective reading and writing strategies rather than simply differentiate the work they provide for each group. Staff development to promote writing tasks that help children explore and reframe ideas to create their own understandings, along with strong encouragement for teachers to use them in responsive rather than mechanistic ways, would benefit writing standards and raise attainment across the curriculum.

Target-setting has encouraged headteachers to see that promoting effective language teaching is a cornerstone of quality management. However headteachers, despite being responsible for the curriculum and for monitoring standards of teaching, have largely been overlooked in the curriculum-development loop. Some now feel less knowledgeable than their staff. To create a professional climate in which teachers rather than programmes and resources drive the curriculum, headteachers need to see that good management involves helping teachers acquire the knowledge to adapt and use schemes and worksheets appropriately and creatively rather than mechanistically. To do this, the headteachers need risk-free and open-ended opportunities to discuss and develop their own understandings of language, literacy teaching and the relationship to learning.

REFERENCES

Fraser, H., MacDougall, A., Pirrie, A., and Croxford, L. (2001) Early Intervention in literacy and numeracy: key issues from the national evaluation of the programme *Interchange 71*, Edinburgh: SEED.

Glasgow Education Authority (2000) *New Horizons in Teaching Writing*, Glasgow: Glasgow City Council.

Scottish Committee on Language Arts (1975) *The SCOLA Survey*, Edinburgh: COPE.

Ellis, S., and Friel, G. (1998) *Learning to Write, Writing to Learn – Teaching Writing 5–14*, Dundee: SCCC.

HMI (1998) *Improving Reading in the Early Stages of 5–14*, Edinburgh, SOEID.

HMI (1999) *Improving Writing 5–14*, Edinburgh, SEED

37

Environmental Studies

Rae Condie

Environmental Studies was established as one of the five broad areas of the curriculum within the 5–14 development programme, the national guidelines for curriculum and assessment in Scottish schools between the ages of 5 and 14 years (SOED, 1991). The Environmental Studies guidelines were the last of the five to be published and the first to be revised (SOED, 1993; SEED, 2000).

The term 'environmental studies' was first given currency in 1965 in the government policy document *Primary Education in Scotland* where it was stated that:

> they [environmental studies] have in common the twofold aim of fostering in the child a desire to know more about the world around him [sic] and of training him in the skills he needs to interpret it. (p. 126)

This document, the 'Primary Memorandum', defined Environmental Studies as the integration of a number of curricular areas (primarily History, Geography and Nature Study but also Mathematics), advocated working in groups and promoted the 'project' as an important approach to learning and teaching. It advised focusing on the needs of the individual child and active learning rather than the acquisition of 'exhaustive factual information' (p. 37), that is a child-centred rather than a subject-centred philosophy. While the place of Environmental Studies in the primary curriculum was thus established in policy, classroom practice responded slowly. In the Scottish curriculum, a distinction has been made between 'Environmental Studies' and 'Environmental Education' where the latter focuses on society's responsibility for the health of the environment, developing concepts such as pollution and conservation, and is regarded as permeating the learning experiences of pupils.

POLICY INTO PRACTICE

In 1980, fifteen years after the memorandum, Her Majesty's Inspectorate of Schools (HMI) reported that only 25% of the Scottish primary schools visited displayed high standards of learning and teaching in Environmental Studies (SED, 1980). In 75% of schools, Environmental Studies received 'scant attention or were ineffectually taught' (p. 25).

Pupils were not receiving a balanced experience of the three subject areas with Science, which had replaced 'Nature Study', faring particularly badly. According to HMI, many teachers appeared unconvinced that an integrated approach could be made to work and experienced considerable problems in planning, organising and managing topic studies. It was considered that, unless adequate support was provided, teachers would be 'tempted to settle for something less demanding' (p. 23).

Other contributory factors listed included: the absence of any coherent policy at primary school level, particularly one which had relevance for the associated secondary school; a lack of co-ordination across stages within the primary school; and a lack of confidence, and a need for guidance, in the primary teachers themselves. While broadly endorsing the main themes of the Primary Memorandum, HMI concluded that there was a need to review the whole notion of Environmental Studies, its aims and constituent parts and its relationship to other subject areas. The report also noted that teachers were under pressure to introduce new subject areas to the curriculum and questioned whether these could be accommodated without decisions on priorities and balance.

The 1980s saw a flurry of reports and activity, with Environmental Studies increasingly regarded as embodying important aspects of education with long-term implications for Scotland's economic position in the world. In 1983 the Committee on Primary Education (COPE) identified Environmental Studies as an area of the curriculum requiring a major initiative. The Primary Education Development Project (PEDP) was launched shortly thereafter with the aim of producing support materials for the learning and teaching of Environmental Studies which, by this time, had expanded to include Health Education. A number of topic packs, advocating practical activity within a problem-solving approach, were produced and trialled in schools. In 1987 COPE was disbanded and the PEDP was phased out in favour of the whole curriculum approach of the 5–14 development programme, under the management of the restructured Scottish Consultative Council on the Curriculum (SCCC). The Review and Development Group (RDG) which was set up to develop guidelines for environmental studies had a membership of twenty-three and included representatives of all relevant areas of the curriculum, in both primary and secondary sectors. The resultant draft document, *Working Paper 13*, was last of the five curricular consultation documents to be issued by the Scottish Office Education Department (SOED).

That it took so long to produce may well reflect the difficulties of achieving a consensus in such a diverse group. However, *Working Paper 13* also caused greater debate than any other RDG publication, primarily because it contained a foreword by the then Minister for Education in Scotland, Michael Forsyth. In this, he set out his views on education in general and Environmental Studies in particular. Much of his comment was at odds with what was regarded as 'good primary practice' by practitioners, with a rejection of integration and topic work, particularly in the later stages of primary school, an emphasis on a subject-centred approach and the suggestion that 'some form of specialism' in teaching should be introduced at the upper primary stages (p. iii).

The ensuing debate focused on this statement and the values which seemed to underpin it, diverting attention from the actual content of the guidelines. While there was some concern amongst secondary specialists that individual subject areas were inadequately represented, much of the argument from the primary sector echoed the philosophy of the 1965 Primary Memorandum. The final version of the Environmental Studies guidelines emerged in 1993, without further consultation and in a much altered form. It essentially consisted of three main components, Science, Social Subjects and Technology, set out as a series of age-related levels attainment targets. Health Education formed a fourth component and Information Technology (intended to be regarded as integral to the other four) completed the document. Overall, 25% of class time was to be allocated to Environmental Studies.

In 1998, an extensive consultation exercise was undertaken by the SCCC (now Learning and Teaching Scotland) as part of a review of the 5–14 programme at the request of the minister with responsibility for education. As a result, the Environmental Studies guidelines were extensively revised. Environmental Studies became Science, Social Subjects and Technology. The Information and Communications Technology (ICT) and Health Education components were removed from Environmental Studies and a set of guidelines produced for each. The new guidelines for Environmental Studies were revised 'to provide a clearer, more manageable framework that will support teachers as they plan, teach and assess programmes (. . .) across the 5–14 age range' (SEED, 2000, p. iii). The framework of knowledge and understanding, skills and developing informed attitudes remains but the three broad stage-related attainment bands of the 1993 guidelines have been replaced by the six 5–14 levels, A – F. A *Guide for Teachers and Managers* provides guidance on the kinds of learning experiences that might be provided across the strands and levels.

A METHODOLOGY FOR ENVIRONMENTAL STUDIES

In 1984, the Scottish Curriculum Development Services (SCDS) published *Learning and Teaching: The Environment and the Primary School*. This encouraged teachers to consider the environment as 'something to learn from, learn about and be responsible to' (p. 10), to adopt an active methodology to learning and teaching and to provide first-hand experience of the environment. Three kinds of approach were advocated: the subject-specific topic, where a single area of the curriculum was the main focus for learning; the general topic, involving a number of subject areas; and the provision of a series of planned learning steps for the direct teaching of specific skills and processes. In each, a 'theme' was identified and pursued through a range of activities, drawing on knowledge and skills from Language, Mathematics and the expressive arts.

The general topic was initially the most widely adopted approach although a 'topic' varied significantly in length and in the degree of integration with other subject areas. In the early years, 'mini-topics' have provided contexts for the acquisition and development of concepts and skills across the curriculum. These tend to reflect events in the wider community, such as seasonal changes and festivals, or relate to the immediate experiences of the pupils, within their families or the school. However, since the introduction of the 5–14 programme, a move towards subject-specific topics, particularly in the upper stages of the primary school has been detected (Harlen, 1995).

Unfortunately topic studies have sometimes been used as a means of organising the curriculum so that a number of subject areas are 'covered' rather than developing learning opportunities where links are natural and relevant. In addition, activities (things to do) rather than learning outcomes (things to learn) can dominate the planning. *Some Aspects of Thematic Work in Primary Schools* (SCDS, 1987) illustrated this with the topic 'The Sea' where the Vikings were listed alongside the Romans (History), seashells (Mathematics and Art), the fishing industry (Geography) and Fingal's Cave (Music): high on coverage, low on coherence!

Traditionally Scottish primary teachers have tended to structure the school day so that English Language and Mathematics are tackled in the morning when the children are more likely to be alert and receptive, while the other curriculum areas are scheduled for the afternoon. The core areas of the curriculum have been well supported by text books and published schemes of work, providing a degree of coherence and progression which has been lacking in other elements of the curriculum. In recent years, the growing political emphasis on accountability, attainment and quality assurance has led, in turn, to increased prescription by education authorities on what is to be taught, when and how. In Science, for example, several authorities have invested in the development of subject-oriented 'units of study', sometimes with boxes of apparatus and materials to support these. The units are designed to be completed in a specific time period for example twenty hours, and consist of a series of teaching sessions on specific concepts and skills within a more structured, subject-oriented timetable of teaching and learning in the primary school.

ASSESSING ENVIRONMENTAL STUDIES 5–14

Concern over the limited attention given to assessment by primary schools grew during the 1980s; one of the main criticisms of the PEDP was the lack of guidance on assessing progress. Since the introduction of the 5–14 programme, teachers have been expected to undertake the assessment of pupils' progress in all areas of the curriculum, including Environmental Studies, and to report that progress in terms of the six levels (A-F).

This is demanding on primary teachers who have tended in the past to rely mainly on their own judgement of the day-to-day progress of pupils in their classrooms as evidence of performance and progress. The 5–14 programme demands a more structured approach and teachers are expected to assess conceptual understanding, practical and process skills and attitudes in areas of the curriculum where they lack confidence in teaching, far less assessment (Harlen, Holroyd and Byrne, 1995). As a result, there are important staff development implications if reports of pupil progress are to be reliable and valid.

General guidance on assessment is included in the 5–14 documents and the SCCC has produced materials designed to support teachers in implementing Environmental Studies. In addition, the SOEID's Assessment of Achievement Programme (AAP) provides advice on assessing Science, as well as English Language and Mathematics. In 2002, the Scottish Executive Education Department launched the 'Assessment is for Learning' programme with the aims of establishing coherent and unified national systems of assessment and supporting teachers in developing strategies for assessment within schools.

DISCUSSION

Environmental Studies 5–14 occupies an uneasy position in the Scottish primary curriculum. On one hand it has been presented as a way to integrate areas of the curriculum in a way that reflects the child-centred approach cherished by many primary teachers. Now, whilst the Environmental Studies label has been retained, the guidelines are sub-divided such that Science, Social Studies and Technology are set out independently, albeit with some guidance for teachers and managers on how these might be linked. The introduction of time allocations for each curricular area (ES – 15%) and the increasing pressure to show performance and progress against national levels of expectations may mean that, in order to meet the expectations, teachers will similarly sub-divide their practice, disaggregating Environmental Studies into its constituent parts. While it appears that there has been some reduction in what constitutes 'Environmental Studies', in practice, Environmental Education, Sustainability and Aspects of Citizenship are all increasingly seen as related if not permeating aspects of Environmental Studies.

Since 1965 there has been considerable expansion of what constitutes Environmental Studies, putting pressure on (generalist) primary teachers to have a command of a greater number of knowledge bases. In addition, integrating these subjects to provide a coherent learning experience for pupils has been a challenge that only a small proportion of teachers has been judged as meeting effectively. Given that HMI were reporting difficulties with three subjects in 1980, the need to acquire even more and deeper knowledge of Environmental Studies let alone the management and organisational skills to provide integrated learning experiences, poses considerable challenges for teachers, and the pre-service and continuing professional development providers.

The Primary Memorandum introduced Environmental Studies in the belief that an integrated approach held greater relevance for children and reflected the ways in which they learned, not in discrete subject areas but as a series of inter-related concepts, growing from what they already knew and could do. Such a view is in accordance with what a constructivist approach would advocate today. However, government concerns about performance levels and standards and the pressure to meet targets and progress through the 5–14 levels, across an increasingly diverse curriculum, cannot be readily reconciled with such a philosophy.

REFERENCES

Harlen, W. (1995) *Interchange 35: Putting 5–14 in Place*, Edinburgh: SOEID.

Harlen, W., Holroyd, C. and Byrne, M. (1995) *Confidence and Understanding in Teaching Science and Technology in Primary Schools*, Edinburgh: SCRE.

SCDS (1987) *Some Aspects of Thematic Work in Primary Schools*, Edinburgh: SCCC.

SED (1980) *Learning and Teaching in Primary 4 and Primary 7*, Edinburgh: HMSO.

SEED (2000) *Environmental Studies: Society, Science and Technology 5–14 National Guidelines*, Edinburgh: LTS.

SOED (1993) *Curriculum and Assessment in Scotland: National Guidelines: Environmental Studies 5–14*, Edinburgh: SOED.

38

Expressive Arts

Pam Robertson

> 'Why can't it always be like this?' asked one, 'instead of having to teach to narrow targets?' No
> one answered but we knew that we had achieved the best expressive arts of the year without
> producing a teaching plan or assessing our music and drama outcomes. (Toner, B. Scottish
> Opinion, *Times Educational Supplement Scotland*, 12 July 2002)

So writes a primary headteacher, describing the reactions of his staff following a
successful musical production. In so doing, he is exemplifying the thoughts of many
primary teachers throughout Scotland, and providing evidence supporting the study carried
out by Ross and Kamba (1997), who found that 'teachers see themselves as battling against a
hard-nosed, market-led tendency to boil the aesthetic way of knowing into little nuggets of
cognitive gains which can be ticked off for assessment.' Positive indications, though, from
this and similar articles, are that the arts continue to provide enjoyment, generate
enthusiasm and influence camaraderie between both staff and pupils, and by their very
nature, will always hold an important place in schools.

However, whilst much excellent work of this type goes on in both nursery and primary
contexts, there are real dilemmas confronting teachers with regard to Expressive Arts:
spontaneity versus linear progression, individual creativity versus the documented path of
development, enjoyment versus accountability. It could be argued that this situation has
come about mainly as a result of the publication, assimilation, and application of the
National Guidelines 5–14 Expressive Arts (1992). Prior to this, teachers were able to be
more spontaneous, and decide upon the content and time taken for the arts. On the other
hand, it was not until 5–14 that the arts had a documented and therefore secure place on the
primary curriculum, and there were no real standards or statements of developmental
achievement to which all Scottish teachers could refer. Strides have been made with regard
to assessment of the arts, the best practice placing it as an integral part of learning and
teaching but, as the original quotation evidences, this can make for a narrowing of activities.
The swings and roundabouts with any published documentation of this kind will have these
inevitable effects, and to be fair, advice from the guidelines does stimulate and encourage
teachers to continue to use the arts for enjoyment as well as scaffolding for children's
learning: 'A school's expressive arts policy should seek to further this curiosity and
excitement in learning; to encourage this positive attitude to trying and the sheer enjoyment
of doing' (SOED, 1992, p. 11).

LOOKING MORE CLOSELY

The Expressive Arts in pre-school and primary education in Scotland currently comprise four elements: Art and Design, Drama, Music, and Physical Education. The history of these subjects within Scottish primary education is well documented: Hanlon's summary (1993) offers a detailed description of the historical pathway and philosophies. Today, however, teachers are asked to ensure a broad and balanced programme in these four areas, together allocated 15% of the total curriculum time in primary, which offer pupils new ways of knowing – essentially in the four subject areas – and which can also support, stimulate and enhance learning in other curricular areas. The 5–14 guidelines sought to rationalise planning and teaching of Expressive Arts and identified three attainment outcomes and six strands (regarding investigation, the use and application of media and materials, creation and design, communication, and critical observation) which all four subject areas share.

In practice, it would be fair to say that the primary curriculum revolves around the main areas of Language, Mathematics, and Environmental Studies, and that the 15% afforded to the arts mainly supports learning in these areas – or at least the topic choice influences the work done, certainly in Art and Design, Drama and Music. Whilst this makes educational sense and provides links in learning for the child, the dangers of revisiting skills and activities under a different guise without proper planning for skill based development are all too prevalent. The nature of Physical Education lends itself more to an independent, progressive content, which is discussed in more detail below.

Impressions given by the Audit Report (1993) which considered the learning and teaching of all four Expressive Arts – measured against the 5–14 documentation – suggest that many primary schools at that time were tackling the Expressive Arts curriculum well; but that out of the four subject areas, Drama was the one causing most concern, with only 45% of Drama lessons seen being judged as 'good'. Historically, this reiterates the reflections of earlier documentation, and even today, it is generally considered that Drama is the least well-supported of the arts in primary and pre-school, with the least number of visiting specialists being employed by local authorities, compared with the other disciplines. Broadening the picture, recurring comments from the report included: excellent opportunities for pupil self-expression in Art and Design, but greater rigour required for the upper age group; Drama programmes needed greater cohesion across the school; Music continued to be dominated by singing, and more opportunities for creative work still needed to be afforded to pupils; and Physical Education was the most consistently well-developed area of the Expressive Arts with many teachers using assessment and recording procedures. This was the official picture in 1993.

A BALANCED ARTS CURRICULUM?

Despite the exhortations found within the national guidelines, a balanced arts curriculum in practical terms still cannot be guaranteed in nursery or primary years of education. This imbalance begins with pre-school documentation (1999), where 'physical development and movement' is placed alone as a curriculum area, thereby affording it more importance than the others (rightly, many would argue), which are grouped together under 'expressive and aesthetic development'. Physical Education has maintained the strong lead over the other arts in curricular access, especially with the emphasis on health and the encouragement to lead healthier lifestyles. The present Scottish Executive is to some extent encouraging this bias, with the setting up of the Physical Activity Task Force (June 2002), and a National Strategy for Physical Activity which recommends, amongst other things, a review of the status and content of Physical Education curriculum and resources. Additionally, and significantly, though, a recent report targets this one area, setting it apart from the other Expressive Arts (*Improving Physical Education in Primary Schools* (2001), HMI report on PE) (www.scotland.gov.uk/hmie). It states that 'only about one third of schools had very good programmes for physical education', and provides comments about what teachers, schools and local authorities should do in order to improve in this area. It would seem from this that either the standards of Physical Education in primary schools have gone down over the past few years, or that the writers of the report are being more demanding on what is expected. It is worth noting here too, that the place of dance in Scottish education is different from elsewhere in that it is subsumed within Physical Education (as a core area, alongside gymnastics and games), but targeted by a recent helpful publication by HMI ('*Dance in the Community – Traditional and Contemporary Dance in Community Settings*, 2000 – which contains contacts and case studies), dance will continue to thrive in settings both within and outwith schools.

STAFFING: WHO TEACHES EXPRESSIVE ARTS?

The philosophical argument continues to occupy minds as to whether the class teacher or a specialist teacher is the best person to teach Expressive Arts. If the priority is the holistic development of each child, then the class teacher is best placed for this task; indeed, the guidelines are clear that this is the case, but that additional support in terms of visiting specialists, artists in residence, instrumental instructors and parents should be embraced as appropriate. In practical terms, there is certainly a great reliance from many class teachers upon 'external' support for teaching the arts, as documented regularly in local and national newspaper features, particularly the *Times Educational Supplement Scotland*. Some reasons for this are explored below.

It would be fair to say that very few class teachers enter the profession with personal confidence in all four arts areas. The place of Expressive Arts in initial teacher education (ITE) institutions gives much cause for concern. In recent years, all teacher education institutions in Scotland have merged with geographically convenient universities, and the ensuing faculties of education have had to face up to challenging decisions with regard to (for example) modularisation, modes of delivery and means of assessing students. Evidence collected through interviews suggests that this has had a detrimental effect upon Expressive Arts, and it is feared that if this continues, the arts will become even more marginalised, especially in pre- and primary school settings. Institutions throughout Scotland offer quite different experiences to ITE students under the guise of Expressive Arts in terms of number of hours allocated, spread of activities/workshops, and opportunities for personal development within any of the four areas, whether studying on a four–year BEd or a one-year Postgraduate degree programme. Certainly in one such institution, during four years of study, the student contact with Expressive Arts is limited to eight hours of workshops (for each of the four areas) plus seminar support in year two, and the opportunity to study one expressive art at a personal level in year three. These beginning teachers thus cannot possibly plan and provide for adequate experiences for their pupils in all four Expressive Arts, with subsequently detrimental effect on their pupils. It could be argued that more expertise would be gained through continued professional development when they have graduated, but this will be haphazard and reliant upon enthusiasms.

As exemplified in the HMI report *Visiting Teachers in Primary Schools* (Edinburgh: HMSO, 1993), Scotland has a history of regional arts specialists being employed to teach in primary schools. However, there is no obligation for any regional authority to employ arts specialists (unlike the refreshingly different philosophy operated in Reggio Emilia, Italy, where, for nursery age children, a visual art specialist is available for every teacher), and thus there is a huge disparity as regards the number and deployment of specialists throughout Scotland. Headteachers who currently have devolved school budgets do 'buy in' specialists in a number of ways (for example, Glasgow has a pool of Physical Education teachers who can be bought in to teach PE in primary schools) but this is dependent upon geographical circumstances, personal enthusiasms and priorities. Where specialists are employed, though, generally they are highly thought of, and manage their increasingly heavy and unwieldy workloads with goodwill, expertise, and enthusiasm. Moreover, it has been recognised (HMI, 1993) that where class teachers and visiting specialists plan and team-teach, the quality of children's experiences are the best achievable.

Highland, Grampian and Scottish Borders Regions continue to provide as cohesive a specialist support system as can be found in Scotland, although here, still, specialists in Drama (particularly) are thin on the ground. The picture looks increasingly gloomy, however, with visiting specialists always 'in the first line of fire' when regional authorities have to make cuts in the education budget (which is common), and the uncertainty of the posts, together with the continued threat of redundancy and idiosyncratic staffing arrangements has meant the loss of quality staff from many schools, with the resulting downward trend of staff confidence and, ergo, the quality and nature of children's education in the arts. The continued threat, too, to music instrumental instruction is worrying. Derek Johnston's review upon the current situation makes interesting reading (Scottish local government reform and instrumental music instruction, *Scottish Educational Review*, 33:2, Nov. 2001), as he points out that the newly formed unitary authorities failed to take account of outdoor education and music instruction as core curricular activities, and that these areas have been adversely affected.

EXTENSIONS OF GOOD PRACTICE AND NEW INITIATIVES

Perhaps one result of the fluctuating staffing arrangements for specialist staff (in schools and education advisory services), and mostly inadequate training for class teachers, other means of support and teaching the arts have flourished. Examples of this include the following, some of which have been built up over the years, and others showing a real burgeoning of activity in this area:

- the production of high quality printed and web-based support materials: for example, National Grid for Learning (NGfL: www.ngflscotland.gov.uk/5–14/guidelines/);
- initiatives taken by staff especially from secondary schools that work together with colleagues in primary;
- artists working in schools, and the creation of educational outreach programmes and posts: for example, TAG and Borderline theatre company;
- pupils visiting specially designed exhibition and activity centres;

- new arts education centres being created and/or adapted for primary pupils: for example, Dancebase (Edinburgh);
- new kinds of appointments to support the arts (often initiated and jointly funded by the Scottish Arts Council (SAC)).

ISSUES

Summarising challenges for the future, it would seem that:

- the arts will remain if only to provide the end-of-term performances, and therefore the danger of an overemphasis on product rather than process remains;
- Physical Education will continue to dominate the arts in curricular terms, and may eventually be set apart to combine with Health;
- children's artistic growth in all four areas of the arts will continue to be overlooked; and that
- the huge potential for learning from and through creative but purposeful activity will remain largely untapped.

Finally, unless or until significant changes are made with regard to national and regional funding, and both quality and quantity of experiences in undergraduate training, many pupils will be short-changed with regard to diverse yet progressive Expressive Arts in primary, and the precious, important and much-documented links between upper primary and secondary education will remain tenuous, with pupils arriving in S1 with quite disparate experiences.

REFERENCES

Audit Unit Report (1993) *Standards and Quality in Scottish Schools*, Edinburgh: HMSO.

Hanlon, M. (1993) 5–14 and the role of Expressive Arts: 1950 – 93, *Scottish Educational Review* 25. (2), 97–104.

Ross M. and Kamba M. (1997) *State of the Arts*, School of Education: University of Exeter.

SCCC (1999) *Curriculum Framework for Children 3–5*, Dundee: SCCC.

Scottish Executive (2002) *Let's Make Scotland More Active - A Strategy for Physical Activity – A Consultation*, Physical Activity Task Force, Edinburgh: HMSO.

SOED (1992) National Guidelines: Expressive Arts 5–14, Edinburgh: HMSO.

39

Mathematics

Effie Maclellan

CURRENT POLICY

The Mathematics curriculum in Scottish primary schools is determined by advice from the Scottish Executive Education Department. This advice is manifest in the framework document, *Curriculum and Assessment in Scotland: National Guidelines on Mathematics 5–14*, (Scottish Office Education Department, 1991) and delineates four aspects of mathematics:

- number, money and measurement;
- information handling;
- shape position and movement;
- problem solving and enquiry.

While the official curricular guidance is advisory rather than mandatory, all primary schools in Scotland appear to develop mathematical policies with this advisory document as their principal source. Despite the lack of enforcement of a centralised curriculum, it would seem that the advice by local authorities on how to implement the guidance, the wholesale use of national testing to confirm teachers' decision making, and the publication of reports by Her Majesty's Inspectorate on the inspection of schools, render current policy and practice statutory in all but name. There is no specialist Mathematics teaching in primary schools, with the class teacher expected to teach all aspects. Progression through the Mathematics curriculum is integrated with assessment as it is recognised that pupils learn at different rates.

INFLUENCES ON EVOLVING POLICY

The official conduit through which policy decisions are made is SEED which, in turn, consults principally with local authorities, Learning and Teaching Scotland and HMI (and, to a lesser extent, with academics) to inform its decision making. Collectively, these agencies seem to advise:

- direct, interactive teaching;
- number and mental computation;

- an increased frequency of Mathematics lessons which explicitly refer to the learning which is intended in each of the four mathematical strands;
- the importance of supplementing the commercial scheme with other tasks and resources.

This has resulted in SEED's declaration that raising standards of attainment in numeracy is of priority. In the *National Statement for Improving Attainment in Numeracy in Schools* (SEED, 2002) numeracy includes competence with numbers, and the use of graphical, numerical and statistical skills to interpret, communicate and apply quantifiable information to everyday (and more abstract) contexts and problems. In preparation for formal schooling, an initial start on numeracy is to be made in pre-school education as expressed in *A Curriculum Framework for Children 3–5* (SCCC, 1999).

WHAT COUNTS AS CURRICULUM CONTENT

Before 1965, the Mathematics curriculum was exclusively concerned with practising and perfecting numerical computations. While the Primary Memorandum (SED, 1965) espoused the provision of a wide variety of practical problem-solving contexts to trigger mathematical learning, Her Majesty's Inspectors noted in *Learning and Teaching in Primary 4 and Primary 7* (HMI, 1980) the continued domination of arithmetical computation with as much as seven hours per week being spent on pencil-and-paper exercises. Current recommendations are for 225 minutes per week to be spent on Mathematics although there are no extant data on how this time is, or should be, apportioned to each of the four aspects. While reports such as *Improving Mathematics Education 5–14* (HMI, 1997), *Standards and Quality in Primary Schools: Mathematics 1998–2001* (HMI, 2001) and *Early Intervention 1998–2000* (HMI, 2001) imply that the Mathematics curriculum is now wider, they focus largely on the topic of numeracy with only cursory reference to topics such as shape, data handling and measurement. In spite of the rich research literature on mathematical problem-solving, which points to effective problem-solving as a critical mechanism through which individuals can construct mathematical meaning, the primary Mathematics curriculum in Scotland is conceptualised very narrowly, as a utilitarian tool for accurate and speedy computation. While mathematical literacy is of itself important, an emphasis on 'social arithmetic' at the expense of mathematical reasoning and genuine engagement in problem-solving is, arguably, an inadequate conceptualisation of Mathematics for full and equitable participation in a technologically advanced society (Hoyles et al, 1999).

WHAT IT MEANS TO TEACH AND LEARN MATHEMATICS

The initial difficulties which teachers had (noted by HMI in 1980) in implementing a differentiated approach to teaching have now been resolved (according to HMI in 1997). But now 'good teaching' is conceived of by the inspectorate as:

- moving from mixed ability grouping to some form of setting by ability;
- moving from individualised approaches to learning to more teacher-led whole class activity;
- reducing dependence on the calculator and allowing its use only for well-defined purposes;
- increasing pupils' facility in mental calculation.

Although group and individual teaching is still appropriate at times, greater emphasis on whole-class teaching and the practice of setting pupils (which allows greater use of whole-class teaching) is seen as emulating the teaching in high performing TIMSS countries. Indeed the model of effective Mathematics teaching which is implied in *Improving Mathematics Education 5–14* (HMI, 1997) and in *Early Intervention 1998–2000* (HMI, 2001) suggests that the teacher:

- begins a lesson with a short review of previous learning and a brief indication of learning outcomes/objectives;
- presents new material in small steps, providing for extensive practice at each step;
- gives clear and detailed instructions and explanations;
- asks large numbers of questions to check for pupil understanding;
- provides systematic feedback and correction;
- gives guided practice in tasks to promote the desired performance;
- monitors pupils individually in terms of their achievement of these tasks.

However unarticulated, theoretically, this model of teaching might be, it is clearly grounded in the view that pupils learn by receiving clear, comprehensible, and correct information about numerical procedures and by having the opportunity to consolidate the information they have received through practice. The teacher provides this information, and so has the mathematical authority for determining what is right and wrong. Classroom instruction is organised around the transfer of information from knowledgeable teacher to uninformed pupil. The implementation of such instruction means that Mathematics is delivered as a discrete subject and where there are applications to other curricular areas, these are seen as affording the opportunity to consolidate mathematical skills rather than as providing an authentic context for mathematical conceptualisation. Regrettably, there is no adequate recognition that this traditional view of learning is questioned by those who view learners as active constructors/organisers of their own learning.

MATHEMATICAL PERFORMANCE

Although national testing is a distinctive element of the Mathematics curriculum, there is no collation of national test results to create a picture of mathematical competence in Scottish primary schools. Rather, there is an annual national survey, *5–14 Attainment in Publicly Funded Schools* by the Scottish Executive Education Department (SEED). The survey reports on the numbers of pupils in P2–P7 and in S1 and S2 who can perform at each of the attainment levels specified in the framework document. National testing confirms a large percentage of these statistics. However, because the declared purpose of national testing is to confirm teachers' judgements, it is highly unlikely that testing is conducted uniformly across schools. This raises questions about the validity of any comparisons made between and among the statistics. A further difficulty with the publication of these statistics is that they refer globally to Mathematics without reference to the four aspects of mathematical attainment. However, more detailed indicators of competence come from two sources:

- *Assessment of Achievement Programme* (AAP): *Sixth Survey of Mathematics* (SEED, 2002).
- *Achievements of Primary 4 and Primary 5 Pupils in the Third International Mathematics and Science Study* (TIMSS) (SCRE, Edinburgh, 1997).

Selected findings from the data in these surveys include:

- Over 80% of the primary 4 pupils tested at level B (the level which should be attainable by most in P4) were accurate in their computation of addition, subtraction and multiplication but when these operations were contextualised, accurate performance dropped to as low as 25%.
- Around 90% of the primary 7 pupils were accurate in their computation of whole numbers but when fractions, percentages or ratios of numbers were included in the assessment tasks, accurate performance dropped to about 40%.
- The achievement of primaries 4 and 5 pupils in relation to that of 9-year-olds in more than forty other countries was well below the international average.
- The performance of Scottish pupils was relatively strong in geometry and in data analysis and relatively weak in numbers and operations compared to the performance of pupils from other countries.

The AAP survey showed performance at primaries 4 and 7 to be significantly better than previously, although improved performance in problem-solving was not as strong as in the other aspects. Notwithstanding this improvement, the dominant message from both of these studies is that Scottish pupils' facility in mental calculation is weak. Disappointing as this is, it is perhaps not surprising, given that mental calculation is a more complex concept than casual consideration might suggest. Mental calculation is not a 'skill' that is independent of the situation(s) in which it is being used. Rather it is a richly connected web of knowledge of computation and estimation which, through use, reflects how number is understood. This knowledge is influenced by the child's:

- knowledge of number relationships;
- facility with basic facts;
- understanding of arithmetical operations;
- ability to make comparisons between numbers;
- and possession of base-ten place value concepts.

Furthermore, as knowledge of computation and computational estimation develops so it can facilitate the development of number sense (Maclellan, 2001a and 2001 b). So, for example, the child might effect the operation 73–36 in one of various ways:

1. $73 + 3 - 36 - 3 = 37$
   (This requires knowledge of number bonds and place value. The operational sequence is one addition followed by two subtractions.)
2. $36 + 4 = 40$ and $40 + 30 = 70$ and $70 + 3 = 73$ and $4 + 30 + 3 = 37$
   (This requires knowledge of number bonds to fill in the missing addends. The operational sequence is three complementary additions followed by a final addition.)
3. $(60 + 13) - (30 + 6) = (60 - 30) + (13 - 6) = 30 + 7 = 37$
   (This requires knowledge of number bonds. The operational sequence is one subtraction then an addition followed by another addition).

While no one of these ways is necessarily superior, it is the child's determination of what is effective that is important because in this determination the child decides:

- how the numbers in the operation can be structurally translated so that they can be addressed by the knowledge and skills that the child already has in his/her repertoire;
- which operational sequence(s) will be consistent with the structural changes made to the original numbers and will also observe the integrity of the original operation.

Herein lies the cognitive demand of mental calculation.

WHAT IS PROBLEMATIC?

While the importance of understanding and applying mathematical ideas is recognised by SEED as necessary for our socio-economic survival and progress, our attempts to improve the relatively poor mathematical performance amongst Scottish pupils can best be described as adopting a blunderbuss approach. This is powerfully illustrated in part of the Early Intervention Programme.

Launched in 1997, with the particular purpose of raising standards in early numeracy as well as literacy, *Early Intervention 1998–2000* (HMI, 2001) reports the programme to be successful. However, there are few documented evaluations of the programme with respect to numeracy, allegedly because intervention in numeracy is much less well developed than that in literacy. The one notable exception, by Fraser et al. (2001), reports no significant improvement in attainment amongst children in primary 3 between 1998 and 2000. Indeed, attainment in Mathematics, as determined by Performance Indicators in Primary Schools (PIPS tests), was lower in 2000 than in 1998 in some schools. While this might seem to be disappointing, it is not surprising. Many HMI audit reports attest to the relatively successful start that children make in school Mathematics. According to the literature (e.g., Nunes & Bryant, 1997) most children's early success is attributable to their robust, intuitive understanding of additive reasoning (which begins to develop long before children enter school) so while the Early Intervention Programme is designed to try to obviate the difficulties which manifest themselves from P3/4 onwards, its efforts would seem to be wrongly targeted. The well documented problems which develop from the middle of the primary school onwards (lack of understanding of common and decimal fractions, of ratio and proportion, of percentages and of the relationships between all these numerical representations) are rooted in the child's difficulty in making a qualitative shift in thinking from additive to multiplicative reasoning; an achievement which we would appear to be poor at supporting children through. However, to enable children to make this type of progress (and hence improve attainment in numeracy) requires a theoretical analysis of what the elements of numeracy actually are. While the Early Intervention Programme is credited with increasing parental participation and the resourceful use of mathematical games and activities (a conclusion that also emerges from the self-reports of many of the Scottish local authorities), this is hardly a professional response to a pressing problem. Teachers need to know the extent of children's achievement in, and their difficulties in developing, all of the components of numeracy including:

- counting principles and procedures;
- written arithmetical symbolism;
- place value;
- word problems;
- the translation between concrete, verbal and numerical formats;

- arithmetical estimation;
- memory for number facts and the use of derived facts and strategies for calculation.

It is when we have comprehensive diagnostic and pedagogical responses to these components that we can properly claim that interventions are having an effect. Furthermore, rather than view such components as a list of targets to be met and 'ticked-off', the research evidence makes clear that these components refer to fundamental understandings which need to be addressed iteratively as the child's conception of number develops from the naïve natural number to the sophisticated rational number.

Such disregard by policy makers both for evidence and for mathematical analyses of what would be helpful to pupils means that the curriculum is pragmatic rather than theoretically driven. This is exacerbated by the somewhat outdated view of Mathematics, a transmission view of teaching and the passive-reception view of learning held by policy makers, as evidenced in the official documents reviewed here. At the same time, however, teachers experience their reality as the external requirement to cover certain amounts of mathematical content in order to fulfil the demands for public accountability. For as long as the Mathematics curriculum continues to be designed, developed and delivered on the basis of personal models of what are considered appropriate rather than on explicit empirical evidence for what is effective, our attempts to improve attainment are likely to fail, although we doubtless can maintain current, depressing standards.

Finally, in addition to an evidence-based curriculum, achievement of improvement has to be based on a developed understanding of learning and teaching. Innovation and development cannot simply be transmitted to teachers who will passively absorb the decreed changes and then implement them in the classroom. Teachers' own beliefs as to what curriculum change should be together with their understandings of what government-driven policy desires it to be are powerful mediators in their own practice. If radical improvement is to be achieved, teachers and policy makers must work in tandem to gain mutual understanding of what is possible and what is desirable.

REFERENCES

Fraser, H., MacDougall, A., Pirrie, A. and Croxford, L. (2001) *Early Intervention in Literacy and Numeracy: Key Issues from the Evaluation of the Programme*, Edinburgh: SEED (Interchange 71).

Hoyles, C., Morgan, C. and Woodhouse, G. (1999) *Rethinking the Mathematics Curriculum*, London: Falmer Press.

Maclellan, E. (2001a) Mental calculation: its place in the development of numeracy, *Westminster Studies in Education*, 24, 2, 145–54.

Maclellan, E. (2001b) What counts as numeracy? *Scottish Education Review*, 33, 2, 157–68.

Nunes, T. and Bryant, P. (1997) *Learning and Teaching Mathematics: An International Perspective*, Hove, East Sussex: Psychology Press.

40

Modern Languages

Lesley Low

FROM PILOT TO NATIONAL EXTENSION OF MODERN LANGUAGES IN THE PRIMARY SCHOOL

The phased national introduction of Modern Languages in the Primary School (MLPS) began in September 1994 when the first cohort of 370 purposely trained primary teachers began teaching a foreign language (FL) to P6 and P7 children within their schools. Eight subsequent cohorts of primary teachers have completed the national in-service training programme and it is estimated that over 95% of Scottish primary schools currently have at least one MLPS-trained teacher. The predominant primary FL is French although a minority of teachers has been trained in German, Spanish or Italian. Although funded directly by the Scottish Office/Executive, places on the training course are allocated to volunteer primary teachers by individual local authorities, responsible for organising the MLPS training in their areas. Teachers typically undergo twenty-seven days of training over a period of a year, usually October to September, but those with prior experience or qualifications in the FL may undertake a reduced version of the course.

The twenty-seven-day national training programme was one of the key legacies of the pilot phase of the MLPS development which was initiated in 1989 by the then Minister for Education, Michael Forsyth, as part of a package of measures to expand the teaching of FLs in Scotland's schools. The main impetus behind this political interest was the need to prepare for the European single market in 1992 by ensuring a pool of young people with good FL skills to help Scotland take advantage of this economic opportunity. The measures to achieve this, set out in January 1989 in the Scottish Office Circular 1187, included making a FL part of the curriculum of all secondary students up to the age of sixteen and piloting the introduction of MLPS.

In setting up the twelve pilot projects (secondary schools and their associated primaries) HMI had two main priorities. The first was to opt for a language acquisition rather than a language awareness model. The aim was to give students an extra year or two in which to develop their foreign language competence rather than simply to develop insights into the general patterns and structure of language or cultivate positive attitudes towards the future learning of another European language. The second priority was to avoid the mistakes that had led to the failure of the earlier experiment of teaching French at primary in the 1960s and early 70s. Evaluations of this first attempt had found no evidence of a lasting advantage to students who had begun their foreign language learning in primary (see Johnstone, 1994, pp. 43–4 for a review of these findings) and FL teaching had all but disappeared from mainstream Scottish primary schools as a result.

Success for the renewed attempt was to be achieved by ensuring an appropriate primary methodology and continuity of learning experience into secondary school through the evolution of a partnership model of secondary visiting FL teachers and primary class teachers (see Giovanazzi, 1992). The partnership model ran from 1989–1995 and was replicated in parallel regional pilots across Fife, Lothian and Strathclyde. The national pilot phase of MLPS was subject to independent evaluation by researchers at the University of Stirling and extensive findings on the workings of the partnership model, classroom processes and children's attainments are published in two reports (see Low et al., 1993 and Low et al., 1995). The Scottish Office/Executive Education Department has retained its interest in the FL attainments of primary and early secondary students throughout the national extension phase of MLPS, and has commissioned two surveys of French and German at P7 and S2 as part of the national Assessment of Achievement Programme (AAP). The first was a pilot study in 1998, findings from which were used to inform the development of the revised 5–14 National Guidelines for Modern Languages (see John-stone et al., 2000 at http://www.cilt.org.uk/research/aap.htm). The second AAP was a full survey conducted in 2001, findings from which were expected to become available in 2003.

The approach to the piloting phase was a pragmatic one and each of the pilot projects was free to develop its MLPS programme within the parameters of the partnership model but, in the event, one particular approach emerged which quickly assumed the status of best practice. This approach became known as 'embedding' and advocated the use of the context of the primary classroom and the areas of the primary curriculum as the basis for the FL content. Everyday routines such as taking the register and dinner numbers, doing mental arithmetic, talking about the date and the weather, and a range of class themes involving, for example, the body, healthy living, food, animals, clothes and sports, could be exploited as a means of introducing and reinforcing the FL (see Johnstone, 1994 for a fuller discussion of this approach). The national extension of MLPS moved away from the pilot model of visiting specialists and primary class teachers in partnership to one where primary teachers would assume sole responsibility for the FL teaching. This change was justified on educational grounds by Staff Inspector for Modern Languages, J. Boyes, and Strathclyde Regional Council Director of Education, F. Pignatelli, who argued that the primary class teacher was the best-placed person to deliver the embedded approach to MLPS, given appropriate training and support. (*Scottish CILT Info 1: Modern Foreign Languages in Primary Schools*, Scottish CILT: Stirling, 1993).

The authors of the national training programme for MLPS had been very involved in the pilot phase of the initiative as, for example, National Development Officers or Regional Modern Languages Advisers. They drew extensively on the pilot experience to compile the training materials, which they based around a list of ten competences that primary teachers would need to acquire. The emphasis was on gaining a confident command of key areas such as the sound system and basic structures of a particular FL, core language (personal, descriptive and affective) and language for the classroom (including daily routine, organis-ing activities), as well as the language required to deliver some basic Art, Craft, Home Economics, Science, Technology, Drama and PE activities through the medium of the FL, and an appropriate methodology for young FL learners including games, songs and story telling. The primary teacher would also develop the ability to use a FL dictionary appropriately, and to write labels and captions accurately and acquire an awareness of the culture and background of the country whose language was being taught (MLPS, *The Training Programme*, 1993).

Teachers were encouraged to take materials from the MLPS training course such as the visuals, cue cards, stories and card games for their FL teaching and to use these resources flexibly within their own learning and teaching programmes. The aim was to put children at the centre of the learning process. Where the MLPS-trained teacher was also the P6 or P7 class teacher, the embedded approach was feasible, but this was difficult to maintain if the MLPS-trained teacher found her/himself as a 'drop-in teacher' to P6 and P7 classes within the school, a model which has become increasingly common. Drop-in arrangements typically consist of a once- or twice-weekly visit by the MLPS-trained teacher and more often or not means a class swap between the two teachers concerned.

During the period 1996 –98, HMI monitored the implementation of MLPS as part of their routine inspections in forty-two primary schools and included findings from these visits in their report *Standards and Quality, Primary and Secondary Schools 1994–1998: Modern Languages* (1998). The key strengths which they noted in primary included: the enthusiasm and motivation of almost all students, high attainments by some very able students, examples of good and very good teaching in 85% of schools and very good organisation of resources and classroom display (p. 8). However, they also found a number of 'major weaknesses', notably that the study of a FL was not necessarily included in the curriculum of all students in P6 and P7; and there was great variation across schools in the time allocated to the FL and in the levels of support and time available to MLPS-trained teachers to maintain their skills, prepare work and consult with other teachers, including those in the local secondary school. As well as these structural and management issues there were other concerns about teaching and learning practices such as the absence or down-playing of the skills of Reading and Writing, the recording of students' attainments and making appropriate links with other curricular areas, particularly English Language (p. 8).

It was widely acknowledged that many of these concerns stemmed from the lack of appropriate 5–14 Guidelines for modern languages. The original curriculum guidelines, published in 1993, pre-dated the national extension of MLPS and related to the secondary stages of S1 and S2 only. As part of her response to the HMI Standards and Quality Report, the Minister for Education, Helen Liddell, instructed Learning and Teaching Scotland to set up a review and development group to devise new 5–14 Guidelines for modern languages. This group would operate alongside and liaise with an Action Group on Languages (AGL), brought into being by the minister in December 1998 with the remit to secure the place of Modern Languages in Scotland's schools. Following a consultation process with the profession and other interested parties, the revised Modern Languages 5–14 National Guidelines were published in 2000. Their distribution to schools, however, was delayed until the autumn of 2001 to coincide with the Scottish Executive's response to the recommendations of the AGL, first published in December 2000 in their report *Citizens of a Multilingual World*.

ISSUES OF CONCERN

Two of the fourteen recommendations of the AGL have particular bearing on the future of MLPS. Recommendation Two states that as part of an eleven component package of entitlement, all students' experience of language learning should begin no later than P6, build on their prior experience of first and other language development and be continuous and progressive in the same language. The new 5–14 National Guidelines for Modern Languages (2000) include an over arching strand of 'knowing about language' and advocate the concept of 'language to languages', aspects which should allow FL teachers to make a real contribution to children's literacy development, a national education priority of the present administration. However, in the introduction to *Citizens of a Multilingual World, Scottish Executive Response* the Minister states that there are elements (unspecified) of the new 5–14 guidelines 'which primary teachers will be unable to implement without further training'. (September 2001, p. 3.) Anecdotal evidence arising from the 5–14 national road show organised by Learning and Teaching Scotland to promote the new guidelines seems to indicate that among the concerns which primary FL teachers have expressed, assessing and reporting on children's FL attainments would be one such element. Primary teachers have always been keen to ensure that secondary colleagues are in a position to build on the FL achievements that primary children bring to S1, and assessment and reporting within the framework of 5–14 should be a means to this end. That said, there is also concern that the enjoyment and experiential learning which has characterised the MLPS development thus far could be put in jeopardy if FL teaching at the primary stages were to become too formal, too focused on the written word and largely attainment-oriented.

It will fall to individual local authorities to consult on, devise and organise the kinds of in-service provision which primary teachers and their secondary colleagues will need in order to implement the 5–14 guidelines in their schools. Ringfenced funding for Modern Languages will continue to be made available to local authorities from the Scottish Executive Education Department (SEED) over the next two to three years to enable them to meet these and other demands in relation to AGL recommendations. The response of local authorities to these challenges will inevitably be variable. In the three-year gap between publication of the HMI Standards and Quality Report and the issuing of the new 5–14 Guidelines and Scottish Executive response to the AGL report, a number of local authorities have been very proactive in relation to MLPS. Some have instigated authority-wide initiatives such as producing new materials for primary languages (e.g. Glasgow City and Angus), operating visiting specialist schemes to support MLPS-trained teachers (Clackmannanshire) or launching 5–14 implementation strategies (Edinburgh City). Others are supporting experimental approaches to earlier FL starts in individual schools in their areas such as pre-school provision (e.g. in North Ayrshire, North Lanarkshire and Renfrew) or partial immersion programmes from P1 (Aberdeen City).

The new agenda of flexibility in the curriculum (SEED Circular 3/2001, August 2001) will no doubt have an impact on the interpretations which individual local authorities and possibly even individual schools may make of the AGL recommendation on entitlement. Individual local authorities have already indicated an interest in shifting the balance of entitlement to FL learning into the primary, starting in P4 and concluding at the end of S2. This would immediately raise the stakes in relation to teacher training and supply in the areas affected but this remains a key issue nationally in the medium and long term. Recommendation ten of the AGL report advocates that all initial teacher education (ITE) courses for primary school teaching should include a core Modern Language component that is coherent, progressive and sufficient to deliver the revised 5–14 guidelines (p. 16). The AGL acknowledges that this would require a radical alteration to such courses but argues that it is the only way to solve the problem of teacher supply for languages at primary school. Not for the first time, the issue of a FL as a core component of the primary BEd has been referred and deferred. This time it is to the national committee currently reviewing

ITE provision across the board in Scotland which will only consider the issue once the national debate on education is complete in autumn 2002. After nearly ten years of MLPS implementation there is still no firm commitment to or prospect of primary teachers entering the profession in numbers sufficient to secure the unique achievements of the last decade and able to respond flexibly to the future demands of FL teaching in primary.

REFERENCES

Giovanazzi, A. (1992) *Foreign Languages in Primary Schools, Sense or Sensibility – The Organisational Imperatives,* paper given to the British Council Triangle Conference, January 1992: Paris.

Johnstone, R. (1994) *Teaching Modern Languages at Primary School, Approaches and Implications,* Edinburgh: SCRE.

LTS (2000) *Modern Languages 5–14 National Guidelines,* Edinburgh: Scottish Executive.

Low, L., Duffield, J., Brown, S., and Johnstone, R., (1993) *Evaluating Foreign Languages in the Primary School,* Report to SOED, Stirling: Scottish CILT.

Low, L., Brown, S., Johnstone, R., and Bankowska, A., (1995) Foreign Languages in Primary Schools, Evaluation of the Scottish Pilot Projects 1993–95, Final Report to SOED, Stirling: Scottish CILT.

SOEID (1993) *Modern Languages in the Primary School, The Training Programme,* Glasgow: Strathclyde University, Jordanhill Campus.

41

Personal and Social Education

David Betteridge

> There are few things which I can desire to do . . . which do not depend upon the active co-
> operation of others. We need one another to be ourselves. (John Macmurray, *Persons in Relation*,
> London: Faber, 1961)

STATUS, DOCUMENTS AND RECOMMENDATIONS

Personal and Social Education occupies an important position in current thinking about the
aims and curriculum of Scottish schools. It had considerable status and publicity given to it
when, in 1993, the Scottish Office Education Department (SOED) issued a set of national
guidelines devoted specifically to personal and social development, and when, in 1995, the
Scottish Consultative Council on the Curriculum (SCCC) published its aptly titled *The
Heart of the Matter*, reviewing and reflecting on emerging policies.

Looking back, there is an interesting history to tell. MacBeath (1988) documents the
variety of banners and initiatives under which personal and social aspects of education were
treated in Scotland in the decades prior to the launching of the SOED's guidelines. He
identified the Advisory Council on Education's report, *Secondary Education* (1947) as being
particularly significant. An essential purpose of all schools, according to this often cited but
under-implemented report, is the provision of a setting conducive to young people's
'progress towards social selfhood'. These last two words nicely encapsulate a notion that is
central to a form of personalist philosophy running, sometimes subterraneously, through
Scottish policy debates.

The SOED's strategic outline of aims and curriculum, *The Structure and Balance of
the Curriculum 5–14*, published in 1993, also gave prominence to personal and social
matters, but, interestingly, did not count them as constituting one of its five main areas
for curriculum planning. Rather, the personal and social development of pupils was seen
as being a fundamental aim of education to which work in the framework areas of
Language, Mathematics, Environmental Studies, the Expressive Arts, and Religious and
Moral Education should contribute. Not only the content of these five areas, but also the
very experience of learning were deemed to be proper vehicles for promoting development. Originally, when the research and development group charged with the remit
for Religious and Moral Education was set up, it was intended that it should incorporate
aspects of social education in its work. However, it rapidly became apparent that the
complexity of the field could not effectively be addressed in this way. A case was made

to the Scottish Office for a separate set of guidelines for personal and social development, and this was agreed.

The guidelines differed from those provided in other curriculum areas in that they did not use an A to E (later A to F) format for the grading of levels of targets. Rather they proposed a framework of three broad developmental stages as an aid to understanding how children progress, emphasising the active role that schools need to adopt in the areas of pupils' self-awareness, self-esteem, inter-personal relationships, and independence/inter-dependence. Significantly, the guidelines sought to establish a timetable niche for the teaching of personal and social development against any possible superficiality or margin-alisation that the *Structure and Balance* document might encourage in the unwary or uncommitted. So, whilst reiterating and endorsing the point that 'personal and social development is embedded in all learning', the guidelines urged the management team of a school to ensure, not only time for cross-curricular approaches, but also for what it called the 'special focus approach'. By special focus approach was meant concentrated work on 'issues which pupils have identified and raised as being important, or which others have identified as being important for the pupils'.

Besides the special focus and cross-curricular approaches there was a third that the guidelines identified, namely the creation of 'a warm, caring, supportive atmosphere in which all individuals, pupils, staff and parents, know that they are valued' – the whole-school approach. Other sources than the guidelines brought the whole-school approach to the attention of schools. In place of the guidelines' 'atmosphere', the term 'ethos' began to gain currency, becoming a focus of concern in Her Majesty's Inspectors of Schools' reports and in their Audit Unit's set of performance indicators for schools' self-evaluation, *How Good is Our School?* (SOED, 1996), revised and reissued under the same title in 2002, with performance indicators redesignated as 'quality indicators'.

The importance of Personal and Social Education has been highlighted with each new curriculum initiative since 1993, as, for example, in the revised edition of *The Structure and Balance of the Curriculum* (Learning and Teaching Scotland, 2000). Here, personal and interpersonal skills are described as being among a set of 'core skills and capabilities' along with language and numeracy, 'widely recognised as essential for a healthy lifestyle, responsible citizenship and, in time, employment and successful lifelong learning'.

Further impetuses have been received from initiatives in the areas of social competence, social inclusion, anti-bullying, anti-racism, child protection, the health-promoting school, citizenship, values education, and school ethos – all areas for development posited on the notion of 'social selfhood'.

PRACTICES, ACHIEVEMENTS AND DEVELOPMENTS

It is unlikely that any two schools arrive at the same set of practices in Personal and Social Education, even given an equal commitment to the sorts of recommendations reviewed above. Schools can only progress from the contingencies of their present positions, 'taking account', as the 5–14 guidelines acknowledge, 'of local circumstances, priorities and resources'. Further, school staffs' own views vary, leading to the giving of different degrees and kinds of priorities. In a progress report to the Scottish Executive Education Department, *Educating the Whole Child*, (SEED, 2000), HM Inspectors concluded that:

Overall, the picture emerging from general inspections is that almost all schools made good provision for personal and social development through whole-school ethos arrangements. A majority of schools afford appropriate special focus programmes, but fewer schools recognised the full scope for cross-curricular links (p. 9).

A considerable body of resources is becoming available for all approaches. Within a few years of the 5–14 guidelines' publication, Ashton (1996) was able to catalogue an impressively long list of books, packs, posters and videos, and of contact addresses, including The Advisory Council on Alcohol and Drug Education (TACADE), one of the best known sources of support for schools. It is interesting to note that, despite starting with a particular social and personal ill, TACADE's authors also address broader concerns of rights and responsibilities, caring and sharing, community and communication, self-esteem, feelings, friendship and values. Books and staff-development courses by Jenny Mosely, Noreen Wetton, Norma Black, Alex Rodger and others have similarly pursued a whole-child, whole-school approach in their developing of sound teaching–learning strategies. Education authorities have played an enterprising role in spreading necessary interest and expertise, as in the case, to take one example, of Glasgow's Positive Inclusion Partnership.

Across Scotland, thus resourced and encouraged, a burgeoning of initiatives can be seen, including mixed-aged peer support systems, for example, buddying; parental and community involvement; study of playground use, leading to pupils' involvement in rule-making; strategies to develop emotional literacy; experiments with class and school councils or parliaments; re-examination of incentives, rewards, and sanctions, and the moral economy that underlies them; and the use of circle time, designed to provide space in which pupils express thoughts and feelings freely, and are listened to. A detailed account of how one school developed circle time to meet a wide range of purposes is given by Campbell and Dominy in *Sharing Good Practice*, edited by Lloyd and Munn (Edinburgh: Moray House Publications, 1997). Here, the authors describe how circle time evolved from being a tactic used initially to tackle particular social difficulties to 'a key plank in our general personal and social development programme'.

The most successful practice appears to be achieved when a school guarantees a specific time allocation for Personal and Social Education, when rich and relevant resources are available, and when regular evaluations are undertaken by staff, including the headteacher, to ensure that whole-school, cross-curricular and special focus approaches are all employed in a judicious mix. Further, as Luby (1993) argued in his study *Democracy and the Classroom* (MPhil thesis, University of Strathclyde), the ethos of a school needs to be such that it fosters a measure of self-direction on the part of pupils. Teachers, too, if they are to extend the scope of their work, benefit from a supportive school ethos, and from a network of friendly and critical fellow practitioners. One network showing the attributes described by Luby is the Scottish Schools Ethos Network, co-ordinated from Moray House Institute of Education, University of Edinburgh.

SHORTFALLS, DIFFICULTIES AND CHALLENGE

The extent to which schools can approach a full programme of Personal and Social Education depends on their capacity to address a number of difficulties. With mounting demands from government and public for schools to be accountable in particular ways, the temptation is to give more and more attention to the more readily tested aspects of the formal curriculum. Cross-curricular work, including work that incorporates a personal and social dimension, can then all too easily and unnecessarily slide into neglect. There is nothing particularly new, or Scottish, in this Gradgrindian fallacy. Pring (1984) warned of it in an earlier time and place of educational change, as others did before him, when he urged teachers to be vigilant in defence of 'humanistic values' against what he perceived as an 'increasingly pragmatic and utilitarian approach to education' (p. 169).

Questions concerning values constitute a further set of difficulties to be addressed. In a survey of teachers' perceptions of values, a Scottish Council for Research in Education team concluded that 'there is not an established discourse for values education' and that many teachers spend little time with their pupils considering 'the processes involved in acquiring knowledge and understanding and reaching a personal values stance' (Powney, 1995, p. ix). It also appeared that there was a tendency to concentrate on those values that 'encourage pupils' development as social beings, especially so as to fit in to the social context of the school'. Promoting debate addressed to long-term issues appeared to be less common. However, given the extent of recent development work, much of it building on initiatives undertaken under the aegis of the Gordon Cook Foundation, shortfalls in the area of values can more readily be tackled.

After values clarification, and their application, there remains the matter of appraising and reforming the approaches to teaching and learning that are employed, addressing, as Pring (1984) put it:

> the effect of the school and the curriculum . . . upon young persons – upon their sense of personal worth, upon their self-confidence and sense of achievement, upon the relationship of trust and co-operation between teacher and pupil and between pupil and pupil (p. 168).

This 'effect' that Pring speaks of includes the so-called 'hidden curriculum' of schools, usually far from hidden from the pupils who experience it. A discussion paper published by the SCCC, *Teaching for Effective Learning* (SCCC, 1996) posed a comprehensive set of questions relating to this. Three questions in particular serve very well to illustrate the scale of their challenge:

- How often do I encourage learners to think for themselves and to try out new ideas?
- In what ways do I demonstrate to young people that I respect and trust them?
- How do we promote, recognise and value the achievement of all young people? (p. 33)

To what extent, then, can Personal and Social Education be judged to be successful? HM Inspectors came to a positive conclusion in their progress report, referred to earlier (SEED, 2000, p. 3): 'Almost all schools recognise the importance of personal and social development in the education of the whole child, and give it good attention.' However, other analyses, taking broader social contexts and outcomes into account, lead to a more pessimistic view. Thus, for example, in the Scottish Executive's Discipline Task Group's report, *Better Behaviour – Better Learning* (SEED, 2001), the unfinished business that faces education looms large: unfinished business, that is, as indicated by shortfalls from such targets as the Scottish Executive's 'five key outcomes for education' (November, 2000). These include 'values and citizenship' and 'learning for life'. The old conundrum about schools and whether or not they can compensate for society remains to be weighed afresh. While it is remarkable that so much is attempted in the name of Personal and Social Education, the inequalities, dysfunctions, and anxieties that perennially damage pupils' and teachers' lives greatly limit schools' capacity to deliver.

ACKNOWLEDGEMENTS

The author would like to acknowledge the value of discussions with Lynn Bennett, Kay Dickson, Mary Doyle, Bryce Hartshorn, Margaret McGhie, Agnes McIntyre, Neena Mahal, Kathleen Millar, Elaine Miller, Maggie Milne, Ruby Pillay and Khushi Usmani.

REFERENCES

Ashton, T. (1996) *5–14 Catalogue: Personal and Social Development*, Dundee: SCCC.
MacBeath, J. E. C. (1988) *Personal and Social Education*, Edinburgh: Scottish Academic Press.
Powney, J. et al. (1995) *Understanding Education Values in the Primary School*, Edinburgh: SCRE.
Pring, R. (1984) *Personal and Social Education in the Curriculum*, London: Hodder and Stoughton.
SEED (2000) *Educating the Whole Child: Personal and Social Development in Primary Schools and the Primary Stage of Special Schools*, Edinburgh: SEED.
SEED (1993) *Personal and Social Development 5–14*, Edinburgh: SOED.

42

Religious and Moral Education

James C. Conroy

> . . . if at the Church they would give us some Ale,
> And a pleasant fire, our souls to regale;
> We'd sing and we'd pray all the live-long day,
> Nor ever once wish from the church to stray.
>
> William Blake, *Songs of Innocence*

The authors of the curriculum and assessment guidelines for Religious and Moral Education in Scottish Primary schools (SOED, 1992) might well have penned Blake's words for him insofar as they wished to retain a healthy attachment to traditional forms of Christianity while recognising that socially, culturally and religiously many of their students have already 'left' for the Ale-house.

This chapter attempts to delineate the evolution, purposes, nature and distinctive qualities of Religious and Moral Education in the Scottish primary school as well as comment on some of the complexities and most evident contradictions etched into the national framework.

HISTORICAL INFLUENCES

The 'modern' era for religious education in Scotland can be traced back to the Scottish Education Department report (SED, 1972), *Moral and Religious Education in Scottish Schools*, commissioned by the then Secretary of State for Scotland. Subsequently known as the Millar Report it both diagnosed the state of religious education then available and offered a prescription for future development. Prior to this, provision in Scottish schools was based on notional assent to the legislation first enacted in the Education (Scotland) Act of 1872, and re-affirmed in subsequent Acts and Memoranda between 1918 and 1980, which required that Religious Education be the only compulsory subject on the curriculum. Unlike its English progenitor it did not preclude Religious Education from being taught in accordance with a particular denominational formulary. Thus an inspectoral report of 1878, quoted in the SED 1943 *Memorandum with Regard to the Provision made for Religious Instruction in the Schools in Scotland*, could state that 'The public schools are to all intents and purposes denominational schools. Public and Presbyterian are practically interchangeable terms' (p. 7). Despite subsequent Education Acts, Religious Education remained effectively denominational up to and beyond the publication of the Millar Report. Catholic schools and 'non-denominational' schools taught Religious Instruction in accordance with the tenets of Catholicism and Presbyterianism respectively.

The Millar Report, on non-denominational education, indicated that the vast majority of Religious Instruction at the beginning of the 1970s continued to focus on biblical knowledge. This practice largely ignored the emerging insights of scholars such as Ronald Goldman and Ninian Smart. Goldman applied the insights of developmental psychology to the study of religious attitudes in the young and realised that they were frequently taught from texts which they were certain to misconstrue because of their stage of growth. Smart wished to promote a 'scientific' study of religion which relied on the student being a dispassionate observer rather than a participant in the religious experience and discourse.

At the time of the report 78% of schools indicated that they never or rarely used any text other than the Bible in their Religious Education lessons. Little or no provision was made for any Religious Education which was not scriptural and not Christian. Paralleling developments in England, the Millar Report opted to promote a more developmental and child-centred approach. It also distinguished the task of the school from that of the home and other (Church) institutions in children's religious development. Nevertheless Religious Education was to go on serving a social function with a continuing emphasis on the fundamental and formative place of Bible stories in the growing moral life of children. Thus in public primary schools Religious Education was no longer to be seen as 'denominational'. It was, instead, to reflect and promote a generally ethical form of Christianity as the basis of the public good. Indeed the explicit wedding of Moral and Religious Education by the curriculum planners in Scotland marked out one continuing distinction between the Scottish and English approaches to curriculum development. This may simply have been a consequence of the more distinctively religious character of Scottish civic life as shown in G. Davie's work *Religion in Britain since 1945* (Oxford: Blackwell, 1994).

Religious Education in Roman Catholic primary schools during the 1970s was influenced by the journal, *Lumen Vitae*. Its primary aim remained the preparation for sacramental participation in the life of the Church enhanced by new pedagogical and methodological considerations. These new methods paralleled those evident in non-denominational schools and were developed to promote a new vision of relevance in pupils' lives. However, the important distinction adumbrated in the Millar Report between the school on the one hand and the parish and home on the other was not replicated in the thought patterns of Catholic primary educators. Rather, school-based nurture was seen as a fulfilment of one's obligations to the Church. Syllabuses were generated locally at diocesan level and approved by the bishop so that significant variation in the quality of provision was to be seen across Scotland. One syllabus produced by the diocese of Paisley demonstrated the anxiety felt by many in the Catholic community that the 'modern', less doctrinally focused approaches were leading to confusion. As a counter measure the syllabus juxtaposed the 'new modern text book complete with work books . . . [with] a compendium of doctrine extracted from the Catechism of Christian Doctrine' (Diocese of Paisley, undated).

THE MODERN ERA

Despite the clear distinctions in approach between denominational (largely Roman Catholic) and non-denominational schools, there was Roman Catholic representation on the new Scottish Central Committee on Religious Education (SCCORE) established in

1974. Although the systems were, and remain, discrete there has been more traffic in ideas between the two than is often acknowledged. The Catholic sector has learned much from developments in the professional management of Religious Education while the non-denominational sector has begun to rediscover the place of the interior life and narrative in the study of religion which has always been maintained in Catholic approaches to Religious Education. The first SCCORE publication (HMSO, 1978) promulgated a view that the common ground across all sectors should be that whatever was provided should be 'educational'. This merely served to suppress an issue which was to re-emerge in the early 1990s with the advent of the national guidelines for 5–14 Religious and Moral Education (SOED, 1992). The issue was and remains centred on a disagreement as to what is to count as 'educational'.

For non-denominational education, the view which emerged from SCCORE *Bulletin One* was that the Bible should continue to hold a significant place but should be approached developmentally. The example offered explored three ways of examining the life of David. For the early stages the focus was to be on David's becoming King, for the middle years pupils were deemed to be interested in David's warrior/guerrilla phase and pupils in the upper phase might wish to discuss why David refused to kill Saul. While such an approach begs as many questions as it answers, taken with the more general recognition of the importance of rooting conceptual and religious development in children's growing yet actual experience, the methods advocated were similar to those which might be seen anywhere in the curriculum.

A number of major national courses on Religious Education held in the late 1970s and early 1980s helped establish the practical force of the 'scientific' study of religion. The approach in primary schools, as seen in a variety of local authority policy guidelines and materials, was to bring about understanding and not commitment, yet the undertow was unequivocally Christian with the, still compulsory, requirement for religious observance being characterised as an opportunity for the school to affirm its Christian identity. Thus a confusion of purpose remained, however subliminally.

Parallel developments in Catholic education saw the replacement of diocesan syllabuses by a nationally approved programme published in Ireland. This programme, *Leading Our Children to God*, by Melody et al. (Dublin: Veritas, 1987) was more systematic and extensive than anything heretofore used in Scottish Catholic education. The Veritas pedagogic philosophy was developmental. It was also consistent with the catechetical principles centred on revelation (God's gift) and faith (the human response) promulgated in the documents of the Second Vatican Council. The developmental element was manifest in the choice of annual themes which covered life, friendship, community, growth, building/creating, communicating. These themes were used at each stage to communicate Christian revelation experientially, doctrinally, morally and sacramentally.

On 1 January 1983 Religious Education was opened to inspection across all sectors of Scottish education, though in Roman Catholic schools the inspection could only deal with structural and systemic issues and could not refer to the content of what was being taught. This major change to Religious Education resulted in a number of insightful and studied reports by both Her Majesty's Inspectors of Schools and local education authorities on the state of Religious Education during the 1980s and 1990s. The first of these (SED, 1986) indicated a general lack of awareness of the issues raised by the Millar Report and SCCORE *Bulletin One* even among a majority of headteachers. Where religious education did occur, by no means universal despite its statutory position, whole-class teaching of Bible stories continued to dominate; the other staple being 'moral' lessons. The introduction of Veritas as the nationally approved syllabus appeared to offer Roman Catholic schools a more coherent approach to Religious Education, but here too the report found that all was not as it should be since many were using the Veritas programme as a basis for a more traditional catechetical approach which failed to reflect the spirit or structure of the original. In recent years this programme has been updated as *Alive-O* and has further eschewed a doctrinal approach, opting instead for an increased emphasis on religion as a form of relationship.

In the years following the publication of the 1986 report, local authorities provided guidance and materials for primary schools which generally laid stress on an implicit religious approach through the study of life, living and growing in the early years. A more systematic and explicit approach was taken in materials developed for the upper primary school with the emphasis remaining on Christianity though some material was being developed by local authority advisers for the study of other faiths, mainly Judaism and Islam.

The 1991 SED consultative paper, *Curriculum and Assessment in Scotland: A Policy for the 90s: Religious and Moral Education* demonstrated that local authorities gave significant attention to staff development and that a majority of schools had policies on Religious Education and observance which derived from earlier local authority documents. Despite this, confusion as to purposes and practices remained with considerable variation in the quality of planning and monitoring of Religious Education. 'Religious education was commonly seen as an area of difficulty and uncertainty' (p. 15).

CURRENT ISSUES

The development of the national guidelines in Religious and Moral Education (SOED, 1992) marked a further decisive moment in the development of the subject in the primary school. In the debate leading to the publication of the draft guidelines much had been made of the need to grapple with Religious Education as process rather than product as well as the need to develop a more rigorously 'scientific' approach which demanded no personal commitment. Yet, in the end, the attainment targets and programmes of study were heavily content-laden. The guidelines indicated, for the first time, that 10% of class time should be devoted to Religious Education.

Attainment outcomes were also cast in terms of knowledge and understanding, skills and attitudes in relation to Christianity, other world religions and personal search. Thus other world religions takes a central place in the primary curriculum for the first time and general dispositions take the place of personal commitment. However, despite the substantial increase in available materials which could assist in delivering the 5–14 targets on teaching faiths other than Christianity, neither sector has made the hoped for progress. According to a report of Her Majesty's Inspectorate in 2002, *Standards and Quality in Primary and Secondary Schools:1998–2001* the teaching of Christianity has remained strong in many instances but that of other world faiths had significant weaknesses in approximately 45% of schools. Given the importance attached in the guidelines to the role of Religious Education in the personal development of pupils, assessment emerged as a crucial issue. Some suggested that it should provide opportunities for reporting on the individual's growth in matters moral and religious; others perceived this to be both impossible and inappropriate. For now the latter view holds sway though the discussion continues.

Inherent contradictions re-emerge since it is not at all clear what such general dispositions might look like; pupils are invited, as a central aim of the programme to develop their own beliefs and attitudes, moral values and practices while at the same time appreciate common values. Carr (1995) and others suggest that it is difficult to hold that there are common values to which presumably everyone should subscribe and at the same time suggest that all values are a matter of personal clarification and preference. The explicit alignment of moral and religious education, the continued emphasis on Christianity, the preserving of religious observance, all point to a culture which knows not its own mind.

On the publication of the guidelines it was generally thought that the Roman Catholic sector, which had been represented on the original research and development group, would accept the guidelines as being applicable to Catholic schools. However, in June 1992 the Catholic Education Commission rejected the SOED guidelines and the Catholic Church, in collaboration with the Scottish Office Education Department, drafted a parallel document (SOED/CEC, 1994), which reflected the structure of the original while replacing the aims and content with others more consistent with the traditions of Catholic education. Other world religions remained in the Catholic document but with a reduced emphasis. Nevertheless the inclusion of the study of other faiths represented a significant development in Catholic primary religious education. A further important difference was the omission of moral from the title of the Roman Catholic document since it was unequivocally held that the moral life could not be divorced from ultimate beliefs.

The more focused approach offered by the guidelines has resulted in primary Religious Education dealing with some of those areas in the study of religion which were traditionally the domain of the secondary phase, especially in the teaching of other faiths. This may say something about educators' perceptions of fundamental changes in the developmental patterns of pupils as well as changes in wider political and social culture. *A Gift to the Child*, developed by Hull et al. at the University of Birmingham (Hemel Hempstead: Simon and Schuster, 1991), is indicative of a contemporary approach which draws on story, song and meditation from different religious traditions as a basis for an affective as well as a cognitive approach to Religious Education. Utilising artefacts, videos and visits to places of worship, Religious Eeducation also provides a place where others' festivals and celebrations are both re-enacted and understood. There must, however, be some doubt about the possibilities of continued progress in the field, with the publication of the Learning and Teaching Scotland revised paper, *The Structure and Balance of the Curriculum 5–14* (Scottish Executive, 2000) where the specific focus on Religious and Moral Education must now be deemed under substantial threat given its new structural relationship to both Health Education and Personal and Social Development. Coupled with the drive to promote citizenship education, these arrangements are likely to put increased pressure on an area of the curriculum where many teachers are in any event deeply insecure.

CONCLUSION

Many confusions and contradictions remain in Religious and Moral Education. Some of the most important which have yet to be resolved include the indecision about the purpose of moral education. Is it to introduce students to the 'good life' or to promote good behaviour? In the aftermath of the introduction of the 5–14 curriculum there was much unsureness as to the advisability of integrating religious and moral education. This can only be exacerbated by the revised curriculum time allocations and structural arrangements.

Further, despite differences from English models, Scottish Religious Education continues to draw heavily not only from the same insights but also from its structures. There remains an opaqueness about whether or not the aims are religious or educational and confusion as to what extent the stance adopted makes any difference. Above all, religion embodies two competing impulses – the conservative tendency and the disruptive tendency. Scottish primary Religious Education reflects the former but assiduously avoids the latter. All these and the other issues raised here represent the contrary forces manifest in Blake's poem which make the task of the primary school religious educator in Scotland a challenging one indeed.

REFERENCES

Carr, D. (1995) 5–14: a philosophical critique, in G. Kirk and R. Glaister (eds), *5–14: Scotland's National Curriculum*, Edinburgh: Scottish Academic Press.

SCCRE (1978) *Bulletin 1: A Curricular Approach to Religious Education*, Edinburgh: HMSO.

SED (1972) *Moral and Religious Education in Scottish Schools*, Edinburgh: HMSO.

SED (1986) *Learning and Teaching in Religious Education: An Interim Report by Her Majesty's Inspectors of Schools*, Edinburgh: HMSO.

SOED (1992) *Curriculum and Assessment in Scotland: National Guidelines: Religious and Moral Education: 5–14*, Edinburgh: SOED.

SOED/Catholic Education Commission (1994) *Religious Education: 5–14 Roman Catholic Schools*, Edinburgh: SOED.

VII

Secondary Education:
Organisation and Management

43

Organisation and Management in the Secondary School

Frank Lennon

A PERIOD OF CHANGE

Since 1996 secondary schools in Scotland have had to deal with change on an unprecedented scale. Apart from the reorganisation of local government into thirty-two local authorities and the inauguration of the Scottish Executive Education Department (SEED) within the newly established Scottish Parliament, there have been several other major initiatives culminating in the publication of *A Teaching Profession for the 21st Century* (Report of the McCrone Committee, HMSO, 2000) which has heralded the biggest restructuring of the teaching profession in Scotland for thirty years. Schools could be forgiven for thinking that teaching in Scotland is like being on a kind of educational Pianosa (the fictitious island setting of Joseph Heller's *Catch 22*) where insensitive and out-of-touch superiors keep raising the number of missions. It now seems that the destiny of the Scottish secondary school is to be largely determined by two of these factors: the McCrone agreement which aims to restructure the profession by 2006 and the New Community Schools initiative currently in its second phase which aims to re-culture the schools.

LEADERSHIP OR MANAGEMENT?

Leadership and management of the highest order will be required at local authority, but more importantly at school level if all of this is to be successful. It seems unlikely that the performance management model of the last decade with its focus on accountability as measured by so called 'hard' indicators, whether of 'Quality' (as in the recently revised *How Good is Our School?* document, SEED, 2002) or 'Performance', (as in the unrevised *How Good is Our School?* document) will survive this tide of change. There are signs that a deeper understanding of the nature and complexity of leadership in education is developing, much of it based on the work of Daniel Goleman and his contemporaries, which stresses the importance of multiple intelligences, particularly emotional intelligence, in leadership. Their work is uncovering strong evidence of the relationship between 'leadership and the brain's design' (Goleman, 2002, p. 26–9). They have investigated in particular 'the open loop design of the limbic system' (p. 7) suggesting, amongst other things, that there is in organisations, such a thing as a 'group IQ' defined as 'the sum total of everyone's best talents' which 'resonant leaders' are able to harness. This they relate to the 'feel' of a company (comparable with the 'ethos' of a school) and suggest that 'despite the great value business culture often places on an intellect devoid of emotion' there is now a logarithm to quantify the impact of a company's 'feel' on its bottom line: 'For every 1 percent improvement in the service climate, there's a 2 percent increase in revenue' (p. 15).

But schools are not commercial companies and, although in education we seem obsessed with quantification, it is axiomatic that what counts in a school often cannot be counted, and that what can be counted, often does not count. A key task for school leaders is to know which is which and that requires a philosophy of education. A case in point is the distinction, often made when discussing the 'effectiveness' of schools, between 'hard' and 'soft' indicators. This is not just unfortunate but confusing and even hypocritical. When such a distinction is made by a school or an authority ostensively committed to the development of 'the whole child', their 'whole child' commitment is rendered spurious by stressing that one aspect of a child's achievement (that which can be measured by so-called 'hard' indicators) is more important than the other. Schools and authorities which adopt the rhetoric of values when stating their aims, yet routinely make this kind of distinction when discussing their 'performance', are contributing to disillusionment and de-motivation. If the aim is to develop staff committed to the idea that every aspect of a child's development should be valued, the routine discourse on school effectiveness should not suggest otherwise.

VALUES

Education then must be centrally concerned with values. This is a matter for leaders in education and it is therefore primarily with the leadership rather than the management of schools that we should now be most concerned. The recent introduction of the Scottish Standard for Headship and its Qualification (SQH), suggests that Scotland may be going in the right direction. It provides a useful framework for professional development and has a welcome component on 'values'. In general, however, too little attention has been paid in recent years to the development of values. We have been immersed as a profession in successive waves of curricular and structural development from Standard Grade and TVEI to 5–14 and Higher Still, much of it dominated by the processes and procedures of assessment and accountability. Little has been done to focus on the development of people in education, their values, attitudes and relationships. Until the introduction of the SQH, attempts at providing coherent programmes of leadership development have been conspicuous by their absence even as the importance of leadership in education has become increasingly recognised – few heads (or Directors of Education for that matter) survive a negative HMI inspection. Yet HMI Inspections of Scottish secondary schools judge the standard of leadership (as with the standard of lessons taught) to be 'good' or 'very good' in the vast majority of cases; but that does not mean that there is no need for development, it just means that a serious and radical look at the kind of leadership development is required. Put simply, a model for leadership and staff development is needed which is values-based rather than skills-based; which focuses on people rather than policies; personal growth rather than professional competence; philosophy rather than practice; and which is sustainable rather than sporadic. We need leadership development that not only takes account of its importance at all levels in the school from classroom teacher and support staff to the senior management team (SMT), but also takes account of schools, not as organisations devoted to the most efficient 'delivery' of services to individuals; but as essentially communities of values, each with a collective sense of its purpose and destiny.

As with the SQH, the introduction of the new grade of Chartered Teacher (CT) offers some exciting possibilities in this regard. Like the SQH, the standard for Chartered Teacher includes a definition of professional values. If however, some of the immediate responses to the introduction of this new grade come to set the pattern for its future development, a real opportunity will have been missed. The increasingly prevalent notion for example, that the CT grade is merely a way of rewarding skilled subject teachers (in return for some as yet unspecified CPD) for work already being done, is potentially damaging. It is damaging for two reasons: firstly it is difficult to see a 'whole child' rationale here if this grade comes be seen as a reward for increasing subject expertise and specialism. This could have the profoundly negative effect of encouraging teachers to see themselves as essentially teachers of an increasingly complex curriculum rather than as essentially teachers of increasingly complex adolescents. Secondly it could lead to increased fragmentation in staff development terms by encouraging teachers to feel they have two roles – teaching their classes during the pupil working week on the one hand, and accumulating CPD credits from a registered provider during the additional contractual time, on the other. It is absolutely essential here that there is a values-based, whole child core element to all CPD for the CT grade, otherwise we run the risk of creating a subject-led, content-based, competence-driven model of staff development at the very time when the McCrone agreement explicitly states that 'teachers have a responsibility to work co-operatively with colleagues and others to pursue the overall objectives of the service' (para. 2.4).

Setting 'the overall objectives of the service' is fundamentally a leadership issue. It is for local education authorities and schools to define them. If they are defined narrowly to include only measurable outcomes or some other performance indicators there will be little development. The objectives should be values based and, if authorities feel constrained here because of concerns about whose values they should be, then they might want to take a look at the new Parliament's mace which has the words 'WISDOM, JUSTICE, COMPASSION, INTEGRITY' carved on it. These four 'national values' might offer more for the future of Scottish education than the five National Priorities. A professional environment in which teachers feel compelled to continually to focus on operational details for fear of some accountability measure being used as a stick to beat them with, will result in a professional culture in which discussion of values and principles is greeted with derision. It would be a sad day indeed if talk of the ideals and idealism that led many to take up a career in teaching were to become a cause of embarrassment in the staff room. It may be of course that such a day has already arrived in some schools. If that is the case then it may merely point to the fact that, overwhelmed by pressures of accountability to 'outsiders', some Scottish schools have long since ceased to be communities driven by values and principles. This is not to say that staff capable of such idealism are no longer in these schools – it is merely to state that schools may feel that they can not afford to spend time on philosophical reflection when there is so much to be done. The problem is of course that a lot of what has 'to be done' has very little to do with values and principles and a great deal to do with systems, procedures and policy implementation.

ACCOUNTABILITY

Secondary schools are increasingly places where policies are implemented not made, where headteachers are now so pressurised by an accountability agenda, set nationally and driven with varying degrees of rigour by local authorities, that they seem constantly to be looking over their shoulders. Headteachers are in the front line. Their professional lives are riddled with accountability: on a day-to-day basis to their own pupils and parents; more formally to their school board (and perhaps to a parent teacher association); to the officers and the elected members of their local authority; to Her Majesty's Inspectorate of Education (HMIE); to SEED; to their local MSPs and MPs. As the number of local authorities in Scotland has multiplied, so have the mechanisms for accountability. Indeed for many schools, the predominant characteristic of their relationship with outside agencies including (sometimes especially) their own local authority is accountability. Schools are well used to authority pressure to undertake certain courses of action but it is always disappointing when the main rationale provided is that, 'the HMIE recommend it'. Even more disappointing is the soon to become regular refrain, 'it's in the legislation.' This is new in Scotland, where the impact of legislation in schools was felt, but never immediately, rarely directly and always discreetly. Now, if the first three years of the Parliament are anything to go by, there is a danger that it is to be immediate, direct and public, with local authorities being reduced to little more than a policing role.

Section 23 of the recently revised Standards in Scotland's Schools etc. Act 2000 (Edinburgh, HMSO) illustrates this. It sets out the role of school boards and though it removes their right to add or delete names from short leets for senior promoted posts, it gives parents (and pupils) the statutory right to be consulted on the school's development plan (also now, a statutory requirement). That statutory right, unthinkable a generation ago, entered the legislation in 2000 and was enacted the following session. It should surprise no-one therefore, if as a result of constantly having to look over their shoulders, schools (and Headteachers in particular) have difficulty focusing on the way ahead.

Moreover, working in a secondary school at a time when, in the words of Eric Hobsbawm (The crisis of today's ideologies, New Left Review 92, 1992.)

> Human societies, and the relations of people within them, have undergone a sort of economic, technological and sociological earthquake within the lifetime of people who have barely got beyond middle age (p. 57)

is additionally challenging. The tremors from this 'earthquake' have been felt in every classroom. Indeed there are teachers who would argue that its epicentre has been schools. One of the traditional pillars of our education system – that of the teacher as an autonomous professional in charge of his/her own classroom – has been profoundly shaken. The school as a collection of autonomous professionals working in splendid isolation has virtually ceased to exist. However, the autonomy of the school as a distinct organisation is now also under threat. This is one of the great paradoxes of Scottish education at present. The rhetoric, both national and local, suggests more diversity and risk-taking is required, while simultaneously, each local authority seeks to use its schools to develop its corporate identity, and the Executive continues to seek to influence schools directly through Target Setting, the National Priorities and legislation. A cynic will say that we might end up with schools as branch offices of SEED plc. But then secondary schools are used to operating in a mixed message universe: they are constantly urged to act co-operatively and share good practice on the one hand, only to be repeatedly set against one another and compared (often by the very people who urge collegiality) for the purposes of accountability. Nevertheless the growing emphasis within schools on teamwork, collaboration and collegiality is not only welcome but necessary, if only as a response to the pressures of accountability.

VALUES AND ACCOUNTABILITY

Central to accountability is the recently revised HMI document *How Good Is Our School?* (SEED, 2002). When it was first published in 1996, it looked for a moment as if Scottish schools were going to be given a statement of the values at the heart of Scottish education. The choice of the word 'good' in the title of this important document, in preference perhaps to the more predictable choice of 'effective', seemed to suggest a 'values' approach. In spite of its title, however, there are no 'indicators of goodness' included. Any attempt at such an inclusion, in any event, might well have been greeted with howls of protest from one quarter or another. For pluralistic, liberal, democratic societies like Scotland in the twenty-first century then, there may be great disagreements over values which may result in publicly funded state schools being unable to assume the truth of, far less 'promote', any particular set of values. This may result in such schools seeking to base their values on principles broadly acceptable to the citizens of society as a whole. Inevitably perhaps, on matters of significant disagreement, schools may seek to achieve what has been called a 'principled forbearance of influence' whereby they seek to shape neither the beliefs nor the personal qualities of the pupil in line with any particular notion of 'the good'. Whereas schools may promote 'social morality' and 'civic virtue', they may do so only insofar as they are widely accepted by society at any given time. Thus, in this approach there is no easily discernible 'overall point of view' – no holistic vision. Yet in Scotland we have publicly funded denominational schools educating around 20% of the population which vigorously promote a holistic vision based on Christian values. The fact that these schools in Scotland tend to be more 'effective' when comparisons of similar schools are made using standard statistical measures such as examination figures and exclusion rates, has not escaped national attention. At a time of increasing concern over such 'effectiveness', there is surprising reluctance in Scotland to investigate fully precisely why this should be so. Instead the debate continues to focus on whether they should continue to exist at all.

A PROFESSION OF VALUES

The profession continues to struggle with this central issue of values. In *Professions, Standards and Competence: A Survey of Continuing Education for the Professions*, C. A. Madden, and V. A. Mitchell (Bristol: Bristol University, 1993) defined a profession as:

> A discrete body of individuals applying advanced learning or scientific knowledge and expertise to provide a service to clients and bound together by a membership of a professional body which assumes responsibility for monitoring professional standards and which confers benefits and may impose sanctions on members (p. 8).

Although in Scotland such a professional body does exist (The General Teaching Council), this definition of what it is to be a professional teacher is inadequate for the twenty-first century. Jon Nixon by contrast offers this definition (Teaching as a profession of values, in J. Smyth (ed.) *Critical Discourses on Teacher Development*, London: Cassell, 1995):

> Teaching is a profession only insofar as the educational values it espouses in theory are professed in – and through – its practice. The prime task for teachers as professionals, therefore, is to work

out their educational values, not in isolation and abstraction but in collaboration with colleagues and amid the complexities of school life. (p. 220)

Clearly these values are more than just narrow 'educational values' in Nixon's terms but they articulate the sense that just as the school community is about more than just 'effectiveness', 'attainment', 'achievement' and educational development, so teaching is about more than just 'applying advanced learning or scientific knowledge and expertise'. So, far from accepting the notion that teaching as a profession is merely about providing 'a service to clients', we need to challenge the assumption that teaching can somehow be separated out into a series of technical operations or competencies. Staff development therefore, in this reading, ceases to be centrally concerned with 'sharing good practice' but rather with 'sharing values': it is to do with personal growth, attitudes and relationships rather than with skills, competencies, processes and procedures. There is evidence from Scottish schools that a more explicit commitment to values by the school as a whole community might, in any case, help deliver some of the elusive 'effectiveness'. We may not be able to change the fact that we live in the midst of an 'economic, technological and sociological earthquake' but we may be able to change the way in which we respond to its various upheavals.

The passing of the new Standards in Scotland's Schools etc. Act 2000 is seen by some as one such upheaval. Following on from the Scottish Executive's New Community Schools initiative it has focused attention on the issue of inclusion in education. What for many years has been a rather tired debate about the relative advantages and disadvantages of main-stream education and special schools has been transformed into a philosophical issue about values in education and specifically about the rights of the child. Peter Mittler's view is uncompromising in this regard: 'The process of working for inclusive education can be seen as one expression of the struggle to achieve universal human rights' (Mittler, 2000, p. 12). He goes on to speak about this as a 'global priority' and one in which the UN has provided leadership. For Mittler, the international context is important. He describes it, beginning with the UN Convention on the Rights of the Child (1989), through the Jomtien Conference (1990) and the Salamanca Conference (1994), to the establishment of the European Agency for Special Needs Education. Developments in this area have been given particular significance for the Scottish educational community because of the passing of the Standards in Scotland's Schools etc. Act 2000. In this Act is an explicit reference to education as a right. This piece of legislation provides, for the first time in Scotland, a legal definition of the rights of all children to an education. In fact it goes further. Sections 1 and 2 of the new Act define a child's right to an education as follows:

> It shall be the right of every child of school age to be provided with school education . . . [and] . . . it shall be the duty of the authority to secure that the education is directed to the development of the personality, talents and mental and physical abilities of the child or young person to their fullest potential.

Children in Scotland must, as of right, have a school education that is 'directed to the development of [their] personality, talents and mental and physical abilities . . . 'to their fullest potential'. This right to an education is not conditional upon the child's socio-economic status, racial origin, cultural background or religious belief; it is a human right in the same vein as that outlined in the UN Convention. The question of whether such a right should extend to the type of education a child receives and whether or not this has to be 'inclusive', might have been conveniently side-stepped by the legislators and left out of the Act. In fact, perhaps somewhat surprisingly, section 15 of the Act is boldly entitled: 'Requirement that education be provided in mainstream schools.'

The clear principle here is that education in a 'mainstream' school is a right for all children unless certain circumstances exist. Although these circumstances are set out in the Act, section 15, subsection 3 ends with the statement: 'it shall be presumed that those circumstances arise only exceptionally.' Here, therefore, the commitment to an integrated education is unambiguous; but taken with the explicit commitment, mentioned above, to an education aimed at developing the personality, talents and mental and physical abilities of the child. This takes further the statement in *How Good is Our School?* (SEED, 2002, para. 4.1 – Support for Pupils) which speaks only of 'the emotional, physical and social needs of individual pupils'.

It is clear then that 'inclusive education' is being promoted by this, the first Education Act of the new Scottish Parliament. Not only that, but the Act requires schools to take account of the views of pupils when decisions are being taken about matters which affect them. In this sense it is a truly visionary piece of legislation which is already having an impact on Scottish schools. All the more disappointing then is the requirement that schools produce annual development plans and progress reports. It is disappointing and perhaps portentous, that alongside the vision of children's rights to a mainstream education and to be consulted on matters which affect them in schools, should sit such relatively petty bureaucratic prescriptions on operational matters. There is no clearer evidence of the changed political and litigious environment in which Scottish schools now find themselves operating than the new Parliament's eagerness to legislate and with such alacrity. At least strenuous efforts were made to consult and to consult not only the educational community but the wider Scottish community. This is a notable feature of the current national debate where evidence is being taken from every aspect of Scottish society including pupils currently in Scottish schools. The legal requirement to consult pupils in schools was also paralleled at a national level two years ago when two S6 pupils were asked to join the ministerial review group following the SQA debacle of 2000. Local authorities not only have a policy of every school having a pupil council but many have pupil representation on their education committees. These are developments that would have been unthinkable a generation ago and with their focus on including young people seem to bode well for the future of participatory democracy in Scotland.

INCLUSION

Paradoxically however, the exclusionary impact on children of their learning difficulties is a growing problem in secondary schools particularly when so many of the same children experience other exclusionary pressures because of their socio-economic circumstances, racial origins, cultural background or gender. A major challenge facing the educational community, if not the Parliament, in the early part of the twenty-first century is to develop structures, practices and curricula in mainstream schools capable of including all children. The inclusion issue has been challenging policy makers ever since the Warnock Report in 1978 introduced the concept of needs into the government literature on educational provision (*Special Educational Needs: Report of the Enquiry into the Education of Handicapped Children and Young People* (Warnock Report), Department of Education and

Science, London: HMSO, 1978). The 'presumption of mainstreaming' now enshrined in Scots law makes us face up to it more urgently. The education systems of both England and Scotland have been struggling with this issue and the publication in June 2001 of the report of the discipline task group, *Better Behaviour Better Learning*, set up by Jack McConnell as part of the McCrone Agreement (SEED, 2001) has focused attention on how provision for particularly challenging pupils is managed within the mainstream setting. The fact is that the 'child-deficit' model criticised by Warnock over twenty years ago has been reinforced by generations of teachers and remains part of the general consciousness of almost everyone who works in Scottish education. For many teachers this is still a powerful determinant of their professional attitude to the pupil with learning difficulties who continues to be seen by them as a barrier to the effective teaching of the subject or course. Such attitudes are not going to 'go away' merely because we now have a new parliament issuing prospectuses on New Community Schools or passing new Education Acts. Serious thought needs to be given to the kind of staff development required to move things forward in this regard.

Nevertheless we do now live and work in an educational environment where 'inclusion' is at the heart of education and social policy. Not only do we have the new Act, the Scottish Executive's New Community Schools initiative is currently being implemented across the country. Phase 2 was launched in session 2000–1 with committed funding for at least two more years. Here the intention is to provide a structure for the implementation of the 'inclusive' philosophy, integrating not only educational but social work and health provision, perhaps on single campuses located within specific communities. Some authorities have gone further with the establishment of children's services in which education, social work and health provision are integrated. This begs the question of course about whether 'integration' and 'inclusion' are the same thing. The terms are often used in the current debate about education and social policy as if they are interchangeable. There are however real differences of values as well as of practice between them. Clarity in this area is an important prerequisite not only for policy makers but also for managers in schools. Ainscow (1999) complains that the tendency is still to think of inclusion as being about pupils with disabilities moving to mainstream schools, with the implication being that they are included merely by being there. Rather he prefers to see inclusion as 'a never ending process, rather than a simple change of state, and dependent on the continuous pedagogical and organisational development within the mainstream'.

For many mainstream schools the concept of 'continuous pedagogical and organisational development' may not be new: many teachers in the forty-plus age category feel that is precisely what they have been involved in for most of their careers. However the proposition here is that such developments have not taken as full account of the range of pupils, their needs and abilities as might have been supposed. Notwithstanding the massive changes that have undoubtedly taken place in education since Warnock in 1978, little has changed as far as the child with special needs is concerned. It may be that more such children are attending their local comprehensive, but the common view of inclusive education as existing when a child attends the neighbourhood school is challenged by Ainscow as being not only mistaken but potentially dangerous.

Over and above any problems which might have been overcome by the local school, for instance in terms of providing physical access, such a school may be anything but inclusive in terms of its practices, structures, section and class composition policies, and in the attitudes of its staff. He argues that inclusion implies that 'all teachers are responsible for the education of all children' irrespective of their needs and abilities. The full implications of such a philosophy are far-reaching for secondary schools in particular. The notion that teachers in secondary schools should be teachers of children first and of their subjects second is one which is struggling to gain general acceptance. Indeed it could be argued that in fact this is the major issue as far as inclusive education is concerned – to effect significant attitudinal change amongst staff in schools.

In many Scottish secondary schools this will require nothing short of a transformation of the professional culture of the school. The relatively small number of schools involved in the early phases of the New Community Schools initiative may be the first to experience some of this cultural change but the scale of the challenge here extends beyond the targeted few schools to the many who need to review not just their structures and practices but their whole philosophy. It may be that a combination of McCrone restructuring, New Community Schools initiative and the new legislation will be the driving force behind such developments; but there are significant dangers. There is a deepening tension between policy and practice both at authority level and in schools. Authorities are keen to pursue integrated working practices and inclusive policies in schools but seem all too often to be oblivious to the fragmentation that can result. This may manifest itself in tensions being created within education authorities and, more worryingly, within individual schools.

Schools are now under pressure to do seemingly contradictory things: to show evidence of reduced exclusions and truancy on the one hand and raised attainment and achievement on the other. In this they are encouraged to apply for funding that may result in the creation of new posts, new projects and new 'units'. However tempting and however desirable such additional resources may be in terms of increased resources and/or staffing levels, they nevertheless bring with them problems of fragmentation. This can be seen most clearly 'on the ground' where it is quite common now for an individual S1/S2 pupil with specific learning difficulties in a Scottish comprehensive to have sixteen subject Teachers, a guidance teacher, a support for learning teacher, a behaviour support teacher, an educational psychologist and an attendance officer involved with him/her at school. In addition he/she may have a social worker, a health worker and a community outreach worker working with him/her in the community. Developing genuinely inclusive education can be difficult if the school structures and care arrangements seem to encourage professional rivalry based on the competitive need for the various professionals involved to justify their funding by demonstrating how essential is their particular contribution to the young person. In all of this any concept of the 'whole child' gets lost amid the inevitable professional 'turf wars' over who is responsible for what.

This kind of confusion, now part and parcel of everyday life for many vulnerable pupils and their carers, is a product of a philosophical vacuum at the heart of the whole operation. Put another way, those involved in the day-to-day operational aspects of such a system need to share a clear vision of its value and purpose. A multi-disciplinary approach does not of itself produce a more inclusive service – it might just as easily result in the opposite. Indeed the proliferation of 'specialist' personnel, each with their own 'expertise' to offer in support of the individual child, is proving to be increasingly challenging to secondary school senior managers anxious to improve their school's figures in the accountability stakes. The national Target Setting initiative has served only to exacerbate this problem in many schools where support for vulnerable pupils has become atomised into individual educational programmes for pupils whose difficulties are increasingly seen as requiring specific types of support from a range of 'specialists' recruited for that purpose. Managing such provision inevitably leads to pressure to extract certain children for 'one to one' or small group support often in a 'base' or 'unit' established for that purpose. While such support may at its best be considered 'integrationist' it frequently falls far short of what would be understood as inclusive.

ENLIGHTENMENT

Scotland at the start of the twenty-first century has a historic opportunity to redefine itself through its education system. The new Parliament has refocused attention on the great importance Scotland has historically attached to education. We are the inheritors of a rich educational legacy which stretches back to the School Act of 1696 which led to Scotland being the first country in the world to have an education system that could legitimately be called 'national'. This concern for education was taken up by Francis Hutcheson, Adam Smith, David Hume and others in the Scottish Enlightenment and led eventually to the the the Argyll Commission of 1865 and the great Education Act of 1872. The Standards in Scotland's Schools etc. Act of 2000 sits comfortably within that enlightened tradition. It is a heritage that schools can honour by putting values back at the centre of our education system. If there is uncertainty about what these values should be, teachers would do well to remind themselves of the Parliament's commitment to 'WISDOM, JUSTICE, COMPASSION, INTEGRITY'.

REFERENCES

Ainscow, M. (1999) *Understanding the Development of Inclusive Schools*, London: Falmer Press.
Booth, T. (1999) Inclusion and exclusion policy in England: who controls the agenda? in D. Armstrong and L. Briton (eds) *Inclusive Education: Policy Contexts and Comparative Perspectives*, London: David Fulton Publishers.
Goleman, D. (2002) *The New Leaders*, London: Little, Brown.
Mittler, P. (2000) *Working towards Inclusive Education: Social Contexts*, London: David Fulton Publishers.
SEED (2002) *How Good is Our School?* Edinburgh: SEED.
SEED (1999) *New Community Schools: Prospectus*, Edinburgh: HMSO.

44

Ethos and Discipline
in the Secondary School

Pamela Munn

Imagine the following scene. An English teacher is meeting her class of thirty 14-year-olds for the first time. It is August 1997 and the start of a new school year. She begins: 'Hello, everyone. My name is Mrs Brown and I'm really looking forward to getting to know you all. I've heard great things about you from Mr Black, about the play you wrote and produced last year and about the terrific poetry you can write. Now we are all going to need a bit of time to get to know each other, and it is important that we work well together. So the first thing we need to decide is the four or five rules that we are all going to stick to. Can you divide into five groups of six and we'll spend ten minutes deciding what these are.'

This vignette contains several elements that are known to contribute to positive relationships and therefore to good discipline. A key feature is Mrs Brown's high expectations of the standard of work she will encounter – 'I have heard great things about you.' Equally important is her pleasure at meeting the class for the first time. She is looking forward to getting to know her pupils – signalling that they are people as well as pupils. Finally, she wants to involve class members in decision making about classroom rules. Their decisions about rewards and sanctions would no doubt follow. Mrs Brown's approach is based on the well-founded belief that if she transmits her interest in and liking for her pupils, involves them in decision making and takes their views seriously, she is likely to motivate them to work hard and to behave well. While the scene is idealised, in that few teachers would embark on group work with a class they didn't know, it nevertheless is not too far removed from the practice of many teachers. There has been a growing realisation of the importance of feelings of self-esteem in pupils if they are to be motivated to learn and there has been an increasing awareness of the influence of the so-called hidden curriculum on pupils' (and on teachers') learning and behaviour. Thus school customs, routines and physical environment send messages, intentionally or not, about who and what is valued. Encouraging teachers to explore these features and to gather views about them from pupils, parents and members of the local community is a recent feature of Scottish schools. The days when pupil–teacher relationships were characterised by intimidation and fear through the use of the belt and other degrading punishments are gradually disappearing.

This chapter begins with a brief consideration of the importance of school ethos and discipline before going on to describe discipline in Scottish secondary schools today. It outlines the main sanctions and punishments used by schools but also draws attention to efforts to promote positive discipline, locating these in an increasing understanding of the ways schools themselves influence pupils' behaviour for good or ill. It concludes on an optimistic note but warns against the stigmatising of pupils displaying troubled or troublesome behaviour and their segregation from mainstream schools.

THE IMPORTANCE OF DISCIPLINE

Standards of pupil behaviour and discipline were identified as in need of improvement in the national debate on education conducted by the Scottish Executive in 2002. This is hardly surprising. There has been a steady stream of newspaper reports about violence in schools, the expulsion of pupils for taking or pushing drugs and most tragically the suicide of a small number of pupils who have been bullied. It would be easy for the casual observer to conclude that schools were a battleground where pupils fought out their disputes with each other and with teachers. Is this the case? Pupil behaviour has long been a concern to Scottish society. For example, in 1675 the Synod of Aberdeen asked its presbyteries to demand only three questions of the school master: 'whether he makes the bairns learn their catechism, whether he teaches them prayers for morning and evening . . . and whether he chastises them for cursing, swearing, lying speaking profanietie; for diobedience to parents and what vices appeares in them'.

School discipline is generally regarded as having two related purposes. One purpose is a means to an end, to provide a necessary condition for learning. Children cannot concentrate on the academic curriculum if there are, for example, unacceptable levels of noise, rowdiness or verbal or physical aggression in the classroom. So reports about indiscipline fuel concerns that the learning of the majority of pupils is being compromised. A second purpose is that of socialising pupils to behave in certain ways and to realise that they are part of a larger society. In this sense discipline is an end in itself, an outcome of schooling. Indeed this socialising function of schools was highlighted in responses to the national debate. There was little support for distance education – now made possible by modern communications technology–largely on the grounds that young people need to learn how to live together.

A description of school discipline then, tells us a great deal about a society's values as well as about the behaviour of young people and their teachers. The little that can be gleaned about discipline in eighteenth-, nineteenth- and even twentieth-century Scotland, for example, paints a rather depressing picture. The main features seem to be an emphasis on conformity, typified by the widespread use of rote learning by pupils and payment by results for teachers; respect for authority through intimidation of pupils by corporal punishment and of teachers through inspection of their competence by local presbyteries and the inspectorate; and moral rectitude as evidenced by the teaching of the catechism, the Bible as the main text in use and the emphasis on the religious orthodoxy of teachers.

Thus discipline can be seen as instilling values not only about acceptable social behaviour but about the very nature of learning. Teachers were the embodiment of both moral virtue and of academic learning. Their job was to transmit these accepted virtues and bodies of knowledge to the next generation, who were expected to absorb them unquestioningly or be punished.

DISCIPLINE IN SCHOOLS TODAY

Discipline remains a key concern. In 2000 a discipline task group was set up by the then Education Minister, Jack McConnell, in response to the continuing concerns of teachers about declining standards of pupil behaviour. The group's report, *Better Behaviour, Better Learning*, contained thirty-six recommendations aimed at schools, local authorities and central government. These highlighted the need for curriculum flexibility, so that courses could be offered which better motivated pupils, increased resources so that pupils with problems could be better supported within mainstream schools and a greater recognition of the range of pupil achievements. The over-reliance on pupil attainments in public examinations as an indicator of school effectiveness was given as a reason for mainstream schools being unwilling to keep pupils with behavioural difficulties. The so called 'league tables' of pupil performance highlighted the public accountability of schools for pupils' academic attainment, and meant that schools were cautious about admitting or retaining pupils who threatened their position in the league.

A number of key developments in contemporary Scottish schooling provide the context in which current concerns about discipline should be understood. First, the raising of the school leaving age to sixteen in 1972–3 (ROSLA) stimulated a concern about truancy and indiscipline, leading to the setting-up of a national committee on these issues. It was recognised that part of the discipline and attendance 'problem' related to the inadequacy of curricular and assessment provision for those now obliged to stay on at school. Indeed there was a more general concern about the curriculum for 14- to 16-year-olds which resulted in a radical overhaul of curriculum and assessment for this age range and the replacement of O Grade by Standard Grade in the 1980s. This reform, followed by the 5–14 programme introduced between 1987 and 1993, provided a common curriculum and assessment for all. Secondly, corporal punishment was abolished in state schools in the United Kingdom as a result of a legal action. Thirdly, the conceptualisation, categorisation and treatment of children seen as having special educational needs changed. There was encouragement for these children, including those who might be classified as having social, emotional and behavioural difficulties, to be educated in mainstream schools rather than in separate specialist provision. Thus teachers in contemporary Scotland are teaching a wider range of pupils than has been the norm. Fourthly, legislation was enacted giving local authorities power to exclude children from school on very general grounds. Fifthly, the government's policy on social inclusion identified education as a key determinant in life chances and in promoting social cohesion. Policy developments in education for citizenship, now one of the five national education priorities, have emphasised the importance of schools in sustaining liberal democratic values in a post-modern world. Teachers are being asked to take forward an ambitious agenda. They frequently complain that they are being asked to cure the ills of society and are being set impossible targets. In this context there have been a number of attempts to measure the nature and extent of indiscipline and so provide evidence on which to base policy developments.

The Pack Report of 1977 on truancy and indiscipline was unable to report on the extent and nature of indiscipline in schools because of the slippery concept of indiscipline and confined itself to the itemising of contexts likely to create problems for teachers. In 1987 the Scottish Office commissioned research on understanding effective discipline in schools. Part of the study included a survey of secondary school teachers' perceptions of indiscipline, involving almost 1,000 teachers in 112 secondary schools (Johnstone and Munn, 1992). A follow-up survey was commissioned in 1996 by the Educational Institute of Scotland (EIS), the largest teaching union (Johnstone and Munn, 1997). This survey included primary as well as secondary teachers. Both surveys revealed that it was the wearing effect of constant minor disruption which concerned teachers and there had been very little change in perceptions over time. The most frequently encountered misbehaviours were 'talking out of turn', 'hindering other children from working', 'eating in class' and in primary schools, pupils getting out of their seats without permission. Physical or verbal aggression towards the teacher were reported as rare. However, 69% of primary teachers and 50% of secondary teachers surveyed reported encountering physical aggression towards other pupils at least once during the week specified by the survey, and around two-thirds of both primary and secondary teachers reported encountering verbal abuse towards other pupils at least once during the week. About one-third of teachers saw indiscipline as a serious or very serious problem. Although the most commonly reported behaviours could be seen as relatively minor, they could nevertheless convey troubled classrooms, especially given pupil–pupil verbal and physical aggression. The cumulative effect on teachers was summed up by this typical comment from a primary teacher:

> Major incidences of indiscipline, I find, are usually the easiest ones to deal with, eg pupils can be excluded, referred to a senior member of staff, parents can be called to the school. It is the continuous minor infringements during the normal day-to-day running of the class which probably cause the most disruption and take most time . . . Almost any method of trying to deal with and improve poor behaviour over a long period of time takes a significant amount of time and adds to the workload. (Johnstone and Munn, 1997, p. 10)

This comment also indicates the range of the reactions to bad behaviour that is now available. No one punishment is universally effective, and there is a greater awareness of the need to prevent disruption in the first place. This is part of the rationale underlying the promoting positive discipline initiative launched by Scottish Office Education and Industry Department (SOEID) in 1997, in the establishing of the Scottish Schools Ethos Network in 1995 and in the production of a CD ROM 'Dealing with Disruption' which was distributed to all schools in Scotland in 2001.

Worries about pupil–pupil verbal and physical aggression were reflected in the prominence given by the government to the development of anti-bullying policies and strategies in schools. Research by Andrew Mellor, a principal teacher of guidance, revealed that 50% of a sample of 942 pupils surveyed had been bullied once or twice during their school careers and a quarter said they had been bullied more frequently. These findings, together with the tragic deaths of a small number of young people reportedly because of bullying, resulted in the Scottish Office funding the development of anti-bullying support packs for schools and the establishing of the post of anti-bullying development officer in Scotland. Most secondary schools now have anti-bullying policies in place. More importantly, most recognise that bullying is a serious issue which schools can tackle productively. The attitude that bullying is a normal part of growing up and doesn't do any harm is on the way out. School and local authority developments are encouraged and supported by the Anti-Bullying Network, funded by SEED, which shares research and practice based knowledge on how to prevent and tackle bullying.

PROMOTING POSITIVE DISCIPLINE

Our understanding of the causes of and hence the 'cures' for troublesome and troubled behaviour has grown over the years. In the past most explanations were rooted in the individual child who was seen as either mad or bad. Thus in the advisory council report

1950–2 dealing with the education of handicapped children, four residential child guidance clinics were suggested as meeting the needs of 'pupils who are maladjusted because of social handicap' (quoted in Petrie, 1978). The treatment provided by these clinics was in terms of psychiatric or psychological approaches. A different emphasis was that of the biological causes of disruption, of children who showed an abnormal incapacity for sustained attention, restlessness, and 'fidgetiness'. There is much debate about the meaning, cause and treatment of this condition which is currently called attention deficit and hyperactivity disorder. A contentious treatment is the use of drugs to aid concentration and attention span. More recently, however, sociological explanations of pupil disaffection have drawn attention to the role schools and teachers play in promoting positive behaviour in pupils. Areas such as curriculum organisation in terms of setting or streaming, curriculum provision, teaching approaches, systems of praise and rewards for positive behaviour and pupil involvement in decision making about school and classroom rules, rewards and punishments have all been highlighted as ways in which schools and teachers influence discipline. These sociological explanations, then, focus attention on things which school can do to promote positive behaviour and provide a counterbalance to medical and psychological explanations which see the causes of bad behaviour as located firmly in individual children and their families.

Two initiatives launched by the Scottish Office in the 1990s are underpinned by the notion that there are steps which schools can take to promote positive discipline. These are the Scottish Schools Ethos Network and the Promoting Positive Discipline in Scottish Schools initiative. Both these initiatives have as their starting points a belief in the importance of positive relationships between pupils and teachers, in the benefits of pupils, teachers, parents and others being actively involved in policy development and in pupils of all abilities being valued.

The Scottish Schools Ethos Network was established to encourage schools to share ideas and experiences about developing a positive ethos. A range of research studies has highlighted the importance of school ethos in the context of raising standards. The findings of all these studies suggest that without attention to the culture and organisational conditions of the school, real improvement in terms of behaviour and attainment is unlikely. The Scottish Office commissioned a group of researchers to identify key aspects of school ethos and to help schools investigate these aspects taking account of the views of the staff, pupils and parents. This work has been reinforced by the Scottish Executive publication *How Good is Our School?* (2002) which identifies a number of features of ethos. Thus ethos can be broadly conceived as encompassing the entire school culture and relationships, or it can be subdivided into features such as the physical environment, the way learning is organised, relationships, leadership style, belief systems and the policy framework. The key point is that schools are being encouraged to evaluate their ethos, taking account of the views of pupils, teachers, parents and others, and to identify aspects for improvement.

The network grew out of the schools' use of the ethos indicators, their desire to share experience of using them and to exchange information about strategies for bringing about change and improvement. The network has over 1,000 school and local authority members. Members receive a regular newsletter, case studies of school experiences of improving their ethos, and can attend regular seminars and an annual conference. An important aspect of ethos is the disciplinary climate. Schools have shared experiences about, for example, using 'buddy systems' whereby older pupils befriend younger pupils to induct them in the school;

pupil councils as a way of involving pupils in decision making; anti-bullying strategies; using praise and reward systems to recognise positive and caring behaviour; and developing the playground to encourage constructive play, thereby helping to avoid anti-social behaviour.

The Ethos Network includes school discipline in its activities but it is not its sole focus. The Promoting Positive Discipline initiative focuses on strategies adopted by schools to combat the low level, minor disruption which teachers report as a feature of life in most schools. Working with local authorities, the initiative encouraged schools to write brief case studies of positive and successful practice, to reflect on key features of their culture which promote good discipline and generally to raise awareness within authorities and nationally about innovative developments. The initiative recognised that good practice in promoting positive discipline takes place in many schools but that there is no obvious method for disseminating and discussing it. Small amounts of funding were made available through the initiative to release staff to write about the ways in which their school promotes positive discipline, to visit other schools, and to take forward new approaches.

Both these initiatives stress the importance of positive and inclusive approaches to promoting good discipline rather than a negative regime of a hierarchy of sanctions to punish unacceptable behaviour. Such sanctions exist, of course, and it is to these that we now turn.

PUNISHMENT AND SANCTIONS

The typical form of punishment for unacceptable behaviour for most of the history of Scottish schooling was corporal punishment. The 'belt' was a feature of the school system until the 1960s and 1970s. In the writer's own school days a class of 11-year-olds was belted by a music teacher because no-one would 'own up' to some minor misdemeanour. In secondary, a French teacher habitually wore his belt over his shoulder, under his gown, and flourished it at any pupil making impertinent remarks. The conventional wisdom is that corporal punishment had little beneficial effect on 'real troublemakers' although it intimidated the majority of pupils, pupils unlikely to misbehave in the first place.

The abolition of corporal punishment brought reliance on a wider range of sanctions to punish unacceptable behaviour. These included a telling off from the teacher, extra homework, lines – for instance, writing a hundred times 'I must behave well in class', detention – staying in school over break, lunchtime or after the end of the school day, withdrawal of privileges such as being refused a place on a school outing, reference to a higher authority in the school, and involving parents. As reported above, surveys of teachers reveal that no one sanction or punishment is seen as universally effective. Indeed teachers report using punishments such as extra work or lines knowing that they do not work. The most effective reaction to misbehaviour is seen as using humour to defuse the situation, thus avoiding the escalation of minor incidents into more serious confrontations.

The 1975 Education (Scotland) Act and subsequent regulations defined the local authority's power to exclude children from school. Exclusion was justified if the pupil or his parents refused to comply with school rules or if the pupil's continued presence in the school posed a threat to the safety and welfare of others. Unlike England and Wales, the Scottish legislation does not stipulate minima or maxima for fixed term exclusion; nor does it endorse permanent exclusion whereby the pupil is refused readmission to his or her original school. Indeed research has demonstrated considerable diversity in local authority policy and practice in regard to exclusion in Scotland. There are thus no comparable statistics between Scotland and England in terms of the number of pupils permanently excluded from school. There is growing concern south of the border at the number of permanently excluded pupils, estimated to be over 11,000 in secondary schools and 1,800 in primary schools in England. The absolute numbers are worrying in themselves, but of greater concern is that numbers are growing with a 45% increase between 1993 and 1994 and 1995 and 1996 in primary schools and an 18% increase over the same period in secondary schools. Numbers are beginning to decline but there has been an accompanying protest about schools having to readmit pupils whose behaviour is unacceptable in order to conform to the present government's social inclusion agenda. Statistics for Scotland have recently begun to be collected on a regular basis but it is too early to identify trends.

Scottish research (Cullen et al., 1997) revealed that in a sample of around 200 schools, of the 4,500 pupils who were excluded in an eight-month period, most were excluded only once and for three days. Nevertheless a substantial minority, 30%, were excluded for longer and over 1,000 young people had been excluded for six days or more. The kinds of offences for which most pupils were excluded seem relatively trivial, or low key. They include the rather general categories, breaking the rules and insolence. More dramatic offences were recorded in a minority of cases. For example, twenty-six pupils were excluded for physical assault on staff; nineteen for possession of an offensive weapon and forty-five for the use or sale of drugs. These pupils came from forty-one different schools. Provision for long-term excludees varies across the country and ranges from the minimum of an hour a week home tuition to placement in a day or residential establishment for pupils with social, emotional and behavioural difficulties. Thus, for some schools, a short-term exclusion might be seen as replacing corporal punishment in the absence of other effective sanctions. Longer-term exclusion might represent a lack of expertise in meeting the needs of children with social, emotional and behavioural difficulties, and perhaps an unwillingness, in some cases, to recognise how the school itself might be contributing to these difficulties.

This is not to deny that troubled children cause problems for schools. A number of local authorities now adopt an inter-agency approach to children evincing serious behavioural problems, whereby social workers, educational psychologists and doctors collaborate with teachers in diagnosing the causes of such problems and suggesting ways forward. The evidence is overwhelming that, as with other social ills, poverty and other forms of social disadvantage are associated with children excluded from school on a long-term or permanent basis. Lawrence and Hayden (1997) found that in a sample of excluded primary school pupils almost all had experienced trauma. This included one or more than one of the following: family breakdown; time in care; multiple moves; disability/bereavement; violence/abuse; major accident/incident; special needs; previous serious exclusion; no member of household in paid work. Thus school discipline inevitably bumps into issues of social welfare and there are clearly limits of resources, expertise and sometimes will, to tackle these. Some schools recognise that they can be a haven for troubled children and hold on to them; others are less willing to do so. We once again encounter the importance of school ethos in explaining the differences in exclusion rates from schools with very similar kinds of pupils. Schools can be identified as 'inclusive' or 'exclusive' in culture. For example inclusive schools tend, among other things, to emphasise social as well as academic development and have a senior management team who believe in the duty to educate all children not just the well motivated and well behaved.

CONCLUSION

Discipline in secondary schools has gradually been transformed as understanding about the 'causes' of and 'cures' for disaffection increases. The days of harsh, oppressive and authoritarian regimes are all but over and it is easy to forget how far we have come in a relatively short time in establishing more positive and constructive relationships between teachers and pupils.

A series of major changes in the 1970s and beyond have begun to influence the way we view schools and teacher–pupil relationships. The most important of these changes have been those in curriculum and assessment whereby there is now a common curriculum for all pupils between the ages of five and sixteen. This entitlement curriculum is now under threat, paradoxically as a consequence of the social inclusion agenda. The needs of all children are not being met and there are demands for greater flexibility and choice. One of our greatest challenges is to develop a set of principles on which flexibility and choice could be based which also protect equality of opportunity. Few want to return to the days when only the privileged few benefited from an academic curriculum.

Most schools in Scotland are now more relaxed and friendly places than they used to be. Relationships between pupils and teachers are generally positive, based more on mutual respect than on fear and intimidation. The trend is to involve parents and pupils more in decision making areas such as school rules, dress codes, anti-bullying strategies and the like. Furthermore there is increasing awareness of the need to recognise and value positive behaviour as well as having systems of sanctions and punishments. Thus many schools now have 'pozzies', statements by teachers about the positive behaviour of pupils, merit certificates and awards for positive behaviour, and 'I am special' badges for younger pupils to celebrate particular achievements.

In addition, techniques such as social group work and anger control originally used with severely troubled and troublesome youngsters are being recognised as having educational value for all pupils.

Optimism is tempered with concern, however, about continuing social inequality, poverty and racism in Scotland. Clark (1997) notes that there are high levels of poverty in some areas:

> In 1995 about 20% of the school population were entitled to free school meals; this varied from about 6% in Borders region to about 40% in the City of Glasgow. In Glasgow in 1993 one in three children lived in households dependent on income support and one in two of all primary-school children received clothing grants.

These figures have not changed much and the gap between rich and poor is widening. It can be difficult to motivate and involve parents, living in such circumstances, in their children's education. It is easy to label parents, who do not attend parents' evenings, or who do not ensure their children's regular attendance at school, or who fail to respond to their children's exclusion from school, as inadequate and/or uncaring and to write them off. Many schools are aware, however, that they provide an important source of stability and security in the lives of troubled youngsters and resist the provocation to exclude which is sometimes offered. Such schools work with their local communities and with other agencies such as social work and community police to maintain an inclusive ethos and to prevent the ratcheting up of the spiral of disadvantage for their pupils.

The balance between a welfare approach and one which emphasises a 'get tough' response to indiscipline will continue to be a major dilemma for government, education authorities and schools. An exclusive emphasis on an attainment culture, whereby schools are judged only by the numbers of pupils achieving particular numbers of passes in public examinations, may encourage an undue reliance on punishment. Scotland has managed to avoid some of the worst effects of a quasi-market approach to schooling evident in rising numbers of children permanently excluded from school in England and Wales. It is clearly important that, in a drive to improve standards of attainment, schools are not placed in direct competition with each other. If they are, the temptation to exclude children with special needs involving social, emotional and behavioural difficulties will be strong. These pupils will be seen as depressing a school's position in performance tables and as making a school an unattractive choice for parents.

Scotland prides itself on its commitment to high quality education for all and comprehensive education has strong roots. Moreover there are numerous examples of successful inclusive approaches across the country. Such approaches need to be widely disseminated and built on so that positive relationships between teachers and pupils are the reality experienced by all pupils and teachers in our schools.

This chapter draws on Munn, P. (2000) Discipline in Scottish schools, in H. Holmes (ed.) *An Ethnology of Scotland*, vol. 11, Edinburgh: Scottish Ethnological Research Centre.

REFERENCES

Clark, M. (1997) Education in Scotland: setting the scene, in M. Clark and P. Munn (eds) *Education in Scotland: Policy and Practice from Pre-School to Secondary*, London: Routledge.

Cullen, M. A., Johnstone, M., Lloyd G. and Munn, P. (1997) *Exclusion from School in Scotland: Headteachers' Views*, Edinburgh: Moray House Institute of Education.

Johnstone, M. and Munn, P. (1997) *Indiscipline: A Survey of Scottish Primary School and Secondary School Teachers*, Edinburgh – confidential report to the Educational Institute of Scotland.

Johnstone, M. and Munn, P. (1992) *Discipline in Scottish Secondary Schools*, Edinburgh: SCRE

Lawrence, B. and Hayden, C. (1997) Primary school exclusions, *Educational Research and Evaluation*, 3(1), pp. 54–77.

Petrie, D. S. (1978) The development of special education in Scotland since 1950, in W. Dockrell, W. Dunn and A. Milne (eds) *Special Education in Scotland*, Edinburgh: SCRE, pp. 1–15.

45

Guidance, Personal and Social Education and Pastoral Care in the Secondary School

David J. McLaren

THE ORIGINS OF GUIDANCE

Many would argue that the system of guidance which existed up until the publication of the McCrone 'Agreement' document (SEED, 2001) originated with the publication of the Scottish Education Department's paper *Guidance in Scottish Secondary Schools* (SED, 1968), and to some extent that argument has some currency in that the issue of 'pupil guidance' had come to the fore as a result of the move away from junior/senior secondary education towards the comprehensive model. Historians might well argue that Scottish schools had always been concerned with the welfare of their pupils but the move to comprehensive education in the 1960s was the first time that the education system as a whole had had to face up to the challenge of S1–S6 all-through secondary schooling. There had always been such schools in rural areas of Scotland, but throughout the country many large secondary schools were created which catered for a much wider ability range and socio-economic mix than ever before. The problem of how to accommodate pupil needs was as contentious then as it is now.

Embedded in the notion of comprehensive education itself was the commitment to ensuring the best provision possible for the individual, meeting individual needs and recognising that pupil 'potential' was a much wider concept than academic achievement. By offering the wide and varied curriculum which larger schools could offer at the appropriate levels and by encouraging a wider social mix, elitism and divisiveness would become things of the past and there would be a new emphasis on equality of opportunity.

Leslie Hunter, in his book *The Scottish Educational System* (Oxford: Pergamon Press, 1972), observed at the time that where a curriculum was characterised by variety and flexibility, 'the need for guidance of pupils arises'. He noted that some large schools had introduced a house system:

> where house masters are expected to know every pupil in their house – his or her abilities, weaknesses, interests, family circumstances, proposed career and so on. (p. 20)

Many schools had had a House system before this time, but Hunter was echoing the spirit of the SED's paper which also identified 'personal', 'vocational' and 'curricular' guidance – terms still used today. In 1968, 'personal' tended to mean discussing vital problems of the day, while 'vocational' had to do with careers information, (as opposed to work experience, self-assessment etc.) and 'curricular' tended to focus on option choice at S2. Each pupil had the right to receive advice or help from a teacher who had 'a special and continuing responsibility for him' and, most importantly, guidance was for all pupils, not only for those who had problems. The guidance system might be organised vertically (house groups) or horizontally (year groups) and staff would require training. Little or nothing was said about the appropriateness or otherwise of having potentially competitive house groups in the new system.

In anticipation of the raising of the school leaving age in 1972, a promoted-post structure was introduced as a further recognition of the importance of guidance in dealing with increasing numbers of pupils who were having to stay on at school. It is highly significant that the promoted post structures in guidance and 'subject' (introduced at the same time) were almost identical and that these parallel structures remained largely unchanged for some thirty years.

However, there was still considerable confusion as to what exactly guidance was all about, not least among newly-appointed guidance staff themselves. By the mid-1970s, HM Inspectors had become involved and, while they reiterated the importance of personal, curricular and vocational guidance, they stressed the need for other, non-promoted members of staff to become involved. This principle is likely to be strongly reinforced, perhaps by default rather than by design, in the post-McCrone era. There was also a growing recognition in the 1970s and 1980s that the formal subject curriculum was insufficient preparation for the world outside school and that 'social education' classes were required to deal with such matters as relationships, health, work and so on. Guidance staff, with their cross-curricular approach and their concern for the whole pupil, were seen as appropriate staff to devise and deliver social education programmes.

By far the most important influence on the aims, objectives and practice of guidance was the SCCC position paper *More than Feelings of Concern* (1986). This was the first real attempt on a national scale to define aims and objectives for guidance. It tried to identify the characteristics of a 'caring' school. It argued that guidance was more than just good intentions: it was, or ought to be, an active, on-going process which required planning and eight objectives were suggested as an aid to such planning. In addition to reinforcing earlier messages about personal, social, vocational and intellectual development and the need to ensure that each pupil was known personally by at least one member of staff, it included objectives covering the following areas:

- raising pupil awareness of and responsibility for their own development;
- identifying and responding quickly and appropriately to individual pupil needs;
- good teacher–pupil relations;
- liaison with home/support and welfare services;
- effective record-keeping.

The paper also attempted to define the remits of promoted guidance staff and, on a wider level, it discussed the relationship between guidance and the discipline system, assessment, the subject curriculum and careers education. Inevitably, it emphasised the need for more time and training for guidance staff and was at pains to point out that all staff have a guidance responsibility.

This report was a seminal piece of work, not necessarily for its intellectual depth or its great vision, but for its practicability. It provided a major stepping stone into the educational world of the 1990s and gave guidance an enhanced status and a much surer footing on which to contribute to important contemporary issues such as school ethos, quality and performance in guidance, school effectiveness, profiling, inter-agency collaboration and education for personal and social development – issues which the 1986 paper could not be expected to envisage. It is a testament to its durability that its eight original objectives were described by HMI in 1996 as being 'as relevant today as they were 10 years ago'.

WHAT DO GUIDANCE TEACHERS DO?

As will be discussed in more detail later, it is uncertain what form the new guidance arrangements will take, given the curricular and structural reforms which will emerge in the next few years. However, it is absolutely certain that schools will continue to have a duty of care towards their pupils and that 'guidance', if not in name, then in nature, will continue. What then, has been the nature of guidance work in the last thirty years?

Based on their guidance inspections in some 250 Scottish schools, HMI outlined a 'Guidance calendar' of whole-school or year-group activities (SOEID, 1996) With some amendments to include more recent developments, it is useful to use this as a starting point.

Year specific activities included:

- S1/S2 primary/secondary liaison programme, reception of S1 intake and S2 course choice process;
- S3/S4 careers advice, work experience, monitoring S3 subject progress, SQA presentation checks and post-exam consultation, post-16 options /Higher Still Guidance Entitlement;
- S5/S6 advice on study skills/decision making, monitoring, 16+ progress, careers advice, university applications, guidance entitlement;
- S1–S6 whole-school activities – pupil interviews, profiling/national record of achievement (NRA) or progress file activities and reporting to and meeting with parents.

It is obvious that any one of the above activities involves a great deal of time and effort on the part of guidance staff. For example, the reception of S1 intake is often a process which begins in P7 and extends throughout the first few months of S1 and involves (or should involve) frequent individual interviews and group activities with new pupils. Similarly, option choice programmes at S2 will often require guidance staff involvement in PSE classes on self-evaluation, in collating subject reports, interviewing pupils, arranging careers information and further interviewing of pupils and parents. In S4, the option choice and career planning process has become so complex that a major investment of time, training and resources has been required to implement the post-16 Guidance Entitlement.

The 'calendar' above can reveal only some of the many and varied activities involved in guidance – a fact recognised, to some extent, by HMI. What is equally significant is the wide range of duties which do not feature in the calendar but which are crucial in guidance work. One or two examples will illustrate the point. Guidance staff spend an enormous amount of time dealing with matters relating to attendance and latecoming. While these tasks might appear to be mundane (if time-consuming), they point to the larger issue of the involvement of guidance staff in creating and maintaining a positive school ethos and in supporting individual pupils – in helping pupils to feel valued by the institution. Guidance staff also spend a lot of time (some would say an inordinate amount of time) dealing with 'crisis' guidance, that is helping young people cope with the whole range of traumatic experience which may be part of their lives – family traumas such as separation, divorce and bereavement, relationship issues, health matters and the like. It is also essential to note that most schools see guidance staff as the first point of contact for parents and for the support agencies. Until recently, a principal teacher of guidance might have had responsibility for some 200 pupils, S1–S6, and would have not only dealt with parental enquiries but would also have been proactive in liaising with parents. In addition, many pupils may have involvement with one or other of the support agencies for instance social work, psychological services, or the Reporter to the Children's Panel. Liaison with these agencies, including case conferences, pupil contracts, individual pupil support, action planning and target setting, are all crucial if a pupil is to benefit from a coherent inter-agency approach and while it is true to say that these issues affect every teacher in every classroom, they are, or have been, the specific responsibility of the promoted guidance staff.

Guidance staff require to liaise closely with other members of staff in this respect. There is little point, for example, in guidance staff, psychological services, and social work agreeing a strategy on behaviour management or special needs provision if guidance staff do not make subject staff aware of the issues and discuss with them how this strategy might operate in the classroom. While this may be particularly true of the relationship between school and social work/psychological services, it is equally important in relation to other support agencies such as the careers service. This is particularly relevant since research indicates that careers officers have felt excluded from the S2/S4 options process.

THE STRUCTURE OF GUIDANCE

As with the previous section, this section describes the guidance/pastoral care structure which will pertain until 2003. The situation beyond that is currently the subject of much debate and some of the issues will be picked up in the second half of this chapter.

The number of promoted guidance posts varies from school to school, although as a general rule, most schools still follow the guidelines in the 1971 paper, that is one promoted post per 150–200 pupils on the roll. It is worth noting that the variability has increased in the last few years as schools have accepted greater responsibility for the management of resources previously controlled by the local authority. Normally, the overall responsibility for guidance will rest with an AHT or depute. A management team which wishes to emphasise the work of the guidance team may well appoint more than the recommended minimum number of staff and may recognise the contribution of guidance to a positive school ethos by allowing more time for unpromoted staff to work with guidance staff in such areas as option choice, or work experience. However, the converse may also be the case, depending on the priorities of the senior management team.

With the development of what might be called the 'quality agenda' in recent years, most schools and local authorities attempted to evaluate their guidance and pastoral care systems by using performance (now 'quality') indicators. While many would argue that these indicators are highly subjective, they did and still do provide a useful means of gathering evidence and there is no doubt that some of the restructuring of guidance teams and remits has come about as a result of documents such as *How Good is Our School?* (HMI, 1996; HMIE, 2002a) and *Taking a Closer Look at Guidance* (HMI, 1998).

In very large schools, a horizontal or year group system may operate, where guidance staff are responsible for age stages and may stay with these pupils for the duration of their schooling. In such schools, assistant heads can be responsible for guidance in S1/S2, S3/S4, or S5/S6. In smaller schools, horizontal systems will be managed by guidance staff only, responsible to one AHT/DHT. However, many schools operate a vertical or house system, where each House comprises pupils from S1–S6, usually grouped by alphabetical order of surname and again managed by one or more AHTs. There are hybrids of these systems and much depends on the number of pupils on the roll but more schools tend to favour the vertical system. This system has several benefits. From a parental viewpoint, all members of the same family will be in the same house and so parents will have to deal with only one member of staff who will know the family circumstances. From a staff perspective, a vertical system offers a wider range of guidance work and a more even spread of workload, while still allowing individuals to develop specialisms or additional management responsibilities. In both vertical and horizontal systems, there is an important pastoral and spiritual role played by the school chaplain, most obviously in denominational schools.

These additional whole-school or cross-curricular management responsibilities are often undertaken by principal teachers of guidance, as distinct from APTs, although remits vary enormously from school to school. Some schools distinguish PT/APT remits purely in terms of numbers of pupils, while others attempt to separate functions and activities. Remits have always been something of a grey area, particularly given the emphasis in recent years on guidance as a whole-school responsibility and the increasing role of first-level guidance staff, that is register/form teachers or volunteer helpers. With the removal of APT posts in 2003 and the probable expansion in first-level guidance and pastoral care, this question of remits will be crucial.

Staff development, training and time allocation will be discussed later, but for the moment it is sufficient to note that at the time of writing, guidance staff in most schools are employed first and foremost as subject staff and spend the majority of their time teaching the school subject for which they were trained. In 1994 the School Census indicated that there were 1,123 principal teachers and 1,072 assistant principal teachers of guidance and that in each category, only one-third had a guidance-related qualification (certificate, diploma, or masters), although it should be noted that the vast majority of guidance staff will have some experience of in-service training, often provided by the local authority (SOEID, 1996, p. 5). The GTC in Scotland recommended that promoted guidance staff should be required to work towards the Certificate in Guidance. (GTCS, 1998) There is no statutory allocation of time for guidance but a generally accepted minimum is forty minutes per fifteen pupils for whom guidance staff have a direct responsibility. Many schools do not even reach this minimum allocation and the competing claims of guidance work and subject teaching have been a major source of stress for guidance staff.

PERSONAL AND SOCIAL EDUCATION

Most whole-school guidance policies will indicate a strong guidance commitment to PSE (also referred to as personal and social development (PSD), or education for personal and social development (EPSD)). It is worth noting in passing that, while the commitment may be strong, the relationship between the guidance process and PSE has often been unclear, at least beyond the timetabled PSE element.

The Scottish Office's 5–14 document noted that PSD was 'essentially concerned with the development of life skills. All aspects of a child's experience at home, in school and outwith school contribute to PSD.' (SOEID, PSD 5–14, 1993, p. 1).

Similarly, the SCCC's *Heart of the Matter* (1995) offered the view that education for personal and social development had to do with:

> developing certain qualities and dispositions which will help them to make sense of an increasingly complex world and to respond in a pro-social way to the diversity of circumstances, systems and working environments they face in their lives. (p. 1)

These (personal) 'qualities and dispositions' tend to refer to positive regard for self and others, increasing responsibility for a pupil's own life, self evaluation, target-setting and decision making skills, although the list is potentially endless. The 'social' element tends to include such factors as social responsibility, participation in a democratic society and moral and ethical decision making.

Guidance staff, with their close involvement in individual pupils' personal, social and vocational development can clearly have a major impact here, particularly in individual interviews and in the process of recording achievements for the progress file and similar profile documentation.

On a wider level, any school has to consider how it might achieve these and many other PSD objectives, taking into consideration the socio-economic context of the community in which the school operates and, just as importantly, the ethos of the school and its staff. A few schools deal with PSE by 'embedding' certain PSE topics (e.g. health education) in certain curricular subjects and they try to ensure that other PSE qualities and dispositions (e.g. core skills) permeate classroom teaching.

While it is desirable that the aims and objectives of PSE should be present in all aspects of classroom life, it is a challenging way to organise a structured, coherent and progressive PSE programme and most schools opt for timetabled PSE, usually one period per week, S1–S6. Topics covered are many and varied and will reflect the needs of the pupils in their local community. Most schools will cover topics such as health education, careers education and study skills, and the classes will normally be smaller than subject sections with a more active, learner-centred methodology.

Guidance staff are seen to have a particular role to play in PSE. In addition to the personal guidance mentioned above, the guidance team is often responsible for devising and delivering the PSE programme although, since this is timetabled time, many other staff will be involved. There are clearly important issues here regarding staff development for all involved, since PSE/guidance issues are not afforded much time in the initial teacher education process, despite the fact that a very large percentage of beginning teachers will take classes in PSE within a few weeks of joining a school or during supply work. The issue of certification of PSE in Higher Still also raises major questions. For example, how appropriate is it for schools to be grading pupils (with the inevitable norm-referencing which will occur) on their personal awareness and development? If a pupil has a Higher in PSE is she/he more aware and developed as a person than a pupil with Intermediate 1?

CURRENT ISSUES IN GUIDANCE/PSE

In a short chapter such as this, it is clearly impossible to discuss major issues in any great detail. There are simply too many of them. However, even if it were possible to discuss them all, they would have to be subsumed under one major heading. The first part of this chapter was concerned with the origins of guidance. This second section has to deal with the future of guidance because at the time of writing, guidance in Scottish secondary schools is facing its biggest challenge and if this challenge is not met and seized as an opportunity, then it is no exaggeration to suggest that pupil support will be set back a decade or more.

This situation has been brought about largely because of the McCrone Report's failure to include guidance in its deliberations. The report and the agreement document which followed it concerned themselves exclusively with 'teaching', 'the classroom' and a flatter management structure. In both documents an entirely traditional view of the teacher is outlined – one who is subject and classroom based. Indeed, the subsequent documentation on chartered teacher status takes largely the same view of a teacher's professional development – subject and classroom are at the core of everything while guidance, pastoral care and pupil support are marginalised.

The agreement document, which will form the foundation structure and practice for many years to come, has basically only two things to say in passing about guidance and PSE. Firstly, more unpromoted staff and register teachers should involve themselves in pastoral care. Secondly, there is brief mention of the duties of a promoted member of staff, referred to (but not discussed or rationalised) as PT pastoral/guidance. These duties include the responsibilities for leadership, good management and strategic direction of pastoral care in the school; assisting in the management, deployment and development of pastoral care staff and so on.

At first sight there appears to be little difficulty. For many years, successive guidance documents have emphasised the need for all staff to have a 'guidance related' remit, that is to involve themselves in the pastoral care of their pupils. Similarly, the duties of the PT above are well established in good schools already.

However, there are major problems with this approach. The documents give no indication of how pastoral care might be structured in a new system. Worse, guidance and pastoral care are not discussed at all in the haste to reorganise the management of subjects while retaining a wholly traditional view of teaching and the classroom. In addition to this, all posts of APT (including guidance) are to disappear. At a stroke, it would appear (and readers are left to infer from the McCrone recommendations) that guidance/pastoral care is to have a broader base, no middle layer of management, and be managed by a small team of principal teachers.

Inevitably, discussion in local authorities and elsewhere has begun to consider seriously the concept of the full-time guidance teacher – long resisted by some guidance staff themselves. Others (including the author of this chapter) have argued for some time that the appointment of full-time guidance staff was the only conceivable way to deliver quality guidance and pastoral care. However, no-one has ever seriously suggested that 'full-time guidance' should mean the removal of all APT posts and a reduction in the number of PT posts, and yet that option is the one which is currently under active consideration by many local authorities.

It is difficult, if not impossible, to see how a full guidance support remit could be offered by the removal of at least half of the promoted team, even allowing for the fact that the remaining members would be full-time. A broader base of first-level support teachers whose subject is their priority is no substitute for a dedicated team of trained staff who know all there is to know about individual pupils and their families. Fundamental (and hard-won) principles of effective pupil support are at risk if there are too few full-time guidance staff.

The problem for local authorities and for schools is to ensure from the outset that the full-time team is large enough to offer full personal, curricular and vocational support to each pupil. It is worth noting in passing here that much of the language of 'support' in these days of targets and league tables has come to mean curricular monitoring and subject progress at the expense of personal guidance or pastoral care. Personal guidance requires a major re-emphasis, as staff who dealt with pupils affected by the SQA exam debacle, for example, will testify. Similarly, 'support' will necessarily require the additional services of learning and behaviour support staff as part of a team.

If the full-time team is large enough, then full-time guidance and pastoral care can and should work. It is not, per se, a new idea. More than one local authority in Scotland has experimented with this approach. However, it will take time and clearly there will be some issues to be resolved. For example, there will still be a need for all staff to have a pastoral role and to retain the principle and practice of first-level guidance. Also, the perennial issue of training requires attention. If there are to be full-time guidance staff, when and how are they to be trained? If they are to have no subject commitment, then a number of related issues arise. Firstly, it will need to be clear whether staff require to 'opt into' guidance after some years of subject teaching, probably through first-level work and if so, what kind of training will be required. If this approach is adopted, it is likely to replicate the existing tensions between subject and guidance if first-level staff need to take on more guidance work in order to become a PT. This tension would also exist if there were to be a route through the chartered teacher programme.

A more radical option would be to train guidance/PSE staff at the ITE stage. Prospective teachers will require training in these areas and it might be possible to qualify students in guidance/PSE work only but this would require schools to have a full-time team of guidance staff which included unpromoted posts. These are crucial issues, not least because they hit at the heart of traditional Scottish teaching – the subject specialist and the credibility of guidance staff among their peers.

It seems clear also that guidance/pastoral care and PSE cannot exist in a vacuum. They are part of a function and process which cross subject boundaries and affect the whole school. The term 'pupil support' might well describe this whole-school function and would necessarily include the learning and behaviour support staff amongst others, as suggested in recent reports. (SEED, 2001, HMIE, 2002a and 2002b). This kind of integration is long overdue although team work need not and ought not to preclude specialisms within the team.

PERSONAL AND SOCIAL EDUCATION

Personal and social education also faces challenges. Some of these are similar to those faced by guidance and pastoral care and some are unique to PSE. There is little doubt that for a number of years PSE struggled to find its feet in terms of quality and status within the profession. HMI noted as much in 1996.

> Inspection evidence indicates that the importance of PSE programmes [was] not reflected in a consistent quality of provision in schools. There is good practice in some schools but overall standards are too variable. PSE is often accorded low priority in terms of staffing and timetabling. It frequently fails to elicit a positive response from pupils or from their parents. Teachers need to apply the same standards and rigour in PSE as they do in their own specialist subjects. There is, therefore, a need for many schools to review and improve their provision of PSE (SOEID, 1996, para 8.9).

HMI identified the traditional issues in PSE – relatively low status in a subject-oriented curriculum and uncertainty among staff as to direction and purpose. There had also been historical tension between PSE as a slot or subject as opposed to PSE permeating other areas of the school and curriculum (a problem which currently faces health education and citizenship).

However by early 2002, PSE had improved considerably. The inspectorate reported that PSD courses in S1–S4 were very good in 80% of schools, although courses in S5 and S6 were less well developed. The best courses were well designed and balanced but there was some 'inconsistent development of skills from stage to stage and lack of systematic assessment of pupils' attainment and progress'. Some schools needed to involve pupils more in evaluating PSD courses (HMIE, 2002b p. 22).

PSE/PSD here is defined in terms of a curricular slot or programme and the apparent improvement might be due to a number of factors. For example, schools have had a number of years now to familiarise themselves with PSE and while there may still be a reluctance in some quarters, schools have been strongly encouraged by the self-evaluation movement to consider specific 'quality' indicators related to PSE.

However, there is something of a conundrum in the fact that these indicators were devised and presented by the then inspectorate. The same inspectorate then tended to report on the extent to which the schools applied these indicators. In effect, HMI were devising policy and then reporting on the success of their own policy. This conflict, real or imagined, was resolved when the First Minister removed the policy-making remit from the inspectorate.

Even accepting that PSE has improved in recent years, there are several significant issues which remain unresolved and which will be brought into sharper focus in the post-McCrone era. PSE/PSD is in danger of becoming another subject in the curriculum. However, unlike traditional subjects, it is often taught by staff who have little training in this area but who are willing (and sometimes unwilling) volunteers. There are some schools with principal teachers of PSD but these are in the minority. If PSE/PSD has indeed improved then it is a testament in part to the work of subject staff who have taken on an extra commitment, but it is surely no way to run a programme of personal and social development.

The relationship between guidance and PSE has remained somewhat uncertain. The guidance quality indicators have included a section on PSD (HMI, *Taking a Closer Look at Guidance*, 1998) and these suggest, not unreasonably, a close link between guidance work and PSD. However, the leading role of guidance staff in the development and the delivery of PSE programmes has more recently been called into question. The most recent version of *How Good is Our School?* (HMIE, 2002) takes a much broader view of PSD as a whole-school function, not necessarily tied exclusively to guidance. In addition to this, health education and citizenship, both areas which might previously have been included as elements within a PSD programme, have developed as curricular and developmental issues and priorities in their own right.

CONCLUSION

It is evident then, that guidance, PSE and pastoral care face major challenges in the aftermath of the McCrone Report. Given the curricular and structural uncertainty which has resulted, it is difficult to predict what hard-pressed local authorities will do. A 'comprehensive review of the nature and purpose of guidance . . . and the training of guidance staff ' was recommended by the Scottish Executive's Discipline Task Group

(SEED, 2001). However this suggestion appeared well after McCrone and any subsequent report is unlikely to appear before 2003. Local authorities cannot afford to wait until then. Indeed, it may be that SEED's review of guidance will report after August 2003, intentionally separating the McCrone arrangements from the review of guidance, making some kind of academic and unsustainable distinction between the two processes. If this is the case, SEED can expect major criticism from the guidance community and local authorities.

In the interim, local authorities are on their own and it seems likely that some will opt for full-time guidance/pastoral care posts where there is a teaching commitment to PSD. There would be some advantage in this as responsibilities would be clear but there are major issues of training. It is difficult to see how a full guidance remit could be achieved unless there were significant numbers of full-time guidance staff. Other local authorities may opt for a pupil support model, combining guidance, PSE, learning and behaviour support staff. New Community Schools, where they exist, may consider a more integrated approach to include support agencies such as social work.

Whatever structures evolve, it is essential that individual pupils are at the centre. With the increased emphasis on raising attainment and exam performance, there is a real danger that what used to be known as personal guidance will be replaced by performance monitoring. Attainment can only be genuinely raised and real discipline (i.e. self-discipline) can only be genuinely achieved where pupils are actively encouraged and supported and where pastoral care is at the heart of the system. Where local authorities move towards full-time posts in this field, they will need to ensure that such staff are sufficient in number and that they are properly trained and resourced.

REFERENCES

GTCS (1998) *Making the Difference. A Policy Document on Guidance in Schools*, Edinburgh: GTCS.

HMIE (2002a) *How Good is Our School? Self-evaluation using Quality Indicators*, Edinburgh: HMIE.

HMIE (2002b) *Standards and Quality in Primary and Secondary Schools: 1998–2001*, Edinburgh: HMIE.

SCCC (1986) *More than Feelings of Concern*, Dundee: SCCC.

SEED (2001) *Better Behaviour, Better Learning. Summary Report of the Discipline Task Group*, Edinburgh: SEED.

SOEID (1996) *Effective Learning and Teaching: Guidance*, Edinburgh: SOEID.

46

Classroom Management in the Secondary School

Margaret Kirkwood

An issue at the heart of effective classroom management is differentiation, through which teachers seek to address pupils' individual learning needs. Identifying learning needs and addressing them effectively presents a considerable challenge to secondary teachers. While in some subjects such as English and Mathematics teachers may see most classes daily for about an hour, in others contact may be much less frequent or prolonged, for example when the social subjects are rotated in the S1/S2 timetable, making it more difficult for teachers to get to know their pupils. Also, according to research on S1/S2 conducted in Angus schools by Brian Boyd and Mary Simpson (2000), it is extremely difficult for secondary schools to take an overview of pupil learning across the range of subjects studied, for teachers to build on learning done elsewhere, and for pupils to hold a 'big picture' of how one subject relates to another, all of which pose problems for incorporating coherence, continuity and progression into pupils' learning. These important issues arise from the organisation of secondary schools which differs from that in primary schools, thus affecting the transition of pupils from P7 to S1.

Class size is a relevant factor in relation to teachers' ability to differentiate instruction. A research review conducted by the Scottish Council for Research in Education (SCRE) on the effects of class size on teaching practice and pupils' behaviour and attainment (see Wilson, V., *Does Small Really Make a Difference?*, Edinburgh: SCRE, 2002) concludes that reducing class size does have a positive impact on pupil attainment, especially in the early years of schooling, for those from ethnic minority groups, and when there is a large reduction to below twenty pupils to one teacher. In most studies, teachers of smaller classes reported that these are quieter and more easily managed, and therefore potential discipline problems are prevented from arising. In terms of impact on classroom practice, teachers reported less stress and were better able to cope with workload; however they did not always organise their classes differently. In a feature on class sizes (see the *Scottish Educational Journal*, 86 (5), 2002, pp. 8–9) Lindsay Paterson highlights the need for more research on the most effective teaching styles for small classes and on whether reductions in class size might also be worthwhile in the later years of schooling. In the same feature, Pamela Munn highlights that in smaller classes pupils get more individual attention, their strengths and weaknesses are better known, it is easier to build up knowledge of pupils as people which can lead to good relationships, it is harder for pupils to hide lack of commitment or failure to understand, and pupils can more easily develop a sense of identity and belonging. What is preventing progress, she observes, is money.

Adopting a particular form of class organisation will not, in itself, create the conditions for effective learning. Establishing order, an ethos of achievement, and an inclusive and supportive learning climate in the classroom are three important prerequisites. Providing interesting, worthwhile and challenging learning activities to promote active, engaged learning is another. It is important to encourage and support pupils to become self-regulated learners, since schools have a crucial role to play in promoting lifelong learning. The development of pupils' thinking skills and their dispositions to use them, whilst being important for gaining a deeper understanding of syllabus topics and thus raising attainment, also has wider implications, since the exercise of critical judgement and creative thinking can lead to more effective problem solving and decision making in all aspects of life. Above all, it is necessary for teachers to be caring and to establish relationships of trust with pupils to ensure that pupils' emotional and cognitive needs are met, and that learning and teaching become a genuinely shared enterprise. These specific goals accord with the National Priorities in School Education, particularly in relation to achievement and attainment, inclusion and equality, and learning for life.

WHAT HELPS PUPILS TO LEARN?

The task of identifying and responding to individual learning needs would be impossible if pupils did not share some common characteristics. Researchers who have asked secondary pupils about what makes a good teacher get consistent responses. For example, when Sally Brown and Donald McIntyre investigated what it is that S2 pupils say their teachers do well, the pupils' statements showed a considerable appreciation of what their teachers were trying to do (see *Making Sense of Teaching*, Buckingham: Open University Press, 1993). The different things which pupils mentioned were: creating a relaxed and enjoyable atmosphere in the classroom; retaining control; presenting work in a way which interests and motivates pupils; enabling pupils to understand the work; making clear what pupils are to do and achieve; judging what can be expected of each pupil; helping pupils with difficulties; encouraging pupils to raise their expectations of themselves; developing personal, mature relationships with pupils; and displaying personal talents (subject related or other).

Research into learning has identified a number of key conditions which optimise learning (see Simpson in Kirkwood (ed.), 1997, p. 4):

- New learning happens best when it is related to what individuals already know, understand and can do.
- Learning is enhanced when individuals are clear about its purpose and about their specific learning goals.
- Learning happens best when individuals are confident and motivated.
- Learning can be enhanced when individuals are enabled to take more responsibility.

When Mary Simpson and Jenny Ure asked secondary pupils about the factors which made a difference to how well they did at school, these turned out to be remarkably similar (see *What's the difference? A Study of differentiation in Scottish Secondary Schools*, Aberdeen: Northern College, 1993). These included the teacher building on strengths and addressing weaknesses, identifying targets and criteria for success, promoting the belief that attainment can improve and sharing the management of learning.

These opinions demonstrate the capability of young people to comment meaningfully on issues affecting their learning in school. Jean Rudduck gave the keynote address at the Scottish Educational Research Conference 2002 on the theme of consulting young people about teaching, learning and schooling. She discussed how some teachers are now consulting pupils in order to 'build a more inclusive and participatory community where young people can offer constructive critiques of teaching and learning, help design units of learning, act as mentors to their peers, and work with teachers to tackle persistent problems, such as bullying'. She argued that if consultation and participation are developed at a whole-school level then schools may benefit through a practical agenda for change that has pupil backing, a more inclusive culture, and the realisation of teacher/pupil partnership in learning. Furthermore pupils experience the principles of democracy enacted in the daily life of the school. This latter point is echoed in a recent paper *Education for Citizenship in Scotland* (see www.LTScotland.com/citizenship/paper/) which proposes that schools should model the kind of society in which active citizenship is encouraged by providing all young people with opportunities to take on responsibilities and exercise choice. The need for more active participation by pupils in school decision making, and more flexibility and pupil choice in the curriculum has been highlighted by Pamela Munn in her summary of the interim findings of the national debate on education. How these ideas can be enacted in the classroom is an important point for the teaching profession to reflect on.

In the context of discussing how teachers can consciously design their classrooms to enable each child to be a full participant in classroom activities and also to feel valued as a class member, Andrew Pollard (see *Reflective Teaching: Effective and Evidence Informed Professional Practice*, London: Continuum, 2002) draws a contrast between classes in which the strengths and weaknesses of each child are recognised and the child's particular level of achievement is viewed as a starting-point, and classes in which the stress is on levels of attainment rather than the effort which children may have made. Of the latter, he comments:

> relative attainments become institutionalized through inflexible 'ability' grouping systems; the ethos becomes competitive rather than co-operative; and the success of some children is made possible only at the cost of the relative failure of others. The overall effect is to marginalize and exclude some children whilst the work of others is praised and regarded as setting the standard to which other children should aspire. This can have very negative consequences for children's perceptions of themselves as learners. (p. 128)

The issue of ability grouping will be discussed more fully later in this chapter. In relation to how pupils can feel valued as members of society, the poor condition of many school buildings is surely of relevance. It is commendable that Glasgow City Council and some other local authorities have now embarked on new school building programmes.

THE IMPLICATIONS OF DIFFERENT CONCEPTIONS OF LEARNING

It is clear there is a great deal the teacher can do to enhance learning and therefore to raise pupils' achievements. This contrasts with the traditional view of school learning, in which variations in attainments between pupils are 'explained' as a natural consequence of pupils having different amounts of general ability, and general ability is perceived as something intrinsic to the pupil and beyond the teacher's influence (Drever, 1985). Benjamin Bloom has dismissed this explanation as 'no explanation'. Eric Drever explains Bloom's ideas as follows:

> But how do we know that they differ in ability? As a rule we infer this from the differences in attainment. The 'explanation' is no explanation. But what it does is important: it allows us to take for granted the quality of our *instruction*. (p. 60)

Bloom substitutes a different model in which the idea of general ability is abandoned in favour of specific abilities. He argues that a pupil's chance of success in a learning task will depend on three things: whether the pupil has already learned the specific skills and knowledge that the task requires; whether the pupil has an interest in learning from the task; and on various aspects of instruction. The attainments that result from the task add to the pupil's stock of specific abilities and raise the chances of future successes. The important point about Bloom's model is that it deals with variables that can be altered rather than with a fixed quantity (general ability). He argues that if we can identify the variables that can make a difference to children's learning, this will do much to explain the learning process and even more directly to improve teaching and learning processes in schools.

From experience of investigating Bloom's model with teachers working with S1 and S2 classes, Eric Drever concluded that, in spite of teachers' well grounded concerns about Bloom's 'utopian vision' (for example, that it overplays the formal, cognitive curriculum and does not give adequate recognition to the affective domain) there was no reason to doubt Bloom's central premise. Also whenever teachers could be induced to suspend belief in 'general ability' and act instead on Bloom's hypothesis, they began to look critically at curriculum and assessment and to experiment creatively in their classrooms, and they reported an improvement in pupils' motivation and performance.

It has been found that pupils also hold different conceptions of ability or 'theories of intelligence' which affect how they approach learning tasks and what they hope to gain from them (Dweck and Elliott, 1983). The first theory (the 'entity' theory of intelligence) involves the belief that intelligence is a rather stable, global trait that can be judged to be adequate or inadequate. This trait is displayed in one's performance, and the judgements of that performance can indicate whether one is or is not intelligent. The second theory ('incremental') involves the belief that intellectual competence consists of a repertoire of skills that can be endlessly expanded through one's efforts. While most older children understand both views of intelligence it appears that different children, independent of their actual ability, tend to favour one or the other. As one would predict, entity theorists prefer tasks that afford opportunities to avoid mistakes and to be judged competent, whereas incremental theorists prefer tasks that afford them opportunities for learning, and they will happily immerse themselves in enquiry ('How can I do it?' 'What will I learn?').

Teachers can influence pupils towards holding an incremental view of intelligence by treating pupils' errors as natural and useful events rather than as evidence of failure, providing opportunities for pupils to engage in problem solving and enquiry, acting as a resource and guide rather than as a judge, and applying flexible and longer-term performance standards which enable progress towards targets to be recognised. Unfortunately, the burden on teachers to 'cover' syllabuses – a problem acknowledged recently with the 5–14 curriculum (see *Times Educational Supplement Scotland*, 8 November 2002) – and the assessment pressures associated with Higher Still create the kind of circumstances which prevent many pupils from experiencing the satisfactions of learning for its own sake and which limit the opportunities for teachers to be flexible and creative. Teachers realise that it takes longer for pupils to think and discover things for themselves, therefore when time is at a premium their pedagogy shifts towards didactic approaches.

Howard Gardner's theory of multiple intelligences has been influential in shaping thinking about learning. The theory identifies that there are at least seven relatively autonomous intellectual capacities each with its own distinctive mode of thinking. In addition to linguistic ability (using words and language) and logical–mathematical ability (working with numbers, recognising abstract patterns and thinking and reasoning in a logical and deductive manner) there are abilities of other kinds which traditionally get less emphasis in schools: such as visual–spatial, musical, interpersonal, intrapersonal (which is concerned with self-reflection and self-awareness) and kinesthetic (which is related to physical activity). The implications are far reaching:

> We should spend less time ranking children and more time helping them to identify their natural competencies and gifts and cultivate these. There are hundreds and hundreds of ways to succeed, and many, many different abilities to help you get there. [This quotation from Gardner is taken from a 1996 SCCC publication, *Teaching for Effective Learning*, which discusses a range of influences on thinking about learning.]

Daniel Goleman's book, *Emotional Intelligence* (London: Bloomsbury 1996) has helped to raise awareness of the role of emotions and feelings in children's education:

> when too many children lack the capacity to handle their upsets, to listen or focus, to rein in impulse, to feel responsible for their work or care about learning, anything that will buttress these skills will help in their education. (p. 284)

Goleman suggests that emotional lessons can be woven into the fabric of school life. The school ethos and classroom atmosphere are important to establish the conditions for emotional intelligence to develop, which Goleman defines as:

> abilities such as being able to motivate oneself and persist in the face of frustration; to control impulse and delay gratification; to regulate one's moods and keep distress from swamping the ability to think; to empathise and to hope. (p. 34).

At the SCRE Forum 2002, Encouraging Positive Behaviour and Learning, many of the contributions focused on this aspect, and a key priority of government is to explore alternatives to school exclusions.

In an excellent introduction to the research literature on teaching thinking, John Nisbet stresses the importance of the emotional dimension of learning:

> We need to build on the satisfactions of thinking, not be preoccupied with the difficulties or the shame of failure. Resolving a difficulty, understanding a complex topic, the flash of insight in solving a problem: these are (or should be) deeply satisfying experiences. Confusion and inability to comprehend are frustrating and quickly erode the will to learn or even to try (*Spotlight No. 26*, Edinburgh: SCRE, 1990, p. 4).

Enabling all learners to succeed in worthwhile tasks is vital for their motivation and self-esteem. This point is well illustrated by a case study on developing S3/S4 pupils' problem solving and thinking skills within computing studies (Kirkwood et al. in Kirkwood (ed.), 1997, pp. 22–8). Pupils' sense of satisfaction and of growing intellectual competence were evident when they succeeded in solving a complex programming problem:

> I enjoyed working on this problem mainly because it required a lot of thinking and testing. It took me a bit longer than some other programs . . . but was a lot more interesting. Every time I ran the program I would discover another bug but eventually I managed to . . . get the program working. I learned that [to] have a detailed design to work from really does help, and I think that had I not used a design I would have had a lot more errors. (Carol)
>
> I felt that it was really MY (underlined twice) work. I would not have felt this if the program had been in the book and I had only copied it. (Carol again, discussing a different problem)

The advice they offered to learners embarking on learning programming was insightful:

> Don't expect it to be easy.
> New things may seem hard, but they become clear after a few tries.
> Go through it one step at a time, don't try to do the whole thing at once.
> Try to solve problems yourself first to help you later, instead of giving up and asking the teacher.
> Be prepared to accept help from other pupils . . .

Inevitably, difficult work will provoke anxiety amongst pupils who are not confident about their abilities:

> like compared to a lot of the people in the class – everyone is away on topic . . . I don't know – I'm just a bit behind, I think. (Marie)

You're more [further on] than me! (Annette)

Annette's willingness to empathise with Marie is striking in this brief exchange. The main factor that enabled pupils such as Marie and Annette to cope with anxiety and to achieve good grades was the support – both practical and emotional – that pupils gave to each other (which came about by design through the teacher's active promotion of collaborative learning) and the individual support provided by the teacher. An important commodity was additional time, secured through a variety of means, to enable pupils' understandings to emerge naturally without attempts to rush the process and to cover the programming content.

There is an increasing emphasis on developing pupils' thinking and learning skills in Scottish secondaries. A recent education forum had as its theme Teaching Thinking Skills and addressed questions such as, 'What are thinking skills?', 'How can they be useful?', and, 'Can they be taught?'. It was informed by a review of research on teaching thinking (see Wilson, V., *Can Thinking Skills be Taught? A Paper for Discussion*, Edinburgh: SCRE, 2000). A range of approaches to teaching thinking is in place, some of which use questioning strategies, others of which focus on specific learning strategies and study skills taught within personal and social education but with the intention that the skills learned will be applied across the curriculum, and others of which (like the example above) link the development of thinking skills to an area of the curriculum.

HOW SECONDARY CLASSROOMS SHOULD BE MANAGED

Classroom management was a major focus of official reports during the 1990s: *The Education of Able Pupils P6–S2* (SOED, 1993); *5–14: A Practical Guide* (SOED, 1994); and *Achievement for All* (SOED, 1996). *Achievement for All* examined the efficacy of current arrangements at S1/S2 with reference to findings from school inspections and national and international surveys of achievement. The evidence from school inspections indicated that pupils were not being stretched, insufficient account was being taken of their primary school experiences, there were weaknesses in attainment (notably in aspects of English Language and Mathematics), better assessment was required including the use of national tests, homework needed to be used more effectively, and organizational structures got in the way of effective teaching:

> Frequently the organisational structures adopted in schools complicate the task of teaching and restrict teachers' opportunities for direct teaching. Too much of teachers' time is consumed managing resources and explaining what is to be done. (p. 22)

However the downside of direct teaching has been observed recently by Brian Boyd and Mary Simpson in their research on S1/S2, where, in some lessons:

> direct teaching meant delivering the lesson to the whole class through teacher exposition of the subject material; the interactive element comprising only closed questions posed to elicit and expose the correct answer to the questions set in the workbooks (Boyd and Simpson, 2000, p. 35).

Insufficient progress in learning between P7 and S2 was revealed in English Language, Mathematics and Science from the results of the national Assessment of Achievement Programme (see Chapter 87). However the findings of the OECD's Programme for International Student Assessment (see Executive Summary, Scottish Executive Education Department, 2002) which surveyed the performance of 15-year-olds in Reading, Mathematics and Science in 2000 reveal a much brighter picture, with better performances than 9- and 13-year-olds in earlier international studies, and Scotland being in the top third of countries in all subjects assessed. Taken alongside the relatively high proportion (50.4% according to the published Age Participation Index 2000-1) of school-leavers who continue on to university full-time, there are surely grounds for some optimism about the earlier stages of schooling which pave the way for future successes.

Achievement for All examined three forms of class organisation – streaming, mixed-ability and setting, and a range of 'within class' organisations. It recommended that attainment grouping should be the preferred form of organisation for most teaching purposes in S1/S2, and indeed the recent trend is towards this (see also chapter 4). This is a highly contested area and the topic of much hot debate in the press.

Streaming

Streaming was a form of organisation common in the 1950s and 1960s which was used both to assign pupils to secondary schools and to group them into classes. Pupils would be in the same class for all subjects on the basis of an overall assessment of their ability arrived at through testing. The aim was to provide each stream with appropriate educational experiences. Pupils in the top streams were given what was regarded as a more academic curriculum and they were expected to learn at a faster pace. The curriculum for the top streams was also better resourced and planned. The main challenge to streaming was on social grounds and came with the introduction of comprehensive education in the late 1960s, which was founded on the desire to have equality of educational opportunity and to provide a shared educational experience for all. There was no recommendation in *Achievement for All* for any return to streaming.

Current organisations – mixed-ability versus setting

The two main forms of class organisation currently used in secondary schools are mixed-ability, in which pupils within a year group are assigned to classes to create a mix of ability; and setting, in which pupils within a year group are assigned to classes for a given subject on the basis of their prior attainment in that subject. A consequence of setting is that pupils may be in different sets for different subjects, and an assumption underlying setting is that learning and teaching in each set will be different, particularly with regard to the pace of learning. A variant of setting is broad-banding which is sometimes used in subjects where there is limited assessment information available to guide the process of allocating pupils to sets. In *Achievement for All*, the main argument in favour of setting was as follows:

> In secondary schools, setting offers teachers the opportunity to reduce significantly the time spent on organising and managing learning for a wide range of attainment within one class. It also eases the pressures of having to be constantly responsive to very wide differences of pupil demands and needs . . . The efficiency gains can be spent on direct teaching and on ensuring that pupils work effectively on tasks which challenge them appropriately. (p. 22)

However the conclusions of a review of research conducted by SCRE on setting and streaming did not support the increased use of attainment groups in secondary schools: 'There is no consistent and reliable evidence of positive effects of setting and streaming in any subjects or for students of particular ability levels' (Harlen and Malcolm, 1997, p. 40). Effective differentiation emerged from the review as the key issue:

> The challenge is to find some way of catering for pupils' individual needs. The research . . . shows that for many, ability grouping reduces both their motivation and the quality of the education they receive. On the other hand, mixed-ability teaching which denies the differences between high- and low-ability pupils is not the answer (SCRE Newsletter, Spring 1997, pp. 8–9).

The authors recommended that urgent action was needed to identify and study methods of adjusting the content, pace and support of classroom work to suit individual needs, but not much appears to have happened since in response to this recommendation. The conclusions of a research review by Susan Hallam (2002) on ability grouping, although not identical to those of Harlen and Malcolm, also signal the importance of factors such as teaching quality:

- In general, more able pupils benefit from ability grouping (either setting, banding or streaming) while the personal and social outcomes of less able pupils are adversely affected.
- There is a tendency for ability grouping to increase differences in performance between the more and less able.

- When setting is in operation, the lack of progress between sets means that early placement can determine entry levels to examinations because lower sets may not cover the required course materials.
- Ability grouping can be beneficial in raising the attainment of the more able if the curriculum is differentiated, allowing faster progress and more in-depth work.
- Where grouping structures lead to low expectations, a reduced curriculum and teaching which is focused on control rather than learning, lower ability groups are likely to do worse.
- Neither of the above two scenarios is inevitable. Teaching in the top sets may be too time-pressured and competitive to enable in-depth understanding for some pupils, leading to poor performance. In the bottom sets, teachers with high expectations who have positive relationships with pupils, engender high levels of motivation and set interesting, challenging work are likely to improve performance.
- The way in which pupils are grouped is only one of several factors affecting the learning environment; the quality of the instruction and the curriculum are central, and both may mediate the effects of pupil grouping.

Hallam argues that the issue is not merely whether ability grouping is effective, but for whom, in what ways and whether anyone else suffers as a result. It is worthwhile to note that the review discusses educational practices in the UK as though they operate within one unified (English) system. A related point is that very little research on ability grouping has been conducted in Scottish schools.

Within class organisations

Grouping by ability is a less common practice in secondary classrooms than in primary. In *5–14 A Practical Guide* is the advice that teachers should identify one group as the teaching group and give each group a turn, and give the other groups clear instructions for working on their own (SOED, 1994). While this makes group work more manageable for the teacher, it can only work successfully if pupils are given quiet work to do which can be accomplished with limited teacher input.

Because of the recent push towards direct teaching, resource-based and individualised learning have become less common forms of organisation at S1/S2; however they may become better established in the upper secondary in response to the demands of bi-level teaching (for example, when pupils working towards two adjacent levels of award are combined in one class) within the Higher Still programme. These organisations enable pupils to work at a pace that is suited to their needs, and to gain a measure of independence from the teacher which is necessary for developing self-regulated learning. However, three common criticisms are that the management of the materials consumes the teachers' time, monitoring of pupils' progress is complex, and pupils tend to work in isolation from each other and the teacher (*Achievement for All*, SOEID, 1996). These problems are mainly located in the design of the materials and the learning environment, and it is apparent that many existing 'schemes' are not well designed. They are over-elaborate and therefore difficult for everyone to manage; collaboration may not have been planned for so that pupils lose the benefits of learning from each other; and teachers may attempt to do all of the checking of pupils' work during the lesson, which is not practicable. An important missing element in the overall equation has been training for teachers on the design, appraisal and use of such materials. Another important new dynamic is technology which is breaking free from the computer lab into the classroom, but will all teachers possess the knowledge and skills to use it effectively to enhance learning?

CONCLUSIONS

Enough is known about the potential advantages and pitfalls of ability grouping for schools to make reasonably well informed choices about how to form classes and groups within classes. However it is imperative that they monitor the effects of such arrangements, and also that any decisions are taken democratically, for example, by consulting parents, pupils, and teachers in other departments.

Differentiation and classroom management should become major focuses of teacher education programmes from pre-service to chartered teacher level. It would be highly regrettable if 'direct teaching' became equated in teachers' minds with whole class teaching, and current advice led to a narrowing of teachers' skills and an abandonment of mixed-ability teaching and resource-based and individualised approaches.

Teachers need time and more opportunities to examine, both collectively and individually, their beliefs and assumptions, to share knowledge of the curriculum and teaching approaches across subjects, to appraise research evidence and policy documents, and to experiment. It is only through such thoughtful and practical engagement that real and lasting improvements in pupils' learning will occur.

REFERENCES

Boyd, B., Simpson, M. (2000) *Developing a Framework for Effective Learning and Teaching in S1/S2 in Angus Secondary Schools*, Arbroath: Angus Council Education.

Drever, E. (1985) Mastery learning in context, theory and practice, in S. Brown and P. Munn (eds.), *The Changing Face of Education 14 to 16: Curriculum and Assessment*, Windsor: NFER-Nelson, pp. 58–68.

Dweck, C. S., Elliott E. S. (1983) Achievement motivation, in E. M. Hetherington (ed.), *Socialization, Personality and Social Development* (vol. IV of P. H. Mussen (ed.) *Handbook of Child Psychology*) New York: Wiley, pp. 643–92.

Hallam, S. (2002) *Ability Grouping in Schools*, London: University of London Institute of Education.

Harlen, W. , Malcolm H. (1997) *Setting and Streaming: A Research Review*, Edinburgh: SCRE.

Kirkwood, M. (ed.) (1997) *Differentiation S1 to S4: The Ways Forward, Report on a One-day Conference at Jordanhill Campus, Strathclyde University*, Glasgow: University of Strathclyde.

VIII

Secondary Education: Curriculum

47

The Structure of the Secondary Curriculum

Tony Gavin

BACKGROUND

The introduction of comprehensive secondary schooling in the 1960s was of fundamental influence in shaping the Scottish secondary school curriculum in the ensuing decades. Those responsible faced the very real challenge of providing quality education for 12–18-year-olds of all abilities and of diverse aspirations. Education authorities were ill prepared to meet this imposed change, teachers had little real understanding of its likely impact, many were less than enthusiastic and few understood its potential benefits.

Recognition of the increasing need for pastoral and vocational support to sustain pupil learning resulted in the introduction into schools of guidance staff. These are subject specialist teachers who undertake additional remits for providing pastoral, curricular and vocational support for pupils. Faced with the real and practical task of providing for all young people, schools expanded their subjects. Courses in economics, accountancy, modern studies, drama, personal and social education, outdoor education and, later, computing, graphic communications and technological studies became more common. New specialist departments were often established to accommodate these new courses.

In 1972 the raising of the school leaving age from fifteen years to sixteen years significantly increased the pressure to introduce new learning experiences relevant to meeting the perceived needs of these new clients. This usually meant courses of a vocational nature as opposed to the established core of academic subjects. The inadequacies of the provision created a demand from teachers for an agreed curricular rationale, particularly for the secondary third and fourth years of secondary school, together with a national curricular and assessment framework to provide for all pupils.

These tasks were addressed by two committees set up by the Scottish Education Department (SED). The committee chaired by James Munn addressed the curriculum (*The Structure of the Curriculum in the Third and Fourth Years of the Scottish Secondary School*) and that chaired by Joe Dunning examined issues relating to assessment and certification (*Assessment for All*). These reports, published in 1977, were to shape the post-14–16 secondary curriculum leading to the introduction of Standard Grade courses and certification for all within a commonly accepted curricular framework based on eight modes of learning.

In 1986 the SCCC published a discussion paper entitled *Education 10–14 in Scotland*. This report identified the desirable outcomes of education over the 10–14 age range expressing them in terms of behavioural and attitudinal characteristics of young people. The 'fresh start' philosophy for pupils transferring from P7 to S1 was firmly rejected and the report challenged the then widening gap between the primary and secondary sectors caused by their different approaches to curricular innovation. In rejecting the more widespread use of middle schools for the 10–14 age group the report supported the retention of the established primary and secondary sectors whilst emphasising the need for these sectors to work closely together.

The report was influential in nurturing a national debate which, in turn, influenced and shaped the 5–14 development programme. A number of innovative ideas proposed in the report quickly became normal practice in schools and colleges. The committee's proposals regarding the use of criterion referenced assessments to promote learning, and for improved forms of recording pupil progress and reporting to parents, found a place in school development planning in the 1990s. Recommendations regarding pupil care which clarified the roles of teachers, parents and support agencies were later reflected in education authority schemes designed to support vulnerable children through the use of inter-agency groups involving teachers, social workers, health officers, psychologists and community education personnel.

Pupils entering the S1 stage of a typical Scottish secondary school are faced with an exciting but sometimes bewildering diet of different subjects, teachers and learning experiences. In the majority of schools between twelve and sixteen different subjects contribute to the S1 curriculum. Usually this is organised and delivered through a timetable by allocating a number of periods each week to the discrete subjects. This results in pupils being taught by up to 16 different teachers. The curriculum modes common throughout the S1–S4 years and within which the various subject specialisms provide courses of systematic and active study were defined in guidelines published by Scottish Consultative Council on the Curriculum (SCCC).

At the S1/S2 stages of the secondary school, English, Mathematics, Modern Languages and Science usually have a more generous time allocation than other subjects. Some schools also include one or more additional elements from Modern Studies, Drama, Celtic Studies, Economics, Classical Studies and Outdoor Education. Schools which provide these additional elements may choose to leave them until the S2 stage or provide them by a process of extracting pupils from the timetabled courses for short periods of time. Some schools, recognising the obvious disadvantages of such a fragmented learning experience, use timetabling devices such as rotations of History and Geography, Music and Art and Craft Design & Technology and Home Economics in order to reduce the number of different teacher contacts experienced by the individual pupil during the course of a week. This situation creates a tension between the advantages of increased choice, which in turn creates a fragmented learning experience, and the pursuit of the educational advantages of personalised pupil teacher relationships.

Schools use the term 'common curriculum' when describing that range of subjects, determined by the school, which is provided for all pupils. Its introduction in the late 1960s was in keeping with a philosophy which promoted equal access for all and rejected any notion of curricular elitism. New ways of addressing issues arising from the introduction of the common curriculum such as effective differentiated learning, the individual pace of learning and appropriate use of prior attainments in primary school are still to be effectively ~d.

~velopments designed to raise pupil attainment levels require collaborative and curricular planning between secondary school and associated primaries. These are impacting on teaching content and approaches in both the upper primary stages and in S1/S2, most noticeably in mathematics, languages including foreign languages and in the use of creative arts to promote better learning. These developments continue despite growing professional concerns on the value and indeed the validity of the present arrangements for national testing.

THE CURRICULUM IN THE FIRST AND SECOND YEARS

The SCCC guidelines suggest the S1/S2 curriculum should allow opportunities for pupil choice. In practice this is often limited to selecting one from a choice of two modern languages and some project activities within some subjects. The curriculum for pupils in S1 and S2 is seen mainly as a continuum but with some degree of increasing subject specialisms becoming more distinctive. Schools, for instance, which offer an integrated science course in S1 move to discrete Biology, Chemistry and Physics during S2. Taking advantage of the circular (*Learning and Teaching Scotland Circular 3/2001*) allowing greater curricular flexibility some schools now provide an element of subject choice for pupils entering S2. At least one education authority is planning to offer national framework courses at Intermediate levels to pupils entering S2.

This new flexibility together with the relaxation of the SQA regulations governing when pupils can be presented for national certification could allow schools to provide much greater diversity in the curriculum while including activities which young people find relevant and valuable and which at present are provided on the periphery of the mainstream curriculum.

THE CURRICULUM IN THE THIRD AND FOURTH YEARS

The S3/S4 curriculum is designed to meet the general aims of the development of knowledge and understanding, the development of cognitive, interpersonal, psychomotor and social skills and the acquiring of behavioural attitudes and insights into the world of work. Pupils have an increased element of choice when embarking on their two–year course of study in S3 and S4. A typical pupil aged fourteen to sixteen years will study seven or eight subjects leading to Standard Grade awards selected from a curriculum framework designed to ensure a broad and balanced education. This is done in accordance with the SCCC guidelines which recommend that subjects are grouped into categories representing eight modes of learning.

At the S3 and S4 stage languages and Mathematics are allocated a minimum of 20% and 10% of the available time. The language component includes the study of another modern European language as well as English. Scientific Studies, Social Studies, Technological and Creative/Aesthetic activities each receive 10% of the time with Physical Education and Religious and Moral Education each receiving a minimum of 5%. This leaves the remaining 20% for student choice. In practice this freedom of choice for any individual is limited to the range of subjects offered in their particular school.

In addition to the subjects which make up the eight modes of learning, pupils commonly follow a special course in social education devised by the school. This accommodates careers education, aspects of health education, care of the environment, learning about rules, rights and responsibilities and guidance relating to living and employment. Schools also use the device of syllabus inserts or permeation across subjects to deliver this element of the curriculum. Religious and Moral Education can be provided through the use of permeating, syllabus inserts and special courses. The majority of S4 pupils in Scottish secondary schools undertake a period of planned work experience. This is organised by extraction from the school timetable for a continuous period of between five and ten school days.

Some schools no longer require all pupils to study a modern language beyond S2. It is increasingly difficult to justify a compulsory modern language for all pupils aged fourteen to sixteen when so few students are choosing to continue to study modern languages at the post 16 years stage. To provide improved progression routes into S5 and S6, schools are increasingly using Intermediate 1 and Intermediate 2 courses in S3 and S4, while some offer access to Standard Grade courses or their equivalent at the end of S1 so providing an accelerated route to National Qualifications for some of their pupils.

As mainstream secondary schools continue in increasing numbers to enrol children with special needs, schools providing an alternative curriculum designed to meet the individual needs of such children are becoming more common.

SCOTTISH EDUCATION DEPARTMENT'S 16–18 ACTION PLAN (1983)

This initiative, which came from the further education sector, successfully rationalised much of the non-advanced post 16 provision in colleges of further education into modular form and established a national system for modular course assessment and certification under the newly formed Scottish Vocational Education Council (SCOTVEC). In the secondary school the arrangements for Higher Grade and the Certificate of Sixth Year Studies remained unaffected. However, with post 16 staying-on rates rising schools working both collectively and individually began to develop and offer a range of modular courses derived from the SCOTVEC catalogue. These courses were used to create progression routes from Standard Grades level 3, 4 and 5 to provide for some students a suitable bridge between Standard Grade and entry to Higher Grade courses in their second year of post 16 education.

The disadvantages of having two distinct examining bodies, namely the Scottish Examination Board and SCOTVEC, became increasingly frustrating to students and teachers as well as creating some confusion among parents and employers. The system accentuated the academic vocational divide and it proved difficult to arrive at clear agreements on such matters as credit transfers across the two distinct systems. By the late 1980s the need for one examining authority to cover all post-16 non-advanced education in Scotland was very evident, but, as thinking progressed, moves to create such a system awaited the implementation of the Higher Still programme.

In the early 1980s, as the recommendations of the Munn and Dunning Committees were being translated into acceptable curricular guidelines and assessment and certification for all in S3 and S4, the impact of computer technology began to influence the thinking and practice of teachers. Clearly the use of such technology will continue to impact on society and has exciting possibilities for learning and access to learning.

The implementation of the Standard Grade programme brought benefits to all pupils in secondary stages S3 and S4. Paradoxically this led to increased dissatisfaction with school provision for the post- 16 age group. An SOED committee under the chairmanship of Professor John Howie of the University of St Andrews proposed two broad post-16 routes, namely that of the Scottish Certificate (SCOTCERT) with exit routes at the end of one year or two years and the Scottish Baccalaureate (SCOTBAC) providing a separate three-year programme leading to entry into higher education. Schools agreed strongly with the need for change and the rationale underpinning the report. Considerable disquiet was expressed at the potentially divisive nature of the proposed progression routes and the absence of coherence with provision in further and higher education. Taking cognisance of the responses to the Howie Report the SOED produced in 1993 further proposals for post-16 provision. This time the vision was for one structure to provide for all post-16 non-advanced education in Scottish schools, FE colleges and adult centres catering for all ages, abilities and aspirations and leading to awards from one newly formed examination board to be called the Scottish Qualifications Authority (SQA). With school staying on rates rising and pressure from government to meet the target set by the Advisory Scottish Council for Education and Training Targets (ASCETT), the prevailing mood was for action.

In late 1993 the SOEID established the Higher Still development programme. This set out to revise all Higher and Certificate of Sixth Year Studies courses together with all additional courses provided at levels between Standard and Higher Grades.

To provide progressional routes for all to continue with relevant and successful study at a level appropriate to the individual student, five levels of courses were identified: Access; Intermediate 1; Intermediate 2; Higher; and Advanced Higher. The programme stressed the importance of core skills to the development of the individual learner defining these as communication, numeracy, problem solving, information technology and working with others. Student achievements in these skills are assessed and certificated. Group Awards were devised to minimise the academic and vocational divide.

The Scottish Qualifications Authority became responsible for all assessment arrangements and certification for all courses within the new National Qualifications framework which commenced in August 1999, with the first certificates issued in August 2000.

Following the implementation of the Higher Still programme and the introduction of the National Qualifications framework the current model of post-16 curricular provision commonly found in Scottish Secondary Schools consists of Higher in S5, Advanced Higher in S6, Intermediate 2 in S5 progressing to Higher in S6 and for a minority of students Intermediate 1 in S5 progressing to Intermediate 2.

Students negotiate an individual curriculum appropriate to their needs, interests and aspirations. Using this approach schools go some way to provide for all their students while ensuring that those who choose to leave school at December or June in their fifth year do so having acquired national certification appropriate to their level of attainment in their chosen subjects.

The widening opportunities offered by the introduction of the National Qualifications framework of courses and levels has resulted in a significant increase in SQA awards to the 16–18 age group. Increasing numbers of school students are choosing courses in Psychology, Sociology, Hospitality and Care while Science and Technology courses remain relatively less popular. The Scholar programme managed by Heriot-Watt University provides progression routes for Science and Engineering students from Advanced Higher directly into second year of university study. This is an interesting and welcome example of a Scottish university recognising an Advanced Higher award as the equivalent of an end of first year university award.

THE TECHNICAL VOCATIONAL EDUCATION INITIATIVE (TVEI) (1984–96)

TVEI was a programme through which education authorities throughout the United Kingdom could access funding from the Department of Employment (later the Department of Industry) to promote change in the education of 14–18-year-olds. The aim was to effect changes in the school curriculum designed better to equip young people for the demands of working life in a rapidly changing technological society. This was to be done by relating what is learned in schools and colleges to the world of work and by improving skills and qualifications in the areas of science, technology, information technology and modern languages. The programme criteria required that young people be provided with real work experience and supported by counselling and individual action planning.

There is evidence to show that the TVEI programmes significantly influenced the curriculum (SOED, 1994) through enhancement of technology, problem solving inserts, the development of personal and social development (PSD) courses, work experience and enterprise education and the introduction of national records of achievement. Teachers identified TVEI as having a major influence in bringing about changes in teaching methods, and, by promoting pupil centred learning, differentiation and flexible learning.

Through the process of curricular development planning and review schools are now addressing the National Priorities for education as identified by the Scottish Executive. The relaxation from a rather heavily prescribed core curriculum S1–S4 together with the imaginative use of the National Qualifications Framework, now provides further opportunities for the local authorities and individual schools to promote inclusion and equality through more active participation of young people in decisions and activities that are part of their schooling, through increasing access to courses by promoting values and dispositions for citizenship and by promoting the acquisition of the core skills of problem solving and working with others. These can be delivered and accessed at all stages of the secondary school through identified courses within the National Qualifications framework or through personal and vocational education programmes. Some specific examples can be found in the success stories publication (*Success Stories 11*, Scottish Executive, 1999).

EDUCATION – INDUSTRY LINKS (EIL)

The importance of education industry links have been highlighted in national policy statements: *Education for Work; Education Industry Links in Scotland* (SCCC, 1994) and *Education for Work in Schools* (HMI, 2000).

The extent of these activities within Scottish schools varies from the occasional school visitor from the world of work to well managed and creatively developed school programmes which influence both the content and nature of the learning experienced by pupils. Programmes of Education for Work encompass a range of activities such as enterprise projects, mock interviews, work experience and work shadowing, placements for teachers with corresponding business personnel placements in schools and joint projects with industry and commerce designed to enrich specific subject courses.

The Scottish Executive has identified Education for Work as a priority and as one of the key purposes of the curriculum enabling young people to face the challenges of life and operate confidently and effectively in the changing world of work and the flexible labour markets of the future.

SOME CRITICAL ISSUES FOR THE FUTURE

Managing change in the secondary curriculum

In any education community change is an essential part of growth. Such change is necessary to ensure the stability and the survival of the institution as an organisation capable of achieving its aims and objectives. The idea that a period of no change within a school will provide stability is dangerously misleading. Change is a natural state in human affairs. Schools exist within dynamic communities and to fulfil their functions change is both endemic and essential. Practising teachers are continuously changing their approaches in order to meet their perceptions of the needs of their pupils. The origins of change derive from a range of sources including the school classroom, the partnerships between schools, parents and employers and from the wider interface between the education establishment, education authorities and central government. All of these groups initiate and influence change to varying degrees. Successful change in secondary schooling requires these key players to come together, to negotiate the change programme and jointly to take responsibility and accountability for the change process. The real issues for schools are those relating to the direction, pace and management of change. Schools exist to serve people and are staffed and managed by people. Even though they desire a degree of change, the participants are often cautious. Successful implementation in schools requires, therefore, a high level of professional management of people including the ability to maintain the confidence and commitment of students, teachers, parents and employers during the change process. For the parties involved this process is never risk free. It is important, therefore, to learn from our successes and failures over the past decades.

Successful programmes for change include the introduction of Standard Grade, the TVEI programme in Scotland and the Higher Still development programme. These were all characterised by a number of common features. To manage change successfully it is important to provide a clear and easily understood rationale for the change and to focus the nature of the development in such a way that the people involved understand their role within the process and are clear as to the expected outcomes. People grow and develop within this change process.

Change invariably requires additional resourcing but usually not as much as might be supposed by teachers and administrators. More important is the careful targeting of resources to promote change and the attention and time given to monitoring and reviewing. The involvement of practitioners in the whole process of planning, developing, monitoring and reviewing is essential in reflecting ownership, in maintaining confidence and in influencing the direction of change. Change is a natural state in human affairs but it neither adopts a linear pathway nor is it a one issue phenomenon.

The subject-centred promoted post structure in secondary schools

A typical secondary school of 900+ pupils is staffed with approximately sixty-six teaching staff, more than half of whom hold a promoted post within the school. About twenty of these promoted posts are allocated to principal teacher subject (PT) and assistant principal teacher subject (APT). The remaining promoted posts will be allocated to guidance support (six), senior teacher posts (five) with four or five positions being occupied by the assistant headteachers, one depute headteacher and the headteacher. This arrangement, whereby the majority of promoted posts are created within the subject departments, has existed since the 1950s and 1960s and was further expanded as new courses found a place in the secondary curriculum. During this period the structure served the development of the secondary curriculum reasonably well with new courses in areas such as business studies, computing and religious education all being accommodated and supported by the appointment of new subject PTs and APTs. However, this predominantly subject-centred promoted post structure, driving a subject content curriculum is unlikely to prove effective for the delivery of a coherent and progressive secondary school curriculum in the coming decade.

In the secondary school the present structure has not proved to be sufficiently flexible to respond to the 5–14 development programme. Cross-curricular courses such as health studies, social and vocational skills, media studies and personal and social education have been slow to become established within the secondary curriculum. What is needed is a structure which motivates teachers and principal teachers to embrace curriculum management responsibilities across a number of subject specialisms, placing the acquisition of knowledge rather than information as central to learning.

It could be argued that the present structure has not only hindered the development of the 5–14 programme, particularly in the areas of environmental studies and the expressive arts, but has also contributed to the fragmentation of the curriculum in S1 and S2. The structure does not fit easily within the modal arrangements in S3 and S4; indeed ensuring a technological entitlement for all pupils in S3 and S4 could not be guaranteed through the established core courses in Science and Mathematics. The present subject-centred structure has underpinned the development of individual Higher Grade subjects. However the future at the post-16 stage is now likely to be one of wider access to modular courses and units with students building credits across a range of these. This will require co-ordinated planning and development with student needs and progression routes central to this process.

The implementation of the recommendations in the McCrone Report is likely to bring significant change to the present management structures within secondary schools. School subject departments are likely to be reorganised into faculty structures. The appointment of school business managers and classroom and administrative support personnel will remove many of the financial, building management and administrative tasks from senior and middle school management and teachers. The resulting new promoted post structures should be better placed to promote and manage cross-curricular activities with appropriate attention paid to quality assurance issues and tracking and monitoring pupil learning.

The role of the Scottish Qualifications Authority

There is frequently a healthy tension between the aspirations of curriculum planners and innovators and the demands of the examination board. Society rightly expects that pupil attainments are recognised through the award of qualifications approved by a national body which commands public confidence. However, an examination board's course arrangements can determine not only the content of a course but, on occasions, the methodologies deployed in the teaching of the course. For example in a science course any change in the examination board's arrangements to increase or decrease the weighting given to the assessment of practical skills can lead to significant changes in the teaching of that subject for all pupils. These changes are not necessarily in the best interests of all pupils in terms of their motivation and attitudes to learning.

Many teachers take the view that a major factor in the perceived declining standards of arithmetical skills among Scottish pupils is directly related to the former Scottish Examination Board's decision to remove arithmetic as a separate course leading to a national award for pupils at the end of their fourth year in secondary school. Presently there is concern over the SQA's proposals for assessing English writing. Clearly it is important that curricular planners and examination subject panels enjoy a shared and collective understanding of each other's aims.

Subject choice within the secondary curriculum

The SCCC curricular guidelines (1989) place considerable emphasis on opportunities for pupil choice in S1 and S2 with an increasing element of choice in the succeeding years. Many teachers and parents regard pupil choice as an important factor in sustaining motivation and in meeting career aspirations although it is debatable whether or not such a view can be substantiated. The practice of presenting pupils with increased choice can lead to uncertainties and even stress among pupils and parents listening to the competing claims from subject specialists. Increasing choice creates resourcing problems for all but the largest of schools and these are exacerbated as students seek to pursue subject specialisms in S5 and S6. Do we know that increasing pupil choice in secondary schools results in higher quality education?

A case can be made for rationalising the S1/S2 curriculum to achieve less emphasis on individual subject specialisms and for reducing the range of subjects available in S3 and S4 while still meeting the principles of breadths, balance and coherence, so providing a curriculum which aims to provide knowledge and understanding while promoting sound social and cognitive learning. Such a curriculum could also be sufficient to ensure the maintenance of post-16 progression and career routes. Is the way to quality education not more a question of how learning and teaching takes place within a broad and balanced curriculum rather than that of pupil choice from a widening range of subject specialisms?

As schools strive to address the National Priorities greater curricular diversity across schools is likely. A strong theme emerging from the current national debate on Scottish education is a concern about whether secondary education is pursuing appropriate curricular objectives and whether the institution of the secondary school is presently designed to meet the needs of all young people.

It is clear that the Scottish Executive, for social and educational reasons, is now targeting funding to promote youth participation in sport and the creative arts. This at a time when teachers themselves are becoming better informed of the value of sports and the arts in promoting effective learning.

Parents and the secondary school curriculum

The past decade has witnessed a raft of initiatives to promote partnership between parents and schools. Some, like the publication of examination results, attendance figures and school cost statistics have become established practice while school boards are promoted, regulated and even constrained by legislation. Although many of the traditional barriers to school–parent partnerships have been lowered the initiatives themselves are not as yet widely supported by parents and are viewed with some suspicion by some local councils.

The significant focus for school partnerships with parents must be to further effective teaching and learning. Some radical thinking is required with a view to engaging the attention, co-operation and participation of all parents in the education of their children. Statistics relating to attendance at school parent evenings, to parental involvement in homework and extra curricular activities might prove a useful starting point for reflection. There are now untapped skills and resources among the over-50 age group in all our local communities. These could be harnessed and directed to assist our young people to be enthusiastic learners. The curriculum must not be the sole prerogative of the education professionals nor should employers have undue influences. The curriculum, to be effective, must belong to everyone.

REFERENCES

HMI Report (2000) *Education for Work in Schools*, Edinburgh: Scottish Executive.
Learning and Teaching Scotland (2002) *Education for Citizenship in Scotland*, Dundee: LTS.
SCCC (1989) *Curriculum Design for the Secondary Stages – Guidelines for Headteachers*, 1st rev. edn, Dundee: SCCC.
SCCC (1995) *Education Industry Links in Scotland 5–18 – A Framework for Action*, Dundee: SCCC.
SOED (1992) *Upper Secondary Education in Scotland* (The Howie Report), Edinburgh: HMSO.
SOED (1994) *School for Skills Report*, Edinburgh: HMSO.

48

Art and Design Education

Glen Coutts

Most people think of Art and Design as a practical subject with pupils engaged in 'hands on' activities using the media and process of art; still life, drawing and painting or sculpture. For many years that was true, but the subject today focuses to a greater extent on developing creative thinking, aesthetic judgement and problem solving skills. The art curriculum, originally designed to develop hand and eye co-ordination for those who would work in factories, today promotes awareness of the influence of art and design on pupils' lives at home, in school and within the wider community.

In this chapter, three key developments of the past thirty years or so are highlighted; the working party report of 1971, the introduction of Standard Grade in the late 1980s and reforms to Higher Grade in the late 1990s. The chapter concludes on an optimistic note. Art and Design is thriving; it is compulsory in the first two years, the most popular subject in the 'Creative and Aesthetic' mode in third and fourth years (in 2001, 21,027 Standard Grade presentations or 34% of the national cohort) and consistently in the top eight subjects (in 2001, 6,843 presentations) at Higher Grade (SQA, Annual Statistical Report, 2001 p. 64).

IN THE BACKGROUND

During the 1960s and early 1970s art teachers in Scotland, and around the world, had much more autonomy. Two major developments however, the introduction of comprehensive education in the early 1970s and the raising of the school-leaving age in 1972, presented significant challenges for secondary schools. How would art education respond to the demands of the expanded cohort of comprehensive schools?

In 1968, a working party was set the following remit:

> To consider the position of art in the secondary school, in providing a continuing experience in creative expression through the visual arts and in fostering a sense of responsibility towards the creation of a visually satisfying environment. (HMSO, 1971, p. viii)

The committee's report (HMSO, 1971), retained emphasis chiefly on practical fine art and craft activities. Art education in the 1960s and 1970s, in the first four years at least, was just that – mainly art (and perhaps craft) education and this remained the case until the introduction of Standard Grade.

History of art was usually reserved for the Higher course and the focus tended to fall on male Western European artists and architects. The contributions made by the arts of other cultures; women artists, lens, time-based or site-specific work received scant coverage. Work by contemporary artists rarely informed the curriculum and visiting artists or trips to art galleries were infrequent. The history of art was somewhat one-dimensional and design may have been limited to repeat pattern or simple graphics exercises, but an excellent grounding in drawing, painting, printmaking and clay work was offered in the typical art department of the 1960s and 1970s. In retrospect, one wonders how well art education served the majority of the average class for whom art was something they had to do in first and second year, or who were allocated a non-certificate course in third and fourth year. What did they learn about the artist or designer's role in society? On leaving school, would they ever visit a gallery or museum? How well did art education serve these students? After all, only a small proportion of the school population would pursue art or design as a career, but all would be consumers of the products of artists and designers.

Almost thirty years later, MacDonald (1999, p. 447) reflected that the effect of art in the secondary school was largely to reinforce the status quo of free expression and visual analysis. During the 1970s therefore, talk was of art in the secondary school, the national certificates cite Ordinary Grade or Higher Grade 'Art'; design was viewed simply as part of 'art' and, by implication, not such an important part. In addition, the notion that a rounded art education should take cognisance of what Robinson (1990, p. 50) referred to as 'reflecting and responding' in addition to 'doing and making' activities was not to fully take root in Scottish art education for almost another twenty years.

A SHIFT OF FOCUS

During the late 1980s Standard Grades replaced Ordinary Grades. The introduction of Standard Grade marked a paradigm shift for Art and Design education. The title of the document setting out the arrangements for Art and Design (SEB: 1985, 1987) was, in itself, significant; there had been growing recognition that design had not been given its proper place. Standard Grade has a structure consisting of three equally weighted elements:

- Design Activity
- Expressive Activity
- Critical Activity

Pupils follow units of work that are either Expressive or Design in focus; within each unit Critical Activity is embedded and is closely related to the practical work. Design, for the first time, was given equal status in terms of the hours allocated within each of the two years, but interestingly Design was, and remains, assessed internally; the other two elements are assessed externally (SQA).

Without doubt, the element that gave rise to most concern amongst art teachers was the introduction of Critical Activity. The arrangements had this to say:

> Encouragement of a critical appraisal of one's own ideas and opinions and those of others is an important aspect of pupils' experiences in both Expressive Activity and Design Activity and helps pupils to gain insights into the role of visual arts and design in society. (SEB, 1987, p. 4)

The implications of Critical Activity for schools were spelled out; the aim was to set the practical studies in a real life context. A unit of work might focus on either Expressive or Design Activity, but it had to include Critical Activity:

> Critical Activity should be presented as an opportunity for active investigation. Where possible school-based audio-visual resources, museums, libraries, galleries, teacher resource centres and other agencies should be utilised. Direct contact with artists, designers, architects and their work would also authenticate the activity. (SEB, 1987, p. 12)

Few art teachers would argue with the educational merits of Critical Activity. However during the late 1980s, a major problem for many teachers was the cost of resources and access to works of art or high quality reproductions. An additional problem is geography. Some schools in the Highlands or Islands would find it very difficult to gain access to museums and galleries. Teaching methods today include independent and supported study using books, catalogues, reproductions and, increasingly, CD-ROM or Internet sources. Departments have developed resource banks, and pupils have a degree of autonomy in terms of when and how they integrate Critical Activity within a unit. Bargain bookshops and the information technology revolution have made high quality reproductions and virtual visits a realistic possibility within the budget of even the smallest (or most remote) school.

Before Standard Grade there was, of course, much good practice. Many departments rightly argued that a balanced and coherent course at Ordinary Grade, included design and critical appraisal of artists' or designers work. The problem was that provision, particularly in design and critical studies, was not coherent across the country. Standard Grade was therefore an attempt to spread good practice.

However, many art teachers complained about the extra administrative work Standard Grade entailed, a perceived loss of autonomy and the extra resources necessary to deliver the courses (though working groups did provide exemplar materials). In short, some thought the course over prescriptive, perhaps looking back to the 'freedom' of the 1971 report:

> Formal class methods and inflexible schemes of work have no place in the art department . . . The creative process, the personal experience and the practice and understanding of the activity is as important as the final result. (HMSO, 1971, p. 6)

This writer would argue that Standard Grade has not limited the freedom of the teacher, threatened the process-based approach or endangered the 'workshop atmosphere of the art room'. Rather, Standard Grade sets practical work in context and allows individual teachers scope to offer a broader range of activities using the project-based, pupil-centred methodology that has always characterised good art teaching. Two major achievements of Standard Grade have been firstly the emphasis on balance between Design and Expressive modes and secondly recognition of the contextual importance of critical studies.

ISSUES AND CHALLENGES

Over the past twenty years, the 'middle years' have proved to be the most stable:

Most departments provide well-planned and effective Standard Grade courses. The quality of courses at S1/S2 (ages 12– 14) and S5/S6 (ages 16– 18) is more variable. (SOEID, 1998, p. 42)

The model adopted for Standard Grade has had a direct influence on curriculum design for other stages. Art in the primary school and the first two years of secondary education has also been subject to reform. The national guidelines cite three attainment outcomes:

- using materials, techniques, skills and media;
- expressing feelings, ideas, thoughts and solutions;
- evaluating and Appreciating. (SOEID, *Expressive Arts 5–14*, 1992, p. 4)

The publication of the guidelines for Expressive Arts was an attempt, for the first time, to provide a coherent and progressive curriculum for art and design at ages 5 –14. In that sense it was a very welcome development, but it's fair to say that the guidelines have had more impact in primary schools than secondary art departments. Many departments are working at closer articulation with primary art experience, looking at not only what is learned, but also how it is learned; the project based, active learning model underpinning good secondary art education shares much with methodology in primary schools.

A TEMPORARY LOSS OF FOCUS?

The most contentious issue in recent years has been reform of the post-16 curriculum. As with many other subjects, the arrangements for Art and Design met with fierce criticism. The influence of Standard Grade on the new courses replacing first the Higher then Revised Higher is clear. Students are required to complete an Expressive unit and Design unit, both of which should contain 'art and design studies' – to set the practical activities in the wider social and historical context.

After a rocky start, Standard Grade is now working well. However, for many art teachers, the reforms to the generally well-regarded Revised Higher course were the straw that broke the camel's back. During the consultation process for the new courses teachers complained about multi-level courses, assessment burden and lack of exemplification in the documentation. Such was the concern, that the Art and Design courses were amongst the last to be implemented (HSDU, 1998).

At the time of writing, the new courses are being taught amidst a monitoring process and several changes to the original arrangements, mainly in the area of assessment. Between January and June 2000, the SQA carried out a review of the initial implementation of the National Qualifications (Phase 3 subjects). The highest number of responses received was for Art and Design. The volume of internal assessment was thought to be unnecessary, time consuming, unrealistic and placing too great a burden on teachers and students. As a result, a fundamental review of the Intermediate, Higher and Advanced Higher courses is to be carried out, with particular emphasis on the volume of assessment and the inter-relationship of external and internal assessment.

Given the history of reform in Art and Design, and tendency for art teachers to disagree with each other, the furore that surrounded the introduction of the new Higher and Advanced Higher courses was predictable. However the professionalism, creativity and enthusiasm of art teachers continues to produce courses extremely popular with pupils as Table 48.1 shows:

Table 48.1: Art and Design presentation 1997–2001 (SQA, 2001, p. 64)

	1997	1998	1999	2000	2001
Standard Grade	20,172	19,728	20,119	20,647	21,027
Higher Grade	7,400	7,271	7,377	7,424*	6,810

*Candidates presented for both old and new Higher.

BEYOND THE ART ROOM

Curricular reform in Art and Design over the past thirty years or so has led, in this writer's view, to a more relevant, inclusive, balanced and coherent educational experience for young people. In addition, the changes have encouraged teachers and pupils to look beyond the immediate school environment to resource and enhance learning and teaching. Many departments invite local artists, crafts people or designers to talk to classes. Opportunities for visits and workshops exist through sources such as local authorities or other arts organisations.

Several 'artist, designer or architect in education' programmes have emerged over the past fifteen years or so – some have been the initiative of enthusiasts within art departments, others have been funded by the Scottish Arts Council or National Lottery. Links between higher education institutions and schools also provide fruitful partnerships. Increasingly, the 'boundaries' are being crossed between primary and secondary schools and the formal and informal sectors of art education, for instance art students in training or community artists working with art teachers and associated primary schools to focus on an environmental design problem.

CONCLUDING REMARKS

For a visitor to an art class today, it might seem that not much has changed; the still life class goes on. The difference now is that students are required to reflect on their own and other artists' work and will engage in critical evaluation from their first to last year in the subject. The chances are the room will be full of objects for drawing with walls displaying pupils' work and reproductions; observational drawing, design projects and other process-based work will be much in evidence. Pupils will engage in active problem solving and often work together in small design teams. Assessment will be based on folios of work using grade related criteria with categories such as 'investigation and research', 'considering possibilities' and 'evaluation'.

There will probably be at least one computer; most departments will have one or two with internet access. A few larger departments may have a computer suite. Industry standard graphics software, scanners, digital still and video cameras are becoming commonplace, but they tend to be used primarily for research, investigation or documentation of finished work rather than for producing artwork. There are exceptions however, like the department that sets a design brief for students to produce animated introductions for television programmes; all of the work is completed digitally and the students' final work is stored on a CD-ROM. A challenge for the future will be to take full advantage of the digital and information age and harness it to existing good practice in active, problem-based learning for the benefit of all pupils.

Our visitor will witness classes taught by a balance of male and female staff. More than one teacher might teach classes during the week, perhaps one for Design and another for Expressive Activity. It's just as likely that the visitor will meet a teacher who trained in a design discipline as one trained in fine art. Unless it is in a remote school, the department will probably have links with local galleries, workshops and businesses.

Many art teachers would argue that Art and Design education in Scotland has never been healthier. Rapid advances in new technologies provide opportunities to access reproductions of great works of art from many cultures. In a crowded curriculum, Art and Design offers unique practical and theoretical learning experiences. The visitor would leave with a feeling that pupils, regardless of ability, are engaged in purposeful activity rooted in real life contexts. Art and Design education clearly has a central role in a balanced curriculum.

REFERENCES

HMSO (1971) *Art in Secondary Schools: Curriculum Paper 9*, Edinburgh: HMSO.

HSDU (1998) *Higher Still Subject Guide: Art and Design*, Dundee: SCCC and Higher Still Development Unit.

MacDonald, S. (1999) Art and design education, T. G. K. Bryce, and W. M. Humes, (eds), *Scottish Education*, Edinburgh: Edinburgh University Press, pp. 447–51.

Robinson, K. et al. (1990) *The Arts 5–16: Curriculum Framework*, London: Oliver and Boyd.

SEB (1985–1987). *Standard Grade: Revised Arrangements in Art and Design at Foundation, General and Credit Level*, Dalkeith: SEB.

SOEID (1998) *Effective Learning and Teaching in Scottish Secondary Schools: Art & Design*, a report by HM Inspectors of Schools, Edinburgh: SOEID.

49

Biology Education

Nicky Souter

The emergence of Biology as a major subject in the Scottish secondary curriculum took place during a comparatively brief period. Prior to the publication of the 'new' syllabus for Biology in 1968, fewer than 1,000 candidates were being submitted for examinations in various combinations of Botany, Zoology, Agriculture and Horticultural Science, Chemistry and Physics. The SQA statistical report 2001 indicated that Biology remained sixth in popularity at Standard Grade: around 23,000 candidates and more than 12,000 for all subjects at Higher Grade. This apparent success masks, however, a disturbingly progressive gender imbalance within the subject. Clarke et al. (1974) reported that the ratio of girls to boys at Higher Grade was 2:1; by 2001 70% of the cohort was female. This trend is mirrored at Standard Grade and, incidentally, reversed for Physics. Although plausible explanations might be offered, course selection in the sciences at Standard Grade and beyond appears to be a case of gender inequality. An extended enquiry remains overdue. The popularity of biological sciences extends into higher education and according to the UCAS statistics (2001) more than 13% of applicants to Scottish universities are in biological disciplines although the gender imbalance is less profound with 40% of applicants being men.

The initial growth in popularity of biology may have been a response to the following four factors:

- *Nature of subject*
  Modern Biology is a heterogeneous subject with more than one million original research papers being published each year. The traditional divisions of Zoology, Botany and Microbiology that relied on observational, morphological and physiological studies have been supplanted by disciplines that bring together the characteristics, instrumentation and techniques of other sciences, enabling previously unimagined insights into the processes of life. One consequence of such insight and associated technological innovation is increasing public concern about the social, moral and economic impact of issues such as biodiversity, global warming and genetically modified organisms. According to the Institute of Biology, 'the pace of biological research and the potential impact of recent discoveries show that biology will play an increasingly important role in wealth creation and improved quality of life.'

- *Graduates from UK universities*
  During the 1960s increased numbers of Biology graduates entered teaching during a period of curricular expansion which was associated with a statutory raising of the school-leaving

age. An enthusiastic and recently qualified teaching force undertook the implementation of the 'new Biology' course. This coincided with the introduction of an 'integrated science course', based on *Curriculum Paper 7, Science for General Education*, HMSO, 1969, that gave parity to the three sciences, as well as formalising the scope and extent of Biology taught in the first two years of secondary school.

- *International and domestic climate*
  Perrott et al. (1968) acknowledged the impact of the American Biological Sciences Curriculum Study. She described the impetus this gave to the 1962 Nuffield Science Teaching Project, 'a British curriculum study which was initiated by the desire of many individual school teachers and organisations for renewal of science curricula and for a study of imaginative ways of teaching science subjects.' Such was the climate that led to the publication of the first syllabus for biology by the Scottish Certificate of Education Examination Board in 1968.

- *Primary teachers' confidence and understanding*
  Traditional 'Nature Study' has been assimilated into aspects of science in the primary school and subsequently into the national guidelines for Environmental Studies, Society, Science and Technology, (Learning and teaching Scotland, 2000). These have defined the scope and range of life science for that age range. The subject area has some advantage and Harlen et al. (1995) reported that primary school, teachers were reasonably confident with the biological content of the 5–14 curriculum.

THE EARLY YEARS –
BIOLOGY COURSES AT ORDINARY AND HIGHER GRADE

These courses, continuous from Ordinary into Higher Grade, were based on 'the establishment of concepts and principles which are common to all life' (*Biology, Ordinary and Higher Grades*, SCEEB, 1968). They involved integration of the existing Botany and Zoology courses and demanded a commitment towards experimental and investigative approaches. The laboratory and field based 'systems approach' to Biology, rather than studying the 'whole organism', involved the establishment of biological generalisations about 'systems' such as gas exchange, osmosis, sexual reproduction and inheritance. The syllabuses gave a representative introduction to the breadth of Biology. During their early years the subject accelerated to its current level of popularity.

National examinations at Ordinary Grade included multiple-choice questions with item banks kept confidential to the examiners and with one exception were not released. Concern was repeatedly expressed by teachers regarding their inability to respond to and prepare candidates for public examination without appropriate insight into the assessment instruments. The robust Ordinary Grade syllabus nevertheless prevailed, with minor amendments, from 1968 until the implementation of Standard Grade in 1988. During its final years it was evident that syllabus revision was required due to subject advances, notably in the fields of molecular biology, biotechnology and genetics. Higher Grade was subsequently revised to articulate with Standard Grade courses in 1991. Further revision of Higher and provision for all the post-compulsory stages took place as part of the Higher Still reform.

CERTIFICATE OF SIXTH YEAR STUDIES (CSYS)

CSYS Biology was introduced in 1977, somewhat later than other CSYS subjects. During the final years of the award roughly half the presenting centres in Scotland entered around

1,250 candidates. Syllabus revision progressively reduced the number of topics and prior to the introduction of Advanced Higher candidates selected two from; chemistry of life; developmental physiology; behaviour; microbiology; diversity of life; man; organisms and environments. Assessment was equally divided between external examinations and an extended laboratory or field investigation as well as a laboratory notebook on each topic studied.

SCIENCE FOR ALL

Munn's curriculum (SED, 1977) demanded a scientific mode of study and the 'distinctive methodology depending heavily on an empirical approach, based on hypothesising and experimentation'. This determined the shape of Standard Grade courses. Munn also suggested that the social impact of science be a component of Standard Grade courses.

STANDARD GRADE BIOLOGY

The derivation of Standard Grade from Ordinary Grade courses is evident with significant content retention. Standard Grade Biology included a more detailed specification of the anticipated learning within four course elements of knowledge and understanding; problem solving; practical abilities; and attitudes. The first three elements are assessed formally. 'Suggested learning activities' at General and Credit levels indicate appropriate contexts, resources and approaches for learning and teaching. The 'learning outcomes' describe the basis of examinable content at each level. This close specification does, however restrict examiners' and teachers' choice in syllabus interpretation.

The philosophy of Standard Grade Biology is derived from three general aspects: the biological basis for life; relationships; applications of biological principles in work, health and leisure activities. Each of the seven topics covers a major area of biology: the biosphere; the world of plants; animal survival; investigating cells; the body in action; inheritance and biotechnology. The 'systems approach' was not incorporated and fewer opportunities arise to generalise fundamental processes. Working parties throughout the country developed a comprehensive range of support materials including worksheets, games, simulations, computer software, and some guidance on management, teaching and learning. Teacher's guides provide useful analysis and supply a foundation for varied classroom experience. The topic resources were designed to be used flexibly by departments and to promote a range of learning approaches. Revised versions remain widely used throughout the country. While HMIE generally comments favourably that resources are considered realistic to suit modern needs and that field work is performed in a variety of suitable locations, teachers report that delivery of all courses is limited by time, financial and training constraints.

ASSESSMENT AT STANDARD GRADE

Internal assessment involves grading practical abilities and estimating performance for 'knowledge and understanding' and 'problem solving'. Two components of practical abilities are assessed, 'practical techniques' and 'investigations'. The first involve laboratory or field procedures that may subsequently be applied to 'investigations' which are performed as structured tasks that are derived from the TAPS investigative skills objectives (Bryce et. al., 1991). Each structured investigation conforms to a prescribed format. It is disappointing that field based investigations are not supplied within published exemplars. Each investigation is based on a model of physical sciences where it is possible to isolate and test single variables. This is not always possible in a field investigation. Since 1999 the assessment of practical abilities has adopted identical approaches in sciences at Standard Grade with reduced weighting from 33% to 20%. Practical abilities' status has diminished in consequence. External assessment involves written examinations combining knowledge and understanding and problem solving with separate papers at General and Credit levels, each lasting one and a half hours and including multiple choice, short answer, extended answer and interpretation questions.

REVISED HIGHER GRADE BIOLOGY AND HUMAN BIOLOGY

Arrangements for Higher Grade were published for first examinations in 1991 with clear progression of content and problem solving from Standard Grade. Higher Biology incorporated topics on cell biology, genetics and evolution, control of growth and development, regulation of biological systems and adaptation. A parallel course on Human Biology was introduced in 1992 to replace a previous course in Anatomy, Physiology and Health, which had not been included in the Standard Grade development programme. Human Biology included topics on cell function, continuation of the species, life support mechanisms, the biological basis of behaviour, and population growth and the environment. This has proved a popular inclusion in the curriculum and has grown to almost 3,000 presentations each year. The practical abilities within these courses sat somewhat uncomfortably between the structured investigative approaches of Standard Grade and the extended open-ended investigation of CSYS with the inclusion of compulsory course practical, assessed by mandatory questions in the final examination. This provided limited opportunities for individual competence to be demonstrated beyond a formalised, procedural response to set questions. The final examinations took place in 2001.

Academic quality in Higher Biology was assured when Devine et al. (1996) suggested that: 'There were some statistically significant differences in individual skill areas between years, but no consistent pattern to indicate any overall change in standards.'

LIFE SCIENCE TODAY IN THE SCOTTISH CURRICULUM

The Scottish curriculum includes the study of life sciences from infant stages in primary school to the National Qualifications framework and is generally well served. Coherence is at points lacking and Standard Grade courses are currently the object of closest scrutiny. The recently published revised guidelines for 5–14 Environmental Studies (2000) and the drive to improve standards of attainment has focused attention on transition from primary to secondary schools as well as introduction of National Certificate courses at S2, S3 and S4. Although the guidelines claim to be progressive and coherent, anomalies are embedded within them.

Many schools are choosing to replace Standard Grade Biology with units and courses from the National Qualifications framework (NQF). SQA (Annual Statistical Report, 2001) indicates that 20% of Intermediate 2 and 12% at Intermediate 1 levels are aged fifteen or under, demonstrating uptake prior to S5.

The content of biology units and courses in the NQF has been taken from previously existing courses or modules. The principle of minimal change that was exercised during the Higher Still development has been well received by teachers. Revision recognised that the scope of existing provision was satisfactory. Courses and units are currently available in Biology, Human Biology and Biotechnology at four levels.

Biology at Intermediate 1 incorporates units in health and technology, biotechnological industries, growing plants. The Intermediate 2 units replicate much of the content of Standard Grade and while this may be an unsatisfactory 'resit' for those progressing from a General level pass at Standard Grade it will provide an appropriate entry point for students entering the subject for the first time. The three units of Higher Biology are cell biology, genetics and adaptation, control and regulation. Higher Human Biology includes units on cell function and inheritance, the continuation of life, behaviour, populations and the environment. Extensive overlap exists between the 2 'cell' topics.

Biotechnology courses have comparatively poor uptake with few presentations reported in 2001, mainly from the FE sector. The low uptake of biotechnology in schools highlights the problem that too many units are being offered in life sciences. With six units available at Intermediate 2 level and nine at Higher Grade SQA should explore routes by which courses can be tailored to schools and candidates needs.

The Advanced Higher course includes two mandatory forty–hour units, cell and molecular biology, environmental biology, two half credits including an investigation and a unit selected from biotechnology, animal behaviour, physiology, health and exercise. It is anticipated that this will remain as popular an option as the Certificate of Sixth year Studies has been for students.

BIOLOGY TEACHERS

Biology teachers are active across a full range of extra-curricular and cross-curricular activities with conservation, outdoor, health education and horticulture groups being amongst the most popular. It is evident that the age profile of teachers has changed. Clarke et al. (1974) reported that 35% of teachers had ten or more years' experience. The 1998 school census indicated more than 90% have more than ten years' teaching experience. The average age of Biology teachers was reported as forty-four, which was amongst the highest reported. Future recruitment will be at high levels over a short period to correspond to the retiral of those who entered during the infancy of Biology as a secondary school subject.

INTO THE FUTURE

The SCCC discussion paper *Science Education in Scottish Schools* (1996) presented innovative and challenging postulates within the five aspects of 'scientific capability' (curiosity, competence, understanding, creativity and sensitivity). Little evidence of this is apparent through the 'Higher Still' reforms or the 5–14 revisions. This is disappointing. A responsive and progressive curriculum is required that will contribute to pupil achievement as well as remaining a popular choice, and for all pupils.

REFERENCES

Bryce, T. G. K., McCall, J. MacGregor, J. Robertson, I. J. and Weston, R. A. J. (1991) *How to Assess Open-ended Investigations in Biology, Chemistry and Physics*, Oxford: Heinemann Educational.

Clarke, R. A., Cruikshank, G., Haddow, J. F., Sloss, H. and. Taylor, D. G (1974) *Biology in Scottish Secondary Schools*, Dundee: Dundee College of Education.

Devine, M., Hall, J., Mapp, J. and Musselbrook, K. (1996) *Maintaining Standards: Performance at Higher Grade in Biology, English, Geography and Mathematics*, Edinburgh: SCRE.

Harlen, W., Holroyd, C. and Byre, M. (1995) *Confidence and Understanding in Teaching Science and Technology in Primary Schools*, Edinburgh: SCRE.

Perrott, E., Martin, E. Campbell, I. (1968) *Biological Sciences in Scottish Secondary Schools*, Stirling: University of Stirling.

SED (1977) *The Structure of the Curriculum in the Third and Fourth Years of the Scottish Secondary School*, Edinburgh: SED.

50

Business Education

Barry Finlayson

The 1980s saw significant changes to the Business Education curriculum for young people in the final two years of compulsory education (S3/S4). New, differentiated, Standard Grade certificate courses were introduced encouraging a pupil-centered approach to teaching and learning and introducing new methods of assessment. Changes to the S3/S4 curriculum had a knock-on effect to fifth and sixth year courses (S5/S6) and in the 1990s the S5/S6 curriculum was radically reshaped to ensure an effective progression from S3/S4 into the new post-16 courses. Courses were broken down into units which were assessed and credited to the student as he/she progressed through the course. Teachers were made responsible for administering and grading the unit assessments. Students were also required to take a terminal external assessment designed to ensure understanding of the content of the whole course and show ability to identify inter-relationships between elements of the content.

These developments placed many new demands on Business Education staff at a time when local government reorganisation removed the support traditionally provided by specialist subject advisers. This has proved to be a serious loss to Business Education departments.

THE BUSINESS EDUCATION CURRICULUM

The curriculum in Business Education is optional and young people can choose to study in the Business Education area at the end of their second year (S2). The four subjects that currently comprise this optional curriculum are Accounting and Finance, Administration, Business Management and Economics. Administration and Business Management are often regarded as 'general' business courses providing young people with a broad understanding of business and how it is administered. Accounting and Finance, and to a lesser extent, Economics, are seen as more 'specialised' courses. It is not common to find all the subjects on offer in a school and hard decisions about the menu of subjects have to be made. Recently the trend has been towards offering the 'general' courses, that is. Administration and Business Management. While aiming to provide young people with knowledge and understanding about the business component of society, the Business Education curriculum also seeks to develop transferable business skills, for instance problem solving, decision making and, in particular, practical abilities in using information and communication technology (ICT). Each Business Education subject is designed to contribute to these aims in the following ways.

- Accounting and Finance develops an understanding of how all types of organisations are financed, the importance of being accountable and managing financial resources in a prudent manner.
- Administration introduces young people to the range of administrative activities which must be undertaken for any organisation to function effectively.
- Business Management develops an understanding of the business and information environment, how organisations operate and the main functions they perform.
- Economics is designed to give young people an understanding of the economic forces that shape/will shape their lives as consumers, workers and citizens.

These subjects are offered to young people in S3 as Standard Grade courses designed to suit three ability levels, Foundation (F), General (G) or Credit (C). Since young people have had no prior work in the department, the norm is to delay the final decision regarding ability in the subject until the latest possible time. In larger departments, able to attract sizeable numbers, setting into F/G and G/C groups is often possible once performance is established. However, in smaller departments mixed ability groups are the norm.

A growing number of departments, anxious to offer young people in S1/S2 short inputs in Business Education, have used the support of the 5–14 programme. While this does not specifically recommend widening the curriculum particularly in favour of Business Education, it does suggest including elements of ICT. The importance of these guidelines and their impact on the S1/S2 curriculum and also the content of S3 courses has been recognised by Business Education departments. As a result many departments offer short courses in basic ICT skills with particular emphasis on keyboarding, simple word processing, database/spreadsheet construction and internet investigation. Some departments also offer contributions to other areas including general business, money management and enterprise skills. The vocational nature of the subjects also makes them attractive to students in S5/S6 who might begin their studies of Business Education by taking one of the post-16 courses with a view to a business career .

The post-16 developments of the late 1990s resulted in differentiated courses for all in Business Education and offered at four levels, Intermediate 1 (Int 1), Intermediate 2 (Int 2), Higher (H) and Advanced Higher (Adv H) levels. Access level courses are also available in Administration and Business Management for young people with learning difficulties. Progression routes from Standard (S) Grade courses into post-16 courses are shown in Table 50.1.

Table 50.1: Progression in the Business Education curriculum

S3/S4		S5		S6		FE/HE
F level	→	Int 1	→	Int 2	→	HNC/D → employment
G level	→	Int 2	→	H	→	HNC/D → employment
C level	→	H	→	Adv H	→	HNC/D → employment
						Degree

It should be noted that each Business Education subject, to a greater or lesser extent, contributes to the development of the nationally identified and important general (core) skills of communication, numeracy, problem solving, ICT and working with others.

TRENDS IN THE BUSINESS EDUCATION CURRICULUM

While Business Education subjects are popular in secondary schools, the total number of young people choosing the subjects is relatively small compared to the main school subjects, for example English and Maths where roughly 60,000 candidates take these courses annually at S Grade (SQA, Annual Statistical Report, 2001 Table SG1). Consequently a very large proportion of pupils leave school without any knowledge of the importance of business and how it operates. The actual numbers of young people being presented for S Grades is shown in Table 50.2 below. While it is difficult to draw firm conclusions at a time when the curriculum is changing, the figures nevertheless help to identify interesting trends.

Table 50.2:   Young people taking S Grade Business Education subjects

		1997	1998	1999	2000	2001
Office & Information Studies	Total	17,520	16,670	16,172	15,370	6,442
	Female					5,028
	Male					1,414
Administration	Total	–	–	–	–	8,771
	Female					6,837
	Male					1,934
Accounting and Finance	Total	5,614	4,777	4,703	4,225	4,003
	Female					2,105
	Male					1,898
Business Management	Total	–	–	875	2,799	4,357
	Female					2,307
	Male					2,050
Economics	Total	1,518	1,488	1,166	953	772
	Female					291
	Male					481

Administration was introduced in 1999 with the first examination in 2001. Business Management was introduced in 1998 with the first examination in 2000.
Source: SQA Annual Statistical Report, 2001
Note: No available gender breakdowns before 2001.

The most popular subjects are Administration and Business Management. The success of Administration is encouraging and derives from the practical and vocational nature of the subject. The large ICT component also increases its appeal to pupils. All Business Education departments see this course as their 'core business'. Since its introduction in 1998, the numbers taking Business Management have increased five-fold. Business Management is also likely to become 'core business' in the future. Smaller numbers opt for Accounting and Finance and Economics. As Table 50.2 shows, while Accounting and Finance is still a popular subject in many schools, the numbers opting to take it have been falling progressively. Economics is regarded both as a social subject and a business subject and so is taught in some schools through Social Subjects and in others through Business Education. However, the majority of young people do so through the Business Education department and with additional pressures many departments have been forced to reappraise their offerings, often at the expense of Economics.

Table 50.2 also shows the gender balance across the subjects and identifies a high proportion of females taking Administration – although a larger proportion of males take Administration than was the case with its predecessor, Office and Information Studies – while the balance is more equal in Accounting and Finance and Business Management. In Economics, males outnumber females by almost 2 to 1.

The introduction of differentiated courses post-16 means that there are now appropriate courses for students of all ability in S5/S6. The replacement of the old H Grade Secretarial Studies with Administration and Management and Information Studies with Business Management offered at Intermediate 1, 2, and H and Advanced H levels has ensured appropriate progession for all students after S Grade and encouraged wider participation. With the exception of Economics, these changes have increased the numbers taking the subjects as Table 50.3 shows:

Table 50.3: Percentage change in numbers taking post Higher Grade courses in Business Education, 1997–2001

	% change on 1997
Accounting and Finance	+ 18%
Administration	+ 68%
Business Management	+ 76%
Economics	– 24%

Table 50.4 illustrates the actual change in absolute numbers of students taking post-16 courses. The popularity of Administration and Business Management is maintained with Accounting and Finance holding up but Economics still failing to maintain its numbers. While the figures are not shown here, there is also a healthy interest in Advanced H Grade in all of the subjects including Economics.

Business Education departments have thus emerged from a period of massive change with reasonable numbers of young people taking a menu of relevant courses suited to their ability levels. In the face of these developments, full credit should be given to Business Education departments and staff who have not only maintained but have expanded their presence in the post-16 curriculum.

CLASSROOM PRACTICE IN BUSINESS EDUCATION

The fact that Business Education is perceived by young people as relevant, practical and vocational, helps to make the teaching both challenging and interesting. Teachers are also positive about their role and feel that they are teaching something of value. Nurturing and maintaining this early enthusiasm is achieved through teaching and learning which is active, relates the content knowledge and skills to the real world and uses real business illustrations, case studies and examples to support and deepen understanding. While teaching methods vary to some extent across the subjects, in the main the approach is pupil centered, practical and activity-based, involving the regular and progressive practice of new skills to maintain interest and develop confidence. 'Teacher chalk and talk' has been replaced by interactive teaching involving group work and activity learning set in a business context where groups,

Table 50.4:   Number of young people taking post-16 Business Education subjects

	1997	1998	1999	2000	2001	Totals for 2001
ACCOUNTING AND FINANCE						
Intermediate 1				455	423	
Intermediate 2				338	510	
Higher (Old)	3,145	2,841	2,773	501	10	
Higher (New)				2,141	2,726	
Advanced Higher					42	**3,711**
ADMINISTRATION						
Intermediate 1				492	986	
Intermediate 2				952	2,830	
Higher				678	2,991	
Advanced Higher						**6,807**
BUSINESS MANAGEMENT						
Intermediate 1				104	122	
Intermediate 2				793	1,035	
Higher				4,971	5,833	
Advanced Higher					19	**7,009**
ECONOMICS						
Intermediate 1				–	3	
Intermediate 2				118	146	
Higher (Old)	1,813	1,700	1,488	199	23	
Higher (New)				1,139	1,160	
Advanced Higher					44	**1,376**
MANAGEMENT & INFORMATION STUDIES*	3,910	4,289	4,482	347	6	
SECRETARIAL STUDIES*	4,220	3,946	3,715	2,742	5	

* Old Higher Grade courses. Management and Information Studies was replaced by Business Management, and Secretarial Studies was replaced by Administration, both in 2000.

pairs and/or individuals often work with prepared resources to develop their knowledge and use that knowledge to suggest and present solutions to business problems. The growing confidence of teachers in the use of ICT as an aid to learning and the enthusiasm with which young people embrace ICT has resulted in learning situations where knowledge can be developed through pupils undertaking investigative tasks using the internet to find out about particular aspects of business organisations. The computer is also used to run business simulations.

Looking to the future, it is not impossible to envisage Business Education courses in schools being web-based and allowing young people home access. Teaching about business is often reinforced by referring to illustrations from the current business world through the press and television, and learning is often further enhanced by visits to organisations to see aspects of business in action and hear at first hand about the world of business from invited speakers. Perhaps the biggest challenge to all teachers arising out of the developments at S Grade and post-16 levels involve multi-level teaching. In the majority of schools the numbers cannot justify setting and mixed ability classes normally use a core plus extension model. Courses are supported by centrally produced differentiated course materials which provide the essential core knowledge in the form of notes on the key ideas along with student tasks/activities.

Post-16 courses present similar problems of multi-level teaching. With the exception of Administration and Business Management, numbers are typically low and multi-level teaching inevitable. The problem is helped to a certain extent by Int 2 and H Grade courses in Accounting and Finance, Business Management and Economics having similar content and providing the possibility of the two levels being taught to one group. Differentiation between the levels is achieved by task complexity. The more practical nature of the Administration course at Intermediate 1 and 2 has resulted in the recommendation that these two levels be taught together while those students taking the Higher Grade, with its greater emphasis on knowledge and understanding, be taught as one group. All post-16 Business Education courses are also supported by centrally produced and differentiated course notes and pupil tasks but multi-level teaching is still seen as challenging.

Assessment has a profound effect on what is taught and how it is taught. Among the S Grade courses, Accounting and Finance and Business Management both involve teachers assessing one of the elements of the course. Staff are required to administer an SQA instrument of assessment during S4. This involves setting aside class time to carry out the assessment, marking and grading each on a 7-point scale and reporting the grade for each pupil to the SQA normally by March of the session. The internal assessment process in each school is moderated on a regular basis by the SQA. The SQA also administers an external examination in May which assesses the remaining elements of the course. The final grade awarded will usually be the average of the grades for each element.

In Accounting and Finance, the internal assessment takes the form of an accounting project completed over a period of fifteen hours of class time involving the application of ICT in the recording and presenting of accounting information. This is normally under-taken towards the end of the course. With Business Management, the internal assessment instrument is a computer-based business simulation from which relevant business in-formation can be extracted in response to questions assessing problem solving and analytical abilities. The final award is the average of the grades achieved for the elements of the course in both the internal assessment and external examination.

The assessment of Administration is slightly different in that young people undertake a number of ICT tasks in school using fifteen hours of class time, normally towards the end of the course. While teachers do not have physically to mark the tasks (this is done by the SQA centrally) they do have to submit an estimated grade indicating the level at which each young person is performing. One issue of concern is that many young people sitting the external examinations involving ICT activities are penalised because their keyboarding skills are not sufficiently developed and consequently they fail to complete all the questions adequately. Internal assessment was removed altogether from S Grade Economics in 1999. Until then an internally written investigation of an economic issue was administered and graded in the school. However, the investigation often proved challenging for 15-year-olds and was replaced by an external examination, which now assesses all elements of the course.

At post-16 level, there is a large amount of internal assessment and detailed recording of student performance to be undertaken. Each course normally comprises three units to be delivered over one academic session. Each unit has three to five learning outcomes to be assessed and each learning outcome normally has one assessment instrument with marking guide and grading instructions provided centrally from the National Assessment Bank (NAB). Each student's success on a NAB is recorded by the teacher and once a student has successfully completed all the NABs for the unit it will be added to their academic record. This has a positive effect in motivating students who are rewarded immediately. Failure to complete a NAB instrument successfully requires further attempt(s) and the process of tracking students and organising additional attempts can be a nightmare for teachers. Recording student performance carefully for communicating to the SQA as well as retaining evidence for moderation purposes can also take time, particularly when the class is large. Pressure can also build up on students undertaking a number of post-16 courses, all requiring course assessments to be undertaken continuously throughout the session. There is a feeling among teachers that while the developments have much to commend them, there really is too much assessment. Teachers teach to the assessment and often narrow their teaching to cover only the content of the assessment instrument; much of the enjoyment for both teachers and students has been lost through the pressure to continuously assess. A National Qualifications task group was recently set up to review the introduction of post-16 National Qualifications and recognised (August 2002) that the assessment load for both teachers and students should be reduced in order to minimise the disruption to teaching and learning. The group also recommended moving towards a more holistic approach to assessment.

Post-16 courses also contain terminal external assessment in the form of a final two and a half hour examination which is designed to test the knowledge, understanding and skills developed through the units. The ability of students to integrate knowledge and understanding in order to solve problems is tested normally by means of interpretation and extended answer questions.

FUTURE PROSPECTS AND CRITICAL ISSUES

There is a concern over the trends identified in Tables 50.2 and 50.4, which show declining numbers taking both Accounting and Finance and Economics. Will these subjects lose their place in the curriculum altogether? It would surely be unacceptable to deny young people these courses and the opportunity to develop knowledge and understanding which would help to equip them for post-school society. In the case of Economics, competition among Social Subjects departments for pupils at the end of S2 and the fact that many potential clients feel that Economics may be a 'hard' subject, have all conspired to deny many young people the opportunity to understand the day-to-day economic issues that affect their own and the nation's life. Also the success of Business Management has not helped Economics. During session 2001–2, for the first time since the beginning of teacher training in Economics at the University of Strathclyde's Faculty of Education, the PGCE course in Economics could not be offered since only one applicant was able to meet the rigorous entry requirements. The situation is unchanged for session 2002–3. Although the numbers of young people at post-16 level interested in taking Accounting and Finance has increased recently (see Table 50.4), the relentless decline at S Grade continues. The fact that the S Grade course Business Management does offer a limited amount of Accounting and Economics is no argument to support the removal of these two subjects from the curriculum. For departments faced with a range of subjects to offer and limited staffing, it might be expected that the future of these two subjects is certainly threatened. The individual enthusiasm of departments and their ability to convince school management of their value to young people will determine their future.

A further issue of concern surrounds the current debate over the replacement of S Grade with post-16 courses. While such a development would certainly bring the benefits of the post-16 structure to young people in S3/S4, there is a concern that the interest of less academic students and teacher enthusiasm for teaching the different levels may be difficult to sustain when the content of the courses is similar and differentiation is by task only. The growth in the importance of ICT and the fact that young people are coming into Business Education departments often with a high skill level in ICTs, means that both the ICT elements and the skill levels of Business Education teachers has to be regularly reviewed and enhanced. The growing focus of ICT in Business Education subjects and the introduction of a new Computing course (Information Systems) at post-16 level with elements of ICT not dissimilar to those which are taught in Administration, has encouraged a number of local authorities to appoint one principal teacher (either a Business Education or Computing specialist) in charge of a department of Information Technology. The increasing number of graduates in training and opting to qualify in both Computing and Business Education will sustain this trend and also increase the opportunities for an expanded presence in the S1/S2 curriculum.

The failure of some universities to accept H Grade Administration for entry is not acceptable and denies Business Education departments access to those students whose curriculum is always determined by what universities will accept. This has an obvious effect on the number of young people taking the course and influences the spread of ability in class groups. In response, changes have been made to the H Grade examination in Administration to make it more challenging and acceptable to those universities currently unwilling to consider it appropriate as an entry qualification and it is hoped that these changes will persuade those universities who have rejected it as unworthy to think again.

The future of the Business Education curriculum is in the hands of teachers who have successfully accommodated the significant developments over the last twenty years and seen their job change radically. They hear from politicians and planners that they are teaching subjects important to the future economic prosperity of the country but too often these positive statements are not followed up by curriculum planners at national and local authority level. Also, school managers themselves do not seem to afford the same priority to the subjects as the politicians. It therefore falls to individual departments to be proactive and confidently promote the value of the Business Education curriculum to young people, their parents and school managers. Many successful departments have done this in the past; all must do so now!

51

Career Education

Cathy Howieson and Sheila Semple

RECENT DEVELOPMENTS

The publication of *Career Education in Scotland, A National Framework* in November 2001 (Learning and Teaching Scotland, 2001) represents a significant advance in the position of career education in Scottish education. It means that for the first time there is national curriculum guidance on career education. For many years there was no agreed definition of 'careers education': its definition, aims, content and resource allocation could be decided at authority or indeed at school level. The result was considerable variation in pupils' experiences of career education (Howieson and Semple, 1996). The national framework set out to define career education, give guidance about content and set out learning outcomes for students to achieve at different stages of their education with the aim of improving coherence and progression. The framework also extended the age range of students who should receive career education to include primary and pre-school children, specifying a 3–18 age range. The title of the framework included what might seem a small change from 'careers' to 'career' but the document makes it clear that this was considered to be a significant change:

> The term 'career education' is used in preference to the more traditional 'careers education' normally used in secondary schools. This signals a move from a narrower definition of 'career' to a broader one more appropriate for a wider age range that includes younger children.
>
> *Careers* education has often been seen as primarily concerned with helping young school leavers make a decision on an occupational route. The broader view of *career* education includes the development of knowledge, understanding, skills and dispositions for future career development over an extended period. Such a view is appropriate in a changing world of work in which individuals are likely to experience several changes in their career during their working lives. (Learning and Teaching Scotland, 2001, p. 1)

EXPECTATIONS

Most young people think that a key role for secondary education is helping them to prepare for their future role in working life (perhaps after time spent in college or university). This view is shared by their parents. Many see it as the clear justification and motivation for being at school, and research suggests that it is a key area of anxiety for both parents and young people; not enough, they say, is being done (Howieson and Semple, 1996; Howieson, Semple and Paris, 2002).

For schools, career education can help young people see purpose and relevance in their education, can improve motivation and raise aspiration in their pupils and help to link core skills to their future use. For governments, career work in schools is critical for the economic performance of the country: employers and the economy need well motivated young people with a sense of direction, who can make appropriate choices, manage their career development and be committed to learning and training throughout their lives.

CONTENT AND DELIVERY OF CAREER EDUCATION

The national framework for career education built on existing frameworks in use in different parts of Scotland: these were mostly based on the DOTS model developed in the 1970s as an analytical tool for career education and guidance (Law and Watts, 1977). But the framework moves beyond existing practice, reflecting a wider view of career education and of young people's career decision-making.

The national framework sets out four broad areas, each with sub-elements:

> *Awareness of self* – being able to identify and assess personal values, aspirations, strengths and development needs and to apply these to choosing and implementing career paths.
> *Awareness of opportunity* – being able to acquire information and to evaluate information and its sources to gain an accurate, up-to-date picture of education, training and work opportunities locally, nationally and internationally.
> *Understanding decision-making* – being able to handle decision-making strategies in a career context, taking account of differing styles of decision-making and the influences of family, friends, school/college and community on choice.
> *Understanding transitions* – understanding the career demands of life changes, transitions and stages, and being able to access guidance, information and actual opportunities in order to implement career action plans. (Learning and Teaching Scotland, 2001, pp. 6–7)

While these four areas as described above bear some relation to existing practice, they extend and develop it in several respects. Firstly, the lifelong aspect of career development is emphasised throughout the 'understanding transitions' theme, and also through the introduction of career education into primary and pre-school curricula. Secondly, gaps in pupils' understanding and knowledge of the opportunity structure (that is, their understanding of post-school education, training and employment) have increasingly been identified (Howieson, Semple and Paris, 2002) and these aspects of a career education programme are given extra emphasis. Thirdly, pupils' decisions about their futures are known to be heavily influenced by the advice, information and perceptions of parents, families, friends and community members – the skills required to handle these influences effectively are included in the strand on decision making. And lastly, the importance of the acquisition of employability skills and their relationship to core skills underpins the progression described across the whole framework.

In practice, only a minority of Scottish schools will yet have developed a consistent programme which covers all the content listed above and which has clear progression in its content and approach. Most schools deliver career education as part of a rolling programme of personal and social education (PSE), with a number of weeks devoted to career education, followed by some weeks covering health, records of achievement etc; some have a discrete career education programme and a very small number deliver career education through other subjects in the curriculum. Overall, the extent to which career education articulates with other parts of PSE is often limited.

Historically, the main focus of career education has been S2 (when Standard Grade subjects are being chosen) and S4 (when post-16 choices are being considered). A clear difficulty for schools is the provision of career education in S5 and S6. The considerable variation in students' academic attainment, career intention, choice of post-school route and vocational maturity is very noticeable at this stage making career education difficult both to design and to deliver. Ideally it requires a short compulsory programme combined with a choice of subsequent inputs based on the individual's needs. This requires a clear identification of needs which is likely to be a complicated and time-consuming task; and a more individualised programme is difficult for schools to deliver within the twin constraints of resources and the timetable.

Although a member of the school's senior management team will have overall responsibility for the career education programme (normally within the context of the whole PSE programme), individual guidance teachers are likely to have responsibility for different aspects, for instance the S2 PSE programme, work experience, the S5/S6 career input. The extent to which guidance teachers delivered career education to their own guidance caseload has been variable in the past, but it is possible that the implementation of the McCrone Agreement and the resulting move in several areas to have full-time guidance teachers may lead to more career education by pupils' own guidance teachers.

In most schools, career education is delivered in a variety of ways. A great deal is presented through classroom work, with discussions, worksheets and, in some cases, video material used. More imaginative approaches, such as career simulations like 'The Real Game' are being developed in some areas. A key part of the programme is often the preparation, and debriefing, of one-week's work experience with a local company.

LINKS TO OTHER ASPECTS OF EDUCATION FOR WORK, TO PSE, TO GUIDANCE SYSTEMS AND TO CAREERS SCOTLAND

The national career education framework was published under the banner of Education for Work. The Education for Work initiative was launched in 1997 by the Minister for Education and Industry to assist in preparing pupils for the world of work in the widest sense. The importance of Education for Work is made clear in HMI inspections (Scottish Executive, 2000):

> The report underlines the central importance of education for work for all Scottish schools. It recognizes education for work as one of a small number of key priorities, such as personal and social development, health and citizenship, which should permeate education at all stages. (Scottish Executive, 2002, p. 5)

Career education is one of three stands within Education for Work, the other two being education industry links and enterprise. In addition to career education, aspects of the Education for Work programme include work experience, work shadowing, enterprise activities, industrial inputs into subjects in the curriculum and events such as industry awareness days. Considered in conjunction with work experience, career education is the aspect of Education for Work which is most likely to be experienced by the majority of pupils (Semple et al., 2001). It comes closest, therefore, to meeting any core entitlement for Education for Work. As noted earlier, it is also very closely linked in practice to PSE provision, being designed, delivered and managed by guidance and PSE staff rather than by those with a formal remit for Education for Work. There is a need to use the strength of career education to support Education for Work in schools and to provide the necessary links to PSE provision so that young people can see the links between other Education for Work experiences and their own personal development and decision making. But clarification of the uncertain position that career education currently occupies between PSE and Education for Work is necessary to enable it to fulfil this role. At the time of writing (August 2002) the summary of the minister's review of Education for Work is imminent. It is likely to recommend an increased focus on enterprise activities but it does not appear likely to clarify the position of career education.

In April 2002, careers service companies, education business partnerships, adult guidance networks and local learning partnerships came together to form Careers Scotland. Career guidance interviews given by careers advisers require good career education in order to be effective and Careers Scotland, therefore, has a considerable interest in helping schools to develop their career programmes. It has appointed a development manager with responsibility for the curriculum (including career education) and will support much of the implementation of the career education framework in conjunction with Learning and Teaching Scotland. This will be done centrally and also in partnership with each school's careers adviser, which is likely to have the effect of continuing the trend for careers advisers to act as consultants in the design of career education rather than being directly involved in its delivery.

ARTICULATION WITH PRIMARY, FURTHER AND HIGHER EDUCATION

The development of career thinking starts very early, continuing throughout adolescence and being refined and reviewed in adult and working life. At one end, primary and pre-school provision can begin to extend pupils' knowledge of the working world beyond that of their family and community through project work and visits; at the other end, further education colleges include career education units (SQA accredited) in many courses; and some universities now run career development classes as part of undergraduate and postgraduate courses. An on-going difficulty has been that such inputs have rarely linked to each other or provided recognised progression. The introduction of a national framework covering the 3–18 age range offers the basis for improved articulation and progression, at least in respect of this age group.

KEY ISSUES

The aims of career education need continuing review in the light of the changing nature of work, training, education and vocational routes. Career education programmes need to reflect the world as it is and will be, and not as it was. How are those delivering career education to be kept up to date? Not only does the content and balance of career education need review, but so also do the methodologies used. Young people respond well to special events (such as equal opportunities days), open discussions and case studies, work experience, outside speakers (especially those with credibility, such as previous school-leavers discussing their experiences and revisiting their career decisions) and to computer-generated information and guidance. They respond less well to class-based worksheets, and to heavily teacher-centred approaches. There are clear issues here relating to the design of career activities and lessons; to training in student-centred methodologies; to the provision of appropriate classroom accommodation to allow flexible teaching; and to the availability of computers capable of handling the range of career guidance and information databases, including those produced to support the new National Qualifications.

A problematic issue is the extent to which the career education programme challenges pupils' views of their choices and their aspirations rather than merely reflecting pupil interests and ideas (which may be limited by prejudice, narrowness or limited experiences and expectations). Policy makers have ever-increasing expectations of career education – to address the social inclusion agenda through giving young people a positive view of the world of work to integrate them more effectively into their communities; to raise aspiration to learning and training; to ensure easy transitions into post-school opportunities and so on. But the challenging of rigid views of the future is not easily done, and requires time and effective resources.

There is also an issue about the balance between the acquisition of knowledge and the learning and practising of skills within career education. Career education cannot be only about 'learning facts about how many exam passes you need to be an accountant' but about the gathering of employability skills and career management skills.

While the recent introduction of the national framework for career education is a positive development, its implementation poses a number of challenges. Firstly extension of coverage of career education to primary and pre-school children will require the provision of support materials to help teachers and others tease out career-related learning in the 5–14 and pre-school curriculum. Secondly, there is the need for support materials for secondary schools to ensure more innovative delivery of a career programme and to encourage the new perspectives (such as an orientation to lifelong learning and career development) which the framework requires. Thirdly, new quality assurance measures are required to make career education programmes more effective in the interests of young people and their communities.

REFERENCES

Howieson, C. and Semple, S. (1996) *Guidance in Secondary Schools*, Edinburgh: Centre for Educational Sociology.

Howieson, C., Semple, S. and Paris, M. (2002) *A Longitudinal Study of Young People in Ayrshire*, Glasgow: University of Strathclyde.

Law, B. and Watts, A. G. (1977) *School, Careers and Community*, London: Church Information Office.

LTS (2001) *Education for Work: Career Education in Scotland, A National Framework*, Dundee: LTS.

Scottish Executive (2000) *Education for Work in Schools, A Report by HMI Inspectors of Schools*, Edinburgh: Scottish Executive.

Semple, S., Paris, M., McCartney, P. and Twiddle, B. (2002) *Learning Gains from Education for Work*, Edinburgh: Scottish Executive.

52

Chemistry Education

Douglas Buchanan

ABOUT CHEMISTRY COURSES

In the first two years of most Scottish secondary schools, Chemistry forms clearly identifiable sections of an integrated science course that is predominately based on the national guidelines for Environmental Studies 5–14. This material, first published in 1993 and recently reviewed by the Scottish Executive Education Department (SEED, 2000) has provided a framework to support primary teachers with the introduction of aspects of Chemistry to programmes of work and, in turn, has given secondary teachers the opportunity to review learning and teaching of the subject within an integrated context for students up to age fourteen. In what is seen as an attempt to provide a more challenging experience for students, a small but growing minority of schools teaches Chemistry as a separate course, mainly in second year.

In years three and four, in line with national policy for all students to study at least one science subject, Chemistry can be taken as a two-year Standard Grade course. Information about this highly popular option, attracting over 23,000 students, is described in the Scottish Qualifications Authority (SQA) *Arrangements* (1997). Unlike Science but in common with Biology and Physics, Chemistry at Standard Grade is on offer at Credit and General levels only. While students tend to be taught in General/Credit classes, in a small but increasing number of schools, proper attention to differentiation leads to students being placed in classes according to likely attainment of awards.

For fifth and sixth year students, courses from Access 3 up to Advanced Higher within the Higher Still programme (SQA, 2000) provide opportunities for students with all levels of achievement to continue with their studies of Chemistry as well as catering for 'fresh-starters'. Progression from Standard Grade Credit level is to a one-year Higher course for students in fifth year and then the Advanced Higher in sixth year. As with Standard Grade, the origins of these courses are well-established and they have a healthy uptake with approximately 10,000 studying at Higher and just under 1,600 taking Advanced Higher, making Chemistry at this level second in popularity to Mathematics.

Recently introduced courses have extended the range of suitable provision at levels below Higher. While it can be seen as a valuable qualification in itself, for example as part of a broad science experience, the Intermediate 2 course is primarily designed as a two-year route to Higher, mainly for students with achievement at Standard Grade General level but also for students who wish to undertake an academic study of Chemistry for the first time.

With the content of the units at Intermediate 2 quite different from those at Higher, unless numbers are very small, there are practical difficulties with bi-level learning and teaching and this has restricted uptake in fifth and sixth years at Intermediate 2 in schools unable to attract the necessary numbers for viable class sizes.

For less academic students, the Intermediate 1 course gives prominence to a practical, applications-led approach to the study of Chemistry. The units of the Access 3 course are designed to meet the needs of students who may find achievement at Intermediate 1 difficult and since it is likely that students working at this level have a low long-term retention span, there is no end-of-course examination at Access 3. Unlike Higher and Intermediate 2, the content of the units at Intermediate 1 and Access 3 are almost the same and the two levels are differentiated by their outcomes. As with Intermediate 2, numbers in fifth and sixth years undertaking a study at Intermediate 1 or Access 3 are still relatively low.

RATIONALE

In the early 1960s, practical work by students tended to be limited and there was a heavy emphasis on theory combined with illustrative demonstrations by teachers. Copying from the blackboard, taking down dictated notes and memorising facts were common student activities. However, while public interest in science, aroused by events such as the early achievements of space exploration, initiated support for the reform of Chemistry education at the classroom level, it was the 1980s Standard Grade development programme (SGDP) that provided the spark for the revolution of learning and teaching of the subject in Scottish schools. What has been the effect of the key aspects of the innovation on classroom practice?

- The acquisition of knowledge and understanding of essential chemical theory, processes and reactions continues to be an important activity. However, in view of the added emphasis given to problem solving and the time required for the assessment of practical work (see below), the introduction of new courses have been accompanied by a significant reduction in content.
- Much greater prominence is given to the assessment of 'conventional' problem-solving skills such as concluding and explaining, generalising and predicting, as well as 'related' skills, for instance selecting, presenting and processing information. As a result, to develop these skills in the classroom, students engage in practical problem solving that is likely to involve designing and planning investigations and evaluating results as well as paper-and-pencil exercises that require students to decode written information about unfamiliar chemistry. Where appropriate, many students use problem-solving approaches to acquire the essential knowledge and understanding.
- In a similar way, the assessment of practical skills has given added importance to selected course experiments, for example preparation of an ester and redox titrations at Higher, 'basic' chemical techniques, for example producing and collecting a precipitate, volumetric titrations at Standard Grade as well as practical investigative work at all levels.
- Theoretical chemical knowledge and understanding is made more relevant by giving prominence to social, economic, environmental and industrial applications, for instance at Standard Grade students cover topics on fossil fuels, acid rain, corrosion, plastics and synthetic fibres and fertilisers while the Higher course, influenced by the Salters Advanced Chemistry Project (University of York, 1988), includes the study of such new materials as Kevlar, poly(ethenol), polyvinyl carbazol and biopolymers as well as covering the general principles of the modern chemical industry.

- 5. Chemistry teachers have always taken a commendable interest in their role in the development of 'core' skills for their students and the SGDP further sensitised this interest. Many teachers give more careful thought to communication skills as well as numerical work and opportunities to use information and communications technology (ICT). In addition, the increasing use of group methods has promoted the development of personal skills.

APPROACHES TO LEARNING AND TEACHING

To cope with the wide variety of student needs and abilities, Chemistry teachers continue to recognise that effective learning and teaching requires judicious use of the complete range of methods. As a result, within the context of 'direct teaching', there continues to be a place for exposition and whole-class question-and-answer sessions, accompanied by memorable demonstrations of illustrative practical work and increasing use is being made of the microcomputer and a data projector for power-point presentations. However, activity sheets generated as part of the course materials by different teams of teachers are now commonly used in many classrooms to support more pupil-centred approaches. Students, usually working in groups, make regular use of textbooks, leaflets and posters, as well as models and video facilities, and schools are encouraged to use microcomputers in a wider variety of ways, for instance to simulate experiments, for self-teaching programmes and to interface with scientific equipment. It says much for the commitment and ingenuity of Chemistry teachers that there is such a wide choice of course materials; indeed Chemcord, RISE and Complete Chemistry are three examples of 'cottage industries', set up by teachers to produce and distribute a range of resources on a commercial basis, which have become familiar features on the Chemistry landscape.

QUALITY OF COURSES AND ATTAINMENT

The recent report, *Standards and Quality in the Sciences* (SEED, 2001) points to well-designed Chemistry courses in the third and fourth years with students thoroughly prepared for the Standard Grade examination. The overall quality of attainment was found to be good or very good in 75% of the departments inspected and 59% of students taking the subject achieved an award at the Credit level with a further 32% achieving an award at the General level in 2001. An equally encouraging picture is painted for fifth and sixth years with the overall quality of attainment judged to be good or very good in 65% of the departments visited and the percentage of students achieving a Band A award and a 'pass' is 17% and 71% respectively for Higher level.

However, in keeping with national and international studies that have highlighted concerns about the quality of students' science education, particularly attainment, the report demonstrates that for 12–14-year-olds, both courses and assessment need to be improved, for instance to take account of students' prior experience at primary school and recent developments in the subject.

CURRENT CHALLENGES

For the chemistry community in Scotland there are perhaps two challenges that stand out – the recruitment of teachers and the provision of modern accommodation and equipment.

With regard to the former issue, the workforce in this country is very well-qualified with approximately 75% of teachers with an honours degree but it is also very experienced with approximately 35% and 15% over the ages of fifty and fifty-five respectively. This means that while at the moment supply meets demand, the steady decline in applications for initial teacher-training strongly suggests a severe shortage in the near future unless effective action is taken.

With regard to the latter issue, the Standards and Quality Report (SEED, 2001) indicates that too many laboratories present a dull and depressing learning environment and the use of out-dated equipment is not uncommon. Indeed, most departments are poorly supplied with modern equipment for ICT, restricting opportunities for interfacing, simulating experiments and the development of subject knowledge, understanding and skills. Recent investments by both the Scottish Executive and local councils have been welcomed but there is still much work to be done if all students are to experience accommodation and resources that provide a safe working environment, designed to meet the needs of modern Chemistry courses.

A LOOK INTO THE CRYSTAL BALL

The innovations that started in Scottish chemistry education in the 1980s continued into the 1990s and it is difficult to foresee other than further change in this new century. Already a significant number of schools have replaced Standard Grade Science with Intermediate 1 Chemistry in combination with other science subjects at the same level. Also, a growing number of schools are beginning to consider Intermediate 2 Chemistry to be more attractive than the present provision as a 'stepping stone' to Higher, particularly for the more able. With the added impact of the ongoing reforms in the first and second years, there can be little doubt that the very future of Standard Grade Chemistry as well as Standard Grade Science would appear to be under threat.

What is perhaps even more surprising is that there is now a debate about the future of the new Higher level course, just two years after its introduction. This has been catalysed by a wide variety of complex and inter-related factors including the steady decline in student numbers in the school population, the clear difficulty of the subject at this level and perhaps most important of all, a near collapse in the number of university students following the discipline. This downward trend, recognised as 'a worldwide problem' by the Royal Society of Chemistry, could undermine the chemistry contribution to the Executive's objective, set out in *A Science Strategy for Scotland* (ELLD, 2001), to 'ensure that enough people study science to a standard which will enable the future needs of the country to be met'. Of course, simple solutions will not be found but it is suggested that to produce a school Chemistry curriculum that meets the needs and challenges of the twenty-first century, consideration of the following would be a useful starting point:

- a further reduction in the content of what students regard as overloaded courses;
- more opportunity for students to research and discuss relevant issues in Chemistry;
- more practical work, especially practical work that is relevant and truly investigative.

The last point may present particular challenges since the recent outcomes of attempts to promote practical work through its assessment have not been notably successful.

However, regardless of the changes that lie ahead, one image in the crystal ball allows a safe prediction to be made – chemistry teachers will surely continue to cope successfully with subject developments and meet the needs of the students in the new millennium.

REFERENCES

ELLD (2001) A Science Strategy for Scotland, Edinburgh: EELLD.
SEED (2000) *Environmental Studies 5–14*, Edinburgh: SEED.
SEED (2001) Standards and Quality in Secondary Schools 1995–2000: The Sciences, Edinburgh: SEED.
SQA (1997) Amended Arrangements in Standard Grade Chemistry, Dalkeith: SQA.
SQA (2000) Arrangements for Higher Still Chemistry Courses, Dalkeith: SQA.

53

Classics Education

Tony Williams

Classics is the object of more hostility and indifference than any other subject in the Scottish curriculum. Behind these two attitudes lies a swathe of ignorance about Classics and its syllabuses currently available to pupils. This chapter should therefore begin with a clear definition of what Classics means.

Classics comprises the three subjects of Latin, Greek, and Classical Studies.

- Classical Studies is a study of the great civilisations of Greece and Rome which represent the cultural ancestry of modern day Western European civilisation. It can include literature, drama, politics, social issues, science and philosophy, Art and architecture and all things that a whole society embraces.
- Latin and Greek are the languages in which were written the great literatures of Rome and Greece. Latin in particular has a massive influence both on English (for whichit is the single largest source of words) and modern European Romance languages, but both languages open the door to a study of the great literatures of the civilisations which are our cultural heritage.

Please note that the account which follows covers Latin and Classical Studies. Greek is a very small (though very precious) subject in the Scottish curriculum and most of what is said about Latin can be taken to apply to Greek also.

THE FIRST CHALLENGES

There were two main challenges which comprehensive schools posed for Classics Education.

The first arose because of the 'common course' rationale of S1 and S2 which dictated that no pupil could study any subject that was not studied by all pupils. It could be stated thus:

> If Classics was to have a place in the first two years of secondary schooling, classicists would need to produce material which avoided the intrinsic difficulties of Latin and was accessible to all.

The second challenge emerged because linguistically able pupils who might have been expected to pursue Latin with success were a much smaller proportion of the cohort than in grammar schools thus rendering class sizes too small. In addition, the most commonly used beginners' Latin course book of the late 1960s, *Approach to Latin* (published 1939!) was based on the faulty assumption that the prior learning of grammar automatically developed the skills of translating and reading. The second challenge could be expressed thus:

> If Classics was to be viable even after the common course, classicists were going to have to produce beginners' course book material in Latin both more accessible to pupils and better designed to promote reading skills.

1970 – THE CHALLENGES MET

The answer to the first challenge, to produce material which was accessible to all pupils in S1 and S2, was so very simple, or so it seems now. If it was hard to envisage pupils of the whole ability range enjoying the languages of Greek and Latin, it was very easy to imagine them caught up in the worlds of Greece and Rome – especially since young children respond so well to stories of the gods, heroes, and monsters of Greek mythology. Thus it was that Classical Studies was born. Just as the main challenge to Classics in S1 and S2 had come in the west of Scotland, so it was in Strathclyde Region that Classical Studies' foundation material was now produced. The main sources of the material were the civilisations of the Minoans and Mycenaeans. This meant that not only could pupils discover the myth of Theseus and the Minotaur and the legend of the Trojan War but they could be introduced to archaeology as well, including the palace of Cnossos on Crete and the Mycenaean sites on mainland Greece and Turkey. Thousands of pupils worked at this material over the years. The first challenge seemed well and truly met.

As for the second challenge, to produce beginners' course book material in Latin more accessible and more relevant, a new course emerged in England at the end of the 1960s that seemed purpose designed to meet the challenge – the Cambridge Latin Course. It was very closely followed both in time and philosophy by its Scottish counterpart – *Ecce Romani*. The writers of the Cambridge Course rejected activities such as learning grammatical tabulations and translating English sentences into Latin as irrelevant to the development of reading skill. In both these courses it was evident that pupils almost immediately had the satisfaction of reading a continuous story in Latin. Grammatical analysis was minimal in Cambridge and not much more than that in *Ecce Romani*. Both courses rejected Roman history in favour of a Roman family as the focus of their continuing storyline. The effect – both north and south of the border – was startling. Latin teachers found they were able to attract and retain more pupils in their classrooms. The second challenge seemed also to be met.

THE PROBLEMS OF THE 1970S

Alas, the very solutions which answered the early challenges themselves proved problematical.

Strathclyde's Classical Studies material comprised a series of information sheets and accompanying worksheets. The latter made it very clear that the whole point of the material was to fill pupils up with facts and then to check that these had been learned. Pupils were asked what a minotaur was, how many Athenians Minos fed to the Minotaur each year, how Ariadne helped Theseus to kill the Minotaur and escape the labyrinth – and so on. Opportunities to use the myth to stimulate imaginative responses ('how do you think

Theseus would feel as he left his old father in Athens for the dangers of Crete?') or arouse intellectual curiosity ('How might the archaeological discoveries at Cnossos suggest that "Theseus and the Minotaur" is more than just a good story?') were nearly always lost.

As for the Cambridge Latin Course and *Ecce Romani*, whilst few people criticised the attractiveness of the material or the storylines, doubts were emerging about the lack of structure in the presentation of language material. In the present writer's view, the new courses had been right to suggest that the reading of Latin should normally come before grammatical comment but wrong to believe that pupils did not require the grammar to be structured at all if they were to read the literature of an inflected language. Even the Scottish course, *Ecce Romani*, which was more explicit about grammatical rules and even occasionally presented a grammatical tabulation after a reading passage, failed to ensure that the bits and pieces of the tabulation occurred sufficiently in the reading passage for the teacher to make the vital connection between grammatical knowledge and reading skill.

Other problems at this time concerned Scottish Examination syllabuses.

- As yet there was no certificate (O Grade) examination in Classical Studies which remained a subject confined to S1 or S2.
- The O Grade examinations in Latin and Greek had been designed on the assumption that pupils would begin study in S1. As has been explained the common course meant that in the maintained sector an S2 or even an S3 start was becoming the norm. As a result the examination was proving too difficult for many pupils. Not surprisingly this was particularly the case with the unseen passage of Latin for translation into English. The effect was very demoralising for pupils and teachers alike.
- Prescribed literature was assessed either by the requirement to translate a block of lines (which some pupils – without the ability to translate – coped with by learning a translation of the whole prescription by heart) or by the requirement to answer factual questions on another block (which suggested that the author had written a mini-encyclopaedia rather than a piece of literature).
- Finally, the last section of the O Grade Latin and Greek papers was a 'Classical Studies' section in which pupils answered questions from a choice of topics such as 'Hadrian's Wall' or a book of Ovid's *Metamorphoses* in translation. Here there were two problems. Firstly the questions were depressingly factual again (e.g. 'What was the width of Hadrian's Wall?'). Secondly, teachers were uncertain about the coverage required in some topics. For instance, they may have spent a lot of time introducing pupils to the design of forts, mile castles, and turrets on Hadrian's Wall only to find that in the examination paper the questions required a knowledge not of the shape of a fort but of the particular troops which manned it.

THE TRIUMPHANT 1980S AND 1990S

In view of the solutions which soon emerged to solve the problems just listed, it does not seem an exaggeration to use the adjective 'triumphant' of the years from 1981.

It was in that year that the first candidates took O Grade Classical Studies. The examination board had finally agreed that an examination in the subject could proceed. Candidates had to answer questions on a whole range of topics but the most important thing about the examination was that questions demanding factual recall ('What law had Antigone broken?') were at long last balanced by questions which demanded some analysis and evaluation by candidates ('What is your view of the arguments which Antigone uses to justify her action?'). There was criticism as well as great praise for the syllabus and examination. Some teachers felt that the style of questions made the examination too difficult for S4 pupils. Unfortunately the examination had to meet the standards of a certificate (O Grade) which had always been geared to the top 30% of pupils academic range. However, O Grade's days were numbered (Classical Studies was one of the last syllabuses to be approved) and Standard Grade was already on the horizon. Any discontent would not last for long.

It was also in 1981 that a first consultative panel for Classics was set up within the Consultative Committee on the Curriculum in Scotland (now the SCCC). It had set out the four main skills developed by the learning of a classical language:

- translation (of Latin into English);
- interpretation (of Latin literature);
- investigation (into the Roman world); and
- language awareness (insight into English and modern Romance languages on all of which Latin was the chief influence).

The working party devising the Standard Grade Latin syllabus adopted the first three of these as its main elements, correctly regarding the fourth as an excellent by-product of the learning of Latin. Because of this and the fact that it was offered at Foundation, General, and Credit levels (and so to a far wider academic range of pupil than ever before) the following solutions to previous problems were almost automatic:

- Translation would be assessed by the requirement to turn an unseen passage of Latin into English. The passage would be rigorously controlled so as to be translatable by pupils after only two years of Latin. Passages in English would cue pupils into the context, and a Standard Grade vocabulary was produced to inform teachers and pupils about the words to be known.
- Interpretation skills would require pupils not only to understand what a writer was saying but to appreciate how he was saying it ('Why does Catullus use the words *lux* (light) and *nox* (darkness) to refer to life and death in poem V?') and to give their own opinions on the result. Prescribed literature was being treated as literature for the very first time and those privileged to mark papers could see how much pupils were enjoying it.
- Investigation skills were defined not simply as gaining knowledge of the Roman world but as evaluating evidence, making comparisons with the modern world, and presenting results. Since it was felt that an examination could not easily assess such things, the natural decision was to require an investigation or report from pupils produced as a piece of their own research under teacher supervision. Immediately pupils could choose a topic that they found interesting and teachers no longer had to worry about predicting the questions that would be asked in an examination room. It is hard to overestimate the enthusiasm created by this element alone.

Standard Grade Classical Studies was to follow and this preserved the balance between knowledge and evaluation first demonstrated by the O Grade exam but now came with the advantage that it was available at Foundation and General as well as Credit levels – in fact to pupils of the whole ability range.

Needless to say, the Standard Grade skills or elements of Latin, Greek and Classical Studies were continued into Revised Higher and CSYS syllabuses – thus ensuring progression.

In 1991, the Latin 5–14 report was issued, setting out the standards to be achieved by pupils in the first two years of secondary schooling. Not surprisingly the working group returned to the very elements of Latin identified by the consultative panel of ten years earlier. However, since it was right that interpretation as well as translation should be developed even on the synthetic Latin young pupils were reading, these two elements were brought together for this age group. And since many of these pupils would end their study of Latin before reaching real literature, the knowledge about language element was elevated to a main aim. Thus the three outcomes were:

- translating / interpreting texts;
- knowledge about language;
- the Roman world.

The 1990s proved to be the decade in which Classical Studies made its greatest strides. As a school subject it was included in the Social Subjects mode of the Scottish curriculum. This means that it can be taken by pupils as part of their core curriculum up to S4 (even though the number of pupils following the course is restricted by the fact that the subject was a relative latecomer into the crowded S3/S4 curriculum). In the Higher Still development programme Classical Studies was developed in its own right (and quite separately from Classical Languages) with its own national development officer and specialist group. In particular, Higher Classical Studies in which pupils study great classical plays such as *Medea* and *Antigone* and can gain special insights into important issues such as the rights and responsibilities of citizens in a democracy or the place of women in society, has gained increased popularity with the numbers of pupils exceeding those who take Standard Grade. In the Universities of St Andrews, Edinburgh and Glasgow it is now possible to embark on degrees in Classical Studies as well as Classical Languages. The next logical step – that it should become a recognised subject for teacher training in Scotland (as has been the case for many years elsewhere) – took place in 1999 with the announcement that, as for other 'new' subjects in Higher Still, appropriate teachers should be produced. Since then, fifteen out of twenty-one Classics teachers qualifying at Jordanhill Campus have been trained in Classical Studies.

As for Classical Languages, the Secretary of State – in a circular of 22 January 1988 – had made it possible in appropriate circumstances for a classical language to replace a modern European language as the foreign language to be studied by pupils up to S4. Another SOED (now SEED) document (Circular 1178) issued in July 1988 included the following statement:

> The Classical Languages . . . represent an important part of our heritage and provide a valuable educative experience. It is right that opportunities for their study should continue to be available and encouraged. I shall therefore be asking education authorities to ensure that *some schools in each area* [italics added] continue to offer these languages.

CONCLUSION

The main problem is that – whatever the expressed wishes of the government as outlined above – it is not the case that some schools continue to offer classical subjects in each area of Scotland. There are one or two regions where outwith the independent sector Classics is not offered at all. In others it continues in only a small number of schools.

The reason for this stark contrast with the government's own statements is the hostility and indifference mentioned at the start of this chapter. It seems that just a single individual – be it a headteacher or someone of influence in a local authority – can on personal whim just remove the subject from school curricula. This means that whole cohorts of pupils in widespread areas of Scotland do not have the opportunity even to decline to opt for the subject – it does not appear on their menu of choices at all. At the same time, there is clear evidence that where classical subjects are still offered to pupils in schools they don't simply continue to exist but are seized upon by very enthusiastic pupils. Can it really continue to be dismissed as naivety (economic or otherwise) when people (the present writer included) complain that the government simply looks on (or looks away?) when there is so evident an example of inequality of opportunity throughout the land?

Of course there is always the possibility of a pendulum swing. As recently as 4 April of this year, *The Scotsman* carried a report on the large number of applicants for Classics courses in Scottish universities starting in 2002–3. No doubt for some of these students absence has made the heart grow very fond! A slow but sure recovery seems to be taking place south of the border where until only a few years ago the position of the subject was far weaker than in Scotland. As for continental Europe, it seems to appreciate fully classical subjects and what they can do for the linguistic and cultural heritage of children. Classics is going from strength to strength there. It is to be hoped that urgent action can be taken soon in Scotland. For it is not Classics which is the loser but the educational experience and enrichment of all Scottish pupils.

REFERENCES

Cambridge School Classics project (1970, 1982, 1990) Cambridge Latin course, Cambridge: Cambridge University Press.

Consultative Panel on Classics (1982) *The Needs for Development in Classics in the Secondary School* (A report to the Committee on Secondary Education), Dundee: CCC.

Scottish Classics Group (1971, 1982) *Ecce Romani*, Edinburgh: Oliver and Boyd.

SOEID (1992) *Latin 5–14*, Edinburgh: HMSO.

SQA (1997/8) *Higher Still arrangements for Classical Languages and Classical Studies*, Dundee, SCCC.

SQA (1986–93) *Revised Arrangements in Latin, Greek and Classical Studies at Standard Grade*, Dalkeith / Glasgow: SQA

SQA (1988–94) *Revised Arrangements in Latin, Greek and Classical Studies at Higher Grade*, Dalkeith / Glasgow: SQA

54

Computing and Information Systems

Tom Conlon

Scottish secondary schools began to take computing seriously during the second half of the 1980s. The Scottish Examination Board introduced Computing Studies courses at Standard Grade (1986), Higher Grade (1989) and CSYS (1993) levels. Guidelines for learning in IT for the 5–14 stages were incorporated within the 1993 documentation for Environmental Studies. In 2000, the Higher Still programme split the subject into two course families named 'Computing' and 'Information Systems'. Also in that year was published a vastly revised and entirely separate set of guidelines for 5–14 IT (now rebadged as 'ICT').

Truly, the pace of curricular change for Computing teachers has seemed as dramatic as the pace of change of the technology itself.

S1/S2

The year 2000 guidelines for the 5–14 stages offer 'advice to assist teachers to develop ICT capability fully in young people and to realise the potential of ICT as a teaching and learning tool' (LTS, 2000). The advice takes the form of a highly elaborate framework that is claimed to promote 'the integration of ICT into existing classroom practice'. At its centre are 102 attainment targets categorised into seven strands of activity and six levels (A–F) of development. For level E – expected to be attainable by some pupils in P7–S1, and by most in S2 – seventeen targets are specified, a representative sample being as follows:

- interpret simple computer specifications such as speed and memory;
- understand the costs of accessing network services;
- create a multimedia presentation or web pages working independently;
- analyse problems, implement and evaluate solutions using database and spreadsheet;
- use a computer to collect and process data from the environment.

Such targets are described as being based on existing good practice, although critics have attacked them variously as over-prescriptive, unrealistic and of dubious value. What is clear is that schools are presented with a strategic problem – to what extent should 5–14 IT be addressed by discrete IT courses at the S1/S2 stages, as opposed to approaches based on cross-curricular permeation? Although the guidelines contain several attractive examples that point towards the latter, the very existence of all those targets for IT, disembodied from mainstream curriculum contexts, seems rather likely to encourage the former. This is especially the case in secondary schools where interdisciplinary co-operation is uncommon.

But discrete IT courses are no panacea. Not only will they have to justify themselves against the goal of 'integration' but also they will face difficulty in matching the needs of learners whose prior experiences in IT may be extremely diverse.

STANDARD GRADE

Standard Grade Computing Studies (SGCS) consists of three main topics – computer applications (sixty hours), computer programming (forty hours) and computer systems (twenty hours) – together with a project. The study of computer applications is based on word processor, spreadsheet, database and other generic software types, typically exemplified by packages such as Apple Works or Microsoft Office. For programming, such languages as BASIC or the once compulsory COMAL are sometimes used but authoring systems such as Hyperstudio are permissible alternatives and perhaps more widely adopted. The study of computer systems introduces fundamental concepts concerned with the role of system software, operating systems and hardware.

Measured by pupil numbers, SGCS has been a considerable success. In 2001 its examination was taken by over 21,000 candidates or around 35% of the year group. This makes computing the eighth most popular Standard Grade, a little behind Biology, History and Geography but ahead of Physics and Art. SGCS easily surpasses all other 'technology mode' subjects such as Craft and Design. It is markedly more popular than its nearest counterpart in England, the GCSE in IT, which was taken by 16% of the year group in 2000.

Two problems should be mentioned. The first is that SGCS suffers from a gender skew in which boys outnumber girls by almost two to one. The skew actually becomes more

Figure 54.1: Percentages of female Computing pupils (2001)

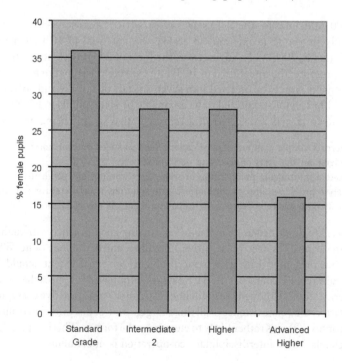

pronounced in subsequent courses, as shown by Figure 54.1 which reflects entries for 2001 in Computing. (The situation in Information Systems, for which 31% of Higher candidates were female, is hardly any better.) Yet those females who did undertake SGCS performed well – 46% of them gained Credit awards compared to 42% of males.

The second problem is that the computer applications topic which forms the backbone of SGCS looks increasingly dubious. Whether pupils realise it or not, much of its content duplicates work that is earmarked for the 5–14 stages. Of course, there is plenty of scope to expand the programming and systems topics but whether this could be done whilst maintaining the broad appeal of the course is uncertain. At present, programming is regarded by teachers as difficult and where there is a choice (for example, to select programming-based projects), SGCS pupils are commonly steered in other directions.

HIGHER STILL

Figure 54.2 outlines the Higher Still courses (SQA, 1999) with which Computing departments have been most preoccupied. Except where shown, units are of forty hours duration.

Figure 54.2: Outline of Higher Still courses

	Computing			Information Systems		
	Int 2	Higher	Adv Higher	Int 2	Higher	Adv Higher
Recommended entry requirement	Standard Grade (General level) or Int 1 Computing	Standard Grade (Credit level) or Int 2 Computing	Higher Computing	Standard Grade (General level) Computing Studies or Int 1 Computing	Standard Grade (Credit level) Computing Studies or Int 2 Info Sys	Higher Info Sys
Mandatory units	Computer Systems Software Development Computing Project	Computer Systems Software Development	Software Development (20 hours) Computing Project (60 hours)	Computer Application Software (Int 2) Database Systems (Int 2)	Database Systems (H) Info Org (H)	Database Systems (AH) 20 hours Information Systems Project (AH) 60 hours
Optional units	N/A	Artificial Intelligence Computer Programming Computer Networking Multimedia Technology	Artificial Intelligence Computer Systems Data Communications	Applications of IT in Society (Int 2) Multimedia (Int 2) The Internet (Int 2)	Computer Application Software (H) Expert Systems (H) Hypermedia (H)	Multimedia (AH) Natural Language Processing (AH) Systems Analysis and Design (AH)
Unit assessment	11 hours	10 hours 45 minutes	20 hours	6 hours 45 minutes	14 hours 30 minutes	18 hours 40 minutes
Examination	1 hour 30 minutes	2 hours 30 minutes	2 hours 30 minutes	1 hour 30 minutes	2 hours 30 minutes	2 hours 30 minutes examination

   In all subjects, a central aim of Higher Still was to provide a set of courses suited to the needs of a broad range of learners. Figure 54.3 shows that the new Intermediate 2 courses in Computing and Information Systems were taken by more than 5,000 pupils in the 2001 session. Also, compared to 1999 there was a large increase in the numbers taking a course at Higher level. However, a proper comparison must acknowledge that schools in 1999 additionally submitted more than 30,000 entries for IT-based stand-alone modules, a category that practically disappeared in 2001. When these are taken into account, and allowing for the modest numbers of pupils who in 2001 took courses at Intermediate 1 level, the total amount of certification pre- and post- Higher Still looks quite similar. The change arguably amounts to the absorption of many pupils, who formerly would have taken stand-alone modules, into Intermediate and Higher courses. Furthermore, none of the new courses comes close to the popularity of some of the former IT modules – for example Word Processing 1, which attracted 10,540 school candidates in 1998.

Figure 54.3:   Candidate numbers for 1999 (pre-Higher Still) and 2001 (post-Higher Still)

| | 1999 | | 2001 | | | |
	Higher	CSYS	Int 2	Higher	Adv Higher	CSYS (final diet)
Computing	4,873	303	1,836	4,604	105	184
Information Systems	N/A	N/A	3,284	2,512	51	N/A
Total	4,873	303	5,120	7,116	156	184

   The Higher Still development for this subject area was particularly fraught and some of the main points of contention can be mentioned here. First, critics argued that the division of the subject into separate Computing and Information Systems streams had no convincing rationale. Although curricular diversity was welcome, it would be better implemented by a unified, flexible course design that offered a wide variety of optional units under a common title (probably Computing). Second, there was disagreement about the extent to which the proposed framework enabled progression and coherence. Critics argued that for progression, each topic should have a representative unit at each level. For coherence, each unit should reflect concepts of programming and systems since these topics constitute the foundations of the subject. Third, the framework was accused of failing to make a sufficiently sharp distinction between the roles of 'tool-user' and 'tool-designer'. As IT tool use becomes ubiquitous, the argument ran, courses based on mere operational skills will become redundant. Future-oriented computing courses should therefore situate learners firmly in the role of tool designers (Bird et al., 1996).
   But it was the issue of assessment that caused most dispute. Computing and Information Systems developers tended to pack units excessively with content. This problem was compounded by an insistence upon explicit and mainly separate assessments for every outcome, performance criterion and range statement of each unit. The result, as shown by the time estimates (which are the SQA's own) in the two final rows of Figure 54.2, was courses that carried an astounding burden of assessment. This burden was later admitted to be far greater than that required by other subjects (SQA, 2001).

TEACHING AND LEARNING

The literature on teaching and learning in Computing Studies in Scotland is threadbare. Academics and researchers have published very little. The school inspectors have produced two reports (SOED, 1993 and Scottish Executive, 2001). The older of these is generally reassuring but bland (for example: 'Pupils are generally well motivated', 'Staff and pupils are punctual and hardworking'). The newer report claims to be based on inspections of forty-six computing departments but such a wealth of observation has produced a document that is surprisingly thin (thirty pages of large type, widely spaced).

In the 2001 report, inspectors rate the quality of teaching as very good in 10% of departments, good in 65% and 'had important weaknesses' in 25%. Weaknesses were especially evident at the S1/S2 stages where only 50% of departments were regarded as meeting pupils' needs well or very well. The problems included failure to take account of pupils' prior experience in primary school; lack of challenge for abler pupils; lack of pace in teaching and learning 'due to insufficient direct teaching and an over-dependence on undemanding worksheets'; and variable quality of support for less able pupils. Although almost all departments had enough computer systems, these were mostly near the end of their useful life. The inspectors recommend that schools should provide more up-to-date computers and more spacious accommodation.

COMPUTING TEACHERS

Although the problem seems less severe in Scotland than in England, the development of Computing has certainly been affected by a shortage of qualified teachers. The PGCE programmes that represent the main entry route into Scottish secondary teaching have typically had far less competition for places in this subject than for subjects such as Biology and History. Although some excellent applicants have been recruited, there has been concern about overall quality. The pioneering teachers who established computing in the 1980s were exceptional in vision and drive and they will be hard to replace.

It has to be said that Computing teachers have seldom managed to develop an effective collective voice. Where other subjects have professional associations that can articulate specialist concerns and interests, Computing has none. Lacking their own conferences, publications, and recognised spokespersons, Computing teachers have sometimes given the impression of being lightweight as a professional group. One instance of this was the ease with which the school inspectors and others were able to brush aside teachers' expressions of doubt during the Higher Still development.

FUTURE PROSPECTS

Compared to other countries, Scotland's investment in Computing as a school subject has been heavy. At its best the subject has provided a marvellous new vehicle for the development of widely respected skills in problem solving, communication and design. However, the volatility of the technological base and the near-permanent state of curriculum upheaval has at times threatened to exhaust the resources of schools and extinguish the enthusiasm of teachers.

It will be clear even from this brief account of the subject's development that no respite from change is likely. In the S1/S2 stages, the new ICT guidelines present a formidable challenge regardless of whether the teaching approach adopted is one of discrete courses, permeation, or some combination of the two. At Standard Grade, the subject continues to attract huge numbers to an applications-based course but whether this can – or should – be sustained as the applications become ubiquitous is doubtful. A move towards a course philosophy that situates learners as 'tool designers' rather than 'tool users' could demarcate the subject's distinctive content but, unless expertly handled, the result might be a meltdown in pupil numbers.

As for the Higher Still courses, these are already under full-scale review at the time of writing and changes to their assessment arrangements are announced almost on a weekly basis. As any software engineer will explain, programmes that are badly designed invariably need lengthy debugging thereafter. In the long run, it makes more sense to build soundly from the start.

REFERENCES

Bird, D., Conlon, T. and Swanson, S. (1996) Computing and Information Technology in Higher Still: Let's get it right, *Scottish Educational Review*, 28 (1), 3–15.

LTS (2000) *Information and Communications Technology: 5–14 National Guidelines*, Dundee: LTS.

Scottish Executive (2001) *Standards and Quality in Secondary Schools: Computing 1995–2001*, Edinburgh: The Stationery Office.

SOED (1993) *Teaching and Learning in Computing Studies*, Edinburgh: SOED.

SQA (1999) *Computing Advanced Higher, Computing Higher, Computing Intermediate 2, Information Systems Advanced Higher, Information Systems Higher, Information Systems Intermediate 2*, Dalkeith: SQA.

SQA (2001) *National Qualifications Review Report: Computing* and *National Qualifications Review Report: Information Systems*, Dalkeith: SQA.

55

Drama Education

Paul Dougall

DEVELOPMENT AND AIMS

Drama as a teaching discipline is influenced by two competing ideologies:

- the utilisation of drama method to develop interpersonal and social skill;
- the development of aesthetic understanding as mediated through theatrical performance.

The attempt to encompass both ideologies in a coherent and progressive curriculum is discussed in this chapter.

Drama as a specialist teaching discipline in Scottish secondary schools was introduced in the late 1950s when the whole philosophy and practice of secondary teaching and learning was entering a period of radical review and revision. The impulse to create a curriculum which would be more pupil centred than previously produced the necessity to seek ways in which the nurturing of the pupils' social and emotional development became a necessary complement to the development of intellectual skills.

The earliest proponents of Drama in the curriculum such as Way (*Development through Drama*, Harlow: Longman, 1967) defined the essential purpose as the development of the whole person, which would:

- encourage pupils to explore the variety of human emotions;
- assist pupils to gain confidence in their own abilities, particularly to communicate verbally and non-verbally;
- develop in pupils the capacity to work together to solve human and practical problems;
- permit pupils to explore the differences between right and wrong in simple moral dilemmas posed through Drama.

Thus, Drama can be seen as being in the vanguard of a progressive ideology which sought to encourage pupils to negotiate possibilities actively with their peers and their teachers. One definition of the central intention of Drama in the curriculum is the development of personal competence and social awareness in pupils. Having established the essential principles, it became necessary in Drama, as in other subjects which shared the same progressive impulse, to develop a methodology.

Throughout the 1960s and 1970s teachers of Drama in secondary schools sought to sustain the principles of active negotiated learning while accommodating to the need to construct a curriculum which could define the particular skills that would be developed through activity in the Drama room. One particular problem confronting the teacher was offering evidence that the Drama process had verifiable learning outcomes. The nature of the Drama process results in important developmental activity happening in the Drama room but the outcome remains ephemeral. The formative nature of teaching and learning in Drama has created a measure of ideological conflict among specialist teachers of the subject.

In the initial development of Drama methodology the necessity to sustain the purity of the driving principles resulted in the subject remaining on the margins of the school system. The formative developmental process became associated with those pupils who would not be able to cope with the academic curriculum and thus Drama became, to a degree, colonised as a teaching methodology which had a social value but lacked the intellectual dimensions of other more traditional subjects. Those additional dimensions were clearly cited in the assessment practices of the National Certificate programmes in which Drama as a subject was excluded. Advantageously, even the most traditional of secondary subjects by the 1970s were actively seeking ways to reflect pupil centred activity in their teaching and learning patterns. The challenge to Drama teachers was to refine the formative teaching programme to incorporate the more flexible summative assessment instruments that were being incorporated into the national examination systems. By accepting this challenge Drama has in the 1990s moved from the periphery to a more central position within the school system. The opportunity afforded to pupils of all ability ranges to undertake a variety of certificate awards in Drama has greatly enhanced the status of the subject.

Conversely, many of the principles and methodological practices incorporated into the teaching methods of other disciplines have been derived from the principles and practices that define Drama methodology, especially its exploratory, experiential approach to learning. Drama has made a signal contribution to teaching methodology across subject boundaries and has, in return, developed a more pragmatic sense that a curriculum must be taught and not merely caught (see Heathcoate and Bolton, 1995). The tension between ideological purity and pragmatic necessity informs the ongoing dialogue in Drama as in other subjects.

The opportunity for the pupil to experience the Drama process has increasingly been understood in terms of the necessity for discrete skills to be defined, developed and evaluated. The emotional shock to many Drama teachers, when they understood that to be more firmly rooted within the secondary sector required of them a comprehensive review of the principles and practices that were driving what they were doing in their classrooms, was palpable. It was realised that a key aspect of the process of teaching and learning was to differentiate between pupils within defined frames of reference, and not merely accommodate to the needs of all pupils as a group.

METHODOLOGY

Since all teaching and learning operates within finite space, time and finance, the teacher of any subject designing a curriculum must address the following questions: who does what? with whom? where? when? why and for how long?

While Drama existed on the margins of National Certificate assessment the curriculum framework was, as noted above, formative in nature, and located within a number of exploratory opportunities which became defined as the Drama process.

At this time limited attention was placed on the aesthetics of Theatre performance since that would entail critical commentary and an interpretation of texts. Essentially, the study of Theatre as a performance discipline was regarded as extraneous to the needs of the particular pupils undertaking Drama programmes. By involving more pupils, the subject has had to incorporate the study of Theatre as an aesthetic discipline as a complement to the study of the Drama process.

The key thing to note about the distinction between Drama process and Theatre process is that although they might share similar vocabularies their purposes are actually quite different. In the Drama process, the group's acting out the improvisation is a sharing of emotional dynamics of the dilemma which becomes the point of focus for the pupils undertaking the task. The evaluation of the activity resides in the interplay of the engagement and exploration by the pupils. Have they been supportive of each other in the task; have they addressed the task demand appropriately? Essentially, the process of exploration is more important than the performed statement.

In contrast, when pupils engage in developing the skills that pertain to theatrical representation, the evaluation relates to the pupil's capacity to represent the appropriate stylistic feature of movement, voice, characterisation in interpreting the part being acted.

STAGE BY STAGE

In S1 and S2 the primary aim is to introduce pupils to the Drama process through improvised activity. As noted above, the Drama form is utilised to mediate the social or moral theme being explored.

The pupils explore the concept of dramatic tension through role play activity. Again it should be stressed that role play is not an end in itself but a means of exploring different attitudes and behaviours. The participants develop an imaginary situation either as self or as another person in order to explore behaviours and values in a safe and constructive environment. The development of role play activity aligns the intention to assist the pupil to explore the social and imaginative world from a number of perspectives with the developing capacity to take on and sustain a number of roles using appropriate language and movement. Integrated with the role play activity, there are discrete lessons which focus on developing skills in voice, speech and movement which will assist the pupil to work more confidently in the different registers which inform the role play activity; and create the basis of technique which will be necessary in the later years when the focus becomes the interpretation of dramatic text.

By the end of S2 pupils should be able to develop convincing roles in specific situations; create and take part in improvised scenes in order to explore particular issues which could have practical, social or moral dimensions; and carry out dramatic intentions with a clear but unforced control over movement and voice.

By the S3/S4 stage there is the further consolidation of the basic skills in voice and movement and a more formalised and sophisticated structure to the improvised activity. Groups of pupils are given more autonomy over the constructions of the dramatic narrative they develop through working on characterisation, which is the investigation and portrayal in depth of a specific role.

Characterisation is the bridge between the role play activity of S1/S2 and the acting skills necessary in S5/S6. The movement from Drama form to Theatre form is articulated through developing pupil skills in characterisation (Neelands, 1990). In addition, the improvisatory work on characterisation is complemented by the interpretational study of text in order to strike a balance between the construction of a more sophisticated group improvisation and the deconstruction of theatre texts; and finally theatre performances.

The assessment of both modes of activity informs the Standard Grade Certificate which incorporates the three dimensions of: creating, presenting, knowledge and understanding.

By the end of S4 the impetus towards interpersonal development has merged with an understanding of the essential conventions of theatrical representation. The pupil will, it is hoped, have enhanced his/her interpersonal skills and performance skills. In summary, the pupils should be able to appreciate dramatic ambiguity (i.e. when language and action work in opposition), and call on a range of subtle skills in voice, posture, movement and gesture in order to sustain, and develop, dramatic action.

The bridge between the interpersonal and the performance is difficult for some pupils and philosophically problematic for some teachers. There is on-going debate between those who feel that training in theatrical representation (i.e. acting) should begin at an earlier stage while others claim that the ideological purpose of working in the drama form is corrupted by the sudden switch to developing theatre performance skills (Hornbrook, 1989).

By S5/S6 the focus is on Theatre and the development of critical skills in relation to specified texts. This theoretical approach is complemented with practical workshop activity which seeks to exemplify the key stylistic features of performance skills directed to designated audiences, and theatre skills which monitor the pupil's ability in theatre arts and technology. Role play has become acting; improvisation has become investigative drama towards a performance; and exploration has become critical commentary and literary analysis.

The National Qualifications framework, as moderated by the Scottish Qualifications Authority, has provoked a review of the locus and focus of Standard Grade at S4; by seeking to recast the S5/S6 curriculum in a way which will articulate more coherently with post-school provision.

The development of a range of differentiated programmes customised to the perceived needs and aspirations of the S5/S6 cohort articulates two points of bias within the Drama curriculum being progressed. For some pupils in the cohort (i.e. those undertaking the Access; Intermediate 1 and Intermediate 2 programmes) the bias will be towards consolidating drama and theatre production skills; while for other pupils in the cohort (i.e. those undertaking Higher and Advanced Higher programmes) the bias will be towards critical analysis and theories of performance.

This pluralism of provision, notwithstanding its intention to forge essential linkages and clearer points of articulation with a range of post-school providers, has, at the time of writing, created as yet unresolved points of tension between Drama teachers and the increasingly prescriptive Scottish Qualifications Authority in relation to matters of ideology, pedagogy and human and financial resources.

In concert with other disciplines there has been concern expressed regarding the balance between internal and external moderation within the new framework; and distress regarding the ways in which established points of synergy between the practical and critical aesthetics of Drama established in the traditional Higher have been diffused through separated modes of provision.

Drama teachers, over the past fifty years, have shown themselves to be both imaginative and pragmatic in relation to designing relevant programmes and efficacious assessment frameworks. The subject has influenced, and continues to influence, progressive pedagogy by establishing itself in the vanguard of innovation at the teaching/learning interface (Taylor (ed.), 1996).

Notwithstanding the present local difficulties alluded to above the grounded precepts of secondary school Drama will find an appropriate accommodation with required practices to the benefit of pupils passing through the Drama programmes. The future holds for Drama in Scottish schools more challenges than fears.

REFERENCES

Heathcote D. and Bolton G. (1995) *Drama for Learning: Dorothy Heathcote's Mantle of the Expert Approach to Education*, Portsmouth: Heinemann.

Hornbrook D. (1989) *Education and Dramatic Art*, Oxford: Blackwell.

Neelands, J. (1990) *Structuring Drama Work*, Cambridge: Cambridge University Press.

O'Neill, C. (1995) *Drama Worlds: A Framework for Process Drama*, Portsmouth: Heinemann.

SCCC/SFEU (1997) *Subject Guide: Drama* Edinburgh: SCCC.

Taylor, P. (1996) (ed.) *Researching Drama and Arts Education, Paradigms and Possibilities*, London: Falmer Press.

56

English Language Education

James McGonigal

HOW SECONDARY TEACHERS APPROACH ENGLISH TEACHING: PHILOSOPHIES AND PRACTICE

The teaching of English occupies a complex position in culture and curriculum. In Scotland as in England, English teaching seemed to draw controversy to itself in the 1990s during a period of sustained reshaping of what should be taught and assessed. Such reshaping benefits from a broadly accepted sense of structure and direction, and perhaps the controversy around English arose partly from the multiple or even contradictory nature of the subject's purposes in secondary schools.

Is English mainly to be concerned with developing pupils' confidence and authenticity in written and spoken expression, for example, or with meeting their presumed adult needs within a global market's demand for an increasingly literate workforce? What of the role of English as school service provider of literacy skills for other curricular areas; or as bearer of traditional literary and cultural values enshrined in key texts; or even as deconstructive questioner of that culture, using a wider range of media and minority texts alongside the canon of great literature in order to help the next generation 'read' more acutely the society that they inherit? Views on exactly what the balance and blend of such purposes should be can vary quite widely across the present cohort of teachers of English (as well as among parents, of course, and teachers of other subjects). In any case, English teaching has proved not to be easily or passively conformable to the modular framework preferred in the design of Higher Still arrangements, towards which all secondary teaching now tends.

The resulting sense of impasse, delay, revision and frustration was felt the more keenly in many schools where teachers of English were already beginning to respond to other initiatives relevant to young people's learning in the modern world: developing, for example, classroom techniques to improve motivation and concentration, particularly among boys; more specific use of targets and assessment in learning; and new approaches to the teaching of reading and writing, including electronic literacy.

In the midst of such educational change, of course, the basic work of teaching must go on, and Scottish teachers of English do share a rationale that would be broadly recognisable to their counterparts elsewhere. Briefly, English teachers endeavour to 'bring texts to life' by creating an active engagement between their pupils' growing minds and hearts, on the one hand, and the meanings implied in the words or images of the text in question, on the other.

Choice of text and also teacher performance in enactment and interactive exploration are crucial to effective learning here.

But English teachers must also 'bring life to texts', by structuring active and social responses to what is read or heard: pupils' first reactions are refined through being expressed in group or whole-class discussion; a more reasoned or reflective individual response then follows, frequently in writing, which may itself become the occasion for further discussion, or redrafting, or publication. Such writing can take a variety of forms, often literary or personal, less frequently transactional or functional. Ideally, both formative and summative assessment are natural elements in this dialogic process, as learners develop towards more confident self-awareness and control in language.

Such broad similarity of approaches to English teaching, however, can mask quite deep differences between teaching in Scotland and elsewhere. The very term 'English Language' is problematic, where Scottish English, Scots Language and, in some areas, Gaelic are spoken in the local community, a linguistic mix enriched by ethnic minority languages such as Urdu or Punjabi. Such dialects and languages are not merely spoken alongside Standard Scottish English in the context of group work, but also read or written about. Classroom texts by Scottish authors often include linguistic and cultural features which would be misunderstood in England, and are selected for study precisely because they do provide opportunities for insight into Scottish experience, urban and rural, past and contemporary. Performances or workshops by local writers and storytellers can also enhance Scottish elements of the secondary curriculum in English.

Yet deriving perhaps from eighteenth-century Scottish rhetorical study of English belles-lettres, there has also remained in Scotland a desire to support competence in Standard English as much as personal or local identity, and to enable young people to move beyond their dialectal boundaries through a traditional focus on the skills needed for academic work, and subsequent educational or economic advancement.

METHODS AND ASSESSMENT S1–S6

The elder generation of Scottish teachers educated in the 1950s or 1960s can still recall the hierarchical, academic lines on which English was organised, with the study of canonical texts of (chiefly) English literature combined with model compositions for imitation and decontextualised grammatical exercises for completion. Methods and assessment in the 1970s and early 1980s developed in reaction to such rigidities, and aimed to right the balance between directive teaching and active learning.

Accordingly, most S1–S2 classes in English came to be taught in mixed-ability sets of about thirty, often sub-divided into friendship or ability groups for discussion activities. During their three to four English lessons per week (about 200 minutes in total) pupils often experience a two-stage lesson, with initial teacher recapitulation or context-setting leading to individual or group follow-up on a focused task or diversified project. Group talk can also be used quickly at the start, to involve pupils in the day's agenda by eliciting initial reactions to the topic, which the rest of the lesson will unpack or refine. Over the last several years, there has been some experimentation with setting or broad-banding arrangements, based on early assessment of pupils' attainment in national testing, or with the use of differentiated texts or groupings to try to ensure a continuum of development and challenge in English.

Contexts for both talk and writing are most frequently created from a literary text appropriate to the pupils' level of maturity, with subsequent discussion arising from its conflicts and characters. Such texts are mainly by twentieth-century authors, although often set in a recreated past or imagined future. (Recent HMI reminders note the range of older classic texts, including Scottish texts, being neglected in the process.) Quite often a social or personal issue, such as fears and conflicts, is explored thematically, combining a variety of factual or autobiographical texts and media resources with literary genres to explore its different facets. Teaching and learning are often structured in month-long units of work, developed by departmental or local authority staff, with photocopiable worksheets linked to a variety of language purposes, often supplemented by publishers' anthologies of texts and activities, sometimes created for the Scottish context.

Within such mixed-ability or broad-banded English classes, the teacher's role in making texts and tasks accessible is vital. Differentiation may occur simply through accepting variation in the response of individuals to the same task; or by the creation of a hierarchy of tasks for different groups; or by additional texts or assignments to be tackled in extension work; or by the level of support offered through simplified worksheets, word-processing, or increased teacher contact, including co-operative teaching by learning support staff in the classroom. A Scottish study of differentiation (Simpson, M. and Ure, J., *What's the Difference? A Study of Differentiation in Scottish Secondary Schools*, Aberdeen: Northern College, 1993) found positive pupil reaction to the kinds of whole-class interactive support featuring in English classrooms more frequently than in the tightly differentiated task-sheets of more 'linear' scientific subjects. Nevertheless, group approaches to the reading of different novels, graded in terms of difficulty but clustered around common themes, have allowed some teachers recently to stretch more able readers while supporting the inclusion of the less able.

Evidence of attainment in S1–S2, increasingly gathered into folios reflecting a range of the language purposes and skills codified in the *English Language National Guidelines 5–14* (1991), is used to set pupils into S3–S4 classes aimed broadly at Foundation/General or General/Credit levels in the Standard Grade examination. Differences between these sets now become more evident in the depth and complexity of texts studied, and the techniques of close reading taught, which will include literal, inferential, stylistic and evaluative understanding at varying levels, as well as reasoning skills. Assessment of talk, both solo to an audience and within group discussion, will count towards the final grade along with reading and writing, so more opportunities for practice are given, sometimes using video tapes of pupil performance to help clarify skills and also the grade-related criteria being applied.

Much pupil (and teacher!) effort in S4 goes into the drafting and redrafting of a Folio for external assessment, which contains both discursive/informational and imaginative/personal writing together with three extended responses to literary or media work in different genres. This folio, presented in term two, is internally and externally assessed, and combined in term three with external examinations in Writing and Close Reading, and the internal assessment of talk, to give a final award. The past ten years have seen a steady rise in attainment in this examination, which is achieved at some level by about 95% of the complete cohort of secondary pupils, including some in special schools and secure units.

Formerly, a Credit award in Standard Grade English was followed by a one-year Higher English course, and a General or Foundation grade by a two-year course, which combined SCOTVEC modules in Communication and Literature in S5, in preparation for a possible Higher English in S6. The ungainliness of this twin-track 'system', which had developed gradually in response to increasing school rolls post-16, and recognition of the motivational benefits for less academic students of shorter, separately assessable modules, led to Higher Still developments towards a more unified system with a staged modular approach, ranging from Access courses for those with learning difficulties, through two Intermediate stages (corresponding broadly to Standard Grade English General and Credit levels), to Higher English and Communication and then Advanced Higher (replacing the Certificate of Sixth Year Studies for the 6% or so specialising in English beyond Higher). This combined National Qualifications system was also expected to facilitate progression of students between school and various further education courses involving communication skills.

During the Higher Still staff development programme for English and Communication, however, real ideological divisions appeared between the vocationally oriented and skills-based modular approach suited to FE courses, and the more literary emphasis valued by school teachers of Higher English, where depth and complexity of texts and critical analysis have been central. When Higher English had been revised in 1991 to take account of Standard Grade advances, optional 'set texts' were included, with some initial teacher resentment at this 'right wing revision' of a liberal curriculum. But certain advantages of such predictable texts were gradually recognised, in the preparation of candidates whose aptitude and motivation were more varied than formerly, and in the range and variety of new texts, including Scottish works, and the assessment exemplars encountered by staff and students.

Higher Still arrangements now abandoned set texts in English, but stipulated that at least one Scottish text should be studied. This appeared too much like nationalist special pleading to some English teachers, and too much like tokenism to others. Since Scottish texts had regularly been set at both Higher and Sixth Year Studies level, the use of Scottish literature now had wider currency in the classroom, and the conflict perhaps signalled more about teacher stress than ideology. Widespread professional concerns were voiced about course coherence and value, the workload implications of multi-level teaching and assessment arrangements, and the shifting balance of internal and external assessment, particularly of talk and listening (a new departure for Higher).

Implementation of English was delayed a year, and finally, after SQA problems in processing modular results, a small non-consultative review group was set up by the Education Minister, which recommended reduction in course content and assessment. Unfortunately, some innovative elements of the new English courses were abandoned in the process: Scottish texts, language investigations, critical listening. The assessment of writing too was effectively downgraded. What remained seemed truncated, a poor return for the massive investment of staff development time and energy over years.

INNOVATIONS AND CHANGE OVER THE PAST TWENTY YEARS

The last twenty years, then, have seen almost continual 'assessment-led curriculum development', in which traditional concern for examination results has been used to extend classroom strategies and materials. An early and successful focus on the needs of less able learners shifted in the late 1990s towards the need for teaching that extends and challenges all, including those gifted in language and those (particularly boys) who show less commitment to the subject.

Initiatives in interactive language use for learning underpinning the Bullock Report (1975) provided a rationale for staff development that occurred powerfully through the central provision in the early 1980s of exemplar materials for Standard Grade courses: units of work to illustrate how the 'new' purposes for reading, writing, talking and listening were to be addressed and assessed; national publications on the development of oral skills, redrafting in writing, and group methodologies. Imaginative resources were also created at regional level by working parties, advisory staff and media development officers.

The then Scottish Examination Board brought out graded exemplars of talk, reading and writing, so that teacher confidence and skills in assessment grew steadily. This openness to sharing of assessment criteria has had a powerful impact at many levels: from national conferences on the HMI's *Effective Learning and Teaching in English* (1992) which outlined the findings of some 200 departmental inspections in the previous ten years, to focused classroom use of grade-related criteria with pupils, aimed at improving performance. *Standards and Quality in Scottish Secondary Schools 1994–97: English* (HMI, 1999) went on to outline a staff development agenda in English that included interactive close reading of texts, more frequent and purposive writing, explicit teaching of knowledge about language, and cross-curricular literacy needs.

Yet, paradoxically, progress in professional awareness also made some assessment and curriculum change in the mid-1990s less welcome in secondary schools. Whereas primary teachers appeared generally to welcome the 5–14 formulation of a language curriculum in terms of key outcomes, strands and stages, many secondary English departments considered that the progress they had made in structuring the subject coherently (in terms of Standard Grade modes and purposes) was being disrupted by new terminology and assessment procedures. The perceived loss of progression from S1 to S4 clearly ought to be counterbalanced by greater (and probably more vital) continuity from P6 to S2, but that happened slowly and patchily across the country and was further delayed as the focus of change shifted to the upper stages with Higher Still developments.

That 5–14 guidelines had been further extended in the later 1990s from Level E (attainable by most pupils in S2) to Level F for those already working beyond Level E in S1–S2, with performance criteria abutting S4 Standard Grade English, suggested that this latter tried and tested area of national assessment was being squeezed out by two different and relatively untried systems in the early and later stages of secondary. Recognising what seemed inevitable, some departments began to replace Standard Grade arrangements by National Qualification assessment at Intermediate levels 1 or 2.

What had made this transition more difficult was the loss of a relatively consensual approach to curriculum change characteristic of the Standard Grade development programme of the 1980s. The sheer pace of change in the 1990s, and the fact that the break-up of larger regional education authorities often led to loss of English specialist advisors capable of linking policy and practice in a credible way, meant lack of enthusiasm for reform. Such changes in turn led to a greater use by local authorities and schools of written policies and target-setting to achieve planning aims. Although not in themselves unhelpful, these represented a marked change in outlook for most English departments.

While the future for teachers of English presents a renewed focus on literacy and language skills to sustain into secondary the attainments in reading emerging from investment in early education, and an extension of their work into information handling and desktop publishing, perhaps the greatest challenge will be to maintain one key finding from HMI inspections: that the vast majority of youngsters clearly enjoy learning English, for the stimulus to thought and expression that their teachers manage to create and sustain.

REFERENCES

HM Inspectorate of Education (2003) *Improving Achievement in English Language in Primary and Secondary Schools*, Edinburgh: SEED.

Peacock, C. (1990) *Classroom Skills in English Teaching*, London: Routledge.

SOED (1991) *English Language National Guidelines 5–14*, Edinburgh: SOED.

SOED (1992) *Effective Learning and Teaching in Scottish Secondary Schools – English*, Edinburgh: SOED.

57

Geography Education

Donald MacDonald

CURRICULAR CHANGE

Secondary school Geography has been a curricular element in Scotland since the latter part of the nineteenth century. When the Scottish Leaving Certificate examination was first instituted in 1888, Geography appeared at both Higher and Lower Grades, although responsibility for its teaching lay with non-specialists, often members of the English department (MacDonald, 1989, p. 60). Throughout much of the twentieth century, Geography has not been a high status subject, partly because of the naive rationalism on which it was founded, and partly because of the ossification which quite quickly pervaded the subject. Testimony to that process lies in the remarkable longevity of the pioneering textbooks produced by Scots such as Archibald Geikie or A. J. Herbertson, whose *Man and his Work*, first published in 1899, was still in print into the 1960s. Geography lessons were for the most part what one English HMI described in 1904 as 'a dreary recitation of names and statistics', with a major emphasis on rote learning of facts, some of them highly questionable, about world regions, around which the Geography curriculum was organised.

By the mid-1960s, however, the quantitative approaches which were becoming prevalent in academic geography, particularly in Sweden and the USA, began to influence in-service courses for secondary school teachers. The 'new' geography elicited a divided response in the pages of professional journals, but the Geography panel of the Scottish Certificate of Education Examination Board, as it then was, tended to support the waxing positivist paradigm, with its emphasis on data collection, hypothesis testing and model building. In 1972, syllabus reforms based on these novel notions were circulated to all Scottish secondary schools, in the form of a proposed Alternative 'O' Grade examination syllabus, followed a year later by suggestions for an Alternative Higher. In subsequent years, quantitative elements, such as descriptive statistics, have discreetly vanished from the Geography syllabus. Meanwhile, pedagogic innovation has taken precedence over academic innovation during the Standard Grade revolution and during the introduction of 5–14 Environmental Studies.

CURRENT PHILOSOPHIES

Contemporary documentary evidence about Geography in Scottish secondary schools suggests two major influences. The first is an epistemology which is rationalist–empiricist, concerned with amassing facts, while the second is learning theory of the associationist or behaviourist variety. At the core of the subject lies the assumption that one can recognise human and physical factors operating together on the surface of the earth, and that the interactions between these factors can usefully be studied, as the Effective Learning and Teaching Report (ELTR) indicates (SOEID, 1995, p. 2). What results from such study, it is claimed, is an understanding of the world. But whether any such understanding can be formed without some detailed knowledge of specific places is, at the very least, debatable. Traditionally, Geography used the regional approach to amass descriptive data about countless places, but offered no accompanying structure of comprehensive explanation. Yet, since the demise of that form of Geography over the past three decades, various reports by organisations such as the Gallup Poll have indicated an alarming absence of place knowledge among the general public. Partly in response, the National Curriculum in England and Wales has statutorily reinstated knowledge of locations and of the character of different places. No such move has occurred in Scotland, where the syllabus focuses simply on describing and explaining selected physical and human themes, rather than on the diverse nature of particular places. Yet whatever understanding of the world is thus developed, it is done through the acquisition of knowledge and skills (SOEID, 1995, pp. 3–4). Knowledge, in school Geography, is still viewed as propositional and largely unproblematic. As ever, textbooks present data as 'objective evidence to be accepted by pupils, and not as something constructed and selected by people' (Healey, M. and Roberts, M., Human and regional geography in schools and higher education, in E. M. Rawling and R. A. Daugherty (eds), *Geography into the Twenty-first Century*, Chichester: John Wiley & Sons, 1996, p. 296). Meanwhile, the subject does also aim to contribute to the development of certain general transferable skills, including those of enquiry, analysis, evaluation and communication, the latter incorporating mapwork, widely held to be the only skill peculiar to Geography.

METHODS AND STRATEGIES

Geography teaching has progressed considerably from the heavy didacticism of the 1960s, although the ELT Report (SOIED, 1995, p. 26) was still noting a 'divergence in approach' between student-centred activities and more teacher-directed methods. However, it is on the former that we will focus here. Most teachers of Geography acknowledge that different pupils have different learning styles, and that a variety of learning experiences must therefore be organised, under the general label of enquiry or investigative activity. Yet it has to be conceded that enquiry is not always as active a process as it may superficially appear. After all, it is the teacher who is likely to choose the question for enquiry, to identify the sources from which data will be drawn and to organise the use of time. On the other hand, teachers are free to slacken control over those aspects of enquiry, whether cognitive or organisational, within which they wish to maximise opportunities for learning.

Student-centred learning depends heavily on a wide range of resources, including maps, atlases, textbooks, televisual aids, and fieldwork sites external to the school. Microcomputers have appealed strongly to a minority of Geography teachers, while the majority make rather cautious use of information technology, though that technology can support the enquiry approach by providing access to secondary sources, including CD-ROM data on countries, digitised Ordnance Survey maps and electronic atlas pages. Again, investigations into weather phenomena, for example, can use data from automatic weather stations or from

MetFax satellite images. As Robinson (1996, pp. 223–7) has shown, students working with data-handling packages can create their own maps and diagrams to illustrate geographical concepts and themes within specific regions.

CLASSROOM ORGANISATION

The emphasis on student-centred or enquiry approaches brings its own advantages and disadvantages. Not least among the latter is that some teachers have put the role of resource organiser ahead of that of stimulating pupils' thinking processes. As a result, lessons can occasionally, as Leat (1997, p. 144) has described, become a mindless plod through seemingly endless worksheet questions linked to exercises in class textbooks. Where repetitive and time-consuming tasks induce neither motivation nor challenge, the result can be a tacit conspiracy in which the pupils work rather than mutiny, while the teacher accepts minimal standards of completed work.

On the other hand, the student-centred classroom offers commendable opportunities for different forms of classroom organisation. Individuals, at their own pace, can interpret maps, whether on the larger local scale or on the small scale of the atlas. Group work, by contrast, encourages pupils to accept shared responsibility for their own learning, but places a correspondingly greater onus on the teacher to differentiate the learning activities. Differentiation has been one of the major advances in Geography over the past decade. In some cases, groups of pupils move around a set of resource stations, each station linked to tasks organised at core and extension levels. Acknowledging variations in the manner and also in the rate of learning, Geography teachers routinely differentiate by expecting different responses to similar tasks, by organising graded tasks or by providing different sources to support a single common task.

ASSESSMENT, RECORDING AND REPORTING

Throughout most of the twentieth century, the dominant form of assessment in Geography has been psychometric, dictated by external examinations and emphasising knowledge outcomes. In recent years, however, classroom practitioners have moved rapidly towards more authentic educational assessment, in which learning and assessment are integrated, rather than kept apart. On the other hand, formative assessment for diagnostic purposes has been encouraged, albeit indirectly, by the criterion-referenced attainment targets now identified for pupils in the first four years of secondary Geography. Diagnostic tests have been most fully developed in those areas of geographical learning, notably mapwork, where a sequential development of skills can be clearly outlined. On the other hand, the programmes for Standard Grade Geography and for 5–14 Environmental Studies have encouraged teachers to assess samples of course work on a regular basis, without recourse to specially devised tests. In practice, some teachers keep a day book in which they enter brief descriptive comments about the performance of individual pupils. Observing and inter-acting with pupils, teachers gather evidence to supplement the annotated checklists and the marked collections of course work which all combine to produce a valid record of attainment.

Meanwhile, summative assessment continues as a key feature of Standard Grade and Higher courses, in which Geography ranks as one of the options most commonly followed. The external assessment of these courses remains the responsibility of the Scottish

Qualifications Authority, as does the modular programme of post-16 courses which will be the basis for entry into higher education in the early 2000s (Hunter, 1996 p. 243).

CONTEMPORARY ISSUES

The 1995 government report on effective learning and teaching in Geography identified a number of issues concerning the future development of the subject. One is an improvement in knowledge of place, which is arguably the central concept of all geographical study. Another is the concern that continuity of learning experience be maintained in the transition between primary and secondary school programmes. Alongside these, one might also consider the four which follow:

Attainment

The HMI Report *Standards and Quality in Secondary Schools 1995–2001: Geography*, (HMI, 2001) suggests that a significant minority of Geography courses (perhaps one-third at S1/S2 and one-fifth elsewhere) are characterised by remediable weaknesses. Pupil attainment seems to be constrained by such factors as over-dependence on worksheets from which important learning points do not clearly emerge. Furthermore, the type of learning tasks set are, even where differentiated, too often insufficiently challenging for the most able pupils. That such practices continue is testimony in part to inadequate monitoring and evaluation of attainment by subject leaders and senior managers responsible for quality assurance. Performance indicators, unloved though they may sometimes be, can at least be useful aids in the systematic audit of attainment and in the self-evaluation of Geography departments. Audit, after all, will identify weaknesses such as using a narrow range of teaching approaches, setting too sluggish a pace for progression or failing to place lessons in context. Hence, a major outcome for development planning at departmental level is to build on identified shortcomings by setting targets and timescales for improvement, most especially in standards of attainment.

Environmentalism

Environmental Education has been identified, over the past forty years or so, as that area of educational endeavour which raises awareness of environmental issues, while seeking means to effect improvements. More recently, it has mutated towards the formation of a sense of personal responsibility for living in a sustainable fashion. Geography and Environmental Education have much in common, since both are concerned with interactions between society and the biophysical environment. Yet, while Environmental Education is prepared to recognise an ethical component in learning, whereby some human actions can be seen as less justifiable than others, Geography teachers have been generally reluctant to go that far. Thus, questions about acid rain, greenhouse gases, atmospheric lead and toxic dumps are routinely examined in class, without much reference to the rights and duties of the human agents involved or to the political contexts within which such problems arise. Similarly, where Environmental Education draws attention to, inter alia, individual behaviour and to the cumulative repercussions of personal choices, Geography has been slow to follow. The result is that, where secondary Geography might have been the main vehicle for learning about sustainable living, that area is but patchily developed.

Schools and Higher Education

There was, at one time, a discernible cycle of events in Geography teaching. Senior pupils underwent a curriculum which, for a tiny minority, led on to a comparable but more advanced curriculum at university. From there, some students went on to practise selected aspects of the curriculum in teacher training courses, before proceeding to teach the same themes in secondary schools. Some, indeed, returned to their own original schools, fitting in seamlessly to an unchanging curricular fabric.

But no more. School Geography became decoupled from higher education during the 1980s. University courses became more esoteric. Physical Geography studied palaeoclimatic patterns, for instance, or the modelling of glaciotectonics, while in Human Studies emerging specialisms included electoral and entrepreneurial geographies. Pupils proceeding to university found themselves following lines for which school had not prepared them, and conversely some student teachers found their new repertoires of knowledge to be inadequate for classroom purposes. One price of these discontinuities is that there has been, during the 1990s, virtually no university-led conceptual development in school Geography, to balance the plethora of pedagogic developments.

Teacher training

There has been a major decline in the role of geographers in teacher training over recent decades. Where once there were nine college of education departments staffed wholly or partly by a total of fifty geographers, the number of specialist staff currently involved in initial teacher training does not even reach double figures. Meanwhile, the number of Geography teachers has been gradually declining. In 1998 there were 1,130 of them, and their average age (forty-five years) was exceeded only by that of History teachers. These gloomy patterns have been exacerbated by the demographic decline in secondary school intakes which, coupled with local education authority financial constraints, have effectively reduced the annual recruitment of new Geography teachers to a handful.

In those teacher training programmes which survive, the perennial tensions between theory and practice continue. But as training becomes more school-oriented, it may be that faculty tutors, teachers and student teachers can resolve some of these tensions by sharing more of the critically reflective paradigm (Lambert, 1996, p. 239), emphasising the thoughtful, open-ended reconstruction of classroom experiences, viewed from the different perspectives of teacher and learners. That paradigm will, in turn, be more workable when the classroom experiences of student teachers become part of schools' ongoing improvement plans.

REFERENCES

Hunter, L. A. (1996) Geography in the Scottish school curriculum, in E. M. Rawling and R. A. Daugherty (eds), *Geography into the Twenty-First Century*, Chichester: John Wiley & Sons, pp. 235–45.

Lambert, D. (1996) Understanding and improving school Geography: the training of beginning teachers, in M. Williams (ed.), *Understanding Geographical and Environmental Education*, London: Cassell, pp. 230–41.

Leat, D. (1997) Cognitive acceleration in geographical education, in D. Tilbury and M. Williams (eds), *Teaching and Learning in Geography*, London: Routledge, pp. 143–53.

MacDonald, D. (1989) Values in Geography teaching, unpublished MEd. dissertation, Glasgow: University of Glasgow.

Robinson, A. (1996) Interactive computer-assisted learning in Geography in Scottish schools, in T. Van Der Zijpp et al. (eds) *Proceeding of the Commission on Geography Education, 28th Congress of the International Geographical Union*, Amsterdam: The Free University Press, pp. 253–7.

SOEID (1995) *Effective Learning and Teaching in Scottish Secondary Schools: Geography*, Edinburgh: HMSO.

58

Health Education

Joan Forrest

A HOLISTIC CONTEXT

Traditionally, Health Education focused on encouraging the individual to change behaviour; little consideration was given to the wider social and environmental influences that can affect health. However, it would be unrealistic to consider the curricular aspects of Health Education without setting their contribution within the broader, more holistic setting of the health promoting school. The health promoting school concept embraces a combination of curricular contributions and all other contextual factors that need to be taken into account to promote the health and well-being of those within it. The emphasis has shifted from an individual responsibility for lifestyle to a recognition that the development of 'supportive environments conducive to the promotion of health' involves all members of the school community and partners in the wider community (see World Health Organisation (WHO), *The Overall Progress of the European Network of Health Promoting Schools*, 1995).

THE HEALTH PROMOTING SCHOOL

Scotland was at the forefront of the health promoting school movement in the 1980s and became a member of the European Network of Health Promoting Schools (ENHPS) in 1993. The early work focused on three main components: Health Education as an integral part of the formal curriculum; the 'hidden' curriculum or school ethos; and links with family and the community. However, more recently, schools have been taking account of a set of principles defined by WHO which emphasise democracy, participation, empowerment, partnership, collaboration and supportive environments (see WHO, *Conference Resolution from the 1st Conference of the European Network of Health Promoting Schools*, 1997).

These principles articulate the reality of schools as 'real-life social settings', where the overall ethos, organisation, management and environment have an impact on the whole school community (Inchley et al., 2000). The WHO principles encourage a genuine commitment to participation. This can be demonstrated through meaningful involvement of the young people themselves in decision making within the school as well as involvement of parents, carers and community members as partners within the health promoting school. As early as 1979, evidence was emerging that schools can make a difference; if young people believe that school is a good place to be, then that will have a discernible impact on their lives (see Rutter, M. et al. *Fifteen Thousand Hours: Secondary Schools and their Effects on Children*, London: Open Books 1979). John MacBeath's research into school effectiveness provides a similar strong message (see School Effectiveness and School Improvement in *Scottish Education*, Chap. 89, 1999). More recent research offers a tentative suggestion that schools may influence health and health behaviours. For example, differences in smoking rates between schools may be influenced by the presence of written policies on smoking; one study linked pupils' perceptions of smoking levels in schools to the degree of application of smoking bans (Griesbach et al., 2002). Apart from the potential effect of written policies, other aspects of school life, such as the existence of an ethos which promotes self-respect and respect for others, is emerging as an influencing factor in young people's sense of well-being. The debate on 'school effects' is current and firm conclusions cannot be drawn at this time.

NATIONAL STRATEGY

In 1998, New Community Schools (NCS), with their focus on meeting the needs of all children, were initiated. An integral part of the development was the requirement for each NCS to become a health promoting school. Partnership and co-operation between school staff, pupils, parents/carers and other community members, has become central to the success of NCS. Gradually, this development is building up in Scotland with some authorities designating all schools as NCS. There is now a strong momentum in Scotland for the health promoting school and all it embraces. Additional support for all schools in Scotland for the development of the health promoting school is evident in the publication of performance indicators to enable schools to review and improve their own practice. *A Route to Health Promotion* (1999) provides a structured approach to self-evaluation and is based on good practice in health promotion identified by HM Inspectors in schools and local authorities across Scotland. A commitment has been made to update this document, including revised and new quality indicators. To assist schools in self-evaluation relating to health issues, quality indicators with a specific focus on education about drugs and personal relationships and responsible sexuality have been developed.

The Government's White Paper *Towards a Healthier Scotland* (HMI, 1999) emphasised a commitment to reducing inequalities and improving health, and indicated the contribution that the health promoting school can make to overall health strategy. There is clearly national commitment and increasingly evidence of similar commitment at local authority and school level. The health education curriculum still remains a key component of the health promoting school. Following extensive consultation, and taking account of the government's overall strategy for improving health, the decision was made to remove Health Education from the Environmental Studies guidelines and to provide separate guidelines for schools. This recent change has provided an opportunity for Health Education to have a more prominent place in the school's overall curricular provision for personal and social development.

CURRICULAR PROVISION

5–14

Health Education aims to provide young people with opportunities to develop knowledge and understanding of a range of health issues, to develop personal and interpersonal skills and to explore and clarify their beliefs, values and attitudes. It is an integral part of their personal and social development, encouraging them to believe in themselves, value themselves and gain in confidence to take responsibility for their own health and to become active citizens in their community.

All schools in Scotland are required to provide a Health Education programme and the development of the 5–14 curricular framework enables schools to plan a flexible, yet coherent, programme across the primary and initial secondary stages which matches the maturity levels and meets the needs of their pupils.

The *Health Education 5–14 National Guidelines* (LTS, 2000) provide a single attainment outcome: 'taking responsibility for health' and three interrelated strands:

- physical health, which focuses on the knowledge, skills and attitudes required to understand physical aspects of health;
- emotional health, which focuses on the knowledge, skills and attitudes needed to understand emotions, feelings and relationships and how they affect mental well-being;
- social health, which is concerned with the knowledge, skills and attitudes required to enable young people to understand the interaction of the individual, the community and the environment in relation to health and safety.

The developmental aspects of the guidelines ensure that, as young people mature, they are able to consider a number of perspectives relating to specific health issues such as nutrition, safety, substance use, sexual health and relationships. Far from focusing on ill-health, the guidelines provide opportunities for the development of emotional well-being, with self-worth and self esteem central to all development. It is worth noting that the focus is not only on individual health behaviours, but also on encouraging pupils to consider their roles as members of families and communities and how communities and the environment support them. The social and emotional context is important; often, health-related decisions are influenced by interactions with others and therefore the development of personal and interpersonal skills is an essential element of Health Education. Many aspects of the guidelines interrelate with key aspects of the 5–14 guidelines for Personal and Social Development and to a lesser extent with the 5–14 guidelines for Religious and Moral Education. Although it is too early to evaluate the impact of the new Health Education guidelines, there is a clear sense that the more prominent status is welcome in Scotland.

Many secondary schools incorporate Health Education into their personal and social education (PSE) programme for all six years. As these programmes are carefully planned, it is normal to see health-related aspects as 'slots' within the overall programme. In many schools, PSE is taught by the guidance team and members are supported by a team of teachers who show a willingness to contribute to this area. In some instances, teachers are allocated to the PSE programme, rather than elect to be part of the team. Alternatively, a cross-curricular approach is taken, with subjects such as Home Economics, Science,

Physical Education, English and Religious and Moral Education contributing. This enables young people to reflect on health issues within a range of contexts. Careful co-ordination and regular monitoring is essential. An effective approach adopted by one school, for example, incorporates 'complementary contributions', healthy leisure activities and accredited achievements through certificated short courses (HMI, 1999). The McCrone report indicates that all teachers have a responsibility for young people's education for personal and social development, of which PSE courses are but one element. This approach reflects the philosophy behind the 1995 Scottish Consultative Council on the Curriculum document, *The Heart of the Matter*.

Post-S2

Health Studies short courses, introduced in 1989 for pupils in S3 upwards, are now incorporated as National Units within the Higher Still programme as part of group awards. There has been a decline in use within schools from a total uptake of 2,738 in 1998, to a total of 1,076 in 2001. Provision of formal awards for age fifteen upward is found within the Higher Still Personal and Social Education programme. The course comprises three forty-hour units in three main contexts: personal awareness & development; social awareness & development and vocational awareness & development. Within the personal awareness & development unit, there is opportunity for pupils to select a sub-context of health-related issues. While there is no further specific health focus in the units, there are elements of a broad approach to health within the community area of the unit social awareness & development. Uptake of the course is minimal with fifteen pupils undertaking the Higher level in 2000, and sixty-nine undertaking it in 2001. The Intermediate 2 level has risen from nought in 2000 to thirty-five in 2001. Provisional figures for 2002 indicate a very small change in numbers.

Further contribution to health-related issues can be found in some units of the Higher Still programmes relating to Physical Education, Home Economics and Science. However, not all schools make use of structured courses and provision of Health Education, beyond the age of fourteen, while increasingly being seen as integral to PSE, varies greatly throughout Scotland.

There are different views within the teaching community regarding assessment of Health Education. While it can aid monitoring of students' progress and quality of provision, this may not always be appropriate. On the one hand, assessment can be used to measure changes in health knowledge and skills development; on the other hand, there is a view that it may not be appropriate, or indeed possible, to assess values and attitudes. At the time of writing (Autumn, 2002), a general review of assessment is taking place. One of the ideas being considered by the Health Promoting Schools Unit, and which in turn may prove helpful to the review, is of the importance of 'discerning comment' about all aspects of a young person's development and of the role of all education, including Health Education, in helping young people to make discerning choices about their own lives for themselves.

RECENT DEVELOPMENTS

Several developments have taken place over the last two years that will have an impact on health education and health promotion in schools.

As a commitment to the Scottish Health Plan, the Health Promoting Schools Unit has been created as a partnership between the Health Education Board for Scotland (now NHS Health Scotland), Learning and Teaching Scotland and the Convention of Scottish Local Authorities. The unit will provide leadership and support to local authorities, schools and National Health Service Boards in the development of health promoting schools throughout Scotland.

Following the intention to repeal section 2A of the Local Government Act 1986, the Executive announced a package of safeguards to be put in place to address concerns expressed by the public, parents and teachers. This resulted in guidance to local authorities and schools from the Executive's working group on, for example, the principles and aims of sex education and on effective consultation with parents. Schools are expected to consult parents and carers about their sex education programme and to give pupils the opportunity to identify their own needs. Guidance on responding to incidents of drug misuse, on policy development and on drug education in schools has been developed through the Executive's School Drug Safety Team and made available to all schools in Scotland.

As part of Scotland's strategy for addressing health priorities, an Expert Panel on School Meals has been initiated. The panel plans to improve the provision, presentation and nutritional content of school meals. Of particular importance, and in line with the inclusive nature of health promoting schools, the stigma attached to taking free school meals will be addressed. Also, a national Physical Activity Co-ordinator has been appointed following a recommendation of the Physical Activity Task Force (established to consider strategy for raising physical activity in children and young people in Scotland).

MEETING YOUNG PEOPLE'S NEEDS

One of the greatest difficulties for schools is ensuring that Health Education is relevant to their pupils' needs. Health-related issues are complex and can be very sensitive and personal; too often, adult perceptions of needs do not match those of the young people; decisions about curricular content are not adequately consulted upon although there is increasing consultation with senior pupils above age sixteen years within schools. Society has changed a great deal over the last twenty years; social and media pressures are quite different and more complex; peer pressure is a reality but often, young people experiment and take risks because they want to. The teaching of health-related issues has to be set within a realistic context and be sensitive to the diverse backgrounds and needs of young people. If teachers are to provide opportunities for young people to discuss their feelings and explore a range of health issues, learning and teaching approaches have to be conducted in a more open and interactive style where activities are designed to engage students in learning together and reflecting on their learning in a supportive and safe environment. Often, this student-centred approach can create difficulties for teachers who have a relatively didactic style of teaching for their own subject and who are expected to switch to a more facilitative role.

TEACHERS' CONCERNS

For many, the teaching of sensitive health-related issues such as sexuality and relationships, drug misuse and body image can be problematic. Many teachers lack confidence for a number of reasons. Often, embarrassment, lack of knowledge and concern regarding parental views can impinge on effective learning and teaching. In addition, it is concern over conflicting values and the parameters for personal disclosure which contributes to teachers' anxieties. Often, the perceived conflict between teachers' values, pupils' and parents' values and the values of the school and society lead to moral dilemmas for individual teachers (Powney and Lowden, 2001).

PARTNERSHIPS

Many schools work in partnership with other professionals and external agencies, often relying on them to contribute in the classroom where the teacher feels support is required. While a planned and coherent approach can only benefit young people, there are issues that remain unresolved. In the first instance, health professionals have differing codes of confidentiality and this has the potential for causing conflict (for example, when giving advice or information about personal matters). Secondly, funding for external visitors is often outwith the education budget and therefore 'vulnerable to changing priorities' (Powney and Lowden, p. 87). However, experience of multi-agency working in New Community Schools should help to provide guidance for collaborative working in all schools.

BACK TO THE FUTURE

There is commitment to Health Education nationally. Also, local authorities and schools are increasingly developing partnerships to support strategies to make the health promoting school a reality. However, while curriculum provision has developed over the last few years and schools are receiving appropriate support and guidance, one must be cautious about the impact that a few hours devoted to Health Education can have on young people's health behaviours and lifestyle. The whole-school approach to health promotion has to be emphasised. Within a holistic definition of health, incorporating the physical, social, emotional and spiritual aspects of health, there is a need to consider the range of policies and support mechanisms that are active within schools such as: anti-bullying network, social inclusion, positive behaviour, citizenship, ethos network. The concept of the health promoting school embraces all of these and can be a tremendous influence on young people's thinking and feelings about all aspects of their lives. This broad concept is the starting point for schools.

REFERENCES

Griesbach, D., Inchley, J., and Currie, C. (2002) More than words? The status and impact of smoking policies in Scottish schools, *Health Promotion International*, 17 (1), 31–41.

HMI (1999) *Health Promotion: Issues for Councils and Schools*, Edinburgh: Scottish Executive.

Inchley, J., Currie, C., and Young, I. (2000) Evaluating the health promoting school: a case study approach, *Health Education*, 100 (5), 200–6.

Powney, J. and Lowden, K. (2001) From information to moral issues: dilemmas in drug education, *Scottish Educational Review*, 33 (1), 84–92.

Scottish Executive and LTS (2000) *Health Education 5–14 National Guidelines*, Dundee: LTS.

Scottish Office Department of Health (1999) *Towards a Healthier Scotland, A White Paper on Health*, Edinburgh: The Stationery Office.

59

History Education

Peter Hillis

RECENT DEVELOPMENTS

Since the late 1980s developments in History Education have often created a mixed economy of consistent and inconsistent initiatives, some with perhaps unforeseen consequences. The introduction of Standard Grade History in 1988 marked a departure from traditional methods which had emphasised the acquisition of knowledge and understanding, but it included new elements of evaluating and investigation. The syllabus for Standard Grade defines evaluating as 'evaluating sources with reference to their historical significance, the points of view conveyed in them and to the relevant historical context' (SEB, 1993, p. 9). Within investigating, pupils had to complete a historical investigation on an issue of their choice relating to developments in Scottish History in the context of Scotland or Britain, or to connections between Scotland and other countries. While this pupil investigation may have satisfied demands for 'real History' involving planning, research and reporting, it foundered on the rocks of workload, authenticity and fairness. Many pupils exceeded the recommended word limit to produce mini-theses in excess of 3,000 words at a time when other subjects required a similar report, folio or investigation. Moreover, there was no fully effective method of preventing some pupils receiving considerable outside help with the exercise. Consequently, the investigation was criticised for favouring pupils from more supportive home backgrounds. Following a consultation exercise by the Scottish Qualification Authority the pupil investigation was removed from the syllabus in 1999 and replaced by a new section in the external examination. This new section contains an issue, related sources followed by questions which test pupils' ability to evaluate and reach conclusions. The most favourable comment on this exercise would be that it bears a passing resemblance to the original aim of allowing pupils to experience a more investigative approach in learning about the past. The change also introduced an element of inconsistency between Standard Grade, 5–14 Environmental Studies and Higher Still.

Environmental Studies 5–14 refers to History as 'people and the past', a term which drew complaints from organisations such as the Scottish Association of Teachers of History since the subject is known, recognised and popularised in its traditional nomenclature. However, the original 5–14 report published in 1993 met with more serious criticisms, most notably those concerning the unwieldy number of assessable strands and targets. These covered knowledge, understanding, planning, collecting evidence, recording/presenting, interpreting, evaluating and developing informed attitudes, each to be assessed across all levels from

A to E. The revised report, published in 2000, reduced the number of strands to knowledge, understanding and enquiry with the last sub-divided into preparing, carrying out and reviewing/reporting on tasks. Nevertheless, the general tenor of each report appeared to favour an investigative approach with, for example, targets at Level E including 'the selection and use of suitable methods to access information', followed by 'presenting findings . . . in a report'. However desirable these methods, they were introduced at a time when the similar process was being dropped from Standard Grade.

Higher Still courses at Intermediate, Higher and Advanced Higher also combine elements of knowledge, understanding, evaluating and investigating. Investigating at Higher History takes the form of an extended essay where pupils research an issue of their choice and prepare a plan for a related essay of approximately 2,000 words. Pupils write the essay under examination conditions which alleviates some of the concerns regarding workload and authenticity raised over the investigation at Standard Grade. The 'investigation' at Advanced Higher is a dissertation of 4,000 words on a topic relating to the syllabus. Despite the variation in approach, each of these 'investigations' incorporates planning, collecting evidence and presenting the outcome and as such relate to the skills required by 5–14 Environmental Studies. Consequently, Standard Grade follows a different strategy from 5–14 and Higher Still in the approach to investigating.

INFLUENCE OF RECENT DEVELOPMENTS

The Teaching of History

The emphasis on evaluating sources has produced a more consistent approach across the curriculum than for investigating. In order to develop evaluative skills History teachers use a wide variety of primary and secondary sources including written sources, photographs and cartoons. For example, a lesson on 'Lenin and the Russian Revolution' at Standard Grade might include evaluation and comparison of the following descriptions of Tsar Nicholas:

Source A is a description of Tsar Nicholas by Alexander Kerensky, written in his memoirs *Crucifixion of Liberty* published in 1934.

Source A: The daily work of a monarch he found intolerably boring. He could not stand listening or reading long reports prepared by his ministers. He liked ministers who could tell an amusing story and who did not weary his attention with too much business. When it came to defending his right to rule he became cunning, stubborn, cruel and merciless at times.

Source B is a view of the Tsar by his wife the Empress Alexandria.

Source B: My poor Nicky's cross is heavy, all the more so as he has nobody on whom he can thoroughly rely and who can be a real help to him. He has had so many bitter disappointments, but through it all he remains brave and full of faith in God's mercy. He tries so hard and works with such effort.

In comparing these sources pupils must make reference to content and authorship with a more straightforward source evaluation on, for example, the usefulness of Source A, examining features such as date, authorship, content, bias and the wider context. However, the particular emphasis on evaluating has often produced the arguably unforeseen consequence of rote type answers to questions asking pupils to comment on the usefulness/ reliability/accuracy of a source. Pupils can produce formulaic answers without showing a full understanding of the source's wider context. This in turn has led to the Scottish Qualifications Authority producing a hierarchy of acceptable responses from Foundation level to Advanced Higher. While clear guidance can be helpful, it is hoped that this does not stifle the more imaginative uses of sources and subsequent pupil answers which have featured in *Teaching History*, the journal of the Historical Association.

Nonetheless, the use of primary and secondary sources encourages a variety of teaching strategies. The majority of lessons combine teacher-led discussion and pupils working on related materials either individually or in groups. The stations approach offers a variation on this strategy since it allows pupils, usually in groups, to examine a range of evidence on a particular topic. A lesson on conditions in the trenches during the First World War could utilise a range of sources including poetry, archive film, war diaries, textbook accounts and photographs with each allocated a particular station. Groups of pupils move round each station answering specific questions to compile a profile of life in the trenches.

Information and communication technologies have begun to influence teaching methodology, but not to the extent foreseen by many politicians and educationalists (Munro, 2000), Programmes relevant to Scottish History incorporate primary sources such as census information within a database so allowing pupils to develop their research and ICT skill by carrying out relatively complicated search routines. Other uses of ICT include pupils designing websites, searching the internet for information and multimedia products. The increasing availability of hardware helps teachers integrate ICT into lessons, but provision varies from school to school. Nonetheless, ICT influences teaching and learning with the teacher becoming a facilitator alongside the more traditional role as the main source of information.

History teaching has also benefited from an increasing choice of attractive and relevant textbooks, especially those relating to Scottish History. A notable example has been the series on Scottish History from Ancient to Modern Times produced by Heinemann in 2002.

COURSE CONTENT

Here the impact has been less radical and more consistent than for evaluating and investigating. Environmental Studies 5–14 lays down general guidelines for History courses. These must cover each of the main historical eras, but not necessarily in chronological order:

- The Ancient World;
- Renaissance, Reformation and the Age of Discovery;
- The Age of Revolutions;
- The Middle Ages;
- The Twentieth Century.

Pupils study three units at Standard Grade which focus on modern History and covering: Scotland and Britain; international co-operation and conflict; and people and power.

Within each unit schools choose from a range of contexts. For example, within international co-operation and conflict one of the following contexts is studied:

- A 1790s–1820s;
- B 1890s–1920s;
- C 1930s–1960s.

A substantial part of course content in Standard Grade developed from earlier syllabuses, but Higher History provides the opportunity to widen the chronological framework. Within the Higher course one of three periods must be studied:

- Medieval;
- Early Modern;
- Later Modern.

Each option contains a combination of prescription and choice as illustrated by the third, Later Modern, where Britain 1850s–1979 must be studied alongside at least one other unit from either growth of nationalism or the large scale state. Moreover, one special topic must be selected from a choice of four units. The most popular special topic is Appeasement and the road to war, to 1939. In Advanced Higher pupils chose one field of study from a choice of thirteen ranging from Northern Britain from the Romans to AD 1000 to Britain at war and peace, 1939–51. The most popular field of study is Germany: Versailles to the outbreak of World War Two.

ASSESSMENT

The move away from a solely knowledge-based curriculum influences assessment which now tests skills of evaluating and investigating. At Higher Still the extended essay/report and dissertation count towards the final award which places greater emphasis on 'course work', but from Standard Grade to Advanced Higher the external examination remains the main determinant of pupil attainment. Examinations assess knowledge and understanding and evaluating, with examination papers containing two broad categories of question. Knowledge and understanding is tested by questions requiring pupils to write a short paragraph or an essay, with the exception being Foundation level at Standard Grade where a list of points or short sentences is accepted. Examinations test evaluation skills by incorporating a range of primary and secondary sources, including cartoons and photographs, with questions relating to the content, context, point of view, accuracy and reliability of the source or sources. As a means of preparing pupils for the external examination, departmental methods of assessment reflect those used in examinations.

STANDARDS OF PERFORMANCE

In a recent overview of standards and quality of History teaching throughout Scotland between 1995 and 1999, Her Majesty's Inspectors of Schools recorded generally good or very good performances between S3 and S6, (SEED, 2000b). HMI expressed concerns over aspects of teaching, learning and attainment in S1 and S2, especially the need to improve extended writing skills and set more demanding tasks for able pupils. These findings are reflected in reports on individual departments where in one school some of the work was not challenging enough for abler pupils, (*Standards and Quality in Scottish Schools, 1995–1998*, Edinburgh: Scottish Executive, 1999). Such criticisms must, however, be read in the context of History receiving very little time, approximately one period, per week, in the S1 and S2 curriculum making it difficult for pupils to develop the skills demanded by HMI. Moreover, most HMI reports comment favourably on general standards within departments, as shown by one school where 'learning and teaching were consistently of high quality. There were many examples of very good direct teaching and well focused questioning. Homework was set and marked regularly. Nearly all pupils were well motivated and making good progress' (SEED, 2000b). The inspectorate have also commented favourably on learning and teaching which include the following characteristics:

- effective direct teaching;
- good use of pupils' own experience;
- systematic extended questioning which gave pupils the opportunity to express their views;
- brisk pace of learning with challenging tasks and carefully planned homework;
- suitable opportunities for pupils to take responsibility for their work;
- varied activities and resources. (SEED, 2000b).

These factors help explain the relative popularity of History at a time of falling school roles. In 2001 there was a drop of 6% in entries at Standard Grade History compared to 8.4% in English, 16.8% in Geography and 8.7% in Modern Studies. By way of contrast Intermediate 1 and 2 History saw increases of 5.14 and 10.7% respectively in the number of candidates in 2001.

Pupil performance in external examinations reflects the favourable HMI reports on teaching and learning from S3 to S6. In 1998, 40% of candidates gained a Credit award at Standard Grade compared to 41% in both Geography and Modern Studies. At Higher level in 1998, 14% of candidates were awarded an A Grade compared to 17 and 16% respectively for Geography and Modern Studies. History is also among the most successful subjects in converting relatively low grades at Standard Grade into passes at Higher. Approximately 33% of pupils gaining a level 3 award at Standard Grade go on to pass Higher History with this conversion rate partly explained by high standards of pupil work in the extended essay. Nonetheless, the advent of amended examinations at Higher Level brought in by the Higher Still programme has given rise to serious concerns which remain one of the key issues for the future.

KEY ISSUES

Assessment

Before the first round of Higher Still examinations in 2000, pupil performance across the three Social Subjects was relatively comparable. However, in the examinations held in 2000, 12% of pupils gained an A pass at Higher History compared to approximately 20% in both Geography and Modern Studies. In 2001 the gap between A passes at History compared to Geography and Modern Studies was reduced to approximately 5%. History is now seen as a relatively difficult subject by many pupils and teachers. Much of this difficulty, it is argued, stems from the requirement in the examination that pupils write two essays marked out of twenty-five. In 2001, only 12.4% of pupils produced A-rated essay answers in the examination compared to 14.7% in paper 2, the source-based paper, and 17.5% for the extended essay. History stands almost alone in demanding essays of this type which makes the subject more difficult per se while also providing reduced opportunities for pupils to develop the necessary skills across the curriculum. Teachers have suggested various alternatives: dividing the twenty-five-mark essay into two smaller tasks; easing the marking instructions; and reducing the marks allocated to twenty. Those in favour of the essay point to its value in preparing pupils for essay-related tasks in higher education. One way forward may lie in a review of the wording of questions to make them more straightforward taking into account pressures caused by examinations and the limited time available to compose each essay, approximately forty minutes. For example, the question, 'How important was the role played by political pressure groups in the growth of democracy in Britain between 1860 and 1914', which featured in the 2001 examination, could be replaced with 'In what ways did Britain become a more democratic country between 1860 and 1928?'

The comparability of performance across the Social Subjects presents only one of several concerns over assessment within Higher Still. The demands of internal assessment place additional pressures on pupils, especially those studying a relatively high number of subjects. Internal assessment viewed in a more positive light motivates some pupils by giving opportunities to develop essay-writing and source-handling skills under examination-type conditions. However, some questions in the internal assessment at Intermediate 2 have proved too difficult for many pupils, but a proposal to amend the external examination to mirror more closely these internal assessments addresses the problem from the wrong direction. Further difficulties have been created by different marking instructions between some internal assessments and the external examination. Key issues for the future, therefore, remain the role of internal assessment and levels of difficulty in many test items.

Concerns over assessment spread across the curriculum and feature prominently at 5–14. This is an assessment-driven programme which ten years after its inception is only now beginning to provide concrete examples of assessment and associated exemplars of pupil work. This delay has made it difficult for teachers to relate their pupils' work to a generally agreed standard for each 5–14 level. Higher Still and 5–14 also illustrate the current preoccupation with assessment and measuring pupil performance. Assessment has assumed a greater importance than is justified within teaching and learning. Furthermore, it has moved the focus onto output when a greater emphasis on input would have proved more beneficial to the pupil experience.

Curriculum Flexibility

When the first edition of this book was produced in 1999 the curriculum framework was relatively uniform across Scotland. In the intervening period schools and local authorities have developed different policies regarding class organisation and subject/course choice. Some schools have replaced Standard Grade History with Intermediate courses in the belief that they offer intrinsically more interesting topics and create a stronger foundation for Higher. Other schools have dropped Standard Grade altogether replacing it with Higher and Advanced Higher. In S1 and S2 the concerns raised about pupil attainment have led to the move away from mixed-ability classes and the reintroduction of setting.

In 2000 the Scottish Executive relaxed the requirement that pupils must choose subjects within each of the eight modes which has led to History becoming an increasingly optional choice in some schools. Greater flexibility increases the demands on department managers at a time when their position is under review as part of the McCrone agreement on teachers' pay. Issues relating to the place of History within the curriculum, the courses offered from S1 to S5 and the management of the History curriculum will become increasingly important in the years to come.

A National or A World View

A 1995 survey into pupils and trainee-teachers' knowledge of Scottish History revealed an apparent knowledge gap in many key areas. This survey sparked considerable debate about Scottish History's place in the curriculum and a review group under the auspices of the Scottish Consultative Council on the Curriculum was asked to report on the teaching of Scottish History. The report advocated a balance between local, Scottish, British, European and global themes, but the draft framework for Scottish History is biased towards Scottish and British themes. One exemplar contains thirteen history topics between P1 and S2, eight of which feature Scottish and/or British History. The exceptions include: the French Revolution; the British Empire and Russia from revolution to the Cold War (SCCC, 1997). This debate raised the profile of History, but the Scottish Association of Teachers of History made strong representations for a balanced rather than a nationalistic approach to the History curriculum while recognising that debates over course content are intrinsic to History teaching.

CONCLUSION

Despite the difficulties created by reforms at 5–14, Standard Grade and Higher Still, History has retained and in some areas increased its relative popularity which stands as a tribute to History teachers and their pupils. It is also a reminder that the quality of learning and teaching in the classroom should be the main focus of debates on education. Future reforms at a national level must take into account the total pupil experience from upper primary to S6 to create a coherent, consistent and well resourced curriculum which will allow teachers and pupils to develop their enthusiasm for History.

REFERENCES

SCCC (1997) *Scottish History in the Curriculum, A Paper for Discussion and Consultation and Draft Frameworks for Scottish History in the 5–14 Curriculum*, Dundee: SCCC.
SEB (1993) *Standard Grade, Amended Arrangements in History*, Dalkeith: SEB.
SEED (2000a) *National Guidelines: Environmental Studies 5–14*, Edinburgh: SEED.
SEED (2000b) *Standards and Quality in Secondary Schools, 1995–99, History*, Edinburgh: SEED.
Munro, R. K., (2000), Information and communication technology in History education, in Peter Hillis (ed.), *History Education in Scotland*, Edinburgh: John Donald.

60

Home Economics Education

Karen Bryce

> Home Economics is an unfortunate title for a course that has such an impact on your life and the life of others. It suggests something a bit dry and old-fashioned. Whereas the reality of this course is founded in contemporary, bang up-to-date thinking, giving you the necessary information to enable you to build the foundations of a healthy and fulfilling life. (Nick Nairn in the Introduction to MacGregor, A., *Home Economics: Standard Grade Course Notes*, 2002)

CHANGING LIFESTYLES: CHANGING SUBJECT

Nick Nairn is right on both counts and while the profession seems unable to fix the name of the subject, its content certainly has changed greatly since the days of O Grade Food and Nutrition and Fabric and Fashion. The main emphasis at that time was on practical 'life skills' (even then conspicuously appropriate to a conventional family household with the woman in the home making role) and very traditional methods of acquiring knowledge and understanding. Now the subject is directed towards achieving a healthy diet and lifestyle and to the acquisition of vocational skills vital to the hospitality, caring, food and fashion industries. The practical skills learned in Home Economics are geared to future employment and not just the home. Pupils working on design briefs (often concerning food preparation) learn to take decisions and are encouraged to analyse, investigate and evaluate across a wide range of topics. Information and communication technology (ICT) skills are central to the classroom; pupils draw upon and further develop ICT skills learned in other subjects.

A number of changes in society have shaped current Home Economics courses. Firstly, significant social trends have taken place: more woman than men now work; there is more technology in the home; generally speaking there is more disposable income; debt and poverty nevertheless are increasing in many homes; traditional family units are less common. Secondly, eating patterns have changed: people actually cook less than they used to; there are more takeaway foods; more fast food restaurants; more hotels and restaurants of all kinds; more people travel abroad (with raised expectations in consequence); a large range of cook-chill and ready-made meals are available. With respect to fast food, the 'McDonaldisation' of the world is sadly under-way. According to Schlosser, there are now more than 30,000 McDonald's burger 'restaurants' in the world with approximately 2,000 new venues opening each year. 'An estimated one out of every eight workers in the United States has at some point been employed by McDonald's' (Schlosser, 2002, p. 4).

Thirdly, the UK faces a range of diet related health problems, as spelled out in the James Report (SOHHD, 1993). Recent reports show that it has the highest rate of heart disease in Western Europe; diabetes is increasing rapidly; the incidence of diet-related cancers and strokes is on the increase; overweight children and teenagers abound – with Scotland worse on most indicators than elsewhere in the UK. Fourthly, there has been a significant change in employment patterns; notably with the rapid growth in the hospitality and tourism, and care industries (two of Scotland's major employers); the expansion of the food industry, especially in food product development; and the growth of the fashion industry. At its peak, some 40,000 people were employed in ship-building on the Clyde; today more than 50,000 work in tourism-related jobs in Greater Glasgow and Clyde valley alone. A fifth factor was of course the introduction of the Sex Discrimination Act in 1975 which led to all boys and girls studying Home Economics (and Technical Education) in Scottish Schools. Courses in S1 and S2 in particular have had to undergo considerable change to counter the gender and cultural biases of traditional courses. It would be fair to say that in all of the programmes in Home Economics – 5–14, Standard Grade and more recently Higher Still – there have been rapid revisions to catch up with a changing world.

COURSE CONTENT: S1 AND S2

Home Economics forms part of the common course in secondary years S1/ S2. It is one part of Environmental Studies 5–14: Society, Science and Technology which hopes to develop 'technological capability' in young people. This is defined in LTS (2000, p. 65, para. 2) and aspects are summarised in the paper *Technology Education in Scottish Schools: A Statement of Position from Scottish CCC* (SCCC, 1996). The 5–14 programme did not change the content of Home Economics courses, but it did change how it was taught and assessed. Most units contain a variety of food and textile work covering topics such as nutrition, dietary targets, food hygiene, food product development, consumer issues, use of fabric equipment, fabric construction, properties and use. The recently produced Home Economics pack for 5–14 distributed by Glasgow City Council and to be made available to other authorities (Bryce and Liveston, 2001) encourages teachers and pupils to use a wide range of equipment and resources relevant to everyday circumstances. The most significant change in the delivery of the course relates to the skills strand. To achieve the attainment targets within this strand it is necessary to carry out a 'design and make task' and pupils learn to 'analyse, research, plan, develop ideas, create solutions, test and evaluate' working from design briefs. These tasks enable pupils to work individually, in pairs and in groups. This allows them to share ideas and 'develop informed attitudes' by using the knowledge gained and by discussing work with their peers and the teacher. All pupils work on the same topics but are able to work to their highest level. As stated in LTS (2000): 'At the heart of technology education is the engagement of children with practical tasks that lead to products that serve a need, solve a problem or, in a word, "work" ' (p. 65). This sense of purpose is widely recognised as having led to boys showing more interest in all aspects of Home Economics. The use of CD-ROMs, the internet, mind maps, peer assessment, self-assessment, target setting, stations and particular cross-curricular links allow pupils to develop and use transferable skills. Support is also available for pupils with the use of writing and note-taking frames or templates; these aid the thinking, planning and organisational skills required for writing (see Liveston, D. et al., *Environmental Studies 5–14. Home Economics. Literacy Support S1/S2. Teaching for Effective Learning*, Glasgow:

Glasgow City Council, 2001). With so much emphasis on achieving attainment targets it is important to remember that Home Economics is at least 50% practical. Timetable rotations with Technical Education are common and cut the number of periods pupils have in Home Economics. The HMI report stating that it is preferable that pupils in S1 and S2 should have contact with fewer teachers has also led to cuts in Home Economics time (see SOEID, Achieving Success in S1/S2, 1996). Time is a significant factor in the delivery of courses with double periods making it easier to cope with the course content and the organisation of lessons. Auxiliary help is essential. Assessment should be holistic; the teacher needs to interact with pupils constantly to be able to assess confidently; Home Economics is very much a pupil-centred subject.

COURSE CONTENT: STANDARD GRADE IN S3 AND S4

There are three assessable areas at Standard Grade. The knowledge and understanding objectives in S3 and S4 for Standard Grade require pupils to recall and apply knowledge across a number of areas: nutrition; dietary targets; individuals' dietary needs; food hygiene; safety; design; family needs; money matters; consumer issues; environmental matters; fabrics. The area of study which pupils find most difficult is nutrition and clearly it is important that pupils do not just memorise facts to pass the final examination. Teaching methods and links to practical work are essential to help pupils put what is learnt into practice. By adapting part of the course it is possible for them to sit the Royal Environmental Health Institute of Scotland (REHIS) examination and gain a certificate for food hygiene, needed for working in any aspect of the food industry. (The certificate can also be gained via the Intermediate 1 Food Hygiene unit.) This puts theory into practice in ways highlighted by the Pennington Report (1997), *Food Safety and Hygiene* (London: the Stationery Office). The handling information element is important for developing decision making skills. For this the pupil has to make an informed decision or an evaluation of a product or service for a given case study.

Practical and organisational skills are internally assessed. This involves regular practical exercises intended to develop a high level of practical, planning and organisational skills. These exercises allow pupils to discuss and decide their own level of work; they motivate pupils and give a sense of achievement; importantly they encourage pupils to think independently. Within the practical element there is a course objective concerned with carrying out an assignment (CO7). Arguably, the assessment arrangements have reflected some lack of confidence among Home Economics teachers regarding this 'practical' subject, for the final grade has been given for the written report of the assignment. Pupils who do not cope well with external written work can often have high levels of practical skill but their final grade is lowered by the assignment. However from 2002 it has been reformulated to enable the practical work within the assignment to be assessed; the new format should bring about pupil progression throughout the technological process and allow movement from 5–14 into the new National Qualifications in Home Economics. The proforma which pupils must use is complex and demanding on language skills. Time will tell if the changes are enough.

The recent publication of *Home Economics Standard Grade Course Notes* (MacGregor, 2002) is an excellent resource which should help to raise levels of attainment. In one sense however, it may have come too late. A general feeling among Home Economics teachers now is that Standard Grade is old-fashioned and does not offer progression between the effective new 5–14 courses and Higher Still course provision (see below). Some schools are offering Intermediate 1 and 2 Health and Food Technology instead of Standard Grade (though the Intermediate 1 course itself needs to be rewritten to enable progression to take place). Changes have been made to take effect in 2003–4.

COURSE CONTENT: NATIONAL QUALIFICATIONS (HIGHER STILL, S5 AND S6)

For many Home Economics teachers, the real strength of the subject lies in the new National Qualifications courses, begun as Higher Still in 1999–2000; these have taken Home Economics into the twenty-first century. A large number of courses are offered in schools (listed in *Conditions and Arrangements for National Qualifications for Session 2002–2003*, or the SQA website www.sqa.org.uk). Too much may have been taken on at the start but it is to the credit of the Higher Still development unit's work for the subject that a large volume of materials and support packages were ready for the first round of Higher Still in 1999–2000. In 2001–2, 709 pupils studied Higher Health and Food Technology and 289 took Intermediate 2. In these pupils have to study nutrition, diet and food-related diseases in depth. Excellent support is given from the British Nutrition Foundation, who run courses for teachers, produce materials and have an extensive website (www.nutrition.org.uk). The introduction of food product development was completely new for Home Economics teachers. Links with the food industry, new textbooks, interactive CD-ROMs and regular packages from the British Meat Education Service (BMES) have helped keep the teacher ahead of the pupils and link learning to the real world. (Regrettably, BMES is scheduled to cease its operations, at the time of writing.) The Consumer Studies unit involves understanding the effects of social trends and the products that are developed to address them. Using cross-curricular opportunities (e.g. with Biology for food experiments; with Art for textile work) can lessen the load of new areas of study and raises awareness of what is happening in Home Economics.

The technological project required at Higher/Intermediate 2 demands that pupils use all the knowledge of the course to develop a food product from a choice of two briefs. The challenge for the teacher is when to start the project, as so much prior knowledge is needed. Although an arduous task, the project puts the pupils through a process similar to that in the food industry. The pressure on teachers to teach towards assessment is considerable as the technological project embraces many of the learning outcomes of the units. Combined with the sheer number of end-of-unit assessment tests, this pressure is also felt by pupils. It can reduce the opportunity to learn through practical work, which is one of the improvements of the new Higher. In 2002, in response to these problems, evidence requirements have now been reduced. In some respects the course content for the new National Qualifications courses is easier for newly trained teachers than for long serving teachers, as it is corresponds to some of the work they will have recently studied at university.

With the recent cuts in staffing in schools in 2002 the problem of teaching composite Intermediate 2 and Higher classes will continue. Lifestyle and Consumer Technology is an alternative course and in 2002, ninety sat Intermediate 2 and 123 sat Higher. Fashion and Textile Technology is offered in schools where teachers have the expertise. The uptake numbers at Higher (forty-eight) reflect the lack of skill now found among teachers in this area and the fact that Standard Grade contains very little fabric work makes progression difficult. Intermediate 1, with 225 pupils taking it in 2002, is more popular because it is mostly practical. The sheer number of courses available means it is important for departments to choose the courses which will yield the highest numbers of pupils. Those who do offer Fashion and Textile Technology make use of the high-tech computerised machines and industrial appliances now commonly available; these allow pupils to use construction methods more suited to the fashion industry. Some of the units lend themselves to useful enterprise exercises, helping to counter earlier HMI criticism which noted that 'the use of the local environment is under-exploited in the majority of departments' (SOEID, 1996). Links with colleges running fashion courses, and fashion designers, and involvement in fashion shows bring work experience into the classroom. Advanced Highers are offered by some schools in all three subjects.

The most exciting and revolutionary course to come out of Higher Still is Hospitality – Practical Cookery Intermediate 2. In 2002, 2,356 pupils studied this with a pass rate of 91.8%. Its purpose is to provide young people with increased knowledge and skills which will not only lead to a better standard of personal life, but allow them to make a focused decision about pursuing a career in the hospitality and tourism industry. Finally, Home Economics has had the confidence to create a truly practical course. The practical work is demanding for the teacher as food is prepared for four and presented as in hotels and restaurants; auxiliary help is therefore essential. The course is expensive as a wide variety of foods is used including international cuisine; catering equipment and outfits are needed to give a more 'real' experience. It all has to be high profile and school management teams must be aware of the importance and relevance of the course when funding and curriculum decisions are being made.

Links with the hospitality industry make this possible. The Culinary Excellence scheme, set up by Frances Gallagher, the Glasgow Adviser for Home Economics, gives pupils the opportunity to be trained by top city chefs in their hotels and restaurants. After the course is completed many are offered job opportunities. Hotels and restaurants are keen to take on skilled employees and send application forms out to schools. One inspired example of an education-industry partnership, also involving cross-curricular activity, has been set up in 2002–3 in a Glasgow school: the pupils will train in a top restaurant, study Italian for work; an Italian assistant will be part of the Hospitality class and in June the pupils will work for a week in a hotel in Florence. Soon every Glasgow school should be linked to their own hotel.

Home Economics teachers must encourage work experience co-ordinators to find suitable work experience for S4 pupils. Staff from Springboard Scotland (an independent organisation which promotes career opportunities in the hospitality and tourism industry) come out to schools to keep pupils informed about openings in Scotland and offer summer schools every year. The Glasgow College of Food Technology helps to train pupils and teachers in the specialised skills required. It has been necessary for Home Economics teachers to learn a new approach to practical work but the possibilities that the course presents to young people and the changing attitude towards Home Economics from parents, pupils and staff is motivation itself. In 2002–3 the course structure will be amended to make it even more skills based.

CHALLENGES AND THE WAY AHEAD

Spreading the word

It is not possible to read about what is happening in Home Economics without being struck by how much it has changed 'since I was at school'. However the good opportunities provided by the new courses are expensive to run. At a time when school budgets are being cut, heads of Home Economics departments should be mindful of in-school politics. They must take account of criticism in the *Effective Learning and Teaching* report on the subject where HMI said that 'too many principal teachers do not take full account of the importance of good communication outwith their departments, with damaging consequences for prestige, uptake of courses and opportunities for pupils' (SOEID, 1996). Guidance teachers must be kept regularly informed about the new courses, progression paths and career opportunities. The senior management team should be regularly invited to the department to be involved in the testing of design briefs, in tasting sessions, in the presentation of certificates. Development plans should articulate the forward thinking of the department and the relevance of the new work on offer. Teachers from other departments can be invited to sensory evaluate dishes for Hospitality. Photographic evidence of all levels of work and projects should be used to inform pupils, staff, parents and visitors to the school. Fashion shows provide a vehicle for displaying work, cross-curricular activity, local community involvement, education–business links, communicating with staff. They normally motivate pupils and increase numbers.

Initial Teacher Education

The success of the new courses resulting in an increased up-take in the subject has caused problems owing to the current shortage of teachers. This is due to the limited number of teacher training places in the one-year PGCE(S) course (only offered by Strathclyde and Aberdeen Universities) and the lack of a dedicated Home Economics degree. Students who initially take degrees in Consumer Management Studies rarely intend to enter teaching. Increasing numbers of boys taking Home Economics alone underlines the need for more male Home Economics teachers. (In 2000–1, the number of pupils taking Access, Standard Grade, and Intermediate 1 and 2 Home Economics courses was 10,539 (2,169 boys and 8,343 girls). The pass rates were 85.6% for boys and 91.9% for girls *SQA Attainment in Scottish Schools: 2000–01*, News Release, 12 March 2002 (www.scotland.gov.uk/stats/ educ.htm). With 8,192 pupils sitting Standard Grade alone in 2002, numbers are on the increase. Currently there are about 1,200 Home Economics teachers in Scotland; six are male. Also, as with many other subjects, the age profile is towards the upper end. Home Economics needs an injection of youth. Many probationer teachers have to take extra courses in their own time to train in the skills they are lacking. This problem needs urgent attention as these skills are at the heart of the success and growth of the subject.

The bigger picture.

Scotland's poor health record and the increase in food hygiene problems lie in stark contrast to the nation's ever-increasing interest in food programmes on TV, videos, recipe books and food magazines. To some, the contrast is something of a paradox but it does present opportunities to the nation which go beyond just schools and education. Finland used to have the worst record of heart disease in the world but in the 1980s concerted efforts were made at a national level involving several government departments, to change that nation's diet. It is beyond the scope of this chapter to analyse what it took and to venture a Scottish equivalent. However it will be clear from what has been written here that Home Economics teachers have the potential to contribute significantly to any nationwide programme which might be put in place by determined MSPs seriously concerned by Scotland's health, diet and welfare.

Note: SQA figures for attainment have used pre-appeal statistics; final figures (not available at the time of writing) would be slightly higher.

REFERENCES

Bryce, K. and Liveston, D. (2001) *Environmental Studies 5–14. Home Economics. Smart Start Fabric Unit*, Glasgow: Glasgow City Council.

LTS (2000) *5–14 National Guidelines. Environmental Studies: Society, Science and Technology*, Dundee: LTS.

MacGregor, A. (2002) *Home Economics: Standard Grade Course Notes*, St Andrews: Leckie & Leckie.

Schlosser, E. (2002) *Fast Food Nation*, London: Penguin Books.

SOEID (1996) *Effective Learning and Teaching: Home Economics*, Edinburgh, SOED.

SOHHD (1993) *Scotland's Health: A Challenge to us All – The Scottish Diet*, Report of a working party to The Chief Medical Officer for Scotland (The James Report), Edinburgh: HMSO.

61

Information and Communication Technology

Robert Munro

Information and Communication Technology (ICT) is not a discrete subject in the Scottish secondary school curriculum. ICT is, however, a ubiquitous resource which comprises an apparently ever-expanding set of sophisticated, powerful, yet increasingly easy-to-use learning tools. These can be applied right across the curriculum, in any subject area. Teachers and pupils can use this sophisticated toolkit to identify, locate, access and collect all manner of digital information. They can then use it to manipulate, process and make sense of this garnered information to discern particular characteristics, trends, patterns and relationships and build knowledge. Finally it can be used to facilitate the effective presentation and communication of the conclusions of their examination and assessment of the information. Fortuitously, ICT can be deployed to support individual, paired, group and whole-class activity both within and between classrooms. Consequently, ICT has become a pivotal teaching and learning resource.

This integral relevance and importance to the curriculum is evidenced by the inclusion of ICT as a key component area within the national guidelines for 5–14. It is considered a core skill within post-16 qualification initiatives and is an essential competence government has decreed trainee teachers must acquire. ICT is at the heart of government strategies to create an information society and is the raison d'être of the National Grid for Learning (NGfL). The quest to develop ICT in schools has led to enormous expenditure on infrastructure, hardware provision and in-service teacher training programmes.

CHARACTERISTICS AND CONSEQUENCES OF RAPID GROWTH

Secondary school pupils have grown up in the information age. Most are conversant with many aspects and uses of ICT. For their teachers it is a very different story – many have struggled to assimilate and then effectively introduce ICT into their classrooms to reap its alleged educational benefits. They have had to cope with exceptionally rapid and wide-ranging development. In a little over twenty years ICT has been transformed from rarity status to commonplace resource, dragging in its wake unprecedented attention, debate, activity and investment in every sector of education. Twenty years have been characterised by accelerating change – in hardware, in software, in applications, in level of provision, even in the title of this vital resource. From the primeval soup of educational computing emerged information technology (IT) and later, when the synergistic benefits and increased range of potential uses and applications afforded by the fusion of information technology with communications technology were appreciated, ICT became the buzz-word.

This rapid evolution spawned a bewildering set of previously unimagined applications and processes. It is difficult for many people to appreciate these are so recent and fundamentally innovative. Word processing, spreadsheets, computer aided design, e-mail, multimedia, hypermedia, videoconferencing, the internet, the world wide web (www), avatars – as well as simulations, databases, CD-ROMs, DVDs, digital cameras and 3G phones – are now commonplace terms and technologies we take for granted. None of these powerful tools which can be deployed to help support and extend teaching and learning is more than twenty years old! Hardware platforms have changed markedly. Systems more than three years old are viewed as obsolete. Memory and storage capacity, functionality and speed of program execution drive remorselessly forward. Software development, always dependent on commercial rather than educational criteria, reflected the desire to enhance performance and versatility. This led to short-lived software cycles, a plethora of outdated packages, software of limited direct subject value and the creation of ultra-sophisticated applications overloaded with facilities seldom relevant to, and never fully utilised by, teachers and pupils in schools.

Not surprisingly, most teachers have found it difficult to respond effectively to such rapid and ubiquitous change. They have tried to incorporate and integrate the best aspects of ICT into their teaching and learning strategies – usually without rigorous assessment of the potential of ICT in advance of its use, or evaluation of its impact and contribution after the event. Teachers have lacked support, guidance and advice on how ICT might be most effectively implemented. It is surprising that most colleagues involved in education are enthralled by ICT and enthusiastically, almost evangelically, promote its continued and expanding use in schools without offering conclusive evidence that it enhances teaching and learning. They maintain ICT extends the range of teaching and learning strategies deployed in classrooms, enhances the flexibility of these strategies to accommodate pupils with diverse learning difficulties, stimulates the exploitation of distance and open learning opportunities and enriches the learning experience of their pupils.

It certainly cannot be said that many ICT-oriented experiences offered within the secondary curriculum have been enriching, that schools offer a full and judiciously integrated range of experiences to their pupils, or that pupils have benefited much thus far from their school-based experiences. The increasing availability of computers in the home may not be complementing ICT experiences in school, rather it may be offering more enriching experiences and promoting pupil dissatisfaction with school provision. ICT use in Scottish schools, following the vanguard deployment of twenty microcomputers in 1979, has been unco-ordinated, patchy, uninformed and frequently inappropriate. There has been scant evaluation of ICT use or assessment of the success of any use – instead evaluation has been obsessed with numbers and distribution of computers or the measurement of teacher/pupil grasp of technical expertise. The period has been a journey of radical, unplanned experimentation, constantly thrown off course by waves of innovation. Twenty years on, millions of pounds later, the returns on ICT investment look pretty meagre.

EXPONENTIAL GROWTH AND THE ODD QUANTUM LEAP

IT was introduced courtesy of a government initiative in 1981 to put a microcomputer into every school. A 50% grant helped finance the purchase of one of three systems –

Sinclair Spectrum, BBC or Research Machines 380Z – together with a supporting educational software pack. Short training courses were offered to selected teachers charged with cascading this newly acquired expertise throughout their schools. The systems represented cutting-edge technology (today they would be regarded as primitive) and were extremely expensive (the RM 380Z cost £1600 in 1981), yet schools, parent teacher associations and local authorities, concerned they might miss out on the widely publicised revolution, invested uncharacteristically heavily in this unproven, rapidly obsolescent technology. Schools then bought additional PC and Apple systems and a chaotic patchwork of provision emerged with contiguous local education authorities (LEAs) – even contiguous schools – favouring markedly different hardware. Initially the BBC ruled supreme but eventually the PC, and to a lesser extent the Apple Macintosh, superseded the vanguard generation.

Early educational software producers – commercial publishers, educational organisations, subject bodies and even enthusiastic amateurs – created a range of largely subject-specific programs. Most had clear educational objectives, thanks to practising teacher input, and were targeted at specialised areas of the curriculum. For teachers lacking ICT experience, but who were expected to integrate ICT into classroom teaching as just another resource, such classroom-focused and group-oriented software resources were invaluable. Despite many shortcomings they helped establish concepts or reinforce skills.

To complement these packages more open-ended software was available – database handling, spreadsheets and text processing. Many were useless without supporting datafiles on, for example, socio-economic data of countries of the world, the characteristics of the elements of the atomic table or nineteenth-century population census data. The Social Subjects and the Sciences were seen as key areas where databases and spreadsheets might be effectively exploited but, despite alleged classroom potential, few teachers were sufficiently motivated to establish and integrate data handling activity into curriculum work. Databases, particularly, failed to enthuse teachers and pupils long term. Datafile creation was incredibly time consuming and the query interface, which allowed the user to design questions which could extract information and relationships from the data, was too complex for many pupils. Other software which could be used across the curriculum as a newspaper-format reporting device or to support creative and functional writing was more enthusiastically adopted.

As the hardware advanced so the software focus changed. Easy to use subject-based, curriculum-specific software was eclipsed on one front by truly open-ended generic packages – increasingly integrated suites of programs (today typified by Microsoft Office) incorporating word processor, database, spreadsheet, graphics and communications functionality. On another front a technological quantum leap brought sophisticated, topic-based software on CD-ROM. Huge amounts of digital information, drawn from diverse sources – text, graphs, charts, maps, pictures, photographs, sound, video, even software – could be welded into complex, interlinked, multimedia/hypermedia resources for investigative activity in the classroom or the school library.

In the early 1990s official documents started to offer guidance to teachers on how computers might be deployed. In 1993, SOED's 5–14 Environmental Studies guidelines identified the key aspects of IT (no communications at this stage) to address in S1/S2:

- text handling;
- information handling;
- position, movement and control;
- modelling (including simulations and adventures);
- image and sound handling;
- applications of IT in society.

Hard on its heels SCET published *Describe IT* (1994). This offered a comprehensive framework on which schools might develop a progressive and coherent IT policy. Unfortunately both documents made little real impact on the secondary sector.

It was hardly surprising. During the 1980s hardware provision was limited and distribution was disproportionate. Departments of Computing Studies and Business Studies attracted the bulk of school hardware and their students enjoyed lavishly equipped rooms featuring the latest and best technology whereas Geography or English might only have access to one or two trolley-mounted systems wheeled around all their classes. What chance was there of developing creative writing and stimulating redrafting of texts and reports in English? How many pupils could follow the Oregon Trail in History or research the characteristics of underdeveloped countries in Geography? Schools also appeared unable to decide who should teach basic ICT skills and frequently offered an S1/S2 course to familiarise pupils with various applications – often their only in-school experience of computers. While policy documents preached the ethos of cross-curricular computer use in practice most pupils encountered the technology but fleetingly in their secondary school career.

In 1995 schools were still floundering about trying to match ICT philosophy with educational practice when they were beset by another quantum leap. Suddenly communication technologies assumed centre stage and the internet, with its world wide web component, emerged as the information delivery system. This was the vehicle to the promised land! Schools were exhorted to join the communications revolution, get on-line, enter cyberspace, ride the superhighway and surf the web. The web dominated ICT.

Later that year the UK Education Departments' Superhighways Initiative evaluated twenty-five projects, two in Scotland. Modern Communications for Teaching and Learning in Argyll and Bute explored, in particular, the potential of video-conferencing. The Superhighways Teams across Rural Schools (STARS) project used e-mail and computer conferencing to involve able children, drawn from small rural schools, in a range of collaborative science-based activities designed to develop critical and creative thinking. The Scottish findings confirmed that electronic communications can benefit teaching and learning, especially where the technology is integrated into the curriculum and electronic networks build upon shared interests. Evaluators found that rural areas could derive great benefits from ICT through linking of small schools, shared approaches to topic work and collaborative pupil activities. They concluded, however, that rural schools risked being left behind when narrow-band technology is superseded by expensive broadband networks – a consideration currently exercising the Scottish Executive.

Key proposals of the Stevenson Report (Independent School Commission, 1997) were adopted as policy by the incoming Labour government. Late in 1997 the government committed £100m to UK schools to buy advanced computers and acquire the necessary infrastructure to facilitate access to the NGfL. This comprehensive web resource was designed to be electronically accessible to all UK educational establishments – schools, colleges, universities, libraries, museums and galleries. Deals were struck with various service providers to ensure that all Scottish secondary schools would enjoy established internet links. Problems associated with copyright, pornography and cost were addressed. Many schools have arranged filtered access to the web – a policy which removes many problems but restricts resource availability. It also conflicts with decisions taken in other European countries.

To reflect the changes in technology and ICT practices in schools the Scottish Executive published ICT guidelines:

> designed to provide a framework for the integration of ICT into existing practice so that all pupils become skilled, confident and informed users and gain the maximum benefit in using ICT in other curricular areas. (LTS, 2000a).

A partner document (LTS, 2000b) offered excellent guidance for teachers and managers – comprehensive, sensibly written and replete with exemplar material. To complement these initiatives regulations which tentatively sought to ensure all student teachers were ICT-literate on leaving teacher education establishments were introduced. These reflected national research findings into the ICT competence and confidence of student teachers (Simpson et al., 1998). Other research into the ICT skills of practising teachers (Williams et al., 1998) undoubtedly helped the release of £25m of New Opportunities Funding (NOF) to support in-service training in ICT.

THE SCENE TODAY – A MOSAIC OF DEVELOPMENT

This rapid and uncontrolled development has resulted in a disparate picture of ICT use in secondary schools across Scotland. While all schools have a considerable number of computers and a selection of associated peripheral equipment, these resources vary widely in type, in age and in capability, and are unevenly distributed, both across the country and within individual schools. However, the commitment to purchasing advanced computer hardware and reducing the computer–pupil ratio (1:5 in 2002) has paid dividends.

In some authorities specific initiatives have resulted in excellent resource provision. Glasgow's Project 2002, a major school refurbishment and rebuilding programme, has led to generous provision of suites of advanced computers and flood-wiring. All departments have access to these suites and to dedicated departmental hardware. An independent service provider manages the ICT resource and is responsible for repairs, upgrades and software access. In addition, in three secondary schools, PDA devices have been provided for all pupils in specific year groups. Evaluation of this project will give interesting pointers towards the potential and value of ubiquitous computing. North Lanarkshire has established an interactive learning centre for digital media and the arts at Bellshill Academy. This community resource, equipped to the highest specifications and featuring training suites, specialist video-editing, animation and sound engineering studios, aims to support the development of digital media skills through process-based and outcome-enhancing learning. St Andrew's High School, Kirkcaldy, is one of three European sites in the Apple Classrooms of Tomorrow (ACOT) project – mission statement 'To change the way teachers think about using technology for teaching'. Work has focused on integrating ICT in Mathematics, English, Science and Modern Languages in S1 and S2. Innovative uses of ICT are explored in upgraded, highly resourced classrooms. In the Highlands one rural secondary secured funding to give all S4 Modern Studies pupils their own laptop and in Edinburgh many schools are experimenting with wireless networks. Unfortunately, there is no national co-ordination of these innovative and developmental activities.

Software availability, outwith provision of conventional suites like Microsoft Office, is quite limited. There is a dearth of subject-specific and curriculum-relevant software. Most teachers have an imperfect knowledge of the software available for their subject or curricular area and few have surplus departmental finance for software purchase. Often LEA purchasing policy precludes the acquisition of anything other than a tightly specified, agreed set of materials. Some agencies still produce a dribble of appropriate software, notably Learning and Teaching Scotland and the Scottish Interactive Technology Centre at Edinburgh University, but the Scottish market is small and nobody will make a fortune out of a software package for, at most, 400 schools.

However, there is no doubt that such resources are desperately needed, as the success of the tightly curriculum-focused History software created at the University of Strathclyde by Dr Peter Hillis illustrates. His resources develop history concepts in 10–16-year-old pupils, deal with many aspects of nineteenth-century urban life in Scotland and offer exciting opportunities and strategies for integrating ICT into the History curriculum. SEED should support the development of this type of software and facilitate the creation of similar software in all curriculum areas that exemplifies underlying educational rigour, integrates the skill of the teacher in its design and utilises the capabilities of the technology to the full.

The main reason so little software of this type is produced is because of the availability of open-ended software and the growing pervasiveness of the web. Teachers have been short-changed by decision makers who have encouraged them to exploit open-ended software and produce individualised pupil resources or involve pupils in the creation of 'presentations'. Few individualised resources have materialised. They are difficult and time-consuming to produce. Pupils have, however, authored an unco-ordinated rash of indifferent reports, stories and multimedia shows. These demonstrate that pupils can arrange and integrate text, graphics, sound and stilted animation into predictable presentation templates but do not illustrate acquisition of deep knowledge, understanding of the issues, topics and concepts they present, or thoughtful appraisal and redrafting of content.

The web has become the Holy Grail. Every teacher wants to use it in his/her classroom. So do all the pupils but not for the same reasons. The web is a classic indicator of how teachers have been stampeded into using ICT without considering how it might best be used. Most teachers have yet to formulate ways of using the web which exploit its educational potential. All too frequently they simply direct pupils to particular sites and engage them in interpretation tasks. If pupils are to get anything from the web they have to know how to search, know which search engines and search techniques produce the most effective results and be able to read accessed information with understanding (detecting bias and gauging authenticity). This is a difficult and demanding set of skills. When should pupils acquire them? Who is going to teach them – the primary school, the Geography teacher, the Computing Studies Department, the librarian? These issues have to be urgently addressed and resolved before the use of the web can transcend that of an elementary fact-gathering vehicle. Indeed, some educationalists consider pupils would understand and learn more from studying a carefully selected set of resources on CD-ROM rather than using the web – arguing there would be less distraction as pupils could focus on a few, carefully chosen, key concepts.

Despite its pivotal importance, ICT is but one resource, one element in teaching and learning. The key to its effective use and deployment is the teacher. ICT is a difficult area in which to acquire expertise because of the constant change and advancement and the bewildering number of applications and potential areas of use with which teachers have to become familiar. They must gain this familiarity before they can make informed decisions on whether, or how, they should proceed to try to integrate ICT into their teaching and learning to the benefit of their pupils. Teachers get very little detailed help and assistance from colleagues in school or others connected with the education business. All schools, local authorities and government bodies have produced extensive, but generalised, policy documents about how to use ICT. These are of little direct help to a teacher wanting to use ICT to introduce a topic like photosynthesis, explore the role of pressure groups in environmental issues, create a montage or support a visit to an old folks home. It is to the great credit of many teachers that there are numerous, excellent exemplars of imaginative and creative integration of ICT in curriculum work.

In addition to support from policy documents and assistance from colleagues, teachers need imaginative, quality pre-service and in-service training. Critically they need time to reflect on and develop expertise related to this training. Pre-service teacher training courses currently provide insufficient guidance and direction on the pedagogical uses of ICT. None requires students to display confidence and competence in ICT use on school placement. The NOF programme offered to all teachers has been a limited success. Many trainers had no experience of using ICT in the classroom, materials used in the courses concentrated on technical skills development rather than pedagogical skills refinement, and there was no apparent commonality of approach between the various courses offered by training providers. Once again, a substantial investment appears to have been wasted.

THE WAY FORWARD?

The development of ICT in Scottish secondary schools has been eventful and, in most respects, nowhere near as successful as had been anticipated. To date the full potential has certainly not been realised. Scottish education must urgently address, and resolve, four key issues. Without their prompt resolution the expanding potential offered by ICT will never be achieved, our education process will be the poorer, and generations of pupils will have been sold short.

A fresh, imaginative vision for ICT is essential – a vision which embodies realisable, concrete results! To date development has been patchy, hasty and reactive. Education has consistently failed to articulate where pupils should be on an ICT skills and competences continuum during, and on completion of, their secondary school education. No progressive, coherent set of ICT skills and competences has been identified for secondary school pupils, far less a specific framework illustrating where and how they should acquire and might refine them. Teachers need to know exactly how ICT can support the curriculum and how best it should be deployed in classrooms.

Achieving this vision requires the creation of an educational environment where all pupils have the opportunity of using ICT as and when desired. Pupils need not necessarily have their own computer – although that may prove the most appropriate way of resourcing and realising the vision! They must have access to adequate, appropriate ICT resources in all school locations. Under-resourced departments require considerable investment and their staff need help to identify ways that new resources could most profitably be deployed. The current disparity in investment favours particular departments and curricular areas, not to mention hotbeds of innovative activity. This must be redressed. Such massive investment will require joint initiatives between education, government and commerce.

There is a desperate need for ICT-related staff development in secondary schools and teacher education institutions (which are being surpassed by developments in schools). The NOF programme should be extended and the funding closely targeted at enhancing the pedagogic skills of the teaching force. All staff should be encouraged to examine and evaluate their use of ICT more rigorously. ICT is but one facet of secondary school education and should always be used purposefully – where it complements, or preferably enhances, more traditional or conventional educational methods or processes, where it more effectively establishes conceptual understanding, or where it offers a unique tool or experience to the pupil. Once staff have identified if, and how, ICT can help them they need support, assistance and advice and should be allocated time to reflect and to develop expertise.

A national team should be charged with the identification of software needs of the secondary education sector. Then a development programme to create fresh educational software resources, which support and complement those currently available and maximise the benefits from web-sourced information, should be established. These software resources should be free to schools.

The target for Scottish secondary school education must be the realisation of the potential of ICT. If the aforementioned components are addressed and tackled positively and coherently then this target can be realised. If not then education will stand guilty of wasting phenomenal sums of money, years of teacher and pupil time and of massive underachievement. If all pupils have unfettered access to information, and all facets of ICT are used imaginatively within teaching and learning strategies, pupils really could transform base information into the gold of knowledge.

REFERENCES

LTS (2000a) *Information and Communications Technology 5–14 National Guidelines*, Glasgow: LTS.

LTS (2000b) *5–14 National Guidelines, Information and Communications Technology 5–14, Guide for Teachers and Managers*, Glasgow: LTS.

Simpson, M. et al. (1998) Using information and communications technology as a pedagogical tool, *Journal for Teacher Education*, 7 (3), 431–6.

The Independent ICT in School Commission (1997) *Information and Communication Technology in UK Schools 1996/7*, London: The Independent School Commission.

Williams, D. et al. (1998) *Teachers' ICT Skills and Knowledge Needs*, Aberdeen: Robert Gordon University.

62

Mathematics Education

Jim Wilson

The current Mathematics curriculum in Scotland stems from a number of national initiatives and guidelines, aimed at ensuring that Mathematics, as a subject, includes pupils of all abilities.

PACE OF WORK / AGE AND STAGE

Until fairly recently the secondary Mathematics curriculum in Scotland would have been discussed in terms of 5–14 in S1/S2, Standard Grade in S3/S4, and the National Qualifications: Access; Intermediate; Higher; and Advanced Higher, in S5/S6. However, there are reports (HMI, 1997, 1999) highlighting the necessity to increase pace of work. These together with the relaxation of restrictions on when pupils can be presented for examinations, and Intermediate being mooted in some quarters as a replacement for Standard Grade, have blended to produce a much more complex and dynamic situation.

There is no longer a 'norm' in terms of the timing of mathematical progression for pupils. Although some departments may not be affected, an increasing number of departments are receiving pupils into S1 who have already commenced level F (the final 5–14 level), or will shortly do so. If these pupils have achieved this through an increase in pace of work at primary school, it would be nonsense to hold them back in secondary. Therefore pupils are now commencing Standard Grade in S2, or even S1 in a small number of cases. This has a knock-on effect. For example, the most able pupils may complete the Higher course before the end of S4. There is also the possibility that pupils from S3, S4, S5 and S6 are all working on the same course. Not only can this create timetabling and resource problems, it also raises the question of whether we should group pupils together in terms of ability, or age.

Does it even have to be Standard Grade after 5–14? As mentioned above, some departments have taken the view that the Intermediate 1 and Intermediate 2 courses are more appropriate, in terms of progression to National Qualifications, than Standard Grade General and Credit. This view is in part based on the unitised structure of the Intermediate courses, which they feel dovetails better with the similar unitised structure in Higher. For less able pupils, some departments are using Access 3 as a replacement for Foundation. The support materials available, language skills required, and the entirely school based assessment procedures are viewed as advantageous.

5–14

The National Guidelines on Mathematics 5–14 are aimed at ensuring that all pupils experience a 'coherent, continuous and challenging programme of work' (SOED, 1991, p. 1)) from the start of primary schooling through to the end of year two at secondary school. As pupils starting secondary school have already had seven years of mathematical experience, and have often covered different amounts of work at varying levels, a 'fresh start' approach is not applicable, nor should pupils 'tread water'. Therefore, Mathematics departments liaise with their associated primary schools to obtain/discuss pupil transfer information, in order to determine the appropriate continuation point at the start of S1.

Individualised learning approaches are no longer as prevalent as they once were. Various reports by the inspectorate highlight the need for an increase in direct teaching in S1/S2 (HMI, 1997, 1999). As departments implement these recommendations, many find that setting or broad banding in both S1 and S2 make direct teaching approaches more effective. However, classes still contain pupils with a range of abilities, albeit narrower.

National testing is an 'integral part' of 5–14. These tests, from levels A through to F, consist of four units. Each unit in the test is related to a specific 5–14 Mathematics outcome. The 5–14 outcomes in Mathematics are: number, money and measurement; information handling; shape, position and movement; problem solving and enquiry (this outcome is integrated with the other three outcomes for testing). The national test result should confirm the teachers view of the level at which the pupil should now work.

There has been concern raised about the validity and value of national tests. A number of local authorities have introduced 'standardised testing' in P4, P7 and S2. Advocates of this approach argue that standardised tests give a more detailed and accurate picture of the progress that pupils are making within 5–14. Detailed statistical data can be produced for each 5–14 outcome, pupils, classes, schools, and so on, allowing tracking from P4 onwards. This information allows departments to identify both strengths and weaknesses in their 5–14 provision. However, there is concern in some quarters that the benefits of this may be overshadowed by their possible use as a league table.

STANDARD GRADE

There are three levels within Standard Grade Mathematics: Foundation, General and Credit.

Foundation level covers mainly arithmetical concepts with some basic mathematical ideas included. General level introduces pupils to the basic concepts in algebra, geometry and trigonometry. Credit significantly extends this into more abstract concepts. It is important to note that pupils often work between two levels, for example, working on some of the Credit material, but not all of it. The SQA have identified some easier content in each level, allowing pupils the opportunity to extend their grade without covering all the material at that level.

The Standard Grade arrangements document for Mathematics, revised for 2001 on-wards, gives detailed guidance on content and methodology. There are now two assessable elements: knowledge and understanding (KU); and reasoning and enquiry (RE). The internally assessed investigative element has been removed from all three levels of Standard Grade. The removal of the investigative element should not be viewed as a devaluing of the merits of investigative approaches. On the contrary, instead of viewing problem solving as a 'bolt on', it is clearly set at the heart of Mathematics. The first paragraph of the revised arrangement document identifies the essential aim of Mathematics:

> to help pupils learn how to describe, tackle and ultimately solve problems which require the use of mathematical knowledge and techniques . . . it is recommended that the main approach to teaching and learning mathematics should be firmly based on problem solving. (SQA, 1999, p. 4)

Although not a requirement, pupils are usually presented for external assessment at two levels, Foundation and General, or General and Credit. There are two papers set for each of the three levels: the first is a non-calculator paper, and in the second, a calculator may be used. Each paper assesses both of the assessable elements, that is, KU and RE. There are seven possible grades (1–7) for each assessable element, with 1 being the highest. An overall grade 1 or 2 gives a Credit award, grade 3 or 4 a General award, grade 5 or 6 a Foundation award. A grade 7 signifies that the course was completed, but the standard specified by the grade related criteria has not been met.

NATIONAL QUALIFICATIONS

The Higher Still programme was designed to produce a more coherent progression from Standard Grade. The courses implemented as a result of the Higher Still programme have been rebadged as National Qualifications (It should be noted that Standard Grade is also classed as a national course). They include: Access 2, Access 3, Intermediate 1, Intermediate 2, Higher, and Advanced Higher.

The course for each qualification consists of three units (usually two mandatory and one optional), each of forty hours duration, with an additional forty hours that is used for induction, support, consolidation and preparation for external assessment. At the end of each unit, pupils undertake a unit assessment set at 'minimum competency' level. These assessments are internally assessed within the department. Pupils failing to pass any unit assessment have a further opportunity, and, in exceptional circumstances, a third attempt to pass. Pupils are required to pass all three of the unit assessments, and the external SQA examination in order to receive a course award. Overall course awards are made at level A (1 or 2), B (3 or 4) and C (5 or 6). Should a pupil 'just miss' a level C award, they will receive a level A award in the course below.

Departments are advised by the SQA to ensure that pupils are tested beyond minimum competency for both examination practice and appeal purposes. The external assessments, in line with Standard Grade, have both a non-calculator paper and a paper where a calculator may be used. Overall, approximately 60% of the questions are at level C, with the remainder testing ability at levels A and B. The Access qualifications do not have an external examination component.

ADVANCED GRAPHICS CALCULATORS

In general, Mathematics departments have found it difficult to fulfil the 5–14 guidelines in terms of information handling and access to computer packages. There are often a number of reasons for this including rooming availability, number of computers in school, lack of software, timetable constraints, and teacher reticence to use technology. As the ratio of computers to pupils continues to improve within schools, Mathematics departments will have increasing opportunities to ensure all pupils can access technology.

In response to concerns over a perceived drop in standards of calculation skills, nearly all departments include a mental Mathematics component in their 5–14 courses, and practise mental skills in S3/S4. Pupils are also assessed on their mental skills in the non-calculator papers of national courses. Although it would appear to be a misnomer, the advanced graphics calculator can be used by the teacher as a learning and teaching aid for mental calculation skills. For example, a software program like 'Countdown', which is based on the television programme of the same name, can be displayed on a screen. Pupils then undertake the role of participants in attempting to find calculations that will produce the displayed target number.

At the same time it is also recognised that advanced graphics calculators can be of considerable benefit by helping pupils to establish a firm understanding of a number of mathematical concepts. However the calculators are not used to provide unnecessary support, nor are they a substitute for the development of personal proficiency in Mathematics (SCCC, 1998). At present calculators, which perform symbolic manipulation via a computer algebra system (CAS), are not permitted in examinations. As it is almost impossible visually to distinguish between a numerical method and a CAS calculator, it can only be a matter of time for their use to be permitted. In the interim period, these CAS calculators are very useful for teaching algebra, calculus and geometry to the more able pupils. Advanced graphics calculators which use a numerical process, as opposed to symbolic, may be used in examinations where calculators are permitted. The use of these calculators as learning and teaching tools is growing each year as teacher confidence in their use grows, and more shareable resources are produced.

ACHIEVEMENT AND ATTAINMENT

In order to improve attainment, it is essential to look at what has already been achieved. One major programme, which looks at pupil performance, is the assessment of achievement programme (AAP). The Scottish Office introduced this programme in 1981, in order to monitor the performance of pupils in English Language, Mathematics, and Science. In order to monitor pupil progression, the assessments are carried out on a three-yearly cycle on P4, P7, and S2 pupils.

The sixth AAP Mathematics survey was carried out in 2000. In terms of S2 pupils, although there was improvement in nearly all strands assessed, compared to the 1997 AAP, there were still areas of weaknesses. Despite considerable improvement in pupil mental skills, fractions, percentages and ratio are still unsatisfactory, that is, the overall mean score of pupils was less than 50%. The survey noted that although S2 pupil performance is improving, it still has some way to go. The survey also identified problem solving as being an area of particular concern. Despite being set at the core of learning and teaching, pupils are still having difficulty in this area. The AAP suggests that this may be a consequence of the number of words contained in problem solving items, and the comprehension and interpretative skills required as much as pupils mathematical skills. (SEED, 2000)

In addition to the national AAP surveys, Scottish pupils were involved in the Third International Mathematics and Science Study (TIMSS). This extensive survey looked at the attainment of over half a million pupils from more than forty countries. At age thirteen, Scottish pupils were less successful in five out of six reported topic areas than those from many other countries. The only area in which these pupils exceeded the international mean was data handling and probability (Andrews, 2000). This would appear to make bleak reading. However, there have been many criticisms levelled against the TIMSS study in terms of its structure, sampling procedures, test design and implementation, but Andrews argues that to deny there is a problem and criticise the manner of the study would be to miss an opportunity to move forward.

NEXT STEPS?

Only around two-thirds of Mathematics departments have fully implemented the 5–14 guidelines. In order fully to evaluate progress, many argue that full implementation of 5–14 takes place as a matter of urgency.

The improvement of pupil mental skills is encouraging, and continued effort should take place to extend the good work that is undertaken in this area; in particular, to widen the use of computers and advanced graphics calculators with all year groups.

Despite a number of recommendations and support from nearly all local authorities and manufacturers, few departments appear to have made effective use of advanced graphics calculators. It is clear therefore that, to date, many departments have either not been convinced of the benefits of using the calculators, or have not received the funding necessary to allow pupils access to them. This requires to be addressed, before a substantial, ongoing national initiative to convince staff of the learning and teaching benefits of the calculators commences.

There is a strong argument to suggest that more departments would place problem solving at the heart of learning and teaching if they could be convinced that this approach would not be at the expense of their examination results. Perhaps the additional time that can be 'created' by increasing pace of work will allow departments more opportunities to explore the varied uses of Mathematics. At present there is often a rush to cover course content.

The winter diet of SQA examinations was withdrawn after its pilot year due to the small number of candidates. Presently, pupils completing a national course in, say, September or October, must wait until May/June the following year to be assessed. Is this good educational practice? If there is to be flexibility in the curriculum, surely it must be matched by flexibility in assessment.

The Mathematics curriculum has greatly altered over the last twenty years or so. Those who have been involved have often wished that things could be 'left alone'. It is impossible to predict what changes the next twenty years may bring. However, one factor that can be guaranteed to remain constant is the high profile that Mathematics will continue to receive.

REFERENCES

Andrews, P. (2000) *Mathematics Education and Comparative Studies: A Rational Model for the Future*, paper prepared for the Scottish Teachers of Mathematics Conferences.
HMI (1997) *Improving Mathematics Education 5–14*, Edinburgh: SOEID.
HMI (1999) *Standards and Quality in Secondary Schools 1995–1999: Mathematics*, Edinburgh: SOEID.
SOED (1991) *Curriculum and Assessment in Scotland, National Guidelines, Mathematics 5–14*, Edinburgh: SOED.

SCCC (1998) *Advanced Calculators in Mathematics Education*, Dundee: SCCC

SEED (2000) *Assessment of Achievement Programme, Sixth Survey of Mathematics 2000*, Edinburgh: SEED.

SQA (1999) *Standard Grade Arrangements in Mathematics: Foundation, General and Credit Levels in and after 2001*, Glasgow: SQA.

63

Modern Foreign Languages

Richard Johnstone

The backcloth to Modern Languages in Scottish secondary schools features two conflicting forces. One is the seemingly irresistible advance of English, the dominant language of globalisation. This influences attitudes to all other languages in Scotland including minority languages (e.g. Gaelic, Scots, Punjabi) and foreign languages. English is the most widely taught foreign language in continental schools and is prominent in business and the media. The other and opposing force arises from the determination of policy makers, academics and others abroad to ensure that the identity of the emerging Europe is shaped by a firm commitment to cultural and linguistic diversity.

The tension between these two forces makes it impossible to forecast how the 'languages game' will be played in the new millennium. Will all Europeans eventually share a common language (an evolved form of English)? If so, how necessary will it be for speakers of English to learn another language at all? Or, on the contrary, will all Europeans, Scots included, need to master at least three major languages, as is argued in an EC White Paper (1996)?

1950S TO LATE 1990S

It is against this unpredictable backcloth that the major thrust of languages policy for Scottish secondary schools over the past fifty years must be considered: the attempt to make a foreign language accessible to the full range of students. Before the mid-1960s it was taught to an academic elite, with emphasis on grammar, translation, writing and literature rather than on spoken language. Reflecting this view, the 1950 SED report on Modern Languages in secondary schools stated that the process of language learning should provide a general linguistic training which would give pupils a surer appreciation of the value of words and help them to use their own language more effectively.

By the end of the 1960s, however, most S1/S2 pupils except for a so-called 'remedial' minority were learning a foreign language. To confront the challenge of teaching this wider social range, including pupils living in areas of major social deprivation, Languages teachers turned to language laboratories, audio-lingual courses and worksheets. Unfortunately, these generally drew on a psychology of language learning that (with Chomsky's attack on Skinnerian behaviourism) had been discredited at the very point at which they were being introduced to schools. In consequence, throughout the 1970s, pupils' learning was based on the repetitious drilling of situational dialogues. In addition, S1/S2 course books tended to feature a family (white) with parents (married), a boy (mischievous, sporty) and a girl (well-behaved, good at school) living in a house (middle-class, detached), and presented thereby a travesty of the cultures in which the particular foreign language was spoken.

It is not surprising that this first attempt to cater for all pupils had run out of steam by the end of the 1970s. An SED-funded research project (Mitchell, R. et al., 1981 *The Foreign Language Classroom: An Observational Study*, Monograph 9, Stirling: University of Stirling, 1981), found that in S1 over 98% of the French spoken consisted of 'practice language' with less than 2% consisting of 'real communication', and the Munn Report (1977) could not justify a place for a foreign language in its core curriculum for all pupils in S3/S4.

A second attempt was launched in the late 1970s through the CCC national French project and regional initiatives. With encouragement from the Council of Europe, teaching became more functional, with the foreign language used for everyday purposes and pupils expressing their real selves, often in interaction with their peers. Differentiated materials offered a chance of success at some level. Another SED-funded research study by Mitchell in 1988, (*Communicative Language Teaching in Practice*, London: CILT) confirmed that by the early 1980s teachers had assimilated tactics such as paraphrase, simplification, L1-cognates and mime for communicating meaning through the foreign language. Drawing on inspections from 1984–1988, HMI (1990) stated in *Effective Teaching and Learning in Scottish Secondary Schools: Modern Languages* that many of the new-style course books lacked cross-reference material and that many schools were not allowing pupils to take their books home, thereby failing to support them adequately in their learning. However, they also identified 'clear signs of greater participation and enjoyment on the part of pupils who are showing increasing capability in using and understanding the spoken language. These are distinct gains which accord with present-day needs' (para. 9.15).

Standard Grade was welcomed because it allowed the new approach to be extended to S3/S4. The 1987 SEB Standard Grade arrangements saw the primary objective as 'real language in real use'. This meant confronting pupils with authentic rather than contrived texts and encouraging gist extraction, inferences, use of a dictionary, confidence, self-reliance and social strategies for dealing with others, as well as 'proper attention to appropriate grammatical structures'. The same objectives formed the basis of the Modern Language modules in the National Certificate. To create and implement a Standard Grade framework of three levels embracing six grades required national support, provided through exemplar materials in five languages for Standard Grade and beyond.

As the end of the 1980s approached it could be claimed that these developments had achieved much progress towards enabling the full range of pupils to profit from foreign language study. Despite this, SCCC (1989) remained 'persuaded that the study of a foreign language should not be a compulsory part of the curriculum post S2 now or in the immediate future'. They believed that to make it compulsory 'would not find favour with parents or with a broad range of professional interests within and outwith education' (p. 12), though research was not commissioned to inform this assumption.

However, a major policy-change occurred soon after, resulting from a 'campaign for languages' by teachers but also endorsed by political will. In Circular 1178 (SED, 1989) the Secretary of State for Scotland's wish was stated that 'the study of at least one language other than English, and preferably a modern foreign language, should normally be pursued by all pupils throughout the third and fourth years of compulsory secondary school' (para. 7). Political will also legitimised the reintroduction of Modern Languages in primary schools. Within a short space of time, therefore, the ultra-cautious view of SCCC had yielded to an ambitious prospect of six years study (P6–S4). Behind politicians' thinking was the advent of the Single European Market (due in 1992) where languages skills would be vital for exports. To encourage larger numbers to maintain their language beyond Standard Grade, a Revised Higher was introduced that dispensed with prose translation and brought greater authenticity and relevance into assessment tasks.

A comparison of presentations in French, German, Spanish, Italian and Russian in 1976 and 1996 tells two starkly different tales. The 29,684 presentations at 'O' Grade in 1976 became 60,525 presentations at Standard Grade in 1996, as a result of 'languages for all', with over 95% of the population being presented. By contrast, the 11,313 presentations in 1976 at Higher (S5/S6) had declined to 5,563 by1996. The only slightly bright spot was Spanish, where presentations at Higher increased from 1976 to 1996, but the percentages taking Spanish in comparison to French and German were so small that they made no real impact on the general trend. National research was commissioned to investigate the factors lying behind the alarming drop in uptake at Higher. The report (McPake et al., 1998) identified 'a climate of negativity' in Scottish society towards languages, for instance in the media, and also a strong feeling on the part of the most high-attaining students in S4 that their Modern Languages curriculum in S3/S4 had been lacking in intellectual excitement and was not enabling them to feel confident that they could actually put their languages to real use to the extent that their peers on the continent were able to achieve.

FROM 1998 INTO THE NEW MILLENNIUM

The 1998 HMI report on Modern Languages was widely perceived as being critical. True, it acknowledged an increased willingness in pupils to speak and it praised the efforts of many teachers to make Modern Languages accessible to pupils of all levels of ability. At the same time, though, it stated that 'significant improvements are needed in standards and quality' and that 'there was evidence in S1/S2 and S3/S4 of a marked decline in the quality of courses'. Following immense and generally negative publicity in the media, a ministerial action group on languages was established in order to address these negative factors and to secure the place of Modern Languages in the curriculum. Their report *Citizens of a Multilingual World* (December, 2000) sets out a radical new agenda for Languages, including a 'rationale' which embraces the notion of preparing all Scottish pupils for the 'mobility across Europe' to which all citizens of the European Union have a funda-mental right. It also sets out a 'languages entitlement for all within education 5–16' which contains eleven different components.

Regrettably, the notion of 'entitlement' has been variously interpreted to suit different ideologies. As intended by the action group, all pupils are recommended to take a modern language to age sixteen, and the eleven components of the 'entitlement' set out what they have a right to expect. By stark contrast, as intended by those who oppose a 'language for all', the proposition becomes 'You don't have to learn a modern language but you are entitled to do so, if you wish' – a travesty of the original intention. SEED Circular 3/2001 (August 2001); dealing with flexibility in the curriculum has been interpreted by many as legitimising this latter erroneous view. The full Scottish Executive response to the action group (September, 2001) and subsequent information bulletins have sought to limit the damage by locating the 'entitlement' within a continuing 'languages for all' policy, but nonetheless considerable doubts remain as to how the 'entitlement' will be interpreted and implemented on the ground across the country.

It is still too early to predict what will be the sustainable effects of the new Higher Still arrangements, but two signs of promise are welcome. First, the Access and Intermediate 1 curricula seem to many teachers to be more motivating for students than their Standard Grade counterparts. Second, the 2001 presentation figures for Higher in Modern Languages went up for the first time in many years.

WHAT OF THE FUTURE?

Four priorities seem evident: to increase motivation (including among high-attaining students); to encourage maximum up-take (in an era of increasing uncertainty as to the status of 'languages for all'); to achieve a greater degree of diversification of languages-learning (with an increase in Spanish being particularly desirable, not only because of its attractiveness but also because of its global importance); and to promote higher levels of proficiency among students in actually using the modern language they are learning. In Scotland, students of languages do well in their national examination attainments but perceive their real-life proficiency in the language as relatively low. There seems merit therefore in locating Scottish students of languages not only on a national attainment scale via SQA but also on an international proficiency scale, and in this sense it may prove useful to draw on the Council of Europe framework which contains six levels of proficiency covering all member states and many different languages.

In order to make progress on these priorities, it will not suffice simply to address issues of languages learning and teaching, as was perhaps read into the 1998 HMI report. It will in fact be necessary to address four main types of factor: 'societal' factors (such as public attitudes to languages and to other cultures; the influence of the media; business perceptions of the need for languages), 'education provision' factors (such as ensuring an adequate supply of appropriately trained teachers; providing the full entitlement to languages so that all pupils benefit from all eleven components of this; providing Scottish pupils with increased access to native speakers of the languages they are learning, including at least some from their own age-group, whether by real or by virtual means), 'institutional' factors (such as whether or not the school has a multicultural, multilingual ethos; creating working links with schools in other countries which enable students to engage in joint projects; committed to a strong version of 'languages for all' and offering support for modern languages in local primary schools), and 'process' factors (not only including processes of teaching, learning and managing but also more internal processes of elaborating new strategies and of forming a multiple, international, multicultural identity which values 'difference' and 'otherness'). It is reasonable to expect languages teachers to assume major responsibility for 'process' factors, but national and local authorities, and schools as institutions, must surely accept major responsibility for ensuring that the 'societal', 'provision' and 'institutional' factors are appropriately addressed – at present much remains to be done in this area. Moreover, 'process' factors apply to teachers as well as to students, and much remains to be achieved in helping Languages teachers regain their morale after the perceived shock of the 1998 HMI report, the bad press they received with the news that presentations in Modern Languages at Higher had dropped substantially between 1976 and 1996, and the confusion surrounding 'languages for all' which has arisen from misguided interpretations of the notion of 'entitlement'.

A variety of measures is already coming into play and some signs of up-turn are becoming evident, including initial indications that the numbers of presentations at Higher have ceased to drop. A consortium of three local authorities (East and North Ayrshire, Argyll and Bute) have gained Excellence Fund support to develop a virtual languages college covering all secondary schools, based on innovative use of several integrated new technologies supplemented by visits abroad, and with initial results which seem highly promising. Another Excellence Fund project at Shawlands Academy, Glasgow, includes 'community' as well as foreign languages. A national Innovation Fund for languages has been created which, it is hoped, will trigger further and more widespread initiatives, though each on a smaller scale.

In more general terms, three complementary strategies deserve encouragement. First, teaching other subject-matter through the medium of a foreign language. In 1994, over 140 German secondary schools were teaching Biology, Geography, History and other subjects through the medium of English, French, Spanish, Portuguese or Russian. The same is beginning to happen in England with students taking Business Studies to GCSE level through the medium of Spanish. The gains in motivation and proficiency appear to be substantial. Second, exploiting the Internet and e-mail in order to connect people across the world through their use of a language of their choice. Creating 'virtual communities' for particular languages will afford learners and their teachers increased exposure to and interaction in the language in question. Third, exploiting EC programmes such as COMENIUS which enable schools to engage in transnational collaboration for various educational purposes, thereby creating opportunities for multilingual communication. In their different ways, developments such as these will increase two factors which are fundamental to successful language-learning, namely 'time' and 'intensity'. The 'time' factor will increase to the extent that languages are used out of class as well as in class, and the 'intensity' factor will increase to the extent that students engage not only in language-learning but also in meaningful language use (something the high-attaining students at Standard Grade strongly wanted but felt they were not receiving). If these factors can be increased, then Modern Languages will have broken their mould as a school subject and become instead part of the culture and everyday processes of schools – in which case they might well fly.

REFERENCES

HMI (1998) *Standards and Quality, Primary and Secondary Schools, 1994–1998: Modern Languages*, Edinburgh: SOEID.

McPake, J., Johnstone, R., Low, L. and Lyall, L. (1998) *Foreign Languages in the Upper Secondary School: A Study of the Causes of Decline. Final Report to SOEID*, Edinburgh: SCRE.

Ministerial Action Group on Languages (2000), *Citizens of a Multilingual World*, Edinburgh: Scottish Executive.

SCCC (1989) *The Provision of Languages other than English in Primary and Secondary Schools*, Edinburgh: SCCC.

Scottish Executive (2001) *Citizens of a Multilingual World. Scottish Executive Response*, Edinburgh: Scottish Executive.

SEED (2001) Circular 3/2001, *Guidance on Flexibility in the Curriculum*, Edinburgh: SEED.

64

Modern Studies Education

Henry Maitles

In a relatively short time, some forty years, Modern Studies has had a marked effect on the curriculum in most Scottish schools, being seen by educators, pupils and parents as a meaningful addition to Social Subjects. Indeed, it has in many schools and areas achieved parity with the two other major Social Subjects, History and Geography and, taking FE college presentations into count, there are now more presentations at Higher level in Modern Studies than in History or Geography. Although it is not yet taught as a discrete subject in all schools at S1/S2 (about 50% in S1 and about 70% in S2), as far as Standard Grade, Higher Grade and university entrance are concerned, it is regarded as equal to the other Social Subjects. The crowded curriculum in S1/S2 has meant that some schools do not teach Modern Studies in the primary school, although the revised 5–14 Environmental Studies 'People in Society' guidelines (SEED, 2000) will make aspects of the subject area compulsory, as well as ensuring that there is some level of knowledge and understanding and skills in the area being developed in the primary school.

WHAT IS MODERN STUDIES?

The subject initially was an amalgam of History and Geography with some politics thrown in, as the early exam papers showed. In the first 'O' Grade in 1962, as well as questions of topical interest, there were some on the Great Depression, the rise of the Nazis, the Bolsheviks and map work questions. In its infancy, the subject was seen as being of most value for the less able as it related more directly to their immediate experiences, but fairly quickly the subject was seen as having value for all pupils. By the time, though, of the first 'H' Grade in 1968, the emphasis had shifted towards current affairs. The massive expansion of Politics and Sociology in the universities and the realisation that these subjects were central to an understanding of the complexities of modern societies has meant that since the 1988 Standard Grade arrangements, the subject has as its main aim the teaching and development of political literacy, 'through a framework of analysis and a core of concepts adopted from the social sciences of politics and sociology (p. 4).' Indeed it was this aim of giving the pupils and students the tools to analyse complex societal questions that most Modern Studies departments saw as being particularly distinctive about the subject in a series of national consultation exercises organised by the HMI in 1994. The report of these consultations (*Effective Learning and Teaching in Modern Studies: Conference Report*, St Andrew's College, Glasgow SOED,

1994) suggested that the distinctive role of Modern Studies in the curriculum was to enable pupils to:

- develop social and political literacy;
- develop skills, which will enable pupils to access, handle and evaluate information about the society, and world in which they live;
- understand the society and world in which they live;
- promote citizenship, responsible participation in and respect for democracy;
- foster open-mindedness, participation and co-operation within society;
- develop an interest in and an understanding of current local community, national and international affairs;
- develop social skills;
- develop the ability to arrive at informed opinions and to reflect critically on society.

With these aims at its heart, Modern Studies has been seen as important by Scottish educationalists, particularly as there seems to be so much disaffection by young people towards politics as such, or at least organised democratic politics, despite a marked increase in involvement in single issue campaigns. It is fair to say that the least apathetic, most politically interested young people in the school will be likely to have taken Modern Studies. That is not to say that there has been universal agreement over how political literacy should be taught in the schools, indeed whether it should be taught in the schools at all, as a glance at the debates of the early 1980s would show. There were those who believed that teaching political/sociological material would destroy democracy and others who believed that teaching it would bolster capitalism! Indeed, the whole area of bias is one that has led some to believe it should not be taught to younger children as there is left-wing bias inherent in the subject, although others have argued that areas of politics should be introduced as early as possible and that there is a greater problem of teachers 'sitting on the fence' when controversial issues are discussed (Ashton and Watson, 1998). The Scottish Executive appears to have endorsed the importance of political education through its 5–14 Environmental Studies proposals. Further, the decision to introduce education for citizenship (LTS, 2002), will deepen the whole move towards political literacy teaching. The knowledge and skills associated with Modern Studies go much towards this important strand of citizenship.

Modern Studies as presently organised is structured around a number of key concepts, seen as central to the development of the subject. These concepts – equality, rights and responsibilities, ideology, participation, need, power, representation – are believed to be the core of the subject and give the scope for analysing the subject and events in the real world. As pupils progress, there is a move from relatively simple to much more complex content. Whilst there is Scottish Qualifications Authority prescribed content at Standard (S) Grades and Higher (H) Grades (albeit with choices at H), mainly of a sociological/political nature, a survey of departments shows a wide range of content in S1/S2, most of it now relating to the 5–14 guidelines. Topics such as representation and laws, participating in society, media bias, human rights, multicultural society, the USA, developing world, law and order, Europe, comparison of local area with another country or culture, United Nations Organization are typical, have an obvious relationship to both S and H Grades and are clear content areas in terms of the development of political literacy.

THE DEVELOPMENT OF SKILLS IN MODERN STUDIES

The skills developed in the subject are now encapsulated in the term 'enquiry', involving both evaluating and investigating. Evaluating is the promotion of pupil ability in the critical appraisal and evaluation of information about social and political institutions, processes and issues through:

- recognising lack of objectivity;
- making comparisons and drawing conclusions;
- expressing support for a personal or given point of view.

These are clearly central to the development of political literacy at any level; progression from S1 to S6 involves the use of increasingly complex, subtle and abstract sources. For the Higher, pupils are expected critically to analyse and evaluate complex sources and to show, through a decision-making exercise, how their evaluating skills can be applied in other specific contexts. Investigating involves the processes of planning, recording, analysing/synthesising and reporting, and again is a vital skill for political literacy.

In addition, Modern Studies has a distinctive and important role in attempting to develop positive attitudes amongst pupils/students. This should include at all levels:

- respect for truth and reason;
- willingness to accept that other views and beliefs can have validity;
- willingness to accept the possibility of, and limits to, compromise;
- confidence and enterprise in pursuing information and communicating views.

This is often seen in pupil activities and course content towards issues such as poverty, the elderly, development issues and civil and equal rights. Where dealing with controversial issues, Modern Studies teachers should be allowing pupils to examine evidence relating to a range of views.

This summary of what is taught in the subject misses out a central feature of the subject – its dynamism in the classroom. The teaching and learning of Modern Studies has since its development as a distinctive sociological/political subject been characterised by the enthusiasm of the teachers and novel methodologies. Central to this has been the use of dialogue in the classroom. Indeed, debate, role-play, dialogue, group work, stages work and the varied use of media and IT have been central to its delivery, especially around elections and participation, in particular. Modern Studies teachers are aware that the content of the subject means that many pupils will be coming to the classroom with some experience that they can give to the lesson. As HMI noted in 1992: 'Most teachers encouraged a classroom atmosphere in which open questioning and challenging of opinion was common-place' (SOED, *Effective Learning and Teaching in Scottish Secondary Schools: Modern Studies*, Edinburgh). The most recent HMI report on Modern Studies (HMI, 2000) claims that in some 85% of departments there was an ethos characterised by 'high expectations . . . a brisk pace of work . . . challenging tasks' and, further, that staff made a valuable contradiction to the wider school and community 'through organizing mock elections, debates, displays and excursions'.

ISSUES OF CONCERN AND DEVELOPMENT

The real world and change

What then of the future? The world is an ever-changing and increasingly complex phenomenon and this offers tremendous opportunities and excitement for a subject like Modern Studies. It is a constant challenge to update content and, indeed, whole curricular areas depend on events in the real world. The fall of the dictatorships of Eastern Europe, the ending of eighteen years of Tory government in Britain, the development of constitutional change in Britain, involving Scottish Parliament and Welsh Assembly, and new electoral systems, the ending of apartheid in South Africa, privatisations in the Welfare State, the events in the Middle East and the Gulf, the development of the Euro, the events of September 11, 2001 and its aftermath and other political events mean that Modern Studies teachers are having to revise course content regularly. This, of course, adds greatly to workload but also keeps the subject relevant, dynamic and interesting and goes a long way to explain the popularity of the subject with S6 pupils and FE students.

Curricular developments

There are widespread curricular developments covering every area of schooling – the nature and indeed future of S Grade, the development of the Higher Still programme and the 5–14 'People in Society' guidelines. All of these offer great opportunities but also have potential difficulties.

The 5–14 proposals throw up the possibility of Modern Studies issues being taught from P1 to S2 and, in particular, those secondaries who have refused so far to implement Modern Studies in S1 and/or S2, whether for reasons of crowded curriculum, perceived unsuitability for young people or inertia to change, will now have to find ways of doing so. Modern Studies teachers and the Modern Studies Assocation (MSA) are arguing hard that this should be done through the appointment of Modern Studies specialists where there are none at present, preferably organised in Modern Studies departments, although there is a worry that in some of these schools there will be a temptation, for reasons of staffing, to deliver the Modern Studies elements through History and Geography.

The 5–14 Environmental Studies document does introduce 'understanding people in society' into the primary school, where explicit Modern Studies themes will be taught, based around the following key ideas of:

- people and needs in society;
- rules, rights and responsibilities in society;
- conflict and decision-making in society.

This offers tremendous opportunities for Modern Studies. Apart from collaboration between feeder primaries and secondaries which will be in itself fruitful, Modern Studies departments in the secondaries will be able to expect pupils arriving with some experience and knowledge of the subject, hopefully meaning that planning and progression can be enhanced. For all departments, though, there will be the necessity of auditing courses, throwing out some parts and developing new units to fit the guidelines but, as argued earlier in the chapter, most departments have already started this process and are finding that much of what is in the courses is relevant.

The Higher Still developments have been generally welcomed, although there are, in common with other subjects, worries over assessment, workload and the issue of more bi-, or even multi-, level teaching and consequent poorer learning experiences for pupils.

IS MODERN STUDIES EFFECTIVE?

One of the central aims of Modern Studies, as shown above, is the development of political literacy. Is Modern Studies useful in terms of developing this body of knowledge and skills? There has been some research in this area. Mercer (*Political Education and Socialization to Democratic Norms*, Glasgow: University of Strathclyde, 1973) found little difference in terms of knowledge/understanding and values of pupils taking Modern Studies and those not. However, as has been pointed out, the nature of the subject in its early days (in particular its relationship to History and Geography) perhaps were central to these results. More recently, Maitles (1999, 2000, 2001) has found a marked difference in terms of knowledge, political interest and trust/cynicism levels between pupils studying Modern Studies and those not. This can be comforting for the subject, although, as a caveat, it must be noted that the 'better' Modern Studies scores can be explained by the fact that more politically knowledgeable and interested pupils may choose Modern Studies rather than the subject itself instilling the knowledge and interest. In terms of values/attitudes, the results suggest that there is not a marked difference, with Modern Studies students 'more positive' in some areas and History or Geography students 'more positive' in others.

EXPANSION AND LIMITATIONS

Whilst it is undoubtedly true that Modern Studies is expanding in some areas and developing anew in some schools, there are a few schools where Modern Studies has been virtually eliminated as a subject in the middle school (S3 and S4). Worryingly, this has tended to be in schools with a larger percentage of lower ability pupils and is justified on the somewhat spurious educational basis of reducing choice and improving quality for these pupils by creating larger groupings in Geography and History. Fortunately, the practice is not widespread.

COMMON SOCIAL SUBJECTS COURSE IN S1/S2

Another area of concern, in common with the other Social Subjects, although also with some positive features, is the trend in some schools to have a Social Studies course in S1 (and sometimes in S2) where History, Geography and Modern Studies are taught by a single teacher, often uncertificated in one or two of these subjects. This can work well in situations where there have been full talks and timetabled meetings and there are committed teachers with ownership of the course, and has the added advantage of reducing the number of teachers with whom each pupil has contact. But often, when staffing is the major consideration, there is a lowest common denominator effect leading consequently to poorer courses on offer.

HMI FINDINGS

The detailed HMI reports outline many strengths in Modern Studies teaching, particularly in terms of methodology, as outlined earlier in this chapter. Further, the most recent report (2000) also notes 'pupils enjoyment of Modern Studies and their good relationships with teachers' and 'high levels of commitment by teachers and good teamwork'. The inspectorate also raised areas of concern that needed attention, such as the issue of progression in skills and content, planning in relation to assessment, and ensuring that pupils have a clear awareness of what is expected of them and thus being able to plan schemes for improvement. At least part of the problem of these areas relates to an earlier concern – the fact that not all schools have Modern Studies principal teachers with the management time to deal with these weaker areas. There is plenty of evidence to show that where there is a Modern Studies department and structure the weaknesses are far less and where existing are much more easily eliminated. The McCrone settlement, which will limit further the number of subject-specific heads of department, will need to be monitored carefully to ensure that these weaknesses do not increase.

THE NEW MILLENNIUM

The future is thus one of optimism tempered by realism. The subject is tremendously popular with pupils, parents, FE students and professionals alike and this is very important. The last twenty years have seen the development of a conservative consensus by governments over the direction of education in general and this has fuelled a rethinking of exactly how political literacy, one of the central areas of citizenship, can be developed within our education system, and within this perspective, Modern Studies clearly has an important central role.

REFERENCES

Ashton, E. and Watson, B. (1998) Values education: a fresh look at procedural neutrality, *Educational Studies*, 24 (2).

HMI (2000) *Standards and Quality in Secondary Schools: Modern Studies*, Edinburgh: SEED.

LTS (2002) *Education for Citizenship in Scotland: A Paper for Discussion and Development*, Dundee: LTS.

Maitles, H. (1999) Political Education in Schools, *International Journal of Inclusive Education*, 3 (2).

Maitles, H. (2000) Thirty years of teaching political literacy in Scottish schools: how effective is Modern Studies? in R. Gardner (ed.) *Citizenship Education*, London: Cassell.

Maitles, H. (2001) Political literacy: the challenge for democratic citizenship, *The School Field*, X1 (3/4).

65

Music Education

Mark Sheridan and Charles Byrne

Prior to the 1980s the Music curriculum consisted of class-singing, sol-fah deciphering and music appreciation. Typical resources were the piano, the Curwen modulator, numerous sets of song and sight-reading books (to suit single gender class groupings) and a record player. More enlightened teachers would have some percussion instruments or recorders in the classroom and, from the 1970s, the odd guitar. The Scottish Examination Board 'O' Grade examination at the end of year four was designed to be taken by pupils who had expertise on an instrument or in voice to the equivalent of Associated Board Grade 5, tuition on which was given outwith the classroom while the teacher concentrated on historical study, rudiments and analysis. Such elitism fuelled growing disillusionment in pupils and many teachers who experienced a different world of music in their private lives (Witkin, 1974).

Significant and effective change came in 1978 with the publication by the Scottish Education Department of the highly controversial Curriculum Paper 16, *Music in Scottish Schools*. This was the dividing line between past practices and future developments which radically changed the way in which music was taught and which clearly focused music teachers' and educators' energies and ideas. It encapsulated many of the ideas and innovations which had been forming in Britain through the work of Paynter and Aston (1970), Witkin (1974) and in the USA since the 1960s (Choksy et al., 1986) and placed them into a Scottish context. This provided the impetus for a root and branch overhaul of the curriculum which would reshape music in the classroom into an action-based experience, open to all children, regardless of their musical or academic ability. In the contexts of both primary and secondary schools, Curriculum Paper 16 recommended syllabus content and teaching and learning strategies, the review of assessment approaches and most significantly, staffing, resource and accommodation requirements to enable 'music for all' to be implemented. These recommendations gave teachers and headteachers the tools and impetus to make demands on local authorities to fund the developments appropriately.

CURRICULAR OVERHAUL

The next ten years was a time of radical change in the classroom, of experimentation with different types of music and alternative approaches to teaching and learning against a backdrop of serious industrial unrest and anxiety for teachers. Practical music-making activities were introduced as pupils engaged in ensembles of pitched percussion instruments, recorders and guitars for the first time. 'Creative music' experiments were developing in schools and teachers were genuinely seeking a positive way to enliven and brighten the musical diet of their pupils. A Grand Central Committee on Music oversaw a number of national courses for teachers and educators and produced numerous 'occasional' papers and other texts written by practising teachers which raised awareness of new teaching techniques and practical approaches in the classroom. These papers were disseminated to all secondary schools, colleges and universities and enabled a broad ranging debate to take place. Following the recommendations of the Munn and Dunning Reports in 1977, the SEB in consultation with the Scottish Education Department began the task of redesigning the curriculum at the hub: the reframing of the old 'O' Grade examination. *The Standard Grade Arrangements in Music* document (SEB, 1988) was the distillation of this process, in which the aims of practical music-making for all pupils was enshrined. Performing, inventing and listening, taught within an integrated, conceptual framework, represented a very different approach to the curriculum, while a criterion-referenced assessment strategy based on these ensured that pupils were rewarded for their positive attainments rather than their failings and shortcomings.

Controversy, however, raged as it had done in 1978. Teachers were unhappy about assessment for all pupils on two instruments (in both solo and group performance which were included as separate components), the necessity to teach across a wide range of abilities in the same classroom, and the compulsory teaching and assessment of inventing. The last was the most contentious area of the new curriculum and one which would remain so, despite the rationale for its inclusion in the curriculum: 'Inventing develops ideas principally through imaginative response . . . It offers pupils a training in discrimination and perception and in the words of the Munn Report provides for "deep imaginative satisfaction"' (SEB, 1988, p. 10). The members of the working party that produced this report and other revisions to the curriculum continued to ensure the presence of inventing in the syllabus. Parallel to the developments in Standard Grade, modularised SCOTVEC courses created a similar diet of music courses for students at colleges of further education, and some schools, based on a building block approach. The elements of music could therefore be studied separately and assessed by means of diaries and recorded attainment strategies rather than by examination.

The result of all of these changes was the rapid growth of numbers of young people taking Music and the transformation of the Music department's largely classical sound-world to one which included folk, rock, pop and jazz. The multi-instrumental nature of the classroom activities and the mixed ability range of the pupils made further demands on Music teachers, many of whom were ill-prepared to deal with the new order. Consequently, a central support group in music (1986), set up under the direction of the Scottish Consultative Council on the Curriculum, in collaboration with local authorities, was directed to produce a significant body of materials to aid teachers. Both curricular and staff development materials gave teachers at least the basis on which to plan and implement the new course. A guiding principle of these developments was to ensure that the philosophy was embraced and that an integrated, practical approach was achieved.

PHILOSOPHY AND PEDAGOGY

It is likely that the innovative teachers in the 1970s and early 1980s, a number of whom were architects of Standard Grade, were unaware of some of the precedents which had been set in creating an integrated curriculum. The authors would assert that Comprehensive Musicianship would appear to be the main, if somewhat indirect, influence on the Scottish framework. Comprehensive Musicianship grew from three significant developments in the USA: the young composer's project (1959); contemporary music project (CMP) for creativity in music education (1963); and a subsequent seminar at Northwestern University in 1965. The fundamental aim of the first two projects was to enhance and develop the teaching of contemporary music in the American classroom, but the event at Northwestern University refocused the direction towards a broad based, all-encompassing, inclusive music curriculum. David Woods (1986) writes: 'A CM approach to music study from preschool through university advocates that students develop personal musical competencies through a balance of experience in:

> Performance: reading and recreating music written by a composer
> Analysis: describing the music through perceptive listening
> Composition: understanding and utilising compositional and improvisational techniques.' (in Choksy et al.,1986, p. 110)

Given that the new curriculum has its origins in such a well-founded philosophy, it is surprising that the approach to curriculum development in Scotland has been somewhat parochial. While teachers and educators would have been well aware of, and to some extent practised in the classroom approaches of Kodaly, Orff and Jacques Dalcroze, the tendency has been to assimilate and draw on these approaches and philosophies within the individual classroom. This has created a colourful national picture, but one which is hard to pin down to a particular approach or philosophy. It is probable that, faced with such a sea of change in the last twenty years, hard-pressed teachers have ignored or dismissed debate on the philosophy and basis of the curriculum in favour of quick fix remedies designed to help them cope with the needs of the classroom (Byrne and Sheridan, 2001). It is undeniable, however, that the philosophy exists. Now that teachers have implemented the difficult changes required of them, they may be better placed to address some of the broader educational issues which would doubtless support understanding of the processes in which they are involved.

FRAMEWORK AND PROGRESSION

Having set the cornerstone of the new curriculum in Standard Grade, the creation and articulation of the Revised Higher (1990) and Certificate of Sixth Year Studies (1992) reinforced the integrated approach, while a greater degree of choice and specialisation gave students the freedom to develop skills and interests best suited to their own aspirations. This curricular choice was possible through selection of extension work in one of the three elements while maintaining core provision for the other two. Performing predominated pupils' selection at these levels of study, while listening and inventing appeared to be less popular although still present in the pupils' experience. This integrated building block approach enabled the music education community to deal with the task of realignment demanded by two further national initiatives: the far reaching 5–14 National Guidelines on Expressive Arts (SOED, 1992) and the Higher Still development programme (1995–8). While 5–14 addressed the primary school curriculum and the necessity more effectively to bridge the gap to secondary, Higher Still reframed and relabelled the ladder of progression created by Standard Grade, Revised Higher and Certificate of Sixth Year Studies. These developments created further challenges for teachers. Despite the heavy handed nature of the 5–14 report and the contrived nature of its language, the programmes of work and the assessment strategies paved the way for possible articulation with existing provision.

The Higher Still initiatives gave teachers and educators the opportunity to revisit some of the issues which arose during the process of curricular overhaul in the 1980s. Literacy and the study of rudiments, for a long time areas of controversy (deemed to be means to ends in the new approaches in Standard Grade), have been addressed in Higher and Advanced Higher levels. Similarly, effective preparation of able pupils for entry to higher education (which seemed to be one of the aims of the original elitist Higher Grade) was for some regarded as a casualty in the new order. Greater collaboration and communication between higher education institutions and schools was encouraged to help alleviate some of the challenges in this area. The impressive flourishing since the 1980s of the use of a broad range of highly sophisticated ICT facilities for performing, composing and recording has greatly expanded pupil access and enhanced achievement in the classroom. The innovations of MIDI, CD-ROM and internet technologies were probably the most significant developments in music in the twentieth century, and while many of their uses and applications still need to be rigorously examined and researched, this revolution has opened up new frontiers and experiences in music for all pupils and teachers. Singing, on the other hand, the most fundamental means of musical expression, has undoubtedly been damaged by rapid change in the classroom. Teachers have argued that the implementation of a largely instrumental curriculum, the reduction in size and the creation of mixed gender classes have created difficulties which have seriously undermined singing in many schools. It may also be true that, as one of the most taxing aspects of the musical diet, it was easy prey for teachers to expel it from the curriculum. The result, however, is that community and church choirs have suffered in recruitment of young members and despite efforts to address the problem by bodies such as the National Youth Choir of Scotland, the British Federation of Youth Choirs and local authorities, the plight of singing in schools still needs to be addressed.

ASSESSMENT

Highlighted previously as an area of concern, the inventing element is the one which appears to have been least successful in implementation. Research has shown that the Standard Grade examination results between 1991 to 1996 reflected a worrying trend:

> Pupil attainment in performing which has traditionally been well taught and learned, with awards at Credit level in Solo . . . and Group . . . now reaching 63% (from 53%) and 60% (from 45%) respectively. Attainment in listening has been improving steadily . . . (45% to 50%). The percentage of pupils achieving grades of 1 or 2 for . . . Inventing are the lowest, starting from 36% in 1991 and rising slowly to a peak of 43% in 1996 (Byrne, C. and Sheridan, M., Music: a source of deep imaginative satisfaction? *British Journal of Music Education*, 15(3), 295–301).

The authors have since examined this phenomenon, outlining and reviewing some potential causes of this inconsistency in attainment. While a number of factors such as teachers' own lack of training in creative music making, the appropriateness of classroom activities and inappropriate assessment criteria may be significant, it is likely that the fundamental problem is the manner in which creativity is assessed. Inventing was included in the assessment process, giving it status and value, in the hope that teachers would embrace the underpinning philosophy of Comprehensive Musicianship and deliver it appropriately. It may be that this very inclusion compromises the nature of the creative attainment it was designed to measure and that assessment in music needs a radical reappraisal (Sheridan, M. and Byrne, C., The ebb and flow of assessment in music, *British Journal of Music Education*, 19(2), 133–141).

Despite these challenges, more and more young people are voting with their feet and taking up Music in school with the result that demand for Music teachers and places in higher education courses is greater than in the past. The range of opportunities now available to study all kinds of music is now extensive and confounds the popular myth that curriculum changes of the late 1980s onwards would adversely affect the number of musicians entering higher education. The proliferation of college and university courses in popular, rock, jazz and traditional music has created a sustainable structure which supports and nourishes the quality of music making across the country.

REFERENCES

Byrne, C. and Sheridan, M. (2001) The SCARLATTI Papers: development of an action research project in music, *British Journal of Music Education*, 18(2), 171–83.

Choksy, L., Abramson, R. M., Gillespie A. E. and Woods D. (1986) *Teaching Music in the Twentieth Century*, Englewood Cliffs: Prentice-Hall.

Paynter, J. and Aston, P. (1970) *Sound and Silence*, London: Cambridge University Press.

SEB (1988) *Scottish Certificate of Education: Standard Grade Arrangements in Music*, Dalkeith: SEB.

SOED (1992) *Curriculum and Assessment in Scotland, National Guidelines, Expressive Arts: 5–14*, Edinburgh: SOED.

Witkin, R. W. (1974) *The Intelligence of Feeling*, London: Heinemann.

66

Outdoor Education

Peter Higgins and Bob Sharp

The term 'Outdoor Education' is likely to conjure up vivid and diverse images. In most Scottish schools Outdoor Education is an established feature of life and yet few have a specialist Outdoor Education teacher. This would be inconceivable in curricular areas and is difficult to understand in the context of the technical aspects and safety considerations of Outdoor Education. Such a situation is somewhat paradoxical and warrants attention.

Despite established provision definitions are elusive. Outdoor Education has often been considered to be an educational approach which can permeate many curricular subject areas. However it is now seen within the sector as both an approach and a subject in its own right drawing on three integrated areas of 'outdoor activities', 'environmental education' and 'personal and social development' (Higgins and Loynes, 1997). (See Figure 66.1). The themes of outdoor, adventure and education are all important in the process. An experiential approach to learning is a central tenet of Outdoor Education and in this context 'adventure' is seen as a way of maximising the learning effect of the experience.

EARLY DEVELOPMENTS

The combination of variable climate, geological, social and cultural history and the resulting topography provide both the physical circumstances for outdoor recreation and educational possibilities for outdoor education. Little wonder that Scotland was one of the first places in the world where outdoor education became formalised. The 1944 Education Act and the 1945 Education (Scotland) Act encouraged the use of the outdoors for environmental and nature studies (Cook, 1999), and the rise of the 'progressive' education movement through the twentieth century gave support to an experiential approach.

The 1944 Education Act emphasised the value of experience of the outdoors and encouraged local education authorities to establish appropriate 'camps'. During the 1970s they did so and many bought and converted old mansions as residential bases for outdoor activities and field studies. This was the heyday of Outdoor Education provision in Scotland. Most Scottish Authorities offered extensive and progressive outdoor educational opportunities and some (e.g. Lothian and Strathclyde) were world leaders. Outdoor Education teachers and others organised activities from schools and used centrally funded staffed and unstaffed residential centres. To meet the demand for teachers and instructors, Outdoor Education courses were established in UK colleges and universities. This move was given extra impetus by the death of five Edinburgh school children in the Cairngorm

Mountains in November 1971 and was significant in the development of the first specialist courses in Scotland (Moray House and Dunfermline Colleges) in 1973.

Early arguments for outdoor adventure experiences lay in Kurt Hahn's philosophy for Gordonstoun School and the Outward Bound movement, which emphasised physical fitness, endurance, craftsmanship and community service. However, the early programmes at Scotland's National Outdoor Training Centre (Glenmore Lodge – established in 1948, and funded for some years by the Scottish Education Department) placed emphasis on experimental approaches to education and field nature study (Nicol, 2002).

ON THE NATURE OF OUTDOOR EDUCATION

The traditional image of Outdoor Education is of outdoor activities, often at a residential centre where the emphasis is on skill acquisition and personal/social development, fails to present a complete picture. An outdoor educator working anywhere from school grounds to mountain ranges or the sea will be presented with boundless opportunities for learning about the natural heritage, social history, rural culture, sustainable living and citizenship. Movement through and living in the landscape provides opportunities to work with others and reflect on personal strengths and weaknesses, encouraging respect for self, others and the environment. Also, most activities can be carried on into later life, bringing significant health benefits from long–term participation.

The view taken in this chapter is that Outdoor Education provides opportunities for individuals to develop personal and social skills, to become active, safe and skilled in the outdoors, and to care about and protect the environment. The implicit expectation (note Figure 66.1) is that subjects are addressed holistically with outdoor educators shifting emphasis as opportunities arise. In broad terms this might be considered as education 'in',

Figure 66.1:   The range and scope of Outdoor Education

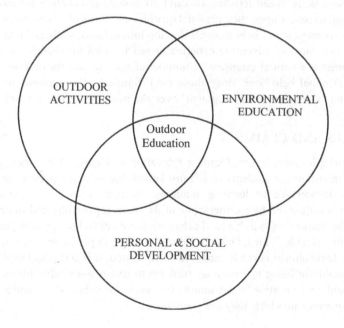

'through', 'about' and 'for' the natural heritage, the last being important for sustainability. The intention is always to maximise opportunities presented to encourage intellectual, physical, emotional, aesthetic and spiritual development. This is not so much a claim as an aspiration for professional practice.

Outdoor activities

The rich and diverse natural heritage of Scotland stimulated the development of many outdoor activities (e.g. mountaineering, climbing, sailing, canoeing) which formed the traditional basis of Outdoor Education, though recently other activities have become popular. All can be pursued for educational and recreational purposes. Outdoor educators are normally qualified through the relevant national governing bodies (NGBs) for each activity, and teach within well established safety guidelines.

Environmental education

Direct contact with the natural heritage has the potential to allow students to increase their knowledge of and develop relationships with the environment. It is not simply knowledge about the environment, but also understanding the relationship between natural systems and sustainability. This relationship extends to appreciation of natural and cultural heritage ('sense of place') and of global sustainability issues. The potential for building positive links with other school curricular subjects is obvious, but it is the integration of these in an interdisciplinary fashion where this is perhaps greatest.

Personal and social development

Practical outdoor activities often require co-operation with others, problem solving and decision-making skills. When activities are carefully devised and skilfully reviewed, students are encouraged to reflect upon their personal qualities and those of others. Such experiences can raise self-awareness and help students develop interpersonal skills and relationships.

The idea that outdoor adventure experiences can be used for therapeutic and rehabilitative purposes is a natural extension. A number of agencies use the outdoors in this way (to address criminal behaviour, drug abuse etc.). Similarly, the outdoors has been used extensively for 'management development' over the past ten to fifteen years.

PRINCIPLES AND CLAIMS

Common principles serve to give Outdoor Education its identity. First, there is always an educational intention for students to acquire knowledge or develop views and attitudes. Second, the importance of learning outdoors contrasts with the 'classroom' as the environment is influenced by weather, time of day/year, topography and so on. This does not need to be 'remote' or 'wild'; a local urban environment (school grounds, canals, parks) can be equally valuable. Third, Outdoor Education engages people in practical, interactive experiences. Involvement is rarely mediated or simulated; it is active and explicit with the role of the facilitator being to encourage students to take responsibility for learning. Each aspect of Outdoor Education is not unique (cf curricular subjects), as much as the wide variety and manner in which they are encountered.

Research in Outdoor Education is limited, perhaps because of the difficulty in monitoring and assessing changes in personal and social qualities. As recently as (1995) Barrett and Greenaway commented that there were few rigorous studies of Outdoor Education from the UK or elsewhere. However, there is now an increasing body of philosophical and empirical work published in specialist international journals. In Scotland a study carried out with North Lanarkshire pupils who had experienced a short outdoor programme designed to 'raise achievement' revealed changes in self-confidence and social competence. In England and Wales, the national DfES scheme 'Summer Activities for 16year-olds' showed similar positive outcomes.

RELATIONSHIP WITH THE CURRICULUM

Whilst the value of Outdoor Education has been noted in the 5–14 guidelines there is no statutory requirement for Outdoor Education to be taught in Scottish schools and so its status is open to interpretation by education authorities and headteachers. Outdoor educators have argued that it provides a valuable means of addressing many of the requirements of the personal and social development, expressive arts and environmental studies guidelines (Loynes, Michie & Smith, 1997). Furthermore, the guidelines on structure and balance in the curriculum expect schools to encourage a range of dispositions, most of which (respect and care for self and others, sense of social responsibility, sense of belonging) are central to the purposes of Outdoor Education.

It plays a role in Standard Grade Physical Education through delivery of water-based activities (sailing, canoeing and windsurfing) and other outdoor pursuits (orienteering, hillwalking, climbing and skiing). Outdoor activities also feature in Higher Grade Physical Education, but to a lesser extent.

Outdoor Education sits well alongside many government priorities such as the social inclusion agenda, health education and promotion, community development, education for citizenship, sustainable development, lifelong learning and education for work. In various councils in Scotland these are invoked as a rationale for Outdoor Education.

PROVISION FOR OUTDOOR EDUCATION

Whilst schools are the traditional locus for Outdoor Education in Scotland, changes in local government, in funding and staffing, have led to a decrease in qualified staff (Higgins, 2002). Although many centres continue to operate, most in the public sector have reduced central funding and have taken a more commercial approach (Nicol, 2002). A number of commercial and charitable-trust centres vie for 'business' as do an increasing number of freelance outdoor providers.

Although some school pupils may experience just three or four days of Outdoor Education in their whole school career, the overall scale of provision is significant. Around 200,000 to 300,000 Scottish student-days per year are spent in some form of Outdoor Education (Higgins, 2002). Whilst some councils have reduced provision others have made new investments. Fee-paying schools have a long tradition of provision (often through the Duke of Edinburgh Award Scheme) and many extol their commitment to the outdoors and assert its personal development potential.

Most young people now pay for any Outdoor Education experience based away from school. Even centres funded by councils make significant (albeit subsidised) charges for their courses and these are not simply for food and accommodation. This raises important ethical issues associated with the nature of public education, equity and opportunity. The situation is compounded by the policy of devolved management of resources to schools and the fact that few councils now operate a disadvantaged pupils fund to ease the financial load for those in need.

Although most Outdoor Education is provided by the Education Departments, in some councils responsibility lies in 'community education' or 'recreation' although extent of provision is varied. Social work departments have traditionally used Outdoor Education too.

A number of UK and Scottish agencies (e.g. Fairbridge, Venture Scotland) work with young people who are considered 'disadvantaged' or 'at risk'. In most cases the programmes on offer are broad-based but all involve some use of the outdoors. Some agencies focus their efforts on 'inner city youth' to encourage them to take part in outdoor projects. Despite the unpredictable nature of charitable funding most agencies manage to fund programmes. The Scout and Guide movements continue to have influence in introducing many young people to the outdoors, although interest in these organisations appears to be decreasing.

Recent New Opportunities Funds (£87m over three years) for 'PE, sport and out of school hours activities' can be accessed for outdoor activities (www.nof.org.uk). Although welcomed by the outdoor sector, there is disquiet about the time-limited nature of the funding.

WHO SPEAKS FOR OUTDOOR EDUCATION?

At present there is no national framework for the management of Outdoor Education in Scotland although a number of bodies represent aspects of the sector. The 'Scottish Advisory Panel for Outdoor Education' is a forum for those who hold an advisory position within the thirty-two Scottish councils. The Association of Heads of Outdoor Education Centres is similar but for centre managers. The National Governing Bodies (NGBs) devise and manage leader/instructional awards in outdoor activities, and these have been adopted as standard and thereby implicitly validated by the sector. Whilst there is no single body to integrate these efforts, a membership organisation, Outdoor Learning Scotland, has attempted to do so and establish a political voice.

CURRENT ISSUES IN OUTDOOR EDUCATION

A 'culture of fear'

There is evidence that in modern society 'risk' is considered something to be minimised or eliminated. The expectation that those who have responsibility for others must manage risks has shifted towards 'risk-avoidance'. This has had serious implications for the outdoor sector leading to exaggerated anxieties amongst parents, teachers and policy makers. Consequently, those involved in Outdoor Education now have their own anxiety, that of litigation. Counter-concern has been voiced that children are over-protected, have diminished childhood experiences and become incapable of properly assessing risks. The situation is clearly unsatisfactory and Outdoor Education has been suggested as one way to teach the skills of risk management.

Licensing and Regulation

In 1993, four school children died whilst sea kayaking in Lyme Bay. Although they were led by unqualified staff, and the centre owner was imprisoned under existing health and safety law, new legislation was enacted (The Activities Centres (Young Persons' Safety) Act (1995)). This led to the establishment of the Adventure Activities Licensing Authority (AALA). The purpose of the authority is:

> to give assurance that good safety management practice is being followed so that young people can continue to have opportunities to experience exciting and stimulating activities outdoors while not being exposed to avoidable risks of death and disabling injury. (www.aala.org)

The AALA has responsibility for licensing agencies offering adventure activities to those under eighteen years of age for commercial gain. It has had significant impact on Outdoor Education, bringing into focus the experience and qualifications of leaders/instructors, safety management by providers and oversight by councils. Although schools and voluntary youth groups do not require a licence they would, in the event of an accident, be expected to have met the AALA standards. Whilst some argue that these groups should be licensed and the scheme extended, others believe that the scheme is unnecessary. It is currently under review by the Department for Education and Skills.

Some councils have training schemes which enable teachers to operate at local venues (e.g., particular hills or crags). These are based on experience and qualifications and the internal safety systems of the centre, school and so on. Some of these pre-date AALA and in most cases adequately meet council requirements.

Access to the countryside

Outdoor recreation, which has grown due to increased leisure time and recognition of the health benefits of physical activity, currently generates around a third of all tourist income to Scotland (Higgins, 2002). Yet until recently Scotland was one of the few countries in Europe where public access to the countryside is not enshrined in law. Recent efforts to address this have led to the Land Reform (Scotland) Act 2003, which confirms a right of recreational access to the countryside. After considerable debate commercial and educational access was also included in the final stages of the Bill. This is fortuitous as outdoor educators will have a central role in teaching aspects of the rights and responsibilities of access, and this can only lead to greater understanding of the countryside and the natural heritage.

Teaching qualifications in Outdoor Education

Undoubtedly the lack of a clear understanding of what Outdoor Education is has led to a range of interpretations amongst policy makers. What is perhaps of greater significance is the lack of a Scottish teaching qualification (TQ). Consequently those who teach Outdoor Education in schools are either qualified in a different subject or completed training south of the border.

Outside schools there is no requirement for a teaching qualification and various approaches are taken. The range of practical competencies demanded of an outdoor educator can be wide, and the sector has adopted the standards of the relevant NGBs.

Anxieties over safety have led to NGB awards being seen as standard qualifications of outdoor educators. However, this is unsatisfactory as NGBs are concerned largely with the development of outdoor activities as sports rather than their relevance to Outdoor Education *per se*. Tertiary level training is available in Scotland with colleges delivering courses leading to NC, HNC and HND awards in Outdoor Education. Undergraduate courses are available at two universities (Edinburgh and Strathclyde) and postgraduate programmes (Diploma/MSc) at Edinburgh. Doctorates in Outdoor Education have now been awarded at both.

There have been several attempts to introduce a TQ in Outdoor Education. In the early 1990s a working group was convened by the Scottish Office Education and Industry Department to prepare detailed proposals but the qualification was never instituted. When, following local government reorganisation in 1996, local authorities were asked for their views, the unequivocal response was positive. In 2000 the Minister for Education asked the Scottish Executive to review the situation. The review group which included the Scottish Advisory Panel and the GTC recommended establishment of an additional teaching qualification (ATQ). Deliberations over the McCrone Report halted progress, and now the Scottish Executive plans to reconsider it during the 'review of initial teacher education'. A positive decision to introduce an ATQ seems the only way to address safety concerns and capitalise on the potential of Outdoor Education in schools.

WHY INDOORS?

The images invoked at the start of this chapter are likely to have a common dimension – that of the outdoors. One common but not explicit theme of most of 'Scottish education' is that education takes place 'indoors'. The belief of those who pursue Outdoor Education as a discipline is not that there is something inherently 'wrong' with the school, or that schools do not teach in an experiential fashion. Rather, that it is illogical and inequitable to confine all education to the school as this ignores important learning opportunities to be found outside the classroom, and fails to acknowledge the range of learning styles students employ in the pursuit of understanding. Finally, it is always instructive to consider a new perspective. In the case of Outdoor Education, illumination may result from simply thinking of 'education outdoors' instead.

REFERENCES

Barrett, J. and Greenaway, R. (1995). *Why Adventure? The Role and Value of Outdoor Activities in Young Peoples' Personal and Social Development: A Review of Research*, Coventry: Foundation for Outdoor Adventure.

Cook, L. (1999). The 1944 Education Act and outdoor education: From policy to practice, *History of Education*, *28*(2), 157–72.

Higgins, P. (2002) Outdoor education in Scotland, *Journal of Adventure Education and Outdoor Learning*, 2: 2, pp. 149–68.

Higgins, P. and Loynes, C. (1997). On the nature of outdoor education, in P. Higgins, C. Loynes and N. Crowther (eds), *A Guide for Outdoor Educators in Scotland*, Penrith: Adventure Education, pp. 6–8.

Loynes, C., Michie, C. and Smith, C. (1997) Justifying outdoor education in the formal and informal curriculum, in P. Higgins, C. Loynes, and N. Crowther (eds), *A Guide for Outdoor Educators in Scotland*, Penrith: Adventure Education, pp. 15–22.

Nicol, R. (2002) Outdoor education: Research topic or universal value? Part One. *Journal of Adventure Education and Outdoor Learning*, 2 (1), 29–42.

Endnote: Much of the primary material drawn upon for this chapter is referred to in Higgins (2002) and Nicol (2002).

67

Physical Education and Sport

Bob Brewer

This chapter gives selective scrutiny to the fundamental curriculum changes apparent in Physical Education and the effects of these on teachers and pupils. It also anticipates the influence of contemporary accounts linking Physical Education with programmes that are attempting to align participation in youth sport with healthy lifestyles.

PHYSICAL EDUCATION AND CERTIFICATION –
THE REDEFINING OF A SUBJECT IN SCOTLAND

It is of little surprise that recent commentaries about youth participation in physical activity and sport have included as part of their treatise a critique of Physical Education (Scottish Executive, 2002). Implicit in such accounts has been a concern regarding the nature of Physical Education and especially the consequences for the subject as it moved towards formal assessment and national certification in S3–S6. The subsequent evolution into post-16 qualifications and the combining of SEB/SCOTVEC award schemes has meant a dramatic transition of remit for Physical Education teachers. The Munn Report's endorsement of 'physical activity' as one of 'eight modes of activity' for S3/S4 pupils and the description of it in terms of skills, enjoyment, personal interests and physical well-being, was much appreciated by teachers of Physical Education. Munn's evaluation of 'physical activity' afforded it a firm place in the curriculum, a comforting endorsement for the status of the subject, but it barely hinted at the course of action that was to unfold, or indeed how such a rationale for physical activity was to be embodied in courses and pupil experiences. While the Munn course diet provided Physical Education with options to pursue (two year certificated work, creative and aesthetic studies, health studies short courses) its teachers were faced with a period of uncertainty, as the fundamental constructs of Physical Education were being centrally driven and redirected.

The introduction of Standard Grade Physical Education (SGPE) in 1988 was a case in point. Scotland's first examinable two-year course in Physical Education broke the mould of a subject unconstrained by external, formalised requirements. In its review of school inspections such developments prompted HMI to comment that 'many Physical Education teachers were, for the first time, directly affected by influences on the curriculum which they had not previously encountered' (SOEID, 1995). Germane to this was the way a rationale for Physical Education was being devised. That it strongly asserted its educational validity through claims about knowledge and the nature of practical experiences and how these might be authentically assessed was the stuff of contest. Clearly sensitive to the significance of such developments for Physical Education, particularly during a period of hiatus over teacher pay and conditions, HMI, in combination with SEB and SCCC, took explicit steps to consult with the profession regarding change. This was often a difficult audience to satisfy. As Green (2000) portends, teachers tend to feel they are marginalised in such developments where, as he puts it, interest groups merely 'talk past one another'.

The significance of SGPE should not be underestimated for a number of reasons. Firstly, it heralded the move towards a certificated Physical Education curriculum based on assertions about course tenets that were also to inform Higher Grade Physical Education (HGPE) and the five course levels at Higher Still (HSPE). Such trends continued despite cautionary advice notably from 'Framework for Decision' whose insert that ' subjects like Physical Education will continue to make their main contribution through non-examined courses' was regularly trumpeted by the Educational Institute of Scotland Central Advisory Committee on Physical Education in their trenchant claims for protecting core programmes for all secondary aged pupils. While this committee's development of a 'Manifesto for Physical Education' was never realised, it merits mention here, not just for its attempts to politicise the issues about priorities in Physical Education, but as a reminder also that current views about core time and programmes for physical activity have an enduring and recent history.

A second set of issues arising from Physical Education's increased commitment to certificated curricula involved the way teachers were required to manage and prepare for such developments. The expectancy of centrally provided exemplars of new course practice, schemes of work and guidance on assessment, had become the givens as the explicit clauses of a newly achieved conditions of service agreement were invoked. While these materials were not exactly 'off the shelf', by the time of the Higher Still development teachers considering its implementation knew what they wanted and were not slow to inform the reference group for HSPE charged with organising such information. This cascading and dissemination of various forms of text for HSPE, while it apparently overcame the content and assessment shortfalls seen in the brief history of HGPE, did escalate the administrative load on its teachers. Additionally, the extended advice regarding the nature of knowledge and understanding underpinning HSPE began to threaten teacher confidence to deliver the appropriate detail of required content. This was significant because of the inroads made on teachers' capacities and inclinations to develop core Physical Education and to support the extra-curricular dimensions of school life. Many have seen this as a defining period for the way Physical Education teachers perceived their professional role. The repercussions therein for sports development have continued to solicit regular reporting, with the McCrone recommendations regarding teacher's hours and conditions of service once again raising the spectre of teacher commitment to the extended curriculum (Scottish Executive, 2002).

The managing of curriculum development through 5–14, SGPE and HGPE to HSPE, increasingly became beholden to centralised resources and, as a consequence, government budgets for HSPE materials went well beyond previous initiatives. While this can be construed as a genuinely sympathetic form of support for its teachers, arguably it was a further indication of teachers being called to account, with politicians establishing funding priorities merely to progress courses devised and approved 'from above' (see for example, Niven, G. (1998) The process of developing the Higher Grade Course in Physical Education, *Scottish Journal of Physical Education*, 26 (2), 14–21). This drift to certification inevitably had its consequences for Physical Education, symbolised by the tide of concern for how the subject was to find its place in the timetable guidelines informing headteachers (issued by SCCC) as well as in the explicit changes to the essential character of its teaching and learning.

WHAT CHARACTERISES PHYSICAL EDUCATION NOW?

HMI overviews of Physical Education in Scotland provide an indication of how teachers were to centre their philosophy and pedagogical practice (SOEID, 1995). Framed around three key themes of performance, knowledge and understanding, and personal and social development, this report summarises the thinking behind curricula statements of rationale for all Physical Education through 5–18. More recently, evaluations of teacher methods and school support for primary school Physical Education (HMIE, *Improving Physical Education in Primary Schools*, 2001) have produced assertive insights into 'good' and 'weak' practice. What therefore characterises Physical Education in 2002 is a sense of unease as these varying accounts of 'what teachers should be doing' sway back and forth across familiar discourses relating to educational worth, health and fitness, and talent identification and sports development. That Physical Education remains a 'site of struggle' is hardly a surprising summary of such affairs.

One characteristic feature of the unease in Physical Education is the extent to which statements made about it have reassured the profession. The nature of the certificated and examinable syllabus concerns observers like Reid who, in a series of papers (notably 1996), questions the basis upon which 'official policy documents' for Physical Education had narrowed its scope of study (especially at HGPE). In becoming pre-eminently concerned with an account of knowledge in Physical Education deemed to be recognisable as of educational worth, Reid's critique of such documentation is a thesis on how the reduction of such knowledge to forms of analytical frameworks based on a largely scientific construction of performance was really something of an assault on the pluralistic essence of the subject (Reid, 1996). On a number of counts Physical Education's quest for 'theoretical tidiness' was inherently problematical for those leading its development, as exemplified by the way priorities switched between an Expressive Arts nomenclature at 5–14 to a performance-related curriculum in 14–18 courses.

As teachers continue to grapple with the pedagogical implications of linking performance-led knowledge to the personal improvement of pupil performance (in HSPE), a further characteristic of unease in Physical Education is how the teachers craft has become polarised as 'theory' and 'practice', a problem compounded by the unitisation of courses witnessed in HSPE. Teaching timetables where 'theory lessons' have their clear designation, bears testimony to the view that the nature of assessment and the relative weighting given to the constituent parts of SGPE and the units of HSPE have made their mark on teachers' organisation of content and practice. It is important to note the tension that this brings to teachers and the teaching of Physical Education. While documentation for Physical Education since SGPE (1988) has made positive reference to critical and imaginative practice, practical and experiential learning, the concerns for evidence of achievement relative to the public scrutiny of examination results appear to act as a constraint to teachers practice. Thus the tendency to fulfil the knowledge and understanding obligations of SGPE and HSPE syllabi in detached classroom contexts has become something of a pragmatic reality, even to the extent of warranting comment approaching rebuke from HMI reporting on 'chalk and talk' teaching (SOEID, 1995).

Whether such methodologies can change is a matter of conjecture. Thorburn's analysis (1999) of SQA results in Physical Education and his review of the implications of these for teaching certificated classes may be more reflective of hope than conviction regarding teachers' future practice and how it might evolve into genuine performance-led contexts. Indeed when linked to Curtner-Smith et al. (2001) and their findings on why teachers of the national curriculum for Physical Education (England/Wales) pursue direct, reproductive teaching styles, such trends of teacher practice, as they are influenced by externally set protocols, clearly requires the profession's scrutiny. In Scotland, understandably, it is hard for teachers to reconcile the competing claims of a rationale proclaiming the practical, experiential nature of Physical Education while at the same time supporting an assessment culture that has a minimum 50% weighting towards written forms of assessment (in SGPE, and, above Intermediate 1 levels at HSPE).

THE CHALLENGE OF SPORT AND HEALTH AGENDAS

There has been an increasing emphasis placed on schools to review how its programmes contribute to the development of children's interest in sport, more especially in the way that this can impact on pupils becoming physically active as part of the broader concerns about encouraging healthy lifestyles (Scottish Executive, 2002). Indeed, partly as a consequence of both a vibrant research literature and its reporting of depressed levels of physical activity in youth groups, allied to the concerns of sport-scotland and the national governing bodies of sport regarding the provision of school sport, this has become an initiative-rich area of both policy and implementation. Top-Play, Top-Sport, (the) Active Primary School, school-sport co-ordinators are current aspects of such policy, all enabled through government agency vetting and support via the National Lottery. More recently the view that schools should be afforded the opportunity to specialise its sports talent (among others) has made its mark in Glasgow and North Lanarkshire schools in varying formats, while research elsewhere is being fostered to verify how talent identification and development schemes with the school-aged population can be properly validated. Clearly the lobby for sport, in alliance with claims being made for its benefits to health and as a vehicle for more socially inclusive practices, is having something of a political moment.

As Green (2000) points out, Physical Education teachers still implicitly endorse sport (generally in the form of team games) as the underlying philosophy of 'what they do' and on this basis current sports-based initiatives might find favour with its departments. It may also be argued that the connections between sport and Physical Education are already an embedded context for some pupils – the youngster in HSPE pursuing 'effective performance in challenging contexts' is little different in intent (at least) from the Olympian. The task for Physical Education and its teachers in schools is to calculate where the priorities lie in dealing with such agendas. In what ways, for example, can any initiative in school formal or extra-curricular contexts encourage children to be willing and active participants in the activities shared by sport and Physical Education? Should school-sport co-ordinators be encouraging participation or competition in their brief? Views that such programmes can foster lifelong learning is a particularly testing remit for the advocates of youth sport policies who continue to seek some reverse to the trends of decline in participation. This latter issue continues to invite animated advice, especially in the way opportunities are afforded to girls where the concerns over lack of enrolment and lower achievements in certificated Physical Education have prompted not only SQA research into the matter, but have rekindled debates in school departments about the selection and presentation of activities along with the organisation of pupils into co-ed or single sex classes.

LOOKING AHEAD

The influences acting upon Physical Education continue to be diverse. An impending review of Physical Education initiated by Scottish Executive ministers will no doubt confirm the range of school sport-healthy lifestyle issues that pervade current analysis (see, for example, Houlihan, B. and White, A., *The Politics of Sports Development – Development of Sport or Development through Sport?* London: Routledge, 2002). Anticipating what might lie ahead for Physical Education in the immediate future will be a function of two foci. Firstly, moves towards a more flexibly managed curriculum where schools are encouraged to advance the particular strengths of pupils may influence one way or another a pupils' entitlement to Physical Education. This begs the view that any proposals for a core Physical Education programme and the reasons for compelling pupils to do it has to be well informed by the research associated with young peoples' views on physical activity. Currently there is little doubt that government will pursue this in a health conscious-'sports can be good for you' context. Secondly, linked to such accounts of the core qualities attributed to Physical Education, will be the ways the subject finds its political voice in the national debate on any future strategy for Scottish Education. Physical Education rose to the challenge of curriculum development in the certificated era as a consequence of assertive central directives led by HMI and SEB, SCOTVEC and SQA regulation. However in the years ahead, paradoxically, given the consistent rise in pupil entries to SGPE and HSPE, it has to now avoid being trapped by certification. Clearly these are not courses for all the school population and current inclinations to download HSPE or 'fast track' SGPE to younger age groups appear misdirected. How children are to realise some form of positive fulfilment through physical activity remains an enduring aspect of school Physical Education and with the demise of its advisorate, the lack of a professional association to voice its concern, and the rechannelling of HMI responsibilities, quite who will take the lead for pursuing joined-up policies for Physical Education and sport remains a major challenge for Scotland.

REFERENCES

Curtner-Smith, M. D., Todorovich, J. R., McCaughtry, N. A. and Lacon, S. A. (2001) Urban teachers' use of productive and reproductive teaching styles within the confines of the National Curriculum for Physical Education, *European Physical Education Review* 7(2), 177–90.

Green, K. (2000) Exploring the everyday 'philosophies' of Physical Education teachers from a sociological perspective, *Sport, Education and Society*, 5(2), 109–29.

Reid, A. (1996) The concept of Physical Education in current curriculum and assessment policy in Scotland, *European Physical Education Review*, 2(1), 7–18.

Scottish Executive (2002) *Lets Make Scotland more Active – A Strategy for Physical Activity – a consultation* – Physical Activity Task Force.

SOEID (1995) *Physical Education: Effective Learning and Teaching in Scottish Secondary Schools*, a Report by HM Inspectors of Schools: Edinburgh: SOEID.

Thorburn, M. (1999) Is it real Physical Education today?: Knowledge and understanding in Standard Grade, Higher and Higher Still Physical Education, *Scottish Journal of Physical Education*, 27 (1), 19–29.

68

Physics Education

Rothwell Glen

PHYSICS FROM 1960 TO THE 1980S

Physics, as a certificated, discrete Science subject, was introduced into the curriculum for Scottish schools in the early 1960s. The main influence on the nature of the course developed during this time was the Physical Science Study Committee Physics Course from USA. This placed emphasis on presenting physics not as a mere body of facts but as a continuing process by which humans seek to understand the nature of the Physical world. In S3 and S4, Physics was taken as a two-year Ordinary Grade course and progression was then to a one-year Higher Grade course.

In the mid-1980s the Higher Grade arrangements document was changed to take into account the impact of modern developments in physics such as electronics and telecommunications. This document was the first occasion where the syllabus content was specified in terms of learning outcome statements – what students should be able to do. This format has had an influence on teaching, learning and assessment and was well received by Physics teachers and looked upon jealously by teachers of other subjects. In the late 1960s, a one-year course for S6, the Certificate of Sixth Year Studies (CSYS) was introduced.

PHYSICS FROM THE 1980S TO 1999

During the 1980s it became obvious that Physics as a school subject was facing a number of problems. The major areas of concern were:

- the physics being taught was dated in comparison to developments in technology that impacted on physics;
- some concepts were seen to be too difficult for many pupils in S3 and S4 and needed to be moved to a higher level or removed completely;
- the majority of pupils who took Physics were boys despite many attempts to address the gender balance;
- Physics was not seen as relevant to society at large either in work or at leisure.

With this in mind the courses in Physics at Ordinary Grade, Higher Grade and CSYS were revised.

For S3 and S4, Standard Grade Physics was introduced in 1988. This course was seen as being modern, relevant and useful to people in everyday life. The course was designed to be delivered via an applications-led approach – the application came first followed by the physics principles involved. The relevance of the physics being studied was emphasised. The course was offered at two levels – General and Credit. At Credit level, students were expected to know more and to problem solve in more complex situations. There was no Foundation level course and so less able pupils were, for the most part, unable to choose Physics in S3.

At Higher Grade and CSYS, revised syllabuses were introduced. Although not 'applications-led' as at Standard Grade appropriate contexts, applications and illustrations were included in the syllabus to emphasise situations where the principles of physics were used. This, like the learning outcome statements, has had an influence on teaching, learning and assessment.

At this time SCOTVEC Modules were introduced as alternative courses in Physics. These modules were aimed at students who found it difficult to cope with the pace and demands of a Higher Grade course or who wished to study Physics for the first time in S5 and S6.

PHYSICS FROM 2000

By the mid-1990s it was apparent that very few students were leaving school at the end of S4 and were returning to pursue courses in Physics that were inappropriate to their needs. In S3 and S4 Standard Grade continued to be offered. In S5 and S6, Access 3, Intermediate 1, Intermediate 2, Higher and Advanced Higher have been introduced as a part of the Higher Still National Qualifications programme. Access 3 and Intermediate 1 deal with the same body of knowledge and are designed to meet the needs of students who wish to study Physics in contexts that relate to their vocational or leisure aspirations. At Intermediate 1 level, students are expected to apply their knowledge in more complex contexts.

Intermediate 2 covers the content of Credit level at Standard Grade. Some concepts are studied in greater depth, compared to Credit level, to act as a bridge to Higher Physics. This will give students who have attained a General level award at Standard Grade Physics the opportunity further to develop the skills needed to pursue the Higher Physics course. It will also provide more able pupils, who have not studied Physics before, with a suitable basis for further study in Physics.

The content of the course at Higher Physics is basically as it was after revision in 1991. However, the opportunity was taken to expand some areas of the syllabus. Advanced Higher, although less demanding mathematically than CSYS, still aims to provide a challenging experience for those who wish to study Physics to a greater depth and to cater for those who wish to proceed with its study at college and university.

All of the courses under the Higher Still arrangements are made up of mandatory units. Each unit can be studied independently from the others. The study of the units as separate, independent entities is valuable, however, it is recognised that students will gain considerable additional benefit from studying the units as components of a course. Pursuing a course in Physics involves opportunities for the integration of skills developed through the study of the units and for problem solving of a more complex nature. This provision does not apply to Access 3 where no course award is available.

All of the syllabuses are described in terms of 'learning outcome statements', now called 'content statements'. These statements specify the knowledge and understanding delivered by the course content. Appropriate contexts, applications, illustrations and activities are included in the syllabus specification. The syllabuses are designed to enable the development of the student's knowledge and understanding, problem solving skills and practical abilities.

ASSESSMENT – STANDARD GRADE

The examination at Standard Grade is at two levels – General and Credit. The duration of the General level paper is one and a half hours and for the Credit level paper it is one and three quarter hours. Both papers assess knowledge and understanding and problem solving with equal weighting given to both elements. There is no choice in either paper. Practical abilities is assessed for the purpose of certification. Originally this contributed to one third of the overall grade awarded but has now been reduced to one-fifth. This assessment is carried out internally and moderated by the examining authority, the Scottish Qualifications Authority (SQA).

ASSESSMENT – NATIONAL QUALIFICATIONS – UNITS

Knowledge and understanding and problem-solving skills are assessed using a closed book test. Practical abilities are assessed through the completion of a report on an activity that allows the student to demonstrate the ability to collect and analyse information. All of the unit assessment is carried out internally and is externally moderated by SQA. Advice and assessment material are provided by SQA through the National Assessment Bank (NAB).

ASSESSMENT – NATIONAL QUALIFICATIONS – COURSES

Table 68.1 below shows the duration of the external examination and the percentage of the total marks allocated to questions assessing knowledge and understanding and problem solving skills.

Table 68.1:   National Qualifications

Course	Duration of examination	Percentage of total marks available	
		Knowledge and understanding	Problem solving skills
Intermediate 1	1½ hours	50%	50%
Intermediate 2	2 hours	50%	50%
Higher	2½ hours	40%	60%
Advanced Higher	2½ hours	40%	60%

At Advanced Higher, there is an additional twenty-five marks allocated to a report of an investigation based on the work carried out in the Physics investigation unit. There is no choice in any of the question papers. To gain the award of the course, the student must achieve a pass in all of the component units for that course as well as in the external examination.

METHODOLOGIES IN PHYSICS

All of the courses in Physics, and the support materials provided, have been designed to allow teachers to use the full range of teaching and learning methods that can realise course objectives and best meet the needs of all students. The variety of methods used includes exposition, discussion, consolidation, practical investigations, problem solving, homework, and diagnostic and summative assessment. The course materials available include nationally developed packages for both students and staff, commercial packages, on-line material such as that provided by the BBC, the Scholar programme developed by Heriot-Watt University, computer assisted learning programmes and a number of text books. On-line materials and other computer assisted learning programmes should allow students to take some responsibility for their own learning.

DIFFERENTIATION

Standard Grade Physics is a bi-level course. Nationally produced materials and those developed by individual Physics departments provide for differentiation in both teaching approach and support for learning and assessment. This allows students to study at a level appropriate to their abilities. The content statements provided in the units at both Access 3 and Intermediate 1 are identical. Students who fail to achieve a pass in the unit assessment for Intermediate 1 can then attempt the less demanding unit assessment for Access 3. The courses at Intermediate 1, Intermediate 2, Higher and Advanced Higher are designed as separate courses and not bi-level as at Standard Grade. In some schools it may not be possible to timetable these courses separately and multi-level teaching may be the solution to this problem. Computer assisted learning programmes are useful tools for assisting in multi-level teaching.

STANDARDS OF PERFORMANCE

Table 68.2 below shows the presentation number and percentage of awards gained in the Scottish Qualifications Authority diet of examinations in 2001. This information is taken from the appropriate principal assessor reports supplied by SQA.

It is likely that the number of entries at Intermediate 1 and Intermediate 2 will increase as more students recognise the value of these courses in catering for a range of needs and abilities. It is significant that the percentage of A–C passes at Higher and Advanced Higher have increased. It may be that the students following these courses are the students for which the courses were designed.

PHYSICS IN THE FUTURE – ISSUES TO CONSIDER

Arrangements documents evolve to keep pace with developments in physics. It is important, therefore, that teachers continue to be given the opportunity to engage in professional development to extend and update their knowledge base. This is particularly necessary because the age profile of Physics teachers is skewed towards the late forties.

Table 68.2: **Standard Grade**

Entries		Awards	
Number	Trend 1999–2001	Credit	General
19,271	fairly constant	60%	33%

Intermediate 1

Entries		Awards			
Number	Trend 2000–1	A	B	C	Total A–C
147	increase	35%	19%	14%	68%

Intermediate 2

Entries		Awards			
Number	Trend 2000–1	A	B	C	Total A–C
1,850	slight increase	14%	19%	26%	59%

Higher

Entries		Awards			
Number	Trend 2000–1	A	B	C	Total A–C
10,065	fairly constant	31%	23%	20%	74%

Advanced Higher

Entries		Awards			
Number	Trend 2000–1	A	B	C	Total A–C
1,026	increase	23%	23%	23%	69%

Impact of 5–14 Environmental Studies

Some of the concepts relating to Standard Grade are now introduced in S1 and S2. This may well lead to an increase in the number of schools which timetable discrete Science subjects in S2 in place of the traditional integrated Science course. It is argued that this will allow the 'subject specialist' to teach the subject and may give pupils a more focused specialist preparation for S3. However this approach may mean that students will meet three separate Science teachers rather than one and the unity of Science as a subject may be lost.

Intermediate Level versus Standard Grade

An increasing number of schools are now considering replacing Standard Grade Physics, and more often Standard Grade Science, by Physics courses at Intermediate 1 and Intermediate 2 level. It is argued that this would allow classes to be set by ability thus narrowing the range of abilities in a particular class and so allowing the teacher to concentrate on the needs of individual pupils. This may also allow all pupils, at the end of S2, a free choice as to which Science subjects to pursue at a level that suits their ability. It is also felt that Intermediate 2 is a better preparation for Higher since some concepts met at Higher, such as momentum, are introduced. Standard Grade Physics, however, is a course that is well received by both staff and students. It is still regarded as a useful, relevant course that allows students to appreciate the diversity of the applications of physics.

Internal assessment

In Higher Still courses, students are required to achieve a pass in all the component units before a course award can be granted. Most staff accept that the on-going internal assessment of knowledge and understanding and problem-solving skills are of benefit to the students in terms of motivation, commitment and work ethic. This requirement means that any student who achieves a course award has a basic knowledge and understanding of the content of all of the component units. However, factors such as administration time, work load and management demands for internal assessment are sources of concern for some teachers. SQA have taken measures to reduce the burden of internal assessment but only time will tell if this satisfies the concerns expressed.

Resources

The impact of microcomputers on Physics courses and Physics teaching has been great over the years. Their use in interfacing, gathering and analysing data, simulation, lesson presentation, consolidation and revision has made it essential that all Physics laboratories are suitably equipped to carry out this kind of work. There will be a need to ensure that laboratory facilities are maintained and updated so that there is a modern, stimulating, teaching environment. Up-to-date resources require appropriate technician and administrative support so that teachers can make full use of advances in technology to help in the delivery of effective learning and teaching.

Women in Physics

Despite the efforts of individual Physics departments and national initiatives, Physics is still perceived to be a male orientated subject. This may be due to the fact that the majority of Physics teachers are male as are most high profile physicists. However, even in Physics departments where female staff have a high profile, female students are high performing and considerable efforts are made to allow students to come in contact with women who have done well in Physics, or related subjects, the gender imbalance still continues. Further initiatives are required to encourage female students to pursue Physics as a career subject.

Physics – is it really difficult?

Considerable time and effort is spent in making the teaching and assessment of Physics more accessible to all students. Despite this, Physics is still looked upon by many students as being a 'hard' subject. This may be due not only to the difficulty of some of the concepts that need to be understood but also the belief that excellent mathematical skills are essential to be successful in Physics. Many students lose sight of the physics of a problem because of their lack of belief in their mathematical skills. Physics teachers, with careful thought, planning and perseverance, can overcome these problems and allow the majority of students to be successful in Physics at a level that meets their needs.

THE FUTURE

Physics education has evolved over the last thirty years both in content and teaching approaches. There is much high quality teaching and effective learning taking place within the Scottish educational system. The Standard Grade Physics course has had a major influence on how the nature of the subject is perceived and in developing an awareness of how the applications of physics impact on society. Those involved in Physics education must continue to enhance the appeal of physics and show its relevance in work and leisure. Continual monitoring of how Physics is taught, learned and assessed at local and national level will be essential to ensure that the importance, relevance and impact of the subject is maintained and developed.

REFERENCES

Bryce, T. G. K., McCall, J., MacGregor, J., Robertson, I. J. and Weston, R. A. J. (1991) *TAPS 3 Assessment Pack: How to Assess Open-ended Practical Investigations in Biology, Chemistry, and Physics*, Oxford: Heinemann Educational.

SOED (1994) *Effective Learning and Teaching in Scottish Secondary Schools: The Sciences*, Edinburgh: SOED.

SQA (1997) *Standard Grade Arrangements in Physics*, Dalkeith: SQA.

SQA (2002) *Arrangements for Access 3, Intermediate 1, Intermediate 2, Higher and Advanced Higher*, Dalkeith: SQA.

SQA (2002) *Monitoring Standards in Highers – Physics*, Dalkeith: SQA.

69

Religious Education

Alex Rodger

PHILOSOPHY

In 1970 the goal of helping young people 'to come to a personal faith in Jesus Christ as Saviour and Lord' (Scottish Joint Committee on Religious Education) was regarded as broadly acceptable for Religious Education in both non-denominational and Roman Catholic schools. An important sub-theme of development since then concerns how these two sectors have negotiated the dialogue between educating young people for understanding and living within a modern pluralist society and equipping them to be reflectively committed within specific traditions and communities of faith.

In 1996 the Scottish Joint Committee on Religious Education was reconstituted as the Scottish Joint Committee on Religious and Moral Education. Its previous membership representing educational organisations and the churches was extended to include representatives of the different faith communities as full members. More recently, the Scottish branch of the Christian Education Movement has reconstituted itself as the Religious Education Movement Scotland. These changes can be seen as reflecting significant developments in Religious Education in Scotland in the last quarter of the twentieth century.

This chapter deals mainly with mainstream developments. The comment (SOED, 1994) that, 'Since the 1970s religious education has benefited from a much more professional approach and now has an educational value that is recognised in all major national developments that have taken place since that time', is equally applicable in 2003. The dramatic development during that period was precipitated by the Millar Report (SED, 1972). Its statements, 'Religious education is no longer aimed at producing assent to one particular faith' (para. 5.1); and 'The teacher is not there to convince pupils of specific religious beliefs . . . children should be exposed to a number of different attitudes and beliefs without the weight of "authority" being ultimately thrown behind any one of them' (para. 5.3); signalled a radical shift in the understanding of the subject.

Important distinctions were marked also between the contributions made by the home, the church and the school to the religious education of young people. The goals of school religious education were to be 'enlightenment rather than conversion, understanding rather than discipleship' (para. 3.3).

The phrase 'rather than' safeguards the educational purpose against indoctrinative or proselytising intention. It does not, however, resolve the important question as to how religious education can be both educational and religious: that is, how it can engender informed and sensitive appreciation of religion(s) in pupils without seeking to determine their own personal responses and commitments. In various forms this issue continues to preoccupy those involved with religious education in Scotland.

The present working consensus as to the aims of religious education derives from the work of the Scottish Central Committee on Religious Education (SCCORE) (1974–86), expressed in its Bulletin 2, *Curriculum Guidelines for Religious Education* (1981), as follows:

1. to help pupils to identify the area of religion in terms of the phenomena of religions and the human experiences from which they arise
2. to enable pupils to explore the nature and meaning of existence in relation to the questions religions pose and the answers they propose
3. to encourage pupils to develop a consistent set of beliefs, attitudes and practices which are the result of a personal process of growth, search and discovery (para. 3.2)

This represents the general view that has shaped national curriculum guidance for the subject throughout the intervening years.

The distinction between two interrelated aspects of (and objectives for) the subject – 'those related to religions and other stances for living, and those related to the pupil's search for meaning, value and purpose in life' (para. 4.2) – proved to be important in identifying what are called the 'assessable elements' of the subject and, therefore, in developing examinations in Religious Education. The ability to foster pupils' own 'personal search' has proven more elusive.

INNOVATION AND CHANGE

In addition to providing an educational view of Religious Education, the Millar Report generated activity and reflection which were to transform Religious Education in the last quarter of the twentieth century. It led to:

- the appointment of local education authority advisers in religious education;
- the introduction of a teaching qualification in Religious Education for secondary teachers;
- the inspection of the subject by Her Majesty's Inspectors of Schools;
- National Certificate examinations in Religious Studies.

These developments were crucial in enabling Religious Education, for the first time, to become an integral part of the curriculum provision in Scottish schools. The principle was established by the Scottish Education Department's response to the Millar Report. The outworking in practice of its implications constitutes the greater part of the subject's development in the last quarter of the twentieth century.

Prior to 1974 there was no secondary teaching qualification in Religious Education, the subject being taught by 'volunteer' teachers of other subjects. In the year 2003 the vast majority of secondary schools have at least one registered teacher of Religious Education; a growing number of schools have more than one; and in many schools – particularly Roman Catholic schools – the Religious Education teacher leads a team of non-specialist teachers each devoting a small amount of time to teaching the subject.

HMI reports reveal an accelerating development in professionalism among Religious Education teachers since 1986, as indicated by departmental subject handbooks; course planning which takes account of balance, continuity, progression and coherence of courses to reflect the subject appropriately for pupils at different stages; awareness and use of a wider range of resources to enhance subject learning; differentiation of courses to match pupil needs and abilities; use of open learning and resource-based learning approaches, with corresponding adaptation of teacher role; the introduction of procedures for monitoring, evaluation, review and development of courses; and an increasing uptake of certificate examinations in Religious Education and Religious Studies, with consequent transfer of (teacher) learning to benefit non-certificate courses in Religious Education.

The inspection of Religious Education, first introduced in 1983, had a dramatic effect on the professionalisation of the subject – supporting teacher development, spreading good practice, ensuring that curriculum principle increasingly shaped its planning, content, methods, assessment and development – bringing balance, continuity, progression, differentiation and coherence towards the realisation of the vision of a subject provided systematically and developmentally throughout the pupil's school career; addressing educational and personal search needs; assuming a broad understanding of religion as the clearest manifestation of the persistent human search for meaning, value and purpose in life; and ensuring that content is broad and balanced and the approach open and disciplined.

Curriculum Design for the Secondary Stages (SCCC, revised edn, 1999) prescribed for Religious and Moral Education (RME) the following time allocations (actual provision shown in brackets):

- S1/S2 5% of curriculum time (provided in about half of schools inspected between 1995 and 2000)
- S3/S4 eighty hours over the two years (met in 73% of schools in 1983; 88% in 1991; just over 50% in 1995–2000; 15% of schools did not provide RME for all pupils in S3 and S4.)
- S5/S6 a continuing element within the context of personal and social development (done in 56% of schools in 1983; 53% in 1991; less than half in 1995–2000.).

At each stage, Roman Catholic schools consistently provide at least the minimum recommended allocation of time. It follows that the provision in non-denominational schools is significantly lower than these percentages suggest.

Courses of study currently undertaken are as follows:

- S1/S2 Courses based on the national guidelines for Religious and Moral Education 5–14. Each school to devise its own course to meet the attainment outcomes' guidelines' in relation to Christianity, other world religions and the pupil's personal search; within a framework of outcomes for knowledge and understanding, skills and attitudes. Roman Catholic schools have much more detailed diocesan syllabi.
- S3/S4 Around 50% of pupils receiving RME follow a course devised by the school. Upwards of 40% follow Scottish Qualifications Authority courses – Standard Grade, Short Courses or (increasingly) National Units – leading to a National Qualification.
- S5/S6 Almost half of schools offer Higher or a programme of National Qualification Units at Intermediate 1 and 2 levels; a very few schools offer Religious Studies for the Advanced Higher.

Despite the upward influence of the 5–14 Religious Education programme, HMI reports still call for greater variety of teaching methods, especially in S1/S2. From S3 on, the demands of certification have broadened the awareness of teachers and extended their skills in such things as course construction, differentiation, variety of method, individual and group work and whole-class teaching, assessment, the use of pupil investigative activities and the development of effective study skills in pupils.

Assessment raises peculiar issues for Religious Education, with fears of any 'test of faith' or intrusion into pupils' personal convictions. SCCORE's view of the dual nature of Religious Education – dealing with the phenomena and with the learner's personal search – opened the way for the identification of 'assessable elements' which avoided that charge, while still involving the learner's reflective activity and evaluation of things studied. Although few would claim that this is altogether successful as yet in enabling pupils to avoid both uncritical acceptance and premature, ill-informed or insensitive judgements, school inspections reveal that much progress was made in this direction during the 1990s. Attention is also being given currently to enabling RME teachers to provide more effective support for the pupils' personal search. Credit must be given to professional religious educators both for the courage to tackle such issues, which have been too long shirked, and for the determination to pursue them in the face of inevitable criticism.

It is to be expected that such a range of interacting changes as is sketched above will be uneven in its introduction and its effects. Nonetheless, it is entirely realistic to view the subject today as fully a part of schools' educational provision, accepting the same educational obligation and deserving of the same resources and support as other subjects. On current evidence, it is well able to continue to progress in the direction of providing a coherent and developing whole-school experience which enhances the academic and personal development of young people in religious and moral understanding.

There are, at this crucial stage, some questions hanging over the effective completion of this task. Recent appointments of advisers with composite remits – for example, RME/PSE/ guidance; and of similar (post-McCrone) arrangements for principal teachers of subjects to be replaced by heads of departments responsible for several subjects within schools – may result in less, and almost certainly less specialist and less well informed, support for the teaching and development of RME.

UNFINISHED BUSINESS

The vigour and commitment directed to the development of Religious Education over the last thirty years encourages, rather than disallows, the following comments. They are premised on a job well begun, rapidly advancing, but with challenges still to face.

In a situation where many non-specialist teachers are involved in teaching RME it is unsurprising – though regrettable – that a significant proportion still lack a holistic vision of the subject which internalises its root principles. Sometimes this is betrayed by lack of awareness of the contribution a specific course makes to the balance and range of pupils' experience and learning of the subject over one session; more often, in a failure to see the opportunities for continuity and coherence over the pupil's secondary school experience (far less its progression from learning in the primary school). To have a firm grasp of the approved framework for the subject within the curriculum is not the same thing as to have a coherent philosophy of the subject, or a clear and generous view of its potential contribution to the human development of the learner. Important as the former undoubtedly is, it is the latter two which inform the teaching that conveys life and engenders growth in both learner and teacher. Without them, the pupil's religious and moral education will be the poorer.

There are criteria we should seek in a teacher of Religious Education which are not similarly required in teachers of others subjects (though there may be parallels in some subjects). The requirement is not that the Religious Education teacher be better (morally) or more religious than other people; and not that she/he be a Christian, or committed to some other specified faith. The requirement, in addition to appropriate academic and professional insight and competence, has to do with the teacher's own commitment to 'the search for meaning, value and purpose in life' in some recognisable form, and a corresponding commitment to let the view of 'the nature of things' she/he holds have appropriate expression in her/his life. Without some such reflective experience of a personal stance for living there can be no 'insider' appreciation of the significance of the subject matter.

In keeping with this understanding of the subject, schools professing to cater for the educational needs of the children of all citizens in a pluralist society are compromised in their educational integrity if they provide religious education, or insist on participation in worship, of a kind which presupposes that Christianity (or any other faith) is 'correct' – with the unspoken corollary that others are wrong.

Scotland has moved away from the indoctrinative intention for the subject that is now called Religious and Moral Education. It has not yet been possible to reach a position which removes grounds for legitimate complaint from those of faiths other than Christianity – particularly in relation to the specious claim that the new understanding of the subject can, on educational grounds, support the legal requirement for a compulsory act of ('mainly Christian' – whatever that means) worship within non-denominational schools. At the time of writing, a review committee appointed by the Scottish Executive is preparing a report on religious observance in schools, including advice for schools on how to provide 'religious observance' which is inclusive of pupils (and staff) of different – religious or non-religious – persuasions.

This belated official recognition that the search for meaning, value and purpose in life is not the monopoly of religions, but a fundamentally spiritual preoccupation of human beings as such, will – if it is serious – entail the facing of related questions that responsible educators in Scotland can no longer avoid at the beginning of the third millennium. These include:

- What are the purpose, the nature and the place of this area of study in an education designed to prepare the young for participating fully as human beings – not simply as citizens – in a democratic and pluralist society?
- What is the nature and scope of the subject matter with which Religious and Moral Education is concerned? And what are its relationships to other contributions such as Social Education, Health Education, Personal and Social Development, Values Education and – the latest arrival on the scene – Education for Citizenship? Can we avoid perpetuating miseducative 'construction kit' approaches to this complex but holistic area of human experience?
- Can we cater maturely in the educational process for the recognition of the limits (without diminishing the wonder) of all human knowledge and accomplishments, and make room again for the persistently mysterious and the awesomely transcendent elements in human experience?
- Will such questions be addressed during the development and implementation phases of the Scottish Executive's National Priorities for education, specifically in relation to Priority 4 – Values and Citizenship? Will the lessons learned in the progress of RME sketched above be carried forward?

A persisting obstacle to finding helpful answers to such questions arises from the fact that, despite the recent resurgence of interest in spirituality both within education and more widely within our nation, we are as a people largely religiously and spiritually illiterate. Thankfully, the damage inflicted on the education of the human spirit in the twentieth-century Western world by the conflict between doctrinaire philosophical dogmas and doctrinaire religious reaction is now widely recognised as something to be lamented. Yet it will take time for any healthily mature outlook to prevail, whereby children are educated to a sensitive understanding of those stances for living in which human beings have found faith to live fully and courage to die well. Nothing less can discharge the school's responsibility to contribute to the education of human beings for the challenge of living humanely in relationship to themselves, to each other, to the world they inhabit and to the cosmos they wonder at, even while they are a part of it.

In addition to time, such an outcome will require that people listen to each other more than has been the case; that they listen to the world's faiths and philosophies; that they learn from its ancient wisdoms and their contemporary expressions; and that they attend to their own awareness of what it is to live in this mysterious world. In the community of learners people may thus find words which help them to engage with their too-often inarticulate experience, and be helped to come for themselves to insights and recognitions which give new life to otherwise dead words inherited from others. Such informed, reflective and responsive attention to what is the case, with no insistence that it issue in any predetermined outcome, is at the heart both of education and of religion when they are worthy of their names.

REFERENCES

HMIE (2001) *Standards and Quality in Secondary Schools: Religious and Moral Education 1995–2000*, Edinburgh: Astron.

Kincaid, M. (1991) *How to Improve Learning in RE*, London: Hodder and Stoughton.

SED (1972) *Moral and Religious Education in Scottish Schools* (The Millar Report), Edinburgh: HMSO.

SOED (1992) *Religious and Moral Education 5–14*, Edinburgh: HMSO.

SOED/SCEC (1994) *Religious Education 5–14: Roman Catholic Schools*, Edinburgh: HMSO.

SCCC (1995) *Religious and Moral Education: 5–14 Exemplification*, Dundee: SCCC.

70

Science Education

John MacGregor

SCIENCE AND THE INDIVIDUAL SCIENCES

The study of Science, as a single coherent subject in its own right, was originally advocated by the Scottish Education Department in the influential Curriculum Paper No 7 *Science for General Education* (SED, 1969). Science was to be taught, to S1 and S2 pupils, not as the separate disciplines of Biology, Chemistry and Physics, but as a fully harmonised Science course delivered to a class by one teacher rather than three: this format, it was argued, reinforced the unity of the subject and created the opportunity for consistent teaching and assessment.

Over the past three decades an integrated Science course has been the norm in the vast majority of schools. Moreover, the emphasis in the teaching of Science has gradually moved away from the acquisition of factual knowledge and towards the development of general competence in the cognitive and practical processes of science, identified by labels such as 'problem-solving abilities' and 'investigative skills'. Consequently one might expect teachers today to feel more comfortable wearing a Science hat than they did previously and more attuned to the notion of 'scientific capability' as advanced by the Scottish Consultative Council on the Curriculum in their discussion paper *Science Education in Scottish Schools – Looking to the Future* (SCCC, 1996).

SCIENCE S1/S2

The original integrated Science course has now been superseded by the Science component of Environmental Studies, which forms part of the common syllabus for all pupils from age five to age fourteen. This national course was conceived with the worthy aim of providing progression and continuity in pupils' learning from P1 to S2 and was first published in 1993. Implementation of the guidelines was fairly slow as teachers grappled with the new structures. Progress was then reviewed by Her Majesty's Inspectorate (HMI) and changes in the delivery of the Science element were advised in the report *Improving Science Education 5–14* (SEED, 1999). The whole syllabus was then revised and re-presented in the form of *5–14 National Guidelines–Environmental Studies* (SEED, 2000). Each component of Environmental Studies is described in terms of attainment outcomes for knowledge and understanding, skills and the development of informed attitudes. There are three attainment outcomes in Science: living things and the processes of life; energy and forces; and earth and space. The Science skills to be developed are collected under one or other of three broad strands: preparing for tasks; carrying out tasks; and finally reviewing and reporting on tasks.

The introduction of Science 5–14 has stimulated a review of existing practice in S1/S2 and a reappraisal of methodology. Previously, teachers adopted a 'clean slate' approach to pupils entering secondary school. It was assumed most pupils would have, at best, a relatively superficial knowledge of Science and the safest policy was to teach the subject from scratch. This view is no longer tenable. Most pupils entering S1 are expected to have had a broadly similar experience in Science, at least in terms of subject content and investigative skills. On the other hand, these pupils will differ in the progress they have achieved so far and this will be reflected in the assessment levels which have been assigned to them, at the end of P7, by their primary teachers. Secondary science staff have to find effective strategies for teaching classes whose members are already differentiated with respect to their scientific comprehension and skills. Change in tactics, for whatever reason, has been slow, according to HMI who noted, in their report *Standards and Quality in Secondary Schools 1995–2000: The Sciences* (SEED, 2001), that ' little account was taken of pupils' prior experience in primary school and most departments adopted a fresh start approach'. Hopefully, the increasingly productive partnerships, developed between secondary schools and their feeder primaries, with regard to science provision, will soon enable the progress of each child to be systematically maintained across the P7–S1 interface. As pupils progress through 12–14 Science inspectors have also perceived some tailing-off of commitment, particularly among the more able pupils. Recommended remedial measures include more groupwork, more setting and more demanding extension activities. Level F content and new attainment targets dealing with aspects of genetics and heredity, astronomy and microelectronics have been introduced to the revised syllabus in order to provide extra topical and challenging material.

S3/S4 SCIENCE

Science, or at least one of the individual sciences, is a compulsory subject for pupils in S3/S4. Pupils are assessed in S2 and advised as to the most suitable courses for them to follow in S3. Currently about a quarter of the S3 cohort takes Standard Grade Science. Course content consists of four compulsory core topics, namely healthy and safe living; an introduction to materials; energy and its uses, and a study of environments.

While Biology, Chemistry and Physics offer certification at General and Credit levels only, Science caters for the full spread of ability and includes certification at Foundation level. Standard Grade Science classes tend to be composites; Foundation/General or General/Credit. Standard Grade Science is the only option available for pupils who were relatively unsuccessful in S2 Science. As a result Science has to overcome the perception that it is the 'poor relation' of the individual sciences in order to attract the more able pupils who would be candidates for Credit level awards. A second factor which dissuaded the more academic pupil from choosing a Credit Science course was the lack of a follow-on course such as 'Higher Science'.

SCIENCE BEYOND S4

Higher Still developments in the late 1990s redesigned and brought together the various Scottish Examination Board (SEB) academic courses and Scottish Vocational Educational Council (SCOTVEC) modules to form one coherent framework for the Sciences.

Implementation of the proposals appeared to redress the problem of Standard Grade Science being a course with a 'dead-end'. Pupils with that particular qualification could now progress into Intermediate 1, Intermediate 2 or even Higher courses depending on the grades which they achieved. An Intermediate 1 course in a Science subject is the natural progression for a student with a Foundation award from Standard Grade Science. In some cases a more appropriate step would be into Access 3 Science, a coherent group of modules comprising telecommunications, practical electricity, health and technology and everyday chemistry.

Paradoxically one of these follow-on courses for Standard Grade Science is emerging, instead, as a serious competitor to it. Although Intermediate 1 was conceived as a course for S5 pupils it is now being taken up, in S3, as an alternative to Standard Grade Science. Many teachers feel the latter course has become 'tired' and consider Intermediate 1 courses in Biology, Chemistry or Physics as more likely to motivate pupils. However such a move is opposed by other teachers who feel that any shift towards greater specialisation is not in the best interests of the average Science pupil.

ASSESSMENT, REPORTING AND CERTIFICATION

S1/S2 Science

There is no national external assessment of pupils in 5–14 Science. Schools administer continuous assessment for the purposes of recording progress and reporting to parents. Pupils' achievements are monitored and reported in terms of levels of attainment A – F, in both knowledge/understanding and skills. The average pupil would be expected to attain level E by the end of S2.

S3/S4 Science

A pupil's performance in Standard Grade Science is assessed under three distinct elements: knowledge and understanding (KU), problem solving (PS) and practical abilities (PA). Questions in the external examination papers are weighted equally between KU and PS. A candidate can be entered for two external examination papers: either Foundation and General or General and Credit. The pupil would be awarded the higher grade achieved.

Pupils tend to score more highly on the internally assessed practical abilities element where their capacity to carry out two open-ended investigations and eight simple laboratory techniques is measured. This is hardly surprising, given the clearly specified nature of the exercise and the opportunity for extended practice. In the mid 1990s it was felt that the typically higher grade obtained in PA distorted the overall profile, which included KU and PS, and thus produced an aggregate grade which was possibly a misleading measure of the pupil's capacity to handle more advanced study in the subject. As a result of consultation with schools and discussion between Scottish Qualifications Authority (SQA) Science Subject panels, it was decided to reduce the weighting of the practical abilities element weighting to one-fifth of total marks rather than one-third.

As with any internal assessment scheme on a national scale there is always pressure to ensure a level playing field and to avoid suspicions that school X is not applying the criteria as rigorously as school Y and thereby giving its pupils an unfair advantage. The moderation process is designed to regulate the process: teachers would wish to have full formal moderation to validate their internal assessments but have to accept considerably less, on the grounds of cost.

EVIDENCE OF THE LEVEL OF PUPILS' COMPETENCE IN SCIENCE

The Scottish edition of the *Third International Mathematics and Science Study (TIMSS) Report* (SOEID, 1996) compared the Science knowledge and understanding of S1 and S2 pupils with that of 13–year-olds in other countries. Results from any international survey have to be viewed cautiously, as there will never be completely identical opportunities for demonstrating achievement across countries. For what it is worth, Scotland's overall ranking was twenty-fifth out of thirty-eight countries at S1 and twenty-fifth out of forty countries at S2. According to the report, the Scottish pupils spent less time doing Science homework and less time exposed to whole class teaching than their counterparts in almost every other country. On a more encouraging note the study revealed that Scots 13–year-olds were relatively good on practical skills and came fourth out of a field of nineteen countries: a reflection, perhaps, of the importance attached to providing our Science pupils with abundant 'hands on' experimentation and the restriction on class size to twenty pupils. The most recent TIMSS survey was carried out in 1999 but this time Scotland was not one of the participating countries and so updated comparisons are not possible.

National surveys such as the assessment of achievement programme (AAP) help to provide a continuous monitoring of standards, over time, within the one country. The most recent AAP survey of Science indicated that two out of three pupils at P4 and P7 achieved the appropriate attainment targets set for them, whereas at S2 only half the pupils demonstrated the desired level of competence. Even more disappointing was the observation that performance in P7 and S2 showed no improvement from 1993. One trusts that, as the 5–14 Science course gradually beds down, teaching will have a sharper cutting edge and learning will be more focused, leading to a sustained enhancement in pupil achievement.

SOME ISSUES IN SCIENCE

Worksheets

Most Science courses have been organised, within the classroom, around a resource based learning (RBL) model. The movement to a pupil-centred rather than teacher-centred mode received its initial impetus with the publication of Curriculum Paper 7 and the subsequent national worksheet scheme which was produced to support the Integrated Science course. The introduction of worksheets was intended to relieve the teacher of much practical instruction and to create the opportunity for differentiated teaching and learning. It was envisaged that each pupil would progress smoothly through a programme of work at a level and at a pace commensurate with his/her ability. However, over the years concern has been expressed at the increasing reliance on the worksheet as the major learning resource at the expense of other methods. The HMI report, *Standards and Quality in Secondary Schools1995–2000* (SEED, 2001), reiterated official concern about this over-dependence on worksheets in S1/S2 and urged teachers to 'provide more direct teaching and a broader range of more challenging and interesting tasks'. Curtailing the controlling influence of worksheets will, it is hoped, encourage teachers to take more individual ownership of what goes on in the classroom and direct responsibility for the learning achieved.

Specifying pupils' learning

The identification of numerous specific objectives for the Integrated Science course in 1969 signalled the first change from norm to criterion referencing. A decade later a similar list of learning outcomes was identified for the Standard Grade Science course. More recently this commitment to the detailed specification of outcomes has continued into the 5–14 Science syllabus. The more precise the formulation of what pupils should be learning at any stage, the more valid and reliable the subsequent assessment can be. On the debit side, the more prescriptive the syllabus the less likely teachers and textbooks may be to add flesh to the bare bones of any topic. In the current competitive climate between schools 'teaching to the test' is easy to justify and not confined to Science. Embellishment of subject matter, with interesting but non-assessed material, is likely to increase pupils' general enthusiasm for Science and thus improve motivation towards learning the basic outcomes. However, in an already congested course, teachers would have to be fully convinced of this quid pro quo.

Thinking skills

Over the past two decades computers have had a major effect on Science teaching. Teachers can access all sorts of useful educational material from the world wide web, word-process paperwork for lessons in attractive fashion and use data projectors to do professional presentations. Nevertheless care has had to be taken to prevent the study of Science becoming prey to information overload and science teaching concentrating on polish at the expense of punch. In the HMI report (SEED 2001) S1/S2 teachers are requested to provide 'more opportunities for pupils to practise and develop investigative skills, problem solving and thinking skills'.

In Standard Grade Science investigative and problem-solving skills have featured for some considerable time now but their development in pupils has suffered, inevitably, from the heavy hand of national assessment. This has tended to constrain much of the open-ended aspect of investigations and overplayed the more mechanical components of problem solving, for instance graph drawing. The time has probably come to develop, not new courses but new material and activities which will genuinely motivate pupils critically to appraise evidence, look for flaws in reasoning and so on, in order to prepare them adequately for dealing with scientific and other related issues in everyday life.

REFERENCES

SCCC (1996) *Science Education in Scottish Schools – Looking to the Future*, Dundee: SCCC.
SEB (1987) *Standard Grade Arrangements in Science*, Dalkeith: SEB.
SED (1969) Curriculum Paper No 7 *Science for General Education*, Edinburgh: HMSO.
SEED (1999) *Improving Science Education 5–14*, Edinburgh: SEED.
SEED (2000) *5–14 National Guidelines – Environmental Studies*, Edinburgh: SEED.
SEED (2001) *Standards and Quality in Secondary Schools 1995–2000: The Sciences*, Edinburgh: SEED.
SOEID (1996) *Third International Mathematics and Science Study (TIMSS) Report*, Edinburgh: SOEID.

71

Technology Education

John R. Dakers and Robert Doherty

THE CONTENT OF TECHNICAL EDUCATION

Technical departments in Scottish secondary schools offer a range of courses that contribute principally to the Environmental Studies area of the 5–14 curriculum and the Technological Activities and Applications mode of the middle school curriculum (14–16). In addition technical subjects make a noticeable contribution to the Creative and Aesthetic mode within the middle school secondary framework and to ICT skills and processes across all stages. Post-16 provision within the Higher Still framework offers progression and access to recognised group awards in career and vocational areas. All courses offered in Technical departments are linked together conceptually, and to national curricular frameworks through the overarching concept of technological capability. Technological capability is defined as, 'understanding appropriate concepts and processes; the ability to apply knowledge and skills by thinking and acting confidently, imaginatively, creatively and with sensitivity; the ability to evaluate technological activities, artifacts and systems critically and constructively' (SCCC, 1996, p. 7).

Current curricular arrangements result in pupils in S1 and S2 following a common course within Technical departments. This common course reflects the requirements of the Environmental Studies curriculum and its assessment regime. Such courses are designed to give pupils an opportunity to understand and use the design process and to develop creativity, craft and graphic skills, in addition to developing confidence using machinery and equipment. An understanding of the role of technology and its impact on society and the use of technology (frequently the integration of discrete technologies), to solve problems and meet human needs are important dimensions of learning. The curriculum also calls for the development of informed attitudes and a capacity to understand and question the social and ethical implications of technological change. The middle school curriculum allows provision for choice and pupils within the present framework can typically choose to study one or two Standard Grade technical subjects. At present Technical departments offer up to three courses at Standard Grade: Craft and Design, Graphic Communication and Technological Studies.

Courses in Craft and Design (C&D) allow pupils to understand and use the design process and to develop craft skills together with knowledge and understanding of related materials and processes. Using timber, metal and plastics, and their associated processes and tools, students complete a serious of projects and models. Models are planned and structured to allow and support different aspects of craft skill development, the flexible use of the design process and study of relevant materials and processes. One-third of the final assessment is established through a school-based project which requires students to demonstrate their use of the design process as evidenced through the production of a design folio. The craft skills of students are assessed through the manufacture of their design. Both elements are internally assessed by the school using criterion referencing whilst the third element of the course, 'knowledge and understanding', is externally assessed by examination. The internal assessment elements across the three Standard Grade courses are also subject to external moderation.

Graphic Communication (GC) is concerned with the communication of graphical information in an engineering, technical or commercial context, the presentation of ideas and designs and knowledge of conventions pertaining to the interpretation of drawings and graphics. Students also develop manual and computer-based skills in drawing and graphic production. The course combines engineering drawing with elements of design and presentation, thus allowing opportunities for creativity. A folio of pupil work, assembled over the duration of the course, is used to assess the skills dimension of the course. This folio is then internally graded in relation to given criteria whilst learning outcomes relating to aspects such as knowledge and drawing ability are assessed externally by terminal examination.

Courses in Technological Studies (TS) aim to offer students an experience of 'modern technology' and an opportunity to develop knowledge, understanding, reasoning, numerical analysis and informed attitudes. The course explicitly promotes the development of interest in technology and related careers. It includes the study of system theory, pneumatics, applied electronics, programmable control, energy and mechanical systems. It incorporates practical tasks and problem solving, assessed internally through what are designated 'application of technology assignments.' Although TS first appeared on the curriculum in 1988, arrangements for the course have recently been revised. One outcome of this revision has been a reduction of differentiation from three levels to two, with the result that the subject is no longer on offer at Foundation level.

COMMON PRACTICE IN TECHNICAL EDUCATION

Whilst approaches to teaching in Technical Education are predominantly characterised by whole-class teaching and teacher demonstration there are also frequent opportunities to set pupils individual tasks and learning activities. Thus a mixture of direct teaching, demonstration, activity and resource-based learning is evidenced across all stages of Technical Education. Less rigid assessment arrangements allow common courses in S1 and S2 greater flexibility to support learning through tasks which are centered around small group processes. Specialised equipment and accommodation are used to support learning, generate pupil interest and support creativity and skill development. Differentiation within the technical curriculum is characterised by approaches focused on pupil product, on learning tasks and extension materials. In S1 and S2 common courses, differentiation is frequently by product, with mixed ability classes undertaking the same project or learning activities with differing levels of teacher support and pupil outcomes. Within Standard Grade arrangements, differentiation strategies are present in relation to content, learning tasks and outcomes distinguished by Foundation, General and Credit levels (although significantly this is currently no longer the case with TS, as will be discussed later). Within this predominantly three-level framework, learning tasks, content and the product of project work are differentiated in an attempt to meet the needs of individual pupils. Generally technical subject classes are of mixed ability although there are departments which employ a policy of setting. There is a significant gender imbalance in favour of boys across the middle school and upper school curriculum.

As part of a series of reports on effective learning and teaching in Scottish schools, Her Majesty's Inspectorate (HMI) published a report on Technical Education (SEED, 1999) which drew upon inspection evidence from 200 Technical departments. Whilst it is acknowledged that HMI views the world through a particular set of lenses, this is in some respects a useful document. It links pupils' positive experiences to teaching styles, opportunities to be creative, levels of challenge and opportunities to work independently. It is critical of the predominance of Craft in S1 and S2 courses and highlights the need to move toward a fuller implementation of the 5–14 Environmental Studies framework. Assessment practice within Technical Education is also highlighted as an area which requires development.

CURRICULUM REFORM AND THE RISE AND FALL OF TECHNOLOGICAL STUDIES

A reflective view of the technical curriculum reveals a genealogy with clear roots in its industrial and vocationally oriented past. The content of contemporary courses in Graphic Communication can be traced back through antecedent courses in Engineering and Building Drawing. The discrete subjects of metalwork and woodwork merged and evolved into working with combined materials (Integrated Craft). The efforts of a movement of individuals and organisations advocating design education (Design Council, 1980) led ultimately to integrated craft developing into courses in Craft and Design. Arguably the most radical curricular reform to Technical Education, however, can be seen in the introduction of Technological Studies. This modernising turn produced a new course distinctive from its forerunners, namely Applied Mechanics and Engineering Science, both historically marginal courses within the technical curriculum. The content of Technological Studies, with its emphasis on the integration of technologies, encourages the implementation of project work, resource-based learning and using technology in a problem-solving context. These factors combine to characterise the distinctiveness of this development.

A large proportion of teachers in Technical Education traditionally came from a background in industry. The new direction intended for Technical Education was therefore, of necessity, accompanied by a concomitant innovation in initial teacher education as new degree courses were developed to replace the long established Diploma in Technical Education. The provision of teachers able to deliver courses in Technological Studies was thus a major influence in the development of the new courses which were informed in part by an assumption that there would be a rationalisation involving a merger between Graphic Communication and Craft and Design at Standard Grade. The fact that these rationalisations failed to materialise was principally due to a combination of practitioner resistance, political lobbying and the mobilisation of industrial opponents.

From its launch in 1988, Technological Studies enjoyed an initial surge of popularity. This was supported in part by the availability of funding from the UK government programme, the Technical and Vocational Education Initiative. Presentations at Standard Grade in 1994 were consequently running at 6076, although significantly, by 1999 presentations had fallen to 3,649 (see Table 71.1).

Table 71.1:   Trend in entries for each subject at Standard Grade

Subject	1994	1995	1996	1997	1998	1999
C&D	11,649	12,578	13,431	13,992	13,613	13,783
GC	5,778	6,670	7,118	7,543	7,319	7,860
TS	6,076	5,978	5,258	4,897	4,282	3,649

Whilst this obvious decline cannot be explained by reference to a single causal factor, a number of contributing elements can be suggested. These include:

- a reluctance by practitioners to reduce Technical Educations' range of courses;
- a natural decline in interest in the subject following an initial surge of popularity;
- the inadequate and uneven provision of professional development to support teachers already in service;
- the unfortunate choice of kits and equipment to support the resource-based learning and project dimensions of the course. (This led to management and storage problems accompanied by very high replacement costs);
- wider pressures on school managers for rationalisation of the curriculum to maximise efficiency. (In this respect, advice to school managers appeared to be directed against the provision of Technological Studies, particularly in schools in the West of Scotland.);
- delays by the SQA and its predecessor in making the revisions necessary to address issues of content, and course sustainability, and to ensure that the course reflected continuing technological development;
- competition with more established and 'prestigious' courses such as Physics within the context of an already crowded curriculum.

The decline of TS occurring ironically in a period of concern over technologically mediated economic globalisation and the advent of knowledge economies (Peters, 2002), has resulted in deep disquiet among practitioner supporters and the inspectorate. This may help to explain the pragmatic, perhaps elitist, direction that has been taken in search of a remedy. TS has been relaunched, with the first cohort due to complete the new course in 2003. It is now, however, a selective course, available to pupils at only Credit and General level. Pupils who are perceived to be capable only of Foundation level are consequently 'directed' to develop their technological capability in other subjects. The potency of this strategy to halt the decline of TS will be a focus of future interest, although this may sit uneasily with those who hold on to the more egalitarian strands of Scottish education.

IMPACT OF HIGHER STILL

The aim of the Higher Still framework was to make provision for groups of pupils who were not catered for by the established Scottish Higher examination system. The intention was to establish a coherent post-16 curriculum that provided routes for progression. This has had some important implications for Technical departments. As a consequence of subject uptake in the upper school and quotas on viable class sizes, for example, it is common to find pupils in the same class studying at Higher and Intermediate levels. Multi-level teaching, therefore, is a recurring challenge for Technical teachers arising from Higher Still

(HS). In commo
Still, moreover
and staff by
modularised
Scottish Hi
cumbersor
inal exam
of SQA
Standard
and Adv
Qualifica
consult o

In the a
support, o
cally four p
Majesty's Ir
Scottish Co
Teaching Sc
and working
Association.
example of th
development o
remove Higher
produce a new
resultant reductio.
and resources whilst simu.
for most institutions. Practitione.
included the addition of a new course, i.

Higher Still courses at Intermediate levels 1 and
Standard Grade) are now being provided by Technica.
Scottish Executive Education Department (SEED) to allow s.
pupils in S3 and S4 has opened up the potential for divergence in.
curriculum and has shrouded the future of Standard Grade in uncertainty. This
holds certain harmful implications for the future of Design education within the midui.
upper school curriculum as new courses in PCS can now be offered in place of CD.

The 'arranged marriage' of Craft to Design has not been without its tensions as the long
established Craft tradition had to make accommodations to its new more creative partner.
The teaching of Design, its assessment, and its integration with Craft skills has not as yet
found an optimum balance in Technical Education and this has left a proportion of students
not entirely convinced of the benefits of the design dimension. Courses in PCS have no
Design element, are continually assessed and are inherently skills based. This particular
curriculum reform could therefore be interpreted as a retrospective dilution and revoca-
tionalisation of the curriculum, or conversely, as a broadening-out of provision which allows
teachers greater scope to respond to the educational needs and preferences of diverse groups
of pupils. Whilst the risks of forecasting curricular futures must be acknowledged, the trend
of departments offering PCS alongside C&D, or indeed in place of C&D, looks set to
continue at the expense of Design education.

nsions will shape the future of Scottish
early discernible tension arising from the
d the wider curricular aim of developing
form the Technical curriculum are suitably
unities and experiences, within what could be
, and to contribute to the development of such a
fers diverse learning opportunities ranging through
ommunication, design, and ICT to electronics and
owledge, understanding and skills contained within the
is simultaneously an educational virtue and an Achilles'
esourcing, management and development demands.

chnology in support of Technology learning is an approach
have shown a willingness to embrace. It seems therefore
nical departments are not as yet being designed with multiple
dard practice. Such ICT is not only essential to the provision of
content, but critically, is in itself an excellent medium for supporting
ch of the Technical curriculum. The development of a progressive
ulum is in many ways arrested by the economic implications of providing
chers with appropriate levels of ICT infrastructure. Integrated Computer
n and Computer Aided Manufacture (CAD CAM) is currently an area of
omission with respect to present curriculum content.

rger southern neighbour has a more focused and privileged Technology curri-
which has attracted international attention. Whilst Scotland has traditionally taken
e in the distinctiveness of its own education system, the direction of Technical
ucation would seem at this juncture to mirror concerns being engaged with in other
countries and to be facing similar challenges from wider international policy discourses.
Technical Education in Scotland is in something of an identity crisis. Schools are at present
witnessing curriculum realignment. There is a displacement of recent design and technological innovations and reforms and a reassertion of a vocational and skills-based tradition.
This is in conflict with a global modernising turn going beyond craftwork and industrial arts
towards a Technology Education located in design and contemporary technologies. The
task of resolving such tensions and questions of identity is an immediate one for all who hold
a stake in the future of Technical Education.

REFERENCES.

Design Council (1980) *Design Education at Secondary School Level*, London: The Design Council.
Peters M. A. (2001) National education policy constructions of the 'knowledge economy': towards a critique, *Journal of Educational Enquiry*, 2 (1) (www.education.unisa.edu.au).
SCCC (1996) *Technology Education in Scottish Schools: A Statement of Position from Scottish CCC*, Dundee: SCCC.
SEED (1999) *Effective Learning and Teaching in Scottish Secondary Schools: Technical Education*, Edinburgh: SEED.
SQA (2000) Annual Statistical Report, Glasgow: SQA.

IX

Further and Higher Education

72

Current Priorities

Joyce Johnston

STILL THE CINDERELLA SECTOR?

The further education sector is of relatively recent origin. Founded largely in the earlier part of the twentieth century to meet the apprentice training needs of Scottish manufacturing, technical colleges metamorphosed in the latter half of the century into institutions offering continuing education for all of the post-16 population. With approximately half of their activity accounted for by full-time students, and offering educational provision ranging from basic literacy and numeracy skills through to degree and postgraduate courses, the forty-four colleges now offer a local, accessible, 'second chance' for post-school education and training. Because of their focus on vocational education, delivered through the National Qualification (NQ) and Higher National Certificate/Diploma (HNC/HND) curriculum, colleges constitute an alternative to S5 and S6 in school for many young people. Similarly, because of a rich network of articulation agreements, which permit students to progress from HNC/HND courses into the later stages of degrees, the colleges constitute a local and affordable alternative to undergraduate years one or two at university. Colleges have also increasingly extended their mission to help those in the community who need a second chance to learn.

This continuum of educational provision offered by further education (FE) colleges is one of their strengths. Conversely however, it presents one of their major challenges, as the overlap with other sectors means that the FE sector has a weaker discreet identity in the national consciousness than other sectors, particularly schools and universities. Given also that education policy makers are in the main products of universities, it is perhaps understandable that those in the FE sector have long believed their comprehensive role to be unrecognised and under-valued. The advent of more local strategic management of the sector, via a Scottish Parliament and knowledgeable MSPs, is perhaps now redressing this situation.

Colleges point to the successes of the sector in the last fifteen to twenty years – a new, competence-based, accessible curriculum satisfactorily introduced, major contributions to government skills targets being made, access to higher education facilitated and increased, huge growth in the numbers of adult students engaging in lifelong learning, efficiency and effectiveness improved, local communities supported in their regeneration – and look with a growing sense of identity and destiny towards their future. This chapter considers some of the principal issues and priorities which at present confront the further education sector in preparing for and shaping its destiny.

PARTNERSHIPS

Further education is unusual in the Scottish education system in that, while it offers a continuum of vocational education and training opportunities for the post-16 population, all parts of its provision overlap with other sectors. It therefore operates within a complex pattern of relationships, within which it has been beneficial to develop collaborative alliances. These partnerships are generally predicated on mutual benefit, and a need to rationalise the use of scarce resources. The pattern of relationships is illustrated and described below in terms of types of provision and main providers. (See Figure 72.1)

Figure 72.1:   Relationships in further education

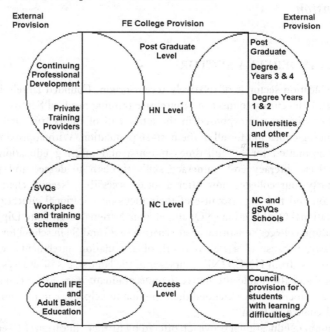

The maintenance or development of these partnerships is a priority for the sector. Each is now examined in its context.

Partnerships – schools

Vocational education and training as offered by further education colleges was radically altered in the 1980s by the introduction of the National Certificate (NC) – a competence-based, modularised curriculum which permitted colleges autonomy to develop courses to meet local needs, and which introduced internal continuous assessment and student-centred teaching methods. The 'Higher Still' initiative, which reformed upper secondary schooling in Scotland in the late 1990s, also impacted on the FE non-advanced curriculum, in that it aimed to integrate vocational and academic streams for post-16 students into one framework with parity of esteem throughout. The resulting National Qualifications (NQs) reintroduced the practice of external assessment, where it was deemed appropriate, to FE programmes. The conversion by FE of full-time NC programmes into NQs however is proceeding only slowly. Concerns about a loss of flexibility, both in the design of programmes and in the timing of assessments, have made many FE staff reluctant to move away from the former NC programmes which are seen as meeting the needs of local employers.

Approximately 70% of the volume of learning activity delivered by colleges is at non-advanced or FE level – although the proportion varies widely among colleges (SFEFC, 2000–1)

National Qualifications are also provided in schools for pupils aged sixteen and over, and colleges and schools have worked together to use NQ units to enrich the school curriculum. In many parts of Scotland partnerships have been established between schools and colleges, with pupils attending a portion of their week in the local college to undertake units or courses not available at school. NQ Group Awards continue this trend. They provide a common framework for full-time courses across the country, incorporating vocational units and core skills, with delivery which may be partly in school and partly in college. This shared delivery model is as yet limited in uptake, but is likely to be built upon as the NQ framework is fully implemented.

The future of this shared provision is not certain however, as there exists a question about the retaining of the existing facilitative funding arrangements. Staffing structures in schools are related to pupil numbers; the recurrent funding of colleges depends upon their success in attracting students. The prospect of competing for students therefore remains. The possibility of local authorities reducing school staffing to reflect pupil numbers attending college also remains, as does the prospect of the SFEFC choosing to prioritise its funding elsewhere. School staff are required to be registered with the General Teaching Council (GTC); college staff are not so required (although many have registered), and this can complicate issues of who teaches what and where. It is to the credit of both sectors in the partnership that generally the patterns of school/college attendance remain determined by the needs of students, rather than such difficulties.

Partnerships – Higher Education Institutions (HEIs)

The relationships between higher education institutions (HEIs) and FE colleges are also at a significant point in their development. It has been a phenomenon of the last ten to fifteen years, when SCOTVEC (now part of the Scottish Qualifications Authority) introduced local flexibility for the development of unitised HN courses, that colleges have responded to increasing demand for higher education by a large-scale development programme at HE level. At approximately the same time the Scottish Wider Access Programme (SWAP) facilitated growth in the extent of FE/HEI links. From these activities a rich network of articulation agreements between the two sectors has developed.

At the present time, it is common for any one FE college to have articulation links with several universities, such that students from HN courses have the opportunity to progress into the second (from HNC) or third year (from HND) of a degree course at a choice of universities. In addition, some FE colleges have obtained validation from a university to deliver degree level work. This is usually at Ordinary degree level, as a third year following successful completion of an HND. Such provision operates under the university's quality assurance mechanisms.

The creation of the Scottish Credit and Qualifications Framework (SCQF), launched in December 2001, has to some extent formalised these agreements. It allows for HNC and

HND qualifications to be regarded as equivalent to levels 7 and 8 on the framework – that is degree year one and two respectively. The framework is not as yet fully implemented, in that automatic recognition of its equivalences is not guaranteed by all institutions. Once fully implemented however, it will negate the need for bilateral articulation agreements, and will be a powerful instrument for integrating the HE work of colleges and universities for the benefit of students.

The quantity of full-time HE work undertaken in FE colleges now constitutes some 19% of all HE in Scotland, and a considerably higher percentage (43%) in part-time modes of attendance (Scottish Executive, 2002). Its high rate of increase, and consequent increase in the cost of student support, led to a cap on full-time growth which was instigated in 1994–5 academic year, and which persists to date. Part-time numbers have continued to increase.

In some instances, articulation developments such as those described above have led to the creation of formal, even exclusive, association agreements between a university and an FE college, and it has been mooted that such agreements might be the precursor to a future merger of institutions, and in time of the two sectors. The University of the Highlands and Islands is an interesting model of development in this context, as the university is emerging from the combined HE activity of a consortium of institutions, mainly FE colleges.

A major impetus to the development of FE/HE relationships came from the committee of inquiry into higher education, chaired by Lord Dearing in 1996. The report of this committee gave substantial and significant support to the role of FE colleges in providing a cost-effective alternative route into and through higher education, and recommended that the cap on HN growth be lifted immediately in FE. For Scotland, the report also recommended the creation of a Scottish Further Education Funding Council (SFEFC), which was viewed as possibly an interim arrangement, leading to the eventual creation of a tertiary education funding council. These recommendations of the committee were generally welcomed in the FE sector, and did lead to the creation of the SFEFC (see later section).

Also relevant to the development of FE/HE partnerships is the current major review of higher education, under way at the time of writing and led by the Scottish Executive. Government policy decisions as a result of the review will be major determinants of the shape, structure and nature of FE and HE provision in Scotland in this new millennium. Many senior staff in further education in Scotland see potentially strong parallels with the 'two–plus–two' structure of higher education in the United States, where community colleges provide the first two years of HE for local students, who can then progress to a regional university for the remaining two years of a degree.

Partnerships – industry, Unitary Councils, and Local Enterprise Companies (LECs)

Local industry, local councils, and LECs constitute the other major agencies with which colleges work in partnership.

The Further and Higher Education (Scotland) Act 1992, under which incorporated colleges operate, requires that at least half of the members of college boards of management be representatives of local employers. Colleges, since the days of apprentice training, have a long history of close links with industry in planning and delivering programmes to meet employers' needs. Colleges often operate through a strong structure of advisory committees to seek involvement by local companies in course review and development. It is common also that they actively seek involvement in the development and support of the small business sector through representative organisations such as chambers of commerce and the Federation of Small Businesses. Development of course provision to ensure that successful students are equipped with the knowledge and skills required by employers is a constant priority for colleges. It is also a requirement for SQA approval of courses.

The reorganisation of local government in Scotland in 1996 accorded greater significance to colleges' relationships with local authorities. Colleges increasingly identify themselves as having a major role in local economic regeneration and development, and seek to co-operate with councils in community development initiatives. Activities in support of regeneration can include support for small business development, provision of 'incubator' units for new businesses, enterprise elements in course curricula, participation in inward investment initiatives, and the provision of training for community activists.

Councils are also often major employers in a college's locality, and hence significant customers, as well as continuing since pre-incorporation days to be providers of services such as payroll, legal and property maintenance. The development or maintenance of a harmonious and mutually-helpful relationship with the local council is therefore of importance to any college.

Similarly LECs are significant agencies for colleges. As organisers of major national training programmes for young people and for unemployed adults, LECs are a source of business and hence finance for many colleges. The cordiality of relationships between colleges and LECs however varies considerably across Scotland, and strategic partnerships are rare. Colleges generally believe themselves to be under-valued by the local enterprise network, and even where there is significant joint endeavour, colleges seek to strengthen and improve the relationship.

In the case of both local councils and LECs, legislation demands co-operation. It is a required part of colleges' development planning procedures that they consult with both agencies when drawing up the strategic plan for the college for the next three years. Similarly legislation requires that there be a LEC representative on the boards of management of colleges.

In recent years, the above relationships have been set within the context of local community planning processes, and the advent of a Local Economic Forum. Both brainchildren of the Scottish Parliament, these new structures and processes require partnership behaviour within a range of forums and co-ordinating groups which are responsible for local social and economic development. FE colleges are recognised as a central part of these processes, and participate fully in them.

NEW MASTERS (OR PARTNERS?) – THE SCOTTISH PARLIAMENT AND THE SCOTTISH FURTHER EDUCATION FUNDING COUNCIL

Undoubtedly the most significant external developments for the FE sector in recent years have been the creation of the Scottish Parliament and the SFEFC. Following its election in 1999, the Scottish Parliament chose to structure its policy development through a set of important committees, with FE and HE being dealt with by an Enterprise and Lifelong Learning Committee (E&LLC). However other committees of the Parliament, such as the Audit Committee, are also having an impact on the sector.

Members of the Scottish Parliament (MSPs) have varied backgrounds, and many have experience and expertise in aspects of lifelong learning. All have more time to spend in their constituencies than is possible for MPs, and many have chosen to spend some of this time getting to know their local college(s). The result of these factors is that policy development for the sector is now led by a knowledgeable and deeply interested group of individuals. Already the Committees of the Parliament, and the decisions of ministers made in response to committee recommendations, have had an impact on colleges which is seen by the sector as largely favourable. A response to the chronic under-funding of the sector (both revenue and capital) has been made available, as have funds to expand student numbers within a social inclusion agenda. It is due to the E&LLC review of economic development that colleges are more widely recognised and valued as members of the Local Economic Forums, and the Audit Committee's focus on the financial health and governance of colleges has, while resulting in an extraordinary volume of audit, strengthened these arrangements.

In 2001–2, the E&LLC conducted a major review of lifelong learning. Its interim consultative report, published in April 2002, presented a series of potential policy developments which could have very significant impact on colleges; the transfer of responsibility for government training programmes from LECs to colleges; the full implementation of the SCQF; the harmonisation of funding for colleges and HEIs up to and including level 8 of the SCQF. The final report of the committee is currently awaited with much interest by the sector.

The SFEFC was also created in 1999. An independent council, but sharing a joint executive with the Scottish Higher Education Funding Council, it inherited from the Scottish Office a sector where unbridled growth and encouragement towards competition had been permitted to continue for too long, with consequences of financial plight and resulting difficult industrial relations in many colleges. Its first major task has been to implement a new funding methodology intended to bring improved financial stability and health to the sector, while at the same time encouraging development and improvement of practice.

The council is now moving into what might be described as a second and more strategic phase of its operation, where issues of the quality, distribution, and adequacy of supply, and resourcing the future nature, shape and size of the sector predominate. A major national study of FE supply and demand is being used as a vehicle to promote an extension of inter-college collaboration, particularly in estates developments, while at the same time more detailed studies in some areas – particularly Glasgow – are paving the way for college mergers. At present the Ccuncil is seeking to adopt a non-interventionist and facilitative role in determining the future strategic direction of any one college, preferring instead to respect the autonomy of college boards. Where a board is deemed by the council to be failing in its task however, the council has of late been swift to intervene. Maintaining a balance between the roles of partner and master will be an increasingly difficult task for the council as it addresses national strategic needs.

COMPETITION AND COLLABORATION – TOWARDS THE TERTIARY INSTITUTE?

In the period after incorporation colleges developed considerable autonomy, and responded dynamically to the pressure to expand. This pressure was exerted partly by demand for their services, but also by a funding methodology designed to smooth the wide variation in levels of funding discovered when colleges emerged from local authority funding. Recurrent funding was determined on a historical basis by colleges' success in attracting and retaining students. Colleges became considerably more efficient, delivering a higher volume of work at a lower unit of funding.

In those first years after incorporation, and in the absence of any controlling influence as had been exerted by local authorities, pressure to increase the volume of activity in colleges resulted in considerable intra-sector competition. This was particularly the case in some areas of Scotland where several colleges are in close proximity, such as Glasgow and Ayrshire/Renfrewshire. However in many instances colleges also sought to collaborate in joint developments (e.g. Glasgow Telecolleges Network, Fife colleges in FAST-TRAC – the local variant of SkillSeekers), and at national level they formed the Association of Scottish Colleges. The association became active and successful in providing a national voice for the sector, and in coordinating its influence on policy.

The SFEFC has acted robustly to end the era of damaging competition, and through the introduction of a new non-competitive funding methodology and the use of Challenge Funds has created a much more collaborative climate. Across the country there are now many examples of colleges working together to share such activities as curriculum and staff development, and in some instances to create joint facilities and shared posts – mainly in senior administrative roles. These developments in turn throw up points for future resolution: for the colleges concerned, there are issues of maintaining identity and local 'ownership' when institutional boundaries are being blurred, and for the council there are issues of adjusting information collection and college reviewing regimes to reflect joint operations. More strategically, there is the major question of the direction of collaboration – intra-sectoral as described above, or perhaps reflecting the likely future merger of the two Funding Councils into one Tertiary Education Funding Council.

Competition however also continues. In the main it is healthy competition, where colleges vie with each other and private training providers for employer-based training or other contracts which are not subsidised by the public purse. Funds obtained from such sources can be used to assist with the development of facilities within the college, and to improve an institution's financial health. An appropriate balance of collaboration on core (subsidised) activity, and competition for commercial activity is close to being established in many areas.

GOVERNMENT TRAINING SCHEMES

Further education colleges have an extensive record of involvement in government training schemes, particularly those directed at raising skill levels and tackling unemployment in a period of rapid social and technological change. From the early days of the Training Opportunities Scheme in the 1970s (a programme for unemployed adults), through the Youth Opportunities Programme and the Youth Training Scheme in the 1980s, and Training for Work, Skillseekers and the New Deal in the 1990s, to name but a few, colleges have played a significant role in working in partnership with government agencies to modernise the country's skills base. This has been at a cost.

The brief list above gives a flavour of the short-term nature of all government training schemes; the accompanying funding arrangements have often meant that colleges have had to take a short-term view of investment in human and material resourcing. Capital funding for buildings and equipment in particular has been absent. Despite these resourcing difficulties, however, colleges have been responsive and provided a large proportion of the off-the-job training needs of trainees on a variety of schemes. At present, these typically involve the delivery of Scottish Vocational Qualifications (SVQs), perhaps packaged into Modern Apprenticeships.

Colleges have however become increasingly frustrated by the regulations and administrative requirements of such training schemes. Centrally-derived rules often make it impossible to tailor training to the needs of the trainee and employer, while the need to maintain a parallel set of reporting and claiming arrangements alongside those for SFEFC is costly. Colleges have argued that better value for the public purse would be obtained by merging the schemes with the training and education which they are already providing for this clientele. The imminent ELLC report may address this issue.

THE MISSION OF WIDENING PARTICIPATION

There is ample research evidence to show that education and training post-school has been largely demanded by and provided to those who have already achieved reasonable levels of qualification (Steedman and Green, 1996). Clear links exist between lack of educational achievement and social disadvantage. Moreover, low levels of economic activity are linked to low expectations of or plans for future participation in learning (NIACE, 1996). It is argued in the Kennedy Report that the social case for widening participation in learning is irresistible, both because of the transformative power of learning to the individual, and because of the damage to the fabric of the community from the existence of a growing underclass (FEFC, 1997).

Together with community education services, further education colleges constitute the sector of the education system which can and does address this issue. Colleges have long made provision for disadvantaged groups in the community – disabled people, women returners to education, ethnic groups – and many operate outreach centres in community facilities which are designed to create an unthreatening and welcoming first step back into learning activity. The National Institute for Adult and Continuing Education (NIACE) report noted above however shows that there is enormous unmet national need, with 53% of individuals in social classes D and E taking no part in learning since leaving school, compared to 19% in social classes A and B. While many in the further education service cherish this societal service aspect of their role, the difficulties for colleges in expanding activity to meet needs lie in the high financial cost of such provision (often necessarily delivered in small groups), and the financial problems of the students themselves.

Recent action to promote wider participation in learning has been three-fold. An element of funding has been introduced which rewards colleges for recruiting students from the postcode areas identified as the 20% most economically deprived, and FE statistics show a very positive result from this incentive. Secondly, the creation of learndirectscotland (the brand name of the Scottish University for Industry), and its accredited learning centres, as well as the more recent development of Careers Scotland, has increased awareness of, guidance about, and access to learning opportunities among a wider segment of the population. Finally, steps have been taken to attempt to improve the arrangements for student financial support.

STUDENT SUPPORT

Financial support for students attending a further education college at present may come from a wide variety of sources. There are bursaries administered by the college, student grants administered by the Student Awards Agency for Scotland, student loans administered by the Student Loans Company, hardship funds provided to colleges for disbursement to needy students, a mature students' bursary fund, child care funds, local council and other hardship funds, scholarships, Job Seekers Allowance, Income Support, Disabled Student's Allowance, housing benefit, and other benefits. To this list must be added the support arrangements available to different categories of students under the New Deal.

While no one student is eligible for all of the above, for any individual student there is often a confusing range of potential sources of finance. These interact on one another, sometimes, because of their regulations, in unexpected ways. Leaving to one side the adequacy of support in terms of amount of money, the confusion of arrangements constitutes a significant disincentive for adults to return to learning, particularly if they have dependants. It is greatly to their credit that so many adult students do attempt to penetrate this maze by returning to learning.

Over the last five years there have been sincere attempts to clarify and strengthen student financial support, the most notable of these stemming from the work of the Cubie Committee. From 1998, full-time higher education students were required to contribute towards the cost of their tuition, on a means-tested basis. At the same time, student grants began to be phased out and replaced only by means-tested loans. There were serious concerns within the FE sector, as elsewhere, that this requirement constituted a further major disincentive for adults to return to learning. Political concerns such as these led to the appointment in 1999 of an investigative committee under the chairmanship of Andrew Cubie. The committee's report recommended a return to grants, with subsequent repayment of fees through income tax later in life once an income threshold had been reached. Government however did not fully adopt this approach. Loans for higher education study were continued, but with augmented amounts of hardship funds able to be disbursed by institutions to those most in need. Further education fees however were abolished for all full-time study, thus creating an affordable entry point for lifelong learning.

The introduction of a UK system of Individual Learning Accounts (ILAs) in 2000 expanded further the financial support for lifelong learning. Designed to be available for all learners, wherever their learning took place, they provided £150 towards the cost of a course of learning, with the balance of fees intended to be provided by the individual and/or their employer. After a slow start, ILAs became very successful, with an uptake of some 110,000 – in Scotland by December 2001. However in that year it had also became apparent that the ILAs were the focus of some fraudulent activity in England, and they were withdrawn at the end of 2001. The loss of these was lamented in FE in Scotland, as they were seen to be very successful in widening participation in learning. A successor is promised, no doubt with tighter controls.

The above brief history makes it apparent that, while laudable efforts have been made to improve financial support for students, and more money is definitely available, the variety of mechanisms and their associated rules mean that the system remains a complex and confusing one for the potential student.

THE FUNDING OF FURTHER EDUCATION –
THROUGH INSTABILITY AND INADEQUACY TO PRUDENCE

In 1993, on incorporation, further education colleges moved from funding by local authorities to funding by the Scottish Office Education and Industry Department. Due to the wide variation in funding levels provided by the authorities, (from £140 to £280 per SUM in 1993–4), it was necessary to develop a new funding methodology based on a common unit of measurement – the SUM (student unit of measurement – equivalent to forty hours of student study time). The methodology was a distribution mechanism, allocating shares of the total quantum of funds available for FE according to each college's share of the national total SUMs in the previous academic year (e.g. allocations for 1997–8 were based on SUMs delivered in 1995–6). Given the historical variation in funding levels described, the immediate and full implementation of this methodology would have resulted in a major redistribution of resources across the sector, with catastrophic consequences for some colleges. Ministers of the then government therefore adopted a cautious and gradual approach to implementation, over a period of five financial years.

While aiming to achieve, and obtaining, stability in the sector as a whole – (defined as no college closures) – the implementation of the methodology created instability for individual colleges. One of the effects was to create heavy pressure for growth, with consequent demands on staff for higher productivity. In this regard policy makers regarded the methodology as successful, with substantial increases achieved in the vast majority of colleges. For many however this pressure to grow was applied at the same time as the need to cut costs, and industrial relations throughout the sector suffered from the unrelenting drive for efficiency.

Systematic planning for the medium to longer term proved impossible, as the outcome of each funding round depended not only on a college's efforts, but on the success of all other colleges too, and was impossible to predict. At the same time, the overall funding quantum being made available to the sector was declining. Small wonder therefore that as the end of the twentieth century approached, most colleges were either in financial difficulties, or were financially weak. This was the situation inherited by the SFEFC in 1999.

The post-incorporation funding regime had achieved its objective of harmonising the funding per SUM for all colleges, and the SFEFC was able to build upon this in developing a new and more real-time methodology. The new system is now a contractual one, in which the SFEFC contracts with each college to deliver a specified number of SUMs at a price of £x per SUM. The contract is conditional upon the college meeting a range of policy requirements, chief of which is that its provision must be of acceptable quality, as measured by HMI review. This contractual mechanism has enabled the SFEFC to control the volume of activity delivered by colleges, and thus bring to an end the era of uncontrolled growth.

The introduction of a three-year planning cycle for government expenditure, with resulting advice from the SFEFC about anticipated future levels of growth, has meant that meaningful forward planning is now more a reality in colleges. Both the first and third comprehensive spending reviews have introduced substantial rises in spending on FE in Scotland, and the extra funds (although to a large extent tied to growth), together with the firmer planning context, are resulting in a general movement towards more robust financial health. The Audit Committee of the Scottish Parliament, alarmed by the financial difficulties of some colleges, has given strong direction to the SFEFC that it must ensure financial health across the sector. The next few years therefore are seen as a period of prudence and reserve building, towards a more robust financial future.

Capital funding for estates is also provided by the SFEFC. An early task of the council was to establish some concept of the scale of need in this area, and a survey of the funding necessary to bring all college estates up to a minimum safe standard identified this to require around £116m. This total did not reflect improvement or modernisation costs, which were estimated at some £390m. The council has put in place a system by which colleges can bid for funds for major estates projects. However the council contribution is normally limited to 50% of costs, and difficulty in sourcing the balance has meant that few colleges have been able to advance projects. Meanwhile many further education colleges are housed in buildings with substantial refurbishment and repair needs. Student facilities continue to be suitable only to the needs of the former part-time population of colleges, rather than to the present full-time, often mature, substantially HE, population. From the crumbling concrete of 1960s buildings, to the rotting windows of Victorian edifices, there exists an extensive catalogue of unaddressed need. The modernisation of college estates, within a context of highly limited funds, is one of the major challenges for college management and the SFEFC.

Another is the need to generate investment in IT in order to keep pace with technological change, to enhance flexibility of provision, and to establish wider networked links to the home and workplace.

USE OF ICT IN DELIVERING LEARNING

Teaching practice in further education colleges is on the brink of considerable change, fuelled in part by the need to increase efficiency, but also by the rapid development of new information and communications technologies (ICT). These are underpinning significant developments in flexible learning. Colleges have long been involved in open or distance learning, and since the mid-1980s have operated in consortia to produce (mainly paper-based) open learning packages. Flexible learning approaches are now in use to combine distance learning with resource-based learning in college, often provided in drop-in units.

Developments in ICT, and particularly widespread use of the internet, have now made possible an exciting range on on-line services and products to support learning, that is the delivery of multimedia learning packages 'down-the-wire', with tutor support available by e-mail or by video-conferencing, and through student-student contact via e-mail and discussion groups.

Supported by specific grants from the SFEFC, colleges have in the last three years made significant advances in implementing ICT strategies to create robust networks to support such e-learning. Broadband access through the Joint Academic Network (JANET) has been made available to all colleges. National initiatives including UK consortia are producing high quality on-line learning materials in quantities which, although still limited, are growing rapidly. FE students now have a much wider choice of methods of learning. These might include inputs from a computer or other media at home, or in a drop-in resource base, or from tutorials and formally taught classes. Tutor support may be available face-to-face, by e-mail, video conference, correspondence, or telephone. New methods of delivering learning require changed behaviour from teaching staff; many colleges are presently engaged in major staff development activity to underpin these new developments.

BUSINESS-LIKE PRACTICE WITHIN A PUBLIC SERVICE – EFFICIENCY, EFFECTIVENESS AND QUALITY

Incorporation brought many challenges to colleges and their managers. As noted above, pressure for growth within a diminishing quantum of funds resulted in increased efficiency, often achieved by adopting business-like practices – for example, benchmarking, using competitive tendering procedures to buy in services, contracting out services, and collaborating in bulk purchase schemes. The need for efficiency and business-like practice has not diminished under SFEFC 'rule'. It also remains equally vital to ensure that increased efficiency is achieved with no lessening of the quality of a college's provision. Competition within the sector, and rising expectations from an increasingly consumerist customer base may themselves have been sufficient to ensure no diminution of the quality of college provision. Audit by a multiplicity of agencies however has been added to these forces. Colleges are subject to regular review by HMI, whose comprehensive reports on a college's provision are made available to the public. LECs and SQA also regularly audit quality in colleges, using the Scottish Quality Management System – a tool designed in a (vain) attempt to reduce the audit burden. Auditors or assessors from the European Social Fund, European Regional Development Fund, National Audit Office, Audit Scotland, SHEFC and HEIs also visit colleges, together with the college's own internal and external auditors. The sector has estimated that any one college will on average be hosting a visit from auditors/assessors for two days in every week.

Colleges have been able to demonstrate to all of the above agencies that they place considerable emphasis on maintaining and improving the quality of their provision. Recent HMI reports on the sector confirm that national standards are secure. Extensive internal quality assurance systems have been developed which check upon and assure assessment standards, and curriculum review and development are continuing processes. Performance indicators, including customer satisfaction, are calculated, used internally as part of the process of curriculum review, and can be published externally in college annual reports. The increasing maturity of quality assurance mechanisms in colleges has been recognised by HMI, who are now placing greater emphasis on self-evaluation in the inspection procedures.

The continuing challenge for college managers, who now lead business-like organisations that provide a public service, is the task of achieving even greater efficiency while at the least maintaining existing levels of customer satisfaction and continuing to operate to rigorous academic standards. This challenge has implications for management and institutional development.

INSTITUTIONAL DEVELOPMENT, MANAGEMENT AND GOVERNANCE

Given the need in recent years to improve their financial situation, colleges have become increasingly entrepreneurial in their efforts to widen their income base. In addition to the core activity of ensuring quality provision of training and education to appropriate standards, colleges are entering into contracts for other activities, for instance employment-related services, and business development consultancies. The organisational structures of colleges, and the portfolio of qualifications and experience of their staff, are changing as institutions develop in these new directions.

The role of managers in further education colleges is considerably different from pre-incorporation. Financial pressures, and the need to operate in a business-like manner, mean that much management attention is now devoted to marketing, accounting issues, human resource considerations, information presentation and interpretation, and estates management. These are all activities which in the past were provided by local authorities and which now require attention in addition to the core activity of ensuring a substantial volume of teaching to high standards. Almost all senior managers in colleges have reached their positions from a background in FE teaching, often with no planned programme of management development to assist them in preparing to discharge these responsibilities. It is therefore a priority for the sector to ensure better preparation of its succeeding generations of managers. Performance management techniques, internal and external staff development events, and a programme of external and work-based learning offered by the Scottish Further Education Unit are all used to meet this need.

The strategic management of a college is the responsibility of its board of management, a group of twelve to sixteen individuals who are deemed to be representative of the local community, and who employ the staff of the college. As well as representatives of employers, it is also essential that the board includes the principal of the college and at least two staff members and one student representative. Given national hostility towards quangos, the concerns about standards in public life that led to the establishment of the Nolan Committee, and the financial concerns of the Audit Committee of the Scottish Parliament, it is unsurprising that the operation of boards of management in colleges has been scrutinised several times since incorporation. The most recent such published study (MVA Consultancy, 1997) found that generally boards were operating satisfactorily, and discharging their strategic role of directing colleges with integrity. A further review of governance arrangements is however under way at the time of writing. Instigated largely because of Audit Committee concerns, it focuses on the powers of the SFEFC to intervene where a board is perceived to be failing. It also addresses issues regarding recruitment to boards. It is often difficult for colleges to attract appropriate senior industry personnel into involvement on boards, but the standing and continued development of the sector require that this must happen.

CONCLUSION

This chapter has analysed the current issues and priorities for the further education sector. Emerging themes from the analysis are the accessibility, diversity and flexibility of provision within the sector, the wide range of partnerships within which colleges operate in order to secure this provision, and the unrelenting pressure for efficiency which has been applied by government.

Two major and related strategic deficits for the sector have been identified – the lack of a national identity, and the need for a strategic framework which defines and clarifies the sector's role. It could be argued that the absence of the latter has been the cause of the former.

With the concepts of lifelong learning and a learning entitlement now at the forefront of Scottish government policy, an increasing belief that a degree is not the only worthwhile qualification, the view that education can be both liberally enriching and vocationally useful, and an increasingly active Scottish Parliament to turn these principles into policies, there is a prospect that the distinctive mission of the further education sector could be clarified, firmed, and accorded the value it deserves.

Thus, while the equivalent chapter in the first edition of this volume named further education 'the Cinderella sector' – a description familiar to many Scottish commentators – there exists now a recognition of the significance of the sector which may mean the end of this epithet.

REFERENCES

FEFC (1997) *Learning Works – Widening Participation in Further Education – A Report for the Further Education Funding Council* (The Kennedy Report), Coventry: FEFC.

MVA Consultancy (1997) *Survey of Further Education College Boards of Management,* report commissioned by SOEID, Edinburgh: MVA.

Neil, A. and Mullin, R. (1996) *Scotland's Colleges – Relationships with Businesses and International Communities,* report commissioned for the Association of Scottish Colleges and Scottish Enterprise, Stirling: ASC.

NIACE (1996) *Creating Two Nations?* Leicester: NIACE.

Scottish Executive (2002) *Standard Tables on Higher Education and Further Education in Scotland 2000–2001,*(National Statistics Publication) Edinburgh: Scottish Executive.

SFEFC (2000–1) *InFact Database –* www.sfefc.ac.uk/infact/

Steedman, H. and Green, A. (1996) *Widening Participation in Further Education and Training: A Survey of the Issues,* London: Centre for Economic Performance.

73

Liberal, Academic and Vocational Strands in Further Education

John Halliday

There was a total of 487,341 student enrolments recorded on courses in Scotland's forty-seven further education colleges during the academic year 2000–1. Of these the majority were said to be on vocational courses (88%). Of vocational enrolments 17% were on courses leading to Higher National Qualifications (defined by The Further and Higher Education (Scotland) Act 1992 as higher education (HE)). The remaining 83% of vocational enrolments were in further education (FE) as defined by the above mentioned Act. According to the Further Education Funding Council (FEFC), the body that supplied these statistics:

> A vocational course is defined as a course primarily designed to prepare students for, or to increase their knowledge, skill or proficiency in, an employment or profession. Other courses are regarded as non-vocational and are generally concerned with a hobby or recreational pursuit. (FEFC, *Student Enrolment Statistics in FE Colleges in Scotland 2000–2001*, Edinburgh: FEFC, 2002.)

In the light of these statistics and these definitions it appears obvious that Scotland's FE colleges are primarily concerned to provide a vocational education that enhances people's ability to perform paid work. The term 'non-vocational' suggests a form of recreation such as flower arranging the educational benefit of which is secondary. While the terms 'academic' and 'liberal' are used in the contexts of secondary schooling and university education, they hardly feature in policy and other documentation concerned with further education. In this chapter it is argued that they should and that a further education should always be and sometimes is concerned with a broad conception of vocational education that includes liberal and academic strands. At present the precise balance that is struck between these strands depends upon the values of particular lecturers and students, their colleges and the groups within which they work. Little is written either in policy documents, theoretical texts or in the descriptions of staff development activities to suggest that what amounts to a fundamental concern with the value of a further education receives much collective attention.

A scrutiny of policy documents published between 1980 and the formation of the Scottish Parliament indicates an over-riding concern with efficiency and quality of procedures in FE. For example a letter sent to college principals sets out the 'key purposes of FE' (SOEID, Funding Methodology Review Group: letter to principals dated 5 June 1997, (ref. VEY/ 37/2) with attachments FMRG 97/1, Edinburgh, Further Education Funding Division, 1997.) under the headings of participation, efficiency and quality. According to this document FE should increase student numbers with particular regard to 'local labour markets and economic development strategies'. This increase should be achieved within 'a culture of continuous quality improvement' by seeking 'efficient use of resources' and by maximising 'non-grant income'.

The absence here as elsewhere of mention of those fundamental values that should inform a further education might be attributed to there being a consensus on such evaluative matters. If there were such a consensus then it would be pointless to rehearse what everyone knows. Alternatively this absence might be attributed to the dominance of neo-liberal thinking about further education in which it is assumed that through market-mechanisms, the values of the sector are equivalent to what potential and actual students want to learn. This attribution roughly coheres with the belief that any form of learning should be supported for those over the age of sixteen providing that resources are available to provide that support. Finally this absence might be attributed to a general worry that conflict is inevitable when fundamental evaluative concerns are put at the centre of policy formulation.

While all three attributions are reasonable, the last worry is particularly important in a country in which consensus within a policy-making community is valued highly. As Humes has pointed out on a number of occasions but most notably in *The Leadership Class in Scottish Education* (John Donald: Edinburgh, 1986), this community does not tend to encourage inclusive evaluative debate about fundamental aims, values and purposes. Yet as college principal Michael Leech warned some time ago, 'F.E. has got to get to grips soon with the question of its role and purpose.' He went on:

> If as a sector we do not have a curricular philosophy we will be in a position of drift, exposed to the possibility of becoming training centres, with universities and schools picking off the cream of our present work. (*TESS* 17 November 1995, p. 24)

Such drift might be the result of a failure to face up to inevitable disagreement that arises when answers are sought to the fundamental question 'What is a further education for?' The question might appear innocuous enough until it is realised that the rational allocation of limited funds is bound to favour those colleges that best satisfy the preferred answer. Moreover as college principal Johnston suggests in this volume (Chapter 72) the sector as a whole still suffers from a weak sense of identity. This weakness puts the sector at a disadvantage in the distribution of what must be a limited educational budget overall.

It is not hard to see why concern might be focused on means, methods or techniques as these seem to be amenable to objective determination in the light of prescribed inputs and outputs. Yet further education no less than any other sector of education is centrally concerned with values. Ongoing evaluative deliberation is logically necessary not only for the rational allocation of resources within the sector but also to inform debate about the kind of society that Scots want to develop. Operational efficiency within accepted criteria for quality is only important insofar as it contributes to what actually is believed to be the most worthwhile aims, values and purposes for the sector. Learning is an under determined concept and cannot constitute an end in itself. One can learn to be a bricklayer or a thief and thieves can operate efficiently and effectively. Deliberation about what ought to be learnt in the light of what can be afforded cannot be avoided.

Since the formation of the Parliament, there have been moves to try to deliberate in this way and to try to build some kind of consensus on the fundamental evaluative issue. At the time of writing the parliamentary committee concerned with further education (the Enterprise and Lifelong Learning Committee (E&LLC)) is concluding a major enquiry into lifelong learning (E&LLC, interim report on the lifelong learning inquiry, Edinburgh: Scottish Parliament, 2002). The committee is concerned to bring about greater social inclusion and it believes that further education has an important role to play in this by ensuring some degree of equal access to formal education after school for everyone.

> Learning can provide an important route out of poverty for individuals, their families and communities, as well as help narrow the gap between rich and poor in society. Therefore new and better ways have to be found to help ensure that those who could benefit most from learning are actively encouraged and supported in doing so. (E&LLC, 2002)

It seems likely that among other things, the committee will recommend that everyone should have an entitlement to a certain amount of such education where the amount is determined by 720 points in the Scottish Credit and Qualifications Framework.

This recommendation may well lead to greater social justice, as it is intended to do. It is worth exercising some caution, however, about the extent to which it will do so. In the first place the notion of entitlement is unclear. To partake in some formal education always requires some other activity to be dropped at some differential cost. It is not clear how costs could ever be equalised even though the committee recognises that there is a need to try and do so. Moreover different forms of learning do not lead to the same benefits and that is precisely the danger with the idea that a further education should be a narrowly focused vocational education. A further education may not lead to rewarding and satisfying employment in a field of the student's choice. Indeed it is clear from a perusal of the Scottish Economic database (Scottish Executive, *Scottish Economic Statistics*, Edinburgh: Scottish Executive, 2002) and the FE student database (FEFC2002) that all too often it will not.

The former database indicates a roughly stable distribution of the numbers employed in the various occupational categories, the numbers unemployed but seeking work within those categories, and the numbers of notified job vacancies in those categories. In contrast the latter database indicates massive fluctuations in the numbers enrolled on FE courses supposedly leading to employment in the occupational categories. For example there was a 64% increase in the numbers enrolled on basic skills courses between the years 1999–2000 and 2000–2001 yet 33,559 people were already claiming unemployment-related benefits during the year 2000 under the category of 'elementary occupation'. It might be claimed that many of those enrolled on such courses go on to more skilled and specialised courses. To take a further example, however, there was a 57% increase in the numbers enrolled on sport and leisure courses during the same period with little possibility of employment for all at the end of those courses.

Especially for those who are bound to be disappointed in this way but for others too, it seems reasonable to hope that a further education would be liberal in the sense that it liberates students from the confines of their present circumstances. Such a further education would focus on the fundamental and the generalisable and would have concern for the intrinsically worthwhile as well as that which is immediately useful. Paradoxically perhaps such a liberal form of vocational education may also be vocationally useful as the world of work is expected to be subject to fairly frequent changes. As stated in the Green Paper *Opportunity Scotland* (Edinbrugh: Scottish Office, 1998, p. 4),

> Change is everywhere and we need to learn to cope with it in different aspects of our lives. Jobs are changing with continually developing technology and pressures to keep up with foreign competitors. Daily life is changing with faster communications and more technology in our homes.

ACADEMIC STRANDS

Despite the policy rhetoric, further education may also be seen to be concerned with an academic education. For example, many of those writing in this volume have had what might best be described as an academic education which is the very precondition for them earning their livings within educational institutions of one sort or another. Moreover as Winch (2002, p. 113) points out,

> the traditional view in the UK, that 'non academic' youngsters should be 'warehoused' in school until they were ready to enter unskilled jobs at the age of 15 or 16 is now thankfully discredited . . . Every parent nowadays is aware of the pressure on schools and children to gain academic qualifications so as to fit them for work.

In other words an academic education is a very effective vocational education for some people. As I have argued elsewhere (Halliday, 1996), if there is a basis to draw a distinction between the academic and the vocational then it is on the basis of the tools that are used to learn. In the case of academic learning, the tools are mainly books, pens, word processors and papers. In the case of vocational education, other tools are used and vocational simply means practical in many cases.

The distinction between academic and vocational education is intended to be dissolved within the Higher Still developments (see Chapter 81). As is pointed out in Chapters 11 and 12, there are two committees of the Parliament and two departments of the Executive that are mainly concerned with education. Further education is the responsibility of ELLD even though some one in five of the enrolments in further education are from people under eighteen who might also have chosen to stay in school and who would have been the concern of the Education Department. In time it is envisaged that there will be an increasing interchange of school age students between colleges of further education and schools. Not only is the further and higher interface becoming increasingly blurred as was indicated earlier, but also the further and secondary interface is far from clear. Practically as well as conceptually it is worth questioning whether further education could ever be exclusively concerned with the vocational strand.

LIBERAL STRANDS

If all that there was to further education was to induct people into certain practices so that they can earn a living, then it might be expected that further education would decline as more employers offered training to employees directly. Mechanisms are available for employers to secure grants through the Enterprise Network and through initiatives such as Modern Apprenticeships to help them with 'on the job' training and employees can be awarded Scottish Vocational Qualifications (SVQs) as they develop their vocational competence. Private training agencies too offer lower cost routes to qualifications validated by the Scottish Qualifications Authority (SQA). Such agencies are often able to undercut colleges of further education because they pay their trainers less than further education colleges pay their lecturers. The economic advantages of 'on the job' training seem obvious. Despite this competition however, most further education colleges continue to attract an increasing number of students year on year, as they are encouraged to do through the funding methodology used by the Scottish Further Education Funding Council.

There might be a number of reasons why students are attracted to further education and it would be wrong to assume that they expect to get something other than a narrow vocational preparation. Further education is notoriously under-researched and it is simply not known what attracts students to the colleges, where they go after college and whether their expectations of further education were realised. (Coffield, 1996) Nevertheless it seems reasonable to assume that they have a right to expect a further education to do more than prepare them for a specific employment opportunity which might or might not materialise when they leave college. To prepare people for just one occupation without being able to guarantee that employment opportunities will arise within that occupational area is unwise and probably ethically indefensible. Moreover as Howieson et al. (1997) point out, the desire for a high skill base within the Scottish economy requires all workers to have a high level of general education rather than an ability to practise in one limited area.

As indicated earlier, the ability to move beyond what is most immediate and particular towards what might be possible and generalisable is a characteristic liberal strand in education. As recent research (Halliday, 1997) illustrates, there are a number of people working in Scottish FE who demonstrate a commitment to a form of liberal education which attempts to enable students to see beyond the instrumental aim of achieving prescribed statements of vocational competence. At the same time these people do not denigrate the vocational – far from it. What they are seeking to do in different ways might perhaps best be summarised by Pring who writes:

> There seems no reason why the liberal could not be conceived as something vocationally useful and why the vocationally useful should not be taught in an educational and liberating way. (Pring, 1995, p. 183)

Yet liberal strands in further education seem not to be encouraged within the policy rhetoric, the *National Guidelines on Provision Leading to the Teaching Qualification (Further Education) and Related Professional Development* (Edinburgh: SOEID) or the current funding methodology. The desire for funding to be tied to some measure of quality which might include the quality of what is learnt has in part been thwarted by the number of Scottish colleges in serious financial difficulty which prompts the Funding Council to have to offer supporting funds (see Circular 56/2001 (Circulars may be accessed electronically from the FEFC website www.sfefc.ac.uk)). It has also been thwarted by a long-standing disagreement on how different subjects that could be learnt should be differentially funded (see Circular 8/2002). Practically however, as Standish points out in Chapter 79, 'the claims of liberal education are apt to sound reactionary, ill-defined, and perhaps rather dull.' The current discourse of quality within Scottish further education seems ill-suited to include such aims and liberal strands have been marginalised.

Prior to Action Plan (Edinburgh: SED, 1983) which introduced a modular curriculum in FE, every course with a vocational aim included some 'liberal studies' to reflect the view that narrow vocationalism was mistaken. As Connelly makes clear in Chapter 74, such studies were never entirely satisfactory and they began to disappear as Action Plan was implemented. It was not clear what the content of liberal studies should be, these studies were not examined and many students saw them as a distraction from their aim of securing permanent employment. It is hardly surprising that students did not choose liberal studies when they were given the opportunity to select a programme of study from a catalogue of modules and when the economic climate was such that the securing of permanent employment seemed paramount.

Of course curriculum designers were well aware that something important had been lost in the demise of liberal studies and that something more general needed to be added to the cafeteria-style curriculum of the modular catalogue. While the terminology has shifted over the years, the notion of core skills has come to the fore as a vehicle for preserving something of the general and liberal in a further education. In addition students on general SVQ courses are required to complete a project in which they show that they can integrate the various modular components of their study along with these core skills into the design of a project of their own choosing. Again there is scope here for some imaginative teaching that goes beyond the immediate and particular competencies that are prescribed and which encourages students to design projects which are actually useful to them and their communities.

The language of core skills does not immediately suggest a liberal strand in FE however. Skills such as personal effectiveness, problem solving, communication, numeracy and information technology which are preferred core skills within FE do not immediately suggest that students should be encouraged critically to engage in a broad range of educational activities. Nevertheless the notion of critical thinking which is embedded within problem solving skills provides a vehicle for some students to see their predicament as something more complicated than a search for a job. While the desire for employment might be uppermost in many students' minds, skilled teachers can encourage students to see their predicament against a wider background of educational possibilities and institutional constraints.

VOCATIONAL STRANDS

Virtually everyone who is employed in colleges of further education has been employed previously in industry and commerce. Many of them are suspicious of those modes of reasoning that seem to neglect economic considerations in education. They believe that public sector institutions, no less than private institutions, should be concerned with economic realities. The analogy that colleges of further education share some similarities with service or production industries is attractive to many of those who have earned their living in such industries. They value commercial and industrial enterprise as a necessary part of liberal democratic society and have little time for suggestions that such enterprise is necessarily illiberal.

Some of those who work in FE have earned their livings by engaging in manual work. The dignity of such work and the dignity of those who perform it informs an egalitarian sense of inclusion for them. Hospital cleaning, for example, has intrinsic value for those who do it well in addition to the extrinsic benefit that such work brings to those who benefit from it. Hospital cleaners no less than solicitors can value work for its own sake in addition to the increased private freedom that remuneration in employment brings. To communicate the intrinsic value of doing a job well is a central aim of some people in FE. The logical point behind this aim seems obvious. Unless students come to appreciate that there is something other than the monetary exchange value of their employment then they are bound to perform at the lowest level that is consistent with their being paid. If they do perform in this way then they require constant monitoring and the set of human relationships that might sustain their work disintegrates. This logical point applies equally to those who work within colleges of further education too and many managers realise that it is not wise to ignore it.

There is a deeper reason for coming to recognise the intrinsic value of practices however. Without such recognition students remain bound by what must be an incomplete chain of instrumental reasoning. They are impoverished not only because they cannot recognise what intrinsic goods might be within a particular practice but more especially because they cannot understand the kind of deep practical engagement that others seem to enjoy. To come to understand such engagement is a form of moral education for some of those who study in FE (Halliday, 1996).

FE offers a second chance to those who for whatever reason were unsuccessful at the primary opportunity to become engaged in learning at school and to take the first steps on the road to a job. Of course a further education cannot increase the number of jobs that are on offer unless it enables people to start businesses which do not lead to the closure of other business. The use of technology might be seen to be important here and it is worth remembering that many colleges were called colleges of technology at one stage. Now such titles have been dropped although the idea that colleges are sites where people have access to new and old technology remains important even if such access is difficult to resource.

The funding methodology for Scottish further education does make some allowance for the differential costs involved in keeping different sorts of technology up to date. These differentials do not in many cases accurately reflect the difference between classroom-based and workshop-based study hence some of the ongoing disagreement about this matter that was reported earlier. While this disagreement persists, academic drift results as students are encouraged to write about doing something rather than actually doing it. (Halliday, 1996). Such drift might be more of a problem in Scottish FE than its English counterpart because there is proportionately more Higher National Certificate and Higher National Diploma work in Scottish colleges. This work has tended to be associated with an increasing ability with the pen rather than more refined practice in wider and more varied contexts that require deeper thought and more honed skills. Academic drift may also have been encouraged by the tendency for Higher National courses to form the entry to study at university which often does require higher levels of writing skill. There has been a tendency as illustrated in the White Paper *Raising the Standard* (Edinburgh: SOEID, 1996) to suggest that the value of a further education is determined by the extent to which it is an entry to a higher education.

Those areas of the further education curriculum that have been able best to resist academic drift are those areas where the cost of technology can be subsidised through the business ventures that serve also as vehicles for study at Higher National level. For example departments of Hospitality Studies may purchase advanced restaurant and hotel facilities to provide both a realistic context for learning and funds to update those facilities. Without such commercial ventures within further education and without the idea that a further education is valuable in itself and not only the means to a higher education, academic drift might continue unchecked.

INSTITUTIONAL CONSIDERATIONS

It has been argued that both academic drift and narrow vocationalism should be resisted and that there is a need for the further education sector to develop a much stronger sense of identity which promotes the idea that a further education is worthwhile in itself. A number of developments have weakened the possibilities for such resistance however. First in some quarters there is a corrosive cynicism which is based on the view that any attempt at resistance is little more than window–dressing for a deep–seated managerialist culture which values only that which can be measured and funded. Such cynicism might be more widespread in England rather than Scotland although in both countries there have been a number of industrial relations problems. Referring specifically to England, Coffield notes:

> All is far from well in a system where a Memorandum entitled 'Twenty Ways to Harass your Staff' is circulated from the Employers Forum to College Principals with the aim of coercing lecturers into signing contracts which reduce their terms and conditions. (Coffield, 1996 p. 6)

A second development might be attributed to some of the literature and statements put about by SQA which is the sole body in Scotland responsible both for accrediting awards and validating programmes of study. Despite the best intentions of some of its officers, this body is often perceived to be caught between the aim of encouraging diversity in provision and the aim of ensuring consistency in standards. These aims are not necessarily incompatible but they are easily misinterpreted by those obsessed with the idea that the statement of standards precludes forms of teaching that encourage anything other than the stated performance criteria. A predecessor of SQA, SCOTVEC, not only prescribed curriculum outcomes but also made recommendations about the time that it should take to teach those outcomes and the teaching methods that should be used. These recommendations were accepted in most colleges and formed the basis of the lecturers' contractual obligations. Thus many lecturers felt that they had no room for manoeuvre as both the product and the process of their work seemed prescribed by one awarding body. The legacy of this sentiment lingers on. Yet paradoxically there is far more diversity in the Scottish FE curriculum overall than in the English counterpart where there is a multitude of awarding bodies. Courses in Applied Christian Theology, Rock Musicianship and Complementary Therapies are just some examples within Scottish FE of how SQA has enabled colleges to respond to what students want to learn.

It is interesting to consider some possible reasons for this apparent paradox. First SCOTVEC was set up by government to encourage competition between different educational providers of which the colleges were just one. Therefore it needed to specify pretty tightly what providers were supposed to do in order to try to standardise the curriculum product, as it were, and to enable an educational market place in FE. There is also an equity consideration in the drive to standardise. Plainly it is unacceptable for students to be deceived into believing that courses and qualifications are equivalent when in reality different providers teach and assess in quite different ways. Whereas in the case of the academic curriculum standardisation is ensured through the use of set examinations administered and marked under strict conditions at set times, this option is not available for further education. In FE practical assignments and projects are often the most valid forms of assessment and assessment takes place at various times to suit those who are treated increasingly as customers and clients.

SQA does not operate in isolation from other validating and awarding bodies in the UK. It would be very odd if SVQs and English National VQs in the same curriculum area were wildly different. It is not plausible to suggest that vocational competence in Scotland is radically different from that in England. Moreover the VQ competence framework was developed partly in response to European requirements for trans-national mobility of labour based on equivalence of qualifications. It would also be odd if two countries sharing a common language could not agree on equivalence arrangements. SCOTVEC might have been dragged along in the wake of what were predominantly English concerns over the roles of the employment and education departments within government. It is possible to argue too that the liberal vocational distinction was itself much more relevant to England where a tradition of specialism and disdain for manual work might support the academic inter-pretation of a liberal education. In Scotland the desirability of breadth in knowledge and practical skill remains influential.

CONCERN WITH QUALITY

In many ways a move now to include some measure of and significant reward for quality could provide a focus for debate about an appropriate balance between liberal, academic and vocational strands in FE. It is clear that many within FE have been aware for some time that such inclusion could be desirable. A research project was commissioned from Coombe Lodge, the then staff college and predecessor of the Further Education Development Agency (FEDA) to explore the mechanisms by which high quality provision could be recognised, encouraged and rewarded. Responses to the findings of this research were invited in Circular 8/95 but no clear consensus emerged from the consultation (Circular 21/ 95).

The Coombe Lodge research raised a number of issues which have not as yet been resolved. For example which approach to measuring quality should be dominant, quality management processes or educational processes? Should any reward be based on value added or actual achievement? It is on this issue of quality that value concerns become most apparent and the flight to an apparent value neutrality becomes most attractive to those wishing to discourage evaluative deliberation. In Circular 21/95 it was reported that:

> any of the methods of measuring quality were seen as being fraught with methodological
> problems and value judgements, and therefore unlikely to underpin a system perceived to be
> objective and fair.

This circular is revealing because in it value judgements are associated with subjectivity and unfairness. So long as such association persists, it seems likely that there will be a proliferation of quality audits that are mainly paper-based attempts at objectivity. Her Majesty's Inspectors (HMI) are bound to be limited in the extent to which they can fulfil their role as evaluators of the educational quality of provision unless they can appeal to some shared notion of what a further education is for. Similar limitations apply to students, lecturers and others who work within FE.

If such a shared notion could be developed, then not only might the sector develop a much stronger sense of identity with all the external benefits that that would bring, but also there might be a real basis for talking meaningfully about educational quality within FE. It is widely accepted that the distinctions between academic, vocational and liberal are deeply damaging and that the enhanced status that academic awards presently enjoy is a product of an outdated class system which privileged a leisured elite. The response to this ought not to be a championing of a narrow vocational education. Rather as Pring (1995) and others argue the response ought to be the recognition that everyone has a right to a liberal education which is concerned to develop the ability to think, understand and appreciate the best that has been said and done by others. Such an education may also be vocational and may include academic strands.

Typically further education prepares people to be hairdressers, builders, joiners, computer technicians, laboratory assistants and other forms of employment in which the use of tools other than pens is central. But it also prepares people to be legal assistants through initiation into the practice of law. Thus it is possible to study law as part of a vocational practice but also as part of what might be a disinterested pursuit of truth. Similarly people might learn to be flower arrangers primarily to earn a living or because they simply like arranging flowers and some florists enjoy earning their living through what for them is a kind of 'calling' or vocation. The distinction made by SFEFC between vocational and non-vocational is far from unproblematic and probably unhelpful.

There is nothing logically necessary about the practice of chemistry for example, which makes it either vocational or non-vocational. Rather it is the primary purpose of Chemistry students at any particular time which determines the appropriateness of the adjective. Pragmatically it makes little sense to induct people into the same practice in two separate streams as it were and this pragmatism has informed thinking about Higher Still which was referred to earlier. On egalitarian grounds too there are good reasons for designing an inclusive curriculum framework which suggests that carers, cooks, hairdressers and plumbers are as important members of society as chemists, theologians, philosophers and linguists. There is also the economic argument that high skill economies require workers who are adaptable, flexible and good at working in teams. All these arguments indicate the desirability of curricular breadth for all students so that they can identify with others who have different special interests. Such breadth might encourage them to be able to make connections quickly between different practices and to relate easily to other people. Arguably in an age in which specific information is available 'at the touch of a button' as it were, people do not so much need to know specific facts associated with particular practices. Rather they need to know how to make connections between those practices and to be able to get on with one another both at work and as fellow citizens.

It has been argued that a further education ought to be concerned both with enabling people to earn their living in useful ways and to look beyond what is immediate and obviously useful. It indicates that practical skills as well as the ability to write, interpret and read to a reasonable standard is both vocational and liberally enriching. Such a conception of a further education has the advantage that it enables a higher skill economic base, the social cohesion that is necessary for individual private flourishing and the ability to take part in political democratic debate. It may be that what Wolf calls *The Tyranny of Numbers* (London: Institute of Education, University of London, 1997) will always deem certain qualifications to have less status than others but that is not immediately an educational concern. In the long term however people are both formed by and form the society of which they are a part. The privileging of academic qualifications and the balancing of academic, liberal and vocational strands are not logical matters. They are centrally concerned with the values embedded within the liberal democratic state. Inclusion within institutions of formal education may well be a precondition for the development of greater social justice. To encourage lifelong learning, broadly conceived as that which is vocationally useful, personally liberating and socially cohesive could be Further Education's contribution to such development.

REFERENCES

Coffield, F. (1996) Introduction and overview, in Coffield, F. (ed.), *Strategic Research in Further Education*, Newcastle: University of Newcastle.

Halliday, J. S. (1996) Values and further education, *British Journal of Educational Studies*, 44 (1), 66–82.

Halliday, J. S. (ed.) (1997) *Exemplars of Values in Further Education*, Stoke on Trent: Trentham.

Howieson, C., Raffe, D., Spours, K., Young, M. (1997) Unifying academic and vocational learning: the state of the debate in England and Scotland, *Journal of Education and Work, 10:1, 5–35.*

Pring, R. (1995) *Closing the Gap: Liberal Education and Vocational Preparation*, London: Hodder and Stoughton.

Winch, C. (2002) The economic aims of education, *Journal of Philosophy of Education*, 36:1, 101–17.

74

Curriculum Development in Further Education

Graham Connelly

> If they hadn't learnt much from him, he had been able to go home in the evening with the
> knowledge that he had gained something from them. (*Wilt on High*, by Tom Sharpe, 1984)

Wilt muses that in twenty years' teaching Liberal Studies in a technical college, he has been
unable to get anyone to tell him clearly what he is supposed to be doing. His dilemma
typifies the identity crisis of further education during the 1960s and 1970s expansion and
highlights the precarious position of non-vocational subjects in the curriculum of technical
and commercial courses. Following the adoption of a modular, outcome-based approach to
the further education (FE) curriculum in the 1980s and a raft of reports on lifelong learning
during the 1990s, college lecturers in post-devolution Scotland find themselves as key
players in a deliberate government strategy to widen access to post-school education and
thus meet the changing economic and social demands of the new millennium. This chapter
explores the genesis of these changes, and analyses current issues impinging on curricular
provision.

CURRICULUM DEVELOPMENTS POST-1945

In the immediate post-war years, theory evening classes for craft apprentices and office
workers were conducted mainly in school classrooms under the auspices of local authorities.
In the mid-1950s, the FE college building programme expanded amid concerns that
workers were not equipped with skills required by industry. Employers were encouraged to
release young apprentices and trainees on a day per week basis or for longer blocks of study.
The new colleges had better practical facilities and students were prepared for external
examinations of the English-based City and Guilds of London Institute (CGLI) and Royal
Society of Arts (RSA), and the Scottish Council for Commercial Education (SCCE). The
syllabuses were strongly vocational, emphasising expertise in practical skills. (See Hunter,
S. L., *The Scottish Educational System*, Oxford: Pergamon Press, 1971, Chap. 10.)

The Brunton Committee (*From School to Further Education*, Edinburgh: SED, 1963)
examined the effect of FE expansion on secondary school provision. The committee's
members were asked to recommend ways of better co-ordinating the last year of compulsory
schooling with FE programmes. Two concerns were identified: avoiding students having to
'waste time on work with which they are already familiar'; and integrating general education

within vocational courses, 'aimed at all round development of the individual'. The aim was to complement vocational education with teaching in literacy, numeracy and 'general studies', in a way that was relevant and not detached from the student's life experience. The language of Brunton now seems at best quaint, at worst stereotypical and uninformed. For example, FE students were said to be, 'not interested in academic learning and [to] prefer physical activity to thinking'; teachers were advised to keep in mind the 'verbal limitations' of their students. Vocational courses were in familiar occupational areas, such as building, agriculture and fishing, but also included 'girls' occupations', mainly retail and office work. The report's authors seemed content to leave the curriculum in vocational areas to the awarding bodies, like CGLI, but they did attempt to describe the general studies curriculum. All students, they argued, should be helped to become more proficient in written and oral English, to develop the capacity to understand instructions, convey information, and make notes and other types of records. They should also know about 'industrial relations, personal finance and budgeting, personal relations in an adult world, and about the local community and the facilities and opportunities it affords for the development of personal interests and for service' (p. 32). Committee members acknowledged resistance from employers to general studies in the curriculum, particularly if the subjects seemed to have no immediate utility in the workplace. The report concluded, somewhat liberally, that teachers should identify their own and students' interests and, thus, 'it would be fruitless to prescribe a detailed syllabus in general studies.'

In 1962 the Scottish Association for National Certificates and Diplomas began to administer post-school technical education and in 1966 the Scottish Council for Commercial, Administrative and Professional Education was established. These bodies reviewed National Certificate courses and standardised entrance qualifications. The Industrial Training Boards also influenced the curriculum of vocational courses, their work funded by a levy on firms. (See Robertson, I., *Recurrent Education and the Work of the Industrial Training Boards*, Association for Recurrent Education, Occasional Paper 3, 1979.)

The Scottish Technical Education Council (SCOTEC) and the Scottish Business Education Council (SCOTBEC), formed in 1975, together provided a broader range of vocational certificates and diplomas. (These organisations merged in 1985 to form the Scottish Vocational Education Council (SCOTVEC), which subsequently merged with the former Scottish Examination Board (SEB) to form the Scottish Qualifications Authority (SQA). See Chapter 83 'The Scottish Qualifications Authority'.) The decade of the 1970s was a time of growing youth unemployment and the government responded with a series of short-term and largely unsuccessful initiatives, such as the Youth Opportunities Programme (YOP) and Work Introduction Courses (WICs). It was also a time of change in assumptions about employment, and there was an acceptance that adults would no longer remain in a single occupation for life and a growing awareness that students should learn transferable skills. (See Ryrie, A. C., *Changing Student Needs in Further Education Colleges*, Edinburgh: SCRE, 1984.)

FE, created to provide qualifications for specific jobs and particular industries, now found it had little to offer students requiring a more general preparation for eventual work, assuming the economy improved, or, pessimistically, long-term unemployment. There were structural problems in the system too. SCOTEC and SCOTBEC had different entrance requirements for courses, different programme lengths and different standards for their qualifications. Finally, the uneasy relationship with general studies remained unresolved. The examination bodies seemed content to leave teaching in Art, Physical

Education, Music and English to colleges but students and employers continued to question the value of these unexamined elements of the curriculum. There was considerable variation in practice between colleges and in many cases the standard of provision was poor and under-resourced. College lecturers of general and aesthetic subjects in particular felt isolated from their secondary school colleagues and had limited access to in-service training.

THE MODULAR CURRICULUM

In 1979 the Scottish Education Department began an extensive consultation exercise culminating in the publication of the 1983 report, *16–18s in Scotland: An Action Plan*, which radically changed the nature of FE provision in Scotland (Edinburgh: SED, 1983). What had been initially concerned with the first two years of post-compulsory education in Scotland and the preparation for life of 16–18-year-olds, paved the way for a radical revision of further and higher education for young people and adults of all ages. The Action Plan's authors concluded that 'there should be no abandonment of broadly-based education, and where specialisation is necessary it should be sought through appropriate emphases' (p. 9). They envisaged a broad curriculum, stressing personal and social development, with strong vocational influences supporting the application of theory and skills and helping to maintain student motivation. Flexibility became a byword and students were to be offered choice in putting together programmes of study, incentives to achieve and increased freedom to move between programmes and institutions.

The consultation indicated a major problem in FE concerning the independent construction of courses largely based on occupational disciplines like engineering. This meant there were separate syllabuses for fundamental subjects like Science and Mathematics in different vocational programmes. Apart from being wasteful, it was difficult for students to move between courses and colleges, and between part-time and full-time education. The solution adopted was a framework based on a curricular component with standard design characteristics. This 'modular' curriculum was to be based on forty-hour blocks of course time and modules would be available at different levels of attainment to facilitate progression, with students entering at the level appropriate to their existing attainment or experience. Modules would be taken as free-standing units of study, combined to form unique programmes for individual students, or grouped to make up vocationally-recognised awards. Finally, module 'descriptors' would contain statements describing student outcomes and these would form the criteria against which performance should be assessed. This process of 'criterion referenced' assessment was advocated because attainment could be reported 'not in relation to the better or poorer performance of others, but in relation to success in achieving what the course was intended to provide' (SED, 1983, p. 40). The assessment process was to be applied internally by teaching staff, subject to external monitoring.

SCOTVEC assumed responsibility for developing a National Certificate programme, based on modules and in 1989 extended the modular principles to Higher National Certificate (HNC) and Higher National Diploma (HND) courses. An important influence on modular curriculum development was the work of the newly established Curriculum Advice and Support Team (CAST) in producing teaching packages and running workshops for lecturers. This centralised activity was designed to reduce duplication of effort and was arguably highly influential in speedily moving the FE curriculum – in general studies and communication at least – from a fairly permissive position to one characterised by a high degree of prescription.

When HM Inspectors conducted a review of the National Certificate, they concluded that the unified modular system had been a major achievement: 'the National Certificate can be used to provide a delivery system which offers flexibility and choice in content and in mode and pace of learning' (*Six years On: Teaching, Learning and Assessment in National Certificate Programmes in Scottish Further Education Colleges*, Edinburgh: SOED, 1991, p. 54). They found the planning of learning and teaching had improved and teaching had become more student-centred. Most students appeared to enjoy their college experiences and this satisfaction was attributed to a combination of increased choice, more active learning and units of study with clear, short-term targets.

Nevertheless, this initial review identified problems. The move to internal assessment presented several professional and organisational difficulties. Designing assessments and interpreting standards had become major activities for lecturers and assessment began to overshadow the learning process. HMI advocated 'approaches which integrate the assessment of a number of learning outcomes or which embed assessment in learning and teaching, so as to counter over-use of a "teach-test" approach to module delivery' (pp. 55–6). They also noted a need for more effective internal moderation to ensure consistency of standards between staff and within colleges, and staff development in assessment for new and part-time staff. Teachers and students had apparently adopted the culture of modules with enthusiasm, but the inspectors called for more 'coherent integrated programmes', an aspect of curriculum planning they felt had been neglected.

In the mid-1990s schools and colleges began offering packages of National Certificate modules in vocationally relevant areas, including an emphasis on core skills such as communication and information technology. These Scottish Group Awards are offered at three levels where qualifications at the first, general, level are known as National Certificate Group Awards, while the more vocationally specific levels 2 and 3 are given the title of General Scottish Vocational Qualifications. Of the 3,021 students gaining Scottish Group Awards in 2001 (including, for example, 479 in Engineering and one in Shipbuilding) virtually all (98%) were presented by FE colleges. However, student success rates in these awards have been poor compared to other qualifications. For example, only 33% of candidates presented in 2001 gained a level 1 award and 43% were successful in the higher levels (compared with a 79% mean success rate in HNC and 75% in Highers). Scottish Groups Awards were under review in mid-2002.

INFLUENCES ON THE CURRICULUM

Before modularisation, vocational elements of the curriculum were prescribed in syllabuses of awarding bodies, in consultation with trades unions, employers, professional bodies and confederations of industrial and commercial interests. Teaching was left to college lecturers, qualified in their subject or trade, who might have gained a teaching qualification by part-time secondment. After 1985 several factors together influenced the view of both the curriculum and course design in further education, of which one important factor was undoubtedly the influence of SCOTVEC. In post-devolution Scotland, whilst the school sector has maintained a very clear separate identity within the UK in relation to curriculum and staff development, FE has had to adjust to both Scottish and UK initiatives. This duality of outlook is exemplified on the one hand by the uniqueness of Higher Still and the

Scottish Qualifications Framework, and on the other by the dependence of Scottish Vocational Qualifications (SVQs) on standards developed by UK-wide National Training Organisations (NTOs).

Occupational competence and vocational qualifications

The Conservative government initiated an ambitious standards programme in 1987 to establish levels of achievement on youth and adult training programmes in the UK. A massive development programme to specify statements of occupational competence began. The rationale for this complex exercise was two-fold. Firstly, changes in workplaces meant that an increasing proportion of workers could expect to change jobs in their working lives and therefore needed skills, transferable between different jobs, even in quite different industries. Secondly, if common definitions of competence in skills could be agreed, then it might be possible to facilitate credit transfer between qualifications and encourage recognition of competence in different occupational sectors.

The process by which statements of competence were written involved analysing job functions of experienced employees, a cumbersome task typically undertaken by consultants. This work was overseen by UK-wide committees, known as 'lead bodies', representing significant occupational groups. The then Employment Department advised lead bodies to express standards of competence in 'unit' form – influenced by the Scottish experience of modules – ideally describing a separate role or function within an occupation, to encourage credit transfer. The tasks of monitoring the quality of unit writing, avoiding duplication and standardising statements of competence in broad skills, were given by the government to SCOTVEC and the London-based National Council for Vocational Qualifications (later to become the Qualifications and Curriculum Authority). The bodies co-operated to approve units of occupational competence, identical throughout the UK. Scottish Vocational Qualifications (SVQs), and their counterparts in the rest of the UK, National Vocational Qualifications (NVQs), made up of lead body units which assess students or employees against standards of performance recognised by employers, were introduced in 1989. SVQs are awarded at five levels, corresponding to an increasing degree of autonomy in the employment context. Units at level 1 describe competence requiring a minimal degree of independent work, skills typically needed by operatives, while level 4 units describe the competences of professionals in work generally associated with degree-level entry qualifications. An example of an SVQ at level 3 (where candidates perform complex tasks and may have responsibility for others) is On Licensed Premises Supervision, which has six mandatory units, one of which is 'Create effective working relationships', with three performance criteria, including 'Gain the trust and support of colleagues and team members'.

Around 50% of SVQs are provided by colleges, with work-related competences assessed through placements or in simulated work environments. In *Opportunities for Everyone: A Strategic Framework for Scottish Further Education* (1999) the Scottish Executive determined that funding for FE colleges should be targeted towards social and economic priorities, including 'narrowing the gap in unemployment' and 'improved demand for high quality in-work training.' Nevertheless the Parliament's Lifelong Learning Committee in March 2002 criticised the local enterprise company (LEC)-funded Skillseekers programme for being overly concerned with meeting LEC training targets and recommended a more flexible approach to meeting employers' skill requirements and individuals' personal development needs. Researchers Cloonan and Canning (2000) found it impossible to ascertain accurate completion rates for SVQs because of the poor quality of the data available. Their case study research supports a view of SVQs as problematic when used in association with government training schemes. Better completion rates are achieved where candidates are in full-time employment or where the employer commitment is high, as in the modern apprenticeship programme, widely regarded as successful.

The interface between further and higher education

The Scottish Wider Access Programme (SWAP) was set up in 1988, in response to the 1987 White Paper, *Higher Education: Meeting the Challenge*, which invited higher education institutions to attract more adult students. SWAP set out to improve participation by older students and those lacking qualifications, to target traditionally under-represented groups in higher education and encourage collaboration between further and higher education. The Scottish Council for Research in Education (Munn et al., 1993) studied the work of SWAP and found access courses were succeeding in opening up higher education to people who might otherwise have missed out, but had limited success in attracting students from traditionally under-represented groups. For example, Connelly and Chakrabarti (1999) studied the uptake of places on access courses in Scottish FE colleges and while they noted general acceptance of the principle of positive action by colleges, they found little evidence of strategies likely to prove effective. Nevertheless the success of strategies for broadening participation in higher education in Scotland is very dependent on the FE sector, due to the high proportion of students doing higher education in colleges, and due to collaboration arrangements with universities.

FE has a key role in the Executive's flagship social justice policy because of the importance of individual achievement and community development in combating disadvantage. Colleges, because of their location in the heart of communities, because of their close links with community education, enterprise bodies and voluntary agencies, and because of their highly developed student support systems, have arguably been successful in challenging cultural beliefs about the possibility of embarking on a college education. However, two particular problems require to be tackled. One problem relates to continuing barriers to participation, such as the difficulties faced by adults with dependants, the persistent inability to attract students from very low income backgrounds and the complexities of the different programme options. The other is the problem of 'reluctant' students, such as those compelled to accept FE as an alternative to unemployment under the New Deal programme (see Gallacher et al., 2000 for a fuller discussion).

The appeal of FE lies in the omnipresence of colleges within communities and in a nurturing role which encourages adults, often juggling study with complex private lives, to believe in their capacity for personal achievement. But what brings students to colleges in the first place? In a study of 700 new entrants to ten Scottish FE colleges, Connelly and Halliday (2001) found that the single most important factor influencing students' decisions to study at their local college was an 'employment reason'. However, despite this instrumental motivation, the research suggests that while the broad area of study is important to students, they are less interested in the precise details of the competences they are supposed to be acquiring than in the general thrust of their learning. For many students, the value of FE is measured in terms of satisfying social relationships, good teaching and developing confidence, rather than in the detail of the curriculum.

ISSUES IMPINGING ON CURRICULUM DEVELOPMENT

Modes of learning

The expansion of FE during the 1990s resulted in a more varied student population requiring more varied approaches to teaching and learning. FE's ability to respond to these varied needs was arguably hampered by the restrictions of a highly-prescribed, outcome-based curriculum. Also FE, compared with HE, faced significant disadvantages in resource terms: it typically offered more modest library provision, came late (2001) to the broadband communication infrastructure (JANET) and, crucially, several colleges were in severe financial difficulties. However, across the sector a range of developments, heavily based on information and communications technology, began to impact on teaching methods. These developments happened at three levels. Firstly, colleges developed approaches to address the access needs of adult students, including establishing satellite campuses in neighbouring towns, forming teaching partnerships with community education, and establishing flexible learning units where students can work independently using text-based and on-line materials with tutorial support as required. Secondly, in the changed political climate post-1997, there was a return to encouraging collaborative activities between colleges, for example in sharing distance-learning materials and in supporting local broadband networks. Thirdly, the sector became involved in government or agency-driven developments, such as Individual Learning Accounts, the Scottish University for Industry (SUfI) and the University of the Highlands and Islands Millennium Institute (UHI). Despite FE's reputation for responding quickly to changing demands, the sector has been criticised for lagging behind universities in developing new methods of learning and teaching (see Pieda Report, *Demand and Supply in Further Education in Scotland*, Edinburgh: SFEFC, 2002), and the Enterprise and Lifelong Learning Committee of the Parliament in the spring of 2002 called on the Executive to develop a more strategic approach to e-learning across both FE and HE.

Staff development and curriculum development

The changing demands on FE have produced challenges in the area of teaching staff training, particularly in supporting part-time lecturers, and in developing skills in pedagogies and the use of ICT. While less than 4% of permanent lecturers are classified as 'unqualified' in that they do not hold the minimum entrance requirements for a teaching qualification in further education (TQFE), over 12% of temporary staff, who make up more than half of the total head count of FE teachers (SFEFC, 2002), are unqualified. Only 56% of the head count hold a recognised teaching qualification, though 80% of permanent lecturers are teacher trained. Teacher training is not a requirement of employment in FE but SFEFC has set an exacting target of having 90% of FE lecturers teacher trained and the shortfall led the Enterprise and Lifelong Learning Committee (SFEFC, 2002) to describe FE, along with HE, as retaining 'too much of an amateur status'.

Prior to 1998, the TQFE was provided exclusively by the Scottish School of Further Education (SSFE) specifically set up for this purpose in 1968 at the former Jordanhill College. The SSFE in its prime was a large semi-autonomous unit within Jordanhill providing a broad range of services, including conferences, in-service training, research and consultancy, but in the period leading up to and since the ending of its monopoly status it became a very small department within the University of Strathclyde's Faculty of Education, with a rather low profile within Scottish FE. The TQFE, jointly approved by the Executive and the General Teaching Council for Scotland, is now also offered by the Universities of Dundee and Stirling, with both institutions using a range of new technologies to support the teacher training of lecturers in colleges around Scotland. However, the resource restraints on universities in the early 2000s have constituted a serious barrier to expansion and innovation of CPD provision in support of FE. Colleges, however, have been active in responding to their own local CPD needs: one interesting example being the MA in Professional Development run within the UHI network and validated by both the Open University and the Institute for Learning and Teaching in Higher Education (ILT); another is the provision of credit within TQFE programmes for SQA Professional Development Awards (PDA) gained by lecturers for assessed CPD in their own workplaces.

Another significant provider of CPD is the Scottish Further Education Unit (SFEU) which was set up in 1991, initially to support management training for senior FE staff in advance of 'incorporation' of colleges in 1993. The SFEU was formed by refocusing the activities of the former Curriculum Advice and Support Team (CAST) in the SSFE to support the new modular curriculum. The SFEU is an independent agency, funded by government and income from commercial activities. It operates from a base in Stirling, providing staff training, consultancy and conferences, supporting specialist interest groups and originating publications and curriculum materials in vocational further and higher education. The SFEU collaborates with the University of Stirling in offering postgraduate courses in tertiary education management and it hosts an impressive website, which also acts as a portal to other web-based resources. It has been unquestionably influential in developing both the breadth and quality of FE provision but its physical relocation severed the link between the initial pedagogical education of lecturers and development of the FE curriculum which had been a cornerstone of the SSFE.

Support for students

The success story of further education is the development of a system that is generally regarded as being student-friendly and supportive, offering a broad range of opportunities and encouraging individual progression. A negative effect is confusion about the plethora of courses, programmes and schemes, and their appropriateness for individual students given their aspirations and the local employment situation. The need for newly-incorporated colleges to market their courses aggressively in the mid-1990s produced a degree of tension between guidance advisers and teaching departments anxious to fill course places. Colleges became adept at providing pre-entry advice and on-course support, but successive HMI inspections have highlighted variations in the quality of provision between colleges and indicated the need for colleges to become more sophisticated in their guidance and student support provisions.

Inappropriate pre-entry guidance, restricted choice within programmes, and poor opportunities for student progression from outreach to mainstream programmes meant that the needs of some students were not being met adequately. There was also a need in some cases to establish more effective links with employers, ensure early identification of the learning support needs of students and provide on-going guidance in less reactive ways. (See *Meeting Learner Needs in Scottish Further Education Colleges*, HMIE, 2001, p. 1)

The Enterprise and Lifelong Learning Committee has recommended that the idiosyncratic infrastructure of adult guidance provision should be simplified and if this happens colleges will arguably become even more important providers of information and guidance about initial and continuing opportunities. Nevertheless, it is unreasonable to expect colleges to be completely impartial in providing guidance about course opportunities. In this regard, the success of the new Careers Scotland agency in driving a national strategic approach to all-age guidance (see Chapter 51) and of significant partners, including FE and HE institutions and LECs, in achieving effective local collaboration, will determine whether school-leavers and adults can expect to receive high quality advice and progression guidance in future. Some recommendations for the way forward for colleges are contained in a consultation report on guidance in Scottish FE (GTCS, 2002). The report's authors advocate, for example, that all learners should have access to timetabled guidance integral to their courses, that colleges should expand partnerships and work more closely with specialist support agencies, that there should be clear allocation of staff time for guidance and support duties, revision of the funding methodology by SFEFC to recognise the key role of student guidance, clarification of the guidance role of lecturers, and provision of continuing staff training in guidance skills.

THE FE CURRICULUM IN THE FUTURE

The modern FE college in Scotland has been given a pivotal role by the Executive in supporting lifelong learning and in driving the ideals of social justice through widening access to post-school education. The revolution in the curriculum which began with Action Plan has made FE courses at the start of the new millennium more structured, varied, and vocationally oriented. However, the developments have also left the sector, as ever, somewhat uncertain of its identity. Some colleges will aim to emphasise the higher education aspect of their provision, though it seems unlikely that they will be permitted to follow Bell College's example by moving entirely into the higher education sector. The impact of new technology will inevitably produce different kinds of relationships between colleges and their students, though the changes are likely to progress slowly. Wilt's successors are more likely to be on temporary or part-time contracts, and teaching students with a broader range of personal and learning needs, with significant implications for staff development. A major challenge for curriculum development lies in understanding the important distinctions between vocational and personal motivations for studying and attending college. The qualification system may change at the margins but its broader influence will not diminish. However, loosening of the constraints of a target-driven approach to matching students to courses, a greater emphasis on the strengths of the community college, and reinforcement of the importance of good teaching might be good ways forward.

REFERENCES

Cloonan, M. and Canning, R. (2000) Completion rates of Scottish Vocational Qualification (SVQ) courses: a research study, *Scottish Educational Review*, 32 (1), 55–67.

Connelly, G. and Chakrabarti, M. (1999) Access courses and students from minority ethnic backgrounds, *Journal of Further and Higher Education*, 23 (2), 231–44.

Connelly, G. and Halliday, J. (2001) Reasons for choosing a further education: the views of 700 new entrants, *Journal of Vocational Education and Training*, 53 (2), 181–92.

Gallacher, J., Crossan, B., Leahy, J., Merrill, B. Field, J. (2000) *Education for All? Further Education, Social Inclusion and Wider Access*, Glasgow/Stirling: Centre for Research in Lifelong Learning.

GTCS (2002) *Guidance within Scottish Further Education*, Edinburgh: GTCS.

Munn, P., Johnstone M. and Lowden, K. (1993) *Students' Perceptions of Access Courses: A Survey*, Edinburgh: SCRE.

75

Teaching and Learning in Further and Higher Education

Rebecca Soden

As has been pointed out elsewhere in this volume, there is considerable overlap between further and higher education in Scotland. Pedagogy in both sectors is changing, influenced by interacting factors such as the impact of communications and information and technology (C & IT), diminished per capita funding, greater emphasis on the idea that education should prepare people for the world of work, burgeoning research on post-school learning, and initiatives to widen participation to a more diverse student population. Analysis of this changing context can be found in an independent report by PA Consulting Group titled *Higher Education in Scotland: Orchestrating an Adaptive Knowledge Based System* (2002), commissioned by and available from the Scottish Higher Education Funding Council (SHEFC).

PEDAGOGICAL PRACTICE

What emerges from articles in the pedagogically oriented journals mentioned later in this chapter is that both university and further education college staff tend to adopt a theoretically eclectic approach influenced by the content of their discipline. Plainly, assessment methods such as final examinations, oral presentations, essays and project reports encourage different approaches to teaching and learning. With the exception of final examinations, all these assessment methods are used widely in both sectors. In SQA accredited programmes, which account for the vast majority of provision in the further education sector, students are assessed continuously, with no final examinations. In universities examinations are common. Typically, there, students learn through participation in lectures, tutorials, workshops and projects, supported by individual library work. All of these methods are common in the further education sector too, with the exception of the mass lecture. Often, further education lecturers combine exposition, questions, discussion and written work in a way that resembles secondary school class teaching but conducted in an atmosphere of much less formal staff–student relationships. This is practicable because the class numbers are often under twenty-five and popular with students because it offers them opportunities to seek clarification while the information is being presented. Some ways of implementing these methods are described by Fry, Ketteridge and Marshall (1999).

INFLUENCE OF COMMUNICATIONS AND INFORMATION TECHNOLOGIES (C & IT) ON PEDAGOGICAL PRACTICE

SHEFC has continued to support strongly the development of learning packages involving web-accessed input, computer-based assessment, electronic support mechanisms and tutorial groups established on the world wide web. In the university sector students are now commonly supported by electronic communication of information designed to help them prepare for lectures, tutorials and assessment and to guide them in their individual library work. Students are expected to access electronically lecture notes, tutorial task guidelines, suggested follow-up articles, explanations of assessment criteria and past examination questions. They often use e-mail to seek academic help from their tutors.

Diminishing per capita funding has provoked a search for ways of managing small-group tutorials/seminars more effectively and efficiently. C & IT are often suggested as an answer to financial challenges but academics have argued that much research is necessary before C & IT can be used to support traditional university methods such as small group work. This point is well made in the research that is currently being funded by Learning and Teaching Subject Networks (LTSN). Interesting examples of such research can be found on the LTSN Psychology website (www.psychology.ltsn.ac.uk). The LTSN is a major network of 24 subject centres based in higher education institutions throughout the UK and a single Generic Centre. This network aims to promote high quality learning and teaching through the development and transfer of good practices in all subject disciplines, and to provide a 'one-stop shop' of learning and teaching resources and information for the HE community. The website of the ASTER project (assisting small group teaching through electronic resources): http://cti-psy.york.ac.uk/aster/ offers further illustration of the kind of research that has been done in this area.

Many examples are appearing of the potential of C & I T to enable radical innovation in teaching and learning. For example, some course teams in universities have attracted development funding for setting up suites equipped to enable lecturers to plan half-day sessions in which students engage in a variety of activities such as listening to brief periods of exposition, watching video clips, conducting electronic searches for articles relevant to prescribed tasks, participating in individual and collaborative web based tasks and face-to-face group discussions. Colleges of further education have relatively recently received substantial financial support from the Scottish Further Education Funding Council to develop an infrastructure to support e-learning. As yet it is hard to find examples but it is anticipated that, within the next few years, colleges will capitalise on this investment in infrastructure to develop schemes for e-learning and e-assessment. Comprised of colleges of further education, the University of the Highlands and Islands is likely to do more of this because of its remote and diverse locations.

Such applications of technology have altered the role of staff in many university departments from lecturing towards preparing course materials and monitoring student activities. Continuing growth can be expected in technology assisted, interactive, self-paced learning materials providing a combination of ideas, questions, repeatable experiments, work based simulations and tasks to provoke independent thinking about the content. These materials will be supported by video tutorials and accompanied by frequent monitoring of students' progress with learning tasks. Techniques such as video-conferencing will open up possibilities for students to discuss their ideas with people around the world who have made significant contributions to a shared area of interest. The development of technology has stimulated inter-institutional collaboration in the development of innovative methods of course delivery.

It would be wrong to assume that such innovation depends entirely on high technology. For example as a response to diminishing per capita funding, and legitimated by particular interpretations of ideas about independent learning, the trend towards packaging of learning materials in the ways described above is likely to continue in a basic way. In the further education sector students often learn from packages consisting of print materials, with access to lecturers, many of whom are on part-time, temporary contracts. Lecturers across a section or department are encouraged to produce for each module a pack containing learning, teaching and assessment materials. This trend has spread to some parts of the university sector where modest reductions in staff/student contact time are achieved by using such packages to support students in independent study and student managed group work.

EDUCATION FOR WORK:
INFLUENCES OF CORE AND KEY SKILLS ON PEDAGOGY

Plainly, the extent to which teaching approaches promote worthwhile learning is influenced by what has to be learned and how that is described to teachers and students. Demands for greater flexibility in the workforce have led to calls for further and higher education to promote the development of 'core' and 'key' skills that are assumed to be transferable from the context in which they were learned to other contexts. In National Certificate courses in the further education sector 'core skills' include communication, numeracy, information technology and problem solving. Further education lecturers are required to teach core skills in all programmes leading to General National (or Scottish) Vocational Qualifications, a national competency-based curriculum. In the higher education sector a parallel emphasis on transferable skills arose from recommendations in the Dearing Report (1997) that all undergraduates should develop 'key skills', which include communication, numeracy, the use of information technology and learning how to learn. Since 1997 key skills policies and strategies have proliferated in the higher education sector. Institutions are now expected to identify 'key skills' in all programme specifications and to record attainment of key skills for every student. Consequently, forms of student-centred approaches similar to those used to develop 'core skills' in the further education sector are now widely used in parts of the university sector. The terms 'transferable skills' and 'core' and 'key' skills often are used interchangeably.

The core skills agenda has helped to legitimate particular forms of student-centred approaches. Typically, these skills are taught through small group work during which students seek, assemble and present information to peer audiences. Martin Bloomer (1998) reported that much student activity on courses in the further education sector was being expended on tasks that were often trivial, tightly prescribed, closely supervised and rarely involved critical enquiry. ('They tell you what to do and then they let you get on with it': The illusion of progressivism in GNVQ, *Journal of Education and Work*, 11 (2), 167–168). In Teaching critical thinking in social care, *Instructional Science*, 29, 1–32, Anderson, Howe, Soden, Halliday and Low (2001) reported a similar finding in courses leading to Scottish National Vocational Qualifications. While it is increasingly acknowledged that lecturers in both sectors should help students to think well in work related contexts, just what this means has not been clearly delineated. The pedagogy to be used for achieving these ends has been more amenable to description than the nature of the ends themselves.

STAFF DEVELOPMENT

In neither sector is initial teacher training a requirement of employment. The changing nature of further and higher education has inevitably stimulated developments in staff training. The recommendation in the Dearing Report that all new higher education lecturers undertake teacher education courses led to the setting up of the Institute for Learning and Teaching (ILT). Most universities encourage lecturers to achieve membership and special admission arrangements are offered to experienced university lecturers. New lecturers can achieve membership by completing a course accredited by ILT or through submission of a portfolio which evidences the applicant's developing competence in supporting learning. The ILT website (http://www.ilt.ac.uk) offers a wealth of resources on which members can draw to support their engagement in continuing professional development. These resources include the ILT journal *Active Learning*, seminars, an annual conference and a members' resource area.

SHEFC invests substantial sums each year to support teaching. Accountability and quality improvement are secured by the quality assessment system for which the council is responsible. Examples of SHEFC-funded projects include support materials that raise interesting questions on topics such as effective learning, teaching and assessment, curriculum design, student support and quality control. These resources are intended to encourage further discussion within Scottish higher education. Recently, SHEFC made available additional funding to support a range of staff development activities to promote wider use of C & IT for learning and teaching throughout the sector. From the SHEFC website (http://www.shefc.ac.uk) a picture of the extent and nature of its involvement in staff development can be constructed.

Kember (1997) points out that many studies point to the very strong influence on practice of lecturers' conceptions of learning and teaching. Yet staff development activities in further and higher education often are designed to change teaching behaviours rather than to provoke lecturers to reconstruct their conceptions. But, unless educators understand why they prefer one account of learning to another, they are little more than technicians severely disadvantaged when faced with new contexts. From a meta-analysis of relevant research, Kember proposed that conceptions of teaching can be summarised in terms of two broad orientations labelled student-centred/learning oriented and teacher-centred/content oriented. The teacher-centred orientation describes the views of lecturers whose predominant conceptions of teaching are that it is about transmitting structured knowledge. The student-centred orientation is described as one which is more likely to be based on beliefs that teaching is about facilitating understandings, promoting conceptual change and intellectual development. This orientation is more compatible with notions of good practice implied in pedagogical research literature outlined in the next section. Although most provision for further and higher education lecturers claims to enhance participants' understanding of learning, a requirement to engage in critical examination of frameworks is not apparent in all programmes.

Lecturers in both sectors usually access the burgeoning research literature on learning, teaching and assessment through staff development activities that, increasingly, are accredited. Thus, providers are in a powerful position to influence lecturers' theoretical preferences. In both sectors there has been a tendency in staff development provision to present fragments of theories about learning together with specific applications rather than to pose questions about the extent to which different perspectives provide adequate accounts of learning. Pressures to make staff development activities 'relevant', and the many other calls on lecturers' time, predispose those who design such activities to choose parts of theories which seem to promise a quick pay-off. Such an approach seems to dilute the explanatory power of theories and to have little potential for suggesting to lecturers conceptions of learning which have wider scope and plausibility than their own narratives. It seems that the extent to which theories about learning become influential depends not only on their overall coherence and explanatory power, but also on other factors such as their congruence with society's conceptions of the overall purposes of education and the resources which can be allocated to pursuing these purposes.

RESEARCH ON TEACHING AND LEARNING

Current research on teaching in post-school education is driven by constructivist accounts of learning that have their psychological roots in Piagetian and Vygotskian research. Although there is significant variation in the many theoretical positions described as constructivism, there is general agreement about its basic tenet: that knowledge is not passively received from others, but is actively built up by individuals through organising and adapting it to the world. Vygotskian ideas have helped to develop a social constructivism, which asserts that the construction of knowing is not a matter of individual, solitary construction of understanding, but a dialectical process firmly grounded in a system of social relations. Such ideas have helped to promote a view that teaching should be about helping students to construct and test conceptualisations of the physical and social world, drawing on the intellectual tools that their culture offers. Constructivism, described often as a vexed and messy landscape, is well explained in Light and Cox (2001), together with discussion of approaches derivable from this general framework. Other useful discussion of Constructivism can be found in Fox (Constructivism examined, *Oxford Review of Education*, 27 (1) 23–35, 2001).

Radical constructivists might design courses in which most of the students' class contact time was occupied by debating interpretations of prescribed and chosen pre-reading in their subject, exploring implications and identifying issues which merited further critical analysis. Pre-reading would have a pivotal role in the course to reflect the Piagetian notion that the construction of knowledge is driven by perceived disparities or conflicts between the individuals' existing ways of thinking and the intellectual demands and opportunities of the environment: such conflicts seem more likely to be provoked by a serious reading programme. Tutors would act in accordance with the constructivist assumption that knowledge is not received from others, even from authoritative sources, by restricting their input to introducing tasks and supporting participants in clarifying and performing these tasks. Such acts are difficult to implement unless course teams are allowed to determine patterns of class contact and unless students gain sufficient experience of working in these ways to disturb typical conceptions that learning is transmitted through lectures and that tutors will do all that is required to ensure that the transmission has been successful.

Their courses would also depend for their success on open ended assessment tasks that are more difficult to design in the competency based further education sector. Assessment in this sector rests on prescriptions of a narrow range of acceptable responses to tasks, an approach that delivers high reliability in grading but discourages intellectual risk taking by students. A literature on authentic assessment has appeared that fits well with approaches informed by Constructivism. An authentic assessment task is one that has some use beyond the assessment requirements and generates new knowledge through engaging in disciplined enquiry. Thus, psychology students might authentically be assessed on their knowledge of enquiry methods by compiling and presenting to an audience of education students an evaluation of research on the influence of television violence on children's behaviour.

Constructivism encourages students to find questions worth pursuing, to pursue their questions through self-directed search and interrogation of knowledge and to debate their emerging views with others. Practices claimed to be optimal for these purposes have been well described in the texts cited in this chapter and in journals such as *Teaching in Higher Education*, *Active Learning*, *Psychology Teaching Review*, *Learning and Instruction* and *Educational Action Research*. Such practices are informed by the idea that teaching approaches should encourage learners to be more self-directed and autonomous. Such self-direction resonates with the idea that post-school education should develop abilities appropriate to lifelong learning and to employment. Harvey and Knight (1996) report research which suggests that the main factor determining student learning is individual study outside the classroom and that teachers should give much more attention to supporting students in working independently and purposefully on worthwhile tasks that help students to develop broad intellectual competences connected with employability and citizenship.

Commitment to constructivist accounts of learning and belief in the value of self-direction led to the development of an approach described as problem-based learning, which has become very influential. It starts with a problem that, as far as possible, is presented in the same context as in real life, rather than with disciplinary knowledge. For example, first year medical students might start with a short case study about people who experience certain symptoms during foreign travel near tropical swamps. This approach often means that traditional discipline boundaries are crossed. What has to be learned is identified by addressing the problem and by reference to resources, some of which may have been provided, and some of which may have been located by the students themselves. Students work in small groups, which allocate knowledge gathering tasks, and which serve as a forum for discussing progress with their problem. Lecturers become designers and facilitators of activities and discussions. Research on problem-based learning can be found in the journals mentioned in this chapter and in books by leading researchers in this area. (For example, see Boud, D. and Felleti, G., *The Challenge of Problem-based Learning*, 2nd edn, London: Kogan Page, 1997).

The value of these approaches has been contested but some of the reported difficulties might be addressed by an on-going institutional strategy which ensures effective staff development and encourages content integration across modules and substantial credit in assessment systems for critical reflection. Bennett, Dunne and Carre's (2000) review of research into abilities which improve performance at work suggests that the most suitable graduates are those who are flexible, adaptable and quick to learn, and who can use skills such as analysis, critique and synthesis to the benefit of their organisations. When the approaches outlined in this section are properly implemented they are likely to promote these abilities, often summarised as the capacity and the disposition to engage in good thinking.

These forms of independent learning will not achieve their intended goals unless students use effective approaches to learning. One of the most important and influential research findings in this area has been the articulation of deep approaches to learning and conditions that encourage or impede development of such approaches. (e.g. see Marton, Hounsell and Entwistle, 1997). Students adopting a deep approach make effective efforts to understand and transform content through critical engagement with ideas: they appraise the evidence offered and the conclusions associated with it; they offer arguments and conclusions. Research suggests that the factors which influence students to adopt a deep approach are the student's own purposes in studying, his or her previous experiences of education and beliefs about learning, together with the teaching and assessment encountered on the course. If students feel overburdened with work, if assessment requirements are inappropriate, and if authoritarian relationships between tutors and learners prevail, students tend to adopt ineffective surface approaches to studying. Kember (1997) reported evidence from a wide range of studies that students are less likely to use deep approaches to learning when their lecturers work with conceptions that knowledge can be transmitted unproblematically from one person to another. Measures to encourage deep approaches to learning are particularly relevant in the further education sector, which has a key role in widening participation in higher education, and therefore in helping students to develop approaches that will serve them well when they move on to universities.

This strand of research on deep and surface approaches to learning differs from the 'learning styles' literature. Useful insights can be derived from both, provided that the reader is suitably sceptical of evidence that 'learning styles' are immutable traits which transcend subject matter. Embedding ideas about 'learning styles' within an ambitious 'triarchic' theory of intelligence developed in teaching students at Yale, Robert Sternberg discusses in his article (A comparison among three models for teaching psychology, *Psychology Teaching Review*, 8 (1), 37–42, 1999) how teaching can be done in ways that encourage students to capitalize on strengths, such as a tendency to 'practical' or 'creative' thinking and to compensate for or to remedy their weaknesses, such as a disinclination towards 'analytical' thinking. More dubious characterisations have become influential in the further education sector (Fry, Ketteridge, and Marshall, 1999). Harvey and Knight (1996: p.125) say that 'learning styles' is a seductive construct which suggests that people have preferred styles of learning regardless of the task. They report studies which cast doubt on this idea. Yet complex issues about promoting cognitive development have been reduced, in some parts of both sectors, to achieving a match between teaching approaches and students' presumed 'learning styles'. In addition to debates about difficulties in establishing whether enduring styles exist and how they are to be identified, there are questions about whether it is in the students' interests to encourage particular styles which might not be appropriate for dealing with their academic tasks. Sternberg's ideas for helping them to extend their existing repertoires seem sensible. Perhaps students should be involved in departmental discussions about such matters.

The notion of metacognition, that is knowing and thinking about one's own knowledge and thinking processes, has had a central role in research on enhancing students' ability to learn and think. Various aspects of metacognition have been distinguished: for example, one can know about one's own knowledge of people, of tasks and of learning strategies. Examples of these aspects of metacognition would be: knowledge that one's own rationality is affected adversely by the behaviour of certain others; knowledge that one is unsure of what counts as critical thinking in essays, knowledge of the range of one's own cognitive resources which are appropriate for the task. The last includes knowledge of effective strategies for different tasks, knowledge that enables adaptation of strategies, and monitoring and control of one's own progress with the task in hand. According to research literature, all approaches should provide for the development of students' metacognition but there is little evidence that such provision exists. Possible reasons are that the concept of metacognition is not often encountered by lecturers in staff development programmes and that its development requires a good deal of time for students to talk about their thinking.

ISSUES

Although many sound ideas have emerged from research on learning and teaching, in both sectors there is a substantial gap between research and practice. Many of the better ideas about good practice rest on the assumption that an important purpose of further and higher education is to enhance students' ability to think critically about whatever they are studying, but pursuit of this goal is not sufficiently guided by research on its nature and its course of development. Employability and citizenship seem to be well served by a capacity to arrive at reasoned judgements by weighing up evidence in the light of multiple and often conflicting criteria, and by a growing understanding that knowledge is neither entirely objective and certain, nor is it simply a matter of opinion. Employees often are expected to help to prepare position papers, a task that requires not only selection of relevant information but working with appropriate criteria to evaluate available evidence on which a position can be reached. Although there is a vast literature on this dimension of thinking, it is largely ignored in delineations in curricula of the 'key' and 'core' skills that were introduced to enhance employability. Nor is much account taken of well founded challenges to the assumption that what is learned in one context transfers unproblematically to others.

A fundamental difficulty with the characterisation of 'core' and 'key' skills is that not enough account is taken of research which suggests that competency in exercising the abilities assumed to be transferable is likely to be strongly affected by the individual's knowledge of the domain in which they are to be exercised. Cognitive research on expertise implies that thinking is intimately bound up with the individual's knowledge of fundamental ideas from relevant disciplines and the interconnectedness of these ideas. Such knowledge enhances and accelerates further related learning. For example, people in senior administrative posts probably communicate and think effectively in their jobs because they build up deep understanding of the broad issues on the agenda of various committees, not because they have had quick-fix training in the so-called transferable skills.

Thus, it is not surprising that the student-centred approaches noted above lacked any provision for inquiry that was genuinely critical. Nor is it surprising that many lecturers find it difficult to distinguish 'core' and 'key' skills from competencies and other attributes that they felt were desirable before skills talk came to dominate. In science education, for example, teachers encourage students to solve problems and to communicate findings from laboratory work. The traditional student task of addressing essay questions invites them to justify their views on the basis of a variety of interpretative considerations, thus demanding much more than is described in the 'key skill' of written communication. It is important to note that many university lecturers especially, but further education lecturers too, define themselves and their identity in terms of a subject specialism and they are not lightly going to give up that identity in favour of what they see as a spurious and sometimes unhelpful discourse.

The idea that further and higher education should promote intellectual development is reflected in current funding of research that investigates how learners can be helped to think effectively about whatever they are studying. In 2002 a Scottish university was awarded substantial funding from the Learning and Skills Development Agency (LSDA) to research pedagogies for enhancing students' thinking in the post-school sector. The LSDA intend to invite tenders in 2003 for a follow-up three-year research programme. The Economic and Social Research Council (ESRC) has funded similar research through its Teaching and Learning Research Programme. It is encouraging that both funders valued highly proposals that included the kind of conceptual and analytical work that might make sense to lecturers. Substantial support from the Scottish Further Education Funding Council Strategic Development Fund was secured by a group of Scottish colleges of further education for an initiative to help staff to try out ideas from research on thinking skills. An important task for researchers in this area is to connect their research on the nature of thinking and how it might be developed with 'key skills' initiatives in higher education. A possible route to achieving this is discussed by Bennett, Dunne and Carre (2000).

Curricula often are inconsistent with the ends discussed above and pedagogical research reviewed here probably depends on quite radical changes. Soden and Halliday (Rethinking vocational education, *International Journal of Lifelong Education*, 19 (2) 171–82, 2000), argue for a radically different division of labour between further education colleges and other institutions in which students live and work. They draw on the theoretical perspective known as 'legitimate peripheral participation' expounded by Lave and Wenger, in *Situated Learning – Legitimate Peripheral Participation* (Cambridge: Cambridge University Press, 1991). What they argue is that vocational preparation should take place through engaging in real work, rather than through the current, widespread use of project work in colleges of further education that is centred on imaginary tasks, and which rests on dubious assumptions that transfer of what is learned in classrooms to culturally different workplaces is relatively unproblematic. The role of the further education lecturer would change from teaching occupational knowledge to one of promoting intellectual development through prescribing reading and engaging students in informed, critical reflection on their work experience. Learning activities in the college could include discussions about how students might determine their chosen work, what overall they wanted from real work, why they valued certain outcomes and why they preferred to pursue them in one way rather than another. These discussions could lead into talk about questioning what might be taken for granted, about having some idea of how the questions one raises might be answered, about grounds on which people might justify their preferences. Soden and Halliday argue that this can be more worthwhile for the development of employability, educational interest and community.

Although the development of good thinking is implicit in the stated aims of SQA accredited programmes, this is not given priority in performance criteria and accreditation that are prevalent in further education. Current psychological literature no longer supports the idea of fixed ability but rather suggests that intellectual development is related to the kind of activities in which people engage. If students' achievements on entry to further education imply underdeveloped capacity for good thinking it would be logical to give greater rather than less emphasis in the further education curriculum to the development of thinking. This is not to say that university lecturers are better than their further education counterparts at facilitating the development of their students' thinking but rather that it is easier for them to do so when assessment criteria are written in a way that allows students to earn substantial credit for thinking critically about what they are studying.

Research interest in developing learners' ability to think effectively about what they are studying is consistent with the developing consensus that lecturers should develop an orientation to helping students with their learning rather than committing themselves to a specific set of teaching techniques. If students are to benefit fully from the growing enthusiasm for self-managed, technology assisted learning, they need to be carefully initiated into all that is involved in informed analysis and critique. This requires sufficient time for face-to-face interactions which offer opportunities for a tutor to judge a student's current state of understanding, to form some notion of what it might become and to engage the student in dialogue aimed at achieving the transformation. Peer tutoring and peer critiquing also have a part to play in this process, but their productive use may well depend on investment of time in developing students' ability to engage effectively in such activities. There is great scope for research in these areas.

Research is likely to turn to the interrelationships between two conceptions of learning which often are treated independently of the other: a conception of individual learning, emphasising the acquisition of knowledge and cognitive skills as transferable commodities and the socio-cultural conception of learning as a collective participatory process of active knowledge construction, emphasising context, interaction and context. These two perspectives on learning interact in synergistic ways. There is considerable support for the view that it is not enough to direct one's own learning as an individual, and that learning should be directed towards several purposes: to learn from and with others; to draw the most from cultural artifacts other than books; to mediate others learning not only for their sake but for what that will teach oneself; to contribute to the learning of a collective.

The challenge now facing post-school education is that of designing courses promoting the integration of what students learn not just in colleges and universities, but in work experience and in pursuing their lives in the wider community. What has been argued in this chapter is that the effectiveness of learning environments which help students to transform themselves and society is intimately related to the purposes of post-school education and that their design should be informed by research which takes proper account of social and cultural factors that influence individual values and cognitions. What is likely to improve learning and teaching is research which goes beyond finding out how policies can be implemented efficiently and engages in critical analysis of the conceptions, assumptions and values underlying proposed policies.

REFERENCES

Bennett, N., Dunne, E. and Carre, C. (2000) *Skills Development in Higher Education and Employment*, Buckingham: Society for Research into Higher Education and Open University Press.

Fry, H., Ketteridge, S., Marshall, S. (1999) *A Handbook for Teaching and Learning in Higher Education*, London: Kogan Page.

Harvey, L. and Knight, P. (1996) *Transforming Higher Education*, Buckingham: Society for Research into Higher Education and Open University Press.

Kember, D. 1997, A reconceptualisation of the research into university academics' conceptions of teaching, *Learning and Instruction*, 7 (3), 255–25.

Light, G. and Cox, R. (2001) *Learning and Teaching in Higher Education*, London: Paul Chapman Publishing.

Marton, F., Hounsell, D. and Entwistle, N. (1997) *The Experience of Learning*, Edinburgh: Scottish Academic Press.

76

Institutional and Curricular Structures in the Universities of Scotland

Richard Shaw

Classification is a means of bringing order to a subject. In this chapter the approach will be to use broad and hopefully simple categories but with the reminder that differences in ethos may differentiate just as effectively as differences in formal structures.

OLD AND NEW UNIVERSITIES: MISSIONS AND CHARACTER

Historically with varying emphases the primary functions of universities were the creation of new knowledge through research and scholarship, and teaching and learning. These continue as the primary functions but in recent years they have been joined by the public priorities to promote social inclusion and to transfer knowledge into the wider economy through the commercialisation of research.

The simplest categorisation is that between the old universities – those created pre-1992 – and the new universities – those created as a result of the Further and Higher Education (Scotland) Act 1992. The latter group, the post-1992 universities, share similar missions and many structural features. The former group, the pre-1992 universities, while being readily identified as distinct from the post-1992 universities, are in practice much more diverse in their history and character.

THE PRE-1992 UNIVERSITIES

As indicated in Chapter 6, this group may be sub-divided into the four 'ancient' universities: St Andrews, Glasgow, Aberdeen, and Edinburgh founded between 1411 and 1583; the four '1960s' universities: Dundee, created by demerging from St Andrews; Strathclyde and Heriot-Watt evolving from their previous status as Scottish Office funded 'Central Institutions'; and the one completely new 1960s university, Stirling, established on a greenfield site in 1966.

All eight pre-1992 universities, as well as being arguably still primarily teaching institutions for undergraduate and postgraduate students, regard themselves as being research universities. In the latest 2001 Research Assessment Exercise (RAE) two-thirds or more of the academic staff of each of these institutions were included in their submissions as being 'active in research'. There is a clear expectation that all, or at least most, academic staff will be active researchers and an aspiration that they should contribute to assessment ratings denoting international research excellence. As is clear from Table 2 in Chapter 6 their success in achieving that aspiration inevitably varies.

While emphasis on research is a common characteristic, differences in history, location, size, subject profile and academic structure make for substantially differing institutions. Put simply, Edinburgh, Glasgow, and Strathclyde are very large (over 14,000 full-time equivalent students) city-based universities covering the vast majority of subject disciplines. At the other end of the spectrum, Stirling and St Andrews are much smaller (around 7,000 students) universities situated in smaller communities and covering a wide but nevertheless relatively restricted range of subject disciplines. Only Aberdeen, Dundee, Edinburgh and Glasgow have full medical faculties with pre- and post-clinical medicine, while Stirling and St Andrews do not have engineering faculties. Heriot-Watt and Strathclyde retain a strong emphasis on science and engineering reflecting their origins as technological institutions. Although other institutions have recently adopted a modular structure within a semester system, only Stirling began life in the 1960s as a modular university and as such was unique in Scotland until the 1990s.

In any sketch of the pre-1992 universities it would be wrong not to refer to both their Scottish character, built on a tradition favouring a broad general education, and their commitment to being also United Kingdom and international universities. Recent statistics show that around 22,000 students from elsewhere in the UK are enrolled at Scottish higher education institutions. These students are largely concentrated in four universities: Dundee, Edinburgh, Stirling, and St Andrews. In addition, overseas students add a distinctive character to most of the pre-1992 universities.

THE POST-1992 UNIVERSITIES

The five post-1992 universities were created from existing institutions. Prior to the abolition of the binary line they were all degree and postgraduate level institutions with their awards being made under the Charter of the Council for National Academic Awards (CNAA). Up to the creation of the Scottish Higher Education Funding Council (SHEFC), the five post-1992 universities were all directly funded by the Scottish Office Education Department (SOED) which strongly encouraged them in their commitment to vocationally oriented programmes of study and to widening access to higher education.

While all five institutions were committed to, and engaged in research and scholarship broadly defined by CNAA, their essential character was defined by their vocationally relevant teaching mission. Most of the institutions' research was applied and targeted at being relevant to the needs of local and regional industry, commerce and public services. SOED, as the funding body, did not explicitly fund research in these institutions and indeed discouraged research activities unless they could be shown to be in support of the vocationally relevant teaching mission. This history is reflected in the submissions to the 2001 RAE in which between 19% and 30% of academic staff in the five post-1992 universities were included as being 'active in research'. Thus, while the post-1992 universities are expanding their research activities, by comparison with the pre-1992 universities, the new universities are still focused much more clearly on learning and teaching and less on academic research. The five are Abertay, Glasgow Caledonian, Napier, Paisley and Robert Gordon.

INSTITUTIONAL STRUCTURES: FACULTIES, SENATE AND COURT

Although there are significant differences in detail, the formal academic management and governance structures in the Scottish universities are generally very similar. The supreme body responsible for the overall character, mission and management of the universities is the governing body, in most cases called the court. The formal responsibilities of the courts are laid down in the constitutional documents of the universities, legislation, and in some particulars reinforced by the financial memorandum between SHEFC and the individual institutions. Although not part of the management and governance structure, all the universities have a titular head, the chancellor. The office of chancellor is primarily ceremonial involving presiding over degree awards ceremonies and other formal functions. The chancellor may also act as an ambassador for the university, assisting in the promotion of external contacts.

As the supreme body, the court, or board of governors, is ultimately responsible for the good management and financial health of the university. Although the detailed composition varies between the universities, the general pattern is of a court of between twenty-five and thirty people with a majority of lay members but including, as well as the executive head of the university, the principal, other appointed or elected members of staff, and students. In the four ancient universities: Glasgow, St Andrews, Aberdeen and Edinburgh, a lay rector elected by the students chairs the court. In the other universities, pre- and post-1992, the chairperson is appointed by court itself and is always a lay member. The lay members are largely drawn from the business, commercial and professional world and will normally include at least one representative from local government.

The court, or board of governors, is supported by a committee structure that generally includes finance, audit, senior staff remuneration, and nominations committees. Not surprisingly, given the differing histories of the institutions, there is some variation in the committee structure though it is now a condition of funding through the financial memorandum with SHEFC that all institutions have audit, and senior staff remuneration committees. Following the Nolan Committee reports on standards in public life (summarised at www.archive.official-documents.co.uk/document/parlment/nolan/nolan.html) there is also a strong recommendation that there is a nominations committee relating to membership of the court.

While formally supreme, the court shares the responsibility for the university with the chief administrative and academic officer, the principal and vice chancellor, and with the senate, the senior academic committee. The nature of this 'partnership' has varied from time to time and from institution to institution. This will be the subject of later discussion.

The academic government of universities is formally the responsibility of senate, or academic board (council). This body normally has overall responsibility for the academic programmes of study, the admission of students, the assessment of students, and the granting of degrees and other awards. The senate, or academic board, is chaired by the principal. Senates vary enormously in size – from around twenty-five to over 200. This variation, as well as partly reflecting the size of the university, mainly results from the number of professors since in the older universities all professors may be members of senate by right. In the newer universities, as well as there being far fewer professors they do not always have an automatic right to membership of senate. In addition to professors, senates have ex-officio categories of membership including the principal and some other senior officers, heads of academic departments and deans, student representatives and elected members.

Senate, or academic board, like court is supported by a committee structure. The normal pattern involves two strands: subject-based and specialist committees. The latter will include committees with special responsibility for university wide functions such as the library and information services, and monitoring academic standards. The subject-based committees include faculties responsible for groupings of academic subjects such as Medicine, Business, Humanities, Science, and Engineering, and academic departments responsible for particular subjects. Naturally, there is considerable variation in the detailed arrangements including the number of tiers involved in academic government. Thus one of the post-1992 universities, Abertay Dundee, has abolished faculties as an intermediate tier between senate and academic departments, and reorganised the latter into small groups of schools. Most recently (2002) Edinburgh has adopted a three-college system replacing the former faculty structure. Indeed there has been a trend towards a reduction in the number of faculties and academic departments as part of a rationalisation process in academic management structures.

THE JARRATT COMMITTEE: RELATIONSHIPS BETWEEN ACADEMIC STRUCTURES, COURT AND EXECUTIVE MANAGEMENT

An inquiry into the management of universities chaired by Sir Alex Jarratt, *Report of the Steering Committee for Efficiency Studies in Universities* (1985), accepted the central role of senates as 'the main forum for generating an academic view', playing 'an essential role in decisions affecting academic questions', and 'coordinating and endorsing the detailed work carried out on their behalf by Faculty Boards, departments and committees', (p. 24, para. 3.50f). The Jarratt Committee endorsed the role of committees in 'academic matters (e.g. curricula, examinations)' – 'decision taking by committees is both desirable and necessary for sound functional reasons', (p. 25, para. 3.53).

However, the Jarratt Committee was concerned that the collegiate structure, heavily dependent on committees, was inadequate to sustain successful universities in an era of change. The committee was concerned with the pre-1992 universities throughout the United Kingdom, and wished to see a stronger role for courts (councils in England) with their lay membership in the sphere of strategic and financial planning. It questioned the role of committees concerned with 'non-academic functions (e.g. catering, residences)', arguing that 'decision taking might normally be assigned to individual managers or officers either with or without committee involvement or aided by consultative committees', (p.25, para. 3.53). It further noted that 'the tradition of Vice Chancellors [principals] being scholars first and acting as a chairman of the Senate carrying out its will, rather than leading it strongly, is changing. The shift to the style of chief executive, bearing the responsibility for leadership and effective management of the institution, is emerging and is likely to be all the more necessary for the future' (p.2 6, para. 3.58).

While acknowledging the central academic purposes of the universities, the Jarratt Committee pointed to the need for strategic and financial planning, and the use of professional management structures and techniques to manage complex institutions responsible for thousands of staff and students and millions of pounds of public and private money. The committee was concerned that what they identified as 'the relative decline in the exercise of influence by Councils [courts] has increased the potential for Senates to resist change and to exercise a natural conservatism' (p. 24, para. 3.50h).

The committee's recommendations were taken seriously not only in the pre-1992 universities but also through the Scottish Office in the higher education institutions it funded. In addition there was a developing agenda for government in increasing the professionalism of management throughout publicly funded institutions. As a result, and strongly aided by an increased pace of change in higher education, there were pressures to increase the chief executive officer role of principals, and to expand the role of courts relative to senates. Among the changes that enhanced these pressures were a series of major switches in government policy creating turbulence, uncertainty and financial pressure. The government first created financial incentives for the universities to expand student numbers and then suddenly imposed a period of consolidation with student numbers capped. It also implemented a continuing policy of squeezing real funding per student leading not only to efficiency gains but also to what ministers have recognised as a crisis in higher education funding. In addition, changes in student finance involving the reduction and elimination of maintenance grants for the majority of full-time students, the introduction of student loans, the introduction of fees and their partial replacement in Scotland by the Graduate Endowmnent, served to heighten the transition of students into students and customers.

The changes outlined have been accompanied by others which have sharply altered relationships between the institutions. In the 1980s, government policy towards higher education embraced the competitive model: universities were encouraged to compete firstly for public research funds from both the research councils and through competitive research assessment exercises, and then for students, and also for private funds to support research, teaching, students and building/projects, and indeed any university activity. In this competitive environment the government moved to a position of encouraging mergers emanating from the institutions themselves. From the mid-1990s the strategic direction was shifted towards emphasising the merits of collaboration but still encouraging mergers as well as strategic alliances. To date, mergers have been confined to those between individual universities and smaller and more specialist institutions including all the former teacher education colleges. Strategic alliances have taken a variety of forms including teaching collaborations; social inclusion access partnerships; and research alliances including a wide-ranging 'synergy' alliance between Glasgow and Strathclyde Universities. Despite these significant developments which seem likely to multiply, the competitive ethos has become deeply embedded in the psyche of higher education.

In these pressured circumstances it is not surprising that both executive managements, led by principals and courts have seemed to exert more influence and authority relative to senates and the academic committee structure. Courts in particular have been encouraged by SHEFC to use their authority. Despite this, much of the collegiate ethos of academia survives, as indeed it must in support of the central teaching, learning and research purposes of the universities. It is on those central academic purposes that attention is next focused.

THE MANAGEMENT OF ACADEMIC AFFAIRS

As already indicated, the senate sits at the top of the academic committee structures. Generally, senates are concerned with broad matters of policy and academic regulation, with the detailed matters concerning individual students, assessments, curricula delegated firstly to faculty boards and then to academic departments, subject committees and examination boards.

As suggested by Jarratt, committees play a crucial role in debating and deciding on academic issues. Deans, who lead faculties, and heads of departments normally chair the main faculty boards and departmental meetings respectively. However, deans and heads of department are also managerially responsible for their faculties and departments. In securing the effective management and administration of their respective responsibilities, they will generally assign duties among academic staff so that academic management is shared with several or indeed many colleagues. Thus there may be admissions officers, examinations officers and examinations board chairpersons, course leaders, subject area leaders, research convenors, and so on, drawn from the teaching and research staff within the faculty and department.

While there is considerable similarity in the general approach between the pre- and post-1992 universities there are at least two major differences. The first arises from the historically much greater autonomy of the pre-1992 universities with their own degree awarding powers contrasting with the original dependence of the post-1992 universities on the authority of CNAA. In the latter, CNAA regulations governed academic procedures and practices prior to the achievement of the universities' own degree awarding powers under the Further and Higher Education (Scotland) Act 1992. The second arises from differing employment contracts in the two groups of universities: fixed term 'rotating' academic management posts in the pre-1992 universities contrasting with 'permanent' academic management posts in the post-1992 universities. The effects of the two differing practices are examined in turn.

Academic autonomy has meant that universities decide for themselves the structure of their degree and other programmes, the regulations and practices under which individual programmes may be developed and offered, and of course the curricula and teaching and learning approaches. At the most general level, the university, through senate, determines the regulations for the award of degrees, honours degrees and the various postgraduate awards. Within those regulations, academic programmes are normally developed by or between academic departments, subject to approval by faculty boards and or senate. In the pre-1992 universities this traditionally meant that there was little or no external-to-the-university scrutiny of individual academic programmes prior to their being offered to students, except in cases involving preparation for membership of professional institutions, for example, in accounting or engineering. In the post-1992 universities, on the other hand, historically new academic programmes could not be offered until they had been validated or approved by a process involving external scrutiny in accordance with CNAA regulations. Despite their newly gained academic autonomy, the post-1992 universities retained the tradition of external scrutiny as part of the approval process required before offering a new academic programme. This general approach was reinforced by the vocational education mission of the post-1992 universities that led to a higher proportion of academic programmes than in pre-1992 universities also leading to membership of professional institutions. The latter naturally impose their own scrutiny external to the university before accrediting an academic programme as part or whole of the requirements for professional membership. This of course applies to pre- and post-1992 universities alike. Notwithstanding the influence of the professional institutions, there still remains a difference in ethos between the pre- and post-1992 universities with the latter accepting more readily external involvement of both employers and other academics in the design and approval of programmes.

A more subtle effect of both the CNAA inheritance of the post-1992 universities and their vocational character has been the emphasis on programme rather than subject discipline. Since each academic programme is approved, monitored and periodically reviewed, the academic management structures typically are based on the programme or course. Thus there are course leaders, course committees and examination panels linked specifically to each programme. In contrast, in the pre-1992 universities the emphasis has been more on the academic discipline and its subject health. Correspondingly, course management structures, while clearly important, have a less prominent role in the academic management of departments.

The differences in programme approval and management outlined above were very clear in the early and mid-1990s; however, more recent developments suggest some measure of convergence in the practices of the pre- and post-1992 universities. This is considered below in the context of other changes after a discussion of the differing academic management employment practices in the pre- and post-1992 universities.

In the pre-1992 universities, the deans and heads of department do not hold permanent appointments. Typically they hold office for around three years, possibly with reappointment, and then revert to their substantive post of professor or senior lecturer. In the post-1992 universities historically the heads of department, and in most cases the deans, held permanent appointments. The managerial style of these permanent office holders obviously varies from those emphasising a collegiate approach to those emphasising a more hierarchical approach. Of course, within the pre-1992 universities the apparent collegiality of 'rotating' heads of department may not be so real in cases where one or more senior staff dominate particular departments. Nevertheless, the presence of permanent officers from vice principal through deans to heads of department in the post-1992 universities has created a more managerialist ethos and practice than exists in the pre-1992 universities.

Whatever the ethos, pressures have grown in recent years to develop more effective leadership and managerial approaches in all universities. These include the advent of the research assessment exercises and teaching quality assessments and audit together with increasing financial pressures, and the rapid developments in information and communications technology. Put simply, the performance of colleagues in publishing research, in the effectiveness of their teaching and support for their students can no longer be a matter of mild interest. The reputation and financial health of the department, and the working environment for the individuals within it, depend on the effectiveness of its members. Instead of being administrative units within which academics exercise their freedom and skills to teach and research, departments have become, in pre- and post-1992 universities alike, closer to businesses. Departments seek to succeed academically through their recruitment of students and teaching and learning strategies, and through their research, both supported by the attraction of external funds where possible. Success may be assessed formally or informally against a series of performance indicators. These may include: student numbers; completion rates; proportion of students attaining a 'good' degree classification; research assessment grading; external income; net financial surplus; cost per student; employment rates for graduates. The pressures outlined are common to all universities and, just as importantly, the externally managed mechanisms and criteria for teaching quality assessment and audit, and research assessment are identical for pre- and post-1992 universities. Inevitably, identical external processes and criteria of assessment and audit have led to convergence in internal procedures and practices in response.

While the detailed responses vary between universities, and indeed between individual departments and faculties within universities, there are some common themes. The pre-1992 universities have developed a much more coherent teaching and learning quality management framework at university and faculty levels than had existed prior to the introduction of teaching quality assessments and academic audits in the early 1990s. The post-1992 universities already had university-wide frameworks with, for example, an academic standards committee as part of the quality assurance requirements of the CNAA. Conversely, both the teaching quality and research assessments have created pressures for the post-1992 universities to move towards pre-1992 university practices in giving greater emphasis to subject health rather than focusing more narrowly on individual course or programme management. It is likely that this process of convergence will continue.

Two other developments may reinforce this process. These are, firstly, a trend towards modularisation of academic structures and programmes designed to increase flexibility and student choice; and secondly the associated development of credit accumulation and transfer both within institutions and as a national framework. Both modularisation and credit accumulation and transfer developments strengthen the need for university-wide strategies and regulations. While not all Scottish universities have adopted these developments, those that have cross the pre- and post-1992 divide.

CURRICULAR STRUCTURES

Any discussion of curricular structures in Scotland must start with the recognition of the traditional emphasis on breadth of study particularly in the early years and the distinction between the Scottish 'ordinary' degree which seeks to retain breadth in later years and the Scottish honours degree involving both an extra year of study and normally a greater emphasis on specialisation in the later years. Within these traditions, students may study between three and five different subjects in their first year before opting for continuing breadth or increasing specialisation. These are powerful traditions with continuing support within both pre- and post-1992 universities. Both the Dearing and Garrick Reports added their support as is clear from one of the recommendations in the Dearing Report (Recommendation 15, p.1 32):

> We recommend that all institutions of higher education should, over the medium term, review the programmes they offer:
> – with a view to securing a better balance between breadth and depth across programmes than currently exists;
> – so that all undergraduate programmes include sufficient breadth to enable specialists to understand their specialism within its context.

Breadth of study is cherished both for its educational value and increasingly for the flexibility that it affords students to taste before choosing or indeed to change direction.

However it would be wrong to overemphasise the current place of breadth in the curriculum as many students choose vocational and professional courses such as those in Law, Medicine, Nursing and professions allied to Medicine, Accountancy, Engineering, Teacher Education. In such cases the curriculum may or may not be broad depending on the requirements of the professional institutions as well as on academic views. While achieving breadth may be a consideration, the main focus tends to be on the preparation to enter a particular career path. Nevertheless, the Garrick Committee was anxious to promote the merits of broad based degrees and recommended that institutions should develop a new Scottish bachelors degree combining breadth of study with a strong emphasis on the skills required by employers.

One trend, whatever the nature and structure of the degree programme, has indeed been the increasing emphasis on its merits as a preparation for employment. This reflects pressure from both the 'student market' and the 'employer market'. Both the expansion in numbers of graduates and diplomates and, at times higher general unemployment levels, have created a much more explicit concern among school leavers and mature entrants to higher education for the employment prospects arising from successful completion of particular programmes at different universities. This trend has almost certainly been given a further boost by the decline in student maintenance grants, the increase in student debt and the elimination of most grants and the introduction of contributions to fees. Employers, too, have become more demanding and increasingly asking not only for traditional graduate accomplishments such as the ability to analyse, to think critically, and work independently, but also for other transferable skills in communication, team working, numeracy, information technology and problem solving. Certainly universities have responded to these growing demands as the Dearing Committee recommended: 'All institutions of higher education should aim for student achievement in key skills – communication, numeracy, the use of information technology, and learning how to learn – to become an outcome for all programmes.' (p. 135, para. 9.25).

Consistent with their advocacy for key skills, the Dearing Committee also strongly endorsed the value of work experience as part of academic programmes. There has been a long tradition of work experience in Scottish higher education particularly in the professional and vocational areas such as engineering, computing and business, where, in the post-1992 universities, sandwich degrees including one year in relevant employment have formed a major part of course provision. In other areas such as nursing and midwifery, social work and teacher education, professional work placements are compulsory parts of the academic and professional awards. However, as both the universities and the Dearing Committee recognise, the constraint on developing and implementing work experience programmes can be the lack of opportunities offered by employers. This is ironic since employers are often the first to stress the value of work experience in academic programmes.

A particular feature in the majority of the post-1992 universities is the existence of Higher National Certificate (HNC) and Higher National Diploma (HND) programmes. These are typically vocational programmes with designed sub-degree exit points after one year, HNC, or after two years, HND. However, there has been an increasing tendency for the successful students to progress to a third year leading to a first degree. Aside from the delivery of HNC and HND programmes in the post-1992 universities, there is the very important trend of increasing numbers of students completing HNCs and HNDs in the further education sector transferring directly into the second and third years of degree programmes in the universities. This trend reflects an increased commitment to improving access to higher education in the universities.

So far, the discussion has focused on the curriculum designed primarily to meet the needs of school-leavers entering universities to study full time for three or four years, or even longer in the case of dentistry, medical and veterinary students. In 2000–1 approximately 115,000 students fell into this category. However, the total number of all students in the Scottish universities, including those taking short courses either part or full time was over 180,000 in that year, according to the Higher Education Statistics Agency. Even this may be an underestimate as it probably excludes large numbers attending workshops and other very short courses. It is difficult to do justice to the variety of programmes offered to meet the needs of the broad spectrum of people involved. Nevertheless, a brief review will seek to draw out the main features.

The first main group are the 40,700 postgraduates. These divide into research students and those studying on taught postgraduate programmes. For the 11,000 research students, the core of their work is directed to individual research programmes leading up to the presentation of a thesis. A relatively recent development has been the institution of taught research preparation or 'training' courses as part of the masters or doctoral programmes. These courses may be offered at departmental, faculty or university wide levels. They may also be offered co-operatively by two or more universities.

Taught postgraduate programmes may be designed as advanced courses for those already having studied a subject, or a closely related subject, to first degree level. Alternatively, the programmes may be designed as 'conversion' courses for graduates from a wide range of disciplines. In the 'conversion' course category the largest groupings are in business and information technology. Somewhere between the advanced course and the 'conversion' course categories, come the postgraduate certificate teacher education courses which build on the graduate's first degree subject, but whose primary function is to prepare the student for entry into the teaching profession. Indeed a key characteristic of most taught postgraduate programmes is their role in preparing graduates either to enter the employment market or to advance their careers through professional development.

For the large numbers of continuing education students there again have been three different traditions. Firstly, in the pre-1992 universities, the continuing education departments have offered a vast range of part-time non-credit bearing and non-assessed courses, often of short duration, in the liberal arts tradition. Secondly, and particularly, but not exclusively, in the post-1992 universities, there have been clearly vocational short continuing professional development courses. Typically, these too have been non-credit bearing. Finally, there has been the development of continuing education using the SCOTCAT credit accumulation and transfer framework (see Chapter 106). This development, pioneered in the post-1992 universities, is increasingly being adopted as a way of providing a very flexible approach of accessing credit-bearing courses to suit both the liberal arts and the professional development needs of mature students. While many students are content to study individual modules as either a hobby or for a specific career development need, many others are using credit accumulation and transfer also as a way of progressing towards the award of a degree, honours degree or even a postgraduate award.

The SCOTCAT credit accumulation and transfer framework, to which all the universities are signatories, formed the basis of the qualifications framework for Scotland recommended by the Garrick Committee and is now incorporated in the resulting Scottish Credit and Qualifications Framework. How this will impact on the structure of academic awards in universities remains to be seen, but there seems little doubt that the Dearing Committee's desire for a better balance between breadth of study and depth will be a source of argument among the curriculum designers for years to come.

FINANCIAL AND RESOURCE MANAGEMENT

According to the Jarratt Committee (1985) 'It is in the planning and use of resources that the universities have greatest opportunity to improve their efficiency and effectiveness' (p. 16, para.3.27). Despite, in the intervening years, very large real cost reductions per student, impressive growth and adaptation, significant achievements in research, earnings from overseas students and attraction of private funding, the Garrick Committee (1997) believed that further progress was possible.

Both the Jarratt and Garrick Committees highlighted issues such as formal structures and responsibility for planning and decision taking, quality and extent of management information including benchmarking against other institutions, and the importance of the effective and efficient use of resources. The last include most importantly staff but also the estate and equipment. The Jarratt Committee's criticism included a lack of long-term planning and use of performance indicators, an inadequate awareness of the full cost of activities and 'a strong emphasis on maintaining the historic distribution of resource' (pp. 2 1–2, para. 3.40).

The force of the Jarratt Committee recommendations was generally recognised. Both the pre-1992 universities, to whom the report was addressed, and the institutions that were to become the post-1992 universities, developed long-term planning processes and indeed are required by SHEFC to submit strategic plans to the council. These plans involve not only issues of strategic direction but also an integration of the academic, financial and physical (estates, space, equipment) aspects of university development. In addition SHEFC have strongly promoted effective planning in areas such as estates, equipment purchasing and management, and information technology. For example, all institutions were required to develop a five-year strategic estate plan in 1994 and are expected to update this plan continually. More recently, similar planning approaches are now required relating to human resource management partly stimulated by the Bett Report (1999).

Similarly, although as anticipated by the Jarratt Committee solutions have varied, universities have reviewed their financial allocation mechanisms. There has been a strong tendency to adopt more devolved budgetary practices with faculties or planning groups becoming responsible for the whole of their budget, including staffing, running costs, space costs and non-recurrent equipment expenditure. Aside from giving scope to faculties, or planning groups, to adjust their expenditures to meet local needs, the central allocation procedures have had to become more transparent. Indeed the explicit student numbers based formula funding model adopted for teaching and the formula driven research funding allocation adopted by SHEFC have substantially undermined tendencies to historical distributions of resource.

Despite these changes, the Garrick Committee expressed disappointment that 'ten years on, awareness of costs and full cost charging, appears to have progressed slowly in the institutions' (p.74, para. 5.18). The committee also advocated greater collaboration between institutions 'ranging from administrative services to research facilities and teaching and learning materials and programmes' (p. 76, para. 5.27) and in areas such as communications and information technology as well as in extending credit based teaching into the summer.

The external pressures exerted by SHEFC and reports such as those of the Jarratt and Garrick committees, together with the 'continuing funding crisis in higher education' (COSHEP, 1997) are causing the universities to review carefully their procedures and practices in financial and resource management. They are only too aware that their deteriorating financial situation requires a continuing search for improved effectiveness and efficiency in the use of resources. Universities, however, are concerned that, without additional resources, the vision of 'higher education in the learning society' painted by the Dearing and Garrick Committees, will be unrealised.

REFERENCES

COSHEP (1997) *Response to the Report of the National Committee of Inquiry into Higher Education*, Glasgow: COSHEP, Glasgow.

HESA (2002) *Students in Higher Education Institutions 2001–01*, London: HESA.

Independent Review of Higher Education Pay and Conditions (1999) (The Bett Report), London: the Stationery Office.

National Committee of Inquiry into Higher Education (1997) *Higher Education in the Learning Society*, (The Dearing Report), Chairman Sir Ronald Dearing, Norwich: HMSO.

National Committee of Inquiry into Higher Education (1997) *Higher Education in the Learning Society*, (The Garrick Report), Norwich: HMSO.

Shaw, R. W. (1997) Catch 22: the newest universities, in R. Crawford (ed.), *A Future for Scottish Higher Education*, COSHEP, Lasswade: Polton Press.

Steering Committee for Efficiency Studies in Universities (1985) *Report for the Committee of Vice Chancellors and Principals*, (The Jarratt Report), London.

77

Beyond the Ivory Tower: the Changing Social Role of the Scottish University

George Kerevan

DEMOCRATIC INTELLECT OR DEGREE FACTORY? THE CHANGING CIVIC AND CULTURAL PLACE OF THE UNIVERSITY IN SCOTLAND

In 1961, George Davie published his now famous treatise on the Scottish universities, *The Democratic Intellect*. Scottish higher education is only now coming to terms with its legacy (Edinburgh: Edinburgh University Press). Davie purported to show how, starting in the nineteenth century, the anglicisation of traditional Scottish higher education, with its alleged over-specialisation and middle-class elitism, had destroyed not just a world-renowned university system but seriously undermined Scottish culture. Davie's book became a nationalist bible, preaching of a lost golden age both of university education and cultural independence. There was only one problem. Davie's analysis was, for the most part, historical invention.

Scotland's traditional universities – St Andrews (1411), Glasgow (1451), Aberdeen (1495) and late-comer Edinburgh (1582) – were originally actually hybrids of secondary school, adult education class and university. Thus male, adult, skilled artisans routinely took non-graduating classes, diffusing essentially secondary school education much wider than in England. Davie's lamented nineteenth-century reforms actually changed this for the better, separating out higher education, raising teaching standards and professionalising research. This resulted in genuine world-class academic institutions as we now know them. In fact, working-class participation in taking full degrees expanded because philanthropist Andrew Carnegie funded a scheme that by 1910 covered much of the fees for half of all Scots undergraduates. The distinctive Scottish generalist MA grew in importance and demand only after the modernisation which Davie criticised.

However, Davie's book, coming when it did, had a political impact: it helped usher in the trend to mass vocationalism – as opposed to generalism – which Scotland has taken further than England. Scotland began the 1960s with 18,500 students in four universities. No new university had been established for over half a millennium. It ended the decade with 38,000 students in eight universities. This proved the single most revolutionary institutional and economic reform between the Second World War and the advent of the Scottish Parliament. It initiated a continuous expansion of higher education till the present day when there are over 170,000 students enrolled on courses leading to qualification or credit at Scottish higher education institutions. That is one in two of the relevant age group, in a population still the same size as it was in 1960. Long gone are the days of the shipyard apprentice making tea in a tin can. Today his equivalent drinks coffee in the student union and is more likely to be female: 54% of today's undergraduates are women.

Davie's emphasis on a bogus democratic era of higher education, supposedly lost, helped to justify this new university system. But this model, while socially worthy and economically justifiable, has produced its own frictions. As a result, the early years of the twenty-first century have seen an emerging cultural crisis in the civic role of the Scottish university. What might be called the 'consensus' of the mythic Davie model (i.e. the universal notion of the ideal Scottish university as the open, classless, independent, and meritocratic guardian of the national culture) is collapsing. Three major fissures have appeared:

- For the first time, rightly or wrongly, the general public and the modern student body have begun to question the quality and validity of attaining a university degree, as a result of the mass extension of higher education.
- The close relationship between the state and the university sector is being reviewed. On the Tory right, the 2001 Westminster general election saw a revolutionary proposal to end direct funding through state grants, and replace this with individual university endowments. Subsequently, the Labour Ggvernment has toyed with the idea of top-up fees, presaging more autonomy and differentiation in university income.
- Relations between the Scottish universities have become more abrasive, with accusations from leading figures in some of the newer, polytechnical institutions of class elitism in some of the older universities.

None of this should be surprising or, indeed, cause for concern per se. It was inevitable that the vast expansion of the university sector (a quarter bigger in Scotland than in England by relative student population in 2001) would alter the social and economic standing of higher education. This chapter seeks to outline, somewhat schematically, some of the major issues that are emerging in this nascent process, with reference to some of the interesting experiments that are evolving.

REAL WORLD OR IVORY TOWER? UNIVERSITY LINKS WITH BUSINESS

Today, 40% of all Scottish undergraduates are studying business-related degrees. Proof of academic dumbing down? Or a sign that Scottish universities are robustly engaging with the real world? To answer these questions it is important to grasp that Scottish universities have never suffered quite the separation from the commercial world found in England. The strength of Scotland's business and engineering tradition – a tradition that might be christened the Scottish Practical Intellect – rests on the unique links the traditional Scottish universities always maintained with the commercial and civil world, as distinct from the English Oxbridge ivory tower tradition. During the English industrial revolution and even after, classics and theology predominated over science and medicine at Oxbridge. Things, however, were different north of the border. Newton's ideas were taught in Scotland before Cambridge accepted them. As early as 1800, Edinburgh University had twelve chairs of science and medicine. At Glasgow University, Joseph Black, one of the most renowned chemists of the eighteenth century, concentrated on applied industrial research. His influence on the university's instrument maker – a certain James Watt – helped stimulate Watt's invention of the modern steam engine, the power source that created the industrial revolution.

This seamless interaction between academia, business and middle-class culture bred the Scottish Practical Intellect – as opposed to George Davie's notion of the Scottish Democratic Intellect, which identified the centre of Scottish education with a broad-based, liberal arts tradition. The Scottish Practical Intellect meant that from the eighteenth century, universities collaborated with practical businessmen and vice versa on a terrain of mutual respect and understanding – something not so true down south during the long years of Oxbridge supremacy. The Scottish Practical Intellect also inspired a generation of teaching and research institutions that would form the precursors of the four new Scottish universities of the 1960s: Strathclyde, Heriot-Watt, Dundee and Stirling.

Today Strathclyde teaches some 20,000 degree students, including around over 10,000 postgraduates, plus another 40,000 people on distance learning, short courses and continuing professional development. That makes it the UK's largest provider of postgraduate and professional education. In a country with a falling population and next to full employment, the local labour market would long since have frozen rigid without this powerful retraining tool. The tradition of the Practical Intellect is also central to Heriot-Watt, named after James Watt himself. It is second among all UK universities in terms of industrial and commercial funding per member of academic staff. A solid 45% of Heriot-Watt's income, over £30m, comes from the research, training and commercial services provided to business. Some 75% of its science and technology units received top gradings in the most recent research assessment exercise, with more top-graded engineering departments than any other Scottish university. Meanwhile, Glasgow Caledonian University (GCU) claims the largest business school in Scotland (a crown disputed by Napier) and the fourth largest in the UK. GCU's Health Faculty is the biggest in Europe and turns out one in five of nurses and health care professions in Scotland.

All of this suggests that there has been no dumbing down of academic rigour in order to accommodate a turn to vocational subjects per se. What Scottish universities teach today is very much in their own technical and commercial tradition – the question is rather whether the vast numbers being sucked into the system can be adequately taught and find a job when they graduate.

THE UNIVERSITY PLC? GROWING COMMERCIALISATION

Has the contemporary drive to make links with the business world perverted research interests? The most interesting model for developing research and funding collaboration – not to mention successful – has been the experience in Dundee. Despite its location in a non-central, declining industrial centre with high unemployment, Dundee University is now world renowned for its medical and biological research, principally its work on cancer under Sir David Lane. He was the world's seventh most highly cited scientist from 1990 to 1997, and the second most highly cited UK-based scientist of the 1990s. His colleague, Sir Philip Cohen was third. Scientists at the University of Dundee are more often cited in the areas of biochemistry, biology and molecular biology than scientists in any of the UK's other 100 universities. Dundee's biomedical research has received top five star ranking ever since the UK national research assessment exercise was introduced in 1986, producing almost the highest research income in the UK. With this growing reputation has come a rise in student numbers. In the five years to 2001 it has doubled in size, to some 12,500 students and over 3,000 staff.

How did Dundee achieve this? The salient lesson is that it had very little to do with the

Scottish Executive and everything to do with an American-style approach from the university itself. The key has been a fierce determination to bring the best research minds in the world to Dundee. The lynchpin was the biochemist, Sir Philip Cohen, who came to Dundee in the early 1970s by way of the University of Washington in Seattle. Cohen fell in love with Dundee and Tayside and determined it would become research Eden. It was Cohen who courted the Wellcome Trust, one of the world's biggest research sponsors, to fund activities. In 1994, the trust made a donation of £10m towards a new, 70,000 square foot medical sciences institute, then the largest single charitable donation ever given to a Scottish university. This now employs over 200 scientists gathered from all round the globe. It was also Philip Cohen who relentlessly went after the top life sciences researchers in the world – never taking no for an answer – and eventually persuading them to come to Dundee. He enticed people like Sir Alfred Cushieri, the pioneer of 'key-hole' surgery, and David Lane, who was previously principal scientist at the Imperial Cancer Research Fund in London and discoverer of the p53 gene that controls the growth of tumours in many common cancers.

The perennial problem which holds back British universities competing for staff with their American counterparts is the inability to match US salaries. UK universities remain tied to common salary scales which makes it difficult to offer world class remuneration to top academics. But Dundee University has a secret weapon that has helped it circumvent this dilemma. The Wellcome Trust tops up normal salaries in medical research and life sciences with special fellowships, meaning Dundee University can play in the world league.

The Dundee example is interesting proof that a rigorous commercial attitude does not mean the sacrifice of cherished freedom or, indeed, of academic achievement. On the contrary, it is proof that escape from state tutelage and academic standardisation can make an institution world class. But how far is it possible to escape reliance on the state? On this issue, a new debate is emerging.

PUBLIC OR PRIVATE?
THE ENDOWMENT DEBATE AND ALUMNI RELATIONS

At the start of the twenty-first century Scottish universities are getting about 40% of their funding in core grants from the state (much of the rest comes from private and public research grants). The Executive plans to raise university spending in Scotland to some £660m per annum by 2004. But to put this in perspective, the annual grant to only the Scottish Enterprise development agency is over £400m. In fact, as Scottish student numbers doubled over the decade of the 1990s, expenditure per student declined sharply. Since 1989, funding per student in the UK fell 37% in real terms, with Scotland hard hit by the relatively greater increase in student numbers compared to England. This financial squeeze doubled the staff–student ratio, and led to 'tutorials' of thirty students in some of Scotland's ex-polytechnic universities.

The option of increased student fees was rejected by Scottish universities at the time of the Cubie Report in 1999 (see Chapters 6 and 13). As a result, Scottish universities – especially the older ones – have sought to protect their international reputations by heavy borrowing, thereby deferring the funding problem. Edinburgh University – which is budgeting for a £12 million shortfall over the period 2000–4 – has borrowed £40m through a bond issue to the Prudential. But there is another model – alumni giving, pioneered in America.

Scotland has played an important role in the recent expansion of alumni giving in the UK. The seminal name here is the late Henry Drucker. Born in New Jersey, Drucker completed a doctorate in Political Philosophy at the London School of Economics before moving to Edinburgh University in 1967. In the 1980s he set up Edinburgh's fledgling development office, drawing on the American model of structured alumni funding.

The US Ivy League universities are not state-funded, although federal research monies are very important. Instead they depend heavily on student fees and alumni giving. Harvard received nearly half a billion dollars in private donations in 1999 alone – more than the Scottish Executive aims to spend per annum on all the Scottish universities by 2004. Of course Harvard is exceptional but the spirit of private giving to one's university is central to how America runs its higher education. Of US private universities, some twenty-six receive more than a $100m per year each from their former students. The picture is the same in the public-sector universities. The University of Wisconsin at Madison received $ 245m in personal giving in 1999.

As a result of generous giving over the decades, US universities – especially the Ivy League – have built up huge endowments. Harvard has over $15b in income-bearing assets. Texas A&M, doyen of the American public sector universities, has some $350b. Over 100 of the top public universities in the United States can boast endowment funds in excess of $100m. Rice University, for instance, has an annual endowment income of around £700,000 per student. Edinburgh and Glasgow have only around £500 per student.

It was this kind of alumni giving that Henry Drucker first sought to import into Edinburgh University back in the 1980s. On the basis of this early successful experiment, he was invited to become director of development at Oxford University in 1987. He launched the Campaign for Oxford in 1988 with the ambitious target (for then) of £220m. It closed in 1994 having raised £341m. Drucker introduced into British and Scottish staples of alumni relations that now seem obvious: the database, the alumni magazine, and dedicated staffing.

Nevertheless, though all Scottish universities now have structured alumni giving projects – Edinburgh remains the most successful, following Drucker's lead – the income remains marginal to need. Edinburgh University gets around £2m per year in donations and trust monies. Glasgow University initiated a very professional fund-raising campaign in the early 1990s which has raised some £6m – good by UK standards but not in the American league. Partly this is due to the lack of a philanthropic culture in the UK. Partly it is the continuing dominance of state support. And partly it is the failure of Scottish universities to grasp the sheer scale of the resources needed to extract significant alumni giving on a sustainable basis. Sir Alan Langlands, the principal of Dundee University, refers to the prestigious Johns Hopkins University, where he is a member of the advisory board of their Bioethics Institute. Hopkins has an endowment of $580m and a team of 200 staff solely devoted to running the alumni giving department. Langlands says Scottish universities are 'light years away' from this kind of set-up.

One place where the American approach to alumni giving is being vigorously pursued is Aberdeen University, under the guidance of Duncan Rice, its principal since 1996. A Scot, Rice taught History at Harvard and Yale and saw at first-hand how tenacious the US universities are at seeking donations from alumni. At New York State he helped in a campaign to raise $1b. Now, under his leadership, Aberdeen is planning to raise £150m by 2010 – it has already raised over £40m. It already matches bigger Edinburgh in capturing annual donations and legacies.

One delightful aspect of the new awareness of grooming alumni has been the explosion in granting honorary degrees to a much wider selection of former students (and sometimes just to the great, rich and famous with some tenuous connection to the local area). The once staid Glasgow University handed out thirty-two honorary degrees to celebrate its 550th anniversary in 2001. Those receiving them included motor racing legend Sir Jackie Stewart, TV presenter Kirsty Wark, the Cabinet minister Lord Macdonald, American astronaut John Young, and Britain's Chief Rabbi, Dr Jonathan Sacks. At an earlier celebration that summer, Glasgow also conferred an honorary degree on the comedian Billy Connolly. To some, this is just Davie's *Democratic Intellect* in a populist guise. To others, it is a crude attempt at publicity combined with a brazen pandering to rich celebrities who might open their wallets. Harry Reid, former editor of the *Glasgow Herald*, was recently awarded two honorary degrees, one from Glasgow University, the other from Edinburgh. He commented: 'To receive one honorary degree is ostentatious. To receive two is vulgar.'

HOW BIG IS BIG?
SOCIAL INCLUSION AND THE QUEST FOR STUDENT NUMBERS

In June 2000, while still Minister with Responsibility for Higher Education, Henry McLeish took time to denounce Edinburgh, St Andrews and Aberdeen Universities for failing to take more students from 'lower social-income groups'. Despite the fact that Scotland graduates a higher proportion of its population than any other European country, the class bias, or otherwise, of its university system remains an extraordinarily sensitive topic.

In fact, Scotland is leading the UK by a substantial margin in tackling social exclusion: 17% of all students in Scotland come from low participation neighbourhoods compared with a UK average of 12%. Scotland's performance on social inclusion is also improving at a faster rate than the rest of the UK. In 2002, there was a 0.7% rise in Scotland in young students from low participation neighbourhoods compared to a 0.2% rise in the rest of the UK.

The emphasis on social inclusion comes from politicians but it is hard to find much evidence that most Scottish universities, rooted in dense, industrial conurbations, have ever been anything but socially open. This has also been facilitated by the traditional, broader-based approach at secondary school. The inclusion policy has found an open door at university management level with the ready introduction of part-time courses, modular courses, open and distance learning provision; and by running access initiatives such as summer schools, collaboration with schools and further education and outreach programmes.

But the real key to social inclusion came in 1992, when five new independent universities were created out of their former polytechnic chrysalis: Glasgow Caledonian University (GCU), Napier University in Edinburgh, the University of Abertay Dundee, Paisley University, and the Robert Gordon University in Aberdeen. Size predominates in these veritable Peoples' Universities. GCU now claims 14,000 students, Napier over 12,500, Paisley over 10,000 and Robert Gordon over 8,000. These 1992 polyversities (with later additions such as Queen Margaret University College) now provide half the university places in Scotland. Servicing largely their own local labour markets, these bodies have the theoretical ability to tailor degree courses to fast-moving local needs. For instance, the unexpected emergence of Scotland as an international base for designing computer games has spawned a serious research institute at Abertay and a degree course at Paisley. But their main forte lies in the standard vocational primers of late twentieth-century post indus-trialism: business studies, communications, hospitality management, health studies and computing.

However, despite this massive development, it is nevertheless true that the richest seventh of Scotland are still five times more likely to go into higher education than the poorest seventh. There is no evidence that this is due to deliberate exclusion by universities. More likely, given the mass penetration of universities in Scotland, the problem lies outside higher education altogether – at secondary level where many students still fail to gain the necessary entry qualifications for university or learn the skills for advanced study.

There is also a reverse side to a social inclusion policy based on crude numbers enrolled. Firstly, it ignores the drop-out rate. In the late 1990s, the highest drop-out rates were found in Glasgow Caledonian, Paisley and Napier, all of which attract large numbers of students from deprived backgrounds. The standard explanation for high drop-out rates in the Scottish universities is student poverty. But another valid reason is that marginally performing students in a mass teaching environment will have special learning difficulties. In 1938, the big four traditional Scottish universities had 10,000 students between them. The number was still only 18,599 in 1960. But in 1998–9, Glasgow and Edinburgh each had to manage over 15,000 undergraduate students. This ballooning of students numbers inside each university is in stark contrast to the political injunction in the primary and secondary schools for ever lower class sizes.

Secondly, degrees for marginal students don't automatically lead to good jobs, or even any job. According to the Higher Education Statistics Agency, nearly 20% of those who graduated from British universities in the summer of 2000 could not find a job immediately. Two of the three worst institutions for poor graduate employment were Scottish: Paisley, with an unemployment record of 14%; and Dundee Abertay, with 12%. Paisley and Abertay could reasonably counter that both service local labour markets with higher than average unemployment and that they have a preponderance of immobile, local students. But it also suggests that prioritising university degrees over shorter, flexible HNCs or HNDs is not always the best way to go when it comes to meeting local labour market needs.

Thirdly, the huge Scottish student population is also having an effect on outward migration. Almost 85% of Scottish-domiciled students obtaining a first degree enter work, training or further study in Scotland. That suggests that something like 15% every year are leaving the country with a portable skill. And that may help explain why Scotland is the only region of the UK with a declining population. Finally, the emphasis on undergraduate education has been at the expense of postgraduates.

TO CHARGE OR NOT TO CHARGE? THE TOP-UP DEBATE

The social inclusion debate returned with a vengeance in late 2002. Prime Minister Tony Blair announced the government would seek to raise English student participation at university to the 50% level found in Scotland. The financial demands this would make led to a proposal from Margaret Hodge, the English Higher Education Minister, that universities should be allowed to set individual top-up fees. This was effectively a deregulation of fees designed to make middle-class families contribute more towards the cost of undergraduate tuition. Another advantage claimed was for science courses, where existing state subventions usually fail to cover marginal teaching costs because of the need for sophisticated equipment.

Immediately, there were voices in Scotland which rejected the idea of top-up fees. Some argued it was an irrelevant issue north of the border as, unlike England, most undergraduate students are currently exempted from fees regardless of family income. The Scottish Executive made it plain it had no interest in sanctioning top-up fees while David Caldwell, Director of Universities Scotland (the umbrella body representing twenty-one Scottish universities and colleges of higher education) wrote in *The Scotsman* (20 November 2002):

> Wider participation will suffer unless students from poorer families continue to be exempted from payment for tuition. If they are not, the consequence will be that they are largely excluded from the universities charging the highest fees, creating a system that is more and not less socially divided. Some universities charging high fees would cater mainly for students from wealthy families, and others charging lower fees for the remainder. Universities cannot be expected to resolve this problem by varying their fees in relation to family income: redistribution is a political decision for government to take, not a matter to be delegated to the higher education system.

This was the long arm of Davie's *Democratic Intellect* argument in contemporary guise: universities, as the cradle of citizenship, should be free to enter (if only theoretically). But the price exacted in the modern world is domination by the state and the loss of academic freedom – thus Caldwell was forced to end his article with the standard denunciation of the Executive for under-funding the universities. There is also the suspicion that lurking in Caldwell's arguments is the fact that Scottish universities are loath to enter competition with each other.

Besides, his argument that top-up fees necessarily lead to class differentiated universities is belied by the US experience. As was seen in the discussion over endowments, in the American Ivy League student admission is by a 'needs-blind' process. They want the most able students, so the university will only discuss finance with the applicant once they have been accepted. A package of grant, loan and campus employment can then be arranged towards the cost of tuition and board, paid out of the Ivy League's huge endowment income.

The significant thing about the top-up debate is the fact that it produced no new thinking on the part of opponents, barring to ask for more taxpayers' cash. Britain invests far less of its national income in higher education than France, Ireland, Australia, Canada, or the US. As a result, only eighty of the world's most cited scientists work in Britain. Short of a truly massive switch in resources, this funding gap is set to continue. Inevitably, perhaps with the advent of economic recession, the fees debate is certain to reappear.

CONCLUSIONS: THE 'SCOTTISHNESS' OF SCOTTISH UNIVERSITIES

In the late 1970s, only one Scottish institution opposed the principle of devolution – the combined Scottish universities. Here was the heartland of the Scottish psyche. Here was Davie's *Democratic Intellect* incarnate. And here lay the bastion of the middle-class professions – lawyers, accountants, teachers, clerics – who stood to gain if there was a Scottish parliament to protect their separate Scottish fiefdoms. But the universities succeeded in their campaign to be excluded from the remit of the ill-fated 1979 Assembly project. Why did the universities turn traitor, as some were wont to put it? More to the point, why did they change their minds?

The gut reaction on the nationalist side was to see the universities as having been anglicised. This was crudely put down to the influx of non-Scottish staff and students after the great expansion of the 1960s. On the Labour devolutionary left, the explanation was the supposed class elitism of the universities. Neither argument held much water. Scottish universities were as dominated by Scots students and academics. Indeed, heavyweight academic immigrants like Professor Chris Smout, at Edinburgh University, were immediately incorporated into the local culture: Smout's *A History of the Scottish People* (Glasgow: Collins, 1969) can be seen as the renaissance of modern Scottish historiography and therefore views on national identity. The American Henry Drucker was the mentor of Gordon Brown and a fierce polemicist for devolution.

The real explanation for the anti-devolution stance was money. The shift towards state funding had begun in 1918 with the creation of the all-UK University Grants Committee. In the era of expansion in the 1960s and 1970s, the Scottish universities opposed a separate Scots funding body because they were concerned they would receive fewer resources than their English counterparts. But come Mrs Thatcher, the entire Scottish establishment, including the universities, decided that devolution was a better way of protecting local interests than integration with UK bodies. Paradoxically, it would be the Conservative government of John Major that finally devolved Scottish higher education (in 1992) with the transformation of the Scottish polytechnics into universities and their merger with the existing universities under the new Scottish Higher Education Funding Council (SHEFC).

This episode explains much about the cultural and political significance of the universities in Scottish society: far from being English cultural incursions they remain the beating heart of the Scottish establishment. Take the case of Sir William Kerr Fraser. Between 1978 and 1988, he was the Permanent Under Secretary at the pre-devolution Scottish Office. From there he moved to become the principal and vice chancellor of Glasgow University. Subsequently, on retirement, he became the university's titular head as chancellor. From 2003, Glasgow's principal will be none other than Sir Muir Russell, the first Permanent Secretary at the new Scottish Executive. This smooth transition between public and university civil service provoked much press comment. The *Scotsman* leader noted: 'To some, this will smack of the kind of Scotland that devolution was supposed to end: administration by an anonymous elite.' Others would suggest this was precisely what devolution was meant to ensure. At any rate, it indicates that devolution has not reduced the social role of Scotland's universities, quite the reverse.

Aside from the narrow, mechanistic debates over social inclusion and job creation, what evidence is there that the universities are playing a radical intellectual role in the new Scotland as they did during the Enlightenment period? Here the jury is still out. While the Scottish universities have maintained a global presence in high technology research, their international impact in the arts and social sciences has diminished. The technical revolution in free market and liberal economics of the past thirty years failed to gain much of a local academic foothold outside of St Andrews, condemning the home of economic science to a virtual backwater. The Scottish history departments are influential at home but stand accused of a cosy parochialism which justifies a corporatist, self-satisfied view of the nation, despite its low economic growth and collapsing population.

In the new media, institutions like Abertay can point to their swift involvement in computer games animation teaching and research. But where is the Scottish film school after a century when that medium has dominated culture? And the universities remain dominated by the Central Belt. If there have been other failures in respect of a debt owed to

Scottish culture, one of the most glaring is the scandal and chaos surrounding the creation of the University of the Highlands and Islands. After much managerial muddle the project is in danger of being scaled down to an archipelago of rural colleges.

George Davie's concept of the *Democratic Intellect* was a mythologising of the Scottish dream – middle-class and working-class – that a good education was an infallible passport to the good life. But the Faustian bargain of mass university expansion has been a dependency on state financing and state educational targets. Post-devolution, the Scottish universities are being forced to rethink that bargain. Their ultimate choices will reshape not just themselves but the Scottish nation.

78

Current Priorities in Higher Education

Stewart Sutherland

EXTERNAL AND INTERNAL PRESSURES

Priorities come from two sources, external and internal. If they are really serious they come from both directions simultaneously.

The major priority facing Scottish higher education is serious in just that way: the need to define its corporate and several individual identities. In the United Kingdom over the last twenty-five years or so a process of displacement has been sweeping through higher education and what has been displaced is the sense of worth and identity. The old certainties of what universities and colleges were, and were for, have been washed out of the system by successive tides of change and revolution. With these certainties have gone the sense of self-direction and self-definition. Whether this is good, bad or indifferent is not the point: all three terms apply to different aspects of the process. What is clear, however, is that in this respect, the experience of Scottish higher education institutions has been no different from that of cousins south of Hadrian's Wall.

The changes which have brought this about are well documented elsewhere in this volume. The expansion of the number of Scottish universities in one lifetime from four to thirteen, plus the Open University and others in the offing, is dramatic. In the same post-war period, the age participation rate measuring the proportion of the 18-year-old cohort experiencing higher education has increased from just over 2% immediately after the war to around 50% in Scotland currently. The size of the largest individual Scottish university now tops 20,000 students.

These changes in themselves, largely driven from outside, but compliantly accepted, have had several significant but often unnoticed implications which affect the internal character of the institutions. It is now impossible for members of staff, academic or otherwise, to know more than a minority of colleagues by appearance, let alone as fellow members of a recognisable collegiate community. If Newman's account of the 'Idea of a University' ever had wide application, it is virtually unrecognisable now.

The consequences for self-regulation and what has now come to be recognised, albeit reluctantly, as the need for management, has inevitably changed the character of internal relations. Significantly increased student–staff ratios have altered the once reasonably intimate nature of teaching, and research has become too closely identified with the funds necessary to carry it out.

Basically, the higher education system in Scotland and the United Kingdom has become

mass higher education. The people affected have yet to adjust fully to the meaning of this –
and 'people' includes universities, employers, parents, and governments and their funding
agencies. The central current priority is to adjust to this changed situation and in essence
this means reconstructing a sustainable account of what a university is, what a higher
education system is meant to be as well as to do.

Universities have become increasingly reactive over the last twenty years or so. Instead of
helping to form national and international agenda they have reacted to the place defined for
them in these agendas by others. In part this is a result of having to pay the price of
becoming heavily dependent on the public purse, and in part a result of the corollary of
what came to be seen as the burden which this created – a steady but compound slicing of
the unit of resource. Gradually the focus of university activity was adjustment to downward
financial pressure which took the form of an academic version of genteel middle-class
decline, patching a tutorial programme here and stitching together the overstretched
laboratory budget there. A particular issue that continues to trouble university principals
and their staff is whether to introduce top-up fees to supplement income from the public
purse and other sources. This opens up the prospect of a seriously divided system, with
students of modest backgrounds being unable to attend the best universities. Interestingly,
the Cubie settlement in Scotland (see Chapters 6 and 13) is now being looked at as a possible
model for arrangements throughout the UK.

Whatever the future of university funding, survival in one form or another has become
the order of the day. In fact most universities are becoming rather street-wise and, within
limitations, moderately successful in adapting to harder times. In the process, however, the
acquired skills of coping with a little bit of this and a little bit less of that have become the
replacement for a self-confident participation in national agenda-setting.

REDEFINING THE PURPOSE OF HIGHER EDUCATION

If the central priority for now is definition of the nature and future of higher education,
what is the detailed shape of the questions which that raises? A visual aid which bears some
resemblance to a completed game of noughts and crosses may offer some help.

            T   R   X
            R   N   I
            T   R   C

Old hands at the game of university acronyms will recognise the first line, T, R and X.
These are the letters used by David Phillips in the mid-1980s to open up a debate about the
academic focus of various universities and university departments. Some, it was implied,
would be research-led (R), some would lay particular emphasis upon teaching (T), and
others (X) would have a mixed focus of, in the case of institutions, having some departments
research-led and others focused primarily on teaching.

Part of the search for definition must be for each institution, and each sub-section, to
define themselves and their aspirations against such benchmark terms and realities. That
has difficulties of its own: but even more difficult, although at least as necessary in a
Scottish context, is to take a view of the emphasis of R, X and T across the system. The
advantage which Scotland has is that, granted the size of the system, this is an achievable
aim. The fundamental questions are essentially of definition. What should a Scottish higher

education system be? And then, what should it look like? In part those questions come with increasing force from the system. But equally importantly they should and do come from within. It is necessary to ask how academic staff and activities should have altered as the system increased the number of degree awarding institutions from four universities to thirteen plus several other colleges. Equally should the menu offered to nearly 50% of the age cohort be uniformly the same throughout the system, and simply a cheaper form of what was offered to 3% of the age cohort fifty years ago?

Such questions should be asked of itself by any respectable higher education system, as well as of themselves by each of its members. One thing is sure: the questions will be pressed from outside as will unsuitable answers if there is a failure of resolve to tackle them. Another certainty is that individual universities as well as faculties and departments will have to set priorities which define roles and individualities. It is not best use of scarce resource and talent if everybody tries to do everything.

REGIONAL, NATIONAL AND INTERNATIONAL ROLES

This leads appropriately to the second line of noughts and crosses. Here (R) stands for Regional, (N) stands for National and (I) stands for International. Universities must define themselves in terms of regional, national and international focus. Whom do they serve? Where do graduates seek employment? What are the continuing education and professional development activities which should be part of the institution's profile? Where should research and development activity find its external partners? Is the profile realistic and compatible with what else is on offer in the region or city?

The issues of regional and national strategies and roles have been shuffling steadily to the forefront of the stage over the last fifteen years or so. In one sense they are not unannounced, for old and new universities and colleges have played important local roles for, in some cases, hundreds of years. But there is a new edge to this as the political frontiers of both Scotland and the United Kingdom change. In Scotland, the rebirth of the Scottish Parliament has brought renewed focus and scrutiny to the contribution which the totality of higher education makes to the health and well-being of the Scottish nation and its economy. The answers already given are very positive, but there is no doubt that the questions will become sharper and more insistent. Some questions may even be misdirected, but for institutions to say so and be convincing will require a stronger sense of self-identity than they possess now.

Each university in Scotland has a regional focus: all have a national role and the variations in the forms which each of these takes will be complemented by an even wider variation of international profiles. The process of self-definition which is the precondition of a sense of identity will involve institutions clarifying, department by department, whether the nature and extent of regional and national commitments does or should include international dimensions. They cannot all be, indeed perhaps none of them can be, the Harvard of the East Atlantic, but areas of some institutions should have the aspiration and confidence to set such benchmarks against which to measure progress and development.

What Scotland certainly does have is the mass higher education system of the East Atlantic and the corollary of that is that there is a need for the variety and diversity of the most experienced and successful mass higher education system in the world. One startling statistic from there: of the 3,000 or so accredited degree-awarding institutions in the USA only 10% are licensed to award doctoral degrees. Now that is diversity with attitude. It is not being suggested that the same proportions would be transportable to Scotland, but at least there is a question to be asked.

COMMUNITY

The third line of the puzzle has a different set of questions, but a set which none the less encompasses much that has gone before. (T) stands for teaching and (R) for research, and these are the two terms around which most academics would seek to construct a redefinition of institutional identify. These surely lie at the core of higher education activities and hence of institutional identity. Of that there is no doubt, and what remains is to define individually for each institution where the balance between these lies.

However, to restrict the enquiry to these two categories in self-definition has perhaps been one of the ways in which institutions have played a part in side-tracking themselves from broader involvement. 'Involvement in what?' is a reasonable rejoinder to that claim. The answer is contained in (C) – (C) for community.

There are several key points here. The first is that in focusing upon (T) and (R) in the account of identity, universities abstract themselves, or at least seem to do so, from context. There is no context-free social institution. To leave space for such a misconception – either internally or externally – is to leave room for all the tedious, but dangerously alive metaphors of ivory towers. Aristophanes' portrayal of a philosopher living in a barrel on top of a long pole was meant to be a joke, not a model for academic success! In reality a philosopher who lives on top of a pole is not long for this world: the same is true of institutions which sought to be ivory towers. The fact that universities, after cathedrals, are European civilisation's most enduring institutions shows the fallacy of the ivory tower jibe.

However, if an attempt is made to define identity without reference to the communities in which universities are located – by reference to teaching and research alone as if they were abstract and abstractable activities – they give credence in many minds, including some within the institutions themselves, to the view that they exist outside or above society. This has shown itself in a number of ways. Most obvious has been the wish to bring universities to heel. Certainly until recently this was a widely shared perception amongst some politicians who regarded universities as too aloof, amongst some industrialists and officials of, for example, such quangos as Scottish Enterprise, who wished to blame universities for any perceived weaknesses in the Scottish economy.

It is a perception which universities have shared as they have responded to the parallel external wish to clip wings by cutting public resources, by defining the relationship to communities in terms of 'Them' unjustly denying 'Us' the necessary funds to carry out teaching and research in a traditional manner. That way lies increasing isolation and poverty.

The counter-proposal is once again to recognise as one of the planks in the platform of self-definition that universities belong to communities and that the only healthy future lies in dialogue and conversation, no doubt robust at times, as members of that community. The University of Edinburgh, for example, was founded as the 'Tounis' university as was the University of London a creation of citizens of London in the 1820s, self-consciously drawing upon the Edinburgh experience of two centuries and more earlier. Each university can recount relevant chapters in its own history and the point is that these chapters are not historical accidents, they are founding and defining events.

It is not, of course, being argued that the way to redefine identity is to become some sort of academic fundamentalist, with universities defining themselves purely historically by what has been. Quite the reverse. The stress on community is stress upon what is living, moving and changing. A university must define itself within, as well as beyond (and possibly against), that community.

The trick, in part, is to decide what for any institution counts as 'its' community. (R), (N) and (I) are all selectively relevant here and again the mix will vary for each institution and in some cases for each department. The point is that in the model which has been offered, (C) is a variable, but it is not an optional extra.

The fundamental plea as a first and almost all-consuming priority, is for a restatement of the identity of institutions as members of a community with a distinctive contribution to bring to that community. That contribution is in part defined as helping the community and its members to flourish, but not simply as providing the means to predetermined ends: rather also to take part in the continuing debate about ends and means and in the definition and setting of ends. Universities have lost their place in such a discussion and this is a sign of the extent to which they have been complicit in their own gradual devaluation. They must start regaining that place not by standing off and shouting, but by first reassuring themselves about their own identity and by responding positively to the opportunities opened up by post-devolution Scotland.

79

From Adult and Continuing Education to Lifelong Learning

Paul Standish

'We will work closely with our partners to provide a safe, welcoming and supportive environment where you can make guided choices about what, how and when you learn.' This, the pledge of leandirectscotland, invites you to 'get into learning the pain free way . . . Whether you want to learn for work or for yourself we have thousands of learning opportunities for you to choose from. Have a look at our *learning opportunities search* to find one that's right for you.' And if you are not sure where to start there is advice available: to help you find the type of learning that's right for you, whether in a classroom, in a learning centre, at work or at home; and to consider the learning style that suits you best.

Learndirect was established by the Scottish Executive Enterprise and Lifelong Learning Department. Much has been written about the now common connection between enterprise, industry and education, as reflected in institutional structures in Scotland and south of the border. The related change that has occurred in organisations that ten years ago styled themselves as centres for 'adult' or 'continuing education' is no less marked. The ubiquitous use of 'lifelong learning' means that these terms are fast becoming anachronisms. At the time of writing only one university in Scotland has a department retaining the former terms in its title. 'Lifelong learning' is, of course, an emotive and contested term, one that raises critical questions about what is to come under its name. But it enters an educational discourse in which the practices and their boundaries have never been easy to define.

For many the phrase 'adult and continuing education' most readily brings to mind the work of the university extra-mural department, an arm of the institution reaching out beyond its body of mainstream courses to extend educational opportunity at university level to members of the wider community. In some respects this has seemed an epitome of liberal education – non-examined, subjects pursued for their own sake, committed university teachers sharing their enthusiasms. Plainly this is a paradigm under threat. But this is but one of the range of ways that adults are, and have been, educated in Scotland. If we look again at the terms in question here, this will help to lead beyond the university to other types of provision.

Let us ask then: what is adult education? How appropriate is it to write about adult education as a discrete entity? Before considering the importance of adult education, or the desirability that it should be 'continuing', it should be recognised that the categorisation raises problems of two kinds. First, how clear is it as a category? The category of 'adult' is itself problematic: the legal definition of the age of majority does not correspond with the various distinctions that have commonly been made in educational practice. There is a vast range of circumstances in which adults are engaged in education and the gap between this and the way that adult education is often understood needs to be emphasised. (Statistics in this field should then be regarded with a degree of caution.) The second, however, is ethical and political: how desirable is it to maintain the use of the category? What's in a name, one might be inclined to say? But inasmuch as this and the range of related overlapping terms are names for institutional practices, this stabilises and strengthens differentiations of funding, organisation, pedagogy, and self-conception. So the terminology does have a bearing on how adult education develops. Where different terms are linked with different organisations, disputes about who is in control and who-is-to-pay-for-what can become critical. It is worth asking who has the responsibility and who has the power, and this needs to be done in terms of the evolution of the practice.

The early history of adult education in Scotland reveals a variety of developments. In the early eighteenth century an important role was played by small local libraries and by night classes in parish schools. In the universities pioneering work was done first by John Anderson at Glasgow University and then by George Birkbeck at the Andersonian Institute (now Strathclyde University). While Birkbeck's lectures for artisans did not always receive due recognition from the universities themselves, it is clear that there was an enthusiastic response from his students. After four years, Birkbeck moved to London to continue his work, and the continuing reputation of Birkbeck College in the University of London is a tribute to his success. In 1821 the first independent Mechanics' Institute (later to become Heriot-Watt University) was established to 'afford instruction to the labouring classes'. By 1850 there were fifty-five such institutes (compared with 610 in England – significantly fewer in proportion). According to Birkbeck, Scots were in a better position to take advantage of adult education than the English. They were more likely to have had a sound basic education (through the parish schools) and there was a stronger tradition of adult learning. For example, more than one-tenth of Gaelic school pupils in the Highlands in 1849 were over twenty years of age. In the middle of the century there were 438 evening schools in Scotland catering for around 15,000 adult pupils. Following Birkbeck's lead, two other Scots, James Stuart and Patrick Geddes, also played important roles in the development of university extra-mural education. Stuart, while at Cambridge, established the University Extension Movement. Geddes organised the first international summer school in Europe, which was held in Scotland in 1887. Later growth in adult education was slow, relative to that in England and Wales, perhaps in part for reasons of geography and accessibility. This needs to be seen, however, in the light of the surprising difference in participation in university education between Scotland and England and Wales. In 1868 the Argyll Commission found that in Scotland proportionately six times as many students received a university education, one-fifth of all Scottish university students having working-class origins.

In the latter half of the twentieth century, the climate has become progressively more favourable to adult education, although this progress has not been without its setbacks and distortions. Generalisation here is difficult because of the diversity. In the decades following the Second World War adult education was offered by a wealth of smaller voluntary organisations with developing services on the part of museums and art galleries, the library service, and public broadcasting. But four main providers stand out. Local education authorities' provision constituted the largest share of the work, while this was consistently complemented by that of the Workers' Education Association and the university extra-mural departments. The Education (Scotland) Act (1945) led to the evolution of the youth and community service, which attempted to offer a comprehensive service for young people and adults. This service developed outside of and as a complement to the mainstream provision of schooling, further education, higher education, and many aspects of adult education. The relationship between these providers and the Community Education Service has not always been harmonious – because of difficulties of demarcation and disparate administrative structures, but also as a result of a difference in outlook, the Community Education Service being committed more to setting up programmes within the community and building on community initiatives. This illustrates well the way that a term can be pivotal for practice, and it suggests the kinds of consequences that may follow too insistent an emphasis on 'adult education'. For all the considerable merits of the Community Education Service, certain uses of the term 'community' themselves undermined the possibility of more inclusive conceptions of community involving mainstream provision through schools and colleges (see Chapter 96).

The diverse opportunities that emerged in the decades towards the end of the twentieth century represented the passage of adult education from margin to mainstream. Adults came to be welcomed in all sectors of secondary and tertiary education. Adult guidance services developed. Company training was extended and broadened. Tax relief was provided for non-advanced vocational education and career development loans for those training on their own initiative. Research into adult education became a major priority for public funding. Perhaps most dramatic of all was the increase in adult participation in mainstream university courses.

It is worth pausing to consider how and why this comparatively recent growth came about. A key document that laid the way for change is the Alexander Report, *Adult Education: The Challenge of Change* (1975). Appointed in 1970, the committee was given the following brief:

> To consider the aims appropriate to voluntary leisure time courses for adults which are educational but not specifically vocational; to examine the extent to which these are being achieved at present; and with due regard to the need to use available resources most effectively, to make recommendations.

A starting point for the committee's extensive deliberation and consultation was the recognition that, while there had been increases in participation in the preceding two decades, many people, and certain sections of the population especially, were not benefiting from adult education. By 1973 only 4.45% of the adult population was participating. Most of the students were female and there was an imbalance between young and older adults (15% were under twenty-five while 25% were over fifty-five years old); only 0.2% of young working-class males attended adult education classes. Moreover, over 80% of participants were in the top three socio-economic classes, with most students having educational qualifications higher than average. And the 'iron law' of adult education was demonstrated: that those who receive it come back for more. The restricted nature of that participation was something the committee wanted to address. Much attention was given, therefore, to finding ways in which barriers to access to education might be removed – barriers to do with location and accommodation, with style of teaching, with subject matter, with the timetabling of classes, with lack of crèche facilities, with lack of marketing, and with traditional prejudices.

The committee recognised the need to address the issue of adult education in the light of a changing world. Changes in technology and demography, and increases in leisure time, presented new challenges. New possibilities of a democratic way of life were to be exploited, extending beyond the ballot box to participation in community and workplace organisation. There was a growing understanding of education as continuing and as being something broader than a training of the intellect. The child-centred progressive movements of the 1960s (and before), and perhaps increasing awareness of the work of Paolo Freire, had laid the way for a new commitment to learner-centredness in adult education. Against the subject-based curriculum, a broader approach that would enhance the learner's capability and flexibility was advocated. In addition the increasing demand for higher education – and the need to enhance access to this – was acknowledged. The reaffirmation of individuality through education was seen as an important means of resisting the dehumanising aspects of work and the impact of the mass media. Furthermore, education for change was thought necessary to equip people to deal with the increasing unpredictability of lives lived in a pluralistic society and in an expanding arena for choice. While the growing desire for that choice was again seen as a healthy reflection of democracy, a more rounded sense of what this might amount to was evident in the committee's emphasis on community development, and on social and political education that promoted consideration of the environment, that bridged the educational gap between the younger and older generations, that brought together different professional groups, and that advanced the public understanding of technology and society. It is not surprising that in their recognition of the challenge of change the committee advocated a raised profile for adult education staff with 200 additional full-time posts, better career and training opportunities, and wider awareness of adult education through BEd programmes.

In concluding its statement of aims, the committee quoted the words of Sir Eric Ashby's William F. Harvey Memorial Lecture in 1955:

> We live in a society which confers on the worker (irrespective of whether he is manual or clerical and irrespective of the amount of education he has) political responsibility, civic rights, and leisure. The contemporary problem in adult education is that among many people at all levels of education the leisure is without purpose, the civic rights are without significance, and the political responsibility is assumed without understanding. We are learning the hard way that social emancipation without personal emancipation is of little value. In a world noisy with the organs of mass communication and riddled with propaganda, modern man is hard put to it to preserve his status as an individual. To help preserve this status is the contemporary task for adult education.

The committee judged that, in the twenty years since these remarks had been made, the imperative for change had intensified. With some zeal, therefore, it opposed the prevailing view of adult education as a marginal enterprise and stressed the need for a national policy committed to lifelong education.

When one looks back at the recommendations of the Alexander Report, they seem for the most part unsurprising. Many recommendations were for practices that are relatively familiar today, practices that adult educators have come to regard as their stock in trade. Yet this is misleading on two counts. First, it does not do justice to the visionary element in the report, arising as it did in a context that was very different. But second, it would be equally wrong therefore to conclude that the report immediately ushered in a period of reform. The truth is that there ensued a period of disappointingly slow development, largely because of economic constraints. Attendance at LEA traditional adult classes declined, partly because of increases in fees and the lack of subsidy for non-vocational education. Scottish Office funding was withdrawn from university continuing education departments and from Newbattle Abbey, Scotland's only residential college for adult education. Central government funding for adult basic education stopped. Voluntary organisations came under increased financial pressure. Nevertheless development was seen in some areas: there was a new drive to combat adult illiteracy, in which the BBC played a prominent part; adult participation in formal education – especially university education – increased; and open learning came onto the wider scene as an important innovation and a signal for later developments.

After 1985 the picture brightened. Colleges of further education generally became better adjusted to the needs of those who were previously excluded. Crèches were provided and classes timetabled to suit the needs of parents of young children. Institutions altered their style and their presentation – at reception, in the classroom, in the library, in the canteen – to attract students who lacked confidence or who would otherwise find the institutional environment alien. Participation rates increased substantially with growing provision of adult educational guidance. Research expanded – especially into such areas as access, open learning, the participation of women and ethnic minorities, staff development, learning effectiveness, and the relationship between industry and further and higher education – notwithstanding the closure in 1991, as a result of a reduction in the funding for voluntary institutions, of the Scottish Institute for Adult and Continuing Education. If courses promoting access to higher education were the flagship of development during this period, achievements in extending continuing education at lower levels should not be underestimated, even if there remained much to be done.

The government document most clearly focused on adult education during this period was the HMI Report *The Education of Adults in Scotland*, published in 1992. This report noted approvingly the increased level of collaboration and cross-sectoral cooperation amongst providers, and was particularly influential in bringing to wider attention the importance of regional integrated networks for adult guidance. It encouraged the flexibility of delivery that was becoming more apparent, seeing this as a key factor in the further removal of barriers to access. The report did not set out to comment on vocational education but, in language that would have come less naturally to the authors of the Alexander Report, it did affirm that 'Investment in wider access is likely to be cost-effective' (p. 2). Moreover, progress in terms of flexibility and collaboration was explicitly attributed to improvements in 'marketing, planning, delivery and evaluation of provision'.

It is very much this rhetoric that characterises the 1997 Scottish Office White Paper *Raising the Standard*, proclaimed by Michael Forsyth as 'a radical vision of an education and training system in which schools, colleges, universities, teachers, and training providers focus on quality and standards' (p. 1). Rather than being especially radical, however, the report is characterised by its endorsement of familiar trends. Regarding adult education it follows the 1992 document in stressing the importance of adult guidance and in advocating collaboration between sectors to establish a 'complex grid of relationships making up a forward-looking community education service' (p. 44). Community education here comes to be seen more clearly as part of the common enterprise of the different institutions. In the rhetoric, however, the idea of community education is increasingly subordinated to that of lifelong learning, and this tends to be seen in terms of an emphasis on skills acquisition and qualifications that partially displaces liberal aims. With the change of government the enthusiasm for these changes was unabated. In 1998, introducing *Opportunity Scotland*, Donald Dewar extolled the virtues of lifelong learning as 'a crucial element of the Government's agenda to promote opportunity through tackling social exclusion, helping people back to work and extending new learning opportunities through initiatives such as the National Grid for Learning and the University for Industry'. The document expressed a readiness to celebrate the development that had already taken place: by 1996–7, 53% of FE students were aged twenty-five or over, compared with one third a decade before; 48% of entrants to HE were over twenty-five compared with one in six a decade before; and in an average week 256,000 adults were participating in community education programmes.

Contrary to any suggestions of radical change, however, the trend throughout the last two decades has been towards flexible delivery of a curriculum that is, if not directly vocational, orientated towards the economy, and that is delivered by institutions whose roles are less clearly demarcated. Change has been radical in the incorporation of the colleges of further education, in the rapid expansion of participation in further and higher education, and in the current changes in the financial support of full-time students in higher education. What are the implications of these changes and what issues does the broader development of adult education and lifelong learning raise?

CRITICAL ISSUES

The question asked at the start of this chapter of how far it is appropriate to write about adult education as a discrete entity points to two broad ways in which key issues can be identified and addressed.

The first of these involves locating developments in the education of adults and lifelong learning within a larger picture of changes in education. This approach can be illustrated by way of an example. There seems little doubt that traditional liberal adult education, where subjects are studied or other activities pursued for their own sake, is in danger of marginalisation – the paradigm under threat referred to at the start. Clear indicators of this are the shifting of resources away from uncertificated programmes and the dismantling of continuing education departments. This emphasis on certification is a reflection of the more general credentialism and accountability that increasingly characterise educational policy and practice at every level. It dovetails with the climate of instrumentalism to create the preoccupation with efficiency and effectiveness nicely evoked by Lyotard's term 'performativity'. But these problems are obviously not exclusive to adult education, and any attempt to understand the education of adults will be severely skewed if it does not take this broader background into view.

The second way in which critical understanding can be brought to bear is to focus on the distinctive features of adult education and lifelong learning. Adult education researchers and practitioners have sometimes seen it as important to delineate the special characteristics of this field and to stress its distinctiveness from wider aspects of education. What distinguishes adults from younger people is their experience, it is said, and this has a bearing on the way that they learn and on the kinds of curricula that are appropriate to them. A leading idea in this way of thinking has been Malcolm Knowles' theory of 'andragogy', while other significant influences have been Paolo Freire's liberation pedagogy and the humanistic psychology of Carl Rogers. The emphasis is often on the therapeutic and consciousness-raising potential of adult education, possibilities implicit in the Alexander Report. This approach has surely been motivated in part by the failure of educational institutions adequately to respond to adults – their tendency to confront them again with the oppressive and authoritarian regimes from which the adults have in the past themselves fled, and with an inflexibility of organisation and curriculum delivery that makes no concessions to their different practical circumstances, needs and aspirations. There is no doubt that elements of this alienating regime persist, yet there is a temptation to caricature this the better to affirm the cogency of alternative practice and to legitimate adult education as a discrete area of educational research.

Of course, these two approaches are not mutually exclusive and the challenge must in part be to find a way of recognising and responding to the broader changes in education that remembers those characteristics and needs of adult learners that have often been overlooked.

Whatever the cogency of this second approach, its practical application is inevitably complicated and likely to be reduced where the education of adults is integrated with the education of young people. The growth of access and adult returners' courses has provided new contexts where adults are educated separately, and the implication of the learning society that education will continue throughout adulthood and through work again extends the contexts of adult education. Yet even as these examples are considered, the distinction becomes increasingly blurred. With the dramatic increase in participation in further and higher education, it is not so much that adults are assimilated into the mainstream as that the mainstream changes to become partly adult. And adult education has expanded beyond its own mainstream through the Community Education Service, the LEC, Investors in People, and a wealth of voluntary and private agencies.

The evolution of practice and institutional co-ordination encouraged by policy documents in recent decades makes the categorisation of 'adult' more porous than must have seemed to be the case in 1970 when the Alexander Committee was first convened. Adult education has always been diverse and it is becoming ever less easy to generalise about the kinds of curricula adult students follow and the contexts in which they learn. To some extent the difficulties over terminology and identity here have been superseded by 'lifelong learning', itself a modulation from 'lifelong education', terms that for all their current vogue seem to date back not only to Philip Virgo's celebrated 1981 Bow Paper *Learning for Change: Training, Retraining and Lifelong Education* but to the *Final Report for the Ministry of Reconstruction, Adult Education Committee* (reprinted in Wiltshire, H. (ed.) *The 1919 Report : Final and Interim Reports, 1918–1919*, Nottingham: Nottingham University, 1980). The terms are taken by some to be nothing other than fashionable surrogates for 'continuing education', adult education by another name, though a more generous reading might find in them an exaltation of education throughout life, perhaps in the manner that Dewey advocated – education from the cradle to the grave. That education must be something that people return to repeatedly in the course of their working lives gives the term a slightly different weight, however, while the cognate idea of 'the learning organisation' heralds a world where the work-place itself has become a learning environment, where much education is related to work, and where the vocabulary of corporate finance is humanised (cf. Investors in People). 'Lifelong learning' seems to contrast with 'adult' or 'continuing education' in that, while the latter seem largely descriptive in force, the former implies a certain imperative: 'lifelong learning' is a missionary term.

The evolution of the idea of the learning society through this terminology is related very much to questions of funding, questions crucial to the future education of adults, affecting access, adult basic education, and undergraduate study. Whatever the short-term effects of current changes in policy, the problems of funding further and higher education are likely to lead to a situation in which more post-compulsory education becomes part time, especially as students pay their own fees. The distinction between full and part time is, of course, itself equivocal, being subject to the inconsistent criteria of different funding bodies, and qualified by the need of full-time students to support themselves through paid work. There are numerous and complex distinctions that need to be drawn here and these are easily glossed over. For example, juxtaposing full-time undergraduate education against the vast range of part-time further education and generalising about these matters smacks more of sectarian interests than a contribution to equity and social justice.

In tandem with the concern for efficiency, a rhetoric of greater choice and ownership of learning provides the rationale for replacing anomalous systems of public funding with individual learning accounts. Thus, it seems, education is added to a portfolio of personal financial planning and investment as people increasingly take responsibility for their own development. But how likely is it that those from the lowest socio-economic groups will avail themselves of such opportunities? People from these groups are the most likely to be deterred by the prospect of long-term investments and debts, especially those arising from a good as intangible as education. Moreover, how far does the apparent autonomy encouraged here deflect attention from a reduction in public commitment? Freire wanted to liberate people from the 'banking' conception of learning; ironically today's students may come to rely on the learning bank! The cultural change that appears to have made unacceptable the kind of increase in taxation necessary for sustained public support is also, however, one that may be newly susceptible to marketing initiatives in education. As traditional educational institutions will have neither the expertise nor the goods to market in this way, their place may be usurped by providers more centrally located in the computer industry, with all its alertness to the knowledge economy and its marketing panache.

If these measures do succeed in helping more students to pursue their education as adults, they are very much to be welcomed. But it is difficult to be confident about the wisdom of these changes. The individuation and commodification of learning here can undermine aspects of learning that, precisely because they are not easily recorded, are easily overlooked. For all the systems of advice and guidance and learning support, there is a potential isolation of the learner: the kind of friendship that can arise in the shared pursuit of a subject is eroded in favour of the supposed independence of the individual and the displacement of subject content by an emphasis on skills. Such friendship, and the larger sense of the common good of which it may be a part, are not incidental to learning. Learning that is shared – with teachers, with fellow students, and with what is studied – suggests a form of relationship for which 'community' may seem too woolly and 'stakeholder' too contractual. As several critics have pointed out, to the extent that lifelong learning is concerned with human capital, it runs the risk of exacerbating these problems. It is the richer notion of social capital that recognises the 'networks, norms and trusts' that contribute to the contexts in which individual lives have meaning (for a discussion related especially to Scotland, see Cloonan and Crossan, 2002). Such networks, norms and trusts are further jeopardised where a short-termism driven by accountability leads to the proliferation of temporary contracts and a general deskilling amongst adult educators. To resist these trends is not to eulogise exclusively liberal pursuits: in more vocational terms, the joint projects that arise with networks of trust and expert teams, and upon which industry's research and development can thrive, are also sources of social capital. If this is right it gives all the more weight to the idea of the educational institution as a locus of community. The change in student populations and diversified modes of attendance consequent upon changes in funding may require the university to become more like a college of further education in certain respects – less 'a place apart' and rather more a focal point for the local and regional community, a hub for a region's further education, continuing professional development, and research and development. Such an institution might extend through its satellite stations and outreach provision, and through virtual locations on the net with its cybercafés or 'village halls'. Inevitably there are worries about what must seem a dilution of university life and inevitably there are concerns about the erosion of standards. But the potential gains are easily underestimated – gains in terms not only of the academic benefits of the highly committed and able adult part-time students but of the democratic counterbalance to globalisation that co-operation with local industry might provide.

This section began by considering the fate of liberal education in terms of decisions about funding in a climate of efficiency and effectiveness. But in other respects also the liberal may be in conflict with a number of paradigms that currently dominate policy making and the training and professional development of practitioners. Progressive theory such as that alluded to at the start of this section has supported a therapeutic conception of practice, in many ways typical of late modern reflexivity. Student-centred learning has been partly subverted, however, by a different set of assumptions emphasising a consumerist concep-tion of choice within an extensively managed and systematic curriculum. A second paradigm, which has partly been responsible for this and which tends to shape issues of policy and funding, is the vocational/instrumental. A third, equally involved in this subversion, is the application of information technology. There are immense gains to be made through the imaginative and efficient application of new technology. Such is its seductiveness, however, that there is a danger that artificial intelligence can come to provide the dominant model for human learning, with all the ramifications for curriculum and its delivery that this implies. The extract from the learndirect website with which this chapter started indicates the ways in which ICT comes to affect the development and presentation of policy and the invitation to the potential student.

It is a mistake to think of these approaches as simply misguided. What is necessary is to dispel the hold that certain pictures have on policy-makers, researchers, and practitioners, and to challenge the vocabularies in which they seem increasingly impelled to speak. There is no doubt that we stand in need of a better, more mature, less jargon-laden language in which to speak of education. In the face of the prevailing discourse it is not surprising that the claims of liberal education are apt to sound reactionary, ill-defined, and perhaps rather dull. In defiance of such pressures, it is important that this chapter should end by reaffirming the importance of continuing liberal education.

It may be that, contrary to vocationalist assumptions, the needs of industry are best served by liberal education because this can provide the breadth and imaginative resour-cefulness that employers increasingly seek. It may be that personal growth, contrary to the expectations of many progressive educators, is best realised where students are challenged by the demands of the kind of rich subject matter that is liberal education's concern. This is to suggest the importance of some kind of initiation into those intrinsically valuable practices and forms of enquiry that are part of the cultural inheritance. This is not to uphold the cumbersome dualism of the liberal and the vocational, for the latter, where it is not narrowly instrumental, can incorporate these same qualities. Neither is what is defended here the mere transmission of that inheritance. Against the stuffy and even arcane connotations that this has, the concern here is with education that is dynamically energised: learning is an engagement leading to intense absorption. Its challenge does indeed impose a kind of responsibility on the learner, but this is of an order quite different from the responsibility for one's own learning that pervades the earnest enthusiasms of the advocates of lifelong learning. In the latter there is a kind of 'governmentality', in Foucault's phrase, that is destructive of the very values that education should enshrine and offer, that renders a kind of hollowness in the invitation extended to the student, and that, in its insensitivity to social capital, makes the encouragement to social inclusion subtly authoritarian. In contrast, a liberal education may contribute that renewal of social capital without which inclusion loses its point.

There is no doubt that the advantages offered by the prevailing paradigms seem more immediate and that they are better understood. Moreover, there is no doubting the marketing appeal of 'lifelong learning'. But it is equally clear that the practices the phrase connotes are not lifelong: so this is surely a phrase that is trying too hard, a make-over term masking perhaps a crisis of confidence and value. The task of those concerned with the education of adults must be to reaffirm a central liberal commitment, whatever extrinsic benefits this may have and whatever other activities are also rightly promoted. The picture of the extra-mural class evoked at the start of this chapter may be tinged with nostalgia but the spirit that it implies is to be realised across the broad range of adult education. There are resources within the Scottish tradition for this to be sustained, but 'lifelong learning' now makes them harder to discern.

REFERENCES

Alexander, K. et al. (1975) *Adult Education: The Challenge of Change*, report of a committee of enquiry appointed by the Secretary of State for Scotland (The Alexander Report), Edinburgh: HMSO.
Cloonan, M. and Crossan, B. (2002) Lifelong Learning: exploring the issues in an area of social deprivation in Scotland, *Scottish Educational Review*, 34 (1), 76–85.
HMI (1992) *The Education of Adults in Scotland*, Edinburgh: SOED.
Scottish Office (1997) *Raising the Standard, a White Paper on Education and Skills Development in Scotland*, Edinburgh: Scottish Office.
Virgo, P. (1981) *Learning for Change: Training, Retraining and Lifelong Education*, Bow Paper, London: Bow Publications.

80

The Open University in Scotland

Bob Glaister

THE OPEN UNIVERSITY – A UK PERSPECTIVE

The Open University (OU), which was granted its royal charter in 1969 and admitted its first students in 1971, has been widely hailed as the most important innovation in UK higher education in the last thirty years. Its underlying philosophy is illustrated by its commitment to be: 'open as to people . . . open as to places . . . open as to methods . . . and open as to ideas' (Crowther, 1969).

Established as the 'university of the second chance' and 'the university of the air' – the titles used by Harold Wilson when he first mentioned the idea in public at a Labour Party rally in Glasgow in 1963 – the OU has now developed into the largest university in the UK. It offers more than 550 courses and resource packs to well over 220,000 people every year both in the UK and mainland Europe, and, increasingly, further afield (e.g. Singapore and Ethiopia). In addition, some of its materials are adapted for collaborative use (e.g. in the Open University of Hong Kong and the Arab Open University). In total, over two million students have now studied with the university, and its impact spreads well beyond its student body as attested by the viewing figure of 2.9 million for the first TV programme of a recent OU/BBC series, *Civil War*.

It is hardly surprising that what was then such an innovative concept met with scepticism, even hostility, in some quarters in its early days, particularly because of the generally poor reputation of correspondence education and doubts about the viability of its open access policy. Most of these concerns have long since abated as a result of the recognised quality of its materials and the exit standards demanded of its students. The quality of the OU's integrated multimedia learning materials, which encompass advances in information technology, is assured by the course teams' consideration of several 'drafts', by the testimony of external assessors and, increasingly, by some form of professional accreditation. The standard of student performance, maintained by a comprehensive system of external examiners, is illustrated by the acceptance of OU graduates for postgraduate study in 'traditional' universities around the UK.

While the learning materials have been the focus of attention for academics in assessing the quality of the OU's provision, there is little doubt that, for students, the locally-based tutorial support assumes equal importance. There is a network of thirteen regional centres in the UK which support and supervise the work of nearly 8,000 part-time associate lecturers (ALs) in 300 study centres (and another forty or so elsewhere in Europe). ALs mark assignments submitted by students, provide written feedback, meet students at study centres, and offer additional personal support through correspondence, telephone and in many cases, computer conferencing.

The OU is making a very significant contribution to mass higher education (HE) in the UK by demonstrating that the possession of traditional entry qualifications is not a prerequisite for successful university study; over one-third of the OU's 270,000 graduates did not match the entry requirements for conventional universities when they enrolled. It has shown also that learning and employment can be combined: 70% of OU students remain in full-time jobs while they study. National, and indeed international, objectives for lifelong learning are made practicable. While scale and quantity are defining features of the OU, they are not attained at the expense of quality and scholarship. Indeed it may be that the first pair have been achieved because of the existence of the second. The OU has come through strongly in the comparative assessment exercises with British universities on teaching and research. For example, since 1996, it has gained an 'excellent' rating (i.e. 21 + points) for its teaching in thirteen out of fourteen subjects assessed, placing it on a par with other British universities which operate strict entrance requirements, and, in the 2001 research assessment exercise, sixteen out of twenty-six units gained a 4 or above.

The OU was, for its first twenty-one years, funded directly by government, through the Department of Education and Science (DES), latterly Department for Education and Employment (DfEE). After the 1992 Higher Education Act, it moved into the mainstream of HE funding when, although it was a UK body, it was resolved to reduce complexity and have it funded by only one of the funding councils – the Higher Education Funding Council for England (HEFCE). However, since devolution and the creation of the Scottish Parliament, it was agreed to transfer the funding of the OU's Scottish teaching to the Scottish Higher Education Funding Council (SHEFC) so that the OU's contribution in Scotland could be better integrated with the rest of Scottish HE.

Another outcome of the 1992 Act was the abolition of the Council for National Academic Awards (CNAA) whose role in validation and quality assurance for other institutions was given to the OU, as the only UK-wide institution of HE. Since 1992, OU Validation Services (OUVS) have made over 26,000 validated awards, many at postgraduate level. The university, therefore, contributes to the widening of access to HE through its own provision and by the validation of others.

THE OPEN UNIVERSITY – A SCOTTISH PERSPECTIVE

The OU in Scotland is one of the thirteen Regions mentioned earlier – region 11 – with an office in Edinburgh. There is a core salaried staff of 100, including the Scottish director, four assistant directors, and twenty academic staff representing the eight faculties and schools. There are approximately 600 part-time ALs offering tuition and counselling at the thirty-six study centres.

The OU in Scotland's application rates have, over the years, moved above and below Scotland's proportion of the UK population, 9%, but have, since 1996, steadied at that figure. While the absolute number of OU students in Scotland has continued to rise, its market share of part-time HE students in universities has dropped. There is no doubt that a partial explanation for this dip is the increased access to HE provided by other universities which are 'modularising' and offering part-time routes, placing them in clear competition with the OU for an audience for which it had previously been the only option. In this context, recent developments to extend education provision in rural areas have brought to the fore real issues about competition versus collaboration. For example, the OU is working collaboratively with the UHI Millennium Institute (UHIMI), and the OUVS are validating UHIMI awards, while at the same time UHIMI is openly planning to attract more mature part-time students in order to meet its growth targets. In the south of Scotland, ministers have decided against a university, but have given strong support to the Crichton Campus development in Dumfries as a collaborative and multi-institutional presence, with the OU in full partnership.

One of the most distinctive features of the OU in Scotland's student enrolment in the early years was the lower percentage of teachers than south of the border. Among the first ten cohorts of OU graduates, 44% were teachers, but only 37% in Scotland, which presumably reflects the fact that Scotland has traditionally had more graduate teachers. Also, some OU students already hold a degree and when one looked only at teachers graduating who had not previously held degrees, the Scottish difference was even more marked: UK 41%, Scotland 29%.

More recently, the OU has expanded into the continuing professional development and master's degree sectors. While the OU in Scotland has a very strong record in the under-graduate market, it has fared less well at postgraduate level. The two longest running OU master's degrees, the MBA and MA in Education, each recruit over 3,000 students annually in the UK, but Scotland attracts only some 6% of the total. One explanation of this phenomenon must be the level of competition: Scotland has some very strong business schools, and the four cities have offered part-time MEds (originally EdBs) to Scottish teachers for three-quarters of a century. Another possible factor which is considered more fully in the last section is that the content of these general postgraduate professional awards lack 'Scottishness'. In contrast, the professional qualification in Social Work has recruited very strongly in Scotland, with about one-third of the UK total, by developing a Scottish 'strand'.

Some of the university's newer and more specialised master's degrees, with smaller total numbers, have also recruited well in Scotland – reflecting a technological and scientific interest which has been matched over the years in the undergraduate programme where the OU in Scotland has attracted above average percentages for these areas. Table 80.1, for example, illustrates that strength in Technology in 2001. The OU continues to dominate part-time undergraduate provision in Scotland of Maths/Computing, Science and Tech-nology, with figures ranging from 52% of all part-time study in the physical sciences to 65% in the biological sciences.

Table 80.1: OU student courses in 2001 by academic area

		Scottish registrations as %	UK regs as %
Arts	1,896	11.5	13.5
Business	1,471	8.9	11.4
Education	718	4.4	5.5
Health and Social Welfare	1,670	10.2	6.8
Languages	445	2.7	3.0
Maths and Computing	2,558	15.6	16.4
Science	1,949	11.8	11.7
Social Sciences	2,801	17.0	15.5
Technology	2,942	17.9	16.2

In 1971, only 27% of the new undergraduate students were women, but across the university, including all programmes, the number of male and female students is now virtually equal; indeed there is a higher proportion of women in the undergraduate programme, but countered by a lower proportion in the postgraduate area. Over the years Scotland's share of women students has always been slightly smaller, but in 2000 it too reached 50:50, with the male:female ration in the undergraduate programme being 48:52 and at postgraduate 61:39.

Although Scotland contains only some 9% of the UK population, it is dispersed over an area which amounts to more than a third of the total UK land mass – including four major clusters of inhabited islands. This means that approximately 20% of Scottish OU students are geographically remote, so that the OU's distance teaching 'package' has had to be augmented in the Scottish context. Over the years a variety of approaches have been adopted: part-time staff with more generic roles, location counsellors, location centres (meeting places rather than formal study centres), planned use of 'old' technology, for instance fax or a loud-speaking telephone. Significant use has also been made in Scotland of telephone conferencing; ALs talking with groups of students gathered round loud-speaking phones; or conference calls whereby half a dozen students and an AL can be linked so that they can talk together no matter how widely scattered geographically. There have also been pilot projects involving video conferencing and electronic whiteboards.

Appropriate to the twenty-first century there is now a clear swing towards the use of computer technology. Whether students are geographically isolated or not, the OU has always attempted to offer the same quality of support across the UK and, indeed, to provide access to the same range of courses. Computer technology facilitates better access to a wider range of services for all, and students in remote parts of Scotland benefit; over 4,000 Scottish students are regularly 'on-line'. They are using UK-wide services which are fast expanding of which the following are a sample: one-third of applicant enquiries are now conducted through the OU's website; over 100 courses use computing as an integrated part of the learning experience; more than 160,000 OU staff and students are linked by 16,000 on-line conferences; in 2001, over 250,000 electronic articles were retrieved by OU staff and students through the Open Library service; the principal administrative and operational system processed over 51 million online transactions.

The OU in Scotland has successfully adapted the OU provision and systems to meet Scottish geography over the last thirty years and, while it has generated student registrations on a scale that compares favourably with other Scottish universities, it is still the Open University **in** Scotland and may never be the Open University **of** Scotland. With the new funding arrangements in a new Scotland, the issue for the university is how to be an Open University **for** Scotland.

ISSUES

Competitive pressures have been felt in all areas of HE – in Scotland as well as the UK generally. Most institutions of HE have developed part-time routes: many have entered the OU's preserve of distance education; all are making more intensive use of accommodation so that there is more limited access to it by the OU for study centres, residential schools, exam centres, and so on; and staff have less time to spare to teach part time for the OU. The OU's strength is that it has always adopted a collaborative approach, and while it has been threatened by the competitive ethos, that approach is the means by which it could make an even more effective contribution to HE in Scotland in the new millennium.

Being governed by remote bodies has always been a source of discontent in Scotland. Government of the OU from Milton Keynes has been a major factor impeding the further development of OU provision in Scotland, and indeed has often been a source of frustration for the staff of the OU in Scotland. With the Scottish Parliament and the OU funding transfer, there is a context within which it will be easier for the OU to make a more distinctive contribution and for the Scottish education system to recognise that contribution. The key issues are, therefore, integration and recognition.

A university has two principal activities: teaching and research. In the case of the OU, research is not covered by the funding transfer and therefore is not a primary responsibility of the OU in Scotland. If one breaks 'teaching' into student services generally and curriculum, the OU in Scotland has a clear role in the former while the latter is still more complex.

In the new environment the compatibility of the OU's mission with the Scottish Parliament's emphasis on inclusion and, in particular, on widening participation in education, has embedded the OU's contribution very readily into some areas. The OU has for many years funded low-income students, and the SHEFC fee waiver scheme has enhanced this so that there are in 2000–1 over 2,500 OU students in Scotland receiving help with course fees and study costs. Another illustration grows from the fact that the OU in Scotland has students in almost every postcode so that it is well-placed to support initiatives based outside the Central Belt, for example, supporting widening access in the south-west through the SHEFC-funded Open Road programme. The OU's mission and pedagogy has extended study opportunities to many disabled students and in Scotland in 1999–2000 the OU taught 8.5% of all disabled students in Scottish HEIs. In addition the OU is the largest provider of HE to Scottish prisoners.

By the nature of the university and how it has developed, the OU has contributed strongly to the development of HE in Scotland, in quantity and quality. A research study (Schuller, 1999, p. 150) affirmed the latter: 'When it comes to student support services, the OU's experience and structure also makes its high rating of 64% judging them 'excellent' or 'good' predictable but the gap between this and 17% for universities and 12% for colleges is very striking.' A major challenge for the OU in the future may be to assist Scottish HE in improving the representation of ethnic minorities in the student population. The OU at large has been less successful in this area, but it might be that an invigorated effort by the OU generally could feed through the OU in Scotland to the country more widely to challenge what is sometimes held to be a rather complacent position.

Turning to curriculum, one can look at structures and content, while recognising the OU's distinctive pedagogy. With regard to degree structures, the OU originally offered degrees which developed from the traditional Scottish degree: modular, three-year ordinary, four-year honours. However, in the mid-1990s, the university was persuaded to move to the English model: three-year honours. This tension for the OU as a UK body is now emphasised more strongly with the development of National Qualification frameworks, but different frameworks in Scotland and England. Add to that the details of credit transfer and the issue becomes significant. The OU in Scotland is well represented in the discussions on these topics so that one can argue that its contribution is recognised and certainly it is developing ways, for example, to articulate with FE in Scotland, but the broad issue of integration remains outstanding.

In curriculum content, there is a further tension. In Scotland the university is welcomed because it brings an external perspective to the Scottish curriculum, but it is open to criticism because it is deemed to be English. Some OU provision, for example in Mathematics/Science/Technology, straddles national differences. In other areas, there has been an effort to recognise a Scottish difference: Scottish supplements for some Education courses; Scottish assessors of proposals and draft materials; and resource materials on Scottish history and culture. However, four recent initiatives perhaps point the way forward. Firstly, there has been collaboration between the OU and Dundee University to develop an honours-level course in Scottish History carrying credit in both institutions. Secondly, as mentioned earlier, the OU's Diploma in Social Work has a Scottish strand including a full module on Scottish law. Thirdly, the OU is collaborating with the University of Edinburgh to offer a course in literacy difficulties through two different modes. Lastly, the Learning Schools Programme, a UK ICT training programme for teachers created by the OU and Research Machines, has generated materials for Scottish teachers in partnership with Learning and Teaching Scotland. Where there is a cultural, legal or professional imperative, however, it is apparent that the OU will have to expand its activities in course versioning and in partnership if it is to integrate fully and gain appropriate recognition.

Looking ahead, after three successful decades, the OU's future contribution in Scotland will be evaluated in terms of its capacity to deal with the widening gap between education in Scotland and England, in practice and in policy. It will have to attend to the content of the curriculum as well as the structure and student support. It will have to take account of Scottish priorities like widening access and expanding vocational education, including work-based learning and assessment. The OU is already preparing for further innovation and development so that it can truly be the Open University for Scotland.

REFERENCES

Carr, R. and Glaister, R. (1981) Information Paper 7: The Open University in Scotland, *Scottish Educational Review*, 13 (1) 58–61.

Crowther, G. (1969) Inaugural Address, Royal Society.

Perry, W. (1976) *The Open University: A Personal Account*, Buckingham: Open University Press.

Schuller, T. et al. (1999) *Part-time Higher Education: Policy, Practice and Experience*, London: Kingsley.

Two useful sources are the annual reports of the Vice Chancellor of the Open University and the regularly produced OU Facts and Figures synopses, prepared for the OU as a whole and for Scotland.

X

Assessment, Certification and Achievements

81

Could Do Better?
Assessment in Scottish Schools

Tom Bryce

A CHANGE FROM THE PAST

People remember their teachers for a variety of reasons, not least in their roles as assessors of what they did in school; as evaluators of their learning, and much else besides. A scurrilous jibe ascribed perhaps to the previous generation, would have it that teachers wrote 'could do better' upon pupils' work, thereby neither indicating what they had achieved, nor whether it was any good at all. The remark carried with it a variety of messages: that teachers judge achievement, capability and worth (as professionally they must) and are gatekeepers to future prospects and employment; that assessment was easy to do and therefore required little effort. Perhaps most of all, in that bad old past, that really very little of substance was conveyed by such 'assessment'. And of course the tone of such remarks could provoke resentment; teachers would be seriously disliked if in the eyes of their pupils there was no recognition of their value and potential as a consequence of being so assessed. At worst, assessment could fail its very purpose if pupils were turned off learning as a result. Perhaps rather many adults do harbour such feelings.

In contrast, the present generation will have quite different views of assessment for two different, though inter-related, reasons. First, what teachers actually do now, how they assess and report upon pupils' work, has become the subject of detailed prescription. The attention paid to assessment and reporting in the national developments of the last two decades has ensured that teachers cannot get away with 'could do better'. Through the requirements of Standard Grade, 5–14, and now new National Qualifications (brought in as Higher Still), central government has steered 'good practice' and standardisation in assessment along with changes to the curriculum. The criteria which teachers should use to assess pupils have been made much more explicit and more classroom assessment counts formally towards final qualifications. Second, and in part a consequence of prescriptions of how to assess, there are now very considerable public as well as professional concerns about the amount of assessment required of pupils, particularly of upper secondary pupils in pursuit of certificates. Disquiet arose in Scotland in relation to the 'examinations fiasco' of 2000 with the first wave of Higher Still (see Paterson, 2000 and below) but has been echoed south of the border with the A-level crisis of 2002. For pupils, parents and teachers, assessment has become much more conspicuous than the curriculum taught in schools; assessment is visible and serious and therefore more demanding of teachers.

Scotland has not been alone in introducing changes to assessment, however, and other developed countries have endeavoured, in broadly similar ways, to improve what goes on in its name (see Nisbet, J. Issues/Questions chapter in OECD document, *Curriculum Reform: Assessment in Question*, Paris: OECD, 1993). However, some things are particularly Scottish and it is appropriate to ask whether current policies and practices are sound and satisfactory or whether the system as a whole 'could do better'? The remainder of this chapter reflects on three distinctive shifts in emphasis which have taken place. First, and with an eye to secondary schools, whereas assessment was once confined to an elite (primarily the academic achievers) it is now required for all. Significantly, much of the associated thinking and some of the practice has moved from secondary to primary as a consequence of the order in which the national developments took place. Furthermore, more of that assessment is now internal; teachers control and carry out assessment as part of course work. Some claims can be made that it is more integrated with ongoing work, guiding and informing teaching (and therefore earning the label 'formative'). Second, and perhaps most importantly, in the past both assessment and reporting were 'norm-referenced', that is they focused on how pupils compared with one another and standards were (at best) only implicit in descriptions such as 'average', 'below average' and so on. The focus is now on what pupils are able to do and criteria for achievement (for 'passing' or for particular grades) are now made explicit; assessment is said to be criterion-referenced. Third, and as a consequence of this, assessment has become tied up with grading and the concept of an educational ladder, where grades are labels for rungs, is the predominant metaphor (see Bryce, 1994). Thinking in terms of grades or levels is sometimes helpful, but it can lead to difficulties, as will be shown.

ASSESSMENT FOR EVERYBODY AND MORE INTERNAL ASSESSMENT

A generation ago, assessment was a rather formal affair. It was the prerogative of the more able in secondary schools; written examinations dominated schooling and teaching was the preparation for them. Following the demise (in the 1960s) of the 'qualifying' examination at the end of P7, assessment remained low key in primary schools and did so until the advent of 5–14 in the 1990s. The important secondary examinations, as today, were externally set (by the then Scottish Examination Board) and teachers could enjoin pupils to work with them against the unknown, external examiner, second-guessing what would come up this year, and so forth. Old memories therefore are of the nervous anxiety associated with exam halls and cramming for the fateful day. In this sense, assessment had formalities and rituals; even when not external in the sense of a certificate examination such as a Higher Grade, school examinations were often seen as an end point and external to the processes of class work and teaching.

Preparation for certificate examinations meant preparatory examinations (prelims) and together these are often the only formal examinations which pupils take in today's secondary school. (In some schools there are end-of-year exams in S1–S3.) Rather more informal assessment now characterises life in school. Some of this has come about through the recognition that it is not valid to try to check certain achievements by formal paper-and-pencil examinations. What you can write about is not the same as what you can actually do; the former can be rehearsed on the basis of rote learning, the latter offers greater opportunities and having it checked 'live' is a more valid process. Investigations and projects, problem solving, reading, listening and practical skills, most obviously require alternatives to written test papers and the assessment of such achievements is now properly located in class time and classroom locations, with teachers assuming responsibility for the assessment as a matter of routine.

Two things are evident about this, concerning level of demand and weighting. A factor associated with the first is that while encouraging more internal assessment by teachers, the system has brought greater rigour and systematisation into classroom assessment than was formerly the case. Ensuring that everyone does the same thing and exercises judgements against the same standards has not proved easy, but has raised widespread professional debate amongst teachers where previously there had been little. That is a good thing and it has meant in the long run that how things should be judged permeates discussion with pupils. Assessment is thus more of an integral part of the on-going teaching and learning process (as predicted by Sally Brown, prior to the Standard Grade developments: Brown, S. *What Do they Know? A Review of Criterion-Referenced Assessment*, Edinburgh: HMSO 1980).

However the shift to greater internal assessment has made more demands of teachers. Over a decade ago, Standard Grade course developments looked poised to permit individual subjects to determine the number of assessed elements which would apply to S3 and S4 courses and to allow a wide range of internal assessment strategies to be adopted. Teachers balked at what they saw as unreasonable burdens and an official 'simplification' took place. *Assessment in Standard Grade Courses: Proposals for Simplification* (The SGROAG Report, SED, 1986) ordained that there would be only three elements per subject and curtailed the structured internal assessments to be carried out by teachers. With 5 – 14, developments in assessment have tended to indicate (if not labour the point) that what teachers do by way of on-going, informal assessment need only be made explicit and contribute to judgements made as the internal assessment required for formally recorded achievements. *Assessment 5–14* (SOED, 1991) is a carefully argued document and one would be hard-pushed to fault its philosophy of assessment, though criticism can be levelled at the lack of detailed advice as to how such laudable intentions might be realised. It outlines how assessment should be considered professionally, firmly identifying it as part and parcel of a teacher's planning, teaching, recording, reporting and evaluating. These five elements are not to be thought of as separate or sequential; 'assessment is an integral part of learning and teaching' (p. 12). Indeed right at the start, the guidelines endeavour to reassure teachers (particularly that they need not fear additional workload) thus: 'While some aspects of the 5–14 Development Programme are new for teachers, assessment itself is not. Teachers should approach this assessment with confidence' (p. 3). However, the assessment and reporting demands of 5–14 are quite considerable. Teachers are required to prepare detailed descriptive reports for parents on their children's progress; strengths and developmental needs (weaknesses) must be spelled out and many schools now issue a one or two page report per pupil in advance of the annual or biannual parents' night. Thus pressure has been applied to shift the system towards an increase in internal, more informal assessment (where assessing is part-and-parcel of teaching) but has had to back pedal carefully to avoid the impression that it is too demanding for teachers to undertake.

The second thing which is evident about these changes, refocusing here on secondary, is that despite satisfactory techniques of moderation (checks made by examination boards of the procedures adopted by teachers) internal assessment retains a minority weighting as far as certification is concerned. Indeed that weighting continues to be reduced following early enthusiastic innovations. For example, in the science subjects at Standard Grade, the internal assessment of practical abilities was, for six years, one-third of the total. From 1999 this was reduced from one-third to one-fifth (*New Arrangements for all Sciences*, Dalkeith: SQA, 1997). Once again the change was brought about in response to the concerns of some teachers about the overall burden of assessment. More recently, with respect to Higher Still (see below), decisions have been announced (by the National Qualifications Task Group in September 2002) to reduce the volume of internal assessment evidence required for Science across all course levels in session 2002–3. In this context, it might be said that there is a natural conservatism about teachers' views of their assessment roles – or at least what they are prepared to do in circumstances where very significant additions to workload have been put in place without compensatory gains of any sort. It is interesting also to reflect on the context in which decisions about the balance of internal to external assessment are made. Retaining the largest component of assessment as external to schools might have seemed the safest bet when Standard Grade was launched. However, with the steady increase in staying-on rates beyond S4, some doubts have been raised about the need for national certification at sixteen years. (Indeed in 2002 a few schools indicated their intention to dispense with Standard Grade in favour of the new Higher Still courses.) Nevertheless, recent revisions to the system have not been to increase the school-based component, rather the reverse! Concerns about cheating in project work (see Bryce, 1994) have also been used as a justification for a reduction in internal assessment.

In parallel with the systematic evolution of assessment strategies in the 1980s and 1990s, Scotland has also participated in the UK-wide National Record of Achievement (NRA) initiative. A record of achievement is a document drawn up by a pupil/student, in collaboration with a teacher or teachers, which sets out in summary form that individual's overall achievements. It is deliberately wide in compass; academic achievements are but a sub-set of what is normally included. As the evaluation by Somekh et al. (1996) revealed, the process of drawing up such a record is more important for the learner than the product. The cycle of activities where pupils review and record their achievements, assess their own strengths and weaknesses and set targets, significantly contributes to motivation. The recommendations from the report by Somekh et al. include aiming for the NRA 'to become a standard part of practice in assessment and recording in educational institutions'. A similar initiative – Progress Files – has gained ground with guidance staff in recent years, however it is evident that in Scotland (as elsewhere) there is a significant gap to be closed between conventional academic assessment procedures and those associated with best practice in the integrated use of NRA in teaching (see Chapter 82).

NORM-REFERENCED VERSUS CRITERION-REFERENCED ASSESSMENT

Probably the most striking feature of modern assessment is the existence of published criteria by which judgements are to be made of pupil work. A considerable amount of development time and effort has been spent on the articulation of criteria in all of the recent national initiatives. This first began during the 1980s for Standard Grade with the development of grade-related criteria; followed by the specification of SCOTVEC module assessment criteria; during the late 1980s and early 1990s with the identification of targets for 5–14 achievements; and in the late 1990s with grade-related criteria for the various levels of Higher Still. It is interesting to reflect on what preceded those periods of intense educational activity; when there were no written criteria, did teachers assess pupils without reference to any standards of acceptability? While the answer to this must clearly be no, it is apparent from history that concerns about variation between teachers and between classes in secondary schools became serious during the 1960s and 1970s. Experienced teachers set tests of subject knowledge and understanding largely on the basis of their own subjective judgements of comparability to what had gone before; on the previous year's paper; on tests used elsewhere. Serious drift occurred when something novel was set in a certificate paper, and it was commonly noted that that particular topic or its demands became emphasised in the years which followed. Class examinations, including those for the years prior to certification, experienced a backwash effect with demands altering as a result. Were any particular year group to be brighter or more able in a teacher's judgement, then of course this would present difficulties for the proportions of pupils getting certain marks or grades. The tendency overall must have been for some constraints to be imposed upon year groups' justified 'achievements'.

During the 1970s, when first year intakes to secondary schools were rather higher than they are now, difficulties of comparing subjects (which pupils inevitably encounter, especially at the end of S2 when they seek to choose 'their best subjects' for S3 and beyond) were reduced by the advent of computer programmes for test mark analyses. Prior to the advent of personal computers, computing facilities in local teacher centres and teacher education institutions developed user-friendly programmes to permit norm-referenced computations to be carried out with ease. Typically, raw marks across a set of school subjects could be scaled to a chosen, common average and chosen common spread of marks. Thus a school could submit sets of subject marks with varying raw averages and varying spreads (left uncalculated of course) and have these computed as scaled marks all averaging, say, 55% with common spreads in each subject (say a standard deviation of 15%). Teachers simply chose the desired parameters and had returned to them printed lists of scaled scores. The hard bit was to explain to pupils why their marks had been reduced in those instances where exam questions had been set 'easy' or where marking had been 'generous', relative to other subjects. As well as introducing perceived fairness and the labour-saving facility of printed lists (which could have grades attached, merely by specifying grade-mark ranges: Grade A = 85% +; Grade B = 84% – 75%; etc.) this disguised the 'real' standards being achieved by pupils in subjects and the diversity and variation among those subject demands. It was, however, a period where the philosophy of norm-referencing held sway. Such procedures mimicked what the Scottish Examination Board did with national data, ensuring commensurate proportions of the national population achieving A, B, C and so on at Higher or Ordinary Grade, year on year. (See also Chapter 88.) More recently, the alleged adjustment of grade boundaries took on a much more serious note in England and Wales during the A-level crisis of 2002.

Two important developments took place in assessment during the 1980s. The first, which sought to replace norm-referencing, was initiated in response to the recommendations of the Dunning Report, *Assessment for All* (Edinburgh: SED, 1977) and produced assessment and certification strategies based on pre-determined targets for learning. These were devised by subject groupings of teachers, led centrally by the Scottish Examination Board. The second, related development was the allocation of grade levels to the outcomes of

Standard Grade achievements (either in recognition that only limited progress had been made towards the certification of 'mastery learning', or more plausibly, as a political expedient to match the expectations of the givers and the users of future certificates). Neither of these completely diverted teachers from their traditional thinking about test scores and marks out of 100; but they did build criteria, grades and grading into the heart of the assessment system.

During the development of the Standard Grade curriculum, not only was the content of the curriculum (content in the widest sense) extended and developed to span the entire ability range, but much effort was expended upon setting out descriptive statements of what pupils should know and be able to do. The various working parties which developed these statements inevitably got bogged down in considerable detail, since it is pretty nigh impossible to be both precise and terse. Rather than settle for description associated with a pass requirement for a Standard Grade subject, a compromise was struck to match more closely the traditional thinking of parents, of employers and of teachers, that is to preserve the notion of a scale of achievement from the most to the least able. What resulted was a system of grades 1 to 7, with 1 and 2 representing the Credit band, 3 and 4 the General band and 5 and 6 the Foundation band of Standard Grade (with 7 as 'no award'). Detailed criteria for what pupils should be able to do were distinguished by grade levels and were labelled extended grade-related criteria (E-GRC). Though not frequently used, the more general GRC are claimed to be meaningful to parents and employers. The SEB, and now the SQA, publish the detailed E-GRC as part of the Arrangements document for each subject. As teachers are at pains to say, these 'bibles' set out what has to be achieved by the end of S4. (Figure 81.1 illustrates the differences between Grade 4 and Grade 3 for close reading in English language.) The differences between criteria for different grade levels are sometimes quantitative in character, sometimes qualitative; and there are instances where the distinction is forced and not particularly helpful to the classroom teacher. Furthermore, the thinking which lies behind criteria and targets is to some extent in conflict with current approaches to learning and mental growth: see, for example, Bryce (1993).

Broadfoot has noted the emergence of criterion-referencing in the assessment policies of many advanced countries, detecting flux and tension between the emerging 'pre-occupation with the attestation of competence rather than the regulation of competition as the principal focus for assessment' (Broadfoot, 1996, p. 51). She sees the new demand on teachers to operate internal, criterion-referenced systems for all pupils across the age range as being considerable, though there are significant differences between countries – depending upon what they implement and how they do it, with Scotland faring rather better than England. And she notes the growing and powerful lobby in favour of 'retaining and indeed strengthening traditional pass/fail certificate examinations, evidenced by recent [English] government moves to reduce coursework assessment.' (p. 53). The 'confirmatory' use by teachers of national tests in Scotland (teachers drawing upon the national test bank when they choose) is identified by her as one positive feature, compared with England's mandatory requirements. While the culture of assessment has changed, she does opt for 'oscillation' as a metaphor. Things are swinging back and on a somewhat pessimistic note she states that 'these changes have come about to defuse potential conflict and frustration while at the same time enabling schools to continue their traditional role of selecting and channelling pupils to different levels of the occupational and social hierarchy' (p. 62).

Figure 81.1:   EGRC for close reading in English for grades 3 and 4

NATURE OF TEXTS

The candidate can read texts that are accessible as a whole, mainly related to personal interest and experience, dealing with concrete human relationships or containing clearly presented ideas.

As the nature of the text permits, the candidate can:

- make a clear statement of the main concerns of the text;
- state accurately in his or her own words (where appropriate) individual items retrieved from the text;
- draw a precise inference from a key statement in the text;
- comment relevantly on a clearly defined aspect of the author's point of view, and justify the comment from personal experience and knowledge and from evidence in the text;
- identify individual features of the author's technique and explain their effects.

FACTORS DIFFERENTIATING. GRADES 4 AND 3

Grade 4
While displaying as appropriate the characteristics essential for General Level the candidate's responses are less consistent, less apt in illustration and explanation, and less successful in retrieving, paraphrasing, explaining and justifying than at grade 3. Overall the performance is more uneven than at grade 3.

Grade 3
The candidate demonstrates a clear understanding and a sound appreciation in responding to particular questions on the various aspects of purpose. The responses are more consistent, more relevant and more successful in retrieving, paraphrasing, explaining and justifying than at grade 4.

From Paragraph 7.9.2 of Standard Grade. Revised arrangements in English at Foundation, General and Credit levels in and after 1989, the Scottish Qualifications Authority (2000)

GRADES AND LEVELS

While the incorporation of pupil performance criteria into the assessment system has made for great complexity, the definition of grades 1–7 across the entire ability range for all subject matter can be regarded as a success, at least at school level. SCOTVEC's national modular system did not take its cue from Standard Grade; it did not adopt grades for modules nor did it make distinctions between students. Instead it opted for a set of outcomes per module all to be mastered or non-mastered (thus taking no account of the reality of variations between students in possession of the same module).

The development of Standard Grade was so demanding of the system that when the policy of national curricula spanning the compulsory school years was introduced (and implicit in that was the idea of targets in ascending order) Scotland was compelled to retain

Standard Grade and confine its 'national curriculum' to 5–14. This resulted in serious mismatches in attainment descriptors at different stages. Pupils move upwards through levels A to E (E is 'highest') and must then switch to grades 1–7 (1 is highest) for S3 and S4. Grades or levels then have rather different meanings. In Standard Grade, achieving a grade level 3, say, by the end of S4 may be understood by scrutiny of the E-GRC so indicated – 3 is a final position on a seven-point scale. In 5–14, a level is defined by a collection of the targets which should be attainable by a certain stage of schooling; thus level B targets should be met by most pupils in P4, level D by most pupils in P7, level E by most pupils in S2 (see Figure 81.2). While there are thousands of targets in the 5–14 guidelines, it is intended that a teacher recognise the stage reached for any pupil through scrutiny of the numbers of targets reached.

Figure 81.2:   Targets and levels

In each of the 5–14 curriculum documents, the attainment outcomes have been subdivided into strands, or main aspects of learning. Each strand is set out in terms of targets at five levels, A-E, where:

Level A   should be attainable in the course of the first three years at primary school by almost all pupils

Level B   should be attainable by some pupils in P3 or even earlier, but certainly by most in P4

Level C   should be attainable in the course of P4 to P6 by most pupils

Level D   should be attainable by some pupils in P5 or P6 or even earlier, but certainly by most in P7

Level E   should be attainable by some pupils in P7 or S1, but certainly by most in S2.

(See, for example, SOED, 1991. *Mathematics 5–14*, p. 9)

Thus in Mathematics, for example, the attainment outcome 'information handling' has four strands (collecting, organising, displaying and interpreting information). In respect of the strand 'display information' pupils should be able to display:

at level A   by using real objects, by using pictures; and by drawing simple diagrams

at level B   by using tables, charts or diagrams (such as mapping one to many); by constructing a bar graph (with axes graduated in units and with discrete categories of information)

at level C   by constructing a table or chart; by constructing a bar graph (with axes graduated in multiple units and discrete categories of information)

at level D   by constructing graphs (bar, line, frequency polygon) and pie charts (involving simple fractions or decimals; involving continuous data which has been grouped)

at level E   by constructing straight line and curved graphs for continuous data (where there is a relationship such as direct proportion – travel, temperature, growth graphs); by constructing pie charts of data (expressed in percentages).

The intention of such assessment using grade levels is that parents should receive reports on their children which indicate their progress up the sequential rungs of the national curriculum ladder. However, it also allows comparisons to be made to the achievements of the majority. Thus, for example, D is where most pupils should be by the end of primary school.

The last statement, for example, is not as simple as it looks and it is not simply hair-splitting to note that the precise wording in any of the 5–14 guideline documents is 'by most in P7'. Why and where does this matter? The point is that in trying to steer national assessment through grades and levels, the consequences of some ambiguity of terminology must be lived with. Grades or levels are not easily or sharply defined entities.

The 5–14 curriculum developers opted to attach two years of schooling to each level through their selection of five levels for nine years of schooling (P1–S2). Two years usually constitutes a significant gain in a pupil's knowledge and skills; the many hundreds of targets associated with one grade vary greatly in their compass, difficulty and depth; grade levels such as D therefore cannot constitute some sharply defined end-point. Furthermore, when national test setters try to ascribe test questions to levels or where researchers try to work with levels to estimate the national proportions of children so achieving, difficulties are encountered. In the case of national tests (at the time of writing, set only for English language and Mathematics: see Chapter 85) when test items are judged to be appropriate to assess the attainment of a particular target, they inevitably vary in difficulty. The rule of thumb which seems to have evolved is for the easiest task to be incorporated into the test bank materials as applicable for the particular 5–14 level. In the Assessment of Achievement Programme (see Chapter 87) researchers who have developed assessment tasks linked to the 5–14 levels have worked out different strategies. They too have had to operationalise some of the more vague terms from 5–14. Thus, for example, the team who conducted the fourth science survey in 1996 interpreted 'most' and 'almost all' as 75% and 90%respectively of the national sample; they used indices of achievement of 0.8 and 0.35 (proportions of scores on tasks assessing particular targets) to judge the extent to which national samples of pupils had or did not have 'secure understanding' or were making 'steady progress' respectively, these being the terms used in 5–14 Environmental Studies (Stark, R., Bryce, T. G. K. and Gray, D. (1997) Four surveys and an epitaph: AAP Science 1985–1997, *Scottish Educational Review*, 29 (2), 114–20). In short, terms adopted for targets and levels may appear attractively straightforward (and no doubt give some flexibility and freedom as far as curriculum guidelines are concerned). However, in practice assessors, whether classroom teachers or more formal 'national testers' or 'national monitors' have much interpreting to do. The 5–14 documents offer curriculum guidelines; they do not present assessment blueprints.

The whole question of standards in Mathematics is an interesting case in point in this respect. The 1997 report by HMI *Improving Mathematics Education 5–14* (Edinburgh: SOEID) sets out the concerns for pupils' Maths attainment indicated by school inspections, national (AAP) and international (TIMSS) surveys of pupil achievements, and puts forward recommendations for changes to practice. Part of the argument is developed through comparisons made between teaching methods used in high achieving countries and teaching methods used in Scotland. Scottish teachers are urged to expect more of pupils, to increase the pace; schools are encouraged to set themselves realistic but challenging targets 'beyond national minimum expectations'. Thus HMI now declare that schools should interpret 5–14 targets as 'minimum expectations' (p. 3, para. 2.2). They have observed that schools have used D as marking the end of P7. Can't D mark the mid-point of P7, they ask? Whereas the targets set out in 1991 were for level A to be attained by almost all in P3, level D by most in P7, the disappointing standards (and especially the international comparisons) led to HMI arguing by 1997 that:

> Most schools should aim to complete Level A as soon as possible and expect most of their pupils to have reached it by the end of P2. (para. 2.3)

> There are also many P7 classes where teachers aim only to complete Level D by the end of the session even though significant numbers of pupils should have attained this minimum level sooner, perhaps in P6. By the end of P7, most pupils should be working beyond Level D and some should be well on the way towards completing Level E. (para. 2.4, SOEID, 1997)

One could paraphrase this as 'moving the goalposts' but it would be unfair to argue that it is improper in the long run (though it does pin much hope on the idea that people do always rise to expectations). And as practitioners know, an F level was added in the late 1990s to the 5–14 grade levels; this provided yet further targets for the most able, adjusting upwards the goals that could or should be attained. It is professionally defensible for the system to adjust targets, insofar as a wide range of evidence is taken into account, particularly that deriving from well-conducted surveys like AAP. In other chapters consideration is given to the arguments about teaching methods and standards (for AAP, see Chapter 87), but it is interesting here to note that HMI observe that school guidelines provided in some other (high achieving) countries, like Switzerland, provide better, more detailed guidance to primary teachers about Mathematics programmes. Might one deduce that more effective detail is supplied than that which has been built in Scotland around the 5–14 target colossus?

Perhaps we should conclude that the whole criterion-referencing paraphernalia with targets has been over-ambitious as an assessment device to advance standards and to tackle the primary/secondary interface difficulties (see Chapter 34). As many have observed, outcomes and strands and targets do not constitute linear sequences of advice to teachers; they do not translate into action in real time. Is that what the system sought to avoid by regarding teachers as professionals able to interpret a complex of target milestones strung across the (st)age-range? Would greater progress have been made by simpler, admittedly more directive, advice? Certainly, as far as assessment is concerned, a great deal has been asked of the profession. (Someone has estimated that by dividing the total number of 5–14 targets by the duration of time spent, one can reckon that a child should be achieving a target every fourteen and a half minutes of their 5–14 school life!) The grade level mentality may be here to stay; if it is, all those involved in assessment are making life hard for themselves.

HIGHER STILL AND YET MORE ASSESSMENT

Higher Still, launched in 1999–2000, brought together academic and vocational qualifications into one multi-level framework for S5 and S6 and beyond into further education, essentially a big brother to Standard Grade. The range of qualifications (Access, Intermediate 1, Intermediate 2, Higher and Advanced Higher) extended the ability/attainment levels significantly and they are now referred to as National Qualifications (NQs). In a very real sense NQs were made to reflect a combination of their predecessors (SEB courses which were only ever externally assessed and SCOTVEC modules which were only internally assessed), for they were devised as courses made up of units, usually three in each, where the units are assessed internally and must be passed prior to the candidate being permitted to sit the external examination. National Assessment Bank tests (NABs) are commonly used in schools and colleges to take the pass/fail decisions, either for a unit as an award in its own right, or as the requirement for external presentation. Candidates who fail unit assessments can re-take them, a consequence which adds complexity to the considerable workload pressure upon subject departments as well as candidates. It takes very little arithmetic to see that a pupil taking, say, five courses in S5, will be undertaking very many formal tests long before they reach the May diet of examinations.

The first year of Higher Still turned out to be overwhelming for the SQA, whose systems and procedures were inadequate for the management of the new assessment required nationally. (Chapter 83 outlines the issues as they related to SQA itself.) While the problems were addressed and the 2001 results handled efficiently, there continue to be widespread concerns, both professionally and amongst the public, about the assessment required to make things work. At the time of writing, relatively little has been done to reduce the overall volume of assessment, despite official deliberations and consultations in the interim. Thus, following the parliamentary committee enquiries into the year 2000 disaster, the review commissioned by the Executive came to the conclusion that 'The evidence indicates strong support for the retention of internal assessment, on the basis of the benefits to candidates reported in survey evidence, but also significant concern about the total burden of assessment on both candidates and teachers'(*Review of Initial Implementation of New National Qualifications: A Report by the National Qualifications Steering Group to the Scottish Executive*, Edinburgh: Scottish Executive, June 2001). The review recommended that there should be course-by-course revisions of assessment arrangements and the Executive proceeded to carry out a consultation exercise with schools and colleges. It pointedly asked teachers whether they would prefer a system where candidates' success depended upon external examination alone (though with unit certification as an option), so-called option A; or whether they would prefer to depend upon the internal unit assessments (with an external examination as an option), so-called option B. The first option would lead to less internal assessment and might have been predicted to be favoured by school teachers; the second to less external assessment, possibly to be favoured by FE lecturers (*Consultation on Review of Assessment within new National Qualifications*, Edinburgh: Scottish Executive, 20 September 2001). In the Spring of 2002, in a somewhat low key announcement, Cathy Jamieson, the then new Minister for Education, announced that neither option had attracted a majority and that, although everyone wanted workload and undue pressure on candidates to be reduced, she observed 'a call for stability and time for the new system to bed in' (NQTG Update. *Newsletter of the National Qualifications Taskgroup*. Issue 4, Edinburgh, Scottish Executive, May 2002). This was certainly consistent with the evidence collated by a group at Glasgow University who reckoned that while 215 responses favoured 'option A not B', as against twenty-nine for 'B not A'; 293 responses opted for 'neither A nor B', with 196 wanting the status quo modified by a review process (*Summary of Glasgow University Report Analysing Responses to Scottish Executive Consultation on Review of Assessment within New National Qualifications*, Edinburgh: Scottish Executive, 7 August 2002). Paragraph 10 of that report states that 'External assessment was often closely associated with credibility by respondents; more commonly internal assessment was associated with motivation and support for learning.'

In the meantime another consultation was put in place, namely the 'national debate' on the government's five educational priorities as defined by the 2000 Act. Again at the time of writing, the official analysis of responses to that has not been published, but early signs are that concerns for the amount of assessment in schools (not just with regard to certification and the upper years of secondary) figure significantly. The public has not been convinced that increased assessment is positively influencing classroom learning; indeed many vocal critics argue that it is having a negative effect by constraining the curriculum and narrowing what is taught to that which will be assessed. It is noticeable that among the public calls for less assessment, many commentators state that classroom assessment should be left to formative assessment, at the teacher's discretion and devising. Some use the term accurately; many do not and simply equate the term with formal internal assessment typical of Higher Still. It is probable that many teachers carry out assessment without due regard for any distinction, such being the pressure they are under to record what pupils can do at any time (see the next chapter by Simpson). Although researchers have long argued the positive effects of formative classroom assessment (see Black and Wiliam, 1998) there has been too little recognition of the complexities of classroom learning and the real demands upon teachers in a climate of ever increasing pressure to raise standards.

REFERENCES

Black, P. and Wiliam, D. (1998) Assessment and classroom learning, *Assessment in Education*, 5 (1), 7–74.

Broadfoot, P. M. (1996) *Education, Assessment and Society*, Buckingham: Open University Press.

Bryce, T. G. K. (1993) Constructivism, knowledge and national science targets, *Scottish Educational Review*, 25 (2), 87–96.

Bryce, T. G. K. (1994) Challenges to the management of assessment. Chapter in W. M. Humes and M. L. MacKenzie (eds), *The Management of Educational Policy: Scottish Perspectives*, Harlow: Longman.

Paterson, L. (2000) *Crisis in the Classroom. The Exam Debacle and the Way Ahead for Scottish Education*, Edinburgh: Mainstream Publishing.

Somekh, B., Tinklin, T., Edwards, L. and Mackay, R. (1996) Evaluation of the National Record of Achievement in Scotland, *Interchange No 44*, Edinburgh: SOEID.

82

Diagnostic and Formative Assessment in the Scottish Classroom

Mary Simpson

INTRODUCING A NEW FORM OF ASSESSMENT

> It is insufficient to devise curricular objectives and to find out if they have been attained by each pupil; for those who are not successful the reasons for misunderstandings require to be identified and alternative methods adopted. (The Dunning Report, *Assessment for All*, SED, 1977).

In the mid-1970s, the Dunning Committee first introduced the educational community to the idea that assessment might serve purposes other than merely sorting pupils. They suggested that the new system of criterion referencing should not only be regarded as a replacement for norm referencing as a method of judging pupils' progress against intended outcomes, but also as a means of contributing to the improvement of educational attainment – difficulties were to be diagnosed and instructional action was to be taken when pupils failed to reach specified attainments.

Although this recommendation appeared reasonable and sensible, there was at that time a lack of clarity both in theory and practice on how diagnostic assessment might operate. Was it the case that tests which were criterion referenced to intended outcomes could serve not only the summative function of giving an account of what pupils had learned, but also diagnose the causes of learning difficulties? And what particular instructional action should be taken following pupil failure? In some subjects, notably Science and Mathematics, 'remedial loops' had already been incorporated into instructional materials but many teachers found these difficult to incorporate into the lock-step delivery which was typical of the time, and there was no convincing evidence that the pre-set remedial activities actually addressed the learning difficulties experienced by the individual pupil within the particular learning task in hand. Clearly, considerably more work was needed to inform any changes in practice.

This chapter outlines some of the subsequent interactions between policy, research and practice which resulted in the development of understanding and practice in Scottish classrooms during the 1990s, and which set the scene for new initiatives in the twenty-first century.

INITIAL CONCEPTIONS OF DIAGNOSTIC ASSESSMENT

In response to the Dunning Report's suggestion that 'diagnostic assessment as an aid to pupil learning' should be further investigated, the educational community in Scotland embarked enthusiastically on a programme of research, largely funded by the Scottish Office, and by February 1983, a full edition of the journal *Programmed Learning and Educational Technology* was devoted to reports of a range of Scottish initiatives. For example, two teachers wrote up a case study, in which they sounded a cautionary note on the amount of work involved, and the necessity to undertake 'a long campaign to inform teachers about diagnostic assessment and of the advantages that can accrue from its use' (Black, p. 8). A group of teacher trainers reported on the development of test items which, they argued, 'can be used to provide both diagnostic and summative information' (p. 11). There was a description of the use of a package of mastery learning materials devised by researchers and tried out by teachers – the researchers noted that 'the teachers' general attitudes and expectations seemed little affected by their participation in this study' (p. 43). One article fired the opening shots in what became a long-standing debate between Scottish researchers on the relationship, in theory and practice, between formative and summative assessment, on the nature and origin of learning difficulties and on the appropriate form of assessment which would contribute effectively to their resolution:

> Many learning difficulties can be attributed not to pupil limitations, but to major deficiencies in the subject presentation, e.g. inconsistencies, anomalies and ambiguities, and to inadequacies in instructional strategies, e.g. the failure to provide adequate instruction in pre-requisite concepts, to monitor their development, to detect the incorrect information acquired by pupils, or to define precise teaching objectives (p. 36).

And in a percipient and prophetic overview, the guest editor for that edition, Harry Black, identified the range of problems which could be anticipated in trying to promote the understanding and adoption of this form of assessment in schools: 'Unless a favourable environment is created within which these problems and tensions can be dealt with, diagnostic assessment is likely to be misunderstood and misused' (p. 58).

Both in Scotland and in the wider educational research community, interest had been growing in the underlying causes of pupil learning difficulties, particularly in Science and Mathematics. It had increasingly become recognised that these were commonly traceable to misconceptions which pupils had acquired, undetected, and therefore uncorrected, during their schooling or in the course of everyday life experiences. Such misconceptions were notably persistent, making the understanding and retention of correct information extremely difficult. Exemplar diagnostic tests to help teachers identify these difficulties were compiled by Scottish researchers, covering topics in Science and Geography in which research had revealed the patterns of typical misunderstandings and difficulties. Although these had the merit of being framed within the model of assessment best understood to teachers – that of the set test comprising objective items – there were practical and theoretical reasons why it was argued that the further development of such diagnostic tests was not a profitable way forward. For example, their coverage of the range of learning difficulties was limited and inflexible; time had to be found to apply them; and teachers tended to aggregate scores and treat them as summative tests (Black, 1983). Their use also tended to reinforce the idea that the causes of learning difficulties were located primarily within the heads of the pupils, and hence that the remediation should be directed wholly towards the actions of the pupils, who would be enjoined to listen, revise, read, and practise more than previously. An alternative view suggested that key contributing deficiencies might lie not in the pupils, but in characteristics prevalent in instruction; remediation of the learning failure might thus require the teacher to change, to revise or restructure their whole teaching strategy and, in particular, to listen and pay more attention to the pupils' ideas (e.g. Simpson, M. and Arnold, B., *Diagnosis in Action*, Aberdeen: Northern College, 1984).

Key areas of difficulty were thus identified and discussed at an early stage: the reconceptualisation of the nature and origins of pupil learning difficulties and professionally appropriate and manageable ways of identifying and dealing with them; resolution of the tensions in the perceived relationship between formative and summative assessment; the identification of ways of successfully introducing innovation; the time and effort required for significant change to take place in teachers' thinking and practice; and the complexity of the professional context within which the changes were to take place.

The staff in schools were interested in and clearly stimulated by the debates and publications which were prompted by the policy exhortation and the dissemination of research findings but, daunted by the range of unresolved difficulties of putting largely untested theory into practice, they turned their attention to the other massive requirement set upon them in the 1980s, the task of putting criterion referencing into place in both the national certification system and in their own internal testing. Nevertheless, the term 'diagnostic assessment' had been introduced into the professional vocabulary and had sown the seeds of the idea that ways round learning difficulties might be found, complex and difficult as the route might seem, and that assessment had a key role in this.

By the early 1990s, when policy requirements associated with the 5–14 development programme again focused the attention of practitioners on the use of assessment as a tool to inform teaching and learning, changes in acceptable forms of assessment and in understanding about the complexities of learning had introduced a number of new factors into the arena.

DEVELOPING A FRAMEWORK FOR FORMATIVE ASSESSMENT

The requirement to use assessment to inform instruction was claimed by teachers in both sectors to be largely met by informal assessment based on their routine, on-going observations of pupils' attainments and difficulties. But, because these activities were intuitive, unsystematic and unrecorded, they went largely unexamined and unevaluated, and the traditional concepts of reliability and validity were not applicable. The secondary teachers' acquisition of the skills of criterion-referenced assessment which related to authentic tasks performed within the classroom, workshop or laboratory offered an opportunity for the development of more systematic strategies which identified learning difficulties and informed teaching. Within the primary school, the informal modes of assessment had long predominated, and the requirement to relate teaching and learning activities to the specified learning outcomes within the curricular guidelines of the 5–14 programme gave primary teachers experience of setting specific targets for pupils, against which their actual attainments could be systematically gauged and failure responded to (see Chapter 81).

Thus, in Scotland, the past two decades have seen an evolution of the concept of forms of assessment which have as their main purpose the promotion of learning. The initial assumption that criterion-referenced assessment, which identified particular areas of pupil failure, was in itself sufficient to point towards appropriate remediation was challenged and soon abandoned. The use of the term 'diagnostic testing' set the thinking about learning difficulties within the framework of a medical model, but had the merit of promoting the idea that investigations were necessary to diagnose the nature of the difficulties. The identification of the intended outcomes of the learning activities and of the current knowledge and understanding of pupils – including an exploration of their misconceptions – were seen as key components of this investigative activity. These investigative processes and the informed reactions to the identified difficulties and needs of the pupils, rather than the application of test items, came to be seen as central to diagnostic assessment as a process. In contrast to the use of standard formulae for the determination of validity in traditional tests, the validity of this contextualised assessment was determined by the success of its outcomes in accurately informing the teacher how to assist the pupil to overcome the identified learning difficulty.

These processes of investigation and remediation match fairly well with the standard model of the teacher as the skilled professional who has sole possession of the required specialist knowledge and who determines and controls the transactions within the class-room. However, there has been increasing acknowledgement of an additional, and potentially more problematic requirement if formative assessment is to fulfil its full potential – that of the informed and active participation of the pupils.

It is now clear, in the present period of rapid technological change, that school leavers need more than basic knowledgeability; it is also essential that they gain the capacity to learn throughout life and to adapt to new environments. They have, therefore, to be motivated and committed to continued learning, to be self-determined, to feel they have the power to promote their own development, and to have confidence that they can succeed and continue to progress. This requires the learner to develop attributes of self-motivation, self-monitoring, self-reflection and self-reliance. In order to promote these characteristics, teachers have been enjoined to give pupils a more active and responsible role in the management of their own learning. However, giving pupils responsibility which is effective and meaningful necessarily involves the sharing of professional knowledge and skills – including full and informed participation in the processes of assessment which are central to the guidance of learning. As Black (1993) noted:

> The development of self assessment by pupils and students is still in its early stages, but within the framework of formative assessment as an integral part of learning, it seems a natural, almost essential development, as well as a potentially powerful source for the improvement of learning. (p. 82)

And he identifies the key characteristics of an effective self-assessment scheme which include: clear, shared criteria; giving students more responsibility for determining their own learning goals; and assessment procedures and recording schemes which are sufficiently clear and economical that students can work them for themselves. Ideas derived from research, and increasingly made accessible to teachers, also suggest that children are born with much greater potential than hitherto acknowledged and that considerable limitations on school learning outcomes may be set by the standard practices and expectancies of classroom settings. The implications of these ideas go far beyond the fine tuning of current assessment strategies or the simple replacement of one assessment scheme by another. Thus, in Black's view:

To incorporate formative assessment into their teaching would involve teachers in far more than acquisition of the necessary skills. Their view of the aims of the teaching of their own subject might have to change if they are to be close to their students in guiding them. The changes in their classroom practice might also involve profound changes of role, even for teachers regarded by themselves and others as already successful (Black, 1993, p. 79).

It is thus clear why formative assessment has proved difficult to implement in the classroom. What it requires is that assessment is reconceptualised as a process central to the teaching and learning interaction rather than as a procedure at the end of instruction directed judgementally towards the pupil; there must be changes in the teachers' conceptions of pupils' abilities and potential leading to the adoption of the view that all pupils can learn more effectively, given the appropriate context, knowledge, and support; there must be an articulation of the learning goals considered appropriate for pupils in general and for individuals when engaging in particular classroom activities; and finally, there must be a change from pupils being passive recipients of educational instruction, to being knowledgeable and proactive in the pursuance of successful learning strategies. Clearly, the introduction of formative assessment requires significant changes to take place in the thinking and practices of many teachers, and a redefining of their roles and of the relationships between them and their pupils. What incentives, models and support have Scottish teachers been offered from policy makers and from researchers to assist and promote development activities of this type?

PROMOTING THE USE OF FORMATIVE ASSESSMENT IN CLASSROOMS

If teachers are going to engage with the demands and difficulties of developing innovative assessment systems, then certain conditions need to be met. Teachers must have the new strategies explained in professional language which they understand and trust – they abhor 'technical jargon'. They must be clear about the aims of the new strategies and they must perceive the changes as having the potential to solve current problems and deal with present professional concerns – and not as creating more difficulties which are just as formidable as the existing ones. They need to have models of what the new strategies might actually look like in practice, preferably along with examples already in use in classrooms and developed by other teachers. And finally, they need to have enough of a grasp of the underlying principles involved to customise, with confidence, the strategies already available, in order to make them manageable and effective within their own context. To what extent have policy and research provided some of the above ingredients?

The SOED *Guidelines on Assessment 5–14* (Edinburgh: SOEID, 1991) were developed independently from the guidelines on national testing and they promoted many of the characteristics of formative assessment outlined above. They presented assessment as an integral component of learning and teaching; indicated that the purposes of the learning tasks should be shared with pupils; proposed that the intended outcomes of the teaching should be clarified and planned in the light of knowledge of what the individual child had already attained; and suggested that, if the outcomes in terms of learning fell short of expectations, the teaching itself should be questioned and reviewed. They anticipated that engagement in these processes would lead to some indication of the next steps in learning appropriate for the pupil. They presented the ideas in the context of language and processes familiar to teachers – planning, teaching, evaluating, recording and reporting.

In the 1990s, almost twenty years after the Dunning Report, with many more in the profession at an advanced stage in their thinking about the interaction of teaching, learning and assessment, the Scottish Office again funded the production of practical exemplification of how the processes of assessment could be deployed in the classroom to serve the purposes of promoting effective learning, this time within the framework of the 5–14 development programme and therefore largely directed towards and accessible to primary teachers. The materials produced, which were developed by teams of researchers and teachers, were made available to all schools in the form of a series of curriculum focused booklets (relating to Mathematics, Reading, Writing and Science) entitled *Taking a Closer Look* (e.g. Hayward and Hall, 1995). These incorporated the key characteristics of formative assessment indicated above and promoted and exemplified the use of the professional knowledge and skills of the teacher as the central feature of the assessment process, rather than the use of formal schemes or sets of test materials.

To what extent have teachers seen the strategies of formative assessment as contributing to the resolution of other pressing professional difficulties? One of the focal points for the development of formative assessment has been that of differentiation. Emerging from a number of recent Scottish policy initiatives has been a growing concern amongst teachers to develop differentiation – strategies for dealing with pupils who have different levels of attainment, but which are effective and acceptable within the non-selective and equitable philosophy of the Scottish educational system. Traditionally, the focus of differentiation has been the curriculum, either through its presentation at different levels of difficulty, or the requirement for different pupils to respond in different ways to the same task. Research projects set both in primary and in secondary classrooms indicated that the prevailing practices were of limited effectiveness in matching the pupils' levels of attainment to the curricular tasks which teachers allocated, and that the key differences between pupils which were influencing attainment, and of which teachers had to take account, had to go considerably beyond the narrow consideration of attainment levels as measured at a specific point in time (Simpson, 2001).

Teachers were eager to hear of the research findings and in particular of the models of differentiation which focused on the central role of the teacher as responder to the varied needs of learners, rather than as merely a curriculum organiser. However, not surprisingly, many were uncertain as to how to proceed in the development of their practice. A number indicated that, while they clearly needed more extensive and detailed information on pupils' attainments and difficulties in order to differentiate more effectively, the amount of necessary information would very quickly swamp them. Pupils themselves indicated that they would be more motivated and that improvements to their learning would be likely if they were made more aware of what they were supposed to be learning, if they knew not only what their problems were, but how to overcome them, and if they could track their own progress and see evidence of their improvement and progression. It became increasingly clear that mechanisms for identifying and sharing with pupils the key information on the intended learning, the actual outcomes, the difficulties encountered and possible ways forward – in other words, strategies for formative assessment – would fulfil the needs identified by both teachers and pupils (Simpson, 1997).

It would seem then, that despite powerful pressures within the educational system with respect to the development and use of summative assessment, a consistent set of policy initiatives, research information and practical support has prevailed over the past twenty years, all of which, in different ways, have been promoting the adoption of formative assessment. What evidence is available that classroom based developments in formative assessment practices are now beginning to meet the aspirations for its development and use?

CLASSROOM BASED DEVELOPMENTS

It is difficult to quantify the current extent of its classroom application since formative assessment can take a variety of forms in different contexts and is only reliably identifiable at the intimate interface of teaching and learning. However, there are positive indications of change at a number of levels.

M. Simpson and J. Goulder (Implementation of the 5–14 development programme in secondary schools: continuity and progression, *Scottish Educational Review*, 30 (1), 15–28, 1998) suggested that in the secondary schools the 'technical jargon' of assessment had clearly entered the vocabulary of many staff. In their national survey conducted in late 1996, they found that 58% of Science teachers, 62% of Mathematics and 92% of English Language claimed to be implementing assessment procedures which have a 'high formative element'. From their whole school perspective, the learning support staff indicated that since the introduction of the assessment guidelines there had been more integration of assessment into teaching (55%), and an increase in a learner centred approach to assessment (32%).

In the data presented by H. Malcolm and U. Schlapp in the parallel report *5–14 in Primary Schools: A Continuing Challenge* (Edinburgh: SCRE, 1997), there were indications that practice had changed there too: half of the primary headteachers surveyed felt that the guidelines had a very strong influence on practice in their schools; 40% of primary teachers indicated that they were now giving more feedback to pupils, and 45% that they had increased the extent to which they used assessment to identify areas where pupils needed help.

However, it was clear that teachers were claiming to be applying formative assessment when, in a fairly traditional manner, they use any information derived from summative assessment to inform the teaching process. For example in the studies noted above, some of the problems identified by primary teachers appeared to be of a fairly traditional type 'Are they not listening properly . . . Am I going too fast . . . Maybe they've forgotten.' In the secondary schools, many English Language teachers appeared to have a clear vision of the formative nature and value of assessment in which interaction with pupils, rather than the use of tests, forms the central element. In contrast, for many teachers in Mathematics, 'assessment' continued to mean 'testing'; tests were still a matter of pass or fail, and continuous assessment was little more than a staccato form of terminal assessment. For these teachers, sharing the management of learning means allowing pupils merely to mark their own tests and to track their progress by meant of the wall chart that directed them to the next set unit of work; self-assessment meant asking the relatively uninformed pupil 'Do you think you did well in this piece of work?' Despite the elaboration of multi-levelled material within Mathematics, pupils considered that their needs and abilities were better met and matched within English lessons (Simpson, 1997).

Nevertheless, it is increasingly possible to identify a number of innovative developments which, in very different ways, exemplify the key characteristics identified earlier. For example, although it is the case that, as Patricia Broadfoot noted in the 1993 SERA lecture, 'The *Pupils in Profile* project did not have a great impact in Scotland' (Exploring the Forgotten Continent: a traveller's tale, *Scottish Educational Review*, 26 (2), 88 – 96, 1994), there is evidence that some teachers are currently engaging comfortably with the use of pupil profiling. Not only that, they are incorporating strong elements of formative assessment into its frameworks in the form of indications of what is to be learned, criteria which will indicate success, difficulties evidenced by the pupil in the work submitted, and ways in which difficulties can be overcome. Teachers have taken on the responsibility of linking their advice to a variety of 'help sheets ' or other forms of support and pupils are encouraged to consult their records before starting new tasks in the same area.

Teachers involved in a number of classroom-based research and development projects have provided evidence of the variety of strategies which have been devised to share knowledge of the intended learning with pupils, and to help them monitor their own progress; these clearly signal a change in the culture of dependency of the pupil on the teacher: 'One feature of this approach is that pupils will have more freedom to get involved in their own learning. And as a direct spin-off from that, we as teachers have to trust them and have confidence in their ability to do that,' commented one science teacher who had developed a particular format of progress sheets for managing differentiation as part of an SCCC development.

While the recording of attainments within the 5–14 programme is seen by some teachers as a significant, and perhaps unnecessary chore, others, rather than just keeping records of progress in the traditional manner, have devised ways of promoting their active use by pupils and learning support staff. For example, one English departmental plan noted:

> Pupils' record sheets have been introduced, which focus both the teacher's and the pupil's attention on areas of achievement and areas requiring support. Pupils are encouraged to consult their own progress sheets before beginning a piece of work. The progress sheets are used in Learning Support consultation time. [This] encourages the attitude that all pupils have areas which can be improved.

There are signs in many secondary subject departments of the erosion of traditional roles as teachers begin to question their previous well-established practices and share with pupils information about tests – such as the item codes that indicate which skill is being tested – which was once regarded as exclusively within the purview of the teacher; and the strategy of applying only end-of-unit tests is beginning to be seen to be inadequate. In primary classrooms, a range of strategies based on a partnership approach has been devised which incorporate many of the key features outlined above and some teachers have skilfully turned Circle Time to the service of assessment through information exchange and the promotion of confidence, learning strategies and self-esteem. All of these are indicators of small but significant steps in the right direction.

CURRENT DEVELOPMENTS

It is auspicious that the assessment strategies indicated above were initiated by teachers in response to difficulties they themselves had identified in their traditional practices, but they are clearly informed by ideas about learning and teaching cognate with those in the research literature; and are in harmony with, and supported by, policy documents on assessment. However, such innovations typically prove fragile and limited in use, even within the schools of their creators. Throughout the 1990s, debate and activities continued to be dominated by concerns about national testing (see Chapter 85), the outcomes of the national monitoring programme (see Chapter 87) and Scotland's position in the international league tables. The legacy of political and ideological disputes throughout the 1990s had left the summative systems of assessment within 5–14 in chaos and the spontaneous school-based formative assessment initiatives were marginalised and faltering. In 1999 the new Scottish Executive Education Department published a review of the current state of play in assessment in 5–14 and distributed it widely for consultation (HMI, *Review of Assessment in Pre-school and 5–14*, Edinburgh: SEED, 1999). Although the document was primarily concerned with potential reforms to summative assessment procedures, the perceived importance of formative assessment is clearly stated:

> Whatever changes to the overall assessment system are considered necessary, assessment in the classroom as part of effective teaching and learning will continue to be at the heart of effective assessment . . . This kind of assessment, which involves pupils in decisions about their own learning, is likely to be most effective in raising standards of attainment. (p. 29)

This quite striking affirmation within the policy document had been prompted by an extensive review of research into formative assessment by Black and Wiliam in 1998 which had been immediately followed by their widely disseminated publication *In the Black Box: Raising Standards through Classroom Assessment* (available as a pdf file from http://www.ltscotland). This presented an accessible argument setting out the virtues of formative assessment, starting with the simple question of key import to politicians, 'Is there evidence that improving formative assessment raises standards?' And they answered it with 'a clear Yes'. The document was used by those within the policy making system who had retained their commitment to the furtherance of formative assessment to rekindle interest at ministerial level. Responses to the SEED review document confirmed that there was a general commitment to assessment which informed teaching and learning, and, included in the subsequent Assessment Development Programme which was initiated to take forward reforms across the range of assessment procedures, was a significantly funded project: Assessment is for Learning (www.ltscotland.com/assess/). The projects recognised the necessity of the full involvement and commitment of the teaching profession:

> Projects are planned to involve practitioners at all stages of the development work, to ensure that the assessment system that emerges is straightforward and does not make unreasonable demands on their time.

In 2002, the project on formative assessment recruited participation from just over 100 teachers in schools across the thirty-two authorities. These teachers have been allocated attractive funds to be at their own disposal for cover or other development costs; they are brought together on a regular basis to meet, talk, and listen to teachers and researchers who are currently well advanced in similar developments in England taken forward by King's College London (Learning how to learn in classrooms, schools and networks, www.tlrp.org/proj/phase11.html). They are supported by a number of development and higher education staff recruited to assist them with any advice or research information they request to assist in the developments they have selected to take forward within the rubric of 'formative assessment'. This represents a very different model of development from the earlier experiences of interested teachers who were largely left to their own devices. Nevertheless, the familiar ingredients are there – driven by policy, informed by research, generated through practice – but given new direction and impetus through the high profile commitment of SEED and the allocation of significant resources. A new era in the development of formative assessment in Scottish schools has clearly begun!

REFERENCES

Black, H. D. (1983) Introducing diagnostic assessment, *Programmed Learning and Educational Technology* 20 (1), 58–63.

Black, P. J. (1993) Formative and summative assessment by teachers, *Studies in Science Education*, 21, 49–97.

Hayward L. and Hall, J. (1995) *Taking a Closer Look at Reading – Diagnostic Procedures*, Edinburgh: SCRE.

Simpson, M. (1997) Developing differentiation practices: meeting the needs of teachers and pupils, *The Curriculum Journal* 8 (1), 85–104.

Simpson, M. (2001) Differentiation and assessment, in D. Scott (ed.), *Curriculum and Assessment, International Perspectives on Assessment*, vol 1, Westport, CN: Ablex.

SOED (1991) *Guidelines on Assessment 5–14*, Edinburgh: SOED.

83

The Scottish Qualifications Authority

Tom Bryce and Walter Humes

> There are at least four ways of looking at an organisation.
> You can look through its annual reports, mission statements,
> corporate strategies, objectives and job descriptions and
> find out what the organisation thinks it is up to or would
> like others to think it is up to. You can also enquire
> of the organisation's participants, customers, clients,
> suppliers and buyers what they think the organisation
> is doing. Then you can try and find out what it is in
> fact that the organisation is doing. Then you can ask
> the question, is this what the organisation should be doing?
> (Donnelly, D. and Wilkie, R., Policing the police,
> *Scottish Review*, 2 (6), p. 45, 2002)

This statement was made as a preliminary to an analysis of the police in Scotland, but it can be argued that it also has a special significance in relation to the Scottish Qualifications Authority (SQA) following the examination crisis of 2000, when there was a failure to release accurate and timely results to a significant number of candidates. The episode raised serious questions not only about the self-perception of SQA, but about Scottish education as a whole. The present chapter is not concerned exclusively, or even primarily, with what happened in 2000 – though some attention certainly has to be given to the enquiries into the crisis and the fall-out from it – but the four-fold perspective outlined in the opening quotation suggests the need to dig beneath the surface if a proper understanding of the SQA as an organisation is to be approached.

SQA'S ORIGINS, ROLE AND FUNCTIONS

The Scottish Qualifications Authority took over all the responsibilities of its predecessor bodies, the Scottish Examination Board (SEB) and the Scottish Vocational Education Council (SCOTVEC), on 1 April, 1997. The reasons for the merger had become apparent in the course of the preceding decade. Historically, the concerns of upper secondary education (the province of SEB) and further education (FE), vocational education and training (the province of SCOTVEC) had been fairly distinct. However, increasingly the separation of academic and vocational qualifications came to be regarded as inadequate to meet the needs of a society in which knowledge was expanding and changing rapidly, and in which the employment market was demanding new skills over and above traditional forms of understanding. The convergence of these pressures meant that the case for a unified qualifications framework and a single qualifications body was compelling.

Institutional mergers, however, are never easy and in this case were to prove especially difficult. SEB, located in the east of Scotland, at Dalkeith, had established systems and structures geared mainly to the school sector, informed by the professional views of teachers, and based on fairly conservative notions of worthwhile knowledge and the best means of assessing it (see Chapter 80 in the first edition). SCOTVEC, by contrast, based in Glasgow in the west of Scotland, had pursued an agenda that was strongly influenced by the expressed needs of employers in business and industry, and had developed a wide range of modular courses using innovative methods of assessment (see Chapter 81 in the first edition). There was, in other words, a significant culture gap between the two organisations, a culture gap that forms an important part of the backdrop to some of the difficulties that subsequently arose. In the early years of the merger, a substantial amount of time was devoted to the question of how integration of SEB and SCOTVEC procedures could best be promoted. This took place at a time when Higher Still was reaching a critical stage in its implementation. Instead of giving so much attention to internal matters such as structure, staffing, and terms and conditions of service, SQA might have been wiser to concentrate on ensuring that service to its external clients could be delivered efficiently.

On its website (www.sqa.org.uk) SQA describes itself as 'the national body in Scotland responsible for the development, accreditation, assessment, and certification of qualifications other than degrees'. Its functions are to:

- devise, develop and validate qualifications, and keep them under review;
- accredit qualifications;
- approve education and training establishments as being suitable for entering people for these qualifications;
- arrange for, assist in, and carry out, the assessment of people taking SQA qualifications;
- quality assure education and training establishments which offer SQA qualifications;
- certificate candidates.

SQA is also responsible for developing and distributing 5–14 national tests to schools as part of the 5–14 programme.

Overall responsibility for ensuring that these functions are carried out efficiently rests with a board of management which includes the chief executive (David Fraser) and representatives from the school, FE and HE sectors, parents, industry and commerce. The board of management was reconstituted (and much reduced in number) following the difficulties of 2000.

The nature of SQA's work requires it to develop strong partnerships with a number of other agencies, including the Scottish Executive Education Department (SEED), Learning and Teaching Scotland (LTS), the Scottish Further Education Unit (SFEU) and the Association of Scottish Colleges (ASC). LTS is particularly important because it provides curriculum back-up to the assessment system for which SQA has responsibility, and produces many publications of use to teachers and students. One interesting example of LTS's role is the online area it has developed (as part of the National Grid for Learning initiative) specifically devoted to supporting National Qualifications. SQA staff see it as an important part of their work to maintain and develop networks which ensure that they have good lines of communication with the school, college and university sectors of the educational system, as well as with employers, training providers and bodies representing particular industrial and commercial sectors. These links are not confined to Scotland or the UK. Increasingly, SQA participates in a number of international projects – funded, for example, by the European Commission and the World Bank.

The bulk of SQA's income derives from fees chargeable to centres (schools, colleges and other bodies) which present candidates for the various qualifications awarded by the authority. Of these, National Qualifications (including Standard Grade and Higher Still) are the best known and are described extensively elsewhere in this volume. Less well known, but equally important, are Scottish Vocational Qualifications (SVQs), Higher National Certificates (HNCs) and Higher National Diplomas (HNDs). SVQs are based on national standards of performance developed by representatives from industry, commerce and education. They offer benefits to both employers and employees. To employers, the attraction is that SVQs give a focused, on-the-job context for staff training and development. To employees, they provide learning that is directly relevant to work and a marketable qualification that will help their career progression. Nearly all occupations are covered, from forestry to IT, management to catering, journalism to construction. Within the SVQ portfolio, the modern apprenticeship programme deserves special mention. Modern Apprenticeships were introduced to help create a high-calibre workforce and strengthen the training system in Scotland. They are designed for those aged over sixteen and offer the opportunity of paid employment combined with training for jobs at craft, technician and management levels. They have the backing of national training organisations, local enterprise companies and the Trades Union Congress.

HNCs and HNDs are offered by colleges, some universities and other training centres, and are specially designed to meet the needs of employers, both locally and nationally. The range of subjects offered is extensive, including Agriculture, Accounting, Business Administration, Computing, Engineering, and Travel and Tourism. All courses are made up of Higher National Unit credits, with one credit representing roughly forty hours of timetabled learning: HNCs require twelve credits and usually take one year to complete, while HNDs require thirty credits and usually take two years to complete. Chapter 88 presents an analysis of the full range of awards handled by SQA in its early years and by its predecessor bodies in the pre-merger period. The growth in student numbers at all levels over the years is very apparent in the tables given in Chapter 88.

In its corporate plan for the period up to 2001 (produced in 1998), SQA set out a number of goals and values. The five corporate goals were to:

- develop and maintain a comprehensive, coherent and relevant Scottish qualifications system;
- ensure that the award of all SQA qualifications is based on a consistent application of standards;
- consult and respond to the needs of users, and promote SQA qualifications nationally and internationally;
- create an organisational ethos which supports individual development and teamwork, and which enhances corporate performance;
- enhance operational effectiveness and maintain financial viability.

In its list of values, SQA sought to 'provide a quality service', 'observe the highest standards of integrity, impartiality and objectivity', 'be responsive, courteous and helpful to those it serves', 'ensure quality, value for money and accuracy in all its services', and 'be open and accountable'. Later in the chapter a more recent formulation of SQA's values and strategic objectives will be given to indicate the organisation's current priorities. First, however, the event which led to sharp external scrutiny and painful internal self-examination requires some attention.

THE EXAMINATIONS CRISIS OF 2000

With the first diet of the new Higher Still examinations in the summer of 2000, Scottish education encountered a major crisis. Thousands of students received wrong results, late results or, in some cases, no results at all, from the SQA. The scale of the crisis was considerable and public reaction, which started with bewilderment on 'results day' (10 August), turned to anger and hostility as the days unfolded. What had heretofore been a smooth operation for the 'old' Highers and Standard Grades, had gone seriously wrong with the new programme and the immediate prospects for school leavers, particularly those hoping to enter university courses, were put in jeopardy. The events proved to be a serious test for the new Scottish Parliament and several investigations were mounted to determine what had happened, with emergency procedures instigated to check all 147,000 certificates. The Education, Culture and Sport Committee and the Enterprise and Lifelong Learning Committee both set up enquiries; the former looking into all the educational dimensions to the debacle, the latter to questions of accountability. Independently from them, the Parliament commissioned management consultants Deloitte and Touche to undertake a review into the exam results issues concerning the SQA which would 'identify any administrative, procedural or management weaknesses and provide a set of clear recommendations on how to ensure that these problems do not recur in future years' (Scottish Executive, 2000). Paterson has concluded that the parliamentary enquiries achieved four things: they provided a platform which was both open and (relatively) informal; a focus for serious public worries; reasonably rigorous questioning of key players; and introduced a culture of openness in Scottish public affairs (Paterson, 2000). Some of the consequences of these enquiries are referred to elsewhere in this volume (e.g. in Chapter 11 on SEED and the Scottish Parliament; in Chapter 14 on HMIE). With respect to the SQA itself, not only has it had to put its house in order, it has had to do so in a climate of increased watchfulness. Paterson's 'openness' has been accompanied by increased doubt and scepticism.

The Deloitte and Touche enquiry came to a number of conclusions. While the data mishandling was judged to be a critical flaw, there were several deficiencies in the SQA operations; these related to management, process and information systems and they were all interlinked. The report noted that the management had relied too heavily upon structures and practices inherited from the predecessor organisations, SEB and SCOTVEC, and had failed to develop an operational plan for the new challenges encountered in session 1999–2000 with Higher Still. The scale and number of the processes required led inevitably to systematic data handling problems. Too few markers were appointed and the appointment arrangements were found to be wanting. Crucially, a new computer system had been put in place in preparation for the increased volume of data (including internal assessment outcomes) but preparatory operations with it had been inadequate. The report also concluded that 'without the sustained commitment and dedication of the [SQA] staff, particularly within the Operations Unit, the levels of inaccurate and incomplete results would have been greater' (Scottish Executive, 2000, p. 3 of the Executive Summary).

In retrospect, the events of 2000 raise a number of interesting questions about power and responsibility in Scottish education. At the time, there was the unedifying spectacle of all the major players (politicians, SQA staff and Board members, the inspectorate) blaming each other. Understanding of the precise nature of the relationship between the Scottish Executive, SQA and other NDPBs remains sketchy. There is a tendency for politicians to want to remain in control but to make others accountable, particularly when things go wrong. The relationship between the Scottish Executive and the SQA altered in the immediate aftermath of 2000, switching from ministerial action at arms-length (the normal description of relations between government and agency) to ministerial 'vice-like grip', in the words of one observer at the time.

POST-2000 ATTITUDES TO ASSESSMENT AND TO SQA

There can be little doubt that secondary teachers and FE lecturers feel overworked by the assessment load brought about by Higher Still. The final section of Chapter 81 has considered many of the details and the consultation exercise referred to in that chapter (carried out in 2001–2) provided interesting reactions to tentative Scottish Executive proposals for change. Inevitably, teachers' concerns and feelings about a system which requires so much internal assessment as a prerequisite to external assessment spill over into feelings about the body which administers the system. Articles in the *Times Educational Supplement Scotland* (*TESS*) regularly reflect the strength of feeling raised by Higher Still assessment and have done so ever since the events of 2000. Writing in the wake of the Education Committee's report of the enquiry, the late Tony McManus castigated the lack of educational principles in Higher Still: 'Reform must be grounded in genuine educational needs, not a corrupting drive to assessment' (*TESS*, 29 December 2000). Some fourteen months later, Marj Adams commented upon the stress of assessment for her as a teacher and the burden on her teenage daughter as she prepared for the forthcoming diet of examinations in 2002: 'Contempt, derision and sustained savagery towards the SQA may make for impressive verbal pyrotechnics, but Higher Still assessments continue unabated with little prospect of imminent change' (*TESS*, 5 April 2002). And public figures are not at all reticent when it comes to judgements about the effects of modern practices in assessment. Writing in a UK context (but thinking probably more of England), the broadcaster John Humphrys has spoken harshly of how counterproductive exam practice has now become: 'Exams are not the measure of a child, so let's ditch them' (*Sunday Times*, 9 June 2002). The general public grows steadily more sceptical about the complexity of national assessment systems.

A full consideration of the issues concerning the educational and social funtion of an assessment system would require a thorough analysis of the complex relationships between SEED, HMI, SQA and other bodies, much of which is beyond the scope of this chapter. Suffice to say that the whole Scottish community, teachers, parents and pupils alike, find it difficult to distinguish between SQA's organisational responsibilities and its wider social function. With regard to teachers, it would be fair to say that the profession, prior to 2000, held the examination agency, particularly in its previous incarnation as the SEB, in high regard. Had the examination and certification arrangements in that year gone smoothly, there would still be complaints about the weight of assessment apparently required for an effective national system. Parents and pupils have long tolerated what is put before them; they accept what comes with authority (from *the* assessment authority). Employers and the public at large have (so far) accepted that certification has to be the way it is, but serious and more vocal doubts about its complexity are growing.

The appeals procedure, an important reliability check invoked annually in the wake of the national diet of examinations (and critical to SQA's professional-public interface) was also affected by the events of 2000. Before then, only a minority of candidates' results were appealed; now a very considerable number must be checked, requiring manpower and time accordingly. The appeals procedure enables candidates/schools to challenge their results where they consider that their course work and school-based assessment provides evidence of higher attainment than that turned in on the day of the external examination. Thus, following a successful appeal, a candidate's particular Higher result might be regraded from say C to B. The procedure has a long pedigree which indicates that early in the twentieth century, Scottish education had a commitment to teacher-based assessment. (Chapter 80 on the SEB, in the first edition of this book, indicates something of its evolution, even pre-dating the establishment of SEB itself.) Basically, if a school or college subject department is, and has recently been, a good predictor of final examination performance for the candidates it presents, then the benefit of any doubt about a final grade level is given to the candidate in question. Detailed checking is required, of course, the process being commenced by a statistical check of the concordance between the internal and external grades; and the important step being scrutiny of the evidence submitted by the school/college department, the examinations sat, their marking, and so forth. Teachers are accustomed to careful preparations, should appeals be called for. The events of 2000 highlighted the significance and potential benefits of appealing any 'less-than-expected' result. Pupils being street-wise, appeals have now become a regular event; just another step to be tried in a world full of qualification hurdles.

FUTURE PLANS

It is not difficult to see that the SQA works hard to progress and develop its core business. Several steps have been taken to get over the difficulties with marking and markers. In an effort to encourage teachers to act as markers, SQA began a pilot project with East Renfrewshire in 2002 to train teachers who had not served in that role in the past. In defending the experience of marking and its contribution to improved teaching, Anton Colella, a director of SQA, stated in the *TESS* of 3 May 2002: 'When you mark you actually have the opportunity to see a variety of responses that may be different from the response your own candidates will provide. Hearing the experiences of others and comments about how particular questions can be marked all add to a greater understanding of standards.' Also in 2002, SQA expanded its efforts to train markers on-line, a development which could bear fruit; and, separately, commenced a two-year project into whether pupils could take tests on-line and send essays by e-mail to be marked. This so-called 'paperless exam project' is thought to offer ways round some of the marking problems which are encountered annually; some 9,000 markers are appointed each session, mostly drawn from the teaching profession. The project is endeavouring to see whether internal (school- or college-conducted) assessment using ICT can be reliably carried out without risk. Several bodies are involved: the Scottish Executive, SQA, SFEU, LTS, BBC Scotland and the Scottish Centre for Research into Online Learning and Assessment.

During session 2001–2, SQA experimented with an additional winter diet of examinations (largely called for by FE Colleges to cater for part-time vocational courses) but it turned out not to be popular. Announcing an end to the short-lived experiment, Nicol Stephen's parliamentary answer in April 2002 was: '[it] is clear from the number of entries for this year and the projected entries for the second year that continuing to run a winter exam round for such a small number of entrants is not a sensible or cost effective option at this time.' Comments from SQA spokespersons were that SQA would still like to have the option of more all-year-round flexibility on assessment and certification.

In fact there is a much more fundamental debate about assessment taking place amongst educationists and researchers. Wiliam's research on formative assessment in England (see, for example, P. Black and Wiliam, D. *Inside the Black Box: Raising Standards through Classroom Assessment*, London: King's College, 1998) persuades him to see an end to the marking and grading of classwork and homework. He considers that pupils should be given comments and suggestions on how to improve their work; these will lead more directly and effectively to improvement for more pupils, particularly those at the bottom of the class who are often discouraged by low grades. When this work was aired by Wiliam at a Scottish Executive hosted seminar in 2002, reactions varied. Voicing the parent's perspective, Judith Gillespie reacted positively. 'If we focus on education rather than marks, then attainment rises as a by-product. It is a fantastic idea' (*The Herald*, 27 January 2002). The teaching union perspective expressed by Easton of the SSTA doubted the prospects of 'another revolution' in education. Cathy Jamieson, Education Minister in the Scottish Executive was mildly positive in her reaction but predictably uncommitted to any formal move as a result. Were there to be any such change to assessment, the consequences would actually simplify things for a body like the SQA.

In 1999, SQA set up nineteen broad-based advisory groups, each with approximately twenty members 'as a three year pilot on the most appropriate model for stakeholder participation in the SQA'. The intended purpose was to obtain sector-based advice on the long-term development of qualifications. Membership was drawn from interested bodies, including schools, FE and HE, employers, HMIE, and SQA staff; the groups met approximately twice per year. The report drawn up when these groups were wound up (SQA, 2002a) indicates that they were not very successful. Despite the time and energy devoted to the process, attendances declined over the period and meeting agendas were dominated by the crisis of 2000 and recovery from it. Despite the potential for influence from widely represented fields, members did not find themselves able to 'identify strategic issues to which they felt they could effectively contribute'; they did not form into 'active teams' (p. 2), in part because the interests of stakeholders were different (some being more concerned with NQs, some with SVQs, and so forth). Crucially, it was apparent that input and discussion did not materialise in action within SQA itself. The various groups remained confused about their relation to other activities of the SQA. In a country the size of Scotland, nineteen groups with twenty members each amounts to a considerable proportion of the stakeholders in question (more precisely, perhaps, of senior professionals in the areas in question). If such a proportion were too cumbersome, would a slimmer interface work any better?

In November 2002 the Scottish Executive invited applications from people willing to serve on an advisory council, which had been established by Order under the SQA Act 2002. The function of the council is to consider matters relating to qualifications devised or awarded by SQA, to provide advice to the board of management in relation to those matters, and also on other matters, as the council thinks appropriate. Applicants were expected to have knowledge or experience relating to one sector of the education and training system, and also to possess an understanding of the issues facing the various stakeholders in Scottish education. In seeking expressions of interest, the Scottish Executive stated its commitment to the principle of making the appointments to the advisory council 'based on merit and equal opportunities with openness and transparency of process'.

Many teachers in all sectors of education in Scotland currently do attest to the professional way in which staff in SQA go about their business; the determination to get over the past and to be positive about the future is apparent when one interacts with SQA personnel. And it would be proper to record how efficiently examinations and certification were conducted in 2001 and 2002. It can be asked whether there is yet an effective synthesis, organisationally, in the difficult business which stemmed from the separate predecessors of SQA. Organisations traditionally seek to expand their spheres of operation and one might interpret the creation of so many advisory groups, now dismantled, as a step intended to bind the organisation into the complex territory that it must serve. It didn't work and it can be surmised that the internal mechanisms were cumbersome and bureaucratic, thereby not easily leading to effective action and development. It remains to be seen whether, with an Advisory council, the organisation will be any more effective in progressing its relationships with the various bodies and sectors concerned. Whether the latter, through their representations and representatives, will be any different in their networking as a result, is also uncertain.

In October 2002 SQA produced a document entitled *Our Strategy for Action 2002–2007* (SQA, 2002b). In the Introduction, the chairman, Professor John Ward, states:

> The need to link education and training with economic
> and skills development is what places the Scottish
> Qualifications Authority at the heart of Scotland's future
> success. While the delivery of National Qualifications to
> young people of Scotland remains vitally important, there
> are other significant imperatives that drive the wider portfolio
> of products and services that SQA is uniquely positioned
> to provide.

This statement indicates a subtle, but significant shift in SQA's priorities. The school sector – the main user of National Qualifications – will continue to be important, but other areas of SQA activity (NVQs, modern apprenticeships, Skillseekers, HNCs/HNDs) will perhaps receive greater attention in the future. The implication is that perhaps Higher Still has consumed a disproportionate amount of effort and it is now time to move on. The reason for this shift is clear – the economy requires that vocational education and training is given priority. However, it should be noted that some analysts are rather sceptical of the assumption of a straightforward relationship between levels of training and economic prosperity, and point to the fact that currently many employees are over-rather than under-qualified for the jobs they do. They suggest that what is needed is a recognition of the fact that some employers have quite deliberately opted to engage in the production of goods and services which require low levels of skill (and correspondingly low wages). Thus they are not required to invest in training and are also failing to take full advantage of the skills that some of their employees already have. The matching of skill levels, commercial/industrial needs and economic development is a highly complex exercise.

In the 2002 strategy document, the chief executive of SQA, David Fraser, identifies three levels of strategic focus for the organisation over the next five years. The first relates to the qualifications portfolio and expresses a commitment 'to design, assess and quality assure qualifications that meet candidate and customer demand and are fit for purpose, relevant and credible'. The second strategic focus has to do with the management of SQA. Emphasis is placed on the importance of leadership so that staff feel 'empowered' and 'enjoy a high level of morale'. In the light of the events of 2000, this is an understandable concern. As with individual grief, the process of organisational recovery from a devastating episode is bound to take time. External perceptions of SQA provide the third strategic focus. Here there is recognition of the need to provide a high quality of service so that clients are satisfied that information about candidates and qualifications will be 'accurate, accessible and easily managed by all those involved in the process'. As part of this, the desirability of simplifying processes and making them more comprehensible to users is stressed. Taken together, these objectives indicate a seriousness of purpose by the present leadership of SQA. Time will tell whether the aspirations are properly fulfilled.

PERSPECTIVES

The quotation that opened this chapter suggested that it was desirable to view organisations from four perspectives. In the case of SQA, it has been possible to say something about three of these. First, the organisation's view of itself has been represented using its own published statements. This has been balanced by, secondly, drawing on the external views of teachers, academics, parents and employers. A third perspective has taken the form of some observations on what SQA should be doing. What about the fourth perspective – 'what it is in fact that the organisation is doing'? That is the most difficult of all. To convey a sense of the 'reality' of what happens in SQA (or any other large organisation) would require insider knowledge, but all insiders are bound to be partial (and, in any case, their public expression will be limited by the contractual constraints to which employees are subject). Thus the 'truth' of what happens in an organisation is bound to be varied, contested and elusive.

REFERENCES

Paterson, L. (2000) *Crisis in the Classroom: The Exam Debacle and the Way Ahead for Scottish Education*, Edinburgh and London: Mainstream Publishing.

Scottish Executive (2000) *A Review into Exam Results Issues concerning the Scottish Qualifications Authority*, final report, 31 October 2000, Deloitte and Touche, Edinburgh: Scottish Executive.

SQA (2002a) *Review of Advisory Groups – Report to Stakeholders*, Dalkeith and Glasgow: SQA.

SQA (2002b) *Our Strategy for Action 2002 – 2007*, Dalkeith and Glasgow: SQA.

84

Baseline Assessment in Scotland

Linda Croxford

The term 'baseline assessment' refers to the assessment of pupils when they first enter primary school at the age of four to five. Baseline assessment is used for two main purposes:

- to provide teachers with information about the levels of readiness for learning of pupils entering primary one at age four to five, and to identify children who may later have difficulties in school;
- to provide a baseline against which future progress can be measured, so that differences in 'value added' can be identified.

There is some controversy as to whether both of these purposes can be addressed using a single system of baseline assessment and whether the assessment should be based on external tests or assessment based on teachers' professional judgements. This controversy is part of the wider debate over the purposes and methods of 5–14 assessment in Scotland.

For baseline assessment, as for 5–14 assessment more generally, developments in Scotland have been less regulated than in England and Wales. In Scotland the use of baseline assessment is at the discretion of local authorities, whereas in England and Wales baseline assessment on entry to reception classes at age four to five was made mandatory by the 1997 Education Act.

This chapter describes the policy context in which baseline assessment was introduced in Scottish primary schools in the late 1990s, and outlines the advantages and disadvantages of two contrasting methods that are used. The introduction of baseline assessment has produced evidence of social inequalities among pupils entering primary school, and this evidence is summarised briefly. The evidence suggests that there is an important role for baseline assessment in the future to alert practitioners and policy makers of the importance of early education for addressing social inequality.

POLICY CONTEXT

The introduction of baseline assessment in Scottish primary schools occurred at a time when a number of over-lapping policy initiatives were increasing pressure on schools and local authorities to improve systems of assessment, measure and evaluate relative school performance, raise standards of attainment and address social inequality. Early in the 1990s the 5–14 programme attempted, amid continuing controversy, to introduce more systematic methods for assessment into primary schools. The Quality Initiative in Scottish Schools emphasised the need for school improvement using performance indicators. Dissatisfaction with crude league tables led to calls for 'value added' measures of relative school performance as a fairer way of evaluating schools. But in Scotland, value added indicators could not be developed because there was no systematic measurement of attainment prior to Standard Grade examinations at age fifteen to sixteen. The situation in Scotland contrasted strongly with developments in England and Wales where there was mandatory key-stage testing of all pupils.

The impetus for the introduction of baseline assessment in Scotland in the late 1990s came from the Early Intervention Programme (EIP). In 1996 a task force on under-achievement in Scottish schools was set up by the Minister of Education, and recommended that the highest priority be given to the early years of schooling, with the aim:

> to overcome by intervention the disadvantages and inequalities of social and domestic back-ground, and to help all children to reach or exceed a minimum level of performance – in language and number especially – by P3 (Scottish Office, 1996, p. 1).

The task force recommended the development of a method of assessing pupils on entry to school 'so that children in need of interventionary attention can be identified' (p. 1).

The EIP began in 1997. Responsibility for deciding how early intervention should be implemented was devolved to local authorities, and this led to a very varied pattern of approaches to EIP (Fraser et al., 2001). Several local authorities introduced baseline assessments as part of EIP: some, such as the City of Edinburgh Council, devised their own standardised baseline assessments; others, such as Aberdeen City Council, chose systems developed in England. In addition to the various approaches to baseline assessment introduced by local authorities, the Scottish Office convened a team of researchers and practitioners to develop a national baseline assessment strategy for Scotland (Wilkinson et al., 1999, 2001).

WHAT IS BASELINE ASSESSMENT?

The term 'baseline assessment' typically refers to the assessment of pupils when they first enter primary school at the age of four to five. A number of different baseline assessment systems are used in Scotland, some of which focus exclusively on literacy, while others include assessment of a wider range of curricular areas including numeracy, while yet others include measures of personal and social development.

The different systems of baseline assessment that are currently used in Scotland are characterised by two contrasting approaches:

- Assessment based on external tests, such as the Performance Indicators in Primary Schools (PIPS) (Tymms, 1999), and the system devised by the City of Edinburgh Council.
- Assessment based on teachers' judgements, especially the system developed by the Scottish Office/Executive.

Baseline assessment based on external tests

This form of baseline assessment uses a common test in which all pupils are asked the same questions, and correct answers are summed to give a test score. In almost all cases this form of baseline assessment is designed to be carried out twice: firstly during the first few weeks after entry to primary school, and secondly at the end of the P1 stage. The initial test is extended to include further items to allow for growth in learning. They are carried out on a one-to-one basis and can provide an opportunity to identify pupils with specific learning difficulties. Although the word 'test' creates an image of drab paper-and-pencil tests typical of later school years, the baseline assessments currently in use are brightly coloured and attractive to young children. Some baseline assessments make use of a computer, and include amusing graphics and sounds.

Typically, the literacy assessments cover vocabulary (the child is shown a picture and asked to point to named objects); writing (the child is asked to write her/his own name); concepts about print (such as ability to distinguish words from pictures); letter identification (how many letters of the alphabet can she/he identify); reading (ability to read whole words); phonological awareness (ability to spot the onset sound and rhyming of words). Not all baseline assessments include numeracy, but the PIPS system includes ideas about maths (concepts such as bigger, most and tallest); counting; early sums; digit identification.

The main benefit of this approach to baseline assessment is that externally-devised tests provide an objective measure of each pupil's attainment. By using a common test it is possible to ensure that pupils are assessed on the same basis in all classes, and all schools in an authority. Assessments at the beginning and end of P1 provide schools with measures of both initial attainment and relative progress of each pupil during their first year at school. These assessments can help teachers to plan effectively to meet children's learning needs, and can provide indications of children who need additional help. Subsequent analysis of the baseline assessment data by local authorities can provide evidence of socio-economic inequality, and indicate school differences in intake and value-added. Objective measures of differences in progress made by pupils were especially valuable for evaluating the impact of early intervention (Croxford, 2001).

The main disadvantages of externally-devised baseline tests are that they are relatively formal and, if handled badly, can give children the feeling of failure when they are unable to answer some questions. Their content is limited to assessment of literacy (and in some cases numeracy) and they are not suited to assessment of personal and social skills.

Baseline Assessment based on teachers' judgements

A national system for assessment of pupils at the end of the pre-school stage and in the second term of P1 has been constructed by a team of researchers and practitioners on behalf of the Scottish Office/Executive (Wilkinson et al., 2001). The title is now 'transition record', and the assessment is part of a pupil record which is aimed at improving the transition of children from pre-school to primary school. The assessment task involves rating each child on a four-point scale for each of eight aspects of learning:

- personal, emotional and social development;
- expressive communication;
- physical co-ordination;
- listening and talking;
- reading;
- writing;
- mathematics;
- understanding the environment.

The rating of each aspect of learning is based on a list of features. For example, personal, emotional and social development has sixteen features including: 'separates readily from parent/carer'; 'plays independently'; 'is independent in personal hygiene, cloakroom and other routines'.

There are appropriate lists of features for each of the aspects of learning. When rating the child on each aspect of learning, teachers are asked to select one of four attainment statements which best reflects the attainment of each individual child in relation to these features. The attainment statements are:

- The child displays very few of these features. Immediate investigation and structured intervention are essential.
- The child displays some of these features. Most others require attention and planned support.
- The child displays the majority of these features successfully and is making good progress with most of the others.
- The child displays almost all of these features consistently and with confidence.

This approach to baseline assessment has many advantages: it covers the whole breadth of young children's development and learning rather than being confined narrowly to literacy and numeracy, and is therefore consistent with the traditions of early childhood education in Scotland and the 5–14 approach to assessment; it builds on teachers' professional judgements and knowledge of each child over a period of time; it helps teachers to highlight each child's strengths and weaknesses, and identifies areas of the curriculum in which the class needs further development.

Potentially, the numerical coding of attainment statements can provide a quantitative score for value-added performance monitoring, but as yet the predictive capacity of the measures has not been established. However, the main disadvantage of this approach is that the results may be perceived as less reliable than measures derived from external tests because of the scope for differences between teachers in the rating of each child. At the pilot stage it was evident that pre-school staff had different expectations of pupils, and applied different grades from P1 teachers (Wilkinson et al., 1999, page 48). Subsequently, the baseline assessment was limited to the spring term of P1, allowing teachers two terms to judge their pupils' capabilities. However, this late timing of baseline assessment renders it inappropriate for evaluation of progress over the course of P1.

ISSUES OF CONCERN

Whichever approach is used, the introduction of baseline assessment at the beginning of primary school raises some issues of concern. There are fears about the effects of assessment on young children: if assessment is conducted or reported insensitively, is there a danger that pupils' self-esteem may be damaged by low assessment results? Some teachers involved in piloting the system of assessment developed for the Scottish Executive expressed anxiety that the use of attainment statements would lead to harmful 'labelling'. On the other hand, do some teachers give too much help to the child so that they will attain a more favourable result? Could baseline assessment lead to differential labelling of children and reinforce socio-economic inequalities?

There are problems associated with workload; the process of baseline assessment, whether using external tests or systems based on teachers' judgement, is very time consuming because each pupil is assessed individually. This leads to concerns about how the process of assessment should be resourced.

Further issues relate to the use of assessment information. Baseline assessment is intended to provide information to support teaching, but it is not clear at present that teachers are making full use of the assessments for pedagogic purposes. There may be problems arising from lack of experience and/or training in the use of assessment-based evidence by early-years staff. In some cases there has been resistance to the use of baseline assessment because staff do not feel 'ownership' of the assessments, and are suspicious of their use in monitoring systems.

Although baseline assessment is intended to form part of a system of value-added performance monitoring, this presupposes that there are appropriate assessment systems at later stages, and at the time of writing this is the case in only one or two local authorities using externally-devised tests. In the short term there has been a policy vacuum at the Scottish Executive with respect to assessment, and the intended national system of baseline assessment has been left in limbo, with no evidence as to its suitability for predicting attainment at later primary stages.

USING BASELINE ASSESSMENT TO MONITOR
INEQUALITY AND EVALUATE EARLY INTERVENTION

Good quality baseline data is essential for monitoring the effects of social inequality on educational attainment and evaluating the impact of policy interventions. An example of the value of baseline assessment is provided by an evaluation of the EIP in Aberdeen City using a 'value-added' type of analysis (Croxford, 2001). Over a three-year period, PIPS baseline assessment at the start and end of P1 was linked to background information about pupils and schools. Analysis of these data identified significant inequality in attainment at the start of P1 associated with age of pupils, first language, entitlement to clothing grants and local-area deprivation. Further analysis showed that after taking account of baseline attainment, pupils had made less progress by the end of P1 if they were male, had a clothing grant or attended a school with high levels of local-area deprivation. Evaluation of the consequences of early intervention over the three-year period found a dramatic rise in average reading scores at the end of P1, but the effects of social inequality were not diminished. Although pupils with clothing grants and pupils attending schools with high levels of deprivation shared to some extent in the overall improvement in reading, the increase in average attainment for these groups was not as great as the increase for other pupils.

This analysis provides important evidence about the reinforcement of social inequality by schooling and the differential impact of a major policy intervention. It could not have been achieved without good-quality baseline data. If policy makers genuinely seek to address issues of social justice in education it is important to monitor the impact of policies, and to do this, robust assessment data is essential.

THE FUTURE OF BASELINE ASSESSMENT IN SCOTLAND

At a national level, baseline assessment, as with other forms of 5–14 assessment, has been in a policy vacuum since the Scottish Office announced a review of assessment practice in 1998. In summer 2002 a programme entitled 'Assessment is for Learning' was announced by Learning and Teaching Scotland, including projects to improve professional practice in formative assessment, and to create new national assessments to replace national tests (see Chapters 82 and 85). The role of baseline assessment in the new programme is unclear.

In the meantime, in the absence of an agreed national system, more local authorities have begun using externally-devised baseline tests. The main increase has been in the use of PIPS, which is now employed by one-third of Scottish local authorities, and has a Scottish base at Aberdeen University. It seems likely that for the foreseeable future the use of baseline assessment will not be nationally prescribed but will vary according to local authority priorities. The absence of a national system makes it difficult to compare pupil intakes across Scotland, and this has some drawbacks. But in view of evidence from south of the border of the negative impact of mandatory national assessment of pupils throughout schooling, perhaps the slightly messy assessment pattern in Scotland is confirmation that things are better north of the border.

REFERENCES

Croxford, L. (2001) The impact of the Early Intervention Programme in Primary 1, *Education in the North* 9, 26–32.

Fraser H., MacDougall, A., Pirrie, A. and Croxford, L. (2001) *National Evaluation of the Early Intervention Programme: Final report*, Edinburgh: University of Edinburgh.

Scottish Office (1996) *Improving Achievements in Scottish Schools*, Edinburgh: The Stationery Office.

Tymms, P. (1999) *Baseline Assessment and Monitoring in Primary Schools*, London: David Fulton Publishers.

Wilkinson, J. E., Napuk, A., Watt, J., Normand, B. and Johnson, S. (1999) *The Development of Baseline Assessment in Scotland: Pilot Procedures, Final report to SEED*, Glasgow: University of Glasgow.

Wilkinson, J. E., Johnson, S., Watt, J., Napuk, A. and Normand, B. (2001) Baseline assessment in Scotland: and evaluation of pilot procedures, *Scottish Educational Review* 33 (1), 33–47.

85

National Testing and National Assessments

Lillian Munro

5–14 NATIONAL TESTS

National testing is in a transition phase. The system which was originally developed in the early 1990s and which continued, with minor additions, improvements and amendments for a decade, will be discontinued from August 2003. It will replaced by 'second generation' national tests, or national assessments as they will be known, performing much the same function, but with a different genesis and delivery mechanism. Much has still to be decided about the new system and therefore most of this chapter is devoted to putting national testing in its historical and contemporary contexts and describing the background to the changes which are about to take place.

National tests in English (Reading and Writing) and Mathematics are designed to assess the competence of pupils in primary school and the first two years of secondary school. In effect they are a large bank of materials at six levels of difficulty, from which teachers may request units of their choice at any time during the school year. Tests are currently chosen from a catalogue, circulated to all primary and secondary schools in Scotland at the start of each school year with packets of paper copies despatched to schools on request. The tests have both a summative and a diagnostic value within certain specified limitations. These tests correspond roughly to key stages 1–3 in England, Wales and Northern Ireland but have greater flexibility in their use and administration.

HISTORICAL PERSPECTIVE

National Testing and the 5–14 Development Programme

The 5–14 development programme which spanned the years from 1987 to the mid-1990s, sought a redefinition of the curriculum from age five, when a pupil starts primary school, to the end of the second year of secondary schooling at age fourteen. Its aim was to create a more coherent and consistent framework for the curriculum, and for assessment and recording policies and their implementation. A series of national curriculum guidelines addressing the five curricular areas of English Language, Mathematics, Environmental Studies, Expressive Arts and Religious and Moral Education set out advice to teachers on planning the curriculum and on appropriate programmes of study. Pupil attainment was defined at five levels of increasing demand from A to E using a common framework of attainment outcomes, strands and attainment targets. A sixth level, F, was added in 1999 to provide suitable programmes of studies for pupils achieving level E before the end of S2. Attainment outcomes are similar in concept to attainment targets in the English national curriculum, while attainment targets accord to statements of attainment. There is no English equivalent to strands which represent different aspects of learning within curricular areas such as 'reading for enjoyment' or 'spelling' or 'money' or 'add and subtract'. While the national curriculum in England and Wales is a statutory curriculum, which all schools are required to deliver, the curriculum guidelines in Scotland continue a long-standing tradition of education by consensus with Her Majesty's Inspectors providing quality assurance.

The guidelines introduced for the first time explicit, if somewhat generalised, statements about expected levels of attainment. Thus level B was defined as being attainable by most pupils in P4, level D by most pupils in P7, and level E by most pupils in S2. Level A was somewhat more loosely defined in terms of the attainment of pupils 'in the course of P1–P3', and similarly level C by most 'in the course of P4–P6'. Only a 'few' pupils in S2 were expected to achieve level F. Alongside the guidelines for each curricular area, additional guidance was developed on the structure and balance of the curriculum, assessment and reporting. The overall assessment strategy sought to ensure that pupil progress at the 5–14 stages would be systematically assessed by teachers in relation to the stated outcomes, strands and targets in the curricular guidelines. Testing at a national level in the key areas of English Language and Mathematics was introduced as an integral part of these new assessment procedures, to help inform judgements about the progress of individual pupils in relation to the five (later six) levels of attainment and to do so in relation to nationally agreed and understood standards.

Originally, it was intended that testing should be confined to all pupils in P4 and P7, paralleling to some extent key stage 1 and key stage 2 testing in England and Wales. A pilot round of national tests was carried out in March and April 1991 with the first proper round scheduled for the academic year 1991–2. There was widespread opposition to statutory testing at these two particular stages and despite changes to the testing arrangements made in response to representations by teachers following a moderation of the test procedures and of the marking (*Report of Moderation*, Edinburgh: SOED, July 1991), this opposition continued. Following a boycott by a large proportion of teachers and the withdrawal, by parents, of pupils from the testing process, the system was reviewed and the arrangements for national testing were amended. Revised proposals were set out in a consultation paper by the Scottish Office Education Department (May 1992).

Political background

Opposition to national testing amongst teachers and parents has already been alluded to and any review of national testing in Scotland must also include reference to the political background to its introduction, as this impinged heavily on the first few years of its development. It was in 1988, during the Conservative government's second term in office, and with Michael Forsyth as Under-Secretary of State with responsibility for education, that the government first announced its intention to introduce testing in primary schools in Scotland. It had already announced plans to introduce end-of-key stage testing in England and Wales and was determined to extend some sort of external assessment system in all areas of the United Kingdom to cover the primary years of schooling which had previously been assessed only by teachers with no external input. Early in 1989 the Scottish Examination Board (SEB) was given the task of developing test materials and implementing the testing process under the policy initiatives of the various committees set up to oversee the 5–14 programme. A small unit, called the Primary Assessment Unit, was established to carry out this task.

Reactions to Testing

There was a good deal of hostile interest from the media, from the teaching profession, the teaching unions and from parents and parents associations (see Chapter 19). At the same time there was also a good deal of criticism of the proposals from the research community. This scepticism was directed towards the notion of setting national standards and the effects this might have on pupils taking the tests. Among parents and teachers testing awoke atavistic memories of the 'Qualie' and the personal and social traumas which it created. The Qualifying Examination was once taken by all pupils in P7 and, in the days prior to comprehensive schooling in Scotland (pre-1968), determined which type of secondary school a pupil would attend. Many of the education authorities resented the implication that their own methods for monitoring and communicating standards were inadequate. Parents frequently said that they wanted direct access to class teachers for information about their children rather than an explicit comparison with a notional national standard. The resentment of teachers was also directed at the expense (around £600,000 initially) which, they maintained, could be better spent on materials and new teachers. Teachers also objected to the fact that the tests were being introduced before the curricular guidelines were properly in place and to the time taken to administer and mark the tests for the purpose of arriving at a judgement which usually confirmed their own more subjective one.

Beneath all the specific complaints there was a recurrent feeling that testing was an English response to a specifically English problem. Standards of performance in English schools were perceived by politicians to be seriously low, but there was no such vocal complaint in Scotland. Resentment against a Conservative government, for whom a substantial majority of the electorate had not voted, was fuelled by testing, the educational equivalent of the Poll Tax.

Development and Piloting

Serious work to develop tests began in October 1989 and continued over the next two years. Only one of the twelve education authorities at that time raised little or no objection and co-operated positively in piloting. Some authorities allowed an approach to be made to their schools so that piloting could progress but few schools agreed; other authorities simply would not give permission for their schools to be approached. Consequently the first round of piloting in year 1990–1 was somewhat restricted.

At this time, the Educational Institute of Scotland (EIS), the main teacher's union, issued a document for parents which spelt out their opposition to the whole idea of testing. During 1990 and 1991, Peter Kimber, the director of the Primary Assessment Unit and Douglas Osler, the Depute Senior Chief Inspector at the then Scottish Office responsible for the 5–14 development programme, were involved in a long-running series of meetings with local authorities, teachers and parents, often with EIS representatives present to articulate opposition to testing. Formal opposition from parents was channelled through the

Scottish Parent Teachers' Association and through the Parents' Coalition formed by Diana Daly in Aberdeen and Judith Gillespie in Edinburgh, who led arguments on behalf of parents opposing the government proposals. Together they raised a very considerable degree of parental awareness, fostered by the EIS and the more hostile education authorities. In the academic year 1990–1 hostility to testing gradually increased. The government tried to persuade authorities to co-operate voluntarily but there was flat refusal to do so. The government therefore decided to introduce regulations to ensure that testing would take place. This is the only time in the history of Scottish education that such a measure has been taken.

The regulations requiring authorities to implement testing came into force in August 1991. Strathclyde Region responded by pointing out a conflict between the regulations and the Education Act which required authorities to educate children in accordance with the wishes of the parents. If parents did not wish their children to be tested, presumably they had the right to withdraw them. Many authorities took this opportunity to avoid testing children where the parents formally asked for them to be withdrawn. At least one authority provided printed letters to this effect and gave them to children, suggesting that parents should sign and return them. At the height of the opposition it was reported that 66% of parents nationally had withdrawn their children. This was the position in the run-up to the 1992 general election, when it was widely expected that a Labour Government would be returned with the promise that national testing would be withdrawn.

In the event this did not happen and the returning Conservative government, with another change in the minister responsible for education, quickly negotiated new agreements with authorities. In return for greater flexibility of administration and professional judgement on the part of teachers, authorities and unions agreed to co-operate and implement the tests as soon as teachers could be prepared. Circular 12/92 issued by SOED in November 1992 became the agreed basis for the implementation of national testing, following which testing was gradually introduced.

Arrangements for National Testing (January 1993 to August 2003)

Three significant changes were made to the arrangements for national testing as a result of Circular 12/92. Firstly, the statutory regulations governing national testing were rescinded. Secondly, instead of pupils being tested only in P4 and P7, pupils were to take a test when the teacher's own assessment indicated that the pupil had largely achieved the attainment targets at one level and was ready to move from that level to the next. Thirdly, the new testing arrangements were also to apply to pupils in secondary schools in S1 and S2. These revised arrangements, described in the *Framework for National Testing* (SEB, 1993), were implemented in primary schools from January 1993 and in secondary schools from January 1994. A test catalogue, issued to schools annually between 1991 and 2002, provided a range of test contexts for national tests from which teachers could choose test units to suit the interests and level of maturity of their pupils. The 2002 catalogue contained some seventy Reading units, forty Writing units and 120 Mathematics units covering the six levels of difficulty and providing a variety of contexts and tasks which schools could order at any time. A significant proportion of the units in the catalogue was replaced each year, to provide new contexts for testing and to ensure that fresh material was always available for testing. Test units were printed in bulk and stored in a warehouse facility run by the SQA.

REVIEW OF ASSESSMENT, 5–14

By the end of the 1990s, national testing was firmly established in schools and the whole climate of antagonism to testing had largely dissipated to be replaced, in some instances, with claims that the tests were not sufficiently rigorous. This was coupled with an increased demand for accountability, the measurement of 'value added', target setting and a desire to improve the ranking of Scotland in international surveys of achievement.

In November 1998, the pre-devolution Minister for Education, Helen Liddell, asked HMI to conduct a review into all aspects of the assessment of pupils' progress from age three to age fourteen, covering pre-school, primary and the first two years of secondary education. Specifically:

> To review the scope, coherence and effectiveness of current Scottish arrangements for assessment, testing and national monitoring in pre-schools, primary schools and S1/S2 and to make recommendations for their improvement.

It was left to the new Scottish Parliament to take the review forward under the first Scottish Minister for Education, Sam Galbraith.

One year later, HMI published a lengthy (sixty page) *Review of Assessment in Pre-school and 5–14* and sent it out to education authorities, schools, pre-school centres and other interested bodies. Parents, school staff and pupils were also invited to respond. A much shorter summary and a parents' guide were also published. The consultation documents were published in December 1999 with responses invited by the end of March 2000. The review covered the different purposes of assessment, contrasting the needs of assessment to inform teaching and learning for individual pupils with that of assessment for monitoring and evaluation at school, authority and national level. The review also acknowledged both the expansion of pre-school education and the importance of assessment within the early stages of education, and the increased demand for reliable information on national standards particularly at the end of key stages of education. How could these diverse and sometimes conflicting demands best be met?

HMI drew on its own experience, observing that in primary schools assessment was identified as requiring improvement in 70% of inspection schools. Further evidence of the need to improve the consistency of assessment across schools was provided by the first survey of attainment carried out in 1998 as part of the government's Setting Targets initiative. Schools were asked to report on the number of pupils achieving the different levels at different stages in the key areas of Language and Mathematics. One third of schools' data was unusable due to inconsistencies. Experience from inspectors also pointed to a scepticism among secondary schools about primary teachers' judgements, often reflecting inconsistencies in reported assessment levels across primary schools, while primary teachers felt that assessment information which had been gathered with care and attention was being ignored.

The review document emphasised repeatedly the need for consistent and reliable assessment information and suggested a number of approaches to changes which might be adopted. These were wide ranging: more support to help teachers make judgements; a common system for record keeping and reporting, particularly at key stages; developing performance criteria/ exemplification of levels; improving on national tests and extending to other areas of the curriculum; providing a bank of items/tasks; extending the Assessment of

Achievement Programme (AAP) and participation in international surveys; introducing external tests at a fixed time.

It was another year before the response to the consultation was published in December 2000. There was widespread support for an assessment system whose prime aim was to support teaching and learning, for a common national system and format for recording and reporting, for consistent assessment terminology and for clear assessment guidelines for staff. Staff development, along with the production of performance criteria and exemplification, was supported by virtually all respondents as a means of improving assessment practices. Moderation as a means of sharing standards and improving consistency was more favoured by education authorities than schools. There was less agreement about aspects of assessment related to national testing and the AAP. Changes to national tests were wanted by 48% of respondents, to make them more valid and reliable, 53% wanted them extended to other areas of the curriculum and 44% of respondents supported some extension of the AAP. Some sort of externally set and marked tests were supported by 44% and fixed point/stage assessment and reporting by 45%. Overall, 58% favoured minor changes to the current national system, stressing the need to provide better support for teachers, while 38% favoured fundamental changes, for instance to improve the validity and reliability of national tests or to strengthen formative assessment. These results must be viewed in relation to the number of responses. Responses numbering 258 were made including fifty-nine schools (of which eighteen primary and twenty-nine secondary), thirty-one EAs (all but one), twenty-one other organisations and 108 teachers. (There are some 2,600 primary schools and 400 secondary schools in Scotland.)

RESPONSE TO RESULTS OF CONSULTATION

With the publication of the report on the consultation (Hayward, Kane and Cogan, 2000), the ball was back in the court of the Scottish Executive to decide how to take things forward. In the meantime there had been considerable changes in the wake of the examination crisis of 2000. The inspectorate had been distanced from SEED and a new Qualifications, Assessment and Curriculum (QuAC) division (albeit with a seconded inspector leading the assessment branch) was now responsible for advising the minister on education matters. On the political scene too, the ground was constantly shifting. Jack McConnell took over from Sam Galbraith as Minister of Education in October 2000, and in due course became First Minister in November 2002 following the resignation of Henry McLeish. The review of assessment was not at the top of the political agenda! Eventually things began to settle down and Cathy Jamieson took over as Minister of Education. Although she was clearly passionately committed to education at the early stages, she left the chairing of the Assessment Action Group to the Liberal Democrat Deputy Minister, Nicol Stephen.

OUTCOME OF THE REVIEW

While waiting for a decision from the Minister, the 5–14 Assessment Unit had been advised by SEED to suspend their normal test preparation cycle; it was likely that the system was about to change but until the minister pronounced, the nature of the change could only be guessed at. No new tests were processed beyond those included in the 2001 catalogue which then remained in effect for 2002.

At the end of August 2001, reports in the *Scotsman* newspaper suggested that the minister was about to introduce a new form of national testing which would be more rigorous than the current system. A previous implacable opponent of testing, Fred Forrester of the EIS, acknowledged that he had been wrong to fight against testing and that it was proper to have objective and reliable means of measuring pupil attainment in 5–14; meanwhile Gordon Jeyes, general secretary to the Association of Directors of Education in Scotland, was reported as supporting the introduction of standardised tests in literacy and numeracy.

Eventually, on 20 September 2001, Jack McConnell, an ex-teacher and at this point still Minister for Education, issued a statement to the Scottish Parliament which proposed that the best way to achieve a coherent system of assessment was to improve the consistency of reporting on pupils' progress, to give support to teachers in making judgements about pupils' learning, to improve national monitoring of achievement in key areas, and to create a unified system for record-keeping. All this was to be taken forward through an assessment development programme under the guidance of an action group comprising a wide range of stakeholders.

This Assessment Action Group met for the first time in November 2001, by which time the vision of an integrated assessment system had taken on some structure but the flesh had still to be added. Ten years earlier, such groups taking forward major educational policy initiatives were carefully directed by HMI. With the distancing of HMI from policy making to concentrate on policy and standards monitoring (see Chapter 14), politicians were more ready to take an active role in policy implementation and Nicol Stephen, the Deputy Minister for education, assumed the role of chair of the Assessment Action Group. At this point it is difficult to talk about national testing in isolation as it was now seen as only part of a much larger assessment initiative which covered the different assessment purposes identified in the *Review of Assessment*, although it is perhaps significant that the parliamentary debate following on from the minister's statement focused almost exclusively on the idea of assessment as testing.

The minister had stated that the aim was to build on current good practice and to create 'improved second generation national assessments, which will be developed from the current national tests, to confirm their judgements and improve consistency across Scotland'. He also suggested that Science might be added to the new assessments. Alongside these new national assessments, he proposed that the Assessment of Achievement Programme (AAP) should also include cores skills within its remit and that there should be a link between AAP and the annual survey of 5–14 attainment. How was all this to be done? 'I intend to establish a unified bank of national assessments that teachers and the Executive can draw on for the new national assessments and the AAP surveys. We will use the AAP results each year to validate and confirm the reported results of national assessments by schools.'

The overall assessment development programme called Assessment is for Learning covers three overlapping phases from April 2002 to December 2003. This ambitious programme involves ten different projects covering classroom practice, quality assurance, monitoring and evaluation, and the commitment to the delivery of personal learning plans for all pupils by 2003. One of these projects is dedicated to the development of new national assessments in the form of an on-line bank of assessment materials, based on AAP tests and tasks, to replace the current national tests.

DIFFERENCES BETWEEN
NEW NATIONAL ASSESSMENTS AND OLD NATIONAL TESTS

At the time of writing, no firm specification for the new style assessments was available, however certain aspects were clear.

- Initially the new assessments will be restricted to Reading, Writing and Mathematics, although extension to other areas such as Science will be considered at a later date.
- The assessments are to be available to schools from August 2003.
- The purpose of the assessments will remain confirmatory.
- Teachers will choose when to administer the assessments and to whom.
- There will be some degree of choice.
- The primary mode of delivery will be electronic (but not on-line testing).
- The reliability of the tests will be ensured by the use of AAP items.
- The appearance of the tests might differ, reflecting the different styles of AAP and national test items.

From the point of view of the teacher, the main change would be the mode of delivery, although having on-line availability opens the possibility of, for example, on-line marking support, such as exemplification of writing.

Critics of the old national tests argued that they were inconsistent and unreliable and that they were not a true reflection of pupils' capabilities. Supporters would argue that the system was successful in doing what it was intended to do, namely to confirm teacher judgement of a level, and that detractors were often expecting of the tests something they had not been designed to do. Items included in national tests were subject to a rigorous process of scrutiny to ensure concordance with the guidelines. Despite these procedures and despite statistically equating threshold scores after pre-testing, some tests appear intrinsically more difficult or easier than others at the same level. Will assessments drawn from the AAP prove any more valid and reliable? AAP items, based on nationally representative samples of pupils, will have an assured pedigree in terms of item information and therefore should be able to be used with a high degree of confidence. However, tasks and individual items will still vary in difficulty and threshold scores will still have to be set. Whether teachers' perceptions of the usefulness and reliability of the tests will be different remains to be seen.

RETROSPECTIVE AND PROSPECTIVE

Has national testing achieved its objectives? It is now well over a decade since the first proposal to introduce national testing in Scotland was made. National testing has been almost fully implemented in primary schools for many years with approximately half the pupils being tested each year. In secondary schools it took target setting to provide the impetus for implementation in many schools. Secondary schools are also more likely to test whole classes or even year groups at fixed times while primary schools more faithfully embrace the testing-when-ready philosophy. The stated aims of national testing were to provide an additional source of evidence about pupils' attainment in Reading, Writing and Mathematics, by defining pupil achievement in relation to nationally agreed standards, and to provide teachers with exemplification of the levels and thus help to ensure consistency between teachers in their interpretation of what levels mean. It has become an integral part of assessment procedures and, in the area of assessing Writing in particular, it has introduced a system of assessment using a single set of criteria throughout the country. However, the system has had its detractors and a substantial number of teachers remain unconvinced about the positive benefits of testing. Malcolm and Schlapp in their research into the implementation of 5–14 in primary schools (SCRE, 1997) reported that 85% of headteachers in their sample were satisfied with national test procedures in their schools at that time (spring 1996). Teachers' views on the value of national tests as part of their assessment strategy were somewhat more equivocal with over half (53%) stating that the tests were of limited or no value in this regard and only 37% stating that they were of considerable value or very valuable. The more recent *Review of Assessment*, previously referred to, indicated that there has been no substantial shift in attitude since then. For most teachers, the tests confirm what they knew already about pupils. There seems to be a lack of recognition on the part of teachers that one of the stated purposes of national testing was to provide just such a confirmation or to recognise that such a confirmation, using common standards, is a professionally acceptable objective.

The SCRE research gave evidence of differences in teachers' understanding of standards associated with the different levels, indicating that there was then a case for the monitoring function of national tests in relation to teachers' own assessments. The more recent response to the review indicates that teachers remain uncertain about the standards implicit at different levels and would value more support in making these judgements.

The distinctive nature of national testing in Scotland whereby teachers choose, from an essentially 'open' assessment bank, test units to confirm their own judgement with respect to individual pupil's progress has attracted considerable interest from outwith Scotland. Many visitors from England express their envy at the liberal approach to testing which contrasts so starkly with the examination format required by the Department for Education and Skills in London. They admire the recognition that teachers are professionals with a detailed familiarity with their pupils' work. The specified role of testing is to confirm – or otherwise – the judgement of teachers and this contrasts markedly with the perceived lack of confidence in teachers south of the border. Visitors from abroad also review the Scottish system with interest, although some, accustomed to more centrally controlled and strictly regulated education systems, find an 'open' testing system a difficult concept to appreciate.

What then of the future? It would be wrong to call the Assessment is for Learning programme a new departure. In large measure it is based on the intentions first articulated in the Assessment and Reporting document published a decade earlier. What has changed over these ten years is an increased requirement for consistent and accurate information about pupils' progress, and that at an earlier age. What has changed too is that parents who ten or fifteen years ago were ready to accept teachers' judgements on their children's progress, are increasingly calling that judgement to account. At a political level too, the need for proven returns for educational investment are accepted by all parties, and such returns are, at least in part, measured in terms of raised educational standards. The teaching profession, which has had to adapt to and deliver on each new initiative, may be less than enthusiastic about some of the requirements introduced to measure educational outcomes. While few would argue against the laudable aim of raising standards, the increased accountability which this entails is seen by many as detracting from the core business of teaching and learning.

REFERENCES

Hayward, L., Kane, J. and Cogan, N. (2000) *Improving Assessment in Scotland: Report of the Consultation on the Review of Assessment Pre-School and 5–14*, Glasgow: Faculty of Education University of Glasgow.

HMI (1999) *Review of Assessment in Pre-school and 5–14*, Edinburgh: SOEID.

Malcolm, H. and Schlapp, U. (1997) *5–14 in the Primary School: A Continuing Challenge*, Edinburgh: SCRE.

SEB (1993) *The Framework for National Testing*, Dalkeith: SEB.

SOED (1992) Circular 12/92, Edinburgh: SOED.

SQA (annually) *Catalogue of National Test Units*, plus *National Tests in Reading: Information for Teachers*; *National Tests in Writing: Information for Teachers*; *National Tests in Mathematics: Information for Teachers*, Dalkeith: SQA.

86

Scottish School Pupils: Characteristics and Influences

Brian Boyd

CHRIS'S STORY: THE JOURNEY BEGINS

Christopher was born on 21 December 1986. His formative years have been spent in East Kilbride, a New Town on the outskirts of Glasgow in the Central Belt of Scotland. His parents are professional people, both involved in education, and so could be described as middle class. He is an only child. Christopher did not qualify for pre-5 or nursery provision, a non-statutory service available, at that time, by right only to those who meet a set of needs-based criteria. Now, the Scottish Executive has pledged to provide a free nursery place for all three-and four-year-olds whose parents want it.

Christopher, along with other Scottish children between the ages of four and a half and five and a half, began his schooling in August 1991, in his case at the age of four years and eight months. As he entered P1 in Mossneuk Primary School with a roll of 550, his class of thirty pupils could look forward to seven years of education with their peers, largely taught by one (generalist) teacher at each stage. Aged eleven years and eight months, Chris (as he now likes to be called) moved to a secondary school – a comprehensive school, which, in common with all Scottish state secondaries, takes all of the pupils from the associated primary schools, without any form of selection.

There he encountered up to seventeen different (specialist) teachers in each of the first two years, following a 'common course', most often in mixed-ability classes. Uniquely, at that time, he made choices at the end of S1, dropping three subjects, before narrowing down the subjects even further at the end of S2 (in common with all schools in Scotland) to around ten, eight of them leading to national certification at Standard Grade. During these two years he was put into 'sets' according to attainment in a number of subjects, and was, in due course, presented for his examinations at Foundation, General or Credit levels. Like the majority of his peers, he will stay on at school to pursue courses leading within the Higher Still programme. Although the statutory leaving age is sixteen, Chris could not have left before Christmas in S5 because he is at the 'young end' of the year group. For him, the prospect is that he might leave at the end of S5, or, given his age, stay on for a sixth year, perhaps moving on to higher education, employment or further education.

But Chris is not necessarily a typical pupil – and at almost every stage of this process there are exceptions to the above pattern. Some parents will have chosen, exercising their right under the 1981 Education (Scotland) Act, to send their child to a school other than the one closest to them for a range of reasons which include child-care (in Chris's case to be closer to his grandparents' home); perceived quality of the schools; and so on. According to Willms, parents of higher social class are more likely to exercise choice, though the majority of all parents, nearly 90%, do not make placing requests (Willms, 1997). For some the choice will be an independent (or fee-paying) school, though across Scotland such schools account for around 4% of the pupil population (*The Herald*, 24 January 2002) A small, but growing, number of parents choose to educate their children at home.

Around half of the 3,000 or so primary schools in Scotland have pupil rolls of fewer than 100, and so mixed-stage or composite classes become the norm rather than the age-stage relationship of larger schools. These smaller schools are mainly rural. And, of course, many of Chris's contemporaries attend denominational (mainly Roman Catholic) schools, catering for between one-sixth and one-fifth of the pupil population, funded by the state since the 1918 Education Act.

Chris's parents have made choices on his behalf, not least to have him educated in the state sector. In the past, when the system was selective, social class was a factor as in Liz Lochhead's poem, *The Choosing*:

> I remember the housing scheme
> where we both stayed.
> Same houses, different homes,
> where the choices were made.

Lochhead reminds the reader too of the gender dimension which influenced many working class fathers: 'He didn't believe in high school education, especially for girls, or in forking out for uniforms.' Now, paradoxically, in Scotland as in the rest of the UK, it is underachievement among boys which is the subject of national concern.

In most areas of Scotland, outwith the cities, there was, historically, no choice, and no selection, as the secondaries were omnibus schools, taking in all of the pupils in the area. Since the publication of examination results in the early 1990s and the subsequent compilation of league tables published in the press, a movement from 'unsuccessful' to 'successful' schools has taken place. The philosophy of market forces initiated by the then Conservative government enshrined choice as the guiding principle and believed that competition among schools would lead to higher standards. As jobs became scarce in the 1980s and early 1990s, more young people stayed on beyond the statutory leaving age of sixteen, and more and more went on to some form of further or higher education.

An outside observer might think that in Scotland, a small country with only 5.1 million people, an observer might think that the experience of schooling must be fairly uniform for all pupils, and that it has probably, in a country with such a proud educational tradition, always been so. But the reality is somewhat different. While Chris has enjoyed a relatively stable childhood, there are many vulnerable children in Scotland. In 2001, the Scottish Executive published *For Scotland's Children*, as part of its 'commitment to improving the quality of life for Scotland's children and defeating child poverty' (p. 2). It highlighted the needs of looked-after children, young people excluded from school and children of asylum seekers. It also cited examples of good practice with initiatives such as internet links with 'base' schools to enable the children of travelling families to maintain links with formal education (see Chapter 93).

While Chris has attended schools which have positively welcomed young people with

special educational needs, the teaching profession as a whole is uneasy about the government's policy of inclusion, particularly as it relates to young people with challenging
behaviour. The barrier to meeting the needs of these young people remains the lack of
commitment to inter-agency working and the perceived lack of training for teachers and
support staff (Hamill and Boyd, 2001). Indeed, many councils are beginning to realise that
the curriculum in its present form may not enable all young people to succeed and are
exploring alternatives for the most challenging young people.

PRE-1970S – SELECTION, THE STRAP AND FULL EMPLOYMENT?

For a start, Chris and his fellow pupils don't speak Scots – officially – and Gaelic is only
now beginning to make a comeback outside its Western Isles heartland. Indeed, the culture
of Scotland as a nation has long been subjugated under the influence of its larger neighbour,
England. Notwithstanding Scotland's separate legal, educational and religious traditions, its
languages have long been left, if not at the school gate, then certainly at the classroom door.
Standard English, the language of the establishment, has ruled, and the grammar taught in
Scottish classrooms was Latinate and traditional, leaving little room for the vernacular.

Often it is in the literature of a nation that life is most graphically depicted. In William
McIlvanney's *Docherty*, (Edinburgh: Mainstream, 1997) the fear inspired by an inhumane
system comes to life as the central character, Conn, still at primary school, is brought before
Mr Pirrie, accused of fighting:

> 'What's wrong with your face, Docherty?'
> 'Skint ma nose, sur.'
> 'How?'
> 'Ah fell an' bumped ma heid in the sheuch, sur.'
> 'I beg your pardon?' . . .
> In the pause Conn understands the nature of the choice, tremblingly, compulsively, makes it.
> 'Ah fell an' bumped ma heid in the sheuch, sur.'
> The blow is instant. His ear seems to enlarge, is muffled in numbness. But it is only the dread of
> tears that hurts. Mr Pirrie distends on a lozenge of light which mustn't be allowed to break. It
> doesn't. Conn hasn't cried.
> 'That, Docherty, is impertinence. You will translate, please, into the mother-tongue.'
> The blow is a mistake, Conn knows. If he tells his father, he will come up to the school. 'Ye'll
> take whit ye get wi' the strap an' like it. But if onybody takes their hauns tae ye, ye'll let me ken.'
> He thinks about it. But the problem is his own. It frightens him more to imagine his father
> coming up.
> 'I'm waiting, Docherty. What happened?'
> 'I bumped my head, sir.'
> 'Where? Where did you bump it, Docherty?'
> 'In the gutter, sir.'
> 'Not an inappropriate setting for you, if I may say so.'

Thus, in one short, highly-charged episode is encapsulated many of the elements which
characterised middle-class teacher/working-class pupil relationships in the past. The
inherent politeness of the pupil ('Sur'); the use of the dialect firstly as a natural response,
then as a gesture of defiance ('the nature of the choice'); the use of Standard English in a
disciplinary context ('I beg your pardon?'); the male fear of being seen to be weak, already

present in Conn ('the dread of tears'); the inherent respect for the teacher's authority of the working class parent but the moral code which will accept 'official' corporal punishment ('the strap') but not unofficial ('takes their hauns tae ye'); the use of sarcasm to degrade and control the pupils ('Not an inappropriate setting . . .'); all of this flies in the face of the myth of the 'lad o' pairts' (McPherson and Raab, 1988) where every pupil had an equal chance of educational success.

Ask Chris's parents about their own experience of schooling and they will almost certainly recount stories about 'the strap', about 'the Quali' and possibly about individual teachers, of the charismatic or autocratic type. Up until the 1970s, selection was a defining feature of the Scottish education system. Pupils in P7 sat an examination ('the Quali'), having previously taken IQ tests, and on the basis of these would be selected for a junior (vocational) or senior (academic) secondary school. This represented an advance from the pre-war situation where some pupils would never be deemed suitable to receive a secondary education at all. The move towards 'age promotion', albeit with the type of schooling still determined by measures of ability, was not universally welcomed in official circles:

> Especially with pupils promoted solely on account of age, many of whom are semi-literate, there are often other tendencies to counter besides ignorance; some of these pupils harbour feelings of resentment that they are still under tutelage and prevented from being wage-earners (SED, 1951, quoted in McPherson and Raab, 1988, p. 248).

This very negative view of children is interesting and may help explain the heavy-handed discipline which was a feature of many junior and senior secondary schools during this period. The notion of 'contest mobility' (McPherson and Raab, 1988) meant also that on arrival in one of the two types of schools pupils would be 'streamed', that is. organised into classes on the basis of general ability. Thus a pupil might find herself in 1A in the senior secondary experiencing a largely classical education while her peer might find himself in 1M (for 'modified') in the junior secondary experiencing a largely practical curriculum with a 'watered-down' version of some of the academic subjects (though not Classics or Modern Languages). Selection had a finality about it, mobility between the sectors was minimal and parity of esteem non-existent.

Thus, Chris's parents were among the 40% or so who enjoyed an academic education (a higher percentage than in England and Wales) and had a thorough grounding in the subjects necessary to secure entry to university and the professions. Along the way, they had access to excellent extra-curricular activities and to the most highly qualified teachers. They did well in the main, though with streaming, the wastage rate was high, with pupils leaving at the then statutory age of fifteen, before the national exams at the end of S4. Meanwhile, the young people who went to the junior secondary had largely less highly qualified or even 'uncertificated' teachers (though official policy was that all secondary teachers should be certificated), were in buildings less well equipped and had no access to national examinations. They too were streamed, with the 'modifieds' or 'remedials' being the lowest. In the best of these schools, future workers would be given a good grounding in technical skills, while for the girls, Domestic Science would help prepare for motherhood!

But by the 1960s the case for the abolition of selection became unstoppable. The 'mute, inglorious Milton' argument, the pool of talent going to waste, the inequity of such selection based on discredited psychometric testing, was overwhelming, and in 1965 the Labour government signalled its intention that all local authorities should submit plans for the ending of selection.

It is unlikely that Chris will encounter a Mr Pirrie in a Scottish school today. Corporal punishment was abolished, as a result of a European ruling, in the early 1980s. The place of Scots has become less marginalised, with Scottish texts now a compulsory element in the Higher English (sic) examination, and with the publication of a *Scots Kist* (see Chapter 24 for the place of the Scots language in education). Gaelic-medium education has expanded to the Central Belt of Scotland, with national broadcasting having been given an injection of funding to promote the language.

SCOTTISH SCHOOLING FROM 1970 TO THE PRESENT

What do Scottish pupils make of their experience? In *Tell Them From Me* (Gow and McPherson, 1980) pupils who left school in the second half of the 1970s wrote about their experiences. The authors chose to concentrate on the views of the 'non-certificate' pupils – those who had not been deemed suitable to sit national examinations. Their writing was characterised by 'qualities of insight, vigour and expression . . . evoked by experience of failure and rejection' (p. 17). The book had a significant impact on Scottish education, and made the case that policy makers should 'acknowledge that the views of all pupils are important'. The words of the pupils told a powerful story of second-class treatment for those who were not 'academic':

> I didn't like school as it was biased towards the intelligent people. (p. 30)

and they talked of labelling:

> While in school I was treated like an idiot not only by my teachers but by my headmaster. (p. 31)

They felt that the school marginalised them:

> the school was short staffed we more or less spent our time sitting our-selves. (p. 36)

The views of the certificate pupils were much more positive, more focused on the curriculum and on passing examinations. All groups had some positive things to say about teachers, but the overwhelming effect of the book was the inequity of the treatment of the pupils.

But those were early days of comprehensive schools, and pre-date the national revision of the examinations system. A quarter of a century later, *The 1994 Leavers* (Edinburgh: SOEID,1996) survey reported that:

> Successive cohorts of school leavers seem to be increasingly positive about their experiences at school. For example, the proportion who agreed that school had helped give them confidence to make decisions rose from 57% of 1992 leavers to 61% of 1993 leavers and 63% of 1994 leavers. (p. 3)

The term non-certificate has now disappeared from Scottish education and, while issues remain about the relative status of Credit, General and Foundation awards, many of the old divisions have gone.

Chris has enjoyed his experience of school to date, and surveys show that most Scottish pupils like school; they like their teachers, 72% in the Leavers Survey believing that teachers had helped them to do their best. Most secondary pupils felt that teachers had helped them to make subject choices. The highest percentage was found to be in response to the statement 'School work was worth doing', with 81% of leavers agreeing – by any standards a high level of 'customer satisfaction'. However, some 16% felt that their teachers did not care about them, and 32% said some teachers could not keep order in class. Equity is a key issue for pupils everywhere and most Scottish pupils feel that boys and girls are treated equally.

While Scottish pupils, in the main, are positive about school and feel that their treatment is fair, there has been concern about discipline within the teaching profession to the extent that a task force was established and produced a report entitled *Better Behaviour – Better Learning* (Edinburgh: The Stationery Office, 2001), offering advice to schools on promoting better discipline. Bullying, too, has emerged as a key issue in Scotland and studies have indicated that around 40% of pupils experience bullying at least once in school. The issue of school ethos is one which is taken seriously in Scottish schools. Following on from the seminal work by Rutter (*Fifteen Thousand Hours*, London: Open Books, 1979) which associated positive relationships (ethos) with effective schools, the Scottish Office Education Department published a pack for primary and for secondary schools under the title *Ethos Indicators* (1992). It urged schools to ask their pupils, their staff and the parents how they felt about aspects of school life, and suggested that ethos was something which ought to be the result of good management at every level in a school. The Scottish Ethos Network was established in 1995 to enable schools to share and celebrate good practice and to become eligible for an award for innovative approaches to the establishment of a positive ethos. At a conference on Study Support at the University of Strathclyde in 1997, a senior pupil from DASH – Dumbarton Academy Seniors against Harassment – spoke eloquently to an audience of teachers about the persistent low-level activity which goes on unknown to them, and argued that 'harassment' was a more appropriate word than bullying, with its connotations of violence. Thus, name-calling, exclusion from games, skipping the queue for lunch, pushing and shoving in the corridors, laughter, and so on may well go unnoticed and make the lives of some pupils miserable. DASH is one of many such interventionist schemes growing up in schools which have declared themselves to be 'bully-free zones' or which have a policy of 'zero tolerance' of bullying. While Scotland is less ethnically diverse than many parts of England, nevertheless racial and racist problems can arise. After some highly publicised difficulties in the 1980s centred on a Glasgow school, Strathclyde Regional Council produced its Tackling Racist Incidents within Educational Establishments policy, with an emphasis on counselling rather than punishment for victims and perpetrators. Thus while organisations like Childline continue to urge vigilance, citing 550 calls to their helpline in one month (*The Herald*, 21 October 1997), most schools, and most pupils, believe that the situation is being tackled well in most cases.

In 1993, the HMI report on *The Education of Able Pupils P6 to S2* challenged schools to ask themselves if they had 'an ethos of achievement', thus recognising the link between the cognitive and the affective domains. It is this area of achievement and ethos which offers the best context in which to look at the experience of the modern Scottish child.

POVERTY, HEALTH AND UNDERACHIEVEMENT

By far the most contentious issue at present facing Scottish education is underachievement, and in particular the association of underachievement with economic and social disadvantage. Put more directly, at the beginning of the twenty-first century, can it be denied that the young person from a family which is experiencing the effects of poverty, setting out on the journey through schooling, is less likely to be successful than her more affluent, or middle-class counterpart?

Lochhead's explanation (*The Choosing*) for how she and her former classmate, and rival in learning, drifted apart, 'I don't know exactly why they moved, but anyway they went. Something about a three-apartment and a cheaper rent', at once introduces the issue of social class and poverty. Since those days of relatively full employment, however, unemployment has become a key issue in many areas of Scotland, particularly, though not exclusively, in the inner cities and large peripheral housing estates. Poverty, as defined in terms of having 50% or less of the national average income, had trebled since 1979. Around 33,000 children a year are part of households which apply to councils as homeless; around 5,000 young people sleep rough every year and Scotland has the third highest teenage pregnancy rate in the Western world. A report by NCH Scotland revealed that 20% of children attending the Sick Childeren's Hospital in Glasgow showed signs of malnutrition (*The Herald*, 23 January 2002).

This report confirmed that poverty is not equally distributed across Scotland. It exists in pockets, and these pockets are served by local schools. In the early 1970s, teachers were persuaded to teach in such 'designated' schools by being offered additional money and travel expenses. Later, under Strathclyde Region's Social Strategy, such schools received extra resources in the form of staff and per capita funding. The link between poverty and attainment is well established in the educational literature, but what is challenging for educationalists is the finding that:

> inequalities in almost all areas of educational attainment are . . . in almost all cases larger than class differences in measured ability at the age of 11 years would predict (Gray, McPherson and Raffe, p. 227).

And their conclusion that 'Scottish education since the war has been neither meritocratic nor equal', is one which must cause concern.

Thus, unlike Chris, the pupil who arrives in P1 from an area of social and economic disadvantage, from a home where neither of the parents (if there are two) has had success in education, where there is unemployment, lack of money and low aspirations, where education is not valued and where authority is perceived as threatening, may struggle to realise her potential. In Glasgow, some 17% of young people go on to further or higher education while in the more affluent East Renfrewshire the figure is 50%. If added to this picture is the fact that Scotland has one of the worst health records in the developed world, and that the urban poor have similar health profiles to some developing countries, the picture of the Scottish pupil begins to take the form of a continuum, from the advantaged, middle-class, conformist, polite, hard-working, high-achieving pupil to the disadvantaged, malnourished, underachieving and eventually disaffected young person. In *Health Behaviours of Scottish Schoolchildren* (Edinburgh: Health Education Board for Scotland, 1993), the authors argue that:

Socioeconomic factors are clearly an important influence on young people's health behaviours . . . including eating patterns, smoking, alcohol consumption and patterns of physical activity (p. 26).

The challenge for schools, in the view of the authors, is how to take account of this where the school has a mixed intake of pupils, especially when:

Young people who are in conflict with the school, as expressed in terms of their dislike for school, are more likely to smoke regularly, drink alcohol, regularly get drunk, do little voluntary exercise and suffer frequent psychosomatic symptoms (p. 26).

These are international issues. In a lecture at the University of Strathclyde in 1996, Dean Corrigan, a leading American academic, argued for the principle of 'no rejects' and proposed that education, particularly in areas of disadvantage, should be 'child-centred; family-focused; community-based and culturally sensitive'. His ideas have been influential in the creation of New Community Schools in Scotland and his philosophy is in keeping with the principle of inclusion which the Scottish Executive has promoted since its inception.

ACHIEVEMENT – STANDS SCOTLAND WHERE IT DID?

Chris was the first of the 5–14 generation, and his parents attended seven parents' evenings at his primary school on the Strengths – Development Needs – Next Steps model. Now that he has reached the later stages of secondary school, Chris has had ascribed to him a bewildering set of levels – which may have become labels – 5–14 provides a possible progression through level A (at around P3) to level E (at around S2). Standard Grade then offers (an at first apparently logical) stage covering F (Foundation), G (General) and C (Credit). The new Higher Still courses offer awards at Access, Intermediate I and II and then Highers where achievements are graded from A to E (though this time A is highest) – see Chapter 81 for details. If he goes to university he may get a degree which is a first; an upper second; a lower second; a third; or a mere general or ordinary degree. The propensity to categorise is immense.

But while qualification levels continue to rise, continuous improvement is demanded by government. League tables are no longer an official part of policy, though the publication of examination results allows the press to create their own, highly misleading comparisons of school effectiveness. This comparison extends even to individual departments within and across secondary schools. International comparisons in the early 1990s, especially of attainment in Mathematics, caused concern and led to HMI reports on achievement generally (1996) and specifically in Maths (1997) which called for more testing, more internal selection and more whole-class teaching. Indeed, the issue of internal selection has re-emerged as one of the most contentious, with one secondary school re-introducing streaming by general ability (as opposed to setting by attainment in a specific subject), ironically just at the same time as evidence against such practices has been published (Ireson and Hallam, 2001). Chris has never been streamed but he has been set – though neither his nor his parents' views on the subject were ever sought.

LISTENING TO YOUNG PEOPLE'S VOICES?

After *Tell Them From Me*, the voice of the child in Scottish education was seldom heard. In the mid-1990s the Improving School Effectiveness Project (ISEP – see Chapter 90) surveyed two cohorts, one in primary and one in secondary across a total of eighty Scottish schools and interviewed small groups of pupils in twenty-four of these schools. The pupils' comments tended to cluster round key themes:

- pupil engagement with school;
- pupil self-esteem/self-efficacy;
- perceptions of teacher expectations of pupils;
- relationship with teachers;
- pupil–pupil relationships;
- pupil empowerment;
- equitable treatment of pupils;
- support for learning for all – praise, recognition, information.

Pupils from P2 to S6 had a lot to say about school, and most of it was positive. They liked school and they thought their teachers did a good job. But they did not generally feel that their views were listened to.

The transition between primary and secondary is the critical point, where many pupils claim that no-one seems to know them, that their learning over the previous seven years is not built upon, and that they are not treated as 'real people'. In the primary school they will most likely have had a variant of 'Circle Time' – structured opportunities to discuss issues affecting them in schools. This is almost non-existent in the secondary, where, at best, there may be an elected pupil council which is rarely perceived to offer the pupils a real voice.

Primary schools place great emphasis on praise and reward, while some secondaries place unfair pressure on pupils to achieve and perform. Equity is an issue, especially in the secondary schools. In the ISEP study most pupils felt most teachers were fair, but were very critical of those who weren't. It was clear, too, that pupils in schools which had had new headteachers were very aware of changes and of why the changes were being made. In other words, pupils' insights might be of as much value in individual schools as they were nationally in 1980.

If underachievement is a matter of failure to learn successfully, then it seems logical that the child-as-a-learner should be the starting point. Publications emanating from the SCCC (*Climate for Learning*; *Teaching for Effective Learning*, 1996), on the impact of recent research on the brain and on the proliferation of new technology, have begun to reach teachers through in-service training and staff development. Scottish teachers might be said to be conservative, and Scottish schools, as HMI found in their review of the P4 and P7 curriculum in 1981, were never wholly won over by the more 'progressive' developments of the 1960s. Instead they married the best of the new to the best of the old. In the primary Chris could be chanting his times-tables in the time-honoured way one minute and be using a concept keyboard the next.

The future, therefore, may include a commitment to staff development for teachers which recognises them as reflective professionals. In turn they may be persuaded that theory and research are part of their professional commitment and a rationale for learning and teaching which focuses on achievement may emerge. Accelerated learning and thinking skills may break free from their 'alternative' (as in alternative medicine) status, and Scottish pupils may enjoy an experience which begins with the premise that they can all be successful learners and that any barriers to the achievement of their potential need to be removed, not reinforced. *Achievement for All* may then become the goal, with learning styles, multiple intelligences, emotional intelligence and high expectations for all being norm.

In 2002, the Scottish Executive launched a national debate on education. It involved a commitment to listening to the voices of young people. When the pupils of Largs Academy were asked in 1997 to discuss in small groups 'what makes a good teacher?', they responded in a way which suggests that they are worth listening to on the issue school improvement:

A 'good' teacher . . .
    is competent and achieves the best results from his pupils;
    is able to generate mutual respect;
    is able to mix discipline with fun;
    is adaptable, communicates well and has empathy for all his pupils;
    is enthusiastic, knowledgeable and compassionate;
    is genuinely interested in young people;
    is patient, well-organised and self-disciplined;
    makes time for individuals;
    has a likeable personality and allows it to come through;
    takes part in the wider life of the school.

Chris, meanwhile, having had an almost entirely positive experience in Mossneuk Primary School and having successfully negotiated the first four years of secondary, stands poised to take his Higher Still courses and, possibly, move on to higher education. He is, without doubt, one of the winners in the Scottish education system. The challenge remains to create a system in which those young people who historically have been losers can fulfil their potential. The aim must be not simply to raise attainment but to close the gap between those who currently succeed and those who do not. In that way, the Scottish education system will begin to meet the aspirations of a people beginning to make demands on its parliamentarians. Scottish children in the twenty-first century will face the same challenges as their counterparts across the world. They deserve an education which will equip them to meet those challenges.

REFERENCES

Gow, L. and McPherson, A. (eds) (1980) *Tell Them From Me*, Aberdeen: Aberdeen University Press.

Gray, J., McPherson, A. F. and Raffe, D. (1983) *Reconstructions of Secondary Education: Theory, Myth and Practice since the War*, London: Routledge and Kegan Paul.

Hamill. P. and Boyd, B. (2001) Rhetoric and Reality? Inter-agency provision for young people with challenging behaviours, *Journal of Emotional and Behavioural Difficulties* 6 (1), 135–149.

Ireson, J. and Hallam, S. (2001) *Ability Grouping in Education*, London: Paul Chapman Publishing.

McPherson, A. and Raab, C. D. (1988) *Governing Education: A Sociology of Policy since 1945*, Edinburgh: Edinburgh University Press.

Willms, J. D. (1997) *Parental Choice and Education Policy*, CES Briefing, Edinburgh: Edinburgh University.

87

The Assessment of Achievement Programme

Rae Condie, Isobel J. Robertson and Angela Napuk

In recent years, concerns over educational standards, nationally and internationally, have driven curricular and assessment policy decisions in Scotland, as in many other countries. However any debate on standards, whether in regard to education in general or specific subject areas, must be informed by significant objective evidence on what pupils know and can do rather than subjective impressions gleaned incidentally and haphazardly.

This requires the deliberate and systematic collecting of such evidence and the Assessment of Achievement Programme (AAP) was established in the early 1980s, by what is now the Scottish Executive Education Department (SEED), for precisely such a purpose. Drawing on a range of experience, not least that of the Assessment of Performance Unit (APU), which undertook national surveys of performance in England and Wales in the early 1980s, a rolling programme of national monitoring in English Language, Mathematics and Science was established in Scotland. The AAP has continued to monitor performance through the implementation of the government's 5–14 development programme, a policy development introduced in 1987.

AIMS AND ORGANISATION

The main aims of the AAP are: to provide a picture of the performance levels of pupils at certain stages, within specified curricular areas; to gather evidence of any change in performance over time; and to provide feedback to education authorities, curriculum developers and teachers which will contribute to the improvement of learning and teaching.

In 1987, a system of national testing in English and Mathematics was introduced as an integral part of the 5–14 development programme (see Chapter 85). The tests focused on the individual pupil and were designed to complement the formative assessment by teachers of pupils, providing confirmatory evidence of levels of attainment. By contrast, the AAP is not concerned with the individual but with a nationally representative sample of pupils, and surveys measure and monitor national performance levels at important stages in the primary and early secondary school. Thus national monitoring and national testing have different purposes and, to a degree, different audiences and they have evolved as two separate systems.

All AAP surveys operate two-stage cluster sampling to obtain nationally representative samples of pupils, stratified by local authority and school size. Until 2002, each AAP survey involved pupils aged eight to nine years (P4), eleven to twelve years (P7) and thirteen to fourteen years (S2). P4 has been regarded as the earliest stage at which pupils can satisfactorily cope with the demands of the assessment while the other two groups are at significant stages in their education. The younger pupils (P7) are reaching the end of their primary education and S2 pupils have selected the subjects which they will study for national certification at the end of S4. Table 87.1 shows the pattern of surveys established to date.

Table 87.1: Surveys in the Assessment of Achievement Programme

Survey	Year of Survey					
Mathematics	1963	1988	1991	1994	1997	2000
English Language	1984	1989	1992	1995	1998	2001
Science	1987	1990	1993	1996	1999	

The SOEID (the predecessor of SEED) funded and managed each project, appointing a project committee to support and advise each team. These were chaired by subject specialists from Her Majesty's Inspectorate of Schools (HMI) and membership included teachers from both primary and secondary sectors, advisers and a principal research officer of the SOEID. Project teams were given a wide remit and considerable responsibility. They were required to develop the survey design and select appropriate assessment materials as well as being encouraged to develop new techniques and tasks for each round of monitoring. Teams appointed and trained assessors to work in schools and markers to evaluate and code pupil responses. Work culminated in the preparation of reports and the drafting of dissemination materials.

In 1996, the organisation of the AAP changed significantly when a national co-ordinator was appointed to oversee all surveys. Subsequently surveys were managed centrally with subject expertise contracted as necessary. Further significant changes took place in 2002 when the decision was taken to extend the number of curriculum areas included in the AAP. In addition, the programme moved to a four-yearly cycle of monitoring and shifted the focus to include pupils in P3, P5, as well as P7 and S2. Science, which was scheduled for 2002, was postponed for one year and its place in the cycle was taken by Social Subjects (History, Geography and Modern Studies). In addition, an AAP reference group was established, drawing on practitioners in each subject area, and assessment extended to include the assessment of attitudes, numeracy, literacy and ICT skills within a context. A range of practical tasks was developed alongside the more traditional written assessments, as appropriate. The combination of school stages and the four year cycle allows genuine longitudinal comparisons to be made, with individual pupils tracked across surveys and their performance compared at, for example, P3 and P7.

The specific aims of each survey include:

- to determine what pupils know and can do in agreed aspects of the subject areas;
- to measure performance in relation to the curricular levels defined in national guidelines as part of the 5–14 programme;
- to provide comparisons of the performance of pupils at each of the stages identified;

- to provide comparisons by gender;
- to provide comparisons of pupils' performance over time.

While each survey has a number of common features, the procedures and techniques developed by project teams reflect the specific nature of each subject area.

ASSESSING ACHIEVEMENT IN MATHEMATICS

The Surveys

The first survey (1983) was undertaken by the Scottish Council for Research in Education and the second (1988) by Macnab, Page and Kennedy at Northern College. The third (1991) and fourth (1994) were directed by Robertson and Meechan at what is now the Faculty of Education (Jordanhill Campus) of the University of Strathclyde. An assessment framework based on consultative documentation for national guidelines was prepared for 1991 and modified to allow robust comparisons with published 5–14 achievement targets in 1994. In matching performance against expectations – defined as what 'most pupils' should be able to do – 'most' was interpreted as $\geqslant 67\%$ of samples. The fifth survey (SOEID, 1997) aligned reporting categories more closely with 'strands' and used 'mean percentage correct' to report on all items contributing to one 'strand' at one 'level', with performance rated through five descriptors ranging from 'excellent'($\geqslant 80\%$) to 'poor and a cause for concern' ($< 50\%$). The sixth survey (SEED, 2000) provided comparisons with targets at level F. Category descriptors were reduced to four, ranging from 'very good – major strengths' to 'unsatisfactory – major weaknesses' (describing $\geqslant 80\%$ and $< 50\%$) with 'good – strengths outweigh weaknesses' applied to means of 66.7% – 79.9% and 'fair – some important weaknesses' to those of 50% – 66.6%. Additionally, pupils were given 'scores' for levels with 'mean scores' compared to 'cut-off scores' of 50%, 60% and 70%.

Innovation and collaboration

The 1991 written survey introduced test booklets with items set within contextual themes, attractively illustrated to minimise reading load and this practice has continued. Prior to 2000, surveys included practical assessment, carried out by field officers using one-to-one oral presentation and circuits of tasks. In 1991, a computerised testing feasibility study was carried out in primary schools. For the 1994 survey, techniques were developed for individual assessment of extended practical problem solving, based on 'starting', 'doing' and 'reporting' tasks. These were used in the 1997 survey which also focused on calculator skills and mental calculation. The 1994 survey included a collaborative study with France attempting comparisons of P4 and P7 with French CE2 and Sixième (6è) stages (Robertson, 2000). Some collaboration with Holland was undertaken in 1997.

The assessment framework

The basic framework has provided a structure for reporting a decade of Mathematics surveys and has allowed acceptably valid and reliable comparisons over time. The 'attainment outcomes' in national guidelines form the major organisers with number, money and measurement most prominent, comprising in 2000, eight reporting categories/

strands. Those assessed at all three stages were range and type of number (including estimate and round); patterns and sequences (incorporating functions, equations and formulae); add and subtract and multiply and divide (incorporating whole and decimal numbers and 'no context' and 'with a context' items); fractions, percentages and ratio and measure (including perimeter and scale). Time (including speed) was assessed at P7 and S2 and algebra at S2. Information handling has two reporting categories, namely, interpret (assessed at all stages) and probability (assessed at S2). Shape, position and movement was assessed at all stages as range of shapes and symmetry and position and Movement and Angle. Problem solving (within the problem solving and enquiry outcome), was assessed in 2000 by short, written response items relating to number, money and measurement.

Findings on performance and influence on practice

In 1994, at P4, almost 60% of items at (target) level B were performed successfully by 67% pupils. At P7, this was true for under 40% of items at (target) level D and, at S2, under 50% of items at level D and less than 20% at (target) level E. These findings, together with publication of the Scottish results from the Third International Mathematics and Science Study (TIMSS) in 1996, were strongly influential in the recommendations made by HMI in 1997 for changes to be made to practice in schools and pre-service teacher education. *Improving Mathematics Education 5–14* recommended 'setting' or 'broad banding' of pupils in secondary schools and, in both primary and secondary sectors, more direct and interactive teaching. Time spent on mental arithmetic was reported to be low compared with many other countries and the widespread use of calculators at variance with practice in countries which had performed well in the TIMSS.

The 1997 survey reflected on the 'dip' in performance in comparison with 1991 and suggested that this might have been caused by the curriculum being squeezed by the pressures of a wide range of other reforms. The report identified some signs of improvement at P4 but difficulties at P7 with fractions, percentages and ratio and multiply and divide and a significant fall in performance on shape, position and movement. Performance at S2 on most of these categories was reported a concern and, although 'mental calculations' were described as 'acceptable', it was suggested that insufficient time was allocated to this aspect of Mathematics. As identified in 1994, using calculators had been found to present few problems at any stage but skills in rounding and approximating remained at a low level. The report of the 2000 survey (SEED, 2001) noted changes in the organisation of teaching Mathematics in both primary and secondary schools since 1997. Primary pupils appeared to be taught Mathematics for longer each week and mental calculation provided daily. Secondary schools were reported to have moved away from mixed ability teaching at S2. It was concluded that, although significant improvement had taken place, performance in 2000 was still not good enough, particularly at P7 and S2, with strands previously identified as 'major weaknesses' remaining so. Using the cut-off score of 60% as an indicator of attainment of their target levels, 77% of P4 but only 52% of P7 and 49% of S2 were considered to have attained these.

Gender comparisons

In 1991 no significant differences in performance were found at P4 and P7, out of line with previous assumptions of better performance from boys. At S2, boys had performed better on number concepts but girls were better on basic processes in *whole number arithmetic*, *fractions, decimals and percentages*, and *position and movement*. The 1994 survey showed a significant difference in favour of girls at P4, for *display and interpret* with no significant differences at P7 or S2. In 1997 no differences were found at any stage and, in 2000, while this remained true at P4 and P7, at S2, a more widely recognised trend – of girls doing better than boys – was evident. The only significant differences were those favouring girls, on *add and subtract* and *multiply and divide* and, overall, on level E items.

ASSESSING ACHIEVEMENT IN ENGLISH LANGUAGE

There have been six surveys of achievement in English Language. The first in 1984 was conducted by a team at the then Dundee College of Education, the next three were based at the University of Edinburgh and the most recent two were co-ordinated by the Scottish Executive Education Department. SEED worked with a specialist project team who helped to plan and implement the surveys, analyse the results and prepare the final report.

The first survey by the Edinburgh team in 1989 took place while national policies for assessment and testing, integral parts of the 5–14 development programme, were still at a formative stage. It was not possible, nor was it part of the team's remit to attempt to link, explicitly, the monitoring project and the 5–14 programme. However, it was considered that the survey would provide a rich source of performance data which could provide some sort of validation of the attainment targets and would contribute to and inform the implementation of the 5–14 national guidelines for English.

The assessment framework

The 1989 survey reflected a shift in emphasis from language as a set of discrete skills towards language as communicative competence. The approach used was purpose based, that is, it began by defining the purposes for which the various language functions are performed and attempted to cover as many of these as possible. The tasks were contextualised in that they formed part of a coherent sequence, with an identifiable justification. The whole sequence attempted to mirror good classroom practice by assessing children, as far as possible, on aspects of language usage in ways which would command the approval of teachers.

This approach to measuring achievement was found to be entirely compatible with the national guidelines and, from 1992 onwards, the surveys were designed to allow comparisons to be made, wherever possible, with these. Only a limited number of the strands could be assessed within the constraints imposed by the survey design and the resources available. In all the surveys, except the 1998 survey, achievement was assessed across the four modes of Reading, Writing, Talking and Listening. These modes are the 5–14 language outcomes, while the purposes are incorporated within the strands.

From 1992, surveys continued to support teachers in interpreting aspects of the guidelines and in developing effective techniques for the assessment of English. Carefully designed frameworks for the assessments of Writing were produced, though, since 1998, the surveys have used the national test criteria for Writing. Criteria for the assessment of Talk were derived from the guidelines and were used in the 1992, 1995 and 2001 surveys.

The 2001 survey, assessing all pupils in Reading and Writing, and a subset of these pupils in Listening and Talking, differed in several significant ways from the previous survey of

1998 which was concerned only with performance in Reading and Writing. In the 2001 Reading assessments, tasks (i.e. the text and the associated questions) were categorised as being at a specific level rather than reflective of performance at a stage, neither were they seen to be part of a contextualised package of assessment tools but rather as a discrete skill. Reading items were also designed to reflect the categories of understanding, analysis and evaluation. New approaches to the assessment of Writing were used which included classroom writing and the completion of a more focused piece of writing. Changes were made to the ways in which Listening and Talking were assessed; though the 1995 survey Talking and Listening tasks were used to provide comparison over time. Listening included a metacognitive component with its focus on the knowledge about language strand. These changes were seen as reflective of the evolving nature of assessment in English Language, especially in the context of a national survey, though the administration of the survey became more complex. The final report from this survey is due to be published in 2003.

Findings on performance

The 1992 AAP findings, although tentative, appeared to indicate that the attainment targets might have been set rather high for 'most pupils'. They seemed to apply to 'just over half', as far as can be ascertained from the imprecise definitions provided. While it was established that, for English, 'most' meant at least three-quarters of pupils, in this survey, at all stages and across all four language modes, the proportion of pupils achieving the appropriate level ranged between one half and three-fifths of each sample cohort.

The incorporation of the national guidelines into classroom practice, particularly in the primary sector, was reflected in the 1995 survey with marked improvements in a number of specific curriculum areas. Standards at P4 for all four language outcomes appeared, for the most part, to be in line with level B; the majority of P7 pupils were competent talkers, attaining level D, while approximately half were working to level D in Listening and Writing albeit with some difficulties in Reading. At S2 performance in both Listening and Reading was reasonable, although Talking, particularly in groups, needed some attention and for many pupils attainment in Writing was well below the expected level E.

Performance for the 1998 survey showed that the majority of P4 pupils were attaining level B or better in Reading and Writing, though a substantial minority were still yet to attain their level B target. At P7, a sizeable majority of pupils were attaining level D or better for Reading but, in Writing, only a minority of pupils attained level D. Less than half the S2 pupils were achieving the target level E for Reading and less than a quarter of pupils for writing.

The specialists have continued to have reservations as to the precise nature of a level of attainment. Reporting overall achievement in terms of the attainment targets and interpreting the levels should not, in their opinion, be viewed as an exact exercise.

Performance over time

Comparisons between performance over time were made from consecutive survey data although no direct comparison could be made between performance in 1989 and 1995. Overall, there was no general change in the level of performance between 1989 and 1992, though some variation of performance occurred in respect of particular skills at P4 and at S2. Comparison between 1992 and 1995 showed significant declines in Reading at all three stages but, at P4 and P7, Writing skills had improved and at P7 there was a significant improvement in some aspects of Talking. Listening and Talking data were unavailable for 1998 but there were small significant improvements in Reading between 1995 and 1998 at both P4 and S2 and in Writing at P7 and S2.

Performance between stages

Comparisons were made between P7 and S2 stages only. In 1995, S2 pupils performed significantly better on all Listening, Reading and Writing tasks bar one (imaginative writing) and in 1998 they again performed significantly better on all Reading and Writing tasks.

Gender

In 1993, across the four language modes, P4 girls performed significantly better in five skills, P7 girls in seven skills and S2 girls in two skills. In 1995 the girls at P4 were significantly better in thirteen skills, at P7 in fourteen skills and at S2 in eighteen skills. These significant differences were most noticeable in both Reading and Writing; at S2 the girls were consistently performing better in all aspects of Writing. The 1998 results showed that girls were performing consistently better than boys and that the differences seem to increase with age. At both P4 and P7 girls performed significantly better on four of the ten Reading tasks and on eight of ten Writing tasks. At S2, girls were significantly out-performing the boys on nine of the twelve Reading tasks and on all but one of the Writing tasks.

Cross curricular projects

Cross-curricular issues, in particular the use of English Language across the curriculum, have formed a vital part of recent SEED publications. Although the English Language specialists have always been aware of the need to respond to such concerns and to develop relevant and valid contexts for the assessment of language skills and, in this spirit, became involved in collaboration with the AAP Science 1993 and Mathematics 1994, no further collaborations have been undertaken.

ASSESSING ACHIEVEMENT IN SCIENCE

The first project in 1987 was essentially a feasibility study, an attempt to determine whether it was possible to conduct national monitoring of Science using both practical and non-practical forms of assessment. Conducted prior to the introduction of the 5–14 programme and national testing, the political stakes were low and the AAP was not perceived by teachers as threatening. In addition, attempts were made to avoid imposing additional burdens on teachers with minimal intrusion into the day-to-day work of the class and no teacher involvement in task development or marking. Schools participated readily and the survey was regarded as fairly successful.

The assessment framework

The initial assessment framework (1987) was derived from an analysis of curricular and policy documents and through consultation. It had the approval of the project committee and met the expectations of the majority of teachers, primary and secondary, whose pupils were involved. A combination of practical and written tasks were designed to assess specific skills and concepts and integrated tasks (practical investigations) required pupils to draw on a range of science concepts as well as practical and process skills. A commitment to Science as an active, participative area of the curriculum was a significant feature of the first four Science surveys although the practical investigations element was not included in the fifth survey in 1999.

Following the publication in 1993 of the guidelines for Science, a component of Environmental Studies 5–14, the 1996 survey was the first to attempt to measure performance in Science against the expectations of the 5–14 programme. Three attainment outcomes, which drew on the three main science disciplines of Biology, Physics, and Chemistry, outlined the content and contexts for learning Science and five strands reflected the levels of knowledge, skills and processes expected across the 5–14 age range. In addition, guidance on the development of informed attitudes was included. The strands were set out in the 5–14 levels while the statements of content and context (the 'key features') are grouped by (st)age into three broad bands: P1–P3, P4–P6 and P7–S2. The key features and strands were combined in the 1996 assessment framework (Table 87.2).

Table 87.2: The 1996 assessment framework

CATEGORY	SUB-CATEGORY	
Knowledge and Understanding (KU)		
Planning (P)	P1:	Question raising
	P2:	Identifying information sources and resources
	P3:	Sequencing plans
	P4:	Planning for recording and reporting
	P5:	Anticipating problems
	P6:	Planning for safety and hygiene
Collecting Evidence (CE)	CE1:	Recognising similarities and differences
	CE2:	Recognising changes
	CE3:	Extracting information
	CE4:	Using simple techniques
	CE5:	Estimating and measuring
	CE6:	Collecting evidence fairly and safely
Recording & Presenting (RP)	RP1:	Recording in a variety of formats
	RP2:	Presenting in a variety of formats
Interpreting & Evaluating (IE)	IE1:	Identifying relationships
	IE2:	Evaluating evidence

The revision of the Environmental Studies guidelines in 2000 removed the three broad stage-related bands and replaced them with the six levels A – F (SEED, 2000). The strands were grouped under the heading 'Skills' and presented as the three phases of investigating: preparing for tasks; carrying out tasks; and reviewing and reporting on tasks. A Guide for managers and teachers was published to exemplify the targets and support teachers in the learning and teaching of science.

The findings

Summaries of findings are, of necessity, broad brush statements which can, and do, mask considerable variation in performance within and across the key features and strands assessed. With that in mind, in 1996 P4 pupils were judged to have attained level B on the assessment tasks and P7 pupils came close to meeting the level D targets. At S2, however, performance was poor with attainment reaching level D rather than the level E anticipated. Overall, at all three stages, girls tended to outperform boys, particularly on process and practical skills and where the content/context was drawn from the biological sciences. Boys produced superior performances on knowledge and understanding where the focus was on the physical sciences.

Over the series of surveys 1987–96, the P4 pupils showed some improvement, P7 stayed fairly steady but S2 performance levels declined, more so amongst boys than girls. In 1996, the P4 pupils who had been involved in the 1993 survey were, where feasible, included in the P7 sample, introducing a truly longitudinal element in an attempt to gain greater insight into the issue of progression through the primary stages. The findings indicated a clear progression in attainment, with some evidence of a growing gap in the performance levels of low and high achievers over time.

International comparisons

In the 1995 TIMSS survey, two samples of pupils in Scottish schools were involved, one with an average age of nine years and a second with an average age of thirteen years. The younger pupils were ranked at approximately the mid-point for all aspects of Science assessed across twenty-six countries. An analysis by gender indicated that, in Scotland, boys did better than girls at both stages although the differences were not significant.

The 13–year-olds were drawn from the S1 and S2 grades in Scottish schools and, overall, were ranked twenty-fifth. Analysis by gender showed that, in all countries, boys performed better than girls at the lower grade and the differences were significant in twenty-six of them (Edinburgh: SOEID, *Achievements of S1 and S2 Pupils in Mathematics and Science: TIMMS*, 1996).

The gender-related data appears to conflict with the AAP findings but it should be noted that in TIMSS the focus was on knowledge and understanding where boys also tended to outperform girls in the AAP survey. Overall, compared with the other TIMSS countries, the performance of 13–year-olds in Scotland was poor, although relatively good for the 9–year-olds tested.

DISCUSSION

When the national curriculum and national testing arrangements were introduced in England and Wales, the government disbanded the APU and determined that measurements of whether or not pupils in schools knew and could do what was expected of them would be based on the collation of national test data. This was not an option for Scotland where the arrangements for the assessment and testing of primary and early secondary pupils were, and remain, quite different. While in England both the national curriculum and national testing are mandatory, the status of national testing in Scotland – non-statutory, exclusively pencil-and-paper and of relatively small samples of the curriculum – would render the collation of test data for monitoring purposes unreliable and lacking in validity (see Chapter 85).

The technical knowledge required for national monitoring (the 'how') has evolved considerably over the last fifteen years and is more than adequate to ensure that the statistical procedures are accurate and appropriate. However, as Dockrell points out, the most contentious issues in national monitoring (as with national testing) are the 'what' and the 'why', both of which are value-laden and, in consequence, should be the real issues for discussion (Dockrell, 1979).

The 'what' in the AAP is given by the 5–14 programme. The curricular guidelines should ensure a degree of commonality in the learning experiences of children across the country. However, the guidelines reflect a particular view of each subject area and embody values which may not be acceptable to all. In addition, there are significant difficulties in reaching a consensus in the interpretation in many of the targets, a problem common to those attempting to reconcile national test data and national expectations in England (Massey, 1995).

Developed primarily for purposes of learning and teaching, the targets within the 5–14 guidelines are mainly expressed as broad general statements rather than specific learning objectives; the degree of generality varies with the subject area. This avoidance of prescription was deliberate in that it would allow teachers to interpret the statements in ways which would more readily meet the needs of their pupils and to develop programmes of study which would reflect the local environment.

This flexibility creates problems for national monitoring (and classroom assessment) as targets can contain some ambiguous statements, considerable variation in conceptual demand and a lack of clarity in specifying how progress can be recognised. It is not a straightforward task to identify unambiguously what pupils should know and be able to do and to develop tasks which accurately tap the targets. (See also Chapter 81.) The AAP has continued to assist in clarifying and interpreting the language of the strands and the targets as well as the criteria used to define the 5–14 levels.

To date, the AAP has assessed widely across each subject area: Listening and Talking in English, practical investigations in science and practical applications of mathematical skills. In addition, it has tried out new techniques and developed alternative approaches to assessment. However, such a commitment is expensive in time and resources and impossible to sustain in the face of diminishing budgets.

It would have been unfortunate if, as a result, the AAP had resorted to what is cheap, that is pencil-and-paper assessment, and easy to test, for instance knowledge and understanding, thus reducing the breadth of coverage and the range of modes of assessment used. Quite apart from the loss of innovative assessment opportunities, the profession could come to believe that only that which is tested is important and, as a result, pupils might experience a narrowing of the curriculum. The recent inclusion of the AAP in the well-resourced Assessment Development Programme should protect against this.

The government's concern with performance levels (the 'why' of monitoring standards) is driven, in the main, by economic and political considerations. Any policy of national monitoring and/or testing attracts critics and much of that criticism tends to be concerned with the values which people perceive to underlie the development of such policies. Concerns include the potential misuse of test results, the mismatch of the test to the local curriculum, teaching to the test, the use of restrictive or narrow testing formats and the potentially divisive consequences of labelling children as a result of assessment.

To date, the AAP has been relatively free of such criticisms. The multi-matrix, light sampling techniques do not place a significant burden on individual pupils and the analysis is designed such that no individual pupil, school or local authority is identified.

In maintaining two systems of assessment, national testing and national monitoring, policy makers acknowledged that measuring the strengths and weaknesses of individual performance and progress and determining national levels of performance require different approaches, and they have earned credit for matching appropriate assessment instruments to purpose (Brown, 1994). As the AAP continues to evolve, it should be an important source of information in the debate on the effectiveness of the 5–14 programme, contributing to policy making, directly and indirectly, and providing real, practical assistance to teachers in turning policy into practice.

REFERENCES

Brown, S. (1994) Assessment and testing, in G. Kirk and R. Glaister (eds), *5–14: Scotland's National Curriculum*, Edinburgh: Scottish Academic Press.

Dockrell, W. B. (1979) National surveys of Achievement, *Issues in Educational Assessment*, Occasional Papers, Edinburgh: HMSO.

Massey, A. J. (1995) Criterion-related Test Development and national test standards, *Assessment in Education: Principles, Policy and Practice*, 2 (2), 187–203.

Napuk, A., Normand, B. and Orr, S. (1996) *The Assessment of Achievement Programme (Scotland): English Language, Fourth Survey 1995*, Edinburgh: University of Edinburgh.

Robertson, I. J. (2000) Collaboration and comparisons: a bilateral study of mathematics performance in Scotland and France, *Comparative Education* 36 (4), 437–57.

Stark R. Gray,, D. Bryce, T. G. K. and Ellis, S. (1997) *Assessment of Achievement Programme: Fourth Survey of Science, 1996*, Glasgow: University of Strathclyde.

88

SQA Findings on Scottish Achievements

Christine De Luca

This chapter updates the two chapters in the first edition of this book which summarised achievements of candidates certificated by SQA's two predecessor bodies, the Scottish Examination Board (SEB) and the Scottish Vocational Education Council (SCOTVEC). These two national awarding bodies were merged in 1997 to form the Scottish Qualifications Authority (SQA), a statutory body whose main functions are developing and validating qualifications other than degrees and assessing, quality assuring and certificating attainment across the full range of secondary school and adult candidates. It also has an approval function to ensure education and training establishments can fully support the assessment of candidates entered for qualifications and a separate regulatory function for Scottish Vocational Qualifications (SVQs). SQA has a support role in the government's 5–14 assessment programme through provision of assessment instruments and carries out a range of testing and quality assurance services for other bodies, including overseas, on a contractual basis.

SQA has come a considerable way in building a unified qualifications and assessment framework on the basis of the government's Higher Still development programme (Scottish Office, 1994). However, the task was immense: so much so, indeed, that the certification of the first diet of the unified assessment system in 2000 which had to be combined with parallel running of all extant qualifications, overwhelmed data management systems in both centres and SQA. Certification in 2001, while successful, was still very demanding for SQA and its centres. It has taken a further year to be able to plan for the future across all qualifications and to re-establish confidence and support for these developments.

The SEB, from its inception in 1963, concentrated on certificating school candidates in secondary stages S4–S6. Ordinary Grades were introduced for S4 candidates at that time to widen the curriculum and provide a stepping stone to Higher Grade. (Ordinary Grades were deemed equivalent to the Ordinary Level, in the rest of the United Kingdom.) As more pupils stayed on at school there was pressure first of all to extend the reporting of lower attainment within Ordinary Grades (to bands D and E), and then to replace them with a qualification more suited to the full ability spectrum (following the influential Munn and Dunning Reports (SED, 1977a and SED, 1977b)). Consequently new Standard Grade courses were introduced gradually from 1986 at much the same time as the equivalent General Certificate of Education (GCSE) was introduced in England, Wales and Northern Ireland. These qualifications were subject-based courses generally started in S3 and completed by the end of S4. The Certificate of Sixth Year Studies (CSYS), also a subject-based qualification, was added to the available qualifications in 1968. Although the CSYS was designed to prepare candidates for higher education, it was never fully used by higher education as an entry qualification. There were a number of linked reasons for this: one was the status of the Higher as the 'gold standard' for entry purposes; another was the four year honours degree in Scottish universities.

All three types of qualification, Standard Grade, Higher Grade and CSYS, required sustained learning over a minimum of a year (though, in practice, Standard Grade is a two-year course for most pupils). The syllabuses and assessment specifications were detailed and the criteria for awards fairly holistic, with marks being aggregated across the various components of the assessment. They encompassed a wide variety of assessment tasks, often in combination. Thus, for one subject, a candidate might sit an external written examination, complete a folio and undertake a practical assessment. Internal assessment played an important role in both Standard and Higher Grade, and internal estimates were used widely to support several awarding functions: determining pass-marks, prioritising scripts for quality assurance checks, identifying results which merited an appeal on the basis of reliable predictions from centres. The SQA inherited all three qualifications from the SEB, together with a small number of Short Courses designed to broaden the curriculum.

SQA also inherited the full range of qualifications offered by SCOTVEC which had been established as a limited company in 1985 through the merger of SCOTEC (the Scottish Technical Education Council) and SCOTBEC (the Scottish Business Education Council). These councils were particularly known for their Ordinary National and Higher National Certificates and Diplomas (ONCs, ONDs, HNCs and HNDs) which were focused on technician-level skills requiring work experience but were assessed through examinations. SCOTVEC began building a new qualifications system on the principles defined in the government's 'Action Plan' published in 1983. The plan envisaged a new approach to vocational education in which programmes of education and training were built of modules, each of which was based on standards of performance defined in advance and publicly available. Standards were to be encapsulated in outcomes and performance criteria and all assessment was to be internal, subject to various forms of external verification.

During its twelve-year existence, and responding to a range of government initiatives, SCOTVEC extended the Action Plan philosophy to all its qualifications. This resulted in a framework based on three types of modules: National Certificate Units; Higher National Units and Workplace-assessed Units which could be offered as tailored programmes or as qualifications. The main qualifications were National Certificates (NCs), HNCs, HNDs, Professional Development Awards (PDAs), Scottish Vocational Qualifications (SVQs) and General SVQs. National Certificate Clusters, reflecting the growing range of activities offered in schools, were also developed. This modular system had a significant impact on Scottish education and training. Over the years the system for developing qualifications and quality assuring assessments became increasingly devolved to centres through an extensive approval and audit system.

The merger of the two organisations (SEB and SCOTVEC) in 1997 required the merger of two assessment systems where similar modular provision was available (SCOTVEC National Certificate modules and SEB short courses). It also helped align the Higher Still initiative more firmly with further education needs by extending the number, nature and form of assessment of National Courses to include full project-based courses. The embedding of core skills certification in National Courses and the introduction of Scottish Group Awards (SGAs) also helped create links between provision in schools and provision in colleges. However, this has not as yet met all expectations and work continues in an attempt to bridge further the academic–vocational divide.

The following two main sections of this chapter summarise:

- The range of qualifications now available at particular types of centre (schools; further education (FE) colleges; higher education (HE) institutions such as universities; training organisations; employers). The first section also highlights the nature of reviews of qualifications which are under way at the time of writing.
- The achievements of candidates (pupils, students, trainees and employees), in terms of uptake and attainment and in relation to gender. This builds on the first edition (which included data for 1987 and 1996) by adding parallel data for 2001 and data on new levels of qualification.

The final section then considers the critical issues which SQA faces; issues which look like creating a challenging environment over the next decade.

RANGE OF QUALIFICATIONS
National Qualifications

Standard Grade

Standard Grade is a qualification for school pupils. Having started their certificate subjects at the beginning of S3, candidates generally sit seven or, more typically, eight Standard Grades at the end of S4. There are thirty-nine different Standard Grades, each with criteria defining the broad levels of achievement across almost the full ability spectrum, namely Foundation – grades 5 and 6, General – grades 3 and 4, and Credit – grades 1 and 2. Candidates generally sit papers at two adjacent levels. Each course is based on a number of elements (typically three) such as 'knowledge and understanding', 'problem solving', 'performing', 'investigating'. One element is usually internally assessed, with external moderation on a sample basis. The certificate shows, for each Standard Grade, both the grades for individual elements and the overall aggregated award on the same scale. Over the years there has been a move away from internally-generated evidence such as investigations or folios. This was due mainly to workload on candidates and staff but also reflected concerns over the authentication of such coursework.

Scottish Certificate of Education Higher Grade

This qualification has been the Scottish 'gold standard' for university entrance for over a century. It was largely a school-based qualification, but colleges also entered candidates. The year 2001 was the final year for all subjects except English. It is now replaced by the new unit-based National Courses at Higher. Awards were made on a scale of A–D, with D indicating a narrow failure.

Certificate of Sixth Year Studies (CSYS)

CSYS was a school-based qualification geared to preparing candidates for university. Like SCE Higher it is also being phased out, and replaced by the new Advanced Higher. It was available in twenty-three subjects until 2001, with only English available until 2002. Awards were made on a scale of A-E.

National Units, Courses and Scottish Group Awards

The year 2000 saw the introduction of the new National Units, Courses and Group Awards at seven levels: Access 1, 2 and 3, Intermediate 1 and 2, Higher, and Advanced Higher. This initiative grew out of plans to reform the upper secondary school system but gradually expanded to encompass other non-advanced provision, and thus bridge the academic-vocational divide. While uptake of National Courses is mainly by school pupils, there is a small but important group of candidates within colleges. Each National Unit is a stand-alone award, internally assessed and subject to external moderation. Most are forty hours in length. National Units are the building blocks of coherent groups of generally three units (120 hours in total) thus creating 'National Clusters' at Access level and National Courses at the levels beyond Access. Only courses are subject to external assessment. Courses have a built-in additional forty hours (making them a notional 160 hours) to allow for consolidation, integration and preparation for the external course assessment which provides the grading (A–C). All units must be achieved before the full course award is made, but units do not provide marks towards course grades. Unit reassessment is however allowed. Unit assessment is supported by a National Assessment Bank (NAB) of exemplar assessment instruments and marking schemes. While most course assessments include an externally set and marked question-paper as a major component, a significant minority are based on a performance or project: the latter can take the form of a practical assignment, a case study or an investigation.

Units, clusters and courses are available in a range of subjects, namely:

- Access 1 and 2 have been designed with candidates with learning disabilities of different severity in mind. There are currently seventy units covering sixteen subject areas available at Access 1 and eighteen clusters at Access 2.
- Access level 3 is benchmarked against Standard Grade Foundation level. There are twenty-three clusters at Access 3.
- Intermediate 1 is bench-marked against Standard Grade General level, with thirty-eight courses available.
- Intermediate 2 is bench-marked against Standard Grade Credit level, with seventy-six courses available, including twenty-one which are project-based.
- Higher is bench-marked against the former SCE Higher Grade, with 103 courses available, including forty-five which are project-based.
- Advanced Higher is bench-marked against the former CSYS, with thirty-eight courses available.

Given the hierarchical arrangement of these courses across the levels, a near-miss in a course assessment allows for a fall-back award of a grade A at the level below. However, this arrangement may change as it has not been universally welcomed.

Group Awards within the National Catalogue

Scottish Group Awards (SGAs) have design rules which aim to encourage study of particular combinations of courses and units, while allowing some choice. They also require candidates to have a specified minimum core skills profile. In the past, Group Awards have been mainly offered in colleges, but the Higher Still initiative was intended to increase the uptake in schools. So far, however, the new SGAs have not attracted as many candidates as their predecessor group awards, particularly the General Vocational Qualifications (GSVQs) and National Certificates. Colleges have tended to continue to offer their own locally-devised programmes. A review of SGAs is under way to make these Group Awards more fit for purpose.

Review of National Qualifications

Such a major transformation and extension of an assessment system was not without teething troubles. Several consultations during 2000–1 suggested much dissatisfaction, particularly with what was perceived as the burden of internal assessment on both candidates and teachers/lecturers. Indeed, so much so, that the Scottish Executive mounted a major review in 2001 (Scottish Executive, 2001), starting with a summary of the various consultations, and from there suggesting several options for the future as a basis of further consultation. The eventual decision was to avoid major design changes to the system; to concentrate instead on slimming down the assessment, ironing out inconsistencies and clarifying standards. SQA completed a comprehensive subject-by-subject review of unit and course assessment at all levels. These recommendations were quickly published and are currently being implemented.

Higher National Qualifications

Higher National Qualifications are intended for adult candidates studying either full time or part time. At certificate level (HNC) they are equivalent to first year higher education, and at diploma level (HND) they are equivalent to second year. Most candidates are in the college sector (98% of HNC and 92% of HND entries in 2001), with the remainder studying in universities. These qualifications are well respected in their own right, but many also give credit towards a degree programme. Credit transfer agreements are worked out between colleges and individual universities so as to smooth transition for students. HN units can be taken as stand-alone awards or built up into HNC, HND or Professional Development Awards (PDAs). Most of the responsibility for developing and validating these qualifications has been devolved to centres and there are now over a thousand validated Group Award titles. In 1988 there were just ninety-seven titles, all of them nationally devised. Of the current titles, about 180 have been devised nationally by SQA or by consortia supported by SQA. For reporting purposes HNCs and HNDs are grouped into twenty-three 'superclasses' (for example Construction and Property – the Built Environment; Business, Management and Office Studies), corresponding broadly to employment and training sectors. Higher National Qualifications have been under review since 1985 in consultation with centres, and new design rules are currently being piloted. The main changes, which will be subject to consultation before the end of 2002, include:

- Uniformity in size of awards: all HNCs to be fifteen credits (with the possibility of twelve credits where there is a clear rationale) and all HNDs to be thirty credits, that is a further fifteen credits added to the HNC. All HN units will be allocated a level in the Scottish Credit and Qualifications Framework (SCQF).
- All HNCs to include two – and all HNDs four – mandatory Integrative Assessments. These assessments will provide a basis for grading awards at A, B or C. Unit assessments will no longer be graded 'pass' or 'merit'.

- All HNCs and HNDs to have a mandatory section which every candidate for a Group Award will take.

Scottish Vocational Qualifications (SVQs)

SVQs are designed to certificate candidates meeting the National Occupational Standards (NOS) defined by standards-setting bodies (SSBs). The NOS and VQ frameworks are UK-wide with SVQs developed generally in parallel with NVQs for England, Wales and Northern Ireland. The standards for SVQs, like NVQs, are defined across levels. There are five levels in all, SVQ level 1–5 (see Chapter 106). The development of standards and associated assessment strategies for qualifications in the occupational area are the responsibility of the new Sector Skills Councils (SSCs) which are gradually replacing the former more narrowly-focused National Training Organisations (NTOs). However, some NTOs are continuing in this role on an interim basis. SVQs are workplace-assessed qualifications, and there are strict guidelines about:

- how external quality control is achieved (for example by independent assessment);
- which aspects of NOS must be assessed in the workplace;
- what occupational expertise the assessor must have;
- in what areas and in what way simulated assessment can be used to assess competence.

These issues are particularly important for qualifications where funding for providers follows success.

Awarding bodies such as SQA build these standards and assessment strategies into qualifications which then go through an accreditation process. Accreditation of SVQs and of the bodies offering them is carried out by SQA's accreditation unit, which operates independly of SQA's awarding function. In 2001, 90% of SVQ awards were by SQA alone or in partnership with another awarding body.

In addition to SVQs, SQA also offers some workplace-assessed Professional Development Awards (PDAs) – for example, the Certificate for Classroom Assistant – and Scottish Progression Awards (SPAs). Work-place assessed PDAs, like SPAs, are built from SVQ units and, in 2001, represented about a quarter of SVQ-based awards achieved by candidates. SPAs were developed in the late 1990s to address the issue of candidates who had difficulty completing a full SVQ award. This was particularly acute among candidates on New Deal programmes (see Chapter 12). SPAs are similar to a stage 1 of the full qualification and allow candidates to complete the rest of the qualification at a later date. Other important uses of SVQ units are in modern apprenticeships and in customised awards created for particular employers. Like HN qualifications, the list of SVQs is lengthy: there are over 1,100 titles and several thousand individual SVQ units. As the majority of the SVQs awarded by SQA have little or no uptake, a review of what is offered has recently been instituted.

CANDIDATE ACHIEVEMENT: UPTAKE AND ATTAINMENT (1986–1997–2001)

This section updates the data on uptake and attainment included in the first edition (by adding data from 2001 to that for 1986 and 1997). It also provides updated data on achievement in relation to gender. For examination-based qualifications, the year refers to the exam diet in May with certification following in August. For HNs and SVQs where a year is stated (for example, 1997), this refers to SQA's 'data collection year' – that is, the period between 1 August 1996 and 31 July 1997. All data are taken from SQA internal statistical analyses and external publications such as the SQA Annual Statistical Reports, unless otherwise stated.

National Qualifications

Standard Grade

In 2001 there were close on 63,000 Standard Grade candidates, with almost half a million subject entries.

Table 88.1: Number of subjects attempted by S4 candidates Ordinary Grade and Standard Grade, 1987, 1996 and 2001

Number of Subjects	Candidates as % of cohort		
	1987 O Grades + S Grades	1996 Standard Grades (excl. Writing)	2001 Standard Grades (excl. Writing)
none	6%	2%	3%
1	6%	1%	1%
2	6%	1%	1%
3	8%	1%	1%
4	9%	1%	1%
5	10%	2%	2%
6	14%	5%	4%
7	19%	36%	20%
8	19%	51%	66%
9	3%	1%	2%
10	0%	–	0%
11	0%	–	–

Scottish Executive estimate used for candidate stage in 2001

Table 88.1 shows that the introduction of Standard Grade led to a bigger proportion of the age cohort attempting qualifications in more subjects (1986–96), and that while in 1996 just over half the cohort (52%) attempted eight or more Standard Grades, by 2001 this proportion had risen to more than two-thirds (68%). Given that these statistics do not include the separate Writing element in Standard Grade Modern Languages, this represents a demanding curriculum for most, at a time when teachers were expected to incorporate more and more personal and social guidance into the school experience.

'Market share' in this context describes entries in each subject group as a percentage of total entries. Between 1987 and 1996 the main changes were an increase in uptake of Modern Languages (in line with curriculum guidelines at the time), the removal of Arithmetic as a separate subject and the successful introduction of Physical Education as an examined subject. Since 1996 there has been growth mainly in the technological mode, partly due to the continuing popularity of Craft and Design and Graphic Communication, and partly to the introduction of Business Management from 1999. The statistics currently show a stable curriculum.

Table 88.2: 'Market share' of Ordinary Grade and Standard Grade subjects (grouped) for S4 candidates, 1987, 1996 and 2001

'Market Share'	1987	1996	2001*
English	15%	13%	13%
Other languages	8%	13%	13%
Mathematics	11%	13%	13%
Other mathematical subjects	15%	1%	1%
Science subjects	20%	18%	18%
Social subjects and Religious Studies	14%	15%	14%
Technological subjects	13%	15%	17%
Creative & aesthetic subjects and Physical Education	5%	11%	12%

*Scottish Executive estimate used for candidate stage in 2001

Table 88.3: Uptake and attainment by gender at Ordinary Grade and Standard Grade for selected subjects, S4 candidates, 1987, 1996 and 2001

	% Entry Group Female			Mean Grade Difference		
	1987	1996	2001*	1987	1996	2001*
English	53%	49%	50%	+ 0.24	+ 0.42	+ 0.41
French	65%	52%	52%	+ 0.11	+ 0.65	+ 0.60
Arithmetic	51%	n/a	n/a	− 0.12	n/a	n/a
Mathematics	50%	49%	50%	− 0.11	+ 0.10	+ 0.08
Biology	67%	70%	71%	−	+ 0.10	+ 0.08
Chemistry	46%	50%	51%	− 0.01	+ 0.10	+ 0.10
Physics	30%	33%	29%	+ 0.17	+ 0.27	+ 0.33
Geography	40%	42%	41%	+ 0.06	+ 0.32	+ 0.23
History	55%	54%	53%	+ 0.09	+ 0.41	+ 0.38
Computing Studies	31%	35%	37%	− 0.27	+ 0.28	+ 0.16
Office and Info Studies/ Secretarial Studies	96%	83%	n/a	+ 0.33	+ 0.57	n/a
Administration	n/a	n/a	78%	n/a	n/a	+ 0.43
Business Management	n/a	n/a	53%	n/a	n/a	+ 0.17
Art & Design	55%	57%	61%	+ 0.29	+ 0.43	+ 0.47
All subjects	52%	50%	50%	+ 0.02	+ 0.32	+ 0.29

A positive grade difference means that the female candidates in that subject obtained better grades on average than the males, a negative grade difference that the male candidates did better and a dash (−) that there was no significant difference
* Scottish Executive estimate used for candidate stage in 2001

Table 88.3 shows that, in those areas of considerable latitude of subject choice within schools, males and females continue to make somewhat different choices. For example:

- Within the sciences: Chemistry continues to attract relatively equal numbers of females and males; Biology continues to attract more females than males (ratio 7:3); Physics continues to attract fewer females than males (ratio 3:7).
- Within the technological mode: subject choices continue to be related strongly to gender; Computing Studies with 37% of its candidates female; office-based subjects still unattractive to males, with the exception of the new Business Management Course.

The table also shows that females are still attaining better grades in their examinations at this level, approximately one-third of a grade better overall. This would mean that for a typical boy and girl each sitting eight Standard Grades and one Writing element, the girl would achieve an award one grade higher than the boy in three of the subjects. The greatest difference, however, occurred between 1987 and 1996; the gap has closed slightly since then. Although the difference occurs in virtually every element of every subject, it is more marked in some than in others. For example, girls who take Physics, though still in the minority for the subject, do particularly well. In other subjects where girls outnumber boys – such as Administration and Art and Design – they also outperform them; and girls also do relatively better in subjects requiring good written communication skills such as English and History.

Higher

In 2001 there were just over 57,000 Higher candidates, with over 160,000 subject entries, mainly, but not exclusively, in schools.

Table 88.4:   Higher entries and awards in 1987, 1996 and 2001 for
school candidates, by gender (SCE Higher Grade in
1987 and 1996; combined SCE Higher and new Higher in 2001)

S5 candidates	as % of S5 Cohort			as % of Age Group		
	1987	1996	2001*	1987	1996	2001*
Total						
attempted 1+ Higher	85%	77%	73%	42%	52%	49%
passed 1+ Higher	67%	61%	62%	33%	41%	41%
passed 3+ Highers	35%	33%	38%	17%	22%	25%
Males						
attempted 1+ Higher	84%	75%	71%	38%	47%	44%
passed 1+ Higher	65%	58%	58%	29%	36%	36%
passed 3+ Highers	35%	31%	34%	16%	19%	21%
Females						
attempted 1+ Higher	85%	78%	76%	46%	57%	53%
passed 1+ Higher	68%	64%	66%	36%	47%	47%
passed 3+ Highers	34%	35%	41%	18%	26%	29%

*Scottish Executive estimate used for candidate stage in 2001

Table 88.4 shows the changes which have occurred in the proportion of school pupils attempting particular numbers of Higher examinations and – separately – passing them.

The first three columns of numbers show this as a percentage of all pupils staying on beyond Christmas of S5; the final three columns show it as a percentage of the whole age group, based on the number in school in S4 the previous year.

The statistics relating to the age group (columns 4–6) are easier to interpret. They show improved performance overall, particularly with an increase in the percentage passing 3 + Highers. The proportion attempting 1 + Highers has dropped slightly, particularly in the context of the S5 group (columns 1–3). This is because of the increased staying-on rate and the wider range of levels of National Courses now available to this group. At Higher, as for Standard Grade, females continue to outperform male candidates. More stay on to attempt more Highers and more achieve passes, particularly in the 3 + Highers category. In 2001, 21% of males within the age group achieved this level of qualification at the end of S5, while the corresponding figure for the females was 29%. As the table shows, this is a considerable gap which shows little sign of closing despite the introduction of qualifications which are built on incremental steps.

Table 88.5: **Uptake of subjects at Higher (grouped):**
entry rates of S5 candidates in 1987, 1996 and 2001

Market share'	% S5 Candidates			% S4 Candidates		
	1987	1996	2001*	1987	1996	2001*
English	69	54	49	34	36	33
Other languages	20	15	15	10	10	10
Mathematics	37	33	36	18	22	24
Other mathematical subjects	5	4	3	2	2	2
Science subjects	67	60	54	33	40	36
Social subjects and Religious Studies	43	35	38	21	23	25
Technological subjects	23	24	31	11	16	21
Creative & Aesthetic subjects and Physical Education	14	20	25	7	13	16
All subjects	278	243	250	136	163	166

Scottish Executive estimate used for candidate stage in 2001

Table 88.5 shows subject choices across the modes for S5 candidates in the three years shown. The first three columns again show this as a proportion of the candidates staying on beyond Christmas in S5 while the final three columns show this as a proportion of the age group, based on the numbers in S4 a year earlier. Candidates study fewer subjects and tend to specialise more in S5 than in S4. Typically pupils study four or five courses, now at a range of possible levels. The main areas of increased uptake – as for Standard Grade – have been in the technological mode and the creative and aesthetic mode.

Table 88.6 confirms the now well-established pattern of uptake with subjects such as Mathematics, Chemistry and Geography attracting similar proportions of males and females; males dominating uptake in such subjects as Physics; and females in French, Biology, Art and Design. It also shows that the percentage of all Higher candidates who are female has remained fairly static at 54%–56%. The final three columns show the difference

Table 88.6:   Uptake and attainment by gender at Higher in S5
               for selected subjects 1987, 1996 and 2001

	% Entry Group Female			Difference in Pass Rates		
	1987	1996	2001*	1987	1996	2001*
English / English and						
Communication	58%	58%	61%	–	+3%	+4%
French	76%	76%	80%	–	–	+1%
Mathematics	46%	49%	52%	–	+4%	+1%
Biology	70%	71%	72%	–9%	–	+2%
Chemistry	43%	48%	52%	–4%	–	–
Physics	29%	31%	30%	+7%	+9%	+7%
Geography	41%	43%	47%	+5%	+7%	+7%
History	56%	59%	59%	–	+3%	+4%
Modern Studies	52%	63%	65%	+4%	+5%	+3%
Art & Design	64%	63%	72%	+12%	+9%	+8%
All subjects	54%	54%	56%	–	+4%	+3%

A positive difference in pass rates means that the female candidates in that subject had a higher pass rate on average than the males, a negative difference that the male candidates did better and a dash (–) that there was no significant difference
* *Scottish Executive estimate used for candidate stage in 2001*

in the proportion of the males and females passing. To the extent that it is fair to assume that an increase in the numbers of candidates attempting Highers will mean a wider ability spectrum, one might expect a lower pass rate among females. However, overall 3% more of the females who attempt Highers pass them. This varies across subjects somewhat, but is particularly marked in subjects which have traditionally attracted more males such as Physics and Geography.

New levels: Intermediate and Access

Table 88.7:   Uptake and attainment at Intermediate levels:
               for all candidates in 2000 and 2001

	Entries in 2000	Pass rates 2000			Entries in 2001	Pass rates 2001		
		All	M	F		All	M	F
Intermediate 1	8,096	72%	68%	74%	15,981	65%	62%	68%
Intermediate 2	34,590	67%	64%	71%	59,093	70%	67%	73%

Table 88.7 shows that uptake has risen substantially for both Intermediate level 1 and level 2 since they were introduced in 2000. Overall pass rates lie in the 65%-72% zone, and again female candidates outperformed male candidates.

Table 88.8:   Uptake and attainment in clusters at Access 2 and 3:
              for all candidates in 2000 and 2001

	Entries in 2000	Awards in 2000	Awards as % entries in 2000	Entries in 2001	Awards in 2001	Awards as % entries in 2001
Access 2 Clusters	140	123	88%	1,238	676	55%
Access 3 Clusters	111	107	96%	1,892	1,175	62%

Table 88.8 shows entries and awards for Access Clusters at both levels 2 and 3 to have
increased significantly. Whilst the rate of awards has fallen, the figures may be distorted by
the relatively high rate of candidates who leave school without completing the award,
including Christmas leavers.

National Units.

National Units have evolved from what were originally SCOTVEC National Certificate
modules, and former SEB short courses. Some of these were selected to create new courses
mainly at Intermediate levels. To these were added new units based on breaking down
former SCE Higher and CSYS courses to create replacement component units and courses
(as part of the Higher Still development programme). Many units remain in the catalogue as
stand-alone units, or form part of group awards of varying sizes and levels. Most units are
now levelled to improve coherence. However, this complex area is subject to review.

Table 88.9:   Uptake of National Units (and former NC modules or short courses)

	1986			1997			2001		
	Candidates Schools	Other, mainly college	Entries	Candidates Schools	Other, mainly college	Entries	Candidates Schools	Other, mainly college	Entries
NC modules	12,500	69,000	657,000	118,421	108,975	1,161,329			
Short courses	–	–	–	n/a	n/a	46,160 awards			
National Units							129,993	84,765	1,198,999

Table 88.9 shows growth in candidate numbers, both in schools and colleges but especially in
schools in the decade between 1986 and 1997. While the number of candidates in schools has
continued to grow (most taking units as part of courses), the number of college students taking
units appears to have shrunk. However, the basis on which the statistics are reported has
changed and are not directly comparable. (A much higher proportion of these 1997 entries
would not have been subject to an award (approximately 70% completion at that time).)

Table 88.10:   Group Awards in the National Catalogue – 2001

		Entries	% male	% females	Awards	Notes
GSVQ	I	83	75	25		
	II	921	41	59		
	III	1,668	22	78		
	Total	**2,672**	30	70	1,222	98% college based.
National Certificate	Total	3,021	84	16	989	97% college based
National Certificate Clusters	Total	185	43	57	107	24% college based, 43% schools
SGA	Access 2	184	64	36		
	Access 3	31	55	45		
	Int 1	151	38	62		
	Int 2	1,757	51	49		
	Higher	454	36	64		
	Adv Higher	1	–	100		
	Total	**2,578**	48	52	722	79% college based

The four types of Group Award in Table 88.10 vary in size from National Certificate (NC) Clusters of three units to some SGAs of twenty units, with intermediate sized NC Group Awards. Overall, in 2001 there were almost 8500 entries across the four types. The vast majority of entries were college-based, especially GSVQ (98%) and National Certificate (97%). Few of the figures are directly comparable to 1986 or 1997, for the reason given.

Higher National Qualifications – Uptake and Attainment

The number of active HN candidates grew from approximately 17,000 in the 1980s to around 55,000 by 1997. The corresponding number of candidates for 2001 was just over 52,000. Statistics for these awards are not directly comparable across 1986, 1997 and 2001, partly due to the process of modularisation which continued into the early 1990s and partly due to a major database change between 1997 and 2001. Comparative data is given where available.

In 2001, over 300,000 HN units were certificated. Traditionally most HN Units have been undertaken in the context of Group Awards (HNCs, HNDs or PDAs) with many students, particularly older students, studying part-time. Thus, while the completion period is typically three years, it varies a lot and entries and awards for any one year merely give a snapshot of the activity levels within that area. Where entries are greater than awards it suggests the area may still be expanding.

Table 88.11:   HNC's, HNDs and (HN) PDAs – entries and awards in 1997 and 2001

	1997			2001		
	Entries	(%FE)	Awards	Entries	(%FE)	Awards
HNCs	18,619	94%	?	16,294	98%	12,858
HNDs	12,148	88%	?	9,958	92%	6,572
PDAs	1,664	95%	?	1,609	99%	1,274

Table 88.11 shows a continuing healthy uptake of these awards, most of which are now completed at FE colleges. By 2001, 45% of HNC students gaining awards were in the over thirty age group. However, a further 25% were in the 20–24 age group, many having entered directly from school. Of those awarded an HNC in 2001, 60% were female. The position for HND in 2001 was virtually reversed, with 50% of awards made to those in the 20–24 age group, and a further 26% to those over thirty. Awards were more evenly split across males (48%) and females (52%). Both HNCs and HNDs are used increasingly as stepping stones to study for a degree.

Table 88.12:   HNCs and HNDs – highest uptake areas in 2001

HNCs	Entries	Awards	% Awards Male	% Awards Female
Computing	1,708	967	69	31
Social Care	1,318	945	16	84
Child Care & Education	1,253	1,438	1	99
Business Admin	999	859	23	77
Admin & Info Management	988	959	5	95
HNDs				
Business Admin	752	533	33	67
Computing: Support	571	330	74	26
Computing: Software Development	528	296	71	29
Accounting	505	424	30	70
Social Sciences	436	249	32	68

Table 88.12 lists the five highest uptake areas for HNC and HND by entries in 2001. Business, Computing and Care areas were all well represented in the high uptake categories in both 1986 and 1997. However 1986 entries were also high for Electronics and Electrical Engineering. Engineering was still a significant sector in 2001, with almost 19,100 individual unit entries. Uptake was related strongly to age and gender. Younger students were well represented in sports and games, catering, leisure and tourism, performing arts, agricultural/ horticultural and animal care, and in manufacturing/production. Students over thirty, who were more likely to be changing career, improving skills or gaining a professional qualification, were more typically studying in the following areas: IT and

information, business management, office studies, education, training and teaching, health care, medicine, health and safety. Table 88.12 also gives a flavour of gender-related choices. Child care and education, and administration and information management were, for example, almost exclusively female at HNC while computing at both HNC and HND was still more popular with males.

Scottish Vocational Qualifications – Uptake and Attainment

Table 88.13: Uptake and attainment for all SVQs by level in 2001

SVQ's	Entries	% Entries from FE	Awards
Level 1	3,151		2,387
Level 2	19,338		16,437
Level 3	8,305		7,139
Level 4	523		487
Level 5	21		27
All	31,338	37%	26,477
Work-based			
PDA	8,753	39%	8,420
Scottish Progression Awards	108	37%	71

Table 88.13 shows the scale of SVQ uptake and awards in 2001. (Of these qualifications, 90% related to awards made by SQA either alone, or in partnership with another awarding body.) Levels 2 and 3 had by far the highest uptake. The total entries were not dissimilar to 1997 (31,497). In the early days of SVQs (early 1990s) most candidates were in FE colleges. By 1997 the proportion had fallen to 44%. By 2001 the comparable figure was 37%. Workplace training or training by specialist providers is now more typical, given the more stringent rules about simulated workplace assessment. Work-based PDAs are certificated solely by SQA (as are customised awards – not reported). Scottish Progression Awards (designed to certificate significant components of SVQs) have not gained a foothold.

Table 88.14 shows the most popular uptake areas in 2001, with Administration at levels 2 and 3 featuring in the top six. While the uptake across all SVQs was relatively gender-balanced (57% male, 43% female), males and females tended to polarise between different occupational sectors. This reached a peak in the workplace assessed PDAs in which the unit (surely with the longest title in the catalogue!) 'Certification in Excavating, Backfilling and Reinstating of Construction Layers with a Cold-Lay Bituminous Surface' was almost exclusively a male domain.

MAINTAINING STANDARDS

One of the key roles of any awarding body is maintenance of awarding standards, both over qualification blocks and across time. SQA does this by a range of activities, some of the main ones being for external assessments:

Table 88.14: SVQs – highest uptake areas in 2001

	Level	Entries	% Males	% Females	Awards
SVQ					
Administration	2	2,060	19	81	1,964
Performing					
Manufacturing					
Operations	2	1,617	65	35	1,660
Customer					
Services	3	1,475	35	65	1,364
Hairdressing	2	1,031	3	97	587
Care	2	991	12	88	892
Administration	3	987	14	86	904
Using IT	2	959	55	45	760
Overall			57	43	
Workplace-assessed PDA					
Cert for Vocational Trainers and Assessors		1,028	52	48	1,033
Cert for Skills Assessors		770	46	54	804
Cert in Excavating in the Highway		679	99	1	716
Cert in Excavating, Backfilling & Re-instatement of Construction Layers with a Cold-lay Bituminous Surface		614	99	1	659
Cert in Home Care Practice		607	4	96	193

- employing subject experts to design qualifications, to set and vet assessment instruments and marking schemes;
- employing independent invigilators to conduct examinations;
- training experienced, practising teachers to mark randomly-allocated scripts, and having a central team of experienced examiners to quality-assure the marking;
- making grade boundary decisions in the light of both statistical evidence (including comprehensive historical data) and qualitative information;

and for internal assessments:

- approving centres and their internally-generated courses;
- for some units, providing prevalidated assessment instruments and marking schemes;
- moderating assessment instruments and assessment decisions.

SQA also undertakes a standards monitoring programme across all three qualification blocks, and has taken part in several bench-marking exercises both within the UK and with other countries. The most significant bench-marking exercise was carried out against A-level in 1998 (SQA, 1998). The outcome of these exercises has demonstrated the on-going quality of Scottish qualifications and awarding decisions.

ISSUES AND CHALLENGES

Looking to the future there are many challenges facing SQA. Some of the most important are achieving a flexible but credible qualification and assessment system which is fit for purpose, affordable, and which meets the needs of all learners and is capable of under-pinning Scottish economic success. Such a system should:

- Provide quality-assured awards which effectively summarise achievement particularly at critical points of transfer, but which fit with formative assessment carried out by centres to support learning.
- Meet the specific needs of each sector and their learners. While all centres probably want less burdensome systems of assessment and quality assurance, there are sectoral differences: colleges need maximum flexibility (assessment when ready) and preferably assessment systems which motivate candidates who may lack confidence in learning; employers and training providers need less assessment-driven learning systems; and schools need systems which can help motivate the full range of ability, allow specialism yet keep options open.
- Offer qualifications which are responsive to broader changes within society, for example, as the Scottish economy changes, what candidates learn, how they learn and how they are assessed will change.

Other challenges are about achieving access to awards for all learners, recognition for all learning and clear progression routes for learners: This means:

- Ease and equality of access: allowing for affordable alternative forms of assessment to improve access and remove any discrimination whilst maintaining reliability and fairness overall.
- Meeting the needs of individuals in terms of their personal, educational, cultural, community and economic aspirations; in particular addressing the noticeable attainment gap for males.
- Developing flexible, smaller-sized qualifications which build into larger qualifications, to underpin lifelong learning and encourage wider participation among, for example, older age-groups and those in work.
- Implementing the Scottish Credit and Qualifications Framework (SCQF). The SCQF is a twelve–level framework designed to offer a common way of describing different learning and qualifications in the Scottish system. It includes everything from Access 1 units to PhDs. This should allow comparisons across qualification blocks, strengthen national credit tariffs and transfer systems, and provide working links to frameworks of other countries.
- Meeting the growing needs for knowledge-workers in the economy.

It is also important to manage change in such a way that candidates and centres can experience stability. Currently all parts of SQA's portfolio are under review (HN, NQ and SVQ); 5–14 assessment is also changing; and the future role of Standard Grade is part of the current wide-ranging education debate. With apparently constant change, there needs to be responsive planning, risk-assessed and measured implementation and good communication with stakeholders if such change is to be manageable for centres and for SQA.

Additionally, the potential of ICT in assessment, quality assurance and data exchange must be harnessed. Part of this is about changes in the way candidates are accessing learning and the new knowledge they will need; part is about ICT applications to allow on-line assessment and e-moderation, to improve flexibility and access. The development of ever more robust, transparent systems which are capable of scrutiny is a further requirement. Finally, there is a need to maximise common approaches to assessment and quality assurance across subjects and sectors while allowing for necessary differences; for example encouraging holistic rather than atomistic approaches where appropriate, having a flexible – rather than uniform – overall quality assurance system which is responsive to the type and purpose of the assessment, and to each centre's internal quality assurance history. Many of these challenges for SQA can only be met through continued collaborative effort and partnership with others working to make Scottish education and training fit for the twenty-first century.

ACKNOWLEDGEMENTS

The author gratefully acknowledges the help of SQA colleagues in compiling and checking this chapter, in particular David Hurst, Marie McGhee, John Hart and Angus Forrester. Any views expressed are those of the author.

REFERENCES

Scottish Executive (2001) *Review of Initial Implementation of New National Qualifications*, Edinburgh: Scottish Executive.
Scottish Office (1994*) Opportunity for All*, Edinburgh: HMSO.
SED (1977a) *The Structure of the Curriculum in the Third and Fourth Years of the Scottish Secondary School*, Edinburgh: HMSO.
SED (1977b) *Assessment for All*, Edinburgh: HMSO.
SQA (1998) *Comparability Study of Scottish Qualifications and GCE Advanced Levels* (general report and four subject reports: English, Mathematics, History and Physics), Dalkeith: SQA.
SQA *Annual Statistical Reports*.

89

CES Findings on Participation
and Attainment in Scottish Education

David Raffe

For three decades the Centre for Educational Sociology (CES) has been an observer, analyst and critical commentator on developments in Scottish education and training. It has been 'a beacon of broadly-based and collaborative social science research into education' (Richardson, 2002, p. 45). It has studied young people's participation and progression in education, their curriculum and attainment, their attitudes and choices and their destinations on leaving. It has linked this individual level of analysis to the school and national levels: it has studied variation in performance across schools and monitored national performance in relation to system and policy change.

The first section of this chapter briefly outlines the centre's history. The second and longest section then reviews the performance of Scottish education as revealed by the centre's research. This review focuses on secondary and post-secondary education up to nineteen years, and on two main indicators of performance: participation and attainment. It summarises the centre's conclusions on the level and pattern of participation and attainment, the implications of the growth in participation, inequalities, factors which influence participation and attainment, and the impact of policy. However it offers only a partial view of the centre's research, which also covers the history of education, the policy process, curriculum, guidance, student attitudes, and information systems. The final section discusses issues for policy and practice.

THE CENTRE FOR EDUCATIONAL SOCIOLOGY

The CES was founded in 1972, as a research unit within the University of Edinburgh's Department of Sociology, with Andrew McPherson as director. In the 1970s and 1980s it established a reputation for its work on secondary education and post-school transitions, and for its programmes of 'collaborative research' (1975–82) which involved users in the research process and tried to transcend the traditional boundaries between the roles of researcher and practitioner and policy maker. Much of its work was based on, or associated with, the Scottish School Leavers Survey (SSLS), which the centre had founded in the early 1970s and which became a biennial national survey from 1977. In 1985 the survey was enlarged and redesigned as the Scottish Young People's Survey (SYPS). From 1987 to 1996 it was an Economic and Social Research Council (ESRC) research centre, with Andrew McPherson and David Raffe as co-directors until McPherson's retirement in 1995. In 1998 the centre joined the new Faculty of Education, created from the university's merger with Moray House Institute of Education, and in 2001 Jenny Ozga took over as director.

The philosophy which has underpinned the centre's work is summarised in the final chapter of *Reconstructions of Secondary Education* (Gray, McPherson and Raffe, 1983). This acknowledges that the scepticism which is intrinsic to research is inevitably in tension with government's need for authority, but despite these tensions research and government are mutually dependent and need to engage with each other. On the one hand, research needs the authority and resources which only the state can provide; on the other hand, effective and democratic government requires critical scrutiny through research, and it requires wide participation in this research by practitioners with experience and insights into the processes of education. During the 1980s and early 1990s this philosophy brought the centre increasingly into conflict with a Conservative administration which distinguished between its interest as a government and the public interest. As a government it was a consumer of research in its own right, but it no longer accepted an obligation to promote the public interest by supporting access to research among those who might want to criticise its policies. The centre's work on comprehensive education, youth training, school performance and access to higher education did not endorse the government's prejudices. With effect from 1993 the Scottish Office, which had been the main funder of the SYPS, redesigned it as a cheaper operation which focused more narrowly on its own data requirements as it perceived them. Data collection was separated from analysis and contracted out to a London survey agency which could do the job more cheaply and whose ignorance of Scottish education was not considered a handicap. Needless to say, the new survey (renamed the SSLS) did not anticipate the government's longer-term needs, and it had to be redesigned again; the new design introduced in 1997 is similar to the SYPS formerly carried out by the centre.

The centre no longer conducts its own surveys but it continues to analyse data from Scottish and other European youth transition surveys. It also makes extensive use of other research methods. The main focus of its research continues to be the study of education and training in their social and labour-market context, and in relation to social and policy change. Together with core university support, its main funding sources are the ESRC, private foundations, the Scottish Executive, UK government departments and the European Commission. Much of the centre's research has had a cross-national focus, comparing Scottish education with the other countries of the UK as well as with other OECD countries. In the early 2000s this research embraced early intervention programmes, progression from science, school target-setting, educational maintenance allowances, Higher Still, vocational education and training initiatives, the careers service, transitions through post-compulsory education and into the labour market, value added in further education, disabled students in higher education, gender and social inequalities in education, comparative change in the education and training systems in the UK, the design and implementation of cross-national surveys of school leavers, and the application of information systems to data processing and documentation.

PARTICIPATION AND ATTAINMENT IN SCOTTISH EDUCATION

The centre has published numerous studies of participation and attainment in Scottish education, comparing it with other systems, analysing trends and explaining distinctive Scottish patterns. This research reveals a system whose performance is middling by international standards, but improving, and where participation and attainment continue to be highly polarised. This section elaborates the picture of Scottish education that emerges from the centre's research. For reasons of space it does not describe the specific studies on which the discussion draws.

The level and distribution of participation and attainment

Contrary to popular belief, participation in full-time education among 16–18-year-olds has not been consistently higher in Scotland than in the other countries of the UK. Relative participation rates have fluctuated over time, and they depend on the age band, on the types of education that are compared, and on the age basis for comparison. By the more demanding standards of other European countries Scottish participation rates are low on average and strongly polarised. About a half of young people enter higher education (HE) but many others leave full-time education within a year of the minimum age. The Scottish system is geared to getting a large number of young people into HE at a relatively early age, but it fails to retain those who are not HE-bound for very long. Fewer Scots enter full-time technical or vocational education than in most European countries, and most entrants leave within a year or two. A substantial proportion of young people enter part-time or work-based provision, but their participation also tends to be brief. Few Scots continue in education or training beyond eighteen or nineteen years unless they are either in HE or trying to get there.

The distribution of attainments is similarly polarised. Many people do well and gain HE degrees, but many others do poorly. Scottish young people outperform the rest of the UK at the qualification levels corresponding to Standard Grades and Highers, but they lag behind many other countries at these levels. This polarisation is reinforced by the pattern of progression. At nearly all stages beyond the end of compulsory schooling, future participation and attainment are strongly influenced by past levels of attainment. Post-compulsory education in Scotland appears to reflect the principle that further learning is for those who are best at it, rather than for those who are most in need of it.

Part of the explanation for Scotland's distinctive patterns of participation and attainment lies not in the education system itself but in its social and labour-market context. Polarisation in society sustains polarisation in education. Family and neighbourhood deprivation contribute to low participation and attainment. The labour market has encouraged the polarisation of attainments by rewarding higher education while often failing to recognise or reward intermediate level education. It has tended to value occupational experience more than vocational qualifications and in earlier decades it provided incentives for able 16-year-olds, especially boys, to leave education early.

Despite this mixed verdict on its performance, Scottish education is improving. Attainments have risen at all levels. Full-time participation has increased, especially in the fifth and sixth years of school and in HE where participation rates more than doubled within a decade. The CES predicted some of this growth in the 1980s, by showing that parents' education was a strong predictor of whether their children entered HE, and that levels of parental education were rising rapidly. However the growth in participation, both at 16-plus and in HE, has considerably exceeded this prediction; a later CES study estimated that only a third of the increase in staying-on at sixteen could be attributed to 'compositional' factors such as changes in parental education or in other family or personal characteristics of 16-year-olds. Other factors which have contributed to the growth in participation include reforms of compulsory education which have encouraged more positive attitudes to school; changes in the labour market which have reduced opportunities for early leavers; and the structure of school courses which allows decisions to be taken one year at a time and thus reduces the risks associated with staying-on. The growth in participation has been further encouraged by the increased supply of higher education places and by a process of credential inflation, a competitive scramble for the positional advantage which higher levels of education can confer.

Some consequences of the increase in participation and attainment

One consequence of rising participation and attainment is a better qualified workforce, able to meet the higher skill demands of the economy, although rising attainments have meant higher qualifications are needed to enter a given occupational level. However the position of unqualified school leavers has deteriorated as they have become a smaller and more selected-out group; they face a high risk of insecure jobs or unemployment, but few return to education.

A further consequence is academic drift: participation has generally risen faster in higher education and 'academic' school courses than in vocational education and training. This is a vicious circle: employers and university selectors favour students with academic qualifications because they believe that the most able students choose academic rather than vocational programmes. This belief is self-fulfilling: academic programmes offer a positional advantage, and able and ambitious students have an incentive to choose them. No country has achieved parity of esteem for vocational and general education, at least at the secondary or upper-secondary level, but the scale and relative status of vocational education are lower in Scotland than elsewhere in the UK. Ironically, this partly reflects the past success of general education in Scotland in providing opportunities for mobility, in contrast with the 'alternative route' provided by vocational education in England.

The principal victim of academic drift has been work-based training for young people, currently delivered mainly through the Skillseeker programme. The number of trainees has declined since the 1980s, although the development of modern apprenticeships within Skillseekers may reverse this trend. The youth training programmes introduced in the early 1980s failed to develop, as intended, into a work-based route of equivalent stature to the German dual system. However comparisons with Ireland, where there are fewer training opportunities for those who leave full-time education, suggest that the 'mixed' model of provision in Scotland has at least provided a better safety net for the educationally disadvantaged and for those at risk of social and economic exclusion.

As the education and training system expands, assumes new roles and becomes more complex, and its pathways become longer and more interconnected, it has a greater need for mechanisms of co-ordination and coherence. The centre has developed the concept of 'unification' to describe the trend, common to most countries, for divisions between the sectors of post-compulsory education and training to erode. 'Unifying' developments in Scotland include Higher Still, the Scottish Credit and Qualifications Framework (SCQF), and the introduction of more unified arrangements for funding, regulation and quality assurance.

Gender and class inequalities in participation and attainment

Outcomes in Scottish education are not only polarised; they are also distributed unequally across classes, genders and ethnic groups. Table 89.1 is based on the year group which completed S4 in 1998 and was surveyed by the SSLS in 1999 and 2001, when the average age was eighteen or nineteen years. It shows inequalities in the percentage achieving selected participation and attainment outcomes.

Table 89.1: Attainment and participation by gender and social class: 1999 and 2001 SSLS

	% Males	% Females	% Middle Class	% Working Class
Achieved 5+ Credit passes at S grade in S4	33	43	60	28
Truanted 'a day here and there', or more, in S4	24	24	15	27
In S5 (spring)	60	68	83	56
In S6 (spring)	40	46	62	34
Passed at least one Higher in S5 or S6	46	55	73	41
Entered Skillseekers by age 18–19	34	19	15	33
Entered FT FE by age 18–19	23	24	16	25
Entered FT HE by age 18–19	40	49	64	34

Females outperform males both at Standard Grade and at Higher, although their higher attainment still tends to be based on a different mix of subjects (see later discussion). However females are as likely as males to play truant, a possible indicator of disaffection. More females continue to study full time at school and in higher education; however Skillseekers, usually based in the workplace, attracts higher male participation, and similar proportions of males and females enter full-time further education.

Middle-class students do better than working-class students at Standard Grade and Higher. More middle-class students stay on in full-time education; they were nearly twice as likely as working-class students to enter S6 in 1999–2000 or to enter higher education. The vocational routes, by contrast, attract more working-class entrants: more working-class than middle-class youngsters enter full-time further education (a reversal of the pattern of the 1980s) and more enter youth training.

In the late 1970s the CES first produced evidence that class inequality in Scottish education was similar to that in England and other countries. Class differences have not changed dramatically since then, but there are signs that they have become slightly narrower. A CES study showed that staying-on rates increased most among the least qualified 16-year-olds, and this in turn led to slight reductions in social differences. Another study found evidence of declining inequalities in school-leaver entrance to higher education. Reforms such as comprehensive education and Standard Grade have reduced inequality on the margins (see below), although their main effect has been at the lower levels of attainment which have less positional value.

Influences on participation and attainment

Much of the centre's research has been multi-level in character. It has studied educational outcomes and the factors which influence them at student, school and area levels, as well as at the level of the system.

At the student level, factors associated with participation and achievement include family characteristics such as parental education, social class, family size, and number of parents. Gender, as discussed in the previous section, has a pervasive influence. However, it is easier for survey research to describe correlations than to be certain of cause and effect. Even if the characteristics of individual students statistically account for variations in performance, that does not mean that further explanation is not required. The 'effect' of individual characteristics such as gender or social class may be a product, for example, of the way that schools or the social environment provide more encouragement for females or for middle class pupils to perform well.

Different sociological theories variously attribute educational inequalities to the unequal distribution of 'cultural capital', to poverty and other material factors, or to the rational decision making of young people with different goals and different circumstances. At least with respect to participation decisions, the Centre's research challenges the notion that young people's educational decisions are determined by cultural factors which lie deeper than rational analysis. If young people do not take advantage of an educational opportunity in the way they are expected to, it should be asked whether it would have been in their interests to have done so. Young people respond to the incentives and disincentives associated with the available options. They tend to be at least pragmatically rational, to have an instrumental orientation and to seek to maximise their qualifications and pursue long-term advantage in the labour market.

At the school level, CES research has explored the extent to which the 'value added' by secondary education varies across schools. Comparisons of schools' performance need to allow for differences in the prior attainments and social backgrounds of pupils entering each school. Unadjusted league tables which do not allow for differences in intakes place schools in the wrong rank order and exaggerate their differences. This is now well accepted, although it was not when the CES began work in this field. The value added by the school varies less among Scottish schools than among comprehensive schools in England, probably reflecting the greater homogeneity of the Scottish comprehensive system and the lower level of social segregation. Choosing the 'right' school is likely to be a less critical decision for a parent in Scotland than in England – at least on the criterion of maximising attainment.

Much of the value added by the school is due to factors outwith its control. One of the most important of these factors is the 'contextual effect': a student's attainment is influenced by the social composition of his or her fellow students. Another factor is the history of a school: older schools and former senior secondaries tend to do better than newer schools with a history as junior secondaries. A third factor is denomination: other things being equal, Roman Catholic schools perform better than non-denominational schools.

Crude league tables may misrepresent the relative performance of local authorities, just as they do of schools. Most of the differences in performance across authorities can be explained by the differences in the social composition of their student populations. The variation in the value added by schools within a local authority is much larger than the average difference between local authorities.

Other area-level influences on attainment include social deprivation, and the effects of local opportunity structures. Neighbourhood deprivation has a negative influence on the local children's school performance, over and above the effect of their measured ability, family background and school. Local unemployment has encouraged 16-year-olds to stay on in full-time education, although this 'discouraged worker' effect has diminished since the mid-1980s, consistent with the view that the labour-market 'pull' on 16-year-olds has weakened.

The impact of policy changes on participation and attainment

Secondary education was reorganised on comprehensive lines following the publication of Circular 600 in 1965. Reorganisation proceeded unevenly across different areas, but this made it possible to analyse its effects by linking comparisons across areas and over time. Levels of SCE attainment increased, and they increased most among girls and among students of lower socio-economic status. There was 'equalisation' as well as 'improvement'. The effects tended to be greatest in respect of the lower levels of SCE attainment. The level of social segregation of schools was reduced; as a result the 'contextual' effect described above was more consistent across schools, and this may account for some of the effect on equalising and improving attainment. Comparisons with English schools point to a similar conclusion: that the lower social segregation of Scottish comprehensive schools contributes to a lower level of social class inequality in attainment.

The impact of comprehensive education may therefore have been partly offset by the 1981 legislation which extended parental choice of schools. Middle-class and better educated parents have been more likely to exercise choice, and the result has been an increase in the social segregation of schools in some areas, notably in Glasgow. However, parents' choices have been heavily constrained by practical considerations such as travel and have often been negative in nature: many parents have exercised choice in order to avoid the neighbourhood school rather than because they particularly wanted the chosen school. On average, choices have favoured schools serving middle-class catchments and with high 'unadjusted' examination results, but they have not favoured schools which provided high 'added value'.

Another reform studied by the CES was the introduction of a curriculum framework for S3 and S4 in 1983, and the phasing in of Standard Grade to replace 'O' Grade from 1984. The framework reduced the gender gap in Mathematics and Science, as these subjects became almost universal, but it did not remove gender differences within Science: more boys studied Physics and more girls studied Biology. Standard Grade reduced social inequalities in attainment. The relative chances of disadvantaged students achieving an award improved significantly with the introduction of Standard Grade; however their relative chances of achieving an award in bands 1–3 (equivalent to an A–C 'pass' at 'O' Grade) did not improve. In other words, inequalities at the more valued levels of attainment have persisted.

The CES has also studied policy developments in post-16 education. Following the 1983 Action Plan the modular National Certificate replaced most non-advanced vocational education in further education; it also achieved a high take-up in schools where it filled gaps in existing provision. It helped to develop a flexible pattern of post-compulsory courses but it had little immediate impact on total participation levels. The 'intrinsic logic' of the modular system was weaker than the 'institutional logic' of the context in which it was embedded. By the 1990s most upper-secondary school students mixed 'academic' Highers and 'vocational' modules, but this mixing tended to confirm the NC's low relative status and it often led to incoherent curricula, poor attainments and blocked progression opportunities. In 1992 the Howie Report proposed a two-track structure for school and college education beyond fifteen years. The centre's research suggested that this structure would reduce participation and attainment, and in 1994 the government published *Higher Still*, which rejected a two-track approach and announced a 'unified curriculum and assessment system' for post-16 education from 1999. The CES is studying the introduction of this system. The process of bringing different subjects, levels and modes of education into a unified system has been politically fraught, and some of the tensions surfaced during the exam results crisis of 2000. Higher Still has been successful in catering for less-qualified 16-year-olds staying on at school, but at the time of writing it has yet to establish itself as a framework for lifelong learning. There is a danger that the unified system will be incomplete, largely school-based, and that many of the goals of a unified system are being displaced onto the SCQF.

The centre has also studied the attempts since the early 1980s to develop a work-based training route for young people. Training schemes were developed from schemes for the unemployed, and consequently acquired low status and a niche in the less skilled occupational sectors. They helped many people to find jobs, but this depended more on their use by employers to screen and select new recruits than on the content or quality of training. Training schemes achieved high participation, catering at their peak for nearly half of the age group, and they extended training to occupations and to groups of young people where opportunities had previously been scarce. However participation tended to depend on the risk of unemployment and on the vagaries of the market. Rates of qualification and of progression tended to be low. In the 1990s, Fife's FAST TRAC initiative aimed to integrate Skillseekers with college provision for young people; it represented a possible way forward, but it was frustrated by regulations and funding conditions at national level.

ISSUES FOR POLICY AND PRACTICE

The Scottish education and training system has had several achievements over the thirty years covered by the centre's research. Participation has increased. Attainments at all levels of the system have improved. The curriculum has been modernised. A comprehensive system has been successfully established, and is being extended into the post-compulsory stage. Academic and vocational learning have been brought closer together, and opportunities for progression are more open and more flexible than in many European countries. Some aspects of gender inequality have declined, and some educational reforms have reduced social inequality even if the total level of inequality has not improved greatly. The system's clients or consumers report higher levels of satisfaction.

But there are limits to this story of success. Vocational education is weak, and is being further weakened by academic drift. Scotland has high participation and attainment in higher education, by international standards, but it also has a high proportion of early leavers, few of whom return to education. Adult participation is still low and skewed towards the well-qualified. The biggest shortcoming of Scottish education is its failure to bring all young people to the 'intermediate' level of education which all citizens of a democratic society should enjoy, and which many commentators perceive as the key to economic success.

We cannot blame all these problems on education alone. There are wider societal factors, including social inequality and the operation of the labour market. The link between social disadvantage and educational underachievement is similar to that elsewhere, but there is more social disadvantage in Scotland than in many other countries, and partly as a result there is also more underachievement. Scotland's poor achievement of intermediate level qualifications also reflects the failure of its labour market to demand and reward such qualifications, and the low skill demands of some sectors of its economy. Scottish education and training have developed through interaction with their social and economic context; this context has been much more conducive to excellence in higher education than to the development of a system which brings all of its students to a minimum standard of learning.

But the centre's research also points to ways in which the system can be improved, even within these constraints. For example:

- The research shows the pitfalls of organising education and training on market principles. Markets tend to reinforce existing values and hierarchies. A voluntarist market-led policy has merely confirmed the low status of work-based training, and has failed to establish either a high-quality alternative to full-time provision or a means for reversing disadvantage and underachievement. A market-led approach has encouraged a polarised distribution of attainments, in response to the labour market's polarised demand for skills. The extension of market principles through parental choice of schools has not increased participation in more effective schools, but it has increased social segregation of schools and consequently increased underachievement.

- Scottish education should continue to build on the comprehensive principle in planning its future development. Comprehensive education, and complementary reforms such as Standard Grade, have underpinned much of the progress that has been observed in Scottish education; this progress will be extended as the comprehensive principle is extended beyond compulsory education through Higher Still and the development of the SCQF.

- Scotland needs to rebuild its tradition of work-based provision for young people. Work-based training has low status and a marginal role within the system, and is in danger of being further marginalised by Higher Still. But there are strong educational and economic arguments for retaining a substantial work-based route; and it still offers one of the most promising ways to reduce underachievement and to reverse the polarisation of participation and attainment in the Scottish system.

Finally, the experience of the CES points to the need, in a small and enclosed system with a tendency for complacency and self-congratulation, for a research capacity which is at the same time involved in the system but able to offer a critical and reasonably independent commentary and analysis on that system, and for consistent and reliable data on which such analysis can be based.

REFERENCES

CES (1995 onwards) Briefings, http://www.ed.ac.uk/ces/publications/briefings.htm

Gray, J., McPherson, A. F. and Raffe, D. (1983) *Reconstructions of Secondary Education: Theory, Myth and Practice since the War*, London: Routledge.

Richardson, W. (2002) Educational studies in the United Kingdom, 1940–2002, *British Journal of Educational Studies*, 50 (1), 3–56.

A bibliography of publications by members and associates of the CES is available from the Centre for Educational Sociology at the University of Edinburgh, and on http://www.ed.ac.uk/ces/publications/pubindex.htm

90

School Effectiveness, Improvement and Self-Evaluation

John MacBeath

School effectiveness as an idea, a movement, a political instrument, has left no school or teacher in Scotland untouched. It is expressed at the most fundamental level in the learning tasks set for 5-year-olds, whose achievements now have to be accounted for because schools operate in a climate of competitive and relative effectiveness. While the international obsession with attainment cannot simply be attributed to effectiveness research it does rest on three of its key premises. One, that achievement is measured at the level of the individual school. Two, that a school's 'effect' can be gauged by an aggregation of the attainment scores of each of its individual pupils. Three, that these data provide a reasonable evidence base for parents to choose a school for their child.

Researchers, while broadly endorsing these three premises, distanced themselves from the political edifices constructed on these foundations. Some (Peter Mortimore and Harvey Goldstein for example) were publicly vociferous in their attack on government policy. At the same time researchers continued to refine their approaches and extend their research into new international fields, seeking to test the key elements of the effective school in order to identify some universal characteristics.

> We cannot stress this too highly: that factors that make for good schools are conceptually quite similar in countries that have widely different cultural, social and economic contexts. (Reynolds, D. *World Class Schools*, London: Routledge Falmer, p. 279, 2001)

This is a not only a troublesome assertion but, by conceptual sleight of hand, conflates the 'good' with the 'effective', a distinction that has been firmly held to for two decades and more. For many within the movement this stream of research had, after thirty years, run dry. It was time to stop the hunt for the unicorn and turn attention from the 'what' to the 'how', to what schools did, or could do, to become more effective. And so was born, in the house of school effectiveness, a new generation of studies called school improvement. This was, in the event, to prove even more appealing to policy-makers as 'improvement' rested on the premise that schools could make a difference, and that models and mechanisms could be held up as 'good practice', encouraging less effective schools to emulate their success.

School improvement, by commonsensical definition, might be taken to mean making schools better places for children. But theological school improvers (effectiveness people beneath the skin) have held to a tighter definition. The publication of *School Effectiveness*

Research: its messages for improvement edited by Sheila Riddell and
burgh: HMSO, 1991), exemplifies the closeness of that relationship.
ment in these and other documents is demonstrated by raised attainꝴ
added. Papers presented at the Annual International Congress of Sꞁ
Improvement over the years reveal that these two 'movements' are s
and mutually reliant. You can't be an effectiveness aficionaꞁ
improvement, and you can't be an improver without recourse to the ι∪∼
Yet, as the congress has grown in size, scope and international reach, there has emⅇ⍳ɓ
less orthodox current of ideas, and even heresies, challenging some of the essential precepts
on which the whole edifice rests. In the foundations of the movement, in its transformation,
in its policy direction, and in the challenge to orthodoxy, Scotland has played a significant
role and has been an influence on thinking and practice on the world stage. It has earned a
place and voice in the history of effectiveness, improvement, and most significantly in self-
evaluation.

A BIT OF HISTORY

The year 1966 is generally taken as the genesis of the big idea. This was in the reign of the
only US president to have been a school teacher, who presided over the war on poverty, the
Great Society reforms and in his first year of presidency, against strong resistance,
introduced the Civil Rights Act (1964). His administration commissioned the Coleman
et al. (*Equality of Educational Opportunity*, Washington DC: US Department of Health,
Education and Welfare, 1966) research into equality of opportunity, the first time that such
data on inequality, on schools and school performance had been collected, data which was
fundamentally to change, perhaps for ever, the way in which people viewed school
education.

Six years later a follow-up study by a Harvard team reached very similar conclusions. In
their report, *Inequality: A Reassessment of the Effect of Family and Schooling in America*,
they conclude:

> Our research suggests that the characteristics of a school's output largely depend on a single
> input, namely the characteristics of the entering children. Everything else – its budget, its
> policies, the characteristics of the teachers – is either secondary or completely irrelevant. (Jencks,
> C., New York: Basic Books, 1972, p. 256)

The concern of both of these studies was with the role of the school in reshuffling the
social pack. It is significant that the studies were situated in a period in which systematic
data collection was in its infancy and it was seen as politically unwise to collect data which
would disclose sharply unequal outcomes.

This data vacuum was filled by a radical, and often highly subjective, critique of
schooling – Paul Goodman's *Compulsory Miseducation* (New York: Vintage Books, 1964,
John Holt's *How Children Fail* (Harmondworth: Penguin, 1969) and Ivan Illich's *Deschooling Society* (London: Calder and Boyars, 1971), the logical end point of this current of ideas.
This challenge to the central place of schools was taken up in the United States by
Brookover, by Rutter and Mortimore in England, Reynolds in Wales and by a stream of
studies from the Centre for Educational Sociology (CES) in Edinburgh. These produced a
substantial and influential body of work which was to bring a greater sense of optimism to

possibilities of schools as both social and educational agencies. Whereas Coleman and Jencks had focused their attention on the three-quarter empty glass, John Gray and his colleagues at CES took a greater interest in the quarter-full glass. Their Scottish data, while confirming the very powerful effects of factors beyond the control of schools, also demonstrated that individual schools could make a significant difference at the margins. They concluded, in what was to become the popular way of illustrating the school effect, that being in school A as against school B could make one or more 'O' Grades of a difference. It also suggested that schools could be effective along different dimensions in respect of attitude, attendance and attainment.

One of the CES studies by Gow and McPherson in 1980 (*Tell Them From Me*, Aberdeen: Aberdeen University Press) illustrated with graphic effect the powerful influence that school ethos and culture could have, for good or ill, on the attitudes, motivation, self-esteem and achievement of secondary age students. Mining data from the Scottish School Leavers archive, *Tell Them From Me* held up a disturbing mirror to Scottish secondary schools and to policy makers who began to take seriously the ethos question. It was to lead many years later to the creation of the Ethos Network (1995), recognising and rewarding good practice in the development of school ethos. The issue of ethos proved to have deeper roots than simply the superficial feel of a school, the colour of posters in the entrance halls or congeniality of welcome to parents. Doug Willms' 1985 study found that if you were a pupil of average ability your chances of exam success were better in schools where your peers were of high ability than in schools where they were of low ability. This was to become known as 'the contextual' or 'compositional' effect, an indication of something volatile and deep-lying in a school culture but not necessarily within the control of schools.

'The CES team concluded that they did not fully understand the contextual effect, warning that there may be spurious effects due to inadequate statistical models. However, taken together with the evidence from other sources, they concluded that it exists and may even be much more powerful than had been previously thought. Further confirmation for this was found in a study of Grampian schools in 1996 (Croxford, T. and Cowie, K., *The Effectiveness of Grampian Secondary Schools*, Aberdeen: Grampian Regional Council) reporting serious inequalities in pupils' examination results. 'The attainment of an average pupil may be raised or lowered by two or three Standard Grades [GCSE equivalent] by differences in school social context' (p. 5). Further endorsement of the contextual effect came a few years later in the Improving School Effectiveness project (MacBeath and Mortimore, 2001).

Identification of this effect as a somewhat teasing variable did not go far enough to satisfy the critics, however. Writing in 1999, Martin Thrupp takes effectiveness research to task for its failure to deal adequately with this complex issue of 'social mix'. He argues that the key to our understanding of its power is limited by the tools we use, the assumptions we start with and our ability to probe with enough sensitivity the complexity of peer social interaction. Thrupp's thesis receives overwhelming support from Judith Harris (London: Bloomsbury, 1999) in her controversial book *The Nurture Assumption*. She argues, with reference to a substantial body of research, that a child's identity as a person, her capacity as a learner and motivation as a student, come from the way in which she defines herself within the immediate peer reference group. The categories we use in our analysis – sex, race, ability, class – may or may not be salient characteristics of children's identity. These features assume great significance when school structures and the nature of the school social mix push them into social prominence. Her thesis is not only a blow to the more simplistic analysis of school effects but to a view of parents as the prime movers and shapers in children's beliefs and attitudes to school. It also complicates questions of parental choice. On what grounds do parents choose schools and to what extent is it their choice, or that of their children? How do geographical, class, race and religious differences impact on those choices? How useful, or misleading, are league tables?

Lying behind the advent of league tables, issued by the Scottish Office under the banner of the Information for Parents was the belief that these would inform parent choice. CES studies were able to demonstrate that when background factors were applied, a significant reordering of the ranking among schools took place, leading to the conclusion that if parents chose schools on the basis of examination results alone, they would very often choose the wrong school. The implication of this was that as more 'informed' parents withdrew their children they would also deprive schools of parental expertise and influence. This would in turn lend greater salience to the contextual effect.

Other writers referred to the rise of the parentocracy in which a child's education was increasingly dependent on the wealth and wishes of parents, rather than on pupils' abilities and efforts. Michael Adler and his colleagues at the University of Edinburgh showed that, in the early 1990s, differences were already being exacerbated, while four years later were able to offer confirmation of a continued widening of the social class differentiation (Adler, in Willms, D., *Parental Choice and Education Policy*, CES Briefing 12, August 1997).

In an earlier edition of this volume, Bryce and Humes showed that class inequalities had changed little from the 1970s. The performance gap between working-class and middle-class students had, in fact, grown larger between Standard Grade (at 15–16-years-old) and Higher Grade (at 17–18-years-old). While working-class students were now more likely than middle-class students to enter further education, in higher education middle-class students outnumbered working-class students by three to one. Whatever had been achieved by effectiveness studies and the improvement movement, the more things changed, it would seem, the more things stayed the same.

IMPROVING SCHOOL EFFECTIVENESS?

In 1995 two teams, from the University of Strathclyde and the Institute of Education in London, worked with schools across Scotland to unravel some of these contested issues; to further understanding of effectiveness and improvement, and their inter-relationship; and to inform policy development, especially in relation to value added. The study involved eighty schools, primary and secondary, all with a substantial commitment to data gathering at the outset of the project and again two years later. In addition to the four attainment tests in Mathematics and English at P4 and S2, eleven qualitative instruments were used to gather information on ethos, development planning, the management of change, and teaching and learning. Pupil, teacher and parent questionnaires were used as a measure of culture, expectations and change. In addition, twenty-four of the eighty schools were designated as case study schools with the benefit of a member of the research team to act as a critical friend, assisting with the collection, interpretation and feedback of data to staff.

Many of the findings in relation to attainment served to confirm previous Scottish research as well as studies in other parts of the world, while the attitudinal data sprang some surprises. On the attainment side (the classical school effectiveness side) among the extensive findings (described in some detail by Rebecca Smees and her colleagues in the May 2002 edition of *Scottish Educational Review*) were:

- Socio-economic disadvantage was shown to have a strong positive relationship with attainment at P4 and P6 and S2.
- Background factors had less influence in Mathematics than in Reading.
- School effects were stronger at primary than at secondary level.
- In primary, girls were ahead in Reading and boys in Mathematics but by S2, girls were still ahead in Reading and had caught up in Mathematics. By S4, Standard Grade, girls significantly outperformed boys in English and in overall performance across subjects.
- As in prior studies there was a 'contextual' or 'peer group' effect, significant for Reading but not for Mathematics.
- Pupils young for their year group performed significantly less well at all levels than their older peers.

Attitude measures, although only weakly related to social class, showed significant variations among schools and some variation by gender. For example, on the measure 'self-efficacy', girls were markedly less positive than boys. Attitudes of primary teachers were consistently and markedly more positive than their secondary colleagues, but at both primary and secondary level there was a consistently wide gap between teachers' view of their schools as they were and what they deemed to be the characteristics of the effective school. The attainment data, which was fed back to the school, very often came as a surprise and even a shock to teachers who had overestimated the school's performance relative to other schools, but such data did give a focus for target setting and rethinking of approaches to teaching, learning and assessment.

The attitudinal data, however, offered the biggest challenge and, in some cases, the most powerful lever for change. The more innovative aspect of the project was the feedback and use of data by the school itself. Data were processed and returned to schools confidentially together with aggregated data for all the schools in the project. Schools were then able to compare their own results with those of other schools. Much of the interpretative work occurred, therefore, at school level, with guidance and a health warning from the critical friends. It was their job to work alongside teachers and management to plan and implement change while the researcher's task was to document the process and to evaluate the role and influence of the critical friend (MacBeath and Mortimore, 2001). This analysis of itself provided a valuable contribution to the stock of knowledge on how support and change agency works and where the pitfalls lie. Sue Swaffield at the University of Cambridge is now building on this work to examine its application in the context of inspection and advisory services.

Critical friendship demanded a high level of skill in dealing with the defence mechanisms of heads and senior management for whom the data often came as a shock. Data were received by some headteachers, with denial ('I just don't believe this'), with projection ('Well they would say that wouldn't they'), sometimes introjection ('Should I resign now?'), by rationalisation ('Well it was done on a wet Friday in December, what would you expect?'). Others, however, viewed it as important, if uncomfortable, data which they saw could be used to move the school on, to address key issues, in particular those where there was marked dissonance between the views of the staff and those of senior, or middle, management.

Addressing the issues with regard for evidence and reasoned argument illustrated the power of 'soft' data as a tin opener, cutting into some deeply entrenched belief systems operating in a school. 'Learning disabilities are tragic in children but fatal in organisations,' argues Peter Senge (*The Fifth Discipline*, 1992). The ISE Project shed new light on some of the learning disabilities of schools but also showed how schools can learn through a process of feedback with appropriate support and challenge. Helping teachers to question their beliefs and assumptions, to deal sensitively and critically with evidence, to engage in dialogue on effects and improvement, proved to be a vital element in professional development and capacity-building.

SELF-EVALUATION; FILLING THE TOOLBOX

One of the spin-offs of ISEP was the tools which may be used in further research and in school self-evaluation. The questionnaire, developed from previous work in Halton, Ontario has, since ISEP, been further adapted for use in the seven-country study *Leadership for Learning* and in the ESRC research *Learning How to Learn* project (Cambridge, King's College, London, Reading University and the Open University). In both of these research projects a core of questionnaire items has been retained, providing for the future a growing bank of normative data in various national contexts.

From a policy point of view the development of materials for self-evaluation was seen as an important byproduct. Scotland was seen among the inspectorate as at the forefront of development and they wished to maintain its leading edge. *How Good is Our school?* was the instrument by which schools could carry out their own health check, feed into development planning and reduce reliance on an external inspectorate. Launching *How Good is Our School?* (1995) at a series of national and regional conferences, encompassing every Scottish school, HMCI Archie McGlynn argued that if self-knowledge is a mark of the healthy individual, then the same holds true of schools. He presented his model of concentric circles – the pupil and teacher at the centre, the school as the second layer, the education authority as the third, and the international context as the outer circumference. Reflecting on this process McGlynn writes:

> We took the thinking behind the concentric circles and the national guidelines on self-evaluation to every corner of the country and gave every school nationwide the opportunity to join us in the drive towards improving students' performance through self-evaluation at all levels in the system. The publication in 1995 of the guidelines entitled 'How Good is Our School?' marked a turning point. The coming of a nationally-agreed set of indicators of school quality, based on a 'bottom-up' campaign involving schools, education authorities, teacher-researchers and HMI, provided, perhaps for the first time, a set of agreed and robust criteria and gave many teachers and schools the confidence to embrace self-evaluation in a new 'open' way. (*Managing Schools Today*, October 2002)

His article ends with a celebration of the impact that the Scottish approach has had world-wide, in Australia, Hong Kong, Germany and Norway. In some countries *How Good is Our School?* has been lifted in its literal entirety, in Germany for example, where *Wie Gut is unsere Schule?* is a direct translation of the Scottish document. In Norway the six main categories have been used but with some modification of the individual indicators.

There is an important lesson to be learned from this export-import trade. In Oslo teachers were briefly consulted before the introduction of the model, meeting it with a marked lack of enthusiasm and some resistance. The Scottish approach had matured over a decade, had involved extensive consultation with teachers, trialing and redrafting, whereas elsewhere it has simply 'arrived', resting on no more than the singular enthusiasm of a policy maker. The frequent mistake in effectiveness, improvement, or self-evaluation and any other form of cultural borrowing is to confuse the product with the process and to ignore the context in which something is intimately located. What the Norwegians, and others, ought to have borrowed was the process rather than the end product. But then policy makers tend to be impatient people.

PRESSURE FROM WITHOUT

The concentric circle model is highly significant in revealing how policy was moving in the 1990s. The four levels of questions represented by the circles were:

- How good is learning and teaching in my classroom?
- How good is our school?
- How good is the education authority?
- How do we compare with other countries?

In common with other countries, the Scottish Office was as interested in the fourth as in the first of these questions. It wanted to be a part of the international horse race. Self-evaluation was seen as insufficient without benchmarks at every level and if schools were to be effective they were to be effective in international as well as national comparisons. If schools were to be improving they needed to be able to demonstrate year-on-year a trajectory of progress. While the school effectiveness/improvement (SESI) movement may not assume all the credit, or blame, for large comparative international studies of attainment, their research had been instrumental in helping to create the climate and furnish the analytical tools for data gathering on a grand scale. SESI researchers played their part in a rapidly growing industry driven by the OECD, the European Commission, Eurostat and UNESCO, whose successive reports were pored over anxiously by politicians, willing to invest substantial sums of money to be included. The most recent and most widely publicised study by the OECD, the Programme for International Student Assessment (PISA), although specifically purporting not to measure school attainment, was greeted by politicians in every parti-cipating country either as an indictment or vindication of their schools. The Scottish Executive's desire to be distinguished from its southern neighbours resulted in a separately commissioned study involving tests and questionnaires of 2,500 students in ninety-nine schools. The press reports give some indication of the seriousness with which politicians treat international comparisons.

The *Financial Times* of 31 January reported that 'Scotland's long-held view that it boasts a superior education system to that of the rest of the UK has won statistical backing from a 30-country survey'. Triumphantly *The Scotsman* proclaimed that 'Scottish pupils have trumped their English counterparts in an international league table of results for maths and reading' (30 January 2002). Going further still, the *Daily Mail* claimed that 'Scotland's schoolchildren are among the most intelligent in the developed world, according to a major international study' (31 January 2002). Welcoming the findings the Minister for Education and Young People, Cathy Jamieson said:

> These very encouraging results are consistent with the HM Inspectorate of Education finding
> that attainment in S3 and S4 is good or very good in 70% of schools, and with the continuing

upward trend in examination performance and improved attainment of target levels. This report shows there is much to be proud of in Scottish education. (SEED press release, January 2002)

This was welcome news given Scotland's indifferent performance in other international league tables. Scottish performance in TIMSS, the Third Mathematics and Science Study had earlier revealed that twenty-two countries were ahead of Scotland in the international league table on Mathematics (SOEID, 1996).

The tenet on which all of this frenetic interest rests is that school attainment is an indicator of economic performance. It is a belief contested by leading academics such as David Berliner (Berliner, D. and Biddle, B. J., *The Manufactured Crisis*, New York: Addison-Wesley, 1996) and Ernest House (*Schools for Sale*, New York: Teachers College Press, 1998) and in the UK by the Institute of Public Policy Research (1999). The immediate effects are, however, inflows and outflows of educational travellers in search of the ingredients that put a country at the top of the league table. While previous sites of international cherry picking were Japan and Taiwan, interest has now turned to Finland and Korea which topped the 2001 PISA table. What such research studiedly ignores is that achievement rests primarily not on what happens in schools and classrooms but what happens outside them. Ever since Coleman's conclusion that school effects are marginal compared with home and community effects, thirty years of studies have simply confirmed that view. Korea's excellent showing is explained not by the quality of classroom teaching or exceptional teachers but by a culture. Kim, presenting the outcomes of his Korean study (2002) provided data to show that it was parental aspiration, private tutoring and cramming classes outside schools that explained its excellent results.

In England the government's anxiety about its performance internationally resulted in numeracy and literacy strategies designed to raise standards quickly, demonstrably and within the lifetime of a government. The evaluation conducted by a team from the Ontario Institute of Education found that while successful in raising test scores, it had resulted in 'collateral damage' (Earle et al., 2001), a narrowing of the curriculum, an impoverishment of the educational experience. The Ontario team's studies of large scale reform around the world point to the endemic problems of top-down change, simplistic notions of transfer of knowledge and 'best practice', the need for the quick political fix. 'Growth', a word favoured in the Canadian context, is an organic concept, a more grounded sentiment than improvement which carries a more paternalistic connotation. Growth, as Michael Fullan has argued for a decade and more, comes through a subtle blend of bottom-up and top-down, support and pressure, internal and external evaluation. Scotland may claim to be closer to this paradigm than many other countries but that claim may have yet to be proven to classroom teachers, heads, school boards and unions.

The launch of SEED's five National Priorities in 2001 has provided an opportunity to pursue a growth strategy. It has promised to give equal status to the key areas of attainment, citizenship, inclusion and to consult as widely as possible in taking this vision forward. Genuinely to maintain an equilibrium among the priorities may prove a challenge too far in an international context where simple quantitative measures count. It may prove difficult to resist a prime minister who wishes a government agenda to be the 'national' agenda. It will require both determined and distributive leadership.

GROWTH FROM WITHIN

Building from the bottom up means that policy needs to take time out to 'study the ant'; to learn from the small scale miracles which may provide the clues to large scale reform. Some of the most inspiring examples to have come out of Scotland in the recent past have been initiated by individual teachers and groups of teachers, by schools or clusters of schools working together, sometimes with strong authority support, sometimes in the context of research and improvement projects with university or private sector partners. It is reassuring that this strategy is being pursued by the SEED National Priorities team in collaboration with universities and Learning and Teaching Scotland.

One of the most inspiring examples of grass roots growth comes from Scotland's northernmost secondary school, Anderson High School in Shetland. It is a small scale miracle with world-wide ramifications. The brainchild of one teacher and a group of school students, The Global Classroom and The Learning School were two initiatives designed to take the curriculum out of the classroom and to extend self-evaluation beyond the school. The Global Classroom started as a project among schools in four countries sharing curricula, exchanging information, ideas and materials using ICT. Scientific experiments in Shetland could be conducted by video link with a school in South Africa which had no laboratory equipment. History came alive through the accounts of those who were living that history. Languages were learned in use, written and verbal, through international links and 'real' rather than contrived conversations.

At the end of the 1990s the partner schools discussed ways of marking the millennium. An idea that emerged in Anderson High was to invite students from each of the partner schools to form an international study group that would spend the year travelling amongst all partner schools. What they would study was never fully worked out until prompted by a fifth-year student, a keen participant in The Global Classroom from its inception in 1997. While leafing through *How Good is Your School?*, he asked how students' views would contribute to answering that question, leading to a 'virtual conference' among the four countries on possible roles for students in the process of school evaluation. Further impetus for the study group was a comment by a visiting Czech student to Anderson High School which provided the title 'The Learning School'. In reply to a frequently asked question as to why he was attending Anderson High, he answered, 'I'm learning to learn.' It was a comment that went to the heart of what goes on, or ought to go on, in schools, and provided a focus for Learning School projects that were to follow.

Now in its fourth year a new group of Learning School (LS) students from eight countries, many them taking a gap year out of their school, are circumnavigating the globe, living with host families, spending four weeks in each participating school, evaluating learning and teaching, feeding their findings back to the staff, making presentations in conferences (so far, in Copenhagen; Hong Kong; Johannesburg; South Africa; Nara; Japan; Cambridge; and Edinburgh for the Scottish Executive). In October 2002 the book of the project, *Self-evaluation in the Global Classroom*, written almost entirely by the LS students themselves, was published by Routledge Falmer. The Learning School typifies the energy and vitality that exists among teachers and school students who rarely get the chance to escape the conventions and strictures of top down reform. It tells a quite different story from many of the arcane and self-referencing school effectiveness studies.

FROM SCHOOL TO EDUCATIONAL EFFECTIVENESS

The school effectiveness paradigm will enjoy a further challenge as Scottish education moves progressively further away from the black box, nine to four, five day week, subject fragmented school. The creation of New Community Schools, symbolically at the turn of the millennium, is one variant on the traditional factory model of schooling. Based on the American model of full-service schools, New Community Schools are designed to offer a one-door entry (physical or metaphorical) to educational, social and psychological services. In theory they promise a coherent cross-agency, inter-professional approach, although critics (for example, Lindsay Paterson writing in *Scotland on Sunday*, November 1999) cautions that by virtue of their location in disadvantaged areas, they may reinforce rather than ameliorate social class variance (See also Chapter 4.) New Community Schools, home learning and more adventurous alternatives in the 'post-comprehensive' or 'new comprehensive' era will serve to confuse effectiveness researchers because the premise of the 'black box' with measured inputs at one end and outcomes at the other will become increasingly problematic. The more seamless learning becomes, the less easy it is to identify and manipulate the variables. Where is the source of learning – the classroom? Study support? Homework and home study? Mentoring and coaching? Psychological services? Improved health care?

Professionals will have to think again, imaginatively, about how to measure learning. Peter Senge, addressing a Scottish Council Foundation seminar in Edinburgh (May 2002) suggested there was a lesson to be learned from the most successful car company in the world, Toyota. Keep data as close as possible to its source and its prime users. Resist the temptation to aggregate data – to class, to school, to authority, to national, to international level – because at each step essential meaning is lost. It is a sobering counsel and one to be borne in mind as the National Priorities roll out and Scotland comes of age in its evaluation of individual, organisational, and inter-organisational learning.

REFERENCES

Earle, L., Fullan, M., Leithwood, K. (2001) *Watching & Learning 2, OISE/UT Evaluation of the Implementation of the National Literacy and National Numeracy Strategies*, Toronto: University of Toronto.

Kim, S. (2002) The influence of private education on schooling in Korea: High academic achievement and 'school collapse', paper presented at the ICSEI 2002 Conference, Copenhagen, Denmark, January 3–7.

MacBeath, J. and Mortimore, P. (2001) *Improving School Effectiveness*, Buckingham: Open University Press.

Senge, P. (1992) *The Fifth Discipline: The Art and Practice of the Learning Organisation*, Sydney: Random House.

Thrupp, M. (1999) *Schools Making a Difference: Let's be Realistic*, Buckingham: Open University Press.

Willms, J. D. (1985), The balance thesis – contextual effects of ability on pupils' 'O' Grade examination results, *Oxford Review of Education*, 11 (1).

XI

Challenges and Responses:
Education for All?

91

Educational Support for Children with Disabilities

Gilbert MacKay and Marion McLarty

CHANGING DEFINITIONS AND BEYOND

This chapter is written at a time of rapid development in the education of children with disabilities. A significant marker in this development is the absence of the term 'special educational needs' (SEN) from the Education (Disability Strategies and Pupils' Educational Records) (Scotland) Act 2002. Accordingly, the chapter's title has changed from that of its predecessor in the first edition of *Scottish Education*. The change takes account of developments which are in place already, and of others which are predicted.

All systems are fallible and the education system is no exception. It must change perpetually to be effective in supporting, enabling and protecting. The modern Scottish system began with an Act of 1872. A century passed before it recognised every child's right to education, through the Education (Mentally Handicapped Children) (Scotland) Act 1974. The early development of special education in Scotland is given in Dockrell, Dunn and Milne (1978). For this chapter, the Warnock Report of 1978 is a useful starting point. In 1973, Warnock's committee was set the task of reviewing 'educational provision in England, Scotland and Wales for children and young people handicapped by disabilities of body or mind . . .'. The report's ultimate title of 'Special Educational Needs' showed that things had begun to change. UK educational systems moved from recognising handicaps in the 1950s, to rights in the early 1970s, to needs in 1978.

Change was inevitable because of developments in education, health and social policies. By 1978, it was no longer sufficient to respond to disabilities defined in statutory regulations of 1954. 'Needs' became the key to a new rhetoric. Of course, rhetoric does not guarantee understanding. Even today, it is common to hear the equating of needs and disabilities, in comments such as, 'Her special need is hearing impairment.' Who needs a hearing impairment? Just now, education authorities have a duty to keep children and young people with SEN under review if they decide to record their needs formally. Soon, it is likely that the prevailing context will be one of co-ordinated support rather than of recording needs. This chapter is concerned with that section of the school population – currently around 16,000, or 2.1%, in Audit Office statistics – who have a 'pronounced, specific or complex' need for co-ordinated support.

KEY POLICY DOCUMENTS FROM WARNOCK ONWARDS

Warnock still exerts a powerful influence. Its 'areas of first priority' – pre-5 children, young adults and the training of teachers—now receive more attention than they did in 1978. Its recommendations on recording and Named Persons were enacted in 1981. So was the disappearance of official categories of disability, though these have re-appeared in an amended form in documents such as *EPSEN* (see below).

Another document, contemporary with Warnock, exerted great influence in Scotland (HMI, 1978) and is discussed in Chapter 92. It shifted focus from pupils' constitutional difficulties, to difficulties caused by inappropriate teaching and other circumstances not within the child. It recommended a change from thinking about 'remedial' to 'appropriate' education in mainstream schools. Understandably, it also influenced developments in special education, as it pointed out how many problems come from low expectation, insensitive teaching and a weak curriculum. However, it also generated extravagant beliefs about the capacity of mainstream schools to educate pupils with severe disabilities. By extension, special provision for such pupils has often been stigmatised in rhetoric that is seldom grounded in experience.

The 1981 Act disappointed many because it seemed to achieve so little, coming after Warnock which seemed to promise so much. However, SED Circular 1087 (1982) indicated the government's intention to honour the spirit of Warnock. Staged assessment was commended, as was the practice of recording, pre-5 intervention, and early detection of children's difficulties. Parents were given a central place in recording, and the rôle of the Named Person was confirmed. Circular 1087's influence is still evident in *Effective Provision for Pupils with Special Educational Needs* (*EPSEN*), a report by HM Inspectors (SOED, 1994) and the *Manual for Good Practice* (SOEID, 1999), which set out policy on quality standards in specialized support.

At the moment, all education in the first nine years of statutory schooling should conform to the 5–14 curriculum, whether it is delivered in mainstream or special schools. The early documentation of 5–14 shows that it was designed for pupils in the former. However, two developments occurred, aimed at achieving the inclusion of all, irrespective of individual circumstances. First was the issue of *Support for Learning* by the Scottish Consultative Council on the Curriculum in 1994. It proposed five strategies for addressing the 'mismatch between delivery of the curriculum and pupils' learning needs: differentiation, individualisation, adaptation, enhancement and elaboration. The second development was the 'elaborated curriculum' for pupils with complex intellectual disabilities. Its original version consisted of components of elderly developmental checklists, shoe-horned into areas of the 5–14 curriculum. 'Assessment' was equated with 'curriculum', a serious flaw. Perhaps the most positive aspect of the elaborated curriculum is that it has stimulated many schools to devise something better. They can be trusted to do this well, because they have done so before in developing activities, teaching methods and home-school partnerships – often ahead of comparable developments in mainstream schools.

LEGISLATIVE FRAMEWORK

The basic legislative framework for pupils with SEN is given in Scottish Office Circular 4/96 (SOEID, 1996). It will be affected by changes now beginning to appear in legislation, policy and practice. Perhaps the first intimations of a change in the legislative framework, to one which focuses on rights and responsibilities, were the Children (Scotland) Act 1995, and the Disability Act 1995. Then, in 2000, the Standards in Scotland's Schools etc. Act declared that mainstream schooling was the assumed placement of all children, unless unusual circumstances made special schooling appropriate. This aspect of the Act is in line with other legislation including the Disability Act 1995 and the Special Educational Needs and Disability Act 2001. The 2000 Act should also be read in conjunction with the Education (Disability Strategies and Pupils' Educational Records) (Scotland) Act 2002, with its commitment to access, communication and support. There are similar messages in forthcoming legislation, which will replace the Record of Needs with Co-ordinated Support Plans (CSPs). A stronger, more streamlined and flexible system will emerge soon, with 'staged intervention' of school-based support, and with CSPs for children with 'additional support needs' requiring input from more than one agency.

THE ROLE OF SCHOOLS AND OTHER AGENCIES IN IDENTIFYING AND PROVIDING FOR SPECIAL EDUCATIONAL NEEDS

From nursery to further education, teachers are supported by advice in *EPSEN* (SOED, 1994), and the *Manual for Good Practice* (SOEID, 1999). *EPSEN* is an HMI report based on evidence from investigations in mainstream and special schools and other establishments. The Manual is an important part of quality initiatives in Scottish education.

EPSEN has chapters on four educational sectors: pre-5, primary, secondary and further education. A major aspect of its general guidance is the statement of 'ten distinctive features of effective provision for special educational needs', seen as fundamental to good practice. The ten cover the process of response from understanding needs, through identifying and planning for them, to monitoring the effectiveness of intervention. The report's section on pre-school children gives a scheme for determining whether or not to open a Record of needs. It draws attention to the range of people who are essential partners if needs are to be identified and met. This section also commends current Scottish thinking on the structure of the curriculum for pre-school children. Other *EPSEN* sections give guidance on provision in primary and secondary schools. They detail steps in deciding whether or not to open a Record and how to conduct the assessment of future needs. The guidance stresses the importance of family involvement from the earliest stages of investigation.

The progress of pupils, say *EPSEN* and the *Manual*, should be structured by Individualised Educational Programmes (IEPs), a device with roots in a 1975 law of the USA. Scottish educationists should be thankful that it does not have a place in a statutory code (as in England and Wales), and that neither system has the stringent review procedures that have caused anxiety in the USA. Making IEPs work is a delicate balancing act. The danger in having too formal a system, apart from unnecessary paperwork, is that of focusing on experiences which can be expressed in terms of simplistic behavioural goals. The danger in having no system is that children and young people will have poor education. IEPs will probably continue to have a place in the forthcoming CSPs. They invite research. The penultimate section of *EPSEN* deals with further education. It covers those students who have SEN that should be met if they are to benefit from general college courses, and those taking courses specifically for people with SEN. *EPSEN* ends with a review of priorities for development.

EPSEN and the *Manual* are regarded by many professionals as useful, practical statements of principle. Forthcoming changes to the legislative framework are unlikely to differ greatly from the principles in them, and so it is probable that their influence will be evident in future quality standards for the delivery of support.

Other chapters of this volume refer to the Higher Still innovations for the curriculum of secondary aged sixteen to eighteen. From the outset, the Higher Still proposals were inclusive, taking account of the needs of all pupils, from those with the most complex difficulties to those who are most able academically. Higher Still guidance includes pupils and students who have previously been regarded as too disabled to be included in any programme of work leading to accreditation. It is possible for pupils with severe intellectual difficulties to engage with Higher Still levels Access 1 and 2. The programme recognises that pupils working at these levels will require individualised planning and an IEP. It also recognises that some students' difficulties are such that independent completion of even the single outcome units at Access 1 will prove demanding. It is recommended that their progress be described using the descriptors of participation, awareness and experience.

TEACHER EDUCATION

This section deals mainly with experienced teachers, but begins with a brief comment on initial training. For some years, Scottish teacher education institutions have included SEN components in initial training. It is important that all students should develop knowledge, attitudes and skills that will let them respond well to the pupils with SEN they meet on placement or in their first jobs. Achieving this in a crowded timetable continues to cause concern.

Until 1992, there was a well-established route to an additional teaching qualification in SEN. Four teacher education colleges (Jordanhill, Moray House, Northern and St Andrew's) offered a Diploma in SEN (Recorded Pupils) and a Diploma in SEN (Non-recorded Pupils), replacing, respectively, older diplomas in special and remedial education. (Craigie College was also active in the field, but with a less comprehensive provision of courses.) In addition, Moray House, exclusively, ran (and continues to run) courses for teachers working with pupils with visual and hearing impairments. At the present writers' base (the former Jordanhill College), teachers undertaking the 'recorded' diploma were seconded for a full-time one-year course of twelve modules. Those following the 'non-recorded' course undertook part-time study over two sessions. The Scottish Office supported teachers' secondments by a specific grant to the authorities. The diplomas conferred were, first, additional teaching qualifications recognised by the GTC and, second, awards of the Council for National Academic Awards.

A number of changes to the diplomas occurred between 1987 and 1992. First, the recorded and non-recorded diplomas merged, as their distinction was difficult to justify. They are now awards in 'support for learning' (SFL). Second, the colleges capitulated to education authority pressure, and replaced the twelve-module course with four-module certificates and eight-module diplomas taken by day release or evening study. The shortened nature of the courses, combined with the removal of assessed teaching placement, killed off the additional qualification in SEN. It is questionable whether the awards in SFL have offered teachers professional development as good as that in the diplomas they replaced, despite their elevation to postgraduate status. Nonetheless, teachers and teacher educators have adapted to the new system. The current courses attract large numbers of candidates from specialised provision, mainstream classes and support services. Increasingly, teachers are using their diplomas for entry to masters' degrees.

Currently, the major unknown in the delivery of postgraduate education on support for pupils with disabilities is the emergence of the Chartered Teacher scheme. It seems certain that specialised professional development will continue because of the Scottish Executive's commitment to providing a high standard of educational support. Finance may well continue to be ringfenced for professional development which meets that purpose. But can the certificate, diploma and master's degree in SFL survive when teachers have a clear financial incentive to choose one particular form of professional development, namely, chartered status, over the others on offer? Superficially it would appear that relatively minor adjustments to the SFL courses would let them fit seamlessly into the Chartered Teacher framework. However, it is not yet clear that such merging of systems will be acceptable to those who are formulating the framework's regulations.

PARENTAL RIGHTS: RELATIONSHIPS BETWEEN HOME AND SCHOOL

A variety of statutory rights for parents has been defined in and since the 1980 Act. That Act gave parents rights of appeal on the opening of Records of Needs and on their content. Such rights will be overtaken when the co-ordinated support legislation takes effect. It is too early to give an authoritative commentary on opening and maintaining CSPs. However, their anticipation in the Disability Strategies and Pupils' Records Act, and in consultative documents, suggests a concern with values evident in Warnock, such as the right to appropriate support, and with a stronger assertion of the rights of the recipients of services – pupils and their families – to influence the nature and extent of provision.

There has been increasing legislative emphasis on rights and duties since the Children (Scotland) Act 1995. The Scottish Executive report on people with intellectual disabilities, *The Same as You* (2000), and the Adults with Incapacity (Scotland) Act 2000, strengthen the rights of vulnerable individuals. The Standards Act of 2000, and the Acts of 1995, 2001 and 2002 concerned with disability, can be expected to alter and, normally, strengthen the rights of parents and children, but it is too early to be specific about their effects. That is partly because of their recency and partly because the Acts, and other related legislation at the draft stage, have still to be incorporated in practices at service level.

There is a necessary formality about parents' relationships with education authorities in respect of educational law. Relationships are less formal in the daily routines of school. Warnock was a milestone in developing the notion of parents as partners. Yet, partnership is a complex idea. To what extent do parents and professionals have equal powers, rights and responsibilities in the relationship? Does a focus on rôles obscure the importance of the systems and other social dynamics which influence families' and professionals' behaviour and aspirations?

Many professionals value their relationship with parents unreservedly because it gives them understanding which is an essential base for planning and daily decisions. The relationship may be low-key in the form of home–school diaries or an open-door or open-telephone policy. Some schools have parents' groups that meet during or after school to consider matters relating to children and families. More formally, it is standard practice to have parents' attendance at review meetings, which most education authorities carry out annually when pupils have Records of Needs. The creation of this relationship took time to establish as normal, because it challenged long-established social representations of parents, professionals and schools. It probably occurred earlier and with greater ease in special education than did comparable developments in mainstream education. That is a credit to parents and professionals. Perhaps it was also a necessary consequence of recognising that the children and young people involved really do have special and different needs, and that these require a another kind of relationship between parents and professionals from that which can suffice in mainstream schools.

MAINSTREAMING; DIFFERENT FORMS OF INTEGRATION; SEPARATE PROVISION

Mainstreaming is the practice of locating in mainstream schools pupils who might have all or most of their education in segregated special provision because of disabilities. Over many years, Scottish Office statistics have shown that a relatively small proportion of children with disabilities attend segregated provision, with most of them in schools for pupils with intellectual disabilities. It is difficult to predict what changes will occur because of recent legislation. However, it is still useful to return to the generation-old Warnock definitions of integration to set the context for mainstreaming.

Warnock identified three types of arrangement – locational, social and functional. Locational integration includes siting special educational provision on the campus or in the classrooms of a mainstream school. There are many examples around Scotland. Social integration occurs when the children in locationally-integrated provision mix with pupils in the mainstream classes during social activities. Again, there are many examples. Functional integration occurs when pupils with disabilities are full members of mainstream classes. Such practices have always occurred in Scottish schools, particularly when children have sensory, emotional and behavioural, specific learning, communicative or physical disabilities. Challenges to functional integration become greater as pupils' intellectual disabilities increase, or when they have severe difficulties communicating and interacting with others.

Warnock's thinking on integration was influenced partly by world movements in civil rights, as segregated schooling may be interpreted as a barrier to participation in an inclusive society. There are also pragmatic arguments for integration because exposure to the company of other mainstream pupils is an excellent way of learning social mores whether or not one has a disability. In addition, the mainstream curriculum may give access to a wider range of life-choices than may that in segregated provision. Yet, it is necessary to challenge the principle that simplistic integrated education is a universal right, especially where it is no more than locational integration masquerading as 'inclusion'. The same UN charters (1959 and 1989) which assert children's rights to education also assert, as an earlier priority than general education, the right to special education for all children who require it. Also, the influential UN Salamanca Agreement (1994) recognises that differences among cultures do not make it possible to have a single model of inclusive education. Salamanca acknowledges the continuing contribution of special schools and units in countries which have long traditions of such provision. Perhaps the USA's concept of 'the least restrictive environment' can be operationalised more easily than 'inclusion' or 'integration', which often defy definition or description.

The 2000 Act may strengthen expectations that every child should and can be educated in the same mainstream class as their age peers. Such an equating of mainstreaming with inclusion is difficult to accept when little functional integration is present. The conditions for functional integration, and the limits of it, require a basis in evidence rather than polemic, for the sake of the pupils, their peers, families and teachers. Thus, education in mainstream schools is not an easy option for all pupils with disabilities. Also, Scotland has many excellent special schools. Yet, that is no reason for complacency about existing services. Certainly, cross-cultural comparisons can mislead, but it is important to acknowledge that countries such as Canada and Italy can claim to have gone far further towards mainstream education for pupils with disabilities than has Scotland. There is a necessity to challenge existing boundaries. To respond to that challenge, there is a need for a national bank of qualitative and quantitative data on mainstreaming, together with reliable information on practices and policies in other educational systems. That requirement may now be overdue. The presumption of mainstreaming is explicit in the Standards Act of 2000, with its accompanying guidance (Circular 3/2002), effective from 1 August 2003.

RESEARCH FINDINGS ON THE NATURE AND EFFECTIVENESS OF CURRENT ARRANGEMENTS

This chapter's equivalent in the first edition of *Scottish Education* gave details of research in the areas of curriculum and specific aspects of disability. That chapter also referred to research on the Record of Needs by Thomson and colleagues at Edinburgh University in 1989. The Edinburgh study reported aspects of recording which have never been resolved since its inception. Indeed, the study may have been one reason for the forthcoming changes to recording legislation. Considerable differences in the interpretation of the law were evident. For example, recording rates varied widely across the (then) twelve regional and island authorities. Decisions to record seemed predicated on local resources. Later research by Thomson et al. (in 1995), led to proposals of criteria for opening Records of Needs, centring on a matrix of need for determining the nature and extent of support. This was a significant move from Warnock's unconvincing continuum of need, a feature of the 1978 report which Warnock herself (in 1989) described as 'naïve to the point of idiocy'. It is also worth asking if concern about the opening of Records became a priority at the expense of an examination of the effects of recording. Authorities had no requirement to supply statements of action taken in response to the contents of children's and young persons' Records. Warnock set out to change attitudes and policies, and to ensure the proper provision of education for people with special needs. Records of Needs and IEPs had a rôle in formal monitoring. Perhaps the incoming CSPs will enable teachers, families and pupils to set more visionary educational goals than are possible under the current system.

Critical research for developing the nature and effectiveness of special provision in the new century was reported by two committees in 1999, after taking evidence from interested parties. First, the Beattie Report, *Implementing Inclusiveness: Realising Potential*, reviewed the range of needs of young people requiring additional support to make the transition to post-school education, training or employment. People with disabilities were not the main focus of the report, but were among the groups considered. The Beattie website (http://www.scotland.gov.uk/who/elld/beattie.asp) gives details on progress towards 'inclusiveness' in Scotland, as developed by a national action group set up in response to the committee's report. Second, the Riddell Committee's report *The Education of Children with Severe Low Incidence Disabilities* (Glasgow: Advisory Committee, University of Glasgow, 1999) led to *Assessing our Children's Educational Needs: The Wary Forward* (Edinburgh: Scottish Executive, 2001). The influence of that report is evident in new legislation and in guidance for its implementation. The influence is apparent in two areas in particular. Firstly, the new legislation and guidance encourage the creation of a system in which there is maximum inclusion of pupils with disabilities in the routines of mainstream education. Secondly, legislation and guidance on disability strategies and support plans have powerful safeguards for pupils and students who require extra assistance. The committee will have done a good job if it increases understanding of the practicalities of mainstreaming, and of the need for diversity of provision even in an inclusive system of education.

SCOTLAND IN THE CONTEXT OF THE UNITED KINGDOM

The establishment of devolved government has been perhaps the most important structural difference to the United Kingdom in recent years. The differences among the education systems of England, Northern Ireland, Scotland and Wales are still relatively slight, though, in respect of pupils with disabilities. Indeed, the Disability Act 1995 and the SEN and Disability Act 2001 apply to Scotland, England and Wales, because equal opportunities are a reserved power under the Scottish and Welsh devolution settlements. (The 1995 Act, modified, applies in Northern Ireland too, but not the 2001 Act.)

In 1970, England and Wales were four years ahead of Scotland in ensuring that every child, including those with complex and severe disabilities, was entitled to education. There, a 1976 Act also entitled pupils with disabilities to integrated education whenever possible. The Record of Needs is the 'Statement' in England and Wales, and uses less paper than the Record. The time needed to complete Records and Statements has been a problem on both sides of the border.

The mandatory nature of the national curriculum in England and Wales has worried many special educationists (though an important exception was made for deafblind pupils). Officially, the current 5–14 Scottish curriculum is not mandatory, but its adoption is close to universal, and there is pressure at central and local level to ensure that all pupils are 'doing 5–14'. With devolution, all four countries of the UK now have their own national curricula for the first nine years of compulsory schooling. That would appear to create an opportunity to start afresh with the two oldest curricula (the national curriculum and 5–14), and create structures which are designed from the outset to include pupils with disabilities.

In 1994, the English and Welsh system adopted the Code of Practice, a set of legally binding standards for services for those with SEN. Scotland has no code, though *EPSEN* and the *Manual* fulfil a similar function. The critical difference between the Code and its Scottish equivalents is its binding nature, because of its roots in a 1993 Act. It will be interesting to assess the extent to which practices in the four UK systems become more or less distinct as incoming legislation across the countries becomes consolidated towards the middle of this decade.

FUTURE PRIORITIES

Scottish educational provision for pupils with disabilities could be on the brink of the most important developments for at least a generation. The Act of 1974 and the Warnock Report invited the creation of a better system. However, they appeared early in a long period of economic recession when the development of supportive services had a low priority. That period was followed by the 1990s, which were characterised by too much rhetoric about integration and inclusion. Nevertheless, that was also the period of *EPSEN* and of some excellent innovations in special and mainstream provision, across disabilities and across the age range. What is particularly exciting is speculation on what could happen when good practice meets the new legislation, with its imperatives of access, communication, co-ordinated support and the presumption of mainstreaming. How bold will Scotland be in rising to the challenge?

It is certainly time to revisit the vast literature on curriculum development, to reassess current demands in the light of principles such as the structure of subjects, and the value of the curriculum. Scotland does not yet have a curricular framework that is suitable for all pupils in the first nine years of schooling. Perhaps that curriculum cannot or should not exist. The debate has still to take place.

Children and young people from ethnic minorities can have particular priorities. Their special needs may be difficult to discern if the first language at home is not English. Those who are the children of refugees may need additional support because of disruptions in their early childhood experience.

There should be continued development of specialisms which have been addressed only recently as areas of priority for service provision across the whole of Scotland, such as the education of children and young people who have difficulty communicating. They include children with autistic behaviour, which makes exceptional demands on themselves, their families and the education system.

The pre-service and in-service professional development of teachers is still a priority. In some cases, this could be facilitated by joint exercises with other professionals such as speech and language therapists. Models of good practice exist. Can such collaborative professional development find a place in the framework for Chartered Teachers?

More broadly, there must be respect for the different ways of understanding people with disabilities. For more than a decade, the support for learning movement (see Chapter 92) has advocated moves away from what it likes to call deficit and medical models – any recognition that people's impairments can create barriers to participation and to learning. Instead, that movement advocates different models, most commonly misty-eyed hybrids of the social model of disability. This preoccupation with models is not particularly helpful. No model of response is right or wrong intrinsically. They are all legitimate ways of knowing, appropriate in some circumstances and not so in others. Pupils, families, teachers and the general community are done a disservice when the diversity that is normality is simplified as a philosophical, political or fiscal inconvenience.

The last words on future priorities should still come from *EPSEN*, a document which has always seemed to be grounded on common sense, vision and a convincing knowledge of pupils with disabilities. *EPSEN* was written in a spirit of confidence in what has been achieved, and in what might be achieved. Its final sentence states that such achievement should be grounded in a basic aim – enabling people 'to enjoy and derive maximum benefit from their education in school and beyond, and to become fully participating members of their communities'. That is a good place to start and finish.

REFERENCES

Committee of Enquiry into the Education of Handicapped Children and Young People, (1978) *Special Educational Needs* (The Warnock Report), London: HMSO.

Dockrell, W. B., Dunn, W. R., and Milne, A. (1978). *Special Education in Scotland*, Edinburgh: SCRE.

HMIS (1978) *Pupils with Learning Difficulties in Primary and Secondary Schools in Scotland*, Edinburgh: HMSO.

SOED (1994) *Effective Provision for Special Educational Needs (EPSEN)*, Edinburgh: SOED.
SOEID (1996) *Children and Young Persons with Special Educational Needs: Assessment and Recording*, Edinburgh: SOEID.
SOEID (1999) *A Manual for Good Practice in Special Educational Needs*, Edinburgh: SOEID.

92

Inclusion for All?
Beyond 'Support for Learning'

Julie Allan

INTRODUCTION

Considerable progress has been made in the inclusion of children with special educational needs within mainstream schools over the last twenty-five-years. In spite of this, inclusion remains a major source of concern and confusion for policy makers and practitioners, and of dissatisfaction for the recipients of the provision: children and their parents. This chapter explores the conceptual confusion surrounding inclusion and examines the impact of policy and legislative developments on the support for children with special needs in mainstream schools. In particular, the changing demands on classroom teachers, learning support teachers and classroom assistants is considered, as is the inclusiveness of the programmes of curriculum and assessment. Pupils' accounts of their experiences of inclusion and exclusion are also discussed. The chapter draws on findings from a recent Scottish parliamentary inquiry into special educational needs, to which the author was adviser, and on recent research.

FROM INTEGRATION TO INCLUSION

The conceptual confusion surrounding inclusion and special educational needs has arisen partly from the somewhat naive practice by policy makers of introducing new terminology in an effort to change the hearts and minds of teachers. The continued dominance of a rigid special education paradigm has also created confusion and restricted the potential for inclusive practice. The so-called watershed of the 1978 Warnock Report saw the birth of the term 'special educational needs', presented as a more positive way of viewing children than the former categories of handicaps. In the same year, the report from Her Majesty's Inspectorate in Scotland dumped the term 'remedial', again wishing to avoid any negative connotations. 'Support for learning' emerged as the new practice of giving assistance to children within classrooms. Both these documents, enshrined in the 1980 Education (Scotland) Act, as amended, gave rise to 'integration', a practice of increasing the proximity of children with special needs – in locational, functional or social terms – to their mainstream peers.

By the early 1990s, serious reservations were being expressed about the value of integration as a concept and about its operation in practice. Commentators argued that integration was merely concerned with distributive calculus – placing children within mainstream schools – and not with the quality of their experiences (Slee, 1996). Meanwhile, Warnock herself admitted that some of the committee's pronouncements, especially with regard to the assessment and recording of children with special educational needs, had been a big mistake (Allan, 1999). A replacement term was sought and 'inclusion' emerged. Inclusion was intended as a radical alternative to integration by requiring schools and teachers, not only to increase participation, but also to remove some of the exclusionary pressures from within schools and classrooms. These pressures arise from environmental, structural and attitudinal barriers, the last of which is perhaps the most significant. Inclusion was not intended to be directed at a discrete population identified as having special educational needs, but at all children. Inclusion, then, is a political and social struggle which foregrounds difference and identity and which involves whole-school and teacher reform. It has moved from being specific to children with special educational needs to being a central part of the current government agenda, but so far there is little evidence of systemic change taking place. Furthermore, race and ethnicity, gender and social class continue to be largely absent from discourses on inclusion and Almeida Diniz and Usmani (2001) have drawn attention to the highly race-blind nature of inclusion policy and practice within Scotland.

'Social exclusion', one of New Labour's big ideas, has been directed largely at disenfranchised groups, such as the unemployed, the homeless and children who are at risk. The remit of the inter-departmental Social Exclusion Unit, established in 1997, is restricted to England. In Scotland, social exclusion and poverty falls within devolved powers, and the Scottish Executive has elected to establish a social *inclusion* strategy.

Within policy documents, the exclusion of disenfranchised groups and their disengagement from school and society is regarded as a serious problem. Social inclusion policies are intended to avoid deficit models and pathologies but they may contribute to the generation of a core of excluded groups and individuals. Curiously, the joined-up working imperative of the government has not extended to the management of social inclusion and exclusion and, within Scotland at least, these appear to represent two separate strands of policy and strategy, with quite different meanings.

Amid the conceptual confusion that exists around the meaning of inclusion, a strong and rigid special education paradigm continues to dominate policies and, inevitably, classroom practice. This paradigm is characterised by deficit thinking in which the problem is viewed as being located within the child, rather than caused by barriers in the school or classroom. Thus, we have the artefact of the included child, who is distinct and separate from the rest. This extremely powerful special education paradigm is characterised by a degree of certainty among the professionals who drive it and the effect of this is to silence the pupils who receive this provision and their parents.

THE SCOTTISH PARLIAMENT'S 'SPECIAL NEEDS' INQUIRY

One of the first Inquiries of the Education, Culture and Sport Committee focused on special educational needs. Specifically, it set out to:

- examine the diversity of provision across Scotland in special needs education;
- investigate the effectiveness of current integration strategies at all levels of pre-school and school education;

- investigate the effectiveness of transition arrangements for special needs pup
  stage in the school education system;
- consider how effectively the requirements of special needs families are unders
  fulfilled by education services.

The language used here – for example 'integration' and 'special needs families' – suggested that the Members of the Scottish Parliament (MSPs) needed to be alerted to the distinction between integration and inclusion and to understand the significance of the systemic changes implied by the latter. The inquiry began in May 2000 and the report was published in February 2001 (Scottish Parliament, 2001a). A request was made for written evidence and 150 submissions were received from local authorities, professional associations, voluntary organisations, parents and disabled individuals. On the basis of these, selected individuals and groups were invited to give oral evidence to the committee and MSPs undertook visits to a range of establishments.

The findings of the inquiry highlighted the wide diversity of provision across Scotland, amounting for some of the witnesses to a 'geographical lottery' (p .4) which was dependent on the attitutes and policies of schools and education authorities and the availability of funding. Parents complained about an inadequate range of provision and a lack of information and guidance to enable them to select the most suitable placement and some reported that their choices were strongly influenced by local education authorities and their financial agendas. Provision in rural and remote areas was particularly problematic. The MSPs' recommendations in respect of provision were directed at both improving consistency and introducing a greater degree of flexibility, for example through split placements.

The Inquiry took evidence from staff, parents and special schools and MSPs recognised the dilemma faced by parents who, presented with no reasonable mainstream alternative to a special school for their child, were likely to opt for a special school. Grant maintained special schools came in for particular scrutiny, as the Scottish Executive had been considering removing their central funding and was looking to the MSPs to guide their decisions. The evidence in this regard, however, was inconclusive and the MSPs were unable to give a clear steer to the Executive. Nevertheless, they recommended that special schools should be required to justify their existence in terms of how they would contribute to the inclusion of particular children.

The MSPs encountered some good practice in inclusion, usually attributable to the strong commitment of individuals, flexibility and resources, but also identified major barriers within schools, the most significant of which were a lack of resources, inadequate training of staff and negative attitudes. They were also made aware by school staff that the pressures to raise achievement, the publication of exam results and the inspection process had the potential to undermine their efforts to be inclusive. Those giving evidence made it clear that inclusion was about more than mere physical presence in schools and that schools, staff and pupils had to make significant changes. Witnesses also emphasised the importance of inclusion being concerned with the diverse needs of the school population and indicated that schools had to take account of the culture, background and experiences of all pupils and tackle 'institutionalised racism' (Scottish Parliament, 2001a p. 6). The MSPs, in their recommendations, provided a definition of inclusion as: 'maximising the participation of all children in mainstream schools and removing environmental, structural and attitudinal barriers to their participation' (p. 2).

The MSPs also called for systematic monitoring of the placement and educational experiences of minority ethnic pupils.

The training of both mainstream and specialist teachers was reported as inadequate by staff in schools, although the Scottish Executive officials who gave oral evidence argued that there was no shortage of information and support available. Teachers' unions expressed concern about the pressures on its members of having to support increasing numbers of children with significant needs, without adequate training and resources. The MSPs were impressed by those schools which had made use of parents as a source of information and advice to teachers and recommended a more widespread use of this key resource. They also recommended that inclusive education should be a central element within Initial Teacher Education programmes and that the training of all staff should include working with professionals in health and social work settings in accordance with the principles of the New Community Schools.

The formal system of assessing pupils with special educational needs and opening a Record of Needs, which follows them through school and into post-16 provision, came in for heavy criticism. Evidence from school staff, local authorities (including educational psychologists) parents and voluntary organisations identified the procedures as time-consuming, bureaucratic, adversarial, and inaccessible to parents. Furthermore, variation in recording practices across local authorities contributed to the 'geographical lottery' (p. 4) in provision. The MSPs recommended an overhaul of the system, and whilst they did not specify an alternative, suggested a number of criteria which a new approach should meet, including consistency and equity.

Evidence on transition arrangements from the local education authorities indicated some good practice at the various stages of compulsory schooling, but identified problems beyond the formal period. Parents complained that poor communication, a lack of planning and problems associated with the formal Record of Needs procedures compounded transition difficulties.

The inquiry had specified the requirements of 'special needs families' as one of its points of focus, and many of the parents and voluntary organisations supporting parents indicated that this kind of patronising terminology was part of the problem they faced. Parents reported highly negative experiences in dealing with professionals and in attempting to secure adequate provision for children with special needs. They found it difficult to obtain information, were discouraged from expressing an opinion and were put off by the overly formal assessment procedures. Parents' views, and the views of children, were ignored by professionals in spite of the wealth of experience they could offer. The Independent Special Education Advice service reported having to deal with parents who were often 'frustrated, angry and pleading for help' (Scottish Parliament, 2001a p. 9). The MSPs expressed outrage that parents should be treated in this way and recommended that resources should be made available for the provision of independent information, advice and training for parents and to establish informal support networks for them.

The parliamentary inquiry received a considerable amount of evidence from young people with special educational needs, either as part of the formal written submissions, in the parliamentary sessions or during the MSPs' visits to establishments. Disabled adults, who were members of voluntary organisations such as Equity, the Inclusion Group and the Minority Ethnic Learning Disability Initiative also informed the inquiry, and the MSPs concluded that there was much to learn from those with direct experience of inclusion and exclusion. Indeed the evidence provided by two witnesses highlighted the complexity of inclusion for the MSPs and the impossibility of arriving at an easy solution. One individual, now in Donaldson's school for the Deaf, told the committee of how he had 'escaped' from his mainstream school and was now confident and happy. Another individual, however, used the same term to describe leaving a special school. The MSPs' recommendations drew heavily on the perspectives of the disabled children and adults and identified the need to ensure that they are given opportunities to influence future policy and practice.

The MSPs' recommendations, and the subsequent extended debate in Parliament, highlighted the features of inclusive practice which they considered of paramount importance:

- *Parents and children's views guide practice*: 'Parents and children are the key to the solution of special educational needs – not the vested interests of one profession or another, or one party-political interest or another' (Gillon, Labour, Scottish Parliament, 2001b, col. 822).
- *The approach to meeting needs is pragmatic and child centred*: 'We are not asking for a philosophical or high-level commitment to the involvement of parents: we want a response to the blood, sweat and tears – too often and too many – of parents who are battling with the system (Stephen, Deputy Minister for Education, Europe and External Affairs, ibid., col. 772).
- *Inequalities created by conflicting policies, e.g. inspection and target setting, are addressed*: 'It is important that the framework of inspection is revised to take due account of the differences in working practices' (Peattie, Labour, ibid., col. 786); 'Targets need to reflect the nature of the school population. They should not be a deterrent to the development of inclusive practices' (ibid., col. 787).
- *Professionals' need for support is recognised*: Teacher training should ensure understanding . . . 'Teachers need time to share and prepare, to network and exchange information and to develop appropriate methods and materials for lessons' (Peattie, ibid., col. 787).

The MSPs expressed pride in the report of the special needs inquiry, viewing it, and the inquiry process, as allowing them to engage with the major issues affecting their electorate:

The report is another example of Scotland becoming a much better place to live in because of the existence of the Scottish Parliament, which is able to address subjects that would not have been given any kind of political airing under the old political system with which we are all too familiar (McAllion, Labour, Scottish Parliament, 2001b, col. 801).

CLASSROOM PRACTICES

Since the early 1980s, a consistent message has been sent to classroom teachers that they are responsible for all children in their classroom, including those with special educational needs. The intention has been to ensure that they can meet the range of pupil needs, with back-up from learning support specialists. Yet, the dominance of the special education paradigm forces classroom teachers to view children with special needs as requiring specialist help of the kind which is beyond their expertise, rather than accepting responsibility for all children. The mismatch of perceptions, identified in the parliamentary inquiry, between the Scottish Executive officials, who claimed that there was adequate information and training for teachers and the teachers themselves, who said there was not, could be explained as a problem of access by teachers to the appropriate information. On the other hand, it could reflect fundamentally different understandings about what inclusion entails and of the nature of the expertise required to achieve it.

Much emphasis has been placed upon collaboration among professionals as a way of meeting the needs of pupils in mainstream schools. In particular, co-operative teaching between learning support and class teachers was seen as an important way of providing support within the classroom, rather than withdrawing pupils, and sharing the available expertise. Research on these practices, carried out with Sally Brown and Pamela Munn (Allan et al., 1991), identified three levels of co-operative teaching:

- Level one occurred when the mainstream teacher taught the lesson and the learning support (LS) teacher helped a small number of pupils with SEN to cope with classwork.
- In level two the mainstream teacher planned and taught the lesson and the LS teacher helped a wider range of pupils (anyone experiencing difficulties) and provided guidance for the mainstream teacher on individual difficulties.
- Level three was the ideal version of co-operative teaching, whereby both teachers planned jointly the goals of the lesson, teaching approaches and materials to be used. Both taught the lesson.

Level three, the ideal, was rarely observed; levels one and two, with less involvement from the LS teacher, were more common. In some cases, LS teachers indicated that they had been unable even to get a foot in the door of some departments. When mainstream and learning support teachers were asked to talk about co-operative teaching, they seemed to have different perceptions about the role of the learning support teacher. Mainstream teachers valued co-operative teaching and the supportive role of the LS teacher, but saw this person as having specific skills and expertise to help mainly those pupils experiencing difficulty, rather than the class as a whole. Learning support teachers, in contrast, saw themselves as having a much broader educative role, helping mainstream teachers to support all pupils and trying to shift their mainstream colleagues' perceptions. But this was a frustrating endeavour and one LS staff member described herself as having an inverted 'U' shape, through years of bending over backwards to help her colleagues. The main difficulty for teachers working co-operatively related to the need for a fundamental shift in the working practices for each of the teachers and to issues of professional expertise. Some mainstream teachers were simply unwilling to change their lesson planning to involve the LS teacher more fully. One learning support teacher, for example, accompanied a pupil to History and simply sat through a traditional chalk and talk lesson. Another described the futility of going to a lesson where, 'we all just sat there listening to him rabbit on. It was just a complete waste of my time'. Other LS teachers said that they could have helped more if there had been time for planning together. Failing that, if the mainstream teacher had given an indication of his or her intentions before the lesson, the LS teacher could have been able to help with differentiation or adapt materials for particular pupils. Time and other commitments often stood in the way of this, but more often it was simply a case of the mainstream teacher doing his or her 'own thing'.

Special needs auxiliaries or assistants, as they are variously called, are an important source of in-class support. They may be assigned to individual children, as determined by their Record of Needs, or may spread their support out more generally, as a means of reducing the potentially stigmatising effect of intensive support on the individual concerned. Those assistants who have concentrated their support on one child have, at times, created a 'velcro effect' (Allan et al., 1991), which limits the child's social interaction with other pupils and which can hardly be inclusive.

Collaboration is a central strand of the recent New Community Schools initiative, with the expectation that teachers, social workers and health professionals will work together to meet the education, health and care needs of young people. Staff development to support this has, so far, concentrated mainly on activities such as work shadowing and whilst these have proved attractive and interesting to those involved, there is little evidence that practices have changed as a result.

INCLUSIVE CURRICULA?

The major curriculum programmes of 5–14 and Higher Still have had an extremely positive impact on the inclusion of children with special educational needs, particularly with regard to the messages they have carried about a curriculum entitlement. There have, however, been problems with the sub-text of some of these messages. The 5–14 programme of curriculum and assessment was intended to be as inclusive as possible and each of the subject materials contained a section on special educational needs, offering important guidance to teachers on the difficulties which children might encounter in particular subjects. The support for learning materials, which provided more specific guidance, were issued a whole year later than the general materials; this is likely to have communicated to teachers that meeting special needs was a 'bolt on', rather than a central, activity. In addition, the failure to involve learning support specialists in the development of the 5–14 materials appeared to have generated resentment and a sense of marginalisation. During the early stages of the implementation of the 5–14 programme, it became clear that level A was going to exclude some children and that there was a need to establish a pre-level A. Concerns also emerged about the reporting of progress for those children who were working towards level A or who would spend a considerable part of their school career at this stage and about how to avoid communicating failure to parents.

The Higher Still initiative did involve specialists from the beginning and the results were a much more embedded and inclusive curriculum programme, with levels at which children with pronounced special needs could participate and achieve success. Nevertheless, despite the clear message that a national curriculum entitlement was not supposed to be dependent on the location of the delivery, separate documents were produced for managers of special schools.

PUPILS' EXPERIENCES OF INCLUSION AND EXCLUSION

Research on the experiences of pupils identified as having special needs and their main-stream peers (Allan, 1999) revealed a mismatch between the teachers' deficit oriented approach to meeting needs and the desires and interests of the pupils. The youngsters with special needs were highly critical of some of the teachers' attempts to provide support, because of the unnecessarily high visibility of the process, and their mainstream peers endorsed this view. The accounts of the pupils with special needs revealed how they worked hard at trying to be included, and had developed strategies for transgressing against the more visible forms of support. In one example, a pupil spoke of how she had lost her long white cane in a nearby loch, while another refused to undergo rehabilitation training anywhere near the school. These strategies often frustrated the teachers' attempts to provide support and they were, at times, highly critical of pupils who were not 'accepting their condition' (p. 102) or the help that was available.

This clash between the teachers' needs based approach and the pupils' desire to be included in the most invisible way possible was recognised by the mainstream pupils within this research, who expressed anger at teachers who singled out individuals unnecessarily for special treatment, who were patronising towards particular pupils or who 'overprotect them, overtreat them' (p. 41). The mainstream pupils argued that their disabled peers wanted 'to be treated like everyone else' (p. 63), but acknowledged that it was sometimes problematic because not helping someone could make things worse. Their accounts of inclusion suggested that they played a key role as 'inclusion gatekeepers' (p. 31), supporting the process through pastoral and pedagogic strategies, and by allowing certain pupils to break some of the informal rules about pupil interaction. The mainstream pupils appeared to want to support inclusion because of the benefits to individual pupils with special needs:

> They do seem quite immature when they're just in the unit . . . I knew Graham when he was just in the unit, but ever since he's come into our class, he really has matured quite quickly. Because he used to just muck around, make quite a fool of himself . . . He used to hit the girls and tell them to shut up, but he's changed quite a bit now. (p. 37)

They also noted benefits for themselves, in terms of increased understanding of difference and difficulty:

> I think it helps us too to have more respect for them, because I used to think people from the special unit didn't actually have to do anything there, so I didn't have much respect. (p. 37)

> It's good experience for in later life, if there's someone in your job, if there's someone like Brian with Down's Syndrome comes and works with you, it's good experience because you kind of know what to expect. (p. 37)

There were occasions where the mainstream pupils deliberately excluded individuals from games, activities or conversations and justified this on the grounds that the person concerned was unaware that this was going on or did not mind. The pupils who experienced this took a rather different view. On the whole, however, the mainstream pupils were highly supportive of inclusion and their responsiveness to the desires and interests of their peers provides strong grounds for optimism.

LOOKING AHEAD

The parliamentary inquiry identified some clear changes which were necessary in order to achieve an inclusive education system for all pupils. The notion that inclusion was about everyone, and not just those with a specific label was a significant step forward in thinking about inclusion. So too was the directive from the Parliament to tackle the exclusionary barriers in schools alongside attempts to increase participation. The MSPs, in their report, sent out a firm message that inclusion was achievable, but only with major systemic changes and, most of all, strong commitment from everyone.

The inquiry process appears to have created a space for politicians to engage in a more sophisticated form of policy making than has hitherto been the case and to demand greater responsibility from government ministers and officials. The level of understanding about inclusion achieved by the MSPs who served on the Education, Culture and Sport Committee, and by those who spoke at the parliamentary debate, was impressive. Not only did they grasp the point that inclusion required significant change to the culture, ethos and practices of mainstream schools, but they also refused to reduce the debate to simplistic alternatives in the way that so many aspects of educational policy are handled. In addition, some of the groups who provided evidence to the inquiry subsequently expressed their satisfaction that their views had been represented and taken account of. Speaking on behalf of the Minority Ethnic Learning Disability Initiative, for example, Almeida Diniz and Usmani (2001) indicated that the 'open manner in which the Committee conducted itself in seeking to deal with a deeply contested field of social policy is a significant change from previous encounters' (p. 27) and described themselves as 'heartened by its willingness to listen' (p. 27). The MSPs have charged the Scottish Executive with some major tasks and it remains to be seen how they will respond.

The presumption of mainstreaming within the Standards in Scotland Schools etc. Act 2000 has been viewed by voluntary organisations concerned with inclusion as likely to lead to improved practice, at least with regard to school placements. This piece of legislation, in line with Article 12 of the United Nations Convention on the Rights of the Child, also requires schools to develop mechanisms to consult children on matters affecting them within the school. It places a duty on schools to develop pupil participation and active citizenship in the school setting and as part of the schools' development planning process. This legislation is to be welcomed, but it will by no means guarantee that schools will become inclusive spaces.

For inclusion to succeed, it will be necessary for teachers to reconcile their professionally based and deficit orientated approach, which focuses on helping, with the pupils' desire to be included in more subtle and less visible ways. It is also crucial that the voices of those who have the most direct experience of inclusion are allowed to influence any future developments of policy and practice. These include disabled children and adults, minority ethnic groups, voluntary organisations representing marginalised groups and individuals and parents. They amount to an enormous resource which, as yet, remains untapped, but which is likely to provide some much needed insights into what successful inclusion entails.

REFERENCES

Allan, J., Brown, S. and Munn, P. (1991) *Off the Record: Mainstream Provision for Pupils with Non-recorded Learning Difficulties in Primary and Secondary School*, Edinburgh: SCRE.

Allan, J. (1999) Actively Seeking Inclusion: Pupils with Special Needs in Mainstream Schools. London: Falmer.

Almeida Diniz, F. and Usmani, K. (2001) Changing the discourse on race and special educational needs, *Multicultural Teaching* 20 (1), 25–8.

Scottish Parliament (2001a) Official report of special needs inquiry, website: http://www.scottish.Parliament.uk/official_report/session-01/sor0517–02.htm

Scottish Parliament (2001b) Official report of debate on motion S1M–1931: special educational needs, website: http://www.scottish.Parliament.uk/official_report/session-01/sor0517–02.htm

Slee, R. (1996) Disability, class and poverty: school structures and policing identities, in C Christensen and F. Rizvi (eds), *Disability and the Dilemmas of Education and Justice*, Buckingham: Open University Press.

93

Education at the Margins:
Outsiders and the Mainstream

Elizabeth Jordan and Pauline Padfield

THE SOCIAL CONTEXT

The notion of the local comprehensive school, both primary and secondary, which reflects and supports its local community, is seductive and resonates well with the current political agenda on social inclusion. However, a careful examination of Scottish society reveals a lack of cohesion, as indeed might be expected in any community of diverse groups and individuals. How are different aspirations, rights and needs of different people to be met within the local school today? The contradictions engendered by conflicting educational legislation and policy directives expose significant institutional exclusion within the school education system. This chapter identifies some of the limitations operating within the present local comprehensive school, examines the processes by which certain groups of pupils become marginalised and excluded and describes some of the strategies for creating a more inclusive school system.

The new Scottish Parliament has given a clear indication that it intends to create a more socially just society. A raft of policy and legislative documents impacting on state schools reinforces the government's intention to place schools at the centre of the drive for social inclusion. These tacitly acknowledge that the secondary comprehensive school, as presently constructed, is falling short of the ideal that all pupils have equality of opportunity to achieve academically. This inevitably raises questions about the role of schools and the staff in them, concerns that are reflected in the national debate on education, launched in 2002.

Scotland's publicly funded schools educate a diverse pupil population that in September 2000 was officially estimated as 75,221. This figure does not include children and young people educated in 'outwith school' settings, which at any point during the school year 2000–1 was officially estimated as 2,104 (http://www.scotland.gov.uk/stats/bulletins/00135–00.asp). Acknowledging pupil diversity demands changes to accepted routines and practices and challenges the belief that schools are 'good places' and that all pupils should be in them. 'Different' is construed as 'difficult'; the 'lippy', the 'late' and the 'lackadaisical' pupils are often subject to various forms of exclusion. Rejection of such pupils is not solely by school staff. Schools operate within an extended social context, a fact often forgotten by those who simplistically blame teaching staff. In many cases, the wider school community initiates some forms of exclusion.

Much recent research has targeted certain groups of 'failing' or under-achieving pupils and this has led to a greater recognition of the complexity of factors involved, such as gender, ethnicity and different life chances. But a persistent lack of empathy with the values and behaviours of some individuals and social groups, together with the belief that they cause their own educational failure and social exclusion, continues. Conversely, families and communities can have negative perceptions of schools; their lack of previous positive experiences have long-term effects on successive generations, whose aspirations and expectations of being valued by schools are low. The different discourse of schools and their implicit rules of engagement can lead to misunderstandings and pupils believing that they have been treated unfairly. Such miscommunication contributes to confrontational behaviours in class, with minority ethnic groups, in particular, being more at risk.

As an example, Scottish research into Gypsies and Travellers, some of whom claim ethnic status, shows their continuing marginalisation, particularly in secondary schools (Lloyd et al., 1999). These communities have their historical and cultural roots in mobile life styles, but self-identify in different ways; as Gypsy/Travellers, as Occupational Travellers and as New (Age) Travellers (see http://www.education.ed.ac.uk/step/index.html). As yet, there are no published statistics on the numbers of Gypsy and Traveller pupils in Scottish schools. However, in 2002, additional categories relating to Gypsies and Travellers were included within the annual school census forms. These returns, completed by schools, can only provide an indication of the numbers of self-identifying Gypsies and Travellers actually attending schools. They provide no indication of the numbers who do not enrol or who have 'dropped out' of schools. Research in Scotland into Gypsies and Travellers' experiences in accessing and engaging with schools has revealed complex patterns of attendance and very high levels of non-attendance. These experiences are not unique to them; there are others who experience interrupted learning (Jordan, 2001a).

INTERRUPTED LEARNING

A key feature of Gypsies and Travellers that causes concern for schools is their mobility; particularly their unpredictable enrolments and departures, together with frequent absences (Jordan, E., *Traveller Pupils and Scottish Schools, Spotlight 76*, SCRE, 2000. These impact on the smooth running of the school, particularly in the organisation of classes, teaching groups, forward plans and allocation of learning support. Their attendance and attainment levels are relatively low. This pattern can also be seen in homeless families, those in women's refuge facilities, children whose care is shared within extended family arrangements due to parental divorce and remarriage, and, to a lesser extent, within 'looked after' children, 'school phobics' and pregnant schoolgirls (Borland et al., 1998). All share the experience of interruptions to the continuity in and coherence of their school learning.

A new term, 'interrupted learners', has entered the educational lexicon as yet another group of vulnerable learners in schools is identified and labelled. However, within this group there is seen to be an implicit subdivision, the 'deserving' (it is not their fault) and the 'non-deserving' (they bring it on themselves). Such subjective interpretations of absence and a focus on the learner, rather than the institution, influence the responses made within schools and authorities. Support for learning during periods of absence has generally been arranged on a 'grace and favour' basis. Some groups with patterns of disrupted attendance are viewed relatively sympathetically, such as those with chronic illnesses, young carers, travelling showground families and minority ethnic families making extended visits abroad to maintain cultural links and family relationships. They are regarded as members of the school community who will return; books and other resources can be loaned out with an expectation that they will be used and brought back. For those whose attendance is less predictable, there is rarely any continuity in support.

Pupils experiencing interrupted learning have other less obvious problems to contend with. All will have experienced a loss of peer groups and friends, and will have to negotiate entry into an already established set on each return or new enrolment. This process becomes more fraught with age and frequency of moves/interruptions. While teachers normally introduce new pupils and delegate others to support them, there are regular reports of name-calling, bullying and racism in the playground and on the journeys to and from school, especially on the school bus. Few such incidents are taken seriously and parents are often unaware of formal procedures for making complaints.

When pupils move across authority boundaries, some become non-pupils as no-one officially takes direct responsibility for their education, other than their parents who themselves often have more pressing priorities to deal with. A homeless family, for example, may be engaged in a constant search for somewhere to sleep; with no fixed address, enrolment in a school is not only problematic, but also a potentially embarrassing and diminishing experience. As a result, many 'interrupted learners' vote with their feet, and 'drop out' of school (Dobson et al., 2000). Families often give tacit support to their youngster's decision to self-exclude. Such laissez-faire parental attitudes are then identified by schools as the cause of the pupil's behaviour, rather than as a response to deficits within the school system.

SELF-EXCLUSION

In Scotland, a greater awareness of parental rights and responsibilities in relation to children's education has led to increasing use of alternatives to school education, which raises questions about the rights of children within society. Self-exclusion from publicly funded comprehensive schooling, for example, is reflected in an upsurge in the numbers of children whose parents have chosen to 'home educate', officially recorded as 349 in 2002 (http://www.scotland.gov.uk/stats/bulletins/00135–00.asp), but possibly as many as 5,000. Parents make this choice for a range of reasons, which implicitly, if not explicitly, rejects the learning and teaching experiences that schools are currently able to provide for children organised in groups of thirty, by age and by stage. Home educators argue that home education is unconstrained by the demands of a school's timetabled curriculum, that their child's learning is positively shaped by their ability to provide individualised teaching that is directly responsive to their child's learning needs (see, http://www.education-otherwise.org). Nevertheless, home education often provokes negative responses from those in state education. Bias against home education has clear resonance with that expressed about the use of private schools. In the case of minority ethnic and religious families, opting out of state schools arguably preserves cherished values and beliefs. However, these forms of self-exclusion can be viewed by critics as socially divisive and as contributing towards racism and sectarianism. The same critics are likely to see opting out as a rejection of social inclusion.

For children outside the system of public accountability, there are justified concerns about the quality of their academic and social experience, the rights of children to be heard, to be consulted and to have their own peer group. Community and/or peer pressure within some Gypsy/Traveller communities does lead to very high levels of rejection of secondary schools, with many not having the opportunity even to enrol at the transfer stage, despite successful experiences at the primary school. Yet, it can be argued that the option of home education supports diversity in cultural values and, in particular, the role of the family and the home. For some Gypsy/Travellers communities, home education is of paramount importance, particularly at the onset of puberty. Young Gypsy/Travellers are inducted into the families' work and value codes, and ethnic and cultural boundaries are maintained. The next generation is nurtured and prepared to take on its duties and responsibilities to the extended family. Schools report on their very positive strengths: adaptability, entrepreneurship, creativity, resilience, social cohesiveness and mutual responsibility. But there are also families where youngsters remain non-literate and lack the knowledge to gain access to opportunities others take for granted (Jordan, 2001b). This situation has been found in some 'young carers', the 'homeless' and 'school-age' mothers. Self-exclusion here does lead to marginalisation and disadvantage. Section 14 of the Standards in Scotland's Schools, etc., Act (2000), highlights the right of support for some pupils 'outwith school', that is, those with chronic illnesses, young carers and others with unspecified 'extraordinary circumstances'. It also refers to pupils excluded from schools as requiring similar support.

CREATING GREATER INCLUSION
OR SUPPORTING INSTITUTIONAL BARRIERS?

Some authorities and individual schools are trying to create more flexible responses to support diverse pupil populations. They organise and deliver alternative educational provision in a variety of ways, which reflects a professional shift from a traditional 'special educational needs' approach (distinguishing between pupils according to cognitive, physical and/or psychological difficulties) to an educational services' approach. These services have been described in two ways, firstly in terms of 'places', to which pupils must go, and secondly in terms of 'outreach teams' of teachers and others, who go to the learners. At least one local authority has joined its education and social work departments under a single director, as advocated in the Kilbrandon Report (*Children and Young Persons in Scotland*, Edinburgh: HMSO, 1995), to achieve a more focused response to high levels of 'disadvantage', a practice which has since increased. The multi-agency approach has allowed a more flexible and comprehensive response to the complexity of learners' individual situations.

The present authors recently conducted a study of Scottish local authorities' distribution and use of laptop computers as a means of supporting youngsters experiencing interruptions to their education, particularly those in 'outwith school' settings (Padfield and Jordan, 2002). The research aimed to describe the experiences of teachers and pupils with laptops, precisely because the technology has a potential for transcending problems of place and time in accessing curriculum materials. But, in policy and practice, no authority issued laptops to those excluded for disciplinary reasons, or to Gypsy/Traveller pupils; those pupils most distanced from mainstream schools appeared least likely to access laptop technologies. One service, which combined both a places' and teams' approach to education outwith school, supported approximately 100 pupils, yet its staff of over twelve had access to only one laptop. In contrast, another authority provided its teacher of Gypsy/Traveller children with a laptop and portable printer, to facilitate on-site provision for children whose ages ranged from three to sixteen, in numbers that varied dramatically from visit to visit.

Some teachers described laptops as beneficial to their practice. First, because pupils found the materials engaging, and second, because the focus of teaching and learning interaction shifted from pupils and their learning difficulties, to the laptop and its software. Other teachers were less convinced and even fearful of revealing their own technological inadequacies, which led to less than enthusiastic attempts to explore the possibilities offered by the National Grid for Learning and New Opportunities Funding. Overall, these teachers, who supported some of the most marginalised pupils, are effectively cut off from current ICT training and development work.

In the same study, service providers and pupils drew attention to the significance of breakdowns in relationships between pupils and the mainstream schools in their descriptions of alternative educational provisions. Some local authorities, with large pupil populations from backgrounds of 'complex disadvantage' who reject traditional forms of curriculum as irrelevant to their lives, had developed New Community Schools as a response to 'disadvantage'. Frequent examples of pupils they hoped to attract were pupils excluded for disciplinary reasons and Gypsies and Travellers. Education Centres, Community Education Centres, Youth Care Strategy Centres, and some residential schools were carefully distinguished from the New Community Schools. Several respondents described placements in these institutions as a process to help youngsters cope with large pupil populations and teachers, in preparation for their return to mainstream schools. Typically, provision began with one-to-one teaching, moving to small groups of six or seven, and included outdoor education and home-link workers or weekly reporting to parents. Of particular relevance for older pupils, considered unlikely to return to mainstream school, provision included work experience, in the hope of pupils establishing positive contacts within the local employment market. This latter approach was reported to show positive results in some authorities. Nevertheless, service providers stressed that pupils' names remained on their last mainstream school's roll for two reasons, to maintain communication links and to remind schools of their responsibilities towards all their pupils.

Authorities also organised specialist staff into designated outreach services, variously administered from psychological services and/or alternative education centres. Teachers went into schools, but also met pupils in a range of places, literally outwith school, which raises issues of trust and safety for both. Although such support was reported by service providers as initiated by the pupils' schools, examples were given of continuing problems in maintaining 'ownership' of, and contact with, outwith school pupils. These were described as 'slipping through the net' or 'getting lost' from the system, thus making it difficult to monitor an individual's progress. Nevertheless, all authorities claimed that pupils received support according to their individual educational needs. In reality, an authority's capacity to provide this was constrained by available support services. One pupil, for example, understood that 'difficulties with the laddies' was the reason for her alternative placement but, ironically, her eight peers were 15- to 16-year-old boys, each with different, but serious, 'social emotional and behavioural difficulties'.

Service providers considered that attainment levels were inadequate as performance indicators for justifying costly intervention work. Some providers expressed reservations about funding targeted services to achieve greater levels of social inclusion, with excluded pupils and Gypsy and Traveller families being frequently mentioned as non-deserving of extra funding. Others, sensitive to Gypsies and Travellers' general difficulties in accessing services, stated a wish to see a designated person as a 'point of contact', responsible for informing families of the range of provision, including education.

The study highlighted the serious difficulties that service providers faced in presenting 'outwith school' pupils for examinations. Nevertheless, examples were given of schools' support for 'their "outwith school" pupils', whose successful presentation and achievement in Standard Grade examinations involved scarce specialist staff in escorting pupils on and off premises, providing cover for invigilation and supervising them during breaks. One boy, excluded by a school that remained as the presenting centre, had prepared for seven Standard Grade examinations, but was not provided with a timetable or information about where the examinations were to take place. The school had simply forgotten to send the information he needed.

One unintended consequence of having designated examination centres was that the successful work of pupils and teachers in alternative settings was not publicly recognised, as examination attainments were absorbed into the presenting schools' statistics. Staff frequently rejected the use of 'attainment' as an appropriate measure of educational outcomes. They and the pupils argued that 'achievement' was better able to accommodate the links between personal and formal progress. Demonstration of achievement (successful interventions) was illustrated through individual accounts; for example, a pupil, initially described as 'out of control' and not able to achieve formal objectives, after intervention work achieved four modules in an accredited course.

In conclusion, the most marginalised pupils are still at risk of social exclusion despite significant attempts to meet their needs more effectively. Exclusionary processes within school systems, including the fragmented character of support projects, reveal that an integrated approach has not generally been achieved. Whilst national guidance documents advocate 'joined up approaches', their focus continues to be on discrete groups supported by central funding mechanisms that produce piecemeal developments.

REFERENCES

Borland, M., Pearson, C., Hill, M., Tisdall, K. and Bloomfield, I. (1998) *Education and Care Away from Home*, Edinburgh: SCRE.

Dobson, J. M., Henthorne, K. and Lynas, Z., (2000) *Pupil Mobility in Schools: Final Report*, London: University College London.

Jordan, E. (2001a) Interrupted learning: the Traveller paradigm. Support for learning, *British Journal of Learning Support*, 16 (3), 128–34.

Jordan, E. (2001b) Exclusion of Travellers in state schools, *Educational Research*, 43 (2), 117–32.

Lloyd, G., Stead, J., Jordan, E. and Norris, C. (1999) Teachers and Gypsy Travellers, *Scottish Educational Review*, 31 (1), 48–65.

Padfield, P. and Jordan, E. (2002) *Interrupted Learning: Laptops and their Communicative Possibilities*, research report, Scottish Traveller Education Programme: Edinburgh: University of Edinburgh.

94

Psychological Services and their Impact

Tommy MacKay

A UNIQUE STATUTORY FOUNDATION

Educational psychology services in Scotland are unique. They are built on a statutory foundation which is broader than for any other country in the world (MacKay, 1996). Their functions are prescribed in section 4 of the Education (Scotland) Act 1980, with subsequent amendments, as follows:

> It shall be the duty of every education authority to provide for their area a psychological service in clinics or elsewhere, and the functions of that service shall include –
> (a) the study of children with special educational needs;
> (b) the giving of advice to parents and teachers as to appropriate methods of education for such children;
> (c) in suitable cases, provision for the special educational needs of such children in clinics;
> (d) the giving of advice to a local authority within the meaning of the Social Work (Scotland) Act 1968 regarding the assessment of the needs of any child for the purposes of any of the provisions of that or any other enactment.

In a number of respects these duties will be seen as having much in common with the work done by psychologists elsewhere in the UK, but there are several important differences. First, while sharing many aspects of professional practice and development with services in England and Wales, Scottish services are fundamentally different in that all of the above duties are mandatory and not discretionary. While, for example, the contribution of the educational psychologist in England and Wales is generally wide ranging, the duties which must be provided by law are narrow, and are limited to the assessment of children and young people in relation to the Statement of Needs. In Scotland, the psychological assessment for the Record of Needs, far from being the exclusive or even the principal statutory duty of the psychologist, is simply a specific requirement added to the general duties which have been described.

Second, the term 'special educational needs' when used to describe the functions of psychological services is intended to be of very broad interpretation. It is a direct replacement for the older term 'handicapped, backward and difficult children', which it was an attempt to modernise. The population of children and young people embraced by this description has been defined in statutory instruments and official guidance, and includes the full range of psychological problems of childhood, whether educational, behavioural or developmental, and whether occurring in the context of school or elsewhere. Indeed, the single most important legislative statement that can be made about educational psychology in Scotland is that it is not a school psychological service, but provides such a service as part of a wider statutory remit.

Third, the breadth of the psychologist's role outwith the narrower sphere of education is reflected in the reference to the Social Work (Scotland) Act 1968. This relates to another distinctive feature of Scottish legislation, the Children's Hearing system, which operates as an alternative to the court system for children in trouble, and for which the psychologist has a duty to provide assessment and advice.

DEVELOPMENT OF CHILD GUIDANCE SERVICES

Educational psychology is a relatively young profession, and its development in Scotland dates from the 1920s. The context in which it developed was set by its parent discipline child psychology, which had become an established subject in the universities by the end of the nineteenth century. In 1884 Francis Galton had opened in London his anthropometric laboratory for the study of individual differences, and had advocated the scientific study of children. James Sully, a founder member of the British Psychological Society and convenor of its first meeting in 1901, opened a psychological laboratory in 1896. In his classic *Studies of Childhood* (London: Longmans Green, 1896) he outlined the importance of 'the careful, methodic study of the individual child', and teachers and parents were invited to take difficult children to his laboratory for examination and advice on treatment. Sully paved the way for a new kind of specialist to work with children in the educational sphere, and in 1913 Cyril Burt became the first educational psychologist in the UK on his appointment to London County Council.

These events had a significant influence on the development of child guidance services in Scotland (McKnight, 1978). In 1923 the first appointment of a child psychologist was made when Kennedy Fraser was appointed jointly by Jordanhill College to train teachers for schools for the mentally handicapped and by Glasgow Education Committee as a psychological adviser. Meanwhile the Bachelor of Education degree (the EdB, not to be confused with the current pre-service degree qualification, BEd) was established in all four universities, and this provided the background to training in educational psychology for many years. In the late 1920s Boyd established an 'educational clinic' at Glasgow University, while Drever set up a 'psychological clinic' at Edinburgh.

While these were the forerunners of the Scottish child guidance clinics, the first establishment to bear this name was the independent Notre Dame Child Guidance Clinic, founded in Glasgow in 1931. Indeed, it is also the last to use such a description, since the term 'child guidance service' was replaced by 'psychological service' in subsequent educational legislation. The Notre Dame Clinic was established on an American model which favoured a three-member team of psychologist, psychiatrist and social worker, and its main focus was on the emotional and behavioural problems of childhood. Together with the Fern Tower Adolescent Unit it continues to provide a therapeutic service to children and young people in co-operation with health, social work and education services.

THE EFFECTS OF LEGISLATION

The statutory period for child guidance began with the Education (Scotland) Act 1946. Glasgow had established the first education authority child guidance service in 1937, to which it appointed a full-time psychologist, and by the outbreak of the war several authorities had clinics in operation, mainly on a voluntary basis and operating on Saturday mornings. In recognition of these developments the 1946 Act empowered education authorities to provide child guidance services, with a range of functions expressed in almost identical terms to the present statutory duties. The Act also required the Secretary of State to make regulations defining the various categories of handicapped children, and these were set out in the Special Educational Treatment (Scotland) Regulations 1954. This had important implications for psychologists, who developed a central role in determining which of these children required special education.

The functions of the child guidance service became mandatory in 1969, while the Education (Mentally Handicapped Children) (Scotland) Act 1974, by bringing every child in Scotland under the care of the education authority, led to an extended role for psychologists in working with pupils with complex learning difficulties. New legislation in 1981 introduced the Record of Needs for children and young people with pronounced, specific or complex special educational needs of a long-term nature, and again the role of the psychologist was extended to become a central one in co-ordinating the recording process for education authorities.

In addition to the Education Acts, several other pieces of legislation have had important implications for the development of psychological services. Until the early 1970s psychologists worked almost exclusively with children, the main thrust being with those of primary school age and to a lesser extent with pre-school children. During the 1970s there was a rapid development of the service provided to children of secondary age and to young persons. The Record of Needs legislation in 1981 dealt extensively with the position of young persons over sixteen, and following the Disabled Persons (Services, Consultation and Representation) Act 1986 services were renamed as 'regional or island authority psychological services' and had a remit for the population aged 0–19 years. This new term was also soon rendered obsolete, and following the Local Government (Scotland) Act 1994 psychological services faced a period of major reorganisation under the thirty-two new unitary authorities established in 1996. The Children (Scotland) Act 1995 again provided a changing context for the work of psychologists, and extended the rights of children (including those with special educational needs) to have their views taken into account in decisions regarding their education and care. Finally, the Standards in Scotland's Schools etc. Act 2000 made provisions for promoting social inclusion and raising attainments in core skills, and in doing so highlighted areas in which the future contribution of educational psychology would be vital.

QUALIFICATIONS AND TRAINING

The training of educational psychologists has changed dramatically over the years both in structure and in content. Prior to the 1960s psychologists were first and foremost teachers. Indeed, they were frequently listed in Education Department records as 'teachers employed as psychologists', and it was usually recommended that they should have a minimum of two years' teaching experience. Entry to the profession was through the MEd honours degree (formally the EdB), specialising in Educational Psychology. In 1962 a postgraduate course in Educational Psychology was established for graduates with a first degree in Psychology and, to meet the demands for recruitment following services becoming mandatory in 1969, postgraduate courses of this kind were soon operating in Aberdeen, Edinburgh, Glasgow, Stirling and Strathclyde Universities, although several of these have now been closed. They offered the degree of MSc or the Diploma in Educational Psychology (later MAppSci).

There was considerable debate about whether teacher training and experience were to be viewed as necessary qualifications for entry to educational psychology, and for a period many employing authorities continued to demand full General Teaching Council (GTC) registration. It was the profession itself which moved away from this position and recommended new approaches to training. Now the only route into the profession is through an honours degree in Psychology and a postgraduate degree in Educational Psychology. This training recognises that it is the study and practice of psychology itself which best informs the assessment and intervention strategies used by psychologists, and which best equips them to give appropriate advice to teachers, parents and others. A broader experience of the education system than was provided under the former teacher training arrangements is recognised as being an essential aspect of training, and this is provided for within the structure of the postgraduate course. Most entrants to the profession take the four year single honours degree in Psychology at one of the Scottish universities and proceed to the two-year MSc in Educational Psychology at either Dundee or Strathclyde University.

Trainees generally require to spend at least two years following (or prior to) their first degree, gaining additional qualifications or experience in fields relevant to educational psychology. This may be, for example, in children's homes, teaching, research or the voluntary sector. As a result, entrants to the profession have for many years been very highly qualified and experienced in their preparations for beginning work as educational psychologists. Practice tutors from the field are centrally involved in supervising placements in psychological services throughout the two postgraduate years. During this period most trainees are seconded to education authorities and receive a trainee educational psychologist salary through Scottish Executive Education Department (SEED) funding.

The final steps in reaching independent professional status involve a probationary period working under the supervision of an appropriately qualified psychologist, to fulfil the British Psychological Society (BPS) requirements to become a chartered educational psychologist (a requirement for employment to new posts since 2002). Quality and standards of training and induction into employment are monitored by the training committee of the BPS Scottish Division of Educational Psychology. For psychologists in service, local arrangements for further study and training are supplemented by a national programme of continuing professional development supported by SEED, and by the opportunity to study for the recently introduced degree of Doctor of Educational Psychology (DEdPsych).

STAFFING AND RECRUITMENT

The number of educational psychologists employed in Scotland as at September 2001 was a full-time equivalent of 379 (Scottish Executive, 2002). This gave an average ratio of 1:3,269 of the 0–19 population. All of the thirty-two local authorities have their own psychological service, and in almost every case these are under the direction of a principal educational psychologist, supported by senior psychologists except in the smallest services. The average percentage of promoted staff was 42%.

LEVELS OF WORK AND CORE FUNCTIONS

Scottish educational psychology services were the first in the world to have a set of nationally recognised performance indicators (MacKay, 1999). These define levels of work and core functions, together with quality standards which represent good practice. Psychologists work at three main levels: the level of the individual child or family, the level of the school or establishment and the level of the local authority, and they have a key role in facilitating interactions between these levels. They also cover the entire age range of children and young people in both mainstream and special sectors in relation to a full spectrum of difficulties in education, behaviour and development. In addition, they frequently occupy the central role in co-ordinating the work of a multi-disciplinary team from health, education and social work and from the voluntary agencies. The breadth of this work gives psychological services a pivotal role in assisting the local authority in the management and development of resources in the field of special educational needs.

In relation to each of the three levels of work, psychologists have five core functions: consultation, assessment, intervention, training and research. All of these functions operate within an interactive context in which the problems of individual children and young people are assessed as part of a wider environment such as classroom or school. While assessment and intervention therefore may involve the use of a wide range of techniques and strategies directly with the individual, a central part of the psychologist's role is in assisting parents and teachers in supporting children with difficulties. This leads to considerable involvement by psychological services in parenting skills, classroom management strategies and staff training, and in the development of new methodologies for helping young people who experience problems in their learning, behaviour or development.

Although acting frequently in a liaison capacity between the education authority, the school and the child or parent, the psychologist in giving advice and in making recommendations must always act in the best interests of the child or young person. This is required by the Code of Conduct, Ethical Principles and Guidelines of the BPS, which sets strict professional standards and exercises disciplinary powers in relation to its members. One of the key skills of the psychologist therefore in giving independent advice is the ability to negotiate arrangements which will best meet children's needs, and to handle tensions which may arise from the perspective of the school or other agencies or indeed between the child and the parent.

RANGE AND SOURCE OF REFERRALS

The foundation of a psychological service and its predominant activity is casework. This is based on interactive assessment and intervention involving both the children or young people who are referred and the local contexts, such as school or family, in which they function. The range of problems referred is almost certainly wider than for any other branch of psychology. Reasons for referral include all of the traditional groupings within the field of special educational needs – moderate, severe and complex learning difficulties, visual and hearing impairments, physical disability, emotional and behavioural disorders and language and communication disorders. Overall referral patterns reflect an increased interest in and concern with the areas of specific learning difficulties, attention deficit/ hyperactivity disorder, the autistic spectrum and child abuse. Referrals may arise in discussion with a variety of agencies, and in some cases are made directly by parents. Older children and young people have a right to make a confidential self-referral, and this is treated in a way which takes account of age and maturity, and the nature of the problem referred. Nevertheless, since problems do not generally occur in isolation but within a family, social or educational context, the small group of self-referrals would normally be guided towards a position which encouraged liaison with other agencies.

It is the schools themselves, however, which have always accounted for perhaps 80% of the referrals to psychological services across Scotland, and much of the backbone of the work arises from the referrals of pupils with educational difficulties or behavioural problems in the classroom. While this may be the most routine aspect of the work of the psychologist it is often the contribution which is most valued by teachers and others who are seeking to support children with difficulties.

FORMAL PROCEDURES FOR SPECIAL EDUCATIONAL NEEDS

While it is estimated that up to 20% of pupils may have special educational needs at some stage during their school career, a small proportion of these pupils have needs described in the Education (Scotland) Act 1980 as 'pronounced, specific or complex special educational needs which are such as require continuing review'. In these cases it is currently the duty of the education authority to open a Record of Needs, and it is not lawful to do so unless there has been a process of psychological assessment.

It is important to recognise that since this group represents approximately one in ten of all children with special needs (SOEID, Circular 4/96, *Children and Young Persons with Special Educational Needs, Assessment and Recording*), they are not the principal focus of the work of psychological services. However, the arrangements for pupils in this category are of a more formal nature, and involvement in this area has made a considerable impact on the work of the psychologist. In addition to responsibility for the psychological assessment, the psychological service is also responsible in most authorities for co-ordinating the entire recording process, for preparing the draft Record of Needs on behalf of the authority and for planning the placement and other special provisions which the child or young person requires.

CHILDREN'S HEARINGS AND SOCIAL WORK

The Children's Hearings in Scotland were developed as an alternative system to the juvenile courts for dealing with children and young people in trouble. Cases are heard by a panel which has a range of options including home or residential supervision orders, or in some instances referral to the sheriff. Since 1969 one of the statutory functions of psychological services has been to provide reports to the social work department or to the Reporter to the Children's Panel in cases where psychological assessment and advice may be helpful.

The pattern of referrals from the Reporter varies from one area to another, and in some services accounts for up to 12% of the workload. The problems referred may occur mainly in relation to the home, the school or the community, and may centre on issues of child care and protection, criminal offences or school attendance issues. In addition to the cases which reach the Reporter, there is a large number of other situations calling for joint working between psychological services and social work, and the effect of more recent legislation has been to increase the involvement of the psychologist with social work and the Reporter in a wide range of child care issues.

IMPACT ON EDUCATIONAL POLICY AND DEVELOPMENT

As well as fulfilling their central task of assisting children and young people with special educational needs, educational psychology services have made a substantial impact on education authority policy and development. Their contribution has been significant not only in the special needs field but also in relation to education in general. This may be illustrated by reference to four areas.

First, the role of psychologists in shaping policy for special educational needs at national and local authority level has been a crucial one. Most authorities have relied heavily on psychological services in planning and developing their special provision, and in a national context psychologists have contributed substantially to government circulars and guidance in this area. Psychologists have also been the dominant force in promoting a philosophy of social inclusion, and in developing the context which enables special needs pupils to be educated along with their mainstream peers.

Second, through research, training, promotion of good practice and production of resources, educational psychologists have had a vast influence on classroom management strategies, anti-bullying policies, parent partnership, child protection procedures, learning support and school organisation and ethos. It is probably the case that virtually every educational establishment in Scotland at nursery, primary, secondary and special level uses strategies or resources developed by psychological services.

Third, psychologists have been central in highlighting the importance of socio-economic disadvantage as a major dimension in Scottish education. Through published research they have not only emphasised its significance as the principal correlate of educational under-achievement but have also developed a range of interventions for tackling its effects (see, for example, Boyle, J. and MacKay, T. (eds), Responding to the problems of reading failure in schools: a Scottish perspective, *Educational and Child Psychology*, 16 (1), (1999). In addition, in many education authorities they have been instrumental in developing a policy framework which targets additional resources on disadvantaged populations.

Fourth, the work of educational psychologists in Scotland in designing projects for improving children's achievement in literacy has been internationally recognised and has had a major impact on national practice. This contribution has been acknowledged in the design and development of early intervention projects for literacy operating since 1997 in all thirty-two education authorities with SEED funding.

A number of consumer studies have been published through the 1980s and 1990s, in which the views of teachers, parents and others have been surveyed. These have acknowledged the impact of psychological services and their value within the education system.

CURRENT ISSUES

The close of the twentieth century found educational psychology facing a number of fundamental challenges. To address these the Scottish Executive called for a review of provision of services, and established a steering group chaired by Mrs Eleanor Currie, with the author as consultant. The Currie Report (Scottish Executive, 2002) will have major implications for educational psychology in Scotland for many years to come. The most significant issues may be summarised under the headings of recruitment, recording and role.

Recruitment to the profession

The principal issue to be addressed through the Currie Report was a forthcoming recruitment crisis. A widespread and increasing shortfall in staffing had arisen for two main reasons. First, the number of psychologists leaving services each year through retirement and other causes was exceeding the supply of qualified trainees. A national analysis of age and staffing structures indicated that if current trends continued more than half of the workforce would leave the profession within ten years. Second, a number of developments including changes in legislation had led to considerable increases in the work psychologists were required to undertake. By 2001 staffing establishments had increased by 15% since local government reorganisation in 1996. It was envisaged that further increases would be necessary to maintain levels of service delivery and to fulfil statutory duties.

Four main reasons for higher workloads have been identified (Association for Scottish Principal Educational Psychologists, *Local Authority Psychological Services in Scotland: Staffing and Training of Educational Psychologists*, 1997). First, there has been a widened conceptualisation of special educational needs, leading to a very great increase in the number of children and young people identified. This has been associated with a greater awareness of parental rights, higher expectations of service delivery and increased levels of litigation in relation to public services. Second, there has been a broadened scope of applicability of psychological services. Some of this has stemmed from new legislation such as the Children (Scotland) Act 1995, and some from demand from councils for a whole range of new services such as responding to traumatic incidents affecting schools and communities. Third, the benefits to consumers of a more sophisticated, ecological approach to effective assessment and intervention has led to an increased demand for services. By using psychologists for anti-bullying strategies and many other initiatives at whole-school and authority level, councils have benefited from cost-effective and preventative roles for psychological services. Fourth, an extension of the principle of equal opportunities for children and young people has introduced demands on services to achieve new standards of professional and public accountability in a wider range of areas. This is reflected in the increased numbers of pupils with special needs in mainstream schools, a more central place in society for the policy and practice of child-care and the extension of rights directly to children and young people. All of these developments have imposed new levels of demand on services and have required a reappraisal of staffing establishments.

To address the recruitment crisis, the number of training places at Dundee and Strathclyde Universities has been increased from seventeen to twenty-four, with provision for further increases if required. This expansion has implications for finding additional staff who are qualified to teach at postgraduate level, and for securing a sufficient number of field placements for trainees.

The impact of the Record of Needs

Although recording is applicable only to a small proportion of the special needs population for whom the psychologist has statutory responsibilities, and is therefore not the main area of a psychologist's work, it is recognised throughout services that it has potential to occupy a disproportionate amount of time. Psychologists frequently find themselves under considerable pressure to initiate Records, often because it is believed, unsurprisingly, that this will provide access to higher levels of provision and resources. In many services the number of Records has increased to the point where service resources have had to be deflected from other areas of work in which the contribution of the psychologist might be more effective in meeting a wider range of needs.

Recording leads to a number of other tensions within educational psychology. The Record of Needs legislation is based on a static psycho-medical model of assessment where the focus is on deficits within the child. The 1981 Act required a 'psychological examination' of the child, and although in 1986 this was changed to 'a process of psychological assessment', the basic model still reflects a different paradigm from that which generally operates within psychological services. Issues of equal opportunity have also been raised in regard to the Record, as patterns of recording have not appeared to reflect adequately the real spread of needs as indicated by socio-economic and other variables.

These issues represent an important challenge to psychological services in relation to policy development and the planning of effective and equitable service delivery. The Scottish Executive has indicated that some of these difficulties will be addressed in a fundamental review of provision and legislation for special educational needs. Nevertheless, over-involvement in this area still raises concerns for psychological services. The Currie Report has therefore recommended that the servicing of the Record of Needs process, and other demands which take time from psychology, should be reallocated to other services.

The changing role of the psychologist

Educational psychology in Scotland faces two significant challenges in terms of the changing role of the psychologist. First, the profession is in the midst of what has been described as a 'paradigm shift' from a largely medical model of assessment and intervention to one which is largely educational (Kirkaldy, 1997). In the first model the psychologist operates as a separate expert technician who applies a range of psychological tests and techniques, the use of which is restricted to the profession. In this model, responsibility for children's problems is referred on to the psychologist by parents and teachers. In the second model the psychologist is a consultative colleague who works alongside parents, teachers and other key adults who have primary responsibility for assessment and intervention in the child's normal context. In this model the perspective is an interactionist one. It recognises that it is only changes in the social ecology of the child or young person which have sustainable effects on development.

Although this change of models is a pronounced one, it is part of a continuous rather than a discontinuous process. The early work of psychologists in Scotland was subject to two major influences which have had an impact on the development of services to the present day. The first was the influence of the mental testing movement, with its focus on the assessment of individual differences in children. The second was the influence of the child guidance movement, with its focus on treatment of children with emotional and behavioural difficulties. These two emphases point to areas which are still central to the work of psychological services today – careful assessment of the individual child with special needs, and providing specialist help to children with difficulties in their emotional and behavioural adjustment. However, it is the way in which these areas are approached that has been subject to extensive change and development. The early foundations of assessment and treatment may be described respectively as being psychometric and psychodynamic. Central to almost all assessment was the intelligence test (typically the Stanford Binet Intelligence Scale and the Wechsler Intelligence Scale for Children), which was used universally in identifying handicapped and backward pupils and in selection for special schools and remedial education. Underlying treatment was a theoretical framework which focused on dynamic processes within the child, resulting in the need for individual therapy over an extended period.

There is still an important place for counselling and therapy in an appropriate context, and the need for holistic services of this kind has been endorsed in the recommendations of the Currie Report. Nevertheless, the earlier psychodynamic emphasis on individual treatment has been challenged on grounds both of efficacy and economy. Psychometric assessment continues in fact to be widely used by educational psychologists in Scotland, but it would no longer be the significant thrust in the assessment strategies adopted. It too has been the subject of theoretical and practical debate at a level which has challenged its entire foundations. At the same time there has been an increased reliance on psychometric test results in the wider society as educational litigation becomes more common, and this creates a number of tensions. The way in which the profession handles this paradigm shift in its model of assessment and intervention will represent a central challenge for the future.

The second change in the role of the psychologist relates not to the model of working but to the actual range of work that is carried out. The statutory functions of educational psychology relate to children and young people with special educational needs. While this will continue to be a central focus of its remit, the Currie Report envisages a much wider contribution which will be of benefit to all children and young people. This parallels developments in other branches of psychology where the early focus was on problems and disorders, but has been broadened to encompass a contribution to the promotion of well-being and quality of life.

The Education (National Priorities) (Scotland) Order 2000 highlighted priorities which are central to the interests of psychologists. They point the way to a much wider contribution than special educational needs. The Currie Report emphasised opportunities for psychologists in relation to each priority: in raising standards of attainment in the core skills of literacy and numeracy; in supporting the skills of teachers and self-discipline of pupils, and enhancing school environments; in promoting equality and helping every pupil to benefit from education; in working with parents to teach pupils respect for self and one another; and in equipping pupils with the skills, attitudes and expectations necessary to prosper in a changing society. The training and skills of psychologists place them in a key position to make a significant contribution in all of these areas.

THE FUTURE

Educational psychology has addressed significant challenges to its structure and role, and in doing so has redefined its place and purpose within Scottish education. The Currie Report has affirmed its key role as an integral and vital element in the local authority structure, and its extended role in promoting social inclusion and in raising atttainments. At the start of the twenty-first century it is a confident profession which has not only adapted successfully to change itself, but has been the facilitator of considerable change and development within the education system as a whole. From its unique statutory foundation it has developed a pivotal role in shaping policy and provision in the field of special educational needs, and in addressing its current challenges it is well placed to offer an extended range of effective services within local authorities in Scotland.

REFERENCES

Kirkaldy, B. (1997) Contemporary tasks for psychological services in Scotland, *Educational Psychology in Scotland* 5, 6–16.

MacKay, T. A. W. N. (1996) The statutory foundations of Scottish educational psychology services, *Educational Psychology in Scotland* 3, 3–9.

MacKay, T. A. W. N. (1999) *Quality Assurance in Education Authority Psychological Services: Self-Evaluation Using Performance Indicators*, Edinburgh: SEED.

McKnight, R. K. (1978) The development of child guidance services, in W. B. Dockrell, W. R. Dunn and A. Milne (eds), *Special Education in Scotland*, Edinburgh: SCRE, pp. 97–109.

Scottish Executive (2002) *Review of Provision of Educational Psychology Services in Scotland* (The Currie Report), Edinburgh: Scottish Executive.

95

Social Work Services

Mono Chakrabarti and Mel Cadman

This chapter addresses some of the more significant current issues in social welfare provision for members of the community who have needs which they, their families and their other social networks are unable to meet, for a variety of reasons, without additional forms of support. Social work services has been created to help people to meet these social needs and to maintain their ability to function as individuals in relation to other people and their environment. Inevitably, it operates within the broader economic and social systems that society has developed.

Social work services are not so readily identifiable or so widely familiar an aspect of the welfare state as, for example, the National Health Service or the social security and education systems. However, social work is an accountable professional activity which facilitates individuals, families and groups to identify personal, social and environmental difficulties adversely affecting them. Social work assists them to manage these difficulties through supportive, rehabilitative, protective or corrective action. It also promotes social welfare and responds to wider social needs promoting equal opportunities for every age, gender, sexual preference, class, disability, race, culture and creed. It has a legal responsibility to protect the vulnerable and exercise authority under various statutes.

Social workers are part of a network of welfare, health, criminal justice and penal provision. Parliament lays down the legal framework and delineates the powers of statutory, voluntary and private agencies within which social workers practise. Their roles can vary in residential, day care, domiciliary, fieldwork and community settings, but they share a common core of knowledge, skills and values. The workforce involved in delivering this range of service provisions therefore includes, in addition to social workers, other professionals such as occupational therapists, psychologists and community workers.

Even more than most public services, social work is facing a period of major change. Services are being delivered by a growing range of providers outside of local authorities: there is a continuing emphasis both to 'specialise', on the one hand, whilst 'joining up' with other services, on the other hand. For the first time, formal regulatory bodies have been established to develop and monitor consistency of standards in both services and the training and conduct of staff, and a minimum honours degree level of professional training is to be introduced in Scotland in 2004.

The main focus of this chapter is to consider the key services provided and some of the major reasons for these changes and their probable impact in the future. First, however, it is important to look briefly at the historical roots of the development of social work.

HISTORICAL BACKGROUND

Personal social services formed one of the main planks of the Welfare State introduced by the Labour government in 1948 as part of its economic and social reconstruction programmes following the Second World War. Although subject to considerable amendment and refinement since, the principles, purpose and scope of this wide-ranging reform to the major instruments of social policy, which included housing, education, health and social security, are still recognisable today.

Social work services, as they are generally termed in Scotland, have their legacy both in the Poor Law, with its origins dating back to the eighteenth century, and in the philanthropic movements of the late nineteenth century. In the earlier decades of the twentieth century, more systematic intervention and support to vulnerable people, including orphaned and neglected children, people suffering from ill-health and criminal offenders, was made available under the auspices of church-based organisations, charities, courts, hospitals and, increasingly, local authorities. From 1948 onwards, the principle that such support services should be provided in a more comprehensive and less fragmented manner resulted in a process of gradual strengthening of the role of the local authority as the lead body in determining community needs and in organising and making direct provision itself.

Without doubt the landmark development in social work services was the publication in 1964 of the Kilbrandon Report, *Children and Young Persons, Scotland* (Edinburgh: HMSO). Drawing on research from the UK and Scandinavia, its central premise was that the adversarial court system then in place for dealing with young offenders placed far too much emphasis on matters of crime/responsibility/punishment, instead of dealing more appropriately with the psychological and social causes of offending behaviour: the phrase often used to encapsulate this philosophy is a concern for 'need not deed'. The committee recommended the establishment of a body of lay people, the Children's Hearing, to take the place of the juvenile courts and the creation of a Social Education Department within local authorities, whose responsibilities would be not only to provide assessments and supervision to children in need but also to intervene much earlier in the cycle of troubled and troublesome behaviour, that is on a preventive basis.

If not all of the detail of Kilbrandon's recommendations were actually implemented, his legacy of careful analysis of social need, concept of 'preventive' strategy and willingness to challenge conventions and vested interests, had a different and wide-reaching impact, eventually resulting in the passage of the Social Work (Scotland) Act, 1968. Its central purpose was to bring together in one, unified local authority department, services for all those user groups formerly serviced by a wide range of public bodies, and to disband juvenile courts in favour of Children's Hearings. The Kilbrandon philosophy also made its impact in two additional respects. Decisions about children experiencing neglect and abuse became the responsibility of the Children's Hearing and the preventive concept was embedded in the key duty of local authorities to 'promote social welfare'.

Although this basic framework for providing social work services remains current, a substantial range of changes in constitutional, legislative and administrative contexts have altered the pattern. In 1999, the Scottish Parliament assumed responsibility for virtually all welfare services, including social work, and, as in England and Wales, it has promoted the principle of 'joined-up' approaches to service through the development of, for example, one-door access to educational, psychological, health, youth and social work services in the

New Community School. This thinking is also reflected in the assignment of Cabinet responsibilities to ministers who, for example, carry a combined portfolio for education and social work. In concert with the rest of the UK, Scotland has created independent regulatory bodies responsible for both social services staff as well as services themselves, which are planned to ensure clearer standards and more consistency in provision. New legislation which will also impact directly and indirectly on the role of social work services is already in place and, in time, more far-reaching changes in the delivery of services can be anticipated. The consolidation of 'best value' for all public sector services will almost certainly lead to a greater involvement by the independent sector in direct provision of services and a reduction in the volume of services provided by councils.

THE WORK OF SOCIAL WORK DEPARTMENTS

This section considers the main social work services that come under the jurisdiction of social work departments. For convenience, these services will be clustered, under three broad headings, namely, community care, adult criminal justice, and children and families. The juvenile justice system, known as Children's Hearings in Scotland, will be dealt with later.

Community Care

'Community care' is commonly used as shorthand to refer to social services to vulnerable adults, including frail elderly people, people who are mentally ill or have physical or learning difficulties and people with addiction problems, who require substantial, planned support to live successfully in either their own homes, or in supported accommodation. Although the principle of supporting people to live in their own homes has been accepted for some decades, little concerted legislative and policy attention was focused on it until the advent of the National Health Service and Community Care Act of 1990. Prompted by a specific concern to tackle the spiralling cost of automatically funding residential care for the rapidly growing population of dependent elderly people, it established four key policy objectives. The first was a move away from institutions to community based service provision. Keeping people for years in large, depersonalising institutions, such as hospitals, is universally regarded as psychologically and socially damaging, creating major dependency and inhibiting the capacity for independent living. It is also very expensive. Despite this, previous attempts to reduce the substantial numbers of people in long-term hospital wards with both learning disabilities and mental health problems had proved remarkably resistant to change.

The second key objective was placing the lead responsibility for community care with local authorities and enabling a transfer of resources from social security and health to social work. The decision was taken because social work services were better placed both to understand the nature of the needs presented by vulnerable adults and to develop and use resources more appropriately and economically. The third objective was to place a greater responsibility on service users themselves to meet some of their support costs. Essentially, whether service users were charged for using broadly comparable services depended much more on chance and legacy than it did on any clear rationale regarding need. As an example, users of any health services were (and are) provided services entirely free of charge, whereas using a home help provided by a local authority would inevitably attract a charge. There was some evidence to suggest that people were driven to use services provided free of charge rather than those which best matched their needs: this was referred to as the 'perverse incentive'.

The fourth key objective, perhaps the most important, was the development of the principle of the local authority acting in a somewhat different capacity from its customary role as service provider, that is, as an 'enabling' authority. The accompanying roles associated with this were four-fold. First, this role placed the lead responsibility on local authorities to make and publish community care plans on a rolling, three-yearly basis, identifying needs, resources and actions necessary to remedy any shortfall in provision, in conjunction with other agencies like health boards, private and voluntary service providers and service users themselves. The second role emphasised responsibility for assessing individual applicants' needs, including financial capacity to pay for services, and to act as a 'care manager' in accessing, managing and reviewing the relevance and value of the care package to the applicant. The third role involved either providing services directly, or commissioning and contracting services from other providers from the independent sector. Although driven with notably greater zeal in England at the time of its introduction, throughout the UK this objective was clearly the means by which the Conservative government's commitment to introducing an element of privatisation into service provision was most apparent. In a Scottish context, however, the incentive for private sector involvement was much more limited, although the rapidly escalating demand for resources to cope with the closure of long-stay hospital wards and transfer of their patients to community settings, resulted in local authorities essentially choosing to support a major growth of service provision by the voluntary sector, rather than attempt to meet it themselves. The fourth role was that of creating a framework for the registration and inspection of all residential services within the authority's area, primarily to placate the numerous critics who regarded it as inevitable that the pursuit of profit by the private sector would be at the expense of providing services of acceptable quality. This role of registration and inspection is to be assumed by the Care Commission from 2003 onwards (see Regulation of Care (Scotland) Act, 2001 below): although most local authorities had already introduced complaints procedures, this, too, became mandatory.

Despite widespread support for this more coherent framework for delivering community care, numerous criticisms have persisted. Concern was expressed whether central government properly calculated the 'true cost' of providing community care to an appropriate standard from the very beginning. Financially, some better service providers have found it difficult to generate sufficient income to meet their costs and, as the degree of intensive support needed for some service users becomes clear, the shortfall can be considerable. Developing the range and depth of services needed to meet the wide variation in support required has taken longer than anticipated, resulting in well-publicised 'scandals' where improperly supported people returning from institutional care have perished or committed crimes. Primary carers, particularly women, were clearly expected to assume a disproportionate burden of responsibility for community care and, amongst those who have, many are critical of the poor financial recompense available to them. There are also problems in separating out roles within the integrated system with over-emphasis on organisational structures, communication difficulties and over-concentration on contracts rather than service delivery.

Adult criminal justice

If one attempts to think of a generic term for the practice of social work with people who are offending, the main term is likely to be 'probation'. In part, this stems from the previous Scottish organisational arrangements where there was, until 1969, a separate Department of Probation. Since 1969 many and varied arrangements for work with people who are offending have been developed. One important initiative was the development of community service either as a sentence in its own right or as a condition of a probation order.

Social work connections with the sheriff courts are more limited compared with their involvement in the Children's Hearings system (which will be discussed more fully in the next section). When probation orders are made it falls to Social Work Departments to carry them out, but such disposals account for only a very small fraction of sheriff court cases. The preparation of reports for the courts is, however, a large scale activity, mainly because the Criminal Procedure (Scotland) Act 1995 requires the courts to obtain reports about young offenders, that is those under the age of twenty-one, in order to decide whether any method other than detention is appropriate, as well as about older offenders who have not previously been sentenced to imprisonment or detention.

In the search for alternatives to imprisonment, the concept of the community service order has attracted a widespread interest. Offenders, and young adults, may be required to spend a fixed number of hours on some practical, socially constructive task. The supervision of community service orders falls to the social work department, and the staff undertaking this work generally specialise in it.

In 1991, the Scottish Office published a policy document initiating significant changes in the practice of social work with people who are offending, which was amended in 1996. The *National Objectives and Standards for Social Work in the Criminal Justice System*, generally referred to in social work as the National Standards have the overall aim to 'assist the courts to keep the use of custodial sentences to the minimum necessary for the protection of the public and the requirements of justice and to help offenders to stop offending' (Section 28). It achieves this by establishing a framework of clearly defined standards, procedures, and processes which have been widely acknowledged as enhancing the service to the criminal justice system. Regrettably, the aim of reducing use of custody has still not been achieved and Scotland continues to incarcerate offenders more frequently than anywhere else in Europe.

Children and families

Given further impetus by the advent of the women's movement in the late 1960s, much impassioned debate has centred on the appropriate role of the state in providing financial and practical help to children and their parents/carers. The essential need for children to have a caring home life and fulfilling upbringing is beyond dispute, although the traditional view that mothers are inherently better suited to child-rearing is now regarded as invalid and defeatist. Certainly children require a close attachment to dependable adults to survive and prosper, but it is now recognised that a number of people, both men and women, can share this role at no risk to the child and that others, for example childminders, can play an extended and constructive part in child-rearing from an early stage in the child's life. The implications of this changed understanding has also resulted in the wider use of substitute family care, including adoption, for older children who cannot be looked after by their birth families, and whose needs include recuperation with, and attachment to, a new family.

Children and their parents/carers have benefited from numerous changes as citizens and employees since the 1960s: reforms have been stimulated by a wish not only to support child-rearing but also to recruit and retain women workers. From the very residual maternity benefits of the 1960s the state has added: more substantial entitlement to maternity leave, better levels of child benefit paid directly to women, recently improved early years childcare provision and tax incentives designed to reduce the cost of its usage by low-paid workers. Workplaces have generally become more child and 'family-friendly' as employers have increasingly recognised the competitive advantage of promoting such an image when recruiting staff, particularly in areas of labour skills shortages. The better organisations, more often in the commercial than public sector, offer a substantial package of improved maternity pay and leave; flexible, family-friendly working hours; opportunities for complete career breaks with no loss of status on reinstatement; subsidised childcare; paid leave to accommodate children's illness; and so on. Welcome though these changes have been, Britain's support to children and families falls some way short of the best provided by many of its partners in the European Union. From women's perspective, the fact that they still do most of the housework, their average pay is significantly less than men, and that they are poorly represented at senior level in many organisations, illustrates how much still needs to change.

Child care service must feature prominently in any account of social work service provision. Supported by the spirit of what is usually referred to as the 'no order' principle, social work services departments devote much effort to working with children at risk of being looked after by local authorities and, especially, accommodated in residential settings. This work will vary from direct work with vulnerable or challenging parents to working with vulnerable young people in social groupwork programmes. Where appropriate and/or unavoidable, children and young people may be accommodated in either substitute family care, usually the placement of first choice, or in residential care, in most cases with a view to working towards their return home whenever the crisis passes. For the small minority who cannot return to their original families, the growing acknowledgement that children and young people can be psychologically harmed by indecision and 'drift' in care has not yet been matched by either a supportive legal process or an abundance of substitute families willing to foster on a long-term basis or, preferably, adopt.

Residential care provides a minority of placements for accommodated children. Most children live in small units, often housing between three and six children to avoid the prospects of institutionalisation, but an equal number spend sometimes substantial periods of time in residential schools which accommodate larger groups of children. The characteristics of children being accommodated are much changed from the past. They are, on average, older, have experienced considerable disadvantage over a longer time span and many are behaviourally challenging. It is only recently that looking after children and young people in residential care has been fully recognised as a demanding task requiring personal qualities and skills of a very high order, properly supported by training and financial support. A start has been made with both residential care workers and substitute family carers, although much has yet to be done.

A further complication for Social Work Departments is the increase in numbers of one-parent families as a consequence of marital breakdown and divorce, and the growth in the numbers of single mothers who prefer to bring up their own children. Increasing numbers of children are being brought up within lone parent or 'reconstituted' families, sometimes involving a large group of unrelated children and young people. Non-traditional family forms present unique challenges to their members and understanding and meeting these needs more fully remains a continuing challenge, not just for social work but also for the range of services children require, including health, early years intervention and education.

In extreme cases children need to be actively protected from one or both of their parents. The issue of child abuse, or child protection as it is usually described, perhaps more than any other area of childcare policy and practice, has brought the activities of health, education, police and other welfare professionals into considerable public, political and media focus in recent years. During the last few decades well over forty public enquiries in the UK have put the practice and decision making of social workers under the microscope. In many respects the issue has provided the main vehicle for articulating a series of debates about how the state, via its Social Work Departments, responds to the needs of children more generally and intervenes in the private sphere of the family in particular. If one takes an objective reading of various child protection related enquiry reports, one finds a picture which might suggest that social workers and their agencies have been caught in a political crossfire between being criticised, on the one hand, for allowing some children to suffer unnecessarily, sometimes to the point of death, at the hands of their parents or guardians, and, on the other hand, of intervening unwarrantably in other families and removing their children inappropriately.

Such cases can be referred to the Reporter to the Children's Panel and brought before a Children's Hearing. However, as suggested before, given the political sensitivities associated with issues of child protection, Social Work Departments are often having to develop a very complex set of procedural arrangements, involving a whole range of other professional groups in the decision making process. Therefore, it is important to establish a good professional relationship with teachers, in particular with those who carry 'guidance' responsibility, in order to provide effective support to this group of very vulnerable children (see Chapter 45).

THE CHILDREN'S HEARINGS SYSTEM

Scotland is unusual in having a juvenile justice system where a significant amount of professional input comes from social work which is controlled and managed through primary social work legislation. Indeed, as has been explained, the proposal to reorganise Scottish social work services was originally a by-product of the Kilbrandon proposals for the replacement of the juvenile courts by a system of Children's Hearings. The hearing system is based on the principle that the promotion of the best interests of the child should be the primary concern. Hence the welfare objective has received some significant emphasis.

Three agencies can be identified as the principal components of the hearing system: the Reporter, the Children's Panel and the Social Work Department. The police are quite independent of the hearings system but it need scarcely be said that the functioning of the system is heavily dependent on their co-operation.

Social workers have a number of extremely significant responsibilities in relation to children and young people who offend. When such children are brought to the notice of the Reporter she/he will ask the Social Work Department to provide information and assessment in three stages. First, an initial enquiry report will advise of any previously known involvement and/or concerns; if appropriate, an initial assessment report is requested, involving an initial contact with, and assessment of, the child and family's circumstances by a social worker; and only where the Reporter believes 'compulsory measures of care' are required will the final social background report be requested. Its function is to assess the child's circumstances, identify the level of continuing risk to the child, and/or risk of offending, analyse the parents' (or other carers') capacity to support and supervise the child, and, finally, to recommend what assistance, if any, a supervision requirement may give in supporting the child and family with future child rearing.

It is known from research evidence that these reports have an important influence on the Reporter's decision to bring a child before a hearing or not, and, in their turn, help to shape discussion in the hearing as well as exercising a good deal of influence on the outcome. When that outcome is a supervision requirement, social workers are given a central role. The great majority of such supervision orders allow the child to continue to live at home, but a significant minority are separated from their families because of a continuing risk either to themselves, from their parents or carers, or because of their disruptive or offending behaviour in the community and/or at school. Children may be placed in either fostercare homes, residential child care units (commonly called 'children's homes') or in residential schools. Supervision requirements must be reviewed no less than annually, but for children separated from their families, placements must be reviewed by the responsible local authority no fewer than three times in the first year, and no less often than at six-monthly intervals thereafter. Whatever the basis for supervision, social workers must develop a formal 'care plan' in conjunction with the child and his parents/carers, outlining the aim of the supervision provided and identifying how these aims are to be achieved.

Three aspects of this system of 'juvenile justice' are constantly debated. The first is whether the system deals effectively with the small, but significant, number of children who persistently offend, despite supervision. The second aspect is the question of whether the relatively informal process and very limited opportunities permitted for legal advice and representation, constitute a serious infringement of the children's right to be heard fully. Thirdly, there is the question of whether Children's Panel members, all volunteers and 'lay' people, have sufficient knowledge to assess the risks and needs in the complex care and protection cases where they are increasingly asked to make decisions. The first issue has led to the development of 'fast track' access to Children's hearings in cases where children offend persistently, currently on a pilot basis. The second concern has been recently addressed by the provision of an opportunity to make available legal advice and representation at Hearings to children who seem particularly vulnerable to removal from their communities. The third issue has been addressed by the advent of more robust risk assessment, review and reporting systems, together with more widespread access to 'safeguarders'. If these changes do not fully address all concerns, the underlying philosophy and transparent process of decision making continue to command more widespread support than would any reversion to a court-based process.

THE CHILDREN (SCOTLAND) ACT 1995

This Act came into force in April 1996, replacing most of the provisions of the Social Work (Scotland) Act, 1968 and later legislation affecting private and public law for children and families. It was driven by numerous objectives, principal amongst which were consolidation of legislation, clarifying the principle of the 'paramountcy' of the welfare on the child, underlining parental rights and responsibilities, promoting children's rights in terms consistent with emerging standards as represented in the UN Convention on the Rights of the Child and setting out the duties and powers available to public authorities to intervene. The only area of relevant public law which remained unaffected was adoption, still governed by the Adoption (Scotland) Act, 1978

The essential principles behind the Act are: each child has a right to be treated as an individual; each child who can form a view on matters affecting him or her has the right to express those views if he or she so wishes; parents should normally be responsible for the upbringing of their children and should share that responsibility; each child has a right to protection from all forms of abuse, neglect or exploitation; so far as is consistent with safeguarding and promoting the child's welfare, the public authority should promote the upbringing of children by their families; any intervention by a public authority in the life of a child must be properly justified and should be supported by services from all relevant agencies working in collaboration; and the local authority must prepare a children's service plan on a rolling, three-yearly basis.

In support of the above principles three main themes run through the Act. These are:

- the welfare of the child is the paramount consideration when his or her needs are considered by courts and Children's Hearings;
- no court should make an order relating to a child and no Children's Hearing should make a supervision requirement unless the court or hearing considers that to do so would be better for the child than making no order or supervision requirement at all;
- the child's views should be taken into account where major decisions are to be made about his or her future.

In addition, there is a requirement in various parts of the Act for those formally caring for children to have regard to religious persuasion, racial origin and cultural and linguistic background. This reflects an acknowledgement that Scottish society is multi-racial and multi-cultural and that social work service provisions must respond appropriately to the needs of children from minority ethnic backgrounds.

For the purposes of support for children and families, 'child' usually means a person under the age of sixteen years, eighteen years in certain circumstances. 'Family', in relation to a child, includes any person who has parental responsibilities for a child. Similar to the principles enshrined in the earlier Social Work (Scotland) Act 1968, a 'service' may comprise or include giving assistance in kind or, in exceptional circumstances, cash. The duty to safeguard and promote the welfare of children in need falls upon the local authority as a whole, and embraces social work, education, housing and any other relevant services required to achieve that end.

While the introduction of a child protection order offered similar powers of inter-vention to the earlier place of safety order, a child assessment order, requiring parents to have a child medically examined and an exclusion order, preventing an alleged abuser from living in the same household as a child, were added. For a variety of reasons, neither power has been widely used since the Act came into force although their introduction underlines the principle of offering a wider range of appropriate powers to protect children at risk.

Perhaps the most important change resulting from the Children (Scotland) Act, 1995, is the explicit recognition that improving services to children and families requires a collaborative and integrated approach to developing services, transcending the narrow departmentalism which had been the hallmark of services until that point. From 1998, local authorities have had to produce a three-year rolling plan for services to children and families, involving a whole range of interested agencies and children and families them-selves, both inside and outside of the local authorities; it is also updated every year. Its purpose is to identify need systematically, audit existing services and resources against recognised models of effective provision, and indicate how any shortfall might be rectified. The process of collaboration involved in service planning has stimulated a range of inter-departmental and inter-agency initiatives to improve the range, reach and accessibility of services to children and their families, breaking down many of the traditional barriers to integrated provision and creating numerous opportunities for imaginative approaches to supporting the most vulnerable children in the community. The New Community School, providing at its best a 'one-door' access point for all health, early years, psychological, youth and social work services, is but one example of the outcome of this joint planning approach and more such initiatives will certainly emerge in the future.

SOCIAL WORK AND EDUCATION

Despite their inevitably close co-existence in local authorities, relationships between social work services and education have been noted in the past more for their mutual disregard for each other than for collaboration. Thanks to their mutual obligation to participate in joint planning of services (see above), to central government's commitment to addressing social exclusion and, lastly, to the growing recognition that joined-up services have the potential to improve value for money and accessibility, much closer working partnerships are beginning to emerge. The underlying philosophy of the New Community School has been broadly welcomed by local authorities and the pilot schemes considered such a success that this model of integration is to be introduced gradually across many more schools in Scotland. The development of early years' services, home-link support to children and families at critical stages in their transition to formal education, and after-school provision are other examples of support designed to accommodate the needs of children most vulnerable to educational under-achievement.

The needs of children and young people accommodated by the local authority still pose serious challenges to services. Evidence from research published in 2001 illustrates that accommodated children fall far behind the attainment levels of the population as a whole. Amongst a complex array of factors which contribute to this are the pronounced social and psychological problems they have experienced growing up, the frequent disruption and discontinuity in education caused by moves into, and during, periods of being accom-modated by the authority and, notably, the potent belief that educational achievement is of little significance to the accommodated child. Although the developments represented by the concept of the New Community School form an important basis for targeting effective support, no one doubts the profundity or scale of the changes required to make a meaningful improvement in educational achievement or of the continued need for social work and education staff to develop innovative models of work.

REGULATION OF CARE (SCOTLAND) ACT 2001

The Regulation of Care (Scotland) Act, 2001, paralleled by similar legislation for England, Wales and Northern Ireland, brought about a fundamental change to the way both social work staff and the services they provide are regulated, through the creation of the Care Commission – responsible for services – and the Scottish Social Services Council (SSSC) – responsible for staff. These bodies, although partly funded by central government at the outset, are governed by a council representative of, amongst others, service providers, educationists and service users. Under the general umbrella of the Scottish Executive's 'modernisation', agenda, the Care Commission assumed responsibility for setting standards for all social care services, after an exhaustive period of consultation with various service providers, staff and service users, and for registering and inspecting all services provided against these standards. The SSSC, similarly constituted, governed and managed, is charged with developing a professional register of social services staff, with all of its attendant powers to define training levels and institute disciplinary measures; with developing a code of conduct for all social services staff; and with assisting in taking forward the changes to training at the qualifying, post-qualifying and continued professional development levels. It is also responsible for specifying how employers should ensure that these 'professional' standards are upheld in the workplace.

While the SSSC represents a new departure in social services, the principles underlying this development are clearly similar to those which have been in existence for some time for public service staff in law, medicine, teaching and nursing. Somewhat different, however, are the wider range of staff for whom it is responsible, working in residential, day care and community settings. The varying types and levels of qualifications formerly considered relevant to their roles and tasks represent another distinguishing feature. Defining standards acceptable to all of these represents a major task for the SSSC in the coming years.

FUTURE ISSUES

The last years of the twentieth and early years of the twenty-first century pose both serious challenges and many opportunities for social work services. Perhaps the most significant change has been the advent of the Scottish Parliament and its devolved responsibility for social work services. While at present mainly symbolic, the administration's decision to assign Cabinet responsibility for social work amongst three ministers reflects its belief that social work services represents an important, core activity which has an important part to play in the development of a range of closely related services in, for example, education and health. If, as in the past, social work still carries a primary responsibility for promoting social inclusion and for protecting the rights of a disadvantaged and vulnerable minority of Scotland's population, it has also achieved a wider recognition for its success in engaging with service users in ways which, at best, are exemplars of approachability, responsiveness and flexibility. Such participatory models of practice are at the core of the 'modernisation' project of the Scottish Parliament and much of the pioneering work carried out by social work agencies in the past can be applied to other services within local government and beyond. Social work has played a very significant role in participatory approaches to planning and developing services to a wide range of people too. Community care plans, joint health and community care plans and children's service plans have all demanded a capacity and willingness to identify needs, examine critically existing services, share ideas and develop new approaches to service delivery in close partnership with a range of other agencies and service users.

At another level, unrivalled opportunities flow from the arrival of the new regulatory bodies. For the first time, social work services has had to engage in a wide-ranging debate over the role, purpose and function of some key services it provides and, through the development of standards, establish much greater clarity about its tasks and responsibilities. The SSSC's role in defining codes of practice to which staff will be held accountable provides a degree of professional autonomy and credibility clearly absent before. Of course, its work is by no means concluded and concern still remains whether the decisions it reaches will be influenced more by convenience and affordability than by setting standards which offer the prospect of significant improvement in service delivery.

If social work services can be regarded as having dealt with major problems around its decision-making processes, planning frameworks and standards, significant challenges remain. At a very practical level, recruitment to social work training courses has declined sharply over the past few years and agencies experience increasing difficulty in acquiring and keeping the workforce needed to meet their growing commitments. Undoubtedly complex though the reasons are, the absence of student bursaries, together with relatively poor pay and stressful conditions play a major part.

About forty years ago, Kilbrandon presented a clear rationale for social work, in which the themes of integration and prevention were dominant. Current trends, represented by the Scottish Executive's thrust towards inter-agency and collaborative approaches, represent integration at one level, but arguably, at the risk of fragmenting the provision of social work services to all service users within defined communities. Over the past decade, social work offices have become more centralised and distant from the communities they serve, posing obstacles to effective community partnership, as distinct from partnership with other agencies. The key preventive role, reflected in the Social Work (Scotland) Act, 1968, may prove equally difficult to promote, as the preoccupation with service provision may be at the expense of stimulating the pioneering work with community groups usually judged to be the hallmark of effective prevention. At a time of continuing financial constraint, there is a risk that only what is readily measurable and verifiable will command support and that the key mission of social work services to promote the rights of its most disadvantaged citizens will be consigned to the margins.

REFERENCES

Asquith, S. and Stafford, A. (eds) (1995) *Families and the Future*, Edinburgh: HMSO.
Chakrabarti, M. (ed.) (2001) *Social Welfare: Scottish Perspective*, Aldershot: Ashgate.
Iwaniec, D. and Hill, M. (eds.) (2000) *Child Welfare Policy and Practice*, London: Jessica Kingsley.
Parrott, L. (1999) *Social Work and Social Care*, East Sussex: Gildredge Press.
Social Work Services Group (1997) *The Children (Scotland) Act 1995, Regulations and Guidance, Part 1*, Edinburgh: Scottish Office.
Scottish Executive (2001), *Learning with Care: The Education of Children Looked After Away from Home by Local Authorities*, Edinburgh: Scottish Executive.

96

Community Education, Community Learning and Development

Ted Milburn and David Wallace

The chapters of this book detail the comprehensive and diverse educational aspirations of our small nation. The focus inevitably rests on school and the extended opportunities that are provided by institutions of further and higher education. However, a society that values learning and truly promotes opportunity in learning as lifelong requires a more comprehensive and inclusive approach to the concept of education. If this vision looks beyond schooling and encompasses the diversity of non-institutional forms of community based education, and if it is to key directly into humanitarian concerns about inequality and exclusion, then it must also embrace a dynamic and thriving community education sector.

At the time of writing major changes are taking place in the provision of community education in Scotland. A recent review on the future of community education was charged with the task of considering 'a national strategy for community based adult education, youth work and educational support for community development in the light of Government priorities in relation to social exclusion and lifelong learning and advis[ing] Ministers on future arrangements' (Scottish Office, 1998, p. 5). The outcomes and implications of this review are described later in the chapter, but it is necessary to emphasise at the outset that changes set in train by its findings are by no means complete. The new form of community education, 'community learning and development' is still emerging and is finding its expression in local authorities, voluntary organisations and in institutions charged with the professional education and training of community educators. In order to debate these developments effectively, it is important to examine the nature of community education and move on to outline the special place for its values, practices, and methodologies within policies and strategies of community learning and development.

THE BEGINNINGS OF COMMUNITY EDUCATION IN SCOTLAND

Community education is one of the newest expressions of educational development in Scotland, tracing its organisational origins to the publication of the Alexander Report in 1975 (HMSO, 1975). Its conceptual origins go back much further and are to be found in the movements which strove to provide youth work, popular adult education and community development from the end of the nineteenth century to the present day. Many of these providers were, and continue to be, voluntary organisations, deploying volunteer workers.

Their partnership as providers with local authorities is considered a central principle of community education.

The interplay between the developing concept of community education and organisational practice has continued to be one of the tensions in the development of services to local communities. One source of this tension lay in the constituent philosophical and methodological underpinnings of the youth and community service and adult education services. Prior to 1975, almost all local authorities in Scotland had youth and community services, usually located within an education department. These services were generally at that time provision led. Education departments provided a variety of local authority youth centres, clubs and programmes through the deployment of trained sessional staff and full-time workers. Some of the youth work was not very radical, surrendering to education departments whose officials seemed to believe that youth workers should be young enough to know what young people wanted, but old enough to see that they did not get it.

Grants for youth work and youth work training were disbursed by local authority education committees to voluntary organisations whose aims and practice conformed to the best principles of youth work. Community development activity included the provision of support to adult groups who were establishing local activities, organising committees, and campaigning for more community resources. The period from 1965 to 1975 had been a time of expansion in youth and community work, which resulted in the building and upgrading of youth and community centres, the extension of full-time training opportunities and the development of a professional career structure with promotion opportunities.

During this period, the adult education provision of local authorities was also the province of education departments and run separately from youth and community services. Along with provision from university extra-mural programmes and the Workers' Educational Association (WEA), local authority adult education classes were offered in a wide range of community rooms, schools and halls. The focus of those provided by local authorities covered subjects which adults wished to pursue to gain passes in public examinations, social and leisure topics, and recreational activities. Classes which were successful (usually judged by the criterion of high attendance) were often offered again and were multiplied. These were accessed from the marketing which was undertaken through annual programmes and publicity in newspapers or from lists of venues, times and subjects which were advertised in schools and public buildings. The staff for these classes were invariably day school teachers who shared their subject with adults in the evening, and more rarely, with groups which met during the weekend.

Despite the success of many of these groups, this set of programmes was unmistakably provision led and generally relied upon numbers attending to determine assumed community need and educational planning. The mode for marketing relied upon participants being skilled in the identification and consumption of advertising placed in settings which many did not frequent. Small concession was made to expressed client need, attempts to meet the needs of other target groups, or the importance of seeking new contexts and modes of delivery which might attract new groups to adult learning. It was against this backcloth that the Alexander Committee reported and established the community education service.

THE STRUCTURE AND ORGANISATION OF COMMUNITY EDUCATION

The Alexander Report (HMSO, 1975) was essentially concerned with the future of adult education in Scotland and the committee quickly began to consider the issues highlighted in the previous paragraph concerning the focus, targeting, settings, curriculum and the social and economic aims of adult education. Having observed from research, amongst other things, that the take-up rate of informal adult education was approximately 4% of the adult population, and that these participants were predominantly middle class, the committee recommended radical changes to provision and practice. Aware of the strategic community locations of youth and community centres (many of which were in deprived areas), the community contacts of full-time workers and their capacity to identify local need, and the informal nature of existing curricula and settings in work with community groups, the committee recommended that 'Adult education should be regarded as an aspect of community education and should with the youth and community service, be incorporated into a community education service' (HMSO, 1975, p. 35). By establishing an organisational amalgam of separate existing educational services, the Alexander Report set in train methodological and strategic changes.

The new community education services which sprang up in almost every local authority in Scotland in 1975, and which existed until local government reorganisation in 1996, carried out work in three central areas – informal educational work with young people, community based adult education and community development work. In so doing, they created a community work arm of their education departments which allowed, and indeed encouraged, the identification of local need, the design of appropriate programmes and services and the engagement of local people in their delivery. This proved to be an attractive and invaluable strategic advantage to local elected representatives, particularly in areas where they were developing social and economic strategies. Many who had previously perceived education departments of their councils to be distant and professionalised by the concerns of teachers and schools, could see a clear role for community education workers in establishing and supporting local groups and providing local opportunities which the community required.

In almost all geographical areas, with the exception of the most far flung and rural, the community education service of regional councils was at this time delivered through area or neighbourhood teams of between four and twenty-five members of full-time staff, supported by much larger numbers of sessional paid youth workers, community development workers and adult education teachers. It is important to recognise that the full-time workers and their managers were not teachers, but professional community educators, subject to college training and professional socialisation which was very different from that of a classroom teacher.

Although community education was a statutory provision of local authorities from 1975 onwards, in that it was given such status in Education Acts, it was never accorded the mandatory status of primary and secondary schooling. In consequence, community education expenditure has generally never been in excess of 3% per annum of local authority education revenue budgets. At times of economic difficulty and cutback within local authorities in the last twenty years, partly because of this distinction in status, the community education service has been at the centre of targeted reductions which were disproportionate to its size.

CONCEPT AND PHILOSOPHY

The organisational marriage of the youth and community service and adult education which followed the publication of the Alexander Report heralded a period within which existing staff in these services worked hard to become community educators, not only in practice but in attitude and personal belief. Community education was and is characterised as non-formal in style, responsive to popular demand, reflecting local communities, embodying voluntarism, and concerned to stimulate self help which values people's experience. It is seen by Kirkwood (1990, p. 323) as a reaction to the ethos of traditional formal education in Scottish schools, colleges and universities. For those who had been youth and community workers, the emergence of this new service was both exciting and frightening.

The value base of youth work and community development already combined the principles of starting programmes from 'where people are' and using the natural processes of group experience as the basis for social learning. Good youth workers had always seen their work as educational, and used the shop window activities of sport and arts programmes, camping and residential weekends, international youth exchanges and youth councils as the means by which they created learning, sensitively adjusted to the needs of young people within informal settings. The youth work curriculum is not that of schooling, but relates to the creation of opportunities for young people to learn social and life skills; to become more confident and build their own self-esteem; to assist them to make reasoned decisions; to offer opportunities for participation and leadership; to encourage appropriate health choices and become politically aware (Milburn et al., 1995). Many of these principles and intentions also applied to educational work with adults in areas where substantial numbers considered they had failed in their previous educational experience, and for whom social and economic circumstances were oppressive.

The principles of community development were also of direct relevance to the aims of community education in that they turned curriculum development upside down and began with local need. Community development workers had already espoused a professional approach within which they strove to help local people to identify issues and needs which were important to them; to support these local groups as they prioritised the issues; to assist them with resources and advice as they worked to challenge and change local circumstances; and to encourage and nurture local skill and leadership. The principal tenets of the community development approach are based on the assumption that the process through which people move to identify and challenge local issues can be educational, and the gains are not only in community terms but also personal in the growth of skill and ability. Many local people have gained in confidence, developed negotiating and advocacy skills, learned how organisations and bureaucracies work, confronted professional gatekeepers, and become effective organisers and managers through such empowerment.

This marriage of professional philosophies was not without problems, in that there was criticism that the community education service, by espousing a community development model of adult education, was unable properly to develop adult education which was sufficiently cognitive. At the other end of the critical spectrum, others accused that the creation of the community education service was no more than an administrative fix, which joined disparate services. It is true that in the early days of the post-Alexander era, the youth and community service predominantly administered the previously existing adult evening class programme which in many areas was largely, but not exclusively, leisure and subject based. Workers struggled at this time to make changes in role and function, and even made leaps in professional belief and methodology, to work in ways which accorded with the aims of community education. It was not long, however, before key workers, advisors and senior officers began to build adult education and community services together with forms of educational work with young people, which were increasingly community based, issue-oriented, concerned with process as well as content and related to the specific needs of previously unsupported groups.

THE DEFINITION OF COMMUNITY EDUCATION

The definition of community education below, devised by the national validation agency for the training of community educators in Scotland, enshrines these conceptual and methodological principles:

> Community education is a process designed to enrich the lives of individuals and groups by engaging with people living within a geographical area, or sharing a common interest, to develop voluntarily a range of learning, action and reflection opportunities determined by their personal, social and economic and political needs. (SCEC, 1990, p. 4)

Based upon the values of lifelong learning; the plurality of beliefs in local communities; the central role of education in achieving personal and community improvement; and change; the importance of individual and group empowerment and the belief in a more equitable distribution of resources, the concept of community education is distinctive and challenging. Although this concept and philosophy has been linked with the Community Education Service as an organisation, it clearly informs work practices, methodologies and strategies which are not solely owned by departments of education.

THE NATIONAL FOCUS

The changes in professional philosophy and methodology outlined above led inevitably to demands for dramatic changes in the training and professional development of those working in community education settings (McConnell, 2002, p. 31). The establishment of the Community Education Validation and Endorsement (CeVe) Committee in 1989 provided a national focus for the development and endorsement of training for community education workers. In its guidelines for qualifying training, it provided a definition of community education which was adopted across Scotland, a statement of values and principles, and an outline of the competences required by community educators. The competences, which fell within the following key themes, required community educators to:

- engage appropriately with local communities;
- empower individuals and groups;
- develop relevant learning opportunities;
- organise and manage resources;
- demonstrate community education principles, purpose and values in youth work, adult education and community work settings;
- gather and use evaluative data to improve and develop programmes.

On the basis of these guidelines and principles, three universities, one distance learning college and one employment-based apprenticeship scheme provide degree courses to qualify community educators.

A key player in the growth of CeVe and its influence was the Scottish Community Education Council (SCEC) – its parent. Situated in Edinburgh, the council had a central responsibility to advise the Secretary of State and the Scottish Education and Industry Department on all matters relating to community education. Since its original inception in 1979, it was relatively well resourced and was responsible for national community education campaigns and initiatives. In addition, SCEC (later renamed Community Learning Scotland (CLS)) publicised key issues relating to the world of young people, adult education and communities and encouraged local action through very strong links with local community education teams and local authorities. Having both a national and international focus, it spearheaded, amongst other things, initiatives such as the Young Scot card and a survival guide for all school leavers, which has become a model for other European countries. Through national forums in adult education, youth work and community work it maintained a national focus on community education issues and developments.

To the dismay of the board of directors and the concern of many in the field of community education the Scottish Executive closed CLS in the cull of quangos which was undertaken in 2001–2. Effectively this diminished the unitary national focus on community education, threatened some very effective networks and dismantled the national progression of community based adult education, community development and work on youth issues under the community education banner. The community development focus and community learning and development are now being progressed by a new government agency, Communities Scotland. The focus on youth issues and youth policy, formerly progressed by CLS has been incorporated into the expanded national youth work and youth issues remit of YouthLink Scotland.

NEW CHALLENGES

A national pattern no longer exists for the provision of community education across Scotland. The Local Government (Scotland) Bill 1994 heralded a return to local government reorganisation in Scotland, and with its implementation, the reduction of large regional authorities to smaller unitary councils, most with a lower tax-raising capability. All local authority services have been faced with financial restrictions because of this and other changes, but the effect upon the community education service has been dramatic. Many local authorities were forced to cut staff, close community buildings, reduce programmes, and even foreclose aspects of their service such as the delivery of a community based adult education service by community education staff.

In some authorities, often in addition to a reduction in community education resources, the community education service and other council services have been amalgamated, to form new departments such as community and leisure services, neighbourhood services, community services, or community economic and development service. A number of former community education workers no longer work within education departments and new departmental heads will not necessarily see the work which continues as inherently educational, even though it may be life-enhancing to local communities.

New working arrangements have been forged and strategies are being developed with a wider group of professionals. The insights and work of librarians, sports and arts development workers, housing staff and others in these new departments are broadening the understanding of community education workers and the base of their work in local community settings. Community education staff speak positively of the ways in which their expertise is now valued and encouraged. This contrasts with the ways many felt undervalued and discouraged in education departments which were inherently driven by concerns with schools and formal education. Strategically, however, it continues to be a serious challenge to find ways to make meaningful development happen in communities with such large scale problems, when resources have been further diminished.

Methodologically, it will be interesting to see the ways in which community educators relate their practice to the new professional and organisational partnerships which have developed. It was through the fusion of such organisational changes in the last fifty years, that new practices emerged. A central thesis of this chapter has been that community education as a method is not confined to education departments, or to services of community education. Youth work, adult learning and community development do not cease to have educational components because they are delivered by community educators in new organisational contexts or through new departments. One of the central challenges to fieldwork staff in the future is to see that the precepts of that practice are grounded and enhanced. It was principally this type of thinking which led to the emergence of the focus upon community learning and development.

COMMUNITY LEARNING AND DEVELOPMENT

There has been concern amongst policy makers, managers and some field staff about what is considered to be a long-term confusion between community education as a way of working and community education as an organisational amalgam of the fields of community based adult education, youth work and community development. New priorities demand that the particular contribution of the community education approach, where the primary focus is upon the use of educational methods to develop skills, knowledge and capacity in community settings, is made available in a wider range of contexts.

The language of the report of the review group mentioned earlier (Scottish Office, 1998) is an acknowledgement of the transforming and developmental processes which community education can deliver. The report reiterates many of the methodological themes of this chapter which have identified community education processes as potentially transforming and liberating. Emphasis is placed on the focus upon motivation and confidence, personal and group effectiveness, widening access to formal learning institutions and involvement in civic life. In these respects the community education approach is being supported, valued and promoted for the future.

By emphasising that community education is an approach not only applicable to specific areas of community activity (youth work and adult education, for example) but a pervasive approach setting education at the heart of wider political intentions and community services, it drives the community agenda forward. Three fundamental dimensions of practice are highlighted by the review group as the revised functions of community education: to promote personal development; to build community capacity; and to invest, and secure investment, in community learning. These are to be associated with and linked to the need to deliver central governmental policies in the following areas: social inclusion; lifelong learning; and active citizenship. In future, these functions and policy areas will be combined to identify priority community education tasks and become a mechanism for the development of cross-sectoral community learning plans which are currently devised annually as a driving force in achieving local community outcomes. There is the inevitable concern to have clear and public targets, yet the document supports the national obsession with quantitative measures by only specifying examples which relate to the recording of numbers of participants and not the quality of the process.

The danger of seeing community education as simply an approach might be to succumb to the temptation of separating the activity from the principles and values highlighted earlier in the chapter. The redefinition of community education permits it to be seen now as 'part of' the work of other professionals in, for example, sports development, community arts, economic development, further education, social work, the police and health promotion. If this aim is to be effectively achieved, it will be essential for the recruitment and training of such professionals to reflect appropriately the community education ideals outlined earlier in this chapter. An approach which is disembodied from the values, principles and central tenets of the community education process will not bring the same outcomes as those valued by managers, community education practitioners and by local people in communities.

The Scottish Executive, in a circular of 6 June 2002 entitled *Community Learning and Development: The Way Forward* has committed itself to putting community learning and development at the heart of sustainable change for Scottish communities and to mainstreaming its values and approaches.

> The Scottish Executive recommends the adoption of the term – community learning and development – as an educative and developmental approach to community empowerment based around working in dialogue with communities to tackle the real issues in people's lives. We would like to see the term adopted by community planning partners i.e. with respect to community learning and development partnerships, strategies and plans. (para. 12, p. 4)

Despite a commitment to invest in a core of youth workers, community workers and community based adult educators, community learning and development is also seen by the Scottish Executive as a means of ensuring that a wider spectrum of public service disciplines increasingly adopt community education styles of working.

CHANGING PRIORITIES

Increasingly the work being undertaken by community educators is being labelled 'community learning and development' – partly to distinguish it from the previously exclusive link between the term 'community education' and community education services or departments. A central commitment for the future must be the increased involvement in partnership and joint working with other professionals and with community activists. Community educators have a strong interest in the development of joint working and many projects have reflected the value of such an approach. There are currently political, financial, social and professional imperatives which drive the move to expand joint working, and some organisational expressions, such as New Community Schools, attempt to embed these practices. Much more needs to be done in the area of interdisciplinary training and the organisational management of professional power relationships in collaborative work settings. The failure of trainers, managers and practitioners in a range of professions to take this seriously finds its expression in inappropriate interdepartmental point-scoring, the discounting of certain professional groups because of their perceived irrelevance, and attempts to freeze out community groups with behaviours which imply that their views are of no consequence.

The disaggregation of services, with local government reorganisation, into smaller units has had a negative effect upon developmental work with young people and adults in the community. In some authorities it has caused councils to close down the community development aspects of the work of community educators, and in others to withdraw these workers from community based contact with groups and their role in identifying learning needs and building customised learning programmes. Current research about local communities and their involvement in community activity and adult education points to the importance of the maintenance of sound processes of contact and engagement with groups at field level. In the past, inappropriate judgements have been made blaming local people for being apathetic and uninterested in adult education and community initiatives, when at the same time, insufficient credence was given to the importance of engaging with local people in identifying issues which are important to them as the basis for educational and social provision. Although these contractions of service are understandable in terms of the severe financial difficulties faced by authorities, the ramifications of such policy shifts are likely to be dramatic. Something much more constructive, developmental and sensitive is needed, than the simple advertising of educational opportunities to people living in excluded and disadvantaged communities.

TENSIONS IN LOCAL ACCOUNTABILITY

Community educators still working in local communities have, more often than other staff in local authorities and voluntary organisations, almost daily contact with local councillors. Part of the role of community educators is to work with local groups of young people and adults to identify issues around which improvement or change is required. These issues quite often concern such matters as housing, unemployment, sectarianism, racism, crime and safety, the lack of provision of local authority services, and poverty. Many of these are also the focus of the relationship of the councillor and her or his constituents. Community educators are trained and experienced in handling this delicate relationship between the legitimate and required support of local groups in voicing and advancing their concerns, and not becoming a part of the subsequent campaigns which often emerge. Their work supporting community groups and their regular meetings in strategy groups, mean that a trust and mutual understanding must be forged between the officer and the councillor. In times when resources are strained, the expectations of councillors can cause role strain for field staff, especially where councillors expect 'service as usual' from area teams whose resources and deployment strategies have been restricted by changed council policies due to cuts in services. It is not surprising that this process has had some astonishing outcomes, such as the occasion when a community group, in dispute with council policy in Strathclyde Region, occupied a large community centre for three months and locked out community education staff, education officials and local councillors. The campaigning of community groups, which is likely to increase at times when resources become more scarce, and the continued support of community educators in the identification of local issues, may well in the future lead to increasing strain in the relationship between councillor and officer. Community educators will in future need to juggle the competing expectations of community groups, councillors and their own line management with even greater skill.

CONCLUSION

Community education and community learning and development are about cultural change and differing forms of community action. The principles and values which are at the heart of this work relate to the importance of building confidence and self-esteem, enhancing social and life skills, and establishing opportunities for leadership through locally based educational programmes for young people and adults. Although it has provided many formalised educational opportunities through youth programmes and adult groups, the curriculum in community education is essentially rooted in the life experiences of its participants. Learning is therefore seen to begin, and is planned to develop, at the point of engagement with local groups. A bottom-up rather than a top-down approach is taken to learning needs and opportunities, and because of this, the approach of community workers, adult educators and youth workers may appear to exist in contrast to the work of educators in other more formalised agencies. However it complements, and is not in opposition to, the work of schools and colleges, with whom community educators have positive collaborative links. Community education has brought a community and youth work arm to the work of education and other departments in Scottish local authorities, which has given real contact with local needs, acted as a broker between local people and existing educational agencies and has, at times, caused such agencies to change approach. It is essential that community educators retain a clear occupational identity and confidence, shaped by the principles and work methodologies outlined above, which begin with communities first and educational programmes second. It is also essential, as community learning and development pro-gresses, that it retains a central concern with educational processes in community and youth development.

REFERENCES

HMSO (1975) *Adult Education: The Challenge of Change* (The Alexander Report), Edinburgh: HMSO.

Kirkwood, C. (1990) *Vulgar Eloquence. From Labour to Liberation*, Edinburgh: Polygon.

McConnell, C. (ed.) (2002) *Community Learning and Development – The Making of an Empowering Profession*, Edinburgh: CLS.

Milburn, T. et al. (1995) *Curriculum Development in Youth Work – Report to the SOED*, Glasgow: University of Strathclyde.

SCEC (1990) *CeVe Scotland: Pre-Service Training for Community Education Work*, Edinburgh: SCEC.

Scottish Office (1998) *Communities: Change through Learning (Report of a Working Group on the Future of Community Education)*, Edinburgh: HMSO.

97

Disaffection with Schooling

Jeannie Mackenzie

Reports of unruly, unwilling and disengaged students have been common throughout society since schooling began. In the Scottish context, there is a long history of concern around children's misbehaviour and absence, a history that challenges the popular understanding of the current level of disruption and truancy as a modern phenomenon. As early as 1675, schoolmasters were being 'urged to chastise children for "cursing and swearing, lying, speaking profanietie, for disobedience to parents and what vices that appears in them."' (Munn, in Holmes, 2000). Oral histories reveal that truancy, indiscipline, and social exclusion were very much part of normal schooling in the early 1900s (Jamieson, in Holmes, 2000). Patterns of school attendance (especially those that reveal gender differences) have always been subject to greater economic and societal factors. The golden period of Scottish education, when pupils were universally well disposed to formal schooling, owes more to popular mythology than to fact. The cluster of phenomena we now term 'disaffection with schooling' is both chronic and endemic.

DEFINING DISAFFECTION

The term 'disaffection' implies attitudinal characteristics such as estrangement, disengagement, alienation and hostility, yet it has traditionally been more acceptable to consider sets of observable behaviours displayed by those who are deemed to be disaffected, for example truancy, school phobia, defiance of teachers, disruption of lessons, and switching off from being taught. Professional responses have been reactions to these symptomatic behaviours, rather than to disaffection per se. It has been less disagreeable for those who provide schooling to classify and treat symptoms of disaffection rather than consider causes. The very act of defining the issue *for* young people rather than in consultation *with* them creates distance; for example, pupils, unlike teachers, consistently cite bullying as one of the main reasons for disaffection. The unpalatable fact is that many pupils dislike school; some find it has little meaning in their lives and others find the school experience painful and distressing. These are the pupils who have been defined as 'disaffected'. It is less common to define teachers as disaffected, although many also experience negative feelings about schooling.

PREVALENCE

To a limited extent, the prevalence of disaffection among pupils can be traced through statistics on school exclusion and attendance. In response to concerns about the extent of school exclusion, the Scottish Executive Education Department established an annual survey in 1998, to monitor exclusions using a national set of criteria and procedures. The survey reveals an increase both in temporary and permanent exclusions. In spite of clearer guidelines on exclusion and central government funding for alternatives, there are almost 40,000 exclusions a year, an average rate of fifty-one exclusions per 1,000 pupils (Table 97.1). Some groups are more likely to be excluded from school than others; for example, boys are much more likely to be excluded than girls. Children from ethnic minority families are more disproportionately represented in school exclusions, ethnic minorities forming only 1.6% of the total Scottish population, but 2.2% of school exclusions. Other risk factors in exclusion are being in receipt of free school meals, having a Record of Needs or being looked after by the local authority. Contrary to popular myth, schools are not physically violent places; by far the most common reason given for exclusion between 1998 and 2001 was not assault, but 'general or persistent disobedience'.

Table 97.1: Exclusion of pupils from Scottish schools

Year	Total number of exclusions	Number of permanent exclusions	Exclusions of male pupils	Exclusion of female pupils
1998–9	34,839	200	82%	18%
1999–2000	38,769	360	81%	19%
2000–1	38,656	322	81%	19%

(*Source: Scottish Executive Central Statistical Unit, 2002*)

Measuring school exclusion is problematic. It is not unknown for a school or a local authority to 'suggest' to parents that their child's needs would be better met in another school, thus avoiding the need for a formal exclusion. These unrecorded exclusions mirror recorded ones in the rejection of and disruption to schooling. However, in one important aspect they differ – the unrecorded exclusion leaves parents without the right of appeal, and recently this strategy has been challenged in the courts. The growth of pupil support bases may reduce formal exclusion rates, but with many teaching staff feeling ill-prepared to cope with the disaffected, responsibility can be all too easily transferred to specialist staff within the base, an exclusion in all but name (Boyd and Hamill, 2002).

Absence rates in Scotland have remained fairly consistent over the last few years and are low in primary schools – around 5% in 2001, representing an average loss of two weeks' schooling over a year. Although this appears positive, and could be accounted for by normal illness, many children are never absent and some have much more prolonged and persistent absence. Absence at secondary is high at around 11%, equal to more than four weeks' schooling over a year, or more than one half day a week. Absence increases sharply between S1 and S5 (Table 97.2).

Table 97.2: Absence of pupils in Scottish schools

Year	Primary	Secondary
1998–9	5.3%	11.2%
1999–2000	4.9%	10.9%
2000–1	5.4%	11.4%

(*Source: Scottish Executive Central Statistical Unit, 2002*)

Measuring non-attendance is also problematic. Attendance may be recorded as authorised and unauthorised; however the criteria used by schools in classifying particular cases may vary.

These statistics present a useful, albeit one-dimensional, picture of the extent of disaffection. However, statistics do not reveal what factors, apart from normal ailments, keep the pupils away. Nor do they reflect the feelings of the pupils who are physically present, but absent in spirit. An emphasis on rates of absence may disregard the patterns of absence that can affect a young person's schooling. For example, the seeds of low attendance patterns at secondary level are often sown at the primary stage although the rate of absence in primary may appear acceptable. Some pupils follow a trajectory from irregular attendance, through disenchantment to school exclusion, and this route lies through virtually unmapped territory.

Measures of attendance and exclusion do not inform us of those pupils who attend, give teachers little trouble, but who are deeply unhappy at school. Bullying is a major cause of unhappiness, as is low self-esteem (a measure of the variation between a person's aspirations and their assessment of themselves). Low self-esteem, like school exclusion, is gendered; with both boys and girls responding to disaffection in ways which are socially acceptable for their gender – therefore girls' disaffection may be as prevalent, but not so easily measured. Self-harm (for example smoking, cutting and eating disorders) are more often practised by girls, but are less easily observed than the aggressive and violent behaviour more often practised by boys. The invisibility of girls' distress may have serious consequences for them in later life.

Above all, statistics on exclusions and attendance do not reveal children and young people's emotional response to school. Not surprisingly, in a system devised and managed by adults, the right of comment and analysis has largely been reserved for adults. The feelings of pupils are generally given little consideration and less credibility. However, there have been attempts to understand more fully how pupils perceive the schooling experience and its effect on pupils. *How We Feel*, a seminal study of the emotional world of teenagers, explored the feelings of adolescents in secondary schools in Glasgow. Pupils numbering 1,643 took part in a survey on one school day in 1995. The study considered young people's feelings about a range of life issues, but among the results that are pertinent to this chapter are that 19% of these pupils reported feeling 'stressed', 37% described themselves as 'bored', 8% felt 'trapped' and 'useless' and 11% felt they were 'not coping'. Only 11% felt 'successful' and only 20% felt 'confident about the future'. It is important to note that this study did not reach those pupils who had absented themselves on that particular day; this was a cross-section of those attending school. Nevertheless, the accounts of their feelings about school challenge the adult myth of time spent at school as the 'best days of your life'.

While many young people spoke positively about their school experience, the levels of unhappiness and sheer despair recorded by others reveal a bleak picture of schooling for a substantial minority of our secondary school population (Gordon and Grant, 1997).

EXPLANATIONS AND RESPONSES

Explanations for disaffection fall into three broad categories: individual pathology, social exclusion, and social relationships.

Individual pathology

This approach sees the disaffected pupil as experiencing a set of problems, medical, psychological and/or familial. The emphasis is on the individual (and in some cases the family) as a suitable case for diagnosis, treatment and provision. Labelling is an inevitable outcome of this approach, from the 'maladjusted' or 'delinquent' pupil of the 1960s and 1970s to the 'emotional /behaviourally disordered' and 'school phobic' of the 1980s and 1990s through to the current, all embracing 'vulnerable pupil', the 'at risk pupil' or the 'pupil with problems'. Definition seldom involves the views of the pupil, and is rarely straightforward – the distinction between the 'at risk pupil' and the 'pupil with special educational needs' is often clouded. The 5-year old who refuses to sit down in class, disrupts other children's work and is highly distracted may suggest a professional diagnosis of inconsistent parenting, attention deficit hyperactivity disorder or emotional distress. Diagnosis may also depend on the location of original concerns (for example, at home or at school) and the nature of any professional intervention (teacher, psychologist or psychiatrist). The *For Scotland's Children* report cites the case of a pupil who by the age of thirteen had received four labels for his difficulties, 'attention deficit hyperactivity disorder', 'conduct disorder', 'clinical depression' and 'problems with parenting'. (Edinburgh: Scottish Executive, 2001)

Presumptions of individual pathology suggest professional diagnosis and treatment. Such intervention may be provided through the school psychological services, through child and family psychiatric services, social services or primary health care. Benefits may include access to specialised support for the child, the family and the teacher, an increased understanding among school staff of the pupil's special needs and resourcing of specialist staff and equipment.

The most effective interventions come about as a result of professional collaboration and pupil/school/parent partnership in decision making. As early as 1977, *Truancy and Indiscipline in Scottish Schools* (the Pack Report, Edinburgh: SED) recommended multi-disciplinary teams in schools. This advice was elaborated on in the *Young People in Trouble* report commissioned by Strathclyde Region in 1987, then the largest Scottish education authority. More recently, the Scottish Executive report, *Better Behaviour, Better Learning* (Edinburgh, 2001) and the HMIE report, *Alternatives to School Exclusion* (Edinburgh, 2000) strongly advocated collaborative practice. However, collaborative practice remains patchy. Most secondary schools in Scotland and an increasing number of primaries have some form of regular meeting to discuss pupils who are identified as having problems. A range of models has been developed, sometimes more by default than by design. In most cases the school psychological service is represented along with the local social work department, but school management frequently drives the agenda. Health and police services are rarely represented and discussion often takes place without pupil or parents present.

Factors that have been identified as inhibiting collaboration include:

- limited inter-professional understanding;
- limited commitment to pupil and parent participation;
- a tendency to fragment the difficulties the pupil is experiencing (into educational, psychiatric or social difficulties, for example);
- the value placed on inclusive practice compared to other priorities (for example social work statutory responsibilities, school curriculum, clinical practice).

Professionals frequently cite a child's failure to attend, to complete homework and to behave in an approved manner as evidence of inconsistent parenting and neglect. Models of intervention may be disciplinary, medical, educational, or participative.

Disciplinary measures may involve referral by the school to the local attendance council, a body of volunteers comprising school board members. The attendance council can order parents and children to appear in order to explain non-attendance and to be given advice and instruction. Parents may be referred to the courts and fined for failure to send their child to school. The councils may also refer cases to the Children's Hearing system.

Family doctors or the school psychological services may refer a pupil for medical interventions. Possible outcomes are psychiatric assessment and family therapy. Expensive resources, these are rare interventions and ones that normally involve a waiting list.

Educational interventions are based on an assumption that parenting skills are lacking and can be acquired – by teaching, through self-help groups or through modelling good practice. Parenting classes have become very popular with professionals in recent years, but less popular with parents, especially among the most socially excluded groups, who may be less willing than middle-class parents to expose to professionals their lack of confidence in their own parenting skills. Self-help networks for parents, such as Parent Link, take a more parent empowering approach. Issue-based approaches are also used, focusing on aspects of parenting that are generally acknowledged to present difficulty, for example, talking with children about sex and drugs and giving practical advice on cooking nutritious family meals on a low budget.

Educational approaches are also individual and are often offered in the home. In Scotland there is a long tradition of home visiting to provide support to parents with problems with health, social and educational issues and school attendance. Support may take the form of advice and advocacy and, in some cases, practical support and modelling good practice in parenting. Staff involved in such work may come from the health, education, social work and voluntary sectors. Attendance officers, who traditionally have been regarded as having an enforcement role, have increasingly developed the supportive aspects of their remit and this has been reflected in changing titles – many are now known as pupil support workers.

Practice in home visiting is based on two assumptions: firstly, that parents may feel more comfortable meeting with professionals on their own territory rather than in an office, and more able to raise their own agendas at such meetings; secondly, if problems are deemed to stem from the home environment, it makes sense to attempt to resolve them in that environment. There is evidence, however, that some parents find this approach intrusive.

Social Exclusion

Scotland is a deeply divided society. The capital city is the home of the new Scottish Parliament, one of the world's leading arts festivals and some of the highest priced housing in the UK outside London and the Home Counties. Within a mile of the centre, however, lie some of the most desperately poor housing estates in Europe. Almost 18% of Edinburgh school pupils are entitled to free school meals. (Free school meals are only available to families in receipt of Income Support or Income Based Job Seekers Allowance. In spite of the relative poverty suffered by these families, not all children take up the entitlement mainly due to the stigma attached. Lack of take-up is reckoned to be as high as 40% in some areas.)

In spite of Scotland's relative affluence, one-third of households live in or on the margins of poverty. Scotland has some of the highest rates of child poverty in the Western world, with one in five Scottish children entitled to free school meals. In Scotland, 8,000 children under sixteen become homeless every day and 360,000 Scottish children live in accommodation affected by dampness (*For Scotland's Children*, Edinburgh: Scottish Executive, 2001). The consequences of poverty for children are not felt only in access to basic human rights such as adequate food, clothing and shelter, but in the effects on self actualisation – the stark contrast between the expectations of the majority of children and the realities for the large minority.

The bleak disparity in access to resources (physical and cultural) that can stimulate learning, enrich knowledge and allow for the ready acquisition of basic skills has an inevitable effect on young children's ability to maximise what schooling has to offer. In spite of the traditional Scottish belief in the 'lad o' pairts' – the working-class lad who can achieve in spite of lowly origins – an analysis of educational outcomes against social class reveals social class as the single most important factor in academic success. The 'lad o' pairts' may exist, but he is an exception (Paterson, 1992).

It is not only the lack of resources in the home that inhibits academic success in the children of low waged and unemployed parents. The practice of setting (grouping children by ability in a subject area) has become more commonly used in primaries in recent years, and in some cases involves children as young as seven years. This social division further excludes already disadvantaged children by lowering attainment and motivation, especially in female children.

Since 1981, Scottish parents have had the right through the parents charter to request a place for their child in a school other than the one provided for their area, if that chosen school has sufficient places. The right to choose, however, is not straightforward; travel costs to a distant school are not refunded and schools that serve more affluent neighbourhoods may make demands in terms of school uniform, school trips and after-school activities. Subtle signals from school staff and pupils also may also exclude children. The last two decades have seen the 'comprehensive' ideal of Scottish schooling gradually eroded as 'sink' and 'magnet' schools have emerged (see Chapter 4).

Given the magnitude of the barriers that the children of the socially excluded must surmount to access learning, it is unsurprising that for many of them, school becomes a place where they are increasingly ill at ease.

For young people, localised, intergenerational unemployment caused by the contraction of manufacturing industry has led to low expectations and a dislocation from the mainstream of society that may be most evident in schooling, as outlined by Dr Richard

Holloway (formerly Episcopal Bishop of Edinburgh) in his opening address to the Schools for the Future Conference in Glasgow in November, 2001:

> The difficulty our education and training systems face in dealing with the children of the [socially] excluded is that they come from a culture of disintegration that has made them internal exiles in their own homeland. They are neither equipped to absorb the culture of the majority nor do they have the energy to revolt against it in any organised way. Rather than using their anger to generate change, it becomes self-destructive and locks them into cycles of despair. Society keeps them at arm's length and usually only encounters them vicariously through teachers and social workers.

Not only are the children of socially excluded families more likely to disengage themselves from schooling, they are also more likely to be excluded from school. When the uptake of free school meals as an indicator of pupil poverty is plotted against levels of school exclusion for 1999–2000, it is evident that there is a link between poverty and school exclusion, as shown in Figure 97.1:

**Figure 97.1:   Poverty/school exclusion in the
                32 Scottish education authorities, 1999–2000**

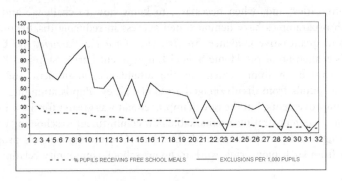

(Source: Prince's Trust (2002) Mapping Exclusion of Young People in Scotland)

Glasgow (1), with the highest rate of free school meals at almost 40%, also had the highest exclusion rate at 109 per 1,000 pupils, while Shetland (31), which had the lowest exclusion rate at two per 1,000 pupils, had the second most affluent pupil population. However, in spite of a strong association between poverty and school exclusion, there is variation between local authority exclusion rates that cannot be explained by poverty alone. An examination of five education authorities that have among the most impoverished pupil populations and share very similar free school meal uptake of around 22%, reveals very different levels of exclusion (see Figure 97.2)

A similar discrepancy can be found among education authorities with more affluent school populations. For example in 1999–2000, Stirling and East Renfrewshire had similar overall populations and similar pupil poverty indicators at 11% and 10.3% respectively, however, Stirling had thirty-six exclusions per 1,000, while East Renfrewshire had twenty. Although social exclusion can explain some of the discord in schools, there are clearly additional factors at work, such as the nature and degree of provision for inclusion.

Figure 97.2:   Poverty/school exclusion in five Scottish education authorities

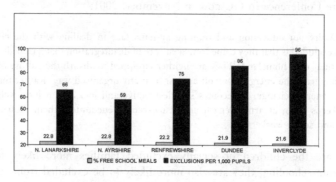

(*Source: Prince's Trust (2002) Mapping Exclusion of Young People in Scotland*)

The barriers to social inclusion in schooling have effectively been breached in some places by the home–school–community movement. Taking an empowering approach, this movement has encouraged parents and children not only to learn together, but to explore new possibilities, to understand and to be confident in co-operating with schools and education authorities, and, when necessary, to know how to challenge and change the system. Such programmes have demonstrated success in reducing disaffection with both qualitative and quantitative evidence. In *Breaking down the Barriers*, the University of Strathclyde's evaluation of the Home School Employment Partnership in 1998, Dr Brian Boyd demonstrated an improvement in the attendance, attainment and post-school destinations of pupils from disadvantaged areas of Paisley. Pupils attending local schools also showed improvements, but the rate of improvement was greater for those involved with the Partnership – demonstrating a remarkable new commitment to schooling on the part of the young people and parents concerned. The New Community Schools programme has learnt much from such pioneering work in home–school–community relationships.

Social relationships

Schools are social settings. They are extremely organised, and have complex hierarchical structures, especially in the secondary sector. The social world of the school operates intricate systems of both formal and informal rewards and sanctions. These are settings where the actors take on roles that are quite different from their roles outwith the school. Moreover, they are social settings that, although liable to considerable external control, also develop within them their own distinctive cultural norms.

Teachers experience considerable role conflict. Societal and political expectations are high and sometimes appear contradictory. In Scottish schools, the current dual emphasis on raising attainment and promoting social inclusion has been seen by some as placing conflicting demands on the role of the teacher. Particularly in the secondary sector, but also increasingly in primary schools, teachers struggle with the perceived contradictions between attainment and inclusion objectives.

Role conflict is also experienced by pupils. A pupil may be regarded as 'oppositional' and 'defiant' within the school, but be accepting of the authority of the parent at home. Other pupils may be classed as having 'low self esteem' and 'poor peer relations' within the school but be confident and sociable members of their local drama club. Pupils experience schools as hugely influential in establishing their perceptions of themselves, their ability and their potential. If the world outside school contradicts sharply with what pupils learn about themselves in school (or worse still, if an already negative construction is further confirmed), there is good reason to develop avoidance and defensive strategies (Mackenzie, 2001).

Pupils negotiate a minefield of conflicting school rules and social codes in striving to meet the competing demands of educational and social inclusion. Moreover, both sets of codes change over time and in different settings; the school's written code of behaviour may be adhered to more strictly by one teacher than another, and what is acceptable and to be admired among friendship groupings shifts as dominance within the group changes. While these struggles are evident in primaries, the effect is more extreme in large secondary schools where it is impossible to know everyone by name and reputations are made in minutes, but can take a lifetime to lose. The social world of the school is also highly gendered: both boys and girls are required by their peers and by their teachers to have gendered characteristics, male and female teachers tending to discipline girls and boys differently (Padfield, 2002).

As the adults in the social world of school, teachers wield considerable power over children and young people. That power differential does not remain uncontested. This is hardly surprising in the secondary sector where most pupils have reached physical and mental maturity, many manage responsible roles outside schools and most are ready to negotiate increasing autonomy. The resistance of disaffected youth creates internal conflict for teachers who expect their dominant role to remain unchallenged.

The emotional response of teachers to that conflict is transparent to the young people in a way it may not be to the adults concerned, and young people are able to make sophisticated evaluations of teacher ability to manage conflict positively. Teachers may use language which suggests a positive approach to encouraging good behaviour, but if these statements are accompanied by 'growling with their eyes', pupils are not deceived. Classroom relationships that are associated with teacher cultures of dominance, didacticism and distance have been shown to be closely linked to teacher/pupil conflict. However, when teachers are able to understand social behaviour, to express emotion and to access and regulate feelings that can aid decision making, then cultures of teacher/pupil negotiation, dialogue and affinity flourish and classroom experience becomes more inclusive. A socio-logical understanding of these processes can help prevent a deficit model of pupil behaviour while at the same time can avoid replacing it with a teacher deficit model. Such an approach will focus less on 'pupils with problems' than on social settings with problems. Interven-tions will empower teachers to use more inclusive pedagogies and to understand their practice as an interactive emotional experience both for the teacher and the learner (Mackenzie, 2001).

ISSUES FOR THE FUTURE

Scottish schools are changing. For some the pace of change will always be too fast; for others it will appear painfully slow. For many of today's pupils, changes will be too little and too late. Three principles that are driving change are particularly relevant to reducing disaffection. These are: a focus on children's rights; an emphasis on the school as a site for health promotion; and the expectation of collaboration in children's services. All three have been given a boost by Scottish Executive directives and the introduction of New Community Schools in 1999. Special funding has been provided to schools and other agencies across Scotland to innovate and trial new approaches at the local level, backed by Scottish Executive support.

The background to some of the changes lies in the staged implementation of the Children (Scotland) Act of 1995, the commitments under the UN Convention on the Rights of the Child and the obligations of European human rights legislation. Of particular importance to this discussion is Article 12 of the UN Convention on the Rights of the Child, which 'asserts the principle that children are full-fledged persons who have the right to express their views in all matters affecting them and requires that those views be heard and given due weight in accordance with the child's age and maturity. It recognizes the potential of children to enrich decision-making processes, to share perspectives and to participate as citizens and actors of change' (Preamble to Article on UNICEF website, http://www.unicef.ir.crc/crc.htm). The degree to which children and young people are participating in decision making within schools varies across Scotland. At one end of the spectrum, there are pupil councils with tightly controlled agendas – these councils give the appearance of consultation, while merely legitimising decisions already taken by school management. At the other end of the spectrum are schools where the vast majority of pupils are actively engaged in decisions on pedagogical issues, new building programmes, the purchase of new resources, and appointing new staff. At the classroom level, participation is reflected in teaching styles that involve negotiation on learning style, pace and content. In cases where schools genuinely listen to and act on pupils' views, there is a noticeable affect on pupil commitment and engagement. The challenge for those that promote pupil participation is to ensure the right to be heard is also extended to the disaffected, and to issues that particularly concern the disaffected. By the very nature of the difficulties these young people experience, they are more likely to be excluded from voicing how they feel – they may be absent from school, absent from class in a pupil support base, or present but disengaged. These pupils are unlikely to be heard unless schools are proactive in seeking their views and ensuring that they are valued and acted upon. Since these views will not always be complimentary, this requires courage and vision.

The Health Promoting School concept, developed by the World Health Organisation, has received a new impetus since the establishment of New Community Schools. The concept is much wider than health education; it also recognises the effect of the physical environment and the contribution of the community, of collaborative practice and the social and emotional well-being of staff and pupils. Among the twelve criteria are some that have direct relevance to disaffection: promoting self-esteem (by demonstrating that everyone can make a contribution); developing good relations between staff and pupils; establishing clear social aims for the school; promoting the well-being of staff; and realising the potential of other services to contribute to the well-being of the school community. The establishment of a Health Promoting Schools Unit in May 2002 will provide more support for all Scottish schools in meeting the criteria. The Scottish Executive has created the unit in partnership with the Health Education Board for Scotland, Learning and Teaching Scotland, and the Convention of Scottish Local Authorities.

Working across professional boundaries is notoriously difficult. Professionalism by its very nature encourages boundary maintenance, and when scarce resources are involved, there is even more temptation to guard jealously the margins between agencies. In the New Community School programme and the Changing Children's Services Fund, the Scottish

Executive has recognised the need to resource integration if services to the most vulnerable children are to work more effectively. The interim evaluation report on New Community Schools suggests significant progress is already being made:

> Evaluation evidence indicates that cross agency liaison and practice have been substantially enhanced. The weight of this finding should not be underestimated as case study analysis highlights the difficulties of initiating and sustaining effective multi-agency working. (*Interchage 76, Edinburgh: SEED, 2002, p. 15,; also available at www.scotland.gov.uk/library5/education/ic76.pdf*)

This evidence of greater collaborative practice is one of the most hopeful indicators that schools are becoming fit places for all of their pupils. There is no evidence that the incidence of disaffection is greater now than before. However, there is ample evidence that Scottish schools are still part of a process that conveys the children of our most socially excluded families on a predicted route via academic disidentification through school exclusion to social exclusion, narrowing their life chances and thereby affecting us all. Schools and teachers cannot reverse this process unaided.

REFERENCES

Boyd, B. and Hamill, P (2002) 'Inclusion or exclusion: a rock and a hard place?' *Scottish Youth Issues Journal*. 4, 87–110.

Gordon, J. and Grant, G. (eds) (1997) *How We Feel: An Insight into the Emotional World of Teenagers*, London: Jessica Kingsley.

Holmes, H. (ed.) (2000) *Scottish Life and Society, Education*, vol. 11, East Linton: Tuckwell Press

Mackenzie, J. (2001) Teachers have to win all the time: new directions in pursuit of social justice in the classroom, *Scottish Youth Issues Journal*, 3, 67–87.

Padfield, P. (2002) What's your reputation at school like?: how social theory can help explain the disproportionate rate of boys' exclusions from school, *Research in Education* 70, Edinburgh: SCER.

Paterson, L. (1992) Social class in education, in S. Brown and S. Riddell (eds), *Class, Race and Gender in School*, Edinburgh: SCRE.

98

Gender and Scottish Education

Sheila Riddell

In Chapter 1 of their edited collection on girls and Scottish education, Paterson and Fewell argued:

> gender inequality is embedded within the structure and texture of Scottish education . . . Its absence as an issue is not because there is no problem, or because any problem is in the process of solving itself, but because until recently its existence as a problem has not been identified. The form and content of gender inequality have therefore remained unacknowledged (Paterson and Fewell, 1990, p. 2).

This chapter considers the extent to which gender still features as an unconscious presence in Scottish educational debate more than a decade later. It begins by examining the general framework within which discussions of gender and education take place, since the naming of problems plays a central part in their understanding and resolution. Thereafter key research projects which have placed gender at the core rather than the periphery of their enquiry are considered. Finally, the chapter focuses on current and future areas of interest to practitioners and policy makers in the sphere of gender and education.

UNPACKING THE NOTION OF EQUALITY

All discussion of gender and education requires some thinking about the type of equality which is being pursued. At times, researchers, policy makers and campaigners have argued that the same education should be provided for all, since all individuals share a common humanity. Within this framework, the idea is to use education to blur differences between individuals and groups. Some groups may require some additional help to achieve the same position as the dominant group, who are implicitly assumed, within the Scottish context, to be male, white and middle class. The goal for all, however, is to iron out difference rather than celebrate or accentuate it. By way of contrast, other accounts of social justice emphasise the importance of diversity and difference between individuals and groups. Within this frame, far from blurring difference, the central goal is to celebrate cultural identity and diversity, recognising that equality policies may well have different goals for individuals and groups. In journals such as *New Left Review*, debates go back and forth between those who favour a project of economic redistribution, implicitly seeking to soften boundaries, and those who promote identity politics and align themselves with a project of recognition, or the celebration of diverse group identities. These arguments may be regarded as overly academic and hair-splitting in an area where there is plenty of room for action rather than words. However, they underline the need for greater clarity of thought around the concept of equality in order to avoid misplaced assumptions, over-simplified recipes for change and inaccurate predictions of the future.

THE NEGLECT OF GENDER IN
MAINSTREAM SCOTTISH EDUCATION ENQUIRY

Reviews of research on gender and education in Scotland (e.g. Brown, A., Breitenbach, E. and Myers, F., *Equality Issues in Scotland: A Research Review*, Manchester: Equal Opportunities Commission, 1994) noted that much work in Scotland has been small scale, conducted as part of masters' programmes within colleges and universities. It has generally failed to address in any detail the relationship between gender, social class, age, region and ethnicity; and ethnographies of girls' and boys' schooling are thin on the ground. A notable exception to the neglect of gender and education has been the steady stream of publications which have been produced by the Centre for Educational Sociology (CES) at Edinburgh University. From 1972 to 1992, CES conducted the Scottish Young People's Survey, which gathered data on the educational outcomes and attitudes of Scottish school leavers. Funded by the Scottish Office and the Economic and Social Research Council (ESRC), such research was used to investigate the relationship between gender and a range of other variables. For example, comparisons of girls' and boys' examination performance revealed that whereas in the early 1970s there were no gender differences, by 1984 there was a considerable female advantage. Analysing these data further, CES researchers maintained that comprehensive reorganisation in Scotland was associated with a general improvement of standards of attainment, with girls and pupils of low socio-economic status being the main beneficiaries. Such data have been very useful as a baseline for the identification of trends in educational outcomes in Scotland (see Furlong and Cartmel, 1997; Croxford et al., 2001).

As will be seen below, over the past four years there has been a marked increase in the amount of research in the area of gender and education. However, the question of why gender was such a neglected area until the mid-1990s demands to be addressed. One obvious reason is that the former Scottish Office, a major funder of educational research, did not regard gender as one of its priority areas, perhaps assuming that there were no issues to address since girls appeared to be performing well in external examinations. Recent nationally-funded work on gender and attainment has conceptualised the problem in terms of boys' under-achievement (Powney et al., 1997; Croxford et al., 2001).

A further explanation for the neglect of gender in discussion of Scottish education may be the on-going dominance of patriarchal attitudes within Scottish society. Hills, for instance, wrote:

> I am a child of the Democratic Intellect; the land of the lad o' pairts. A land famed for its excellent egalitarian education system. This is a strong male myth which has served the women of Scotland ill. Since women have been largely invisible there is a habit of silence. When women seek to break the silence there is no precedent and they are isolated and vulnerable. Gender codes and behaviours are so institutionalised as to go unnoticed. (Hills,

L., The Senga syndrome; reflections on 21 years in education, in Paterson and Fewell (eds), 1990, p. 148).

The Engender collective, a voluntary organisation committed to promoting equality for women, maintained:

> Women and girls in Scotland still experience considerable inequality and disadvantage in economic, social and political life as compared to men and boys. This disadvantage is further compounded by their relative exclusion as a focus of research and the unevenness in the collection and availability of statistics disaggregated by both country/region and gender. (Engender *Gender Audit*, 1997, p.1).

Much, then, remains to be done. However, as suggested earlier, there is some evidence of a recent growth of interest in gender and education in the research community. The directions which this research is taking will now be considered.

RECENT RESEARCH FOCUSING ON GENDER AND EDUCATION IN SCOTLAND

The new focus on gender and education has been paralleled by a wider surge of interest in gender issues, related in part to a sense of the possibilities offered by the Scottish Parliament for women to play a much greater role in Scottish public life than hitherto. The strategy paper *Equality Strategy; Working Together for Equality* (Scottish Executive, 2000) acknowledged the crucial importance of appropriate data, information and research to the development of mainstreaming equality into its policies and programmes, and made a commitment to providing better statistics for different equality groups. Improvements in gathering and disseminating statistical information is likely to make future research much easier in that baseline data will be readily available.

GENDER AND ATTAINMENT

In line with the Scottish Executive's commitment to improving public services and promoting social justice, there is a growing interest in gender and attainment. A literature review on gender and attainment conducted by Powney (1997) at the Scottish Council for Research in Education drew on a range of sources including Scottish Office statistics and international studies. Powney noted that the performance of Scottish girls in many areas of the curriculum was surpassing that of boys. Indeed, Scottish Examination Board statistics show that in 1996 at Standard Grade girls did better in all subjects apart from PE and Science. Girls' superior performance amounted to an average of 0.3 of a grade over all subjects. Between 1991 and 1996, girls performed better than boys at Higher Grade in English, Physics, Geography and Art and Design, and to a certain extent in Mathematics and Craft and Design. Taking all subjects together, the female pass rate was 4% higher than the male (Scottish Examination Board, Annual Report, 1997).

Using more recent data, Croxford et al. (2001) demonstrated that girls gain more Standard Grade awards than boys and the largest differences in performance are found at the highest levels of attainment, with more girls than boys gaining five or more awards at 1–2 (Credit level) and 1–4 (General and Credit level) (see Table 98.1).

Table 98.1:   **Percentage of males and females gaining five
or more Standard Grade awards in 1999**

Level of Standard Grade awards	Males	Females	Difference in favour of females
1–2 (Credit)	29	40	+11
1–4 (General or Credit)	73	81	+8
1–6 (Foundation, General or Credit)	92	94	+2

A similar pattern is found at Higher Grade: 55% of young men compared with 61% of young women completed S5 and S6 with three or more Higher grade passes at A–C in 1999. SQA data from 1999 showed that female candidates performed better than males in every subject they entered, apart from PE, Economics and General Science.

However, it should not be concluded from this that any problem which might have existed for girls is solved and the focus should now be on the boys. Furlong and Cartmel (1997), drawing on data from the Scottish Young People's Survey, analysed patterns of attainment in external examinations by social class and gender. Their analysis revealed that whereas the attainment of most pupils in Higher Grade examinations had improved since 1979, the performance of boys from social class IV and V had remained static. In all social classes, the performance of girls had increased more rapidly than that of boys. Croxford et al. (2001), using SQA data from 1998, noted very large socio-economic differences in Standard Grade attainment. Whilst girls performed better than boys in all groups apart from social class V (Unskilled), the social class gap in attainment was much larger than the gender gap (see Table 98.2).

Table 98.2:   **Percentage of S4 students attaining five
or more Standard Grade awards at Credit level in 1998**

Father's occupation	Professional	Intermediate	Skilled non-manual	Partly skilled	Unskilled
Females	78	62	32	30	23
Males	68	51	22	21	20

A number of points are suggested by these data. First, it is evident that the relative difference in the performance of the most advantaged and least advantaged social groups is considerable and has not been significantly eroded. These statistics are in stark contrast with the myth of the Scottish democratic education tradition and raise questions about the extent to which comprehensive schools have been successful in one of their stated aims, the whittling away of class differences in educational outcomes. Whilst examination results (although not necessarily standards) are improving, social class remains the most powerful determinant of pupils' school achievement, which will in turn play a major role in influencing their future life chances. Another important point is that being female seems to mitigate somewhat the negative impact of low social class (although not for girls in the lowest social group), an effect which has not been systematically investigated in Scotland and demands qualitative research into the family and school culture of working-class girls and boys. Similarly, being female seems to confer additional educational advantage on pupils in the more advantaged social groups, and again this is an effect which demands further investigation.

It is disappointing that school effectiveness research has had so little to say about gender effects. Because such research reveals that schools are always more effective for girls than boys, gender, like social class, is simply regarded as background statistical noise to be controlled for rather than understood. Research conducted by Brown, Riddell and Duffield at Stirling University attempted to unpack some of the classroom processes associated with differential levels of effectiveness in more and less effective Scottish schools. This research confirmed that in the classrooms of the four schools observed, low achieving boys tended to attract more teacher attention, were more likely to participate in question and answer sessions and featured more prominently in teachers' accounts of what had taken place in observed lessons. Some of this attention was negative, associated with pupil indiscipline, but nonetheless the message drawn from these interactions by lower achieving boys was that even if they were not performing well academically, they could still exert power in the classroom through noisy and attention-seeking activity. The most neglected pupils in the class were the lowest achieving girls. This study is one of the few in the UK which has investigated teaching and learning activities in relation to gender and level of achievement and further work of this type would do much to improve understanding of classroom processes (see Duffield, J., 2000, School effectiveness, school improvement and gender issues, in J. Salisbury and S. Riddell (eds) *Gender and Educational Change*, London: Routledge).

A question which also needs to be addressed is the extent to which the educational advantage of girls is translated into post-school advantage. Despite the fact that girls' performance in Highers has been improving more rapidly than that of boys since the late 1970s, this superiority has not been fully reflected in their higher education performance, although Paterson documented the way in which women and those from socially disadvantaged backgrounds gained considerably from the expansion of the early 1990s (Paterson, L. Trends in higher education participation in Scotland, *Higher Education Quarterly*, 51 (1), 29–48, 1997). In 1986, more women graduated from Scottish higher education institutions, when the ratio of women to men was 51:49. Following the reduction of places in colleges of education (which traditionally admitted more female than male students) in line with the shrinking of the school population from a late 1970s high of 400,000 to 300,000 in 1990, the ratio of higher education graduates shifted in favour of men. In 1995, female graduates again outnumbered men, this time by 52:48. Despite this numerical advantage, more men than women get first class honours degrees (8% as opposed to 6%), and gender differentiation of the higher education curriculum remains strong, reflecting gender differences in the school curriculum.

The puzzle which emerges from the data presented above is how girls manage to outperform boys in a school system where boys appear to dominate classroom activity, attracting more positive and negative teacher attention. Part of the reason, as has been seen, is that although educated in co-educational schools, they often self-select into different curricular areas, thus experiencing the school in different ways. There is a strong possibility that this self-selection may represent a survival mechanism for girls in a potentially hostile environment.

GENDER AND THE CURRICULUM

Statistics on the educational attainment of girls and boys might appear to support the contention that, as Macrae argued in an article in the *Times Educational Supplement Scotland* (21 July 1989, p. 14) 'the school system in Scotland, and in Britain as a whole, discriminates against boys.' According to Macrae, feminist dogma should be blamed for blinding people to the obvious truth that girls are doing better than boys in the school system, and have been doing so for a long time. Closer examination of the statistics, however, suggests that the picture is more complex. First, it is evident that gender differences in subject uptake have proved remarkably resistant to change and that in, for example, 'male' and 'female' subjects there has been little boundary crossing. Croxford et al. (2001) noted gender differences in subjects within curriculum modes, although the 1997 report from the Scottish Examination Board notes that the proportion of girls in Craft and Design and Graphic Communication has increased, but not in Technological Studies. There is evidence, therefore, of some female incursion into male territory, but little traffic in the other direction.

Since Science is such an important subject in an increasingly technological age, it is worth looking closely at male and female participation in this area. Croxford, L. (Participation in Science subjects: the effects of the Scottish curriculum framework, *Research Papers in Education*, 12 (1), 69–89, 1997) analysed such patterns over a fifteen year period in the context of the introduction of the common curriculum in the 1980s and the implementation of equal opportunities legislation. Figure 98.1 demonstrates that the proportion of girls aged fourteen to sixteen studying Physics has slowly but steadily climbed from 10% in 1976 to just over 20% in 1990. In Biology, the proportion of boys studying the subject has also increased, from 12% in 1976 to 28% in 1990, although the pattern here is less smooth, with small declines in 1986 and 1988. Croxford concludes that even though the common curriculum in Scotland is presented in gender neutral terms, the opportunities for choice within it result in girls and boys opting for different routes, with their attendant messages about appropriate concerns and future occupations for males and females. This, she suggests, may be attributed to 'deep-seated attitudes that some subjects are more appropriate for girls or boys'. She comments: 'Gender differences in post-compulsory courses and careers would be reduced if there was a larger common entitlement and less choice of subjects for the final two years of each national curriculum' (Croxford, L., Gender and national curricula, in Salisbury and Riddell, eds, 2000).

GENDER AND SPECIAL EDUCATIONAL NEEDS

One of the important but relatively unexplored areas of Scottish education is the relationship between gender and special educational needs. Table 98.3 shows the number of pupils placed in special schools by gender and impairment.

Overall, two-thirds of pupils with Records of Needs are boys and they outnumber girls in almost every category of impairment. Gender differences are greatest in the areas of social, emotional and behavioural difficulties (84% male), autistic spectrum disorder (84% male) and specific learning difficulties (dyslexia) (77% male). How can both these discrepancies and the lack of attention which has been paid to them be explained? Biology might offer a simple explanation, in that boys are more susceptible to genetic damage and trauma. In relation to impairments with a physiological aetiology, that explains some of the variance.

Figure 98.1: Gender differences in Science subjects studied at age 14–16, in Scotland 1976–90

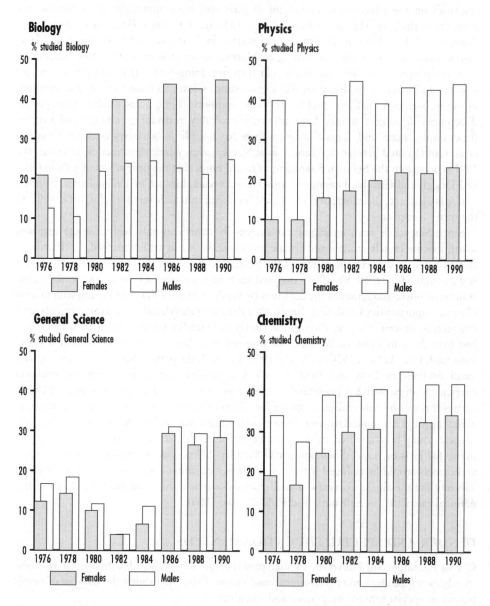

However, the fact that the greatest predominance of boys occurs in areas which are dependent on professional judgement as well as pupil behaviour, suggests that it is also necessary to look to explanations based on social constructionist ideas, that is, that boys are culturally conditioned to behave in ways which are defined as problematic, and that professionals are more likely to judge male behaviour as problematic. Again, these issues require further empirical investigation.

Table 98.3:   Main impairment of pupils with a Record of Needs by gender

Main impairment	No and % male		No and % female	
Hearing impairment	310	(54.7)	257	(45.3)
Visual impairment	217	(53.2)	191	(46.8)
Physical/motor impairment	650	(61.8)	401	(38.2)
Language & communication disorder	714	(76.5)	219	(23.5)
Autistic spectrum disorder	805	(84)	152	(16)
Social & emotional difficulties	504	(84)	97	(16)
Learning difficulties – moderate	2,839	(63)	1,663	(37)
Learning difficulties – severe	589	(58)	430	(42)
Learning difficulties – profound	134	(60)	88	(40)
Learning difficulties – specific	1,146	(77)	334	(23)
Dual sensory impairment	49	(49)	50	(51)
Moderate learning difficulties & others	854	(67)	421	(33)
Severe learning difficulties & others	576	(60)	390	(40)
Learning difficulties & others	310	(56)	239	(44)
Other	686	(68)	328	(32)

5,260 (34)

Source: School Census, September 1999

Despite the clarity of these patterns, gender, as well as social class, has been almost invisible in the world of special needs education, with its focus on the needs of the individual pupil in isolation from his or her social context. The growing field of disability studies has also tended to develop in isolation from special educational needs and from gender studies, since its material analysis has few points of contact with the individual explanations of the former and the feminist accounts of the latter. Research applying the insights of disability studies, with its emphasis on the social creation of disability to the field of special educational needs would help understanding of the relationship between gender, social class and special educational needs.

GENDER AND EDUCATION REFORM –
THE UNINTENDED CONSEQUENCES OF POLICIES

The educational reforms introduced by the former Conservative government throughout the 1980s and early 1990s provided a rich field for the development of policy studies in education. The pursuit of the market-driven agenda of choice and diversity and the new managerialist agenda of effectiveness and efficiency were extensively analysed but the effects of multiple policy innovations, and in particular the impact of market-driven reforms on the emerging equal opportunities agenda, were not widely explored. A piece of research funded by the Equal Opportunities Commission at Stirling University, conducted by Turner, Riddell and Brown (1995), took on the somewhat daunting task of investigating the intersection of these separately conceived policies. The research began by investigating the nature and development of equal opportunities policies in the twelve Scottish regions which were in place in 1995, a year before local government reorganisation. Regions varied markedly in their policy development; urban Labour-controlled authorities tended, unsurprisingly, to have the firmest policies in place encompassing commitment to social change rather than simple compliance with the legal requirement not to discriminate. In 1995 when the research took place, some rural authorities still lacked an equal opportunities policy statement and most authorities published their statements in the early 1990s, a decade after the passage of the Sex Discrimination Act. Due to protracted political wrangling, one large Scottish region managed to publish its policy only six weeks before its dissolution. The second part of the study explored gendered patterns of attainment and subject uptake and these have already been described.

Finally, the researchers investigated the differential impact of policies informed by marketisation and new managerialism in case study schools varying in relation to social class of the pupil population and location. Variations were identified between four schools, two primary and two secondary, in one urban authority with a progressive equal opportunities policy. Broadly, it was found that the curricular reforms had a neutral effect in challenging gender differentiation. Teachers felt that the 5–14 programme and the curriculum of the later secondary years, emphasising the entitlement of all children to a common curricular experience, discouraged active discrimination, but on the other hand did not encourage teachers to adopt radical positive action unless they were so minded.

Management reforms, on the other hand, were seen by the schools in working-class areas to have an overwhelmingly negative effect. The secondary school in the socially disadvantaged area had a well-established reputation for its work in anti-racist and anti-sexist education. The publication of league tables of schools according to their external examination results had accelerated the trend towards falling rolls, reduced resources and low morale amongst teachers, parents and pupils. This meant that energy which had previously gone into anti-sexist education was instead used in maintaining the basic functioning of the school. By comparison, the middle-class secondary was buoyant in terms of pupil numbers and found that its liberal equal opportunities policies were acceptable to parents of girls who wished their daughters to achieve academically, but were not sufficiently radical to upset the parents of boys. In both secondary schools, teachers were anxious about boys' performance relative to that of girls, but in the socially disadvantaged schools these worries were heightened by pressure from the authority not to exclude difficult pupils, most of whom were boys, and indeed to accept pupils who had been excluded from other schools. In the low socio-economic status (SES) case study school, about 50% of pupils, the majority male, were perceived by the teachers to have some sort of learning difficulty, but this was not fully reflected in their allocation of learning support teachers. The primary schools, although less affected by anxiety over test results since these were not in the public domain, were nonetheless affected differently by the proportion of pupils with learning and behavioural difficulties. In the low SES primary school, a significant amount of energy was invested in maintaining an orderly environment, although indiscipline was not construed as a gendered problem. In the high SES primary school, on the other hand, equal opportunities was an explicit part of its agenda and again this struck an approving chord with its clientele, who were predominantly middle class and ambitious.

Overall, it was concluded that the regional equal opportunities policy was implemented very differently in the case study primary and secondary schools, mediated by effects of social class, parent culture and location. These variables also affected the implementation of curricular and management reforms, which in turn shaped the environment in which equality policies were developing. A complex iterative process was thus set in train, with high SES schools judged to be more effective not only in terms of academic performance, but also in relation to their equality programmes. The low SES schools, on the other hand, were pressurised into survival mode, with little space for innovatory work of any kind. There seems to be an on-going need to assess the unintended, as well as anticipated, consequences of educational change, including those associated with gender equality.

Both Westminster and Holyrood governments are committed to the twin agendas of raising attainment and pursuing social justice. The extent to which these policy goals are mutually compatible, and their implications for gender and education, will need to be carefully scrutinised.

FUTURE ISSUES FOR POLICY-MAKERS AND PRACTITIONERS

As a preliminary to this section, it is worth noting the rapid changes which have happened in the position of women in society over the past two decades and the perils of predicting the future. From a position of performing worse than boys at Higher Grade in the mid-1970s, girls of all social classes are now performing better than boys of similar social class in all subject areas, although gender differentiation in the curriculum remains stubbornly in place. In the late 1970s, however, this was not what was predicted. Noting the way in which post-war education reports and legislation had tended to reinforce the provision of different education for boys and girls, Deem predicted that after a brief period of liberalism in the 1970s which saw the introduction of equal opportunities legislation, the advent of Thatcherism was about to herald:

> A gradual return to the education of women for domestic labour, emphasis on the importance of motherhood to the economy and the reproduction of 'suitable' labour power (i.e. that which is prepared to accept low wages and discipline) as the need for women's paid work outside the family evaporates. In many areas, girls leaving school will have little possibility of entering employment at all; if they do find jobs, especially in manufacturing, clerical or secretarial work, it is likely that the microchip will soon begin to eat away at that work. (Deem, R., State policy and ideology in the education of women, 1944–1980, *British Journal of Sociology of Education*, 2 (2), 141, 1981)

Such analysis assumed that women's position in the labour market was more tenuous than that of men, that male labour would be preferred to that of women and that motherhood was foisted on women to serve the needs of the economy rather than something they chose themselves. For the past twenty years, jobs in manufacturing, where man predominated, have disappeared, whilst the service sector, employing more women than men, has expanded. More women with young children are in employment and girls' education is based on the assumption that they will be economically active for most of their lives, as well as shouldering the major responsibility for home-making and child-rearing. So, whilst avoiding the pitfalls of prediction, it is worth concluding with some of the questions for research, policy and practice which demand to be addressed over the coming decade as the Scottish Parliament establishes itself.

Devolution will have many implications for the formation of Scottish identity, often defined in opposition to all things English. Given existing anxieties about boys' performance and their vulnerability to school failure and exclusion, it will be important for schools to use the new focus on the development of a positive Scottish identity to foster new versions of masculinity which reject macho posturing. Tackling male disaffection and violence requires a critical look at popular male culture, rather than seeing the male as norm and the female as in some way lacking. Getting this right in school will clearly not be easy and the tendency to blame women for boys' difficulties will have to be avoided. Male teachers clearly have an immensely important role to play here (though the increasing feminisation of the teaching force runs counter to this). Some attempts to assist boys, such as focusing on transactional writing in single sex classes, may actually do more harm than good by reifying out-dated concepts of masculinity. Interestingly, Murphy (Equity, assessment and gender, in Salisbury and Riddell (eds), 2000) has shown that there is no form of assessment which disproportionately favours girls (girls do better, no matter how they are assessed). Attempts to redress the gender balance by, for example, making greater use of multiple choice rather than coursework, are doomed to failure.

Paying attention to the problems of boys does not mean that girls can now be ignored. In addition to enjoying far less teacher attention than boys, young women may well be the victims of male violence both inside and outside the school. High achieving middle-class girls may experience fear of failure, becoming the custodians of middle-class awareness of risk and danger. The rate of teenage pregnancy is higher in Scotland than the rest of the UK, and yet there is still reticence about the discussion of sexuality in some schools. Issues which have a gender dimension, such as indiscipline, violence and bullying are still often seen in gender neutral terms, despite the evidence that these are perpetrated and experienced differently by boys and girls.

Finally, the gendered impact of a range of policy innovations needs to be explored. These include managerialism and marketisation, promoted by the previous government but still very much in evidence in current educational discourse. Other policies, such as the restructuring of welfare, the new emphasis on the redemptive power of work and the lifelong learning agenda have specific implications for males and females as participants in education and these will need careful examination. Throughout this account, an attempt has been made to draw out the interaction of a range of variables, for it is impossible to understand the effects of gender without paying attention also to the multiple identities which people occupy, based on nationality, ethnicity, age, social class, sexuality and disability. Exploring these avenues while continuing to interrogate the notion of equality will provide much work for researchers and practitioners well into the next decade.

REFERENCES

Croxford, L., Tinklin, T., Ducklin, A. and Frame, B. (2001) Gender and pupil performance, *Interchange 70*, Edinburgh: Scottish Executive.

Furlong, A. and Cartmel, F. (1997) *Young People and Social Change Individualization and Risk in Late Modernity*, Buckingham: Open University Press.

Paterson, F. and Fewell, J. (1990) (eds) *Girls in their Prime: Scottish Education Revisited* Edinburgh: Scottish Academic Press.

Powney, J. (1997) *Gender and Attainment: A Review*, Edinburgh: SCRE.

Salisbury, J. and Riddell, S. (eds), (2000) *Gender, Policy and Educational Change: Shifting Agendas in the UK and Europe*, London: Routledge.

Turner, E., S. Riddell and Brown, S. (1995) *Gender Equality in Scottish Schools: The Impact of Recent Educational Reforms*, Manchester: Equal Opportunities Commission.

99

'Sectarianism':
A Challenge for Scottish Education

Gerry P. T. Finn

The arrival of a new century usually induces speculation about what the future will bring and encourages more than just optimists to hope for very much better times. Tackling those problems subsumed under or, to be more accurate, disguised by the use of the terms 'sectarian' or 'sectarianism' is long overdue. Nonetheless, there can be some little satisfaction that now in the twenty-first century there are signs of growing recognition of the need for action. As the last century began to wind down, three independent events in 1999 combined to mean that the issue could no longer be ignored but instead became a topic that had to be seriously discussed. These concerned Church–state relationships in the UK; the acceptability of anti-Catholic or anti-Irish songs; and the impact of a public lecture at the Edinburgh International Festival.

CHURCH–STATE RELATIONSHIPS AND 'SECTARIANISM'

The first event revealed a tragi-comic element. For the eighteen years between 1979 and 1997 the government of the United Kingdom of Great Britain and Northern Ireland had been undertaken by administrations formed by the Conservative party. Michael Forsyth had been a minister in some of those governments but by 1999 neither he nor his party was any longer in government. So, when Forsyth announced with seeming surprise that it was Britain's 'grubby little secret' that Catholics could not accede to the British throne, it was by then a very belated (and safe) discovery for him to make (cited in Finn, G. P. T., *A Culture of Prejudice: Promoting Pluralism in Education for a Change*, Chapter 5 in T. M. Devine, 2000, pp. 53–88). Nonetheless, his intervention did draw public attention to an unsavoury aspect of the UK state, but this 'secret' is one that should lead to much wider scrutiny of the manner in which Protestantism remains formally at the heart of the state.

Historically the United Kingdom relied on Protestantism to unite most of the different peoples and nations included within it. Anti-Catholic sentiments and prejudices were characteristics of the state. The establishment of Protestant national churches set boundaries which determined religious and political deviance. Today Church and state remain intertwined: the sovereign is the temporal head of the Church of England, the established state Church in England. Monarchs must be Protestant, vow to uphold Protestantism, and are forbidden to marry Catholics. Archbishops and bishops in the Church of England are appointed by the Crown. The upper echelon of this clerical hierarchy has the constitutional advantage of twenty-six seats in the unelected second chamber of government, the House of Lords. In Scotland, the question of state patronage of religion led to theological disputation and eventual division among Presbyterians. Nonetheless, the Church of Scotland was the established national Church for Scotland, and probably, at least nominally, that status remains. Although the present constitutional position is confused, there can be no doubt that the Church has remained in a favoured position in relation to the state. (For further discussion and references: see Finn, in Devine, 2000.)

Although Protestantism does still remain pre-eminent in the British state and, as a result, has a privileged position in the social fabric, other faiths do also contribute an increasing patchwork quality to the make-up of British political life. The state now demonstrates greater recognition and acceptance of other religions and their adherents. The official pre-eminence of Protestantism is no longer intended to denote sanctioned domination over all other forms of religious belief within the state. In the past other religions were marked out as being inferior and their adherents could be excluded from many areas of civil society. Exclusion or subjection was most often directed against Catholicism but at various times there was state discrimination against others, including dissenting Protestant creeds. As a result, these practices should not be seen to have operated only in terms of Protestant-Catholic exchanges. And today, the remaining links between the state and Protestantism, especially that of the establishment of the Church of England, despite internal Anglican critics, have been defended by some from Catholic, Jewish and Islamic religions, as well as by some Protestants affiliated to other churches. They have argued that the link is now important as a symbol of the significance of faith (rather than a specific religion) to British life. Nonetheless, it is important that any links between the state and belief-systems are not, and do not appear, monopolistic. Declarations by Prince Charles, the heir to the throne, that on his own accession he would wish to become Defender of Faiths rather than Defender of the Faith can be seen as another indication that British society may be moving towards genuine religious pluralism. However, further progress towards cultural pluralism will be evident when the state can recognise and accept a range of beliefs, both religious and non-religious.

Yet, it is clear that the role of Protestantism in the UK state has been quietly and slowly changing. Church–state associations have been subject to some quiet reflection, accompanied by some elements of reconstruction and reinterpretation. These incremental changes mark quiet progress in ecumenical and inter-faith relations. This subdued advance has not been much disturbed, even by the loud protests, featuring accusations of treachery to the state and to Protestantism, trumpeted on various occasions by the Reverend Iain Paisley and others of a similar viewpoint. Their identification of Britishness with the interlocking of Protestantism and monarchy means that they see the potential for change as a challenge to the very essence of what it is to be British. Although their stance may appear quaint to many, those who avow this interpretation do represent what was the traditional mainstream position. And that is why the interrelationship of state and Protestantism in Britain, albeit inadequately understood, still remains so important: it offers crucial insights into the roots of religious prejudice and conflict.

CATHOLICS AND PROTESTANTS: SCOTLAND AND IRELAND

In Scotland the Reformation had been relatively bloodless. Attachment to Catholicism proved to be surprisingly weak and, as a result, was soon replaced by an extensive acceptance of Protestantism. Very few Catholics remained, nor did the number grow: by the mid-1750s Catholics were estimated to number fewer than 17,000 people, approximately 1% of the Scottish population. Bloody religious conflicts in Scotland did follow the Reformation. Energy was expended and blood spilt over the form of Church government that should reign. One side supported a Church built up from presbyteries, which were governed by Church elders, including the ministers, who were chosen by the presbyteries: the other accepted government of the Church by bishops, who were judged to have greater knowledge and experience, who appointed ministers to churches. Some opposition to episcopacy was from those who believed it was papacy in disguise or a religious form that would inevitably lead to the return of Catholicism. Even so, these remained disagreements within Protestantism. To the state and its British inhabitants, Catholicism was seen to be 'foreign' and 'alien'. Within the United Kingdom state, that marked out Ireland and the Catholic majority of its population as problems. That also meant that Irish 'immigration' within the supposedly unitary UK state was perceived to be another problem. The Catholic Irish were judged to be a different ethnic community, and at times were subjected to processes of racialisation. In this framework, their racial inferiority was confirmed by their adherence to Catholicism.

MODELS OF PREJUDICE

Now, even to raise these matters runs the risk of being accused of resurrecting old problems that are best forgotten. Critical analysis of these societal arrangements is judged unnecessary, and Church–state relationships are seen by some to be arcane, archaic and now largely irrelevant. However, accusations of this type betray a common misunderstanding of prejudice (Finn, 2000). Dominant lay explanations of prejudice focus on the individual rather than on social systems and rely on notions of ignorance or psychological disturbance. An individualised focus is unhelpful, and neither notion comes even close to offering an adequate account or response. Education and the psychological treatment of abnormality respectively are logically implied to be the appropriate solutions. Presenting prejudice as a form of psychological abnormality misunderstands the range of forms and the power of prejudice. Equally, if prejudice is a function of ignorance then only those who are uneducated must be a concern. Both versions, themselves expressions of other prejudicial beliefs, minimise mundane everyday prejudice. Prejudice is implicitly defined as not being a concern for 'normal' people, but really only a problem for certain (deficient) individuals.

Instead prejudice is much better seen as being an important by-product of inter-group relations. Prejudice is a societal phenomenon that reflects the power structures of that society. Having emerged from these societal structures, prejudice then acts to reinforce, and insist on the validity of retaining, the very same hierarchical arrangements. Prejudice cannot be dismissed as a characteristic of the deviant few. It is so deeply embedded in social culture and societal structure as to appear as certainty, not ignorance. That is evident in the widespread nature of popular beliefs and stereotypical thinking. Top-down societal models therefore have much greater power in explaining prejudice and also, when added to an understanding of the history of relevant inter-group relations, the origins of specific prejudices.

Consequently, the remaining present associations between Protestantism and the UK state are unhelpful. This very public attribute of the state was crucial in sustaining prejudice and apparently giving royal approval to discrimination against Catholics and other religions.

Certainly the identification of Protestantism with the UK state as a whole has been slowly weakening: no longer is the association between the two intended to signify quite the same official view of religion in the United Kingdom. Nonetheless, for the moment, the association remains formally in much the same historic guise. That is what Paisley seeks to maintain. For as long as this association of Protestantism and the state is retained, support is offered for traditional interpretations of religious difference within the UK state. Nor should there be surprise then when that happens. There remain subjects in this state for whom Protestantism continues to be central to the story-line that runs through their narratives of what it is to be a British citizen.

Nevertheless, there are those who have welcomed the subtly changing emphasis in the relationship between state and religion. It is recognition of these subtle soft-focus changes that has drawn unofficial support from within a range of faiths for the retention of the established Church. Opposition to the disestablishment of the Church of England from some members of other faiths is less attractive than it first appears, and should be discounted. Their collective desire is a conservative one: they wish to retain this historic form of state approval, but not in the sense that one religion would be set above other religions. Instead the Church of England, with whom most Christian denominations and other faiths now have reasonable working relations, would retain its established role but somehow come to be seen as representative of mainstream religious beliefs in Britain. The objection is that, if this did come to pass, it might be progress towards religious pluralism, but not pluralism itself. It would merely replace the injustice of State support for one religion over others with state approval of faiths over other forms of thought. The pluralist principle to follow must remain the same. The state's role is to aid the peaceful management of human difference, not to establish hierarchies of power based upon them.

DENIALS AND DEFENCE: NO PREJUDICE IN SCOTLAND

In late May 1999, on their return to the club's stadium, Rangers Football Club justifiably celebrated their Scottish Cup triumph over old rivals Celtic. Later that night, Donald Findlay QC, then vice-chairman of Rangers Football Club, accompanied by the victorious Rangers team, took the trophy to an official supporters' celebration held elsewhere in the stadium complex. There, along with an assembly of team members and fans, he performed a repertoire of supposedly 'traditional' Rangers songs. Findlay's actions can be no surprise to those aware of his earlier publicly stated views.

In 1995, Findlay had doubted that there was a problem of prejudice in Scottish football. He had also made clear his objections to suggestions that Rangers should take action against 'sectarian' chanting and singing.

> In short, I don't think Scottish football has a 'racism' or 'sectarian' problem, although that doesn't mean we should be complacent about it. But to ban chanting on the basis that it is sectarian is not only impossible to implement, it would ruin the game as we know it . . . the regular songs are part of a tradition and no-one has the right to tell someone else that their beliefs are wrong. (*The Glaswegian*, 24 September 1995)

So Findlay's behaviour in 1999 cannot be seen to be a surprise. At the supporters' celebration he acknowledged that others would judge his 'songs' and 'beliefs' to be 'wrong'. He prefaced his remarks by joking that Rangers could no longer be seen to be 'sectarian', and that they had to be careful or they would appear on tabloid front pages. They did: the proceedings were being videotaped by a supporter, who sold a copy to the media. The supporter who did so was publicly castigated for his actions by the leading Rangers fanzine *Follow, Follow*, which also published his home address. Soon he was forced to go into hiding after receiving death-threats from fellow Rangers fans.

The video showed the assembly celebrating by singing many of these 'traditional' songs. Findlay's own actions and his earlier comments show that he found nothing wrong with this repertoire. Some lyrics, however, are taken to convey anti-Catholic or anti-Irish prejudices. In some of these compositions, singers proclaim, 'We're up to our knees in Fenian blood' and issue the challenge, 'Surrender or you'll die'.

Nonetheless, in Scotland, denials of the presence of racism or even 'sectarianism' are surprisingly common. Acceptance of their reality would clash too harshly with the fondly believed myth of Scottish egalitarianism, which is a belief so powerful that McCrone has intriguingly commented, 'It is as if Scots are egalitarian by dint of racial characteristics . . .' (McCrone, D., *Understanding Scotland*, London: Routledge, 1992, p. 90). As a result, actions motivated by prejudice are discounted unless they fall into the extreme range of the spectrum. But then, when extreme actions do occur, they can be dismissed as the product of individual psychopathology or ignorance. So, complacent assertions that there is no real problem in Scotland prove difficult to contradict, leaving the myth of innate Scottish egalitarianism intact. Divorcing the different expressions of prejudice from one another is essential if this evasion is to succeed: on this analysis, songs and talk must be judged to be of no concern. Prejudice instead should be recognised as a continuum of behavioural expressions. A ratchet effect means that increased activity at lower levels of prejudice makes activity by others at higher levels more probable. Talk, songs or chants expressing 'beliefs' excused as 'traditional', therefore, cannot be discounted, which debars the false conclusion that there is no real problem.

Some efforts were made to play down Findlay's actions; however, his celebrity made containment impossible. Because it was Donald Findlay QC, the rector of St Andrews University, the usual strategies to minimise recognition of the widespread nature of prejudice could not be employed to defend Scottish egalitarianism. There was some acknowledgement that there was a social dimension to this form of prejudice. There were also some who grasped the interconnection between different expressions of prejudice: that talk and violence were linked. Tragically, there were those who knew that to be true. Nil By Mouth was created to combat 'sectarianism' by friends and family of Mark Scott, a young Celtic fan murdered in 1995. The title taken by the charity is intended to direct attention to the power of talk and verbal abuse in the creation and maintenance of prejudice. (For a fuller discussion of these issues see Finn, G. P. T., Scottish myopia and global prejudices, in Finn, G. P. T. and Giulianotti, R. (eds.) 2000, pp. 54–99.)

Findlay's performance led to some intriguing interpretations. The association with football led some to claim that this sport was the last remaining area affected or that the prejudice was the responsibility of either Rangers or Celtic Football Clubs or both. For many the allusions to Ireland evident in some 'traditional' songs sung meant that any problem could be made foreign to Scotland. Yet, this displacement ploy can only be successful if the many links between Scotland and Ireland, and indeed Scottish involvement in Britain's relationship with Ireland, are to be repressed. But, if accomplished, the racialisation of the Irish in both Ireland and Scotland can be ignored. Those ever flexible friends, the seemingly omnifarious terms 'sectarian' and 'sectarianism', were even deployed to defend Findlay: it was criticism of his actions that was 'sectarianism'. And, almost inevitably, some commentators were able to attribute responsibility for Findlay's performance to the existence of Catholic schools!

CATHOLICS AND CATHOLIC SCHOOLS

The event with most dramatic impact then occurred at a lecture at the Edinburgh International Festival in August 1999. Internationally acclaimed Scottish composer James MacMillan described how it felt to be Catholic in modern Scotland. He recognised the influence of ecumenism and improvements in inter-faith relations in Scotland. One of his intentions was to build on these developments so that anti-Catholic prejudice could finally be ended. Nor was he concerned only by this prejudice: he wished to see Scotland finish with all other forms of religious and racial prejudice. He detected a 'tendency in Scotland to restrict, to control and to enforce conformity and homogeneity'. MacMillan relayed his bewilderment at the way that Catholics and Catholicism could still face prejudice. One of the most important themes was his concern about the persistent criticism directed against the existence of Catholic schools. Strong criticism of these schools in many responses to his lecture confirmed his fears. In turn, many Catholic responses showed that his anxieties on this matter were firmly shared.

Strange beliefs plague the discussion of Catholic schools (see Conroy, 1999; Finn in the first edition of this book; Finn in Devine, 2000). They cannot be described as 'segregated', as they are open to all children. Indeed one measure of increasing progress towards religious harmony in Scotland is the proportion of pupils from other faiths and none that attend them. They became state denominational schools, along with about sixty Episcopalian Church schools, as a result of the 1918 Education (Scotland) Act. The result of the earlier 1872 Act had been to build a national education system on the schools previously run by the different Presbyterian denominations. The contentious issue of state patronage and religion led to a fudge on the issue of religious instruction. Nonetheless, it was apparent that these schools were effectively non-denominational *Presbyterian* schools. State funded-Catholic and Episcopal schools were introduced as a means of remedying an injustice and ending inequality.

However, the 1920s and 1930s saw an intense racialisation of the Catholic Scots of Irish descent. Irish-Scots were described as being Scotland's equivalent of Germany's supposed Jewish 'problem'. At General Assemblies of the Church of Scotland speakers took care to describe their opposition to the Catholic Irish-Scots as racial, not religious. Other Presbyterian Churches, mainstream right-wing politicians and electorally successful extremist right-wing Protestant parties joined the clamour. Repatriation of these Irish-Scots and expulsion of Catholic clergy were some of the 'solutions' demanded. The supposed power and growing influence of this minority community was claimed to be apparent in state acceptance and support of Catholic schools.

Clearly Catholic schools were not the cause of this ethnic division, but they became a central element in this supposedly 'Protestant' and 'Scottish' cause against the Irish-Scots. The existence of Catholic schools was no more than a pretext for mobilising anti-Irish and anti-Catholic prejudices. But the inherited legacy of the persistent and powerful propaganda of those days has been that Catholic schools are now blamed by many for the echoes of that earlier division. Yet Lindsay Paterson (*Journal of Education and Christian Belief*, 2000) has concluded 'there to be no evidence at all' that Catholic schools create bigotry, division or exclusive communities. Slowly there is now some acknowledgement that these schools and the 1918 Act have had a positive impact on community relations in Scotland. L. Bennie, J. Brand and J. Mitchell judged that: 'As a means of offering an immigrant community a stake in society, acknowledging and accepting religious pluralism, minimising grievance and potential conflict, it is difficult to see the Act as anything other than a success' (*How Scotland Votes: Scottish Parties and Elections*, Manchester: Manchester University Press, 1997, p. 111). MacMillan and other Catholics have a strong case for concern when schools that are successful – pupil exam performance also exceeds statistical prediction – are subject to frequent demands that they should no longer exist.

Inevitably not every point made in MacMillan's lecture was as well considered, but he said much of value in his courageous effort to move Scotland forward. Nonetheless, a great disservice was done to both MacMillan and the development of the debate by partial reporting of the lecture. Further distraction was provided by ill-informed responses to the caricature provided. Inevitably the immediate public response was very mixed and confused. MacMillan was even attacked for 'sectarianism', an accusation which underlines again the omnifarious quality of the term. Yet MacMillan had been inspired to speak by his trust in a stronger Scottish ecumenical spirit, and that the time was right to do so, in a reinvigorated Scotland with its own new Parliament. So it is gratifying that the longer-term impact has been much more positive. That has been helped by the publication of the real speech (in Devine, 2000) and not partial reports. (A range of responses to the speech and analyses of the position of Catholics in Scotland are also contained in this same collection.)

MacMillan's own high profile meant that his comments on the matter were taken seriously. In a number of ways he has been proved correct in his judgement that the time was right to raise the matter. He received personal support and congratulations from ecumenically minded clergy and lay members in other churches (MacMillan, private communication). And, although it may not be directly connected to MacMillan's intervention, it is much to the credit of the Church of Scotland that the 2002 General Assembly heard some public soul-searching and self-criticism of its own role, especially in the 1920s and 1930s, in promoting disharmony in Scotland. Probable legislation by the Scottish Parliament offers further confirmation of his good sense of timing. And even though discussions of the issue by parliamentarians do still lack sufficient clarity of focus, a goverment initiative merits a welcome as a very public statement of intent to tackle prejudice. But what part should education play?

AN EDUCATIONAL RESPONSE

An obvious lesson to be drawn is that only modest claims can be made for the specific role of education in the eradication of prejudice. Statements that education is the key are wrong. If progress is to be made in reducing inter-group conflict, then educational approaches must be part of a wider societal strategy. The brief exposition of Church–state relationships in the context of British–Irish connections is intended to make that clear, and direct attention to the societal dimension to prejudice. In this very restricted sense, education on these matters is invaluable, but only if that aids political mobilisation around an agenda of social change. When the aim is the eradication of a societal prejudice, a multi-level approach is required. Political, legal and juridical strategies, at the very least, need to accompany educational initiatives. In this context, three educational goals are essential. A much wider awareness of the complexity of prejudice and discrimination must be achieved, which has to be accompanied by an understanding of their origins in societal structures, and the consequential recognition that anti-discriminatory strategies cannot be successful if challenged by educational efforts alone. These three aspects will be central to the construction of meaningful anti-discriminatory initiatives and social policies.

Recognition that there is a problem must be followed by identification of what it is. 'Sectarianism' is capable of so many interpretations as to be unhelpful. If the confusion is to be cleared then it must be recognised that the most common usage in Scotland concerns anti-Protestant prejudice and anti-Catholic prejudice. However they are not simply equivalent phenomena. Now this might seem an unnecessarily precise distinction for the victims of either, and in a real and immediate sense the distinction is irrelevant for those left scarred or even worse by an attack motivated by either form. However, the distinction is important if serious efforts are to be made to address them. Anti-Catholic prejudice can be intertwined with anti-Irish racism – which remains a Britain-wide phenomenon to this day (Hickman and Walter, 1997). Moreover, this version of religious prejudice is further complicated by the historical and contemporary societal structures from which it was derived and succoured. As a result, anti-Catholic prejudice remains associated with social and political power in British society. This constellation of factors explains why a broad-based strategy is essential if it is to be tackled.

In a genuinely ecumenical climate, anti-Protestant prejudice is a much less complex social phenomenon: sadly that does not mean that it will necessarily be easier to tackle. Indeed care has to be taken to ensure that analysis of factors contributing to anti-Irish and anti-Catholic prejudices do not fuel a simplistic reversal of some of the elements on which these often interlocking prejudices themselves do depend. A Catholic sense of injustice about the deep-rooted and manifestly societal anti-Catholic prejudice is both understandable and acceptable. However, a dangerously misplaced sense of that injustice can solidify into anti-Protestant prejudice rather than lead to actions in support of social justice. It is the search for a remedy to injustice, not the perpetuation of another that is needed. For these reasons it is tactically appropriate to deal with these forms of prejudice simultaneously, but strategically wrong to judge them to be the same. Moreover, the distinctions between them also need to be recognised and carefully handled within the educational sphere.

The relationship of Britain and Ireland also has to be tackled. Fortunately, the Good Friday Agreement of 1998, despite its vicissitudinous path in Northern Ireland, has transformed this. Moreover, the East–West dimension to the agreement, the Council of the British Isles, has brought about direct contacts between Scotland, the Irish Republic and Northern Ireland. With a remit for mutual development that includes culture, the council could provide at least a useful venue for exploring potential innovations related to both culture and education. Scotland has had cross-migrations with both parts of Ireland. These cultural relationships merit study. The ideal would be the creation of common curricular materials that could be used in all three places. Pupil exchanges and mini-conferences to present the results of their own learning would offer another exciting dimension, but would certainly require very careful preparation and sensitive teaching.

Even greater care would be required in handling the expression of political opinions on Northern Ireland. In this context Donald Findlay has a genuine point of concern about telling people that their beliefs are wrong. Others may judge some or all of these views to be in error, but expression of unionist, loyalist, nationalist or republican views is not illegal. Nor should they be in a pluralist society: they do need to be discussed. The complication is that each position can be mired in religious prejudice. Some also have the potential to be linked with support for paramilitary activity, which is illegal, even when associated political activity is legal. Each of these political positions is also capable of being expressed in unobjectionable terms. Great care will have to be taken in policing this difference, but that will be a critical question for political and juridical approaches. It will be important to distinguish between the valid expression of these political ideas, even if they are unpopular, and those forms that rely on, or are wrapped up in, religious prejudice. This area is an especially tricky one, but the emotionally arousing issue of Northern Ireland (in both historical and contemporary forms) has such a brooding influence on Scottish thinking about Ireland that no effort can simply side-step it and be successful.

Education in the widest sense has much to contribute to an understanding of this conflict. So far it has failed to do so. It is worrying that Michael Forsyth could have progressed through all three levels of Scottish education, and become minister responsible for Scottish education, without recognising the importance of Church–state relationships in the United Kingdom. The religious restrictions that apply to the monarchy have certainly been no secret: progressive politicians and Catholic representatives have frequently identified this injustice. Church–state relationships are relevant to gaining a wider understanding of History, Modern Studies and Religious Education in relation to the United Kingdom, and could very well be pertinent to discussions in Personal and Social Education. And now, when very strong claims are made about the importance of citizenship education, there can be no excuse for failing to teach learners about this constitutional component of the state to which they are expected to owe allegiance. This is an omission to be remedied if education is to play its part in eradicating these prejudices.

The recognition and identification of anti-Irish racism in this complex of prejudices offers a potentially important bridge to anti-racist education. The case of the Irish makes the challenge to dominant beliefs about the validity of 'races' and racialised thinking even more potent. Links can also be made to anti-Semitism, another mix of racism with religious prejudice. Both examples confront 'whiteness' as an inevitable basis for racial categorisation. And this broad context also offers the option of comparisons and contrasts with Islamophobia, in which, depending on the specific ethnicity of the individual concerned, there can also be an accompanying racist dimension.

So what is now required is a formal educational initiative to help address these issues in a coherent manner. That must allow comparisons and contrasts to be made between different societal prejudices, and undertake to provide appropriate curriculum development and training in support of these eventual developments. In relation to conflict between Protestants and Catholics, groups such as Nil By Mouth, Bhoys against Bigotry, Sense over Sectarianism and the Mark Scott Foundation have all developed packages and strategies in the educational work they have pioneered in schools. Some individual schools have started their own programmes, sometimes in association with a local partner school. So there are already practices to be evaluated and built on. However, the absence so far of any nationwide government-led educational initiative is a telling omission.

CHOICE AND DIVERSITY

Perhaps the biggest challenge facing Scottish education (and Scottish society alike) is how to respond to socio-cultural diversity. Many countries struggle to manage human difference. Too often difference becomes confused with division, and acceptance and recognition of difference is then equated with the promotion of division. Instead it is the inability to allow difference that ends in either divisive conflict or, when the drive against difference is successful, usually following a period of intense conflict, the eventual elimination (sometimes extermination) of another cultural identity. In dealing with the challenge of diversity, Scottish myths are even more of a hindrance than usual. The egalitarian myth plays an important role in relation to Scottish education. Consequently, the rhetoric surrounding educational policy and practice must honour this myth. That means that truly egalitarian values are not served. Confusion of difference with division, added to a presumption of a certain Scottish adherence to egalitarian values, has meant that equality is too easily interpreted as meaning no more than uniformity and homogeneity.

The 1918 Education (Scotland) Act was a positive exception to these forces. In 1982, the addition of one Jewish school to the Catholic and shrinking Episcopalian sectors at least extended the potential for the creation of a pluralist schooling system. Recent doctoral research by Akhtar-Saeed Bhutta (University of Strathclyde, 2002) has shown that there is a growing demand for state provision of Islamic schools among Glasgow's Muslim community. Schooling practices devised for the contemporary secularised-Presbyterian norm of most 'non-denominational' schools cannot adequately accommodate the needs of the vast majority of this community. A privately run Islamic school does now operate in Glasgow but many Muslims want state-funded Islamic schools under the same arrangements established by the 1918 Act. Moreover, contrary to the common and simplistic misconception about the positive value of social contact, Muslim parents do not report daily social contact in schools as lessening anti-Islamic prejudice. Instead, repeated questioning of their children's religious practice is judged to be hostile and leaves pupils with no option other than to become 'defenders of the faith' from a very young age.

State-funded Islamic schools would be seen as a momentous advance by most of the Scottish Muslim community. The provision of Catholic schools was an equally important development because it offered Catholics a role in Scottish community *as* Catholics. That is precisely why it became such an important symbol to Catholics and anti-Catholics alike. Regrettably it is only now that the benefits of the Catholic sector are belatedly beginning to be recognised. Similar provision of State schools for Muslims, in accordance with the terms of the 1918 Act, would now offer considerable, and much needed, reassurance to the Islamic population that they are to be accepted as equals in Scotland.

It is unfortunate and unhelpful that Scottish education has had an erratic history of responding to difference. The past treatment of Gaelic, never mind versions of the Scots vernacular, such as Lallans or the Doric, allows another glimpse of the power of this underlying force for conformity. Learning in the medium of the English language was the norm to which all had to conform. After years of political lobbying by Gaelic-speakers, there has been a reversal of past policy and a Gaelic-medium state-funded primary school has been established, with others planned. This development sends out a very welcome message. It makes a very public statement about the value of Gaelic within Scottish society and communicates that Gaelic deserves parity with English as a classroom language of instruction. The establishment of the school recognises that special provision is required to meet the different needs of Gaelic speakers. Recognition of this difference helps protect a Gaelic identity and contributes positively to the maintenance of cultural diversity within Scotland. Perhaps this is a portent of future positive moves towards a truly pluralist model of education.

A genuinely pluralist model of Scottish education would be expected to demonstrate more than religious pluralism. As the Gaelic school example demonstrates, there is no reason why choice should be restricted to faith schools. Various specialist schools, not schools narrowly defined in terms of academic specialities, but those with a different value-system, could be established. If there is sufficient demand for Steiner or Montessori state-funded schools, then why not provide them? And schools based on the principles of A. S. Neill's Summerhill School would be a very welcome antidote to Scottish conformity and uniformity. It is essential that these proposals be distinguished from superficially similar moves in England (Judge, 2001). The sudden discovery of the value of faith schools or proposals for specialist academic schools are motivated, at least in part, by the desire to remove more schools from local authority control. In Scotland these proposals offer the possibility of enhancing a national comprehensive *system* of schooling by offering the prospect of real choice within it.

At present parental choice is closely associated with housing mobility. But, for parents who reject their local school, their selection of the replacement school is largely determined by the high socio-economic status of the school-intake and by unadjusted examination results (Willms, J. D., *CES Briefing No 12*, 1997) – a combination that probably means that the purchase of home tutors has ensured that the 'raw' results are even more distorted and misleading than usual. As a result, parental decisions are only marginally advantageous for their children, but the collective effects on designated local schools can be damaging for pupils (and teachers), and can even result in genuinely good schools being closed. No clamour insists that this form of parental choice be ended, despite the outcome being the concentration of educational advantage and disadvantage in increasingly unequal schools. Indeed, it is revealing to learn what categories of school choice meet with approval and disapproval in Scottish society. However, the introduction of a genuinely pluralist comprehensive system would inject a new social dynamic into Scottish education. Parents would then be offered educationally meaningful choices between schools with different value systems or teaching philosophies. That truly would be a choice worth having.

REFERENCES

Conroy, J. C. (ed.) (1999) *Catholic Education: Inside Out, Outside In*, Dublin: Lindisfarne Books.

Devine, T. M. (ed.) (2000) *Scotland's Shame? Bigotry and Sectarianism in Modern Scotland*, Edinburgh, Mainstream.

Finn, G. P. T. and Giulianotti, R. (eds) (2000) *Football Culture: Local Contests, Global Visions*, London, Frank Cass.

Finn, G. P. T. (2000) Thinking uncomfortable thoughts about prejudice: is educational intervention prejudiced by a prejudice against prejudice? *Psychology of Education Review*, 24 (1), 3–16. (Also see pp. 31–4 and read the responses in the intervening pages.)

Hickman, M. J. and Walters, B. (1997) *Discrimination and the Irish Community in Britain. A Report of Research Undertaken for the Commission for Racial Equality*, London: Commission for Racial Equality.

Judge, H. (ed.) (2001) The state, schools and religion, *Oxford Review of Education* (Special issue), 27 (4).

100

Race Equality in Scottish Education

Rowena Arshad and Fernando Almeida Diniz

The events of September 11, 2001, religious conflict and the 'influx' of asylum seekers and refugees are having a profound impact on communities globally and within the devolved parts of the UK. It has forced 'race' issues onto the public agenda. It is against this contemporary socio-political context, in which 'race', or more accurately racism, is an underlying factor that this chapter focuses on the situation in Scottish education. The overall conclusion is that the 'no problem here' approach, so prevalent in mainstream Scottish thinking, no longer commands political support since the Scottish Parliament was established (Edinburgh: Scottish Executive, 2001). However, major barriers exist in institutional and professional practice in all sectors of statutory and voluntary public services (Netto et al., 2001). The Scottish education system is not immune to such criticism, though there are signs of positive change (Almeida Diniz, et al., 2001).

The first part of this chapter traces key developments in the discourses on multi-cultural and anti-racist education (MCARE) up to the establishment of the Scottish Parliament in 1999. Next, it critically reflects on the agenda for action that the present writers proposed in the first edition of this volume and highlights areas in which progress has been made in policy and practice since devolution. Finally, the chapter identifies issues that continue to cause concern if social justice is to be assured for minority ethnic pupils (particularly visible minority ethnic pupils), in the light of the Race Relations Amendment Act 2000. In order to understand what progress has been achieved, it is necessary to trace the emergence of the discourse and its impact on the education system.

RACE EQUALITY PRIOR TO SCOTTISH DEVOLUTION: POLICY, RESEARCH AND PRACTICE

From assimilation to multi-cultural education to MCARE

The dominant approach in the 1970s in Scotland could be characterised as 'assimilationist' in which the emphasis was on assisting children for whom English was a second language (designated 'ESL children') to 'catch up' with indigenous English speaking peers in their adopted country. The response in many Scottish regions was the establishment of language centres to which children could be withdrawn from mainstream schools for full- or part-time education. Community languages, such as Panjabi, Urdu and Cantonese were deemed of less value and indeed potentially harmful to the cognitive development of the 'ESL child'. Eager for their children to achieve in their 'adopted' country, minority ethnic parents listened in good faith to teachers, whom they credited with knowing best; and as English was to be given priority, they often refrained from speaking their mother tongue to their children at home.

The change in direction to multi-cultural education, which was being introduced in England, was yet to be reflected in Scotland where the emphasis was still on the assimilation of minority ethnic children into a white English-speaking Scottish culture. Multi-cultural education, when it was introduced, concentrated on celebrating exotic aspects of minority cultural traditions with the aim of promoting understanding and tolerance, while ignoring discriminatory barriers in institutional policies and practices.

The most significant initiative to prompt the shift to MCARE was the Swann Report (Department of Education and Science, 1985) *Education for All*. Originally set up to investigate the problems of minority ethnic children, it concluded by drawing attention to the growing underachievement of African-Caribbean pupils in mainstream schools and highlighted the impact of social and economic factors. It was the first government report to mention 'institutional racism' as a problem in British society and urged all schools, irrespective of ethnic composition, to confront the issue of racism as part of political education. The MCARE approach recognised the value of cultural diversity but went further to embrace an analysis of issues of power and social justice, arguing for basic changes in the social structures of society, a view that was consistent with the legal frameworks of the Race Relations Act 1976. This period saw a plethora of courses offered on MCARE to teachers and the production of policies and guidelines for permeation of MCARE into curricula. The prevalence and effectiveness of these discourses have remained contentious and problematic in Scotland where the education community is divided on whether to adopt multi-cultural education or anti-racist education, or both; whether to incorporate MCARE within a generic equal opportunities policy, or to retain discrete policies for each dimension. The picture that emerged from the consultations undertaken by the Centre for Education for Racial Equality in Scotland (CERES) in 1999 concluded that:

- Schools (particularly the primaries) tended to verge on playing 'safe' rather than challenging racism; their curriculum approach reflected multi-culturalism in the choice of resources and an emphasis on festivals and global development education.
- Compartmentalisation and 'bolt-on' approaches predominated, particularly in the secondary sector where the responsibility for MCARE in the curriculum was often located within Religious and Moral Education, English, Modern Studies, History, Personal and Social Education.
- Visible minority ethnic pupils were still viewed as 'incomers', 'foreigners' or alternatively were endowed with an assimilated 'Scots' or 'New Scots' identity; how they defined themselves was not given much attention by curriculum developers and researchers.
- Bilingualism, apart from Gaelic, was still perceived as a problem by teachers; the provision of community language teaching (for example, Urdu, Panjabi, Bengali, Cantonese or Arabic) was sparse despite the well-documented research evidence on the cognitive benefits of bilingualism and the maintenance of mother tongue. This was further aggravated by the shortage of bilingual teachers in general and, in particular, as members of the ESL services in Scotland.
- Few authorities had effective policies for dealing with racial harassment, despite the evidence of racial bullying; some appeared to be reluctant to see the relevance of such policies, particularly for early years or special education sectors.

- The rhetoric of 'parental power, choice and diversity' promulgated by the Conservative government had remained marginal to the interests of minority ethnic parents, who were invisible in many of the policy documents in Scottish education and, more seriously, in decisions about their children's education.

Meanwhile, at policy level, it was widely assumed that Scotland had 'good race relations' and that there was 'no problem' here. Consequently, racism did not become an issue in Scottish political and policy discourse and, by extension, in teacher education institutions or schools. Since then, there was a shift from a stance of total complacency to one that accepted, albeit grudgingly, that racism was not a phenomenon confined to urban areas where high numbers of minority ethnic people resided, such as Birmingham. This situation had led many professionals within the field of MCARE to conclude that while there had been rhetorical encouragement from a few politicians, officials at the Scottish Office Education and Industry Department (SOEID) and other education establishments had, in general, maintained a hands-off approach.

The contribution of educational research to the discourse on race equality in education (pre-devolution)

The possible gap between the official espoused theory of 'all is well here' and the practical reality in schools is made all the more difficult to gauge, given the dearth of research on race equality in education in Scotland. In an attempt to assess the current level and scope of research on race equality in education in Scotland, CERES (1997) instigated a postal survey in which researchers, academics, local authorities and practitioners were invited to submit details of studies, conducted in the 1990s, in which race was a principal focus of analysis; a literature search was also undertaken. Conscious of the limitations in the design of this small-scale enquiry, it nonetheless drew tentative impressions of the position, as follows:

- The majority of the sample of studies which were reported could be characterised as small-scale, locally driven by service providers' needs and rarely published for wider consumption; few of the submissions would meet the conventional criteria for research and even fewer attracted significant amounts of external funding.
- There was an apparent reluctance by the mainstream research community in Scotland to include race and ethnicity as integral components of any social policy research. This 'colour-blind' approach, which was evidenced in much of policy research funded by SOEID, was symptomatic of this dilemma. While researchers may have included minority ethnic members in their samples, they failed to analyse the contributing effects of particular factors (e.g. bicultural and bilingual status, experience of racism) in understanding the social impact of educational policies on diverse racial and ethnic groups.
- Most striking, however, was the absence of minority ethnic communities and organisations in the management of research concerning them. The shortage of minority ethnic educational researchers, teachers and academics at all levels may have more to do with structural barriers to obtaining funding and jobs, rather than a lack of skilled personnel.

RACE EQUALITY POST SCOTTISH DEVOLUTION

In early 1999, when the equivalent chapter in the first edition of this book was first written, an agenda for change for the twenty-first century was called for. It was argued that an impending parliament keen to demonstrate its credentials should consider the following seven areas to progress the area of race equality:

- the drawing up of a national policy for combating racism in education;
- the establishment of ethnic monitoring in data gathering systems within the Scottish Office Education and Industry Department;
- tackling racial harassment;
- developing partnership work with minority ethnic parents;
- raising the numbers of minority ethnic staff at all levels of Scottish education;
- developing a strategy to support community languages and bilingualism in Scottish education;
- developing research that moved beyond a description of minority ethnic people's lifestyles to one that seeks to account for racism and its effects in education.

This section charts some of the events of significance that have taken place since early 1999 and comments on progress on the above action areas.

In 1999, a combination of events, particularly the onset of Scottish devolution and publication of the Macpherson Report (1999) on the Stephen Lawrence inquiry, contributed to a conceptual shift in political thinking and commitment towards equality issues, and particularly race equality. The 'new' Scotland regarded itself as a Scotland where everyone matters. The Macpherson Report challenged Scotland to address the matter of institutional racism. The Scottish Executive (SE) responded by publishing *An Action Plan for Scotland* (Edinburgh: Scottish Executive, 2000) and creating two Scotland-wide groups to take forward its recommendations. One of those groups called the Race Equality Advisory Forum (REAF) prepared a race equality strategy for Scotland, which included a section on education. The REAF education sub-group consulted widely with education practitioners and came forward with fifty-six recommendations covering all levels of Scottish Education. Among some of the key recommendations were ones that called for:

- a thematic inspection of education authorities, schools, colleges and community education services on race equality;
- the introduction of a presumption that all data collection and reporting should be done on an ethnically disaggregated basis and, where appropriate, by religious affiliation, belief and languages used;
- the SE to provide guidance to schools to ensure completion of data returns on ethnicity and to publish an accessible explanatory leaflet to schools and parents on the role and use made of ethnic monitoring information in education;
- the development and publication of a strategy in which English as an Additional Language(EAL – this term replaced the previous term of ESL) and bilingual provision can be maintained, developed and resourced in Scotland;
- providers of courses for continuing professional development of teachers to include race equality issues both as permeative and discrete strands;
- the review of Initial Teacher Education to incorporate an analysis of equality issues, including race equality;
- the General Teaching Council in Scotland to ensure that race equality forms part of the quality control during validation reviews of teacher education courses and in the setting of teacher competences;
- children and young people (pupils) to be treated as active partners in setting the agenda for anti-racist education. Schools in particular need to value the views of young people and

issues around challenging racism should be explicitly addressed in the Education for Citizenship programme.

The REAF recommendations were well received by the education and minority ethnic communities. They provided a clear message to politicians and policy makers on what kinds of action to prioritise in the development of race equality in Scottish education. A few weeks prior to the publication of the Macpherson Report, Her Majesty's Inspectorate published an audit toolkit for schools called *A Route to Equality and Fairness* which provides advice to schools on how to evaluate the effectiveness of their efforts to combat discrimination and achieve equality of opportunity.

The following year (2000) the Scottish Executive Education Department (SEED) commissioned work to develop a staff development CD-ROM and website to assist teachers embed anti-racist education in their work. This work produced by Learning and Teaching Scotland, the Centre for Education for Racial Equality in Scotland and the City of Edinburgh Council Education Department was made available for every school in Scotland by spring 2003 (SEED, 2003). The SE Central Research Unit (CRU) had also commissioned an audit of research on race-related issues within Scotland in the past ten years. The CRU report *Audit of Research on Minority Ethnic Issues in Scotland from a 'Race' Perspective* published in the autumn of 2001 (Netto et al., 2001) also includes an education chapter. The education chapter documents over 100 pieces of research related to race and education. The key findings remain largely the same as documented in the first part of this chapter where most research remains characterised as small-scale university based research or locally driven by service providers' needs and rarely published for wider consumption. In addition, Netto et al. identified main themes emerging for education from this audit:

- Scottish education had largely failed to embed race equality issues within teaching and learning in any systematic way and there was no clear evidence of anti-racist approaches being developed and promoted.
- The potential role of Her Majesty's Inspectorate of Education (HMIE) and Learning and Teaching Scotland (LTS) in relation to the promotion of race equality had been largely neglected.
- In the important area of school ethos, the virtual invisibility of race and ethnicity as key factors was notable.
- There remained a lack of statistics on key areas like attainment, aspirations, participation, experience and outlooks of minority ethnic learners.
- Teacher education courses did not provide adequate training to develop teacher competencies for working within a contemporary multi-lingual, multi-faith, multi-cultural, multi-racial classroom.
- Some of the key barriers for minority ethnic pupils include a largely Eurocentric curriculum, lack of bilingual teachers and staff, lack of access to interpreting services, absence of minority ethnic role models and the apathy of educational establishments in tackling covert racism and racial discrimination.
- There remained serious under-representation of minority ethnic people within the Scottish education workforce in all levels.
- There was possible under-use by minority ethnic communities of early years educational provision.
- Some minority ethnic groups continued to be particularly vulnerable to exclusion; for example, those whose children had special educational needs, those living in dispersed communities, or those from specific minority communities such as refugees and asylum

seekers or Gypsy/Travellers.
- Linguistic and cultural diversity had gone largely unrecognised by educational service
- providers and where they had been recognised they were mainly seen as problems.
- Support for the bilingual learner was underfunded.
- Most research connected to race equality focused on the needs, aspirations and perspectives of one or more minority ethnic groups. Little research focused on the causes of racism or on the effectiveness of anti-racist work with either majority or minority ethnic communities.

The audit did reveal some areas of progress:

- A higher profile had been given to the barriers of learning for minority ethnic people in post-compulsory education, as a result of government priorities on social inclusion and widening access.
- Research related to Gypsy/Travellers in Scotland has been considerably boosted in the past decade as a result of research and work done by Save the Children Fund and the Scottish Traveller Education Programme (see Chapter 93).
- The funding areas of the SE were also taking race equality issues into account. For example, the SE's special educational needs (SEN) Innovation Grants had supported three projects designed to foster institutional change in SEN, within an anti-racist perspective.
- Equality and social justice issues had become more mainstream. This was reflected in the National Priorities, three of which focused on inclusion and equality, values and citizenship and learning for life.
- The SEED research agenda also recognised the need to fund research about minority ethnic communities and to support work on promoting race equality.

LEGISLATION AND THE PACE OF CHANGE

However, nothing propels change more than legislation. The first key change occurred when the first major piece of legislation for education since 1980, the Standards in Scotland's Schools etc. (Scotland) Act 2000 included equal opportunities in its schedules. It required each education authority to include an account 'of the ways in which they will, in providing school education, encourage equal opportunities and in particular the observance of the equal opportunity requirements' (section 5.2b). The inclusion of this statement was hard fought for and a result of the combined effort of effective lobbying from the education community working in partnership with the Equal Opportunities Commission, the Commission for Racial Equality, the Disability Rights Commission and the Equality Network (a non-governmental organisation campaigning for the rights of lesbian, gay, transgendered and bisexual people in Scotland). However the key legislation that was to bring the most wide-ranging change in race equality was the Race Relations (Amendment) Act (RRAA) 2000.

The impact of legislation was swift and the following report of the stance taken by the then Senior Chief Inspector of HMIE showed how structures began to adapt in anticipation of forthcoming legislation.

HMI is to mount an inspection into race equality in Scottish schools next year and report in 2003, Douglas Osler, senior chief inspector, told the *TES* Scotland. The inspectorate has already published a hard-hitting report on race equality in further education colleges and HMI's interest stems from the new statutory obligation to monitor in this area. Inspectors have called in outside consultants to help HMI erase any institutional racism on its part and to advise on staff development. (*TESS*, December 2001)

The RRAA was introduced to strengthen the framework for ensuring that all public authorities provide services in a way that is fair, accessible and non-discriminatory on the grounds of race, ethnicity or colour. The Amendment Act introduced three key provisions:

- It widened and strengthened the anti-discrimination provisions within the Race Relations Act 1976 to include all public functions.
- It extended the range and number of public authorities covered by the Act.
- It introduced a new and enforceable duty on key public authorities to promote race equality in all that they do.

The RRAA imposed a general duty on public authorities in performing their public function to have due regard for the need to: promote equality of opportunity; promote good relations between persons of different racial groups; and eliminate unlawful racial discrimination. This general duty applies to all designated public authorities including the educational services of local authorities, for example, such bodies as the Scottish Qualifications Authority, the Scottish Executive, Her Majesty's Inspectorate of Education, the General Teaching Council, and Learning and Teaching Scotland.

There are also specific duties. These include: the preparation and maintenance of a race equality policy; assessing policies to ensure that race equality issues are mainstreamed; and monitoring policies and publishing the results of any monitoring carried out. There are other duties relating to human resource areas like employment, as well as one on ethnic monitoring.

In Scotland, it is the local authority which is the public body responsible for its schools and it is the local education authority which must produce a race equality policy and be responsible for all schools and nurseries under its management. Schools are then required to implement their local education authority race equality policy. Headteachers need to ensure that the school has a race equality policy (or a section on race equality within an equity/ equal Opportunities/Diversity Policy). This policy should cover: staff; pupils; parents/ carers; the wider community.

This means that all policies and procedures within schools have to be developed, monitored and reviewed to ensure that they do not discriminate against any of the groups identified. Race equality should eventually be mainstreamed into all policies which impact on minority ethnic pupils, staff or parents/guardians (for example, learning and teaching; homework; behaviour; anti-bullying; dress code; communication with parents, and so on).

It remains to be seen whether schools in Scotland will approach this piece of legislation as 'yet another piece of work' or as an opportunity to take a fresh look at equality issues. There is no escape from having to take seriously the key requirements of the Act. An authority or school cannot cite lack of resources, time, staff expertise as reasons for not complying. This Act is not about schools with som,e or high levels of, minority ethnic pupils: it is for all schools regardless of the ethnic composition of the school roll.

The SE response to the Act has been to embrace both its spirit and its requirements, launching a national campaign to raise public awareness in Scotland about racism and the need to challenge racism. The campaign called 'One Scotland: Many Cultures', based on a year's-worth of research and consultation, pushed race equality onto the public agenda and warned Scottish people to reject complacency and to live up to their reputation as egalitarian and internationalist.

Looking back to the 'agenda for the twenty-first century' as called for by the present writers in 1999, the pace of change has been swift and positive. The emergence of the RRAA has begun the process of institutionalising race equality. For example, there is now a requirement to monitor ethnically and this means in future years Scotland will be able to provide ethnically disaggregated data relating to the progress and attainment levels of minority ethnic pupils, the correlation between ethnicity and exclusions, the ethnic profile of the Scottish teaching force, the numbers of minority ethnic parents on school boards, and so on. The SE has also provided guidance, for the first time at a national level, on how to record racist incidents. This guidance will also apply to schools. The clear definition provided by the Macpherson Report, which defines a racist incident as any incident which is perceived to be racist by the victim or any other person, also ensures it will now be more difficult for anyone to ignore racial harassment or to camouflage it under a generic anti-bullying policy.

Though there is no national policy for combating racism in education, strategies are in place which collectively would have been the ingredients of a national policy. In particular, the commitment by HMIE to inspect for race equality will cause a sea change in the way over 4,000 schools address multi-cultural and anti-racist education. Prior to such a move, positive practice in race equality tended to be taken forward in schools where there were higher levels of minority ethnic pupils or where the headteacher and/or senior management team had been particularly committed to the issue. At long last race equality will not be an 'ad hoc' feature of school development planning.

However, the areas of improving partnership with minority ethnic parents, the redressing of under-representation of minority ethnic staff at all levels of Scottish education, the commitment to promote Scotland's community languages within educational frameworks, and the proper resourcing of bilingual service provision in schools, remain to be addressed.

CONCLUSION

It could be said that on the macro level, the educational structures are beginning to change to take on board race equality. One of the key challenges for the future is how to convince school senior managers and ordinary classroom teachers to take up the baton and run the race of change. While Scottish teachers theoretically understand the importance of taking forward race equality issues, there is no general consensus on how to do this. For example, there is still conceptual ambiguity on which approach to adopt if any; should it be multi-cultural or anti-racist or both? Some wish to see discrete elements on race equality in the overall curriculum while others favour a more permeative approach.

There remains a fair degree of confusion over terminology and many teachers are worried that they may use terminology that might offend or which is out of date. For example, there are those who find the term 'anti-racism' to be negative, often confusing it to mean 'anti-race', preferring instead to use softer terms like diversity and inclusion. Yet there are others who feel that unless racism is identified and dealt with as a live and contemporary issue the issue will once again be buried under 'sanitise speak'.

Then there is the issue of incorrect use of terminology such as the term 'ethnic' which is still used as a term to refer to all people perceived as minority ethnic. Yet everyone has an ethnicity and therefore the correct description would be 'minority ethnic' or 'ethnic minority'. It is still very commonplace to hear comments from teaching staff and senior managers such as 'we do not have a problem, we do not have many of them here', equating racism or racial discrimination with the presence of minority ethnic people. Racism requires to be addressed even in the total absence of minority ethnic pupils.

It still remains the case that schools in areas of ethnic diversity are more likely to be active in addressing race equality issues than schools in areas considered 'predominantly white'. Schools with less ethnic diversity are more dependent on the committed teacher or headteacher to take this work forward. One commendable piece of research by Donald et al. (1995), carried out by three Central Region primary teachers, remains a useful example of the kind of study that starkly addresses the importance of pursuing an active anti-racist agenda in schools with low numbers of minority ethnic pupils.

Amidst all this, of course, is the resource issue. The RRAA and its requirements have sometimes been compared with the requirements of the Education (Disability Strategies and Pupils' Educational Records) (Scotland) Act 2002. While the disablity legislation comes with monies from the SE to support work at authority and school level, the RRAA comes with no resources and is reliant upon existing authority/school resources and a great deal of commitment and goodwill by staff. Authorities and schools are stating clearly that they require assistance for staff development, and the creation of relevant multi-cultural and anti-racist learning and teaching resources to enable them to feel confident about meeting the key tenets of the RRAA. However, as yet, little has been forthcoming.

The 'catch up' curve for some teachers and schools in Scotland is quite steep, particularly schools which have not shown much interest in race equality issues and which do not have an abundance of local community networks or groups working with minority ethnic people from which to draw assistance. Much guidance and example for promoting race equality practice hails from England or North America. As a result, while there are useful and highly valuable ideas or lesson templates to draw on, by and large they may not be appropriate to Scottish classrooms unless adapted for local relevance. This requires teacher time and understanding of race equality issues which is not always available.

There must be a commitment from the SE to work with key curricular developers like Learning and Teaching Scotland and the major publishing houses to provide relevant resources for Scottish teachers at all levels. There must be monies available to local authorities (and through them to schools) to provide staff development that will promote staff confidence and knowledge in these areas. There also needs to be a connection to the continuing professional development frameworks, such as the Chartered Teacher programme, if the developments are to be taken up seriously and meaningfully.

Equally, teachers and education managers must be given space to air difficult and sensitive issues that often come with the terrain of diversity such as: working positively with differences in values and approaches because of faith or cultural reasons; the challenges of working with diversity in any one classroom; the juggling of limited financial resources in order to ensure the needs of all pupils are being met; and finding ways to overcome the fear of getting it wrong and being labelled a 'racist'. One of the areas that will undoubtedly require attention over the next few years is the way schools can work with a range of partners (parents, communities, voluntary sector organisations, other professionals) to ensure that race equality work progresses well, as the move towards New Community Schools advances. Teachers and teacher educators have a tremendous opportunity to contribute to this new, inclusive vision of Scotland through what is taught: their choices will play a large part in determining the thinking of tomorrow's leaders and the shape of Scottish society for the next decades.

REFERENCES

Almeida Diniz et al. (2001) Race and the New Scotland: special issue on Scotland, *Multicultural Teaching 20 (1), Autumn 2001,* Stoke on Trent: Trentham Books.

Donald, P., Gosling, S. and Hamilton, J. (1995) *'No Problem here?': Children's Attitudes to Race in a Mainly White Area,* Stirling: Central Regional Council, and University of Stirling. http://www.scre.ac.uk/spotlight/spotlight54.html

Macpherson of Cluny (1999) *The Stephen Lawrence Inquiry* (the Macpherson Report), London: HMSO.

Netto, G. et al. (2001) *Audit of Research on Minority Ethnic Issues in Scotland from a 'Race' Perspective,* Edinburgh: SECRU.

Scottish Executive (2001) *Making it Real: A Race Equality Strategy for Scotland,* Race Equality Advisory Forum report, Edinburgh: HMSO.

Scottish Executive (2002) *One Scotland: Many Cultures.* www.onescotland.com

SEED (2003) *Educating for Race Equality – a toolkit for Scottish teachers.* http://www.antiracisttoolkit.org.uk

XII

Scottish Teachers, Teacher Education and Professionalism

101

Teacher Education Institutions

Gordon Kirk

THE UNIVERSITY CONNECTION

One of the features of Scotland's educational tradition is that the professional preparation of teachers took place in specialist institutions devoted to that purpose. These institutions, some of which trace their roots to the early years of the nineteenth century, have been variously known as 'normal schools' or 'training centres', and have enjoyed varying degrees of collaboration with universities and other institutions of higher education. They evolved as independent colleges of education, a separate sector of higher education with a distinctive role to perform and operating within a framework stipulated by the Secretary of State, whose accountability for the education system as a whole required that he controlled the education and training of teachers. The alternative arrangement, common elsewhere, of locating teacher education in universities was ruled out on two counts. The Scottish Education Department (SED) had no confidence that the universities could provide an appropriate training. One Secretary of the SED disparagingly referred to professors 'walled up in their impenetrable fortresses of academic seclusion' and suggested that, if what was wanted was a strong professional education for teachers, the universities would be the last place to look for it. In any event, the Secretary of State for Scotland had no locus with regard to universities: they were accountable, through the University Grants Committee (UGC), to the Minister for Education in England and Wales.

The most immediate antecedents of Scotland's teacher education institutions (TEIs) are shown in Table 101.1.

Two features of the recent past should be highlighted. There has been a significant reduction in the scale of provision both with regard to the student population (from 10,697 to 7,020) and the number of institutions involved. In 1976 there were ten colleges of education and a small teacher education centre in the Education Department at the University of Stirling, instituted in 1964 on an experimental basis in a new and innovative university. Four of these colleges – Jordanhill, Moray House, Dundee and Aberdeen – were the descendants of the 'provincial committees', which had been established in 1907; two of them – Notre Dame and Craiglockhart – served Roman Catholic students, in keeping with the 1918 legislation, which gave the Roman Catholic Church the right to satisfy itself with regard to the 'religious belief and character' of teachers in Roman Catholic schools; Dunfermline College of Physical Education, founded in 1909, was a response to the national shortcomings in health and physical well-being at that time; and the remaining colleges at Hamilton, Craigie and Callendar Park were established to redress an acute shortage of teachers in the early 1960s.

By the late 1970s, the anticipated shortfall of teachers had become an embarrassing over-supply, thanks to the dramatic decline in the size of the school population. South of the border that same problem was met by institutional amalgamations in which smaller specialist institutions were combined to create large polytechnics. However, the tripartite division of higher education in Scotland ruled out such a response; the only option was closure or merger. In 1981, and again in 1987, in the face of the most severe political trauma, the system was reduced, first to seven and then to five colleges, leaving a widely dispersed configuration of institutions, two of which – Moray House and Northern – operated on a multi-site basis, with St Andrew's becoming the national Catholic college.

Table 101.1: The antecedents of Scotland's teacher education institutions

1976	1981	1987	1990+	2001
Craigie (1964)	→ Craigie	→ Craigie	→ University of Paisley	→ University of Paisley
Craiglockhart (1918) Notre Dame (1895)	→ St Andrew's	→ St Andrew's	→ St Andrew's	→ University of Glasgow
Callendar Park (1964) Moray House (1835)	→ Moray House			
Dunfermline (1907)	→ Dunfermline	→ Moray House	→ Moray House Institute (Heriot-Watt University)	→ University of Edinburgh
Aberdeen (1874)	→ Aberdeen			→ University of Aberdeen
Dundee (1906)	→ Dundee	→ Northern	→ Northern	→ University of Dundee
Jordanhill (1832) Hamilton (1966)	→ Jordanhill	→ Jordanhill	→ University of Strathclyde	→ University of Strathclyde
University of Stirling (1964)	→ University of Stirling	→ University of Stirling	→ University of Stirling	→ Univeristy of Stirling
(10,697)	(5,480)	(5,043)	(6,490)	(7,020)

(The figures in brackets denote total student numbers.)

The second feature of the recent past is the progressive erosion of the monotechnic principle as institutions have formed strategic alliances of various kinds with universities. Even as late as 1985 the institutions themselves had vigorously defended their monotechnic status, maintaining that the preoccupation with teaching was a source of institutional strength, providing a powerful source of student motivation and serving as a focus for research and development work. In addition, autonomous status allowed the colleges the opportunity to maintain strong links with the teaching profession. Following a major national inquiry completed in 1985, the Scottish Tertiary Education Advisory Council concluded that teacher education should continue to be provided in 'thriving specialist establishments' and the acclaim which met that recommendation clearly showed that it reflected a widespread consensus. Yet, seventeen years later, the monotechnic institution has passed away and teacher education has come to operate wholly under the aegis of the university. What has led to that transformation of the institutional context of teacher education?

There is no doubt that, within the colleges themselves, if not elsewhere, the attraction of a richer and more varied institutional context provided by university began to outweigh the benefits of institutional autonomy. It came to be accepted that the association with, or incorporation within, a university would strengthen courses, significantly extend the involvement of staff in research activities, especially with the advent of the research assessment exercise (RAE), and enrich the student and staff experience. Moreover, on the wider international scene, not to mention south of the border, the education of teachers and cognate professionals was already located in universities and appeared to flourish there. If similar arrangements could not be made in Scotland might it not be implied that teacher education was of lower standing and quality than elsewhere, and might that perception, in turn, have a detrimental effect on the recruitment of staff and students? Finally, it was acknowledged that the professional education of doctors, lawyers, engineers, and others was well established in the university while, at the same time, strong links with professional bodies and agencies – so strongly valued in teacher education – were fully maintained. All of these considerations suggested that there were academic grounds for placing teacher education within a university context. Conversely, although colleges of education might be reticent about making the claim, the life and work of the university could be enriched through the incorporation of a strong teacher education faculty, especially since the introduction of formal and independent evaluation of teaching – through the statutory arrangements for assessing teaching quality – forced universities to give greater priority to teaching.

Financial pressures also forced colleges to consider their independent status and to seek some form of strategic alliance with a university. The funding environment that developed in the 1980s and 1990s put maximum pressure on institutions to recruit students. The reduced intake levels determined by the Secretary of State created very serious financial difficulties for institutions which, because of their monotechnic nature, were unable to offset the reduction in funds from teacher education by increased activity in other spheres. The severity of the financial problem of some colleges was such that they required 'safety-net' support to protect them against too substantial a reduction in income. The Scottish Higher Education Funding Council's (SHEFC) intimation that safety-net provision would be withdrawn – mainly because it was seen to be a tax on the rest of higher education – made it all the more difficult for small specialised institutions to maintain financial viability. Incorporation within a larger institution, with the economies of scale and other efficiencies that could be secured, made merger with a university extremely attractive, especially in view of the acknowledged academic advantages that could be realised. While mergers of that kind might have proved extremely difficult when colleges of education and universities were the responsibility of separate ministers, in 1992 the Scottish Further and Higher Education (Scotland) Act repatriated the Scottish universities and brought all of higher education within the responsibility of the Secretary of State for Scotland and the SHEFC.

The legislation of 1992 also disbanded the Council for National Academic Awards (CNAA), the body that had been established to validate courses and to confer awards on students in non-university institutions. The demise of the CNAA made it essential for non-university institutions to establish a relationship with a university to ensure that their programmes were academically acceptable and that students obtained university degrees on qualification.

That combination of factors, some of them originating in changed perspectives within the colleges themselves and some of them reflecting wider changes in the context of higher education, led to the dissolution of teacher education as a separate sector of higher education and to its incorporation within universities.

CURRENT PROVISION

Current provision in the seven TEIs is given in Table 101.2. They differ in size and in the scope of their offerings. In some, teacher education is the sole preoccupation, whereas, in others, there has been diversification into a number of cognate fields, such as social work; community education; speech and language therapy; sports and leisure; and so on.

All courses for prospective school teachers lead either to the Teaching Qualification (Primary Education) or the Teaching Qualification (Secondary Education). In addition, there are two standard routes to each teaching qualification: the one-year postgraduate or 'consecutive' route, and the four-year, or longer, 'concurrent' route. Both approaches have their defenders. The consecutive approach is justified on the grounds that entrants to teaching require a strong academic base, which it is the purpose of undergraduate study to provide. That acquired, the period of professional education – in North America and parts of Australia this extends over not one but two years – is devoted to those studies and experiences which enable students to induct learners into the activities they have mastered. In the concurrent approach, the academic study of subjects proceeds in parallel with educational studies and periods of school placement, thus allowing, it is claimed, a progressive maturing of professional understanding in a way that is extremely difficult in what has been called the 'forcing house' of the consecutive route. The Scottish tradition of teacher education has espoused both approaches. In teacher education circles, there is, perhaps, a preference for the concurrent approach. However, there is merit in retaining the consecutive route as a way of regulating supply more easily than if there was complete dependence on the alternative approach.

In the primary field, the balance between the BEd concurrent route and the PGCE consecutive route has been officially set at 55:45. However, partly in response to calls from the General Teaching Council for Scotland (GTC) and the TEIs, the Scottish Executive Education Department (SEED) has allowed some slippage with the ratio, at one point reaching 75:25 in favour of the BEd, but, more recently, coming closer to 50:50. In the secondary sphere, the one-year postgraduate consecutive route has traditionally been the principal preparation for teaching for those professing the familiar range of university academic subjects. The concurrent route was reserved for such studies as Physical Education, Music, and Technology, all of these normally leading to the award of a BEd degree after four years. When teacher education was introduced at the University of Stirling, the preference was for the concurrent route. That approach, from which the teacher graduates with an academic qualification in a subject as well as a secondary teaching qualification, has attracted increased support in recent years, particularly following incorporation of colleges within universities.

Table 101.2: Current provision in Scottish teacher education institutions

Course	Aberdeen	Dundee	Edinburgh	Glasgow	Paisley	Stirling	Strathclyde
PGCE (Primary)	75	93	157	155	70	–	181
PGCE (Secondary)	177	–	201	175	65	–	472
BEd (Primary)	346	245	492	465	290	–	538
BEd (Physical Education)	–	–	373	–	–	–	–
BEd (Technology)	–	–	34	77	–	–	–
BEd (Music)/ Applied Music	73	–	–	76	–	–	212
Concurrent	3	–	–	24	–	277	73
Further Education	–	–	–	–	–	184	102
Community Education	–	135	96	–	–	–	123
Social Work	–	126	–	–	–	–	131
Leisure/Sport/ Outdoor Education	–	–	213	–	–	–	291
Speech and Language Therapy	–	–	–	–	–	–	116
BA Childhood Studies	–	–	–	–	84	–	–
Total	674	599	1566	972	509	461	2239

A glance at Table 101.2 confirms that the range of provision in the seven TEIs varies significantly: no two are alike. However, all TEIs share two common features. Firstly, they all offer a range of in-service programmes. In the late 1970s, partly in response to the dramatic decline in pre-service students, the Scottish Office designated over 200 FTE staff for in-service work, to be undertaken in colleges or in schools (see Chapter 103). That was an extremely generous and far-sighted policy, for it enabled college of education staff, many of whom were at the forefront of professional practice and who played a leading role in curriculum development, to support the revitalisation of the work of the schools through consultancy and other types of activity. Progressively, that earmarked funding for in-service activities was withdrawn and placed with employing authorities who were then in a position to purchase in-service support, initially from the colleges but ultimately from any source they chose. Predictably, that source of funds became lost in the general expenditure block allocated to authorities. Nevertheless, all TEIs continue to offer in-service support to schools and to offer opportunities for continuing professional development through SCOTCAT– the Scottish Credit Accumulation and Transfer scheme – the national framework of certificate, diploma and master's degree awards (see Chapter 106).

Secondly, all TEIs are committed to strengthening their involvement in research activities. The former colleges of education were allocated an annual 8% staffing allowance for research and development work, another example of forward-thinking on the part of the Scottish Office. Disappointingly, that allowance was withdrawn in 1986 as part of the government's attempt to reduce expenditure on the colleges and to bring them into line with practice in the central institutions, which had not received a research allowance. Despite that, research activity has continued to develop in the TEIs. It has been acknowledged that strong courses flourish in a climate of intellectual enquiry and discussion of the kind that a research culture is able to sustain. Moreover, the financial inducements afforded by the RAE have encouraged a still further involvement in research, notwithstanding the intensity of the competition. The pressure to engage in research is likely to intensify as TEIs become incorporated within the university system, where engagement in research and other forms of scholarly activity is an explicit academic expectation.

STUDENT NUMBERS AND FINANCE

The diversity of TEIs, the variations in provision that occur between them, and the apparent haphazard distribution of courses, may convey the impression that teacher education is inadequately controlled and has been merely allowed to develop according to institutional initiatives or the enterprise of individuals and groups in different parts of the country. On the contrary, teacher education provision is very tightly controlled. The effectiveness of the whole educational system depends on an adequate supply of well qualified and well prepared teachers. Besides, it would be a source of considerable political embarrassment if there were a shortage of teachers. Furthermore, the pressure on the public purse makes it imperative that there is no over-supply: it would not represent a prudent use of scarce resources to train teachers who would merely help to swell the ranks of the unemployed.

Consequently, SEED exercises a tight grip on the numbers admitted to training. Annually, on the advice of an advisory group that includes representatives of the GTC, the education authorities and the TEIs, SEED generates a consultation paper which proposes intake levels for the different courses in the following year, taking account of the birth rate, the size of the school population, non-completion rates on courses, and other factors. Following consultation with interested parties, the First Minister then determines the overall levels for each of the different modes of training. Having made that calculation, the First Minister then passes responsibility for the distribution of the intake among the different TEIs to the SHEFC. That transfer of responsibility is appropriate for it enables the body that is responsible for funding all of Scottish higher education to integrate the distribution of teacher education places into its overall funding model.

That model has two key features. Firstly, the money follows the student: the size of the financial allocation made to an institution relates directly to the number of students it enrols. Institutions are therefore under extreme pressure to recruit to the maximum permitted. Secondly, the funding allocated per student is not based on a direct assessment of costs but, rather, derives from the total sum of money made available by the Scottish Executive to the Funding Council. That is, the institutions are allocated not what they need but their share of the funds made available for the system as a whole.

PROFESSIONAL AND ACADEMIC CONTROL

There are other forms of control of the teacher education system. As has been seen, SEED has the authority to determine the annual intake to courses. SEED is also entitled to approve the content of courses. Since the early 1980s, this responsibility has been exercised by the promulgation, after consultation, of national guidelines for teacher education courses, and TEIs are obliged to ensure that courses offered are compatible with these guidelines. Unless that condition is met, SEED can withhold approval of a course. The

1993 revision of the guidelines contained for the first time a set of competences based on a functional analysis of the teacher's role. These were also included with minor modifications in the 1998 version of the guidelines, and were subsequently incorporated in the Standard for Initial Teacher Education in Scotland. (Quality Assurance Agency for Higher Education, 2000).

That standard is 'a comprehensive and unitary set of benchmark statements which are the requirements for each programme of Initial Teacher Education in Scotland'. Following a recommendation of the Sutherland Report (NCIHE, 1997), it has been decided to create a framework for the continuing professional development of teachers in Scotland, which consists of a series of standards to mark particular levels of professional achievement. The Standard for Initial Teacher Education provides the basic foundation on which subsequent standards – for example, the Standard for Full Registration and the Standard for Chartered Teacher – will build (see Chapter 104).

The specification of competences reflected the Secretary of State's determination to ensure that those who have completed a teacher education programme have acquired the capacities which are judged to characterise competent professional performance. However, the competence approach has attracted criticism. Some feel that it represents a heavily reductionist view of teaching: it is thought to concentrate on the practical know-how of teaching and, as a result of that emphasis, to undervalue the theoretical underpinnings of teachers, the knowledge and insight which enable teachers to adopt a reflective and self-critical approach to their work and to their professional circumstances. There are two rejoinders. In the first place, the national guidelines explicitly require that teachers come to terms with the knowledge and understanding relating to the various competences. Secondly, all of the programmes concerned result in university awards and universities, as the custodians of academic standards, are unlikely to be associated with programmes that are entirely skills-based and do not testify to intellectual and cognitive achievements.

The second form of control is exercised by the GTC. Acting on behalf of the teaching profession, the GTC has to satisfy itself that the work of TEIs is fully in line with professional expectations. It exercises its responsibility in a number of ways: it has the authority to visit TEIs from time to time to scrutinise aspects of provision and, even where it finds that a TEI is unresponsive to its reports, to refer the matter to the First Minister; the GTC also has the authority to ensure that members of staff in TEIs who work on teacher education courses are themselves registered teachers. Finally, the council's most obvious role in initial teacher education is through its accreditation and review of courses. That work is undertaken by panels drawn from members of the council and wider afield. In that way, the council, which includes a majority of practising teachers, is able to satisfy itself that any proposed programme takes full account of the changing demands of the schools. Since 1999, SEED has looked to the GTC to advise it on whether or not teacher education programmes are compatible with national guidelines (see Chapter 112).

Finally, all teacher education courses have to meet the academic standards of the university which confers the award. While practice between the different universities varies, all of them are required to have in place mechanisms to ensure that, before they are offered, programmes undergo a process of scrutiny by peers, that they are subjected to the rigours of the external examining system and are subjected to periodic review. Since the establishment of the SHEFC in 1992, universities have been exposed to other sources of external scrutiny. The SHEFC looks to the Quality Assurance Agency in Higher Education (QAA) to assess and to report publicly on quality of the teaching and learning environment, the standard of university awards and students' achievements, as well as the robustness of their quality assurance arrangements. Finally, all institutions of higher education are under pressure to expose their research activities to the peer review that is sponsored by the periodic RAE. All of these various forms of control, that are extended across the full scope of university studies, are therefore also applied to provision in teacher education.

Teacher education is therefore subject to several levels of external scrutiny. The Sutherland Report considered, indeed, that the process required streamlining. A standing committee for quality assurance in initial teacher education was established and, after consultation, has devised a process of collaborative review in which HM Inspectorate of Education, the GTC, and the QAA co-operate in assessing the quality of provision, relying substantially on evidence generated by the internal review processes of institutions. Collaborative review was piloted in two institutions in the course of session 2001–2. It remains to be seen whether that innovative approach to quality assurance will become standard practice, or whether the price will prove too high and there will be a reversion to the arrangements that were so roundly criticised in the Sutherland Report.

PARTNERSHIP

All teacher education programmes require sustained periods of supervised work in schools, on the assumption that teachers should not only demonstrate a theoretical understanding of teaching but should also demonstrate their capacity to perform competently in real settings. Clearly, it is essential, therefore, to ensure that the institution-based components of a course are closely integrated with placement or school-based activities. If that is to happen, it is essential that there is close collaboration between teacher education institutions and schools.

Over the past decade it has proved frustratingly difficult to develop arrangements in Scotland to match best practice elsewhere, despite the committed efforts of thousands of Scottish teachers to support the professional preparation of their future colleagues. The mentoring initiative introduced in 1992 sought to create a larger role for teachers in the training process by appointing mentors, who would be given special training for their role, and would be freed from some of their teaching responsibilities to undertake that important task. Despite the provision of additional transitional funding and a carefully evaluated two-year pilot study at Moray House, it transpired that the initiative could not command the support of teachers and the scheme was withdrawn. Instead, the GTC was requested, in October 1995, to undertake a study of the ways in which partnership might be developed. The GTC report, published in March 1997, reaffirmed the importance of the principle, maintaining that teachers in schools and TEIs should co-operate across the whole range of functions, including student selection, course planning, student supervision, assessment and course evaluation. The report saw the TEIs and the schools having distinctive but complementary contributions to make to training. That principle of complementarity is taken to imply that it is the function of the higher education institution to ensure that students come to terms with the academic and theoretical underpinnings of teaching through reading and research and discussion, whereas it is the responsibility of the school to draw on the accumulated expertise of experienced professionals and to make that available to students. An effective programme of teacher education is one in which these two knowledge bases are integrated to create a coherent framework of professional preparation.

Conscious of previous difficulties, the GTC report concluded that 'new money should be directed towards schools in order to enhance the teachers' role in initial teacher education'.

Understandably enough, there followed an inquiry into the costs of partnership by Deloitte and Touche, published in 1999. When it transpired that the costs were alarmingly high for all concerned, the report was placed on the web and no other official action followed.

The *First Stage Review of Initial Teacher Education* (Deloitte and Touche, 2001), having carefully rehearsed the arguments on partnership, recommended the establishment of teacher development partnerships (TDPs), which appeared to offer the prospect of comprehensive collaborative arrangements between TEIs and schools from the point of student selection, throughout initial teacher education and probation, and encompassing teachers' CPD. If those now considering the implementation of these proposals fail to take account of the resource implications of TDPs, the report will follow others into the dustbin of educational history. Meanwhile, in other parts of the world, there are now fruitful approaches towards what is called 'collaborative partnership'. In such initiatives, there is a sharing of power between university and schools; ample provision is made for staff development; formal mechanisms for collaboration are put in place; and, finally, initial teacher education forms part of a wider network of collaborative activities. It is to be hoped that in Scotland it will be possible to move towards that kind of partnership and that the creation of such partnership will not be vitiated by a debate on the availability of resources.

ISSUES FOR THE FUTURE

Despite a series of profoundly dislocating changes over the past two decades, teacher education in Scotland has developed significantly (Kirk, 2000). Its quality has been endorsed by the 'highly satisfactory' ratings obtained by most of the TEIs in the 1995 Quality Assessment of Teacher Education, and the extremely positive outcome of the collaborative review pilot which rated provision in both the University of Edinburgh and the University of Strathclyde as 'commendable' in all areas, with significant instances of 'Exemplary' provision. Finally, the Sutherland Report concluded that, 'The structural arrangements for funding and organising teacher education and training have served Scotland reasonably well and, indeed, in many respects they provide a model for other parts of the United Kingdom.'

Gratifying as these endorsements undoubtedly are, there is evidence to suggest that further improvement is required. The McCrone Report (2000) identified a number of areas in which, in the opinion of an undisclosed number of informants, provision could be improved to the extent that a review of initial teacher education was recommended. That review was divided into two stages. The first of these, the Deloitte and Touche review mentioned previously, made helpful recommendations in such areas as ICT, special educational needs, health and sex education, and classroom management, and urged institutions to review their provision accordingly.

It is likely, however, that the Second Stage Review – to be completed after the conclusion of Scotland's national debate on the future of school education – will call for more radical thinking. Assuming that the difficulties concerning quality assurance and partnership can be resolved, the agenda for change is likely to include the following:

- part-time provision;
- the relationship between ITE and in-service provision, particularly in view of the abbreviated form of probation and the introduction of the Standard for Chartered Teacher;

- the need for a teaching qualification which straddles primary and secondary education in response to such developments as the 5–14 programme;
- the need for a teaching qualification which straddles upper secondary and further education in response to the Higher Still programme;
- greater opportunities for specialised study within the BEd (primary);
- introduction of a teaching qualification in personal, social or lifestyle education in response to Scotland's appalling record in health and related matters;
- further development of concurrent approaches.

Perhaps the most important challenge facing the teacher education institutions concerns their full incorporation into the life and work of universities. Some fear that this change may lead to academic drift, in the sense that the TEIs may devote less attention to schools with a consequent blurring of the focus on professional action. There is no doubt that the TEIs will need to accept the obligation to undertake research that is imposed by membership of the university community. However, in responding positively to the new challenges, it will be important to ensure that there is no weakening of the strong links that have been forged with teachers and education authorities. Indeed, given the enhanced role which the profession expects to play in teacher education, these links will need to be strengthened. To that end, arrangements for collaborative partnership must to be established, based on the faculty or institute of education, and strongly committed to academic and professional interchange of various kinds. It is not too optimistic to envisage a culture of professional collaboration in which there are shared understandings between schools and universities about teacher education and training, in which there are joint research initiatives where the expertise of universities is accessed to support school development planning and curriculum evaluation, and in which formal agreements are made on the provision of the continuing professional development of teachers. Through such collaborative partnerships, universities will be able to contribute to the revitalisation of schools and teachers themselves will come to participate more fully in the life and work of universities. The effectiveness of the national arrangements for teacher education in the new era will be measured by the extent to which that vision of partnership is made a reality.

REFERENCES

Deloitte and Touche (2001) *Report of the 'First Stage' Review of Initial Teacher Education*, Edinburgh: SEED.

Kirk, G. (2000) *Enhancing Quality in Initial Teacher Education*, Edinburgh: Dunedin Academic Press.

National Committee of Inquiry into Higher Education, Report 10, Annex A, *Teacher Education and Training: Scotland* (The Sutherland Report), in *Higher Education in the Learning Society*, Norwich: HMSO.

QAAHE (2000) *The Standard for Initial Teacher Education in Scotland*, Gloucester: QAAHE.

Report of the Committee of Inquiry into Professional Conditions of Service for Teachers (The McCrone Report) (2000) *A Teaching Profession for the 21st Century*, Edinburgh: HMSO.

102

Professional Studies in Initial Teacher Education

Donald Christie

Though the detailed curriculum of initial teacher education courses in Scotland varies considerably, not least to reflect durations ranging from thirty-six weeks to four years, their overall structure broadly comprises three common components: direct practical experience of placement in schools; study of the relevant aspects or subjects of the school curriculum; and course element which may go by the title 'professional studies'or some similar label such as 'theory and practice of education' or, put more simply, 'education' or 'educational studies'. In most programmes there is also a fourth component, comprising optional elements, which enable students either to advance their own personal education or to gain a deeper professional insight in an area of special interest. The present chapter examines the historical development and current status of professional studies and considers the implications of issues arising for the future of initial teacher education in Scotland.

WHAT CONSTITUTES PROFESSIONAL STUDIES?

In the words of the working party set up in the early 1980s to review the pre-service training of primary teachers at the time when the former three-year diploma course was about to be replaced by a four-year BEd degree course, 'professional studies' comprises: 'the whole range of studies which give students the knowledge, understandings, skills, insights and attitudes which allow them to operate efficiently in the primary school' (SED, *The New Degree: Report and Guidelines – A Report to the Secretary of State, by the Working Party on Primary Pre-service Training*, Edinburgh: SED, 1983). Such a broad definition clearly permits a wide range of interpretations; in this general sense it refers to the entire curriculum of the initial professional education of teachers. However, as indicated above, it has also been used as a label to attach to a particular part of that curriculum. For example, in the *Guidelines for Initial Teacher Training* first issued by SOED in 1993, professional studies receives the following introduction: 'The professional studies *element* of courses should provide an intellectual challenge for students and have an explicit concern with the classroom and the professional needs of teachers' (p. 2, italics added). The revised version of these guidelines (SOEID, 1998), whose title significantly refers to initial teacher *education* rather than initial teacher training, stipulates that courses must 'contain professional studies, subject studies and school experience' (p. 4), but does not offer any definition of these terms. Nevertheless, the guidelines require course providers to ensure that the three elements are 'carefully sequenced, inter-related and progressively more demanding of students' (p. 4). In considering professional studies in Scottish initial teacher education, the present chapter will consider both the general and the specific meanings of the term.

The character of professional studies in initial teacher education courses can be expected to reflect prevailing views about the nature of teaching as a professional activity. Kirk (1988) advances six propositions which encapsulate the essential features of the professionalism for which initial teacher education must prepare prospective entrants to the profession, namely: that teaching is a vitally important social function; that it is a multi-faceted activity involving many different roles within and beyond the classroom; that teaching is based on an extensive range of theoretical understandings; that it is a problematic and controversial activity; that teaching entails self-evaluation; and that it requires a commitment to professional development. If these propositions are accepted, they provide a framework against which to evaluate professional studies within teacher education courses past and present.

The applicability of the concept of professionalism to teaching is not unchallenged. Humes (1986) draws attention to several flaws in the ideal of professionalism, which are worth bearing in mind as the nature of professional studies is considered. Humes argues that while the rhetoric of professional status may be attractive, the reality is that teachers tend to be motivated not so much by high professional ideals but rather by self-interest. Humes also claims that the enormous variation in the status and level of professional training of teachers undermines the general applicability of the concept of professionalism. However, this argument is now hard to sustain given the tightening of national standards applied to all programmes of initial teacher education and continuing professional self-regulation by the General Teaching Council for Scotland (Kirk, 2000). Nevertheless, examination of the evolution of professional studies over the last few decades shows that there has indeed been ambivalence among those responsible for the funding of initial teacher education towards some of the key features of professionalism delineated by Kirk (1988). For instance, a rational and critical analysis of social and political conditions impinging on education is implied by the idea that teaching should be seen as a controversial activity. However, one might argue that national and local government agencies responsible for the administration of education will in fact select and promote those who conform and do not ask awkward questions. Teacher educators are unlikely to be immune to the influence arising from having to operate in this kind of context, and while over the years one of the declared aims of professional studies programmes has been to foster critical thinking, successful students may instead have been those who learn to display compliance.

It is worth noting that the academic study of education and concern about the quality of preparation of teachers in Scotland has a long and rather contentious history, dating from the early nineteenth century, a period which included in 1876 the appointment of the first professors of education in the English-speaking world at the Universities of Edinburgh and St Andrews. This ambivalence towards academic status for teacher education is an enduring characteristic of the attitude of the Scottish educational establishment. First, the churches and then successive governments through the Scottish Office kept tight control over teacher education by maintaining their own separate training institutions in the form of training centres or colleges of education and allowing only marginal involvement of the universities. However, the turmoil and rapid change in higher education during the 1990s has seen the former separation of initial teacher education from the university sector brought to a dramatic end in a spate of mergers, the result of which is that all initial teacher education in Scotland is now carried out in the universities of Aberdeen, Dundee, Edinburgh, Glasgow, Paisley, Stirling and Strathclyde (see Chapter 101 of this volume and Kirk, 2000). The Scottish Office and subsequently the Scottish Executive Education Department have adopted an uncharacteristically 'laissez faire' attitude to these recent institutional changes. In response to these developments, Scottish teacher educators have had to shift their professional orientation toward the academic culture of the universities. As university academics they are expected to engage in a balance of duties involving research and other scholarly activity in addition to teaching.

During the 1980s as part of a government drive towards improving educational standards in schools, a distinctly utilitarian approach to teacher education emerged which was reflected in the way the desired curriculum for teacher education came to be described. Competences rather than disciplines provided the organising principles around which courses were designed. In place of previously distinct discipline-based units of study in Psychology, Education, Sociology or Philosophy and separate 'methods' courses, guidelines required the colleges of education to provide integrated programmes of professional studies to complement school placement experience and study of the relevant subjects of the school curriculum. By this they were referring to the need for staff in separate departments of Psychology, Education and Methods (which still existed in many Scottish colleges of education at that time) to work in collaboration and to ensure that professional relevance was the paramount consideration in course planning. New course programmes were devised, variously described with labels such as 'theory and practice of education'. New relationships were explored between institution-based study and practical school experience, and tensions were created between concern for the quality of understanding of students in the formerly separate disciplines on the one hand and the call for more staff to participate as generalist tutors supporting students in their teaching practice on the other.

The dichotomy between theory and practice has proved to be a persistent theme in the discourse of teacher education and has implications for consideration of professional studies. According to the traditional, positivist view, practice was expected to be informed or guided by theory: practice referred to classroom experience of teaching and learning; and theory was taken to refer to models or sets of ideas arising out of published research or speculative enquiry. From this perspective, teacher educators were expected to communicate certain favoured theoretical perspectives in such a way as to enable students to apply, say, learning theory in their practice of teaching. A more constructivist view of the relationship between theory and practice would hold that the traditional approach is misguided in that it accords unjustified status to pre-existing published theories and their application. This alternative approach emphasises the process of theorising and ascribes greater value to the personal theories which students themselves construct, derived from practical experiences in the classroom. The latter approach is explicitly or implicitly to be discerned in the declared philosophy of the most recent versions of initial teacher education courses, almost all of which make reference to the need to foster reflective practice, though there is evidence that the ideal of reflection to be found in course documentation is rarely in fact attained by students (Stark, R., 2001, Unpublished PhD thesis, University of Strathclyde).

Attempts to move significantly greater responsibility for teacher education away from the higher education institutions and into the schools, as has been achieved in the graduate and licensed teacher schemes in England and Wales, have so far been thwarted by united resistance from all sides in Scottish education. It could further be argued that the professional and academic status of teachers in Scotland was reflected in the terms of reference of the group set up by the Scottish Office in the wake of the Garrick Report on Higher Education and the Sutherland Report on Teacher Education. This group was asked to examine the implications of new arrangements for delivery and quality assurance for initial teacher education courses, particularly to take account of the inception of the Quality Assurance Agency for Higher Education (QAA). Unlike in England and Wales, where the Teacher Training Agency maintained control over quality assurance, the Scottish Executive and, though somewhat less wholeheartedly, the General Teaching Council, gave their blessing to the idea that initial teacher education in Scotland should be treated as a university 'subject' in its own right by QAA. Recognising that there were several stakeholders with an interest in quality of provision in ITE, the new policy elite within the Scottish Executive responded to injunctions contained in the Sutherland Report by setting up a group, involving teacher educators from the universities, school teachers, local authority education managers, HMI, together with officers of the GTCS and QAAHE, to define the benchmark standards for ITE and to establish collaborative arrangements and procedures for the scrutiny and review of course provision. The resulting Benchmark *Standard for Initial Teacher Education in Scotland* (QAAHE, 2000), described in more detail in Chapter 104 of this volume, is arguably less narrowly defined than the equivalent statements emanating from the relevant training agencies elsewhere in the United Kingdom. National consultations appear to indicate that the Scottish ITE Benchmarks enjoy wide consensual support among teacher educators and the other stakeholders.

TEACHER EDUCATORS: BACKGROUNDS AND VALUES

The distinctiveness and quality of Scottish education have been powerful and persistent elements in the national identity. Clearly associated with these constructs is the respect supposedly accorded to the teaching profession in Scotland (e.g. see Clark, 1997 and Chapter 113 of this volume). Whether such respect is extended in the public perception to those responsible for teacher education is, however, highly debatable. But who are the persons entrusted with the role of providing programmes of studies for intending teachers? What are their qualifications and to what extent are they entitled to claim credit for the quality of professionalism in the Scottish teaching profession? As discussed in Chapter 101 of the present volume, until the mergers with universities which took place during the 1990s and with the exception of concurrent training of secondary school teachers at the University of Stirling, initial teacher education in Scotland has been the province of training centres or colleges of education, which were mainly monotechnic institutions independent of the university sector. The staff in the colleges of education were generally recruited from the ranks of the teaching profession. In the case of secondary teacher education this meant typically that subject specialists in the college sector were drawn from among aspiring principal teachers and members of senior management teams in secondary schools. In the case of primary teacher education, primary 'methods' tutors tended to have been able classroom practitioners who had already begun to progress through the hierarchy to positions of assistant, deputy, or headteacher. Securing a post in the college of education sector was seen as an alternative to gaining further promotion in the schools, entering local education authority structures or joining national bodies such as the inspectorate. There were always exceptions to this pattern allowed in order to recruit people with skills or areas of expertise in short supply at any time, or during times of rapid expansion such as occurred during the late 1960s and early 1970s, when at its peak the sector contained ten teacher education colleges and at Stirling, a university department of education.

While there has always been traditionally a strong representation of psychologists and education specialists among the 'home grown' staff involved in teacher education, the philosophers, sociologists and historians have been fewer in number and more often than not have been recruited furth of Scotland. In recent years the range of options for postgraduate study in education has increased with flexible, modular certificate, diploma and masters programmes becoming available in several faculties of education as well as the research degrees, MPhil and PhD, and with the Doctorate in Education (EdD) now being offered in addition to the MEd Existing staff are under pressure to obtain higher degree qualifications to enhance the academic profiles of the faculties of education and such qualifications are now routinely being sought from applicants for the few available posts in the sector.

The professional credentials of the staff in initial teacher education were an issue which was pursued strenuously by the GTC from its inception in 1965 until the revised regulations governing teacher education in 1987 required all staff engaged in teacher education to be registered with the GTC (Kirk, 1988). Since the late 1990s with teacher education firmly within the universities, this criterion for staff recruitment has inevitably become harder to sustain. Other considerations such as demonstrable research capability have now demanded attention in view of the institutional importance of the SHEFC research assessment exercise. This potential cause for concern for the GTC has perhaps been obscured by the fact that the period in question has been a time of staff reduction in the sector with only a trickle of new appointments being made. New potential problems for recruitment have been posed by the relatively favourable salary settlement for teachers contained in the McCrone Agreement (SEED, 2001). Sharp (2001) argues that the resulting imbalance in salary levels will make it hard to attract teachers who have achieved any kind of promotion in the primary or secondary school sectors as candidates for initial teacher education posts in Scottish universities. While there seems little evidence to date of difficulty on the part of the faculties and institutes of education in filling any vacancies arising, at the time of writing the full implications of the introduction of the status of Chartered Teacher have yet to be felt.

Staff in the Scottish university institutes and faculties of education remain deeply committed to providing teaching of high quality and have been accustomed to a high level of external accountability. However, with the proliferation of new courses at both the undergraduate and postgraduate level, they find themselves facing an increasingly diverse and demanding teaching load and at the same time having to endure, together with their university colleagues in other disciplines, significant cuts in resources. As a consequence, it is not unusual to hear colleagues sharing fears about their ability to continue to deliver teaching of the quality they would wish. When the additional pressure to produce publishable research is taken into account, some have found their changed circumstances almost intolerable. By contrast, for others, the new context has been seen as providing welcome opportunities simultaneously to pursue both scholarly research as part of a university community and professionally worthwhile activities within the field of education. Moreover, diminishing resources are seen by some as a stimulus to find imaginative new methods of course delivery.

Generally speaking the values of teacher educators lie within the humanistic, egalitarian tradition. A strong commitment to notions of social and moral responsibility is also to be discerned both implicitly and explicitly in course materials. However, there could also be said to be a degree of cautious conservatism, or even anti-intellectualism, evident in the stance adopted by staff in the sector. This may be part of the wider tendency in Scottish professional life to seek consensus rather than confrontation, as documented by Humes (1986). It may also be to do with a reluctance to take risks in the face of subtle forms of centralised control, which engender both compliance and complacency. The influence of the Scottish Executive on most aspects of teacher education, while arguably less overt than that of the former Scottish Office, remains pervasive, including: course approval; the setting of quotas; the financing of the sector (indirectly since the inception of SHEFC in 1992); and, of course, the setting of priorities for, and funding of, any research into teacher education. Hence it is, perhaps, understandable that teacher educators, despite their new-found status as university academics, are taking time to shake off their reluctance to be overtly critical with respect to Scottish Executive policies.

CONTENT OF INITIAL TEACHER EDUCATION COURSES

Teacher education courses operate on the basis of some explicit or implicit conceptualisation of what constitutes good teaching. Analysis of course documentation from the 1970s until the early 1990s suggests the prevailing models had a shared origin in systematic behavioural approaches to learning applied pragmatically to what were seen as the essential steps in the teaching process, and a common function which was to provide a way to sharpen the focus of both the teacher educator and the student teacher. Such models are less conspicuous in more recent course validation documents, apparently considered no longer to convey the multi-faceted nature of teaching nor the complexity of the social context in which teaching occurs. Essentially they have been supplanted by the set of competences for the beginning teacher declared by the SOEID (1998) guidelines and the QAAHE (2000) Benchmark statements. A cynical view might see this as pragmatic compliance with the Scottish Executive. However, a more positive interpretation is that course planners have in general been comfortable with these guidelines since the definition given of competence is not a narrow one. The vision of the newly qualified teacher portrayed in the Benchmark *Standard for Initial Teacher Education in Scotland* (QAAHE, 2000) is of someone who 'can function as an effective facilitator of pupils' learning, is committed to professional development and reflection and is able to engage collaboratively with colleagues in the profession, with other groups and agencies, and with the various members of the communities served by education' (p. 1). Kirk (2000) argues that Scotland has succeeded in ensuring that initial teacher education is appropriately focused on the skills of teaching but 'without the excessive prescription that has so alienated teacher educators in England' (p. 21). Course programmes in Scottish initial teacher education must also aim to provide students with relevant theoretical perspectives and opportunities both to question practice, to develop their own personal theories and to articulate their value positions with respect to education. Course planners can use their own discretion and ingenuity to strike what they see as the optimum balance between these arguably more challenging professional aspirations on the one hand and the acquisition of practical classroom skills on the other. Precisely where this balance should be struck is an issue on which there is continuing debate in the sector and there have been many attempts to resolve the problem by integrating practical and theoretical elements.

The overall design of the curriculum of ITE programmes is now shaped by the requirements of the QAAHE (2000) Benchmark Standard that they should, among other things, draw on a wide range of intellectual resources, theoretical perspectives and academic disciplines to illuminate understanding of education and the contexts within which it takes place; encourage students to engage with fundamental questions concerning the aims and values of education and its relationship to society; provide opportunities for students to engage with and draw on educational theory, research, policy and practice; develop in students the ability to construct and sustain a reasoned argument about educational issues in a clear, lucid and coherent manner; and promote a range of qualities in students, including intellectual independence and critical engagement with evidence. In the new faculties of education, these challenging requirements provide a framework within which academically demanding and intellectually stimulating course programmes can be developed and offered as fully-fledged degree courses in their own right, or which can be made available as options to students of other disciplines, as well as providing the professional studies component of an initial teacher education course.

While there is now in place a common Benchmark Standard covering initial teacher education across pre-school, primary and secondary sectors, course programmes continue to diverge along the traditional lines. Pre-school and primary teachers undertake either the four-year BEd degree or the one-year PGCE in primary education. Despite their different durations both of these courses of study aim to achieve the same challenging outcomes in terms of knowledge and skills across the whole curricular spectrum, since all primary teachers qualifying in Scotland must be competent to teach children aged three to twelve across all areas of the primary curriculum as outlined in the 5–14 programme (see Section VI of this volume). Initial teacher education for intending secondary school teachers continues to be based on curriculum specialisms modelled on the existing subject boundaries in Scottish secondary schools and with entry limited to those who meet stringent requirements in terms of the subject focus of their previous degree level qualifications. There have been calls to break down the rigid boundaries both between primary and secondary sectors and between the subjects in secondary schools, but as yet these barriers have proved highly impregnable.

In order to avoid confusion between the general and specific meanings of professional studies, some faculties of education are reverting to the use of the label 'education' or 'educational studies' to describe the course element which can be distinguished from school experience and curricular programmes. This has been seen as particularly appropriate where units of study in education or educational studies are offered to a wide range of different groups of students, not all of whom will be destined for the teaching profession. The menu of modules in such educational studies programmes typically include: aspects of child development; topics in the area of pedagogy; and ethical, political and structural features of the educational system. Some such programmes also include significant elements dealing explicitly with personal and professional development. How closely integrated these topics are with school experience and, correspondingly, how congruent the tutor teams involved in modules in these areas are with the teams of tutors who visit and assess students in schools, varies quite widely among the teacher education institutions in Scotland.

INITIAL TEACHER EDUCATION UNDER THE SPOTLIGHT

Initial teacher education did not escape critical scrutiny in the fundamental review of the teaching profession instigated by the Scottish Executive in the late 1990s. The soundings taken by Professor McCrone and his committee yielded several highly critical comments from students, probationers and registered teachers about the quality of the initial teacher education they had received. Such comments were reflected in *A Teaching Profession for the 21st Century: Agreement Reached Following Recommendations in the McCrone Report* (SEED, 2001), which included a commitment by the Scottish Executive to review initial teacher education. It was decided that the review should be conducted in two phases, the first to address a series of quite specific points and the second to be more wide ranging and to be conducted in the context of a broader national debate on education. To satisfy the perceived need for a degree of independence and in keeping with the Scottish Executive's preference for partnerships between the public and private sectors, the contract to conduct the review was awarded to the firm of consultants, Deloitte and Touche. The issues addressed in the first phase for early action were: quality of provision of student placements in schools; partnership arrangements between education authorities and teacher education institutions; the lack of recent classroom experience among initial teacher education staff alleged in the McCrone Report; the use of information and communications technology; and the degree of preparation students receive in classroom behaviour management, special educational needs and health education. In addition, the team from Deloitte and Touche were asked to map current structures and practices and to prepare the ground for the more fundamental second stage of the review which in turn was expected to lead to 'structural and strategic changes' (Scottish Executive, *First Stage Review of Initial Teacher Education: Action Plan*, Edinburgh: Scottish Executive, 2001, p. 2).

   The issue of perceived lack of recent classroom experience among staff in teacher education institutions produced what the review team refers to as a 'virtual polarity' of views between the TEI staff and the other stakeholders (Deloitte and Touche, *Report of the 'First Stage' Review of Intital Teacher Education*, Edinburgh: Scottish Executive, 2001). The McCrone Report had unequivocally recommended, 'TEI staff should be required to update their experience with periodic spells in a school teaching environment as appropriate.' This recommendation was based on what it described as the widely held view among students and school staff that 'an insufficient number of the lecturing staff in the TEIs had recent experience of working in a school, and that they were, therefore, sometimes out of touch with recent curriculum developments and the problems and requirements of the job as it is now' (Scottish Executive, *'A Teaching Profession for the 21st Century': The Findings of the McCrone Inquiry*, Edinburgh: Scottish Executive, 2000, para. 3.4). Having investigated the issue, however, the review team found it impossible to support the McCrone recommendation. The team confirmed that school teachers and students did indeed feel that ITE staff could do with more recent and relevant classroom experience. However, they were also persuaded by the arguments offered by TEI staff: that they do indeed keep in touch with current practices and had continuing contacts with schools through student supervision, providing school-based in-service and carrying out field research; and that making regular secondments back into schools a requirement would neither be feasible nor particularly effective. The conclusion reached was less threatening to the TEIs than might have been expected. Acknowledging that there was some existing good practice in 'secondments and classroom based research', the uncontroversial recommendation was simply that this should merely be 'extended and encouraged where possible' (Deloitte and Touche, 2001, para. 6.4.1). One aspect of current practice, particularly in the concurrent degree programme at Stirling University, which was commended by the Deloitte and Touche report, was the idea of bringing leading practitioners into the TEIs on a part-time basis as 'teaching fellows'. This was seen as conferring the dual benefit of importing contemporary expertise and hence gaining greater credibility for the ITE programme among students and at the same time allowing greater flexibility in overall staffing arrangements.

INTERPROFESSIONAL COLLABORATION AND 'SHARED LEARNING' IN INITIAL TEACHER EDUCATION

Initial teacher education is now recognised as having to prepare students for an extended professionalism operating in a much wider domain than that which can be contained by four classroom walls (Kirk, 1988). An important area of competence in this context is the ability to communicate effectively with others, since teachers are increasingly required to collaborate professionally and to develop partnerships with parents and other professionals. The requirement for all professions concerned with the welfare of children to collaborate effectively is enshrined in the Children (Scotland) Act 1995. The skills of professional collaboration, already included in the SOEID (1998) competences and firmly located in the QAAHE (2000) Benchmark Standard, have secured a place in the professional studies programmes of most of the teacher education institutions in Scotland. However, there is considerable diversity among the institutions and among different courses within institutions in the nature and extent of provision in this area, not least when one compares one-year PGCE and four-year BEd courses.

During the period of expansion which took place in the 1960s, colleges of education began to diversify and develop courses for other professions, most notably for community education and for social work. The faculties and institutes of education offer, to a varying degree, opportunities for direct contact with other professional disciplines, during the pre-service phase of professional training, for example, in Dundee and Strathclyde Universities, enabling student teachers, social work and community education students to come together to share common learning experiences. Shared interdisciplinary learning experiences have provided a model for the development of common units of study across the entire range of undergraduate courses in the faculties of education. The political priority accorded by the Scottish Executive to social inclusion has spawned a series of educational initiatives which have given additional impetus to inter-professional approaches within courses of initial professional education. In particular, the prospectus for the New Community Schools initiative sets out a clear future agenda for initial professional education across several disciplines. Integration of professional services has become imperative.

ISSUES FOR THE FUTURE

Thus far in the chapter several major concerns for the future of initial teacher education have been identified; these can be set against the propositions of Kirk (1988) which were considered at the outset. Firstly, there is the continued tension between theory and practice. Adopting the fashionable constructivist view of theory as process may fail to recognise the need to bring prospective teachers into contact with an extensive range of theoretical understandings. A related issue is the continuing exercise in semantics which has characterised successive course reviews. Merely tinkering with the labels attached to course programmes will not clarify their essential purposes. Secondly, the recent orthodoxy of reflective practice may prove hollow unless students are genuinely allowed the space to evaluate their own professionalism and to consider teaching as a problematic and controversial activity. Thirdly, while the new arrangements for probation and the induction year have removed the initial uncertainty which formerly faced those who emerged from initial teacher education, continuing concerns about longer-term employment prospects militate against students and newly qualified teachers innovating and asking awkward questions about the education system. The new framework for the continuing professional development of teachers in the post-McCrone era demands that teacher educators must strive to instil in student teachers a commitment to professional development. Encouraging students to take more responsibility for their own learning is desirable on educational grounds and, in view of developments in the sector, this will increasingly become a practical necessity.

New challenges for professional studies in initial teacher education also come from the changing demands faced by teachers. Significant among these is the introduction during the late 1990s of large numbers of para-professionals into schools. As part of their attempt to raise standards and alleviate social exclusion through a series of 'early intervention' initiatives, the Scottish Executive has provided the resources for local authorities to employ classroom assistants, particularly in primary schools. Calder (2002) in her paper, 'The place of classroom assistants in Scottish primary schools', delivered at the Scottish Educational Research Association annual conference, reported a very wide range of practice and varying degrees of confusion in schools in relation to the evolving professional relationship between teachers and classroom assistants. The ITE Benchmark Standard (QAAHE, 2000) makes clear reference to the need for students to be prepared for the broader responsibilities of working with others in the classroom. Programmes of initial teacher education will have to find ways to tackle the issue of managing relationships in the classroom so as to equip students for what is a significantly changing role.

The absorption of teacher education into the universities has considerable implications for the curriculum of teacher education courses, implications which are all the more profound given that the universities themselves have entered a period of radical reform following the Dearing and Garrick Reports in 1997. Courses are expected to become fully modularised and to be delivered in ways designed to be both efficient and effective in terms of the quality of student learning experiences they provide. The recommendations are that student choice should be maximised and innovative modes of course delivery should be employed. Imaginative approaches are called for to make best use of the opportunities offered by full integration into the university structures. Sharing of generic modules is expected to provide valuable opportunities for dialogue between sectors, such as secondary and primary PGCE students, and between professions, such as student teachers and students undergoing initial training in social work. However, any move towards sharing modules with students on other courses is perceived by some as a threat to the professional integrity of those involved in initial teacher education who still have to satisfy the demands of the General Teaching Council, the Scottish Office and the employing authorities for maximum professional relevance and the maintenance of high professional standards of attainment. Can the increased flexibility inherent in these new approaches be reconciled with the need for appropriate, dedicated courses of professional education? Perhaps if teacher educators were prepared to accept the full implications of adherence to the ideal of the self-monitoring, reflective practitioner, this apparent conflict might in fact prove to be illusory. Nevertheless, maintaining quality and professional integrity while at the same time relinquishing a measure of control over student learning will provide a continuing challenge for all concerned in initial teacher education in Scotland.

REFERENCES

Clark, M. M. (1997) The teaching profession: its qualifications and status, in M. M. Clark and P. Munn (eds), *Education in Scotland: Policy and Practice from Pre-school to Secondary*, London: Routledge, pp. 98–114.

Humes, W. (1986) *The Leadership Class in Scottish Education*, Edinburgh: John Donald.

Kirk, G. (1988) *Teacher Education and Professional Development*, Edinburgh: Scottish Academic Press.

Kirk, G. (2000) *Enhancing Quality in Teacher Education*, Edinburgh: Dunedin Academic Press.

QAAHE (2000) *The Standard for Initial Teacher Education in Scotland: Benchmark Information*, Gloucester: QAAHE. (Also at http://www.qaa.ac.uk/crntwork/benchmark/ITEScot/introduction.htm)

Sharp, S. (2001) The McCrone Report: some staffing implications for initial teacher education in Scottish Universities, *Scottish Educational Review* 33, 123–33.

SOEID (1998) *Guidelines for Initial Teacher Education Courses in Scotland*, Edinburgh: SOEID.

103

The Professional Development of Teachers

Aileen Purdon

Since the first edition of *Scottish Education* was published in 1999 the world of professional development for teachers in Scotland has changed considerably – a pattern that looks likely to continue. This chapter therefore focuses on current issues and implications for the future; the equivalent chapter in the first edition provided a more detailed exploration of the historical background.

The first part outlines the current context of teachers' continuing professional development (CPD). It should be noted, however, that the present situation is the result of a number of complex and interwoven events, and cannot therefore be described neatly in a sequential or linear order. The second part of the chapter draws together some of the issues raised in part one and analyses them in a more critical manner, focusing particularly on future concerns in teachers' CPD.

THE CURRENT CONTEXT

A national framework of continuing professional development for teachers in Scotland had been under consideration for some time, highlighted as a recommendation in the Sutherland Report (HMSO, 1997) with a national consultation taking place shortly thereafter (SOEID, 1998). However, 2000 proved to be a particularly significant year in terms of CPD for teachers. In July 2000 the first Education Bill to pass through the Scottish Parliament – Standards in Scotland's Schools etc. Act 2000 – was given royal assent. The Act made statutory provision for the General Teaching Council for Scotland (GTCS) to expand its remit to consider 'career development'. While this historically significant and wide-ranging Act was being debated and developed, the teaching profession was campaigning for changes to pay and conditions. This campaign led to the establishment, in September 1999, of the Independent Committee of Inquiry into Professional Conditions of Service for Teachers, chaired by Professor Gavin McCrone. The committee's recommendations (the McCrone Report) were published in 2000, with subsequent agreement (the McCrone Agreement) reached in 2001.

Professional development redefined: The McCrone Agreement

The McCrone Report (SEED, 2000), and the subsequent agreement (SEED, 2001) addressed issues under several sub-headings, one of which was 'professional development'.

Improved opportunities for career-long professional development were to be seen as part of a package of measures designed to enhance the teaching profession, both in terms of its own esteem and capabilities and its public perception. In keeping with the emphasis on career-long professional development, the recommendations began with initial teacher education (ITE), where it was suggested that greater emphasis be placed on certain practical skills, staff in teacher education institutions (TEIs) should 'update their experience' and consideration should be given to greater quality assurance in school placements. Of all the recommendations in the final agreement, the ones relating to ITE were seen as having least credibility, in the main due to the lack of clear evidence upon which they were based. However, the recommendations led to SEED commissioning a two-stage review of ITE, part one of which has been completed at the time of writing.

The induction of new teachers was an area in which the McCrone Report used some of its most emotive language, stating categorically that the current situation was 'little short of scandalous' (SEED, 2000, p. 7). The resulting agreement (SEED, 2001) guarantees new teachers a one-year training contract with a maximum class commitment of 0.7 FTE; the remaining time to be used for professional development. Significantly, it also makes provision for support and mentoring time.

Under the McCrone Agreement all teachers will have an additional contractual thirty-five hours per year for CPD (this particular recommendation is scheduled to be implemented in full by August 2003). CPD is to be seen as a condition of service and should be 'applicable and accessible' (p. 16) to everyone. Nonetheless, there is still much debate over the status of CPD: is it an entitlement or an obligation? This issue will be considered in more detail in the second part of the chapter.

Teachers will have an annual professional review, resulting in an individual CPD plan. They will be expected to maintain a CPD portfolio, which will be a prerequisite for entry to the Chartered Teacher programme. The Chartered Teacher programme, part of the McCrone Agreement, is designed to recognise and reward good classroom practice, and to ensure that such teachers can develop their careers without leaving the classroom. After embarking upon the programme, progression through the Chartered Teacher scale will be by qualification. It is, however, acknowledged that transition arrangements will need to be put in place to deal with what could be a substantial number of teachers who are already meeting or are near to meeting the standard required for the award of Chartered Teacher.

The developing CPD 'framework'

There are various components of what is increasingly commonly referred to as the 'CPD framework': sets of standards and procedures covering initial teacher education, induction, Chartered Teacher and headship, as well as arrangements for on-going staff development and review. The extent to which these various components are actually, or indeed should be, classed as a framework is debatable. First, it is necessary to look more closely at the origins and progress of each of the framework components.

In November 1999, in the wake of the national consultation on CPD, SEED announced that it was going to create a new framework for the continuing professional development of teachers, and that a ministerial strategy committee for CPD would be established to oversee the development and implementation of a national strategy. The committee draws its membership from a variety of stakeholders in education and business, and has a number of sub-groups charged with particular responsibilities, including: the development of the

Chartered Teacher programme; professional review and development; education inclusion; and leadership and management. However, while the strategy committee for CPD now has a role in overseeing the development of the CPD strategy, it should be noted that many of the constituent parts were well under way prior to its establishment.

One such example is the development and implementation of the new benchmarks for ITE, which have in turn impacted on other developments. While university courses leading to teaching qualifications have always been subject to quality assurance by the GTCS, changing quality assurance arrangements in the university sector as a whole led to the need for new Quality Assurance Agency benchmark statements to be developed – these were published in 2000. Student teachers are required to meet the standard for ITE in order to gain a teaching qualification and provisional registration with the GTCS.

The next stage in a teacher's career is induction, an area which had been acknowledged as long overdue for review. The new Standard for Full Registration was officially launched in June 2002, with guidance about the implementation of the induction year being issued by GTCS shortly thereafter. However, work on the development of a Standard for Full Registration and a new framework for induction had begun in 1998. The Teacher Induction Project, funded jointly by the GTCS and SEED, initially envisioned a standard based on the *Guidelines for Initial Teacher Education Courses in Scotland* (Edinburgh: SOEID, 1998). As it became evident that there would be a new standard for ITE, the remit of the teacher induction project changed to accommodate this, the justification being that the profession would expect coherence, and that the Standard for Full Registration would need to be based on the equivalent ITE standard.

Interestingly, the same argument has not been articulated for the Standard for Chartered Teacher, where the Standard has been developed in a quite different way. Rather than a development officer being employed, answerable to individual officers in the employing bodies (SEED and the GTCS in the case of the development of the SFR), the Chartered Teacher project was put out to tender. The tender was awarded to a consortium from Arthur Andersen consultants together with the Universities of Edinburgh and Strathclyde, the project team being directly responsible to the ministerial strategy committee for CPD. The brief in developing the Standard for Chartered Teacher was to start with the identification of the qualities and characteristics of the Chartered Teacher and to develop a Standard based on this evidence. This approach contrasts markedly with the equivalent brief in the induction phase where the key focus was to build on an existing Standard. Indeed, not only have the approaches to developing Standards for Full Registration and Chartered Teacher been quite different, but the processes used to develop the frameworks have also been contrasting. The development of the Chartered Teacher programme has been subject to wide and varied consultation by the project team and has been debated in the educational press. In marked contrast, the framework for the implementation of the new induction requirements was developed by the GTCS, and was put out to schools and employers as a fait accompli.

The development of what is now known as the Chartered Teacher programme, however, is not entirely straightforward. Its origins can be tracked back to questions in the 1998 consultation on CPD surrounding issues of 'standards to give recognition to very good classroom teachers' (Edinburgh: SOEID, 1998, p. 13): the term 'the expert teacher' was coined as short-hand for this notion. In early 2000, the Arthur Andersen consortium was awarded the tender, the main brief of which was to develop a standard and associated programme for the award of 'expert teacher'. However, with the publication of the

McCrone Report in May 2000, and the subsequent McCrone Agreement in 2001, the brief of the project team changed, and 'Chartered Teacher' developed a specific definition of its own, allied not only to CPD, but also to salary and conditions.

The complex nature of Chartered Teacher status, in terms of CPD, pay and conditions, has led to significant debate about the role, purpose and rewards attributable to such teachers. One of the more public debates has concerned the nature of the Chartered Teacher programme itself. Many of the significant players in contemporary Scottish education have raised their heads above the parapet (for example, 'Rift over chartered status', *Times Educational Supplement Scotland*, 15 March 2002) to declare allegiance to either the 'professional' or the 'academic' route to Chartered Teacher status – particularly in relation to the transition phase where many serving teachers will want to make claim for having already met the Standard. Significant debate has been generated on whether this claim should be made on the basis of academic qualifications such as the postgraduate diploma, MSc and MEd, or on verification or evidence of good classroom practice. The very fact that this debate has surfaced indicates the confusion that exists over what can, or should, be considered to constitute professional development, and ultimately what its purpose is.

The ministerial strategy committee for CPD recognised that while Chartered Teacher status would be attractive to many teachers who wish to remain in the classroom and be recognised and awarded accordingly, there are others who aspire to management roles in schools. It therefore established the Leadership and Management Pathways Sub-Group (LAMPS) to look at a parallel route of CPD for such teachers. It is interesting to note, however, that there is no directly corresponding recognition in terms of pay and conditions for teachers following this route – other than the enhanced likelihood of eventually securing a management position. The route will ultimately lead to the Standard for Headship, for which the Scottish Qualification for Headship (SQH) is currently the only route. While the SQH has established itself fairly successfully, it is now recognised as being at variance with the rest of the CPD framework, not least because the Chartered Teacher programme will be based on the modular masters system of SCOTCAT accreditation (see Chapter 106), with full Chartered Teacher status being equivalent to a masters degree, whereas the SQH is currently the equivalent of a postgraduate diploma. With the Standard for Headship, there is yet again variance in the status of the constituent components of the CPD framework in terms of obligation and/or entitlement. In December 2001 it was announced that the Standard for Headship would become mandatory for all headteachers by 2005. Routes to achieving the Standard, though, will be flexible and not restricted to the SQH.

While the above stages mark significant components of a teacher's career, it is recognised that not all teachers will seek promoted positions after attaining full registration, and others, while perhaps aspiring to Chartered Teacher status or headship at some point in the future, will be happy to teach as ordinary grade teachers. These teachers make up a significant percentage of the teaching workforce, and if the philosophy of CPD as a commitment to lifelong learning is to be truly meaningful, then these teachers must also be considered within the framework. The ministerial strategy committee for CPD has been looking at this aspect and has recently consulted on proposals to update the existing staff development and review guidelines to take account of the McCrone Agreement.

SEED priorities in CPD

The rhetoric evident in most documents relating to the CPD framework promotes flexibility and local adaptation to suit particular circumstances. Nonetheless, expectations are also evident that Government priorities such as ICT training for teachers and the meeting of the National Priorities should be achieved through the CPD framework. Indeed, the definition of National Priority 2, 'Framework for learning', includes the intention 'to support and develop the skills of teachers'. It is intended that a performance measure will be developed to monitor progress in teachers' continuing professional development, possibly including the measurement of quality of formal provision, access to CPD, impact of CPD, or completion of the additional contractual thirty-five hours. Schools and local authorities will be obliged to produce evidence of their progress in meeting the National Priorities; it is therefore vital that any 'performance measure' is considered carefully in terms of its validity.

In contrast to the visible, published priorities there are also policy agenda priorities which can be detected through examination of the policy development process, but which are not necessarily publicly acknowledged as such. Most prominent in the field of teachers' CPD is the way in which a standards-based framework has been embraced, relying principally on a competence-based approach to measuring the (sometimes immeasurable) quality of learning and teaching in schools. This agenda takes as its foundation a business approach to education where performance management and target setting dominate, and where the ultimate goal of education could crudely be described as producing citizens for tomorrow who will have the knowledge and skills to help the country to compete in the global economy. While it cannot be said that economic prosperity is not important for a country, the exclusion of other educational aims is of concern. This policy trend can be tracked beyond CPD issues, but it is particularly visible here in the terminology used: standards, competences, benchmarks, attainments, target setting, quality indicators and so on. Yet as Humes (2001) claims, as with any dominant discourse, this approach has now been more or less accepted as the norm, and is therefore rarely challenged at a fundamental level.

Current CPD practice in local authorities and teacher education institutions

Local government reorganisation in 1996 had a significant impact on the range of professional development opportunities available to teachers, with the smaller local authorities being particularly disadvantaged due to their inability to maintain an extensive educational support service (see Chapter 17). However, more recently the effects of devolved management of resources to schools and the introduction of specific funding streams under the Excellence Fund (since session 1999–2000) have allowed schools to consider a wider range of opportunities for staff, which relate closely to school priorities as well as to national priorities. There is a growing trend in using a wide variety of course providers including local authorities, universities, private consultants and commercial companies. However, the emphasis is still very much on courses as opposed to other forms of professional development – a situation that raises concerns over the diversity of professional development opportunities currently undertaken by teachers. Interestingly, there is also growing demand from local authorities for accreditation, in terms of SCOTCAT points, for courses they deliver to their teachers; particularly for probationers and in relation to potential claims for accreditation of prior learning towards Chartered Teacher status. This means the strengthening of partnerships with higher education institutions. Such partnerships have always existed to some degree, particularly in relation to initial teacher education, but are now being looked at afresh in relation to CPD. However, there is a certain ambiguity surrounding the role of teacher education institutions (TEIs) in teachers' CPD: while they undoubtedly have (at least for the time being) a key role to play in initial teacher education, the role beyond that has never really been explored or articulated in any significant way.

The Sutherland Report (1997) recommended that a more coherent and transparent national system of CPD for teachers be developed, and that higher education should play a significant part in this given that it already had a structure in place which could be developed to accommodate teachers' CPD. Sutherland was even more specific about the need for higher education, in partnership with the GTCS, to 'consider the practicality, and implications, of developing a national programme of induction' (p. 37). While this recommendation has been taken forward in part, the partnership has essentially been between the GTCS and local authorities, rather than GTCS and higher education.

In the intervening years between the Sutherland Report being published in 1997 and the writing of this chapter, there has been no formal agreement or articulation of a role for TEIs in teachers' CPD beyond the ITE phase. That is not to say that TEIs are not involved, as individual institutions and their neighbouring local authorities are currently developing CPD relationships which will be of benefit to both parties. However, as this is taking place at local level, between existing players, with no particular overall strategy in mind, the danger is that the traditional way of doing things – local authorities commissioning TEIs to deliver in-service courses on particular themes – will continue to dominate to the exclusion of more innovative, and potentially more effective ways of working. There currently exist unique opportunities for CPD partnerships which would go some way to bridging the often bemoaned theory/practice divide. Teachers in schools could access a wider variety of opportunities such as mentoring, action research, working with students and staff in TEIs, whereas greater and more diverse opportunities for TEI staff to work with schools and employers would go some way towards counteracting the claims asserted in the McCrone Report that many TEI staff are out of touch. It is unlikely, however, that such partnership will become widespread if it continues to be planned on an ad hoc basis, without intellectual or financial investment. Financial restraints, not helped by the lack of surety from year to year regarding intake numbers to ITE courses, help to perpetuate a situation which limits the longer-term strategic planning and investment necessary to be innovative in CPD involvement.

DEBATING THE ISSUES

The developing framework: coherence or coincidence?

The establishment of a national CPD framework was announced in 1999, with the ministerial strategy committee for CPD, created in 2000, now having responsibility for 'setting out a vision of the direction that CPD should take'. However, while all CPD-related issues are now channelled through this group, many of the current initiatives were instigated well before its establishment. For example, work on the development of a standard for full registration and a new induction framework began in 1998, and while the idea of the 'expert teacher' was introduced by SOEID in the late 1990s, the Chartered Teacher programme really took its shape from the McCrone Agreement. Arrangements for the re-evaluation of the current staff development and review guidelines have also been driven by the McCrone Agreement. Finally, the SQH was already in existence, but in a form that does not articulate clearly with other component parts of the CPD framework.

It is therefore questionable whether SEED can seriously claim that what is now in existence is the result of a vision that has been considered, debated, developed and shared by all the major stakeholders. The use of the term 'framework' does imply some form of strategic planning and resulting consistency and coherence, but it also implies the notion of control by the group or organisation with responsibility for its development.

Diversity in CPD

In order to agree on a 'Standard' for any particular stage of teaching, it is reasonable to assume that there is some agreed notion of the nature and purpose of teaching. In pursuing this line of argument, it stands to reason that if there is an agreed notion, then other concepts of the nature and purpose of teaching might not be encouraged within the agreed framework. This could limit the diversity of opportunities that teachers consider as appropriate. If, as has also been argued, CPD is about teacher accountability, then the diversity of opportunities will be limited to those activities that can be translated into measurable units, to be credited to the individual teacher.

The extent to which teachers' own personal professional needs or aspirations are catered for within a national framework should also be considered. There is the potential for conflicting demands on the framework according to whether teachers' CPD is ultimately about fulfilling personal needs and aspirations, meeting the development plans of schools and local authorities, or fulfilling government priorities. Ideally all of these priorities could be met through effective CPD, but it is essential that a balance be struck between them.

Funding is another issue that has an impact on diversity of CPD opportunity. If an employer is funding CPD, whether it be funding for cover, or for materials or resources, or to pay for a course, then there is naturally some obligation on the part of the teacher to ensure that the CPD activity is of direct benefit to the employer. However, if the opportunity is funded by the individual teacher, then teachers should surely have the right to exercise more choice. Employers currently fund most CPD activity, although with the Chartered Teacher programme, which teachers will fund themselves, that traditional pattern looks set to change. Whether or not this will have an impact on the sorts of demands teachers, as consumers, make of the programme remains to be seen.

Current debate over possibilities for a register of CPD providers indicates a perception that CPD should be provided for, and delivered to, teachers. It also means that there might be a greater degree of control over the diversity of opportunities available to individual teachers. Naturally, the organisation with the responsibility for maintaining the register might have its CPD agenda as priority, which could well be reflected in the range of providers approved.

It should be remembered that there are enormous opportunities for professional development that do not necessarily need a provider; for example, the establishment of communities of enquiry, group or individual research activities, participation in conferences and seminars, peer observation and discussion, teacher exchanges and participation in working groups, to name but a few. The competence-based approach to CPD, where standards are developed for various career stages, encourages the view that CPD is about accountability, and that all CPD activities and opportunities can necessarily be measured and related to a particular standard. The focus on measurability of CPD opportunities limits some of the more innovative approaches where neither the input nor the output is as easily quantifiable.

Another growing trend in education, the use of commercial consultants, might also have an effect on the diversity of CPD activities, a recent example of which is the Chartered Teacher project being awarded to the Arthur Andersen consortium. It could be argued that in bringing in organisations from outwith teaching, a fresh perspective might encourage new ideas and greater opportunity for diversity. However, the status of such consultants as commercial businesses also brings with it the risk that a business model will be applied, perhaps inappropriately, to an educational setting, thereby shifting the focus of the agenda from educational to economic.

The nature of consultation

While it could not be contested that most aspects of the CPD framework hitherto have involved an element of consultation, there are questions to be asked about the nature and purpose of that consultation. For example, if the framework is genuinely designed to be coherent and consistent, then why have the development and consultation procedures been so variable? When the ITE benchmarks went out to consultation (see Chapter 104), despite general acceptance of the draft document, there was an overwhelming body of response claiming that the package was an extremely demanding standard to expect of newly qualified teachers and that some of the content could be moved into the induction year. However, there was little substantive change from the draft to the final document. Following the development of the ITE Benchmark document, it was decided that the Standard for Full Registration should follow on from the ITE standard to ensure coherent progression, thereby ignoring the very point that had been raised so strongly in the ITE consultation – that there needed to be greater consideration of what could be reasonably expected in initial teacher education and what could reasonably be kept for the induction year. It could be argued that with different groups having responsibility for different aspects of CPD, the transfer of consultation data across groups was simply not possible. This surely has implications for the claim that what is being developed is a coherent framework.

While there was again consultation on the draft Standard for Full Registration, there was very little substantive change between the draft and final documents. It is interesting, though, that while the Standard was subject to consultation, the actual framework for the induction year has not been consulted on; indeed, there has been very little communication about the development process. However, in stark contrast to consultative procedures used in the development of the induction phase, development of the Chartered Teacher programme has been held up as an example of thorough and open consultation. It is important to recognise that, whereas the Standard for Full Registration is a statutory requirement, the pursuit of Chartered Teacher status is voluntary and consumer driven. This may account for the different approaches to consultation – the Chartered Teacher programme had to have appeal.

Nevertheless, a pattern is beginning to emerge: public consultation on the content of the standards – but no consultation on whether or not standards themselves are the best approach to promoting quality CPD. The coherence argument appears to have won the day in that there now seems to be not just an acceptance, but an expectation that such an approach should apply to all aspects of CPD; that is the Standard for Full Registration must be consistent with the ITE Benchmarks, regardless of whether or not that is the most appropriate approach in the first place. It could therefore be argued that the consultative process was not truly open, as those being consulted had not necessarily had the opportunity to consider fully or to comment on the principles contained in the draft documents, rather they were encouraged to make comment on the operational feasibility of proposals which had been designed to fit a particular predetermined approach.

When the summary of responses to the 1998 consultation on the development of a national framework of CPD was published, it stated that while the majority of respondents were in favour of a national framework, there 'were different interpretations as to what it might include'. How can it then be claimed that teachers have had the opportunity to contribute to open debate on CPD if they have not yet had sufficient opportunity to inform their thinking on it? It could be argued that respondents being asked the extent to which they agree with a particular policy solution laid out in front of them is not actually consultation; rather it is an attempt to gain public validation of the policy.

CPD: the beneficiaries?

Much of the recent consultation on CPD-related matters provides evidence that the majority opinion supports the development of a national CPD framework. However, what is also evident is that there is no clear, shared understanding of what constitutes CPD and what its purpose is. While most people with an interest and involvement in Scottish education would say that CPD should ultimately enhance the standard of learning and teaching in schools, and that it should have a positive impact on pupils' experience, the issue is much more complex. For example, perhaps the main impetus for the most recent focus on CPD is the McCrone Agreement – an agreement reached as a result of disquiet within the profession, relating principally to pay and conditions. In this context CPD could therefore be seen as something which improves teachers' desire to remain in the profession and indeed makes it an attractive option for new recruits – so CPD could be seen to be about the recruitment and retention of teachers. Undoubtedly the government is concerned about issues of recruitment and retention, and success in these areas could be seen to improve voter approval.

However, it would be unfair to suggest that recruitment and retention are the only, or indeed primary, motivators in developing a national framework. It could also be argued, that through CPD, teachers become more effective, resulting in pupils becoming more effective learners. Improved learning leads to better attainment and better attainment leads to a bigger pool of skilled and able employees on which the economy so heavily relies. However, the nature of this learning and attainment must be questionned. Are some subjects and pedagogical approaches favoured above others? If so, then through a national CPD framework policy makers could be working towards an economic agenda in which the purpose of schooling is to facilitate the global economy. A coherent, standard, nationalised framework of CPD has the potential to limit diversity and support the prioritising of educational aims that have not been debated or agreed explicitly. It also has the potential to curb teacher autonomy by limiting the diversity of opportunities available within the framework and indeed the need for teachers to develop and articulate their own conception of teaching. If, on the other hand, CPD is actually about enabling the intellectual liberation of teachers, then it is likely that there will be much more debate within the profession about the objectives and underpinning philosophies of education policies. Would it be in the interest of the educational establishment to encourage this?

In conclusion, then, while much has changed in teachers' CPD over the past two or three years, it is evident that there is still much work to be done. Through CPD, teachers have the opportunity to become even better at what they do, to try new approaches, to develop and to share ideas about the nature and purpose of teaching. However, with many different agendas driving the development of CPD policy, only time will tell where the balance of control will eventually settle.

REFERENCES

Humes, W. (2001) Conditions for professional development, *Scottish Educational Review*. 33(1), 6–17.

SEED (2000) *A Teaching Profession for the 21st Century: Report of the Committee of Inquiry into Professional Conditions of Service for Teachers* (The McCrone Report), Edinburgh: HMSO.

SEED (2001) *A Teaching Profession for the 21st Century: Agreement Reached Following the McCrone Report*, Edinburgh: HMSO.

SOEID (1998) *Proposals for Developing a Framework for Continuing Professional Development for the Teaching Profession in Scotland*, Edinburgh: SOEID.

Sutherland, Sir Stewart (1997) Report 10 – Teacher Education and Training: A Study (The Sutherland Report) in National Committee of Inquiry into Higher Education *Higher Education in the Learning Society*, Report of the National Committee, Norwich: HMSO.

104

Competences, Benchmarks and Standards in Teaching

Donald Christie

In keeping with the importance of education as a facet of national identity, it is generally assumed that teachers have historically been accorded a higher degree of professional status in Scotland than elsewhere in the United Kingdom. However, in order to define itself as a profession and to ensure comparability with other learned professions, the teaching profession has to be able to meet a number of key criteria. These conventionally are taken to include possession of specialised knowledge, ability to apply a high level of skill or technical expertise, a commitment to an ethic of service and the capacity to exercise both individual autonomy and collective self-regulation. Whether teachers in Scotland can indeed meet these conditions and lay claim to professional status is not a question that can be answered without considering the level of their specialised knowledge, the nature of their skills or the degree of professional and personal commitment they display. Eraut (1994) traces a historical shift in the prevailing ideology of professionalism from a traditional, functionalist view emphasising unique expertise and trustworthiness towards a more client-centred view in which the concepts of quality and accountability hold sway. The tension between these conflicting views provides the backdrop for the present chapter, which will examine the discourse of teacher professionalism as it relates to the definition of standards within the evolving framework for professional development in Scotland, a framework which now encompasses initial teacher education, the probationary period, full registration as well as lifelong learning through continuing professional development.

THE DRIVE TO DEFINE PROFESSIONAL STANDARDS

Concern with standards in education and associated close scrutiny of the performance of teachers has become a global obsession. During the last few decades, government and independent agencies in all parts of the world have embarked on a quest to define and monitor standards for teaching. In the United Kingdom this trend towards increased professional accountability was given added impetus by the emergence of a 'new right' orientation in the prevailing political climate during the period of Conservative government from 1979 to 1997. In addition to the emphasis on accountability for the quality in service provision, high priority was accorded to consumer choice in education in order to bring the discipline of the free market into play. Also emphasised was the achievement of high educational standards in order to enable the economy to compete in the global market place.

While the New Labour administrations in both Westminster and Edinburgh have provided an additional dimension in their professed concern for social justice, the commitment to choice, quality, standards and achievement has continued. The development of a framework of standards for the teaching profession in Scotland during this period provides a vivid illustration of some of the key features of the Scottish education system as discussed elsewhere in this volume. The present chapter examines how attempts were made to ensure that the vocabulary for the definition of standards was derived collaboratively in order to reflect what might be assumed to be consensus among those seen as relevant stakeholders; and considers the extent to which the resultant statements provide a distinctively 'Scottish' vision of teaching as a profession. It is also important to assess the extent to which the rhetoric of consensual standards may merely be a disguise for control and compliance.

The period of reform of professional education of teachers spanning the last two decades of the twentieth century has seen several attempts to define the core competences of teachers. Since competence by definition consists of the combination of attributes, such as knowledge, abilities, skills and attitudes, which underlies successful professional performance, any attempt to define the core competences of the teaching profession requires some kind of consensus around what constitutes successful teaching. However, critics have argued that any set of competences must be intrinsically flawed in that it is based on the erroneous assumption that it is possible to reach a consensus on something as complex and problematic as the nature of the task of the teacher. Stronach et al. (1994) in their critique of the first set of these competences assert that in order to make them acceptable to the stakeholders, the competences have been written in such bland terms as to render them technically meaningless in any case. All such criticisms have been put to the side, however, in the plethora of documentation which has been generated by various bodies and task groups set up by Scottish Executive in pursuance of the objective of creating a comprehensive framework of standards for the eponymous *Teaching Profession for the 21st Century*.

THE EMERGENCE AND ACCEPTANCE OF COMPETENCES IN INITIAL TEACHER EDUCATION

The first set of competences for the newly qualified teacher was issued in 1993 (SOED, *Guidelines for Teacher Training Courses*, Edinburgh: Scottish Office). Following a brief period of turbulence in the form of strident criticism from the academic community, the guidelines surprisingly quickly entered a calm period of implementation during which the competences became embedded into the course documentation, the school experience assessment schedules and the finishing student profiles issued by most teacher education institutions (TEIs). This could be construed as yet another instance of the compliance of a sector of the Scottish education system under close central control. However, an alternative interpretation can be offered. When TEI staff studied the detail of the competences carefully, it became clear that they represented no threat to their established practices. Some of the initial objections were over the form rather than the content: the competences resembled behavioural objectives and hence were viewed with suspicion by those imbued in the liberal tradition. The tone of the guidelines and the content of the competences in fact, however, reflected a broader conception of teacher professionalism which referred to 'knowledge, understanding, critical thinking and positive attitudes as well as to practical skills' (SOED, 1993, p. 1).

While it should be acknowledged that some of the most critical views expressed initially were directed at the blandness of the competence statements (Stronach et al., 1994), the authors of the 1993 guidelines may be entitled to credit for their skill in crafting a document which so skilfully avoided offending any of the stakeholders. Any subsequent arguments during the period of implementation of the guidelines tended to be focused not on the content of the competence statements themselves, but on issues such as whether it is possible to grade the level of attainment of the competences. Nevertheless, the guidelines were revised in 1998 and some minor changes were made in the detail of the statements; for example, to include specific reference to the responsibility of all teachers, regardless of whether they teach at pre-school, primary or secondary level, to contribute to the development of pupils' literacy and numeracy, and to update the 1993 reference to selecting appropriately from 'radio and television broadcasts' as resources for learning to refer to 'ability to use information and communications technology'.

FROM COMPETENCES TO BENCHMARKS

Soon after their introduction in 1998, the revised guidelines (SOEID, *Guidelines for Initial Teacher Education Courses in Scotland*, Edinburgh: SOEID), containing the now widely accepted competences were overtaken by the radical overhaul of the system of quality assurance in teacher education which took place in the wake of the Dearing and Garrick Reports on higher education in general and the recommendations of the Sutherland Report on initial teacher education in particular. The Scottish Executive's response to the recommendations was to set up a Standing Committee on Quality Assurance in Initial Teacher Education (SCQAITE) which was carefully constituted to ensure representation of all the key stakeholders, namely, the higher education institutions (HEIs), local authorities, schools, the Scottish Higher Education Funding Council (SHEFC), the General Teaching Council for Scotland (GTCS), HM Inspectors of Schools – later to become HM Inspectors for Education (HMIE), the Scottish Executive and, crucially, the Quality Assurance Agency for Higher Education (QAA). The significance of the involve-ment of QAA should not be overlooked: this signified that initial teacher education was to be treated in the same way as other university 'subjects', such as Law, Chemistry or Engineering, all of which were to be subjected to 'benchmarking'. Normally this entailed QAA identifying a group of experienced academic staff from the HEIs who were given the responsibility to draft a statement of the Benchmark Standard to be applied to all HEI courses in their particular discipline. Such a group had been established, for example, to determine the Benchmark Standard for Educational Studies courses.

The situation as far as ITE was concerned was somewhat more complex. Whereas the Benchmark Standards for all other subjects were established for the whole of the United Kingdom, the proposed Benchmark Standard for Initial Teacher Education was devised for use only in Scotland, since in England and Wales the Teacher Training Agency retained complete control over all aspects of quality assurance and QAA was given no part to play in ITE. Therefore, the conditions were set for a uniquely Scottish approach. In order to accommodate the demands of the QAA procedures, SCQAITE needed to establish a group to create a Benchmark Standard for Initial Teacher Education in Scotland against which the quality of ITE course provision could be reviewed. In good Scottish tradition, the ITE Benchmarking group was collaborative in nature, comprising: a representative from each of the teacher education institutions (TEIs); two representatives from GTCS; two head-teachers, one primary and one secondary; a representative from the local authorities; an

HMI (representing SEED – prior to the change to agency status); and a representative from the QAA's Scottish regional office, acting as an observer. As a member of the benchmarking group, the present author is able to confirm that a collaborative approach was indeed adopted, informed by three guiding principles. Firstly, it was decided that the new Standard for Initial Teacher Education should be a demanding one, based on a vision of the newly qualified teacher, which reflected high professional expectations. Secondly, it was felt important to create a single, generic Benchmark for all ITE programmes, irrespective of whether they were four-year BEd honours degree courses or 36–week postgraduate certificates in education, and regardless of the stage of pre-school, primary or secondary education they were designed to prepare students to teach. The third principle adopted by the group was to ensure that all of the existing competences would be subsumed within the new Benchmark Statements. After much discussion in the Benchmark group and a series of consultative meetings including a national seminar, a draft standard was issued for a somewhat uncontentious national consultation exercise involving all the local authorities and other key stakeholders. The final document (QAAHE, 2000) presented the necessary Benchmark information in the form of a new Standard for Initial Teacher Education in Scotland.

THE BENCHMARK STANDARD FOR INITIAL TEACHER EDUCATION

The Standard essentially describes a series of twenty-four Benchmarks, defined as statements specifying the design requirements for programmes of initial teacher education, each of which is prefaced by the phrase, 'The programme of initial teacher education will enable students to . . .'. The Benchmarks are organised under three so-called aspects of professional development: professional values and personal commitment; professional skills and abilities; and professional knowledge and understanding. The Benchmark statements are each accompanied by a number of more specific statements, referred to as 'expected features', which describe aspects of student performance any ITE programme should be designed to achieve. It is at the level of the expected features, numbering a total of eighty-eight statements, that direct comparisons can be made with the competences in the 1998 guidelines and cross references are provided to show that all of these are indeed subsumed in the new standard. It was anticipated that the expected features would serve the purpose of assisting HEI staff to design appropriate assessment strategies. However, mindful of some of the earlier criticism of the competences, great care was taken during consultation meetings to dispel the notion that the expected features should operate in any way like a behavioural check list. Indeed considerable emphasis was placed on the proposition that the statements were rather to be considered as indicative or illustrative. However, during the consultative phase, several critics expressed concern about what they saw as an inherent logical inconsistency. How, they asked, could something be 'expected' and at the same time only be 'illustrative'? While the label, 'expected feature' is retained in the published version, the commentary gives the less stringent meaning, namely, that the statements were 'intended to clarify and illustrate' aspects of student performance. This softer line is also indicated in the stress placed on the discretion and latitude given to HEIs in the design and specification of ITE programmes. The final element in the Benchmark Standard is a set of ten 'transferable skills,' defined as generic skills derived from and integral to the Benchmark Statements, for example, 'develop and mange effective relationships with others' and 'be systematic, well prepared and capable of planning ahead' (QAAHE, 2000, p. 22). Such statements were included to ensure that the Scottish Standard for ITE complied with the general QAA requirements governing all Benchmark Standards.

The Benchmark Standard includes a model (see Figure 104.1) which was intended to convey the idea that, while all ITE programmes will develop all three aspects of professional development (symbolised by the triangle), they will be the result of unique interactions among these aspects (indicated by the circle in the centre), each with a 'distinctive balance and emphasis' (QAAHE, 2000, p. 7). The placing of professional values and personal commitments at the apex of the triangle is also worth noting, since some had said that the equivalent element in the SOEID (1998) guidelines appeared tacked on at the end of the list almost as an afterthought.

Figure 104.1:   Model of the interrelationships among the three key aspects of professional development identified in the Scottish initial teacher education benchmark standard (QAAHE, 2000, p. 7).

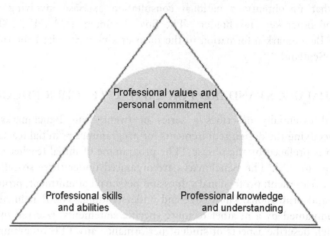

It can be seen that great pains were being taken to strike the difficult balance between, on the one hand, the need to create a uniform standard against which the quality of all programmes of initial teacher education may be judged and, on the other, a concern not to undermine the academic integrity of the HEIs. At the same time, the interests of the other stakeholders also had to be safeguarded, including the local authorities, as the prospective employers of newly qualified teachers emerging from ITE programmes, and GTC Scotland, as the body with overall responsibility for protecting standards in the profession.

To most staff involved in ITE, at the time of its introduction, there was much that seemed familiar in the new Benchmark Statement, since it incorporated the existing SOEID Competences. However, several new elements were introduced in order that the standard could serve as a Benchmark for a programme of higher education and not just professional preparation. For example, within 'professional knowledge and understanding', in addition to the familiar requirements in terms of curricular knowledge, knowledge of education systems and knowledge of professional responsibilities, the following benchmark statements are included under the subheading of 'Principles and Perspectives':

- Draw on relevant principles, perspectives and theories to inform professional values and practices; and
- Acquire an understanding of research and its contribution to education.

The second of these has the following two expected features:

- Know how to access and apply relevant findings from educational research; and
- Know how to engage appropriately in the systematic investigation of practice (QAAHE, 2000, p. 13).

Such statements clearly extend the range of capabilities being addressed when compared with the previous Competences which were more exclusively focused on performance in the classroom. Similarly, within 'professional skills and abilities', in addition to the familiar skills of teaching and learning, classroom organisation and pupil assessment, the skills associated with 'professional reflection and communication' receive new emphasis in the Benchmark Standard with the inclusion of three Benchmark Statements, accompanied by nine expected features, referring to skills associated with academic scholarship as well as skills related to extended professionalism, such as accessing professionally relevant literature, constructing and sustaining reasoned arguments and reflecting on and acting to improve the effectiveness of practice. Within the set of statements describing 'professional values' and 'personal commitment', social justice and engagement with the community are mentioned and the idea of commitment to continuing professional development, present in the Competences, receives renewed emphasis.

The primary purpose of the Standard for Initial Teacher Education was to provide the essential points of reference against which the quality of ITE course programmes might be assessed as part of the so-called 'collaborative review' procedures devised especially for the Quality Assurance of Initial Teacher Education in Scotland. It was seen as necessary to replace the general QAA procedures for academic 'subject review' with this distinctive approach in order to meet the needs of all the stakeholders. A unified, collaborative approach had been called for in the Sutherland Report to replace what were seen as the unsatisfactory arrangements surrounding the previously separate processes of course approval, (historically the responsibility of the Scottish Office), course accreditation (the responsibility of the GTC) and teaching quality assessment, which had been the responsibility of various embodiments and sub-groups of the universities' funding agencies. A second working group established by the standing committee produced a detailed and comprehensive handbook for collaborative review, which was successfully piloted in 2001–2 in the Universities of Edinburgh and Strathclyde. The future of this particular approach, originally intended to be fully implemented from 2003, was put into some doubt by the decision taken by QAAHE at a national level, in the light of complaints about the burden of subject-based review, to move towards an institutional review process. Doubts have also emerged from the GTCS concerning whether their needs, as far as course accreditation is concerned, can be met in a single review exercise, simultaneously dealing with all teacher education courses offered by any institution, since in the larger teacher education institutions there could be as many as ten or twelve different course programmes to consider.

THE STANDARD FOR FULL REGISTRATION

During the same period as saw the development of the ITE Benchmark Standard, the GTCS had initiated a review of the arrangements for probation. The experiences of many successive cohorts of newly qualified teachers in Scotland, while serving the mandatory two-year probationary period before becoming eligible to be fully registered with GTCS, had become a matter of concern due to the large numbers of probationers who found themselves on teacher supply lists and working for short periods in a large number of different schools. As part of the review exercise, GTCS undertook the task of creating a standard to be attained by the end of probation. It quickly became clear that it would be desirable to draft the Standard for Full Registration (SFR) in a form that was compatible with the Standard for Initial Teacher Education. Purdon (2002) in a paper, 'Consultative approaches: standards for full registration and for Chartered Teacher', presented to the Scottish Educational Research Association Annual Conference in Dundee, based on an analysis of records of meetings and other documents, has questioned the manner in which pressure might have been brought to bear by the Scottish Executive on the GTCS to bring its SFR into line with the ITE Benchmark Standard. In any event, when the SFR (GTCS, 2001) was finally published, again following a period of national consultation, it was clear that the two Standards were identically structured around the same three aspects of professional development, namely, values and commitments, knowledge and understanding and skills and abilities. The detailed statements contained in the two Standards were also very similar, with most of the elements of the SFR being identified in the document as consolidating or extending the relevant expected features contained in the ITE Benchmark statements. Some distinctive terminology is to be found, however. For example, instead of the term 'Benchmark' there are statements listed under the heading, 'The Professional Standard' and instead of 'expected features' there are 'Illustrations of professional practice.' There are some additional features incorporated, for example, in the statement referring to registered teachers having the knowledge and understanding to meet their responsibilities to teach cross-curricular aspects, such as core skills, sustainable development and citizenship. Of key importance to this development was the introduction of the one-year probationary period and the guaranteed induction year of employment for all newly qualified teachers in Scotland.

STANDARDS FOR CONTINUING PROFESSIONAL DEVELOPMENT?

A significant element in the McCrone Agreement (SEED, 2001) was the recognition given to the importance of continuing professional development (CPD), both as a professional entitlement and a professional obligation (Purdon, 2001; see also Chapter 103). A contractual commitment to an additional thirty-five hours of CPD per annum was accepted by teachers as part of the agreement. Teachers were also encouraged to maintain a personal CPD profile documenting their professional development activities. As demanded by the agreement, a new CPD framework was created, in which professional standards, defined at different levels, play a central role (Scottish Executive, 2002a). A particularly significant innovation in the McCrone Agreement was the introduction of a new grade of teacher, the new qualification-based professional status of the Chartered Teacher. This was seen as a means of rewarding teachers who wished to pursue a challenging career and gain promotion, without taking on a management role, while remaining in the classroom. The Scottish CPD framework could, therefore, now be organised around three standards, The Standard for Full Registration, the Standard for Chartered Teacher and the pre-existing Standard for Headship.

Compared with the rather modest exercises which yielded the Benchmark Standard for Initial Teacher Education and the Standard for Full Registration, the present author can, as a member of the team involved, assert that the process of defining the Standard for the

Chartered Teacher (SCT) was more elaborate, certainly more empirical and, arguably, more thorough. Firstly, a comprehensive international literature review was conducted to explore the many other formulations of the qualities of professional accomplishment in teaching which have appeared in recent years in what seems to be a global quest to define Standards across the professions. Secondly, two rounds of focus group interviews were conducted with groups of teachers and other stakeholders: the first in order to examine general issues surrounding the Chartered Teacher programme, involving twenty groups comprising a total of 300 individuals; and the second gathering views about the essential elements of accomplishment in teaching, involving seventeen groups comprising 235 teachers, TEI staff, pupils, parents and HM Inspectors. Thirdly, a series of intensive interviews were conducted with nineteen class teachers identified as being particularly accomplished practitioners. During the interviews, the practices of these accomplished teachers were probed in considerable depth in order to gather instances of good practice and an insight into their underlying professional priorities, reasoning and decision-making processes. Fourthly, information was gleaned from a national consultation exercise in which views were sought by means of questionnaires issued to all 60,000 serving teachers. Careful content analysis of the collated information from all these sources yielded a draft Standard which could be claimed genuinely to reflect views expressed by Scottish teachers and the wider educational community. This was then subjected to a further full national consultation exercise again involving all serving teachers in Scotland, this time being issued with a copy of the full draft standard document. In addition, copies of a fuller supplementary paper were circulated. The evidence from the consultation process clearly demonstrated strong support for the Standard for Chartered Teacher in the profession.

THE STANDARD FOR CHARTERED TEACHER

When the *Standard for Chartered Teacher* was finally published (Scottish Executive, 2002b) it had been subjected to only minor modifications following the national consultation exercise, including the addition of an explanation of the inter-relationships among the key professional standards for teachers in Scotland, namely, the Standard for Initial Teacher Education, the Standard for Full Registration and the Standard for Chartered Teacher. In essence the three standards provide a comprehensive and progressive framework for the professional development of teachers in Scotland encompassing both the pre-service stage and continuing professional development. There is a high degree of continuity resulting from the use of a common language. The three aspects of professional development from the ITE Benchmark Standard and SFR have been extended and adapted to become the four 'key components' of the Standard for Chartered Teacher, which are as follows:

- professional values and personal commitments;
- professional knowledge and understanding;
- professional and personal attributes; and
- professional action.

  The dimension of values and commitments is again given central importance and is articulated in terms of four core elements: effectiveness in promoting learning in the classroom; critical self-evaluation and development; collaboration and influence; and educational and social values. The rationale for the Standard (Scottish Executive,

2002b) asserts, 'Accomplished teaching of the kind reflected in the Standard for Chartered Teacher is teaching in which the four central values and commitments permeate the work of the teacher in the classroom, the school and beyond' (p. 3). Key features of this Standard are the references to improving practice, moral and social values and working collaboratively. Terminology familiar from other educational contexts is apparent. The four components, it is asserted, should serve as the four major quality indicators when candidates, making a case for the award of Chartered Teacher status, are preparing evidence.

The Standard for Chartered Teacher outlines nine forms of professional action which characterise accomplished teaching:

- effect further progress in pupils' learning and development;
- create and sustain a positive climate for learning;
- use strategies which increase pupils' learning;
- evaluate practice and reflect critically on it;
- improve professional performance;
- ensure that teaching is informed by reading and research;
- contribute to enhancing the quality of the educational experience provided by the school and to the wider professional context of teaching;
- relate teaching to wider school aims and social values; and
- articulate a personal, independent and critical stance in relation to contrasting perspectives on educational issues, policies and developments.

Each of these forms is illustrated in the text by more specific examples of professional action to provide a detailed portrayal of accomplishment.

COMPARISONS WITH DEVELOPMENTS IN ENGLAND

There are several points of comparison that can be made between the new framework of standards for the professional development of teachers in Scotland and the evolving standards framework in England. The Teacher Training Agency (TTA) in 2002 issued a revised statement of its *Standards for the Award of Qualified Teacher Status* (QTS), which serves the equivalent function to the Standard for Initial Teacher Education in Scotland. The TTA QTS standard shows some similarities, but there are several important differences. The TTA standard has three components: professional values and practice; knowledge and understanding: and teaching, similar to the three aspects of professional development identified in the Scottish Benchmark Standard. Within the first component are similar statements about, for example, having high expectations of all pupils, but there is no mention of wider commitments to the community beyond the school in the TTA document. Under knowledge and understanding there is in the English standard a much more prescriptive list of requirements closely tied to elements of the national curriculum and a reference to the controversial QTS skills tests in numeracy, literacy and ICT. The third component, teaching, which is subdivided into three parts to do with planning, assessment and class management, respectively, contains many similar statements to those in the 'professional skills and abilities' component of the Scottish Benchmark Standard, but none of the wider capabilities associated with the academic demands of university study is mentioned. Not only are there important differences in terms of content, the provenance and purposes of the two standards are also different. Quality Assurance for ITE in Scotland involves collaboration among several stakeholders including the higher education institutions and QAAHE, and the Benchmark Standard is fundamentally concerned with the quality of ITE course provision. In England, control over quality assurance and all other matters to do with ITE lies with TTA alone. Moving beyond qualification from initial teacher education, new induction standards have also been issued by TTA, which are largely a consolidation of the QTS with some degree of extension of capability expected of the newly qualified teacher during the induction period. In this respect there is some similarity to the Scottish Standard for Full Registration, but the TTA documentation is far less detailed than the guidance issued by GTC Scotland.

Entering further into the realm of continuing professional development there are further comparisons to be made, but the degree of similarity becomes even less marked. Teachers in England have the opportunity after a number of years service to apply for a performance-related salary enhancement of £2,000 and access to further incremental scales by subjecting themselves to a 'threshold assessment'. Teachers have to provide evidence of their performance over a two- to three-year period prior to making the application, against the Threshold Standard which comprises five components, 'knowledge and understanding', 'teaching and assessment', 'pupil progress', 'wider professional effectiveness' and 'professional characteristics'. The Threshold Standard has some surface similarities with elements of the Standard for Chartered Teacher, but there are very significant differences. The emphasis on pupil progress has led to a perception that this is simply payment by results, a perception reinforced by the fact that the assessment of applicants is carried out by their headteachers. There is an additional standard and status available in England which may also be compared with the Chartered Teacher in Scotland, namely, the 'Advanced Skills Teacher' (AST). The standard for AST is set out against a list of ten main teacher characteristics. Indeed all of the standards in the English framework are progressively articulated against this common set of headings, but with some of the characteristics being deemed only relevant for the more demanding standards. While Threshold status is in the gift of the headteacher, the assessment of whether an individual is entitled to the status of AST is carried out in a one-day visit to the applicant's school by an educational consultant from a private consultancy firm and is also contingent on there being a particular post established for the candidate. The process is under the control of DfES whose documentation indicates that only around 3%–5% of teachers nationally will be eligible. Advanced Skills Teachers have strict contractual obligations requiring 80% class teaching to be complemented by 20% outreach work in other schools. In contrast, Chartered Teacher status will be achieved in Scotland by means of a qualification in the form of a masters degree awarded by a university and professionally accredited by the GTCS. All teachers who have reached the top of the salary scale will be eligible to enter the programme of twelve modules, which in addition to core elements, will include a choice of options and a work-based project. Progress through the programme will be rewarded with a salary increment for each two modules completed. Financial recognition will not be in the gift of line management as in the case of threshold payments in England. Important provision is made within the programme for the accreditation of prior learning. Some contentious issues remain unresolved at the time of writing. In particular the question of fee payment for the modules is causing considerable concern in the profession and among the other stakeholders.

ENHANCED OR RESTRICTED PROFESSIONALISM

From the detail of the Standards, which now make up the framework for the professional development of teachers in Scotland, it can be strongly argued that they provide a basis for the enhancement rather than the restriction of teacher professionalism. One particular illustration of this is the place occupied by research and enquiry in the standards framework. As well as the inclusion of firm references to the professional importance of research in the ITE Benchmark Standard and the Standard for Full Registration, there are clear expectations in the Standard for Chartered Teacher that accomplished teachers will turn to 'reading and research for fresh insights' (Scottish Executive, 2002b, p. 3) and engage in 'professional enquiry and action research' (p. 10). An enhanced professional role for teachers is also indicated by the expectations that Chartered Teachers will 'collaborate with and influence' others within and beyond the school, that they will 'build positive relationships and partnerships in the community' and that they will 'contribute to the literature on, and public discussion of, teaching and learning and education' (p. 11). It should be pointed out, however, that such statements are not written as requirements, but rather as examples of ways in which the core professional commitments might be illustrated in the professional actions of individual teachers.

The development of a framework of standards for the teaching profession put in place at the start of the twenty-first century can be interpreted in two different ways. On the one hand, it might appear that the very act of defining such standards in a sense diminishes the status of any profession so defined. This kind of interpretation can be linked to the traditional, deferential view of professional status carrying a certain mystique and relying heavily on trust rather than accountability (Eraut, 1994). One important assumption lying behind this view, however, is about who controls the processes of definition and application of the standards in question. A cynical view might be that, despite the trappings of professional involvement, the collaborative approach which has characterised these developments merely masks central control by a policy elite dominated by the Scottish Executive. Such a view might find support from those who would point to the close similarities between the Scottish framework and the equivalent set of standards in England, produced in a more openly centralised manner. Ian Stronach, in his 1999 SERA lecture, described this kind of underlying similarity between educational structures (even where Scottish educationalists like to celebrate distinctiveness), as Scotland having the 'ghostly equivalents' of whatever applies in England.

On the other hand, it is possible to argue that the creation of the framework of standards is a necessary and even a desirable part of a process of enhancement of the professionalism of teachers. The involvement of members of the profession in the process was significant, particularly in the development of the Standard for Chartered Teacher. The professional involvement of teacher education staff was central in defining the Benchmark Standard for Initial Teacher Education. The Standard for Full Registration was primarily the responsibility of the GTCS as the relevant professional body. It is could be claimed that those who oppose the very idea of attempting to define standards are merely seeking to protect the notion of professional mystique as a way of avoiding accountability. The manner in which the standards have been developed, and the model of professionalism which they convey mean that the framework for professional development now in place is a genuine opportunity for the teaching profession to maintain and enhance its status in Scottish society.

REFERENCES

Eraut, M. (1994) *Developing Professional Knowledge and Competence*, London: Falmer.

Purdon, A. (2001) New teachers' perspectives on continuing professional development: accountability or professional growth, *Scottish Educational Review*, 33 (2), 110–22.

QAAHE (2000) *Standard for Initial Teacher Education in Scotland: Benchmark Information*, Gloucester: QAAHE.

Scottish Executive (2002a) *Continuing Professional Development*, Edinburgh: Scottish Executive.

Scottish Executive (2002b) *Standard for Chartered Teacher*, Edinburgh: Scottish Executive.

Stronach, I., Cope, P., Inglis, B. and McNally, J. (1994) The SOED competence guidelines for initial teacher education: issues of control, performance and relevance. *Scottish Educational Review*, 26 (2), 118–23.

105

The European Dimension

Kay Livingston

While politicians continue to debate the advantages and disadvantages of the European Union, the reality is that there is an on-going process of integration and an increasing number of supranational policies. Decisions are made at a European level which impact on the lives of all citizens and necessitate change. These changes represent both a challenge and an opportunity for education.

The argument for including a European dimension as part of international education focuses on the need to prepare pupils for life as European citizens with rights and responsibilities within an international community. Social reality plays a decisive role in the determination of educational priorities and the fact that citizens are living in a more interdependent world should be reflected in the educational process. Young people need to have knowledge and understanding of international issues and the necessary skills to enable them to participate actively and responsibly in twenty-first century life.

EUROPEAN RESOLUTIONS, TREATIES AND POLICIES

The idea of a community of European nations grew out of a desire to maintain peace after the Second World War. The political plan focused on establishing economic ties and in 1957 the Treaty of Rome established the European Economic Community (EEC). With the enlargement of the Community over the following years (the UK joining in 1972), there was a growing realisation that European integration was more than a political and economic process. It was recognised that to establish a union of people, policies needed to extend beyond political and economic co-operation. The later change in title from EEC to European Union (EU) reflected this broader view.

The Single European Act in 1986 stepped up the momentum of the integration process by introducing provision for greater economic and social cohesion and this had an impact on education and training. The role of education as a means of assisting changes in an evolving European society was gradually recognised and the first action programmes in the field of education were put in place. For example, the ERASMUS programme was adopted in 1987 and promoted the mobility of university staff and students and the development of inter-university co-operation.

A resolution in 1988 by the Council and Ministers of Education gave further emphasis to the inclusion of a European dimension in education. It highlighted the need to strengthen in young people a sense of European identity and prepare them to take part in the economic and social development of the Community. The resolution set out a range of proposals for encouraging and developing the European dimension in schools and through initial and in-service teacher education. At Community level, the European Commission took action in the area of teacher exchanges and encouraged the formation of networks of teacher education institutions and university departments responsible for training teachers throughout Europe. The member states were invited to take initiatives within the limits of their own specific educational policies and structures. For example, the resolution exhorted the member states to develop curricula, devise teaching materials, train teachers and support measures to promote contacts between pupils and teachers of different countries.

In November 1993 the Treaty on European Union, often known as the Maastricht Treaty, came into effect. The Treaty is noted as the one that provided for closer European integration in terms of economic co-operation and freedom of movement of goods, services and people. However, the impact that it had on education may not be as widely recognised. The treaty marked a new stage for action at European level by giving a legal basis to Community action in the field of education for the first time.

Article 126 of the treaty stated that the Community shall contribute to the development of quality education by encouraging co-operation between member states and, if necessary, by supporting and supplementing their action, while fully respecting the responsibility of the member states for the content of education and the organisation of their educational systems. The accent on raising the quality of education throughout the Union centres on the 'added value' that European co-operation can bring, through the exchange of ideas and methods, and the sharing of experiences. According to the European Commission, harmonisation of education systems is not proposed and the principle of subsidiarity set out in the treaty ensures that the content of teaching and its implementation remain the responsibility of the member states.

The position of vocational training is different: it has been included in European policies since 1957 and there has been a wide range of initiatives taken in this field. However, Article 127 of the treaty gave the EU the competence to implement a vocational training policy and consolidated action towards mutual recognition of qualifications across all member states.

Although European Commission documents continue to uphold the value of diversity in education systems, co-operation on policy issues has increased. According to the EU Directorate-General for Education and Culture, the challenge is to preserve the best of the diversity of educational experience in Europe, while harnessing it to raise standards, remove obstacles to learning opportunities and meet the educational requirements of the twenty-first century. The European Council of Ministers meeting in Lisbon in 2000 set out a new strategic objective for Europe to become the most competitive and dynamic knowledge-based economy in the world capable of sustainable economic growth with more and better jobs and greater social cohesion. A detailed work plan (Brussels: Report from the Commission: *The Concrete Future Objectives of Education Systems*, 2001) has been prepared to strengthen European co-operation in education. The Commission's intention is that this work plan will pave the way for coherent policies in areas such as education where a 'common policy' does not exist but where they wish to develop what they call a 'European educational area'. This process of convergence has already begun with the agreement of the European ministers responsible for higher education to create a European Area of Higher Education by 2010 (Bologna Process). While the EU cannot intervene directly in the educational matters of the member states, the series of resolutions, treaties and working papers have led to closer European co-operation and national education systems increas-ingly have to plan and implement new initiatives taking account of actions at an inter-national level.

EUROPEAN ACTION PROGRAMMES

The key instruments used to translate the EU policy discourse into action are the European action programmes. The SOCRATES and LEONARDO programmes (Brussels: European Commission, 1995) represented the first concrete implementation of Articles 126 and 127 of the Maastricht Treaty. They aim to extend the development of the European dimension to all sectors of education and training and to strengthen the spirit of European citizenship. The LEONARDO programme aims to implement a common vocational and training policy by supporting work experience periods in businesses or training organisations in other EU countries.

In the first phase (1995–9) the SOCRATES programme was implemented in the fifteen member states of the EU and those countries covered by the European Economic Area agreement (Iceland, Liechtenstein and Norway). Since 1998 it has also been open to a number of countries which have applied to join the EU (Cyprus, Romania, Poland, Hungary, Czech Republic and Slovakia). Bulgaria, Slovenia, Estonia, Latvia, and Lithuania came into the programme in 1999. The programme comprised action in higher education (ERASMUS), in school education (COMENIUS), and in the promotion of language skills (LINGUA). It also included action in open and distance learning and in the promotion of information exchanges. The school education programme COMENIUS was the most innovative, as schools were the focus of European policy for the first time. It was divided into three actions, to encourage the creation of multi-lateral partnerships between schools, to promote an intercultural dimension and to develop and run transnational in-ervice courses for teachers.

The results of phase 1 show that the SOCRATES programme has made a significant impact on raising awareness of the European dimension in many universities, schools and other educational institutions. The second phase of SOCRATES (2000–6) will add Malta and Turkey to the list of eligible countries and will continue many of the activities already established while introducing some new initiatives. The new activities focus on the promotion of lifelong learning and opening up access to knowledge. The growing number of countries eligible for funding through the programmes will inevitably raise the profile of international education by widening the geographical spread and encouraging the development of a European dimension with a greater number of people. However, the new eligibility has already increased the complexity of the application forms and may limit the amount of funds available for individual activities. Enlargement of the EU presents many challenges, not least the administration of the SOCRATES and LEONARDO programmes.

WHAT IS THE EUROPEAN DIMMENSION IN EDUCATION?

The rhetoric of European treaties and resolutions calls for the promotion of a European dimension in education. However, its definition is not made explicit. Knowing what the European dimension in education is and understanding what form it might take are difficult problems. There is no single definition that everyone would easily agree on, nor one clear set of strategies to implement a European dimension.

A broad view of the concept of a European dimension is possible. It could be described as opening up and broadening pupils' horizons and making them more aware of other European cultures. However, such a general definition is likely to hinder the effective implementation of a European dimension. Teachers may not include it in their work because it is not easy to identify a starting point, or because it is so generic that it is unclear whose responsibility it should be to ensure that it forms part of the education process. The opposite extreme would be to restrict the definition to very specific aspects. A curricular insert on the infrastructure of the European Parliament would be one example. Knowledge about Europe is necessary, but it is just one element of the European dimension.

A broad definition as opposed to a narrow one provides a simplistic description of two poles of thought. It does not take account of the many definitions that fall between the extremes. These definitions need not be in competition with one another: employing one does not mean eschewing others. The European dimension is a multi-faceted phenomenon which does not have a simple common denominator.

To add to the difficulties, it could be argued that even a broadly-defined European dimension is inadequate. Europe's interdependence with the rest of the world means that an international dimension is more meaningful. Aspects such as tolerance of others, raising awareness and understanding of other cultures and promoting democratic values extend beyond the boundaries of Europe and are relevant within an international context. In today's global society international education is important but as European citizens it is necessary for young people to have an understanding of the EU and how it impacts on their lives. They need to know how to participate actively in an integrated European community in an informed, enlightened and responsible manner.

The ambiguity and lack of consensus concerning the definition, the place of a European dimension in education and the methodology for implementation creates uncertainty for teachers. However, the teacher's task is not about putting forward one solution to all the questions or identifying one definition for a European dimension. It is the process involved in finding answers that is important. Education should act as a mediator, not to integrate people into a particular social structure, but to provide them with knowledge and understanding to make their own reasoned judgements. Discussion, debate, negotiation and compromise are some of the main features that a European dimension seeks to bring to education. Facilitating pupils to think for themselves, to be aware of similarities and differences and seek, in a democratic way, solutions to conflicts which arise, are central to the development of a European dimension in education.

While this may represent a step forward in understanding the multi-faceted nature of the concept, it is not particularly helpful for planning its implementation. Links exist between values education, citizenship education, intercultural education, European and global education. However, a curriculum dominated by subject divisions does not make it easy to develop overlapping educational processes effectively. What is needed is an operational framework that enables teachers to analyse where opportunities already exist to develop a European dimension, identify the gaps and co-ordinate what has to be included in the curriculum (formal, informal and hidden) in a developmental and coherent way. Without such a framework there is a danger of the European dimension being nothing more than a collection of vague and disjointed inserts on Europe.

Shennan (1991) proposed a three-dimensional model which provides a helpful structure for aiding curricular design. The first dimension suggests that a European element should include learning about Europe, learning for Europe and learning through Europe. The second dimension identifies the components: knowledge, skills, attitudes and values. For example, knowledge is required about Europe's geography, its people, history and cultures. Certain skills are required to prepare young people for life in Europe, where effective communication skills and the ability to solve problems and react to changing circumstances are essential. To live and work together with other Europeans, attitudes and values need to be explored. Judgements may be based on stereotypical snapshot images. The European dimension should focus on the deconstruction of these pre-formed and often long-standing images of European regions, nations and people. Pupils need to go beyond a superficial understanding of other European countries. Learning through Europe, by getting to know 'real' people in other countries, is an important step. This does not necessarily mean an exchange trip. New communication technology may be utilised to create class to class links and enable pupils to share and exchange information. However, there can be no question that geographical mobility of pupils and teachers will lead to deeper mutual understanding and greater co-operation. Seeing and experiencing enhances learning. The acquisition of knowledge and skills must go together with the acquisition of values and dispositions.

Shennan's third dimension suggests that Europe is encapsulated in culture, time and area. Culture includes particular features of society and the creative heritage of civilisation. Time refers to the past, present and future. Area is not restricted to the EU countries. Exploration of shifting borders and the impact of international changes is needed to understand the dynamic and evolving nature of Europe within a global society.

Although there is no unique prescribed route for implementing a European dimension, Shennan's model presents a structure that could be used to consider how a European dimension might be integrated in the curriculum in a systematic way.

A whole-school or institutional policy is needed which includes a statement of aims for international education with specific objectives for inclusion of a European dimension, a management strategy, identification of staffing and resource implications and a development plan. Such an approach is necessary to assure the quality of a European dimension in education.

A EUROPEAN DIMENSION IN SCOTTISH EDUCATION

Since 1972 there has been an office of the Central Bureau for Educational Visits and Exchanges in Edinburgh and it has been active in promoting European links and exchanges (a function now taken over by the British Council). The gradual development towards establishing the single European market gave impetus to the discussions concerning the role of education and sharpened the focus on trying to promote a European dimension in Scotland. Added to this, the 1988 resolution prompted a response from the UK Government (DES, 1991) which included Scotland. The policy statement set out the government's objectives for the European dimension which were in line with those of the resolution. It created an official framework whereby the government's legislative role relates to taking appropriate central initiatives to assist and encourage the dissemination of good practice. The policy also encouraged support for language learning and teaching, bilateral links and exchanges, and facilitation of the implementation of EU action programmes.

The strategy of the Scottish Office Education and Industry Department (SOEID) – now Scottish Executive Education Department (SEED) – was developed within the framework of the UK government's policy. In 1990, the Scottish Office set up an International Relations Branch (IRB) – now International Relations Unit (IRU). Two of its first objectives were provision of easy access to information about the EU and establishment of a number of networks to facilitate the development of the European dimension. In 1994, the SOEID published *Scottish Education and the European Community – Policy, Strategy and Practice*. This set out the government's policy and priorities, the legal basis for European Community action and the SOEID's strategy. It also included a chapter on the European dimension in practice, which covered all levels of education. The paper concluded with a useful checklist for institutional self-assessment, which used the framework: education through Europe; education for Europe; and education about Europe.

In the 1990s the emphasis was on raising schools' awareness of the events in Europe and the first priority was to provide guidance to encourage schools to develop a European dimension. This was done through a series of conferences and key publications. For example, *Thinking European: Ideas for Integrating a European Dimension in the Curriculum* (SCCC, 1993) was published, followed by a partner publication, *Sharing Responsibility* (SCCC, 1995). Both include examples of good practice. A supplement, *Thinking European* (SCCC, 1997), provided further case studies of European activities in secondary and primary schools. These publications provided practical help for classroom teachers as well as providing evidence of the work going on in Scotland.

The responsibility for implementation is placed with the local authorities. They have allocated resources for the development of international education, including an international co-ordinator. In many cases the task of developing international education is just one of many of that person's responsibilities. Nevertheless, several authorities have experienced co-ordinators and some have set up awareness groups to produce policy statements and action plans. The education authority co-ordinators meet regularly with the IRU to ensure a two-way exchange of information. Staff from the British Council also work with the coordinators to promote international activities, including the European action programmes within schools.

During the early 1990s the General Teaching Council (GTC) supported the need to encourage a European dimension in Scottish schools. It recognised the central role that teachers should have in developing a European dimension and that change within the system would only be effective if those responsible for delivering the curriculum were well trained. The council issued a paper, *The European Dimension in Initial Teacher Education* (Edinburgh: GTC, 1990), which stated that the objectives of the resolution should be achieved through the provision of a systematic and structured programme of training for the teachers who would deliver the curriculum. It recommended that all courses of initial teacher education for primary and secondary teachers should incorporate a European dimension from the start of 1992–3. This resulted in a number of the teacher education institutions making an effort to include a European dimension either through a permeative approach, through course inserts or through student/staff exchanges with other European teacher education institutions. An up-dated GTC statement would help to reactivate thinking about the development of international education in schools and in teacher education.

At national level there has been increasing cognisance of the need to include international education in the curriculum of Scottish schools. Devolved government in Scotland means that for the first time there is a Scottish minister with specific responsibility for Europe and External Affairs. All Scottish ministers are now responsible for ensuring that EU obligations, mainly in the form of European Commission directives, are implemented through legislation in the Scottish Parliament. The Scottish Executive has already expanded its range of contacts in the EU and has substantially increased its participation in the EU councils and working groups. The recent publication, *An International Outlook* (SEED, 2001) says that devolution means that a positive, close engagement with Europe is a top priority for the Scottish Executive. However, the publication demonstrates that the emphasis is on encouraging international education in Scottish schools with the inclusion of a European dimension as a part of the initiative. It says that the aim is to broaden the minds of young people towards global citizenship, building on previous developments in the education system by expanding beyond the European dimension into the rest of the world. Similarly the publications, *The Global Dimension in the Curriculum* (Dundee: LTS, 2001) and *Education for Citizenship in Scotland* (Dundee: LTS, 2002) point to the connections between European, international and global issues and the need to provide pupils with the necessary skills to enable them to participate in an interdependent world.

ISSUES, CONCERNS AND DEVELOPMENTS

The structure of implementation of a European dimension in Scottish education has been a combination of limited centralised guidance and grassroots initiatives in some schools, colleges and universities. The emerging picture is one of pockets of good practice, driven by the interest and enthusiasm of motivated individuals. There are examples of schools that regard international education as an important part of their work and understand that it is cross-curricular and multi-disciplinary. They are well aware of the opportunities that exist to participate in EU programmes and have established good links with other schools in Europe. As case studies demonstrate, their teachers have recognised the value that can be derived from partnerships with other European schools.

Since the start of the COMENIUS programme there has been a steady increase in the number of Scottish primary and secondary schools applying to and participating in joint European projects. The programme provides benefits for teachers as well as pupils: it offers opportunities to work with a team of teachers from at least two other European countries to develop curricular work. Finding out about other systems and other ways of working enables teachers to reflect on their own methods, it broadens experience and generates new enthusiasm. Set against this, it is necessary to invest time and energy and requires the backing of the management team. The complexity of applying for funding and reporting on a European project is daunting. If the European Commission adopted a more streamlined approach, this might encourage more schools to take up the opportunities that European programmes offer.

Although many schools have recognised the benefits of a European dimension, there are many more that have not. Some are still at the stage of wondering what it is about, whether it should be included in the curriculum, and if so, how it should be done. They appear to lack information and have no understanding of the funding possibilities or the advantages that may be gained from European links.

As in society at large, not all educationalists believe in the construction of a European Union or support the notion of European citizenship and it may appear to some that promoting a European dimension would be synonymous with a pro-European approach. They may feel that including a European dimension in education has more to do with political and economic issues than educational ones. However, the educational process must prepare pupils for the reality of Europe and enable them to develop a critical consciousness. Experiences should provide them with opportunities to discuss advantages and disadvantages and explore the concept of European citizenship. Critical thinking should be both the means and the outcome of developing a European dimension.

In the past the purpose of education has often been linked to 'nation-building'. Some teachers may feel that they play a major role in maintaining cultural traditions and values and see a tension between promoting European citizenship and national citizenship. However, strengthening an understanding of European citizenship does not mean adopting a Eurocentric approach or doing away with cultural diversity or national identity. There is no suggestion that a European dimension is about creating a melting pot of European cultures. The European treaties and resolutions seek to promote an understanding of Europe as a multi-cultural, multi-lingual community. Their purpose is not to eliminate differences, but to encourage people to learn to understand and appreciate them. Learning about other nations, regions and cultures and communicating with pupils in other European countries will enable pupils to reflect on their Scottish and regional identity and how these relate to being a citizen of the EU within a global context.

The fact that Europe is multi-lingual emphasises the need for more and better language teaching to enable participation in a mobile multi-cultural world. However, Scotland is on the edge of Europe and crossing national, cultural and linguistic boundaries is not a regular occurrence for most people. Added to this the 'lingua franca' in cross-cultural communication is usually English; this inevitably reduces the need and consequently the motivation for people in Scotland to learn another European language. Since language is closely linked to culture and identity, this lack of competence in languages continues to create a barrier not just to communication, but to understanding others. The publication *Citizens of a Multilingual World* (Edinburgh: SEED, 2001) reinforced the importance of language learning for all pupils in Scottish education. It is important that continuous development of languages throughout the educational process remains high on the priority list of policy-makers.

At pre-service level, all the teacher education institutions would claim to include elements of international education in their course work with four-year BEd students, but not all do so in any co-ordinated way. Similar to the situation in schools, there are examples of good practice, with a range of activities included in the curricular work either as a permeative feature, a specific module or an elective course. However, pressures on course content are also evident: opportunities for students on a one-year PGCE course to gain experience in the development of international education are much more limited. A small number of Scottish students have benefited from short placements in teacher education institutions in another country. However, demand for other European students wishing to study in Scotland is far higher. While students from other European countries view an exchange as a positive advantage, Scottish students appear to be reluctant to take time out of their courses. They do not seem to have grasped the value of a study period in another European country. There are many factors which contribute to this situation, not least the perceived effect on employment prospects. Student teachers need to be provided with clearer information regarding the benefits of a European profile and the value of international education.

The Standards in Scotland's Schools, etc. Act 2000 led to the identification of five National Priorities for education. These priorities point to the need to provide a rich diet of educational experiences. Priority four emphasises the need to teach pupils to respect themselves and others in an interdependent society and teach them the duties and responsibilities of citizenship in a democratic society. Priority five relates to the need to provide pupils with the skills, attitudes and expectations necessary to prosper in a changing society. These priorities add weight to the rationale for international education incorporating a European dimension. However, if the European dimension is presented as another subject to be squeezed into an already packed curriculum, teachers may be reluctant to take it on. It must be understood as a way of enriching the existing curriculum and extending it beyond a Scottish context. Adding opportunities to learn through Europe will require additional work to establish links and set up exchanges, but will ultimately benefit pupils and teachers in ways which often have a lasting impact on their lives.

To implement a European dimension effectively teachers need to be equipped with the necessary knowledge, skills, attitudes, values and teaching approaches. An immediate target for action is staff development for teachers and teacher educators. An effective monitoring and evaluation system is needed in order to identify areas for professional development. The publication, *How Good is Our School?* (HGIOS) (HMIE, 2002) sets out a comprehensive list of quality indicators, many of which are relevant to international education. A new series of documents to complement HGIOS is currently being produced. One of the series relates to evaluating international education (*International Education*, HMIE, 2003). This publication will encourage schools to reflect more systematically on the ways that international education, including a European dimension, is incorporated in their work and it will provide a clearer picture of teachers' needs for continuing professional development in this area.

IN CONCLUSION

International education, including a European dimension, is gradually gaining a higher profile in Scottish education. An increasing number of policy-makers, teachers and parents are aware that the global nature of society means there is an urgent need to alter the curriculum to meet the needs of a changing world. However, paradigm shifts are not easy, particularly when they challenge taken-for-granted beliefs about the way things are usually done. Changing traditional models that limit the possibility of cross-curricular learning will require new ways of thinking and working and require improved communication between teachers to enable shared decision making. A clearer understanding about the needs of pupils growing up in a more integrated, rapidly changing world must be the starting point for change.

The implementation of international education which includes providing pupils with an understanding of their role as a European citizens can make a valuable contribution to the change process needed more generally in Scottish education. A key factor in the successful implementation of a European dimension will be a new conceptual understanding of it. Its inclusion in the curriculum creates new possibilities for learning and teaching and offers different perspectives of education. For example, a link with another European school can provide a collaborative learning environment which requires active engagement in the learning process. Through a European dimension, critical and reflective thinking, decision making, conflict resolution, problem solving and communication skills can be developed in order to increase pupils' confidence, motivation and ability to participate more effectively as citizens in a democratic society.

There are many hurdles to surmount to ensure that Scottish pupils are prepared to meet the challenges of an integrated European community within a global society. New personal, professional and vocational skills, competences and attitudes are required, which in turn demand different learning and teaching approaches. Scottish education in the twenty-first century has a crucial role to play in preparing young people to survive, make a living and give sense to their lives in different social contexts in a unifying Europe. Much more needs to be done in all sectors of education to extend the existing frontiers of educational practice beyond an insular view.

REFERENCES

DES (1991) *The European Dimension in Education – A Statement of the UK Government's Policy and Report of Activities Undertaken to Implement the EC Resolution of 24 May 1988*, London: DES.
SCCC (1993,1997) *Thinking European*, Dundee: SCCC.
SCCC (1995) *Sharing Responsibility*, Dundee: SCCC.
SEED (2001) *An International Outlook*, Edinburgh: SEED.
Shennan, M. (1991) *Teaching about Europe*, London: Cassell.
SOEID (1994) *Scottish Education and the European Community – Policy, Strategy and Practice*, Edinburgh: SOEID.

106

SCOTCAT and SCQF Arrangements

Joan Menmuir

THE SCOTCAT FRAMEWORK

In the early 1990s, the extension of the university system led to the replacement of the National Council for Academic Awards (CNAA) by the Higher Education Quality Council (HEQC) as the body responsible for quality assurance and quality improvement of academic programmes. In 1997 HEQC in turn became the Quality Assurance Agency for Higher Education (QAA). The early responsibilities of HEQC included the development of credit systems, begun by CNAA in response to the need for more open and flexible systems of higher education (HE). In 1991 the Scottish Credit Accumulation and Transfer (SCOTCAT) framework was established as the national credit framework for HE in Scotland, considerably ahead of any national agreement in England and Wales.

The framework was based on the recognition of a number of key principles: agreement on a common system of credit points and levels; and agreement to co-operate in the development of credit-based learning including links with employment-based learning and programmes of continuing professional development. By early 1992 the SCOTCAT framework had the formal agreement of all HE institutions in Scotland and was being increasingly adopted as the basis for organising provision.

In 1993 the Scottish Advisory Committee for Credit and Access (SACCA) was set up jointly by the Scottish Committee of Higher Education Principals (COSHEP) and HEQC to advise them and the higher education sector generally on matters relating to credit and access. From it, the SCOTCAT development group and various subject-based specialist fora evolved and began to undertake a variety of activities to support the development and quality assurance of credit based learning and access across the sector.

PROFESSIONAL DEVELOPMENT OPPORTUNITIES FOR TEACHERS

In 1990 Jordanhill College of Education (now the Faculty of Education of Strathclyde University) with the approval of CNAA and in anticipation of the establishment of the SCOTCAT framework, established a flexible modular continuing professional development (CPD) framework for teachers and other professional workers. By 1993, the other HE providers in Scotland with an interest in teacher education had all developed their own specific modular approaches to accrediting CPD opportunities. Providers complemented the traditional, non-assessed and very practical in-service course provision by a range of opportunities to gather postgraduate academic credit for professional development work undertaken. The accredited provision was in the main at postgraduate level since all teachers in Scotland already had first degrees or their equivalent along with or including their initial qualification. There was however considerable variation from institution to institution in the composition and requirements of a postgraduate award.

During 1994–5 the SCOTCAT development group led the development of the SCOT-CAT *Quality Assurance Handbook* that gave further definition to the SCOTCAT framework (HEQC, 1995). This was used by the SCOTCAT Teacher Education Group (STEG), one of the SACCA specialist fora, as it worked with the teacher education sector to develop an agreed Scottish framework for the provision of postgraduate credit rated professional development opportunities for teachers at masters level. STEG was established in 1993 and its members were drawn from all the institutions in Scotland with a role in initial teacher education and continuing professional development. It also included representation from the Scottish Office Education and Industry Department (SOEID) and from the SCOTCAT development group. Particular issues like definitions of level and effort, progression within awards, and accreditation of prior learning were discussed by the group, and agreed understandings emerged. Agreement about collaborative arrangements for joint provision, with local authorities for example, and how these could be quality assured was more difficult, but the SCOTCAT framework proved helpful and reassured HE providers that participation in such arrangements did not undermine the autonomy of individual institutions. Publication by SOEID of a teachers' guide to SCOTCAT followed (Thomson, Partington and Menmuir, 1996).

The level of collaboration achieved has meant that, since 1996, all providers of postgraduate CPD masters awards for teachers in Scotland have adopted the SCOTCAT framework to define their awards. Benchmark statements for quality of work at masters level facilitate programme planning by institutions and individuals and explicit criteria for recognising the quality of work have also been developed. The awards have a twelve-module structure with each module credit rated at fifteen Scottish Masters (SM) points and requiring 150 notional hours of student effort. There are exit points at certificate (sixty SM points) and diploma (120SM points) for the achievement of appropriate learning outcomes and the masters award is achieved by the accumulation of 180 SM points of credit. Each module has a general credit rating attached to it, based on the SCOTCAT tariff and set by the awarding institution, and other institutions can make judgements about how much specific credit to award the learning if a teacher wants to transfer credit into one of their awards. Currency and relevance of the learning to the chosen award are the criteria used in determining specific credit. This arrangement means that teachers can transfer credit from one institution to another while, at the same time, individual institutions can maintain their autonomy. More recently the SCOTCAT framework has been embedded within the new Scottish Credit and Qualifications Framework (SCQF) and SM is now referred to as SCQF level 11.

ACCREDITATION OF PRIOR LEARNING (APL)

One of the key principles of SCOTCAT is that appropriate learning, at higher education level, wherever it occurs and provided it can be assessed, can be given credit towards an academic award. This principle provides opportunities to link the traditionally academic content of courses with the more sharply focused requirements of the world of work.

Using this principle, it is possible to look back on a professional career and identify previous learning, normally defined as being within the last five years, which can be used to gain credit within a current academic award. Institutions decide how much prior formal learning (APFL) and prior experiential learning (APEL) credit to allocate in this way though the amount is normally defined at a maximum of 50% of any award. Where the learning has not previously been formally assessed, but has been derived from professional experience in the workplace, the learning can still be assessed. This is done using, for example, a portfolio of evidence or by undertaking pre-specified assessment tasks which map the prior experiential learning onto the outcomes of an existing part of a current award. As a way of gaining academic and professional recognition for work undertaken in the recent past, this approach is now widely accepted and recognised in the HE sector and has been a key principle of developments in teachers' CPD provision. It is now beginning to be discussed in relation to initial teacher education.

ACCREDITATION OF WORK-BASED LEARNING

Just as it is possible to look back to prior learning as a source of credit, it is also possible to look forward and use current or planned learning in a similar way. This offers opportunities for relevant current work-based activity that is not being assessed in another way to gain credit within an award. Different institutions have different mechanisms available to credit such learning but most use some form of work-based learning agreement as the basis for a work-based project.

Unlike the accreditation of prior learning, the proportion of an award that can be achieved through the accreditation of current or planned learning is less likely to be limited and in some cases an entire award can be gained through project activity of this type. A SHEFC sponsored development project in 1996 with Strathclyde University, Paisley University and St Andrew's College (now incorporated into the Faculty of Education of Glasgow University), produced a guide for schools about professional development through work-based learning agreements (Thomson et al., 1996). This was then followed by a guide for teachers themselves (Menmuir et al., 1998). These guides contributed to the work-based learning principles developed in CPD provision for teachers, most recently in the Scottish Qualification for Headship (SQH) and the Chartered Teacher (CT) initiative. Although not currently conceptualised in the same way, the principles are already well established in the school experience strand of initial teacher education where planned school-based learning is assessed and credit rated.

THE SCOTTISH CREDIT AND QUALIFICATIONS FRAMEWORK (SCQF)

In 1997, the National Committee of Inquiry into Higher Education in 'Higher Education in the Learning Society' (The Dearing Report, Norwich: HMSO) recommended the adoption of a framework for all higher education qualifications. The framework would recognise achievement, encompass vocational and academic qualifications and facilitate the development, understanding, and uptake of lifelong learning opportunities. The Scottish Committee Report (The Garrick Report) of the National Inquiry had, in its submission to the main Committee, described the work already undertaken in Scotland to develop such a framework. In 1998 a Scottish Office Green Paper (*Opportunity Scotland*) emphasised the importance of a lifelong learning agenda for Scotland and included the development of the

SCQF as one of its action points. It proposed that the SCQF would build on the existing framework used by the SCOTCAT system for credit arrangements in higher education. Early in 1999 a consultation paper was produced by the SCQF partners (COSHEP, SOEID, QAA, SACCA, SQA) and by the end of the year the SCQF was in place.

Table 106.1: The Scottish Credit and Qualifications Framework

SCQF level	SQA National Units, Courses and Group Awards	Higher Education	SVQs*	SCQF level
12		Doctorates		12
11		Masters	SVQ 5	11
10		Honours Degree Graduate Diploma/Certificate**		10
9		Ordinary Degree Graduate Diploma/Certificate**		9
8		Higher National Diploma Diploma in Higher Education	SVQ 4	8
7	Advanced Higher	Higher National Certificate Certificate in Higher Education		7
6	Higher		SVQ 3*	6
5	Intermediate 2 Credit Standard Grade		SVQ 2	5
4	Intermediate 1 General Standard Grade		SVQ 1	4
3	Access 3 Foundation Standard Grade			3
2	Access 2			2
1	Access 1			1

The positioning of the SVQs in the table gives a broad indication of their place in the framework. Like most Group Awards, SVQs are likely to be made up of units at a number of levels. The current placing of SVQ3 at level 6 is based on the way in which SVQs are positioned in statutory documents and national targets. However there is a view that in some sectors SVQ3 could be placed at level 7. Further work with the Scottish Council of NTOs and individual NTOs will clarify this within an overall UK context.

**These qualifications are differentiated by volume of outcomes and may be offered at either level.*

The SCQF has twelve levels, reflecting the current Scottish system of education and training (see Table 106.1). It embraces and integrates all post-16 qualifications whether delivered in school, in further education, in universities, at work or in professional practice. Although the SCQF has the potential to accommodate all forms of post-compulsory provision and achievement, it does not impinge on the autonomy of the different awards streams like HE awards or vocational qualifications, nor does it provide automatic credit transfer or establish artificial equivalence between awards. A set of level descriptors was designed by the SCQF partners to be useful for all awards, academic, professional and vocational, as they aligned themselves with the evolving framework (Scottish Executive Education and Lifelong Learning Department (SEELLD), QAA, Universities Scotland and SQA, 2001). These level descriptors are intended to act as a guide to locating level of outcome and they have an academic and professional focus. One of the most significant benefits of the general debate about qualifications which has been promoted through the introduction of SCOTCAT and SCQF arrangements in Scotland has been the need to think closely about the links between academic, vocational and professional development. All those concerned with quality and standards in teacher education are currently involved in this debate.

CHALLENGES FOR THE CONTINUING PROFESSIONAL DEVELOPMENT OF TEACHERS

By 1996, Scotland had developed a national system for teachers gathering CPD credit at masters level which was competitive in terms of choice and availability of opportunities but where the competition was conducted within a co-operative and enabling framework which had clear and accountable quality features. However, although SCOTCAT arrangements had helped to define the academic standards for provision, national agreement on professional standards for CPD had still to be reached. This meant that masters awards did not always offer a systematic approach to professional development that identified professional needs, was coherent and progressive in meeting these needs, and that focused on professional action and the impact made on practice.

Since 1996 national professional Standards have been developed for Initial Teacher Education (2000), for Full Registration (2002), for Chartered Teacher (2002) and for Headship (2000, and soon subject to review). Chapters 103 and 104 give the background to these developments. But setting the Standards is only the start. As new teachers begin as probationers, gain some initial experience in the classroom and then begin to think about specialising in management or teaching and learning how can their professional learning be supported? The challenge will lie in opening up the range of opportunities to support teachers' professional development, while still assuring the quality of the opportunities provided. Arrangements will vary according to teachers' stage of development with the first few years of provision for teacher development providing a link between undergraduate initial education and the immediacy of the world of work. Current masters awards (MSc and MEd) focus on the academic and professional development of teachers taking the next step and beginning to think about specialisation. These awards are defined through SCQF level and volume of learning but at the moment they do not always link to the new continuing professional development standards that have been developed. The need to locate their assessment requirements very clearly in professional practice, in order to meet the Standards, presents a particular challenge for the future.

As part of the Chartered Teacher initiative, the Scottish Executive Education Department (SEED) commissioned development work carried out by a consortium of Andersen Consultants and the Universities of Edinburgh and Strathclyde. This work involved extensive consultation with teachers, employers, parents and pupils to produce the new CT Standard but it also involved the development of an exemplar programme of how teachers could achieve and demonstrate their achievement of that Standard. The exemplar programme used the principles of SCOTCAT/SCQF and brought together the academic and professional expectations set out in the Standard to meet the expectations of a masters level award. SCQF arrangements have also helped to structure the APL and work-based learning opportunities within it.

One of the opportunities for HE in the future will be to show that, along with their partner providers, they can provide masters awards to meet the Standard for Chartered Teacher while still assuring the quality of the provision. Supporting teachers at this stage of their development as they identify their professional needs and use the academic and professional demands of masters awards to make an impact on learning and teaching will be a challenge. And what about the review of the Standard for Headship? Can this other CPD Standard continue to be met through a postgraduate diploma or will early management processes be linked in future to SCQF level 11 and the revised Standard for Headship to a higher level of learning demand? How might it relate, for example, to the EdD (an SCQF level 12 award)? In the past SCOTCAT arrangements have helped define academic demand and ensure quality standards of CPD for teachers when provided by HE, often in partnership with other providers. These arrangements have enabled innovative and flexible approaches to emerge. The challenge now will be to use the strength of SCQF arrangements to build on that success and support teachers as they work towards the new professional standards currently being set.

CHALLENGES FOR INITIAL TEACHER EDUCATION

The SCQF has already begun to exert its influence at undergraduate levels. The framework has begun to encourage more collaboration and information sharing within and between award streams (see Table 106.1). The increasingly common understanding of level across award streams is contributing to a developing debate about relevant specific credit from one award stream being recognised in another. As Higher National (HN) awards, Scottish Vocational Qualifications (SVQs) and other competence-based qualifications begin to be credit rated by SQA, this debate will intensify. Access into the early years of many undergraduate professional education courses like teaching, nursing and social work, which are currently credit rated and delivered in universities, is coming under increasing scrutiny. Initial teacher education courses at undergraduate level are now being asked questions about entry requirements, about APL and duplication of learning effort, and about flexibility for students who change their career aspirations. Similarly, common learning in the initial qualifications of different public sector professionals is now being identified. These developments in turn are contributing to discussions about the content of these professional qualifications, about new ways of meeting their professional standards and about workforce planning and the flexibility required to develop better integrated services for children in Scotland.

The use of SCOTCAT and SCQF in initial teacher education is raising questions for the future, not least the use of the name Postgraduate Certificate in Education (PGCE) for initial teacher education awards. The PGCE awards are postgraduate in time rather than level and do not fit with the new qualification nomenclature of SCQF in Scotland (SEELLD, QAA, US, SQA, 2001). A more important issue, however, is how best the provision of initial teacher education at undergraduate level (whether through an undergraduate degree or a PGCE) can be developed to meet the new Standard for Initial Teacher Education. As employers demand more flexibility from staff and the demand for more integrated services for children develops, how will the profession respond? Can the current dedicated Bachelor of Education four-year honours degree survive in its present form? Is a generic SCQF level 7, shared with other undergraduate degrees, a realistic option or will more radical reconceptualisation be required? How will the provision develop to accommodate common standards and common learning across professional groups?

As students increasingly understand the principles of SCQF they will also exert more influence. They will increasingly expect entry or exemption credit for prior relevant learning and assume flexible provision with a range of choice and progression opportunities. Can the profession realistically continue to say 'go back to the start' to early education and childcare staff with an HNC qualification who ask for their relevant learning to be recognised within the undergraduate teaching qualification? And what about a student nurse part way through a degree qualification or someone with a relevant SVQ4 who wants to transfer to teaching? How will horizontal or lower progression be flexibly accommodated? Whatever else, the processes which are developed must be easy to understand and operate.

Although the standards of initial teacher education have been carefully monitored by the professional body, the General Teaching Council for Scotland (GTCS) over many years, the council will now be drawn into a wider debate with other professional bodies about standards for public service professionals. As progression routes into initial teacher education degrees develop, the emerging standards for para-professional staff who work in schools and whose qualifications will increasingly articulate with those of teachers must also be of interest. Just as with the support offered to teachers in the wide ranging and rapidly changing area of continuing professional development, the council must also support those who aspire to be teachers as they work towards the new professional Standards that have been set.

FUTURE DEVELOPMENTS

The Scottish Parliament's Enterprise and Lifelong Learning Committee (E&LLC) Report on the *Lifelong Learning Inquiry* (2002) placed the SCQF at the heart of the education and training agenda in Scotland. The Interim Report had already raised a number of important issues, not least that old distinctions, such as higher/further, academic/vocational, full-time/part-time, which existed within and between sectors are breaking down and that developments in funding and policy need to reflect this (E&LLC, 2002). The Joint Advisory Committee for the SCQF is optimistic that all those with an interest in education and training in Scotland will work together to maximise the potential of the SCQF. SCOTCAT and SCQF arrangements have already played a considerable part in the success of credit-based learning in teacher education. The next few years will offer the potential for exciting and innovative SCQF developments based on flexibility, inclusivity, credit transfer, learner choice and progression. These are important concepts for those who work in teacher education and the teaching profession can only benefit by using SCQF to meet the professional challenges ahead.

REFERENCES

E&LLC (2002) *Second Report: Interim Report on the Lifelong Learning Inquiry* (www.scottish. parliament.uk).

HEQC (1995) *The SCOTCAT Quality Assurance Handbook*, London: HEQC.

Menmuir, J. G., Thomson, W. P and Stark, M. E. R. (1998*) Partnership in Professional Development: Work Based Learning Agreements: A Guide for Practice*, Glasgow: University of Strathclyde.

SEELLD, QAA, US, SQA (2001) *An Introduction to the Scottish Credit and Qualifications Framework*, publication code AE1243 (also at www.qaa.ac.uk).

Thomson, W. P., Menmuir, J. G., Forde, C. McCreath, D., Forbes, D. and Verth, J. (1996) *Professional Development through Work Based Learning Agreements: A Guide for Schools*, Glasgow: University of Strathclyde.

Thomson, W. P., Partington, R. and Menmuir, J. G. (1996) *Academic Credit and Staff Development: A Teachers' Guide to the Scottish Credit Accumulation and Transfer Framework*, (SCOTCAT), Edinburgh: HMSO (www.leeds.ac.uk/educol).

107

Research and Practice

Pamela Munn and Jenny Ozga

For a long time research, in Scotland as elsewhere, was something done to teachers rather than by teachers. Researchers would typically be commissioned by the Scottish Office to investigate areas causing concern, or be asked to evaluate major innovations in curriculum or assessment or school governance, for example. In addition, researchers themselves would have ideas they wanted to explore and theories they wanted to test. Teachers continue to be involved in these kinds of research projects. They are often subjects of it: they are interviewed, their classroom practice is observed, they are asked to complete questionnaires and the curriculum and assessment materials they use are analysed.

This way of thinking about the design of research has tended to limit the involvement of practitioners in research, and has perhaps inhibited the development of practice routinely informed by research. One reason is that teachers have no real 'ownership' of the research. They have not decided on the topic under investigation and are usually not consulted about how the topic might be conceptualised in such a way as to inform practice. Not surprisingly, therefore, teachers have paid very little attention to these kinds of research as not impinging on matters of direct practical concern to them. Moreover, where the research does, as in the case of the evaluation of curriculum implementation, findings can all too easily portray teachers as 'deficient' in terms of skills and knowledge. Thus research findings can often be presented as identifying things which teachers ought to be doing and are not. Research findings rarely celebrate that elusive phenomenon, good practice, in schools and classrooms and on the few occasions they do, seem not to be concerned with exploring ways in which examples of good practice in specific schools might be useful to schools in general. In addition, research topics and problems are seldom conceptualised by researchers and teachers working in partnership to define and explore an issue of mutual concern. Finally, researchers may give insufficient thought to the ways in which their research findings are communicated to the profession, and their implications for practice explained and explored.

The need to find ways of bridging the gap between research and practice is perhaps more pressing than ever. There are growing policy pressures on researchers to focus on 'useful' research, and teachers are also under pressure to monitor their own performance in order to ensure their maximum effectiveness. These developments take place within the context of the emergent 'knowledge economies' in which teachers – in Scotland, and elsewhere – have a central role to play in developing capacities to design and produce knowledge.

It is possible to foster these professional capacities through involvement in research. Research can be designed and developed in such a way as to incorporate and sustain reflection on practice, and can support reflexivity in teaching. The development of a research orientation among teachers could enable knowledge transfer, so that research practices such as experimentation, scrutiny of results, review of evidence, teamwork, evaluation and the search for improvement in problem solving become explicitly part of classroom practice. This is, perhaps, an 'indirect' relationship between research and practice, in which attention is given to fostering a 'researcherly' disposition among teachers, rather than the direct transfer of knowledge based on research into classroom practice. Arguably, this is the intention of the recently developed Standard for Full Registration of teachers with the GTC and the Standard for Chartered Teacher.

In this chapter, the possibilities for direct- and indirect-research–practice relationships, and the conditions under which they could develop are considered. This is done through exploration of the following questions:

- How has the relationship between research and practice been developed?
- What are the conditions necessary for either a direct (evidence-based) practice or more indirect orientation to research in partnership?
- How does 'action' research fit into this picture?
- Are teacher networks a feasible way of applying research and sharing practice?
- What policy developments in teaching and research would support a partnership relationship?

THE RESEARCH–PRACTICE RELATIONSHIP

Writing on educational research typically distinguishes basic or 'blue skies' research from applied or practical research (Dockrell, 1984; Nisbet, 1988; Hammersley, 1997; Hargreaves, 1997). Basic research, or research for enlightenment, concerns challenging and changing assumptions, for example, about how learning takes place, or about conceptions of ability or about the structure of knowledge. Such research is not intended directly or immediately to affect practice. Rather its function is to contribute to the way the world of education is viewed, 'influencing aspirations . . . and offering new insights' (Nisbet, 1988, p. 17). Research for enlightenment thus has an indirect influence on practice and indeed on policy too, but its prime function is that of extending knowledge for its own sake rather than helping to do current work better. Many commentators would accept, therefore, that a legitimate function of research is to extend knowledge rather than deliberately and immediately to inform and to improve practice

However it may be that this sharp dichotomy between research for 'enlightenment' and research for improvement in practice is in need of modification, in the light of developments in the interface between research and 'real life'. There is a very strong policy interest in the area becoming known as 'knowledge transfer' and considerable efforts are being made to find ways of translating advances in knowledge into outputs or effects that improve effectiveness in many spheres of work and life, including health, education and business development. Whether these developments threaten the integrity of blue skies research, or can be more positively interpreted as progressing a neglected element of research (that is its dissemination or impact) is a matter for debate.

It is certainly the case that in Scotland, and probably elsewhere, there has been an assumption that one purpose of educational research was to inform practice. What is changing is the way in which professionals think about how that can be done. In the past, as is known from research on the origins of the Scottish Council for Research in Education (SCRE), the founders' concerns were that research should raise the level of efficiency in school work (see Chapter 110). Indeed, throughout its existence SCRE has had to take account of expectations of funders and others that the research it conducted would make a practical contribution to solving problems of the day. Nisbet (1988) draws attention to a range of early studies by SCRE with a strong practical slant, such as Studies in Arithmetic, Addition and Subtraction, *Facts and Processes* and *The Writing of Arabic Numbers*. Recent work continues this trend including work on, for example, *An Evaluation of Drug Education in Scottish Schools (2000)* and *Teachers' and Pupils' Days in the Primary Classroom* (1999). Thus the concern that research should be useful is not new. This practical slant is echoed by the Scottish Executive Education Department (SEED), a major funder of educational research in Scotland. It clearly expects some of the research it funds to have an impact on practice. It has signalled this by:

- sponsoring national conferences to disseminate findings and promote discussion;
- funding a series of summaries of research findings, *Interchange*, distributed free of charge to all schools and other appropriate educational institutions;
- commissioning resource packs derived from research for use in schools and classrooms;
- commissioning an evaluation of the use and impact of these resource packs;
- commissioning a study of the relationship between research and staff development.

However there does seem to be a search for new ways of injecting research into the bloodstream of professionals and other 'users'. Major UK funding bodies such as the Economic and Social Research Council (ESRC) indicate that the role of 'users', either in helping to define the research focus or in taking up findings, is an important criterion in securing funding for research. The medical metaphor is apposite, as one way of transforming research use in education is through the development of a more secure evidence base for practice.

EVIDENCE-BASED RESEARCH AS A WAY OF INFORMING PRACTICE?

Harlen describes this approach with reference to the guidelines being used by doctors in Scotland to judge the quality of evidence and thus whether it should be taken more or less seriously in terms of practice. Six levels of evidence are identified. 'At the highest level stands evidence from meta-analysis of several randomised controlled trials; at the lowest level is evidence obtained from expert committee reports or opinions and/or clinical experience of respected authorities' (quoted in Hargreaves, 1997, p. 413). Adapting this approach to classify evidence from educational research it is clear that there is comparatively little evidence at the highest level. Furthermore, there is comparatively little meta-analysis of evidence from case studies, surveys, experiments and so on, regarding particular substantive issues. Recent moves by the Scottish Office to commission research reviews are, therefore, welcome, especially where there is explicit encouragement to move beyond description to critical commentary on the robustness of evidence.

However the adoption of an evidence-based model of professional practice is not straightforward. Some commentators suggest that the idea of the medical profession as a model of research-informed and research-driven practice is more myth than reality. Others point to the difficulty of interpreting evidence in education. In the first place, as already pointed out, the evidence base is underdeveloped, and in the second there is disagreement about interpreting the evidence, because of the strongly value-driven nature of education. For example, although sociological studies of grammar and secondary modern schools did much to contribute to the debate about the desirability of selection at age eleven, this evidence in itself was not sufficient to abolish selection. These kinds of studies helped to raise awareness about the consequences of selection among and within schools and added a different dimension to the debate on selection from that on the validity and reliability of the IQ test as a selection instrument; in themselves they provide a nice illustration of research designed to improve an existing system (IQ testing) and research which challenged assumptions upon which the system rested. The key driving force behind the abolition of selection, however, was the ideological commitment of the Labour governments of the 1960s. Conservative governments of the 1980s and 1990s, with a different ideological stance, changed tack and began reintroducing selection.

Nor can the existence of evidence guarantee that policy and practice follow the direction of that evidence. At the time of writing, the UK government is 'decomprehensivising' in England, with pressures for increased diversity of provision in Scotland, despite evidence of the success of the comprehensive system in raising attainment levels, including among less advantaged pupils (Croxford et al., 2000). As Nisbet (1986, p. 16) points out, research is used to inform policy and practice only 'in non-controversial areas where there is a consensus on values'.

However given that the evidence from the recent national debate on education in Scotland illustrates considerable consensus on a number of key issues of principle in educational provision (including comprehensive organisation) and also expresses concerns about areas of schooling (bullying, academic curricula, citizenship), it might be possible to propose that, where consensus existed, then research-based practice could be more in evidence. It is useful, therefore, to consider the circumstances under which research-based practice could be achieved.

- The research should be on a topic of direct concern to teachers. Research on learning to read, on bullying, on children with visual and aural impairment accessing the curriculum, are but a few examples which readily spring to mind. But this should not be too narrow a field – we know that teachers are interested in, and concerned about, less immediately 'practical' issues such as how to ensure fairness and equity in the classroom.
- Teachers need, therefore, to have a voice in the decisions about the focus of research which is to be undertaken. Hargreaves, in his 1996 Teacher Training Agency lecture, advocated a National Educational Research Forum for this purpose. In the mid-1980s SCRE experimented with a national forum as a way of determining research priorities to be funded via the Scottish Office. It was not a success. It was difficult to reach consensus on priorities; there was perhaps a lack of understanding of the ability of research to deliver immediate answers to problems; and the Scottish Office was unwilling to relinquish control of its research budget. It therefore remained the key player in determining priorities. The National Education Research Forum recently established in England seems to be facing similar difficulties. Perhaps it is more productive to search for a means of enabling three-way dialogue between researchers, funders and practitioners that looks at means of transferring knowledge and evaluating its impact as well as at developing new knowledge.
- Research findings have to be made accessible to teachers. This means that researchers need to think about new forms of dissemination and about working with practitioners in exploring implications for practice that can be spread throughout the system. This has implications for the funding of research.

- Teachers need to be convinced about the validity and reliability of research findings, and the robustness of the evidence on which their practice is based. This means that teachers, in their professional formation and development, need a good grasp of research principles, so that they can make an accurate assessment of evidence. This also promotes the 'researcherly disposition' advocated earlier. There is also an obligation on researchers to engage with practitioners in a more open and informative way.
- Professional researchers and those who fund research should promote replication studies so that a cumulative body of evidence is available on a particular topic, and in an accessible form.
- Time and money have to be provided for meta-analysis.
- Longitudinal work is necessary so that effects of particular strategies can be analysed over time.
- A much more strategic view has to be taken of practical research priorities, rather than the 'one damn thing after another' syndrome which typifies much current practice. The funding of research programmes on a specific area, rather than unconnected short term projects which allow time only for data gathering and descriptions rather than serious analysis, should be the norm, and time and money would also need to be devoted to ensuring impact.
- There would be a move away from the current system of competitive tendering for external research funds which results in more funding being spent on the competition than in doing research. Much of what is being argued for is dependent on fostering partnerships between funders, practitioners and researchers: such relationships are not enabled by competition.
- Better systems of accountability need to be developed within faculties and schools of education for the use of research funds allocated through the government's 'dual support' system of funding for teaching and research in higher education.
- Researchers need to engage in debates that help to build consensus and/or identify conflict about future research directions in education, in collaboration with the profession.

No doubt other conditions might be identified. However, if the above represents the beginnings of an analysis of what might be needed in order for research more adequately to inform practice then a formidable but by no means impossible agenda lies ahead. There are signs that on the funding and research side some movement in the direction outlined is taking place. More needs to be done.

ACTION RESEARCH

So far, the discussion has been in terms of research conducted by professional researchers and its relationship to practice. Many commentators would argue that the way to bring research and practice into closer alignment is for teachers themselves to carry out the research on an issue of direct practical concern to them with the express purpose of bringing about change – that is through 'action' research. In contrast to the concerns about validity and reliability which characterise traditional research:

> Action research is concerned with exploring the multiple determinants of actions, interactions and interpersonal relationships in unique contexts. Its aim is to deepen practitioners' understanding of the complex situations in which they live and work, so that their actions are better informed. Rather than specific 'findings' or 'outcomes' action research generates . . . 'practical wisdom' [or] situational understanding (Somekh, 1995, p. 341).

Action research has become a major feature of many advanced level courses for teachers and almost all education faculties in the UK would claim to be in the business of developing 'reflective practitioners' in both initial teacher training and in advanced certificates, diplomas and degrees. Whether all mean the same thing by 'reflective practice' is open to question. For some reflective practice means teachers being aware of their professional context; for others it means teachers doing a bit of data gathering on a topic of direct practical concern to them and relating their analysis of the data to the relevant literature; for others again it means taking action based on evidence teachers themselves have collected. Action can range from developing a particular technique such as questioning, to challenging the purpose and moral order of schooling. There are thus different 'schools' of action research. Debates about the meaning and purpose of and support for action research have, however, not been evident in Scotland.

In Scotland's teacher education institutions it is commonplace for BEd degree and PGCE students to undertake a substantial piece of action research as part of their studies. In addition, the Scottish Council for Research in Education (SCRE) has established a teacher-researcher network. SCRE also awards a prize each year to teachers carrying out a piece of research outwith accredited advanced level work. The Scottish Educational Research Association (SERA) has supported teacher-researcher groups in various parts of Scotland and has helped to promote annual conferences for teacher-researchers. Teachers research-ing their own practice and that of their school are now features of school improvement programmes. HMI state in their report on *Standards and Quality in Scottish Schools 1992–95*, (1996) that 'the most effective way of improving the quality of education for individual pupils is to expect schools to take responsibility for their own quality assurance by evaluating their performance and making the necessary changes' (Summary, p. 4). To the casual observer, therefore, it might seem that the gap between research and practice has been bridged by the prevalence of and support for action research in the system. This is far from true. There are a number of reasons for this as well as that mentioned above, namely, the lack of critical engagement with the philosophy of action research by the education community in Scotland.

The first is that only a very small number of teachers is involved in action research. The second is that action research is typically a private matter for a teacher, a group, or a school. The work is seldom made public and so cumulative knowledge about specific areas of practice is hard to find. The third reason was alluded to by Donald McIntyre in his Presidential Address to the Annual Conference of the British Educational Research Association in Bath (1996). It is difficult to do high quality educational research. This is so not only for professional researchers but doubly so for teachers when the expertise required to teach well is rather different from that required to carry out a good piece of research. McIntyre is not persuaded of the feasibility of asking teachers to be the front runners in conducting educational research given the other demands on them as teachers. He sees a role for teachers in testing useful theories of educational practice provided by educational research. This, of course, reintroduces questions about who decides on the priorities for the focus of educational research and the role of teachers in this process.

NETWORKING

A possible interpretation of McIntyre's suggestion for the role of teachers in research is the development of networks among schools and teachers on topics where a cumulative body of research evidence exists. Two recent examples in Scotland are the Scottish Schools Ethos Network and the Promoting Positive Discipline initiative.

The Ethos Network takes as its starting point the influence which school culture has on attainment and on behaviour. Research evidence from a range of school effectiveness studies, based on large samples in Britain, the United States and Australia, points to ethos as an important influence. Likewise a range of small-scale qualitative studies has explored the ways in which schools can promote positive behaviour. While some of this evidence does not meet the strongest criteria suggested above, and there is debate about how ethos can most adequately be conceptualised, there is an emerging consensus about the importance of school ethos. The first step, therefore, was to bring this conclusion to the attention of schools and to convince teachers about the evidential base for the importance of ethos. Highlighting the importance of ethos, however, is not much practical help to schools. Ethos by its very nature encompasses much that is taken for granted about school life, the rules, routines and rituals. It was, therefore, important to provide schools with tools to help them analyse and develop their ethos.

The Scottish Office commissioned a group of researchers to develop 'ethos indicators' and to suggest ways in which schools could 'take the temperature' of their ethos. A key feature was that views about aspects of school ethos should be sought from pupils, parents and where possible members of the local community. The network was prompted initially by a number of schools seeking advice about the collection and analysis of data about their ethos. It has grown beyond sharing experience of these technical details to include information and experience about the process of developing a positive ethos and a focus on substantive issues such as involving parents in curriculum work, pupil participation in decision making and raising pupils' self-esteem. The value of teacher research in this context is less as a contribution to theory building than to theory testing. This being so, professional researchers should, over time, be looking for outcomes in terms of improved attainment and improved behaviour and correlating these with a range of activities promoting a positive ethos. With over 1,000 members the network can provide a sample which makes such a study feasible.

Likewise, in promoting positive discipline, it is known from a number of studies that it is the effect of constant minor disruption which teachers find wearying. Talking out of turn, eating in class, arriving without books or materials, and so on, are the discipline problems faced by the majority of teachers, rather than violence, drug dealing and other more serious offences. Also known, from a range of studies, is the importance of teachers praising pupils' work, setting realistic targets for learning and behaviour, and involving pupils in rule setting and accompanying rewards and sanctions. Again, however, simply telling teachers to use praise more frequently or to set targets for behaviour is of little practical help. The Promoting Positive Discipline initiative aims to share experience among schools about the use and effectiveness of a number of strategies including praise and reward schemes, playground development, and particular curriculum strategies such as social skills training. Schools involved in the initiative write up their experience in a three- or four-page case study. Furthermore, local authorities are being encouraged to write about the approaches they are taking to co-ordinate and share information and experience across the authority.

These are examples of initiatives where teachers are involved in sharing experience through writing about the development, monitoring and evaluation of specific practices and in this way testing the relevance and applicability of research findings to their own situation. There are, of course, many other examples of research findings being used to inform practice. Much remains to be done, however, if the conditions that we set out above for more research-based practice are to be met in the future.

POLICY FOR RESEARCH – FUTURE DIRECTIONS?

Although no-one can predict with certainty what the future holds for educational research there are indications of future directions. Perhaps most importantly in terms of concerns about the research–practice relationship, there is a strong policy steer towards 'useful' research that has an impact on practice. The overwhelming government concern with raising standards and school improvement in the UK as a whole will put increasing pressure on research in Scotland to contribute directly to this policy goal. Additional pressure comes from the growing trend towards international comparisons of school performance. Policy makers are thus likely to take a closer interest than ever before in steering research towards their policy goals of improved attainment, and in devising mechanisms for the transfer of officially-recognised evidence into practice. As suggested above, there are problems with a direct relationship between evidence and practice, because of the value-driven nature of education. Policy-makers have their own values which may lead them to select the evidence that points them in the direction that they prefer to take.

Increased competition for research funds is another trend likely to develop in the future. Research is one of the few areas where higher education institutions are reasonably free to increase their income without incurring financial and other penalties. Thus research funds can help to support the running costs of cash-strapped institutions through charging overheads. Furthermore, research income is an indicator taken into account by the research assessment exercise which judges the quality of educational (and other) research in higher education. The quality rating determines the amount of money which institutions receive from central government to support teaching and research. Competing for funds costs money, of course, and a recent account told of 600 applications for a European Union programme. If researchers are competing for funds they are not doing research and the situation could be fast approaching where the net costs to the system of bidding for funds exceeds the funds on offer.

What do these trends – towards increased competitiveness and increased policy 'steerage' of research – imply for arguments about the need for cultivation of a researcherly disposition among teachers and for greater attention to knowledge transfer from researchers? Firstly, they strengthen the case for three-way dialogue between researchers, funders and practitioners. Strong steerage of research by policy makers may threaten the independence and thus the quality of research. If the research is too narrowly defined, then it limits the possibilities for teachers to participate in it as partners, rather than recipients of research. Thus the dual funding mechanism, whereby higher education institutions are funded to undertake teaching and research through a block grant, needs to remain in some form if educational research in the enlightenment tradition is to continue. Research in cognitive science, brain functioning, information technology and the like all need to be supported if learning is to be understood more fully. Similarly, independent policy related research on issues such as gender, race and social class and education, special needs issues and curriculum frameworks, for instance, is needed to supply the grit in the system to provoke change in policy, in provision, and participation. In short, the heightened emphasis on relevance and practicality must leave room for research with broader and more challenging purposes. Nisbet (1988, pp.14 and 22) provides a neat summing up.

> I suggest comparing education to cheese, which has many varieties with different qualities. Research on cheese is complicated by the plurality of tastes and values . . . We must recognise different styles of research and different ways in which it may contribute to education.

In addition, as indicated earlier, there is scope for thinking about better ways of enabling research findings to become part of the professional discourse of teachers. Research and practice are united in their shared concern for improved educational experiences and opportunities for all learners in Scotland. (This is not to limit research to improving attainment.) Much could be achieved through greater dialogue between funders, researchers and practitioners with the aim of strengthening the elements of a 'researcherly disposition' contained in current policy for the teaching profession, and of enabling researchers to contribute to that aim. A key issue for building this future agenda is the development of resources and skills in knowledge transfer. Much excellent research remains unknown to practitioners, or is presented without sufficient development of its implications for policy and practice. Researchers are not currently supported to work with practitioners in developing these implications. A small country such as Scotland is in a good position to take initiatives here, as representatives of the key stakeholders in the school system know each other and already have a strong base on which to build. Perhaps the new sense of self-confidence in Scotland as a country which has accompanied the establishment of a Scottish Parliament means that the time is right to take forward such dialogue.

REFERENCES

Dockrell, W. B. (1984) Practical research, in W. B. Dockrell (ed.) *An Attitude of Mind: Twenty Five Years of Educational Research in Scotland*, Edinburgh: SCRE.

Croxford, L., Raffe, D. and Brannen, K. (2000) *Social Inequalities, Attainment and Comprehensive Schooling: a Home-Internationals Analysis*, Edinburgh: CES, University of Edinburgh.

Hammersley, M. (1997) Educational research and teaching: a response to David Hargreaves' TTA lecture, *British Educational Research Journal*, 23 (2), 141–62.

Hargreaves, D. H. (1997) In defence of research for evidence-based teaching: a rejoinder to Martyn Hammersley, *British Educational Research Journal*, 23 (4), 405–20.

Nisbet, J. (1988) The contribution of research to education, in S. Brown and R. Wake (eds), *Education in Transition: What Role for Research?* Edinburgh: SCRE.

Somekh, B. (1995) The contribution of action research to development in social endeavours: a position paper on action research methodology, *British Educational Research Journal*, 21 (3), pp. 339–55.

108

The Scottish
Educational Research Association

Brian Morris

The Scottish Educational Research Association (SERA) constitution identifies two aims:

- to disseminate educational research findings to all parties interested in education in Scotland;
- to promote co-operation and communication among research workers in various disciplines working in the educational field in Scotland.

It goes on to state that these aims are to be achieved through a wide range of activities to include: the arrangement of conferences, seminars and symposia; the organisation of study groups on specific topics; publication and distribution of monographs, documents, bulletins and reports; the promotion and/or publication of a research journal; the editing and publishing of abstracts of research work; the promotion of research projects. SERA has pursued all of these at various times, but the most prominent recently have been regular one-day conferences on educational topics, a newsletter, a teacher-researcher conference, and most prominently the SERA annual conference. The annual conference, held over three days, has become the most important national event for the dissemination and discussion of research.

Throughout its existence SERA has been keen to promote the existence of a Scottish educational journal. SERA policy is to encourage its members to support the existing independent *Scottish Educational Review* (*SER*, see Chapter 109) through a preferential subscription scheme for SERA members and a regular voluntary donation to *SER*. The association is run by an elected executive which organises itself into task-based sub-committees which reflect the activities identified above. Inevitably, SERA has also developed a representative role for research and researchers in Scotland. It meets twice a year with research staff from the Scottish Executive Education Department to discuss research related issues. Similarly it meets regularly with Learning and Teaching Scotland and sends representatives to the Scottish Civic Forum.

MEMBERSHIP

Membership of SERA, which is individual, is 'open to those actively engaged in education in Scotland and interested individuals resident in Scotland'. Associate membership, which confers the same privileges as full membership is also open to interested individuals 'working outwith Scotland'.

SERA was founded in 1974, its original planning committee containing representatives from higher education, teacher unions, the Scottish Certificate in Education (SCE) Examination Board and research societies in history and sociology. The imminent creation of a British Educational Research Association (BERA) perhaps accelerated the establishment of a research association which would represent the distinctively Scottish educational system (Nisbet, 1995). The original list of members in November 1974 numbered 136 and by the mid-1980s it had settled to around 200. There are now approximately 250 members. As Nisbet (1995) pointed out, this level of membership (250 members: 5 million population) compares favourably with that of the British Educational Research Association (660 members: 56 million population).

A feature of SERA membership in its first few years was its heterogeneity. In 1974, almost one-quarter of members were teachers, about half being headteachers. Just over one-third of members worked in higher education although not all were from education departments, the membership including professors of German and Psychology. Educational psychologists comprised just over 10% of members. Other than those employed by the Scottish Council for Research in Education (SCRE), only six members had the term 'research' in their job title: four of these were from local authorities. By 1978, Nisbet (1995, p. 132) quotes from a SERA source that 'a third of the membership are school-based and almost half are "not the traditional practitioners of educational research"'. However, by 1987 the membership list indicated that almost half (44%) of the membership were employed in higher education. Teachers accounted for only 12% of the membership. There was only one educational psychologist. The number of members with 'research' in their job titles had reached just over 10% of the membership. Due to changes in record keeping practice, comparisons of membership over time is difficult. However, it is apparent that this trend has continued and that there has been a discernible trend towards a membership which is dominated by higher education staff for whom research is an essential element of their professional obligations. The decrease in the number of educational psychologists as members is perhaps explained by the move away from what was once regarded as the 'founding disciplines' approach to teacher education based on psychology, sociology and philosophy. Consequently, representatives from these disciplines are less evident in educational colleges and university departments, or at any rate they are less likely to describe themselves as such.

This change in membership characteristics reflects changes within higher education, schools and local authorities. The integration of initial teacher education within the university system has resulted in increasing pressure on higher education staff to conduct and publish research. This has led to more research activity, as well as more job titles which include the term 'research'. Both of these developments have influenced the form, and to some extent the content, of the annual conferences. The number of papers submitted has increased in recent years and there has been a demand from members for these to be published. Conference papers are now published electronically through the education-line website. There have also been changes in schools which have inhibited teacher participation in SERA. SERA support for teacher research traditionally took the form of support for local teacher-research groups and an annual, later biannual, conference on teacher-research. These no longer take place. This activity was established in a period when relatively few teachers undertook research. However, this has changed with the proliferation of accredited in-service courses being offered by higher education institutions which contain elements of research. The support function for teacher-research might therefore be said to have transferred to individual higher education institutions.

ANNUAL CONFERENCE

From 1979 to 1987, the conference was organised around themes selected by the executive. This practice was superseded in 1987 by an annual 'open' call for individual papers and symposia in the spring. The range of conference papers is comprehensive and includes consideration of methodological issues, research into teaching and learning in schools and higher education, as well as evaluative research of policy-led innovations. While it would be difficult to claim a definitive trend in the subjects covered, this last theme seems to have become increasingly prominent.

However, the striking feature of change in the annual conference is to be found, not in the numbers attending which have held steady in the region of 130 since the 1980s, but rather in the number of papers presented. It is apparent that for a considerable period, the majority of delegates did not give papers. In 1979, 129 delegates attended a two-day conference where twenty-one papers were given. In 1985, the conference programme involving seventeen papers could be printed on less than two sides of A4. In more recent times, more delegates expect to give papers. In 1994, 137 people attended and forty-nine papers were given. In 1997, 145 delegates attended the conference with the equivalent of approximately 100 individual papers being given; a trend which continues to this day. In 2002, 112 delegates presented a total of 62 papers. It might be said that if the original primary task for SERA was to disseminate research to its members, the contemporary task is to disseminate the research produced by them.

FUTURE CONCERNS

The challenge for SERA is to continue to promote its stated aims in a rapidly changing local, national and European context. The European context is, perhaps, the least problematic. SERA has been active in the European Educational Research Association (EERA) since its inception and, in 2000, it hosted the EERA conference (ECER) in Edinburgh. More recently SERA has established formal organisational links with BERA by taking up an offered place on the BERA executive council. This relationship will be kept under review but currently it has opened channels of communication not only with colleagues in England but also in Wales.

There has been recent increased criticism of educational research by some researchers (see Hargreaves, 1996) and by politicians in Scotland as well as England (see Sam Galbraith, *The Scotsman* 22 March 2000; Blunkett, 2000). However, this criticism has been accompanied by a rhetoric which stresses the importance of the role of research in 'evidence-based' (sometimes softened to 'evidence-informed', or even 'evidence-aware') policy making. In response, researchers have argued that the role for research proposed by policy makers limits its nature and misrepresents its relationship to policy making (see Ozga, 2000). In a context where it can be argued that research contracts from SEED are particularly, even disproportionately, important for Scottish educational researchers, Nisbet (1995, p. 76) had historically identified such a development in Scottish research as indicating a general shift of power to the centre. More recently Humes and Bryce have described this new emphasis on research as offering the 'danger(s) of a retreat to a narrow empirical role' (Humes and Bryce, 2001, p. 329).

The wider Scottish educational context has also been subject to recent change. The current government emphasises the relationships between education, economic success, social inclusion and poverty. The New Community Schools initiative involves new professions and new professional relationships in schools. The regular renaming of the bodies responsible for research in schools, shadowing the title changes of ministers responsible for education in Scotland in recent years, seem to have converged to emphasise 'children' and 'young people'. These changes in themselves imply an expanded research agenda.

David Blunkett (2000) has argued for an important role for social science research in social policy making. Given the central role of education in current social policy, this would appear to have implications for who should conduct educational research. In Scotland, Humes and Bryce (2001) distinguish a pattern between 1994 and 1999 where there was a small decrease in the number of research projects being awarded to higher education and a significant decrease for SCRE (29% to 15%) whose Scottish Executive core funding will cease in 2003. In contrast, more SEED educational research is being awarded to the private sector (10%–29%). This apparent political concern to engage with a wider range of research, and researchers, has been accompanied by changes in the political system in Scotland which have the potential for making this engagement more direct. The advent of a Scottish Parliament has created ministers with a policy brief. The removal of Her Majesty's Inspectorate from a policy role could be said, in turn, to have cleared the way for more direct communication between politicians and researchers as well as creating the conditions for a more direct management of research.

Taken together these developments seem to offer SERA an environment where research will become increasingly important politically, and where there will be more immediate political engagement with the research community. However, being granted your wishes is traditionally not without its accompanying difficulties. There is also the potential that research could become narrower in scope and involve researchers outside of the traditional educational research community. A major issue for SERA will be how to engage with policy makers in a way that expands the opportunities for, and use of, research. SERA need not respond to accusations of educational research as inward looking and insufficiently rigorous by accepting an approach to research which can be similarly criticised. In discussion with the Scottish Executive it can emphasise the range of types and purposes of research. However, its activities need not become entirely focused on funding for research from the Scottish Executive. In keeping with its original aims, and recent practice, it can also seek to respond to any potential narrowing by extending the range of individuals and institutions with which it has contact. This expansion could involve researchers, and research societies, in the social sciences who were among its founding members. SERA could also seek to represent Scottish research in relation to a wider range of research funding bodies, particularly the ESRC and SHEFC. The move to 'learned society' status currently being managed by the SERA executive might be seen as a first stage in this process.

Throughout its existence SERA has relied on the considerable voluntary efforts of individuals and some support from educational institutions. The increasing commercialisation of higher education has made support more difficult for individuals and less forthcoming from institutions. SERA will prosper to the extent to which individual educational researchers and institutions continue to realise their community of interest in promoting research in a democratic society.

REFERENCES

Blunkett, D. (2000) Influence or irrelevance: can social science improve government? *Research Intelligence* 71, 12–21.

Hargreaves, D. H. (1996) *Teaching as a Research-based Profession: Possibilities and Prospects*, TTA annual lecture. London: TTA.

Humes, W. M. and Bryce, T. G. K. (2001) Scholarship, research and the evidential basis of policy development in education, *British Journal of Educational Studies* 3, 329–52.

Nisbet, J. (1995) *Pipers & Tunes: A Decade of Educational Research in Scotland*. Edinburgh: SCRE.

Nisbet, S. (1984) Does Scotland need SERA? *Scottish Educational Review* 16 (2), 127–33.

Ozga, J. (2000) *Policy Research in Educational Settings*, Buckingham: Open University Press.

109

Scottish Educational Journals

Willis Pickard

SCOTTISH EDUCATIONAL JOURNAL

> We shall bring before our readers all such information as shall tend to make the bonds of brotherhood closer, smooth down the asperities which have unfortunately too often occurred in the past, and send us out to work with a more cheerful and hopeful spirit.

So the *Educational News* launched itself on 1 January 1876. The journal for the profession was to deal in professional matters and in a positive frame of mind.

Two thousand, two hundred and nine issues later, in the final year of the First World War, the *Educational News* merged with the *Scottish Educational Journal* (*SEJ*), which was the organ of the Educational Institute of Scotland (EIS) and dated from 1852, only five years after the founding of the institute.

The *SEJ*, as it is now usually known, is the longest running of the newspapers and reviews serving the teaching profession. Its prime purpose has always been to form a link between the institute and its members in schools, but it has done so in various ways. Early on it was interested in adult education and published mathematical puzzles and 'harmless entertainment' as well as educational news. As a weekly, it gave space to the young Christopher Grieve (Hugh MacDiarmid) in the 1920s.

In the 1970s it sought to develop into a wide-ranging educational magazine challenging the *Times Educational Supplement*, which had recently started a Scottish edition. Later, responding to the need to communicate with members in the fraught industrial climate of the Callaghan and Thatcher governments, it became more of a union news sheet, published after meetings of the institute's councils and committees and presented in tabloid format for quick absorption in staff rooms.

As general secretary of the EIS from the mid-1970s, John Pollock saw the value of a regular channel of communication with 40,000 members through copies mailed to schools. Especially during the two-year dispute from 1984 to 1986 the *SEJ* helped the union to maintain morale in the face of anti-strike pressure from the government and the local authority employers. The downside was that inevitably the journal reflected the Moray Place headquarters view and appeared to exclude that of more left-wing critics.

In common with other unions, the EIS moved away from industrial confrontation in the late 1980s and the *SEJ* subtly changed tack. The constitution of the institute was changed to give local associations greater autonomy. Under Pollock's successors, Jim Martin and

Ronnie Smith, there was also renewed concentration on an educational agenda, and this was reflected in increased educational content within the *SEJ*. The day-to-day work of schools, and especially that of EIS members, became a regular feature as the journal has developed into a full colour magazine.

TIMES EDUCATIONAL SUPPLEMENT SCOTLAND

Since 1965 the main professional medium for the educational community has been the *Times Educational Supplement Scotland* (*TESS*), which is published every Friday. The separate edition for Scotland was founded at a time of rapid expansion of education, especially at post-school level. The aim was to increase advertising and circulation, which quickly went up from 1,500 a week to 3,000. Ironically, the universities market was soon siphoned off by the stablemate *Times Higher Education Supplement* founded in 1971.

By the time of the Munn and Dunning Reports the *TESS* was selling around 6,000 copies, but in 1978, in common with other *Times* newspapers, it disappeared for eleven months in an industrial dispute. Lost readers were not immediately attracted back to a publication which in many weeks suffered from the production problems of the 1980s that led to the Wapping dispute. The circulation rose rapidly, however, when reform of local government in 1996 brought into being thirty-two education authorities which all used *TESS* to advertise their jobs. The editorial content of the Scottish edition was also increased.

In journalists' jargon the paper is built on 'change pages', that is, pages which are different for *TES Scotland* from those in *TES* itself. From the outset the aim was to give coverage of news from within the distinctive Scottish education system and to stimulate comment and debate on it from both staff contributors and the Scottish education community. Six or seven pages of Scottish news are followed by three of comment. Inserted only in the Scottish edition is 'ScotlandPlus', a 12–16-page supplement with features and reviews, plus coverage of arts in education and school sport. But many readers turn first to the back cover where the Jotter diary gives lighthearted prominence to the sayings and doings of leading figures who, for the most part, welcome the publicity.

The aim of the paper, which employs three staff journalists, plus sub-editorial support in London where the paper is prepared for the press along with the parent *TES*, is to report educational news of significance from every part of Scotland. Much comes from government and local authority sources, but increasingly there is also attention to – and reader interest in – the ways in which individual schools and colleges confront the challenges of a national curriculum and wider ranging forms of assessment. The creation of self-governing colleges of further education in 1993 led to a new feature in *TES* called FE Focus wherein there is also scope for a page devoted to Scottish FE and training.

In attempting to speak for Scottish education, *TES Scotland* adheres to no political party or union line. But it was strongly critical during the eighteen Conservative years of attacks on public sector services and of underfunding of schools and colleges. It also campaigned unstintingly for a Scottish Parliament with education as a principal responsibility.

SCOTTISH EDUCATIONAL REVIEW

While *TES Scotland* ranges across the educational spectrum, there are more specialised (or niche) publications. Among these the twice-yearly *Scottish Educational Review* (*SER*) must take pride of place, not because of its circulation which remains in the hundreds but because it is the main Scottish-based home for research papers and for academic comment on policy and practice. It dates back to 1968 and it started as *Scottish Educational Studies*. Ten years later the title was changed because, as the editor wrote, ' "studies" might suggest to some that type of academic activity pursued by specialists behind closed doors and likely to be of interest only to other specialists.'

But the intention was still 'to continue concern for academic rigour and high standards of critical scrutiny and at the same time to emphasise that studies in education should be viewed in a context of their relevance and value to the educational system and society in general.' This has been reflected in articles assessing government policies of the day as well as research reports. *SER* is not to be found in many school staff rooms but it is important to the research community and since 1977 it has had close links with the Scottish Educational Research Association. Until recently it was published by the Scottish Academic Press but it now looks after its own business affairs and production.

OTHER PUBLICATIONS

While *SER* comes out in spring and autumn, a once-a-year journal *Education in the North* claims to be the oldest existing academic periodical in Scotland. Intended to give a non-Central Belt perspective, it was founded in 1964 at Aberdeen College of Education. After volume 24, it ceased publication in 1988 but was reborn six years later, again at the Aberdeen campus of Northern College (now part of Aberdeen University) where its editors are based. With the subtitle of 'Journal of Scottish Education' it aims to bridge the gap between practitioner and academic, and has a mix of refereed articles alongside lighter ones and book reviews.

The extent to which teachers of individual subjects are served by regular publications varies greatly and has worsened over the past decade or so. There is, for example, no Scottish publication devoted to the primary sector, although primary teachers read UK magazines like *Child Education* and *Junior Education* and the primary coverage in *TES Scotland*.

In the heyday of subject advisers and the curriculum development service of the Scottish Consultative Council on the Curriculum, there were, among others, magazines devoted to the interests of English, History and Modern Languages teachers. They disappeared largely because there was no-one with the time to edit them and to look after advertising, circulation and production. Developments like the secondary aspects of the 5–14 programme and Higher Still suggest that there would be interest among subject teachers in curriculum materials, discussion of assessment and examples of good practice in a more detailed form than would appeal to *TES Scotland*.

Some subjects remain well served. There are journals, at least annually, for Mathematics, Media Studies, Modern Studies and Technological Studies, and no doubt others. Self-help by subject associations tends to have replaced input from a national curriculum base, and it may be that they will find on-line communication the most convenient way of keeping their members regularly updated.

Areas of post-school education have their periodicals, too, though they are vulnerable to changes of institutional structure. *Scan*, which used to be sent to community educators, disappeared alongwith its national parent organisation Community Learning Scotland. On the other hand *Broadcast* flourishes. It belongs to the Scottish Further Education Unit and appears quarterly with a print run of over 4,000. It aims to provide a platform for views on FE and to keep college readers up to date with national initiatives.

The demise of Community Learning Scotland also saw a change at the *Scottish Journal of Adult and Continuing Education*. It is now edited at Stirling University though it belongs to the National Institute of Adult and Continuing Education in Leicester. The word Scottish has been dropped from the twice-yearly publication but the editors say it will continue to have Scottish coverage.

THE IMPACT OF JOURNALS

Assessing the influence of journals is hard. Many teachers say that pressures of the job prevent them reading as widely as they would like. When a group of primary staff were asked what they would like to see in a proposed primary magazine, one said: 'Useful materials for teaching P4.' She was a P4 teacher and, understandably, was looking for practical help. She and the others in the group recognised, however, that they would benefit from the forum which a more general primary journal would offer.

There are about 50,000 school teachers in Scotland. Adding in the further education sector, academics in teacher education and administrators, a total of 60,000 education employees is reasonable. The weekly sale of *TESS* is running at about 9,000 copies, which is higher than at any time, but one that still suggests a limited level of reader commitment. True, staff room copies may be looked at by many non-purchasers of the paper. But leaving aside *SEJ*, which is mailed to schools for EIS members, no regular education publication in Scotland is reaching a mass market.

Influence is not necessarily dependent on sales. *TESS* has greater penetration of the market among senior staff, especially heads, administrators and teacher educators than in the wider profession. It may also be assumed that other publications are most widely read by senior staff or the more ambitious among their younger colleagues.

Therefore the scope for influencing debate is considerable. Quantifying the level of influence is impossible. People make frequent references to items they have seen in *TESS*. Whether the views of contributors on contentious topics of the day affect readers' own opinions is doubtful, and the same applies more powerfully to leading articles, painful though the admission is for an editor.

On the optimistic side, people need knowledge. That is particularly so in an era of national curricula. At one time primary schools in particular could be well run without constant reference to what was happening beyond their gates. That is no longer possible, and the promoted staff at least have to keep abreast of national developments. The education coverage of the daily press, broadcasting and professional publications fulfils an information role.

Changes to government alter needs and outlook. Since the abolition of regions and the creation of thirty-two councils none has been large enough to ignore what is going on in the rest of Scotland. Innovations in one area are eagerly studied elsewhere. So the appetite for news and the scope for disseminating it have grown. Within the Edinburgh Parliament education has a far higher profile than Scottish education could ever have at Westminster. Again, there is a need by those involved in schools and beyond to know what the Executive and MSPs are doing. Their documentation is available on-line but it needs to be sifted and highlighted. That offers a new challenge and role for educational journalists. Perhaps unfortunately, however, the century-old aspiration of the *Educational News* to encourage brotherhood and smooth down asperities is beyond their powers.

110

Scottish Council for Research in Education (The SCRE Centre)

Valerie Wilson

All organisations must grow and adapt if they are to survive in a rapidly changing world. The Scottish Council for Research in Education (SCRE) is no exception and the year 2002 marked the most radical change to have occurred in SCRE's seventy-four-year history. The Scottish Council for Research in Education was established in 1928, at a time when there was no other national educational research council in the world. The founding aims were 'to encourage and organise Research Work in Education in Scotland' (SCRE, *Annual Report*, 1928–9, p. 8) and this SCRE has endeavoured to do. However, who sets the agenda for that research, who funds it, how it should be undertaken and disseminated, how, if at all, teachers should be encouraged to participate, and what should be the relationship with the Scottish Executive and its predecessors, are questions which have bedevilled SCRE's past and to some extent destabilised the organisation. At the time of writing, SCRE's future role is now far clearer. On 1 August 2002, the council became the SCRE Centre within a recently reorganised Faculty of Education in Glasgow University. This change offers opportunities to both parties at a time when SCRE's 'special relationship' with the Executive is due to end in March 2003. This chapter charts the major changes in SCRE's history, from a council in which research was undertaken by voluntary committees to a dedicated research centre staffed by professional researchers within a Scottish university. It describes the services which SCRE has provided for the Scottish educational system, changes in government policy which provoked a funding crisis in SCRE, the options for the future considered by the SCRE board, and the implications for Scottish education.

THE ORIGINS OF SCRE

SCRE has its origins in a collaborative venture between the Educational Institute of Scotland (EIS) and the Association of Directors of Education. The First Annual Report (SCRE, *Annual Report*, 1928–9) describes how in May 1927 the Association of Directors of Education approached the EIS's research committee suggesting collaboration in educational research. A joint meeting convened for 6 May proposed that there should be a Scottish Educational Research Council composed of fifteen members, five from each of the following bodies: the Association of Education Authorities, the Association of Directors of Education in Scotland, and the Educational Institute of Scotland.

It is interesting to note that the founders foresaw two issues which continued to dominate

SCRE's history: finance, and relationships with the Scottish Education Department (SED) (later to become successively, the Scottish Office Education Department (SOED), the Scottish Office Education and Industry Department (SOEID) and the Scottish Executive Education Department (SEED)), which they realised would be crucial to the development of the nascent council. Relationships with SED were addressed directly when a deputation from the three founding organisations met with the secretary of the department in November 1927. Following this initial meeting, the representation of the council was broadened by the inclusion of other interested parties. A further meeting was held with the department in March 1928 when the secretary of the department, while deciding against direct participation in the work of the council, indicated that:

> the Department was prepared to allow individual Education Authorities to make contributions to the Research Council under Section 9 of the Education (Scotland) Act, 1918, and the Association of Education Authorities in Scotland agreed at their Executive Meeting of 19 December 1928 to recommend to the favourable consideration of Education Authorities the Research Council's suggestion that the latter should contribute to the funds of the Council on the basis of 1/4d per pupil. (SCRE, *Annual Report*, 1929–30, p. 6)

The department also expressed the hope that it would be kept informed of the progress of the council's work.

Why was SED less than enthusiastic? Private correspondence released fifty years later, quoted by Harlen and Nisbet (1999), shows that some civil servants feared that researchers, if given encouragement, might challenge the traditional system of deciding policy on the basis of past experience.

While the SED maintained its distance from the newly formed council, the EIS agreed to fund it up to £750 per year. This guaranteed the establishment of the research council and cemented the relationship between the council and the EIS – a relationship which has continued to this day. The first meeting of the new council was held on 23 June 1928 and a constitution was drawn up. The council was formally named 'The Scottish Council for Research in Education' with a membership of thirty-two members nominated by various stakeholder bodies in Scottish education. It agreed that the general aim of the council should be to encourage and organise research work in education in Scotland. By acting through its executive committee, the council would aim:

- to initiate and control special investigations, making the necessary arrangements with Education Authorities;
- to receive suggestions for research;
- to allocate problems to suitable investigators;
- to wholly or partly finance approved investigations;
- to authorise the publication of results and recommendations, and to bear the cost (wholly or partly) for such publications. (SCRE, *Annual Report*, 1929–30, p. 4)

By the end of the first year of its existence, the council's accounts showed an expenditure of £275 0s 6d against an income of £1,430 12s 2d (half of which came from the EIS), leaving a very healthy balance of £1,155 11s 8d. This was largely achieved through an organisational model based upon researchers working unpaid in their spare time as members of voluntary project committees. Dr Robert Rusk, head of the Education Department at Jordanhill College, had been appointed to 'the spare-time post of Director to the Council'

(SCRE, *Annual Report*, 1929–30, p. 13) and the generosity of the EIS in providing accommodation for the council in its building at 47 Moray Place, Edinburgh, was acknowledged.

It is obvious from those early annual reports that SCRE set out to undertake research which would be of value to teachers in Scottish schools. This is reflected in the publications of such reports as: *Studies in Arithmetic* (1939 and 1941); *Studies in Reading* (1948 and 1950); and *Studies in Spelling* (1961) but SCRE also remained firmly embedded in the academic community. It published academic histories of education in Scotland, for example *A History of Scottish Experiments in Rural Education* (1935) and psychological studies such as the one on *Left-handedness* (1957) which established its reputation in the international research community. In addition, there was a clear bias towards educational assessment and testing: one might argue, a reflection of the dominance of psychology in the study of education at that time. Numerous studies were published on achievement tests in primary and secondary schools, for example *Achievement Tests in the Primary School* (1934) and *Tests of Ability for Secondary School Courses* (1936), and on the transition to higher education, such as *The Prognostic Value of University Entrance Examinations in Scotland* (1936). This strand of SCRE's work has been retained to this day. Undoubtedly the largest single project ever organised by SCRE was the Scottish Mental Survey, in which every 11-year-old attending school on 1 June 1932 (44,210 boys and 43,288 girls) sat the Moray House Test – a well-validated mental ability test. A second cohort was tested in 1947. As far as SCRE is aware, no other country collected information about the childhood mental ability differences of almost an entire year-of-birth cohort (SCRE, 1933), which gives SCRE and Scotland a unique resource. Fortunately some funders, such as the Leverhulme Trust and the Scottish Executive's Chief Scientist Office, have now recognised the value of these data and SCRE researchers, working in conjunction with colleagues from Psychology and Medicine at Edinburgh and Aberdeen Universities, are now researching the connections between early mental ability and successful cognitive ageing, seventy years after SCRE's original research.

THE WORK OF SCRE

SCRE has continued to be a centre of expertise for educational research in Scotland. However, it has not been immune to external influences. As Nisbet (1995) noted, the trend towards shorter research projects has been a significant part of the funded educational research scene since the late 1980s. This has, perforce, had an impact on the work of SCRE. In an average year SCRE may undertake up to forty projects. This trend has exacerbated the pressure on contract research staff and fragmented the research process. Smaller projects are less cost effective: they are also very demanding and labour intensive. As a consequence, SCRE can no longer guarantee that researchers will participate in each stage of the research process from searching the literature to reporting the results. Increasing amounts of time, especially of senior researchers, are spent writing proposals in competition with others for disparate research projects funded by numerous funders, time which previously would have been used doing research, reflecting on the process and developing new researchers.

Despite these systemic pressures, SCRE has managed to maintain a wide variety of research, evaluation and consultancy activities, only some of which can really be thought of as 'research', in the narrow sense of that term used by its founders. There is increasing emphasis at a policy level in Scotland on lifelong learning, and learning within communities, and this is reflected in a variety of recent SCRE projects. While not abandoning research in the compulsory school sector, SCRE has widened its interests to include not only lifelong learning but also health, equal opportunities, social inclusion and disaffection. Several projects in progress during 2001–2 fell broadly within the area of health and well-being, giving members of the research team the opportunity to develop the kind of subject-specific research expertise which can be transferred from one project to another. Work continues on health needs related to New Community Schools in Scotland.

In addition, SCRE has increased the amount of work it undertakes outwith Scotland. Ironically, for a Scottish organisation, one of its largest funders is now the Department for Education and Skills in England (DfES). In 2001 a major new study got under way for the DfES, exploring the causes and effects of truancy. This joined existing DfES-funded projects on the impact of age, disability, ethnicity and gender on career patterns in the teaching profession in England, and an evaluation of Progress Files.

Progress was also made in diversifying SCRE's funding base. A two-year investigation was funded by the Diana Princess of Wales Memorial Fund into methods of supporting bereaved young people; an audit of gender equality in the SOCRATES programme for the European Commission; and a project to gather and analyse evidence related to the appointment, retention and promotion of academic staff within higher education institutions in England commissioned by HEFCE.

SCRE's founders recognised the need to evaluate educational provision in Scotland and evaluative research remains a staple part of SCRE's research programme. Evaluations can vary greatly, in their length, scope, and the range of methodologies utilised, but all essentially ask the same questions about whether a particular initiative is working, whether it justifies continued support or expansion, and what specific problems there are to be addressed. SCRE researchers have experience of evaluating programmes and initiatives of all scales: from national programmes to local initiatives, and in a wide range of policy areas. During 2001–2, SCRE researchers were working on evaluations of three major national projects: the Classroom Assistants Initiative, the Higher Still Qualification in Scotland, and the Progress File in England and Wales. In the past, SCRE has played a key role in other major educational reforms, such as the 5–14 guidelines, SCE Standard Grade, and the Technical and Vocational Education Initiative. Depending on the findings, the answers to the evaluation questions can cause funders some discomfort, leading occasionally to the postponement or even cancellation of projects or pressure to postpone publication of the results. Such occurrences are rare but it is important to note that SEED's support comes at a price and whoever pays the piper can indeed call the tune on contract research.

Measuring educational attainment and testing the factors which affect it is a complex area of research and SCRE's team of experienced researchers is involved in a range of projects involving large-scale data collection and statistical analysis, in both national and international studies looking at different aspects of attainment. SCRE remains one of the few research centres in Scotland able to undertake such work. For many years, SCRE was involved in the national Assessment of Achievement Programme (AAP) and maintained a Central Support Unit for this programme, whose role was to provide the AAP with support services and advice in areas common to all main projects. The services included sampling, liaison with schools, distribution and collection of written materials, data preparation, analysis and structuring for the AAP data archive. SCRE researchers also bring to bear their expertise and experience in sampling methods and fieldwork in a number of collaborative international surveys. Three such studies were in progress during 2001–2:

- The Progress in International Reading Literacy Study (PIRLS), involving approximately forty countries, is a study to measure reading literacy achievement of 9- and 10-year-olds.
- The OECD Survey of Upper Secondary Schools is collecting data on the preparation of pupils for transition from school to the workplace.
- The Programme for International Student Assessment (PISA) is investigating pupils' mathematical, scientific, and reading literacy at age fifteen.

However, SEED's recent absorption of AAP activities into the Executive and its agencies and the cancellation of the Higher Still Core Skills evaluation puts SCRE's Central Support Unit under increased pressure and makes it more difficult for SCRE to maintain this centre of expertise.

DISSEMINATION AND PUBLICATION

From its inception, SCRE not only conducted educational research but also played a key role in disseminating findings to teachers, policy makers and other researchers. The value of this function was recognised in subsequent SOEID/SEED service level agreements and the service will continue until the end of the existing contract in March 2003. SCRE aims to promote the use and understanding of educational research throughout Scotland, and research ideas, findings, and applications are disseminated, through a range of services, to practitioners, fellow researchers, parents, students, government, members of the Scottish Parliament, and the media. These include:

Research reports

Five reports were published in 2001–2 arising from diverse projects in SCRE's research programme. Executive summaries and, where possible, the full reports are made available free of charge on the SCRE website (www.scre.ac.uk).

Newsletters

Research in Education, the SCRE newsletter, contains a mix of articles on research projects and methodologies, as well as news about SCRE activities, and other educational research initiatives around Scotland. 2001–2 saw the amalgamation of this title with *Observations*, SCRE's newsletter for teacher researchers, to provide a new and improved forum for communication between the research community and Scottish practitioners. *Research in Education* is published twice per year, and distributed to every school in Scotland. The full text of all articles is also available on the website.

Spotlights

This series of briefing papers provides a platform for more detailed discussion of research topics than space in the newsletter allows. It focuses on the implications of the research in order to engage with teachers and other practitioners.

Databases

The advent of accessible information and communications technology enabled SCRE to develop the Educational Research in Scotland Database (ERSDAT). This is now a key resource for anyone looking for information on current and completed research projects in Scotland.

E-mail news

SCRE provides a news alerting service to notify subscribers free of charge by e-mail of developments at SCRE, including new reports, press releases, and major updates to the website such as the addition of full-text articles and papers. The service continues to be extremely popular: 2001–2 saw over 300 new subscribers.

Enquiries

In 2001–2 approximately 350 responses were made by SCRE's Information Services to enquiries on a wide range of subjects: some concerning SCRE activities, others regarding specific research questions, or seeking assistance with tracking down publications or research information.

Website

SCRE's website is an increasingly important dissemination tool in its own right: more and more reports are being prepared exclusively for the website; reports which it would not be economical to produce in printed form, but which nonetheless deserve to be in the public domain. By April 2002 the website was receiving over 350,000 page requests per month.

SETTING RESEARCH PRIORITIES

After over seventy years' existence as a dedicated research centre, it is clear that SCRE has developed an expertise in Scottish educational research, but the question of who sets its research agenda remains problematic. As Morris (1994), a former Chief HMI, points out 'power to set the research agenda is positive and negative. The former is when the theme is intrinsically valuable. The latter is when the available resources are fully committed, thus preventing something of greater worth from being considered. It involves choice, which may reside in members of the council or its funders' (p. 303). In its early years, SCRE undertook research which was of interest to the members of its council and to teachers. It operated independently from 1928 to 1945 by making its findings freely available and ignoring the SED. By 1958, Robert Rusk, the first director (see Table 110.1) was able to retire content that he had never been beholden to the SED.

By 1945, SCRE had accepted a small grant from the SED but was able to maintain its independence under its next director, David Walker, largely because of residual funds which were available from the Population Investigation Committee which was willing to purchase earlier intelligence survey data and the skills SCRE's researchers had developed in conducting national surveys. However, 1972 marked a turning point when SCRE negotiated an agreement with SED on finance and accepted the Secretary of State's appointees

Table 110.1:   Directors of SCRE

1928–58	Dr Robert Rusk
1958–70	Dr David Walker
1971–86	Dr Bryan Dockrell
1986–90	Professor Sally Brown
1990–99	Professor Wynne Harlen
1999–	Dr Valerie Wilson

to the council. Government funding became the major source of support for SCRE and this inevitably changed the way SCRE operated. The voluntary committees disappeared and the choice of research topics had to reflect the concerns of government in order to justify the expenditure of public funds.

Despite these changes, SCRE was able to operate with considerable autonomy until the mid 1980s. However, by 1984 the SED was able to conduct a 'critical scrutiny' of SCRE's operation. The resulting Freeman Report recommended that the SED 'endorsed the role [of SCRE] as the authoritative national forum for the consideration of educational research policy' (SCRE, *Annual Report*, 1984/5, p. 8), but the price was a new director and senior staff and a programme of policy-related research. Following a further review in 1989 and another change of director, SCRE emerged with a contractual agreement which lasted for the next decade. Its status changed from a Non-Departmental Public Body (NDPB) to a non-controlled body. The new level of contractual funding was set at a figure which was approximately one-third of SCRE's total income. Throughout the next decade the figure hardly changed, thus losing its value in real terms, until by 1999 it was a quarter of SCRE's income, with the rest won by bidding competitively for externally funded projects. This was the situation when the current director, Valerie Wilson, was appointed in 1999. There was no indication at that time that relationships with SOEID/SEED were about to change irrevocably.

RADICAL CHANGE

By 1999, SCRE was experiencing numerous but not insurmountable difficulties: competitive tendering and the trend towards smaller, shorter, funded research projects were beginning to take their toll. In the period from 1985–94, SCRE was not only in receipt of SOED/SOEID funding but regularly won approximately a third of all the money spent on commissioned research in Scotland. But as Harlen and Nisbet (1999) point out, 'SCRE has no favoured status in the scramble for funds, though its position and experience may sometimes give it an advantage' (p. 971). However, a direct consequence of competitive tendering has been to turn former collaborators in Scottish universities and colleges into rivals for research funding with no evidence of improved quality or efficiency of the research output.

SCRE's service level agreement with SEED was declining and the financial contribution of the EIS and the Scottish education authorities had also reduced. Management accountants Deloitte and Touche advised the new director that 'it is clear that SCRE will have to plan its activities within an environment of considerable stringency' (Deloitte and Touche, 1999, unpublished report, p. 7). There had been a tendency for SCRE to respond to increasing financial pressure by reducing the number of its researchers, leaving a disproportionate number of support and information staff, most of whom were on permanent contracts, compared to the researchers who typically were employed on fixed-term contracts. Maintaining the status quo was clearly not an option: managing the expenditure down in line with income would inevitably lead to a loss of SCRE's best researchers, contracts being put at risk through lack of resources, difficulties in resourcing new bids and increased pension costs, largely inherited from the redundancies demanded by SOEID in 1985 but still being paid out of current income fifteen years later. The consultants were unequivocal and wrote: 'our view is that the *status quo* – or minimal change – is unsustainable' (Deloitte and Touche, 1999, p. 18). The SCRE board accepted that a refocusing of the organisation was necessary and put a 'vision' for a reorganised SCRE to SEED.

The intimation that this vision was unacceptable and the signal of a radical change in SEED's relationship with SCRE were swiftly and unceremoniously delivered by fax on 13 March 2000. The head of the Educational Research Unit writing on behalf of the Education Department and the Enterprise and Lifelong Learning Department informed SCRE that: 'the "special relationship" with the Executive will end formally with the completion of the SLA [service level agreement] in March 2003' (SEED, 2000, unpublished letter). SCRE was now free to contemplate its future but minus its infrastructural support. Four options were discussed at board meetings throughout 2000–1: closure, status quo, association or merger, with the board finally agreeing that merger offered the best guarantee for SCRE's long-term future. To aid it, and perhaps as a direct response to the outrage expressed in the education community at the announcement of the ending of SEED's funding, SEED offered some transitional aid. The Executive wrote to SCRE informing it that: 'we [the Scottish Executive] recognise the need for SCRE to restructure if it is to develop as a viable organisation and . . . in view of the "special relationship" which has existed between central government and SCRE, ED [the Education Department] and ELLD [the Enterprise and Lifelong Learning Department] are prepared to consider making a contribution to the costs of SCRE's restructuring' (SEED, 2000, unpublished letter). The process of restructuring, introducing a new financial management system and redressing the balance of research to administrative support staff, commenced. Fortuitously, while the SCRE board was discussing possible mergers, it was approached by Glasgow University. The merger agreement, formalised on 1 August 2002, offered benefits to both parties. The university would gain an experienced research unit in the Faculty of Education; while SCRE's name, reputation and independence from government influence were guaranteed. Both recognise the benefits for capacity building of educational research in Scotland.

KEY ISSUES

Should Scotland have a national educational research centre?

'Why a Scottish research council?' was the question posed by Harlen and Nisbet (1999). How, if at all, is SCRE different from the National Foundation for Educational Research in England or comparable bodies in the Australia, New Zealand or the USA? The aim of SCRE is to 'conduct high quality research for the benefit of education and training in Scotland and elsewhere' but what happens if there are insufficient funds within Scotland to maintain the Council – a situation unforeseen by SCRE's founders – or an unwillingness on the part of SEED to contribute to its upkeep? Prior to 1990, SCRE undertook few projects outwith Scotland, but increasingly it has been forced, by lack of sufficient Scottish funding, to bid for projects from the DfES and the European Commission. Does this make it any less Scottish or is it merely a recognition that research transcends national boundaries and that collaborations with institutions in England, Wales, Northern Ireland or the EU are now part of a global economy? These arguments undoubtedly have merit, but the concept of a 'national' Scottish research council implies a close link with the national educational system in Scotland. SCRE's founders envisaged that the council would be responsive to the information needs of the Scottish education system, and throughout its seventy-four-year history SCRE has remained close to schools and teachers in a way which few others can match. Throughout its numerous transformations, SCRE has been an integral part of the Scottish education system; teachers, directors of education and local authority representatives remained loyal to SCRE, facilitating access for its researchers and trusting its findings. The Teacher/Researcher Network, still co-ordinated by SCRE, is one manifestation of the bond between SCRE and its user community.

It is also ironic that SEED should choose to sever its relationship with SCRE at a time when Scotland has achieved its own Parliament and a host of researchable issues is emerging. Why this occurred has been the subject of much speculation. Had the quality of SCRE's research declined to the extent that it was not worthy of funding? This seems improbable. Was SCRE so inefficient that it could no longer be trusted with public funds? Had SCRE researchers in their evaluations of recent educational initiatives inadvertently offended policy makers? Did the then Minister for Education assume a medical model of research which did not articulate with the one commonly adopted by educational researchers? Was SCRE an 'easy target' unprotected by SHEFC funding, as the HEIs were? Is 'New Labour' a firm believer in the market economy? Some or all of these factors may have played a part in SEED's unilateral decision to end its 'special relationship' with SCRE, but as it has so far refused to divulge a reason the answers are simply not known. The stark reality is that Scotland, unlike England, no longer has a national research council; but Glasgow University has gained an active research unit.

How can research capacity be built up?

How will these changes affect Scotland's research capacity? Traditionally, SCRE researchers similar to those in HEIs have been employed on fixed-term contracts. In theory, contract researchers provide a source of experienced and trained staff who can be deployed if and when funding becomes available. But the iniquities of the fixed-term contract system are now recognised. It creates an insecurity of employment, especially for those who are on very short contracts or near the end of their contract, which is inimical to sustained high quality research. The report writing phase of research projects, when time for reflection is most needed, invariably coincides with contract researchers' frantic efforts to find further employment. A national knowledge-based resource cannot be maintained on this basis and, as a consequence, SCRE has introduced a system of 'rolling contracts' for research staff in order to maintain experienced researchers. Nationally, there is still a problem, and one which is only partially addressed by the adoption of the 1996 Concordat on Contract Research Staff Career Management in HEIs. Efforts to build research capacity in Scotland will inevitably be hampered unless a less stressful and more secure form of employment for researchers is created.

Who should establish educational research priorities?

Who should determine educational research priorities, not only for SCRE but also for Scotland, remains a live issue. In the mid-1980s, SOEID asked SCRE to convene a forum from which priorities would emerge: the resulting meeting was by all accounts unmanageable and was replaced by an annual Educational Research Forum. This became a task for the SCRE board set out in SEED's service level agreement, in which the board acted as a proxy for Scottish educational interests. The members of the board consulted their own organisations and suggested priorities for research funding and discussed feedback from the Educational Forum. Now, however, the SCRE board's suggestions constitute one of a number of factors which may or may not help SEED establish its research priorities. How the opinions of the education community in Scotland inform research priorities remains an unresolved issue. South of the border, the DfES has made attempts to engage with researchers and other stakeholders to develop such an agenda: in contrast SEED has merely issued a three-year research programme, presumably based upon policy makers' information needs.

What does the future hold for SCRE?

Throughout its history SCRE has never claimed to be the only source of research-based information for policy makers in Scotland. It has, as far as possible, within available resources sought honestly and systematically to answer questions and address issues faced by those who work in the Scottish education system. It has also evaluated educational initiatives, disseminated results and trained others, including teachers, in research methods. By so doing, it has not subscribed entirely to an instrumental view of educational research. Many would argue that there is not, and nor should there be, a direct relationship between research findings and policy making. SCRE's research has contributed to the general climate in which educational policy has been formulated in Scotland. Its researchers have attempted to raise issues of concern, contribute opinions based upon evidence, and utilise their expertise independently of education providers and policy makers. The merger with Glasgow University will strengthen these core research activities while affording SCRE some measure of protection within a larger institution. SCRE may have given up its organisational independence, but it has certainly gained a new academic freedom which it now intends to use for the benefit of Scottish education.

REFERENCES

Deloitte and Touche (1999) *The Scottish Council for Research in Education: Key issues Review*, Edinburgh: Deloitte and Touche.

Harlen, W. and Nisbet, J. (1999) The Scottish Council for Research in Education, in T. Bryce and W. Humes (eds), *Scottish Education*, Edinburgh: Edinburgh University Press.

Morris, J. G. (1994) *Scottish Council for Research in Education: 1928–1993*, unpublished PhD., Edinburgh: University of Edinburgh.

Nisbet, J. (1995) *Pipers and Tunes: A Decade of Educational Research in Scotland*, Edinburgh: SCRE.

SCRE (1933) *The Intelligence of Scottish Children: A National Survey of an Age-group*, London: University of London Press.

SEED (2000) Unpublished letter from the head of the Education Department Research Unit.

111

Teachers' Professional Organisations

Fred Forrester

A UNIONISED WORKFORCE

Scottish teachers are a heavily unionised workforce. The reasons for this can be found in the existence of centralised arrangements for the negotiation of salaries and conditions of service and in the personal insecurity felt by many teachers. This latter factor may be seen as surprising in a mainly public sector profession that offers secure employment, but teachers are increasingly vulnerable to complaints from parents, pupils and senior colleagues. Membership of a teachers' union is an insurance policy against such complaints and case work by full-time and lay officers is the most important union service.

THE TEACHER ASSOCIATIONS

The Educational Institute of Scotland (EIS) is by far the largest and oldest of the associations. Founded in 1847 and awarded its first royal charter by Queen Victoria in 1851, the institute has over 50,000 members. Though the bulk of the membership is in primary and secondary schools, the organisation seeks to represent all teachers from nursery education to further and higher education and has special forms of organisation for FE and HE lecturers. Membership is also offered to educational psychologists, education advisers, members of education directorates, adult education tutors, chartered librarians working in education and a limited range of instructors. This is the only teachers' association that aspires in principle to be a professional body, the first objective laid out in the royal charters being the promotion of sound learning.

The Scottish Secondary Teachers' Association (SSTA) has about 8,000 members, almost all employed in secondary schools. Though it has roots in the early part of the twentieth century, it dates in its present form from 1944. It came into being because of a feeling that the EIS was dominated by primary sector interests. It resisted the EIS policy of a common maximum salary for primary and secondary teachers, but, having lost this battle many years ago, it continues to campaign in a more general way for what it sees as the separate interests of secondary teachers. Its position on union with the EIS is that this would require the Institute to reorganise itself as a federation of primary and secondary teacher associations. The SSTA has a rather elitist image and this may explain its having more members in the independent sector than the EIS, though teachers in private schools are much less unionised than their public sector counterparts.

The National Association of Schoolmasters and Union of Women Teachers (Scotland) (NASUWT) is essentially the Scottish end of an English and Welsh teacher organisation. Its membership is probably fewer than 2,000. The male part of it, originally called the Scottish Schoolmasters' Association, was very prominent at the time of the setting up of the General Teaching Council for Scotland (see Chapter 112) in 1965 when it ran a campaign against existing qualified teachers' having to register with the council in order to retain their teaching posts. This campaign had one prominent martyr in the shape of the late Jack Malloch, who forfeited his post in Aberdeen and took his case to the House of Lords, where he lost. The Union of Women Teachers had only a handful of members in Scotland at the time of its amalgamation with the NAS. In Scotland, NASUWT has a profile in the press and media that is out of proportion to its small membership. It takes a hard line on pupil indiscipline, on unruly parents and on health and safety issues and sometimes captures the headlines. Its spokespersons are usually elected members rather than its full-time Scottish secretary. For reasons that are unclear, it is stronger in Catholic secondary schools in the West of Scotland than elsewhere.

The Professional Association of Teachers (Scotland) (PAT) is again an offshoot of an English/Welsh union and has only a small membership (possibly around 1,000). Its presence in Scotland dates from the mid-1980s when the EIS had a period of severe industrial action on pay lasting for the best part of three years (1983–6) and culminating in the Main Report. SSTA and NASUWT associated themselves with the action to the extent of having their own militant campaigns, albeit on a limited scale. The result of all this was that a constituency was created of teachers who wished to belong to a union but were unwilling to take militant action. PAT, which had emerged from a parallel round of industrial action by teacher unions in England, begin to recruit in Scotland on a platform of opposition to industrial action. Since there has been no serious industrial action in Scotland since 1986, PAT has now lost its appeal and its membership has declined. Its continued existence is a reflection of the fact that smaller English teacher unions, once established in Scotland, wish to keep their foothold there and are willing to give financial support to their Scottish offsprings.

The Headteachers' Association of Scotland (HAS) (whose membership includes a good proportion of secondary heads) and the Association of Headteachers in Scotland (AHTS) (which has a smaller proportion of primary heads) both aspire to be fully-fledged teacher associations on the analogy of their counterparts south of the border. However, EIS and SSTA strongly maintain that they represent headteachers and, indeed, a good proportion of HAS and AHTS members are in dual membership of a mainstream teacher union. So far the headteacher associations have been effectively excluded from national negotiations on salaries and conditions of service, though they are part of a panel from which the membership of the Scottish Negotiating Committee for Teachers (SNCT) is drawn. These two associations offer case work services to members, but the legitimacy of separate unions for headteachers remains a matter of acute controversy in both Scotland and England.

The Scottish Further and Higher Education Association (SFHEA) operates in the further education colleges, including those that offer higher education courses, but has only a slight foothold in the higher education institutions. It was founded in the late 1960s on the back of complaints that the EIS paid scant regard to the interests of its further education membership. However, the EIS responded (eventually) by setting up a semi-autonomous College Lecturers' Association (CLA). This put a halt to the SFHEA's membership advance, but in Scottish education breakaway organisations continue, albeit in a truncated form, long after the conditions that led to their establishment have disappeared.

INTER-UNION RIVALRIES

The various unions compete for membership in the sectors where they operate using a variety of recruitment strategies. However, the leaders of the smaller organisations will admit, in unguarded moments, that they struggle against the dominance of the EIS, which is, to use modern computer speak, the default organisation. In most countries, union organisation recognises primary teachers and secondary teachers as separate groups, but the EIS vigorously resists this position and is able to call upon the same inclusivist tradition that informs much of Scottish public life. The main danger for all the unions is that a particular policy decision can lead to a loss of membership. Their leaderships are always aware of this possibility and use their influence to avoid or 'bury' such decisions. A good example would be the issue of the integration of Catholic schools, which was the subject of EIS conference resolutions in the 1980s and 1990s.

The General Teaching Council (GTC) for Scotland, a statutory body whose principal function is to maintain a register of qualified teachers but which has become involved for good reasons in general educational debates, has always been something of a cockpit for union rivalries. For several decades, the main unions offered 'slates' of official candidates in the periodic elections of the GTC. Until 2001, the EIS was successful in obtaining a controlling majority on the council, despite doing less well in the secondary sector than its membership would indicate. However, the 2000 Act of the Scottish Parliament created separate constituencies for headteachers in primary and secondary schools and, in the 2001 GTC election, the EIS lost out in the secondary headteacher constituency to a well-organised HAS slate and ended up in an overall minority position. The consequences of this are not yet fully apparent but may be considerable.

SALARIES AND CONDITIONS OF SERVICE

The EIS dominated the teachers' side of the former Scottish Joint Negotiating Committee and continues to control the teachers' panel of the new Scottish Negotiating Committee for Teachers (SNCT). There were periods of serious industrial action in the 1970s and the 1980s, focused respectively on conditions of service and on salaries.

The 1970s campaign used the groundbreaking idea of unilateral implementation of a set of basic conditions of service contained in the so-called Five Principles. Having failed to persuade the employers to agree to new conditions, the EIS called on its members to implement unilaterally certain class-size maxima, certain amounts of non-class contact time and certain conditions regarding the suitability of teaching accommodation. The employers capitulated one by one and the final outcome, after lengthy negotiations, was a very detailed set of national conditions of service set out in the so-called Yellow Book.

In the 1980s, discontent focused on salaries and the EIS called for an independent one-off review (but not for the kind of standing independent review body that existed in England). This was resisted by the Conservative Scottish Office administration. There was a campaign of determined industrial action focused on the parliamentary constituencies of Scottish Office ministers and involving EIS members going on strike in selected schools on Tuesday, Wednesday and Thursday of each week, with the lost 'take-home' pay of members being reimbursed through a levy on the membership as a whole. This meant that the EIS paid the teachers for three days and the local authorities paid them for the other four, only two of which were working days. From one point of view, this was one of the most successful campaigns by any trade union in Scotland; from another point of view, it was bad for relationships between teachers and the general public, including, of course, the parents. Only the skilled media performances by general secretary John Pollock alleviated what could have been a public relations disaster. However, the government climbed down and set up the Main Inquiry, which followed on from the earlier Houghton and Clegg Inquiries in giving teachers a substantial salary increase. A notable feature of the 1970s and 1980s was that teachers' salaries fell behind in annual negotiations and were then pulled up through the device of one-off inquiries.

The 1990s produced a new wave of discontent in the profession over the relentless decline in the real value of salaries. A newly elected Labour government set up an inquiry into teachers' salaries and conditions under the chairmanship of Professor Gavin McCrone. His report, published in May 2000, was controversial and was remitted to an implementation group consisting of representatives of teacher organisations, local authorities and the new Scottish Executive that had emerged from the election in 1999 of the Scottish Parliament. It is important to distinguish between the McCrone Report (HMSO, 2000) as such and the so-called Agreement (SEED, 2001), though both use the title *A Teaching Profession for the 21st Century*. Certain aspects of the agreement have been criticised or repudiated by Professor McCrone. The agreement reflected the strong wish of the then Education Minister, Jack McConnell, and the Scottish Executive as a whole to put the pre-devolution legacy of teacher discontent behind them. Substantial salary increases were agreed, beginning with an overall 10% in April 2001 and followed by further tranches of 4% in April 2002, 3.5% in January 2003 and 4% in August 2003. Important parts of the package were, however, contingent on teachers' agreeing to substantial changes in working practices over the implementation period.

THE MCCRONE HARVEST

The post-McCrone Agreement was entered into by the various parties partly in good faith but partly also because: on the teachers' side, the money on offer was too good to be refused; and on the management side, there was a strong desire that the first term of the new devolved Labour administration should not be dogged by a long-running dispute with the teachers. Several of the more difficult issues were effectively 'back burner' questions to be tackled over a period of years by a new set of negotiators. The difficulties of some of these issues were glossed over at the time.

- The introduction, from August 2002, of the new 'guaranteed' one-session induction arrangements for new teachers had serious implications, which no-one seemed to notice at the time, for existing probationers and, indeed, for all teachers on temporary contracts.
- The agreement said that all teachers were to have a thirty-five–hour working week from 1 August 2001, but, under Annex D, the detailed arrangements for this were to be settled at school level. These local discussions have been tense because of disagreement on whether the thirty-five hours is an absolute ceiling within which all contractual duties must be capable of being carried out or whether it is more of an indicative target for the purposes of local educational planning, the kind of status it had under the previous Yellow Book. The statement that 'The individual and collective work of teachers should be capable of being undertaken within the thirty-five-hour working week' is open to interpretation.
- There is on-going controversy as to whether the status of Chartered Teacher (carrying with it an increase in salary of up to about £6,500) will be attained mainly through a

teacher's obtaining further qualifications (e.g. a master's degree) or mainly through a teacher performing competently in the classroom over a period and maintaining a folio of continuing professional development. The Chartered Teacher grade is supposed to kick in from August 2003, but the details are currently the subject of tense discussion in a Chartered Teacher project group. Clearly the employers have an interest in putting a ceiling on the number of Chartered Teachers. The GTC is involved in the controversy through developing the standard for Chartered Teacher, one of its four key standards.

- The agreement provided for a jobsizing exercise, this to be completed by 1 August 2003. This will introduce a pay range for principal teachers not based (as at present) on the school roll but on an assessment of the content of each job. It is a fair assumption that principal teachers of large departments will receive more (up to £9,000 more) than those in small departments. It is indicative of the difficulty of this exercise that it has now been farmed out to a firm of educational consultants at a considerable fee.

POLITICAL POSTURE AND THE SCOTTISH 'POLICY COMMUNITY'

The EIS is more involved in mainstream politics than the smaller unions (which tend towards a position of party political neutrality). Though constitutionally it is not affiliated to any political party and its political fund may not be used to support any party, many of its leading activists are Labour Party members, though this is less true now than before devolution. In the 1970s and 1980s, the Trotskyite 'entryism' conflicts within the Labour Party were reflected in the EIS. Now the political dimension of union debates is essentially a three-way contest between New Labour, Old Labour and the Scottish National Party (SNP). The flavour of many debates, for example on public private partnership, is essentially Old Labour, with some tactical voting by SNP supporters and a new element of supporters of Tommy Sheridan's Scottish Socialist Party.

EIS posture since the Second World War has been strongly biased towards a 'Big Tent' approach, even during periods of Conservative government. In other words, the union has always favoured involvement in discussions, working groups, and so on, rather than shouting from the sidelines. This is likely to continue. 'Oppositionism' is a luxury that smaller unions may enjoy, but the EIS always sees itself as being at the centre of educational policy discussions, even when it is hostile to a particular policy prospectus, an approach that was particularly noticeable during the Michael Forsyth years (1990–97, with his greatest influence being when he was Secretary of State, 1995–97) but one that could be increasingly relied on as New Labour policies are developed.

New Labour has arguably reduced the extent to which Scottish educational policies are decided by a small policy community populated by 'the usual suspects' wearing different hats in different policy forums. The old Scottish educational establishment flourished when Scotland was run by a Conservative Scottish Office that was deeply unrepresentative of opinion in the country. Its influence has been weakened by devolution, which has produced a Scottish Executive with a higher political legitimacy. Yet, in truth, the new settlement has not yet been subjected to any serious political test in regard to controversial educational policies. Issues such as dealing with teacher incompetence and the on-going appraisal of teachers have been temporarily submerged, but will come to the fore shortly in the form of new GTC/SNCT procedures for alleged incompetence and for the establishment of the new grade of Chartered Teacher.

REFERENCES

HMSO (2000) *A Teaching Profession for the 21st Century – Report of the McCrone Committee*, (The McCrone Report), Edinburgh: HMSO.

SEED (2001) *A Teaching Profession for the 21st Century* – Agreement reached following recommendations made in the McCrone Report, January 2001, Edinburgh: SEED.

112

The General Teaching Council for Scotland

Matthew M. MacIver

Scotland was arguably the first country in the world to introduce an organisation which would develop the concept of a self-regulating teaching profession. The General Teaching Council was set up by the Teaching Council (Scotland) Act 1965 and the new council met for the first time in 1966. Over the last thirty-seven years many countries, including Commonwealth countries, have sought to establish similar organisations. In the last few years, for example, General Teaching Councils have been set up in England and Wales and Northern Ireland and a Teaching Council will appear shortly in the Republic of Ireland.

These new councils will undoubtedly try to meet specific needs in their own particular countries. In many ways that is what happened in Scotland in the 1960s. The details of the 1965 Act and the powers it conferred on the new council reflected the times. One of the main concerns at that time was the number of uncertificated teachers in Scottish classrooms. There was a danger that the profession could become so diluted in terms of academic qualifications that it would lose the high status it had always enjoyed. Not only that but Scottish pupils could be taught by teachers who had no knowledge of the subjects they were teaching. The new organisation was, therefore, given the power to regulate entry into the profession. The fact that there is now an all-graduate profession in Scotland is some measure of the success of the council in using its power to oversee standards of entry into the profession. In Scotland presently there are just over 79,000 teachers who are registered to teach and, of these, 65,000 are in the classroom every day. Each year around 2,000 new teachers come into the system. All of these teachers must be registered with the General Teaching Council before they can teach in local authority schools.

THE ORIGINAL POWERS OF THE COUNCIL

The power of overseeing standards of entry into the profession was not the only power bestowed on the council by the 1965 Act. The Act gives the council both executive and advisory powers. It is charged with maintaining a register of teachers qualified to teach in local authority schools in Scotland; it advises the government on the supply of teachers and initial teacher education; and it deals with teachers found guilty of professional misconduct. In practical terms these powers have been implemented to ensure that the General Teaching Council for Scotland has the key role in determining what kind of teacher enters the profession in Scotland. It has, for example, a major role in initial teacher education. Through its Accreditation and Review Committee the council scrutinises all initial teacher education programmes being offered by the seven initial teacher education providers in Scotland. It then advises the First Minister on the acceptability or otherwise of each programme. This ensures a consistency of national standards but it also accepts that programmes will reflect the strengths and interests of the different providers. There is not a slavish uniformity of provision.

Just as influential has been the key role of the council in ensuring that a strong system of probation exists in Scotland for new teachers embarking on their teaching careers. Until August 2002 this meant that each probationary teacher in Scotland had to complete the equivalent of two years' service before full registration was granted by the council. The quality of young practitioners is always a good indicator of the health of any profession and that is why the council has taken its role in probation so seriously. Much of its resources has been devoted to developing methods of supporting schools in helping probationers achieve full registration. It has never, however, lost sight of the fact that in a self-regulating profession the final judgement must belong to the profession itself. That is why the full registration of a probationer teacher will always depend on the recommendation of a headteacher.

These professional recommendations are also critical when assessments are made of applicants to the register who completed their professional education outwith Scotland. No one is granted full registration without detailed professional judgements being made. In the same way, of course, teachers are not taken off the register without the same thoroughness and without representatives of the profession being involved in the final decision.

Thus, in 1965, the General Teaching Council was effectively given the power to oversee standards of entry into the profession and also to deal with exit from the profession when dealing with teachers found guilty of professional misconduct. It was little wonder that critics at the time accused it of being little more than a watchdog. A few even went so far as to suggest that it was merely the lapdog of the Secretary of State (see Humes, 1986; Sutherland, 1999).

THE WORK OF THE COUNCIL

The principal aims of the General Teaching Council for Scotland are to contribute to improving the quality of teaching and learning; to maintain and to enhance professional standards in schools and colleges in collaboration with partners including teachers, employing authorities, teacher education institutions, parents and the Scottish Executive Education Department; to be recognised as a voice and advocate for the profession; and to contribute to the development of a world-class educational system in Scotland. Most of the work of the council is carried out through a committee structure which up until the Standard in Scotland's Schools etc. Act 2000 had changed very little since the establishment of the council. The mixture of statutory and standing committees has been a long-standing feature of the organisation. Prior to the Act, the statutory committees were: Investigating, Disciplinary and Exceptional Admission to the Register. The 2000 Act changed that. The Investigating and Disciplinary, Committees have now become sub-committees of the new statutory committee, the Professional Conduct Committee. This committee scrutinises the work of the two sub-committees and responds to appeals against some of their decisions. The Committee on Exceptional Admission to the Register remains. In the recent past, committees such as Communications and Further Education have been subsumed within others but original committees such as Probation, the Probation Appeals Board, Accreditation and Review, Finance and General Purposes and Education have remained. The one new standing committee to appear since the 2000 Act – and there is a significance to its appearance – has been the Policy and Strategy Committee. It gives an indication of where the council sees its future. It wants to set policy initiatives whose implementation will affect the whole of Scottish education.

As the council moves into a new era of development it is clear that some of its long-standing committees will simply not meet the demands that are going to be made of them. The field of continuing professional development, for example, will place demands on the council's committee structure that the council will have to respond to. Similarly, the introduction in August 2002 of a new induction system for probationers will lead to a change in the role of the Probation Committee. It is conceivable also that the assimilation of the former teacher education institutions into university Faculties of Education will inevitably lead to a new remit for the Accreditation and Review Committee or a new committee being established to deal with issues related to initial teacher education.

The tried and tested formula of setting up ad hoc groups, working groups and sub-committees is unlikely to meet the needs of the council. Other ways of structuring the council will have to be considered. It has to be said, however, that the new responsibilities about to be shouldered by the council are so fundamental that new committees will appear at the same time as the old ones will disappear. Other new working practices such as secondments from schools, local authorities and higher education are also likely to take place. The structure and working methods of the council are about to change in quite fundamental ways.

A NEW ERA OF DEVELOPMENT

Some have argued that, over the past thirty-five years, the General Teaching Council has done no more than faithfully follow the logic of its motto *Tutela ac Praesidium* (Guardian and Protector). It has controlled entry into the profession, it has struck off the register teachers who have been guilty of professional misconduct and it has been the guardian and protector of something indefinable called 'professionalism'. In doing so it has lost touch with the profession itself who see it as little more than an organisation to which they have to pay an annual fee. There is some substance to that argument.

It is quite legitimate, for example, to argue that one of the reasons why the council has not really touched the lives of teachers since 1965 is simply because its statutory responsibility lasts only until the end of probation. Since most teachers achieve full registration then spend the rest of their careers teaching in a professional and competent manner, the council becomes irrelevant to their professional lives. Until now that has been an acceptable stance but in the new world it will be unsustainable. The Standards in Scotland's School etc. Act 2000 has made it clear that the role of the council will extend quite significantly and that it will touch the professional lives of teachers in a way that it has never done before. The McCrone settlement has also ensured that the council's remit in certain areas, for instance the new teacher induction system and the continuing professional development of teachers, will be significantly extended.

The Act of 2000 envisages a world where the council will assume extended powers in various areas but especially in the areas of competence and continuing professional development (CPD). The council has always maintained that it should be closely involved in dealing with cases of teacher incompetence. In its response to the government's consultation on the General Teaching Council prior to the passing of the 2000 Act, the council noted 'with satisfaction that the Government recognises professional competence as grounds for deregistration' and welcomed the proposed extension of the GTCS in this area. 'Addressing the issue of incompetence will demonstrate the Council's support for the vast majority of teachers who are the epitome of professionalism in every respect,' commented Dr Sutherland, the registrar at the time. In 2002, the Council produced a Code of Practice on Teacher Competence which has been accepted by the profession as well as the employers. The power to remove a teacher from the register on the grounds of incompetence is, without doubt, a powerful tool.

A significant move towards defining competence has already been taken by the council in producing a Standard for Full Registration (SFR). The SFR, produced in partnership with the Scottish Executive, sets the standard for full registration with the council and thereby sets the benchmarks for competence. The Standard for Full Registration is also a professional standard set jointly by the teachers' professional body and the Scottish Executive. It is an important milestone for the teaching profession in Scotland. It sets out clearly what is expected of new teachers during their induction process and it provides a professional standard against which decisions will be taken on full registration.

But the standard will do more than that. It is also an important element in constructing a national framework for continuing professional development for all teachers. There is, therefore, now a real opportunity here in Scotland to create a continuum of professional development, starting with initial teacher education, being further developed in the new one year induction period and then continuing throughout the rest of a teacher's professional career. The Standard for Full Registration will be one of the key elements of that system along with the Standard for Chartered Teacher and the Standard for Headship. These Standards will be the foundations on which a national system of continuing professional development (CPD) will be based in Scotland (see Chapter 104 in this volume and Purdon, 2001).

Continuing professional development is one of the obvious ways of touching the profession (see Humes, 2001). The council's role in CPD – both in setting national standards and in accrediting programmes leading to the award of Chartered Teacher and headship – will ensure close contact with individual teachers. The intention is that in the coming decade every single teacher in Scotland will know that the council has been involved in developing his/her professional life. It was always going to be the case that the council would be the body to accredit CPD providers and programmes. In a world where all teachers will need to meet certain CPD requirements, it is critical that any national system has credibility with the profession. That is why the teachers' professional body, the General Teaching Council for Scotland, will be at its heart ensuring that satisfactory modules and programmes are available from credible providers. The new system of probation introduced in August 2002 will ensure that the council becomes even more proactive in an area where it has always been active. It will become involved in monitoring and moderating the assessment process in partnership with the employers. The fact that full registration will come after one year's probation and not the traditional two years will mean that the council has to set clear guidelines for probationers, for schools and local authorities.

THE PRESENT SITUATION

There is, at the moment, a professional vacuum at the heart of Scottish education. The inspectorate has been removed from its role as policy maker. Who is then to make policy? Is the teaching profession going to allow others to dictate educational policy? Teachers have a wonderful opportunity to set the agenda as far as curriculum development is concerned. The idea that a knowledgeable profession has really not been utilised in recent years in the development of the curriculum is to be regretted. The role of the teaching profession is not simply to respond to consultation papers; it is to set the agenda. That is why the council has been articulating what the professional parameters should be in relation to other professionals in New Community Schools and what the relationship should be between teachers and the para-professionals who have come into classrooms.

There will also be an opportunity to show how the council is influencing curricular change by what it says in accrediting programmes of initial teacher education. As the arguments widen over access to these programmes as well as their delivery, the council will become the most influential body in determining what tomorrow's teacher will look like. Certain key questions have to be faced in the near future. Is teaching an attractive profession? Is it a welcoming profession? It is worrying, for example, that the profession seems not to welcome the disabled or members of the ethnic minorities. Just as worrying is the fact that males seem not to be attracted to the profession. Considering the profession as a whole, 94% of teachers in the primary sector are female; in the secondary sector the figure is 60%. Statistics from the latest cohort to enter the profession in August 2002 seem to reinforce this trend. Despite various attempts to attract males into the profession 92% of probationers coming into the primary sector in 2002 are female; in the secondary sector the trend is arguably more worrying with 65% of new secondary teachers female. A further breakdown of the figures shows that in session 2002–3 there will be no new male primary teachers in six of the Scottish local authorities; and there will be no new male secondary teachers in three of the local authorities. All of these issues are important and have to be addressed by the Scottish education system. They are not solely for the General Teaching Council but it would also be true to say that the council must be involved in the whole process of resolving them.

THE WAY AHEAD

In the Standards in Scotland's Schools etc. Act 2000, it is explicitly stated that 'in exercising their functions the Council shall have regard to the interests of the public' (para. 45 (4). The public interest is represented on the council. Its membership of fifty consists of twenty-six elected registered teacher members; eighteen appointed members representing local authorities, directors of education, directors of social work, further and higher education institutions, the churches and the Scottish Council of Independent Schools; and six members nominated by Scottish Executive ministers.

The council is an advisory Non-Departmental Public Body (NDPB), but differs from other NDPBs in that it is funded from the annual registration fees paid by registered teachers and not from the public purse. With regard to the public interest, policy statements and general advice issued by the council are made available to the public, and minutes of meetings of the council are made available to the press and, in the near future, will also appear on the internet, subject to confidentiality in the council's case-work. It is, therefore, clear that in a new world of accountability and transparency the council must be seen to be acting in the public interest. Already professional organisations like the General Medical Council have come under attack not just because its bureaucracy has been slow to react, but because its processes are not immediately transparent. The General Teaching Council, therefore, has a role to explain its policy to the public and to ensure that the public understands exactly what its role is in the Scottish education system. The committee structure of the council should not be seen as an inflexible bureaucracy but as a structure that can be accessed by anyone who is interested. By definition, the work of some of the committees (for instance Investigating, Discipline, Probation Appeals Board) is confidential and must remain so. But others such as the Exceptional Admissions Committee should be as accessible as possible to those who are not joining the Scottish teaching profession through the conventional routes.

The council will also have a pivotal role in changing perceptions of the teaching profession. The present perceptions aided by an ambivalent, if not hostile, media will need to be changed. Young teachers have to be recruited. There will be a major responsibility on council to ensure that the profession they enter is a reflective, self–regulating one which has a high status within society. The council will need to engage in that public debate and will have to be very positive in publicising the commitment and high standards found within the profession.

It must also develop partnerships. The relationship, for example, between the council and local authorities will be critical especially in the area of competence. At the time of writing it seems that a review of initial teacher education is imminent. The close relation-ship which presently exists between the council and the teacher education institutions must not be compromised. Neither must the key role that the council plays in accrediting courses of initial teacher education. Above all, the council must drive the professional debate. As the impact of other United Kingdom councils begins to be felt it is important to promote the distinctiveness of the Scottish education system and the high calibre of the Scottish teaching profession. It will not be enough to reach reciprocity agreements with the other councils. There is an all-graduate profession in Scotland; in other parts of the United Kingdom certain teachers are allowed to register without degrees. In Scotland student teachers not only must have practical experience of the classroom but must also study the professional aspects of teaching; in other parts of the United Kingdom that professional element can be omitted. Scotland, therefore, must not allow a dilution of its high standards and accept without question teachers from a less robust system.

In the context of the new Education Act, National Priorities and a McCrone settlement, there now exists the opportunity to restore to the teaching profession the place it should rightfully have in a devolved society. This is a major challenge not only to the GTCS, but to Scottish education as a whole. It is the intention of the GTCS not only to be at the heart of the argument, but to lead it. However, in order to do so, it must be prepared to adopt a more radical stance than it has done in the past.

REFERENCES

Humes, W. M. (1986) *The Leadership Class in Scottish Education*, Edinburgh: John Donald.

Humes, W. M. (2001) Conditions for professional development, *Scottish Educational Review* 33 (1) 6–17.

Purdon, A. (2001) New teachers' perspectives on continuing professional development: accountability or professional growth, *Scottish Educational Review*, 33 (2), 110–22.

Sutherland, I. (1999) The General Teaching Council, Chapter 110 in T. G. K. Bryce and W. M. Humes (eds), *Scottish Education*, Edinburgh: Edinburgh University Press.

113

Scottish Teachers

Bill Gatherer

IMAGES AND MYTHS

The Scots are famously proud of their education system; but its vaunted superiority is not often attributed to the teachers themselves. Yet since the Reformation, with its strong social and religious emphasis on learning, teachers have been entrusted with the important functions of promoting literacy and character formation, and for centuries the schools have been strongly supported by both the authorities and the ordinary people. Teaching has always been regarded as a worthy occupation, albeit not endowed with much social prestige.

The pictures we have of teachers in the eighteenth and early nineteenth centuries fall into three main categories. The local parish schoolmasters, educated at university and appointed by the ministers and the heritors (landowners), were selected for their moral as well as their educational qualifications. These were the respected dominies who abound in biographies and novels as the inspirers of the 'lads o' pairts', the clever boys from poor homes who became successful in later life, carrying throughout the world the image of pragmatic intellectual power which is still cherished as a national characteristic. Scots writers are generous in their praise of their teachers. Robert Burns, Thomas Carlyle, David Livingstone, Hugh Miller, Ramsay MacDonald (himself a pupil teacher until he was eighteen) and countless others testify to the beneficent influences of their schoolmasters: hardworking men of integrity and scholarship, well enough versed in the classics to equip their pupils for higher learning, able to introduce them to the glories of literature and philosophy, powerful role models and religious mentors but themselves as poorly paid and badly housed as the people whose children they served.

Then there were the schoolmasters in the burgh schools and academies in the large towns: men of genuine scholarship, with higher social status and comfortable stipends, able to mingle with their pupils' affluent parents. They could teach Latin and Greek, Mathematics, Philosophy; they wrote scholarly papers and delivered them in the numerous field clubs and literary and scientific societies that met throughout the country; they wrote books; many were doctors of law or philosophy; some became university professors. These schoolmasters were an elite which transmitted an educational heritage and also preserved much of what was best in the national culture.

Then there were the women. In the eighteenth century many parishes had dame schools, run by any decent widow or spinster who could read and write and teach knitting, spinning, sewing and any other accomplishment valued by the parents, and who could put the girls and boys through the agony of Scripture lessons. By the mid-nineteenth century the academies and high schools were appointing ladies to teach the womanly crafts and 'deportment'; but it was not until the large-scale feminisation of the profession in the later nineteenth century that women were perceived seriously as teachers and acknowledged as worthy of training and able to teach important subjects. Many tributes are paid in biographical literature to the women (mostly remembered as 'old') who taught in elementary schools and gave the great majority of Scots the only learning they knew. Hugh Miller fondly remembered Miss Bond in the little school in Cromarty, an accomplished and refined lady who wrote *Letters of a Village Governess*. Another Victorian autobiographer told of old Janet setting aside her pipe and taking up the 'ABC card' and likening it to a key which opens the door to knowledge and shuts it to ignorance. And William Adamson, a leading Labour politician in the 1920s, gave a moving account in one of his last parliamentary speeches of his schooldays in a mining village, with about a hundred pupils of all ages in a single room, and a lone heroic woman in charge. Of course there has been an accretion of myth around the testimonies recorded. The 'lad o' pairts' himself was largely mythical: for every poor, hardworking, intellectually gifted boy who was made into a scholar or a pioneer of empire by the free and thorough schooling he got at the local school there were thousands whose schooling was as threadbare as their breeks, who ended up as half-starved peasants or miners or factory workers. And for every inspiring dominie celebrated in the reminiscences of successful Scots there were hundreds of pedestrian drudges.

But the myths were to some extent true, and though their apotheoses in the tales of the so-called Kailyard writers in Victorian times were larger than life, they were sincerely believed in, and their power has been attested in the great educational charities of such figures as James Dick and Andrew Carnegie. As McPherson points out the myths, as folk stories celebrating dearly-held values, have lived on in many public statements about equality, tradition and dedication to learning in Scottish education (McPherson, in Humes and Paterson, 1983).

Modern Scottish writers seldom draw teachers with much sympathy. The only great masterpiece is Muriel Spark's Miss Jean Brodie, a brilliant portrayal of the teacher's charismatic centrality in the lives of intelligent girls. Alasdair Gray's character, Duncan Thaw, finds his teachers both daunting and ridiculous. James Kelman's Patrick Doyle (in *A Disaffection*, London: Secker and Warburg, 1994) is a teacher at the end of his tether, but his plight has little to do with his job: Kelman wanted to create a character whose working-class origins combined with a high educational and cultural consciousness. Schools and teachers seem to have no intrinsic dramatic potential such as can be found in the professional worlds of doctors and police officers. This is true also of ephemeral writing, where teachers are seldom drawn with respect. An exception was the 1950s television series, *This Man Craig*, which recounted the adventures of a sensitive teacher at a time when Scottish schools were taking on greater pastoral responsibilities. Craig was a 'housemaster' in a city comprehensive school, and each episode dealt with a social problem connected with one of his pupils; he was unconventional, wore a tweed jacket rather than a suit, and he was frequently in conflict with authority because of his commitment to his pupils' needs. That Scottish teachers do not feature often in television fiction is no doubt mainly due to the absence of a commercial market; but there is no reason to doubt that they would be perceived as pompous fools or petty tyrants, as are most of the teachers who feature in British films. Scottish teachers themselves have been entertained for many years by John

Mitchell's comic anti-hero Morris Simpson, whose hapless career is described in regular chapters in the *Times Educational Supplement*. Here is the secondary school brought to life with quiet satire, the recurring educational issues of the day seen through the eyes of a variety of truer-than-life members of staff.

THE DARK IMAGE

There is a sinister aspect to the story of Scottish teachers. Partly because they were virtually second-hand clergymen, expected to bring their pupils to the milk of the Calvinist doctrine by teaching and preaching and chastisement, the parish schoolmasters wielded a harsh discipline. The tawse or belt, described by George MacDonald in the nineteenth century as a 'long, thick strap of horse-hide, prepared by steeping in brine, black and supple with constant use, and cut into fingers at one end', was openly used on children from five years old and upwards. The teacher has frequently been portrayed as a cruel tyrant, ever ready to administer brutal 'justice' for sins as varied as playing truant and forgetting parts of the Shorter Catechism. This continual abuse was sanctioned by supervisors and parents alike in the belief that sparing the rod would spoil the child. MacDonald remembered his teacher in Aberdeenshire in the 1830s as a grim sadist. A hundred years later, in Mallaig, John Alexander MacKenzie's schooling was 'a continual battle with the teacher'; the strap was in daily use and vigorously applied at the slightest excuse (from *A Mallaig Boyhood*, 1996). In *A Scottish Childhood* (1985) Peter Brodie, a Moderator of the General Assembly of the Church of Scotland, remembers a kindly woman teacher in the 1920s, still however armed with the belt and ready to dole out 'three of the best' from a keen sense of duty. In the same book the journalist Magnus Linklater remembers his teacher's strap in the 1950s as 'a weapon of vengeance, black with age and hardened by constant use'.

Many Scots remember their teachers with a mixture of fearful loathing and reluctant respect. Naturally those who did well at school recall their teachers with more gratitude than those whose schooldays were more painful. But despite the scourge of the belt the majority of the less academically successful pupils seem to have considered their teachers fair and considerate, as we learn from the work of researchers such as McPherson and Gow in the 1970s. In *Tell Them from Me* (Aberdeen: Aberdeen University Press, 1980) they report that the belt was used in about a quarter of Scottish secondary schools, and despite the urgings of government officials to use it sparingly and 'as a last resort', in a large minority of schools a large minority of pupils were belted. Despite that, the majority of the pupils surveyed believed that although some teachers were capricious punishers most of them were kind-hearted and forced to use the belt by their circumstances – large classes, bored and resentful pupils and irrelevant curricula.

By 1980 there was a growing groundswell of belief among Scottish teachers that the belt was both demeaning and ineffectual, and some of the local authorities set up panels of teachers to discuss alternative forms of discipline. Advisers and inspectors encouraged schools to dispense with corporal punishment altogether. Hugh MacKenzie tells in his book *Craigroyston Days* (1996) how a 'new atmosphere' and a 'more appropriate curriculum' led to a gradual decline in belting, until in 1981–2 the staff (with only two dissenters) agreed to ban corporal punishment. By the time the government legislated against the use of the belt most Scottish schools had virtually abandoned it, and the vast majority of the teachers welcomed its disappearance.

The ethos of Scottish schools today is kindlier than ever before; inspectors write of a pleasant and purposeful atmosphere, conducive to effective learning. Time and again in their reports they refer to 'the school's ethos' and the 'commitment and teamwork' of the staff' as 'key strengths'.

THE GROWTH OF PROFESSIONALISM

With the formation of the Educational Institute of Scotland (EIS) in 1847, Scottish teachers acquired a formal means of expressing a long-felt desire for a true professional voice. They had long been accorded what amounted to official status: they held their jobs *ad vitam aut culpam*, an enviable security enjoyed by the clergy themselves; they had been officially recognised in government Acts and regulations as important functionaries; but they had always been – at any rate at parish level – under the dominance of the ministers. With the rapid industrialisation and urbanisation of the nineteenth century they saw the destruction of their cosy, if modest, authority. The parish schools could not cope; town schools were built hastily and badly staffed; many thousands of city children could not attend school at all. The interventionist legislation enacted in London and applied to Scotland as well as England and Wales introduced new systems of control which diminished their autonomy: pupil–teacher schemes, inspection, regulation of teaching content. The EIS soon became a vigorous lobby and forum; yet its efforts were unsuccessful in winning either goal of professional authority or political influence (Humes and Paterson, 1983, p. 75 ff). This was because the occupation of teaching was changing radically and irreversibly.

The new city schools had little or no connection with the parish schools of a former age. There was developing a deep historic shift from a world in which teachers were important figures in Scotland's religious culture to a society which was controlled by the state and in which teachers were a secular workforce (Anderson, 1995, p. 296). By the end of the nineteenth century teaching covered a wide range of occupational categories, the schoolmasters giving way to massed ranks of public employees, predominantly female. Midcentury, men made up 65% of the teaching profession; by the end of the century, they constituted 41%; now they are less than a third.

The feminisation of the teaching profession has been one of the most important factors in its development (Humes and Paterson, 1983, p. 137 ff). Last century, women's main entry was through the teacher training institutions, which offered them one of the few available paths to a professional career. The government treated them as cheaper, subordinate teachers well into the twentieth century. The employment of large numbers of women was initially forced by a high demand for teachers. When, during the 1920s and 1930s, there was a surplus of qualified persons, men teachers were nearly always given precedence and women teachers were paid less, had less chance of promotion, and were required to leave when they married. Women could find jobs in secondary schools but it was common for less qualified men to be their heads of department. During the last fifty years there have been periods of staff shortage, when women's presence in the profession has become more powerful, and their status has improved towards equality of esteem and financial parity. But it cannot be claimed that women have won equal security or status: even now, nine out of ten part-time and short-contract posts are held by women, and the great majority of headships and other management positions are held by men. Nevertheless women now constitute an important force in the profession, and it can be expected that their roles will continue to improve.

Teachers' march towards genuine professionalism met with increasing success. Better qualifications and training helped. By 1940 the great majority of teachers had training certificates. The unions worked hard to eliminate uncertificated teachers and this was at last accomplished in the 1970s. Teaching in Scotland is now an all-graduate profession.

The capacity of teachers to participate in policy formation has also increased greatly in recent decades. From the 1920s onwards the Scottish Education Department (SED) included teachers in various advisory councils and negotiating committees; increasingly after 1918 the unions were able to represent their views to government with growing expectation of being listened to; after 1945 their voices were both more powerful and more constructive. The rise of 'experts' in the training colleges and universities, nearly all of them trained teachers with practical experience in classrooms, greatly enhanced the profession's authority: although their claim to a unique professional knowledge was often questioned by civil servants, teachers came to be acknowledged as practitioners of a special kind of craft and the exponents of specialised professional theory. The foundation of the Scottish Council for Research in Education (SCRE) in 1928 (see Chapter 110) created a powerful new partnership between practising teachers and their professional allies (McPherson and Raab, 1988, p. 256 ff). It was the strength of this partnership, sustained by an impressive corpus of research and exposition, which led eventually to a recognition that teachers could efficiently control professional organisations such as a national examination board, teacher training institutions and a General Teaching Council (GTC – see Chapter 112) which administers regulations for professional accreditation, discipline and the maintenance of standards.

The establishment of a Scottish Parliament in 1999 has made governmental policies more reflective of the views of ordinary people; but it has subjected teachers and their managers to closer public scrutiny. Through their unions and professional associations, and in the press, teachers' voices have become more prominent and influential. One of the Parliament's first acts was to set up the McCrone Committee to inquire how teachers' pay, promotion structures and conditions of service should be changed to ensure 'a committed, professional and flexible teaching force which will secure high and improving standards of school education for all children in Scotland into the new Millennium'. The committee's proposals are now being implemented, and the new arrangements will certainly enhance teachers' public status and professional prestige.

IN DEFENCE OF EDUCATIONAL VALUES

During the last forty years there has been a rapid growth of teachers' influence in the development of new educational approaches. At both national and local levels they have been heavily represented in consultative bodies. Their influence was crucial in the 1965 review of the primary school curriculum, and the memorandum it produced provided a reasoned, detailed rationale for the conduct of primary schooling which has long been admired throughout the world. When in 1965 the SED set up the Consultative Committee on the Curriculum (CCC), charged with leading a comprehensive reform of the content and methods of all teaching at primary and secondary levels, teachers were members of the main committee and leading members of its many national development committees (McPherson and Raab, 1988, p. 243 ff). While it is certainly the case that none of these arrangements has come near to realising the claims for true democracy and egalitarianism which are characteristic of Scottish educational rhetoric, the fact remains that teachers gained unprecedented responsibilities and powers.

A large range of progressive approaches continues to be a prominent feature in all Scottish schools. The curricula are now wider and more varied, and teachers can readily introduce new methods and materials. The 'mission statements' of primary schools indicate that children's personal interests as well as their educational needs are of prime concern to the staff. Secondary schools in Scotland are by any standard well staffed with teachers specially trained in a very wide variety of disciplines and activities.

Teachers are always subject to control from external authorities; but although they can recognise the right of politicians to prescribe general educational policies, they have professional values which they are obliged to protect. The first of these is that children's needs and interests must take precedence in any consideration of what should be taught. Another important value is that teachers need a degree of autonomy in determining an individual pupil's educational needs and the best ways of meeting them. Modern teachers are well informed about the psychological characteristics of children and how learning most effectively proceeds, and they demand acknowledgement of their ability to diagnose and prescribe for their students' learning requirements. Unfortunately they are frequently attacked by politicians and journalists who have only subjective prejudice and personal memories of school experience to substitute for professional knowledge. The main planks of the case against modern teaching are crudely simple: education is a service bought by parents; private schools give the best service but are unavailable to the majority, so state-provided schools should be made as like private ones as possible; parents and the providers of schools (the government), not teachers, should stipulate what they want pupils to learn. Successive governments have introduced and maintained arrangements to increase control mechanisms devised by national authorities: performance measurements; the publication of league tables of schools' performance; more control by school boards and governors, giving them power to hire and fire staff; and the introduction of the language of market forces, such as 'development management', 'consumer choice' and 'market power'. In England and Wales these policies were all enshrined in the Education Reform Act of 1987. In Scotland where no government could flout the tradition of consultation and debate, the government issued a paper, *Curriculum and Assessment in Scotland: A Policy for the 1990s* (Edinburgh: SOED), which proposed national prescriptions for the curriculum and making schools more accountable to parents through new school boards, including national testing schemes and the publication of results. The so-called consultation process soon demonstrated a deep and widespread dismay throughout the teaching profession (Roger and Hartley, 1990). It was argued that the curriculum depended almost wholly on the skills and energies of highly trained teachers, and the government's clumsy attempts to invade their autonomy would dangerously impede the development of teachers' professionalism. In the event, some of the more radical proposals were watered down, but the shift of government policy away from consultation and co-operation with teachers still constitutes a sore anxiety for the profession. The last ten or fifteen years have seen continual attacks on their autonomy, combined with increasing requirements for the 'delivery' of externally prescribed curriculum content and teaching methods; and their confidence has been undermined by insistent monitoring of their teaching in accordance with control devices such as 'performance indicators'. It is no wonder that many deplore the 'de-professionalisation' and the 'de-skilling' which come from treating teachers as mere technicians rather than experienced professional educators.

Yet Scottish teachers contribute significantly to the management of what and how they teach. In the 1980s a scheme of development for secondary education and in the 1990s a scheme for primary education have produced a hierarchical structure of tests and examinations along with a complex body of curriculum prescriptions which are still in force; all these have been produced by teachers in working parties supervised by inspectors and 'development officers'. Similarly, for further education colleges and secondary schools, a vast complex of modular courses was produced by working parties of teachers and lecturers. Imposed by government they may be, but the Scottish curriculum and assessment materials and arrangements are undoubtedly the achievement of able practising teachers, and their quality is attested by the widespread interest in them from numerous countries throughout the world. A uniform, integrated curriculum and assessment scheme for advanced level school students is now in place. Scottish teachers nowadays are constantly engaged in devising new learning and teaching approaches at all levels: in their classrooms, in whole school groups and in local and national working parties. This kind of activity was unheard of forty years ago; it can now be asserted with confidence that whatever the authorities propose it will be teachers who finally determine the content and methodology best suited for their students.

TEACHERS, 'GAMEKEEPERS' AND 'REFUGEES'

Generalisations about teachers are inevitably weakened by the immense variety of types contained in the profession. The categories of certificated teachers in Scotland range from nursery teachers who are assisted by nursery nurses (qualified and trained but not teachers), to primary school, special school, and secondary school teachers. All of these are formally attested and certificated by the GTC. In the tiny number of recognised private schools there may be a few untrained and uncertificated teachers, but this is now rare, as parents and governors put a high value on proper qualifications. In further education colleges the majority of the teachers – given the title of 'lecturers' – are formally trained or under part-time training. Only in the universities are there many untrained teachers, and the provision of training and accreditation for university staff is now an agreed priority.

Scottish authorities strongly emphasise the need for formal leadership throughout the education system. Every school and college has a headteacher or principal, and the staff are ranked and functionally labelled; this of course is a universal feature in education systems, but in Scotland there has been an unusual emphasis on hierarchy. The implementation of the McCrone Report will flatten out the structures, but only partially. It is characteristic, too, that outside of schools and colleges there is a large number of persons who have left regular school teaching to assume other jobs. These are variously described as 'leaders' or 'poachers turned gamekeepers', or 'hangers-on' or 'refugees from the chalk-face'. As in all workforces, those who remain at the basic levels of provision look askance at those who have moved away – especially if, as is usually the case, moving away means more power and more autonomy and more pay. The McCrone reforms should give successful class teachers a welcome boost in status and remuneration.

Humes's percipient account of the powers and values of educational leaders in Scotland assigns little authority to teachers at large, except of course in so far as officials such as directors of education, inspectors and advisers are deemed to be teachers; it is evident that, regardless of their professional beginnings, these officials become far removed in their perceptions as well as their functions from the daily tasks of teaching pupils in classrooms. Even leaders of teachers' unions, whose main mission is supposed to be to represent teachers' interests, seem to assume values and purposes which sometimes conflict with those of their rank and file members.

The terms invoked by the 'leaders' – 'partnership', 'co-operation', 'consensus', 'parti-cipation' – can often be exposed as rhetoric at best and, at worst, mere pretence. Humes argues that classroom teaching is regarded as a 'modest rung on the ladder of career advancement', and that success may be partly defined in relation to the ability to secure non-teaching jobs: teachers themselves have endorsed a hierarchical career structure which creates 'a situation in which the more specialist opportunities that arise, the less prestige the unpromoted teacher enjoys' (Humes, 1986, p. 22).

There is a case to be made, however, in defence of those whose jobs are designed to support the teachers by giving them advice, encouragement and in-service training. From the point of view of planners and administrators there are certain constraints on teachers' work that make support services essential. Teachers are relatively stationary: they spend nearly all their time in classrooms, and they have relatively little experience of other schools, so they are less able than professional advisers and supervisors to form impressions and generalisations about the conditions that need to be assessed in order to facilitate change. Teachers, too, are naturally preoccupied by the needs of their own pupils, and they are less able to formulate hypotheses and propositions about young persons in general. It is true that reflective teachers can, over time, build up the wisdom of experience which makes them unequalled as advisors on many aspects of education. But that activity requires time, and lack of time is teachers' greatest constraint. They face classes for several hours each day, every day, coping with the multifarious problems that children bring to them, and they put in many hours every week marking work, preparing lessons and meeting a host of bureaucratic demands. And because teachers are increasingly playing greater roles in the formulation of guidance to all concerned, they need time to do the essential work of researching, describing, devising proposals, consulting others and so on. Guidance and advice must be written and issued; schools must be visited; teachers must be given training and encouragement.

The advisory and support services built up by the regional education authorities between 1975 and 1996 were ultimately accepted by the great majority of teachers as useful and necessary. But the governments led by Thatcher and Major were never enthusiastic about that form of collaborative management. Believing that the education system should be run like a large business, they relied on published regulations and enforced compliance, and they expected the government inspectorates to 'monitor' and 'evaluate' the effectiveness of the workforce in the implementation of the managers' instructions. Her Majesty's Inspectors (HMI) were required to carry out government's policies, and unavoidably they were compelled to apply objectives which had little to do with teachers' professional values. The creation of the Office for Standards in Education (OfSTED) brought, in England and Wales, a system of commercially contracted inspectors whose carefully stipulated functions are almost wholly monitorial, with the few remaining HMIs super-vising the system and preparing reports for the politicians and the public. In Scotland the inspectors' jobs have become much more concerned with formal school inspections and the implementation of government policies. Despite these constraints they have remained essentially loyal to the most central values and concerns of Scottish teachers, as their many published school reports can testify.

The new governmental insistence on control by regulation and overt appraisal has malignly affected Scottish local authorities: in the larger education authorities during the 1980s advisers were to a significant extent replaced by 'adspectors', former advisory officers charged with functions described as 'quality control' and 'assessment'. When in 1996 the government abolished the regions and set up smaller unitary authorities, a large number of advisory posts disappeared for wholly economic reasons, and ad hoc 'quality control' teams are now struggling to provide some measure of advisory support to teachers along with monitoring and evaluation services to the directors. Fortunately the professional expertise of practising teachers is now great enough to promise a new resurgence of development activity and teacher support. A highly effective device is the secondment of skilled experienced teachers to act as 'development officers': both at national and local level these have spent their time – periods varying from two or three months to two or three years – working on innovative programmes, devising teaching schemes and materials, visiting schools to support teachers in their classrooms. This arrangement has been successful in the teacher training institutions, in government projects and in the schools themselves, and the new Scottish Executive has warmly endorsed the idea. Despite the ever-present danger that teachers and lecturers on short-term contracts will be badly treated in terms of pay and conditions of service, and the recurrent suspicion that the authorities will try to use them to reduce costs rather than enhance services, teachers given time out will always prove a blessing to the profession at large.

The truth is that teaching, as a profession, lends itself to constant variety and adaptability. There can surely be no other professional body so full of various talents, so rich in such a wide range of specialist skills, creative ability and versatility. In other professions there are a few specific academic disciplines which yield the knowledge their members need; in education there are dozens of disciplines represented even in the basic jobs. Perhaps that is why teachers so frequently leave the profession – not simply because they may dislike it but because they have talents that allow them to do other things. In Scotland it is possible to list hundreds of politicians, writers, painters, musicians, administrators, business people who have all at one time been teachers – and not always unsuccessful ones. This may reflect the hardships of the job, but it may well also reflect the vitality of the practitioners.

REFERENCES

Anderson, R. D. (1995) *Education and the Scottish People*, Oxford: Clarendon Press.

Humes, W. M. (1986) *The Leadership Class in Scottish Education*, Edinburgh: John Donald.

Humes, W. M. and Paterson, H. M. (eds) (1983) *Scottish Culture and Scottish Education 1800–1980*, Edinburgh: John Donald.

McPherson, A. and Raab, C. D. (1988) *Governing Education*, Edinburgh: Edinburgh University Press.

Roger, A. and Hartley, D. (eds) (1990) *Curriculum and Assessment in Scotland*, Edinburgh: Scottish Academic Press.

XIII

Future

XIII

Future Advances
in Neuropharmacology

114

Scottish Education:
An International Perspective

Michael Peters

All the themes which are dealt with in this chapter are broadly covered by the combination of the terms 'politics' and 'education', for this conjunction brings together issues that can help explain both the distinctiveness of Scottish education, its unique past and the set of challenges that Scotland shares in common with most of the developed world. The responses to these will determine whether the national system of education either will uniquely distinguish Scotland's system or shape it so that it becomes increasingly like others in the West, a game to be played in the international contest of national competitive advantage.

The formal distinctiveness of the Scottish framework, stronger in schools than in universities, is given in terms of separate legislative powers and an institutional set-up that marks it off from England. The Scottish institutional apparatus differs, for example, in terms of school boards (rather than governing bodies), school management, and national bodies like the Scottish Qualifications Authority (SQA) and General Teaching Council (GTC). Yet whether such institutional distinctiveness embodies a particularly Scottish vision of the nature and purpose of education is a moot point. In the first edition of this volume the editors raised issues of resistance to change and lack of leadership, suggesting that a culture of subservience may well be a major factor in the educational policy community's capacity to address the big issues – including social polarisation and the knowledge underclass – in innovative ways. There is nothing surprising about these observations and they may well be taken to characterise educational policy communities anywhere in the Western world. The fact that national education systems comprise a huge proportion of the annual budget and constitute one of the biggest policy portfolios in any government, which is not always reflected in Cabinet rankings, explains why governments are often reluctant to embark on sweeping reform or even to introduce radical policy ideas.

At the same time two points must be recognised. First, the private finance initiative (PFI), originating under the Conservative government and continued (with some changes) by Blair's Labour administration, has been enthusiastically embraced by the Scottish Parliament as a means of funding infrastructure improvements to Scottish schools. This initiative, the impact of which will be difficult to judge for some years, has the power to change the nature and purpose of Scottish schooling and largely in covert ways not explicitly apparent when contracts were originally drawn up. Second, in line with PFI and as a result of the rise of neo-liberalism, especially during the Thatcher–Reagan era, education has seen, perhaps, the greatest change in policy since the Second World War, as Western governments have moved away from the Keynesian principles governing the post-war welfare state settlement to adopt and substitute market and market-like arrangements (the so-called quasi-market) in the allocation of scarce public funds across the public sector (see, for example, Marshall and Peters, 1999; Whitty, 2002).

Underlying these issues is the question of whether Scottish education has a strategic direction for the future based on a sound understanding of the broad social, political and economic forces which are shaping the world. And, as the editors asked in the first edition, if there is a map for the future, who holds it? Viewing Scottish education from an international perspective involves consideration of some of the major pressures for change that have affected educational systems in all developed countries.

DEMOCRACY, EDUCATION AND DEVOLUTION

The initial claim in the opening paragraph of this chapter can be briefly advanced in terms of a number of related themes that concern the watershed represented by the establishment of the Scottish Parliament and, with it, the national responsibility for determining education policy. Thus, consideration might be given, first, to the question of devolution, decentralisation and delegation (three quite different concepts) in terms of the democratic state's three principal functions of the funding, provision and regulation of education. This question uniquely distinguishes Scottish education, although the issue of autonomy remains to be pursued at both the international and regional levels. Given the establishment of the Scottish Parliament, to what extent can it be taken further both within the larger international context of the European Union and within Scottish education itself, with possible devolution of authority (and funding), to individual learning institutions or, indeed, ultimately, to 'learners' themselves? How desirable are such options and what are the primary means through which they might be pursued? The issue of local autonomy, a central notion to both democracy and education, clearly may be pursued in different ways. For example, it can be argued that fully consumer-driven models of education are inimical to principles of participatory democracy.

The restructuring of state education systems in many Western countries during the last two decades has involved a significant shift away from an emphasis on administration and policy to an emphasis on management, a tendency also recognisable in Scotland, although to a lesser extent than England. There has, for instance, been a strong move toward devolved management with increasing emphasis on the new techniques in strategic and development planning, accountability and reporting. There has been an associated tendency to emphasise the concept of educational leadership, as evidenced in the Scottish qualification for headship, even although the distinction between management and leadership is not always obvious. The 'new managerialism' has found a home in Scottish education: while its techniques are enthusiastically embraced, its ideological origins and conceptual basis is rarely appreciated. Effective management and leadership are seen to be the commonsense way to enhance achievement and encourage greater equality, but the possible long-term conflict of the new managerialism with the principles of participatory democracy has not yet been clearly articulated.

The 'new managerialism' in education has drawn theoretically on the model of corporate managerialism and private sector management styles on the one hand, and public choice theory, new institutional economics and human capital theory, on the other. A specific constellation of these theories, sometimes called 'new public management', has been very influential in the United Kingdom, Australia, Canada and New Zealand. These theories and models have been used both as the legitimating basis and policy means for redesigning state educational bureaucracies, educational institutions and even the public policy process itself.

Most significantly, there has been a decentralisation of management control away from the centre to individual institutions permitted by a new contractualism – often referred to as the 'doctrine of self-management' (in education, see Caldwell and Spinks, 1998) – coupled with new accountability and funding structures. This shift has often been accompanied by a disaggregation of large state bureaucracies into autonomous agencies, a clarification of organisational objectives, and a separation between policy advice and policy implementation. The new managerialism has also involved a shift from input controls to quantifiable output measures and performance targets, along with an emphasis on short-term performance contracts, especially for chief executive officers and senior managers. In the interests of so-called productive efficiency, the provision of educational services has been made competitive; and, in the interests of so-called allocative efficiency, state education in many Western countries has undergone marketisation and incremental privatisation.

Features of new public management include: an extensive use of written contracts and performance agreements; a reliance on short-term employment contracts, and emphasis on economic rewards and sanctions; a reduction in multiple accountability relationships, minimising the opportunities for ministerial discretion in the detailed operation of government agencies; the institutional separation of the funding agency from the provider and the separation of advisory, delivery, and regulatory functions; an introduction of accrual accounting; the development of capital charging regimes; a distinction between the state's ownership and purchaser's interests; a distinction between outcomes and outputs; an accrual based appropriations system and an emphasis on contestable provision and contracting out for services. It might be added that there is often a blind ideological emphasis on concepts of choice and diversity, and on the promotion of the quasi-market for the delivery of public services, where the citizen becomes a consumer in a fully consumer-driven model of welfare (see e.g., Whitty et al., 1998).

Yet the managerial literature in education contains little reference to the welfare state or the characteristic modes of thought of its policy makers, administrators and service providers. Social needs, professional standards, deprivation, community and equity have historically played little or no part in the development of the new managerialism. Thus, the transfer, during the late 1980s and 1990s, of managerialism from private sector corporations to welfare-state services changes, and perhaps compromises, the ethos of public service based on norms of impartiality, the protection of social entitlements and rights. The new managerialism blurs the boundaries between the public and the private sectors, raising new ethical and political problems concerning the principles and processes of public contracts and who the stakeholders and beneficiaries are likely to be.

The reform of education and training in the international context must be understood within the wider context of public sector restructuring, and as a sub-set of the reforms of the state sector based on the same principles, just as the restructuring of the public sector must be understood as a part of the radical economic restructuring many governments embarked on during the Thatcher–Reagan years. It is important to note that for neo-liberals there is nothing distinctive about education: it is just another service that can be traded in the market place and is subject to the same market disciplines as other services. Neo-liberals and advocates of New Right in the 1980s increasingly focused their attention on the rising and apparently irreversible tide of welfare expectations. They argued that the welfare state had evaded both investment and work incentives, directly contributing to economic recession during the 1970s. The combined effects of social policies – including guaranteed minimum wages, superannuation, and the growth of spending in health and education sectors – allegedly had strengthened organised labour against capital, augmenting wages as against capital goods. It had also, they claimed, substantially led to increased state borrowings leading to a decline of profitability.

Neo-liberals argue that the so-called 'perverse effects' lead to greater state intervention in both social and economic terms, but the more the state helps the more it will have to help and at diminishing levels of effectiveness. It is alleged that increasing levels of intervention tend in the long term to rob economic liberalism of its vitality. The bottom line is that the perverse effects of economic and social intervention represent to these critics a fundamental threat to individual political and democratic freedom. Aspects of neo-liberalism, including PFI and arguments against the effectiveness of the old welfare state, have been preserved and taken up with renewed vigour and experimentation by Blair's Third Way Labour government. Blair argues that no longer is it possible to hang onto the idea of a monolithic, 'one size fits all' welfare state, and he has signalled the end of the comprehensive school (in England) and the development through PFI of more customised specialist schools that will create diversity and serve individual needs.

New managerialism is also congruent with an emphasis on the reconstruction of education in terms of 'enterprise culture' – as against the so-called 'culture of dependency' allegedly created by the welfare state – with an emphasis on entrepreneurial skills in the curriculum, 'education for work', the development of generic and transferable skills, public private partnerships between universities and business, and technology transfer policies designed to synergise 'blue-sky' research aimed at generating appropriate conditions for the transition to the 'knowledge economy'. The dispersion of education, and competition from non-traditional providers, has been increased by the advent of new communications and information technologies that now promise customised individual learning packages and a new kind of informal learning at home and in the workplace.

Devolution in social democratic theory serves as a metaphor for community, solidarity and increased participation and representation in school affairs. With the reform of educational administration in New Zealand, for example, the originally intended form of devolution was never a genuine option with the reform of educational administration under Tomorrow's Schools. The promise of community and participatory democracy was replaced by a form of delegation and the doctrine of self-managing schools. As delegation, 'devolution' becomes a contract relationship between individuals with delegated powers which is controlled through monitoring performance and applying incentives and sanctions to encourage managers to meet agreed objectives rather than to follow their own opportunistic goals. Thus, the social democratic promise is made hostage to a form of neo-liberal thinking based on principles of abstract individualism and consumer (parental) choice.

In Scotland, the full impact of neo-liberal reforms in education has not taken place to the same extent as it has in England, Australia or New Zealand. In part this is a result of the fact that local councils and intermediary organisations have retained their control. In part, one would like to think that it is also the result of a strong political tradition of equality that makes itself manifest in locally controlled and managed councils which administer and fund schools. A critical question for Scotland is the extent to which it can resist the fully consumer-driven model of education being developed elsewhere in the Western world and strongly advocated by New Labour.

Another important aspect of 'devolution' is captured by the notion of the 'fitness of the state' and the case for effective devolution to local government. In thinking about the future roles of government in Scotland in relation to education, a number of important questions arise. How many levels of government should there be in a relatively small democracy like Scotland? How should various functions of government be allocated between national and local councils? How should sub-national government be organised and structured and what powers and autonomy should it have with regard to the funding and regulation of education? These issues go right to the heart of democratic politics and they impact on questions of 'the politics of choice' and diversity, ownership and governance, and informed citizenship.

In the Scottish education policy network there is an almost complete lack of understanding of either the economics of education or of the way in which theories originating outside education determine both the macro- and micro-economic reality of education policy (at all levels). Economics of education is not taught in education faculties, nor is it approached thematically at national conferences. There seems little understanding of neoclassical economics or recent so-called 'new growth theory'. By this is meant two principal developments: first, the neo-classical economics of the 'third generation' Chicago school, beginning with Friedman, Becker and others, focusing on human capital theory, public choice economics, the economics of knowledge, the economics of information, and of education (the last three specialities are necessary for even a rudimentary understanding of the 'knowledge economy' which Scotland professes to be following in the realm of education policy); and second, 'new growth theory' which now drives governmental concerns about the 'knowledge economy'. New growth theory highlights the role of higher education in the creation of human capital and in the production of new knowledge. On this basis it has explored the possibilities of education-related externalities. In short, there is a consensus emerging in economic theory that education is important for successful research activities (e.g., by producing scientists and engineers), which are, in turn, important for productivity growth; and education creates human capital, which directly affects knowledge accumulation and therefore productivity.

GLOBALISATION, CITIZENSHIP AND NATIONAL IDENTITY

Another issue that is part of the same problem is the question of citizenship, together with the increasingly vexed matter of national identity. Citizenship and its relation to the modern democratic state relates to traditional questions of politics, ethics, and political economy for which Scotland is justly famous. While Scotland has its own Parliament that now addresses many areas of domestic policy, including education, it is still part of the Westminster system of government that involves a centralisation of many governmental functions. At the same time, the Parliament sits within the broader governmental framework of the EU, with its legislative powers and a focus on helping member states to protect and develop the promise of social democracy with an emphasis on a range of economic, social and human rights now intrinsic to the modern idea of citizenship. In the modern era Scotland has an enviable reputation as the home of a distinctive philosophical tradition that began in the time before the Reformation to develop as a significant national tradition contributing to the Age of

Enlightenment (see Broadie, 2000). The Scottish Enlightenment tradition contributed greatly to European political and legal thought, to economic understanding of society, to discussions of human nature, realism or 'common sense', scepticism and ethics. Perhaps one of most significant and enduring contributions, bearing on citizenship, is the Scottish critique of individualism. Adam Ferguson (1723–1816), for instance, in *History of Civil Society* questioned the then prevalent assumptions governing talk of a State of Nature (especially in Rousseau and Hobbes). He was to maintain the inherent sociality of human society on the basis of his discussions of instinct, the family and concepts of friendship and loyalty that disturbed the early contract theorists who wanted to explain sociality in terms of individual reason. Christopher Berry in *Social Theory of the Scottish Enlightenment* (Edinburgh: Edinburgh University Press, 1997: p. 47) writes:

> Having established that humans are social beings, the Scots . . . proceeded to address the consequences that followed. Since humans are social then any acceptable account of human society must start there. It was because much of the prevailing social theory did not appear to do that that the Scots criticised it so wholeheartedly. Individuals we certainly are and rational we certainly are but an individualistic rationalism is inadequate as social theory. The recognition of that inadequacy is what helps to make the Scots historically important.

In one important sense the debate about citizenship finds a conceptual anchor and set of intellectual resources in these thinkers of the Scottish Enlightenment to retheorise and rethink citizenship in the age of globalisation. The themes of individualism and community are motifs that still mark contemporary politics and economics, whether they be forms of rational choice theory, neo-liberalism or New Right notions of individual freedom construed as consumer choice, Third Way politics with an emphasis on the slogan 'market economy but not market society' or contemporary forms of communitarianism (see Peters and Marshall, 1996).

At the beginning of the twenty-first century Europe and, indeed, the world, experiences processes of both integration and disintegration. In particular, the expansion of world markets as a form of economic globalisation can be understood as a process of world economic integration composed of international flows of capital, goods of all kinds, including consumer goods, knowledge and information, and people. The same process is both a form of economic integration and a polarisation of wealth, exacerbating existing tendencies toward greater global inequalities between rich and poor countries and regions. Perhaps now more than at any time in the past with the end of the Cold War, the collapse of the Soviet system, the consolidation of the EU, and the entry of China into the World Trade Organisation, political observers are witnessing an accelerated set of changes – economic, cultural, technological and political – that impinge on one another in novel ways and create new possibilities and dangers for the democratic state and the notion of citizenship that underpins it.

The two terms 'globalisation' and 'citizenship' are not normally juxtaposed in social and political analysis. They appear as contradictory or, at least, conflicting: the former points to an economic and cultural process of world integration, based on unregulated flows of capital and underwritten by developments in new information and communications technologies, while the latter serves as a metaphor for political community. Globalisation seems to threaten the sovereignty of the nation-state and with it the notion of citizenship that developed during the modern era. Within the context of globalisation a crucial question is how people can create a sense of community and local identity to protect and bolster the institutions that provide them with social protection. In advanced welfare states, like Scotland, how are people to defend the entitlements that form part of social citizenship? Even more challenging is the question: what possibilities are there for developing transnational alliances and defining entirely new rights within supranational arenas like the EU?

Answers to these questions crucially involve education at all levels and depend upon understanding a new set of relationships between the terms 'globalisation' and 'citizenship', for globalisation without citizenship is politically blind and citizenship without globalisation is theoretically naive. An important part of advancing the citizenship and capacity building agenda in education depends upon a critical understanding of the new reality of globalisation and the different ways it impinges upon the democratic state.

The modern concept of citizenship implies the existence of a civil or political community, a set of rights and obligations ascribed to citizens by virtue of their membership in that community, and an ethic of participation and solidarity needed to sustain it. Most traditional accounts of citizenship begin with the assertion of basic civil, political and social rights of individuals. The concept has appealed to both conservatives and radical democrats: the former emphasise individual freedom at the expense of equality and see state intervention as an intolerable and unwarranted violation of the freedom of the individual, while the latter stress the democratic potential of citizenship. Increasingly, on the left, the concept has been seen as a means to control the injustices of capitalism. The most pressing question concerns the status of citizenship in the modern state and what kind of political community best promotes it. These are contested issues and impact directly on education.

The classic theorisation of democratic citizenship is to be found in Marshall's famous formulation of three forms of citizenship: civil, political and social. By comparing Marshall's theorisation with that of the Crick Report (*Education for Citizenship and the Teaching of Democracy in Schools*, London: QCA, 1998) it is possible to chart the significant shifts in the definitions of citizenship that have accompanied globalisation, including the breakdown of the compromise between capitalism, democracy and the welfare state, the rise of neo-liberalism and, with it, the expansion of world markets. There have been large shifts from rights to responsibilities, from active state intervention to reduce economic inequalities to active involvement in civic networks, and from political citizenship to political literacy.

Scotland has recently embraced the concept of citizenship education. The *Education for Citizenship in Scotland* paper lays out a framework for the medium term based around four questions, viz.: What is meant by 'citizenship'? Why is 'education for citizenship' important? What should education for citizenship do for young people? What does effective education for citizenship involve in practice – for the curriculum, for schools and early education centres and for communities? (see http://www.ltscotland.com/citizenship/paper/paper_summary.asp). The main contention behind the paper is that young people's education in school and early education settings has a key role to play in fostering a modern, democratic society, whose members have a clear sense of identity and belonging, feel empowered to participate effectively in their communities and recognise their roles and responsibilities as global citizens. The paper develops a set of core and generic skills and contains concrete proposals for development and exploration. It also promotes a form of active citizenship although there is little consideration of how globalisation might impact on citizenship or the ways in which broader reforms in Scottish education conflict with, or are compatible with, a participatory social democratic model of school governance and management. What are the competing discourses for citizenship in Scotland and to what extent are the strands of economic enterprise, moral renewal and civic activism compatible?

Citizenship education within the globalisation frame is also strongly linked with questions of national identity. Some scholars talk of an emerging international youth style based on consumerism that threatens to numb local historical memory, traditions and consciousness and promote blind acceptance of an underlying market individualism based on purchasing power. The fear of cultural homogenisation and a wish to protect the local community is sometimes juxtaposed with the need to develop national cultural strategies to preserve and enhance cultural heritage in the face of globalisation. Clearly, the overlap between education and national cultural strategy in Scotland is a policy area that promises much and deserves more attention, especially in view of what has been promoted under the banner of enterprise culture, education for work and a myriad of schemes designed to foster the development of closer links between education and business. Scotland's National Cultural Strategy *Creating Our Future, Minding Our Past* (http://www.scotland.gov.uk/ nationalculturalstrategy/docs/cult-00.asp) emphasises participation, access and innovation, reconstructing 'creativity' as a national resource, and gives a central place to education in its four main strategic objectives: promoting creativity, the arts, and other cultural activity; celebrating Scotland's cultural heritage in its full diversity; realising culture's potential contribution to education, promoting inclusion and enhancing people's quality of life; and assuring an effective national support framework for culture. It is difficult and too early to judge the effectiveness of these strategies, or the impact and development of culture as an 'industry' or 'sector' promoted by government as a means for deliberately shaping national identity or encouraging innovation and creativity. One might argue since the establishment of the Parliament that there has been a growing self-confidence and a new sense of Scottishness based on the vitality and increase in Scottish literature and the arts.

TOWARDS THE KNOWLEDGE ECONOMY?
LIFELONG EDUCATION, WORK AND SOCIAL INCLUSION

National visions of education are rarely developed in isolation from other policy areas. Perhaps one demand of the new era of policy experimentation in education is the extent to which education can be developed in conjunction with other policy areas of health, housing, culture, media and the economy. The question of educational futures is a critical policy area that points to the need not only for experimentation but also for a medium- to long-term national strategy or sense of direction.

One such candidate is the education policy template recently provided by the concept of the 'knowledge economy' that reinforces and builds upon the concept of 'lifelong education'. The economic importance of education is fundamental to understanding the global knowledge economy. The OECD and the World Bank have stressed the significance of education and training for the development of 'human resources', for upskilling and increasing the competencies of workers, and for the production of research and scientific knowledge, as keys to participation in the new global knowledge economy. Many writers emphasise the importance of the economics and productivity of knowledge as the basis for national competition within the international market place. One commentator Lester Thurow (in *The Future of Capitalism: How Today's Economic Forces Shape Tomorrow's World*, New York: Wm Morrow and Company, 1996, p. 68) suggests that 'a technological shift to an era dominated by man-made brainpower industries' is one of five economic tenets, which constitute a new game with new rules: 'Today knowledge and skills now stand alone as the only source of comparative advantage. They have become the key ingredient in the late twentieth century's location of economic activity.' Equipped with this central understanding and guided by neo-liberal theories of human capital, public choice, and new public management, many Western governments have begun the process of restructuring their national education systems and are redesigning the interface between education and business.

The United Kingdom's White Paper *Our Competitive Future* (Department of Trade and Industry, 1998), for example, begins by acknowledging the fact that the World Bank's 1998 *World Development Report* took knowledge as its theme, citing the report as follows:

> For countries in the vanguard of the world economy, the balance between knowledge and resources has shifted so far towards the former that knowledge has become perhaps the most important factor determining the standard of living . . . Today's most technologically advanced economies are truly knowledge-based. (http://www.dti.gov.uk/comp/competitive/main.htm.)

The UK White Paper also mentions that the OECD has drawn attention to the growing importance of knowledge, indicating that the emergence of knowledge-based economies has significant policy implications for the organisation of production and its effect on employment and skill requirements. The report suggests that already other countries, including the United States, Canada, Denmark and Finland, have identified the growing importance of knowledge and reflected it in their approach to economic policy.

The Scottish Executive released its White Paper *Targeting Excellence: Modernising Scotland's Schools* in 1999 (for a summary of the White Paper, see: http://www.scotland. gov.uk/library/documents-w6/edsp-00.htm). It includes the following statement:

> The knowledge economy will pose challenges and opportunities. Knowledge and know-how are taking over from buildings and machinery as the most valuable assets of business. The speed at which information can cross the globe, the sophistication of modern products and services, and the sophistication of the modern consumer all point to increasing globalisation of the economy, and to increasing customisation of goods and services to meet people's individual needs. Innovation, fresh thinking, the acquisition and application of knowledge, and high levels of customer awareness are likely to be among the critical factors in achievement in the future. Competitive advantage will come from the application of intellect and knowledge to business problems. The skills Scotland will need to be successful can and should be fostered and grown in schools.

The White Paper then lists initiatives already under way, including: the implementation of the National Grid for Learning by 2002; investment in training teachers in the use of ICT; development of the Scottish Virtual Teachers' Centre; the 'Think Business' programme to bring entrepreneurs into the classroom; promoting enterprise skills in schools; support for the National Centre: Education for Work and Enterprise; investment in industry and enterprise awareness for teachers and schools. And it also identifies the next steps as: extension of the National Grid for Learning to enhance lifelong learning, in particular support for community access; new guidelines on improving work experience; new guidelines on careers education; expanding the 'education for work' and 'enterprise' agenda.

This emphasis is repeated and extended in *Research and Knowledge Transfer in Scotland*, Report of the Scottish Higher Education Funding Council and Scottish Enterprise Joint Task Group (2002, available at http://www.shefc.ac.uk) with an accent on technology transfer, mapping and monitoring the flows of technical information, and dissemination between universities and firms.

There are some relatively benign versions of the knowledge economy – versions, for instance, that emphasise the crucial role that the non-sciences and 'soft sciences' can play. However, the dominant notion seems to accept without question that the emphasis should be on science, engineering and technology – a purely instrumental version that does not recognise that many of the new developments supporting the knowledge economy are significantly language-based: developments in telematics, informatics, new computer languages and algorithms, and so on. In other words, there is insufficient understanding of the way in which knowledge becomes part of knowledge systems and how, in turn, knowledge systems become operationalised. Developments in the humanities, social sciences, and creative arts ('soft technologies') are an essential part of the knowledge economy – a fact that instrumentalist, 'scientific' versions ignore.

There has been little attempt to indigenise the concept of knowledge economy or to mark it as a left-wing conception – one that, for instance, focuses clearly upon 'knowledge workers' not purely as human capital but as members of 'knowledge institutions'. There has been little attempt by educationalists to distinguish the notion of the knowledge economy as their own or to suggest how the concept looks different from an educational perspective. Such a version might make the standard distinction between 'knowledge economy' and 'knowledge society', thus emphasising the social and cultural conditions of the knowledge economy and the new citizenship rights associated with information, knowledge and education. New citizenship rights might be seen to include: 'freedom of information', a right that is significantly curtailed under the clause of commercial sensitivity; but also, 'freedom of knowledge' and 'freedom to education'; rights now often jeopardised by a commodification of knowledge and education that leads to the instituting of intellectual property rights.

If the nature of work changes in the post-industrial, service-oriented knowledge economy, what does this mean for work as a basis for social inclusion and for education based upon these concepts? To what extent is the knowledge economy educational policy template compatible with wider educational goals and visions that aim to preserve the distinctiveness of Scotland's system of education and its guiding ethos? To what extent has policy addressed the question of access to knowledge, information and education in terms of the emerging digital divide? To what extent has the issue of the knowledge economy/society been embraced by curriculum theorists and designers? What are the educational visions of the knowledge economy/society in Scotland and how might the distinctiveness of the Scottish philosophical and educational traditions provide an imaginative basis for reinventing social democracy, citizenship, culture and national identity in the third millennium? These are the vital questions that the new Scotland must address with urgency.

REFERENCES

Broadie, A. (2000) *The Scottish Enlightenment: The Historical Age of the Historical Nation*, Edinburgh: Birlinn.
Caldwell, B. J. and Spinks, J. M. (1998) *The Self-Managing School*, London: Falmer.

Marshall, J. D. and Peters, M. A. (1999) *Education Policy*, Cheltenham; Northampton, MA: E. Elgar.

Peters, M. A. and Marshall, J. D. (1996) *Individualism and Community: Education and Social Policy in the Postmodern Condition*, London: Falmer.

Whitty, G. (2002) *Making Sense of Education Policy*, London: Chapman.

Whitty, G., Power, S. and Halpin, D. (1998) *Devolution and Choice in Education*, Buckingham: Open University Press.

115

The Future of Scottish Education

Walter Humes and Tom Bryce

One of the aims of the first edition of this book was to increase the knowledge-base which informs understanding of the Scottish educational system by bringing together in a single volume a vast amount of information and analysis. We hope we succeeded in that aim. However, what has become apparent in the four years since has been the sheer scale and pace of change (social, economic, technological) which impacts on educational provision. Add to this the very different political landscape following the establishment of the Scottish Parliament and the need for an updated and revised text became evident. Education is – and should be – a developing, dynamic process in which existing ideas are examined, criticised and refined, and new ideas are advanced, scrutinised and tested. The Parliament deserves credit for giving education a high priority in its policy initiatives – apparent, for example, in legislative reform, in the setting of National Priorities, and in the mounting of a national debate on the future of Scottish education. Underlying these activities is a belief in the importance of education as a driver in social and economic reform, and in its capacity to raise individual and collective achievements in ways that will promote enterprise, creativity and active citizenship. It is too early to say with any confidence how successful these efforts will be, but few would deny that they are well intentioned. Meanwhile the forces of change continue and the need for educational responses based on evidence and judgement remains. The ideal of a 'period of consolidation' in which things stand still is simply an illusion.

One of the committees of the Scottish Parliament, the Education, Culture and Sport Committee, in 2002 conducted its own enquiry into the future of Scottish education (parallel to, but separate from, the national debate promoted by the Executive), drawing on the views of academic advisers and informed by consultation responses from professionals, organisations and members of the public. A number of key themes were identified. Two of these were 'coping with change and uncertainty' and 'engaging with ideas'. Moreover, a vision of the future of society was seen as a necessary precursor of a vision for education. This was an interesting finding, in contrast to the pragmatism (some would say anti-intellectualism) of the Scottish educational tradition, pre-devolution. There seems to be some (albeit limited) recognition of the need to be more outward-looking in thinking about possible futures for Scottish education. This is to be welcomed. What is known as 'horizon scanning' – that is, trying to predict likely developments and working out possible responses to them – is now a feature of the work of policy analysts in many fields. In the sections that follow, consideration will be given to the shape that future schools might take, the kinds of teachers that will be needed to work in them, areas where further research is needed, and the evolving political context within Scotland. With regard to the last of these, it should be borne in mind that new elections to the Scottish Parliament will have taken place before the publication of this book. However, even if the composition of the Scottish Executive changes, the commitment of all the major parties to education as a political priority seems set to continue.

FUTURE SCHOOLS

In one of an interesting series of publications on education by the independent think-tank, the Scottish Council Foundation (SCF), the question is posed, 'Will the traditional concept of "school" . . . survive long into the 21st century?' (Bloomer, K., *Learning to Change: Scottish Education in the 21st Century*, Edinburgh: SCF, June 2001, p. 12.) This is an issue that is not confined to Scotland. At an international level, the Organisation for Economic Co-operation and Development (OECD), through its Centre for Educational Research, has developed six scenarios for tomorrow's schools. These are not intended to have firm predictive value but to serve as a means of stimulating serious thinking about the direction of schooling over the next few decades.

The first two scenarios are essentially extrapolations from existing systems. Scenario 1 envisages the continuation of 'robust bureaucratic school systems'. These will be resistant to change because of the vested interests of powerful stakeholders. Such systems are likely to be subject to high political expectations but these will not be matched by adequate resources. Despite repeated policy initiatives designed to promote social inclusion, educational inequalities would be likely to persist. Credentialism, in the shape of more examinations, certificates, degrees and other awards, would continue to expand, but the market value of qualifications as passports to economic life would diminish.

Scenario 2 takes the form of 'extending the market model'. It assumes increasing dissatisfaction with state control of education, leading to a reshaping of funding mechanisms and school systems. The involvement of the private sector (already evident in school building programmes, health provision and the prison service) would proceed apace. The outcome would be greater diversity in the nature of educational provision, less uniformity in routes into teaching (with new forms of 'professionalism' emerging), and greater inequalities between social classes. There would be considerable scope for entrepreneurial enterprise in developing new markets and new approaches to teaching and learning. Assessment and accreditation would be demand-driven and would lead to an emphasis on skills and competences rather than knowledge and understanding. The transitions from current practices would be controversial and painful, and would lead to a diminished role for government in the provision of education.

Scenarios 3 and 4 offer 'reschooling' alternatives to the existing system; that is, they redefine the central purposes of schools. In scenario 3, schools are seen as 'core social centres', regarded as the most effective bulwark against social fragmentation and a perceived crisis in values. Such schools would receive high levels of public funding and would enjoy high levels of public trust. They would become focal points for community development, the places where valuable 'social capital' could be formed. Professional barriers would be broken down through shared roles, interprofessional training, and a more flexible approach to the settings in which learning takes place. Education would be seen as a 'public good' (in contrast to scenario 2 where it would be seen as a 'private market').

Diversity would be respected but the community emphasis would increase social cohesion and the hope would be that inequalities would diminish.

The fourth scenario envisages schools as 'focused learning organisations'. They would have a strong 'knowledge agenda', reflecting the needs of the 'learning society' and the 'knowledge economy'. Curriculum specialisms would flourish and there would be openness to innovation in pedagogy and assessment. The use of ICT would be widespread. Professionals would be highly motivated, would routinely engage in self-evaluation, and would have plenty of opportunities for professional development. As with scenario 3, there would be high levels of public trust and funding. The main difference is that, whereas scenario 3 has community as its focus, scenario 4 concentrates on the learning process itself (in all its forms). Schools would thus serve as the lead agencies in promoting 'lifelong learning for all' and would have strong links with other public and private organisations with a stake in enhancing the general level of knowledge and skills in society. The whole enterprise would be underpinned by a belief that it was possible to pursue the goals of quality and equity at the same time.

The final two scenarios involve a move towards different forms of 'deschooling'. Scenario 5 – 'learner networks and the network society' – starts from the premise that dissatisfaction with conventional schools will increase with their perceived inability to meet the needs of complex, diverse societies. The educated classes would begin to desert state provision and, along with other special interest and religious groups, would develop new arrangements in tune with general developments towards the 'network society'. Various 'communities of interest' would emerge. Traditional curriculum structures would decline and much learning would be tailored to meet individual needs. The traditional role of teachers would come under serious threat. Knowledge and skills would be 'shared' in new ways through different network clusters. Many schools would simply cease to exist because of a lack of pupils. A combination of web-based learning, self-help groups, 'surgeries' and home visits would replace them. Some state schools would certainly survive (perhaps particularly at primary level) for children otherwise excluded from learning by the 'digital divide'. Inevitably such a 'system' would lead to gross inequalities. It would also raise serious ethical concerns about the motives of some providers and the abandonment of any commitment to social justice through education.

The final OECD scenario – 'teacher exodus: the meltdown scenario' – is even more dramatic. It presupposes a major problem of teacher supply, deriving from a skewed age profile (retirements outstripping inflows of new recruits), poor rewards compared to other occupations in a rapidly changing job market, and the unattractiveness of the profession because of indiscipline, pupil disaffection, and so on. Policy initiatives would be ineffective because they would take too long to have an impact. Standards of achievement would fall and there would be considerable unevenness across the system. Alternative reactions to this scenario can be envisaged. There might be an ineffective attempt to retrench, by narrowing the aims of schooling (to 'basic skills' perhaps) and trying to hold things together. More optimistically, the crisis might provide a spur to radical innovation, with a range of stakeholders joining forces to introduce far-reaching reforms. However, the level of investment required would be very high and the economy might not be able to sustain it. The political challenge would also be considerable since any effective intervention would require strong central direction – thus reversing the general trend to devolve more decision making to local levels.

Where might Scottish education be located in relation to these various scenarios? It has connections with all of them, though not in equal measure. With the post-McCrone settlement, the 'meltdown' scenario may seem unlikely, certainly in the immediate future. Scottish teachers now have a more secure career structure than before and the financial rewards, while not generous, are sufficient to attract a reasonable supply of new teachers. However, it is quite difficult to recruit high-quality candidates in some subject areas and men are increasingly showing a disinclination to enter teaching: the feminisation of the profession is now evident in secondary schools as well as primaries.

Another respect in which the OECD scenarios may seem to have limited relevance is in the extent to which private enterprise might invade territory previously occupied by the state. In the national debate of 2002, parents expressed general satisfaction with public-sector provision of primary and secondary schools. Moreover, in Scotland public private partnerships so far relate mainly to building programmes, not to the delivery of the curriculum. When it comes to the provision of in-service training, however, many authorities now make use of private consultants who have particular areas of expertise. Similarly, some research and development contracts commissioned by the Scottish Executive go to the private sector, including to companies based outside Scotland. It is not difficult to imagine an extension of this trend, especially in the field of information and communications technology. The real test would be if an attempt were made to offer private-sector options (perhaps through some kind of voucher scheme) to local authority primary and secondary schools. So far there is no evidence of demand for this, but parents whose children attend 'failing' inner city schools may come to feel that such an option would be worth a try. And it should be borne in mind that, in the pre-school sector, there is already a mix of private, voluntary and local authority provision.

The development of New Community Schools in Scotland is consistent with the 'core social centres' scenario as outlined by OECD. Both recognise the need to see education not as a separate form of social provision, but in association with a range of other services. As yet, however, the various professionals involved are still learning how to work together and have not moved far in the direction of interprofessional training. Furthermore, the precise balance between the 'social' and the 'learning' aspects of the curriculum is still being worked out. Related to this, the extent to which the new suite of Higher Still courses is adequate to serve the whole school population is uncertain. There are some grounds for thinking that the needs of a significant minority of secondary school pupils (perhaps as much as a quarter of the total) are not adequately met, and that more in the way of vocational options is required. Other European countries do rather better in this respect.

However, for the foreseeable future, Scotland is likely to stick with its 'robust bureaucratic system'. This is so partly because of its strong institutional structure and the vested interests of powerful groups. Those who enjoy power in the present arrangements are unlikely to give it up lightly. Bodies such as the General Teaching Council, Learning and Teaching Scotland and the Scottish Qualifications Authority are well established and confident that their stewardship of the system is essential. Add to this the role of important players such as inspectors and directors of education, as well as the instinctive conservatism of teachers themselves, and the likelihood of major systemic change in the next few years seems remote. A key question to ask is whether there is sufficient awareness among these groups of the wider economic and technological forces which prompted the OECD exercise. The Scottish tradition has always been inclined to be pragmatic, focused on immediate practical questions and distrustful of theory. This may serve the system reasonably well in times of relative stability, but in periods of rapid change it may be inadequate as a basis for responding to global challenges. The climate of ideas may need to be strengthened if the sort of creative thinking that is required is to be stimulated. One important part of this is a reconceptualisation of the role of teachers and the kind of training and professional development they should receive as the twenty-first century advances.

FUTURE TEACHERS

For the present, the capabilities of teachers may be said to be defined by the competences and benchmarks outlined in Chapter 104. Scottish education has set out what it considers necessary for teachers at various stages of their professional development: initial training; full registration; 'chartered' status; headteacher. Are these the teachers of the future? The foregoing analysis of future schools might suggest some doubt, but much may be a matter of interpretation and emphasis. To be cynical, if the Scottish 'experts' have got it right, then cloning would do the trick. Much more likely is the probability that individual creativity has been underestimated and we have not allowed for what cannot be seen around the corner.

There are also indications that the traditional sector split (primary-trained experts teach primary pupils, secondary-trained experts teach secondary pupils, and so on) might not serve the future; 5–14 has always had the potential to undermine that and it is now a matter of serious debate as to whether and how alternative forms of training might enable individual teachers to specialise in the middle years where, arguably, there should be a better blend of typically primary style pedagogy allied to subject expertise and specialism. Clearly, GTCS support for moves away from conventional patterns will be essential (and the traditional hands of the unions may prevent change). However, blurring the sector basis of training is secondary to the need for multi-professionalism.

Inter-professional collaboration and social inclusion

It is now beginning to be recognised that professionals with different kinds of expertise should collaborate in the interests of effective support to youngsters. Thus teachers, social workers, health experts and community educators have been encouraged to work together in New Community Schools. Several writers in this volume, including ourselves in Chapter 4, have referred to the modest progress being made on this front, it being challenging for professionals with different orientations and priorities to co-ordinate their efforts in the formal setting of school. The social inclusion agenda is demanding for all concerned.

One professional group which has received little attention in this respect is speech and language therapists (SLTs). The majority of teachers will be unfamiliar with the work of SLTs, although some learning support teachers will know of the support that can be given to children with speech, language and communication impairments. For many decades, the locus of SLT activity was in hospitals and clinics, but increasingly SLTs carry out part of their work in schools and in collaboration with teachers. Indeed there is growing body of literature, more familiar to SLTs than to teachers, which deals with the challenges of interprofessional collaboration. The HMI report of 1996 (*The Education of Pupils with Language and Communication Disorders*, Edinburgh: HMSO) noted that 'One of the most critical factors in determining the quality of provision for pupils with language and communication disorders was the quality of the partnership between speech and language therapists and teachers' (p. 3). Many researchers now comment upon the importance of SLTs working in mainstream education and in joint programmes of support and therapy for individual pupils in need. Wright and Graham (1997) are firmly of the view that children gain most from joint working partnerships between SLTs and learning support teachers; the professionals concerned benefit from joint planning, assessment and implementations of their decisions; perhaps significantly, their expectations of each other are more realistic. In commenting upon the challenges presented by collaborative work, McCartney has noted the differing priorities held by health and educational service professionals; which children should take priority for support and treatment? And there are basic problems associated with time-tables, professional schedules and locations for the various activities which are part of people's work patterns (McCartney, 1999).

It is noticeable of course that both groups, SLTs and teachers, have little in common in their initial training. The basic degree (BSc) and professional qualification of SLTs makes little contact with, say, BEd or PGCE courses for teachers, and vice versa. The research in the SLT field calls out for further work to be done and progress to be made on the interprofessional front. Sadly it is little known to teachers, and other staff involved in New Community Schools are probably unfamiliar with it too. Alternative forms of training may however be completely coloured by a matter of serious concern to Scottish teachers.

Jobsizing

At the time of writing, jobsizing was commencing in primary and secondary schools throughout Scotland. One part of the McCrone Agreement was that salary placements should be determined within a new flatter structure of promoted posts through a 'jobsizing methodology'. Rather than responsibility payments being determined solely by school roll, resulting in principal teachers of all subjects within a school being paid the same, the underlying thinking was that the salaries of promoted individuals should be dependent upon the size of *their* responsibility – to be precise, the size of the responsibility of the post they hold. In practice this will affect principal teachers (subject and guidance) and above in secondary schools and all promoted posts in the primary sector, with the designations of assistant headteacher, assistant principal teacher and senior teacher disappearing. The Scottish Negotiating Committee for Teachers (SNCT), consisting of representatives from SEED, COSLA and the teaching unions, contracted PricewaterhouseCoopers to develop a jobsizing methodology and subsequently to oversee the implementation of the exercise. That firm, well experienced in the private, commercial sector, developed the so-called jobsizing 'toolkit', a questionnaire designed to size the jobs of promoted individuals, its administration being undertaken by locally appointed co-ordinators drawn from teaching union and local authority management nominees.

The outcomes of the exercise are scheduled to start from August 2003 (with conserved salaries for existing post-holders who have been in their current post since April 2001). It is claimed that the methodology will assess the relatively factual aspects of what promoted teachers do, their responsibilities, not how well they fulfil them. Four categories are identified: responsibilities for leadership, good management and the strategic direction of colleagues; curriculum development and quality assurance; whole school policy imple-mentation; and working with partners. When the exercise commenced (autumn 2002), no agreement had been reached within the SNCT as to how the responsibilities would be weighted. The fall-out from the exercise is anything but transparent. In fact, it is difficult to detect enthusiasm amongst any of the stakeholders in this complex undertaking. It would be charitable to say that the differentiated pay scales likely to emerge from it will give greater flexibility to school managers and local authorities; that is certainly envisaged through importing private sector thinking into the public service arena. Business men and women may be used to keeping what they earn to themselves and playing the competitive game; teachers are certainly not and, if nothing else, they will talk openly amongst themselves. Many see jobsizing as purely financial cost-cutting, and teachers are extremely negative about any 'faculty' notions (whereby, say, one promoted staff member is to manage expressive arts in a secondary school, in place of PTs responsible, separately, for Art, Music, Physical Education and Drama). The McCrone Agreement may have made jobsizing a legal requirement but it is evident at this stage that nobody is really taking a lead on this issue. As with many other parts of the McCrone settlement, neither government nor unions grasped the full detail and its complications. At this point one can only predict rapid disillusionment in the profession and significant disincentives for future employees, or else a significant retreat from highly differentiated outcomes when it comes to determining the result of the whole exercise. Once again, the Scottish preference for bureaucratic negotiation, rather than 'blue skies thinking', is evident.

Scottish teachers are understandably concerned about how developments in curriculum and assessment, in relations with other occupational groups (such as SLTs), and in their job descriptions, will affect them in their day-to-day work. But they also need to take a longer-term view of the changing nature of teaching as a professional activity. Their social role as the gatekeepers of knowledge is under pressure from a number of directions. The most obvious of these is the information revolution brought about through the use of computer technology and other forms of electronic media. This will change the dynamics of teaching and learning in significant ways. Instead of the teacher-led schools of the present, we may have to think of schools as being only *one* site of learning (albeit an important one), alongside a range of other locations managed by different agencies and offered on a 'lifelong' basis. This pattern of provision may not go as far as OECD scenario 5 ('learner networks and the network society') but it is likely to require teachers to be more responsive to the way learners themselves define their needs than they have traditionally been disposed to. If schools stand still – or even if they change at too slow a pace – then the cultural gap between formal educational establishments and the alternative sources of information in wider society will become so great that teachers might run the risk of simply being left behind in the knowledge revolution. History would judge them harshly as professional dinosaurs, victims of their own inability to read the signs of social change. While it would be wrong to overstate this point, the seriousness of the challenges that face schools and teachers should not be underestimated.

FURTHER RESEARCH

In the first edition of *Scottish Education*, we identified four areas which called for further research and guidance for those who work in schools. These were: the law as it affects the work of teachers; the economics of education; the position of less successful adolescents, particularly disaffected young people; and Higher Still, which in 1999 was on the point of implementation. Some brief commentary on these is in order.

Concerning the law, it is worth recording the appearance in 2001 of an *A–Z of Scots Education Law: A Guide for Parents*, edited by Jackie Welsh and published by the Scottish Consumer Council. Written in plain, non-technical terms, this is indeed a 'handy reference to education law in Scotland . . . [and] aims to equip parents, young people and their advisors with the information they need to get the best out of the education system; whilst helping teachers and headteachers to become familiar with the legal framework in which they work'.

With reference to economics, the chapters by Hartley (26) and Midwinter (27) here represent important contributions to our understanding of finance and economic effectiveness with respect to education; they significantly advance the debate. We hope they will stimulate further work in these areas and that researchers will focus some of their energies upon expenditure and outcomes – not simply in conventional value-for-money terms – but to further unravel the linkages between policy, funding and educational practice; to understand the *realpolitik* and the *realfinanz*.

With respect to disaffection, several of the chapters in this edition have referred to the strong rhetoric on social inclusion apparent in the business of the new Parliament since devolution. Mackenzie's chapter (97) presents a rigorous analysis of disaffection among youngsters, emphasising the social divisions within Scotland and indicating that, for some, their 'culture of disintegration [makes] them internal exiles in their own homeland' (quoting Holloway's words). While there may be no greater incidence of disaffection among youth overall compared to the past, Mackenzie tracks the connections between school exclusion and social exclusion and records the potential benefits of interprofessional working in New Community Schools; teachers alone cannot counter social exclusion. If the rhetoric of parliament is to be translated into more effective action, it should think again about the level of support required in the extension of new community schooling (cf. Chapter 4).

With regard to Higher Still, the final chapter in the first edition turned out to be somewhat prophetic on several counts. We had cited SQA's first chief executive's admission that the integration of SEB and SCOTVEC would be a radical step and that '[the authority must] manage a flexible system while maintaining rigorous standards, which no examination body in the world has been able to do' (speaking in 1998). It didn't achieve that first time round in 2000 (as discussed in Chapter 83) and huge investment of effort, time and money was required to get things effectively operational for 2001. We also indicated that the more successful Higher Still became, the greater would be the washback upon Standard Grade. The take-up figures presented in Chapter 88 do indeed indicate that the numbers taking the sub-Higher levels have risen quickly; so much so that during session 2001–2, some schools were beginning to argue that Intermediate courses should be accelerated in preference to Standard Grade. Such moves are apparent in the more socially advantaged areas where teachers desire to progress able pupils. Other schools have responded by emphasising how successful Standard Grade has been across the ability range; many (but not all) pupils are served well by the certification levels available. Nevertheless, it is clear that this debate will continue over the next few years and it would not be acceptable for system drift to result in what would be more socially divisive. From the perspective of some teachers and subjects, a key point is the content and methodology advances which have accompanied new National Qualifications (Higher Still) courses; these too influence perceptions of the value of their Standard Grade counterparts. Bearing in mind the difficulties which parents, employers and society at large have in knowing about what goes on in the name of courses and certificates, the challenge to SEED to rationalise upper secondary arrangements is considerable. Furthermore, the effects of Higher Still's implementation upon the FE sector has not been unproblematic, as Chapter 5 has set out; there have been gains and losses and much will need to be taken into account in any revisions to the complex apparatus of qualifications which Scotland currently has in place.

Looking to further research, there is much that should be addressed, not only in these four areas but in related areas and in other fields. Sticking first with new National Qualifications, the rapid uptake of Intermediate 1 and 2 courses has a bearing upon the intended 'progression' routes inherent in the original model of Higher Still, where pupils move through S4 to S6 and beyond. Schools and national subject groups are of course reacting to the shifting landscape of study and achievement, but more fundamental questions are raised than simply the articulation of courses. How well served is the actual learning of young people associated with the changing architecture of qualifications? Is the knowledge any less inert than was the case with its predecessors? These are fundamental questions and will require innovative strategies for research. The flip side of learning is teaching and there are corresponding questions to be put about teaching, many of which resonate with those posed earlier in this chapter. Arguably too, the challenges and uncertainties are at their greatest in post-school education. The many training initiatives outlined in Chapter 12 are, rightly, focused upon workplace learning and are concerned with lifelong education, but there is a corresponding need to focus too upon the changing nature of academic learning. Academia needs to research itself and we need to know more about what is possible and valuable, given the ever more constraining circumstances within which lecturers operate. If significant proportions of future generations seriously begin to doubt the worth of education beyond school, despite all that is known about future earnings and the changing nature of work (cf. Chapter 77), then very many of the now-taken-for-granted assumptions will require serious scrutiny.

A different, but not unconnected, area for research relates to the decline in reading in the population, particularly among many young people. The contending stimulants are obvious: electronic media of all sorts, including high quality digitised imagery, widely available; and an associated cultural context which is changing social priorities. Elsewhere, reference has been made to the digital divide which this creates in terms of opportunities – a yet further source of division and exclusion. But overall the challenge to education is a significant one. As youngsters read less, it makes things more than difficult for teachers, of all subjects and in all sectors; the very medium of what is drawn upon for stimulation, for support and practice, for recovery and revitalisation is taken away. It is not at all clear how educators should respond. At the time of writing the packed and demanding 5–14 curriculum is beginning to be questioned (with senior HMIE admitting to their own contribution to overload in *TESS*, 8 November 2002). Have the many varied and enriching targets helped or hindered reading? Or, is that to miss the point that reading strategies must be taken from school *to* home, families being, in reality for some children, and potentially for others, the most powerful educational ally. Must schools work longer and harder, being open at weekends and holidays, in the interests of educating families in ways which might break the cycle of underachievement and exclusion? Such comments would be unwelcome to an already hard-pressed profession; yet they seem to represent the logic of relevant evidence about schooling (not about teachers individually).

The relation between what happens in school and what happens in the home, the community and wider society remains problematic, particularly (but not exclusively) for those youngsters who are not fulfilling their potential. The Scottish Executive has shown a commendable concern for children looked after by local authorities and other marginalised groups (such as the children of Travellers and asylum seekers). This signifies a recognition of the fact that the capacity to benefit from schooling is strongly influenced by the social context in which children live. In the period up to 2000 there was a very heavy emphasis on 'in school' factors which might raise levels of achievement. A great deal of research took the form of studies of school effectiveness in meeting targets, boosting standards, and so on. While this produced many interesting findings, what was lost was a sense of the big sociological factors which limit (but do not completely determine) what schools can bring about. These include, poverty, crime, ill-health, inadequate housing, marital breakdown. Two examples specific to young people and their education will illustrate the point about the relation between schooling and external pressures.

Scotland has one of the highest teenage (school-age) pregnancy rates in Europe. This usually has a major impact not only on the education of the young mothers themselves, but also on the opportunities for their children. (The impact on the fathers is less marked as their education need not be subject to interruption.) When the children go to school the capacity of the mothers to provide support is likely to be limited – partly because of the disruption to their own education, and partly because of other factors. They may, for example, suffer from financial hardship and poor housing, and lack the emotional support of a partner. This is an important intergenerational issue which deserves serious attention from educational researchers.

The second example relates to drugs. Here the legal position is under review. By the time this book is published, changes in the law regarding cannabis may have been implemented, following a UK Cabinet decision made in the summer of 2002. This proposes to reclassify cannabis from class B to class C but to retain powers of police arrest for possession in certain circumstances, 'where public order is threatened or where children are at risk', according to the Home Secretary, David Blunkett. Stiffer sentences would be imposed for class C drug dealing, the Labour government endeavouring to be seen as both liberal with regard to cannabis smoking, yet not soft on possible harm to children.

Whatever finally emerges, schools are likely to find themselves on the front line. There is scepticism about the effectiveness of current drugs education but general agreement that there is a problem. As session 2002–3 began, a senior police officer warned that drug dealers were probably targeting every school in the Strathclyde area (a pupil population of some 250,000) with the full range of drugs, from cannabis to heroin. The *Times Educational Supplement* of 4 October 2002, reporting debate at the annual conference of the Scottish branch of the British Psychological Society (BPS), noted that one in five Glasgow children were now estimated to live in households where drugs are used in combination with drink. The Advisory Council on the Misuse of Drugs estimated that some 50,000 Scottish children have addict parents and, according to Scotland Against Drugs, there are more than 55,000 problematic heroin users in the country. Ellen Moran, at the BPS conference, warned that pupils suffering under addict parents were often 'impulsive, immature and inattentive': she urged that schools need to look out for under-performing children. The capacity of hard-pressed teachers to take on this monitoring role is likely to be limited and there is clearly scope for research in studying the effects of the new legislation.

In both of these examples, it is important not to 'pathologise' the young people – that is, to present the problem as one of individual failure (either their own or their parents) – or to pass negative judgement. Actions which serve to restrict educational opportunities need to be understood in relation to wider cultural, structural, economic and political factors. The reinstatement of those factors as central to educational discourse is an essential requirement of serious debate about where Scottish education should be going as the twenty-first century advances. It is fitting, therefore, that this chapter, and the book as a whole, should end with some reflections on the developing political context in post-devolution Scotland.

THE POLITICAL CONTEXT

There are certainly some grounds for optimism. Education remains high on the political agenda and there is widespread recognition of its importance for future social and economic development. But is there a clear map to guide where we are going? And, if so, who holds it? It cannot be assumed that simply because there is a great deal of activity (in the form of educational initiatives) that progress is being made. There is a difference between 'policy as spectacle' and 'policy as vision'.

On the plus side, there is now more scope (compared with the pre-devolution period) to interrogate the decision makers of Scottish education. The two parliamentary education committees have made use of their powers to conduct a number of worthwhile enquiries (e.g., into SQA, lifelong learning and future strategy). These committees constitute an important structural provision which can continue to offer useful avenues of investigation. In addition, the Scottish Executive website allows many stakeholders (and members of the public) access to information that, under the Scottish Office regime, was less easily obtainable. Whether that would have happened anyway because of advances in technology might be open to debate but, whatever the stimulus, it certainly provides opportunities to keep track of political developments.

This opening up of sources of information means that the 'map' shaping the direction of Scottish education, if it exists, should be possible to locate. Although the move towards greater openness has so far stopped short of a proper Freedom of Information Act, the scrutiny of the Scottish Executive has been aided by a vigilant media keen to report on (educational) successes and failures. In this way, the constituency of informed opinion is gradually increasing and public exchanges about educational proposals are informed by wider debate. Inevitably there are government attempts at 'news management' but, compared with what happens at Westminster, these are amateurish and often ineffective.

These changes can be related to broader cultural movements. One of the most encouraging features of post-devolution Scotland is the growing confidence and visibility of people working in a wide range of fields, for instance literature, music, art, drama, publishing. With reference to the last of these, there has been a significant increase in writing about Scotland and things Scottish, and not in an unreflective, celebratory way. On the contrary, some of the writing has been sharply critical and has taken the form of challenges to Scotland's various establishments (political, legal, religious, educational) – see, for example, Paterson et al., (2001), and Hassan and Warhurst (2002a; 2002b).

In *Tomorrow's Scotland*, Hassan and Warhurst consider 'three tomorrows' for Scotland. 'One is a technocratic, managerial, post-ideological politics defined by the Blairite mantra "what works is what works".' As far as education is concerned, this would present a bleak prospect. So too would the second tomorrow – 'a politics obsessed with constitutional issues, in which arguments over the Barnett Formula, fiscal autonomy and electoral systems became the obsession of the political classes to the marginalisation, even exclusion of everything else'. It is their third tomorrow that would give education a major role to play – a tomorrow which 'would see social democratic Scotland find a new voice and confidence to develop a politics that lives up to the hopes of people pre-devolution and the demands of the twenty-first century'. Those demands will require a highly educated, well-informed citizenry willing to accept responsibility and take on difficult tasks, prepared to question authority and established tradition, and – above all – committed to making Scotland a better place for future generations.

REFERENCES

Hassan, G. and Warhurst, C. (eds) (2002a) *Anatomy of the New Scotland: Power, Influence and Change*, Edinburgh: Mainstream Publishing.

Hassan, G. and Warhurst, C. (eds) (2002b) *Tomorrow's Scotland*, London: Lawrence and Wishart.

McCartney, E. (ed.) (1999) *Speech/Language Therapists and Teachers Working Together: A Systems Approach to Collaboration*, London: Whurr Publishers Ltd.

Paterson, L. et al. (2001) *New Scotland, New Politics?*, Edinburgh: Polygon.

Wright, J. and Graham, J. (1997) Where and when do speech and language therapists work with teachers? *British Journal of Special Education* 24 (4), 171–4.

Glossary of Abbreviations

AALA	Adventure Activities Licensing Authority
AAP	Assessment of Achievement Programme
ACCAC	Qualifications, Curriculum and Assessment Authority for Wales
ACDP	Advanced Courses Development Programme
ACET	Australian Council for Education through Technology
ACOT	Apple Classroom of Tomorrow
ADES	Association of Directors of Education in Scotland
AEAS	Association of Educational Advisers in Scotland
AEF	Aggregate External Finance
AGL	Action Group on Languages
AGM	Annual General Meeting
AHT	Assistant Headteacher
AHTS	Association of Headteachers in Scotland
AL	Associate Lecturer
AME	Annually Managed Expenditure
APEL	Accreditation of Prior Experiential Learning
APFL	Accreditation of Prior Formal Learning
API	Age Participation Index
APL	Accreditation of Prior Learning
APS	Assisted Places Scheme
APT	Assistant Principal Teacher
APU	Assessment of Performance Unit
ARTEN	Anti-Racist Teacher Education Network
ASC	Association of Scottish Colleges
ASCETT	Advisory Scottish Council for Education and Training Targets
ASDAN	Award Scheme Development and Accreditation Network
ASLS	Association of Scottish Literary Studies
ASPEP	Association of Scottish Principal Educational Psychologists
AST	Advanced Skills Teacher
ASTER	Assisting Small-group Teaching through Electronic Resources
ATQ	Additional Teaching Qualification
ATQRE	Advanced Teaching Qualification in Religious Education
AWBL	Assessment of Work-Based Learning
BA	Bachelor of Arts
BBC	British Broadcasting Corporation

BECTA	British Education and Communications Technology Agency
BEd	Bachelor of Education
BERA	British Educational Research Association
BMES	British Meat Education Service
BPS	British Psychological Society
BSc	Bachelor of Science
CAD	Computer Aided Drawing
CAL	Computer Assisted Learning
CAS	Computer Algebra System
CAST	Curriculum Advice and Support Team
CAT	College of Advanced Technology
CBEVE	Central Bureau for Educational Visits and Exchanges
CBI	Confederation of British Industry
CCC	Consultative Committee on the Curriculum
CCEA	Council for the Curriculum, Examinations and Assessment *(Northern Ireland)*
CCETSW	Central Council for Education and Training in Social Work
C&D	Craft and Design
CE	Colleges of Education
CEC	Catholic Education Commission
CERES	Centre for Education for Racial Equality in Scotland
CES	Centre for Educational Sociology
CeVe	Community Education Validation and Endorsement
CGLI	City and Guilds of London Institute
CI	Central Institutions
CIDREE	Consortium of Institutions for Development and Research in Education in Europe
CILT	Centre for Information on Language Teaching
CIPFA	Chartered Institute of Public Finance and Accountancy
C&IT	Communications and Information Technology
CITB	Construction Industry Training Board
CLA	College Lecturers' Association
CLS	Community Learning Scotland
CMP	Contemporary Music Project
CNAA	Council for National Academic Awards
CNAG	Comunn na Gàidhlig
CNSA	Comhairle nan Sgoiltean Araich
COPE	Committee on Primary Education
COSHEP	Committee of Scottish Higher Education Principals
COSLA	Convention of Scottish Local Authorities
COSPEN	Committee on Special Educational Needs
COT	Committee on Technology
CP7	Curriculum Paper 7
CPD	Continuing Professional Development
CRE	Commission for Racial Equality
CRU	Central Research Unit
CSP	Co-ordinated Support Plan
CSR	Comprehensive Spending Review
CSU	Central Support Unit

CSUP	Committee of Scottish University Principals
CSYS	Certificate of Sixth Year Studies
CT	Chartered Teacher
CTC	City Technology College
CTI	Computers in Teaching Initiative
CVCP	Committee of Vice-Chancellors and Principals
CYMS	Catholic Young Men's Society
DASH	Dumbarton Academy Seniors against Harassment
DEdPsych	Doctor of Educational Psychology
DEL	Departmental Expenditure Limit
DENI	Department of Education in Northern Ireland
DES	Department of Education and Science
DfEE	Department for Education and Employment
DfES	Department for Education and Skills
DHT	Depute Headteacher
DMR	Devolved Management of Resources
DSM	Devolved School Management
DSM	Diagnostic and Statistical Manual (*of the American Psychiatric Association*)
EA	Education Authority
EAL	English as an Additional Language
EBP	Education Business Partnerships
EC	Educational Computing
EC	European Community
ECER	European Conference on Educational Research
ECITB	Engineering Construction Industry Training Board
EC&SC	Education Culture and Sport Committee
ED	Education Department
EdB	Bachelor of Education Degree
EdD	Doctor of Education
EDRU	Education Department Research Unit
EDSI	Education Departments' Superhighways Initiative
EEC	European Economic Community
EERA	European Educational Research Association
EfW	Education for Work
EGRC	Extended Grade Related Criteria
EIL	Education–Industry Links
EIP	Early Intervention Programme
EIS	Educational Institute of Scotland
EISP	Education for the Industrial Society Project
E&LLC	Enterprise and Lifelong Learning Committee
ELLD	Enterprise and Lifelong Learning Department
ELTR	Effective Learning and Teaching Report
EMA	Educational Maintenance Allowances
ENHPS	European Network of Health Promoting Schools
EPPE	Effective Provision of Pre-School Education
EPSD	Education for Personal and Social Development
EPSEN	Effective Provision for Pupils with Special Educational Needs
ERSDAT	Educational Research in Scotland Database
ES	Environmental Studies

ESL	English as a Second Language
ESRC	Economic and Social Research Council
EU	European Union
FE	Further Education
FEDA	Further Education Development Agency
FEFC	Further Education Funding Council
FL	Foreign Language
FMRG	Funding Methodology Review Group
FT	Full Time
FTE	Full-Time Equivalent
FTLS	Flexibility in Teaching and Learning Scheme
GAE	Grand Aided Expenditure
GC	Graphic Communication
GCE	General Certificate of Education
GCSE	General Certificate of Secondary Education
GCU	Glasgow Caledonian University
GDP	Gross Domestic Product
GIST	Generic Issues and Strategies for Teaching
GNVQ	(or gNVQ) General National Vocational Qualification
GRC	Grade-Related Criteria
GSVQ	(or gSVQ) General Scottish Vocational Qualification
GTC(S)	General Teaching Council (for Scotland)
HAS	Headteachers' Association of Scotland
HE	Higher Education
HEBS	Health Education Board for Scotland
HEFCE	Higher Education Funding Council for England
HEFCW	Higher Education Funding Council for Wales
HEI	Higher Education Institution
HELP	Health Education for Living Project
HEQC	Higher Education Quality Council
HESA	Higher Education Statistics Agency
HGIOS	*How Good is Our School?*
HGPE	Higher Grade Physical Education
HIE	Highlands and Islands Enterprise
HMCI	Her Majesty's Chief Inspector
HMDSCI	Her Majesty's Depute Senior Chief Inspector
HMI	Her Majesty's Inspectorate
HMIE	Her Majesty's Inspectorate of Education
HMSCI	Her Majesty's Senior Chief Inspector
HMSO	Her Majesty's Stationery Office
HN	Higher National
HNC	Higher National Certificate
HND	Higher National Diploma
HS	Higher Still
HSDP	Higher Still Development Programme
HSDU	Higher Still Development Unit
HSPE	Higher Still Physical Education
HT	Headteacher
HTML	Hyper Text Mark-up Language

IAPS	Independent Association of Preparatory Schools
IASG	Inter-Authority Standing Group for Gaelic
ICT	Information and Communication(s) Technology
IDES	International Design Technology and Enterprise Support Network
IEA	International Association for the Evaluation of Educational Achievement
IEP	Individualised Educational Programmes
IFE	Informal Further Education
ILA	Individual Learning Account
ILB	Industry Lead Body
ILS	Integrated Learning Systems
ILT	Institute for Learning and Teaching
InSEA	International Society for Education through Art
INSET	In-service Education and Training
IQ	Intelligence Quotient
IRB	International Relations Branch
IRU	International Relations Unit
ISC	Integrated Science Course
ISEP	Improving School Effectiveness Project
ISES	Institute for the Study of Education and Society
IT	Information Technology
ITE	Initial Teacher Education
ITQ	Infant Teaching Qualification
ITV	Independent Television
JANET	Joint Academic Network
JISC	Joint Information Systems Committee
JLLG	Joint Lifelong Learning Group
JWP	Joint Working Party
KU	Knowledge and Understanding
LA	Local Authority
LACE	Local Authority Current Expenditure
LAMPS	Leadership and Management Pathways Sub-Group
LAN	Local Area Networks
LASFE	Local Authority Self-Financed Expenditure
LEA	Local Education Authority
LEC	Local Enterprise Company
LMS	Local Management of Schools
LS	Learning Schools
LS	Learning Support
LSA	Local Service Agreement
LSDA	Learning and Skills Development Agency
LTS	Learning and Teaching Scotland
LTSN	Learning and Teaching Subject Network
MA	Master of Arts
MA	Modern Apprenticeship
MAppSci	Master of Applied Science
MAN	Metropolitan Area Networks
MBA	Master of Business Administration
MCARE	Multi-cultural and Anti-Racist Education
MCI	Management Charter Initiative

MEC	Multi-cultural Education Centre
MEd	Master of Education
MEDC	Micro-electronics Development Centre
MEP	Member of the European Parliament
MERU	Management of Educational Resources Unit
META	Minority Ethnic Teachers Association
MLPS	Modern Languages in Primary Schools
MP	Member of Parliament
MPhil	Master of Philosophy
MSA	Modern Studies Association
MSc	Master of Science
MSC	Manpower Services Commission
MSP	Member of the Scottish Parliament
MTHT	Management Training for Headteachers
NAB	National Assessment Bank
NAEIAC	National Association for Educational Inspectors, Advisers and Consultants
NAME	National Anti-racist Movement in Education
NAS/UWT	National Association of Schoolmasters/Union of Women Teachers
NC	National Certificate
NCC	National Curriculum Council
NCET	National Council for Educational Technology
NCH	National Children's Homes (Scotland)
NCIHE	National Committee of Inquiry into Higher Education
NCITT	National Committee for the In-service Training of Teachers
NCS	New Community Schools
NCVQ	National Council for Vocational Qualifications
NDPB	Non-Departmental Public Body
NFER	National Foundation for Educational Research
NGB	National Governing Body
NGfL	National Grid for Learning
NIACE	National Institute for Adult and Continuing Education
NOF	New Opportunities Funding
NOS	National Occupational Standards
NQ	National Qualification
NQTG	National Qualifications Taskgroup
NRA	National Record of Achievement
NTO	National Training Organisation
NUT	National Union of Teachers
NVQ	National Vocational Qualifications
OECD	Organisation for Economic Co-operation and Development
OED	Oxford English Dictionary
OFDL	Open, Flexible and Distance Learning
OfSTED	Office for Standards in Education
OIS	Office and Information Studies
ONC	Ordinary National Certificate
OND	Ordinary National Diploma
OU	Open University
OUVS	Open University, Validation Services
PA	Parent Associations

PA	Practical Abilities
PAT	Planned Activity Time
PAT	Professional Association of Teachers
PC	Personal Computer
PCS	Practical Craft Skills
PDA	Professional Development Awards
PE	Physical Education
PEDP	Primary Education Development Project
PFI	Private Finance Initiative
PGCE	Postgraduate Certificate in Education
PGCE(P)	Postgraduate Certificate in Education (Primary)
PGCE(S)	Postgraduate Certificate in Education (Secondary)
PhD	Doctor of Philosophy
PIPS	Performance Indicators in Primary Schools
PIRLS	Progress in International Reading Literacy Study
PISA	Programme for International Student Assessment
PPP	Public Private Partnerships
PS	Primary School
PS	Problem Solving
PSBR	Public Sector Borrowing Requirement
PSC	Public Sector Comparator
PSD	Personal and Social Development
PSE	Personal and Social Education
PT	Part Time
PT	Principal Teacher
PTA	Parent Teacher Association
QAA(HE)	Quality Assurance Agency (for Higher Education)
QCA	Qualifications and Curriculum Authority
QIE	Quality in Education
QIO	Quality Improvement Officer
QTS	Qualified Teacher Status
QuAC	Qualifications, Assessment and Curriculum
QUANGO	Quasi-Autonomous Non Governmental Organisation
RAE	Research Assessment Exercise
RBL	Resource Based Learning
R&D	Research and Development
RDG	Review and Development Group
RE	Reasoning and Enquiry
RE	Religious Education
REAF	Race Equality Advisory Forum
REHIS	Royal Environmental Health Institute of Scotland
RET	Record of Education and Training
RIU	Research and Intelligence Unit
RME	Religious and Moral Education
ROSLA	Raising of the School Leaving Age
RP	Received Pronunciation
RRAA	Race Relations Amendment Act
RSA	Royal Society of Arts
SAA	Student Awards Agency

SAAS   Student Awards Agency for Scotland
SAC   Scottish Arts Council
SACCA   Scottish Advisory Committee for Credit and Access
SATRO   Science and Technology Regional Organisations
SCAA   School Curriculum and Assessment Authority
SCAMP   Scottish Computer Administration and Management Programme
SCCC   Scottish Consultative Council on the Curriculum
SCCE   Scottish Council for Commercial Education
SCCOPE   Scottish Central Committee on Primary Education
SCCORE   Scottish Central Committee on Religious Education
SCDS   Scottish Curriculum Development Services
SCE   Scottish Certificate of Education
SCEC   Scottish Community Education Council
SCEEB   Scottish Certificate of Education Examination Board
SCET   Scottish Council for Educational Technology
SCETDEX   SCET Indexing system
SCF   Scottish Council Foundation
SCI   School Characteristics Index
SCIS   Scottish Council of Independent Schools
SCOLA   Scottish Committee on Language Arts
SCOSDE   Scottish Committee for Staff Development in Education
SCOTBAC   Scottish Baccalaureate
SCOTBEC   Scottish Business Education Council
SCOTCAT   Scottish Credit Accumulation and Transfer
SCOTCERT   Scottish Certificate
SCOTEC   Scottish Technical Education Council
SCOTVEC   Scottish Vocational Education Council
SCQAITE   Standing Committee on Quality Assurance in Initial Teacher Education
SCQF   Scottish Credit and Qualifications Framework
SCRE   Scottish Council for Research in Education
SCT   Standard for Chartered Teacher
SE   Scottish Enterprise
SE   Scottish Executive
SEB   Scottish Examination Board
SED   Scottish Education Department
SEED   Scottish Executive Education Department
SEELLD   Scottish Executive Education and Lifelong Learning Departmnet
SEERAD   Scottish Executive Environment and Rural Affairs Department
SEJ   Scottish Educational Journal
SEMRU   Scottish Ethnic Minorities Research Unit
SEN   Special Educational Needs
SER   *Scottish Educational Review*
SERA   Scottish Educational Research Association
SES   Socio-Economic Status
SE/SI   School Effectiveness/School Improvement
SFC   Scottish Film Council
SFEFC   Scottish Further Education Funding Council
SFEU   Scottish Further Education Unit
SFHEA   Scottish Further and Higher Education Association

SFIS	School-Focused Inservice
SFL	Support for Learning
SFR	Standard for Full Registration
SGA	Scottish Group Awards
SGCS	Standard Grade Computing Studies
SGDP	Standard Grade Development Programme
SGPE	Standard Grade Physical Education
SHEFC	Scottish Higher Education Funding Council
SIMON	School Initiated Monitoring of Needs
SINA	Scottish Independent Nurseries Association
SJNC	Scottish Joint Negotiating Committee
SLC	Scottish Leaving Certificate
SLT	Speech and Language Therapist
SM	Scottish Masters
SMT	Senior Management Team
SNAG	Schools Nutrition Action Groups
SNAP	Scottish Network for Able Pupils
SNCT	Scottish Negotiating Committee for Teachers
SNP	Scottish National Party
SOED	Scottish Office Education Department
SOEID	Scottish Office Education and Industry Department
SOHHD	Scottish Office Home and Health Department
SOSB	Scottish Office Statistical Bulletin
SPA	Scottish Progression Awards
SPAG	Southside Parents' Action Group
SPIE	Specify, Plan, Implement and Evaluate
SPMG	Scottish Primary Mathematics Group
SPPA	The Scottish Pre-school Playgroup Association
SPTC	Scottish Parent Teacher Council
SQA	Scottish Qualifications Authority
SQH	Scottish Qualification for Headship
SSA	Scottish Schoolmasters' Association
SSB	Standard Setting Body
SSBA	Scottish School Board Association
SSC	Sector Skills Council
SSE	Scottish Standard English
SSFE	Scottish School of Further Education
SSLS	Scottish School Leavers Survey
SSR	Strategic Spending Review
SSRC	Social Science Research Council
SSSC	Scottish Social Services Council
SSSERC	Scottish Schools Science Equipment Research Centre
SSTA	Scottish Secondary Teachers' Association
STARS	Superhighways Teams Across Rural Schools
STEAC	Scottish Tertiary Education Advisory Council
STEG	Scottish Teacher Education Group
STEP	Scottish Traveller Education Programme
STSC	Scottish Teachers' Salaries Committee
STSCC	Scottish Teachers' Service and Conditions Committee

STUC	Scottish Trades Union Congress
SUCE	Scottish Universities Council on Entrance
SUfI	Scottish University for Industry
SUM	Student Unit of Measurement
SVQ	Scottish Vocational Qualification
SWAP	Scottish Wider Access Programme
SYPS	Scottish Young People's Survey
TACADE	The Advisory Council on Alcohol and Drug Education
TAPS	Techniques for the Assessment of Practical Skills (in Science)
TDP	Teacher Development Partnership
TEI	Teacher Education Institution
TES	*Times Educational Supplement*
TESS	*Times Educational Supplement Scotland*
TfW	Training for Work
TIMSS	Third International Mathematics and Science Study
TLTP	Teaching and Learning Technology Programme
TQ	Teaching Qualification
TQA	Teaching Quality Assessment
TQFE	Teaching Qualification Further Education
TQM	Total Quality Management
TS	Technological Studies
TSSE	Teachers Side School Education
TTA	Teacher Training Agency
TUFL	Trade Union Fund for Learning
TUWPLL	Trade Union Working Party on Lifelong Learning
TVEI	Technical and Vocational Education Initiative
UCAS	Universities and Colleges Admission System
UFC	Universities Funding Council
UGC	University Grants Committee
UHI	University of the Highlands and Islands
UHIMI	University of the Highlands and Islands Millennium Institute
UK	United Kingdom
UKERNA	UK Education and Research Network Association
UN	United Nations
UNESCO	United Nations Educational Scientific and Cultural Organisation
UNICEF	United Nations Children's Fund
US	Universities Scotland
USA	United States of America
VLE	Virtual Learning Environment
VQ	Vocational Qualification
WEA	Workers' Educational Association
WHO	World Health Organisation
WIC	Work Introduction Courses
WWW	World Wide Web
YOP	Youth Opportunities Programme
YTS	Youth Training Scheme

Index